HUXFORD'S
OLD BOOK
VALUE GUIDE

Ninth Edition

COLLECTOR BOOKS
A Division of Schroeder Publishing Co., Inc.

The current values in this book should be used only as a guide. They are not intended to set prices, which vary from one section of the country to another. Auction prices as well as dealer prices vary greatly and are affected by condition as well as demand. Neither the Author nor the Publisher assumes responsibility for any losses that might be incurred as a result of consulting this guide.

Searching For A Publisher?

We are always looking for knowledgeable people considered to be experts within their fields. If you feel that there is a real need for a book on your collectible subject and have a large comprehensive collection, contact Collector Books.

On the Cover:

Conroy, Pat. *The Prince of Tides*. Boston: Houghton Mifflin. 1986. 1st edition. NF/NF. $50.00

Perrin, Noel. *Amateur Sugar Maker*. Hanover, NH: University Press of New England. 1972. 1st edition. NF. $8.50

Wallace, Lew. *Ben Hur*. NY: Harper. 1901. 2 volumes. VG. $15.00

Irving, Washington. *Chronicle of the Conquest of Granada*. NY: Putnams, Knickerbocker Press. 1893. 2 volumes. G+. $45.00

Books featured on cover courtesy of:
David & Nancy Haines
Vintage Books
181 Hayden Rowe St.
Hopkington, MA 01748
(508)435-3499

Cover design: Beth Summers

Additional copies of this book may be ordered from:

COLLECTOR BOOKS
P.O. Box 3009
Paducah, KY 42002-3009

@ $19.95. Add $2.00 for postage and handling.

Copyright © 1997 by Schroeder Publishing Co., Inc.

INTRODUCTION

This book was compiled to help the owner of old books evaluate his holdings and find a buyer for them. Most of us have a box, trunk, stack, or bookcase of old books. Chances are they are not rare books, but they may have value. Two questions that we are asked most frequently are 'Can you tell me the value of my old books?' and 'Where can I sell them?' *Huxford's Old Book Value Guide* will help answer both of these questions. Not only does this book place retail values on nearly 25,000 old books, it also lists scores of buyers along with the type of material each is interested in purchasing. Note that we list retail values (values that an interested party would be willing to pay to obtain possession of the book). These prices are taken from dealers' selling lists that have been issued within the past year. All of the listings are coded (A1, S7, etc.) before the price. This coding refers to a specific dealer's listing for that book. When two or more dealers have listed the same book, their codes will be listed alphabetically in the description line. Please refer to the section titled 'Book Sellers' for codes.

If you were to sell your books to a dealer, you should expect to receive no more than 50% of the values listed in this book, unless the dealer has a specific buyer in mind for some of your material. In many cases, a dealer will pay less than 50% of retail for a book to stock.

Do not ask a dealer to evaluate your old books unless you intend to sell them to him. Most antiquarian book dealers in the larger cities will appraise your books and ephemera for a fee that ranges from a low of $10.00 per hour to $50.00 per hour (or more). If you have an extensive library of rare books, the $50.00-an-hour figure would be money well spent (assuming, of course, the appraiser to be qualified and honest).

Huxford's Old Book Value Guide places values on the more common holdings that many seem to accumulate. You will notice that the majority of the books listed are in the $10.00 to $40.00 range. Many such guides list only the rare, almost non-existent books that the average person will never see. The format is very simple: listings are alphabetized first by the name of the author, translator, editor, or illustrator; if more than one book is listed for a particular author, each title is listed alphabetically under his or her name. When pseudonyms are known, names have been cross-referenced. (Please also see the section titled 'Pseudonyms' for additional information.) Dust jackets or wrappers are noted when present, and sizes (when given) are approximate. Condition is usually noted as well.

Fine condition refers to books that are perfect, in as-issued condition with no defects. Books in near-fine condition are perfect, but not as crisp as those graded fine. Near-fine condition books show only a little wear from reading (such as very small marks on binding); they are not as crisp as those graded fine, but they still have no major defects. Books rated very good may show wear but must have no tears on pages, binding, or dust jacket (if issued). A rating of good applies to an average used book that has all of its pages and yet may have small tears and other defects. The term reading copy (some dealers also use 'poor') describes a book having major defects; however, its text must be complete. Ex-library books are always indicated as such; they may be found in any condition. This rule also applies to any Book Club edition. Some of our booksellers indicate intermediate grades with a + or ++, or VG-EX. We have endeavored to use the grade that best corresponded to the description of condition as given in each dealer's listing. If you want to check further on the condition of a specific book, please consult the bookseller indicated. Please note that the condition stated in the description is for the book and then the dust jacket. (Dust jackets on many modern first editions may account for up to 80% of their value.)

In the back of the book we have listed buyers of books and book-related material. When you correspond with these dealers, be sure to enclose a self-addressed, stamped envelope if you want a reply. Please do not send lists of books for an appraisal. If you wish to sell your books, quote the price that you want or negotiate price only on the items the buyer is interested in purchasing. When you list your books, do so by author, full title, publisher and place, date, and edition. Indicate condition, noting any defects on cover or contents.

When shipping your books, first wrap each book in paper such as brown kraft or a similar type of material. Never use newspaper for the inner wrap, since newsprint tends to rub off. (It may, however be used as a cushioning material within the outer carton.) Place your books in a sturdy corrugated box and use a good shipping tape to seal it. Tape reinforced with nylon string is preferable, as it will not tear. Books shipped by parcel post may be sent at a special fourth class book rate, which may be lower than regular parcel post zone rates.

LISTING OF STANDARD ABBREVIATIONS

/ ....and, also, with, or indicates dual-title book
ACS ....advance copy slip
aeg ....all edge gilt
AJA.......American Jewish Archives
AJC ......American Jewish Congress
AJHS...American Jewish Historical Society
Am ....American
AP ..proof, advance proof, advance uncorrected proof, or galley
ARC .....advance reading or review copy
bdg....................binding, bound
decor..........decoration, decorated
b&w ....black & white
bl...blue
blk...black
BC ....any book club edition
BOMC.............Book of Month Club
brd.......................................boards
c ....copyright
ca ....circa
cbdg....................comb binding
chip ....chipped
clip ....clipped price
CMG....Coward McCann Geoghegan
dk ....dark
dj.....................................dust jacket
DSP ....Duell Sloan Pearce
dtd.......................................dated
E ....east, eastern
edit..editor
ed ....edition
emb...............embossed, embossing
Eng.....................England, English
ep...............................end pages
ES..errata slip
ERB ....Edgar Rice Burroughs Inc.
F ....fine
fld.....................folding, folder
ftspc...............................frontispiece
FSC..........Farrar, Straus & Cudahy
FSG ....Farrar, Straus & Giroux
fwd.......................................forward
G ....good
GPO ...Government Printing Office

gr ....green
HBJ .....Harcourt Brace Jovanovich, Inc.
HBW............Harcourt Brace World
hist ....history
hc ....hard cover
HRW ....Holt Rinehart Winston
ils ....illustrated
imp...................................imprint
intl..................................initialed
inscr ....inscribed
Inst....................................Institute
Internat ....International
intro...................introduction
LEC...............Limited Edition Club
lg ....large
Lib ....library
lt ....light
ltd....................................limited
mc ....multicolor
MIT .....MA Institute of Technology
MTI..................movie tie-in
MOMA.....Museum of Modern Art
MPA ....Museum of Primitive Art
mtd..................................mounted
Mus ....museum
N.........................north, northern
NAL ....New American Library
Nat ....national
NEL...............New English Library
nd ....no date
ne ....no edition given
NF ....near fine
NGS ..National Geographic Society
np..........................no place given
NYGS ...New York Graphic Society
obl ....oblong
orig ....original
p...................................page, pages
pc..piece
pb ....paperback
pict......................................pictorial
pl ....plate, plates
Pr..press
pref ....preface
pres..........................presentation
promo..........................promotion

prt.......................print, printing
pub ....publisher, publishing
rem mk...................remainder mark
repro ....reproduction
rpr ....repair
rpt...................................reprint
RS........................review slip
S..............................south, southern
swrp ....shrink wrap
sans ....none issued
sbdg........................spiral binding
sc ....softcover
SF...............................science fiction
sgn.................signature, signed
sm...small
sq ....square
stp................stamp or stamped
supp ....supplement
TB..textbook
teg ....top edge gilt
trans ....translated
TVTI ....TV tie-in
U ....University
unp ....unpaged
UP ....uncorrected proof
VG ....very good
W............................west, western
w/ ...with, indicates laid in material
wht ....white
wrp ....wrappers
xl...ex-library
yel.....................................yellow
#d...................................numbered
12mo ....about 7" tall
16mo ....6" to 7" tall
24mo ....5" to 6" tall
32mo ....4" to 5" tall
48mo ....less than 4" tall
64mo ....about 3" tall
sm 8vo ....7 ½" to 8" tall
8vo........................8" to 9" tall
sm 4to ....about 10" tall, quarto
4to..............between 11" to 13" tall
folio ....13" or larger
elephant folio ....23" or larger
atlas folio ....25"
double elephant folio..larger than 25"

A. TRUMP JUNIOR. *Laws & Regulations of Short Whist With Maxims...* 1880. NY. 111p. VG. S1. $25.00

AARON, David. *State Scarlet.* 1987. Putnam. 1st ed. F/NF. H11. $20.00

AARON, David. *State Scarlet.* 1987. Putnam. 1st ed. VG+/VG+ clip. N4. $15.00

AARON, Henry. *I Had a Hammer.* 1991. Harper Collins. 1st ed. F/F. P8. $75.00

AARONS, Jules. *Solar System Radio Astronomy.* 1965. NY. Plenum. 4to. 416p. xl. VG. K5. $25.00

ABBATE, Francesco. *Egyptian Art.* 1972. Octopus. 1st ed. 8vo. 158p. NF/dj. W1. $14.00

ABBEVILLE, Sanson D. *Introduction a la Geographie.* 1708. Amsterdam. xl. fld maps. G. B5. $250.00

ABBEY, Edward. *Brave Cowboy.* 1993. Dream Garden/Santa Theresa. 1st ed thus. 1/500. M/dj. A18. $125.00

ABBEY, Edward. *Cactus Country.* 1973. Time Life. 1st ed. photos. F/sans. A18. $30.00

ABBEY, Edward. *Desert Solitaire.* 1968. McGraw Hill. 1st ed. author's 4th book. F/dj. S9. $650.00

ABBEY, Edward. *Fool's Progress.* 1988. Holt. 1st ed. M/M. A18. $30.00

ABBEY, Edward. *Hayduke Lives.* 1990. Little Brn. 1st ed. M/dj. A18. $25.00

ABBEY, Edward. *Hidden Canyon: A River Journey.* 1977. Viking. 1st ed. 4to. F/clip. B4. $300.00

ABBEY, Edward. *Monkey Wrench Gang.* 1985. Salt Lake City. 1st ed thus. F/F. C2. $75.00

ABBEY, Edward. *Monkey Wrench Gang.* 1990. Dream Garden. revised ils ed/1st prt. F/F. A18. $50.00

ABBEY, Edward. *Outlet.* 1905. Houghton Mifflin. 1st ed. ils E Boyd Smith. VG+. A18. $75.00

ABBEY, Edward. *Texas Matchmaker.* 1904. Houghton Mifflin. 1st ed. ils E Boyd Smith. VG+. A18. $60.00

ABBEY, J.R. *Travel in Aquatint & Lithography 1770-1860.* nd. np. 2 vol in 1. ltd ed. 1/100. ils. 722p. F. A4. $150.00

ABBOT, Anthony. *About the Murder of the Clergyman's...* 1931. Covici Friede. 2nd. VG. P3. $20.00

ABBOT, Willis J. *Nations at War: A Current History.* 1914. NY. Syndicate. probable 1st ed. 366p. red cloth. VG/VG. B22. $25.00

ABBOTT, Austin. *Select Cases on the Examination of Witnesses.* 1894. NY. Diossy Law Book Co. sheep. working copy. M11. $50.00

ABBOTT, Austin. *Trial Evidence, Rules of Evidence Applicable...* 1900. NY. Baker Voorhis. orig sheep. reading copy. M11. $40.00

ABBOTT, Benjamin Vaughan. *Travelling Law-School & Famous Trials...* 1884. Chicago. Interstate. gilt brn cloth. M11. $125.00

ABBOTT, Bruce. *Sign of the Scorpion.* 1970. Grove. 1st ed. F/F. P3. $20.00

ABBOTT, I.A. *Laau Hawaii: Traditional Hawaiian Uses of Plants.* 1992. Bishop Mus. 4to. photos. 163p. F/pict wrp. B1. $36.00

ABBOTT, John S.C. *George Washington; or, Life in America...* 1875. Dodd Mead. ils. xl. poor. B10. $12.00

ABBOTT, John S.C. *Napoleon at St Helena.* nd. Harper. G. P3. $85.00

ABBOTT, John. *Scimitar.* 1992. Crown. 1st ed. F/F. H11. $20.00

ABBOTT, Maude E. *Atlas of Congenital Cardiac Disease.* 1936. NY. 1st ed. lg 4to. red cloth. VG+. B14. $350.00

ABBOTT, R.T. *Compendium of Land Shells.* 1989. Melbourne. Am Malacologists. 1st ed. 4to. 240p. F/F. B1. $50.00

ABBOTT, Shirley. *Womenfolks: Growing Up Down South.* 1983. Ticknor Fields. 1st ed. F/dj. B4. $45.00

ABBOTT, Twyman O. *Synopsis of the California Vehicle Act & Guide Book.* 1925. Sacramento. Division of Motor Vehicles. 77p. stapled wrp. M11. $15.00

ABBOTT, Winston. *Come Climb My Hill.* 1982. Inspiration. revised. ils Bette Eaton Bossen. VG/VG. B11. $8.50

ABBOTT, Winston. *Sing With the Wind.* 1982. Inspiration. sgn. ils/sgn BE Bossen. F/F. B11. $12.00

ABBOTT & DICKINSON. *Guide to Reading.* 1925. Doubleday Page. VG. P3. $13.00

ABDULLAH, Achmed. *Night Drums.* nd. AL Burt. VG/G. P3. $25.00

ABDULLAH, Morg Murray. *My Khyber Marriage.* 1990. London. Octagon. 1st ed. 8vo. 272p. NF/dj. W1. $20.00

ABE, Kobo. *Ruined Map.* 1969. Knopf. 1st ed. VG/VG. P3. $25.00

ABEL, Kenneth. *Bait.* 1994. Delacorte. ARC. NF/wrp. M22. $15.00

ABEL-SMITH, Brian. *Hospitals 1800-1948: Study in Social Administration...* 1964. Cambridge. 1st ed. 415p. VG/dj. A13. $35.00

ABELLA, Alex. *Killing of the Saints.* 1991. Crown. 1st ed. F/F. A20. $20.00

ABERNETHY, John. *Hunterian Oration, for the Year 1819.* 1825. Hartford. 1st Am ed. extract. 40p. VG. A13. $40.00

ABRAHAMS, Peter. *Fury of Rachel Monette.* 1980. Macmillan. 1st ed. author's 1st book. NF/NF. H11. $40.00

ABRAHAMS, Peter. *Revolution #9.* 1992. Mysterious. 1st ed. F/F. A20. $18.00

ABRO, Ben. *July 14 Assassination.* 1963. Jonathan Cape. 1st ed. VG/VG. P3. $20.00

ACHEBE, Chinua. *Anthills of Savannah.* 1988. Anchor. 1st ed. F/F. M19. $17.50

ACHESON, Edward. *Grammarian's Funeral.* nd. Grosset Dunlap. VG. P3. $15.00

ACKER, Kathy. *My Mother: Demonology, a Novel.* 1993. Pantheon. 1st ed. F/NF. G10. $25.00

ACKER, Marian Francis. *Etchings of Old Mobile.* 1938. Mobile. Gill Prt. unp. F/G. B10. $20.00

ACKROYD, Peter. *Chatterton.* 1987. Grove. 1st ed. F/F. B35. $28.00

ACKROYD, Peter. *Dickens.* 1991. Harper Collins. 1st ed. F/F. P3. $35.00

ACKROYD, Peter. *First Light.* 1989. London. 1st ed. sgn. F/NF. C2. $40.00

ACKROYD, Peter. *Great Fire of London.* 1982. Hamish Hamilton. 1st ed. author's 1st novel. F/F. C2. $200.00

ACKROYD, Peter. *Israel Under Babylon & Persia.* 1970. Oxford. 1st ed. 374p. VG/dj. W1. $18.00

ACKROYD, Peter. *TS Eliot: A Life.* 1984. Simon Schuster. 1st ed. rem mk. F/F. B35. $40.00

ACKWORTH, Robert C. *Dr Kildare Assigned to Trouble.* 1963. Whitman. TVTI. VG. P3. $10.00

ACOSTA, Jorge R. *El Palacio del Quetzalpapaloti.* 1964. Mexico. 1st ed. 85p. F3. $30.00

ADAIR, James. *History of the American Indians; Particularly...* 1775. London. 1st ed. 4to. 464p. contemporary bdg. C6. $1,650.00

ADAM, Peter. *Art of the Third Reich.* 1992. Abrams. ils/pl. 332p. F/dj. A17. $30.00

ADAMCZEWSKI, Jan. *Nicolaus Copernicus & His Epoch.* ca 1965. Phil. Copernicus Soc of Am. 4to. 160p. VG/dj. K5. $30.00

ADAMIC, Louis. *House in Antigua.* 1937. Harper. 1st ed. ils. 300p. F3. $30.00

ADAMIC, Louis. *Robinson Jeffers.* 1938. Ward Ritchie. 1/250. VG+. S9. $60.00

ADAMS, Alice. *Families & Survivors.* 1974. Knopf. 1st ed. F/NF. B4. $65.00

ADAMS, Alice. *Mexico.* 1990. Prentice Hall. 1st ed. 216p. F3. $20.00

ADAMS, Alice. *To See You Again.* 1982. Knopf. 1st ed. F/NF. B4. $45.00

ADAMS, Andy. *Log of a Cowboy: A Narrative of Old Trail Days.* 1931. Houghton Mifflin. 1st ed thus. ils E Boyd Smith. F/VG. A18. $35.00

ADAMS, Andy. *Outlet.* 1905. Houghton Mifflin. 1st ed. ils E Boyd Smith. F. A18. $60.00

ADAMS, Andy. *Texas Matchmaker.* 1904. Houghton Mifflin. 1st ed. ils E Boyd Smith. F. A18. $75.00

ADAMS, Ansel. *Camera.* 1980. NYGS. 1st ed. 4to. F/NF. T10. $35.00

ADAMS, Ansel. *Letters & Images 1916-1984.* 1988. NYGS. 1st ed. 402p. F/dj. A17. $40.00

ADAMS, Bill. *Wind in the Topsails.* 1931. London. Harrap. 8vo. 163p. VG. T7. $30.00

ADAMS, Brian. *Flowering of the Pacific.* 1986. Sydney. Wm Collins. 1st ed. 4to. 16 pl. 194p. F/F. T10. $65.00

ADAMS, Charles Francis. *Autobiography.* 1920. Houghton Mifflin. 7th. 8vo. 224p. gilt blk cloth. VG. T10. $30.00

ADAMS, Charles Francis. *Railroads: Their Origin & Problems.* 1879. Putnam. 12mo. 216p. brick cloth. F. T10. $125.00

ADAMS, Charles True. *Contract Bridge Standardized.* 1929. Chicago. 2nd. 73p. VG. S1. $10.00

ADAMS, Charles. *Charles Adams' Mother Goose.* 1967. Windmill. ils. NF/VG. P2. $55.00

ADAMS, Clifton. *Hassle & the Medicine Man.* nd. BC. VG/G. P3. $5.00

ADAMS, Douglas. *Dirk Gently's Holistic Detective Age.* 1987. Simon Schuster. 1st ed. F/F. P3. $20.00

ADAMS, Douglas. *Hitchhiker's Guide to the Galaxy.* 1987. Heinemann. 3rd. VG/VG. P3. $20.00

ADAMS, Douglas. *Life, the Universe & Everything.* 1982. Harmony. 1st ed. F/F. P3. $20.00

ADAMS, Douglas. *Long Dark Tea-Time of the Soul.* 1989. Stoddart. 1st ed. VG/VG. P3. $20.00

ADAMS, Douglas. *Restaurant at the End of the Universe.* nd. Harmony. 4th. F/F. P3. $15.00

ADAMS, Douglas. *So Long, & Thanks for All the Fish.* 1985. Harmony. 1st ed. NF/NF. P3. $20.00

ADAMS, E.C.L. *Potee's Gal: A Drama of Negro Life Near Big Congaree Swamps.* 1929. Columbia. 1/250. 49p. maroon cloth. VG/VG. B11. $85.00

ADAMS, E.C.L. *Potee's Gal: A Drama of Negro Life Near Big Congaree Swamps.* 1929. Columbia. 1st ed. 1/250. sgn. red cloth. NF/NF. C2. $125.00

ADAMS, Eustace. *Andy Lane: Racing Around the World (#3).* 1928. Grosset Dunlap. 219p. lists 12 titles. VG/dj. M20. $25.00

ADAMS, Eustace. *Doomed Demons.* 1935. Grosset Dunlap. Air Combat Stories for Boys series. VG/poor. P12. $8.00

ADAMS, Frank. *Simple Simon.* nd. Dodge. 4to. pls/text on French-fold paper. VG. M5. $125.00

ADAMS, George I. *Gold Deposits of Alabama & Occurrences of Copper, Pyrite...* 1930. AL U. 1st ed. xl. VG. M8. $45.00

ADAMS, George Worthington. *Doctors in Blue.* 1985. Dayton, OH. 12mo. 237p. VG. T3. $20.00

ADAMS, H. *Golf Course Murder.* 1933. NY. Blk. VG/VG. B5. $27.50

ADAMS, Hanna. *Abridgement of History of New England for Use of Young...* 1805. Boston. B&J Homans. author's ed. 12mo. 186p. leather. poor. B36. $35.00

ADAMS, Harold. *Man Who Missed the Party.* 1989. Mysterious. 1st ed. sgn. F/F. P3. $25.00

ADAMS, Harold. *Naked Liar.* 1985. Mysterious. 1st ed. F/F. M23. $20.00

ADAMS, Henry. *Education of Henry Adams.* 1942. Merrymount. 12 orig etchings. gilt rust buckram. F/case. B14. $200.00

ADAMS, Herbert. *Mystery & Minette.* 1934. Lippincott. 1st ed. VG. P3. $35.00

ADAMS, Hugh. *Art of the Sixties.* 1978. Oxford. ils/biography. 80p. dj. D2. $25.00

ADAMS, James Truslow. *American.* 1943. Scribner. 1st ed. 8vo. 404p. F/NF. T10. $25.00

ADAMS, James Truslow. *Atlas of American History.* 1943. NY. 1st ed. 360p. buckram. G+. B18. $25.00

ADAMS, James Truslow. *Dictionary of American History.* 1940. Scribner. 6 vol. 2nd. 2625p. VG. A4. $245.00

ADAMS, James Truslow. *March of Democracy.* 1955. Scribner. 7 vol. VG. P12. $50.00

ADAMS, John. *Diary & Autobiography.* 1961. Cambridge, MA. 4 vol. 2nd. 8vo. F/djs. T10. $150.00

ADAMS, Katharine. *Gray Eyes.* 1934. Macmillan. 1st ed. 267p. VG+/dj. M20. $25.00

ADAMS, Leon. *Wines of America.* 1973. Houghton Mifflin. 1st ed. sgn. 465p. F/F. T10. $50.00

ADAMS, Mark H. *Bacteriophages.* 1959. NY. Interscience. ARC. sgn Salvadore Lurin. 8vo. ils. VG. B14. $75.00

ADAMS, Maryline P. *Merrie England, a Philatelic Celebration...* 1983. Poole. 1/101. sgn. 25 French-fold p. miniature. F. B24. $165.00

ADAMS, Nancy M. *Mountain Flowers of New Zealand.* 1965. Wellington. ils. VG/dj. B26. $22.50

ADAMS, Peter. *Clipper Ships: Done in Cork Models.* 1929. Dutton. VG/VG. A16. $17.50

ADAMS, Ramon F. *More Burs Under the Saddle: Books & Histories of West.* 1979. OK U. 1st ed. AN/dj. A18. $40.00

ADAMS, Ramon F. *Six-Guns & Saddle Leather.* 1954. Norman. 1st ed. 8vo. F/NF. T10. $250.00

ADAMS, Ramon F. *Six-Guns & Saddle Leather.* 1982. 2491 books listed. hc. F. E1. $60.00

ADAMS, Randolph G. *Gateway to American History.* 1927. Boston. hc. VG. O7. $45.00

ADAMS, Richard. *Day Gone By.* 1990. Hutchinson. 1st ed. VG/VG. P3. $30.00

ADAMS, Richard. *Day Gone By.* 1991. Knopf. AP. 8vo. F/prt wrp. S9. $25.00

ADAMS, Richard. *Girl in a Swing.* 1980. Allen Lane. 1st ed. VG/VG. P3. $22.00

ADAMS, Richard. *Iron Wolf & Other Stories.* 1980. Allen Lane. 1st ed. F/F. P3. $25.00

ADAMS, Richard. *Plague Dogs.* 1977. Allen Lane. 1st ed. F/F. P3. $20.00

ADAMS, Richard. *Prehistoric Mesoamerica.* 1977. Little Brn. 1st ed. 370p. VG. F3. $25.00

ADAMS, Richard. *Shardik.* 1974. Simon Schuster. 1st ed. F/F. P3. $25.00

ADAMS, Richard. *Ship's Cat.* 1977. Knopf. 1st Am ed. ils Alan Aldridge. VG/VG. D1. $45.00

ADAMS, Richard. *Traveller.* 1988. Knopf. 1st ed. F/F. M23. $25.00

ADAMS, Richard. *Tyger Voyage.* 1976. Knopf. 1st Am ed. 30p. F/NF. T5. $25.00

ADAMS, Richard. *Watership Down.* 1974. Macmillan. 1st Am ed. NF/NF. B2. $65.00

ADAMS, Richard. *Watership Down.* 1974. Macmillan. 1st ed. NF/VG clip. M22. $25.00

ADAMS, Robert. *Nil: Episodes in Literary Conquest of Void...* 1966. Oxford. 255p. NF/VG. A4. $35.00

ADAMS, Samuel Hoplins. *Great American Fraud.* 1906. NY. 1st ed. 146p. VG. A13. $75.00

ADAMS, Sherman. *First-Hand Report: Story of Eisenhower Administration.* 1961. Harper. 1st ed. sgn. 481p. bl cloth. F/VG+. B22. $12.00

ADAMS, Susan. *Let's Play Cards.* 1981. Eng. G. S1. $3.00

ADAMS, Thomas R. *Non-Cartographical Maritime Works Published by Mount & Page.* 1985. London. VG/wrp. O7. $25.00

ADAMS, Thomas R. *Rare Americana: A Selection of One Hundred & One Books...* 1974. Providence. VG/wrp. O7. $45.00

ADAMS, Tom. *Agatha Christie & the Art of Her Crimes.* 1981. Everest House. 1st ed. NF/NF. P3. $35.00

ADAMS & ADAMS. *Smaller British Birds.* 1874. London. Bell. 1st ed. 4to. gr cloth. VG. T10. $125.00

ADAMS & CONNOR. *Poisonous Plants of New Zealand.* 1951. Wellington. 1st ed. inscr Connor. 39 pl. 141p. VG/wrp. B26. $22.50

ADAMS & HARBAUGH. *Favorite Torte & Cake Recipes.* 1951. Simon Schuster. 1st ed. sgns. 8vo. 164p. VG/G. B11. $10.00

ADAMS & LLOYD. *Meaning of Life.* 1984. Harmony. 1st Am ed. F/NF. T2. $12.00

ADAMS & LUNGWITZ. *Textbook of Horseshoeing.* 1966. Corvallis. facsimile of 1884 ed. VG/G. O3. $25.00

ADAMS & NEWHALL. *This Is the American Earth.* 1960. Sierra Club. 2nd. 89p. VG/dj. A17. $40.00

ADAMS. *American Controversy: A Bibiliographical Study...* 1980. 2 vol. describes 2350 pamphlets. 1102p. F. A4. $135.00

ADAMSON, David. *Ruins of Time.* 1975. Praeger. 1st ed. 272p. dj. F3. $30.00

ADAMSON, Joe. *Groucho, Harpo, Chico & Sometimes Zeppo.* 1973. NY. 1st ed. photos. 464p. F/dj. A17. $10.00

ADAMSON, Joy. *Born Free: A Lioness in Two Worlds.* 1960. NY. 1st ed. 220p. VG/dj. B14. $55.00

ADBIAN, Jack. *Detective Stories From the Strand...* nd. Quality BC. VG/VG. P3. $10.00

ADDAMS, Charles. *Addams & Evil.* nd. Simon Schuster. 8th. VG/VG. P3. $25.00

ADDAMS, Charles. *Dear Dead Days.* 1959. Putnam. 1st ed. 8vo. VG+/dj. M21. $30.00

ADDAMS, Charles. *World of Charles Addams.* 1991. Knopf. 1st ed. 4to. NF/dj. M21. $45.00

ADDAMS, Jane. *Long Road of Woman's Memory.* 1916. Macmillan. 1st ed. inscr. F. B4. $450.00

ADDEO & GARVIN. *Midnight Special: Legend of Leadbelly by...* 1971. Geis. 1st ed. F/NF. N3. $35.00

ADDINGTON, Sarah. *Jerry Juddikins.* 1926. McKay. probable 1st ed. inscr/dtd 1926. 65p. VG. P2. $35.00

ADDIS. *Through a Woman's I: An Annotated Bibliography...* 1983. 2217 annotated entries. 607p. F. A4. $45.00

ADDISON, William. *English Fairs & Markets.* 1953. Batsford. 1st ed. ils Barbara Jones. VG/VG. M20. $40.00

ADE, George. *Doc' Horne.* 1899. 1st ed. ils McCutcheon. VG+. S13. $12.00

ADE, George. *Fables in Slang.* 1900. Herbert Stone. ils Clyde J Newman. G+. P12. $6.00

ADEN, Paul. *Hosta Book.* 1992 (1988). Portland. 2nd. 133p. sc. M. B26. $18.00

ADLEMAN, Melvin. *Sporting Time.* 1986. IL U. 1st ed. F/F. P8. $35.00

ADLEMAN, Robert H. *Annie Deane.* 1971. World. 1st ed. VG/VG. P3. $20.00

ADLEMAN & WALTON. *Rome Fell Today.* 1968. Boston. 1st ed. 336p. F/dj. A17. $10.00

ADLER, Bill. *Murder Game.* 1991. Carroll Graf. 1st ed. F/F. N4. $22.50

ADLER, Bill. *Murder in Manhattan.* 1986. Morrow. 1st ed. VG/VG. P3. $16.00

ADLER, Frederick Herbert. *Winds & Words.* 1947. Cleveland. Flozari/Pegasus. 8vo. 44p. G/wrp. B11. $10.00

ADLER, Renata. *Toward a Radical Middle: Fourteen Pieces of Reporting...* 1969. Random. 1st ed. 1F/F. B4. $65.00

ADLER, Warren. *Blood Ties.* 1979. Putnam. 1st ed. VG/VG. P3. $15.00

ADLER, Warren. *Casanova Embrace.* 1978. Putnam. 1st ed. NF/NF. P3. $13.00

ADLER & CHASTAIN. *Who Killed the Robins Family?* 1983. Morrow. 1st ed. xl. VG+/dj. N4. $12.50

ADMAS, Henry. *Democracy: An American Novel.* 1880. NY. 1st issue. NF. C6. $750.00

ADNEY & CHAPELLE. *Bark Canoes & Skin Boats of North America.* 1964. Smithsonian. 1st ed. sgn Chapelle. 242p. gilt cloth. F. B11. $100.00

ADONIAS, Isa. *Mapa: Imagens da Formacao Territorial Brasileira.* 1993. Rio de Janerio. Odebrecht. 396p. AN. O7. $275.00

ADRIAN, E.D. *Basis of Sensation. The Action of Sense Organs.* 1928. Norton. 1st Am ed. 122p. VG. G1. $40.00

ADRIAN, E.D. *Physical Background of Perception.* 1947. Oxford. Clarendon. thin 8vo. 95p. VG. G1. $40.00

AESCHYLUS. *Oresteia.* 1961. LEC. 1st ed. 1/1500. ils/sgn Ayrton. F/case. C2. $100.00

AESOP. *Aesop for Children.* 1919. Rand McNally. 1st ed. ils Milo Winter. 112p. G. C14. $25.00

AESOP. *Aesop's Fables.* 1933. Viking. ils Boris Artzybasheff. F/VG. A20. $50.00

AESOP. *Aesop's Fables.* 1941. Heritage. 1st ed. ils Robert Lawson. 134p. VG+. P2. $45.00

AESOP. *Aesop's Fables.* 1982. Franklin Lib. aeg. leather spine. F. P3. $20.00

AESOP. *Aesop's Fables.* 1988. Jelly Bean. 1st ed. ils Charles Santore. 48p. F/F. P2. $25.00

AESOP. *Fables of Aesop.* 1909. Hodder Stoughton. ltd ed. ils/sgn E Detmold. gilt red cloth. scarce. D1. $1,250.00

AESOP. *Some of Aesop's Fables With Modern Instances.* 1983. Macmillan. 1st Am ed. ils Caldecott. VG. D1. $150.00

AFER, Publius Terentius. *Works...* 1822. Lincolns Inn Fields. Pickering. miniature. contemporary calf. F. T10. $100.00

AFRICANO, Lillian. *Businessman's Guide to the Middle East.* 1977. Harper Row. 1st ed. 8vo. 312p. NF/dj. W1. $20.00

AGASSIZ, Elizabeth Cary. *Louis Agassiz: His Life & Correspondence.* 1885. Boston. 2 vol. xl. VG. B14. $150.00

AGASSIZ & AGASSIZ. *Journey in Brazil.* 1868. Ticknor Field. 2nd. professionally rehinged. VG. A10. $125.00

AGEE, James. *Letters to Father Flye.* 1962. NY. 1st ed. inscr. NF/VG. C6. $350.00

AGEE & WALKER. *Let Us Now Praise Famous Men.* 1941. Houghton Mifflin. 1st ed. ils. reading copy. C2. $60.00

AGETON, Arthur A. *Naval Officer's Guide.* 1943. Whittlesey. 2nd. ils. 514p. G+. P12. $15.00

AGNEW, Georgette. *Let's Pretend.* 1927. London. Saville. 1st ltd ed. sgns. ils/sgn EH Shepard. VG/case. D1. $800.00

AGNEW, Spiro T. *Canfield Decision.* 1976. Playboy. 1st ed. rem mk. NF/VG. N4. $17.50

AGUIRRE, Lily. *Guatemala, My Beautiful Country.* 1959. Guate. 160p. stiff wrp. F3. $20.00

AHEARN, Allen. *Book Collecting: A Comprehensive Guide.* 1995. Putnam. 2nd. M. A18. $35.00

AHLSON, Hereward. *Thunderbolt & the Rebel Planet.* 1954. Lutterworth. 1st ed. VG/VG. P3. $15.00

AI. *Cruelty: Poems.* 1973. Houghton Mifflin. 1st ed. author's 1st book. F/VG. M19. $35.00

AI. *Cruelty: Poems.* 1973. Houghton Mifflin. 1st ed. author's 1st book. sgn. NF/NF. C2. $75.00

AICHELE, Dietmar. *Was Bluht Denn Da?* 1973. Stuttgart. ils M Golte-Bechtle. 400p. VG/dj. B26 $20.00

AICKMAN, Robert. *Cold Hand in Mine.* 1975. Scribner. 1st ed. F/F. P3. $40.00

AICKMAN, Robert. *Painted Devils.* 1979. Scribner. 1st ed. NF/NF. P3. $30.00

AIKEN, Conrad. *Blue Voyage.* 1927. Scribner. 1st ed. F/VG. C2. $125.00

AIKEN, Joan. *Castle Barebane.* 1976. Viking. 1st ed. VG/VG. P3. $15.00

AIKEN, Joan. *Foul Matter.* 1983. Doubleday. 1st ed. VG/G. P3. $13.00

AIKEN, Joan. *Haunting of Lamb House.* 1993. St Martin. 1st Am ed. F/F. G10. $25.00

AIKMAN, Lonnelle. *Nature's Healing Arts: From Folk Medicine to Modern Drugs.* 1977. WA. 1st ed. 199p. VG. A13. $25.00

AIMONE, Alan C. *Military History: Biographical Guide.* 1987. West Point. VG/wrp. O7. $20.00

AINSLIE, Kathleen. *Catharine Susan & Me Goes Abroad.* ca 1909. London. Casteel. 1st ed. ils Kathleen Ainslie. VG. D1. $125.00

AINSLIE, Tom. *Anslie's Complete Guide to Thoroughbred Racing.* 1979. Simon Schuster. 1st ed. 470p. gr cloth. NF/dj. B22. $5.50

AINSWORTH, Ed. *California.* 1951. Los Angeles. House-Warven. 272p. VG/worn. P4. $15.00

AINSWORTH, Ed. *Maverick Mayor (Sam Yorty).* 1966. Doubleday. 1st ed. inscr Yorty. 8vo. F/F. T10. $45.00

AINSWORTH, William. *Historical Romances.* 1898. Phil. Barrie. Author's Memorial ed. 20 vol. 8vo. aeg. morocco. F. B14. $750.00

AINSWORTH & AINSWORTH. *In the Shade of the Juniper Tree: A Life of Fray...* 1970. Doubleday. 1st ed. 8vo. 199p. gr cloth. NF. T10. $35.00

AIRD, Catherine. *Most Contagious Game.* 1967. Crime Club. VG/VG. P3. $15.00

AIRTH, Rennie. *Once a Spy.* 1981. Jonathan Cape. 1st ed. VG/VG. P3. $18.00

AITKEN, Robert G. *Measures of 1865 A Double Stars.* 1937. Berkeley. Lick Observatory Bulletin #491. wrp. K5. $25.00

AJILVAQI, Geyata. *Wild Flowers of the Big Thicket.* 1979. College Station. photos/map/glossary. 360p. F/dj. B26. $22.50

AKERMAN, John Yonge. *Remains of Pagan Saxondom.* 1855. London. Smith. 4to. 40 pl/ils. 84p. VG. T10. $500.00

AKINARI, Ueda. *Ugetsu Monogatari.* 1974. U British Columbia. F/F. P3. $30.00

AKINS, Zoe. *Old Maid.* 1935. Appleton. 1st ed. F/NF clip. B4. $350.00

AKSYONOV, Vassily. *Quest for an Island.* 1987. NY. 1st Am ed. sgn. F/NF. C2. $50.00

AKSYONOV, Vassily. *Say Cheese!* 1989. NY. 1st Am ed. sgn. F/NF. C2. $40.00

ALAUZEN & RIPERT. *Monticelli. Sa vie et Son Oeuvre.* 1969. Paris. Bibliotheque des Arts. ils. 471p. cloth. dj. D2. $550.00

ALBA, Victor. *Horizon Concise History of Mexico.* 1973. American Heritage. 1st ed. 224p. dj. F3. $20.00

ALBAUGH, William A. *More Confederate Faces.* 1972. WA, DC. ABS Prt. 1st ed. 1/400. 233p. NF. M8. $175.00

ALBAUGH, William A. *Tyler, Texas, CSA.* 1958. Stackpole. photos. 235p. xl. VG/G. B10. $40.00

ALBEE, Edward. *Box & Quotations From Chairman Mao Tse-Tung.* 1969. NY. 1st ed. sgn. F/F. A11. $35.00

ALBEE, Edward. *Zoo Story, Death of Bessie Smith, The Sandbox.* 1960. 1st ed. MTI. VG/VG clip. S13. $30.00

ALBERT, Alpaeus H. *Record of American Uniform & Historical Buttons.* 1976. Bicentennial ed. 8vo. ils. 411p. VG. T3. $40.00

ALBERT, Herman W. *Odyssey of a Desert Prospector.* 1967. Norman. 1st ed. 12mo. 260p. F/F. T10. $25.00

ALBERT, Susan Wittig. *Witches' Bane.* 1993. Scribner. 1st ed. F/F. M23. $20.00

ALBERT, Virginia. *Peter Rabbit & Jimmy Chipmunk.* 1918. Saalfield. ils Fern Bisel Peat. unp. pict brd. VG. M20. $10.00

ALBION, Robert G. *Makers of Naval Policy 1798-1947.* 1980. Naval Inst. 737p. F. A17. $14.50

ALBION, Robert G. *Seaports South of Sahara.* 1959. NY. 1st ed. sgn. 316p. gilt bl cloth. F. H3. $75.00

ALBRAND, Martha. *Linden Affair.* 1956. Random. 1st ed. VG/VG. P3. $30.00

ALBRAND, Martha. *Manhattan North.* 1971. CMG. 1st ed. VG/VG. P3. $20.00

ALBRAND, Martha. *Mask of Alexander.* 1955. Random. 1st ed. VG/VG. P3. $20.00

ALBRAND, Martha. *Taste of Terror.* 1977. Putnam. 1st ed. NF/NF. P3. $20.00

ALBRIGHT & TAYLOR. *O Ranger!, a Book About the National Parks.* 1982. Stanford. 2nd. 8vo. VG. B17. $5.00

ALCIATUS, Andreas. *Omnia Emblemata Cum Commentariis+Notae per Claudius Minois.* 1589 (1588). Paris. 213 woodcut-bordered emblems. 838p. gilt calf. VG. B14. $1,400.00

ALCOCK, Vivien. *Cuckoo Sister.* 1986. Delacorte. UP. 8vo. NF/wrp. C14. $8.00

ALCOHOLICS ANONYMOUS. *Alcoholics Anonymous Big Book.* 2nd ed/8th prt. F/poor. N3. $20.00

ALCOHOLICS ANONYMOUS. *Twelve Steps & Twelve Traditions.* 1953. stated 1st ed. F/F. H7. $100.00

ALCOHOLICS ANONYMOUS. *Twelve Steps & Twelve Traditions.* 1953. NY. 1st ed. F/poor. N3. $55.00

ALCOHOLICS ANONYMOUS. *Works...* 1948. 12th. G. B5. $125.00

ALCORN, John S. *Jolly Rogers: History of 90th Bomber Group During WWII.* 1981. Temple City, CA. 1st ed. 212p. VG. A17. $40.00

ALCOTT, Louisa May. *Hidden Louisa May Alcott.* 1984. Avenel. VG/VG. P3. $15.00

ALCOTT, Louisa May. *Jo's Boys.* 1886. Boston. 1st ed. gilt brn cloth. VG. M5. $48.00

ALCOTT, Louisa May. *Jo's Boys.* 1925. Little Brn. 1st ed thus. 8vo. ils Clara Burd. F. M5. $42.00

ALCOTT, Louisa May. *Little Men.* nd. Chicago. 357p. F/G. A17. $5.00

ALCOTT, Louisa May. *Little Men.* 1871. Boston. 1st Am ed/1st issue. VG. C6. $250.00

ALCOTT, Louisa May. *Little Men.* 1932. Little Brn. 8vo. VG. B17. $10.00

ALCOTT, Louisa May. *Little Women, Part 1.* 1879 (1868). Roberts. 12mo. gilt gr cloth. VG. M5. $55.00

ALCOTT, Louisa May. *Little Women.* 1912 (1868). Little Brn. 12mo. brn cloth. VG. M5. $25.00

ALCOTT, Louisa May. *Little Women.* 1922. Little Brn. early rpt. ils JW Smith. G. B17. $12.50

ALCOTT, Louisa May. *Little Women.* 1922 (1915). Little Brn. ils JW Smith. 397p. VG. P2. $60.00

ALCOTT, Louisa May. *Little Women.* 1932. Garden City. ils Stein. VG. M5. $25.00

ALCOTT, Louisa May. *Little Women.* 1932. Garden City. 8vo. F/G. M5. $45.00

ALCOTT, Louisa May. *Little Women.* 1947. Grosset Dunlap. ils Louis Jambor. 546p. cloth. VG/dj. T5. $15.00

ALCOTT, Louisa May. *Louisa May Alcott: Her Life, Letters & Journals.* 1889. Roberts Bros. 1st ed. 404p. VG. P2. $100.00

ALCOTT, Louisa May. *Louisa's Wonder Book.* 1975. Central MI U. 8vo. F. B17. $10.00

ALCOTT, Louisa May. *Old-Fashioned Girl.* 1950. Little Brn. late rpt. VG/VG. B17. $6.50

ALCOTT, Louisa May. *Shawl Straps...Aunt Jo's Scrap Bag.* 1873 (1872). Roberts. 12mo. gilt royal bl cloth. VG. M5. $60.00

ALCOTT, Louisa May. *Under the Lilacs.* 1928. Little Brn. 1st ed. ils Marguerite Davis. F. M5. $38.00

ALDANOV, Mark. *For Thee the Best.* 1945. Scribner. 1st ed. VG/G. P3. $15.00

ALDELMAN. *Moving Pageant: A Selection of Essays.* 1977. np. 1/650. inscr. VG. A4. $85.00

ALDERMAN & KENNEDY. *Right to Privacy.* 1995. NY. Knopf. 1st ed. sgn. inscr Caroline Kennedy. dj. B14. $55.00

ALDERMAN & SMITH. *Library of Southern Literature.* 1923. Martin Hoyt. 642p. VG. B10. $35.00

ALDERSON, E.A.H. *Pink & Scarlet; or, Hunting As a School for Soldiering.* 1913. Hodder Stoughton. 4to. O3. $85.00

ALDERSON, W.J.S. *Hints on Sailing Service Boats.* 1907. Portsmouth. G. A16. $20.00

ALDIN, Cecil. *Bunnyborough.* 1946. Eyre Spottiswode. 1st ed. 14 pl. VG+/G+. P2. $125.00

ALDIN, Cecil. *Cecil Aldin Book.* 1932. London. ils. VG. M17. $75.00

ALDIN, Cecil. *Ratcatcher to Scarlet.* 1932. London. Eyre Spottiswoode. binding copy. O3. $20.00

ALDIN, Cecil. *Romance of the Road.* 1928. London. Eyre Spottiswoode. 1/200. sgn. VG+. O3. $695.00

ALDIN, Cecil. *Romance of the Road.* 1928. London. Eyre Spottswode. 1st ed. folio. 10 mtd pl/fld map. VG. B14. $125.00

ALDIN, Cecil. *Time I Was Dead.* 1934. Scribner. 1st Am ed. VG. O3. $125.00

ALDING, Peter. *Man Condemned.* 1981. Walker. 1st ed. VG/VG. P3. $15.00

ALDIS, Dorothy. *Magic City, John & Jane at the World's Fair.* 1933. Minton Balch. 8vo. VG. B17. $7.50

ALDISS, Brian W. *Billion Year Spree.* 1973. Doubleday. 1st ed. F/F. P3. $40.00

ALDISS, Brian W. *Canopy of Time.* 1961. British SF BC. VG/torn. p3. $10.00

ALDISS, Brian W. *Dracula Unbound.* 1991. Harper Collins. 1st ed. F/F. P3. $19.00

ALDISS, Brian W. *Earthworks.* 1966. Doubleday. 1st ed. VG/VG. P3. $35.00

ALDISS, Brian W. *Helliconia Spring.* 1982. Jonathan Cape. 2nd. F/F. P3. $15.00

ALDISS, Brian W. *Helliconia Winter.* 1985. Jonathan Cape. 1st ed. F/F. P3. $30.00

ALDISS, Brian W. *Last Orders.* 1977. Jonathan Cape. 1st ed. F/F. P3. $28.00

ALDISS, Brian W. *Life in the West.* 1990. Caroll Graf. 1st ed. VG/G. P3. $15.00

ALDISS, Brian W. *New Arrivals, Old Encounters.* 1979. Jonathan Cape. 1st ed. F/F. P3. $25.00

ALDISS, Brian W. *Remembrance Day.* 1993. St Martin. 1st Am ed. F/NF. G10. $20.00

ALDISS, Brian W. *Report on Probability.* 1969. Doubleday. 1st ed. VG/VG. P3. $25.00

ALDISS, Brian W. *Rude Awakening.* 1978. Random. 1st ed. VG/VG. P3. $25.00

ALDISS, Brian W. *Rude Awakening.* 1978. Weidenfeld Nicolson. 1st ed. VG/VG. P3. $25.00

ALDISS, Brian W. *Ruins.* 1987. Hutchinson. 1st ed. F/F. P3. $15.00

ALDISS, Brian W. *Seasons in Flight.* 1984. Jonathan Cape. 1st ed. F/F. P3. $20.00

ALDISS, Brian W. *Soldier Erect.* 1971. CMG. 1st ed. VG/VG. P3. $35.00

ALDISS, Brian W. *Soldier Erect.* 1971. Weidenfeld Nicolson. 1st ed. VG/VG. P3. $35.00

ALDISS, Brian W. *Year Before Yesterday.* 1987. Watts. 1st ed. F/F. P3. $17.00

ALDISS & HARRISON. *Decade in the 1950s.* 1978. St Martin. 1st ed. NF/NF. P3. $20.00

ALDRED, Cyril. *Egyptians.* 1984. London. Thames Hudson. revised ed. 8vo. ils. 268p. VG. W1. $18.00

ALDRICH, Ann; see Meaker, Marijane.

ALDRICH, T.B. *Stillwater Tragedy.* 1880. Houghton Mifflin. 1st ed. 324p. gilt bdg. VG. M20. $32.00

ALDRICH & SNYDER. *Florida Seashells.* 1936. Houghton Mifflin. 12mo. sgn Snyder. 11 pl. 126p. G. B11. $15.00

ALDRIDGE, Janet. *Meadow-Brook Girls on the Tennis Courts.* 1914. Altemus. 1st ed. 256p. VG+/ragged. M20. $25.00

ALDRIDGE, Richard. *Maine Lines.* 1970. Phil. 1st ed. 224p. F. A17. $10.00

ALDYNE, Nathan. *Cobalt.* 1982. St Martin. VG/VG. P3. $12.00

ALESHKOVSKY, Yuz. *Kangaroo.* 1986. FSG. 1st ed. author's 1st book in Eng. F. B35. $30.00

ALEXANDER, Archibald. *Biographical Sketches of the Founder & Principal Alumni...* 1851. Presbyterian Brd Pub. 279p. cloth. VG. M20. $32.00

ALEXANDER, David. *Most Men Don't Kill.* 1951. Random. 1st ed. VG/G. P3. $15.00

ALEXANDER, David. *Pennies From Hell.* 1960. Lippincott. 1st ed. VG/VG. P3. $25.00

ALEXANDER, Shana. *Nutcracker.* 1985. Doubleday. 1st ed. F/NF. H11. $20.00

ALEXANDER & JAY. *Federalist: Collection of Essays, Written in Favour...* 1983. Birmingham. Legal Classics Lib. facsimile. modern leather. M11. $75.00

ALEXANDER & O'DEA. *Bibliography of Newfoundland.* 1986. Toronto. 2 vol. 1450. F. A4. $165.00

ALEXANDER & SELESNICK. *History of Psychiatry: An Evaluation...* 1966. NY. 1st ed. 471p. A13. $30.00

ALEXANDER. *Guide to Atlases: World, Regional, National, Thematic.* 1971. np. 671p. xl. VG. A4. $45.00

ALEXIE, Sherman. *Lone Ranger & Tonto Fistfight in Heaven.* 1993. Atlantic Monthly. 1st ed. F/F. M23. $45.00

ALEXIE, Sherman. *Reservation Blues.* 1995. Atlantic Monthly. 1st ed. F/F. M23. $35.00

ALGER, Edwin. *Jacob Marlowe's Secret.* nd. AL Burt. decor brd. G. P3. $7.00

ALGER, Horatio. *Bertha's Christmas Vision. An Autumn Sheaf.* 1856. Boston. Brn Bazin. 1st ed. author's 1st book. red cloth. VG+. B24. $850.00

ALGER, Horatio. *Bound To Rise.* nd. Cleveland. 150p. VG/dj. A17. $5.00

ALGER, Horatio. *Grandfather Baldwin's Thanksgiving With Other Ballads...* 1875. Boston. Loring. 1st ed. inscr/dtd 1875. 125p. NF. B24. $2,250.00

ALGREN, Nelson. *Chicago: City on the Make.* 1951. Garden City. 1st ed. inscr w/drawing of cat. F/NF. C2. $100.00

ALGREN, Nelson. *Galena Guide.* 1937. np. ils/23 photos. 79p. pict wrp. A4. $185.00

ALGREN, Nelson. *Man With the Golden Arm.* 1949. Doubleday. ltd ed. w/sgn leaf. F/NF. B2. $200.00

ALI, Tariq. *New Revolutionaries: Handbook of International Radical Left.* 1969. NY. Morrow. 1st ed. F/F. B4. $85.00

ALIBERT & BALOUET. *Extinct Species of the World.* 1990. NY. Barron. 192p. AN/dj. D8. $30.00

ALLAIN, Maurice. *Atlas Universel Quillet, Physique...* 1933. Paris. Aristide Quillet. 42 hinged maps. blind-tooled bdg. F/pub box. O7. $225.00

ALLAN, John B.; see Westlake, Donald E.

ALLAN, Mae. *Darwin & His Flowers.* 1977. NY. ils. VG+/dj. B26. $39.00

ALLAN, Mae. *Hookers of Kew, 1785-1911.* 1967. London. ils. 273p. VG/dj. B26. $80.00

ALLAN, Mae. *Plants That Changed Our Gardens.* 1974. Devon. Newton Abbot. ils. 208p. F/dj. B26. $29.00

ALLARD, Harry. *Tutti-Frutti Case: Starring the Four Doctors of Goodge.* 1975. Prentice Hall. 1st ed. 8vo. unp. NF. C14. $8.00

ALLARDYCE, Paula. *Adam's Rib.* 1963. Hodder Stoughton. 1st ed. F/F. B35. $30.00

ALLBEURY, Ted. *Alpha List.* 1979. General. 1st ed. VG/VG. P3. $20.00

ALLBEURY, Ted. *Children of Tender Years.* 1985. Beaufort. 1st ed. NF/NF. P3. $15.00

ALLBEURY, Ted. *Crossing.* 1987. Kent. NEL. 1st ed. F/F. T2. $30.00

ALLBEURY, Ted. *Omega-Minus.* 1975. Viking. 1st Am ed. F/F. T2. $15.00

ALLBEURY, Ted. *Pay Any Price.* 1983. Grande. 1st ed. VG/VG. P3. $20.00

ALLBEURY, Ted. *Seeds of Treason.* 1986. Kent. NEL. 1st ed. F/F. T2. $30.00

ALLBEURY, Ted. *Snowball.* 1974. Lippincott. 1st ed. VG/G. P3. $20.00

ALLBEURY, Ted. *Wilderness of Mirrors.* 1988. Stoddart. 1st ed. F/F. P3. $20.00

ALLEGRETTO, Michael. *Suitor.* 1993. Simon Schuster. 1st ed. NF/NF. P3. $20.00

ALLEN, Betsy. *Clue in the Blue.* nd. Grosset Dunlap. VG/VG. P3. $10.00

ALLEN, C.D. *Classified List of Early American Bookplates.* 1894. Grollier. 1st ed. VG/wrp. B5. $90.00

ALLEN, Charles Warrenne. *Radiotherapy & Phototherapy...* 1904. Phil. 27 pl. 618p. red cloth. VG+. B14. $300.00

ALLEN, Dave. *Little Night Reading.* 1974. Schlesinger. 1st ed. F/F. P3. $20.00

ALLEN, David E. *Victorian Fern Craze.* 1969. London. ils/index/biblio. F. B26. $22.50

ALLEN, Edward. *Mustang Sally.* 1992. Norton. 1st ed. author's 2nd novel. AN/dj. M22. $15.00

ALLEN, Hervey. *Israfel: Life & Times of Edgar Allen Poe.* 1926. Doran. 2 vol. 1st ed. 8vo. gilt maroon cloth. F. T10. $75.00

ALLEN, Hugh. *Story of the Airship.* 1942. Akron. 1st ed. inscr. 74p. G/torn. B18. $37.50

ALLEN, James Lane. *Bride of the Mistletoe.* 1909. Macmillan. 1st ed. 109p. VG. B10. $20.00

ALLEN, James Lane. *Flute & Violin & Other Kentucky Tales.* 1910. Macmillan. 6th. 308p. VG. B10. $20.00

ALLEN, James Lane. *Kentucky Cardinal & Aftermath.* 1900. Macmillan. 1st ed thus. 276p. VG. B10/M5. $35.00

ALLEN, James Lane. *Reign of Law: Tale of the Kentucky Hemp Fields.* 1900. Macmillan. 1st ed/2nd state? ils Fenn/Earl. 385p. VG-. B10. $25.00

ALLEN, Jimmy. *Burden of a Secret.* 1995. Nashville. Moorings. 1st ed. sgn. F/F. M23. $35.00

ALLEN, L.J. *Trans Alaska Pipeline, the Beginning. Vol 1.* 1975. Seattle. Scribe. ils. 151p. NF/dj. D8. $30.00

ALLEN, Lee. *Cincinnati Reds.* 1948. Putnam. 1st ed. VG+. P8. $75.00

ALLEN, Leslie. *Liberty: The Stature & the American Dream.* (1985). Ellis Island Foundation. deluxe ed. 304p. padded brn brd. F. B22. $7.00

ALLEN, Mark. *Falconry in Arabia.* 1984. Orbis. tall 8vo. ils/map. VG. W1. $20.00

ALLEN, Maury. *Roger Maris: Man for All Seasons.* 1986. Donald Fine. 1st ed. photos. F/F. P8. $30.00

ALLEN, Paul H. *Rain Forests of Golfo Dulce.* 1986 (1956). Stanford. 2nd. 417p. M. B26. $55.00

ALLEN, Raymond. *Medical Education & the Changing Order.* 1946. NY. 1st ed. 142p. VG/dj. A13. $20.00

ALLEN, Steve. *Funny Men.* 1956. NY. 1st ed. pres. VG/VG. B5. $30.00

ALLEN, Steve. *Murder in Manhattan.* 1990. Zebra. 1st ed. F/F. P3. $19.00

ALLEN, Tim. *Don't Stand Too Close to a Naked Man.* 1994. Hyperion. 1st ed. F/F. H11. $25.00

ALLEN, Warner. *Uncounted Hour.* 1936. Constable. 1st ed. VG. P3. $30.00

ALLEN, William Sheridan. *Nazi Seizure of Power: Experience of a Single German Town...* 1965. Chicago. 345p. G. A17. $9.50

ALLEN, Woody. *Getting Even.* 1971. Random. 1st ed. NF/F. M23. $45.00

ALLEN, Woody. *Play It Again, Sam.* 1969. Random. 1st ed. VG/G. P3. $30.00

ALLEN. *NC Wyeth: Collected Paintings, Illustrations & Murals.* 1972. Bonanza. 4to. 335p. NF/VG. A4. $85.00

ALLEN. *Tennesseana: A Value Guide to Scarce & Rare Books...* 1979. 1/125. sgn/#d. 200p. VG. A4. $265.00

ALLENDE, Isabel. *Eva Luna.* 1988. Knopf. 1st ed. author's 3rd book. F/F. H11. $40.00

ALLENDE, Isabel. *House of the Spirits.* 1985. Knopf. 1st ed. author's 1st book. NF/F. H11. $110.00

ALLENDE, Isabel. *Of Love & Shadows.* 1987. Knopf. 1st ed. F/F. M23. $30.00

ALLENDE, Isabel. *Stories of Eva Luna.* 1991. Athen. 1st ed. F/dj. H11. $30.00

ALLER, Lawrence H. *Astrophysics: Atmospheres of the Sun & Stars.* 1953. NY. Ronald Pr. 8vo. 412p. cloth. G. K5. $30.00

ALLINGHAM, Cedric. *Flying Saucers From Mars.* 1955. British BC. VG/fair. P3. $20.00

ALLINGHAM, Margery. *Cargo of Eagles.* 1968. Morrow. 1st ed. VG/VG. P3. $22.00

ALLINGHAM, Margery. *China Governess.* 1962. Doubleday. 1st ed. VG/G. P3. $30.00

ALLINGHAM, Margery. *Estate of the Beckoning Lady.* 1955. Doubleday. 1st ed. VG/VG. P3. $40.00

ALLINGHAM, Margery. *Gyrth Chalice Mystery.* 1931. Crime Club. 1st ed. VG. P3. $40.00

ALLISON, Annye Lewis. *Dogwood & Iris.* nd. np. sgn. VG. w/sgn Christmas card. B10. $12.00

ALLISON, Annye Lewis. *Foot-Path Way.* 1927. Whittet Sheperson. inscr. 74p. G. b10. $10.00

ALLISON, Clyde; see Knowles, William.

ALLISON, Dorothy. *Bastard Out of Carolina.* 1992. Dutton. 1st ed. F/F. A11. $100.00

ALLISON, Sam. *Wells Fargo & Danger Station.* 1958. Whitman. TVTI. NF. P3. $20.00

ALLISON, William. *Memories of Men & Horses.* 1924. NY. Brentano. 1st Am ed. xl. VG. O3. $35.00

ALLIX, Susan. *Pyramids, an Account by Herodotus.* 1995. London. Allix. 1/12. sgn. M/clasped box. B24. $750.00

ALLMENDINGER, Blake. *Cowboy: Representations of Labor in American Work Culture.* 1992. Oxford. 1st ed. ils. M/dj. A18. $32.50

ALLMOND, Marcus Blakey. *Estelle: Idyll of Old Virginia.* 1899. Louisville. self pub. 56p. G. B10. $35.00

ALLPORT, Gordon W. *Individual & His Religion: A Psychological Interpretation.* 1950. Macmillan. 8vo. pres. bl-gray cloth. G1. $45.00

ALLSOP, F.C. *Practical Electric Fitting Up of Buildings...* ca 1875. London. 12mo. ils/pl. 275p. gilt bl cloth. F. H3. $125.00

ALLYN, Doug. *Cheerio Killings.* 1989. NY. 1st ed. author's 1st book. F/F. H11. $35.00

ALLYN, Doug. *Motown Underground.* 1993. NY. 1st ed. NF/NF. H11. $20.00

ALMOND, Linda Stevens. *Peter Rabbit & Little White Rabbit.* 1935. Platt Munk. 16mo. VG. M5. $20.00

ALOU, Felipe. *My Life & Baseball.* 1967. World. 1st ed. sgn. VG+/VG+. P8. $65.00

ALSON, Lawrence. *Leave It to Beaver.* 1959. Little Golden Book. TVTI. G. P3. $12.00

ALSOP, Gulielma F. *April in the Branches.* 1947. Dutton. 1st ed. sgn. 8vo. 257p. VG/VG. B11. $15.00

ALTER, Dinsmore. *Lunar Atlas.* 1968. Dover. rpt. 4to. 174p. G. K5. $45.00

ALTER, Robert Edmond. *Shovel Nose & the Gator Grabbers.* 1963. Putnam. VG/VG. P3. $35.00

ALTERTON & CRAIG. *Edgar Allan Poe.* 1935. Am Book Co. 12mo. 563p. G. A17. $9.50

ALTIERS, J. *Spearheaders.* 1960. Indianapolis. 1st ed. ils. 318p. VG/VG. B5. $45.00

ALTMAN & MELBY. *Handbook of Laboratory Animal Science. Vol 1.* 1977. Cleveland. 2nd. 451p. 8vo. hc. F. B1. $40.00

ALTSHELER, Joseph A. *Horsemen of the Plains.* 1910. Grosset Dunlap. Thrushwood reissue. 390p. orange cloth VG/VG. T5. $22.00

ALVAREZ, Julia. *In the Time of Butterflies.* 1994. Algonquin. ARC. pres set of fld/gathered sheets. sgn. F/wrp. S9. $40.00

ALVERSON, Charles. *Fighting Back.* 1973. Bobbs Merrill. 1st ed. VG/VG. P3. $20.00

ALVERSON, Charles. *Not Sleeping, Just Dead.* 1977. Houghton Mifflin. F/F. P3. $13.00

AMADO, Jorge. *Gabriela. Clove & Cinnamon.* 1962. Knopf. 4th. 426p. dj. F3. $10.00

AMALGIA, Roberto. *Monvmenta Cartographica Vaticana...Volumen I...* 1944. Citta del Vaticano. lg folio. 56 maps. Samuel Eliot Morison's copy. M. O7. $475.00

AMBEKDAR, B.R. *What Congress & Gandhi Have Done to the Untouchables.* 1945. Bombay. 1st ed. 360p. cloth. VG. A17. $15.00

AMBLER, Charles. *Reports of Cases Argued & Determined in High Court...* 1790. London. Whicldon. 1st/only ed. folio. modern 3-quarter sheep. M11. $350.00

AMBLER, Eric. *Care of Time.* 1981. FSG. 1st ed. VG/VG. M22/P3. $15.00

AMBLER, Eric. *Cause for Alarm.* 1940. Knopf. 1st ed. VG/G. P3. $15.00

AMBLER, Eric. *Dark Frontier.* 1990. Mysterious. 1st ed. F/F. P3. $19.00

AMBLER, Eric. *Dirty Story.* 1967. Bodley Head. 1st ed. VG/G. P3. $20.00

AMBLER, Eric. *Doctor Frigo.* 1974. Atheneum. 1st ed. VG/VG. P3. $20.00

AMBLER, Eric. *Eric Ambler.* 1978. Heinemann/Octopus. F/F. P3. $15.00

AMBLER, Eric. *Intercom Conspiracy.* 1969. Atheneum. 1st ed. VG/VG. P3. $25.00

AMBLER, Eric. *Intrigue.* 1960. Knopf. VG/VG. P3. $20.00

AMBLER, Eric. *Kind of Anger.* 1964. Bodley Head. 1st ed. VG/G. P3. $30.00

AMBLER, Eric. *Passage of Arms.* 1960. Reprint Soc. VG/VG. P3. $8.00

AMBLER, Gifford. *Maxims of Marquis.* 1937. Eyre Spottiswood. 1st ed. ils. 111p. VG/VG. P2. $45.00

AMBROSE, Stephen E. *Eisenhower.* 1990. Simon Schuster. 1st ed. sgn. F/F. M23. $35.00

AMBROSE, Stephen E. *Undaunted Courage.* 1996. Simon Schuster. 1st ed. F/F. M23. $40.00

AMBROSIUS, Ernst. *Andrees Allgemeiner Hand Atlas.* 1914. Velhagen Klasing. lg folio. 24 maps. gr bdg. xl. F. O7. $350.00

AMERICAN STEAMSHIP COMPANY. *How To Make a Steamship Float.* 1985. MI. Harbor House. AN. A16. $10.95

AMES, Clyde; see Knowles, William.

AMES, Delano. *Body on Page One.* 1951. Hodder Stoughton. 1st ed. VG. P3. $20.00

AMES, Delano. *Murder, Maestro, Please.* 1952. Hodder Stoughton. VG. P3. $15.00

AMES, Fisher. *Practical Guide to Whist.* 1895. NY. 7th. 118p. VG. S1. $10.00

AMES, Jennifer. *Flight Into Fear.* 1954. Collins. 1st ed. VG/VG. P3. $20.00

AMHERST, Alicia. *History of Gardening in England.* 1969 (1896). Detroit. 2nd. ils. 405p. yel cloth. F. B26. $55.00

AMIRSADEGI, Hossein. *Twentieth-Century Iran.* 1977. NY. Holmes Meier. 1st ed. 8 pl/2 maps/tables. VG/torn. W1. $32.00

AMIS, Kingsley. *Alteration.* 1977. Viking. 1st ed. G/G. P3. $25.00

AMIS, Kingsley. *Colonel Sun.* England. 1st ed. VG/VG. M17. $22.50

AMIS, Kingsley. *Difficulties With Girls.* 1988. Summit. 1st ed. F/F. H11. $25.00

AMIS, Kingsley. *Egyptologists.* 1966. Random. 1st ed. VG/G. P3. $23.00

AMIS, Kingsley. *Girl, 20.* 1971. Jonathan Cape. 1st ed. VG/VG. P3. $20.00

AMIS, Kingsley. *Girl, 20.* 1972. HBJ. 1st ed. VG/G. P3. $15.00

AMIS, Kingsley. *I Want It Now.* 1968. Jonathan Cape. 1st ed. VG/VG. P3. $23.00

AMIS, Kingsley. *Jake's Thing.* 1978. Hutchinson. 1st ed. F/F. P3. $18.00

AMIS, Kingsley. *James Bond Dossier.* nd. NAL. 5th. VG/VG. P3. $22.00

AMIS, Kingsley. *James Bond Dossier.* 1965. London. Cape. 1st ed. VG/VG. M19. $50.00

AMIS, Kingsley. *Memoirs.* 1991. Hutchinson. 1st ed. F/F. P3. $30.00

AMIS, Kingsley. *One Fat Englishman.* 1963. Gollancz. 1st ed. VG/VG. P3. $30.00

AMIS, Kingsley. *Russian Hide & Seek.* 1980. Hutchinson. 1st ed. VG/VG. P3. $20.00

AMIS, Kingsley. *Stanley & the Women.* 1984. Hutchinson. 1st ed. NF/NF. P3. $22.00

AMIS, Kingsley. *What Became of Jane Austen?* 1970. HBJ. 1st Am ed. F/NF. B4. $85.00

AMIS, Martin. *Dead Babies.* 1975. Knopf. 1st ed. NF/NF. P3. $75.00

AMIS, Martin. *London Fields.* 1989. London. 1st ed. sgn. F/F. A11. $70.00

AMIS, Martin. *London Fields.* 1990. Harmony. AP. 8vo. NF/prt wrp. S9. $35.00

AMIS, Martin. *Other People: A Mystery Story.* 1981. Viking. 1st Am ed. F/F. B2. $60.00

AMIS, Martin. *Rachel Papers.* 1974. Knopf. 1st ed. NF/NF. P3. $80.00

AMIS, Martin. *Time's Arrow.* 1991. Canada. Viking. 1st ed. F/F. P3. $23.00

AMIS, Martin. *Time's Arrow.* 1991. London. 1st ed. sgn. F/F. A11. $55.00

AMIS, Martin. *Visiting Mr Nabokov & Other Excursions.* 1994. Harmony. 1st ed. F/F. B35. $20.00

AMMONS, A.R. *Six-Piece Suit.* 1978. Palaemon. 1/200. 6p. F/stiff wrp. B10. $35.00

AMORY, Cleveland. *Last Resorts.* 1952. Harper. 1st ed. sgn. 527p. VG/VG. B11. $30.00

AMOS, Alan. *Borderline Murder.* 1947. Crime Club. 1st ed. VG. P3. $12.00

AMOS, William. *Originals: An A-Z of Fiction's Real-Life Characters...* 1985. np. 40 photos. 634p. NF/NF. A4. $65.00

AMSBURY, Joe. *Bridge: Bidding Naturally.* 1979. London. 152p. VG. S1. $10.00

AMSBURY & PAYNE. *Bridge: TNT & Competitive Bidding.* 1981. London. 175p. VG/wrp. S1. $10.00

AMSDEN, Charles Avery. *Prehistoric Southwesterners From Basketmaker to Pueblo.* 1949. Los Angeles. Southwest Mus. 1st ed. ils/maps. 163p. F. T10. $75.00

AMUNATEGUI SOLAR, Domingo. *Historia de Chile.* 1925. Santiago. 4to. 259p. rebound Lib Congress bdg. F3. $15.00

AMUNDSEN, Bjorstad. *Kirkenesperda.* 1946 (1942). Oslo. fld chart/photos/maps. 464p. dj. A17. $35.00

AMUNDSEN & ELLSWORTH. *First Crossing of the Polar Sea.* 1928. Doubleday Doran. ils/fld map. 324p. VG. T7. $65.00

AN OBSERVOR. *Archangel American War With Russia.* 1924. Chicago. 1st ed. ils. 216p. VG. B5. $75.00

AN PHILIBIN; see Pollock, John Hackett.

ANANOFF, Alexnadre. *L'Oeuvre Dessine de Jean-Honore Fragonard.* 1961-71. Paris. F deNobele. 4 vol. 1/650. xl. D2. $1,850.00

ANATI, Emmanuel. *Camonica Valley.* 1961. Knopf. 1st Am ed. 8vo. ils. 262p. VG/dj. W1. $20.00

ANATI, Emmanuel. *Palestine Before the Hebrews.* 1963. Knopf. 1st ed. 8vo. 5 full-p maps. 453p. NF/dj. W1. $22.00

ANATOLE, Ray; see Weiss, Joe.

ANBUREY, Thomas. *Travels Through the Interior Parts of America.* 1923. Houghton Mifflin. 2 vol. 1/445. 1st Am ed. 8vo. T10. $225.00

AND, Metin. *Osmanli Senliklerinde Turk Sanatlari.* 1982. Ankara. Kultur ve Turism Bakanligi. 1st ed. VG/stiff wrp. W1. $45.00

ANDERSEN, Hans Christian. *Andersen's Fairy Tales.* 1932. McKay. 1st Am ed. ils Rackham. G+. B17. $80.00

ANDERSEN, Hans Christian. *Ausgewahlte Marchen Gerlach & Wiedling.* ca 1906. Wien Leipzig. ils H Steiner-Prag. VG. D1. $100.00

ANDERSEN, Hans Christian. *Die Kleine Seejungrau.* 1953. Elberfeld. Sulamith Wulfing Pub. ils Sulamith Wulfin. VG/wrp/dj. D1. $125.00

ANDERSEN, Hans Christian. *Emperor's New Clothes.* 1992. Atlantic Monthly. ils Karl Lagerfield. F/F case. P2. $45.00

ANDERSEN, Hans Christian. *Eventyr og Historier. Med Illustrationer af V Pederson.* 1862 & 1863. Copenhagen. CA Reitzels. 2 vol. 8vo. gilt bl cloth. F. B24. $1,500.00

ANDERSEN, Hans Christian. *Fairy Tales.* ca 1920s. Nelson. ils Honor Appleton. gilt bl cloth. VG. M5. $225.00

ANDERSEN, Hans Christian. *Fairy Tales.* 1924. Doran. 1st Am ed. ils Kay Nielsen. 280p. VG. D1. $650.00

ANDERSEN, Hans Christian. *Hans Andersen's Fairy Tales.* ca 1900. Nister Dutton. VG. M5. $60.00

ANDERSEN, Hans Christian. *Hans Andersen's Fairy Tales.* nd. Altemus. thick 8vo. ils A Duncan Carse. VG. M5. $60.00

ANDERSEN, Hans Christian. *Hans Andersen's Fairy Tales.* 1913. Eng. Boots the Chemists. ils WH Robinson. 320p. VG. D1. $250.00

ANDERSEN, Hans Christian. *Hans Christian Andersen's Fairy Tales.* nd. London. 1st ed. ils Jiri Trnka. F/torn. M5. $40.00

ANDERSEN, Hans Christian. *Little Fir Tree.* 1970. Harper Row. 1st ed. ils Nancy Burkert. 36p. F/NF. P2. $35.00

ANDERSEN, Hans Christian. *Little Mermaid.* 1939. Macmillan. 1st ed thus. ils Dorothy Lathrop. VG/torn. D1. $295.00

ANDERSEN, Hans Christian. *Nightingale.* 1984. Picture Book Studio. probable 1st ed. ils/sgn Zwerger. unp. glossy brd. F/F. T5. $55.00

ANDERSEN, Hans Christian. *Old Man Is Always Right.* 1940. Harper. stated 1st ed. ils Rojankovsky. VG. M5. $48.00

ANDERSEN, Hans Christian. *Snow Queen & Other Stories.* 1961. Golden. 1st Am ed. ils Andrienne Segur. 136p. NF. P2. $165.00

ANDERSEN, Hans Christian. *Snow Queen.* 1929. Dutton. ils Katherine Beverly/Elizabeth Ellender. VG. P2. $100.00

ANDERSEN, Hans Christian. *Snow Queen.* 1982. Dial. 1st ed. ils Susan Jeffes. gray cloth. F/VG. D1. $45.00

ANDERSEN, Hans Christian. *Stories From Hans Andersen.* nd. Nister. trans W Angeldorff. ils ES Hardy. aeg. cloth. VG. M5. $40.00

ANDERSEN, Hans Christian. *Wild Swan.* 1981. Dial. 1st ed. ils Susan Jeffers. F/VG. D1. $45.00

ANDERSEN, Johannes C. *Myths & Legends of the Polynesians.* 1986. Rutland. VG. O7. $25.00

ANDERSEN & WEI. *Action for the Defense: When the Enemy Opens the Bidding.* 1980. NY. 245p. VG/wrp. S1. $6.00

ANDERSEN & WEI. *Bidding Precisely: Volume 2.* 1976. NY. 159p. VG/wrp. S1. $5.00

ANDERSEN & WEI. *Profits From Preempts: Bidding Precisely Volume 3.* 1977. NY. 162p. VG/wrp. S1. $5.00

ANDERSON, Anne. *Bitter Green of the Willow.* 1967. Chilton. 1st ed. ils/6 pl. VG/worn. M5. $40.00

ANDERSON, Anne. *Nursery Zoo.* nd. Nelson. 48 pl. VG+. M5. $125.00

ANDERSON, Anne. *Old Old Fairy Tales.* nd. Nelson. 12 pl. 159p. G+. P2. $125.00

ANDERSON, Anne. *Tiny Tot's First Book of All.* ca 1920s. Nelson. 8vo. ils Anderson/Wright/Rees/Reid. fair. M5. $30.00

ANDERSON, Bernice. *Topsy Turvey's Pigtails.* 1937 (1930). Rand McNally. ils Bernice Friend. VG. P2. $75.00

ANDERSON, C.W. *Black, Bay & Chestnut.* 1939. NY. Macmillan. 2nd. obl 4to. VG/dj. T10. $25.00

ANDERSON, C.W. *Filly for Joan.* 1960. Macmillan. 1st ed. VG. O3. $25.00

ANDERSON, C.W. *Horse for Hurricane Hill.* 1957. Macmillan. 2nd. VG/VG. O3. $35.00

ANDERSON, C.W. *Horses Are Folks.* 1950. Harper Row. 15 full-p lithographs. G+. P2. $20.00

ANDERSON, C.W. *Horses Are Folks.* 1950. NY. Harper Row. sm 4to. ils Anderson. tweed pict brd/cloth spine. NF/VG. C8. $65.00

ANDERSON, C.W. *Lonesome Little Colt.* 1963. Macmillan. 4th. G+. O3. $25.00

ANDERSON, C.W. *Phantom, Son of the Gray Ghost.* 1969. Macmillan. 3rd. VG. O3. $15.00

ANDERSON, C.W. *Tomorrow's Champion.* 1946. Macmillan. ils. cloth. VG+. M5. $18.00

ANDERSON, C.W. *Tomorrow's Champion.* 1946. Macmillan. 1st ed. VG/G. P2. $32.00

ANDERSON, C.W. *Touch of Greatness.* 1945. NY. Macmillan. probable 1st ed. sm 4to. ils. pict cloth. F/VG. C8. $85.00

ANDERSON, Charles Carter. *Fighting by Southern Federals.* 1912. NY. Neale. 1st ed. 408p. cloth. G+. M8. $85.00

ANDERSON, D. *Art of Written Forms. Theory & Practice of Calligraphy.* 1969. NY. 1st ed. ils/index. 358p. VG/VG. B5. $45.00

ANDERSON, Frank. *Birds of My Mind.* 1971. Spartenberg. Kitemaug. unp. VG/VG. B10. $15.00

ANDERSON, Frank. *Illustrated Treasury of Cultivated Flowers.* 1979. NY. Crown. folio. 50 full-p pl. AN/dj. A10. $45.00

ANDERSON, J.W. *Ship-Masters Business Companion.* 1911. James Brn. G. A16. $60.00

ANDERSON, James Douglas. *Making the American Thoroughbred.* 1946. Nashville. Grainger Williams. 2nd. VG. O3. $68.00

ANDERSON, James. *Assault & Matrimony.* 1980. Muller. 1st ed. NF/NF. P3. $20.00

ANDERSON, Janice. *Marilyn Monroe.* 1983. Royce. VG/VG. P3. $25.00

ANDERSON, Jervis. *This Was Harlem.* 1982. NY. 1st ed. ils/photos/index. 390p. VG/VG. B5. $25.00

ANDERSON, John L. *Fifteenth-Century Cookry Boke.* 1962. Scribner. ils Adrienne Adams. VG/G. B17. $17.50

ANDERSON, John P. *Book of British Topography.* 1966. Amsterdam. TOT. rpt of 1881 London ed. AN. T7. $55.00

ANDERSON, John Quincy. *Campaigning With Parsons' Texas Cavalry Brigade...* 1967. Hill Jr College. 1st ed. 173p. F/NF. M8. $95.00

ANDERSON, Kenneth. *Black Panther of Sivanipalli.* 1960. Rand McNally. ils/photos. G. P12. $10.00

ANDERSON, Luther A. *How To Hunt a Whitetail Deer.* 1968. Funk Wagnall. photos. VG/G+. P12. $8.00

ANDERSON, Mabel Washbourne. *Life of General Stand Waite.* 1915. Pryor, OK. 1st ed. 58p. ES. VG/prt wrp. M8. $175.00

ANDERSON, Maxwell. *Storm Operation.* 1944. Anderson House. 1st ed. F/F. B4. $125.00

ANDERSON, Oma Carlyle. *I Hear the Lark Singing.* 1982. Brandon, FL. 1st ed. sgn. 90p. F/VG. B11. $10.00

ANDERSON, Per-Olow. *They Are Human Too...* 1957. Chicago. Regnery. ils. 191p. VG/tattered. W1. $28.00

ANDERSON, Poul. *Armis of Elfland.* 1994. Severn House. 1st hc ed. F/F. G10. $25.00

ANDERSON, Poul. *Avatar.* 1978. Berkley Putnam. 1st ed. F/F. P3. $20.00

ANDERSON, Poul. *Boat of a Million Years.* 1989. Tor. 1st ed. sgn. F/F. P3. $25.00

ANDERSON, Poul. *Harvest of Stars.* 1993. Tor. 1st ed. F/F. P3. $23.00

ANDERSON, Poul. *Infinite Voyage.* 1969. Crowell Collier. 1st ed. VG/VG. P3. $25.00

ANDERSON, Poul. *Kinship With the Stars.* 1993. Severn House. 1st Eng/1st hc ed. F/F. G10. $25.00

ANDERSON, Poul. *Let the Spacemen Beware!* 1969. London. Dennis Dobson. 1st hc ed. sgn. F/clip. T2. $35.00

ANDERSON, Poul. *Orion Shall Rise.* 1983. Phantasia. 1/600. sgn/#d. F/box. P3. $45.00

ANDERSON, Poul. *Orion Shall Rise.* 1983. Timescape. 1st ed. F/F. P3. $17.00

ANDERSON, Poul. *Shield of Time.* 1990. Tor. 1st ed. AN/dj. M21. $15.00

ANDERSON, Poul. *Three Worlds To Conquer.* 1982. Sidgwick Jackson. F/F. P3. $22.00

ANDERSON, Poul. *Vault of the Ages.* 1967. HRW. 4th. VG/VG. P3. $30.00

ANDERSON, Robert E. *Story of Extinct Civilizations of the East.* 1904. Appleton. ils/maps. 213p. teg. VG. W1. $12.00

ANDERSON, Robert. *All Summer Long.* 1955. Samuel French. 1st ed. F/NF. B4. $125.00

ANDERSON, Roy. *White Star.* 1964. Prescott, Eng. Stephenson. 58 photos. 236p. VG/dj. T7. $35.00

ANDERSON, Sherwood. *New Testament.* 1927. NY. 1st ed. 1/250. sgn. NF/case. C2. $150.00

ANDERSON, Sherwood. *Sherwood Anderson's Memoirs.* 1942. Harcourt Brace. 1st ed. 507p. cloth. VG/dj. M20. $62.00

ANDERSON, Sherwood. *Sherwood Anderson's Notebook.* 1926. NY. 1st ed. inscr. NF/VG. C6. $150.00

ANDERSON, Sherwood. *Tar, a Midwest Childhood.* 1926. Boni Liveright. 1st ed. 346p. VG/dj. M20. $77.00

ANDERSON, Sherwood. *Windy McPherson's Son.* 1916. John Lane. 1st ed. author's 1st book. later bdg. NF. C2. $75.00

ANDERSON, William D. *Light Gymnastics: A Guide to Systematic Instruction...* 1893. NY. ils. 234p. pict cloth. VG. B14. $45.00

ANDERSON & ANDERSON. *Sailing Ship: Six Thousand Years of History.* 1926-27. NY/London. 20 pl. 211p. VG. T7. $45.00

ANDERSON & EKLUND. *Inheritors of Earth.* 1974. Chilton. 1st ed. VG/VG. P3. $20.00

ANDERSON & HUNTER. *Jack Ruby's Girls.* 1970. Atlanta. 1st ed. VG/VG. B5. $60.00

ANDERSON & MAY. *McCarthy: The Man, the Senator, the 'Ism.'* 1952. Beacon. 1st ed. NF/worn. B2. $25.00

ANDERTON, Philip. *Bridge in 20 Lessons.* 1961. London. 127p. VG. S1. $6.00

ANDRE, John. *Andre's Journal: An Authentic Record of the Movements...* 1903. Boston. Bibliophile Soc. 2 vol. 1/487 on handmade. F. O7. $675.00

ANDREW, Christopher. *KGB: The Inside Story.* 1990. Hodder Stoughton. 1st ed. VG. P3. $35.00

ANDREW, Felicia; see Grant, Charles L.

ANDREW, T.G. *Twelve Wild Ducks: A Tale of the Norse.* 1859. Phil. 12mo. 31p. pebbled brn cloth. VG. H3. $175.00

ANDREWS, Allen. *Pig Plantagenet.* 1981. Viking. 1st ed. VG/G. P3. $15.00

ANDREWS, Arthur E. *Rags: Being an Explanation of Why They Are Used...* nd. Issued by 29 Rag Paper Mfgs. 4to. 30p w/samples. G. B14. $55.00

ANDREWS, Bart. *Story of I Love Lucy.* nd. BC. TVTI. VG/VG. P3. $8.00

ANDREWS, Bart. *TV Addict's Nostalgia, Trivia & Quiz.* 1984. Greenwich. TVTI. VG/VG. P3. $15.00

ANDREWS, Charles M. *Colonial Period of American History.* Yale. 3 vol. later prt. bl cloth. VG. B30. $85.00

ANDREWS, Jean. *Peppers: Domesticated Capsicums.* 1984. Austin. 1st ed. ils. 170p. NF/dj. B26. $37.50

ANDREWS, Luman. *Catalogue of Flowering Plants & Ferns of Springfield, MA...* 1924. Springfield. ils/photos. 221p. wrp. B26. $22.00

ANDREWS, Nigel. *Horror Films.* 1985. Gallery. VG/VG. P3. $20.00

ANDREWS, Raymond. *Appalachee Red.* 1978. Dial. 1st ed. F/NF. B2. $40.00

ANDREWS, T.S. *World Sporting Annual Record Book.* 1928. Milwaukee. 320p. G/stiff wrp. A17. $22.50

ANDREWS, V.C. *Fallen Hearts.* 1988. Poseidon. 1st ed. VG/VG. P3. $20.00

ANDREWS, V.C. *Flowers in the Attic.* 1979. Simon Schuster. 1st ed. VG/VG. P3. $25.00

ANDREWS, Wayne. *American Gothic: Its Origins, Its Trials, Its Triumphs.* 1975. Random. 1st ed. 4to. 154p. T10. $25.00

ANDREWS & KARLINS. *Gomorrah.* 1974. Doubleday. 1st ed. NF/NF. P3. $13.00

ANGAS, W. Mack. *Rivalry on the Atlantic.* 1939. Lee Furman. G. A16. $40.00

ANGEL, Marie. *Beasts in Heraldry.* 1974. Stephen Greene. 1st ed. ils Marie Angel. unp. VG+/box. D1. $85.00

ANGELL, James Rowland. *Intro to Psychology.* 1918. Holt. 282p. dk gray cloth. G1. $40.00

ANGELL, James Rowland. *Psychology: Introductory Study of Structure & Function...* 1904. Holt. 402p. ruled bl cloth. G1. $50.00

ANGELL, Roger. *Baseball.* 1984. Abrams. 1st ed. photos Walter Ioos. F/F. P8. $45.00

ANGELL, Roger. *Day in the Life of Roger Angell.* 1970. 1st ed. VG/VG. C4. $40.00

ANGELL, Roger. *Summer Game.* 1972. Viking. 1st ed. VG+/VG. P8. $50.00

ANGELO, Valenti. *Golden Gate.* 1939. Viking/Jr Literary Guild. 8vo. 273p. ils cloth. VG+. C14. $8.00

ANGELO, Valenti. *Nino.* 1938. NY. 1st ed. ils. 244p. NF/worn. A17. $10.00

ANGELO, Valenti. *Voiage & Travaile of Sir John Maundevile...* 1928. Random. 1/150. folio. morocco-backed oak brd. buckram case. B24. $2,000.00

ANGELOU, Maya. *All God's Children Need Traveling Shoes.* 1986. Random. 1st ed. F/NF. B4. $65.00

ANGELOU, Maya. *And Still I Rise.* 1978. Random. 1st ed. F/F. B35. $40.00

ANGELOU, Maya. *Collapsing Universe.* 1983. Harper Row. 1st ed. F/F. M19. $17.50

ANGELOU, Maya. *Gather Together in My Name.* 1974. Random. 1st ed. sgn. rem mk. F/F clip. B4. $175.00

ANGELOU, Maya. *I Shall Not Be Moved.* 1990. Random. ARC/1st ed. inscr. RS. F/F. B4. $125.00

ANGELOU, Maya. *I Shall Not Be Moved.* 1990. Random. ARC/1st ed. RS. F/F. w/promo material. B4. $45.00

ANGELOU, Maya. *I Shall Not Be Moved.* 1990. Random. 1st ed. F/F. M19. $17.50

ANGELOU, Maya. *Oh Pray My Wings Are Gonna Fit Me Well.* 1975. Random. 1st ed. NF/F. B35. $50.00

ANGELOU, Maya. *Wouldn't Take Nothing for My Journey Now.* 1993. Random. 1st ed. inscr. AN/dj. B4. $85.00

ANGLE, Paul M. *American Reader: From Columbus to Today.* 1958. Chicago. VG. O7. $35.00

ANGLE, Paul M. *Portrait of Abraham Lincoln in Letters by His Oldest Son.* 1968. Chicago Hist Soc. 92p. VG+/dj. M20. $20.00

ANGLUND, Joan Walsh. *Childhood Is a Time of Innocence.* 1964. Harcourt. stated 1st ed. cloth. VG+/G. M5. $25.00

ANGLUND, Joan Walsh. *Christmas Is a Time of Giving.* 1961. Harcourt. 1st ed. ils. F/G. M5. $25.00

ANGLUND, Joan Walsh. *Do You Love Someone?* 1971. HBJ. 1st ed. 16mo. unp. ils cloth. NF/VG. C14. $15.00

ANGLUND, Joan Walsh. *Een Vriend Is Iemand Die om je Geeft.* 1973 (1966). Wageningen. Zomer Keuning. trans Hendrichs. ils cloth. VG. C14. $8.00

ANGLUND, Joan Walsh. *In a Pumpkin Shell: A Mother Goose ABC.* 1960. Harcourt Brace. 1st ed. unp. VG. C14. $12.00

ANGLUND, Joan Walsh. *Joan Walsh Anglund Story Book.* 1978. Random. 7th. VG. B17. $7.50

ANGLUND, Joan Walsh. *Morning Is a Little Child.* 1969. Harcourt. sm 4to. F. M5. $25.00

ANGLUND, Joan Walsh. *Spring Is a New Beginning.* 1963. HBW. 1st ed. 16mo. unp. F/F. C14. $20.00

ANGLUND, Joan Walsh. *Teddy Bear Tales.* 1985. Random. 1st ed. 4to. F. M5. $18.00

ANGLUND, Joan Walsh. *What Color Is Love?* 1966. Harcourt. 1st ed. ils. F/VG+. M5. $30.00

ANIBARRO. *Intento de un Diccionario Biografico...* 1993. 1/1000. 4to. 628p. NF. A4. $125.00

ANNENBERG. *Type Foundries of America & Their Catalogs.* 1975. np. 4to. ils. 245p. F/VG. A4. $300.00

ANNIN, Robert Edwards. *Ocean Shipping.* 1920. Century. ils. 427p. gilt bl bdg. G+. P12. $10.00

ANNO, Mitsumasa. *Anno's Counting Book.* 1975. Crowell. 1st Am ed. ils. unp. F/VG. T5. $35.00

ANNO, Mitsumasa. *Dr Anno's Magical Midnight Circus.* 1972. Weatherhill. 1st ed. ils. 27p. F/NF. P2. $45.00

ANOBILE, Richard J. *Godfrey Daniels!* 1975. Crown. VG/VG. P3. $15.00

ANOBILE, Richard J. *Why a Duck?* nd. Darien. 8th. VG/VG. P3. $15.00
z
ANON. *ABC & Busy Days.* ca 1940. Samuel Lowe. VG/wrp. M5. $25.00

ANON. *Alpine Climbing: Narratives of Recent Ascents...* 1881. London. ils. 237p. new ep. G. A17. $35.00

ANON. *Animal & Train ABC.* ca 1908. London. Dean. ils. NF. D1. $250.00

ANON. *Baby's Red Letter Days.* 1901. Syracuse, NY. Just's Food. ils JW Smith. VG. D1. $120.00

ANON. *Bicentennial Wagon Train Pilgrimage.* 1977. Kenosha. ltd ed. 1/2500. sgn pub. VG. O3. $45.00

ANON. *Boy Mechanic, Book 3.* 1919. Chicago. Popular Mechanics. 476p. VG. D1. $35.00

ANON. *Bunny Cottontail.* (1910). Saalfield. ils. muslin. NF. D1. $60.00

ANON. *Bunty: The Book for Girls 1979.* 1978. London. DC Thomson. ils. 127p. VG+/clip. C14. $15.00

ANON. *Christmas Stories ABC.* ca 1910-20. Chicago. Donohue. 8vo. prt glazed cloth. NF/cloth self wrp. B24. $285.00

ANON. *Circus Fun.* 1946. Whitehall. ils Fiona. 4 moveables. NF/wrp. D1. $48.00

ANON. *Dame Crump & Her Pig.* 1900s. NY. McLoughlin. 4to. VG/gilt wrp. D1. $250.00

ANON. *Die Schonen Ferien Von Biblche.* 1948. Lyon. J Barbe. 1st trade ed. ils Blanchard. VG. D1. $95.00

ANON. *Fairyland Tales & ABCs.* ca 1900. np. linen. VG/stiff wrp. M5. $45.00

ANON. *Fun Faces.* 1914. Chicago. Ideal. 6 die-cut faces. half cloth/pict brd. VG/torn box. D1. $300.00

ANON. *Gay Mother Goose.* 1938. Scribner. 1st ed. ils Francoise. 63p. F. D1. $200.00
Z
ANON. *Half Hours in the Tiny World: Wonders of Insect Life.* 1882. London. 80 ils. 311p. Bickers bdg. A17. $30.00

ANON. *Indoor Polo.* 1931-32. Assn Am Offical Manual. VG. O3. $95.00

ANON. *Little Lucy; or, The Pleasant Day.* ca 1840s. New Haven. Babcock. Chap Book. woodcuts. VG/wrp. D1. $50.00

ANON. *Missa 'O Quam Suavis'...by an Anonomous English Composer...* 1927. Nashdom Abby. Burnham Plainsong. 83p. red cloth. NF. T10. $100.00

ANON. *Mountains & Mountain Climbing.* 1883. London. ils. 415p. gilt gr cloth. G. H3. $65.00

ANON. *Noah's ABC.* 1900s. Dean's Rag Book. 12mo. ils. VG. D1. $135.00

ANON. *Object Lesson ABC.* ca 1890. Donohue. 32p. paper brd. G. A17. $10.00

ANON. *Object Teacher.* (1884). McLoughlin. probable 1st ed. ils CJ Howard. VG-. D1. $285.00

ANON. *Owl & the Pussy Cat.* 1946. Whitehall. ils Eoina. 8 moveables. VG/wrp. D1. $60.00

ANON. *Pets & Playmates ABC.* ca 1900. NY. 2 pl. rem mk. VG/wrp. M5. $45.00

ANON. *Picture Alphabet for Wee Ones.* ca 1890. np. thin 4to. 4 chromolithographs. unp. NF/stiff wrp. T10. $100.00

ANON. *Saddle & Song: A Collection of Verses...* 1905. Lippincott. 1st ed. G+. O3. $25.00

ANON. *Tall Book of Nursery Tales.* 1944. Harry Doehla. ils/moveables. VG. D1. $85.00

ANON. *Ten Little Colored Boys.* 1942. NY. Howell Soskin. ils Emery Gondor. sbdg. VG. D1. $200.00

ANON. *Ten Little Niggers.* ca 1900. London. Dean's Rag Book Co. ils RJ Williams. VG. D1. $300.00

ANON. *Visit to the Tower.* ca 1820. York. J Kendrew. ils. 13p. NF/wrp. D1. $25.00

ANSAY, A. Manette. *Vinegar Hill.* 1994. Viking. 1st ed. sgn. F/F. M23. $45.00

ANSCOMBE, Roderick. *Secret Life of Laszlo, Count Dracula.* 1994. Hyperion. 1st ed. F/F. P3. $23.00

ANSHAW, Carol. *Aquamarine.* 1992. Houghton Mifflin. 1st ed. sgn. F/F. M23. $20.00

ANSON, Adrian C. *Ball Player's Career.* 1900. Era Pub. photos. G+. P8. $450.00

ANSON, Jay. *666.* 1981. Simon Schuster. 1st ed. VG/VG. P3. $15.00

ANSTEY, F. *Vice Versa.* 1911. Smith Elder. 40th. VG. P3. $20.00

ANTEVS, Ernst. *Rainfall & Tree Growth in the Great Basin.* 1938. WA/NY. VG. O7. $20.00

ANTHOLOGY. *After the Darkness.* 1993. Baltimore. Maclay. 1st ed. 1/750. sgn all contributors. F/sans/case. T2. $50.00

ANTHOLOGY. *Antique Gems From the Greek & Latin.* 1901-1902. Phil. Barrie. 1/1000. 11 vol set. VG. A20. $350.00

ANTHOLOGY. *Battle Stations! Your Navy in Action.* 1946. NY. 402p. G. A17. $15.00

ANTHOLOGY. *Black Scenes.* 1971. Doubleday/Zenith. 1st ed. edit Alice Childress. F/VG clip. B4. $45.00

ANTHOLOGY. *Book of the Sixth World Fantasy Convention.* 1980. Underwood Miller. 1st ed. VG+. R10. $15.00

ANTHOLOGY. *Cry at Birth.* 1971. McGraw Hill. 1st ed. F/F. B4. $45.00

ANTHOLOGY. *Decade 1931-1941.* 1941. London. Hamish Hamilton. 1st ed. sgn/dtd Hamish Hamilton. VG. S9. $35.00

ANTHOLOGY. *Editor's Choice: Literature & Graphics From US Small Press.* 1980. np. 500p. VG. R10. $8.00

ANTHOLOGY. *Homes of American Authors.* 1853. Putnam. 1st ed/1st prt. aeg. marbled ep. emb morocco. F. B14. $250.00

ANTHOLOGY. *National Lampoon Tenth Anniversary Anthology 1970-1980.* 1979. NY. National Lampoon. 1st ed. 4to. NF/VG. B4. $100.00

ANTHOLOGY. *New Poems 1942.* 1942. Peter Pauper. 1st trade ed. NF/VG clip. B4. $85.00

ANTHOLOGY. *Night Comes Softly: An Anthology of Black Female Voices.* 1970. np. 1st ed. edit Nikki Giovanni. F/wrp. B4. $125.00

ANTHOLOGY. *Pictorial History of the Second World War.* 1944-46. NY. VFW ed. 4 vol. VG. A17. $35.00

ANTHOLOGY. *Pushcart Prize, II: Best of the Small Presses.* 1977. Pushcart. 1st ed. F/NF. B35. $70.00

ANTHOLOGY. *Story Parade: A Collection of Modern Stories...* 1937. Winston. 8vo. 363p. pict ep. VG. T5. $20.00

ANTHOLOGY. *To Gwen With Love: Anthology Dedicated to Gwendolyn Brooks.* 1971. Chicago. Johnson. 1st ed. F/NF. B4. $85.00

ANTHOLOGY. *Wild Women Don't Wear No Blues: Black Women Writers...* 1993. Doubleday. 1st ed. sgn 4 contributors. F/F. B4. $100.00

ANTHONY, Evelyn. *Albatross.* 1982. Hutchinson. 1st ed. VG/VG. P3. $20.00

ANTHONY, Evelyn. *Anne Boleyn.* 1986. Century. VG/VG. P3. $15.00

ANTHONY, Evelyn. *Avenue of the Dead.* 1981. Hutchinson. 1st ed. NF/NF. P3. $18.00

ANTHONY, Evelyn. *Charles the King.* 1987. Century. VG/VG. P3. $15.00

ANTHONY, Evelyn. *Scarlet Thread.* 1990. Harper Row. 1st ed. F/F. P3. $19.00

ANTHONY, Evelyn. *Stranger at the Gates.* 1973. CMG. 1st ed. VG/VG. P3. $20.00

ANTHONY, Evelyn. *Voices on the Wind.* 1985. Hutchinson. 1st ed. NF/NF. P3. $18.00

ANTHONY, Florence. *Fate.* 1991. Boston. AP. VG. C4. $35.00

ANTHONY, Patricia. *Brother Termite.* 1993. HBJ. 1st ed. author's 2nd book. F/F. G10. $15.00

ANTHONY, Patricia. *Cold Allies.* 1993. HBJ. 1st ed. F/F. M23. $25.00

ANTHONY, Piers. *And Eternity.* 1990. Morrow. 1st ed. VG/VG. P3. $16.00

ANTHONY, Piers. *Demons Don't Dream.* 1993. Tor. 1st ed. F/F. P3. $20.00

ANTHONY, Piers. *Firefly.* 1990. Morrow. 1st ed. F/F. P3. $19.00

ANTHONY, Piers. *Firefly.* 1990. Morrow. 1st ed. NF/NF. M22. $12.00

ANTHONY, Piers. *For Love of Evil.* 1988. Morrow. 1st ed. NF/NF. P3. $18.00

ANTHONY, Piers. *Fractal Mode.* 1992. Ace/Putnam. F/F. P3. $19.00

ANTHONY, Piers. *Isle of Woman.* 1993. Tor. 1st ed. NF/NF. P3. $24.00

ANTHONY, Piers. *Question Quest.* 1991. Morrow. 1st ed. F/F. P3. $20.00

ANTHONY, Piers. *Robot Adept.* 1988. Ace Putnam. 1st ed. NF/NF. P3. $17.00

ANTHONY, Piers. *Shade of the Tree.* 1986. Tor. 1st ed. F/F. P3. $16.00

ANTHONY, Piers. *Total Recall.* 1989. Morrow. 1st ed. NF/NF. P3. $20.00

ANTHONY, Piers. *Unicorn Point.* 1989. Ace Putnam. 1st ed. F/F. P3. $16.00

ANTHONY, Piers. *With a Tangled Skein.* 1985. Del Rey. 1st ed. F/F. P3. $20.00

ANTON, Ferdinand. *Primitive Art.* 1979. Abrams. rem mk. F/dj. B18. $37.50

ANTONELLI, Lisa M. *Virginia: Commonwealth Comes of Age.* 1988. Windsor. 1st ed. ils. 470p. VG/VG. B10. $20.00

ANTONGINI, Tom. *D'Annunzio.* 1938. Boston. 1st Am ed. 583p. NF. A17. $15.00

APPEL, Benjamin. *Heart of Ice.* 1977. Pantheon. ils JK Lambert. 8vo. 58p. rem mk? VG+/G+. T5. $15.00

APPELFELD, Aharon. *For Every Sin.* 1989. Weidenfeld Nicolson. ARC. w/promo material. F/F. B35. $26.00

APPELFELD, Aharon. *Tzili: The Story of a Life.* 1983. Dutton. 1st ed. F/F. B35. $24.00

APPLE, Max. *Free Agents.* 1984. 1st ed. F/F. C4. $35.00

APPLE, William. *Widowmakers.* 1994. Walker. 1st ed. F/F. M22. $15.00

APPLEBY, John. *Bad Summer.* 1958. Washburn. 1st ed. VG. P3. $10.00

APPLER, A.C. *Younger Brothers.* 1955. Frederick Fell. fwd Burton Rascoe. 245p. VG/dj. T10. $28.00

APPLETON, John Edward. *Beginner's Hand-Book of Chemistry.* 1888 (1884). NY. Chautauqua. 8vo. 256p. gilt cloth. G. K5. $50.00

APPLETON, Victor. *Desert of Mystery.* 1953. Children's Pr. 1st ed. VG/G. P3. $15.00

APPLETON, Victor. *Don Sturdy in the Land of Giants.* nd. Grosset Dunlap. VG. P3. $15.00

APPLETON, Victor. *Don Sturdy in the Port of Lost Ships (#6).* 1926. Grosset Dunlap. lists 11 titles. 214p. VG/dj. M20. $40.00

APPLETON, Victor. *Don Sturdy Lost in Glacier Bay (#13).* 1933. Grosset Dunlap. 204p. VG/dj. M20. $72.00

APPLETON, Victor. *Movie Boys at the Big Fair (#16).* 1926. Garden City. 214p. VG/pict wrp. M20. $32.00

APPLETON, Victor. *Moving Picture Boys on the Coast (#3).* 1913. Grosset Dunlap. lists 9 titles. 212p. VG/dj. M20. $25.00

APPLETON, Victor. *Tom Swift & His Electronic Retroscope (#14).* 1959. Grosset Dunlap. 1st ed. 184p. VG/dj. M20. $22.00

APPLETON, Victor. *Tom Swift & His House on Wheels (#32).* 1929. Grosset Dunlap. 1st ed. VG+. M21. $30.00

APPLETON, Victor. *Tom Swift & His Motor Boat.* nd. Keds premium ed. 92p. worn. M20. $275.00

APPLETON, Victor. *Tom Swift & His Television Detector.* 1938 (1933). Grosset Dunlap. 217p. brn brd. VG. B14. $35.00

APPLETON, Victor. *Tom Swift & the Captive Planetoid (#29).* 1967. Grosset Dunlap. lists to this title. 174p. VG+. M20. $20.00

APPLETON, Victor. *Tom Swift & the Caves of Nuclear Fire (#8).* 1956. Grosset Dunlap. 1st ed. 214p. VG/dj. M20. $22.00

APPLETON, Victor. *Tom Swift Among the Fire Fighters (#24).* 1921. Grosset Dunlap. lists to #30. 214p. VG/VG. M20. $55.00

APPLETON. *Appleton's Cyclopaedia of American Biography.* 1888-1889. np. 2 vol. 61 full-p portraits. full calf. VG. A4. $550.00

APTHEKER, Herbert. *Negro in the Abolitionist Movement.* 1941. NY. Internat. 48 p. NF/wrp. R11. $14.00

AQUINAS, Thomas. *Basic Writings of...* 1945. NY. 2 vol. 1st ed. 8vo. gilt pict blk cloth. F/G case. H3. $150.00

ARACHI, J.X. *Weeds: A Monograph on Weeds of Tamil Nadu.* 1978. Tamil Nadu. ils. 104p. F. B26. $17.50

ARBENA. *Annotated Bibliography of Latin American Sport...* 1989. np. 1379 entries. A4. $75.00

ARBER, Edward. *First Three English Books on America.* 1971. NY. Kraus. rpt of 1885 ed. 408p. F3. $45.00

ARBUTHNOT, May Hill. *Anthology.* 1952. VG. K2. $16.00

ARBUTHNOT, May Hill. *Children & Books.* 1957. Scott Foresman. TB. 684p. VG. M5. $25.00

ARCH, E.L. *Bridge to Yesterday.* 1963. Avalon. 1st ed. F/F. P3. $20.00

ARCHBOLD, Rick. *Hindenburg: An Illustrated History.* 1994. NY. ils. 229p. F/dj. A17. $35.00

ARCHER, Jeffrey. *First Among Equals.* 1984. Hodder Stoughton. 1st ed. F/F. P3. $20.00

ARCHER, Jeffrey. *Matter of Honor.* 1986. Linden. 1st Am ed. F/F. N4. $27.50

ARCHER, Jeffrey. *Shall We Tell the President.* 1977. Viking. 1st ed. VG/VG. P3. $20.00

ARCHER, Jeffrey. *Twist in the Tale.* 1988. Simon Schuster. 1st ed. NF/NF. P3. $20.00

ARCHIBALD, Norman. *Heaven High Hell Deep, 1917-1918.* 1935. NY. 350p. G. B18. $22.50

ARCINIEGAS, German. *Germans in the Conquest of America.* 1943. NY. VG. O7. $25.00

ARD, William; see Block, Lawrence.

ARDAI, Charles. *Great Tales of Madness & Macabre.* 1990. Galahad. F/F. P3. $15.00

ARDEN, William. *Mystery of the Dancing Devil.* 1976. Random. 1st ed. VG. P3. $12.00

ARDEN, William. *Mystery of the Laughing Shadow.* 1969. Random. VG. P3. $15.00

ARDIS. *Guide to Literature of Electrical & Electronics Engineering.* 1987. np. 697 annotated entries. 190p. VG. A4. $85.00

ARDIZZONE, Edward. *Little Tim & the Brave Sea Captain.* 1936. NY. 2nd. ils. fair/dj. M5. $25.00

ARDIZZONE, Edward. *Young Ardizzone: An Autobiographical Fragment.* 1970. NY. 1st ed. ils. F/VG. B17. $25.00

ARDOIN & FITZGERALD. *Callas: The Art & Life.* 1974. NY. 1st ed. VG/G. B5. $25.00

ARENSBERG, Ann. *Sister Wolf.* 1980. 1st ed. inscr. author's 1st book. VG+/VG+. S13. $20.00

ARETAEUS. *Extant Works of Aretaeus, the Cappadocian.* 1972. Boston. facsimile of 1856 ed. 510p. A13. $60.00

AREVALO, Juan Jose. *Shark & the Sardines.* 1961. Lyle Stuart. 2nd. index. 256p. dj. F3. $10.00

ARIES. *Centuries of Childhood: Social History of Family Life.* 1962. np. 447p. VG/wrp. A4. $15.00

ARLEN, Michael. *These Charming People.* 1924. Doran. 1st ed? VG. R10. $10.00

ARLINGTON & LEWISOHN. *In Search of Old Peking.* 1935. Peking. 1st ed. ils. 328p. pocket map VG. B5. $95.00

ARMATAGE, George. *Horseowner & the Stableman's Companion.* 1892. London. 4th. 12mo. VG. O3. $25.00

ARMES, Ethel. *Stratford Hall & the Great House of the Lees...* 1936. Richmond, VA. Garrett Massie. 1st ed. 575p. cloth. NF/VG. M8. $275.00

ARMISTEAD, John. *Legacy of Vengeance.* 1994. NY. 1st ed. author's 1st book. F/F. H11. $30.00

ARMITAGE, Andrew. *Owen Sound: Steamboat Days.* 1981. Ontario. Boston Mills. G/wrp. A16. $7.50

ARMITAGE, Merle. *Accent on Life.* 1965. IA U. 52 photos. 386p. VG/VG. A4. $65.00

ARMITAGE, Merle. *Pagans, Conquistadores, Heroes & Martyrs.* 1960. Fresno. VG. O7. $55.00

ARMITAGE, Merle. *Stella Dysart of Ambrosia Lake.* 1959. DSP. 1st ed. 8vo. 160p. F/clip. T10. $65.00

ARMOUR, Robert A. *Douglas Southall Freeman: Reflections by His Daughter...* 1986. Richmond. 30p. VG. B10. $8.00

ARMSTRONG, Charlotte. *Black-Eyed Stranger.* 1952. Peter Davies. 1st ed. G. p3. $10.00

ARMSTRONG, Gregory. *The Dragon Has Come.* 1974. Harper. stated 1st ed. 238p. NF/NF. R11. $30.00

ARMSTRONG, Karen. *Gospel According to Woman.* 1986. Anchor/Doubleday. 1st ed. F/NF. B35. $65.00

ARMSTRONG, Margaret. *Blue Santo Murder Mystery.* 1941. Random. 1st ed. VG. P3. $30.00

ARMSTRONG, Margaret. *Man With No Face.* 1943. Tower. VG/torn. P3. $10.00

ARMSTRONG, Samuel. *Walt Disney's Lady.* 1954. Whitman. MTI. G. P3. $10.00

ARMSTRONG & CRAVEN. *200 Years of American Sculpture.* 1976. Whitney Mus Am Art. ils/pl. 336. cloth. dj. D2. $65.00

ARMSTRONG & LUDLOW. *Hampton & Its Students.* 1974. NY. 1st ed. ils. 256p. G. B5. $125.00

ARMSTRONG. *Nevada Printing History: A Bibliography of Imprints...* 1981. Reno. NV U. 16 pl. 441p. F/F. A4. $50.00

ARNASON, Eleanor. *Ring of Swords.* 1993. Tor. 1st ed. F/F. G10. $25.00

ARNASON, Eleanor. *Woman of the Iron People.* nd. BC. VG/VG. P3. $8.00

ARNESON, Ben Albert. *Elements of Constitutional Law.* 1928. NY. Harper. M11. $35.00

ARNETT, R.H. *Entomological Information Storage & Retrieval.* 1970. Baltimore. Bio-Rand. 1st ed. 8vo. 210p. cloth. F. B1. $18.00

ARNOLD, C.D. *Studies in Architecture at Home & Abroad.* 1888. np. photos. stiff wrp/ribbon ties. VG. M17. $20.00

ARNOLD, Edgar. *Young Refugee: Adventures of Two Lads From Virginia.* 1912. Hermitage. 305p. G. B10. $12.00

ARNOLD, Edwin. *Bhagavad Gita: The Song Celestial.* 1964. Bombay. LEC. 1st ed. 1/1500. ils/sgn YG Srimati. F/case. C2. $75.00

ARNOLD, Edwin. *Japonica.* 1891. NY. 1st Am ed. ils R Blum. cloth. VG. C2. $60.00

ARNOLD, Edwin. *Light of Asia.* 1926. London. 1st ed thus. ils Hamzeh Carr. NF/VG. C2. $50.00

ARNOLD, James. *All Drawn by Horses.* 1985. Newton Abbott. sm 4to. ils. VG. O3. $48.00

ARNOLD, Jean. *Prettybelle.* 1970. Dial. 1st ed. F/F. B35. $30.00

ARNOLD, Lloyd R. *High on the Wild With Hemingway.* 1969. Caldwell. 2nd. 343p. G/torn. B18. $17.50

ARNOLD & GUILLAUME. *Legacy of Islam.* 1952. London. Oxford. ils. 416p. VG. W1. $25.00

ARNOLD. *Concise History of Irish Art.* 1968. Praeger. F/F. D2. $20.00

ARNOSKY, Jim. *Mouse Numbers & Letters.* 1982. HBJ. 5th. ils. unp. tan pict brd. VG+. T5. $12.00

ARNOT, Hugo. *Collection & Abridgement of Celebrated Criminal Trials...* 1785. Edinburgh. Smellie. 1st ed. contemporary tree calf. M11. $750.00

ARNOW, Harriette Simpson. *Hunter's Horn.* 1949. 1st ed. author's 1st novel. VG/VG. C4. $75.00

ARNOW, Harriette Simpson. *Kentucky Trace: Novel of the American Revolution.* 1974. Knopf. 1st ed. F/F. B4. $45.00

ARNOW, Harriette Simpson. *Weedkiller's Daughter.* 1970. Knopf. 1st ed. F/NF. B4. $45.00

ARNTZEN & RAINWATER. *Guide to the Literature of Art History.* 1980. Am Lib Assn. 4to. 634p. F. A4. $80.00

ART INSTITUTE OF CHICAGO. *Radiance of Jade & the Clarity of Water. Korean Ceramics.* 1991. Chicago. 1st ed. photos. VG+. S13. $18.00

ARTAUD, Antonin. *Collected Works, Vol 3.* 1972. London. Calder Boyars. 1st ed. F/wrp. B2. $40.00

ARTHUR, Elizabeth. *Bad Guys.* 1986. Knopf. 1st ed. author's 3rd book. F/NF. B4. $65.00

ARUNDEL, Jocelyn. *Whitecap's Song.* 1982. NY. Whittlesey. 1st ed. ils Wesley Dennis. VG/G. O3. $30.00

ASBOJORNSEN & MOE. *East of the Sun, West of the Moon.* nd. Doubleday Doran. ils Kay Nielsen/25 pl. 204p. NF/VG. P2. $400.00

ASBURY, E. *Horse Sense & Humor in Kentucky.* 1981. Lexington. 1st ed. w/author's sgn pasted in. VG/G. O3. $25.00

ASBURY, Herbert. *Sucker's Progress: An Informal History of Gambling...* 1938. Dodd Mead. 1st ed. 8vo. 493p. NF. B14. $50.00

ASH, Christopher. *Whaler's Eye.* 1962. Macmillan. 200 photos. 248p. VG/dj. T7. $28.00

ASH, Lee. *Serial Publications Containing Medical Classics.* 1961. New Haven. 1st ed. 147p. VG A13. $25.00

ASHBEE, C.R. *Socialism & Politics.* 1906. Campden. Essex House. 8vo. gilt quarter vellum. VG+. T10. $100.00

ASHBEE, Henry Spencer. *Encyclopedia of Erotic Literature...* 1962. np. 3 vol. VG/case. A4. $125.00

ASHBERRY, John. *Fairfield Porter.* 1982. NYGS. 1st ed. NF/NF. S13. $20.00

ASHBERRY, John. *Shadow Train: Poems.* 1981. Viking. ARC/1st ed. inscr/dtd 1981. RS. F/NF. C2. $150.00

ASHBERRY, John. *Wave: Poems.* 1984. Viking. 1st ed. inscr. F/F. C2. $150.00

ASHBROOK, F.G. *How To Raise Rabbits for Food & Fur.* 1951. Orange Judd. 8vo. ils. 256p. cloth. NF. B1. $22.50

ASHBROOK, H. *Murder of Cecily Thane.* 1930. Coward McCann. 1st ed. VG. P3. $25.00

ASHBROOK, H. *Murder of Steven Kester.* 1931. Coward McCann. VG. P3. $20.00

ASHBY, W. Ross. *Design for a Brain.* 1952. NY. John Wiley. 1st Am ed. 260p. VG/dj. G1. $65.00

ASHCROFT. *Ashcroft's Railway Directory for 1865...* 1865. NY. John W Amerman. 8vo. 182p. gilt emb cloth. G. B14. $150.00

ASHE, Geoffrey. *Discovery of King Arthur.* 1985. Debrett's Peerage. 1st ed. VG/VG. P3. $25.00

ASHE, Gordon; see Creasey, John.

ASHER, Benjamin. *American Builders Companion.* 1816. Boston. 3rd. ils/pl. 104p. full leather. G+. B5. $450.00

ASHFORD, Jeffrey. *Double Run.* 1973. Walker. 1st ed. VG/VG. P3. $20.00

ASHFORD, Jeffrey. *Honourable Detective.* 1988. St Martin. 1st ed. VG/VG. P3. $15.00

ASHFORD, Jeffrey. *Question of Principle.* 1986. St Martin. 1st ed. VG/VG. P3. $15.00

ASHLEY, Clifford W. *Whalers, Wharves & Waterways.* 1973. New Bedford. Old Dartmouth Hist Soc. 8vo. 93p. VG/wrp. T7. $35.00

ASHLEY, Franklin. *James Dickey: A Checklist.* 1972. Bruccoli Clark. 98p. VG. B10. $20.00

ASHLEY, Michael. *History of the SF MAgazine 1926-1935.* 1974. NEL. 1st ed. F/F. P3. $35.00

ASHLEY & READ. *Thoroughbred: A Celebration of the Breed.* 1990. Simon Schuster. 1st ed. VG/VG. O3. $35.00

ASHMONT. *Dogs: Their Management & Treatment in Disease.* 1886. Boston. Thayer. 208p. VG. B14. $40.00

ASHTON, Dore. *Philip Guston.* 1960. Grove. Evergreen Gallery Book #10. ils. 63p. D2. $25.00

ASHTON, John. *Romances of Chivalry.* 1887. London. Fisher Unwin. 8vo. ils/glossary. teg. leather/cloth. T10. $250.00

ASIMOV, GREENBERG & WAUGH. *13 Short SF Novels.* 1985. Bonanza. VG/VG. P3. $15.00

ASIMOV, GREENBERG & WAUGH. *7 Deadly Sins & Cardinal Virtues...* 1982. Bonanza. VG/VG. P3. $15.00

ASIMOV, Isaac. *Annotated Gulliver's Travels.* 1980. Potter. 1st ed. VG/VG. P3. $25.00

ASIMOV, Isaac. *Asimov's Galaxy.* 1989. Doubleday. 1st ed. F/F. P3. $18.00

ASIMOV, Isaac. *Asimov's Sherlockian Limericks.* 1978. NY. 1st ed. VG/VG. B5. $27.50

ASIMOV, Isaac. *Before the Golden Age Trilogy.* 1988. Black Cat. VG/VG. P3. $20.00

ASIMOV, Isaac. *Before the Golden Age.* 1974. Doubleday. 1st ed. VG/VG. P3. $25.00

ASIMOV, Isaac. *Choice of Catastrophes.* 1979. Simon Schuster. 1st ed. VG. P3. $23.00

ASIMOV, Isaac. *Counting the Eons.* 1984. Granada. 1st ed. VG/VG. P3. $20.00

ASIMOV, Isaac. *Edge of Tomorrow.* 1985. Tor. 1st ed. F/F. P3. $16.00

ASIMOV, Isaac. *Exploring the Earth & the Cosmos.* 1982. Crown. 1st ed. VG. P3. $15.00

ASIMOV, Isaac. *Fantastic Voyage II: Destination Brain.* 1987. Doubleday. 1st ed. F/NF. N4. $22.50

ASIMOV, Isaac. *Fantastic Voyage II: Destination Brain.* 1987. Doubleday. 1st ed. VG/VG. P3. $19.00

ASIMOV, Isaac. *Far As Human Eye Can See.* 1987. Doubleday. 1st ed. F/F. P3. $20.00

ASIMOV, Isaac. *Far Ends of Time & Earth.* 1979. Doubleday. 1st ed. F/F. P3. $20.00

ASIMOV, Isaac. *Foundation & Earth.* 1986. Doubleday. 1st ed. F/F. P3. $20.00

ASIMOV, Isaac. *Foundation & Earth.* 1986. Doubleday. 1st ed. VG/VG. N4. $17.50

ASIMOV, Isaac. *Foundation's Edge.* 1982. Doubleday. 1st ed. F/F. P3. $20.00

ASIMOV, Isaac. *I Asimov: A Memoir.* 1994. Doubleday. 1st ed. F/F. T2. $30.00

ASIMOV, Isaac. *Isaac Asimov's Book of Facts.* 1979. Grosset Dunlap. 1st ed. VG/VG. P3. $20.00

ASIMOV, Isaac. *Lucky Starr & Big Sun of Mercury.* 1978. Gregg. 1st ed. VG/VG. P3. $20.00

ASIMOV, Isaac. *Measure of the Universe.* 1983. Harper Row. 1st ed. F/F. M19. $17.50

ASIMOV, Isaac. *Nemesis.* 1989. Doubleday. 1st ed. F/F. M23. $20.00

ASIMOV, Isaac. *Opus 100.* 1969. Houghton Mifflin. 1st ed. VG/VG. P3. $50.00

ASIMOV, Isaac. *Opus 200.* 1979. Houghton Mifflin. 1st ed. NF/NF. P3. $20.00

ASIMOV, Isaac. *Our World in Space.* 1974. NYGS. 1st ed. F/VG. M19. $45.00

ASIMOV, Isaac. *Prelude to Foundation.* 1988. Doubleday. VG/VG. P3. $19.00

ASIMOV, Isaac. *Robots & Empire.* 1985. Doubleday. 1st ed. RS. F/F. P3. $20.00

ASIMOV, Isaac. *Robots of Dawn.* 1983. Doubleday. 1st ed. F/F. P3. $20.00

ASIMOV, Isaac. *Satellites in Outer Space.* 1966. Random. decor brd. VG. P3. $20.00

ASIMOV, Isaac. *Today & Tomorrow &...* 1973. Doubleday. 1st ed. VG/G. P3. $30.00

ASIMOV, Isaac. *World of Carbon.* 1958. Abelard. 1st ed. NF/torn. A15. $35.00

ASIMOV & GREENBERG. *Visions of Fantasy.* 1989. Doubleday. 1st ed. F/F. P3. $15.00

ASIMOV & SILVERBERG. *Nightfall.* 1990. Doubleday. 1st ed. F/F. P3. $20.00

ASIMOV & SILVERBERG. *Ugly Little Boy.* 1992. Doubleday. 1st ed. F/F. P3. $23.00

ASINOF, E. *Eight Men Out.* 1963. NY. 1st ed. VG/VG. B5. $45.00

ASKINS, Charles. *American Shotgun.* 1910. NY. Outing. 1st ed. VG. H7. $50.00

ASMUS, Henry. *Farm Horseshoeing.* 1943. Ithaca. Cornell Bulletin #23. VG/wrp. O3. $15.00

ASPLER & PAPE. *Scorpion Sanction.* 1980. Viking. 1st ed. VG/VG. P3. $18.00

ASPRIN, Robert. *Bug Wars.* 1979. St Martin. 1st ed. VG/VG. P3. $20.00

ASTRUP, Elivind. *Lt Rober E Peary, USN's Journey Across Northern Greenland.* 1897. Phil. 8vo. photos. 560p. bl cloth. VG. B14. $55.00

ASWELL, James. *We Know Better.* 1927. Gordon Lewis. 1/500. bdg ils/sgn Don Miller. box. B10. $35.00

ATELEE, Philip; see Philips, James Atlee.

ATGET, Eugene. *Vision of Paris.* 1963. Macmillan. 1st ed. inscr/dtd 1963. VG/dj. S9. $400.00

ATHELING, William. *Issue at Hand.* 1964. Advent. 1st ed. VG/VG. P3. $45.00

ATHERTON, Gertrude. *Ancestors.* 1907. Harper. 1st ed. NF. B4. $50.00

ATHERTON, Gertrude. *Dido: Queen of Hearts.* 1929. NY. Liveright. 1st ed. NF/VG+. B4. $85.00

ATHERTON, Gertrude. *House of Lee.* 1940. Appleton. inscr. NF. M19. $50.00

ATHERTON, Gertrude. *Jealous Gods.* 1928. Liveright. 1st ed. F/NF. M19. $75.00

ATHERTON, Gertrude. *Rulers of Kings.* 1904. Harper. 1st ed. NF. B4. $75.00

ATHERTON, Gertrude. *Sophisticates.* 1931. Liveright. 1st ed. F/NF. B4. $75.00

ATHERTON, Gertrude. *What Dreams May Come.* 1988. Chicago/NY/San Francisco. 1st ed. author's 1st book. NF/wrp/custom case. C6. $350.00

ATKIN, Ronald. *Revolution!* 1970. John Day. 1st Am ed. 354p. dj. F3. $20.00

ATKINSON, Geoffroy. *La Literature Geographique de la Renaissance.* 1968. NY. VG. w/supplement. O7. $95.00

ATKINSON, Oriana. *Big Eyes.* 1949. NY. 1st ed. VG/VG. A17. $9.50

ATKINSON, William. *Physicians & Surgeons of the United States.* 1878. Phil. 1st ed. 788p. VG. A13. $300.00

ATTANSIO, A.A. *Beast Marks.* 1984. Ziesing. 1st ed. sgn. F/F. P3. $45.00

ATTANSIO, A.A. *Hunting the Ghost Dancer.* 1991. Harper Collins. 1st ed. F/F. P3. $22.00

ATTANSIO, A.A. *In Other Worlds.* 1984. Morrow. 1st ed. VG/VG. P3. $20.00

ATTANSIO, A.A. *Wyvern.* 1988. Ticknor Fields. 1st ed. F/F. G10. $15.00

ATTWELL, Mabel Lucie. *Lucie Attwell's Picture Book.* 1936. Whitman. lg 4to. 12 glossy linette p. F/stiff wrp. M5. $165.00

ATTWELL, Mabel Lucie. *Story Book.* ca 1920s. Whitman. 6 pl. G+. M5. $85.00

ATWOOD, Margaret. *Bluebeard's Egg.* 1983. McClelland Stewart. 1st ed. F/F. P3. $25.00

ATWOOD, Margaret. *Cat's Eye.* 1988. McClelland Stewart. 1st ed. 8vo. F/dj. S9. $75.00

ATWOOD, Margaret. *Cat's Eye.* 1989. Doubleday. 1st ed. NF/NF. P3. $20.00

ATWOOD, Margaret. *Dancing Girls & Other Stories.* 1977. McClelland Stewart. 1st ed. VG/VG. P3. $35.00

ATWOOD, Margaret. *Handmaid's Tale.* 1985. McClelland Stewart. 1st ed. VG/VG. P3. $30.00

ATWOOD, Margaret. *Procedures for Underground.* 1972. Atlantic/Little Brn. 1st Am ed. F/NF. M23. $25.00

ATWOOD, Margaret. *Robber Bride.* 1993. London. Bloomsbury. 1st ed. F/F. T2. $20.00

ATWOOD, Margaret. *Surfacing.* 1972. Tor. 1st ed. author's 2nd novel. sgn. F/NF. C6. $150.00

ATWOOD, Margaret. *Wilderness Tips.* 1991. NY. 1st ed. sgn. F/F. A9. $30.00

AUBIER & MORATH. *Fiesta in Pamplona.* 1956. London. 1st ed. folio. F/NF. B4. $125.00

AUCHINCLOSS, Louis. *Winthrop Covenant.* 1976. Houghton Mifflin. 1st ed. F/F. H11. $35.00

AUDEN, W.H. *Academic Graffiti.* nd. England. 1st ed. VG. M17. $20.00

AUDEN, W.H. *Collected Shorter Poems 1927-1957.* 1967. NY. 1st ed. sgn/corrected. F/F. C6. $175.00

AUDEN, W.H. *Enchafed Flood; or, Romantic Iconography of the Sea.* 1979. Charlottesville. VG. O7. $25.00

AUDEN, W.H. *Homage to Clio.* 1960. Random. 1st ed. F/VG. M19. $35.00

AUDEN & ISHERWOOD. *Ascent of F6: Tragedy in Two Acts.* 1936. London. Faber. 1st ed. F/NF. B24. $385.00

AUDEN & ISHERWOOD. *Journey to a War.* 1939. Random. 1st Am ed. NF/NF. C2. $75.00

AUDEN & ISHERWOOD. *On the Frontier: A Melodrama in Three Acts.* 1938. London. Faber. 1st ed. red cloth. F/dj. B24. $400.00

AUDEN & PEARSON. *Poets of the English Language.* 1950. Viking. 1st Am ed. 5 vol. NF/NF. C2. $100.00

AUDOUZE, Jean. *Cambridge Atlas of Astronomy.* 1988. Cambridge. 350 color photos. F/dj. O7. $65.00

AUDUBON, John James. *Delineations of American Scenery & Character.* 1926. NY. Baker. 8vo. 349p. gilt blk cloth. NF. T10. $75.00

AUDUBON, Maria. *Audubon & His Journals. Vol 2.* 1898. London. John Nimmo. ils. 554p. VG. A4. $75.00

AUEL, Jean M. *Clan of the Cave Bear.* 1980. Crown. 1st ed. VG/G. P3. $25.00

AUEL, Jean M. *Clan of the Cave Bear.* 1980. NY. Crown. 1st ed. F/F. H11. $100.00

AUEL, Jean M. *Mammoth Hunters.* 1985. Crown. 1st ed. F/F. H11. $35.00

AUEL, Jean M. *Mammoth Hunters.* 1985. Crown. 1st ed. VG/VG. P3. $20.00

AUEL, Jean M. *Mammoth Hunters.* 1985. NY. Crown. ARC. NF. B4. $45.00

AUEL, Jean M. *Plains of Passage.* 1990. Crown. 1st ed. F/F. G6. $25.00

AUEL, Jean M. *Valley of Horses.* 1982. Crown. ARC. F/wrp. w/promo poster. M19. $85.00

AUEL, Jean M. *Valley of the Horses.* 1982. Crown. 1st ed. sgn. F/F. B35. $40.00

AUGUST, John. *Advance Agent.* 1944. Tower. 2nd. G/G. P3. $8.00

AUGUSTUS, Albert Jr.; see Nuetzel, Charles.

AULT, Phil. *Whistles Round the Bend.* 1982. Dodd Mead. VG/VG. A16. $10.00

AUNT LAURA; see Barrow, Frances Elizabeth.

AURNER, Nellie Slayton. *Caxton: Mirour of Fifteenth Century Letters.* 1926. Houghton Mifflin. 8vo. 16 pl. 304p. F/NF. T10. $45.00

AUSLANDER. *Unconquerables: Salutes to the Undying Spirit...* 1943. np. 59p. F/NF. A4. $25.00

AUSTEN, Jane. *Emma.* 1964. LEC. 1st ed. 1/1500. ils/sgn Kredel. F/case. C2. $100.00

AUSTEN, Jane. *Mansfield Park.* 1959. London. Folio Soc. Sangorski/Sutcliffe bdg. F. A4. $95.00

AUSTEN, Jane. *Pride & Prejudice.* 1951. Bombay. Jaico Books. 1st ed. NF/wrp. A11. $25.00

AUSTER, Paul. *Art of Hunger.* 1992. LA. 1st ed. sgn. F/F. A11. $55.00

AUSTER, Paul. *In the Country of Last Things.* 1987. Viking. 1st ed. F/F. M23. $20.00

AUSTER, Paul. *In the Country of Last Things.* 1987. Viking. 1st ed. VG/VG. P3. $16.00

AUSTIN, A.C. *Story of Diamonds.* 1941. Los Angeles. ils. bl cloth. VG. B14. $30.00

AUSTIN, Alicia. *Age of Dreams.* 1978. Donald Grant. 1st ed. VG/VG. P3. $35.00

AUSTIN, Aurelia. *Bright Feathers.* 1958. np. inscr. 59p. VG/VG. B11. $10.00

AUSTIN, David. *Heritage of the Rose.* 1988. Suffolk. ils. 445p. F/dj. B26. $60.00

AUSTIN, Doris Jean. *After the Garden.* 1987. NAL. 1st ed. F/F. B4. $35.00

AUSTIN, G.L. *Life & Times of Wendell Phillips.* 1884. Boston. 12mo. 431p. gilt brn cloth. T3. $29.00

AUSTIN, J.M. *Voice to the Married...Addressed to Husbands & Wives.* 1847. Boston. 16mo. 402p. emb brn cloth. G. T3. $32.00

AUSTIN, Jean. *Mexico in Your Pocket.* 1937. Doubleday. 1st ed. 140p. F3. $10.00

AUSTIN, Margot. *Churchmouse Stories.* 1956. Dutton. later reprint. VG. B17. $5.00

AUSTIN, Margot. *Gabriel Churchkitten.* Sept 1943. Dutton. 4th. VG/VG. P2. $20.00

AUSTIN, Margot. *Trumpet.* 1943. Dutton. 1st ed. VG+/G. M5. $30.00

AUSTIN, Margot. *Very Young Mother Goose.* nd. Platt Munk. ils. 91p. G+. C14. $8.00

AUSTIN, Mary. *Cactus Thorn: A Novella.* 1988. NV U. 1st ed. fwd Melody Graulich. cloth. M/dj. A18. $30.00

AUSTIN, Mary. *Experiences Facing Death.* 1931. Bobbs Merrill. 1st ed. F. A18. $60.00

AUSTIN, William. *Peter Rugg: Missing Man.* 1948. Comet. 1st ed. F/sans. B4. $50.00

AUSTIN & SHORT. *Germ Cells & Fertilization, Book 1: Reproduction in Mammals.* 1978. Cambridge. rpt. 133p. F. B11. $22.50

AVEDON, Richard. *In the American West 1979-1984.* 1985. Abrams. 1st ed. sgn/dtd 1985. F. S9. $250.00

AVELOT, Henri. *Philibert's Bright Ideas.* 1932. Warne. 84p. VG/VG. P2. $50.00

AVENI, Athony. *Empires of Time.* 1990. London. Tauris. 1st ed. ils. 371p. F3. $25.00

AVERA, Carl L. *Wind Swept Land.* 1964. San Antonio, TX. 1st ed. 89p. pict cloth. VG/VG. B18. $15.00

AVERILL, Esther. *Daniel Boone.* 1945. Harper. 1st ed. 4to. VG. M5. $42.00

AVERILL, Esther. *Voyages of Jacques Cartier.* 1937. Domino. 1st ed. ils Rojankovsky. F/dj. M5. $95.00

AVERILL, Naomi. *Whistling-Two-Teeth & the Forty-Nine Buffalos.* 1939. NY. ils. VG. M5. $45.00

AVIL, Christopher. *Strangers in Paradise.* 1976. Herbert Jenkins. 1st ed. F/F. P3. $20.00

AVNERY, Uri. *Israel Without Zionists: A Plea for Peace in Middle East.* 1968. Macmillan. 1st ed. sm 8vo. 215p. VG/dj. W1. $18.00

AWAD, Joseph. *Neon Distances.* 1980. Golden Quill. 80p. F/VG. B10. $7.00

AXFORD, Lavinne. *Index to the Poems of Ogden Nash.* 1972. Scarecrow. 139p. xl. F. B22. $5.00

AXTON, David; see Koontz, Dean R.

AYER, Frederick Jr. *Man in the Mirror.* 1965. Regnery. VG/VG. P3. $20.00

AYMAR, Brandt. *Pictorial Treasury of the Marine Museums of the World.* 1967. Crown. VG/VG. A16. $22.50

AYMAR, Gordon. *Yacht Racing Rules & Tactics.* 1962. Van Nostrand. VG/VG. A16. $9.00

AYRE, Joseph. *Practical Observations on Nature & Treatment of Marasmus...* 1832. Northampton. 1st Am ed. 220p. contemporary sheepskin. B14. $175.00

AYRES, Noreen. *World the Color of Salt.* 1992. Morrow. 1st ed. author's 1st book. F/F. H11. $30.00

AYRES, Paul; see Aarons, Edward S.

AYRES. *British Folk Art.* 1977. Overlook. F/F. D2. $35.00

AZIZ, Philippe. *Doctors of Death.* 1976. Geneva. 3 vol of 4. VG. A17. $40.00

AZIZ, Philippe. *Man in the Mirror.* 1965. Regnery. VG/VG. P3. $20.00

AZIZ, Philippe. *Mysteries of the Great Pyramid.* 1977. Eds Fermi. decor brd. VG. P3. $15.00

BAADE, Fritz. *Race to the Year 2000.* 1963. Cresset. 1st ed. VG/VG. P3. $15.00

BAALI & WARDI. *Ibn Khaldun & Islamic Thought...* 1981. Boston. Hall. 1st ed. 155p. VG. W1. $28.00

BABCOCK, Bernie. *Hallerloogy.* 1943. self pub. ils/photos. G+. P2. $65.00

BABCOCK, C. Merton. *Wisdom of the Koran.* 1966. Peter Pauper. 1st ed. 16mo. 62p. VG/dj. W1. $12.00

BABSON, Marian. *Murder, Murder, Little Star.* 1977. Collins Crime Club. 1st ed. VG/VG. P3. $20.00

BABSON, Marian. *Pretty Lady.* 1980. Walker. 1st ed. F/F. P3. $16.00

BACH, Richard. *Bridge Across Forever.* 1984. Morrow. 1st ed. VG/VG. P3. $20.00

BACHMAN, Richard; see King, Stephen.

BACHMEYER, Arthur. *Hospital Trends & Developments 1940-46.* 1948. NY. 1st ed. 819p. A13. $75.00

BACON, Francis. *Cabala...Mysteries of State & Government...* 1691. London. Sawbridge. 3rd. contemporary calf. M11. $350.00

BACON, Francis. *Essays or Counsels of Civill & Morall.* 1944. LEC. 1st ed. 1/1500. designer/sgn Bruce Rogers. F/case. C2. $125.00

BACON, Francis. *Philosophical Works of...* 1733. London. 3 vol. old calf/raised bands. G. A17. $250.00

BACON, John. *Liber Regis, del Thesaurus Rerum Ecclesiasticarum...* 1786. London. John Nichols. only ed. contemporary bdg. M11. $250.00

BACON, John. *Town Officer's Guide, Containing a Compilation...* 1825. Haverhill. contemporary mottled sheep. M11. $150.00

BACON, Peggy. *Good American Witch.* 1957. Franklin Watts. 1st ed. 222p. G+/G+. P2. $40.00

BACON, Peggy. *Mystery at East Hatchett.* 1939. Viking. 1st ed. ils. VG/G+. P2. $50.00

BADAWY, Alexander. *Architecture in Ancient Egypt & the Near East.* 1972. Cambridge/MIT. 2nd. ils/map. NF/dj. W1. $65.00

BADER, Barbara. *American Picture Books From Noah's Ark to the Beast Within.* 1976. Macmillan. 1st ed. ils. F/F. A4. $145.00

BADER, Barbara. *American Picture Books From Noah's Ark to the Beast Within.* 1976. Macmillan. 1st ed. VG/VG. P2. $95.00

BADSWORTH. *Principles of Bridge & Laws of the Game...* 1914. London/NY. New ed. 288p. VG. S1. $15.00

BAEDEKER, Karl. *Spain & Portugal.* 1913. Leipsic. VG. O7. $25.00

BAER, Helene G. *Heart Is Like Heaven: Life of Lydia Maria Child.* 1964. PA U. 1st ed. 339p. NF/dj. M20. $28.00

BAERS, Henri. *Les Tables Astronomiques de Louvain, 1528.* 1976. Brussels. Culture et Civililasion. 8vo. 90p. F/F. T10. $25.00

BAEZ, Carlos. *Las Lagrimas de Churun.* 1959. Caracas. Lipografia Londres. 1st ed. 8vo. 124p. VG. T10. $50.00

BAEZ, Joan. *And a Voice To Sing With.* 1987. Summit. 1st ed. sgn. F/F. B11. $40.00

BAGBY, George. *Dead Wrong.* 1957. Doubleday. 1st ed. F/NF. M19. $25.00

BAGBY, George. *Old Virginia Gentleman & Other Sketches.* 1911. Scribner. 321p. VG. B10. $45.00

BAGBY, George. *Two in the Bush.* 1976. Crime Club. 1st ed. VG/VG. P3. $15.00

BAGLEY, Desmond. *Enemy.* 1978. Doubleday. 1st ed. VG/VG. P3. $18.00

BAGLEY, Desmond. *Flyaway.* 1979. Doubleday. 1st ed. VG/VG. P3. $18.00

BAGLEY, Desmond. *Juggernaut.* 1985. Collins. 1st ed. VG/VG. P3. $20.00

BAGLEY, Desmond. *Tightrope Men.* 1973. Collins. 1st ed. NF/NF. P3. $25.00

BAGLEY, Desmond. *Vivero Letter.* 1968. London. Collins. apparent 1st ed? 317p. gr brd. NF. B22. $4.00

BAGNALL, William R. *Textile Industries of the United States...1639-1810.* 1893. Cambridge. Riverside. sold by subscription. 613p. F. B14. $350.00

BAGNOLD, Enid. *National Velvet.* 1935. Morrow. 1st ed. 303p. VG/G. P2. $35.00

BAGROW, Leo. *Die Geschichte der Kartographie.* 1951. Berlin. Safari-Verlag. ils. F/worn. O7. $125.00

BAGSTER, Samuel. *Management of Bees.* 1834. London. Bagster Pickering. 40 woodcuts. 244p. cloth. VG. A10. $350.00

BAHR, Edith Jane. *Nice Neighbourhood.* 1973. Collins Crime Club. 1st ed. VG/G. P3. $15.00

BAHTI, Tom. *Intro to Southwestern Indian Arts & Crafts.* 1966. Flagstaff. KC Pub. ils. 32p. F/thin wrp. T10. $10.00

BAIKIE, James. *History of Egypt From the Earliest Times...* 1929. London. Blk. 2 vol. 1st ed. 8vo. ils. VG. W1. $65.00

BAILEY, Alice Cooper. *Kimo, the Whistling Boy.* 1928. Volland. ils Holling. VG. K2. $80.00

BAILEY, C.S. *Lil' Hannibal.* 1938. Platt Munk. ils. VG. B5. $32.50

BAILEY, Carolyn Sherwin. *Children of the Handcrafts.* 1935. Viking. 1st ed. 8vo. 192p. T5. $30.00

BAILEY, Carolyn Sherwin. *Finnigan II: His Nine Lives.* 1953. Viking. 1st ed. 95p. cloth. VG/dj. M20. $42.00

BAILEY, Edgar H. *Geology of Northern California. Bulletin 190.* 1966. San Francisco. CA Division of Mines & Geology. 4to. F. O7. $125.00

BAILEY, F.M. *Comprehensive Catalogue of Queensland Plants.* 1902. Brisbane. Cumming. 2nd. 8vo. ils/pl. 879p. VG. B1. $120.00

BAILEY, H.C. *Meet Mr Fortune: A Reggie Fortune Omnibus.* 1942. Doubleday Crime Club. 1st ed. 546p. gilt red cloth. VG. B22. $5.50

BAILEY, H.C. *Sullen Sky Mystery.* 1935. Crime Club. 1st ed. G. P3. $25.00

BAILEY, Harriet. *Nursing Mental Diseases.* 1929. 2nd. VG. K2. $10.00

BAILEY, J.O. *Pilgrims Through Time & Space.* 1947. Argus. 1st ed. VG/VG. P3. $50.00

BAILEY, J.O. *Poetry of Thomas Hardy: A Handbook & Commentary.* 1970. Chapel Hill. 1st ed. thick 8vo. 712p. NF/dj. C2. $45.00

BAILEY, James. *God-Kings & the Titans.* 1973. St Martin. 1st ed. ils/maps. 350p. F3. $20.00

BAILEY, Jean. *Cherokee Bill.* 1952. Abingdon/Cokesbury. ils Pers Crowell. VG/G. O3. $22.00

BAILEY, L.H. *Standard Cyclopedia of Horticulture.* 1939. NY. 3 vol. photos. 3639p. A17. $150.00

BAILEY, LAMB & MARKUN. *Pelican Tree & Other Panama Adventures.* 1953. North River. sgns. ils Beaudry. map ep. 96p. F/VG. B11. $50.00

BAILEY, Pearl. *Duey's Tale.* 1975. HBJ. 1st ed. inscr. F/F. B4. $40.00

BAILEY, Percival. *Intracranial Tumors.* 1933. Chicago. ils. 475p. NF. B14. $750.00

BAILEY & BAILEY. *Hortus Second.* 1959. Macmillan. 10th. 778p. cloth. VG. B1. $40.00

BAILEY & KNEBEL. *Convention.* 1964. Harper Row. VG/VG. P3. $18.00

BAILEY & KNEBEL. *Crossing in Berlin.* 1981. Doubleday. 1st ed. VG/VG. P3. $20.00

BAILY, Francis. *Journal of a Tour in Unsettled Parts of North America.* 1969. Carbondale. VG. O7. $35.00

BAIN, Donald. *War in Illinois: An Incredible True Story...* 1978. Prentice Hall. 1st ed. NF/NF. B35. $15.00

BAINBRIDGE, Beryl. *Bottle Factory Outing.* 1975. Braziller. 1st ed. F/F. B35. $20.00

BAINBRIDGE, Beryl. *Harriet Said.* 1972. Braziller. 1st ed. F/F. B35. $20.00

BAINBRIDGE, Henry C. *Peter Carl Faberge: Goldsmith & Jeweler.* 1949. London. 1st ed. 1/750. 126 pl. VG/dj. B14. $150.00

BAINBRIDGE. *Garbo.* 1971. HRW. 1st ed. VG/VG. D2. $35.00

BAIR, Deirdre. *Simone de Beauvoir.* 1990. NY. 1st ed thus. 718p. F/wrp. A17. $10.00

BAKE, William A. *Blue Ridge.* 1977. Viking. photos/map ep. 112p. VG/G. B10. $15.00

BAKELESS, John. *Eyes of Discovery.* 1950. Phil. VG. O7. $55.00

BAKER, Betty. *Great Ghost Stories of the Old West.* nd. BC. VG. P3. $4.00

BAKER, Denys Val. *Family at Sea.* 1981. William Kimber. 1st ed. F/F. P3. $20.00

BAKER, Denys Val. *Mill in the Valley.* 1984. William Kimber. 1st ed. VG/VG. P3. $20.00

BAKER, Denys Val. *Waterwheel Turns.* 1982. William Kimber. 1st ed. VG/VG. P3. $20.00

BAKER, Denys Val. *When Cornish Skies Are Smiling.* 1984. William Kimber. 1st ed. VG/VG. P3. $20.00

BAKER, George. *New Sad Sack.* 1946. NY. 1st ed. VG/VG. B5. $25.00

BAKER, Kenneth. *Turbulent Years.* 1993. London. Faber. 1st ed. ils. 498p. F/F. T10. $50.00

BAKER, Marcus. *Geographic Dictionary of Alaska.* 1906. WA. VG. O7. $125.00

BAKER, Nicholson. *Mezzanine.* 1988. Weidenfeld Nicolson. 1st ed. author's 1st book. F/F. B2. $125.00

BAKER, Nicholson. *Mezzanine.* 1989. London. Granta/Penguin. 1st ed. author's 1st novel. F/NF. A15. $30.00

BAKER, Nicholson. *Room Temperature.* 1990. Grove Weidenfeld. 1st ed. sgn. AN/dj. C2. $75.00

BAKER, Nicholson. *Room Temperature.* 1990. NY. Grove Weidenfeld. 1st ed. author's 2nd book. H11. $45.00

BAKER, Nicholson. *U & I.* 1991. Random. 1st ed. F/F. B2. $30.00

BAKER, Nicholson. *Vox.* 1992. NY. ARC. F/wrp. C6. $40.00

BAKER, Nicholson. *Vox.* 1992. Random. 1st ed. sgn. F/dj. C2. $60.00

BAKER, Richard M. *Death Stops the Rehearsal.* 1937. Scribner. 1st ed. VG/G. P3. $35.00

BAKER, Robert H. *Introducing the Constellations.* 1937. Viking. 1st ed. 8vo. 205p. cloth. G. K5. $10.00

BAKER, Roger. *Marilyn Monroe.* 1990. Portland. VG/VG. P3. $25.00

BAKER, Samuel. *Explorations of the Nile Tributaries of Abyssinia.* 1868. Hartford. VG. w/suppliment sketch. O7. $250.00

BAKER, Samuel. *Ismailia: A Narrative of Expedition to Central Africa...* 1875. NY. ils. 542p. G. B5. $70.00

BAKER, Scott. *Ancestral Hungers.* 1995. Tor. 1st ed. F/F. P3. $22.00

BAKER, Scott. *Night Child.* 1979. Berkley. 1st ed. AN/dj. M21. $25.00

BAKER, Susan. *My First Murder.* 1989. NY. 1st ed. author's 1st novel. F/F. H11. $25.00

BAKER & BAKER. *Water Elf & the Miller's Child.* 1928. Duffield. 1st ed. silhouettes. VG/G. M5. $75.00

BAKER & MURPHY. *Handbook of Marine Science.* 1981. Baca Raton. 8vo. hc. 223p. F. B1. $65.00

BAKKER, R.T. *Dinosaur Heresies.* 1986. Morrow. 481p. cloth. F/dj. D8. $36.00

BALCH, Glenn. *Little Hawk & the Free Horses.* 1957. Crowell. 1st ed. VG/G+. O3. $25.00

BALCHIN, Nigel. *Seen Dimly Before Dawn.* 1964. Reprint Soc. VG/VG. P3. $8.00

BALDACCI, David. *Absolute Power.* 1996. Warner. 1st ed. F/wrp. w/promo material. M22. $55.00

BALDUINUS & NIGRONUS. *De Calcio Antiquo et De Caliga Veterum.* 1667. Amsterdam. Andres Frisius. 1st ed. fld pl/table. contemporary bdg. B24. $1,250.00

BALDWIN, Faith. *Arizona Star.* 1945. Farrar Rinehart. 1st ed. F/VG+ clip. B4. $65.00

BALDWIN, Faith. *Career by Proxy.* 1939. Farrar Rinehart. 1st ed. inscr. F/VG+ clip. B4. $125.00

BALDWIN, Faith. *Golden Shoestring.* 1949. Rinehart. 1st ed. F/VG+ clip. B4. $50.00

BALDWIN, Faith. *Something Special.* 1940. Farrar Rinehart. 1st ed. VG+/VG+. B4. $65.00

BALDWIN, Hanson W. *Sea Fights & Shipwrecks.* 1955. Garden City. VG. O7. $20.00

BALDWIN, J.L. *Laws of Short Whist Edited by Baldwin...* 1866. London. 111p. VG. S1. $25.00

BALDWIN, James Mark. *Development & Evolution Including Psychophysical Evolution.* 1902. Macmillan. 395p. panelled crimson cloth. xl. G1. $65.00

BALDWIN, James Mark. *Genetic Theory of Reality...* 1915. Knickerbocker. 335p. gr cloth. VG. G1. $75.00

BALDWIN, James. *Devil Finds Work.* 1976. Dial. 1st ed. F/F. H11. $55.00

BALDWIN, James. *Evidence of Things Not Seen.* 1985. Holt. 1st ed. F/F. H11. $30.00

BALDWIN, James. *Giovanni's Room.* 1956. Dial. 1st ed. author's 2nd novel. 8vo. F/NF. T10. $350.00

BALDWIN, James. *Giovanni's Room.* 1956. NY. 1st ed. VG/VG. B5. $135.00

BALDWIN, James. *Going To Meet the Man.* 1965. Dial. 1st ed. F/NF. w/promo flyer. M19. $75.00

BALDWIN, James. *Nobody Knows My Name.* 1961. Dial. 1st ed. F/NF. B2. $45.00

BALDWIN, Thomas. *Kick Off.* 1932. Goldsmith. VG/G+. P12. $10.00

BALDWIN, William. *Hard To Catch Mercy.* 1993. Algonquin. 1st ed. sgn. F/F. M23. $40.00

BALDWIN & MEAD. *Rap on Race.* 1972. London. Corgi. 1st ed. pb. 255p. reading copy. R11. $8.00

BALDWIN & STOTZ. *At Bat With the Little League.* 1952. Phil. Macrae. 1st ed. NF/VG+. B4. $65.00

BALET, Jan. *What Makes an Orchestra.* nd. NY. Oxford. 1st ed. 41p. VG. C14. $15.00

BALFOUR, Victoria. *Rock Wives.* 1986. NY. Beech Tree/Morrow. 1st ed. photos Harvey Wang. F/NF. B4. $45.00

BALFOUR. *Life of Robert Louis Stevenson.* 1908. np. 2 vol. ils. VG. A4. $25.00

BALL, Brian N. *Baker Street Boys.* 1983. British BC. 1st ed. VG/VG. P3. $20.00

BALL, J.A. *Mexico.* nd. Mexico. 2nd. 56p. F3. $30.00

BALL, John. *Cop Cade.* 1978. Crime Club. 1st ed. VG/VG. P3. $15.00

BALL, John. *Kiwi Target.* 1989. Carroll Graf. 1st ed. F/F. P3. $16.00

BALL, Robert S. *In Starry Realms.* 1908 (1892). London. Pitman. cheap ed. 371p. cloth. K5. $18.00

BALL & BREEN. *Murder California Style.* 1987. St Martin. 1st ed. F/F. P3. $18.00

BALL & HALBERT. *Creek War of 1813 & 1814.* 1895. Chicago. Donohue Henneberry. 1st ed. 4 pl/fld map. 331p. VG. M8. $350.00

BALLANTINE, Betty. *American Celebration: Art of Charles Wysocki.* 1985. Greenwich. 192p. NF/NF. M20. $30.00

BALLANTINE, Bill. *Clown Alley.* 1982. Boston. 1st ed. F/F. B5. $35.00

BALLANTINE, Henry Winthrop. *California Corporation Laws.* 1932. Los Angeles. Parker Stone Baird. orig buckram. M11. $100.00

BALLANTINE, Sheila. *Norma Jean the Termite Queen.* 1975. Doubleday. ARC. author's 1st novel. F/NF. B4. $50.00

BALLANTYNE, R.M. *Coral Island: Tale of the Pacific Ocean.* nd. London. red full leather. VG. B30. $50.00

BALLANTYNE, R.M. *Hudson Bay; or, Everyday Life in the Wilds of North America.* 1971. NY. VG. O7. $40.00

BALLARD, J.G. *Concrete Island.* 1974. FSG. 1st ed. NF/NF. P3. $30.00

BALLARD, J.G. *Day of Creation.* 1988. FSG. 1st Am ed. F/F. M22. $20.00

BALLARD, J.G. *Hello America.* 1988. Carroll Graf. 1st ed. F/F. P3. $18.00

BALLARD, J.G. *High-Rise.* 1977. HRW. 1st Am ed. NF/VG+. R10. $20.00

BALLARD, J.G. *Kindness of Women.* 1991. FSG. 1st Am ed. NF/VG. M21. $10.00

BALLARD, J.G. *Memories of the Space Age.* 1988. Arkham. 1st ed. F/F. T2. $17.00

BALLARD, J.G. *Running Wild.* 1988. Hutchinson. 1st ed. F/F. P3. $30.00

BALLARD, J.G. *Rushing to Paradise.* 1994. London. 1st ed. sgn. F/F. A11. $50.00

BALLARD, J.G. *Unlimited Dream Company.* 1979. HRW. 1st ed. VG/VG. P3. $25.00

BALLARD, J.G. *Venus Hunters.* 1986. Gollancz. 1st ed. F/F. P3. $20.00

BALLARD, J.G. *War Fever.* 1991. FSG. 1st Am ed. F/F. G10. $12.00

BALLARD, Robert D. *Explorer.* 1992. Turner. ils. F. B17. $15.00

BALLARD, Robert D. *Exploring the Titanic.* 1988. Ontario. Scholastic/Madison Pr. VG/VG. A16. $25.00

BALLIETT, Whitney. *Improvising.* 1977. Oxford. 1st ed. F/NF. B2. $30.00

BALLINGER, Bill S. *Bill S Ballinger Triptych.* nd. Sherbourne. 1st ed. VG/VG. P3. $20.00

BALLINGER, Bill S. *Wife of the Red-Haired Man.* 1957. Harper. 1st ed. VG/G. P3. $15.00

BALLINGER, W.A. *Rebellion.* 1967. Howard Baker. 1st ed. F/F. P3. $15.00

BALLS, W. Lawrence. *Egypt of the Egyptians.* 1920. London/Bath/NY. Pitman. 1st ed. 266p. VG. W1. $20.00

BALTZ, John. *Honorable Edward D Baker, US Senator From Oregon.* 1888. Lancaster, PA. 248p. VG. A4. $125.00

BAMBARA, Toni Cade. *Salt Eaters.* 1980. Random. 1st ed. rem mk. F/F. B4. $45.00

BANCROFT, Betsy Barber. *Wild Honeysuckle.* 1966. Birmingham. Banner. unp. VG. B10. $10.00

BANCROFT, George. *Martin Van Buren: To the End of His Career.* 1889. NY. 1st ed. 239p. VG. B18. $45.00

BANCROFT, Griffing. *Snowy: Story of an Egret.* 1970. McCall. 1st ed. sgn. VG/VG. B11. $10.00

BANCROFT, Hubert Howe. *Literary Industries, a Memoir.* 1891. np. 477p. VG. A4. $85.00

BANDELIER, Adolf F. *Delight Makers.* 1918. Dodd Mead. 2nd. preface Hodge. intro Lummis. gilt gold cloth. VG. B14. $60.00

BANG, Betsy. *Five Tales From Bengal, The Demons of Rajpur.* 1980. Greenwillow. 8vo. ils. F/VG. B17. $5.00

BANG, Molly. *Buried Moon & Other Stories.* 1977. Scribner. 1st ed. 63p. F/F. P2. $35.00

BANG, Molly. *Goose.* 1966. Bl Sky. 1st ed. ils. unp. glossy brd. M/dj. M20. $11.00

BANG, Molly. *One Fall Day.* 1994. Greenwillow. ARC. ils. RS. pict brd. AN/dj. C8. $30.00

BANG, Molly. *Paper Crane.* 1985. Greenwillow. 1st ed. ils. NF/VG. C8. $25.00

BANGDEL & FLEMING. *Birds of Nepal.* 1976. Kathmandu. 1st ed. sgns. VG/VG. B5. $30.00

BANGS, John Kendrick. *House-Boat on the Styx.* 1896. Harper. decor brd. VG. P3. $50.00

BANGS, John Kendrick. *House-Boat on the Styx.* 1902 (1896). Harper. rpt. gilt red cloth. G+. M21. $10.00

BANGS, John Kendrick. *House-Boat on the Styx.* 1903. Harper. 8vo. ils Peter Newell. teg. blk/gilt red cloth. VG. T10. $50.00

BANISTER, Margaret. *Tears Are for the Living.* 1963. Houghton Mifflin. 2nd. 506p. VG. B10. $10.00

BANKHEAD, Tallulah. *My Autogbiography.* 1952. Sears Readers Club. NF. D2. $9.00

BANKHEAD, Tallulah. *Tallulah: My Autobiography.* 1952. Harper. 1st ed. F/F. B4. $85.00

BANKS, Carolyn. *Dark Room.* 1980. Viking. 1st ed. 279p. VG/G+. B10. $15.00

BANKS, Ernie. *Mr Cup.* 1971. Follet. 1st ed. VGVG. P8. $45.00

BANKS, Iain M. *Complicity.* 1995. Talese/Doubleday. 1st Am ed. AN/dj. M22. $20.00

BANKS, Iain M. *Player of Games.* 1988. Macmillan. 1st ed. F/F. P3. $30.00

BANKS, Iain M. *Walking on Glass.* 1985. Macmillan. 1st ed. F/F. M21/P3. $30.00

BANKS, Robert Webb. *Battle of Franklin, November 30, 1864...* 1908. NY/WA. Neale. 1st ed. pres. 88p. cloth. NF. w/prospectus. M8. $475.00

BANKS, Russell. *Affliction.* 1989. Harper Row. 1st ed. sgn. NF/NF. M23. $25.00

BANKS, Russell. *Affliction.* 1989. Toronto. McClelland. 1st ed. F/F. H11. $20.00

BANKS, Russell. *Book of Jamaica.* 1980. Houghton Mifflin. 1st ed. sgn. F/NF. M23. $45.00

BANKS, Russell. *Continental Death.* 1985. Harper Row. 1st ed. sgn. F/NF. M23. $40.00

BANKS, Russell. *New World*. 1978. Urbana, IL. 1st ed. sgn. F/wrp. A11. $35.00

BANKS, Russell. *Searching for Survivors*. 1975. NY. 1st ed. sgn. NF/NF. C6. $40.00

BANKS, Russell. *Success Stories*. 1986. Harper Row. 1st ed. sgn. F/F. M23. $35.00

BANKS, Russell. *Sweet Hereafter*. 1991. Harper Collins. 1st ed. sgn. NF/F. M23. $25.00

BANKS & KENNY. *Looking at Sails*. 1979. Boston. Sail Books. ils Peter Campbell. 143p. VG. T7. $20.00

BANNERMAN, Helen. *Little Black Sambo Animated*. 1943. Duenewald. 8vo. ils/6 moveables. NF. T10. $600.00

BANNERMAN, Helen. *Little Black Sambo Animated*. 1943. NY. Duenewald. ils Julian Wehr/6 moveables. 8vo. unp. sbdg. G+. T5. $200.00

BANNERMAN, Helen. *Little Black Sambo*. ca 1920. Saalfield. 8vo. ils Florence White Williams. fair. M5. $30.00

BANNERMAN, Helen. *Little Black Sambo*. ca 1920s. Chicago. Whitman. Just Right Books. ils C Shinn. 63p. gilt bdg. VG-. D1. $400.00

BANNERMAN, Helen. *Little Black Sambo*. ca 1928. Saalfield. ils Florence White Williams. G. D1. $32.00

BANNERMAN, Helen. *Little Black Sambo*. nd. Whitman. Tell-A-Tale. ils Gladys Turley Michell. VG. C14. $30.00

BANNERMAN, Helen. *Little Black Sambo*. 1942. Grosset Dunlap. ils Robert Moore. VG. M5. $110.00

BANNERMAN, Helen. *Little Black Sambo*. 1942. Saalfield. ils Ethel Hays. fair. M5. $65.00

BANNERMAN, Helen. *Little Black Sambo*. 1943. NY. Duenewald. moveables Julian Wehr. sbdg. VG. D1. $450.00

BANNERMAN, Helen. *Little Black Sambo*. 1948. Simon Schuster. 1st ed thus. ils Gustaf Tenggren. VG. D1. $85.00

BANNERMAN, Helen. *Little Black Sambo*. 1961. Whitman. probable 1st ed. ils Rutherford. unp. G+. T5. $45.00

BANNERMAN, Helen. *Little Black Sambo/Red Hen/Peter Rabbit*. 1942. Saalfield. ils Ethel Hays. VG. D1. $185.00

BANNERMAN, Helen. *Story of Little Black Mingo*. 1902. Londons. Nisbet. ils Bannerman. VG/VG. D1. $225.00

BANNERMAN, Helen. *Story of Little Black Quasha*. 1908. London. Nisbet. ils Bannerman. yel cloth. VG/VG. D1. $225.00

BANNERMAN, Helen. *Story of Little Black Sambo*. nd. Harper Collins. rpt. ils. F/F. T2. $18.00

BANNERMAN, Helen. *Story of Little Black Sambo*. 1903. NY. Stokes. 1st Am ed/lg format. ils Bannerman. VG. D1. $850.00

BANNERMAN, Helen. *Story of Little Black Sambo*. 1959. Western Pub. probable 1st ed. ils Violet LaMont. pict brd. AN. T5. $45.00

BANNERMAN, Helen. *Story of Little Black Sambo*. 1983 (1899). Berkeley. 1/100. ils Maryline Poole Adams. miniature. F. B24. $175.00

BANNING, George Hugh. *In Mexican Waters*. 1925. Boston. Lauriat. 8vo. map/pl. 196p. teg. gilt bl cloth. F. T10. $65.00

BANNING & HUGH. *Six Horses*. (1930). Century. G. O3. $18.00

BANNION, Della; see Sellers, Con.

BANTOCK, Nick. *Sabine Trilogy: Griffin & Sabine...* 1991-93. San Francisco. Chronicle Books. 1st ed. 3 vol. F. C2. $175.00

BANVILLE, John. *Athena*. 1995. London. 1st ed. sgn. F/F. A11. $50.00

BANVILLE, John. *Doctor Copernicus*. 1976. Norton. 1st Am ed. F/NF. B4. $125.00

BANVILLE, John. *Long Lankin*. 1970. London. Secker Warburg. UP. sgn. NF/wrp. B4. $850.00

BARAKAT, Layyah A. *Message From Mt Lebanon*. (1912). Sunday School Times Co. 1st ed. 167p. bl cloth. VG+. B22. $4.50

BARBEAU, Marius. *Pathfinders in the North Pacific*. 1958. Caldwell/Toronto. pres. VG. O7. $75.00

BARBER, John. *Richard Brautigan: An Annotated Bibliography*. 1990. McFarland. 1st ed. sgn. gr cloth. F/sans. C2. $45.00

BARBER, Noel. *Sinister Twilight: Fall of Singapore 1942*. 1968. Houghton Mifflin. 2nd. 364p. F/dj. A17. $10.00

BARBER, Noel. *Sultans*. 1973. Simon Schuster. 1st ed. 304p. VG. W1. $18.00

BARBER, Noel. *Woman of Cairo*. 1984. Hodder Stoughton. 1st ed. 8vo. 592p. NF/dj. W1. $20.00

BARBER, Red. *Broadcasters*. 1970. Dial. 1st ed. sgn. 271p. VG/VG. B11. $55.00

BARBER, Red. *1947: When All Hell Broke Loose in Baseball*. 1982. Doubleday. 1st ed. VG+/G. P8. $40.00

BARBER, W. Charles. *Elmira College: The First 100 Years*. 1955. McGraw Hill. 1st ed. 16 pl. 8vo. F/VG. B11. $25.00

BARBICAN, James. *Confessions of a Rum Runner*. 1928. NY. 1st ed. 12mo. 310p. red stp blk cloth. VG. H3. $45.00

BARBIER, Dominique. *Dressage for the New Age*. 1990. NY. Prentice Hall. 1st ed. F/F. O3. $25.00

BARBOUR, George M. *Florida for Tourists, Invalids, & Settlers*. 1885. Appleton. revised. 8vo. 325p. blk stp gilt red cloth. VG. T10. $150.00

BARBOUR, Paul. *One Man's Family*. 1938. VG. K2. $8.00

BARBOUR, Ralph Henry. *Crimson Sweater*. 1933. Appleton Century Crofts. VG/VG. P12. $8.00

BARBOUR, Ralph Henry. *Joyce of the Jasmines*. 1911. 1st ed. ils Underwood/Holloway. VG+. S13. $16.00

BARBOUR, Ralph Henry. *Right End Emerson*. 1922. Grosset Dunlap. ils Leslie Crump. G+. P12. $8.00

BARCLAY, Bill; see Moorcock, Michael.

BARCUS, Frank. *Fresh-Water Fury*. 1960. Wayne State. 1st ed. maps/ils. VG/dj. A16. $50.00

BARENHOLZ, Edith F. *George Brown Toy Sketchbook*. 1971. Princeton. Pyne. 1st ed. ils George Brown. NF/case. D1. $125.00

BARETTI, Joseph. *Journey From London to Genoa Through England, Portugal...* 1970. Fontwell. VG. O7. $65.00

BARFIELD, Owen. *Owen Barfield on CS Lewis*. 1989. Wesleyan U. 1st Am ed. M/clip. A18. $20.00

BARHEL, Joan. *Death in California*. 1981. NY. 1st ed. F/F. A17. $8.00

BARICH, Bill. *Laughing in the Hills*. 1980. NY. 1st ed. inscr. F/VG+. A11. $60.00

BARJAVEL, Rene. *Immortals*. 1974. Morrow. 1st ed. VG/VG. P3. $20.00

BARKER, Cicely Mary. *Little Book of Old Rhymes*. 1976. London. Blackie. ils. unp. NF/F. C14. $10.00

BARKER, Clive. *Books of Blood V*. 1988. Scream. 1/333. sgn. ils/sgn Harry O Morris. F/sans/case. T2. $75.00

BARKER, Clive. *Cabal*. 1988. Poseidon. 1st ed. F/F. P3. $25.00

BARKER, Clive. *Cabal.* 1988. Poseidon. 1st ed. 1/750. sgn. F/sans/case. T2. $95.00

BARKER, Clive. *Damnation Game.* 1985. Weidenfeld Nicolson. 1st ed. F/F. P3. $30.00

BARKER, Clive. *Damnation Game.* 1987. Putnam. 1st ed. author's 1st novel. F/F. H11. $40.00

BARKER, Clive. *Everville.* ARC. w/photo & promo kit. F/F. B30. $25.00

BARKER, Clive. *Great & Secret Show.* 1989. Harper Row. 1st ed. F/F. M21. $15.00

BARKER, Clive. *Imajica.* 1991. Harper Collins. 1st ed. VG/VG. P3. $23.00

BARKER, Clive. *In the Flesh: Tales of Terror.* 1986. Poseidon. 1st Am ed. F/F. T2. $25.00

BARKER, Clive. *Inhuman Condition: Tales of Terror.* 1986. Poseidon. 1st Am ed. F/F. T2. $25.00

BARKER, Clive. *Thief of Always.* 1992. Harper Collins. 1st ed. F/F. G10/H11. $25.00

BARKER, Clive. *Thief of Always.* 1992. Harper Collins. 1st ed. sgn. F/F. B35. $45.00

BARKER, Clive. *Weaveworld.* 1987. Collins. 1st ed. F/F. P3. $25.00

BARKER, Clive. *Weaveworld.* 1987. Poseidon. 1st ed. F/F. M19/R10. $17.50

BARKER, F. *Oliviers.* 1953. Phil. 1st ed. VG/G. B5. $35.00

BARKER, H.E. *Abraham Lincoln, His Life in Illinois...* 1940. NY. 1st ed. 64p. VG/dj. B18. $17.50

BARKER, John. *British in Boston Being the Diary of Lt John Barker...* 1924. Harvard. 1st ed. 73p. cloth. VG+. M8. $45.00

BARKER, Nicholas. *Catalogue of the Ahman-Murphy Aldine Collection at UCLA...* 1989. U Research Lib. 4to. 21p. 231p. NF/stiff wrp. A4. $95.00

BARKER, Nicholas. *Printer & the Poet: An Account of Printing...* 1970. Cambridge. private prt. 1/500. 4to. 54p. NF. A4. $145.00

BARKER, Ralph. *Blockade Busters.* 1977. Norton. 1st ed. 224p. F/dj. B22. $5.00

BARKER, Samuel W. *Cast Up by the Sea.* 1869. Harper. ils. 419p. VG. T7. $50.00

BARKER, Shirley. *Swear by Apollo.* 1958. Ramdom. 1st ed. VG/VG. P3. $35.00

BARLOW, Roger. *Sandy Steele & Fire at Red Lake.* 1959. Simon Schuster. 1st ed. G+/G. P12. $7.00

BARLOW, Roger. *Sandy Steele Adventures.* 1959. Simon Schuster. 1st ed. G+/G. P12. $7.00

BARLOW, Ronald S. *How To Be Successful in the Antique Business.* 1985. 8vo. ils. 186p. G. T3. $10.00

BARLOW, Theodore. *Justice of Peace: A Treatise...* 1745. London. Lintot Knapton. folio. contemporary calf. M11. $450.00

BARLOW. *Notes on Woman Printers in Colonial America & the US...* 1976. Hroswitha Club. 1/600. 89p. F/F. A4. $135.00

BARNARD, George N. *Photographic Views of Sherman's Campaign.* Dover. facsimile of 1866 ed. ils. G. T3. $15.00

BARNARD, Robert. *Bodies.* 1986. Scribner. 1st ed. VG/VG. P3. $14.00

BARNARD, Robert. *Cherry Blossom Corpse.* 1987. Scribner. 1st ed. VG/VG. P3. $15.00

BARNARD, Robert. *City of Strangers.* 1990. Scribner. 1st ed. sgn. F/F. T2. $20.00

BARNARD, Robert. *Death & the Chaste Apprentice.* 1989. Scribner. 1st ed. sgn. F/F. T2. $18.00

BARNARD, Robert. *Death of a Literary Widow.* 1980. Scribner. 1st ed. F/F. H11. $30.00

BARNARD, Robert. *Death of a Perfect Mother.* 1981. Scribner. ARC. F/F. H11. $30.00

BARNARD, Robert. *Death of a Salesperson & Other Untimely Exits.* 1989. Scribner. 1st Am ed. sgn. F/F. T2. $17.00

BARNARD, Robert. *Political Suicide.* 1986. Scribner. 1st ed. sgn. F/F. T2. $18.00

BARNARD, Robert. *Talent To Deceive: Agatha Christie.* 1980. Dodd Mead. 1st ed. VG/VG. P3. $15.00

BARNERS, Parker T. *House Plants & How To Grow Them.* 1909. Doubleday Page. 1st ed. 12mo. 236p. red/blk stp gilt gr cloth. NF. T10. $50.00

BARNES, Djuna. *Book of Repulsive Women.* 1915. NY. Guido Bruno. 1st ed. author's 1st book. NF/yel wrp. B24. $950.00

BARNES, Djuna. *Vagaries Malicieux.* 1974. NY. Frank Hallman. 1/500. F/glassine. B2. $75.00

BARNES, Eva Salisbury. *Red-Letter Days.* 1908. Hot Springs. photos. 147p. VG. B10. $10.00

BARNES, Harper. *Blue Monday.* 1991. St Louis. Patrice. 1st ed. author's 1st novel. sgn. F/pict wrp. T2. $18.00

BARNES, John. *Kaleidoscope Century.* 1995. NY. Tor. 1st ed/1st prt. photo of ES. F/F. T2. $45.00

BARNES, John. *Man Who Pulled Down the Sky.* 1986. Congdon Weed. 1st ed. VG/VG. P3. $20.00

BARNES, John. *Mother of Storms.* 1994. Tor. 1st ed. F/F. G10. $27.50

BARNES, John. *Orbital Resonance.* 1991. Tor. 1st ed. F/F. G10. $25.00

BARNES, Josiah. *Green Mountain Travellers' Entertainment.* 1860. NY. 360p. G. A17. $10.00

BARNES, Linda. *Dead Heat.* 1984. St Martin. 1st ed. xl. dj. P3. $7.00

BARNES, Linda. *Snake Tattoo.* 1989. St Martin. 1st ed. VG/VG+. N4. $25.00

BARNES, Linda. *Trouble of Fools.* 1987. St Martin. 1st ed. F/F. C2. $75.00

BARNES, NIVEN & POURNELLE. *Legacy of Heorot.* 1987. Simon Schuster. 1st ed. rem mk. F/F. N4. $25.00

BARNES, Ruth. *I Hear America Singing.* 1937. Winston. ils Robert Lawson. VG. M5. $40.00

BARNES, Trevor. *Midsummer Night's Killing.* 1989. Morrow. 1st ed. author's 1st book. F/F. H11. $20.00

BARNES, Trevor. *Pound of Flesh.* 1991. Morrow. 1st Am ed. author's 2nd novel. F/NF. M22. $10.00

BARNETT. *Shipping Literature of the Great Lakes: A Catalogue...* 1992. MI State. ils. 194p. F. A4. $65.00

BARNEY, Libeus. *Letters of the Pike's Peak Gold Rush.* 1959. San Jose. Talisman. 1/975. F/NF. O7. $85.00

BARNEY, Maginel Wright. *Valley of God Almighty Joneses.* 1965. NY. 1st ed. VG/VG. B5. $45.00

BARON & CARVER. *Bud Stewart: Michigan's Legendary Lure Maker.* 1990. Marceline, MO. 1st ed. photos/pl. 227p. AN. A17. $75.00

BARONI, Aldo. *Yucatan.* 1937. Mexico. Ediciones Botas. 1st ed. 211p. F3. $20.00

BARR, Nevada. *Superior Death.* 1994. Putnam. 1st ed. F/F. M22/T2. $45.00

BARR, Nevada. *Superior Death.* 1994. Putnam. 1st ed. sgn. F/F. H11. $55.00

BARR, Nevada. *Track of the Cat.* 1993. Putnam. UP. author's 1st book. F/wrp. B5. $300.00

BARR, Nevada. *Track of the Cat.* 1993. Putnam. 1st ed. author's 1st mystery. F/F. T2. $125.00

BARR & CRANE. *O'Ruddy.* 1903. NY. 1st ed. NF. C6. $100.00

BARR & MALONEY. *Types of Mental Defectives.* 1920. Phil. 31 pl. 179p. red cloth. VG. B14. $225.00

BARRETT, John G. *Civil War in North Carolina.* 1975. Chapel Hill. 1st ed/2nd prt. 484p. cloth. NF/dj. M8. $35.00

BARRETT, John Paul. *Sea Stories: Harrowing Tales of Mystery...* 1987. Gaff. 1st ed. sgn. pict off-wht cloth. VG. B11. $25.00

BARRETT, Neal Jr. *Dead Dog Blues.* 1994. St Martin. 1st ed. F/F. T2. $23.00

BARRETT, Neal Jr. *Hereafter Gang.* 1991. Ziesing. 1st ed. F/F. P3/T2. $25.00

BARRIE, James M. *Farewell Miss Julie Logan.* 1932. Scribner. 1st ed. VG. P3. $20.00

BARRIE, James M. *Margaret Ogilvy by Her Son.* 1897. NY. 12mo. 207p. teg. gilt brd. VG+. C14. $12.00

BARRIE, James M. *Peter Pan & Wendy.* 1930 (1921). Scribner. ils ML Attwell. VG. M5. $65.00

BARRIE, James M. *Peter Pan in Kensington Gardens.* 1910. London. Hodder Stoughton. 7th. ils Rackham. VG. D1. $450.00

BARRIE, James M. *Peter Pan.* 1987. Holt. 1st ed. ils Michael Hague. F/F. B17. $20.00

BARRIE, James M. *Plays of JM Barrie.* 1928. Lodnon. 1st ed. NF/NF. w/manuscript leaf from Half an Hour. C6. $250.00

BARRIE, James M. *Quality Street.* ca 1913. London. Hodder Stoughton. ils Hugh Thomson. 198p. gilt purple cloth. NF. T10. $275.00

BARRINGER, William E. *Lincoln's Rise to Power.* nd. np. 1st ed. 373p. VG/dj. B18. $25.00

BARRON, Greg. *Groundrush.* 1982. Random. 1st ed. rem mk. F/NF. B35. $20.00

BARROW, Frances Elizabeth. *Little Katy & Her Mother, by Aunt Laura.* 1863. Buffalo. 64p. lacks rear ep. B24. $95.00

BARROW, Frances Elizabeth. *Silver Medal, by Aunt Laura.* 1863. Buffalo. 64p. aeg. gilt pink cloth. NF. B24. $110.00

BARROW, John. *Mutiny of the Bounty.* 1980. Godine. new ed. edit Gavin Kennedy. 217p. F/VG. A4. $45.00

BARROWS, Edward M. *Great Commodore: Exploits of Mathew C Perry.* (1935). Indianapolis. ils/pl. map ep. 396p. bl cloth. VG/G. M23. $35.00

BARROWS, Marjorie. *Four Little Kittens.* 1957. Rand McNally. 1st ed. ils Harry Frees. F. M5. $12.00

BARROWS, Walter Bradford. *Michigan Bird Life.* 1912. MI Agriculture College. 70 full-p photos. 822p. wrp. A17. $50.00

BARRY, Iris. *DW Griffith: American Film Master.* 1940. MOMA Film Lib. 1st ed. VG+. B5/D2. $65.00

BARRY, James P. *Fate of the Lakes: Portrait of the Great Lakes.* 1972. Grand Rapids. Baker Book House. 1st ed. sgn. VG/VG. A16. $20.00

BARRY, James P. *Wrecks & Rescues of the Great Lakes.* 1981. CA. Howell-North. VG/VG. A16. $40.00

BARRY, Jerome. *Extreme License.* 1958. Crime Club. 1st ed. G/G. P3. $8.00

BARRY, Jerome. *Fall Guy.* 1960. Crime Club. 1st ed. VG/G. P3. $18.00

BARRYMORE, Ethel. *Memories.* 1955. Harper. 1st ed. inscr. NF/VG+. B4. $250.00

BARTH, John. *End of the Road.* 1958. Garden City. 1st ed. F/F. C2. $150.00

BARTHELME, Donald. *Amateurs.* 1976. FSG. 1st ed. F/F. B35. $30.00

BARTHELME, Donald. *Great Days.* 1979. FSG. 1st ed. F/F. B35. $24.00

BARTHELME, Frederick. *Tracer.* 1985. Simon Schuster. 1st ed. F/F. B35. $24.00

BARTHELME, Frederick. *Two Against One.* 1988. Weidenfield Nicholson. 1st ed. F/F. A20. $17.00

BARTHOLOMEW, Ed. *Houston Story 1836-1865.* 1951. Frontier. 1st ed. sgn. VG. P12. $47.50

BARTHOLOMEW, Roberts. *Manual of Instructions for Enlisting & Discharging Soldiers.* 1864. Phil. 276p. gr cloth. VG. B14. $275.00

BARTLESS, James H. *Restricted Problem of Three Bodies.* 1964 & 1965. Copenhagen. Ejnar Munksgaard. xl. wrp. K5. $50.00

BARTLETT, Arthur. *Game-Legs.* 1928. Cupples Leon. 1st ed. VG/G. O3. $20.00

BARTLETT, D.W. *Heroes of the Indian Rebellion.* 1860. Follett Foster. 456p. cloth. VG. M20. $52.00

BARTLETT, Kim. *Finest Kind: Fishermen of Gloucester.* 1977. Norton. 1st ed. 8vo. 251p. VG/VG. B11. $25.00

BARTLETT, Mary. *Gentians.* 1981 (1975). Dorset. new revised ed. 21 pl. 144p. F/dj. B26. $22.50

BARTLETT, Robert A. *Log of Bob Bartlett: True Story of Forty Years...* 1932. Bl Ribbon. 352p. G/G. B11. $55.00

BARTLETT, W.H. *Jerusalem Revisited.* 1855. London. ils. 202p. 3-quarter leather. B5. $350.00

BARTLETT & WHALLEY. *Derwentwater Sketchbook: A Commentary & Exact Reproduction.* ca 1984. London. Warne. 1/250. 2 booklets. F/F case. C8. $100.00

BARTLETT. *Nathaniel Tarn: A Descriptive Bibliography.* 1987. np. ils. 135p. F. A4. $135.00

BARTON, Clara. *Story of the Red Cross: Glimpses of Field Work.* 1904. Appleton. 1st ed. inscr/dtd 1904. 199p. tan cloth. VG. C6. $500.00

BARTON, F.P. *Barton Variation: The Only Certain Method of Slam Bidding.* 1935. London. 13th. 89p. VG. S1. $6.00

BARTON, Frederick. *El Cholo Feeling Passes.* 1985. Atlanta. Peachtree. 1st ed. author's 1st book. F/F. w/ephemera. H11. $40.00

BARTON, George A. *Archaeology & the Bible.* 1927. Am Sunday School Union. 5th. 127 pl. 481p. VG. W1. $65.00

BARTON, Mary. *Impressions of Mexico With Brush & Pen.* 1911. Methuen. 2nd. ils. 164p. G. F3. $20.00

BARTON, W. *JP Williamson: A Brother to the Sioux.* 1919. Revell. 1st ed. VG+/remnant. A15. $45.00

BARTON, William E. *Paternity of Abraham Lincoln...* 1920. NY. Doran. 1st ed. pres. 414p. VG. M8. $85.00

BARTON, William E. *Women Lincoln Loved.* 1927. London. 1st ed. ils. 284p. G+. B18. $37.50

BARTON & CAPOBIANCO. *Iris.* 1990. Doubleday. 1st ed. F/F. P3. $20.00

BARTRAM, George. *Job Abroad.* 1975. Macmillan. 1st ed. VG/VG. P3. $20.00

BARTRUM, Douglas. *Lilac & Laburnum.* 1959. London. ils/photos. 175p. cloth. VG. B26. $15.00

BARZUN, Jacques. *Catalogue of Crime.* 1971. Harper Row. 1st ed. xl. VG+/dj. N4. $30.00

BAS, C. *Monografias de Zoologia Marina. Vol I.* 1986. Barcelona. Inst Ciencias del Mar. 4to. 432p. pict wrp. B1. $120.00

BASBANES. *Gentle Madness: Bibliophiles, Bibliomanes...* 1995. np. ils. 638p. F/NF. A4. $35.00

BASCOM, Willard. *Crest of the Wave.* 1988. NY. xl. VG. O7. $10.00

BASCULE. *Advanced Auction Bridge (Royal Spades).* 1916. London. 2nd. 232p. VG. S1. $15.00

BASE, Graeme. *Eleventh Hour.* 1988. NY. 1st Am ed. NF/VG+. C8. $25.00

BASE, Graeme. *Sign of the Seahorse, a Tale of Greed & High Adventure...* 1992. NY. Abrams. 1st Am ed. 4to. F/F. C8. $25.00

BASILE, Giambattista. *Stories From the Pentamerone.* 1911. London. Macmillan. 1st ed thus. ils Warwick Goble. 301p. VG. P2. $260.00

BASKIN, Leonard. *Imps, Demons, Hobgoblins, Witches, Fairies & Elves.* 1984. NY. 1st ed. unp. VG+/dj. B18. $12.50

BASKIN, Leonard. *Passover Haggadah.* 1974. NY. Grossman. 1/500. sgn. quarter leather/marbled brd. F/case. w/sgn prt. B24. $500.00

BASLER, Roy P. *Concerning Lincoln & the Declaration of Indpendence.* 1982. Skokie. Blk Cat. 1/249. miniature. 45p. gold bl leatherette. M. B24. $35.00

BASS, Rick. *Deer Pasture.* 1985. College Sta, TX. 1st ed. F/F clip. M23. $125.00

BASS, Rick. *Watch.* 1989. Norton. 1st ed. inscr. F/F. M23. $50.00

BASS, T.J. *Godwhale.* 1975. Eyre Methuen. 1st ed. NF/NF. P3. $40.00

BASSETT, John. *Medical Reports of John V Bassett, MD: The Alabama Student.* 1941. Springfield. 1st ed. 62p. A13. $60.00

BASSETT, Sara Ware. *Within the Harbor.* 1948. NY. 1st ed. VG/VG. A17. $8.50

BASTABLE, Bernard; see Barnard, Robert.

BASTIN, Bruce. *Crying for the Carolines.* 1971. London. Studio Vista. 1st ed. F/wrp. B2. $25.00

BASTOW, Thelma W. *If Only...Story of Henri Peney.* 1964. Dietz. ARC. 250p. VG/G. B10. $15.00

BATCHELOR, D. *Jack Johnson & His Times.* 1957. London. ils. 190p. VG/VG. B5. $45.00

BATCHELOR, John C. *Gordon Liddy Is My Muse.* 1990. Simon Schuster. 1st ed. F/F. A20. $14.00

BATCHELOR, John Calvin. *American Falls.* 1985. Norton. 1st ed. F/F. H11. $40.00

BATCHELOR, John Calvin. *Gordon Liddy Is My Muse, by Tommy 'Tip' Paine.* 1990. NY. Linden. 1st ed. F/F. H11. $20.00

BATCHELOR & HOGG. *Naval Gun.* 1978. England. 1st ed. ils/photos. 142p. F/F. E1. $45.00

BATEMAN, Colin. *Divorcing Jack.* 1995. Arcade. 1st Am ed. author's 1st book. F/F. M23. $25.00

BATEMAN, Ed. *Horse Breaker!* 1947. Seattle. Wilson. 1st ed. photos. 110p. VG. O3. $35.00

BATES, Arthenia J. *Seeds Beneath the Snow.* 1969. NY. Greenwich. 1st ed. sgn. NF/VG. B4. $125.00

BATES, H.E. *Down the River.* 1937. Holt. ARC. ils Agnes Miller Parker. 141p. VG/dj. M20. $155.00

BATHE, Basil W. *Seven Centuries of Sea Travel: From Crusades to Cruises.* 1990. NY. Portland House. VG/dj. A16. $25.00

BATMAN, Richard. *Outer Coast.* 1985. NY. VG. O7. $15.00

BATTELL, Joseph. *Yankee Boy From Home.* 1864. NY. Miller. O3. $295.00

BATTEN, Jack. *Straight No Chaser.* 1989. Canada. Macmillan. 1st ed. F/F. P3. $20.00

BATTLE, Kemp Plummer. *Memories of an Old-Timer Tar Heel.* 1945. Chapel Hill. 1st ed. ils. 296p. VG/dj. B18. $22.50

BATTS, John Stuart. *British Manuscript Diaries of the 19th Century...* 1976. London. Centaur. M11. $35.00

BATTY, E.C. *Americans Before Columbus.* 1951. NY. 1st ed. VG/G. B5. $25.00

BAUCHER, F. *New Method of Horsemanship.* nd. NY. Jenkins. VG. O3. $65.00

BAUDOUIN, Frans. *Pietro Paulo Rubens.* 1977. Abrams. trans Elsie Callander. ils. 407p. cloth. dj. D2. $150.00

BAUER, Margaret Jean. *Animal Babies.* 1949. Donohue. ils Jacob Bates Abbott. VG/G. B17. $10.00

BAUER, Steven. *Satyrday.* 1980. Berkley Putnam. 1st ed. NF/NF. P3. $15.00

BAUGHMAN, Robert W. *Kansas in Maps.* 1961. KS State Hist Soc. 90+ maps. F/worn. O7. $95.00

BAUM, L. Frank. *Aunt Jane's Nieces.* 1906. Reilly Lee. not 1st ed. as by Edith VanDyne. F/NF. A17. $10.00

BAUM, L. Frank. *Dorothy & the Wizard in Oz.* 1920. Reilly Lee. decor brd. G+. P3. $75.00

BAUM, L. Frank. *Emerald City of Oz.* 1939. Rand McNally. G. P3. $10.00

BAUM, L. Frank. *Father Goose, His Book.* ca 1910. Donahue. 6th. ils WW Denslow. unp. VG/dj. D1. $385.00

BAUM, L. Frank. *Lost Princess of Oz.* 1941. Reilly Lee. NF/NF. P3. $100.00

BAUM, L. Frank. *Magic of Oz.* 1931. Reilly Lee. NF/NF. P3. $125.00

BAUM, L. Frank. *New Wizard of Oz.* (1899). Bobbs Merrill. 6th. 8 pl. 208p. VG/poor. P2. $75.00

BAUM, L. Frank. *New Wizard of Oz.* ca 1940. Bobbs Merrill. MTI. ils Denslow. pict ep. VG. M19. $35.00

BAUM, L. Frank. *New Wizard of Oz.* 1939. Bobbs Merrill. ils WW Denslow. 208p. gilt gr cloth. VG/tattered. D1. $275.00

BAUM, L. Frank. *New Wizard of Oz.* 1944. Bobbs Merrill. ils Evelyn Copelman. F. M19. $85.00

BAUM, L. Frank. *Ozma of Oz.* 1907. Reilly Lee. 1st ed/3rd state. ils JR Neill. tan cloth. VG. D1. $875.00

BAUM, L. Frank. *Rinkitink in Oz.* pre-1935. Chicago. Reilly Lee. ils JR Neill. 314p. red cloth. NF/torn. D1. $400.00

BAUM, L. Frank. *Road to Oz.* 1941. Reilly Lee. NF/NF. P3. $100.00

BAUM, L. Frank. *Tin Woodman of Oz.* 1937. Reilly Lee. NF/NF. P3. $120.00

BAUM, L. Frank. *Wizard of Oz.* 1939. Grosset Dunlap. abridged ed. ils Oskar Lebeck. F/VG. P3. $35.00

BAUM, L. Frank. *Wizard of Oz.* 1944. Bobbs Merrill. ils Evelyn Copelman. VG/dj. B30. $12.00

BAUM, L. Frank. *Wizard of Oz.* 1944. Saalfield. moveables Julian Wehr. sbdg. VG. D1. $200.00

BAUM, L. Frank. *Wizard of Oz.* 1991. Jelly Bean. 1st ed thus. ils Charles Santore. F/VG. B17. $8.50

BAUM, L. Frank. *Woggle-Bug Book.* 1905. Reilly Britton. 1st/only ed. ils Ike Morgan. G. D1. $1,600.00

BAUM, Vicki. *Headless Angel*. 1948. Doubleday. 1st ed. NF/NF. B4. $50.00

BAUMGARDT, Carola. *Johannes Kepler: Life & Letters*. 1951. NY. Philosophical Lib. 1st ed. 8vo. 209p. VG/G. K5. $30.00

BAUMGARTL, I. *Sea Gods*. 1937. Chicago. Kroch. 1st ed. ils Gertrude S Ruben. NF/dj. S9. $30.00

BAUMGARTNER & FULTON. *Bibliography of the Poem, Syphilis Sive Morbus Gallicus*. 1935. Yale. ils. 158p. bl cloth. K1. $50.00

BAUSCH, Richard. *Violence*. 1992. Houghton Mifflin. 1st ed. F/F. M22. $25.00

BAUXBAUM, E.C. *Collector's Guide to the National Geographic Magazine*. 1956. Wilmington, DE. 1st ed. NF. H7. $25.00

BAVIER, Bob. *America's Cup Fever*. 1980. Ziff Davis. ils 240p. VG/dj. T7. $20.00

BAXT, George. *Alfred Hitchcock Murder Case*. 1986. NY. 1st ed. F/F. H11. $20.00

BAXT, Geroge. *Neon Graveyard*. 1979. St Martin. 1st ed. VG/VG. P3. $30.00

BAXTER, Betty. *Supposin'*. 1931. Volland. A Sunny Book. 1st ed. sm 8vo. VG. M5. $60.00

BAXTER, Charles. *First Light*. 1987. Viking. 1st ed. F/F. M23. $20.00

BAXTER, Charles. *Relative Stranger*. 1990. Norton. 1st ed. F/F. M23. $20.00

BAXTER, Charles. *Shadow Play*. 1993. NY. Norton. ARC. sgn. F/decor wrp. S9. $75.00

BAXTER, John. *Kid*. 1981. Viking. 1st ed. F/F. B35. $15.00

BAXTER, Lorna. *Eggchild*. 1979. Dutton. 1st ed. VG/VG. P3. $18.00

BAXTER, Richard. *Guilty Women*. 1943. Quality Pr. 7th. NF/NF. P3. $9.00

BAYER, Oliver Weld. *Eye for an Eye*. 1946. Tower. VG/G. P3. $15.00

BAYER, William. *Blind Side*. 1989. Villard. 1st ed. F/F. H11. $35.00

BAYER, William. *Peregrine*. 1981. Congdon Lattes. 1st ed. F/F. A20/P3. $25.00

BAYER, William. *Punish Me With Kisses*. 1980. Congdon Lattes. 1st ed. VG/VG. P3. $15.00

BAYER, William. *Punish Me With Kisses*. 1980. NY. Congdon. 1st ed. NF/NF. H11. $25.00

BAYER, William. *Switch*. 1984. Simon Schuster. 1st ed. F/NF. H11. $45.00

BAYLEY, Barrington J. *Rod of Light*. 1987. Arbor. 1st ed. F/F. P3. $16.00

BAYLEY & MAYNE. *Mouldy*. 1982. Knopf. 1st Am ed. ils Nicola Bayley. unp. M/M. D1. $45.00

BAYLEY & METCALFE. *Golden Calm*. 1980. NY. VG. O7. $20.00

BAYLISS, Marguerite F. *Yearbook of Show Horses*. 1936. NY. Blackwell. 2 vol. 4to. G. O3. $125.00

BAYLOR, Byrd. *Way To Start a Day*. 1978. Scribner. 1st ed. ils. NF/NF. C8. $35.00

BAYLOR, Don. *Don Baylor*. 1989. St Martin. 1st ed. inscr. F/F. P8. $55.00

BAYNE, Samuel G. *Pith of Astronomy...* 1898 (1896). Harper. 19 pl. 122p. ils cloth. K5. $35.00

BAYNES, Ernest. *Sprite: Story of a Red Fox*. 1938. Scribner. 1st Am ed. VG. O3. $25.00

BAYNTON-WILLIAMS, Ashley. *Town & City Maps of the British Isles, 1800-1855*. 1992. London. Studio. 56 plans. AN/dj. O7. $50.00

BAYNTON-WILLIAMS, Roger. *Investing in Maps*. 1969. Clarkson Potter. F/dj. O7. $65.00

BEACH, Bell. *Riding & Driving for Women*. 1912. Scribner. 1st ed in better bdg. VG. O3. $125.00

BEACH, Edward L. *Dust on the Sea*. 1972. Holt. 1st ed. F/NF. H11. $25.00

BEACH, Edward L. *Run Silent, Run Deep*. 1955. Holt. 1st ed. NF/NF. B4. $125.00

BEACH, Harlan P. *Geography & Atlas of Protestant Missions, Volumes I & II...* 1901 & 1903. NY. Student Volunteer Movement for Foreign Missions. 2 vol. O7. $100.00

BEACH, Rex. *Ne'er-Do-Well*. 1911. NY. Harper. 1st ed. 8vo. ils HC Christy. gilt bl cloth. F. T10. $150.00

BEACH, S.A. *Apples of New York*. 1905. Albany. Lyon. 2 vol. pl. VG. H7. $140.00

BEACH, Sylvia. *Shakespeare & Company*. 1959. NY. 1st ed. VG/VG. B5. $35.00

BEADLE, J.H. *Western Wilds*. 1878. Cincinnati. lg map. 624p. marbled ep. half leather. fair. B18. $45.00

BEAGLE, Peter S. *Folk of the Air*. 1986. Ballantine. 1st ed. F/NF. G10. $20.00

BEAGLE, Peter S. *I See By My Outfit*. 1966. Muller. 1st Eng ed. F/F. M19. $75.00

BEAGLEHOLE, J.C. *Life of Captain James Cook*. 1974. Stranford. ils/fld map. 760p. F/dj. B26. $45.00

BEAHM, George. *Stephen King Story: A Literary Profile*. 1991. Andrews McMeel. 1st ed. F/F. T2. $20.00

BEALE, Lionel S. *How To Work With the Microscope*. 1865. Phil. Lindsay Blakiston. 3rd. 8vo. gr cloth. F. B14. $75.00

BEALE, Lionel S. *Microscope: Its Application to Clinical Medicine*. 1854. London. ils. 303p. cloth. VG. B14. $125.00

BEALE, Marie. *Flight Into America's Past*. 1932. NY. Putnam. 1st ed. 286p. G. F3. $10.00

BEAMISH, Richard J. *Boy's Story of Lindbergh: The Lone Eagle*. 1928. Phil. Winston. 8vo. 288p. VG+. C14. $18.00

BEAN, L.L. *Hunting-Fishing-Camping*. 19444. LL Bean. photos/maps. blk stp red bdg. G. P12. $10.00

BEAR, Elizabeth. *Better Flower Arrangements for Home & Exhibition*. 1953. Scranton. Laurel. sgn. G. B11. $7.00

BEAR, Firman E. *Soils & Fertilizers*. 1953 (1924). NY. 4th. ils/maps. 420p. VG. B26. $15.00

BEAR, Greg. *Eon*. 1985. NY. Bluejay. 1st ed. F/F. M23. $75.00

BEAR, Greg. *Eternity*. 1988. Warner. 1st ed. F/F. P3. $17.00

BEAR, Greg. *Forge of God*. 1987. Tor. 1st ed. VG+/NF. M23. $35.00

BEAR, Greg. *Heads*. 1991. St Martin. 1st ed. F/F. M23. $15.00

BEAR, Greg. *Moving Mars*. 1993. NY. Tor. 1st ed. F/F. M23. $40.00

BEAR, Greg. *Psychlone*. 1990. Severn. 1st hc ed. author's 2nd book. F/F. G10. $30.00

BEAR, Greg. *Queen of Angels*. 1990. Warner. 1st trade ed (preceded by Easton ed). F/NF. G10. $15.00

BEAR, Greg. *Tangents*. 1989. Warner. 1st ed. F/F. M23. $30.00

BEAR, Greg. *Wind From the Burning Woman*. 1983. Sauk City. Arkham. 1st ed. 1/3046. F/F. T2. $85.00

BEARD, Henry. *Miss Piggy's Guide to Life*. 1981. Knopf. 1st ed. F/F. B17. $20.00

BEARDSLEY, Aubrey. *Yellow Book: An Illustrated Quarterly.* 1894-1897. London. Lane/Bodley Head. 13 vol. blk prt yel cloth. VG to NF. T10. $1,600.00

BEARDSLEY & GLASSCO. *Under the Hill.* 1959. Grove. 1st ed. ils. dj. A17. $9.50

BEARE, George. *Snake on the Grave.* 1974. Houghton Mifflin. 1st ed. VG/VG. P3. $15.00

BEARSS, Edwin Cole. *Decision in Mississippi...* 1962. Jackson. MS Comm on War Between States. 1st ed. 636p. NF/NF. M8. $95.00

BEASLEY, Conger. *Hidalgo's Beard.* 1979. Andrews McMeel. 1st ed. VG/VG. P3. $20.00

BEASLEY, H.M. *Beasley Contract Bridge System.* 1935. London. 128p. VG. S1. $8.00

BEASLEY, N. *Men-Working.* 1931. NY. 1st ed. ils/index. 296p. VG/VG. B5. $25.00

BEASLEY, Norman *Freighters of Fortune* 1930. Harper. G/dj. A16. $45.00

BEASTON, Bud. *Master Farrier.* 1975. Sperry. OK Farrier's College. sgn. 191p. VG/VG. O3. $25.00

BEATLEY, Janice C. *Vascular Plants of the NV Test Site & General S NV...* 1976. Springfield. photos. F. B26. $42.50

BEATON, Cecil. *Diaries 1955-1963.* 1976. 1st ed. NF/VG+. S13. $20.00

BEATON, Cecil. *Face of the World.* 1957. John Day. photos. 240p. NF. B14. $55.00

BEATON, M.C. *Death of a Hussy.* 1990. NY. 1st ed. F/NF. H11. $20.00

BEATON & TYNAN. *Persona Grata.* 1954. Putnam. 1st Am ed. F/NF. B4. $175.00

BEATTIE, Ann. *Distortions.* 1976. Doubleday. 1st ed. sgn. F/F. B35. $100.00

BEATTIE, Ann. *Falling in Place.* 1980. Random. 1st ed. rem mk. F/F. B35. $20.00

BEATTIE, Ann. *Falling in Place.* 1980. Random. 1st ed. sgn. author's 2nd novel. NF/F. B4. $75.00

BEATTIE, Ann. *Falling in Place.* 1980. Random. 2nd. VG/clip. B10. $25.00

BEATTIE, Ann. *Love Always.* 1985. Random. 1st ed. author's 3rd novel. F/F. B4. $45.00

BEATTIE, Ann. *Picturing Will.* 1989. Random. 1st ed. AN/dj. B4. $45.00

BEATTIE, Ann. *Secrets & Surprises.* 1978. Random. 1st ed. F/F. B5. $75.00

BEATTIE, Ann. *What Was Mine.* 1991. Random. AP. 8vo. F/wrp. S9. $25.00

BEATTIE, Ann. *Where You'll Find Me.* 1986. NY. Linden. 1st ed. sgn. F/F. B4. $50.00

BEATTY, Bill. *Next Door to Paradise.* 1965. Melbourne. VG. O7. $20.00

BEATY, John O. *Swords in the Dawn.* 1937. Longman Gr. 1st ed. ils Henry Pitz. 212p. map ep. F. C14. $12.00

BEATY, John. *Crossroads: Novel of the 20th-Century South.* 1956. Dallas. Wilkerson. VG/G. B10. $12.00

BEATY, Josephine Powell. *Road to Jericho.* 1965. Dorrance. inscr pres. 154p. F/F. B10. $12.00

BEATY, Richard Edward. *Mountain Angels: Trials of the Mountaineers of Blue Ridge...* 1928. Front Royall. self pub. 125p. VG. B10. $25.00

BEAUCHAMP, Loren; see Silverberg, Robert.

BEAUFORT, Duke of. *Driving.* 1889. London. Longman Gr. lg paper ed. 1/250. G. O3. $95.00

BEAUMONT, Charles. *Shadow Play.* 1964. London. Panther. 1st ed. VG+. A11. $25.00

BECCARIA, Cesare. *Essay on Crimes & Punishments, Trans From Italian...* 1801. London. 1st 19th-C ed in Eng. modern quarter calf. M11. $275.00

BECHET, Sidney. *Treat It Gentle.* 1960. Hill Wang. 1st ed. F/NF. B2. $65.00

BECHTEL, CRIBB & LAUNERT. *Manual of Cultivated Orchid Species.* 1981. Cambridge. 1st MIT ed. photos/drawings. 444p. F/dj. B26. $52.50

BECK, Ann. *History of the British Medical Administration of E Africa.* 1970. Cambridge. 1st ed. 271p. VG. A13. $30.00

BECK, Carl. *Roentgen Ray Diagnosis & Therapy.* 1904. NY. 1st ed. 460p. VG. B14. $225.00

BECK, K.K. *Murder in a Mummy Case.* 1986. Walker. 1st ed. author's 2nd book. rem mk. F/F. N4. $17.50

BECK, Richard. *Icelandic Lyrics.* 1930. Bjarnason. Reykjavik. 1st ed. half leather. VG. A17. $30.00

BECK & ROTH. *Music in Prints.* 1965. NY Public Lib. 4to. 120p. F. A4. $85.00

BECK. *Away in the Manger, a Christmas Carousel Book.* 1994. np. fld popups w/ribbon ties. F. A4. $65.00

BECKER, Robert H. *Disenos of California Ranchos: Maps of 37 Land Grants...* 1964. San Francisco. BC of CA. 1/400. folio. AN. O7. $825.00

BECKER, Robert. *Designs on the Land: Disenos of California Ranchos...* 1969. San Francisco. Grabhorn. BC of CA. 1/500. ils/maps. 178p. suede/cloth. NF. T10. $400.00

BECKER, Stephen. *Chinese Bandit.* 1975. Random. 1st ed. VG/VG. P3. $25.00

BECKER, Stephen. *Dog Tags.* 1973. Random. 1st ed. VG/VG. P3. $25.00

BECKER, Stephen. *Last Mandarin.* 1979. Random. 1st ed. VG/VG. P3. $25.00

BECKER, Stephen. *When the War Is Over.* 1969. Random. 1st ed. VG/VG. P3. $25.00

BECKER. *Estelle Donheny Collection.* 1989. NY. Christie's. 4to. 134p. red cloth. F. A4. $85.00

BECKETT, Samuel. *How It Is.* 1964. London. 1/100. sgn. full vellum. C6. $350.00

BECKETT, Samuel. *Rockaby & Other Short Pieces.* 1981. Grove. 1st ed. F/F. B35. $22.00

BECKFORD, William. *Vathek.* 1928. John Day. 1st ed. 229p. NF/ragged dj/worn case. M20. $65.00

BECKMANN, Frank Harrison. *Dust of India.* 1937. Boston. 1st ed. 8vo. 300p. VG/G. B11. $25.00

BEDELL & CREHORE. *Alternating Currents: Analytical & Graphical Treatment...* 1893. NY. Johnston. 2nd. assn sgn. 8vo. 325p. gr cloth. VG. T10. $50.00

BEDFORD, Annie North. *Disneyland on the Air.* 1955. Mickey Mouse Club Book. TVTI. VG. P3. $20.00

BEDFORD, Annie North. *Susie's New Stove, the Little Chef's Cookbook.* nd. Little Golden. 1st/A ed. ils Corinne Malvern. VG. M5. $18.00

BEDFORD, Francis D. *Another Book of Verses for Children.* 1925. Macmillan. 1st rpt. 8vo. stp gray cloth. NF. M5. $65.00

BEDFORD, Sybille. *Aldous Huxley Vol 1: 1894-1939.* 1973. Chatto Windus. VG/VG. P3. $25.00

BEDNAR, Kamil. *Puppets & Fairy Tales.* 1958. Prague. ils/photos. 52p. VG/dj. A17. $20.00

BEE, Clair. *Chip Hilton: Pitcher's Duel (#6).* 1950. Grosset Dunlap. lists 8 titles. VG/dj. M20. $22.00

BEEBE, Lucius. *Mansions on Wheels.* 1959. NY. 1st ed. VG/G. B5. $50.00

BEEBE, William. *Jungle Peace.* 1918. NY. 1st ed. inscr. NF. A9. $50.00

BEEBE, William. *Two Bird-Lovers in Mexico.* 1905. Houghton Mifflin. 1st ed/2nd issue. teg. VG. A20. $85.00

BEEBE & CLEGG. *American West.* 1955. Dutton. 1st ed. 4to. 412p. F/NF. T10. $65.00

BEEBE & CLEGG. *US West: The Saga of Wells Fargo.* 1949. Dutton. 1st ed. 8vo. 320p. red cloth. VG/dj. T10. $40.00

BEEBE & CLEGG. *When Beauty Rode the Rails.* 1962. NY. 1st ed. 222p. G+/torn. B18. $22.50

BEEBEE, Chris. *Hub.* 1987. MacDonald. F/F. P3. $22.00

BEECHER, Elizabeth. *Roy Rogers on the Double-R Ranch.* 1951. Simon Schuster. VG. P3. $15.00

BEECHER, Henry Ward. *Star Papers; or, Experiences of Art & Nature.* 1855. NY. JC Derby. 359p. aeg. gilt full leather. VG. A4. $45.00

BEECHER, Henry Ward. *Theodore Tilton Vs Henry Ward Beecher...* 1875. NY. McDivitt Campbell. 3 vol. VG. M11. $350.00

BEECHER, John. *Collected Poems 1924-1974.* 1975. Macmillan. inscr. VG/VG. w/sgn letter. M19. $45.00

BEECHER, John. *Report to the Stockholders.* 1962. Rampart. 1/300. sgn. NF. M19. $45.00

BEEDING, Francis. *Death Walks in Eastrepps.* 1931. Mystery League. 1st ed. G. P3. $15.00

BEEMAN, Howard. *Veterinary Obstetrics & Zoo Technics.* 1932. Am Remount Assn. 131p. VG. O3. $45.00

BEER & BEER. *Vistas in Astonomy.* 1977. Oxford. Pergamon. 412p. VG. K5. $30.00

BEERBOHM, Max. *Christmas Garland, Woven by Max Beerbohm.* 1912. London. Heineman. 1st ed. gilt bl cloth. F. B24. $125.00

BEERBOHM, Max. *Happy Hypocrite. A Fairy Tale for Tired Men.* 1897. NY. Lane. 1st ed. sm 8vo. 53p. F/prt wrp. B24. $485.00

BEERBOHM, Max. *Letters to Reggie Turner.* 1965. np. photos/caricatures. 312p. F/VG. A4. $45.00

BEERBOHM, Max. *Mainly on the Air.* 1947. Knopf. 1st Am ed. 12mo. 142p. gilt blk cloth. F/NF. T10. $50.00

BEERBOHM, Max. *Peep Into the Past.* 1923. private prt. 1/300 on Japanese vellum. NF/rpr case. T10. $300.00

BEERBOHM, Max. *Rossetti & His Circle.* 1921. Heinemann. 1st ed. 23 mtd pl. gilt bl cloth. NF. T10. $125.00

BEERBOHM, Max. *Things New & Old.* 1923. London. Heinemann. 1st ed. 1/380. sgn. aeg. F/F. w/sgn extra plate. B24. $450.00

BEERCROFT & HAYCRAFT. *Treasury of Great Mysteries. Vol 1 & 2.* nd. Nelson Doubleday. VG/VG. P3. $15.00

BEERS. *Bibliographies in American History: Guide to Materials...* 1938. HW Wilson. nearly 7700 entries. xl. VG. A4. $35.00

BEERY, Jesse. *Four Types of Disposition.* 1921. Pleasant Hill. VG/wrp. O3. $35.00

BEESLEY & HOSTETTER. *It's a Racket.* 1929. Chicago. 1st ed. photos. F/torn. A15. $75.00

BEESON, Leola Selman. *History Stories of Milledgeville & Baldwin County.* 1943. Macon, GA. 1st ed. 1/300. 202p. cloth. NF. M8. $125.00

BEETON, Isabella. *Book of Household Management.* 1892. np. ils. G. M17. $50.00

BEEZLEY, William. *Insurgent Governor.* 1973. Lincoln, NE. 1st ed. 195p. dj. F3. $15.00

BEGIN, Menachem. *Revolt Story of the Irgun.* 1951. NY. Schuman. 1st ed. 8vo. 386p. bl cloth. G. B14. $75.00

BEGLEY, Louis. *Man Who Was Late.* 1993. Knopf. 1st ed. F/F. M23. $20.00

BEHAN, Brendon. *Brendon Behan's New York.* nd. np. 1st ed. F/VG+. N3. $10.00

BEHAN & HOGARTH. *Brendan Behan's Island. An Irish Sketch-Book.* 1962. NY. Bernard Geis. 1st ed. sgns. F/F. A17. $135.00

BEHN, Harry. *All Kinds of Time.* 1950. Harcourt Brace. 1st ed. ils. F/VG+. P2. $35.00

BEHN, Noel. *Shadowboxer.* 1969. Simon Schuster. 1st ed. VG. P3. $12.00

BEHR, M. *Outlines of Universal History.* 1861. Boston. 8vo. 595p. quarter leather/blk brd. G. T3. $17.00

BEHRMAN, Cynthia F. *Victorian Myths of the Sea.* 1977. Athens. VG. O7. $20.00

BEHRMAN. *Three Plays: Serena Blandish; Meteor; Second Man.* 1934. Farrar Rinehart. inscr/dtd 1939. cloth. NF. D2. $40.00

BEIER. *Art in Nigeria.* 1960. Cambridge. F. D2. $25.00

BEITTEL, Will. *Santa Barbara's Street & Park Trees.* 1972. Santa Barbara. ils/5 maps. 94p. photo wrp. B26. $15.00

BELFRAGE, Cedric. *Let My People Go.* 1940. London. Gollancz. 319p. G. A17. $8.50

BELIAEV, Alexander. *Professor Dowell's Head.* 1980. Macmillan. 1st ed. VG/VG. P3. $15.00

DELILES, Mark A. *Thomas Jefferson's Abridgement of Words of Jesus...* 1993. self pub. 72p. VG. B10. $8.00

BELITT, Ben. *Five-Fold Mesh.* 1938. Knopf. 1st ed. 50p. VG. B10. $12.00

BELKNAP, Jeremy. *Foresters: An American Tale.* 1970. Gregg. 216p. VG. A17. $10.00

BELL, Bill. *Saxophone Boy.* 1980. Tundra. 1st ed. sgn. ils. 95p. VG+/dj. M20. $37.00

BELL, Charles G. *Sons for a New America.* 1966. Dunwoody, GA. 78p. VG. B10. $12.00

BELL, Clare. *Ratha's Creature.* 1983. Atheneum. 1st ed. F/F. P3. $11.00

BELL, George Joseph. *Principles of the Law of Scotland. The Third Edition.* 1833. Edinburgh/London. Simpkin Marshall. quarter calf. M11. $225.00

BELL, Gertrude Lowthian. *Letters of...* 1927. London. Benn. 2 vol. 5th. 30 pl/2 maps. VG. W1. $65.00

BELL, Gordon B. *Golden Troubadour.* 1980. McGraw Hill. F/F. P3. $13.00

BELL, John. *Travels From St Petersburg in Russia to Diverse Parts...* 1763 & 1768. Glasgow. 2 vol in 1. early sheepskin. VG. B14. $850.00

BELL, Joseph. *World Series Thrills.* 1962. Messner. later prt. VG/G. P8. $17.50

BELL, Josephine. *In the King's Absence.* 1973. Bles. 1st ed. F/F. P3. $20.00

BELL, Josephine. *New People of the Hollies.* 1961. Macmillan. 1st ed. VG/VG. P3. $25.00

BELL, Josephine. *Wilberforce Legacy.* 1969. Walker. 1st ed. VG/G. P3. $15.00

BELL, Josephine. *Wolf! Wolf! Wolf!* 1980. Walker. 1st ed. VG/VG. P3. $15.00

BELL, Larry. *Works From New Mexico.* 1989. Musee d'Art Contemporain. sgn. French/Eng text. ils/photos. 95p. stiff wrp. D2. $65.00

BELL, Madison Smartt. *Barking Man & Other Stories.* 1990. Ticknor. 1st ed. F/F. H11. $30.00

BELL, Madison Smartt. *Doctor Sleep.* 1991. HBJ. 1st ed. F/F. B4. $45.00

BELL, Madison Smartt. *Save Me, Joe Louis.* 1993. Harcourt Brace. NF/NF. A20. $20.00

BELL, Madison Smartt. *Soldier's Joy.* 1989. Ticknor Fields. 1st ed. NF/F. M23. $20.00

BELL, Madison Smartt. *Straight Cut.* 1986. Ticknor. 1st ed. F/F. H11. $35.00

BELL, Madison Smartt. *Waiting for the End of the World.* 1985. Ticknor Fields. 1st ed. sgn. F/F. B35. $80.00

BELL, Madison Smartt. *Washington Square Ensemble.* 1983. Viking. 1st ed. F/F. B35. $80.00

BELL, Madison Smartt. *Year of Silence.* 1987. Ticknor Fields. 1st ed. 194p. VG/VG. B10. $35.00

BELL, Marvin. *Poems for Nathan & Saul.* 1966. Hillside. 1st ed. 1/350. NF/prt wrp. C2. $350.00

BELL, R.C. *Diaries From the Days of Sail.* 1974. NY. VG. O7. $25.00

BELL, Samuel D. *Justice & Sheriff, Practical Forms for Use of Justices...* 1843. Concord. G Parker Lyon. 1st ed. contemporary sheep. M11. $150.00

BELLADONNA & CAROZZO. *Percision & Superprecision Bidding.* 1975. NY. 237p. VG. S1. $20.00

BELLAH, James Warner. *Ward 20.* 1946. Doubleday. 1st ed. 160p. VG+/dj. M20. $35.00

BELLAIRS, George. *Intruder in the Dark.* 1966. John Gifford. 1st ed. VG/G. P3. $20.00

BELLAIRS, John. *Dark Secret of Weatherend.* 1984. Dial. 1st ed. VG/G. P3. $15.00

BELLAMY, David. *Queen's Hidden Garden.* 1984. Newton Abbott, Eng. ils. 224p. F/clip. B26. $32.50

BELLAMY, Edward. *Duke of Stockbridge.* 1901. NY. VG. O7. $20.00

BELLAMY, Edward. *Equality.* 1897. Appleton. 1st ed. NF. M22. $35.00

BELLAMY, Edward. *Looking Backward.* 1942. Modern Lib. 1st ed thus. VG. M21. $10.00

BELLAMY, Edward. *Looking Backward.* 1945. Tower. 2nd ed. NF/NF. P3. $18.00

BELLI, Melvin M. *Blood Money.* 1956. NY. 1st ed. author's 1st book. F/F. A17. $15.00

BELLI, Melvin M. *My Life on Trial: An Autobiography.* 1976. Morrow. 1st ed. 5-line inscr/dtd 1976. 351p. F. P3. $125.00

BELLOC, H. *Bad Child's Book of Beasts.* nd. Duckworth. ils Basil Blackwood. 48p. VG. P2. $35.00

BELLOC, H. *Cruise of the Nona.* 1955. Newman. 347p. VG/dj. T7. $20.00

BELLOC, H. *Highway & Its Vehicles.* 1926. London. The Studio. 1/1250. 131 pl. VG. T10. $200.00

BELLOC, H. *More Beasts for Worse Children.* nd. Duckworth. 48p. VG. P2. $30.00

BELLOW, Saul. *Adventures of Augie March.* 1953. Viking. 1st ed/1st state. NF/VG+. M23. $115.00

BELLOW, Saul. *Dangling Man.* 1944. Vanguard. 1st ed. author's 1st book. gr-tan cloth. F/brn dj. B24. $1,500.00

BELLOW, Saul. *Dean's December.* 1982. NY. 1st trade ed. F/dj. A17. $10.00

BELLOW, Saul. *Him With His Foot in His Mouth.* 1984. Harper Row. 1st ed. NF/NF. M23. $20.00

BELLOW, Saul. *Him With His Foot in His Mouth.* 1984. NY. Harper. 1st ed. sgn. F/F. B2. $60.00

BELLOW, Saul. *Humboldt's Gift.* 1975. Viking. 1st ed. NF/VG. B35. $35.00

BELLOW, Saul. *More Die of Heartbreak.* 1987. NY. 1st ed. F/F. A17. $12.50

BELLOW, Saul. *Mr Sammler's Planet.* 1970. NY. 1st ed. sgn. VG+/VG. C6. $60.00

BELLOW, Saul. *Mr Sammler's Planet.* 1970. Viking. 1st ed. NF/NF. A20. $28.00

BELLOW, Saul. *Mr Sammler's Planet.* 1970. Viking. 1st ed. VG/VG. P3. $15.00

BELLOW, Saul. *Summations.* 1987. Bennington College. 1st ed. 1/1000. F/prt wrp. C2. $30.00

BELMONT, Bob; see Reynolds, Mack.

BELOTE & BELOTE. *Typhoon of Steel: Battle for Okinawa.* 1970. NY. BC. 384p. F/dj. A17. $7.50

BELT, Elmer. *Leonardo the Anatomist.* 1955. Lawrence. KS U. thin 12mo. ils. 76p. F/NF. T10. $50.00

BELTING, Natalia. *Summer's Coming In.* 1970. HRW. 1st ed. ils Adrienne Adams. 8vo. unp. VG/VG. T5. $30.00

BEMELMANS, Ludwig. *Blue Danube.* 1945. Viking. 1st ed. F/F. B35. $60.00

BEMELMANS, Ludwig. *Castle No 9.* 1937. Viking. 1st ed. VG/fair. P2. $90.00

BEMELMANS, Ludwig. *Father, Dear Father.* 1953. Viking. 1st ed/deluxe issue. 1/151. F. w/sgn drawing. B24. $375.00

BEMELMANS, Ludwig. *Golden Basket.* 1936. Viking. 1st ed. ils. VG+/VG. C8. $200.00

BEMELMANS, Ludwig. *Madeline & the Bad Hat.* 1956. Viking. 1st ed. ils. VG/VG. D1. $225.00

BEMELMANS, Ludwig. *Madeline's Christmas.* 1985. Viking Kestrel. 1st ed. ils. F/F. P2. $50.00

BEMELMANS, Ludwig. *Madeline's Rescue.* 1953. London. Verschoyle. 1st probable UK ed. NF/VG. C8. $175.00

BEMELMANS, Ludwig. *Madeline's Rescue.* 1953 (1951). NY. Viking BC. ils. NF/F. C14. $15.00

BEMELMANS, Ludwig. *Madeline.* 1939. Simon Schuster. 1st ed. lacks ffe. ils. VG/VG. 313. $65.00

BEMELMANS, Ludwig. *Madeline.* 1939. Simon Schuster. 1st ed/1st issue. lg 4to. VG/G ist issue. M5. $225.00

BEMELMANS, Ludwig. *Sunshine.* 1950. Simon Schuster. 1st ed. ils. 42p. NF/NF. D1. $200.00

BEMMANN, Hans. *Stone & the Flute.* 1986. Viking. 1st ed. VG/VG. P3. $20.00

BENCHLEY, Nathaniel. *Monument.* 1966. McGraw Hill. 1st ed. VG/VG. P3. $20.00

BENCHLEY, Nathaniel. *Strange Disappearance of Arthur Cluck.* 1967. Harper Row. 1st ed. 8vo. F/VG+. M5. $25.00

BENCHLEY, Nathaniel. *Visitors.* 1965. McGraw. 1st ed. VG/VG. H11. $25.00

BENCHLEY, Peter. *Beast.* 1991. Random. 1st ed. F/F. B35. $20.00

BENCHLEY, Peter. *Deep.* 1976. Doubleday. 1st ed. 301p. VG/G+. P12. $12.50

BENCHLEY, Peter. *Island.* 1979. Doubleday. 1st ed. NF/NF. B35. $30.00

BENCHLEY, Peter. *Island.* 1979. Doubleday. 1st ed. VG/VG. P3. $18.00

BENCHLEY, Peter. *Jaws.* 1974. Doubleday. 1st ed. F/VG+. B35. $75.00

BENDER, Roger James. *Hitler Albums: Mussolini's State Visit...* 1970. palo Alto. 1st ed. ils. 144p. leatherette. A17. $35.00

BENEDICT, David. *General History of the Baptist Denomination in America.* 1813. Boston. 2 vol. orig full sheep. VG. C6. $300.00

BENEDICT, Elizabeth. *Slow Dancing.* 1985. Knopf. 1st ed. 8vo. F/F. T10. $100.00

BENEDICT, Leonard. *Waifs of the Slums & Their Way Out.* 1907. NY. Revell. 1st ed. NF. B2. $50.00

BENEDICT, Pinckney. *Dogs of God.* 1994. NY. Doubleday. 1st ed. sgn. F/F. M23. $40.00

BENEDICT, Pinckney. *Town Smokes.* 1987. Princeton. Ontario Review. 1st ed. author's 1st book. sgn. F/wrp. C2. $100.00

BENES, MAREK & TUREK. *Fossils of the World.* 1989. Arch Cape. 4to. 800 mc photos/300 drawings. 495p. F/F. B1. $65.00

BENESCH, Otto. *Artistic & Intellectual Trends From Rubens to Daumier...* 1969. np. ils. 176p. F. A4. $65.00

BENESCH, Otto. *Collected Writings. Vol I: Rembrandt.* 1970. London/NY. Phaidon. ils/notes. cloth. dj. D2. $60.00

BENET, Stephen Vincent. *John Brown's Body.* 1928. Doubleday Doran. 1st ed. sgn. 377p. VG. B11. $200.00

BENFORD, Gregory. *Across the Sea of Suns.* 1984. Timescape. 1st ed. F/F. P3. $18.00

BENFORD, Gregory. *Against Infinity.* 1983. Timescape. 1st ed. xl. VG/VG. N4. $10.00

BENFORD, Gregory. *Furious Gulf.* 1994. Bantam. 1st ed. NF/NF. P3. $23.00

BENFORD, Gregory. *Great Sky River.* 1987. Bantam. 1st ed. sgn bookplate. F/F. T2. $25.00

BENFORD, Gregory. *Jupiter Project.* 1975. Thomas Nelson. 1st ed. F/NF. M23. $40.00

BENFORD, Gregory. *Jupiter Project.* 1975. Thomas Nelson. 1st ed. 192p. VG/dj. M20. $37.00

BENFORD, Gregory. *Sailing Bright Eternity.* 1995. Bantam. 1st ed. AN/dj. M22. $20.00

BENFORD, Gregory. *Tides of Light.* 1989. Bantam. 1st ed. F/F. M21. $15.00

BENFORD, Gregory. *Timescape.* 1980. Simon Schuster. 1st ed. VG/G. P3. $30.00

BENFORD & CLARKE. *Beyond the Fall of Night.* 1990. Ace/Putnam. 1st ed. F/F. P3. $20.00

BENFORD & EKLUND. *If the Stars Are Gods.* 1977. Berkley. 1st ed. F/F. P3. $23.00

BENJAMIN, Asher. *American Builders Companion.* 1816. Boston. 3rd. 59 pl. full leather. B5. $300.00

BENJAMIN, Paul; see Auster, Paul.

BENJAMIN & SLIDELL. *Digest of Reported Decisions of the Superior Court...* 1840. New Orleans. E Johns. 2nd. quarter calf. xl. M11. $450.00

BENNET, Robert Ames. *Bowl of Baal.* 1975. Donald Grant. 1st hc ed. F/F. T2. $15.00

BENNETT, Arnold. *From the Log of the Velsa.* 1920. Chatto Windus. 1st ed. sgn. assoc copy. 209p. VG. B11. $75.00

BENNETT, Arnold. *Man From the North.* 1898. London/NY. 1st ed. author's 1st book. VG. C6. $150.00

BENNETT, Charles E. *Laudonniere & Fort Caroline: History & Documents.* 1964. Gainesville. sgn. 191 p. gilt bl brd. F. B11. $65.00

BENNETT, Dorothy. *Golden Encyclopedia.* 1946. NY. 1st ed. ils Cornelius DeWitt. 125p. G. A17. $15.00

BENNETT, Dwight. *Cheyenne Encounter.* 1976. Doubleday. 1st ed. VG/VG. P3. $12.00

BENNETT, E.D. *American Journeys.* 1975. Convent Station. VG/wrp. O7. $20.00

BENNETT, Geoffrey. *Death in the Dog Watches.* 1974. White Lion. VG/VG. P3. $15.00

BENNETT, J.M. *Local Matter.* 1985. Walker. 1st ed. F/F. M23. $20.00

BENNETT, James Gordon. *My Father's Geisha.* 1990. Delacorte. 1st ed. sgn. F/NF. M23. $30.00

BENNETT, James. *Overland to California: Journal of James Bennett...* 1987. Ye Galleon. 1st ed thus. F/sans. A18. $17.50

BENNETT, Rick. *King of a Small World.* 1995. Arcade. 1st ed. author's 1st novel. AN/dj. M22. $20.00

BENNETT, Rowena. *Runner for the King.* 1944. Chicago. apparent 1st ed. ils Fiore Mastri. F/torn. M5. $18.00

BENNETT, Rowena. *Songs From Around the Toadstool Table.* 1967. Follett. 1st ed. ils Betty Fraser. 61p. F/VG+. P2. $15.00

BENNETT. *How To Buy Photographs.* 1987. np. 150 photos. 159p. F/F. A4. $35.00

BENSON, A.C. *Thread of Gold.* 1907. Dutton. 1st ed. VG. P3. $20.00

BENSON, Albert E. *History of the Massachusetts Horticultural Society.* 1929. Boston. 553p. cloth. VG. A10. $60.00

BENSON, L. *Book of Remarkable Trials & Notorious Characters...* 1871? London. Chatto Windus. gr cloth. M11. $175.00

BENSON, Lyman. *Treatise on the Northern American Ranunculi.* 1948. Nortre Dame. 264p. wrp. B26. $50.00

BENSON, Stella. *Kwan-Yin.* 1922. Graborn. 8vo. inscr Grabhorn/Benson. NF. T10. $100.00

BENSUSAN, S.L. *Morocco.* 1904. London. Blk. 1st ed. 74 pl. 231p. teg. xl. VG. W1. $35.00

BENT, A.C. *Life Histories of North America Diving Birds.* 1946. NY. 1st ed. VG/VG. B5. $27.50

BENTHAM, Jeremy. *Fragment on Government; Being an Examination...* 1776. Dublin. Sheppard Whitestone. modern speckled calf. M11. $3,500.00

BENTLEY, BURGIS & SLATER. *Dickens Index.* 1990. Oxford. VG/VG. P3. $45.00

BENTLEY, Gerald Eades. *Jacobean & Caroline Stage.* 1949-1956. Oxford. Clarendon. 5 vol. 1st ed. xl. F/dj. A17. $50.00

BENTLEY, KHOSLA & SECKLER. *Agroforestry in South Asia.* 1993. Internat Science Pub. 8vo. ils. brd. F/F. B1. $35.00

BENTON, Thomas Hart. *Artist in America.* 1937. McBride. 1st ed. VG/remnant. B5. $40.00

BENTON, Thomas Hart. *Thirty Years' View. Volume I.* 1854. NY. royal 8vo. 739p. brn cloth. T3. $12.00

BERCIU, Dumitru. *Romania.* 1967. Praeger. 1st ed. 8vo. 32 pl/10 maps/5 tables. VG/dj. W1. $22.00

BERDAN, Frances. *Aztecs of Central Mexico.* 1982. HRW. 1st ed. 195p. G. F3. $15.00

BERENDT, John. *Midnight in the Garden of Good & Evil.* 1994. Random. ARC. RS. AN/dj. B4. $250.00

BERENDT, John. *Midnight in the Garden of Good & Evil.* 1994. Random. 1st ed. F/clip. H11. $80.00

BERENSON, Bernard. *Arch of Constantine.* 1954. London. 1st ed. photos. VG+/VG. S13. $18.00

BERETON, John. *Brief & True Relation of Virginia.* 1966. Ann Arbor. VG. O7. $20.00

BERGE, Carol. *Couple Called Moebius: Eleven Sensual Stories.* 1972. Bobbs Merrill. ARC. RS. F/F. B4. $50.00

BERGEN, Marty. *Better Bidding With Bergen: Vol I, Uncontested Auction.* 1985. Las Vegas. 1st prt. 199p. VG/wrp. S1. $5.00

BERGER, Melvin. *Early Humans, a Prehistoric World.* 1988. Putnam. ils Michael Welply. rem mk. F. B17. $7.50

BERGER, Raoul. *Federalism, the Founder's Design.* 1987. OK U. M11. $35.00

BERGER, Suzanne. *These Rooms.* 1979. Penmaen. ltd ed. 1/200. sgn. F/F. V1. $35.00

BERGER, Thomas. *Changing the Past.* 1989. Little Brn. 1st ed. F/F. H11. $30.00

BERGER, Thomas. *Crazy in Berlin.* 1958. Scribner. 1st ed. author's 1st book. VG/dj. S9. $225.00

BERGER, Thomas. *Little Big Man.* 1964. Dial. 1st ed. sgn. F/NF. B24. $300.00

BERGER, Thomas. *Little Big Man.* 1964. NY. 1st ed. sgn. NF/VG+. C6. $275.00

BERGER, Thomas. *Nowhere.* 1985. Delacorte. 1st ed. VG/VG. P3. $20.00

BERGER, Thomas. *Reinhart's Women.* 1981. Delacorte. 1st ed. F/NF. H11. $40.00

BERGER, Thomas. *Reinhart's Women.* 1981. Delacorte. 1st ed. VG/VG. P3. $20.00

BERGER, Thomas. *Rhinehart in Berlin.* 1962. Scribner. 1st ed. F/NF. M19. $45.00

BERGER, Thomas. *Who Is Teddy Villanova?* 1977. Delacorte. 1st ed. NF/NF. P3. $25.00

BERGMAN, Andrew. *Big Kiss-Off of 1944.* 1974. HRW. 1st ed. VG/VG. P3. $25.00

BERGMAN, Ray. *Just Fishing.* 1932. Phil. 1st ed. VG/VG. B5. $50.00

BERGMAN, Tamar. *Boy From Over There.* 1988. Boston. Houghton Mifflin. 1st Am ed. 8vo. 180p. F/F. C14. $12.00

BERGSTEIN, Eleanor. *Advancing Paul Newman.* 1973. Viking. 1st ed. inscr. author's 1st novel. NF/VG. B4. $75.00

BERGSTEIN, Eleanor. *Ex-Lover.* 1989. Random. 1st ed. F/F. B4. $35.00

BERKE & WILSON. *Watch Out for the Weather.* 1951. NY. Viking. 8vo. 226p. G/dj. K5. $10.00

BERKELEY, Anthony. *Puzzle in Poison.* 1938. Crime Club. 1st ed. VG. P3. $45.00

BERKELEY, Anthony. *Second Shot.* 1931. Crime Club. 1st ed. VG. P3. $35.00

BERKELEY, Sandra. *Coming Attractions.* 1971. Dutton. 1st ed. xl. F/VG. B4. $35.00

BERKOWITZ, David Sandler. *From Ptolemy to the Moon: Progress in Art of Exploration...* 1965. Waltham. Brandeis. F. O7. $45.00

BERKOWITZ. *In Remembrance of Creation, Evolution of Art...* 1968. Brandeis U. 4to. pl. 300p. NF. A4. $150.00

BERLANT, Jeffrey. *Profession & Molopoly: Study of Medicine in the US...* 1975. Los Angeles. 1st ed. 337p. dj. A13. $30.00

BERLANT & KAHLENBERG. *Navajo Blanket.* 1972. LA Co Mus of Art. 4to. ils. F/wrp. T10. $45.00

BERLINGHIERI, Francesco. *Geographia.* 1966 (1482). Amsterdam. Theatrvm Orbis Terrarvm. folio. 31 double-p maps. AN/dj. O7. $395.00

BERLINSKI, David. *Clean Sweep.* 1993. NY. 1st ed. author's 1st book. F/F. H11. $25.00

BERLITZ, Charles. *Atlantis: The Lost Continent Revealed.* 1984. Macmillan. 1st ed. VG. P3. $15.00

BERLITZ, Charles. *Bermuda Triangle.* 1974. Doubleday. 1st ed. NF/VG. H11. $20.00

BERLITZ, Charles. *Bermuda Triangle.* 1974. Garden City. VG. O7. $15.00

BERLO, Janet. *Art of Pre-Hispanic Mesoamerica.* 1988. Boston. Hall. 1st ed. 272p. F3. $65.00

BERMAN, James Gabriel. *Uninvited.* 1995. Warner. 1st ed. author's 1st novel. AN/dj. M22. $15.00

BERNADAC. *Naked Puppets, Auschwitz.* 1978. np. 12 full-p photos. 308p. F. A4. $45.00

BERNAL, Ignacio. *Olmec World.* 1969. Berkeley. 1st ed. 273p. dj. F3. $60.00

BERNAL, Ignacio. *Tenochtitlan en una Isla.* 1959. Mexico. ils/lg fld map. 147p. VG. F3. $20.00

BERNARD, Claude. *Cahier Rouge of Claude Bernard.* 1967. Cambridge. 1st Eng trans. 120p. VG/dj. A13. $25.00

BERNARD, Claude. *Lecons sur la Physiologie et la Pahtologie du Systeme...* 1858. Paris. 2 vol. ils. contemporary blk sheep. VG. B14. $950.00

BERNARD, George Smith. *War Talks of Confederate Veterans.* 1892. Petersburg, VA. Fenn Owen. 1st ed. 2 fld maps. VG. M8. $175.00

BERNARD, Nelson T. *Wildflowers Along Forest & Mesa Trails.* 1984 (1957). Albuquerque. ils. 177p. sc. VG. B26. $12.50

BERNARD, William. *Jailbait: Story of Juvenile Delinquency.* 1949. Greenberg. 216p. VG. A17. $15.00

BERNATOVA, Eva. *Wonder Shoes.* 1990. FSG. 1st ed. sm 4to. 24p. F/NF. C14. $12.00

BERNAU, George. *Black Phoenix.* 1994. Warner. 1st ed. F/F. H11. $25.00

BERNAU, George. *Promises To Keep.* 1988. Warner. 1st ed. author's 1st book. rem mk. NF/F. H11. $15.00

BERNETT, Lincoln. *Treasure of Our Tongue.* 1964. Knopf. 1st ed. NF/F. B35. $28.00

BERNHARDT, P. *Wily Violets & Underground Orchids.* 1989. Morrow. 1st ed. photos/drawings. 255p. F/F. B1. $19.00

BERNHEIM, Bertram. *Story of the Johns Hopkins.* 1949. Surrey. Kingswood. 1st Eng ed. 274p. VG. A13. $35.00

BERNSTEIN, Burton. *Sinai: The Great & Terrible Wilderness.* 1979. Viking. 1st ed. 8vo. pl/map. 268p. NF/dj. W1. $18.00

BERNSTEIN & FEINBERG. *Cosmological Constants.* 1986. Columbia. 1st ed. VG/VG. K5. $23.00

BERRIE, BERRIE & EZE. *Tropical Plant Science.* 1987. Longman. 8vo. ils/phogos. 410p. pict new cloth. F. B1. $25.00

BERRING & COHEN. *How To Find the Law. Ninth Edition.* 1989. West Pub. gilt gr buckram. M11. $25.00

BERRISFORD, Judith. *Rhodendrons & Azaleas.* 1965. NY. ils/pl. 288p. F/dj. B26. $17.50

BERRY, Arthur. *Short History of Astronomy.* 1961 (1898). NY. Dover. pb. 440p. VG. K5. $10.00

BERRY, Carole. *Year of the Monkey.* 1988. St Martin. 1st ed. F/F. P3. $17.00

BERRY, Charles W. *Arthurian Reverie.* 1939. London. Buckley. lg paper copy. pres. 171p. Zaehnsdorff bdg. T10. $1,200.00

BERRY, Chester D. *Loss of the Sultana.* 1892. Lansing, MI. 1st ed. ils. 426p. G. B18. $150.00

BERRY, Chuck. *Autobiography of...* 1987. 1st ed. VG/VG. K2. $18.00

BERRY, Don. *Moontrap.* 1962. Viking. 1st ed. F/F. A18. $50.00

BERRY, Don. *Trask.* 1961. Viking. 1st ed. F/VG. A18. $50.00

BERRY, Erik. *Honey of the Nile.* 1938. Oxford. 1st ed thus. ils. 224p. VG. P2. $12.50

BERRY, Mike; see Malzberg, Barry.

BERRY, R.J.A. *Brain & Mind; or, The Nervous System of Man.* 1928. Macmillan. 8vo. 608p. xl. G1. $50.00

BERRY, Wendell. *Discovery of Kentucky.* 1991. Frankfort. 1st ed. 1/100. sgn/#d. F. C2. $60.00

BERRY, Wendell. *Farm.* 1993. Larkspur. sgn. VG/as issued. C4. $40.00

BERRY, Wendell. *Gift of the Good Land: Further Essays...* 1981. North Point. 1st ed. sgn. F/F. C2. $40.00

BERRY, Wendell. *Memory of Old Jack.* 1974. Harcourt. 1st ed. F/NF. C2. $125.00

BERRY, Wendell. *Nathan Coulter.* 1960. Boston. Houghton Mifflin. 1st ed. author's 1st book. NF/dj. S9. $150.00

BERRY, Wendell. *November Twenty-Six Nineteen Hundred Sixty-Three.* 1964. Braziller. ltd ed. sgn. F/case. C4. $175.00

BERRY, Wendell. *November Twenty-Six Nineteen Hundred Sixty-Three.* 1964. NY. ltd ed. sgn. ils/sgn Ben Shahn. F. C2. $150.00

BERRY, Wendell. *Recollected Essays 1965-1980.* 1981. North Point. 1st ed. sgn. F/F. C2. $40.00

BERRY, Wendell. *Sex, Economy, Freedom & Community.* 1993. NY. 1st ed. inscr. F/F. A11. $30.00

BERRY, Wendell. *There Is Singing Around Me.* 1976. Cold Mountain. 1st ed. 1/26 lettered. sgn. F. C2. $225.00

BERRY, Wendell. *Unsettling of America: Culture & Agriculture.* 1977. Sierra Club. sgn. F/VG. C6. $75.00

BERRY, Wendell. *Wild Birds.* 1986. Northpoint. 1st ed. F/F. M23. $20.00

BERRY & MASON. *Elements of Mineralogy.* 1968. Freeman. revised. 550p. VG. D8. $15.00

BERRY & MASON. *Mineralogy Concepts, Descriptions, Determinations.* 1959. San Francisco. Freeman. 630p. cloth. VG. D8. $25.00

BERRYMAN, John. *Berryman's Sonnets.* 1965. FSG. 1st ed. F/NF. C2. $50.00

BERRYMAN, John. *Delusions.* 1972. FSG. 1st ed. F/VG. H4. $30.00

BERRYMAN, John. *Dispossessed.* 1948. NY. 1st ed. sgn. VG/VG. C6. $400.00

BERRYMAN, John. *Dispossessed.* 1948. Wm Sloan. 1st ed. NF/dj. B24. $275.00

BERRYMAN, John. *Henry's Fate.* 1977. FSG. 1st ed. F/F. B4. $45.00

BERRYMAN, John. *Homage to Mistress Broadstreet.* 1956. FSC. 1st ed. F/NF clip. C2. $100.00

BERRYMAN, John. *Recovery.* 1973. FSG. 1st ed. VG/VG. A20. $28.00

BERRYMAN, John. *Stephen Crane.* 1950. Wm Sloan. 1st ed. F/dj. B24. $250.00

BERTELSEN, Aage. *October 43.* 1955. London. Mus Pr. photos/map. 160p. VG/dj. A17. $10.00

BERTHOLD, Victor M. *Pioneer Steamer California, 1848-1849.* 1932. Houghton Mifflin. 1/550. 1st ed. 8vo. ils/facsimiles/maps. F/case. T10. $150.00

BERTIN, Jack. *Brood of Helios.* 1966. Arcadia. 1st ed. VG/VG. P3. $13.00

BERTO, G. *Sky Is Red.* 1948. New Directions. 1st ed. F/VG. N3. $15.00

BERTO, G. *Works of God.* 1950. New Directions. 1st ed. VG/VG. M17. $17.50

BERTSCHE & SANDERS. *X Biedler: Vigilante.* 1969. Norman, OK. 3rd. 12mo. 164p. F/VG. T10. $35.00

BESKOW, Elsa. *Pelle's New Suit.* 1930. Platt Munk. unp. cloth. VG/dj. M20. $37.00

BESKOW, Elsa. *Vill Du Lasa.* 1937. Stockholm. Norstedt Soners. 1st reader in Swedish. 160p. VG. P2. $55.00

BESSIE, Alvah. *Inquisition in Eden.* 1965. Macmillan. 1st ed. F/F. B2. $45.00

BEST, Gerald M. *Ships & Narrow Gauge Rails.* 1981. San Diego. Howell North. 2nd. ils/fld map/index. F/dj. T10. $45.00

BESTER, Alfred. *Light Fantastic.* 1977. Gollancz. RS. VG/VG. P3. $25.00

BESTER, Alfred. *Star Light, Star Bright.* 1976. Berkley Putnam. 1st ed. NF/NF. P3. $20.00

BESTER, Alfred. *Stars in My Destination.* 1979. 1/3000. sgn. ils H Chaykin. F. M13. $30.00

BESTERMAN, Catherine. *Extraordinary Education of Johnny Lightfoot.* 1949. Bobbs Merrill. 1st ed. inscr. VG/VG. P2. $35.00

BESTERMAN, Theodore. *Art & Architecture: A Bibliography of Bibliographies.* 1971.. 230p. F. A4. $20.00

BESTERMAN, Theodore. *World Bibliography of Oriental Bibliographies.* 1975. np. revised. 4to. 349p. NF. A4. $65.00

BESTON, Henry. *Starlight Wonder Book.* 1923. Atlantic Monthly. 1st ed. ils Maurice Day. gilt bdg. VG. P2. $75.00

BESTON & COATSWORTH. *Chimney Farm Bedtime Stories.* 1977. HRW. 1st ed. ils Maurice Day. 78p. VG/G+. P2. $25.00

BESTOR, A. *Backwood Utopias.* 1959. Phil. 2nd. VG/VG. B5. $30.00

BETETA, Ramon. *Jarano.* 1970. Austin, TX. 1st ed. 163p. dj. F3. $20.00

BETHEL, L.C. *Compendium & Question Book of Parliamentary Law.* 1892. Columbus. self pub. 69p. prt stapled wrp. M11. $15.00

BETHELL, Nicholas. *War Hitler Won: Fall of Poland, September 1939.* 1973. NY. 1st Am ed. 472p. VG/tape rpr. A17. $15.00

BETTINA. *Goat Boy.* 1966. Norton. 1st Am ed. ils. NF/G+. P2. $28.00

BETTS, Doris. *Beasts of the Southern Wild & Other Stories.* 1973. NY. Harper. 1st ed. F/F. B4. $75.00

BETTS, Edwin M. *Thomas Jefferson's Garden Book, 1766-1824.* 1944. Am Philosophical Soc. 2nd. 704p. VG. B10. $45.00

BETTS, Tony. *Across the Board.* 1956. NY. Citadel. 1st ed. VG/VG. O3. $10.00

BEVAN & PHILLOT. *Mediaeval Geography: An Essay in Illustration of Hereford...* 1969. Amsterdam. Meridian. rpt of 1873 London ed. 3 maps. AN. O7. $55.00

BEVERIDGE, Albert Jeremiah. *Abraham Lincoln 1809-1858.* 1928. Houghton Mifflin. 2 vol. 1st ed. cloth. VG. M8. $45.00

BEWICK, Thomas. *My Life.* 1981. London. Folio Soc. 1st ed. 8vo. ils. F/case. T10. $50.00

BEYER, Harmann. *Analysis of Maya Hieroglyphs.* 1930. Brill Ltd. rpt. inscr. 20p. F3. $45.00

BEYER, William Gray. *Minions of the Moon.* 1950. Gnome. 1st ed. VG/VG. P3. $30.00

BIANCHINI, Francesco. *Complete Book of Fruits & Vegetables.* 1975. 1st ed. 4to. ils. VG. S13. $75.00

BIANCO, Margery Williams. *Poor Cecco.* 1925. Doran. 1st trade ed. ils Rackham. gilt bl cloth. NF. T10. $300.00

BIANCO & COLLISON. *Penny & the White Horse.* 1942. Messner. 4to. pict brd. VG. B17. $12.50

BIBBY, Geoffrey. *Looking for Dilmun.* 1969. Knopf. 1st ed. ils/maps. NF/dj. W1. $18.00

BIBLE. *Bible Alphabet.* ca 1890. np. 8vo. ils. VG/stiff wrp. A17. $12.50

BIBLE. *Bible in English; Common Prayer.* 1837. London. Bell. thick 12mo. fore-edge painting. full leather. T10. $450.00

BIBLE. *Biblia Hebraica.* 1838. Lipsiae. Ex Typis Caroli Tauchnitii. Stereotype ed. 1036p. VG. T10. $150.00

BIBLE. *Biblia Sacra Sive Testamentvm Vetvs...El Testamentvm Novvm.* 1651. Anstelaedami. Ioannis Blaev. thick 12mo. 895p. contemporary bdg. T10. $250.00

BIBLE. *Biblical Drawings With Illustrative Passages...* Dec 1951. Merrymount. 1/500. 100 drawings. 206p. Ruzicka bdg. VG. B14. $100.00

BIBLE. *Book of Psalms From Authorized King James Version.* 1960. LEC. 1/1500. ils/sgn Valenti Angelo. F/glassine/cloth chemise. B24. $225.00

BIBLE. *Book of Ruth.* 1947. LEC. ils/sgn Arthur Szyk. leather/pict brd. NF/gold case. B14. $200.00

BIBLE. *Book of the Prophet Isaiah in the King James Version.* 1979. LEC. 1/2000. sgn Chaim Gross/Franklin Littell. 121p. F/NF case. C2. $150.00

BIBLE. *First Bible.* 1934. Oxford. 1st ed. ils Helen Sewell. 109p. VG/G+. P2. $35.00

BIBLE. *Gospel of St Luke.* 1926. NY. Harbor. 1/20. 12mo. 7p. wht brd. F. B24. $200.00

BIBLE. *Holy Bible.* 1925-27. London. Nonesuch. 4 vol. Authorized version 1611. VG. V4. $75.00

BIBLE. *Holy Bible: Containing the Old & New Testament & Apocrypha.* 1911. London. 3 vol. marbled ep. full leather. VG. B30. $125.00

BIBLE. *Leabhraichean an T-Seann Tiomnaidh Agus an Tiomnaidh Nuaidh.* 1885. London. 8vo. gilt full leather. VG. T10. $350.00

BIBLE. *Nu Testament (in Fonetik Speling).* 1864. Sinsinati. G. V4. $65.00

BIBLE. *Second Chapter From the Gospel According to Saint Matthew.* np. nd. 1/100. ils/sgn Angelo. 10p. F/stiff wrp/dj. B24. $175.00

BIBLE. *Sermon on the Mount.* 1924. San Francisco. Grabhorn. 1/190. folio. 10p. F. B24. $325.00

BIBLE. *Sixth Chapter of St Matthew Containing the Lord's Prayer.* 1961. NY. Hammer Creek. 1/65. ils/sgn Valenti Angelo. 10p. F/stiff wrp. A4. $200.00

BIBLE. *Ten Commandments.* 1947. Winston. 1st ed (so stated). ils Arthur Szyk. gray cloth. VG. D1. $85.00

BICKEL, Alexander M. *Morality of Consent.* 1975. Yale. VG/dj. M11. $35.00

BICKNELL, A.J. *Bicknell's Public Buildings.* 1878. NY. 21 pl. VG. B5. $95.00

BIDDLE, A.J.D. *New Illustrated Do or Die.* 1944. WA. Leatherneck Assn. 108p. G. B18. $15.00

BIDDLE, George. *Tahitian Journal.* 1968. MN. 1st ed. F/NF. N3. $35.00

BIEBUYCK. *Tradition & Creativity in Tribal Art.* 1969. UCLA. F/VG. D2. $45.00

BIENEK, Horst. *Cell.* 1972. Unicorn. 2nd. 8vo. inscr/trans Ursula Mahlendorf. F/NF. S9. $45.00

BIERCE, Ambrose. *Shadow on the Dial & Other Essays.* 1909. San Francisco. Robertson. 1st ed. 249p. uncut. dj. A17. $175.00

BIERCE, Ambrose. *Tales of Soldiers & Civilians.* 1891. San Francisco. Steele. 1st ed. 300p. A bdg/gilt brn cloth. F/case/chemise. B24. $1,650.00

BIERRING, Walter. *History of Dept of Internal Medicine.* 1958. IA City. 1st ed. 116p. VG. A13. $20.00

BIGELOW, Edwin S. *Lowell on the Merrick: An Art Souvenir.* 1892. Lowell, MA. ils. unp. VG. B18. $35.00

BIGELOW, Henry J. *Orthopedic Surgery & Other Medical Papers.* 1900. Boston. 1st ed. 373p. A13. $100.00

BIGELOW, Henry J. *Rapid Lithotrity With Evacuation.* 1878. Boston. ils. 41p. blk cloth. NF. B14. $175.00

BIGELOW, Jacob. *Florula Bostoniensis: A Collection of Plants...* 1824. Boston. 2nd. 424p. modern bl cloth. B14. $150.00

BIGELOW, John. *Life & Public Services of John Charles Fremont.* 1856. NY. 1st ed. 12mo. 480p. olive cloth. G. T3. $55.00

BIGELOW, John. *Life of Benjamin Franklin Written by Himself.* 1879. Lippincott. 2 vol. 2nd. 8vo. gilt bl cloth. VG. T10. $45.00

BIGGERS, Earl Derr. *Black Camel.* 1929. Bobbs Merrill. early rpt. VG. M22. $15.00

BIGGERS, Earl Derr. *Charlie Chan Carries On.* 1930. Bobbs Merrill. 1st ed. G. P3. $20.00

BIGGLE, Lloyd. *This Darkening Universe.* 1977. Millington. VG/VG. P3. $30.00

BILENKIN, Dmitri. *Uncertainty Principle.* 1978. Macmillan. F/F. P3. $13.00

BILGRAY & MARCUS. *Index to Jewish Festschriften.* 1970 (1935). NY. Kraus. rpt. 4to. cloth. VG. W1. $25.00

BILL, A.H. *Beleagured City: Richmond 1861-1865.* 1946. ltd sgn ed. VG/G. B5. $27.50

BILL & JOHNSON. *Horsemen Blue & Gray: A Pictorial History.* 1960. NY. 1st ed. photos. 236p. F/F. E1. $50.00

BILLARD, Jules B. *Ancient Egypt: Discovering Its Splendors.* 1978. NGS. 1st ed. 256p. NF/dj. W1. $45.00

BILLE-D MOT, Eleonore. *Age of Akhenaten.* 1966. McGraw Hill. 1st ed. 24 color pl. 200p. VG/dj. W1. $26.00

BILLINGS, C.K.G. *King & Queen.* 1921. private prt. O3. $45.00

BILLINGS, Donald E. *Guide to the Solar Corona.* 1966. NY. Academic. xl. VG. K5. $30.00

BILLINGS, John S. *Selected Papers of John Shaw Billings.* 1965. Chicago. 1st ed. 300p. VG. A13. $85.00

BILLINGS, M.P. *Structural Geology.* 1972. Prentice Hall. 606p. G. D8. $20.00

BILLINGS & BURN. *Baronial & Ecclesiastical Antiquities of Scotland.* (1045-1852). Edingurgh. Oliver Boyd. 4 vol. lg 4to. NF. T10. $1,200.00

BILLINGTON, C. *Shrubs of Michigan.* 1977. Bloomfield Hills. Cranbrook Inst. 2nd/3rd prt. 339p. F/NF. B1. $27.50

BILLINGTON, Elizabeth T. *Randolph Caldecott Treasury.* 1978. Warne. 1st ed. 4to. 288p. NF/F. T5. $55.00

BILLINGTON, R.A. *Journal of Charlotte L Forten: Early Sea Island Teacher...* 1953. NY. 1st ed. 248p. VG/VG. B5. $35.00

BILLMAN. *Secret of the Stratemeyer Syndicate: Nancy Drew...* 1986. np. ils. 197p. F/F. A4. $65.00

BILYEU, Richard. *Tanelorn Archives.* 1981. Pandora. 1/250. sgn/#d. F. P3. $25.00

BINET, Alfred. *Les Revelations de l'Ecriture d'Apres...* 1906. Paris. Felix Alcan. ils. 260p. G1. $100.00

BINET & SIMON. *Intelligence of the Feeble-Minded.* 1916. Baltimore. Williams Wilkins. 1st Eng-language ed. 328p. VG. G1. $125.00

BINFORD, Lewis R. *In Pursuit of the Past: Decoding the Archeological Record.* 1983. Thames Hudson. 1st Am ed. 8vo. 256p. F/dj. T10. $50.00

BING & ROSENFELD. *Quality of Justice in the Lower Criminal Courts...* 1970. Boston. Lawyer's Commitee for Civil Rights Under Law. 149p. M11. $35.00

BINGAY, Malcolm W. *Detroit Is My Own Home Town.* 1946. Bobbs Merrill. 1st ed. sgn. G+. P12. $30.00

BINGAY, Malcolm W. *Detroit Is My Own Home Town.* 1946. Bobbs Merrill. 1st ed. sgn. 21 pl. 360p. G/G. B11. $50.00

BINGHAM, Helen. *In Tamal Land.* 1906. San Francisco. Calkins. 1st ed. 8vo. 141p. NF. T10. $250.00

BINGHAM, Hiram. *Lost City of Incas.* 1962. NY. 1st ed. VG/VG. B5. $30.00

BINGHAM, Hiram. *Residence of Twenty-One Years in the Sandwich Islands.* 1848. Hartford. Huntington. 2nd. fld map. 616p. F. T7. $220.00

BINGHAM & HAWKEY. *Wild Card.* 1974. Stein Day. 1st ed. F/F. P3. $15.00

BINKLEY, Sue. *Clockwork Sparrow: Time, Clocks & Calendars...* 1990. Prentice Hall. 1st ed. F/NF. G10. $10.00

BINKS, C.J. *Pioneers of Tasmania's West Coast.* 1988. Hobart. VG. O7. $65.00

BINNS, Archie. *Roaring Land.* 1942. McBride. 1st ed. sgn. 284p. VG/VG. P3. $40.00

BINNS. *Introduction to Historical Bibliography.* 1953. London. ils. 383p. VG/worn. A4. $65.00

BINSTOCK, R.C. *Light of Home.* 1992. Atheneum. 1st ed. F/F. M23. $25.00

BIRCH, Franklin. *Pedigrees of Leading Winners 1912-1959.* 1960. London. VG. O3. $85.00

BIRCHMORE, Fred. *Around the World on a Bicycle.* 1939. Athens. 1st ed. photos. 345p. VG. B5. $40.00

BIRD, Isabella. *Hawaiian Archipelago, Six Months Among the Palm Groves...* 1881. np. ils. 318p. VG. A4. $85.00

BIRD, Joseph. *Protection Against Fire & Best Means of Putting Out...* 1873. NY. 278p. xl. gilt brn cloth. G. B14. $75.00

BIRD, Junius. *Excavations in Northern Chile.* 1943. NY. AMNH. ils/tables. F3. $45.00

BIRD, Sarah. *Virgin of the Rodeo.* 1993. NY. ARC/1st ed. RS. F/F. V4. $25.00

BIRD, Will R. *Two Jacks: Amazing Adventures of Major Jack M Veness...* 1955. Phil. 2nd. 209p. dj. A17. $9.50

BIRD & KLINGER. *Kosher Bridge.* 1992. London. 128p. VG/wrp. S1. $8.00

BIRDSALL, Ralph. *Story of Cooperstown.* 1925. NY. 433p. VG. B18. $22.50

BIRKERTS, Sven. *Electric Life: Essays on Modern Poetry.* 1989. Morrow. 1st ed. F/F. M23. $20.00

BIRRELL, Augustine. *Res Judicatae, Papers & Essays.* 1892. np. 308p. VG. A4. $25.00

BISHOP, Chris. *1400 Days: Civil War Day by Day.* 1990. folio. 256p. red cloth. F/dj. T3. $30.00

BISHOP, Claire Huchet. *Pancakes-Paris.* 1947. Viking/Jr Literary Guild. 1st ed thus. 8vo. ils Georges Schreiber. VG+/dj. M5. $22.00

BISHOP, Isabel. *Prints & Drawings 1925-1964.* 1964. NY. Shorwood. 8vo. pict brd. F/partial dj. B14. $55.00

BISHOP, Jim. *Day in the Life of President Johnson.* 1967. Random. 1st ed. 274p. bl cloth. F/F. B22. $4.50

BISHOP, Jim. *Day Lincoln Was Shot.* 1955. NY. 1st ed. ils. NF. B14. $45.00

BISHOP, Michael. *And Strange at Ecbatan the Trees.* 1976. Harper Row. 1st ed. F/F. P3. $15.00

BISHOP, Michael. *Blooded on Arachne.* 1982. Arkham. 1st ed. F/F. P3. $15.00

BISHOP, Michael. *Brittle Innings.* 1994. Bantam. 1st ed. F/F. G10. $25.00

BISHOP, Michael. *Count Geiger's Blues.* 1992. Tor. 1st ed. F/NF. G10. $20.00

BISHOP, Michael. *One Winter in Eden.* 1984. Arkham. 1st ed. 1/3596. F/F. T2. $35.00

BISHOP, Michael. *Stolen Faces.* 1977. Harper Row. 1st ed. F/F. P3. $15.00

BISHOP, Michael. *Transfigurations.* 1980. Gollancz. 1st ed. VG/VG. P3. $20.00

BISSELL, Richard. *My Life on the Mississippi; or, Why I Am Not Mark Twain.* 1973. Boston. 1st ed. sgn. VG/VG. B5. $30.00

BISSON, Terry. *Bears Discover Fire.* 1993. Tor. 1st ed/1st issue. F/NF. G10. $25.00

BISSON & MCCONAUGHY. *Madame X.* nd. Grosset Dunlap. MTI. G. P3. $20.00

BITTING, Katherine. *Gastronomic Bibliography.* nd. np. rpt. 1/150. 8vo. F. A4. $95.00

BITTMAN, S. *Seeds: The Ultimate Guide to Growing Vegetables...* 1989. Bantam. 4to. 243p. F/F. B1. $40.00

BIXBY, William. *Hurricanes.* 1979. David McKay. xl. dj. K5. $7.00

BIXBY, William. *Seawatchers: Oceanographers in Action.* 1967. NY. VG. O7. $15.00

BJELKE & SHAPIRO. *Northern Light.* 1985. Potter. ils. 116p. VG/dj. T7. $30.00

BJORN, Thyra Ferre. *Home Has a Heart.* 1968. HRW. 1st ed. sgn. F/VG. B11. $25.00

BJORNSTAD, Edith. *Wings in Waiting: History of Iowa Methodist Hospital.* 1952. Des Moines. 1st ed. 238p. A13. $20.00

BLACK, Archibald. *Transport Aviation.* 1926. Chicago. 1st ed. 245p. G+. B18. $125.00

BLACK, Campbell. *Brainfire.* 1979. Morrow. 1st ed. VG/G. P3. $15.00

BLACK, Campbell. *Letters From the Dead.* 1985. Villard. 1st ed. NF/NF. P3. $16.00

BLACK, Gavin. *Golden Cockatrice.* 1975. Harper Row. 1st ed. VG/VG. P3. $20.00

BLACK, Gavin. *You Want To Die, Johnny?* 1966. Harper Row. 1st ed. VG/VG. P3. $20.00

BLACK, Jospeh. *Lectures on the Elements of Chemistry...* 1807. Phil. 2 vol. 1st Am ed. contemporary sheep. VG. B14. $600.00

BLACK, Lionel. *Flood.* 1971. Stein Day. VG/VG. P3. $13.00

BLACK, Lionel. *Life & Death of Peter Wade.* 1974. Stein Day. 1st ed. VG/VG. P3. $13.00

BLACK, Veronica. *Vow of Chastity.* 1992. NY. 1st ed. F/F. H11. $20.00

BLACK & LIPMAN. *American Folk Painting.* 1966. NY. rpt. 86 pl. 244p. F/dj. A17. $20.00

BLACK HAWK. *Autobiography of Ma-Ka-Tai-Me-She-Kia-Kiak, or Black Hawk.* 1882. Oquawka, IL. VG. A9. $100.00

BLACKBMAN, R.P. *From Jordan's Delight.* 1937. Arrow. 1st ed. NF/VG. B4. $150.00

BLACKBURN, Henry. *Randolph Caldecott: His Early Art Career.* 1886. NY. Routledge. 1st ed. 172 ils. NF/VG. D1. $150.00

BLACKBURN, John. *Bury Him Darkly.* 1970. Putnam. 1st ed. VG/VG. P3. $45.00

BLACKBURN, John. *Cyclops Gambit.* 1977. London. Cape. 1st ed. F/dj. M21. $35.00

BLACKBURN, John. *Dead Man's Handle.* 1978. London. Cape. 1st ed. F/dj. M21. $45.00

BLACKBURN, John. *Devil Daddy.* 1972. London. Cape. 1st ed. VG/dj. M21. $50.00

BLACKBURN, John. *Gaunt Woman.* 1962. Mill Morrow. 1st ed. VG/VG. P3. $30.00

BLACKBURN, John. *Scent of New-Mown Hay.* 1958. Mill Morrow. 1st Am hc ed. VG+/dj. M21. $35.00

BLACKBURN, Paul. *In. On. Or About the Premises.* 1968. London. Cape Goliard. 1st ed. 1/100. sgn/#d. F/NF. C2. $175.00

BLACKBURN, William. *Love, Boy: Letters of Mac Hyman.* 1969. LSU. VG/VG. B10. $15.00

BLACKER, Brigadier Monkey. *Story of Workboy.* 1960. London. 1st ed. 192p. gilt bl cloth. F/G. H3. $35.00

BLACKER, Irwin R. *Old West in Fiction.* 1961. Obolensky. 1st ed. F/chip. A18. $25.00

BLACKFORD, W.W. *War Years With Jeb Stuart.* 1945. NY. 1st ed. VG/G. B5. $45.00

BLACKMON, Anita. *Murder a la Richelieu.* 1937. Crime Club. 1st ed. VG. P3. $30.00

BLACKMORE, Howard L. *Guns & Rifles of the World.* 1965. Viking. 1st ed. 134p. VG+/dj. M20. $50.00

BLACKMORE, Jane. *Perilous Waters.* 1957. Collins. VG/VG. P3. $15.00

BLACKSTOCK, Lee. *All Men Are Murderers.* 1958. Crime Club. 1st ed. VG/VG. P3. $15.00

BLACKSTONE, William. *Analysis of the Laws of England...* 1762. Oxford. Clarendon. M11. $650.00

BLACKSTONE, William. *Commentaries on the Laws of England.* nd. Oxford. 4 vol. 8th. 8vo. full leather. VG. H3. $1,400.00

BLACKSTONE, William. *Commentaries on the Laws of England. Four Volumes.* 1766-1771. Duplin. 4 vol. mixed eds. contemporary calf. M11. $2,000.00

BLACKSTONE, William. *Commentaries on the Laws of England...* 1790. Worcester. contemporary sheep. M11. $2,250.00

BLACKSTONE, William. *Great Charter & Charter of the Forest...* 1759. Oxford. Clarendon. contemporary reverse calf/rebacked. M11. $3,500.00

BLACKWELL, Alice Stone. *Songs of Russia Rendered Into English Verse.* 1906. Chicago. self pub. 62p. red cloth. VG. B14. $125.00

BLACKWELL, Edward Maurice. *Blackwell Genealogy.* 1948. Old Dominion. photos. 112p. VG. B10. $50.00

BLACKWELL, Leslie. *African Occasions, Reminiscences of 30 Years of Bar...* 1970. Westport. rpt of 1938 ed. 8vo. 287p. gilt red cloth. AN/sans. P4. $17.50

BLACKWOOD, A. *Prisoner in Fairyland.* 1913. np. NF. C6. $95.00

BLACKWOOD, Algernon. *Best Supernatural Tales of Blackwood.* 1973. Causeway. VG/VG. P3. $30.00

BLACKWOOD, Algernon. *Doll & One Other.* 1946. Arkham. 1st ed. F/VG. M19. $65.00

BLACKWOOD, Algernon. *Dudley & Gilderoy.* 1929. Benn. 1st ed. VG. P3. $75.00

BLACKWOOD, Algernon. *Dudley & Gilderoy.* 1929. Dutton. 1st ed. VG/VG. P3. $75.00

BLACKWOOD, Algernon. *Dudley & Gilderoy.* 1951. London. rpt. 12mo. cloth. VG. A17. $7.50

BLACKWOOD, Algernon. *Education of Uncle Paul.* 1909. Macmillan Colonial Lib. VG. P3. $60.00

BLACKWOOD, Easley. *Complete Book of Opening Leads.* 1983. KY. 475p. VG. S1. $8.00

BLAGOWIDOW, George. *Last Train From Berlin.* 1977. Doubleday. 1st ed. VG/VG. P3. $13.00

BLAINE, John. *Magic Talisman.* 1989. Manuscript Pr. 1st ed. decor brd. VG. P3. $25.00

BLAINE, John. *Rick Brant: Egyptian Cat Mystery (#16).* 1961. Grosset Dunlap. 1st ed. 182p. Vg/dj. M20. $37.00

BLAIR, Claude. *Pistols of the World.* 1968. Viking. 205p. VG+/worn. M20. $50.00

BLAIR, Dierdre. *Anais Nin: A Biography.* 1995. NY. Putnam. 1st ed. 8vo. ils/index. 654p. F/dj. T10. $25.00

BLAIR, John M. *Control of Oil.* 1976. Pantheon. 1st ed. 8vo. ils/tables. 441p. NF/dj. W1. $25.00

BLAIR, Maria. *Mathew Fontaine Maury.* 1918. Whittet Shepperson. 1st ed. 13p. NF/wrp. M8. $37.50

BLAIR, Robert. *Grave.* 1808. London. 1st ed thus. 4to. ils Louis Schiavonetti. rare. C6. $1,600.00

BLAIR & SEYMOUR. *Seymour & Blair: Their Lives & Services.* 1868. NY. 12mo. 575p. brn cloth. T3. $15.00

BLAISDELL, Paul H. *Three Centuries on Winnipesaukee.* 1936. Concord, NH. 14 pl. 77p. VG. T7. $60.00

BLAKE, E. Vale. *Arctic Experiences: Containing Capt George E Tyson...* 1874. NY. Harper. 1st ed. ils/map. 486p. VG. B14. $155.00

BLAKE, Forrester. *Johnny Christmas.* 1948. Morrow. 1st ed. map ep. F/VG. A18. $50.00

BLAKE, Michael. *Airman Mortensen.* 1991. Los Angeles. Seven Wolves. 1st ed. F/NF. H11. $25.00

BLAKE, Nicholas. *Head of a Traveller.* 1949. NY. 1st ed. VG/VG. B5. $35.00

BLAKE, Robert. *Disraeli's Grand Tour.* 1982. NY. VG. O7. $20.00

BLAKE, William. *Illustrations of the Book of Job.* 1825. London. Wm Blake. 1st ed. 1/100. 21 engraved pl. watermark paper. calf. F. B24. $36,000.00

BLAKE, William. *Illustrations to the Divine Comedy of Dante.* 1922. London. 1st ed thus. 1/250. folio. loose as issued. C6. $320.00

BLAKE, William. *Jerusalem.* 1951. London. Trianon. 5 vol. facsimile. 1/516. 100 pl. F/bl wrp/clamshell box. B24. $1,500.00

BLAKE, William. *Land of Dreams.* 1928. Macmillan. 1st ed. Ils Pamela Bianco. 42p. VG/G1. P2. $75.00

BLAKE, William. *Marriage of Heaven & Hell & a Song of Liberty.* 1911. NY. Dutton. 12mo. 79p. teg. paper brd/cloth spine. NF. T10. $40.00

BLAKE, William. *Song of Los.* 1975. Paris. Trianon. facsimile. 1/400. folio. half morocco. NF/case. C6. $200.00

BLAKE, William. *There Is No Natural Religion.* 1886. London. facsimile. 1/50. 12 sm engravings. C6. $325.00

BLAKEY, George C. *Gambler's Companion.* 1979. Paddington. 1st ed. NF/NF. P3. $20.00

BLANCHARD, Amy Ella. *Bonny Bairns.* 1888. Worthington. probable 1st ed. ils Ida Waugh. 48p. VG. D1. $325.00

BLANCHARD, Charles. *With Heaps O'Love.* 1925. Des Moines. Nichols Book & Travel. 12mo. 288p. gilt bl cloth. VG. B11. $25.00

BLANCHARD, Fessenden S. *Sailboat Classes of North America.* 1968. Doubleday. G/dj. A16. $20.00

BLANCHARD, John. *H Book of Harvard Athletics 1852-1922.* 1923. Boston. 8vo. photos. 612p. red buckram. VG. B14. $95.00

BLANCHARD & WELLMAN. *Life & Times of Sir Archie 1805-1833.* 1958. Chapel Hill. 1st ed. VG/G. O3. $45.00

BLANCK. *Biography of American Literature.* 1955-1991. Yale. 9 vol. 4to. 5186p. VG to NF. A4. $1,250.00

BLANCK. *Merle Johnson's American First Editions.* 1942. 4th/1st prt. 571p. VG. A4. $200.00

BLANCK. *Peter Parley to Penrod, a Bibliographical Description...* 1974. 159p. VG+. A4. $135.00

BLAND, Edward. *Discovery of New Brittaine.* 1966. Ann Arbor. xl. VG. O7. $20.00

BLAND, Eleanor Taylor. *Dead Time.* 1992. St Martin. 1st ed. F/F. P3. $18.00

BLAND, Henry Meade. *Day in the Hills.* 1926. San Francisco. private prt. 12mo. VG/stiff prt wrp. T10. $45.00

BLAND, Humphrey. *Treatise of Military Discipline.* 1759. London. Longman. 6 fld plans. old calf/rebacked. K1. $350.00

BLAND, William. *Forms of Ships and Boats.* 1917. London. Lockwood. ils. G. A16. $25.00

BLANDING, Don. *Vagabond's House.* 1943. Dodd Mead. inscr. 114p. F/VG. B11. $20.00

BLANK, Clair. *Beverly Gray on a Treasure Hunt.* (1938). Grosset Dunlap. 243p. gr bdg. VG/G. P2. $16.00

BLANK, Clair. *Beverly Gray's Adventure (#14).* 1944. Grosset Dunlap. 12mo. VG/VG. B17. $14.00

BLANK, Clair. *Beverly Gray's Assignment (#17).* 1947. Grosset Dunlap. 1st ed. lists to #16. 212p. VG/dj. M20. $20.00

BLANK, Clair. *Beverly Gray's Challenge (#15).* 1945. Grosset Dunlap. 1st ed. lists to #14. VG/worn. M20. $15.00

BLANK, Clair. *Beverly Gray's Discovery (#23).* 1953. Clover. lists 25 titles. 183p. VG. M20. $15.00

BLANK, Clair. *Beverly Gray's Quest (#12).* 1942. Grosset Dunlap. 1st ed. 220p. VG/dj. M20. $42.00

BLANK, Clair. *Beverly Gray's Secret (#21).* 1951. Grosset Dunlap. 1st ed. 212p. VG/dj. M20. $32.00

BLANK, Clair. *Beverly Gray's Vacation (#19).* 1949. Grosset Dunlap. 1st ed. lists to this title. 212p. VG+/dj. M20. $25.00

BLANKSTEN, George. *Ecuador: Constitutions & Caudillos.* 1951. Berkeley. index/biblio. 196p. F3. $25.00

BLANSHARD, Paul. *Religion & the Schools.* 1963. Boston. Beacon. M11. $35.00

BLANTON, Smiley. *Now or Never: The Promise of the Middle Years.* 1959. Prentice Hall. sgn. 273p. bl cloth. VG/G1. $50.00

BLATT & MURRY. *Origin of Sedimentary Rocks.* 1980. Prentice Hall. 2nd. 782p. NF. D8. $30.00

BLATTY, William Peter. *Legion.* 1983. Simon Schuster. 1st ed. NF/F. H11. $25.00

BLATTY, William Peter. *Legion.* 1983. Simon Schuster. 1st ed. VG/VG. P3. $15.00

BLAU, Bela. *Ten Commandments.* 1965. Los Angeles. Hebrew text followed by Eng trans. 24p. miniature. AN. B24. $395.00

BLAUNER, Peter. *Slow Motion Riot.* 1991. Morrow. ARC. author's 1st book. VG/wrp. S9. $35.00

BLAUNER, Peter. *Slow Motion Riot.* 1991. Morrow. 1st ed. author's 1st novel. F/F. H11. $35.00

BLAUNER, Peter. *Slow Motion Riot.* 1991. Morrow. 1st ed. NF/NF. P3. $20.00

BLAUVELT, Anna. *Piece Bag Book.* 1927. Macmillan. 1st ed. ils. 96p. VG/G+. P2. $35.00

BLAYLOCK, James P. *Homunculus.* 1988. Morrigan. 1st ed. F/F. P3. $30.00

BLAYLOCK, James P. *Land of Dreams.* 1987. Arbor. 1st ed. inscr. F/F. T2. $35.00

BLAYLOCK, James P. *Last Coin.* 1988. NY. Ace. 1st trade ed. F/F. T2. $18.00

BLAYLOCK, James P. *Last Coin.* 1988. Willimantic. Ziessing. 1st ed. 1/750. sgns. F/F/case. T2. $60.00

BLAYLOCK, James P. *Magic Spectacles.* 1991. Morrigan. 1st ed. F/F. P3. $30.00

BLAYLOCK, James P. *Paper Grail.* 1991. Ace. 1st ed. F/F. P3. $18.00

BLEECK, Oliver; see Thomas, Ross.

BLEGEN, T.C. *Norwegian Migration to America.* 1940. Northfield. 1st ed. ils. 655p. VG/VG. B5. $50.00

BLEGVAD & BLEGVAD. *One Is for the Sun.* 1968. HBW. 1st ed. ils. NF/G+. P2. $15.00

BLEVINS, Winfred. *Misadventures of Silk & Shakespeare.* 1985. Jameson. 1st ed. sgn. M/dj. A18. $15.00

BLEWITT, Mary. *Surveys of the Seas. Brief History of British Hydrography.* 1956. London. McGibbon Kee. folio. 67 pl. F. O7. $150.00

BLICHFELDT, E.H. *Mexican Journey.* 1919 (1912). Chautauqua. 280p. VG. F3. $20.00

BLISH, James. *Cities in Flight.* 1970. Doubleday. 593p. F. M13. $35.00

BLISH, James. *Doctor Mirabilis.* 1971. Dodd Mead. 1st ed. NF/NF. P3. $75.00

BLISH, James. *Frozen Year.* 1957. Ballantine. 1st ed. VG/G. P3. $75.00

BLISH, James. *Jack of Eagles.* 1952. Greenberg. 1st ed. VG/VG. P3. $85.00

BLISH, James. *Star Trek Reader III.* 1977. Dutton. 1st ed. VG/VG. P3. $25.00

BLISS, Michael. *Discovery of Insulin.* 1982. Chicago. 1st ed. 304p. VG/dj. A13. $45.00

BLIVEN, Bruce Jr. *Battle for Manhattan.* 1956. NY. 1st ed. ils/map ep. 128p. VG/dj. B18. $20.00

BLOCH, ELLISON & LEIBER. *Book of the Sixth World Fantasy Convention.* 1980. Underwood Miller. 1st ed. VG/NF. R10. $15.00

BLOCH, Robert. *Bitter Ends.* 1987. Underwood Miller. 1st ed. NF. P3. $40.00

BLOCH, Robert. *Dead Beat.* 1960. Simon Schuster. 1st ed. 12mo. VG+. M21. $20.00

BLOCH, Robert. *Final Reckonings.* 1987. Underwood Miller. 1st ed. VG. P3. $40.00

BLOCH, Robert. *Last Rites.* 1987. Underwood Miller. 1st ed. NF. P3. $40.00

BLOCH, Robert. *Night of the Ripper.* 1984. Doubleday. 1st ed. NF/VG. M22. $10.00

BLOCH, Robert. *Opener of the Way.* 1945. Arkham. 1st ed. author's 1st book. VG/VG. M19. $350.00

BLOCH, Robert. *Psycho House.* 1990. NY. 1st ed. 217p. AN/dj. A17. $7.50

BLOCH, Robert. *Psycho.* 1959. Simon Schuster. 1st ed. inscr. NF/NF. B4. $1,200.00

BLOCH, Robert. *Psycho-Paths.* 1991. Tor. 1st ed. F/F. G10. $15.00

BLOCH, Robert. *Screams: Three Novels of Suspense.* 1989. Underwood Miller. 1st thus. NF/VG. M22. $15.00

BLOCH, Robert. *Strange Eons.* 1978. Whispers. 1st ed. F/F. P3. $30.00

BLOCK, Eugene B. *Fabric of Guilt.* 1968. Doubleday. 1st ed. VG/VG. P3. $20.00

BLOCK, Francesca Lia. *Baby Be-Bop.* 1995. Harper Collins. 1st ed. sgn pub bookplate. F/dj. S9. $20.00

BLOCK, Herbert. *Straight Herblock.* 1964. Simon Schuster. 1st ed. ils. G+. P12. $6.00

BLOCK, Lawrence. *Ariel.* 1980. Arbor. 1st ed. inscr. F/NF. T2. $35.00

BLOCK, Lawrence. *As Bad As I Am.* 1960. Boardman. VG/G. P3. $30.00

BLOCK, Lawrence. *Burglar Who Painted Like Mondrian.* 1983. Arbor. 1st ed. F/F. P3. $25.00

BLOCK, Lawrence. *Burglar Who Thought He Was Bogart.* 1995. Dutton. F/F. P3. $22.00

BLOCK, Lawrence. *Burglar Who Traded Ted Williams.* 1994. Dutton. sgn. F/F. A4. $35.00

BLOCK, Lawrence. *Burglar Who Traded Ted Williams.* 1994. Dutton. 1st ed. F/F. M22. $25.00

BLOCK, Lawrence. *Dance at the Slaughterhouse.* 1991. Morrow. 1st ed. F/F. A20/T2. $25.00

BLOCK, Lawrence. *Devil Knows You're Dead.* 1993. Morrow. 1st ed. F/NF. M22. $20.00

BLOCK, Lawrence. *Devil Knows Your'e Dead.* 1990. 1st ed. inscr. F/F. M19. $35.00

BLOCK, Lawrence. *Into the Night.* 1987. Mysterious. 1st ed. sgn. F/F. T2. $20.00

BLOCK, Lawrence. *Private Party.* 1953. Rinehart. 1st ed. VG/VG. P3. $45.00

BLOCK, Lawrence. *Random Walk.* 1988. Tor. 1st ed. sgn. F/F. T2. $20.00

BLOCK, Lawrence. *Sins of the Fathers.* 1992. Dark Harvest. 1st hc ed. sgn. F/F. M19. $45.00

BLOCK, Lawrence. *Ticket to the Boneyard.* 1990. NY. Morrow. 1st ed. sgn. F/F. t2. $25.00

BLOCK, Lawrence. *Walk Among the Tombstones.* 1992. Morrow. 1st ed. sgn. F/F. T2. $25.00

BLOCK, Lawrence. *When the Sacred Ginmill Closes.* 1986. Arbor. UP/ARC. sgn. VG/wrp. M22. $45.00

BLOCK, Thomas H. *Airship Nine.* 1984. Putnam. 1st ed. VG/VG. P3. $17.00

BLOCK & KING. *Code of Arms.* 1981. Mareck. 1st ed. NF/NF. P3. $28.00

BLOCK & KING. *Me Tanner, You Jane.* 1970. Macmillan. 1st ed. VG/VG. P3. $40.00

BLODGETT. *Photographs, a Collector's Guide.* 1979. np. 248p. F/VG. A4. $125.00

BLOM, Frans. *Conquest of Yucatan.* 1936. Houghton Mifflin. 1st ed. ils. 238p. F3. $20.00

BLOMFIELD, E. *General View of the World: Geographical, Historical...* 1807. Bungay. Brightly Binnersley. 10 maps. VG. O7. $120.00

BLOODGOOD, Lida Fleitmann. *Saddle of Queens.* 1959. London. Allen. 1st ed. VG/G. O3. $65.00

BLOODSTONE, John; see Byrne, Stuart.

BLOODWORTH, Dennis. *Eye for the Dragon: Southeast Asia Observed, 1954-1970.* 1970. FSG. 1st ed. F/F. B35. $30.00

BLOOM, Amy. *Come to Me.* 1994. London. Macmillan. AP. author's 1st book. NF/wrp/proof dj. S9. $45.00

BLOOM, James D. *Left Letters: Culture Wars of Mike Gold & Joseph Freeman.* 1992. Columbia. 1st ed. F/F. B2. $30.00

BLOSSFELDT, Karl. *Karl Blossfeldt.* 1994. Koln. Benedikt Taschen. 1st ed. 8vo. F. S9. $35.00

BLOTNER, Joseph. *Faulkner: A Biography.* 1974. Random. 1st ed. 127p. VG/fair. B10. $15.00

BLOUNT, R. *About 3 Bricks Shy of a Load.* 1974. Boston. 1st ed. VG/VG. B5. $17.50

BLOUNT, Thomas. *Fragmenta Antiquitatis; or, Ancient Tenures of Land...* 1815. London. Brooke Paternoster-Row. 3rd. working copy. M11. $150.00

BLOUSTEIN, Edward J. *University & the Counterculture.* 1972. New Brunswick. Rutgers. 1st ed. inscr. F/F. B4. $50.00

BLUCK, Louise. *Proofs & Theories: Essays on Poetry.* 1994. Hopwell, NJ. Ecco. 1st ed. F/F. M23. $35.00

BLUM, Andre. *Les Origines du Livre a Gravures en France...* 1928. Paris. Van Oest. 4to. 78 pl. NF/self wrp. T10. $150.00

BLUM, Ann. *Picturing Nature, American 19th-Century Zoological Ils.* 1993. Princeton. 4to. 442p. F/F. A4. $60.00

BLUM, Daniel. *Pictorial History of the Silent Screen.* 1953. Grosset Dunlap. rpt. 4to. 334p. VG/VG. T10. $25.00

BLUMENTHAL, Joseph. *Art of the Printed Book, 1455-1955: Masterpieces...* 1978. Pierpont Morgan. 3rd. 125 pl. 192p. gilt blk cloth. F/dj. T10. $50.00

BLUMENTHAL, Walter Hart. *Formats & Foibles: Few Books Which Might Be Called Curious.* 1956. Worchester. 1/300. 105p. aeg. Sangorski-Stucliffe bdg. F. B24. $225.00

BLUMLEIN, Michael. *Brains of Rats.* 1990. Scream. 1st ed. 1/250. sgn/#d. F/F/case. T2. $65.00

BLUNDELL, Nigel. *World's Greatest Crooks & Conmen.* 1982. Octopus. 1st ed. F. P3. $13.00

BLUNK, Ira R. *Grouch Pills.* 1967. Dorrance. 1st ed. author's 1st book. NF/F. H11. $30.00

BLUNT, Wilfrid Scawen. *Secret History of the English Occupation of Egypt.* 1922. Knopf. 1st Am ed. 416p. VG. W1. $35.00

BLY, Robert. *Forty Poems Touching on Recent American History.* 1970. Beacon. 1st ed. sgn. F/NF. M19. $17.50

BLY, Robert. *Iron John.* 1990. Addison Wesley. 1st ed. F/VG. A20. $25.00

BLY, Robert. *Light Around the Body.* 1967. Harper Row. 1st ed. sgn. F/clip. B35. $100.00

BLY, Robert. *Loon.* 1977. Ox Head. 1/500. VG/hand-sewn wrp. C4. $40.00

BLY, Robert. *Loving a Woman in Two Worlds.* 1985. 1st ed. VG/VG. C4. $35.00

BLY, Robert. *Sibling Society.* 1996. Addison Wesley. 1st ed. inscr/drawing. F/F. B35. $55.00

BLYTHE, Legette. *Hear Me, Pilate!* 1961. Holt. 1st ed. VG/NF. H11. $30.00

BOARD, John. *From Point to Point.* nd. London. Johnson. 1st ed. VG/VG. O3. $45.00

BOARDMAN, John. *Oxford History of the Classical World.* 1988. Oxford. 3rd ed. F/F. P3. $30.00

BOARDMAN, Tom. *SF Stories.* 1979. Octopus. 1st ed. VG/VG. P3. $15.00

BOAS, Franz. *Handbook of American Indian Languages.* 1911. GPO. 2 vol. 8vo. xl. gilt olive cloth. T10. $100.00

BOASE, Wendy. *Sky's the Limit: Women Pioneers in Aviation.* 1979. NY. 1st ed. 223p. VG+/dj. B18. $25.00

BOCCACCIO, Giovanni. *Decameron.* 1930. LEC. 1/1500. ils/sgn TM Cleland. 2 vol. F/case. C2. $100.00

BOCCACCIO, Giovanni. *Life of Dante.* 1992. Greenbrae, CA. Allen. 1/109. ils. Fortuny bdg. F. w/prospectus. B24. $300.00

BODARD, Lucien. *Green Hell.* 1971. Dutton. 1st ed. 291p. dj. F3. $15.00

BODDAM-WHETHAM, J.W. *Western Wanderings: A Record of Travel in the Evening Land.* 1874. London. Bentley. 1st ed. 12 pl. 364p. VG. H7. $100.00

BODE, Vaughn. *Deadbone.* 1975. Northern Comfort Communications. 1st ed. VG/VG. P3. $100.00

BODE. *New Mencken Letters.* 1977. np. 635p. F/VG. A4. $35.00

BODENHEIM, Maxwell. *Replenishing Jessica.* 1925. Boni Liveright. 1st ed. F/NF. B2. $100.00

BODFISH, Hartson H. *Chasing the Bowhead.* 1936. Harvard. ils. 281p. teg. VG. T7. $110.00

BOEING AIRCRAFT COMPANY. *Flight & Operational Manual for the B-29 Bomber.* 1943. Seattle. ils. 387p. stp flexible leatherette/snap closure. VG. B18. $350.00

BOELDEKE, Alfred. *With Graciela to the Head-Hunters.* 1948. McKay. 1st ed. ils/photos. 166p. F3. $15.00

BOESIGER & GIRSBERGER. *LeCorbusier 1910-1965.* 1967. photos. VG/VG. M17. $75.00

BOGAN, Louise. *Dark Summer.* 1929. Scribner. 1st ed. inscr/dtd 1936. F/VG+. B4. $650.00

BOGGS, Ralph. *Bibliography of Latin American Folklore.* 1940. Wilson. 1st ed. xl. F3. $25.00

BOGGS, Stanley. *Salvadoran Varieties of Wheeled Figurines.* 1973. Miami. 1st ed. 32p. wrp. F3. $20.00

BOGLE, Donald. *Brown Sugar: 80 Years of America's Black Female Superstars.* 1980. Harmony. 1st ed. 4to. 208p. F/NF. R11. $50.00

BOGLE, Donald. *Toms, Coons, Mullatos, Mammies & Books.* 1973. NY. 1st ed. VG/VG. B5. $20.00

BOHN, Dave. *Glacier Bay, the Land & Silence.* 1967. Sierra Club. folio. F/dj. T10. $50.00

BOK, Edward. *Americanization of Edward Bok.* 1922. Scribner. 1/1250. sgn. 15 pl. VG. B11. $50.00

BOK, Hannes. *Beauty & the Beasts.* 1978. De La Ree. 1st ed. NF/NF. P3. $45.00

BOK & MERRITT. *Fox Woman/The Blue Pagoda/The Black Wheel.* 1976. Arno. 1st combined ed. F/sans. G10. $100.00

BOKTOR, Amir. *Development & Expansion of Education in United Arab...* 1963. Cairo. Am U in Cairo. 1st ed. lg 8vo. 3 fld charts. 182p. VG/dj. W1. $22.00

BOLAND, Charles. *They All Discovered America.* 1961. Garden City. VG. O7. $35.00

BOLDREWOOD, Rolf. *Last Chance.* 1905. London. VG. A17. $9.50

BOLIN, C. *Narrative of the Life & Adventures of...* 1965. Palo Alto. VG. O7. $75.00

BOLITHO, William. *Twelve Against the Gods.* 1930. Simon Schuster. not 1st ed. 351p. bl cloth. NF/dj. B22. $4.50

BOLL, Heinrich. *Absent Without Leave.* 1965. McGraw Hill. 1st ed. VG/VG. A20. $22.00

BOLL, Heinrich. *Stories.* 1986. Knopf. 1st ed. rem mk. NF/NF. B35. $24.00

BOLOTIN & LAING. *Chicago World's Fair of 1893: The World Columbian Expo.* 1992. WA, DC. ils/photos. 166p. cloth. dj. D2. $35.00

BOLTON, Herbert E. *Coronado: Knight of Pueblos & Plains.* 1949. NY/Albuquerque. VG. O7. $25.00

BOLTON, Herbert E. *Rim of Christendom: A Biography of Eusebio Francisco Kino.* 1936. Macmillan. 1st ed. 8vo. 8 fld maps/12 pl/3 facsimilies. F. T10. $150.00

BOLTON & COE. *American Samplers.* 1921. Boston. 1st ed. 125 pl. 416p. G. B5. $145.00

BOLTON. *American Book Illustrators, Bibliographic Check Lists...* 1938. np. 1/1000. 302p. VG. A4. $225.00

BOMBECK, Erma. *Aunt Erma's Cope Book.* 1979. McGraw Hill. VG/VG. P12. $6.00

BOMBECK, Erma. *Grass Is Always Greener Over the Septic Tank.* 1976. McGraw Hill. NF/VG. P12. $5.00

BOMMERSBACH, Jana. *Trunk Murderess: Winnie Ruth Judd.* 1992. Simon Schuster. 1st ed. sgn. F/F. T2. $25.00

BONCZEK, Willi. *Essen im Spiegel der Karten: Historische Karten...* 1975. Essen. Richrd Bacht. 93 maps. AN/dj. O7. $250.00

BOND, Beverley W. Jr. *Civilization of the Old Northwest.* 1934. NY. 1st ed. 534p. G/tattered. B18. $37.50

BOND, J. Wesley. *Minnesota & Its Resources, Camp-Fire Sketches...* 1853. NY. Redfield. 1st ed. fld map. 364p. VG. w/edit letter. B14. $125.00

BOND, Michael. *Monsieur Pamplemousse & the Secret.* 1984. Hodder Stoughton. 1st ed. VG/VG. P3. $15.00

BOND, Michael. *More About Paddington.* 1962. dj. K2. $14.00

BOND, Nelson. *Nightmares & Daydreams.* 1968. Arkham. 1st ed. VG/VG. P3. $40.00

BOND, Nelson. *State of Mind.* 1958. Samuel French. 76p. VG. B10. $15.00

BOND & YELLIN. *Pen Is Ours: A Listing of Writings...About African-American.* 1991. Oxford. ils/photos. 360p. F. A4. $40.00

BONDY, Louis. *Miniature Books: Their History From the Beginning...* 1981. ils. 227p. F/F. A4. $165.00

BONDY, Ruth. *Israelis, Profile of a People.* 1969. Funk Wagnall. 1st ed. inscr. 8vo. 320p. VG/dj. T10. $125.00

BONE, David W. *Capstan Bars.* 1931. Edinburgh. Porpoise. 1st ed. sgn. ils/sgn Freda Bone. teg. T7. $85.00

BONE, Neil. *Aurora: Sun-Earth Interactions.* 1991. NY. Horwood. 8vo. 156p. VG/wrp. K5. $15.00

BONER, Harold A. *Giant's Ladder: David H Moffat & His Railroad.* 1962. Kalmbach. 224p. NF/dj. M20. $42.00

BONFIGLIOLI, Kyril. *After You With the Pistol.* 1980. Crime Club. 1st ed. xl. dj. P3. $5.00

BONGE, Lyle. *Photographs of Lyle Bonge.* 1982. Jargon Soc. 1st ed. 4to. sgn Bonge/Williams. AN/dj. C2. $60.00

BONN. *Under Cover, an Illustrated History...* 1982. np. revised. 144p. VG/wrp. A4. $25.00

BONNARD, Andre. *Greek Civilization.* nd. np. 3 vol. 1st ed. photos. VG/VG/VG case. M17. $45.00

BONNECARRERE & HEMINGWAY. *Rosebud.* 1974. Morrow. 1st Am ed. B4. $75.00

BONNER, M.G. *Baseball Rookies Who Made Good.* 1954. Knopf. later prt. G/clip. P8. $8.00

BONNER, Mary Graham. *Adventures in Puddle Muddle.* 1935. NY. 1st ed. ils Kolliker. VG/VG. B5. $45.00

BONNER, Mary Graham. *Magic Journeys.* 1928. Macaulay. ils Luxor Price. 286p. G. A17. $25.00

BONNER, Mary Graham. *365 Bedtime Stories.* 1987. Derrydale. 1st ed thus. 8vo. 302p. F/VG+. C14. $8.00

BONNER, Thomas. *William Faulkner: The William B Wisdom Collection...* 1980. Tulane. ils. 90p. VG. B10. $18.00

BONNET, Theodore. *Dutch.* 1955. Doubleday. 1st ed. VG/VG. P3. $20.00

BONNETTE & ZUBAL. *Gritloaf Anthology.* 1978. Palaemon. 1/500. 44p. F. B10. $35.00

BONNEY, Richard. *Dorchester Old & New in the Old Bay Colony.* 1930. Dorchester. Tercentenary Committee. sgn. 79p. VG/wrp. B11. $20.00

BONNEY, Therese. *Europe's Children 1939-1943.* 1943. np. ltd ed. sgn. 62 full-p photos. F/stiff wrp/dj. S9. $125.00

BONSOR, N.R.P. *South Atlantic Seaway.* 1983. Jersey Channel Islands. Brookside Pub. VG/VG. A16. $25.00

BONTLY, Thomas. *Celestial Chess.* 1979. Harper Row. 1st ed. VG/VG. P3. $18.00

BOOKER, M. Keith. *Dystopian Impulse in Modern Literature.* 1994. Greenwood. F. P3. $50.00

BOOKMAN & POWERS. *March to Victory.* 1986. NY. 1st ed. 340p. dj. A17. $10.00

BOONZY, William. *Big Bill Blues: William Boonzy's Story.* 1955. London. Cassell. 1st ed. F/VG+. N3. $55.00

BOORMAN, John. *Emerald Forest Diary.* 1985. FSG. 1st ed. MTI. F/F. P3. $15.00

BOORSTIN, Daniel J. *Exploring Spirit.* 1976. NY. VG. O7. $15.00

BOOTH, Norman K. *Basic Elements of Landscape Design.* 1983. NY. 4th. ils. 315p. VG. B26. $25.00

BOOTHBY, Guy. *Pharos l'Egyptien.* ca 1910. Paris. La Vie Illustree. 1st ed. 188p. VG. W1. $20.00

BORAH, Woodrow. *Justice by Insurance.* 1983. Berkeley. 1st ed. 479p. dj. F3. $20.00

BORBA, Oney. *Os Iapoenses.* 1986. De Cujo Vale do Iapo. fld map. 239p. stiff wrp. F3. $15.00

BORCHARDT & BORCHARDT. *Egypt: Architecture, Landscape, Life of the People.* ca 1927. Berlin. Wasmuth. 1st ed. 272p. VG/dj. W1. $65.00

BORDONE, Benedetto. *Libro...De Tutte l'Isole del Mondo.* 1966. Amsterdam. Theatrvm Orbis Terrarvm. facsimile of 1528 atlas. M. T7. $300.00

BORG, Scott. *Water Hazard.* 1995. Delacort. ARC. author's 1st novel. NF/wrp. M22. $30.00

BORGENICHT, Miriam. *Bad Medicine.* 1984. Macmillan. 1st ed. F/F. P3. $15.00

BORGENICHT, Miriam. *Don't Look Back.* 1956. Doubleday. 1st ed. inscr. VG/VG. M22. $25.00

BORGENICHT, Miriam. *No Bail for Dalton.* 1974. Bobbs Merrill. 1st ed. VG/VG. P3. $18.00

BORGLUM & CASEY. *Give the Man Room.* 1952. Indianapolis. 1st ed. F/F. B5. $30.00

BORING, Edwin. *History of Experimental Psychology.* 1929. NY. 1st ed. 699p. VG. A13. $45.00

BORLAND, Hal. *12 Moons of the Year.* 1979. NY. 1st ed. VG/VG. B5. $22.50

BORN. *American Landscape Painting.* 1948. Yale. cloth. NF. D2. $60.00

BOROWSKY, Marvin. *Queen's Knight.* 1955. NY. Random. 1st ed. 8vo. F/dj. T10. $75.00

BORRADAILE, L.W. *Animal & Its Environment.* 1922. London. 399p. red cloth. VG. B14. $125.00

BORTON, Elizabeth. *Pollyanna & the Secret Mission (#14).* 1951. Grosset Dunlap. 263p. VG/dj. M20. $20.00

BORTON, Elizabeth. *Pollyanna's Castle in Mexico (#7).* 1934. Page. 1st ed. 322p. red silk cloth. VG/dj. M20. $35.00

BORTON, Helen. *Jungle.* 1968. HBW. 1st ed. 13 double-p ils. G+. C14. $10.00

BOSCAWEN, William. *Treatise on Convictions on Penal Statues.* 1792. Dublin. 1st ed thus. contemporary calf. M11. $450.00

BOSE, Pradodh Chandra. *Introduction to Juristic Psychology.* 1917. Calcutta. Thacker Spink. 424p. ruled fuchsia cloth. G1. $50.00

BOSHER, Kate Langley; see Cary, Mary.

BOSQUET, Alain. *Selected Poems.* 1972. OH U. 1st Am ed. F/NF clip. C2. $35.00

BOSSE. *Civil War Newspaper Maps: A Cartobibliography...* 1993. np. ils/2041 entries. 271p. F. A4. $75.00

BOSSERT, Helmuth. *Encyclopedia of Colour Decoration From Earliest Times...* 1928. Berlin. Ernst Wasmuth. 4to. 120 loose pl+36p text. xl. F/later portfolio. T10. $150.00

BOSTON, John. *Ikenja.* 1977. Nigeria. F/F. D2. $70.00

BOSTON, Lucy. *Enemy at Green Knowe.* 1964. HBW. 6th. 156p. VG/VG. P2. $10.00

BOSTON, Lucy. *Stranger at Green Knowe.* 1961. HBW. 1st Am ed. 158p. VG. P2. $15.00

BOSWELL, H. *French Canada.* 1938. Viking. 1st ed. ils. beige cloth. NF/NF. D1. $75.00

BOSWELL, H. *French Canada: Pictures & Stories.* 1938. Viking. 1st ed. ils. NF. P2. $20.00

BOSWELL, Robert. *Crooked Hearts.* 1987. Knopf. 1st ed. author's 1st book. F/F. H11. $40.00

BOSWELL, Robert. *Crooked Hearts.* 1987. Knopf. 1st ed. NF/VG+. M23. $20.00

BOSWELL, Robert. *Dancing at the Movies.* 1986. IA City. 1st ed. author's 1st book. F/F. C2. $100.00

BOSWELL, Robert. *Mystery Ride.* 1993. Knopf. 1st ed. F/F. M23. $25.00

BOSWELL & FISHER. *Fenway Park Stadium Pop-Up Book.* 1992. Little Brn. 1st ed. M. P8. $25.00

BOTTING, Douglas. *Humbolt & the Cosmos.* 1973. NY. VG. O7. $20.00

BOTTING, Douglas. *Pirates.* 1978. Time Life. ils. 192p. gilt bdg. G+. P12. $12.00

BOTTOMS, David. *Any Cold Jordan.* 1987. Atlanta. Peachtree. 1st ed. author's 1st novel. NF/NF. H11. $35.00

BOTTOMS, David. *Easter Weekend.* 1990. Houghton Mittlin. 1st ed. F/F. H11. $75.00

BOTTONE, S.R. *Radiography & the X-Rays in Practice & Theory...* 1898. London. 1st ed. ils. 176p. VG. B14. $150.00

BOUCHER, Anthony. *Best Detective Stories 19th.* 1964. Dutton. 1st ed. VG/VG. P3. $25.00

BOUCHER, Anthony. *Quintessence of Queen.* 1962. Random. 1st ed. VG/VG. P3. $40.00

BOUCHER D'ARGIS, A.L.G. *Nouveau Dictionnaire Raisonne de la Taxe in Matiere Civile.* 1874. Paris. Billard. worn. M11. $175.00

BOUDINOT, Elias. *Elias Boudinot's Journey to Boston.* 1955. Princeton. VG. O7. $55.00

BOUGEREAU, Maurice. *Le Theatre Francoys.* 1966. Amsterdam. Theatrvm Orbis Terrarvm. facsimile of 1594 ed. M. T7. $150.00

BOULD, John. *Introduction to the Trochilidae...* 1861. London. Prt for Author. revised. folio. pres/dtd 1861. gilt plum cloth. VG. A4. $495.00

BOULGER & BRITTEN. *Biographical Index of Deceased British & Irish Botanists.* 1931 (1893). London. revised/completed AB Rendle. 2nd. 342p. VG. B26. $45.00

BOULLE, Pierre. *Because It Is Absurd.* 1971. Vanguard. 1st ed. xl. dj. P3. $10.00

BOULTON, Alfredo. *El Rostro de Bolivar.* 1982. Caracas. Macanao. ils. 146p. blk vinyl bdg w/raised portrait. D2. $100.00

BOURDAIN, Anthony. *Bone in the Throat.* 1995. Villard. 1st ed. F/NF. H11. $25.00

BOURKE-WHITE, Margaret; see White, Margaret Bourke.

BOURNE, Peter. *Flames of Empire.* 1949. Putnam. 1st ed. VG/G. P3. $18.00

BOURNE, Peter. *Twilight of the Dragon.* 1954. Putnam. 1st ed. VG/VG. P3. $20.00

BOURSIER-MOUGENOT, A. *Doudou Flies Away.* 1937. NY. 1st ed? trans Georges Duplaix. VG. M5. $110.00

BOUTELL, Charles. *Heraldry: Historical & Popular.* 1864. London. ils. 547p. 3-quarter leather. A9. $85.00

BOUTELL. *First Editions of Today & How To Tell Them, Fourth Edition.* 1965. Peacock. revised/ltd ed. 231p. VG. A4. $155.00

BOUTERWEK, Frederick. *History of Spanish & Portuguese Literature.* 1823. London. 2 vol. VG. O7. $100.00

BOUTMY, Emile. *Essai d'une Psychologie Politique du Peuple...* 1901. Paris. Armand Colin. 12mo. 456p. yel wrp. G1. $45.00

BOUVIER, E.L. *Psychic Life of Insects.* 1922. Century. 1st Eng-language ed. trans LO Howard. VG. G1. $40.00

BOUVIER, John. *Law Dictionary & Concise Encyclopedia, Third Revision...* 1984. Buffalo. Hein. facsimile of 1914 ed. M11. $175.00

BOVA, Ben. *Cyberbrooks.* 1989. Tor. 1st ed. F/F. P3. $18.00

BOVA, Ben. *Dueling Machine.* 1969. HRW. 1st ed. sgn. F/NF. G10. $45.00

BOVA, Ben. *End of Exile.* 1975. Dutton. 1st ed. RS. F/F. P3. $35.00

BOVA, Ben. *High Road.* 1981. Houghton Mifflin. 1st ed. VG. P3. $18.00

BOVA, Ben. *Kinsman Saga.* 1987. Tor. 1st ed. F/NF. M22. $15.00

BOVA, Ben. *Millenium.* 1976. Random. 1st ed. NF/NF. P3. $30.00

BOVA, Ben. *Multiple Men.* 1976. Bobbs Merrill. 1st ed. NF/NF. P3. $25.00

BOVA, Ben. *Peacekeepers.* 1988. Tor. 1st ed. F/F. P3. $18.00

BOVA, Ben. *Viewpoint.* 1977. NESFA. 1/800. sgn. F/F. G10. $20.00

BOVA, Ben. *Winds of Altair.* 1973. Dutton. 1st ed. VG. P3. $13.00

BOVILL, E.W. *Niger Explored.* 1968. London. VG. O7. $55.00

BOVIS & HAGUES. *Les Oiseaux ABC.* 1945. Lyon. Agence Gutenberg. 4to. 24p. F/prt red wrp. B24. $250.00

BOWAN & DICKINSON. *Death Is Incidental.* 1937. Chicago. Willett. 1st ed. 111p. dj. F3. $20.00

BOWDEN. *Pop-Up Book for Christmas: A Treasury of Celebrations...* 1994. np. 4 double-p popups. F. A4. $35.00

BOWDITCH, Henry I. *Brief Memories of Louis & Some of His Contemporaries...* 1872. Boston. 37p. VG/prt wrp. B14. $75.00

BOWDITCH, Nathaniel. *American Practical Navigator, 1962.* 1966. np. corrected prt. A16. $35.00

BOWEN, Catherine Drinker. *Yankee From Olympus, Justice Holmes & His Family.* 1944. London. Benn. 1st Eng ed. VG/dj. M11. $45.00

BOWEN, Dana Thomas. *Memories of the Lakes.* 1946. FL. 1st ed. G/torn. A16. $22.50

BOWEN, Elizabeth. *House in Paris.* 1936. Knopf. 1st ed. VG/VG. P3. $20.00

BOWEN, John. *Scale Model Sailing Ships.* 1978. NY. Mayflower. ils. 192p. VG/dj. T7. $25.00

BOWEN, Marjorie. *Kecksies & Other Twilight Tales.* 1976. Sauk City. 1st ed. 1/4391. F/F. T2. $10.00

BOWEN, Robert O. *Weight of the Cross.* 1951. Knopf. 1st ed. NF/NF. B4. $45.00

BOWEN, Sidney R. *Dave Dawson at Singapore.* 1942. Saafield. VG. P12. $6.00

BOWEN, Sidney R. *Dave Dawson With the Air Corp.* 1942. Saalfield. G+. P12. $5.00

BOWEN, Sidney R. *Dave Dawson With the Pacific Fleet.* 1942. Saalfield. G+. P12. $5.00

BOWEN & JUX. *Afro-Arabian Geology.* 1987. London. Chapman Hall. ils. 295p. ils brd. F. B1. $42.50

BOWER, B.M. *Dark Horse: A Story of the Flying U.* 1931. Little Brn. 1st ed. F/clip. A18. $30.00

BOWER & SWANBOROUGH. *United States Navy Aircraft Since 1910.* 1968. NY. 1st ed. 518p. VG/dj. B18. $37.50

BOWER. *Fred Rosenstock: A Legend in Books & Art.* 1976. np. 1/250. ils. 229p. F/case. A4. $125.00

BOWERS, Claude G. *Beveridge & the Progressive Era.* 1932. Literary Guild. M11. $25.00

BOWERS, Claude G. *Thomas Jefferson.* 1945. Boston. 3 vol. 8vo. gilt red cloth. F/G case. H3. $90.00

BOWERS, Claude G. *Tragic Era: Revolution After Lincoln.* 1929. Houghton Mifflin. 1st ed. inscr pres. 567p. VG. B10. $45.00

BOWERS, Fredson. *Principles of Bibliographical Description.* 1949. Princeton. 522p. VG. A4. $185.00

BOWIE, Walter Russell. *Story of Jesus for Young People.* 1937. Scribner. 1st ed. 125p. G+. C14. $8.00

BOWKER, Richard. *Marlborough Street.* 1987. Doubleday. 1st ed. RS. F/F. P3. $18.00

BOWLBY, J. *Charles Darwin: A New Life.* 1990. Norton. 1st ed. 511p. F/dj. D8. $30.00

BOWLE, John. *Henry VIII: A Biography.* 1964. Little Brn. 1st Am ed. 316p. red cloth. VG+. B22. $5.50

BOWLES, Elisabeth Ann. *Good Beginning: First Decades of U of NC at Greensboro.* 1967. UNC. photos. 193p. VG/fair. B10. $15.00

BOWLES, Paul. *In Touch.* 1994. NY. 1/250. sgn. case. C4. $100.00

BOWLES, Samuel. *Across the Continent.* 1966. np. fld map. 42p. B18. $17.50

BOWLES & HAEBERLIN. *Yallah.* 1957. NY. 1st ed. VG/VG. B5. $50.00

BOWMAN, Dan M. III. *Giants of the Turf.* 1960. Lexington. 1st ed. VG/G. O3. $35.00

BOWMAN, Isaiah. *New World.* 1922. Yonkers. VG. O7. $35.00

BOWMAN, Karl. *Sexual Being Versus Governments That Promote Homosexuality.* 1993. Rochester, WA. Sovereign. 50p. prt wrp. M11. $4.00

BOWMAN & CARTEN. *Busy Bodies: The Busy ABC's.* 1959. Rand McNally. 1st ed. 8vo. unp. VG. C14. $9.00

BOWMAN & DICKINSON. *Westward From Rio.* 1936. Willett Clark. sgns. 100 woodblock prt. 351p. VG/VG. B11. $45.00

BOWRA, C.M. *Heroic Poetry.* 1932. London. Macmillan. 1st ed. F/NF. C2. $30.00

BOXER, Arabella. *Wind in the Willows Cookbook.* 1983. 1st ed. ils Shephard. NF/NF. S13. $25.00

BOYD, Blanche McCrary. *Mourning the Death of Magic.* 1977. Macmillan. 1st ed. author's 2nd novel. NF/dj. B4. $50.00

BOYD, David French. *Reminiscences of the War in Virigina.* 1989. Austin, TX. Jenkins. 1st ed. 37p. F/wrp. M8. $25.00

BOYD, Frank; see Kane, Frank.

BOYD, J. *Life of General William T Sherman.* 1891. np. 12mo. 608p. grn cloth. T3. $20.00

BOYD, James. *Long Hunt.* 1930. Scribner. 1st ed. 376p. VG. B10. $12.00

BOYD, James. *Marchin On.* 1927. Scribner. 1st ed. 426p. VG. B10. $25.00

BOYD, James. *Marching On.* 1927. Scribner. sgn. 426p. VG/dj. M20. $32.00

BOYD, John. *Girl With the Jade Green Eyes.* 1978. Viking. 1st ed. VG/VG. P3. $25.00

BOYD, Lizzie Edmunds. *Travel Carol, Being Diary-Record of Two Tours...* 1938. Dietz. sgn. ils Elmo Jones. 111p. VG. B10. $10.00

BOYD, Louise A. *Coast of Northeast Greenland With Hydrographic Studies...* 1948. Am Geographical Soc. 7 maps/5 panora mas. F/case. O7. $55.00

BOYD, Malcolm. *Runner.* 1974. Waco. Word. 1st ed. sgn. 203p. F/VG. B11. $15.00

BOYD, Marion. *Murder in the Stacks.* 1934. Lee Shepard. 1st ed. author's 2nd novel. VG. M22. $25.00

BOYD & PEDERSEN. *Folk Games of Denmark & Sweden for School...* 1915. Chicago. ils/songs/music. 58p. wrp. A17. $15.00

BOYER, Dwight. *Ghost Ships of the Great Lakes.* 1968. Dodd Mead. VG/dj. A16. $20.00

BOYER, Dwight. *Great Stories of the Great Lakes.* 1966. Dodd Mead. 2nd prt. VG/dj. A16. $15.00

BOYER, Dwight. *Ships & Men of the Great Lakes.* 1977. Dodd Mead. VG/VG. A16. $30.00

BOYER, Dwight. *Strange Adventures of the Great Lakes.* 1974. Dodd Mead. VG/VG. A16. $20.00

BOYER, Dwight. *True Tales of the Great Lakes.* 1971. Dodd Mead. VG/VG. A16. $20.00

BOYKIN, Edward. *Between Wind & Water.* 1966. NY. Norton. 1st ed. 207p. VG/dj. T7. $25.00

BOYLAN, Grace. *Kids of Many Colors.* 1901. Jamieson Higgins. ils Ike Morgan. 157p. VG. P2. $135.00

BOYLE, Kay. *Avalanche.* 1944. Simon Schuster. 1st ed. NF/VG. B4. $60.00

BOYLE, Kay. *Generation Without Farewell.* 1960. Knopf. 1st ed. F/F. B4. $50.00

BOYLE, Kay. *Pinky in Persia.* 1968. Crowell Collier. 1st ed. sgn. ils Lilian Obligado. rem mk. F/NF. B4. $150.00

BOYLE, Kay. *Smoking Mountain.* 1951. McGraw Hill. 1st ed. F/G. B4. $45.00

BOYLE, Kay. *Words That Must Somehow Be Said.* 1984. London. 1st ed. sgn. F/F. A11. $35.00

BOYLE, Kay. *Year Before Last.* 1932. Harrison Smith. 1st ed. VG+/dj. B4. $100.00

BOYLE, T. Coraghessan. *Budding Prospects.* 1984. Viking. 1st ed. F/F. H11. $60.00

BOYLE, T. Coraghessan. *Descent of Man.* 1979. Little Brn. 1st ed. author's 1st book. F/F. S9. $550.00

BOYLE, T. Coraghessan. *Descent of Man.* 1979. Little Brn. 1st ed. author's 1st book. rem mk. NF/NF. A15. $125.00

BOYLE, T. Coraghessan. *East Is East.* 1990. Viking. 1st ed. F/F. H11. $35.00

BOYLE, T. Coraghessan. *East Is East.* 1990. Viking. 1st ed. sgn. F/F. C2. $50.00

BOYLE, T. Coraghessan. *If the River Was Whiskey.* 1989. Viking. 1st ed. sgn. F/F. H11. $55.00

BOYLE, T. Coraghessan. *Road to Wellville.* 1993. Viking. 1st ed. AN/dj. B4. $45.00

BOYLE, T. Coraghessan. *Road to Wellville.* 1993. Viking. 1st ed. rem mk. F/F. B35. $30.00

BOYLE, T. Coraghessan. *World's End.* 1987. NY. 1st ed. sgn. F/F. C2. $60.00

BOYLE, Thomas. *Only the Dead Know.* 1985. Stoddart. 1st ed. F/F. P3. $15.00

BOYLSTON, Helen Dore. *Sue Barton, Rural Nurse (#4).* 1939. Little Brn. 4th. 254p. VG+/worn. M20. $60.00

BOYLSTON, Helen Dore. *Sue Barton, Student Nurse (#1).* 1936. Little Brn. 244p. VG/dj. M20. $40.00

BOYS & SMITH. *Poisonous Amphibians & Reptiles.* 1959. Springfield. Thomas. inscr/dtd Boys. 149p. VG/dj. A10. $45.00

BRACHER, Karl Dietrich. *German Dictatorship: Origins, Structure & Consequences...* 1971. London. 1st ed. 553p. VG/dj. A17. $20.00

BRACKEN, Dorothy. *Rodeo.* 1949. Steck. ils Elizabeth Rice. VG. P2. $30.00

BRACKMAN, Arnold C. *Search for the Gold of the Tutankhamen.* 1976. Mason Charter. 1st ed. 8vo. 197p. VG/dj. W1. $16.00

BRADBURN, John. *Breeding & Driving the Trotter.* 1906. Boston. Am Horse Breeder. 1st ed. VG. O3. $45.00

BRADBURY, Edward P.; see Moorcock, Michael.

BRADBURY, Ray. *Dandelion Wine.* 1957. Doubleday. 1st ed. inscr. NF/VG. B4. $650.00

BRADBURY, Ray. *Dark Carnival.* 1947. Arkham. 1st ed. author's 1st book. sgn. blk cloth. F/dj. B24. $750.00

BRADBURY, Ray. *Death Is a Lonely Business.* 1985. Knopf. 1st ed. NF/NF. P3. $25.00

BRADBURY, Ray. *Golden Apples of the Sun.* 1953. NY. 1st ed. 12mo. brn cloth. F/G. H3. $225.00

BRADBURY, Ray. *Graveyard for Lunatics.* 1990. Knopf. 1st ed. F/F. G10. $15.00

BRADBURY, Ray. *Machineries of Joy.* 1964. Doubleday. 1st ed. inscr/dtd 1982. F/F. C2. $200.00

BRADBURY, Ray. *Martian Chronicles.* 1950. Doubleday. 1st ed. F/F. B24. $650.00

BRADBURY, Ray. *Martian Chronicles.* 1974. Avon, CT. ils Joseph Mugnaini. 309p. silvered blk cloth. F/case. T10. $275.00

BRADBURY, Ray. *Medicine for Melancholy.* 1959. Doubleday. 1st ed. inscr/dtd 1982. F/clip. C2. $200.00

BRADBURY, Ray. *Star of Danger.* 1993. Severn. 1st ed. F/F. G10. $15.00

BRADBURY, Ray. *Stories of Ray Bradbury.* 1980. Knopf. 1st ed. VG/G. P3. $22.00

BRADBURY, Ray. *Stories of Ray Bradbury.* 1980. NY. 1st ed. inscr. F/F. C2. $100.00

BRADBURY, Ray. *Toynbee Convector.* 1988. Knopf. 1st ed. F/F. P3. $18.00

BRADBURY, Ray. *Toynbee Convector.* 1988. NY. 1st ed. 275p. VG+/dj. B18. $12.50

BRADDOCK, Joseph. *Haunted Houses of Great Britain.* nd. Dorset. 1st ed. VG. P3. $15.00

BRADDON, George. *Microbe's Kiss.* 1940. Faber. 1st ed. G/G. P3. $30.00

BRADEN, James A. *Trail of the Seneca.* 1907. Saalfield. ils RB Vosburgh. G+/G. P12. $10.00

BRADFORD, Beulah Harth. *Gems of Wisdom.* 1986. NY. Vantage. 1st ed. F/VG. B4. $45.00

BRADFORD, E. *Story of Mary Rose: Henry VIII's Flagship.* 1982. 1st ed. photos. NF/NF. S13. $16.00

BRADFORD, E. *Wall of Empire.* 1966. S Brunswick. VG. O7. $25.00

BRADFORD, Ernie. *Cleopatra.* 1972. HBJ. 1st ed. 279p. VG/dj. W1. $25.00

BRADFORD, Richard. *Red Sky at Morning.* 1968. Lippincott. 1st ed. author's 1st book. NF/NF. H11. $30.00

BRADFORD, Roark. *John Henry: A Play.* 1939. NY. 1st ed. F/F. C2. $50.00

BRADFORD, Roark. *Ol' King David an' the Philistine Boys.* 1930. Harper. 1st ed. 227p. ils AB Walker. VG/G. B10. $50.00

BRADFORD, Roark. *Ol' Man Adam & His Chillun.* 1928. NY. 1st ed. VG. B5. $45.00

BRADFORD, Roark. *This Side of Jordan.* 1929. Harper. 1st ed. 8vo. VG/dj. S9. $35.00

BRADLEY, Alice; see Sheldon, Alice Bradley.

BRADLEY, John. *Best There Ever Was.* 1990. Atlantic. 1st ed. F/dj. H11. $30.00

BRADLEY, John. *Ils History of the Third Reich.* 1978. NY. photos. 256p. G. A17. $15.00

BRADLEY, Marion Zimmer. *House Between the Worlds.* 1980. Doubleday. ARC. sgn. F/F. M19. $45.00

BRADLEY, Marion Zimmer. *Mists of Avalon.* 1982. Knopf. AP. VG/wrp. C2. $40.00

BRADLEY, Marion Zimmer. *Mists of Avalon.* 1982. Knopf. UP. VG/prt wrp. C2. $75.00

BRADLEY, Marion Zimmer. *Mists of Avalon.* 1982. Knopf. 1st ed. inscr. 8vo. VG/F. T10. $300.00

BRADLEY, Mary Hastings. *Trailing the Tiger.* 1929. Appleton. 1st ed. sgn. 8vo. 246p. VG. B11. $35.00

BRADLEY, Muriel. *Murder in Montana.* 1950. NY. 1st ed. VG/VG. B5. $25.00

BRADLEY, Van Allen. *Book Collector's Handbook of Values.* 1975. NY. 8vo. 566p. blk cloth. VG/dj. T3. $10.00

BRADLEY, Van Allen. *Book Collectors Handbook of Values.* 1978. 3rd. VG. S13. $20.00

BRADLEY, Van Allen. *Gold in Your Attic.* 1958. NY. Fleet. 2nd. 8vo. VG+/dj. S9. $45.00

BRADLEY & PACKER. *Checklist of Rare Vascular Plants in Alberta.* 1984. Edmonton. Alberta Culture. 4to. 112p. wrp. B1. $15.00

BRADSHAW, Gillian. *Beacon at Alexandria.* 1986. Houghton Mifflin. 1st ed/1st prt. 8vo. 376p. F/F. T10. $25.00

BRADT & GIACCONI. *X- & Gamma-Ray Astronomy...* 1973. Dordrecht, Holland. 4to. 323p. xl. dj. K5. $30.00

BRADY, John. *Unholy Ground.* 1989. Canada. Collins. 1st ed. VG/VG. P3. $20.00

BRADY, Leo. *Edge of Doom.* 1949. Dutton. 1st ed. VG/G. P3. $13.00

BRADY, Ryder. *Instar.* 1976. Doubleday. F/F. P3. $13.00

BRADY & GARDNER. *Original Photographs Taken on Battlefields...* 1907. Hartford. 126p. professionally recased. VG. B18. $225.00

BRADZIL, Rudolf. *Climatic Change: In Historical & Instrumental Periods.* 1990. Masaryk. 8vo. 362p. VG/dj. K5. $12.00

BRAHMS, Johannas. *German Requiem After Words of Holy Scripture...* 1975. Easthampton, MA. 1/45. ils/prt/sgn Carol Blinn. gilt bdg. F. B24. $850.00

BRAIN, Russell. *Galatea or the Future of Darwinism.* (1927). London. Kegan Paul. 16mo. 95p. bl cloth/paper labels. G1. $35.00

BRAIN, Russell. *Nature of Experience. The Riddell Memorial Lectures...* 1959. London. Oxford. 12mo. VG/clip. G1. $35.00

BRAIN & POLLOCK. *Bangwa Funerary Sculpture.* 1971. Toronto. F/F. D2. $90.00

BRAITHWAITE, John. *History of the Revolution in Empire of Morocco...* 1729. London. Lg Paper ed. fld map. 380p. gilt calf. VG. B14. $480.00

BRAMBLE, Forbes. *Strange Case of Deacon Brodie.* 1975. Hamish Hamilton. 1st ed. F/F. P3. $20.00

BRAMELD, Theodore. *Japan: Culture, Education & Change in Two Communities.* 1968. HRW. dedication to/sgn Matsuura. 316p. VG. B11. $15.00

BRAMHALL, Marion. *Tradedy in Blue.* 1945. Crime Club. 1st ed. VG. P3. $18.00

BRANCH, Douglas. *Cowboy & His Interpreters.* 1926. Appleton Century. 1st ed. 8vo. 278p. prt cloth. T10. $250.00

BRAND, Christianna. *Death in High Heels.* 1954. Scribner. 1st ed. VG/G. P3. $30.00

BRAND, Christianna. *Naughty Children.* 1963. Dutton. 1st ed. ils Ardizzone. 314p. VG/VG. P2. $25.00

BRAND, Max. *Best Western Stories Vol 2.* 1985. Dodd Mead. 1st ed. VG/VG. P3. $14.00

BRAND, Max. *Man From the Wilderness.* nd. Dodd Mead. 1st ed. F/F. P3. $15.00

BRAND, Millen. *Outward Room.* 1937. NY. 1st ed. author's 1st book. F/NF. A17. $15.00

BRANDAE, Ambrosis Fernandes. *Dialogues of the Great Things of Brazil.* 1987. NM U. 1st ed. ils. 385p. dj. F3. $20.00

BRANDER, Bruce. *River Nile.* 1966. NGS. 1st ed. 1 fld map. NF/dj. W1. $16.00

BRANDON, Jay. *Fade the Heat.* 1990. Pocket. 1st ed. author's 1st novel. AN/dj. M22. $40.00

BRANDON, S.G.F. *Ancient Empires (Milestones of History).* 1970. Newsweek. 2nd. 160p. VG/dj. W1. $20.00

BRANDT, Tom; see Dewey, Thomas B.

BRANLEY, Franklyn. *Lodestar Rocket Ship to Mars.* 1951. Crowell. 1st ed. VG/VG. P3. $18.00

BRANSON & TARR. *Introduction to Geology.* 1941. McGraw Hill. 2nd. 482p. VG. D8. $30.00

BRANTLEY, Rabun Lee. *Georgia Journalism of the Civil War Period.* 1929. Nashville. George Peabody College for Teachers. 1st ed. NF/wrp. M8. $250.00

BRASHLER, William. *Josh Gibson.* 1978. Harper Row. 1st ed. F/VG+. P8. $110.00

BRASOL, Boris. *Elements of Crime.* 1931. Oxford. 2nd. ruled bl cloth. VG/dj. G1. $50.00

BRASSEY, A. *Sunshine & Storm in the East.* 1880. London. 1st ed. 2 maps. inscr author's husband. VG. A15. $75.00

BRASSEY, Mrs. *Voyage in the Sunbeam: Our Home on the Ocean...* 1881. Chicago. Belford Clarke. G+. A16. $50.00

BRAUDE, William G. *Pesikta Rabbati: Discourses for Feasts, Fasts...* 1968. Yale. 2 vol. Yale Judaica series. 8vo. cloth. VG/dj. W1. $65.00

BRAUN, Lilian Jackson. *Cat Who Came to Breakfast.* 1994. Putnam. 1st ed. F/F. P3. $20.00

BRAUN, Lilian Jackson. *Cat Who Sniffed Glue.* 1988. Putnam. 1st ed. VG/VG. P3. $18.00

BRAUN, Lilian Jackson. *Cat Who Went Into the Closet.* 1993. Putnam. 1st ed. F/F. P3. $20.00

BRAUN, Thomas. *L'An. Poemes par Thomas Braun.* 1897. Brussels. Lyon-Claeson. 1/1070. sq 4to. woodblocks. F. B24. $3,000.00

BRAUNLICH, Tom. *Pente Strategy.* 1984. NY. 132p. VG/wrp. S1. $5.00

BRAUTIGAN, Richard. *Abortion: An Historical Romance 1966.* nd. Simon Schuster. VG/VG. P3. $20.00

BRAUTIGAN, Richard. *Dreaming of Babylon.* 1977. Delacorte. 1st ed. F/NF. T2. $35.00

BRAUTIGAN, Richard. *Dreaming of Babylon.* 1977. Delacorte. 1st ed. NF/NF. P3. $30.00

BRAUTIGAN, Richard. *Hawkline Monster.* 1974. NY. 1st ed. sgn. F/F. A11. $225.00

BRAUTIGAN, Richard. *Revenge of the Lawn.* 1971. Simon Schuster. 1st ed. F/NF. B2. $100.00

BRAUTIGAN, Richard. *Trout Fishing in America/The Pill Versus Springhill Mine...* 1969. Delacorte. 1st collected ed. NF. M19. $50.00

BRAUTIGAN, Richard. *Willard & His Bowling Trophies.* 1975. Simon Schuster. 1st ed. F/F. H11. $40.00

BRAUTIGAN, Richard. *Willard & His Bowling Trophies.* 1975. Simon Schuster. 1st ed. NF/NF. P3. $25.00

BRAWLEY, Benjamin. *Early Negro American Writers.* 1935. UNC. 1st ed. VG/VG. C6. $200.00

BRAY, Martha Coleman. *Joseph Nicollet & His Map.* 1980. Phil. Am Philosophical Soc. fld map. F/dj. O7. $45.00

BRAY, Wayne. *Common Law Zone in Panama.* 1977. San Juan. 1st ed. sgn. 150p. dj. F3. $20.00

BRAY & CARLTON. *Herreshoff of Bristol.* 1989. Brooklin, ME. Wooden Boat. 250+ photos. 241p. VG/dj. T7. $45.00

BRAYMER, Marjorie. *Atlantis: The Biography of a Legend.* 1983. Atheneum. 1st ed. VG/VG. P3. $20.00

BRAYNARD, Frank. *Famous American Ships.* 1978. Hastings. revised/enlarged. VG/VG. A16. $14.00

BRAYNARD, Frank. *Search for the Tall Ships.* 1977. NY. Operation Ship. sgn. xl. VG/VG. B11. $18.00

BRAYNARD, Frank. *Tall Ships.* 1976. Sabine. portfolio. F. A16. $100.00

BRAZEAU, Peter. *Parts of a World Remembered.* 1983. Random. 1st ed. F/dj. V1. $20.00

BRAZIL, Angela. *Captain Peggie.* 1924. Stokes. 1st ed. 8vo. VG. M5. $20.00

BREASTED, James Henry. *History of Egypt From Earliest Times to Persian Conquest.* 1905. Scribner. 1st ed. 634p. gilt cloth. VG. W1. $65.00

BREASTED, James Henry. *History of the Ancient Egyptians.* 1908. Scribner. 2nd. sm 8vo. 469p. VG. W1. $18.00

BREAUX, Daisy. *Autobiography of a Chameleon.* 1930. Washington, DC. Potomac. ltd ed. sgn. 407p. VG/VG. B11. $50.00

BREBNER, John B. *Explorers of North America.* 1933. NY. VG. O7. $85.00

BRECHT, Bertolt. *Threepenny Opera.* 1982. LEC. 1/2000. intro/sgn Eric Bentley. ils/sgn Jack Levine. F/case. C2. $125.00

BRECKENRIDGE, Sean. *Yuppie Scum.* 1993. NY. 1st ed. author's 1st book. F/F. H11. $25.00

BREDIUS, Abraham. *Rembrandt: Complete Edition of the Paintings.* 1969. London. Phaidon. 3rd. 636p. cloth. dj. D2. $60.00

BREED, Clara E. *Turning the Pages.* 1983. Friends of San Diego Public Lib. 1st ed. NF/NF. B19. $25.00

BREED, W.J. *Age of Dinosaurs in North Arizona.* 1968. Flagstaff. Mus of N AZ. sgn. ils/pl. 45p. F/wrp. D8. $8.00

BREEN, Jon L. *Listen for the Click.* 1983. NY. Walker. 1st ed. F/NF. H11. $30.00

BREEN & COATES. *Pacific National Exhibition.* 1982. Vancouver. VG. O7. $20.00

BREHME, Hugo. *Mexico: Una Nacion Persistente.* 1995. Hugo Breheme. 1st ed. 1/3000. 154p. wrp. F3. $25.00

BREITENBACK, Josef. *Josef Breitenback.* 1985. NY. Temple Rock. 1st ed. 4to. F/wrp. S9. $60.00

BRENAMAN, J.N. *History of Virginia Conventions With Constitution of VA...* 1902. JL Hill. leatherette. G+. B10. $45.00

BRENNA, Virgilio. *Moon.* 1963. Golden. 4to. 104p. laminated pict brd. K5. $20.00

BRENNAN, Joseph Payne. *Adventures of Lucius Leffing.* 1990. Hampton Falls. Donald Grant. 1st ed. 1/1000. sgn. F/F. T2. $30.00

BRENNAN, Joseph Payne. *Chronicles of Lucius Leffing.* 1977. Donald Grant. 1st ed. F/F. T2. $40.00

BRENNAN, Joseph Payne. *Creep to Death.* 1981. Donald Grant. 1st ed. 1/750. sgn. ils/sgn Robert Lavoie. F/dj. T2. $45.00

BRENNAN, Joseph Payne. *Look Back on Laurel Hills.* 1989. Minneapolis. Jwindz Pub. 1st ed. F/prt wrp. T2. $12.00

BRENNAN, Joseph Payne. *Shapes of Midnight.* 1980. Berkley. 1st ed. VG/NF. R10. $5.00

BRENNAN, Joseph Payne. *Stories of Darkness & Dread.* 1973. Arkham. 1st ed. 1/4138. F/NF. T2. $45.00

BRENNAN, Joseph Payne. *60 Selected Poems.* 1985. Establishment Pr. 1st ed. F/F. R10. $5.00

BRENNER, Wendy. *Large Animals in Everyday Life.* 1996. Athens, GA. 1st ed. sgn. F/F. M23. $40.00

BRENNERT, Alan. *Her Pilgrim Soul.* 1990. Tor. 1st ed. F/F. G10. $25.00

BRENT, Joseph L. *Lugo Case.* 1926. New Orleans. 84p. VG. M8. $850.00

BRENT, Madeleine. *Capricorn Stone.* 1980. BC Associates. VG/VG. P3. $10.00

BRENT, P. *Charles Darwin: A Man of Enlarged Curiosity.* 1981. NY. Harper Row. 1st ed. 536p. F/chip. D8. $21.00

BRENTON, M. *La Russie Ou Mours Usages et Costumes.* 1813. Paris. 6 vol. xl. G. B5. $450.00

BRESLAUER & FOLTER. *Bibliography: Its History & Development.* 1984. Grollier. 1/600. ils. 224p. F. A4. $125.00

BRESLER, Fenton. *Mystery of Georges Simenon.* 1983. Beaufort. 1st ed. F/F. P3. $19.00

BRESLIN, Howard. *Silver Oar.* 1954. Crowell. 1st ed. VG/VG. P3. $15.00

BRESLIN, Jimmy. *Can't Anyone Here Play This Game?* 1963. Viking. 1st ed. VG+/VG. P8. $40.00

BRESLIN, Jimmy. *How Good Guys Finally Won.* sgn. VG/VG. K2. $60.00

BRESSON, Henri Cartier. *Face of Asia.* 1972. NY. Viking. 1st ed. 4to. NF/dj. S9. $90.00

BRETT, Simon. *Comedian Dies*. 1979. Scribner. 1st ed. VG/VG. P3. $15.00

BRETT, Simon. *Reconstructed Corpse*. 1994. Scribner. 1st Am ed. rem mk. F/F. N4. $15.00

BRETT, Simon. *Shock to the System*. 1985. Scribner. 1st ed. NF/NF. P3. $14.00

BRETT, Simon. *So Much Blood*. 1976. Scribner. 1st Am ed. VG/VG. N4. $17.50

BRETZ, J. Harlen. *Grand Coulee*. 1932. NY. VG. O7. $85.00

BREWER, David J. *Crowned Masterpieces of Literature*. 1908. Kaiser Pub. 10 vol. ils. 3-quarter leather. G+. P12. $85.00

BREWER, Josiah. *Residence at Constantinople in the Year 1827*. 1830. New Haven. Durrie Peck. 12mo. ils. 384p. contemporary calf/blk leather. K1. $200.00

BREWER, Sydney. *Do-It-Yourself Astronomy*. 1988. Edinburgh. 8vo. 137p. VG. K5. $7.00

BREWER. *Literature of Geography: A Guide to Its Organization...* 1978. np. 2nd. 264p. F/F. A4. $65.00

BREWERTON, George Douglas. *Fitz Poodle at Newport*. 1869. Cambridge. 1st ed. cloth. A17. $15.00

BREYER & POLMAR. *Guide to the Soviet Navy*. 1977. Annapolis. ils/drawings. 610p. F. A17. $25.00

BREYTENBACH, Breyten. *Sinking Ship Blues*. 1977. Toronto. Oasis. 1st Eng-language ed. F/decor wrp. C2. $125.00

BREZHNEV, Leonid I. *Leonid I Brezhnev: Pages From His Life*. 1978. Simon Schuster. 1st ed. 320p. F/dj. B22. $5.50

BRIAN, Denis. *Genius Talk: Conversations With Novel Scientists...* 1995. NY. Plenum. 8vo. ils. 428p. F/F. K5. $23.00

BRICE, Marshall Moore. *Daughter of the Stars*. 1973. McClure. sgn. 309p. xl. dj flaps missing. G. B10. $8.00

BRICKER, Charles. *Landmarks of Mapmaking: An Illustrated Survey...* 1968. Amsterdam. folio. 276p. F/VG. A4. $175.00

BRICKER, Charles. *Landmarks of Mapmaking: Ils Survey of Maps & Mapmakers*. 1989. Ware. Wordsworth. 10 fld maps/350+ ils. AN/dj. O7. $75.00

BRICKMAN, Richard P. *Bringing Down the House*. 1972. Scribner. 1st ed. author's 2nd book. F/NF. H11. $25.00

BRICKTOP & HASKINS. *Bricktop*. 1983. Atheneum. 1st ed. NF/NF. B2. $30.00

BRIDGMAN, Betty. *Lullaby for Eggs*. 1955. Macmillan. 1st ed. ils EO Jones. VG/G+. P2. $32.00

BRIDGWATER & GLOAG. *History of Cast Iron in Architecture*. 1948. London. 1st ed. 4to. 395p. F. T10. $150.00

BRIDWEL, Rodger. *Fidelio: My Voyage to a Distant Shore*. 1986. Dutton. 227p. VG/dj. T7. $20.00

BRIGGS, Lloyd Cabot. *Tribes of the Sahara*. 1960. Cambridge. Harvard. 1st ed. ils. 295p. NF/dj. W1. $45.00

BRIGGS, Philip. *Escape From Gravity*. 1955. Lutterworth. 1st ed. VG/VG. P3. $15.00

BRIGGS, Philip. *Silent Planet*. 1957. Lutterworth. 1st ed. VG/torn. P3. $15.00

BRIGGS, Walter. *Without Noise of Arms: 1776 Dominguez-Escalante Search...* 1976. Flagstaff. Northland. ils/15 maps. F/dj. O7. $75.00

BRIGHAM, C. *History & Bibliography of American Newspapers 1690-1820*. 1947. Am Antiquarian Soc. 2 vol. 4to. VG. A4. $350.00

BRIGHAM, C. *History & Bibliography of American Newspapers 1690-1820*. 1947. Worcester, MA. Am Antiquarian Soc. 2 vol. 8vo. xl. VG. T3. $95.00

BRIGHAM, Carl C. *Study of Error: Summary & Evaluation of Methods...* 1932. NY. College Entrance Examination Brd. 4to. xl. VG. G1. $40.00

BRIGHAM, Clarence. *50 Years of Collecting Americana for Lib Am Antiquarian Soc*. 1958. np. 1/1000. 185p. F/VG. A4. $75.00

BRIM, Charles. *Medicine in the Bible, the Pentatuch, Torah*. 1936. NY. 1st ed. 384p. A13. $130.00

BRIN, David. *Earth*. 1990. Bantam. 1st trade ed. F/F. M21. $20.00

BRIN, David. *Postman*. 1985. Bantam. 1st ed. F/F. H11/P3. $25.00

BRIN, David. *River of Time*. 1986. Dark Harvest. 1st ed. 1/400. sgns. F/F/case. T2. $85.00

BRINISTOOL, E.A. *Fighting Indian Warriors*. 1953. Stackpole. ARC. 353p. cloth. RS. VG/dj. M20. $52.00

BRINK, Andre. *Act of Terror*. 1991. Summit. 1st ed. F/F. P3. $25.00

BRINK, Carol. *Highly Trained Dogs of Professor Petit*. 1953. Macmillan. 1st ed. 139p. F/VG. P2. $35.00

BRINK, Carol. *Lad With a Whistle*. 1943 (1941). Macmillan. 3rd. 8vo. 235p. VG/G. T5. $25.00

BRINK, Carol. *Stopover*. 1951. Macmillan. 1st ed. sgn. 245p. VG/G. P2. $30.00

BRINKNER, Richard M. *Intellectual Functions of the Frontal Lobes*. 1936. Macmillan. pres. 10 pl. 354p. VG. G1. $75.00

BRINNIN, John Malcolm. *Beau Voyage: Life Aboard the Last Great Ships*. 1981. Dorset. VG/VG. A16. $58.00

BRINNIN, John Malcolm. *Sorrows of Cold Stone*. 1951. Dodd Mead. 1st ed. 109p. VG/dj. M20. $47.00

BRINNIN, John Malcolm. *Sway of Grand Saloon: A Social History of North Atlantic*. 1971. Delacorte. 1st ed. VG/VG. A16. $40.00

BRINNIN, John Malcolm. *Sway of the Grand Saloon*. 1986. London. Arlington. 2nd revised ed. VG/VG. A16. $30.00

BRISE, Marshall Moore. *Vagaries in Verse*. 1977. McClure. inscr. 88p. G. B10. $8.00

BRISTOL, George. *Salute Me! The Dilemas of a Second Lieutenant*. 1943. NY. Dial. 1st ed. 172p. VG/chip. A17. $6.50

BRISTOL, Helen O. *Let the Blackbird Sing*. 1952. Exposition. 1st ed. F/VG+. B4. $50.00

BRITE, Poppy Z. *Drawing Blood*. 1993. Delacorte. 1st ed. F/F. H11. $35.00

BRITE, Poppy Z. *Drawing Blood*. 1993. Huntington Beach. James Cahill. ltd ed. 1/274. sgn. F/sans/case. T2. $65.00

BRITE, Poppy Z. *Lost Souls*. 1992. Delacorte/Abyss. 1st ed. author's 1st novel. sgn. F/F. T2. $45.00

BRITT, Albert. *Toward the Western Ocean*. 1963. Barre. VG. O7. $30.00

BRITTIN & WATSON. *International Law for Seagoing Officers, Second Edition*. 1961. US Naval Inst. NF/dj. M11. $35.00

BRITTON, Nathaniel L. *Flora of Bermuda*. 1918. NY. 1st ed. 585p. VG. B26. $95.00

BRITTON, William Everett. *Cases on the Law of Bills & Notes*. 1951. Chicago. Callaghan. worn. M11. $20.00

BROCK, Lynn. *Slip Carriage Mystery*. 1928. Harper. 1st ed. VG. P3. $35.00

BROCK, Rose; see Hansen, Joseph.

BROCK & BUDD. *Farming Once Upon a Time: An Illustrated History...* 1996. Concord. 1st ed. 159p. cloth. M. M20. $25.00

BROCKELMANN, Carl. *History of the Islamic Peoples.* 1947. Putnam. 1st ed. 8vo. 8 maps. VG. W1. $25.00

BROCKETT, L.P. *Woman's Work in the Civil War: A Record of Heroism...* 1867. Phil. Zeigler. 8vo. cloth. T10. $150.00

BROCKMAN, James. *Genesis.* 1924. Soho. Nonesuch. 1/375. lg 8vo. 28p on handmade. blk morocco. box. B24. $1,750.00

BRODER, Patricia Janis. *Hopi Painting: World of the Hopis.* 1979. NY. Brandywine. stated 1st ed. 4to. 319p. F/NF. T10. $75.00

BRODERICK, J.C. *Biographical Memoir of Archibald MacLeish.* nd. Am Phil Soc. F/prt wrp. V1. $25.00

BRODEUR, Paul. *Stunt Man.* 1970. Athen. 1st ed. F/NF. H11. $45.00

BRODIE. *Devil Drives: Life of Sir Richard Burton.* 1967. np. ils. 390p. VG/dj. A4. $35.00

BRODKEY, Harold. *Runaway Soul.* 1992. FSG. 1st ed. F/F. A20. $20.00

BRODRICK, A. Houghton. *Animals in Archaeology.* 1972. NY. Praeger. 1st Am ed. ils/index. F/dj. T10. $25.00

BRODRICK, Alan. *Prehistoric Painting.* 1948. London. Avalon. ils/pl. 38p. F3. $20.00

BRODSKY & HAMLIN. *William Faulkner: A Perspective From Brodsky Collection.* 1979. SE MO St Prt Service. 1/2500. unp. VG. B10. $25.00

BRODY, J.J. *Anazazi & Pueblo Painting.* 1991. NM U. 1st ed. 191p. F/dj. T10. $50.00

BROEN, Johann. *Exercitatio Physico-Medica.* 1675. Leyden. Johannem Prins. 12mo. 249p. contemporary vellum/leather spine label. K1. $275.00

BROGAN, James; see Hodder-William, C.

BROHL, Ted. *In a Fine Frenzy Rolling.* 1992. Vantage. 1st ed. sgn. F/F. P3. $20.00

BROIDY, Thomas Gately. *Rogue's Isles.* 1995. St Martin. 1st ed. F/F. M23. $35.00

BROKAW & STARR. *Putnam's Automobile Handbook: Care & Management...* 1918. NY. 1st ed. photos. 348p. red cloth. F. B14. $55.00

BROMFIELD, Louis. *Few Brass Tacks.* 1946. Harper. 1st ed. F/F. M19. $35.00

BROMFIELD, Louis. *Modern Hero.* 1932. Stokes. 1st ed. 1/250. sgn. red/wht cloth. NF/dj/case. B24. $200.00

BROMFIELD, Louis. *Mr Smith.* 1951. Harper. 1st ed. VG/VG. P3. $29.00

BROMFIELD, Louis. *Out of the Earth.* 1948. Harper. 1st ed. 305p. VG/dj. M20. $30.00

BROMFIELD, Louis. *Strange Case of Miss Annie Spragg.* 1928. Stokes. ARC. sgn. F. M19. $65.00

BROMFIELD, Louis. *Wild Is the River.* 1941. Harper. 1st ed. inscr. cloth. VG/dj. B24. $100.00

BROMFIELD, Louis. *World We Live In.* 1944. Harper. 1st ed. VG/VG. M19. $35.00

BROMFIELD, Louis. *24 Hours.* 1930. NY. ltd ed. 1/500. sgn. VG/VG/VG box. B5. $95.00

BROMHALL, Winifred. *Chipmunk That Went to Church.* 1952. Knopf. 1st ed. 8vo. VG/G. B17. $12.50

BROMLEY, George Washington. *Manhattan Land Book of the City of New York, 1955.* 1955. GW Bromley. Desk & Lib ed. 188 maps. sbdg. NF. O7. $275.00

BRONOWSKI, J. *Ascent of Man.* (1973). Little Brn. 8vo. ils/photos. 448p. rust cloth. F. D22. $6.50

BRONTE, Charlotte. *Professor: A Tale by Currer Bell.* 1857. Harper. 1st Am ed. 330p. VG. A4. $345.00

BRONTE, Charlotte. *Professor: A Tale by Currer Bell.* 1857. London. Smith Elder. 2 vol. 1st ed/1st issue ponts present. purple cloth. T10. $1,000.00

BRONTE, Charlotte. *Shirley: A Tale by Currer Bell, Author of Jane Eyre.* 1850. Harper. 572p. lacks ffe. VG. A4. $695.00

BROOK, Lynn. *Slip-Carriage Mystery: Colonel Gore's Fourth Case.* 1928. Harper. 1st Am ed. VG/VG. B4. $65.00

BROOKE, Keith. *Keepers of the Peace.* 1990. Gollancz. 1st ed. F/F. P3. $20.00

BROOKES, John. *Room Outside.* 1970 (1969). NY. ils/photos/plans. 192p. VG+/dj. B26. $20.00

BROOKES, Owen. *Gatherer.* 1982. HRW. 1st ed. VG/VG. P3. $20.00

BROOKES, Owen. *Inheritance.* 1980. Hutchinson. 1st ed. NF/NF. P3. $25.00

BROOKES, R. *General Gazetteer; or, Compendious Geographical Dictionary.* 1812. London. Ribington. 8 maps. VG+. O7. $195.00

BROOKESMITH, Peter. *Against All Reason.* 1984. Orbis. 1st ed. VG. P3. $13.00

BROOKS, C.E.P. *Evolution of a Climate.* 1925 (1922). NY. Coleman. 2nd. 8vo. 173p. G/tattered. K5. $21.00

BROOKS, Charles Walker. *Rhymes of a Southerner.* 1936. Dietz. 1st ed. inscr. 143p. VG/G. B10. $12.00

BROOKS, Gwendolyn. *Bean Eaters.* 1960. Harper. 1st ed. F/F. B4. $375.00

BROOKS, Gwendolyn. *Maud Martha.* 1953. Harper. 1st ed. F/VG+. B4. $250.00

BROOKS, Gwendolyn. *Very Young Poets.* 1983. Chicago. Brooks. 1st ed. sgn. F/stapled wrp. B4. $75.00

BROOKS, Lester. *Behind Japan's Surrender.* 1968. NY. 1st ed. 428p. F/F. A17. $12.50

BROOKS, Mary E. *King for Portugal.* 1964. Madson. VG. O7. $20.00

BROOKS, Noah. *First Across the Continent.* 1901. Scribner. 1st ed. 8vo. 24 pl/fld map. ribbed gr cloth. F. T10. $150.00

BROOKS, Owen. *Gatherer.* 1982. Holt. 1st ed. F/F. H11. $35.00

BROOKS, Phillips. *Christmas Songs & Easter Carols.* 1904. Dutton/Merrymount. 1/150 on handmade. 48p. F/cb box. B24. $350.00

BROOKS, Terry. *Black Unicorn.* 1987. Del Rey. 1st ed. F/F. P3. $20.00

BROOKS, Terry. *Hook.* 1992. Fawcett. 1st ed. F/F. H11. $25.00

BROOKS, Terry. *Magic Kingdom for Sale! Sold!* 1988. 1st ed. F/NF. M19. $45.00

BROOKS, Terry. *Wizard at Large.* 1988. Del Rey. 1st ed. NF/NF. P3. $20.00

BROSBT & PRATT. *United States Mineral Resources, Geological Survey...* 1973. GPO. 722p. cloth. F. D8. $24.00

BROSSARD, Chandler. *Bold Saboteurs.* 1953. NY. 1st ed. author's 2nd book. F/NF. A15. $50.00

BROSSARD, Chandler. *Did Christ Make Love?* 1973. Indianapolis. 1st ed. sgn. F/NF clip. A11. $40.00

BROTHERS GRIMM; see Grimm & Grimm.

BROTHERUS, V.F. *Contributions to the Bryological Flora of NW Himalaya.* 1978 (1898). Dehra Dun. rpt. 4to. 46p. VG. B26. $15.00

BROTZ, H. *Black Jews of Harlem.* 1964. NY. 1st ed. 144p. VG. B5. $35.00

BROUGHTON, Jack. *Going Downtown.* 1988. NY. 1st ed. 300p. VG/dj. B18. $20.00

BROUSSEAU, Kate. *Mongolism: Study of Physical & Mental Characteristics...* 1928. Williams Wilkins. 18 half-tone pl. 210p. F/worn. G1. $85.00

BROWER, Brock. *Late Great Creature.* 1972. Atheneum. 1st ed. sgn. F/clip. B11. $30.00

BROWN, Alan. *Audrey Hepburn's Neck.* 1996. NY. Pocket. 1st ed. author's 1st book. rem mk. F/F. H11. $35.00

BROWN, Alexander Crosby. *Mariners' Museum: A History & Guide.* 1950. Newport News. Mariners' Mus. 264p. VG. T7. $65.00

BROWN, Alexander Crosby. *Sea-Lingo: Notes on the Language of Mariners...* 1980. Mariners Mus. 40p. VG/stiff wrp. B10. $10.00

BROWN, Annora. *Old Man's Garden.* 1954. Toronto. 1st ed. ils. VG+/dj. B26. $24.00

BROWN, Bob. *Readies for Bob Brown's Machine.* 1931. Roving Eye. 1st ed. 1/300. rpr torn p. NF/prt wrp. B24. $850.00

BROWN, Charles H. *Insurrection at Magellan.* 1854. Boston. VG. O7. $55.00

BROWN, Christy. *Down All the Days.* 1970. Stein Day. 1st ed. author's 2nd book. NF/NF. H11. $20.00

BROWN, Christy. *My Left Foot.* 1st Am ed. NF/NF. B30. $50.00

BROWN, Clair A. *Vegetation of the Outer Banks of NC.* 1959. Baton Rouge. ils. VG. B26. $42.50

BROWN, Dale. *Hammerheads.* 1990. Donald Fine. 1st ed. NF/F. N4. $25.00

BROWN, Dale. *Night of the Hawk.* 1992. Donald Fine. 1st ed. NF/NF. N4. $20.00

BROWN, Dee. *Bury My Heart at Wounded Knee.* 1971. HRW. F/NF. T10. $10.00

BROWN, Dee. *Fetterman Massacre.* 1972. Barrie Jenkins. 1st ed. F/F. P3. $20.00

BROWN, Dee. *Fort Phil Kearney.* 1962. Putnam. 1st ed. 8vo. map ep. F/dj. T10. $35.00

BROWN, Dee. *They Went Thataway.* 1960. Putnam. 1st ed. ils Robert Galster. F/VG+. A18. $35.00

BROWN, Dee. *Westerners.* 1974. Holt. BC? 288p. brn brd. AN/dj. B22. $6.00

BROWN, Douglas; see Gibson, Walter B.

BROWN, Earle B. *Modern Optics.* 1965. Reinhold. 8vo. 645p. VG/laid on. K5. $45.00

BROWN, Edward. *Wadsworth Memorial...* 1875. Wadsworth. 232p. G. B18. $125.00

BROWN, Frederic. *Screaming Mimi.* 1949. Dutton. 1st ed. 12mo. yel brd. F. T10. $275.00

BROWN, Fredric. *And the Gods Laughed.* 1987. Phantasia. 1st ed. F/F. P3. $35.00

BROWN, Fredric. *And the Gods Laughed: A Collection of SF & Fantasy.* 1987. Phantasia. 1st ed. 1/475. sgn Brown/Mack Reynolds. F/F/case. T2. $45.00

BROWN, Fredric. *Before She Kills.* 1984. Denis McMillan. 1st ed. 1/350. intro/sgn WF Nolen. F/F. T2. $100.00

BROWN, Fredric. *Gibbering Night.* 1991. Denis McMillan. 1st ed. 1/425. intro/sgn Joe Lansdale. F/F. t2. $50.00

BROWN, Fredric. *Happy Ending.* 1990. Missoula. McMillan. 1st ed. 1/450. F/F. T2. $50.00

BROWN, Fredric. *Homicide Sanitarium.* 1984. San Antonio. McMillan. 1st ed. 1/300. intro/sgn Bill Pronzini. F/F. T2. $125.00

BROWN, Fredric. *Lights in the Sky Are Stars.* 1953. Dutton. BC. VG/G. M22. $15.00

BROWN, Fredric. *Mrs Murphy's Underpants.* 1965. Boardman. 1st ed. VG. P3. $150.00

BROWN, Fredric. *Office.* 1958. Dutton. 1st ed. VG/tape rpr. P3. $250.00

BROWN, Fredric. *Paradox Lost & Twelve Other Great SF Stories.* 1975. London. Hale. 1st Eng ed. F/NF. T2. $15.00

BROWN, Fredric. *Pickled Punks.* 1991. Macmillan. F/F. P3. $35.00

BROWN, Fredric. *Red Is the Hue of Hell.* 1986. Miami Beach. McMillan. 1st ed. 1/400. intro/sgn Walt Sheldon. F/F. T2. $75.00

BROWN, Fredric. *The Best of Fredric Brown.* 1976. Doubleday. BC. VG/dj. M21. $10.00

BROWN, George E. *Pruning of Trees, Shrubs & Conifers.* 1995 (1972). Portland. ils/photos. 354p. M/dj. B26. $30.00

BROWN, George. *New & Complete English Letter-Writer; or, Whole Art...* 1775. London. A Hogg. 12mo. 216p+8p ads. aeg. F. B14. $250.00

BROWN, Hanbury. *Man & the Stars.* 1978. Oxford. ils/photos. 185. VG/VG. K5. $25.00

BROWN, Harrison. *Bibliography on Meteorites.* 1953. Chicago. 1st ed. xl. K5. $75.00

BROWN, Henry Collins. *In the Golden Nineties.* 1928. Valentine's Manual Inc. photos. G+. P12. $15.00

BROWN, Irving. *Gypsy Fires in America: Narrative of Life...* 1924. Harper. 1st ed. photos. 244p. cloth. NF. B14. $95.00

BROWN, John Gregory. *Decorations in a Ruined Cemetery.* 1994. Houghton Mifflin. 1st ed. F/F. M23. $35.00

BROWN, John K. *Baldwin Locomotive Works.* 1995. Johns Hopkins. 1st ed. 8vo. 328p. F/dj. T10. $45.00

BROWN, John Mason. *Many a Watchful Night.* 1944. NY. 219p. VG. A17. $7.50

BROWN, John. *Bridge With Dora.* 1965. London. 172p. VG/VG. S1. $10.00

BROWN, John. *Horae Subsecivae. Rab & His Friends & Other Papers.* 1862. Leipzig. 340p. half leather. VG. A13. $30.00

BROWN, John. *Rab & His Friends & Marjorie Fleming.* 1876. Boston. Osgood. 12mo. 93p. emb gr cloth. NF. T10. $65.00

BROWN, L. Carl. *Tunisia of Ahmad Bey, 1837-1855.* 1974. Princeton. 1st ed. ils/maps. 409p. NF/dj. W1. $25.00

BROWN, Larry. *Dirty Work.* 1989. Algonquin. 1st ed. F/F. H11/M23. $40.00

BROWN, Larry. *Facing the Music.* 1988. Algonquin. 1st ed. sgn. F/F. A11/C6. $65.00

BROWN, Larry. *Joe.* 1991. Chapel Hill. 1st ed. sgn. F/F. C2. $30.00

BROWN, Lloyd A. *British Maps of the American Revolution: A Guide...* 1936. Ann Arbor. 1/2000. F/NF wrp. O7. $30.00

BROWN, Lloyd A. *Jean Domenique Cassini & His World Map of 1696.* 1941. Ann Arbor. MI U. 236p. xl. F. O7. $150.00

BROWN, Lloyd A. *Story of Maps.* 1949. Little Brn. 2nd. 4to. ils. 397p. VG/VG. A4. $60.00

BROWN, Marcia. *Dick Whittington & His Cat.* 1950. Scribner/Weekly Reader. 4to. ils. unp. VG. C14. $14.00

BROWN, Margaret Wise. *Baby Animals.* 1989. Random. 1st ed. rem mk. VG/VG. B17. $12.50

BROWN, Margaret Wise. *Little Island.* 1946. Doubleday. early ed. as by Golden MacDonald. VG. M5. $30.00

BROWN, Margaret Wise. *Little Island.* 1946. Doubleday. 1st ed. ils Leonard Weisgard. VG/G. P2. $55.00

BROWN, Margaret Wise. *Little Pig's Picnic & Other Stories.* 1939. Boston. DC Heath. ils Disney Studio. 8vo. 102p. VG. M8. $35.00

BROWN, Margaret Wise. *Red Light, Green Light.* 1944. Doubleday Doran. Jr Literary Guild. 1st ed. ils Weisgard. unp. VG. T5. $30.00

BROWN, Margaret Wise. *Red Light, Green Light.* 1944. Doubleday. 1st ed thus. as by Golden MacDonald. F/G. M5. $65.00

BROWN, Margaret Wise. *Runaway Bunny.* 1942. Hale. 8vo. lib bdg. M5. $10.00

BROWN, Margaret Wise. *Two Little Trains.* 1949. NY. Wm R Scott. 1st ed. ils Jean Charlot. unp. xl. G+. T5. $30.00

BROWN, Mark. *Game Face.* 1992. Woodbridge. Ox Bow. 1st ed. author's 1st book. F/F. H11. $40.00

BROWN, Mary. *Unlikely Ones.* 1986. McGraw Hill. 1st ed. F/F. P3. $16.00

BROWN, Maud Morrow. *University Greys Company: A Eleventh Mississippi Regiment...* 1940. Richmond, VA. Garrett Massie. 1st ed. 80p. VG. M8. $175.00

BROWN, Merle E. *Poems As Act.* 1970. Wayne State. 1st ed. assn copy. F/NF. V1. $20.00

BROWN, O. Phelps. *Complete Herbalist; or, People Their Own Physicians.* 1867. Jersey City. hand-color pl. 407p. VG. B5. $60.00

BROWN, Paul. *Good Luck & Bad.* 1940. Scribner. 1/780. sgn. VG. O3. $295.00

BROWN, Paul. *Good Luck & Bad.* 1940. Scribner. 1st ed. 1/780. sgn/#d. ils. NF. C8. $350.00

BROWN, Paul. *Piper's Pony.* 1935. Scribner. 1st/A ed. G. O3. $68.00

BROWN, Paul. *Piper's Pony: The Story of Patchwork.* 1935. Scribner. 1st ed. ils. VG+. C8. $100.00

BROWN, Paul. *Sparkie & Puff Ball.* (1954). Scribner. ils. VG/VG. P2. $35.00

BROWN, Paul. *Ups & Downs.* 1936. Scribner. 1/750. sgn. VG. O3. $325.00

BROWN, R. Haig. *Fisherman's Spring.* 1951. NY. 1st ed. VG/VG. B5. $55.00

BROWN, R.A. *Horse Brasses: Their History & Origin.* 1952. Lewes. 64p. VG/G. O3. $25.00

BROWN, Richard. *Moments in Eden.* 1989. Boston. photos. VG/dj. B26. $25.00

BROWN, Richard. *Voyage of the Iceberg.* 1982. NY. Beaufort. 1st Am ed. VG/VG. A16. $25.00

BROWN, Richard. *Voyage of the Iceberg.* 1985. Bodley Head. 1st ed. 159p. NF/VG. P12. $17.00

BROWN, Rick. *Annotated Index of American Newspaper Editions...* 1992. NCSA. 8vo. 45p. VG. T3. $5.00

BROWN, Rita Mae. *Dolley.* 1994. Bantam. 1st ed. sgn. AN/dj. B4. $45.00

BROWN, Rita Mae. *High Hearts.* 1986. Bantam. 1st ed. inscr. NF/VG+. B4. $45.00

BROWN, Rita Mae. *High Hearts.* 1986. Bantam. 1st ed. 464p. VG/fair. B10. $15.00

BROWN, Rita Mae. *In Her Day.* 1976. Plainfield, VT. Daughters Inc. 1st ed. author's 4th book. NF/wrp. B4. $65.00

BROWN, Rita Mae. *Rest In Pieces.* 1992. Bantam. 1st ed. F/F. H11. $25.00

BROWN, Rita Mae. *Songs to a Handsome Woman.* 1973. Diana. 2nd. 39p. VG. B10. $75.00

BROWN, Rita Mae. *Sudden Death.* 1983. Bantam. 1st ed. 241p. VG/G. B10. $15.00

BROWN, Rita Mae. *Venus Envy.* 1993. Bantam. 1st ed. F/NF. B4. $35.00

BROWN, Rosellen. *Before & After.* 1992. FSG. 1st ed. F/F. H11/T2. $30.00

BROWN, Rosellen. *Cora Fry.* 1977. Norton. 1st ed. F/NF. B4. $50.00

BROWN, Rosellen. *Some Deaths in the Delta.* 1970. MA U. 1st ed. author's 1st book. F/NF. M19. $62.50

BROWN, Rosellen. *Tender Mercies.* 1978. Knopf. AP. NF. M19. $45.00

BROWN, Slater. *Ethan Allen & the Green Mountain Boys.* 1956. Random. Landmark Book. BC. 8vo. 184p. beige cloth. G/G. T5. $12.00

BROWN, Slater. *Spaceward Bound.* 1955. Prentice Hall. VG. P3. $15.00

BROWN, T. *Lectures on the Philosophy of the Human Mind.* 1836. Boston. 8vo. 538p. leather. xl. T3. $12.00

BROWN, Thurlow W. *Minnie Hermon; or, The Night & Its Morning, Tale for Times.* 1854. Auburn/Buffalo, NY. Miller Orton Mulligan. 12mo. 472p. cloth. G. B36. $35.00

BROWN, Tom. *Tracker.* 1978. Englewood Cliffs. 1st ed. VG/VG. B5. $35.00

BROWN, W.N. *India, Pakistan, Ceylon.* 1960. Phil. VG. O7. $45.00

BROWN, William H. *Hand on My Shoulder.* 1962. Vantage. 1st ed. NF/NF. B35. $25.00

BROWN, William Moseley. *From These Beginnings: Life Story of Remmie LeRoy Arnold.* 1953. McClure. 1st ed. inscr Arnold. photos. 634p. VG. B10. $25.00

BROWN, William Robinson. *Horse of the Desert.* 1929. Derrydale. 4to. O3. $325.00

BROWN & BUCKINGHAM. *National Field Trials.* 1955. Harrisburg. ltd ed. sgns. leather. VG. B5. $150.00

BROWN & CONTENTO. *SF in Print: 1985.* 1986. Locus. VG. P3. $60.00

BROWN & KIRMAN. *Trees of Georgia & Adjacent States.* 1990. Portland. Timer Pr. 8vo. photos/maps. 292p. NF/NF. B1. $36.50

BROWN & LOVELL. *Exploration of Space by Radio.* 1957. London. Chapman Hall. 1st prt. xl. VG. K5. $24.00

BROWN & MILLER. *Margaret Wise Brown's Wonderful Storybook.* nd. Western/Golden. 1st Golden Book ed. 4to. 61p. F. C14. $20.00

BROWN & PHILLIPS. *Pre-Columbian Shell Engravings From the Craig Mound...* 1975-1982. Peabody Mus. 6 vol. ltd ed. folio. 360p. map ep. F/sans. T10. $450.00

BROWN & SCHMIDT. *Fighting Indians of the West.* nd. Bonanza. rpt. photos/biblio/index. 362p. NF/G. E1. $45.00

BROWN & SCHMIDT. *Fighting Indians of the West.* 1948. NY. 1st ed. 362p. VG+. E1. $75.00

BROWN & SNIFFEN. *James & John Bard: Painters of Steamboat Portraits.* 1970. Dodd Mead. ils. 272p. VG/dj. T7. $30.00

BROWN & VAN THIEL. *Rembrandt: The Master & His Workshop.* 1991. Yale/Nat Gallery. 288p. F/case. A17. $75.00

BROWNE, G. Waldo. *Young Gunbearer.* 1925. Page. new ed. ils Meynell. 334p. pict cloth. G. A17. $8.00

BROWNE, Georgiana. *Water Babies' Circus & Other Stories.* 1940. Boston. DC Heath. ils Disney Studio. 78p. VG. T5. $30.00

BROWNE, Gerald A. *Hazzard.* 1973. Arbor. VG/VG. P3. $13.00

BROWNE, Harry. *How To Find Freedom in an Unfree World.* 1973. NY. 1st ed. VG/VG. C5. $35.00

BROWNE, Howard. *Pork City.* 1988. St Martin. 1st ed. VG/VG. P3. $17.00

BROWNE, Howard. *Scotch on the Rocks.* 1991. St Martin. 1st ed. NF/NF. P3. $15.00

BROWNE, J. Ross. *Crusoe's Island.* 1867. NY. VG. O7. $75.00

BROWNE, Roland A. *Rose-Lover's Guide.* 1974. NY. photos/drawings. 235p. VG+/dj. B26. $17.50

BROWNE, Thomas. *Religio Medici, Hydriotaphia, & the Letter to a Friend.* 1869. London. 196p. VG. A13. $75.00

BROWNE, Thomas. *Religio Medici.* 1939. LEC. 1/1500. sgn. 4to. 113p. marbled brd/cloth spine. F. B11. $65.00

BROWNE, Thomas. *Works of Sir Thomas Browne.* 1928. London. 6 vol. 1st ed thus. 8vo. F. C2. $100.00

BROWNELL, Elizabeth. *Really Babies.* 1908. Rand McNally. 1st ed. 4to. fair. M5. $25.00

BROWNELL, W.C. *Tributes & Appreciations (Edith Wharton).* 1929. Scribner. 98p. VG. A4. $135.00

BROWNING, Elizabeth Barrett. *Correspondence of...& Benjamin Robert Haydon 1842-1845.* 1972. Harvard. 200p. F/F. A4. $55.00

BROWNING, Elizabeth Barrett. *Elizabeth Barrett Browning: Letters to Her Sister...* 1929. London. John Murray. 1st ed. 8vo. 344p. F/NF. C2. $35.00

BROWNING, Elizabeth Barrett. *Essays on the Greek Christian Poets & English Poets.* 1863. James Miller. 1st Am ed. VG. M19. $65.00

BROWNING, Elizabeth Barrett. *Letters to Mrs David Ogilvy.* 1974. np. ils. 220p. F/NF. A4. $35.00

BROWNING, Robert. *Agamemnon of Aeschylus.* 1877. London. Smith Elder. 1st ed. 12mo. 18p. half crushed morocco. teg. NF. T10. $450.00

BROWNING, Robert. *Agememnon of Aeschylus.* 1877. London. Smith Elder. 1st ed. VG. M19. $125.00

BROWNING, Robert. *Pied Piper of Hamelin.* 1934. London. Harrap. 1st ed. 1/410. ils/sgn Rackham. 45p. F/vellum wrp. B24. $750.00

BROWNSTEIN, Michael. *Highway to the Sky.* 1969. Columbia. 1st ed. F/NF. C2. $50.00

BRUCCOLI, Matthew. *Chandler Before Marlowe.* 1973. Columbia, SC. 1st trade ed. sgn. F/F. A11. $45.00

BRUCCOLI, Matthew. *F Scott Fitzgerald: A Descriptive Bibliography.* 1972. Pittsburgh. ils. 392p. VG. A4. $35.00

BRUCCOLI, Matthew. *F Scott Fitzgerald: A Descriptive Bibliography.* 1987. Pittsburgh. 1st revised ed. F. C6. $50.00

BRUCCOLI, Matthew. *Supplement to F Scott Fitzgerald Descriptive Bibliography.* 1980. np. ils. 234p. F. A4. $55.00

BRUCE, Errol. *Cape Horn to Port.* 1978. NY. McKay. ils. 175p. VG/dj. T7. $22.00

BRUCE, H.A.B. *Riddle of Personality.* 1908. NY. Moffat Yard. 12mo. prt panelled gr cloth. VG. G1. $35.00

BRUCE, Janet. *Kansas City Monarchs.* 1986. KS U. 1st ed. F/VG+. P8. $65.00

BRUCE, Jean. *Deep Freeze.* 1963. Cassell. 1st ed. VG. P3. $12.00

BRUCE, Lenny. *How To Talk Dirty & Influence People.* 1965. Playboy. 1st ed. photos. VG/dj. S9. $30.00

BRUCE, R. *National Road.* 1916. Clinton, NY. 1st ed. sgn. 94p. VG. B5. $65.00

BRUCKER, Gene. *Giovanni & Lusanna.* 1986. Berkeley. sgn. VG. O7. $30.00

BRUETON, Diana. *Many Moons: Myth & Magic, Fact & Fantasy...* 1991. Prentice Hall. 1st pb prt. 256p. K5. $15.00

BRUETTE, William. *American Duck, Goose & Brant Shooting.* 1929. NY. 1st ed. 415p. VG. B5. $60.00

BRUMBAUGH, Florence. *Donald Duck & His Nephews.* 1940. Boston. DC Heath. 1st ed. sm 8vo. Disney ils ep. 66p. ils cloth. H4. $60.00

BRUNA, Dick. *B Is for Bear.* 1977. London. Methuen. 12mo. unp. VG. C14. $7.00

BRUNDAGE, Burr C. *Empire of the Inca.* 1963. Norman. VG. O7. $25.00

BRUNDAGE, F. *Adventures of Jack.* 1921. Stecher. ils. VG/stiff wrp. M5. $55.00

BRUNDAGE, F. *Robin Hood.* nd. Saalfield. 12mo. VG-. B17. $7.50

BRUNEL, George. *Fun With Magic: Amusing Experiments in Physics...* 1901. NY. ils. 175p. cloth. G. A17. $10.00

BRUNHOUSE, Robert. *Frans Blom, Maya Explorer.* 1976. Albuquerque. 1st ed. 291p. dj. F3. $35.00

BRUNHOUSE, Robert. *In Search of the Maya.* 1973. NM U. 1st ed. 243p. dj. F3. $30.00

BRUNNER, John. *Crucible of Time.* 1983. Del Rey. 1st ed. xl. VG/VG. N4. $10.00

BRUNNER, John. *Long Result.* 1965. Faber. 1st ed. VG/VG. P3. $30.00

BRUNO, Anthony. *Bad Luck.* 1990. Delacorte. 1st ed. VG/VG. P3. $19.00

BRUNSON, H. *Oilman Who Didn't Want To Become a Millionaire...* 1955. Exposition. 1st ed. inscr. 84p. cloth. F/chip. D8. $12.00

BRUNT, David. *Weather Study.* 1948 (1942). London. Nelson. 8vo. 215p. G/dj. K5. $12.00

BRUSH, Peter. *Hunter Chaser.* 1948. Hutchinson. G+. O3. $15.00

BRUSSEL, I.R. *Bibliography of Writings of James Branch Cabell.* 1932. Century. revised ed. 126p. VG/G-. B10. $35.00

BRUST, Steven. *Agyar.* 1993. Tor. 1st ed. F/F. G10. $10.00

BRUST, Steven. *Phoenix Guards.* 1991. Tor. F/NF. G10. $10.00

BRUYN, G.W. *Centennial Bibliography of Huntington's Chorea 1872-1972.* 1974. Louvain. 1st ed. 314p. VG/wrp. A13. $40.00

BRY, Charlene. *World of Plants: MO Botanical Garden.* 1989. NY. ils. 191p. F/dj. B26. $32.50

BRYAN, C.D.B. *National Air & Space Museum.* 1979. NY. VG. O7. $35.00

BRYAN, C.D.B. *National Geographic Society: 100 Years of Adventure...* 1987. Abrams. 406 ils. 484p. VG/dj. D8. $25.00

BRYAN, C.W. *From NY to the Hills & Homes of Berkshire.* 1881. Great Barrington. VG/rpr wrp. O7. $35.00

BRYAN, Christopher. *Night of the Wolf.* 1983. Harper Row. 1st ed. VG/VG. P3. $15.00

BRYAN, George S. *Edison: The Man & His Work.* 1926. NY. 350p. red cloth. VG. B14. $50.00

BRYAN, Mike. *Baseball Lives.* 1989. Pantheon. 1st ed. F/F. P8. $10.00

BRYAN, William Alanson. *Natural History of Hawaii.* 1915. Honolulu. Hawaiian Gazette. 117 full-p pl. 596p. xl. VG. T10. $100.00

BRYANT, Billy. *Children of Ol' Man River.* 1936. NY. 1st ed. VG/VG. V4. $85.00

BRYANT, Edward. *Fetish.* 1991. Axolotl. 1/300. sgn. AN/dj. M21. $35.00

BRYANT, Paul W. *Bear.* 1974. Little Brn. 1st ed. sgn. VG/VG. B11. $40.00

BRYANT, Sara Cone. *Epamindas & His Auntie.* 1938. Houghton Mifflin. ils Inez Hogan. VG. M5. $45.00

BRYANT, William Cullen. *Family Library of Poetry & Song.* 1880. NY. Fords Horard Hulbert. Memorial ed. lg 8vo. 1065p. aeg. pict cloth. VG. T10. $50.00

BRYNER, B.G. *Abraham Lincoln in Peoria, IL.* 1926. Peoria. 2nd. 1/1000. 304p. VG. B5. $70.00

BUBBLE BOOK. *Funny Froggy Bubble Book, Harper Columbia Book That Sings.* 1919. Harper. 7th of series. pict brd w/3 records. VG. M5. $35.00

BUBER, Martin. *Tales of the Hasidim: The Early Masters.* 1947. NY. Schocken. 1st ed. 8vo. trans Olga Marx. 335p. VG/VG. H4. $45.00

BUCHAN, John. *History of the First World War.* 1991. Scotland. Lochar. abridged/intro Victor Neuburg. 192p. F/dj. B18. $25.00

BUCHAN, John. *House of the Four Winds.* 1935. Hodder Stoughton. 1st ed. VG. P3. $30.00

BUCHAN, John. *Island of Sheep.* 1936. Hodder Stoughton. 1st ed. VG. P3. $35.00

BUCHAN, John. *Memory Hold the Door.* 1940. Musson. 1st ed. VG. P3. $30.00

BUCHAN, John. *Sick Heart River.* 1941. Musson. 1st ed. VG. P3. $20.00

BUCHANAN, Edna. *Contents Under Pressure.* 1992. Hyperion. ARC/1st ed. VG/VG. N4. $35.00

BUCHANAN, Edna. *Contents Under Pressure.* 1992. Hyperion. 1st ed. sgn. B stp on bottom edges. F/F. H11. $45.00

BUCHANAN, Edna. *Nobody Lives Forever.* 1990. Random. 1st ed. author's 1st novel. rem mk. F/F. H11. $35.00

BUCHANAN, Edna. *Nobody Lives Forever.* 1990. Random. 1st ed. VG/VG. P3. $18.00

BUCHANAN, J.-Brown. *Book Illustrations of George Cruikshank.* 1980. Rutland. 1st ed. 249 pl. F/F. B5. $25.00

BUCHANAN, Lamont. *Kentucky Derby Story.* 1953. Dutton. 1st ed. VG/G. O3. $20.00

BUCHANAN, Marie. *Dark Backward.* 1975. Hart Davis MacGibbon. 1st ed. VG/VG. P3. $20.00

BUCHANAN, Marie. *Morgana.* 1977. Doubleday. 1st ed. VG/VG. P3. $15.00

BUCHANAN, Marie. *Unofficial Breath.* 1973. St Martin. VG/VG. P3. $20.00

BUCHANAN & MCCAULEY. *Roadside Kansas: A Traveler's Guide to Its Geology...* 1987. Lawrence, KS. 1st ed. 365p. NF/wrp. D8. $9.00

BUCHANAN. *Treasure of Auchinleck, Story of Boswell Papers.* 1974. np. ils. 390p. F/VG. A4. $65.00

BUCHARD, Peter. *River Queen.* 1957. Macmillan. 1st ed. 40p. F/VG. C14. $15.00

BUCHHEIM, Lothar-Gunther. *Boat.* 1975. Knopf. 1st ed. F/NF. H11. $35.00

BUCK, Frank. *Bring 'Em Back Alive.* 1930. NY. 1st ed. VG/G. B5. $47.50

BUCK, Pearl S. *China: Past & Present...* 1972. John Day. 1st ed. photos. F/clip. S9. $40.00

BUCK, Pearl S. *Essay on Myself.* 1966. NY. 1st ed. 1/1000. VG. B5. $35.00

BUCK, Pearl S. *Fighting Angel.* 1936. Reynal Hitchcock. 1st ed. NF/VG. B4. $125.00

BUCK, Pearl S. *House of Earth.* 1935. Reynal Hitchcock. 1st ed. NF/VG. B4. $125.00

BUCK, Pearl S. *Stories for Little Children.* 1940. John Day. 1st ed. Ils Weda Yap. VG/VG. C8. $100.00

BUCK, Pearl S. *Water Buffalo Children.* 1943. NY. John Day. 1st ed. ils WA Smith. pict cloth. G/G+. C8. $35.00

BUCK, Pearl S. *Young Revolutionist.* 1932. Friendship. 1st ed. ils. 182p. F/dj. B14. $95.00

BUCK, Peter H. *Vikings of the Sunrise.* 1938. NY. VG. O7. $30.00

BUCK, Peter. *Coming of the Maori.* 1966. Wellington. VG. O7. $65.00

BUCKERIDGE, Anthony. *Stories for Boys.* 1957. Faber. 1st ed. VG/VG. P3. $25.00

BUCKERIDGE, J. *Lincoln's Choice.* 1956. Harrisburg. 1st ed. VG/VG. B5. $65.00

BUCKINGHAM, Bruce. *Boiled Alive.* 1957. Michael Joseph. 1st ed. VG/VG. P3. $30.00

BUCKINGHAM, Nash. *De Shootinest Gent'man.* 1941. NY. 1st trade ed. ils. F/clip. A17. $75.00

BUCKLAND, Raymond. *Ancient & Modern Witchcraft.* nd. Castle. VG. P3. $8.00

BUCKLEY, Arabella B. *Fairy-Land of Science.* 1888 (1878). Lippincott. ils. 244p. G. K5. $13.00

BUCKLEY, Christopher. *Wet Work.* 1991. Knopf. 1st ed. F/F. H11. $25.00

BUCKLEY, William F. *Excerpts From an Address to Conservative Party of NY.* 1964. WA, DC. ltd 1st ed. 1/200. inscr. NF/sans. A11. $65.00

BUCKLEY, William F. *Mongoose, RIP.* 1987. Random. 1st ed. F/F. P3. $20.00

BUCKLEY, William F. *Saving the Queen.* 1976. Doubleday. 1st ed. author's 1st novel. NF/NF. H11. $30.00

BUCKLEY, William F. *Temptation of Wilfred Malachey.* 1985. Workman Pub. 1st ed. 8vo. 45p. F/F. C14. $18.00

BUCKLEY, William F. *Who's on First.* 1980. Doubleday. 1st ed. VG/VG. P3. $20.00

BUCKWALD, Ann. *Seems Like Yesterday.* 1980. Putnam. photos. VG/VG. P12. $5.00

BUD, Robert. *Science Versus Practice: Chemistry in Victorian Britain.* 1984. Manchester. 1st ed. 236p. VG. A13. $20.00

BUDAY, George. *History of the Christmas Card.* 1964. London. Spring Books. 8vo. ils/pl. red brd. F/dj. B24. $25.00

BUDGE, E.A. Wallis. *Mummy: Chapters on Egyptian Funereal Archaeology.* 1894. London. Cambridge. 2nd. 8vo. ils. 404p. xl. G. W1. $30.00

BUDGE, E.A. Wallis. *Osiris & the Egyptian Resurrection.* 1973. Dover. 2 vol. 1st ed thus. VG/stiff wrp. W1. $18.00

BUDGE, E.A. Wallis. *Tutankhamen, Amenism, Atenism & Egyptian Monotheism.* ca 1975. NY. Bell. rpt of 1928 ed. 8vo. ils. F/dj. W1. $18.00

BUECHER, Thomas S. *Norman Rockwell: Artist & Illustrator.* 1970. Abrams. 328p. VG+/dj. M20. $125.00

BUEL & DACUS. *Tour of St Louis.* 1878. St Louis. 1st ed. NF. A15. $75.00

BUELL, John. *Playground.* 1976. FSG. 1st ed. VG/VG. P3. $20.00

BUELL, John. *Shrewsdale Exit.* 1972. FSG. 1st ed. VG/VG. P3. $23.00

BUFF, Mary Marsh. *Dancing Cloud.* 1945. NY. Viking. 3rd prt. ils. 80p. VG/tattered. D1. $32.00

BUFF & BUFF. *Big Tree.* 1946. Viking. 1st ed. ils. F/VG. P2. $75.00

BUFF & BUFF. *Magic Maize.* 1953. Houghton Mifflin. 1st ed. ils. 76p. cloth. VG/dj. M20. $32.00

BUFFETT, Jimmy. *Tales From Margaritaville.* 1989. HBJ. 1st ed. F/F. B35. $22.00

BUFFETT, Jimmy. *Where Is Joe Merchant?* 1992. Harcourt. 1st ed. author's 1st novel. NF/NF clip. M22. $20.00

BUFFIER, Claude. *Geographie Universelle.* 1759. Paris. Giffart. 18 fld maps. 442p. VG. B14. $850.00

BUFFON. *Buffon's Sammtliche Werke, Sammt Ben Erganzungen...* 1837. Koln. 2 vol. pl. half leather/marbled brd. A17. $75.00

BUHLER, Charlotte. *Kindheit und Jugend: Genese des Bewusstseins.* 1928. Leipzig. Hirzel. 307p. prt bl cloth. G. G1. $35.00

BUHLER & THURSTON. *Check List of Fifteenth-Century Printing in Pierpont...* 1939. np. 4to. 1991 entries. 363p. xl. VG. A4. $200.00

BUHRER & ISENBART. *Imperial Horse.* 1986. Knopf. 1st Am ed. F/F. O3. $125.00

BUJOLD, Lois McMaster. *Mirror Dance.* 1994. Baen. 1st ed. F/F. M23. $30.00

BUJOLD, Lois McMaster. *Mirror Dance.* 1994. Baen. 1st trade ed. rem mk. F/NF. G10. $25.00

BUKIET, Melvin J. *Sandman's Dust.* 1985. Arbor. 1st ed. F/NF. G10. $10.00

BUKOWSKI, Charles. *Crucifix in a Deathhand.* 1965. New Orleans. 1st ed. 1/3100. sgn. F/wrp/orig band. w/sgn letter. C2. $250.00

BUKOWSKI, Charles. *Erections, Ejaculations, Exhibitions...* 1972. City Lights. 1st ed. 8vo. 478p. F/photo wrp. S9. $300.00

BUKOWSKI, Charles. *In the Shadow of the Rose.* 1991. Blk Sparrow. 1/750. sgn/#d. F/plain turquoise dj. S9. $175.00

BUKOWSKI, Charles. *Living on Luck. Selected Letters 1960s-1970s. Volume 2.* 1995. Blk Sparrow. 1/200. F/acetate dj. S9. $300.00

BUKOWSKI, Charles. *Longshot Poems for Broke Players.* 1962. 7 Poets. 1/200. author's 2nd book. F/stiff beige wrp. B24. $850.00

BUKOWSKI, Charles. *Love Poem.* 1979. Blk Sparrow. 1/26. sgn/lettered. handbound decor brd. F/F. S9. $200.00

BUKOWSKI, Charles. *One for the Old Boy.* 1984. Santa Barbara. 1st ed. 1/226. sgn. AN. A4. $125.00

BUKOWSKI, Charles. *Poems Written Before Jumping Out of an 8-Story Window.* nd. Berkley. Litmus. F/wrp. B2. $200.00

BUKOWSKI, Charles. *Septuagenarian Stew.* 1990. Blk Sparrow. 1/225. sgn/#d. F/dj. S9. $150.00

BUKOWSKI, Charles. *Shakespeare Never Did This.* 1995. Blk Sparrow. 1st ed thus. 1/326. F/dj. S9. $65.00

BUKOWSKI, Charles. *War All the Time.* 1984. Blk Sparrow. 1st ed. 1/500 hc trade copies. F/acetate dj. T10. $100.00

BUKOWSKI, Charles. *You Kissed Lilly.* 1978. Blk Sparrow. 1st ed. 1/75. sgn. F. B24. $285.00

BULEY, R. Carlyle. *Old Northwest: Pioneer Period 1815-1840.* 1951. IN U. 2 vol. 2nd. maps/pl. VG. A17. $40.00

BULFINCH. *Book of Myths: Selections From Bulfinch's Age of Fables.* 1942. Macmillan. 1st ed. ils Sewell. VG+/VG. C8. $65.00

BULFINCH. *Book of Myths: Selections From Bulfinch's Age of Fables.* 1953 (1942). Macmillan. 4th. ils Helen Sewell. 8vo. 128p. VG/torn. T5. $20.00

BULGAKOV, Mikhail. *Master & Margarita.* 1967. Grove. 1st ed. trans Mirra Ginsburg. NF/NF. B2. $25.00

BULGAKOV, Mikhail. *Master & Margarita.* 1967. Harper Row. 1st ed. VG/VG. P3. $30.00

BULL, Rene. *Arabian Nights.* 1917. Dodd Mead. 8 mc pl. 98 b&w ils. NF. A20. $50.00

BULL & COLEMAN. *Northwest Books, First Supplement...1942-1947.* 1949. np. 276p. VG. A4. $45.00

BULLA, Clyde Robert. *Donkey Cart.* 1946. Crowell. 1st ed. ils Lois Lenski. xl. M5. $35.00

BULLARD, E. John. *Mary Cassatt: Oils & Pastels.* 1972. Watson Guptill. orig ed. 32 pl. 87p. cloth. D2. $45.00

BULLEN, Frank T. *Men of the Merchant Service.* 1900. NY/London. 331p. T7. $45.00

BULLEN, K.E. *Introduction to the Theory of Seismology.* 1965. Cambridge. 3rd. 381p. F/torn. D8. $21.00

BULLER, Francis. *Introduction to the Law Relative to Trials at Nisi Prius...* 1806. NY. Riley. modern half crimson morocco. xl. M11. $225.00

BULLETT, Gerald. *Walt Whitman: A Study & Selection.* 1925. Phil. 1/780. NF/VG. C6. $55.00

BULLOCK, Alan. *Hitler: A Study in Tyranny.* 1962. NY. revised ed. 848p. fair. A17. $6.00

BULLOUGH, Vern. *Sex, Society & History.* 1976. NY. 1st ed. 185p. VG/wrp. A13. $20.00

BULWER-LYTTON, Edward. *Athens: Its Rise & Fall.* 1843. Tauchnitz. G. P3. $40.00

BUNBURY, Henry William. *Annals of Horsemanship: Containing Accounts...* 1812. London. Stockdale. folio. 17 full-p pl. teg. brn morocco/marbled brd. NF. C6. $500.00

BUNCH & COLE. *Warrior's Tale.* 1994. Ballantine. 1st ed. F/F. w/pub letter. G10. $12.00

BUNDY, Walter E. *Jesus & the First Three Gospels.* 1955. Cambridge. Harvard. 1st ed. sgn. 598p. F/G. B11. $50.00

BUNDY & STIMSON. *On Active Service in Peace & War, Vol 1.* 1948. Harper. 1st ed. sgn Stimson. VG/worn. B11. $15.00

BUNKER, M.N. *What Handwriting Tells You About Yourself...* 1951. Cleveland. World. sgn. 240p. VG/G. B11. $6.00

BUNN, Harriet. *Johann Sebastian Bach.* 1942. ils Rafaello Busoni. VG. B30. $10.00

BUNN, Thomas. *Closing Costs.* 1990. Holt. 1st ed. F/F. P3. $10.00

BUNNELL, L.H. *Discovery of the Yosemite & the Indian War of 1851...* 1911. LA. Gerlicher. 4th. ils/map. VG. H7. $75.00

BUNTING, Basil. *Collected Poems.* 1985. Mt Kisco, NY. 1st Am ed. sgn J Williams. w/sgn leaflett. F. A11. $150.00

BUNYAN, John. *Pilgrim's Progress.* ca 1847. London. ils WB Scott after David Scott. Kelliegram morocco. C6. $1,750.00

BUNYAN, John. *Pilgrim's Progress.* 1942. Heritage. ils. case. A17. $17.50

BUPP, Walter; see Garrett, Randall.

BURBANK, Luther. *Harvest of the Years.* 1927. Boston. ils. 296p. VG/VG. B5. $22.50

BURCHAM, L.T. *California Range Land.* 1957. Sacramento. ils/photos/tables. 261p. B26. $30.00

BURDEN, Hamilton T. *Nuremberg Party Rallies 1923-39.* 1967. NY. photos. 206p. VG. A17. $22.50

BURGERS, Thornton. *Burgers' Book of Nature.* 1965. Boston. 1st ed. VG/VG. B5. $50.00

BURGESS, Anthony. *Any Old Iron.* 1989. London. 1st ed. sgn. F/F. C2. $75.00

BURGESS, Anthony. *Any Old Iron.* 1989. Random. 1st ed. F/F. P3. $20.00

BURGESS, Anthony. *End of the World News.* 1983. McGraw Hill. 1st ed. F/F. P3. $20.00

BURGESS, Anthony. *Ernest Hemingway & His World.* 1978. London. Thames Hudson. 1st ed. thin 4to. F/dj. C2. $75.00

BURGESS, Anthony. *Ernest Hemingway & His World.* 1978. Scribner. 1st ed. F/F. B2. $30.00

BURGESS, Anthony. *Kingdom of the Wicked.* Franklin Lib. sgn. VG. M17. $27.50

BURGESS, Anthony. *Kingdom of the Wicked.* 1985. Arbor. 1st ed. VG/VG. P3. $20.00

BURGESS, Anthony. *Napoleon Symphony.* 1974. NY. 1st Am ed. sgn. F/F. C2. $60.00

BURGESS, Anthony. *Pianoplayers.* 1986. Hutchinson. 1st ed. F/F. P3. $18.00

BURGESS, Anthony. *1985.* 1978. Little Brn. 1st ed. VG/VG. P3. $18.00

BURGESS, Gelett. *Burgess Nonsense Book.* 1901. Stokes. ils. 239p. VG. P2. $60.00

BURGESS, Gelett. *Goops & How To Be Them...A Manual of Manners...* 1900. Stokes. 1st ed. 4to. VG. M5. $275.00

BURGESS, Gelett. *Why Be a Goop?* 1924. Stokes. 1st ed. ils. 159p. VG. P2. $110.00

BURGESS, Lorraine. *Garden Art.* 1981. NY. Walker. 1st ed. ils. 187p. F/F. T10. $15.00

BURGESS, Thornton W. *Adventures of Bob White.* 1919. Little Brn. 1st ed. ils Harrison Cady. VG. P2. $75.00

BURGESS, Thornton W. *Adventures of Buster Bear.* (1919). Little Brn. ils Harrison Cady. gray cloth. VG. M5. $30.00

BURGESS, Thornton W. *Adventures of Buster Bear.* 1945. Little Brn. ils/inscr Harrison Cady. VG/VG. D1. $185.00

BURGESS, Thornton W. *Adventures of Buster Bear.* 1964. Canada. Little Brn. decor brd. VG. P3. $8.00

BURGESS, Thornton W. *Adventures of Jimmy Skunk.* 1937. Little Brn. F/G. M5. $45.00

BURGESS, Thornton W. *Adventures of Peter Cottontail.* nd. McClelland Stewart. VG/G. P3. $12.00

BURGESS, Thornton W. *Aunt Sally's Friends...* 1955. Boston. 1st ed. VG/G. B5. $45.00

BURGESS, Thornton W. *Burgess Bird Book for Children.* Oct 1919. Boston. Little Brn. 1st ed. 351p. F. B14. $65.00

BURGESS, Thornton W. *Burgess Bird Book for Children.* 1919. Little Brn. 1st ed. gilt bl cloth. VG. A15/M5. $45.00

BURGESS, Thornton W. *Burgess Book of Nature Lore.* 1965. Boston. 1st ed. VG/VG. B5. $60.00

BURGESS, Thornton W. *Burgess Seashore Book for Children.* 1946 (1929). Little Brn. ils Southwick/Sutton. VG/G. P2. $45.00

BURGESS, Thornton W. *Crooked Little Path.* nd. Bonanza. later rpt. ils Harrison Cady. VG/VG. B17. $10.00

BURGESS, Thornton W. *How Peter Cottontail Got His Name.* 1957. Wonder. ils Phoebe Erickson. VG. M5. $15.00

BURGESS, Thornton W. *Jerry Muskrat at Home.* nd. Grosset Dunlap. VG/G. P3. $15.00

BURGESS, Thornton W. *Littlest Christmas Tree.* 1954. Wonder. ils Hauge. VG. M5. $30.00

BURGESS, Thornton W. *Mother West Wind Why Stories.* 1915. Little Brn. 1st ed. ils Harrison Cady. 230p. VG. P2. $110.00

BURGESS, Thornton W. *Old Mother West Wind, Golden Anniversary Ed.* 1960. Little Brn. ils Harrison Cady. 10th prt. VG/VG. B17. $8.50

BURGESS, Thornton W. *While the Story-Log Burns.* 1938. Little Brn. 1st ed. ils Lemuel Palmer. 195p. VG/VG. D1. $150.00

BURGHEIM, Fanny Louise. *First Circus.* 1930. Platt Munk. ils. 30p. emb brd. A17. $10.00

BURKE, Alan Dennis. *Driven to Murder.* 1986. Atlantic Monthly. 1st ed. F/F. P3. $16.00

BURKE, James Lee. *Burning Angel.* 1995. Hyperion. 1st ed. F/F. M19. $25.00

BURKE, James Lee. *Convict.* 1985. Baton Rouge. 1st ed. inscr. hc. NF. B4. $250.00

BURKE, James Lee. *Dixie City Jam.* 1994. Hyperion. 1/1525. special ed. sgn/#d. case. P3. $100.00

BURKE, James Lee. *Dixie City Jam.* 1994. Hyperion. 1st ed. F/F. A20/H11. $25.00

BURKE, James Lee. *Dixie City Jam.* 1994. Hyperion. 1st ed. inscr. F/F. B2. $40.00

BURKE, James Lee. *In the Electric Mist With Confederate Dead.* 1993. Hyperion. 1st ed. F/F. H11. $35.00

BURKE, James Lee. *Stained White Radiance.* 1992. Hyperion. 1st ed. F/F. H11. $35.00

BURKE, Jan. *Goodnight, Irene.* 1993. Simon Schuster. 1st ed. F/F. A20. $25.00

BURKE, Jan. *Goodnight, Irene.* 1993. Simon Schuster. 1st ed. sgn. F/F. T2. $40.00

BURKE, Martyn. *Commissar's Report.* 1984. Houghton Mifflin. 1st ed. NF/NF. H11. $20.00

BURKE, Pauline Wilcox. *Emily Donelson of Tennessee.* 1941. Garrett Massie. 2 vol. ils. box. B10. $45.00

BURKERT, Nancy Ekholm. *Valentine & Orson.* 1989. FSG. 1st ed. unp. NF/dj. M20. $27.00

BURKHARDT. *Concise Dictionary of American Biography.* 1990. np. 4th. 1549p. F/F. A4. $95.00

BURKHOLDER & CHANDLER. *From Impotence to Authority.* 1977. MO U. 1st ed. 253p. dj. F3. $20.00

BURKHOLZ & IRVING. *Death Freak.* 1978. Summit. 1st ed. VG/VG. P3. $15.00

BURKHOLZ & IRVING. *Thirty-Eighth Floor.* 1965. McGraw Hill. 1st ed. VG/VG. P3. $20.00

BURLAND, Cottie. *People of the Ancient Americas.* 1970. London. Hamilyn. 1st ed. 159p. dj. F3. $20.00

BURLEIGH, Anne H. *John Adams.* nd. Arlington. 437p. bl cloth. F/VG. B22. $5.00

BURLEY, W.J. *Charles & Elizabeth.* 1981. Walker. 1st ed. NF/NF. P3. $13.00

BURLEY, W.J. *Wycliffe & the Tangled Web.* 1989. Crime Club. 1st ed. VG/VG. P3. $16.00

BURLINGAME, Roger. *Of Making Many Books.* 1946. Scribner. 1st ed. 8vo. 347p. gilt beige cloth. NF. T10. $35.00

BURLINGHAM, Gertrude S. *Study of the Lactariae of the United States.* 1908. NY. ils/photos. wrp. B26. $20.00

BURMAN, Ben Lucien. *Blow a Wild Bugle for Catfish Bend.* 1967. Taplinger. ils Alice Cady. VG/VG. B10. $15.00

BURMAN, Ben Lucien. *Owl Hoots Twice at Cafish Bend.* 1961. Taplinger. 1st ed. ils Alice Caddy. VG/VG. B10. $25.00

BURNET, Gilbert. *Vindication of the Authority, Constitution & Laws...* 1673. Glasgow. 1st ed. contemporary sheep. xl. M11. $150.00

BURNETT, Constance Buel. *Shoemaker's Son: Life of Hans Christian Andersen.* 1941. Random/JLG. 1st ed thus. 313p. VG. P2. $12.50

BURNETT, Frances Hodgeson. *Little Lord Fauntleroy.* 1886. NY. Scribner. 1st ed. 8vo. VG/modern case. C8. $225.00

BURNETT, Frances Hodgson. *Little Lord Fauntleroy*. 1936. NY. ils. 236p. VG/tape rpr. A17. $10.00

BURNETT, Frances Hodgson. *Little Princess*. 1905. Scribner. 1st ed thus. lg 8vo. teg. VG. M5. $90.00

BURNETT, Frances Hodgson. *Little Princess*. 1963. Lippincott. early/not 1st ed. gilt gr cloth. F/VG. M5. $35.00

BURNETT, Frances Hodgson. *Little Princess*. 1963. Lippincott. 1st ed. ils/sgn Tasha Tudor. VG/G+. P2. $85.00

BURNETT, Frances Hodgson. *Little Princess*. 1965. Lippincott. 8vo. ils Tasha Tudor. F/F. B17. $12.50

BURNETT, Frances Hodgson. *Making of a Marchioness*. 1901. NY. 1st ed. F/VG+. C6. $225.00

BURNETT, Frances Hodgson. *Secret Garden*. 1911. Stokes. 1st ed. 1 pl missing. fair. M5. $35.00

BURNETT, Frances Hodgson. *Secret Garden*. 1962. ils Tasha Tudor. NF/NF. S13. $25.00

BURNETT, Frances Hodgson. *Spring Cleaning As Told by Queen Crosspatch*. 1973. England. Tom Stacey. rpt. 12mo. 86p. gilt bdg. NF/VG. T5. $35.00

BURNETT, Frances Hodgson. *Two Little Pilgrims' Progress*. 1895. Scribner. 1st ed. 191p. bl cloth. VG. M20. $57.00

BURNETT, Francis Hodgson. *Once Upon a Time Stories, Jingles, Rhymes*. 1915. Cupples Leon. 8vo. 92p. fair. C14. $8.00

BURNETT, Hallie. *Brain Pickers*. 1957. Messner. 1st ed. VG+/VG. B4. $85.00

BURNETT, Virgil. *Towers at the Edge of the World*. 1980. St Martin. 1st ed. F/F. P3. $15.00

BURNETT, W.R. *Dark Hazard*. 1933. Harper. 1st ed. VG. P3. $25.00

BURNETT, W.R. *Goodhues of Sinking Creek*. nd. np 1st ed. ils JJ Lankes. NF/NF. A11. $60.00

BURNETT, W.R. *Iron Man*. 1930. Lincoln MacVeagh. 1st ed. VG+. M22/P3. $30.00

BURNETT, W.R. *Little Caesar*. 1929. Dial. 1st ed. author's 1st novel. VG. M22. $45.00

BURNETT. *Autobiography of the Working Class...1790-1900*. 1984. NY. 1028 entries. 501p. NF. A4. $65.00

BURNHAM, Eleanor. *Justin Morgan: Founder of His Race*. 1911. Shakespeare. 1st ed. hc. VG. O3. $95.00

BURNHAM, Frederick Russell. *Scouting on Two Continents*. 1934. Los Angeles. Ivan Deach. sgn. 370p. gilt bl cloth. VG. T10. $50.00

BURNHAM, Sophy. *Art Crowd*. 1973. McKay. 395p. cloth. dj. D2. $25.00

BURNINGHAM, John. *Mr Grumpy's Motor Car*. 1976. Crowell. 1st Am ed. ils. F/F. P2. $28.00

BURNINGHAM, John. *Seasons*. 1971. Bobbs Merrill. 1st Am ed. VG/VG. B35. $7.50

BURNINGHAM, John. *Where's Julius?* 1986. Crown. stated 1st ed. 4to. ils. unp. VG+/VG clip. C14. $10.00

BURNS, E. Bradford. *Perspectives of Brazillian History*. 1967. Columbia. 1st ed. 235p. dj. F3. $15.00

BURNS, Elizabeth. *Late Liz*. 1968. NY. sgn. VG/VG. B5. $25.00

BURNS, George. *I Love Her That's Why*. 1955. NY. 1st ed. VG/VG. B5. $30.00

BURNS, Olive Ann. *Cold Sassy Tree*. 1984. Ticknor Fields. 1st ed. F/NF. B2. $150.00

BURNS, Rex. *Alvarez Journal*. 1975. Harper Row. 1st ed. VG/VG. P3. $20.00

BURNS, Robert. *Poems, Chiefly in the Scottish Dialect*. 1927. London. T Werner Laurie. facsimile of Kilmarnock 1786 ed. 240p. teg. VG/case. B18. $195.00

BURNS, Tex; see L'Amour, Louis.

BURNS, Walter Noble. *Saga of Billy the Kid*. 1926. Doubleday. 8vo. 322p. reading copy. T10. $25.00

BURNS. *Herbert Hoover: Bibliography of His Times & Presidency*. 1991. np. ils. 290p. F. A4. $70.00

BURNSIDE, H.M. *Noel*. nd. Raphael Tuck. inscr. G/wrp. B18. $17.50

BURR, Fearing. *Field & Garden Vegetables of America*. 1994. Chillicothe, IL. Am Botanist. rpt. 664p. M. A10. $35.00

BURROUGHS, Edgar Rice. *At the Earth's Core*. 1962. Canaveral. 1st ed. VG/VG. P3. $50.00

BURROUGHS, Edgar Rice. *Beasts of Tarzan*. 1916. AL Burt. ils J Allen St John. 337p. VG/dj. M20. $47.00

BURROUGHS, Edgar Rice. *Cave Girl*. 1925. Chicago. McClurg. 1st ed. F/NF. C2. $1,750.00

BURROUGHS, Edgar Rice. *Deputy Sheriff of Comanche County*. 1940. Tarzana. ERB. 1st ed. F/1st issue dj. B24. $650.00

BURROUGHS, Edgar Rice. *ERB Library of Illustration Vol 1*. 1976. Russ Cochran. 1st ed. F. P3. $200.00

BURROUGHS, Edgar Rice. *Escape on Venus*. 1946. ERB. 1st ed. VG/G. P3. $125.00

BURROUGHS, Edgar Rice. *Fighting Man of Mars*. 1933. John Lane/Bodley Head. 2nd. VG. P3. $40.00

BURROUGHS, Edgar Rice. *Girl From Hollywood*. 1923. Macaulay. 1st ed. VG. P3. $55.00

BURROUGHS, Edgar Rice. *Jungle Girl*. 1932. ERB. 1st ed. VG/worn. B5. $150.00

BURROUGHS, Edgar Rice. *Jungle Girl*. 1933. Odhams. 1st ed. VG/G. P3. $75.00

BURROUGHS, Edgar Rice. *Land That Time Forgot*. nd. Doubleday. hc. 249p. F. M13. $20.00

BURROUGHS, Edgar Rice. *Mucker*. 1963. Canaveral. 1st ed. VG/VG. P3. $75.00

BURROUGHS, Edgar Rice. *Pellucidar*. 1962. Canaveral. 1st ed. VG/VG. P3. $50.00

BURROUGHS, Edgar Rice. *Pirates of Venus*. 1940. ERB. VG/VG. P3. $150.00

BURROUGHS, Edgar Rice. *Pirates of Venus*. 1962. Canaveral. NF/NF. P3. $60.00

BURROUGHS, Edgar Rice. *Princess of Mars*. 1917. McClurg. 1st ed. ils Frank Schoonover. VG. M22. $300.00

BURROUGHS, Edgar Rice. *Return of Tarzan*. 1927. Grosset Dunlap. VG/G. P3. $75.00

BURROUGHS, Edgar Rice. *Savage Pellucidar*. 1963. Canaveral. 1st ed. G/G. P3. $40.00

BURROUGHS, Edgar Rice. *Son of Tarzan*. 1917. Grosset Dunlap. ils St John. 394p. VG/dj. M20. $52.00

BURROUGHS, Edgar Rice. *Son of Tarzan*. 1927. Grosset Dunlap. VG/G. P3. $50.00

BURROUGHS, Edgar Rice. *Tanar of Pellucidar*. 1962. Canaveral. NF/NF. P3. $50.00

BURROUGHS, Edgar Rice. *Tarzan & the Ant Men*. 1924. Grosset Dunlap. 346p. VG+/dj. M20. $52.00

BURROUGHS, Edgar Rice. *Tarzan & the Forbidden City*. 1933. ERB. VG. H7. $25.00

BURROUGHS, Edgar Rice. *Tarzan & the Golden Lion.* 1923. Chicago. 1st ed. NF. C2. $75.00

BURROUGHS, Edgar Rice. *Tarzan & the Jewels of Opar.* 1919. McClurg. 2nd ed. VG. P3. $90.00

BURROUGHS, Edgar Rice. *Tarzan & the Lost Empire.* 1929. ERB. 313p. cloth. VG+/dj. M20. $77.00

BURROUGHS, Edgar Rice. *Tarzan & the Lost Empire.* 1932. Cassell. 2nd. VG. P3. $35.00

BURROUGHS, Edgar Rice. *Tarzan at the Earth's Core.* 1962. Canaveral. NF/NF. P3. $50.00

BURROUGHS, Edgar Rice. *Tarzan's Quest.* 1936. ERB. early rpt. F/F. M19. $125.00

BURROUGHS, Edgar Rice. *Tarzan's Quest.* 1936. ERB. ils J Allen St John. 318p. VG/dj. M20. $77.00

BURROUGHS, Edgar Rice. *Tarzan the Avenger.* 1939. Dell/ERB. 192p. VG. B14. $125.00

BURROUGHS, Edgar Rice. *Tarzan the Magnificent.* 1939. ERB. 318p. VG+/dj. M20. $77.00

BURROUGHS, Edgar Rice. *Tarzan the Magnificent.* 1948. Burroughs. F/F. P3. $75.00

BURROUGHS, Edgar Rice. *Tarzan the Untamed.* 1920. Canada. McClelland Stewart. 1st ed. G. P3. $125.00

BURROUGHS, Edgar Rice. *Tarzan the Untamed.* 1920. Chicago. McClurg. 1st ed. NF. C2. $75.00

BURROUGHS, Edgar Rice. *War Chief.* 1978. Gregg. 1st ed. VG/VG. P3. $40.00

BURROUGHS, Edgar Rice. *Warlord of Mars.* 1919. McClurg. 1st ed. G. P3. $75.00

BURROUGHS, Harry E. *Tale of a Vanished Land.* 1930. Houghton Mifflin. 1/1000. sgn. 336p. VG. B11. $40.00

BURROUGHS, John. *Squirrels & Other Fur-Bearers.* 1901. Boston/NY. Houghton Mifflin. sm 8vo. 149p. cloth. VG. H4. $35.00

BURROUGHS, John. *Writings of...* 1904. NY. 15 vol. marbled brd/brn half leather. F. B30. $235.00

BURROUGHS, Margaret T.G. *What Shall I Tell My Children Who Are Black.* 1968. Chicago. MAAH Pr. 2nd. inscr. NF/stapled wrp. B4. $45.00

BURROUGHS, Polly. *Zeb: A Celebrated Schooner Life.* 1972. Riverside, CT. Chatham. 4to. ils. 160p. VG/dj. T7. $35.00

BURROUGHS, Raleigh. *Horses, Burroughs & Other Animals.* 1977. Barnes. pres. F/F. w/sgn letter. O3. $65.00

BURROUGHS, Samuel. *History of the Chancery, Relating to Judicial Power...* 1726. London. J Walthoe. modern full calf. M11. $650.00

BURROUGHS, W.J. *Weather Cycles: Real or Imaginary?* 1992. Cambridge. 4to. 201p. VG/VG. K5. $20.00

BURROUGHS, William Jr. *Map From Hell.* 1978. Red Ozier. rolled w/band. F. V1. $25.00

BURROUGHS, William S. *Cobble Stone Gardens* 1976. Cherry Valley. 1st ed. 1/50. sgn. hc. NF. B4. $350.00

BURROUGHS, William S. *Dead Star.* 1969. San Francisco. Nova Broadcast. 1st ed. 1/2000. sgn. F/prt wrp. S9. $100.00

BURROUGHS, William S. *Exterminator!* 1973. Viking. 1st ed. F/F. M19. $75.00

BURROUGHS, William S. *Last Words of Dutch Schultz.* 1975. Viking. 1st ed. F/F. H11. $55.00

BURROUGHS, William S. *Nova Express.* 1964. NY. 1st ed. F/F. C6. $40.00

BURROUGHS, William S. *Nova Express.* 1964. NY. 1st ed. NF/VG. N3. $25.00

BURROUGHS, William S. *Soft Machine.* 1968. London. Calder Boyars. 2nd Eng ed. F/NF. B2. $50.00

BURROUGHS, William S. *Ticket That Exploded.* 1967. Grove. 1st Am ed. F/NF. B2. $65.00

BURRUS, Ernest J. *Kino & the Cartography of the Northwestern New Spain.* 1965. AZ Pioneers Hist Soc. 1/750. 17 maps. M. O7. $350.00

BURST, Steven. *Gypsy.* 1992. Tor. 1st ed. F/F. P3. $19.00

BURST, Steven. *Phoenix Guards.* 1991. Tor. 1st ed. F/F. P3. $20.00

BURSTEIN & CRIMP. *Many Lives of Elton John.* 1992. Birch Lane. 1st ed. F/F. P3. $20.00

BURT & LEASOR. *One That Got Away.* 1956. Collins. 1st ed. VG/VG. P3. $15.00

BURTON, Mary Kerr. *Serenity & Other Poems.* 1975. Reynolds. 32p. VG. B10. $12.00

BURTON, Miles. *Hardway Diamonds.* 1930. Mystery League. 1st ed. VG. P3. $20.00

BURTON, Steven J. *Introduction to Law & Legal Reasoning. Second Edition.* 1995. Boston. Little Brn. 178p. wrp. M11. $10.00

BURTON, Thomas G. *Tom Ashley, Sam McGee, Bukka White: TN Traditional Singers.* 1981. Knoxville, TN. 1st ed. F/F. B2. $25.00

BURTON, William. *History & Description of English Porcelain.* 1902. Cassell. 1/1200. 8vo. 24 pl. 196p. gilt gr cloth. xl. T10. $100.00

BURTON, Yvonne. *Grady Country, Georgia.* 1981. Danielsville, GA. Heritage. 2nd. inscr. 357p. gilt brd. F. B11. $40.00

BURY. *Cambridge Medieval History.* 1936-1967. Cambridge. 9 vol. maps. xl. VG. A4. $195.00

BUSBEY, Hamilton. *Recollections of Men & Horses.* 1907. Dodd Mead. 1st ed. lacks ffe. O3. $35.00

BUSBEY, Hamilton. *Trotting & the Pacing Horse in America.* 1904. Macmillan. 1st ed. O3. $45.00

BUSBY, F.M. *Long View.* 1976. Berkley Putnam. 1st ed. F/F. P3. $18.00

BUSBY, Roger. *Main Line Kill.* 1968. Walker. 1st ed. VG/VG. P3. $12.00

BUSBY, Roger. *New Face in Hell.* 1976. Collins Crime Club. 1st ed. VG/VG. P3. $20.00

BUSBY, Roger. *Snow Man.* 1987. Collins Crime Club. 1st ed. VG/G. P3. $15.00

BUSCEMA & LEE. *How To Draw Comics the Marvel Way.* 1978. hc. ils. 160p. F. M13. $23.00

BUSCH, Francis X. *Enemies of the State.* 1954. Bobbs Merrill. crimson brd. G. M11. $45.00

BUSCH, Frederick. *Closing Arguments.* 1991. Ticknor Fields. 1st ed. AN/dj. M22. $25.00

BUSCH, Frederick. *I Wanted a Year Without Fall.* 1971. London. 1st/only ed. F/NF. A11. $70.00

BUSCH, Wilhelm. *Max & Moritz.* 1925. Braun Schneider. pict brd. VG. M5. $35.00

BUSCH, Wilhelm. *Max und Moritz.* 1925. Munchen. Braun Schneider. ils. VG. M5. $22.00

BUSH, Caroll D. *Nut Growers Handbook: A Practical Guide...* 1941. NY. photos/drawings. 189p. B26. $25.00

BUSH, Christopher. *Dead Man's Music.* 1937. Heinemann. VG. P3. $20.00

BUSHNELL, Belle. *John Arrowsmith: Planter.* 1910 (1909). Torch. inscr. ils. 115p. G+. B10. $25.00

BUSHNELL, Eleanore. *Nevada Constitution, Origin & Growth. Revised Edition.* 1968. NV U. 201p. prt sewn/stapled wrp. M11. $25.00

BUSHNELL, Sarah T. *Truth About Henry Ford.* 1922. Chicago. 222p. orange cloth. VG. B14. $125.00

BUSHONG, Millard K. *Old Jube: A Biography of General Jubal A Early.* 1988 (1955). Wht Mane. 4th. 343p. AN. B10. $25.00

BUSS, Irven. *Wisconsin Pheasant Population.* 1943. Madison, WI. Conservation Dept. 318p. VG. A10. $45.00

BUTENKO, R.G. *Plant Cell Culture.* 1985. Moscow. MIR Pub. 207p. VG/wrp. B1. $22.00

BUTLER, Benjamin. *Butler's Book.* 1892. Boston. st ed. thick 8vo. ils 1154p. G. T3. $40.00

BUTLER, Charles Henry. *Century at the Bar of the Supreme Court of United States.* 1942. putnam. G/worn. M11. $50.00

BUTLER, Constance. *Illyria, Lady.* 1935. Boston. Houghton Mifflin. 1st ed. NF/VG+. B4. $65.00

BUTLER, Ellis Parker. *Confessions of a Daddy.* 1907. Century. 1st ed. ils Fanny Cory. VG+. M5. $48.00

BUTLER, Gerald. *Kiss the Blood Off My Hands.* 1946. Farrar Rinehart. 1st ed. VG/G. P3. $20.00

BUTLER, Gwendoline. *Albion Walk.* 1982. CMG. 1st ed. VG/VG. P3. $20.00

BUTLER, Gwendoline. *Coffin in Malta.* 1965. Walker. 1st ed. VG/VG. P3. $30.00

BUTLER, Gwendoline. *Coffin on the Water.* 1986. St Martin. 1st ed. VG/VG. P3. $20.00

BUTLER, Gwendoline. *Red Staircase.* 1979. CMG. 1st ed. VG/VG. P3. $20.00

BUTLER, Mann. *History of the Commonwealth of Kentucky.* 1934. Louisville. 1st ed. 8vo. 396p. contemporary bdg. C6. $400.00

BUTLER, Margaret Manor. *Lakewood Story.* 1949. Stratford. 1st ed. sgn. 263p. VG. M20. $22.00

BUTLER, Octavia E. *Adulthood Rites.* 1988. Warner. 1st ed. F/F. B4. $45.00

BUTLER, Octavia E. *Blood Child.* 1995. 4 Walls 8 Windows. 1st ed. F/F. M23. $20.00

BUTLER, Octavia E. *Clay's Ark.* 1984. St Martin. 1st ed. F/NF. M23. $60.00

BUTLER, Octavia E. *Dawn.* 1987. Warner. 1st ed. VG/G. P3. $13.00

BUTLER, Octavia E. *Imago.* 1989. Warner. 1st ed. F/F. P3. $20.00

BUTLER, Octavia E. *Kindred.* 1979. Doubleday. 1st ed. F/NF. M23. $75.00

BUTLER, Octavia E. *Mind of My Mind.* 1977. Doubleday. 1st ed. xl. VG+/VG+. M23. $60.00

BUTLER, Octavia E. *Patternmaster.* 1976. Doubleday. 1st ed. VG+/VG. M23. $75.00

BUTLER, Octavia E. *Survivor.* 1978. Doubleday. 1st ed. F/VG+. M23. $65.00

BUTLER, Octavia E. *Wild Seed.* 1980. Doubleday. 1st ed. F/F. M23. $125.00

BUTLER, Robert Olen. *Alleys of Eden.* 1981. NY. 1st ed. F/F. A11. $65.00

BUTLER, Robert Olen. *Sun Dogs.* 1982. NY. 1st ed. author's 2nd novel. F/F. A11. $50.00

BUTLER, Robert Olen. *They Whisper.* 1994. Holt. 1st ed. rem mk. F/F. H11. $25.00

BUTLER, Robert Olen. *They Whisper.* 1994. Holt. 1st ed. sgn. F/F. B4. $50.00

BUTLER, Robert Olen. *Wabash.* 1987. Knopf. 1st ed. F/F. H11. $35.00

BUTLER, Samuel. *Erewhon.* 1901. LEC. 1/1500. ils/sgn Rockwell Kent. 8vo. striped bl/wht cloth. VG. B11. $100.00

BUTLER, Samuel. *Geographia Classica.* 1831. Phil. VG. O7. $35.00

BUTLER, Samuel. *Hudibras.* 1744. Cambridge. 2 vol. 1st 8vo ed. ils Hogarth. 19th-C morocco. VG. C6. $275.00

BUTLER, Samuel. *Way of All Flesh.* 1903. London. 1st ed. VG. C6. $195.00

BUTLER, William E. *Soviet Union & the Law of the Sea.* 1971. Baltimore. VG. O7. $15.00

BUTLER & WALBERT. *Abortion, Medicine & the Law.* 1986. Facts on File. M11. $35.00

BUTT & LYTHE. *Economic History of Scotland 1100-1939.* 1975. Glasgow/London. 1st ed. 293p. AN/dj. P4. $20.00

BUTTERWORTH, Hezekiah. *In Old New England.* 1895. NY. 1st ed. 281p. emb cloth. F. A17. $10.00

BUTTERWORTH, Michael. *Virgin on the Rocks.* 1985. Crime Club. 1st ed. NF/NF. P3. $13.00

BUTTERWORTH, W.E. *Air Evac.* 1967. Norton. 1st ed. NF/clip. B4. $150.00

BYARS, Betsy. *After the Goat Man.* 1974. Viking. 1st ed. ils Ronald Himler. NF/VG+. P2. $20.00

BYATT, A.S. *Djinn in the Nightingale's Eye.* 1994. London. 1st ed. sgn. F/F. A11. $45.00

BYERS, Horace Robert. *Elements of Cloud Physics.* 1973 (1965). Chicago. 2nd. 8vo. 191p. VG/dj. K5. $20.00

BYERS, Horace Robert. *Thunderstorm Electricity.* 1953. Chicago. 8vo. ils. 344p. cloth. G. K5. $36.00

BYNNER, W. Caravan. *Caravan.* 1925. NY. 1st ed. inscr. NF. A15. $45.00

BYNNER, Witter. *Journey With Genius.* 1951. NY. John Day. 1st ed. NF/dj. H4. $40.00

BYRD, Richard E. *Alone.* 1938. NY. Putnam. 1st ed. sgn. VG. H4. $25.00

BYRD, Richard E. *Big Aviation Book for Boys.* 1929. Springfield, MA. 285p. F/dj. A17. $25.00

BYRD, Richard E. *Discovery: Story of Second Byrd Antarctic Expedition.* 1935. Putnam. 1st ed. sgn. ils/2 maps. 405p. VG. T7. $50.00

BYRD, Richard E. *Discovery: Story of Second Byrd Antarctic Expedition.* 1935. Putnam. 1st ed. 405p. bl cloth. VG. B22. $7.50

BYRD, Richard E. *Skyward.* 1928. NY. 1st ed. 359p. G+. B18. $22.50

BYRNE, J. Grandson. *Studies on the Physiology of the Middle Ear.* 1938. London. Lewis. ils. 289p. panelled red cloth. xl. G1. $37.50

BYRNE, Robert. *Tunnel.* 1977. Detective BC. VG. P3. $8.00

BYRON, Lord. *Childe Harold's Pilgrimage.* 1892. ils Nims/Knight. NF/G. M19. $85.00

BYRON, Lord. *Finden's Illustrations of the Life & Works of Lord Byron.* 1883. London. 3 vol. 126 engraved pl. full levant morocco. NF. C6. $400.00

C.S.S.; see Street, Charles Stuart.

CABELL, James Branch. *Cream of the Jest.* 1917. McBride. 1st ed. G. P3. $35.00

CABELL, James Branch. *Devil's Own Dear Son.* 1949. Farrar Straus. 1st ed. 209p. VG/VG. B10. $15.00

CABELL, James Branch. *Domnei: A Comedy of Woman-Worship.* 1930. McBride. 1st ed thus. ils. 252p. VG/G. B10. $25.00

CABELL, James Branch. *Hamlet Had an Uncle.* 1940. Farrar Rinehart. 1st ed. 169p. VG/fair. B10. $15.00

CABELL, James Branch. *Letters of...* 1975. OK U. 1st ed. 277p. B10/R10. $15.00

CABELL, James Branch. *Silver Stallion.* 1926. McBride. 1st ed. G. P3. $30.00

CABELL, James Branch. *Silver Stallion.* 1926. McBride. 1st ed. 358p. VG/dj. M20. $47.00

CABELL, James Branch. *Something About Eve.* 1927. McBride. 1st ed. VG/VG. P3. $75.00

CABELL, James Branch. *Something About Eve.* 1927. McBride. 1st ed. 1/850. sgn. NF. B4. $175.00

CABELL, James Branch. *There Were Two Pirates.* 1946. Farrar Straus. 1st ed. VG/G. P3. $30.00

CABELL, James Branch. *Way of Ecben, a Comedietta Involving a Gentleman.* 1929. NY. 8vo. 209p. gilt blk cloth. uncut. G+. B14. $100.00

CABELL & COLUM. *Between Friends: Letters of James Branch Cabell & Others.* 1962. HBW. 1st ed. 304p. VG/G. B10. $25.00

CABLE, George Washington. *Grandissimes. Story of a Creole Life.* 1880. Scribner. 1st ed. author's 2nd book. NF. C2. $100.00

CABON, Michael. *Model World.* 1991. Morrow. 1st ed. F/F. A20. $16.00

CADIGAN, Pat. *Dirty Work.* 1993. Shingletown. Ziesing. 1st ed. sgn. F/F. T2. $30.00

CADIGAN, Pat. *Dirty Work.* 1993. Ziesing. 1st ed. F/NF. G10. $20.00

CADIGAN, Pat. *Mindplayers.* 1988. London. Gollancz. 1st hc ed. sgn. F/F. T2. $40.00

CADOGAN, Lady. *Lady Cadogan's Illustrated Games of Solitaire or Patience.* 1914. Phil. New Revised ed. 121p. stiff brd. VG. S1. $10.00

CADUTO, M.J. *Pond & Brook.* 1985. Prentice Hall. 8vo. 276p. rem mk. dj. B1. $15.00

CADY, Jack. *Well.* 1980. Arbor. 1st ed. VG+/dj. M21. $45.00

CAESAR, Sid. *Where Have I Been: An Autobiography.* 1982. NY. Crown. 1st ed. sgn pres. 280p. F/F. H4. $45.00

CAHN, W. *Out of the Cracker Barrel.* 1969. NY. 1st ed. ils/index. VG/VG. B5. $20.00

CAIDIN, Martin. *Cyborg.* 1972. Arbor. 1st ed. F/NF. B4. $350.00

CAIDIN, Martin. *Hydrospace.* 1965. Dutton. photos. 320p. xl. G/G. P12. $4.00

CAIN, James M. *Galatea.* 1953. Knopf. 1st ed. NF/NF. M22. $45.00

CAIN, James M. *Moth.* 1948. Knopf. 1st ed. F/F. M22. $45.00

CAIN, James M. *Moth.* 1948. Knopf. 1st ed. NF/NF. M19. $40.00

CAIN, James M. *Past All Dishonor.* 1946. Knopf. 1st ed. F/NF. C2. $125.00

CAIN, James M. *Postman Always Rings Twice.* 1935. Knopf. correct 1st pb/Borzoi ed. NF/red wrp/VG+ dj. A11. $115.00

CAIN, James M. *Serenade.* 1937. Knopf. 1st ed. VG/G+. M22. $90.00

CAIN, Paul. *Fast One.* 1978. S IL U. 1st ed thus. VG/VG. M22. $60.00

CAIN, Paul. *Seven Slayers.* 1987. Blood & Guts. 1st hc ed. 1/1000. F/F. M22. $30.00

CAIRIS, Nicholas T. *Passenger Liners of the World Since 1893.* 1979. Bonanza. revised ed. VG/VG. A16. $25.00

CAJORI, F. *Sir Isaac Newton's Mathematical Principles...* 1947. Berkeley. 680p. cloth. F. D8. $20.00

CALDECOTT, Moyra. *Tall Stones.* 1977. Hill Wang. 1st ed. VG/VG. P3. $20.00

CALDECOTT, Randolph. *Graphic Pictures, Complete Ed.* 1891. London. Routledge. 1/1250. teal cloth. VG. A20. $95.00

CALDER, Angus. *People's War: Britain 1939-45.* 1969. Pantheon. 1st Am ed. 656p. F/dj. A17. $10.00

CALDER, Richrd. *Dead Girls.* 1992. Collins. 1st ed. AN/dj. M21. $25.00

CALDERON, Hector M. *La Ciencia Matematica de Los Mayas.* 1966. Orion. 1st ed. 1/2000. 134p. dj. F3. $35.00

CALDERWOOD, Henry. *Evolution & Man's Place in Nature.* 1893. London. Macmillan. 12mo. 349p. panelled ochre cloth. NF. G1. $65.00

CALDERWOOD, Henry. *Relations of Mind & Brain.* 1884. London. Macmillan. 2nd. 528p. pebbled ochre cloth. G1. $85.00

CALDWELL, E.N. *Alaska Trail Dogs.* 1950. NY. ils/photos. 150p. G. B5. $35.00

CALDWELL, Erskine. *Jenny by Nature.* 1961. Heinemann. 1st ed. F/F. M19. $45.00

CALDWELL, Erskine. *Men & Women: 22 Stories.* 1961. Little Brn. 1st ed thus. 313p. VG. B10. $12.00

CALDWELL, Erskine. *Some American People.* 1935. McBride. 1st ed. author's 1st nonfiction book. 266p. VG/fair. B10. $100.00

CALDWELL, Guy. *Early History of the Ochsner Medical Center.* 1965. Springfield. 1st ed. 115p. VG. A13. $25.00

CALDWELL, J.A. *Atlas of Ashland County, Ohio.* 1874. Condit, OH. ils. 124p. VG. B18. $175.00

CALDWELL, Steven. *Aliens in Space.* 1979. Crescent. F/F. P3. $8.00

CALDWELL, Taylor. *Earth Is the Lord's.* 1941. Scribner. 1st ed. NF/VG. B4. $75.00

CALDWELL, Taylor. *There Was a Time.* 1947. Scribner. 1st ed. VG/VG. P3. $25.00

CALHOUN, Frances Boyd. *Miss Minerva & William Green Hill.* 1909. Reilly Britton. 212p. VG. M20. $20.00

CALHOUN, Frances Boyd. *Miss Minerva & William Green Hill.* 1919. Chicago. Reilly Lee. 44th. 12mo. F/VG. C8. $55.00

CALHOUN, Mary. *House of Thirty Cats.* 1965. Harper Row. ils Mary Chalmers. 219p. F/F. P2. $18.00

CALHOUN, Mary. *Katie John.* 1960. Harper. possible 1st ed. 8vo. 134p. gr cloth. VG/VG. T5. $30.00

CALHOUN & MCCAFFERY. *Flower Mother.* 1972. Morrow. 1st ed. sm 4to. unp. ils brd. VG/NF. C14. $14.00

CALI, Francois. *Bruges of Cradle of Flemish Painting.* 1964. 1st ed. NF/VG+. S13. $18.00

CALISHER, Hortense. *Journal From Ellipsia.* 1965. Little Brn. 1st ed. NF/NF. B35. $20.00

CALISHER, Hortense. *New Yorkers.* 1969. Little Brn. ARC/1st ed. inscr/dtd 1973. RS. F/dj. B4. $125.00

CALISHER, Hortense. *On Keeping Women.* 1977. Arbor. ARC. inscr. F/F. w/promo material & photo. B4. $100.00

CALKINS, Mary Whiton. *Persistent Problems of Philosophy: Intro to Metaphysics...* 1907. Macmillan. 575p. panelled gr cloth. VG. G1. $50.00

CALL, Deborah. *Art of the Empire Strikes Back.* 1980. Ballantine. 1st ed. F/F. P3. $45.00

CALLAGHAN, Morley. *That Summer in Paris: Memories of Tangled Friendships...* nd. UK. 1st ed. VG/VG. M17. $20.00

CALLAHAM, Robert E. *Heart of an Indian.* 1927. NY. Hitchcock. Autograph ed. 8vo. inscr. 339p. w/color photo. VG. T10. $45.00

CALOGERAS, Jaao P. *History of Brazil.* 1963. NY. xl. VG. O7. $15.00

CALOMIRIS, Angela. *Red Masquerade. Undercover for the FBI.* 1950. Lippincott. 1st ed. F/NF. B2. $40.00

CALTHROP, D.C. *English Costume.* 1925. London. Blk. xl. cloth. G. D2. $20.00

CALVI, Gerolamo. *I Manoscritti di Leonardo da Vinci.* 1925. Bologna. Zanichelli. ils 323p. D2. $65.00

CALVINO, Italo. *Invisible Cities.* 1972. Harcourt. 1st Am ed. F/NF. C2. $100.00

CALVINO, Italo. *Path to the Nest of Spiders.* 1957. Beacon. 1st Am ed. NF/NF. C2. $75.00

CALVINO, Italo. *Silent Mr Palomar.* 1981. Targ. 1st ed. 1/250. sgn. F/NF. C2. $175.00

CALVINO, Italo. *Watcher & Other Stories.* 1971. Harcourt. 1st Am ed. F/NF. C2. $75.00

CALVOCORESSI & WINT. *Total War: Story of WWII.* 1972. NY. 1st Am ed. 959p. cloth. VG. A17. $10.00

CAM, Helen. *Selected Historical Essays of FW Maitland.* 1957. Cambridge. 13 essays. G/worn. M11. $85.00

CAMBPELL, Bebe Moore. *Sweet Summer.* 1989. Putnam. 1st ed. sgn/dtd 1992. F/dj. S9. $55.00

CAMDEN, John. *Hundreth Acre.* 1905. Turner. 1st ed. G. P3. $20.00

CAMERON, Eleanor. *Time & Mr Bass, a Mushroom Planet Book.* 1967. Little Brn/Atlantic Monthly. 6th. 8vo. xl. G. T5. $30.00

CAMERON, Ian. *Mountains of the Gods.* 1984. NY. VG. O7. $35.00

CAMERON, James. *Witness; or, Here Is Your Enemy.* 1966. HRW. 1st ed. mock-up copy w/7 photos. gr cloth. NF. S9. $125.00

CAMERON, Katherine. *Where the Bee Sucks.* nd. Hale Cushman Flint. sm 4to. 12 pl. gilt lettered gr cloth. VG+. M5. $75.00

CAMERON, L.C.R. *Hunting Horn.* nd. London. Kohler. 27p. VG/wrp. O3. $10.00

CAMERON, Lucy Lyttleton. *Warning Clock; or, Voice of the New Year.* 1827. Wellington Salop Houlston. 6th. 3 woodcuts. VG. T10. $35.00

CAMERON, Owen. *Butcher's Wife.* 1954. Simon Schuster. 1st ed. VG/G. P3. $20.00

CAMMELL, C.R. *Aleister Croweley: The Man, the Mage, the Poet.* 1951. London. 1st ed. photos/ils. 230p. G. B5. $45.00

CAMP, John. *Fool's Run.* 1989. Holt. 1st ed. F/NF. M23. $25.00

CAMP, Raymond R. *All Seasons Afield With Rod & Gun.* 1939. Whittlesey. 1st ed. inscr. 8vo. 352p. VG. B11. $50.00

CAMP & FRANCIS. *Making, Shaping & Treating of Steel.* 1951. Pittsburgh. ARC/6th. VG. V4. $75.00

CAMP & WAGNER. *Plains & the Rockies, a Bibliography of Original Narratives.* 1937. revised/expanded. 1/600. 308p. VG. A4. $175.00

CAMPA, Arthur L. *Treasure of the Sangre de Cristos.* 1963. Norman, OK. 1st ed. 8vo. 223p. red cloth. F/dj. T10. $35.00

CAMPAN, Madame. *Memoirs of Marie Antoinette.* nd. Collier. NF. P3. $15.00

CAMPBELL, Archibald. *Survey of the Northern Boundary of the US.* 1878. WA. 1st ed. 7 fld map. 624p. VG. B5. $350.00

CAMPBELL, Bebe Moore. *Brothers & Sisters.* 1994. Putnam. AP. NF/wrp. M19. $35.00

CAMPBELL, Bruce. *Secret of Skeleton Island.* 1949. Grosset Dunlap. VG. P3. $6.00

CAMPBELL, Bruce. *Where the High Winds Blow.* 1946. Scribner. ils P Bear. 215p. VG/dj. T7. $24.00

CAMPBELL, Charles Macfie. *Problems of Personality...* (1925). Harcourt Brace. 434p. gr cloth. G1. $37.50

CAMPBELL, Charles Macfie. *Problems of Personality...* (1925). London. Kegan Paul. 1st ed. 343p. bl-gr cloth. VG. G1. $65.00

CAMPBELL, Douglas. *Evolution of the Land Plants.* 1940. Stanford. ils. 731p. VG. B26. $24.00

CAMPBELL, George. *Eastwood: Notes on Ecclesiastical Antiquities of the Parish.* 1902. Paisley. Alexander Gardner. 154p. VG. T10. $150.00

CAMPBELL, H.J. *Beyond the Visible.* 1952. Hamilton. 1st ed. VG/VG. P3. $25.00

CAMPBELL, H.J. *Case for Mrs Surratt.* 1943. NY. 1st ed. 272p. G-. B18. $25.00

CAMPBELL, J.F. *Leabhar Na Feinne.* 1872. London. Spottiswoode. 224p. gr cloth. xl. VG. T10. $175.00

CAMPBELL, John Lord. *Lives of the Chief Justices of England. Six Volumes.* 1873-1875. NY. Cockcroft. gilt gr cloth. G. M11. $350.00

CAMPBELL, John Lord. *Lives of the Chief Justices of England... Five Volumes.* 1894-1899. Long Island. Edward Thomson. M11. $850.00

CAMPBELL, John Lord. *Lives of the Lord Chancellors & Keepers of the Great Seal...* 1846-1849. London. John Murray. 8 vol. 3-quarter morocco. M11. $1,250.00

CAMPBELL, John W. *Analog 8.* 1971. Doubleday. 1st ed. VG/VG. P3. $18.00

CAMPBELL, John W. *Cloak of Aesir.* 1953. Shasta. NF/VG+. G10. $55.00

CAMPBELL, John. *Black Star Passes.* 1953. Fantasy. 1st ed. VG/VG. M19. $75.00

CAMPBELL, Joseph. *Flight of the Wild Gander.* 1969. 1st ed. VG/G. M19. $25.00

CAMPBELL, Karen. *Wheel of Fortune.* 1973. Bobbs Merrill. 1st ed. VG/VG. P3. $15.00

CAMPBELL, Mary B. *Witness & the Other World.* 1988. Ithaca. VG. O7. $25.00

CAMPBELL, Mary Mason. *New England Butt'ry Shelf Almanac.* 1970. World. 1st ed. ils Tasha Tudor. 302p. VG+/dj. M20. $55.00

CAMPBELL, Ramsey. *Alone With the Horrors: Great Short Fiction of...* 1993. Arkham. 1st ed. F/F. T2. $27.00

CAMPBELL, Ramsey. *Count of Eleven.* 1992. Tor. 1st ed. NF/NF. P3. $20.00

CAMPBELL, Ramsey. *Dark Companions.* 1982. Macmillan. 1st ed. F/F. P3. $60.00

CAMPBELL, Ramsey. *Dark Feasts: World of Ramsey Campbell.* 1987. London. Robinson. 1st ed. 1/400. F/F. T2. $45.00

CAMPBELL, Ramsey. *Demons by Daylight.* 1973. Arkham. 1st ed. 1/3500. F/NF. R10. $25.00

CAMPBELL, Ramsey. *Doll Who Ate His Mother.* 1976. Bobbs Merrill. 1st ed. F/F. P3. $125.00

CAMPBELL, Ramsey. *Height of the Scream.* 1976. Arkham. 1st ed. 1/4348. F/F. T2. $12.00

CAMPBELL, Ramsey. *Hungry Moon.* 1987. London. Century. 1st ed. inscr. F/F. T2. $35.00

CAMPBELL, Ramsey. *Incarnate.* 1983. ARC. NF/wrp. M19. $35.00

CAMPBELL, Ramsey. *Incarnate.* 1983. Macmillan. 1st ed. F/NF. N4. $40.00

CAMPBELL, Ramsey. *Influence.* 1988. Macmillan. 1st ed. rem mk. NF/VG. N4. $17.50

CAMPBELL, Ramsey. *Needing Ghosts.* 1990. London. Century. 1st ed. 1/300. sgn. F/F. T2. $55.00

CAMPBELL, Ramsey. *Parasite.* 1980. Macmillan. 1st Am ed. NF/VG+. R10. $10.00

CAMPBELL, Ramsey *Strange Things & Stranger Places.* 1993. Tor. 1st ed. F/NF. G10. $12.00

CAMPBELL, Ramsey. *Superhorror.* 1976. WH Allen. 1st ed. F/F. P3. $35.00

CAMPBELL, Robert. *Alice in La-La Land.* 1987. Poseidon. 1st ed. rem mk. F/F. H11. $25.00

CAMPBELL, Robert. *Alice in La-La Land.* 1987. Poseidon. 1st ed. VG/VG. P3. $17.00

CAMPBELL, Robert. *Cat's Meow.* 1988. NAL. 2nd. VG/VG. P3. $15.00

CAMPBELL, Robert. *In a Pig's Eye.* 1991. Pocket. 1st ed. F/F. H11/N4. $20.00

CAMPBELL, Robert. *Juice.* 1988. Poseidon. 1st ed. F/F. H11. $25.00

CAMPBELL, Robert. *Nibbled to Death by Ducks.* 1989. Pocket. 1st ed. F/F. P3. $18.00

CAMPBELL, Roy. *Flaming Terrapin.* 1924. Dial. 1st Am ed. author's 1st book. F/NF. B2. $85.00

CAMPBELL, Sam. *Loony Coon.* 1954. Bobbs Merrill. 236p. VG+/dj. M20. $12.00

CAMPBELL, Thomas J. *Jesuits 1534-1921.* 1921. NY. 937p. gilt cloth. A17. $25.00

CAMPBELL, Tony. *Earliest Printed Maps, 1472-1500.* 1987. Berkeley. 222 maps. AN/dj. O7. $85.00

CAMPBELL, W.W. *Biographical Memoir: Simon Newcomb 1835-1909.* 1924. WA, DC. cloth. xl. G. K5. $75.00

CAMPBELL, Will D. *Brother to a Dragonfly.* 1977. Seabury. 1st ed. F/F. B35. $13.00

CAMPBELL & JACCHIA. *Story of Variable Stars.* 1945 (1941). Phil. Blakiston. 2nd prt. cloth. VG. K5. $20.00

CAMPBELL-WALKER, Arthur. *Correct Card on How To Play Whist.* 1878. London. 5th. 79p. VG. S1. $15.00

CAMSELL, Charles. *Son of the North.* 1954. Toronto. 1st ed. ils. 244p. VG/VG. B5. $25.00

CAMUS, Albert. *Exile & the Kingdom.* 1958. Knopf. 1st ed. F/NF. B35. $40.00

CAMUS, Albert. *Happy Death.* 1972. Knopf. 1st Am ed. F/VG. M19. $35.00

CAMUS, Albert. *Lyrical & Critical Essays.* 1968. Knopf. 1st Am ed. F/VG. M19. $35.00

CAMUS, J.M. *World of Ferns.* 1991. London. ils. 112p. sc. F. B26. $22.50

CANBY, Peter. *Heart of the Sky.* 1992. Collins. 1st ed. 368p. dj. F3. $20.00

CANFIELD, Dorothy. *Bonfire.* 1933. Harcourt Brace. 1st ed. NF/VG. B4. $85.00

CANFIELD, Dorothy. *Fables for Parents.* 1937. Harcourt Brace. 1st ed. F/NF. M19. $35.00

CANGUILHEM, Georges. *Ideologie et Rationalite dans l'Histories des Science...* 1977. Paris. 1st ed. 145p. VG/wrp. A13. $20.00

CANIN, Ethan. *Blue River.* 1991. Houghton Mifflin. 1st ed. F/F. B35/H11. $28.00

CANIN, Ethan. *Emperor of the Air.* 1988. Houghton Mifflin. 1st ed. sgn. F/F. B35. $65.00

CANIN, Ethan. *Palace Thief.* 1994. Random. 1st ed. F/F. B35. $30.00

CANNING, Victor. *Dragon Tree.* 1958. Sloane. 1st ed. NF/NF. P3. $45.00

CANNING, Victor. *Mr Finchley Goes to Paris.* 1938. Carrick Evans. 1st ed. VG/fair. P3. $25.00

CANNING, Victor. *Mr Finchley's Holiday.* 1935. Reynal Hitchcock. 1st ed. NF/VG+. B4. $75.00

CANNING, Victor. *Python Project.* 1968. Morrow. 1st ed. F/F. P3. $15.00

CANNING, Victor. *Rainbird Pattern.* 1972. Morrow. 1st Am ed. NF/VG. M22. $15.00

CANNON, Curt; see Hunter, Evan.

CANNON, Peter H. *Scream for Jeeves: A Parody.* 1994. Woodcraft. 1st ed. 1/250. F/F. T2. $45.00

CANNON, Walter Bradford. *Bodily Changes in Pain, Hunger, Fear & Rage.* 1915. Appleton. 311p. ruled panelled russet cloth. VG. G1. $100.00

CANNON & MAYALL. *Annie J Cannon Memorial Vol of Henry Draper Extension.* 1949. Cambridge. Harvard. 2nd. 295p. VG/wrp. K5. $45.00

CANNON. *American Book Collectors & Collecting From Colonial Times...* 1941. np. 402p. VG. A4. $135.00

CANNY & HEARTMAN. *Bibliography of First Printings of Writings of EA Poe.* 1943. np. revised. 295p. ES. VG. A4. $195.00

CANTLEY, Marjorie. *Building a Home in Sweden.* 1931. Macmillan. 1st ed. ils Helen Sewell. G+. P2. $15.00

CANTOR, Norman F. *Civilization of the Middle Ages.* 1994. Harper Collins. 1st ed. F/F. B35. $25.00

CANTOR, Norman F. *Medieval Lives.* 1994. Harper Collins. 1st ed. F/F. B35. $18.00

CANTY, Kevin. *Stranger in This World.* 1994. Doubleday. 1st ed. author's 1st book. F/F. M23. $40.00

CAPA, Robert. *Robert Capa 1913-1954.* 1974. NY. Grossman. 1st ed thus. 8vo. VG/prt wrp. S9. $55.00

CAPE, Tony. *Cambridge Theorem.* 1990. Doubleday. 1st ed. NF/NF. P3. $20.00

CAPEK, Lou E. *West Winds II.* 1974. Vantage. 1st ed. sgn. 216p. F/VG. B11. $25.00

CAPELL, F. *Strange Death of Marilyn Monroe.* 1964. Zarephath, NJ. 1st ed. VG/wrp. B5. $50.00

CAPERS, Ellison. *Confederate Military History: South Carolina.* 1976. Syracuse, NY. Bl & Gray. rpt of 1899 ed. F/NF. M8. $20.00

CAPERTON, Helena Lefroy. *Legends of Virginia.* 1931. Garrett Massie. inscr pres. 74p. VG/fair. B10. $25.00

CAPLAN, W.M. *Subsurface Geology & Related Oil & Gas Possiblities...* 1954. Little Rock. AR Resources & Development Comm Bulletin #20. VG. D8. $16.00

CAPOTE, Truman. *Christmas Memory.* 1956. Random. 4th. VG/box. B10. $12.00

CAPOTE, Truman. *Christmas Memory.* 1989. Knopf. 1st thus. ils Beth Peck. F/F. B17. $8.00

CAPOTE, Truman. *In Cold Blood.* 1965. NY. 1st ed. VG/VG. H7. $15.00

CAPOTE, Truman. *Muses Are Heard.* 1956. NY. 1st ed. NF/NF. C6. $75.00

CAPOTE, Truman. *Music for Chameleons.* 1980. Random. 1st trade ed. sgn. F/F. M22. $95.00

CAPOTE, Truman. *One Christmas.* 1983. Random. 1st ed. 1/500. sgn. F/case. B24. $275.00

CAPOTE, Truman. *Tree of Night & Other Stories.* 1949. Random. 1st ed. author's 2nd book. NF/VG. S9. $125.00

CAPP, Lil. *Best of Lil Abner.* 1978. Holt. ils. 190p. F. M13. $19.00

CAPPON, Lester J. *Atlas of Early American History: Revolutionary Era...* 1976. Newberry Lib. 285 maps. AN/dj. O7. $225.00

CAPPS, Benjamin. *Women of the People.* 1966. DSP. 1st ed. F/VG+. A18. $25.00

CAPUTO, Philip. *DelCorso's Gallery.* 1983. Holt. 1st ed. F/NF. H11. $30.00

CAPUTO, Philip. *DelCorso's Gallery.* 1983. HRW. 2nd. sgn. VG/VG. B11. $25.00

CAPUTO, Philip. *Horn of Africa.* 1980. HRW. 1st ed. author's 2nd book. F/F. B35/H11. $30.00

CAPUTO, Philip. *Horn of Africa.* 1980. HRW. 1st ed. sgn. VG/F. A20. $40.00

CAPUTO, Philip. *Indian Country.* 1987. np. 1st ed. author's 3rd book. F/NF. B35. $21.00

CAPUTO, Philip. *Means of Escape.* 1991. Harper Collins. 1st ed. sgn. B stp on bottom edges. F/F. H11. $50.00

CAPUTO, Philip. *Rumor of War.* 1977. HRW. 1st ed. author's 1st book. F/F. H11. $60.00

CAPUTO, Philip. *Rumor of War.* 1977. HRW. 1st ed. author's 1st book. NF/NF. B35. $45.00

CARCATERRA, Lorenzo. *Safe Place.* 1992. Villard. 1st ed. AN/dj. M22. $50.00

CARCATERRA, Lornezo. *Sleepers.* 1995. Ballantine. 1st ed. author's 2nd book. F/F. H11. $40.00

CARD, Orson Scott. *Abyss.* 1989. Legend/Century. 1st hc ed. AN/dj. M21. $30.00

CARD, Orson Scott. *Call of Earth.* 1993. Tor. 1st ed. F/F. P3. $25.00

CARD, Orson Scott. *Cardography.* 1987. Hypatia. ltd ed. 1/750. sgn/#d. F/F. M19. $125.00

CARD, Orson Scott. *Lost Boys.* 1992. Harper Collins. 1st ed. F/NF. G10. $25.00

CARD, Orson Scott. *Memory of Earth.* 1992. Tor. 1st ed. F/F. G10. $12.00

CARD, Orson Scott. *Prentice Alvin.* 1989. Tor. 1st ed. sgn. F/F. M23. $35.00

CARD, Orson Scott. *Red Prophet.* 1988. Tor. 1st ed. sgn. F/F. M23. $40.00

CARD, Orson Scott. *Seventh Son.* 1987. Tor. 1st ed. F/F. G10. $35.00

CARD, Orson Scott. *Seventh Son.* 1987. Tor. 1st ed. sgn. F/F. M23. $45.00

CARD, Orson Scott. *Songmaster.* 1980. Dial. 1st ed. VG/VG. M21. $50.00

CARD, Orson Scott. *Speaker for the Dead.* 1986. Tor. 1st ed. inscr. NF/F. M19. $125.00

CARD, Orson Scott. *Tales of Alvin Maker Trilogy: Seventh Son, Red Prophet...* 1987-89. Tor. 1st ed. 3 sgn vol. F/dj. C2. $150.00

CARD, Orson Scott. *Treason.* 1988. St Martin. 1st ed. F/F. P3. $35.00

CARD, Orson Scott. *Unacompanied Sonata & Other Stories.* 1981. Dial. 1st ed. F/VG+. G10. $55.00

CARD, Orson Scott. *Wyrms.* 1987. Arbor. 1st ed. F/NF. G10. $15.00

CARD, Orson Scott. *Xenocide.* 1991. Tor. 1st ed. G10/P3. $22.00

CAREW, Thomas. *Rapture.* 1927. Golden Cockeral. ils JE Laboueur. 14p. VG/dj. M20. $112.00

CAREY, Arthur A. *Memoirs of a Murder Man.* 1930. Doubleday Doran. 1st ed. VG. P3. $20.00

CAREY, George G. *Sailor's Songbag.* 1976. Amherst. VG. O7. $20.00

CAREY, Jacqueline. *Good Gossip.* 1992. Random. 1st ed. author's 1st book. F/F. B4. $45.00

CAREY, Peter. *Illywhacker.* 1985. Harper Row. 1st ed. F/F. M23. $30.00

CAREY, Peter. *Oscar & Lucinda.* 1988. NY. Harper. 1st Am ed. F/dj. C2. $50.00

CAREY, Peter. *Tax Inspector.* 1991. Franklin. 1st ed (precedes trade) ed. sgn. F. M19. $50.00

CARFAX, Catherine. *Silence With Voices.* 1969. Macmillan. 1st ed. VG/VG. P3. $20.00

CARGILL, Morris. *Ian Fleming Introduces Jamaica.* 1965. Andre Deutsch. 1st ed. VG/G. P3. $30.00

CARGILL, Morris. *Ian Fleming Introduces Jamaica.* 1965. London. Andre Deutsch. 2nd. F/F. T2. $35.00

CARLE, Eric. *Very Busy Spider.* 1984. Philomel. 1st ed. 8vo. VG. B17. $10.00

CARLSON, Bruce. *Ghosts of Scott County, IA.* 1987. Quixote. 1st ed. sgn. VG+. M21. $20.00

CARLSON, P.M. *Murder Misread.* 1990. Crime Club. 1st ed. VG/VG. P3. $15.00

CARLYLE, Thomas. *Letters to His Wife.* 1953. Harvard. 1st ed. VG+/VG. S13. $20.00

CARLYON, Richard. *Dark Lord of Pengersick.* 1980. FSG. 1st ed. F/F. P3. $15.00

CARMAN & THOMPSON. *Guide to the Principal Sources for American Civilization...* 1960. NY. VG. O7. $45.00

CARMAN & THOMPSON. *Guide to the Principle Sources for American Civilization...* 1962. Columbia. 676p. F/NF. A4. $65.00

CARMER, Carl. *Cavalcade of Young Americans.* 1958. Columbus. ils Howard Simon. 128p. wrp. A17. $4.50

CARMER, Carl. *Farm Boy & the Angel.* 1970. Garden City. 1st ed. VG/VG. B5. $30.00

CARMER, Carl. *Hurricane's Children.* 1937. NY. 1st ed. VG/VG. B5. $25.00

CARMER, Carl. *Pets at the White House.* 1959. 1st ed. ils Savitt. VG/VG. S13. $15.00

CARMER, Carl. *Songs of the Rivers of America.* 1942. NY. 1st ed. VG/fair. B5. $145.00

CARMER, Carl. *Susquehanna.* 1955. NY. 1st ed. VG/VG. B5. $45.00

CARMICHAEL, Harry; see Creasey, John.

CARMICHAEL, John. *My Greatest Day in Baseball.* 1945. Barnes. 1st ed. photos. VG+/VG. P8. $30.00

CARMICHAEL, Robert D. *Theory of Relativity.* 1913. John Wiley. 1st ed. 8vo. 74p. G. K5. $25.00

CARMICHAEL & HAMILTON. *Black Power: Politics of Liberation in America.* 1967. Random. 1st ed. inscr/sgn pres by Carmichael. F/NF-. R11. $70.00

CARMICHEL, Jim. *Modern Rifle.* 1975. Winchester. 1st ed. phtos. NF/VG. P12. $12.50

CARO, Dennis R. *Devine War.* 1986. Arbor. 1st ed. RS. F/F. P3. $18.00

CARPENTER, Don. *Hard Rain Falling.* 1966. Harcourt Brace. 1st ed. author's 1st novel. F/dj. B24. $135.00

CARPENTER, Frank G. *From Tangier to Tripolii, Morocco, Algeria, Tunisia...* 1923. Doubleday Page. 1st ed. ils. 277p. VG. W1. $20.00

CARPENTER, Humphrey. *Tolkien: A Biography.* 1977. Houghton Mifflin. 1st ed. VG/VG. P3. $20.00

CARPENTER, J. Estlin. *Phases of Early Christianity.* 1916. Putnam. 1st ed. 8vo. 449p. VG. W1. $25.00

CARPENTER, Meta. *Loving Gentleman: Love Story of William Faulkner...* 1976. Simon Schuster. 1st ed. 334p. G/fair. B10. $15.00

CARPENTER, R.A. *Assessing Tropical Forest Lands.* 1981. Dublin. 1st ed. 337p. cloth. dj. B1. $30.00

CARPENTER, W.H. *History of Tennessee, From Its Earliest Settlement...* 1857. Phil. 284p. cloth. G+. B18. $35.00

CARPENTER, William B. *On the Use & Abuse of Alcoholic Liquors...* 1850. Lea Blanchard. 1st Am ed. F. N3. $95.00

CARPENTER, William B. *Principles of Mental Physiology...* 1888. London. Henry King. 6th. thick 12mo. 739p. VG. G1. $65.00

CARPENTER & FOWKE. *Bibliography of Canadian Folklore in English.* 1981. Toronto. 3877 annotated entries. 292p. F. A4. $55.00

CARPENTER. *First 350 Years of the Harvard University Library.* 1986. np. 4to. ils. 216p. F. A4. $45.00

CARR, Anthony. *Girl in Green.* 1959. Cassell. 1st ed. VG. P3. $15.00

CARR, Caleb. *Alienist.* 1994. Random. later prt. F/clip. N4. $22.50

CARR, Caleb. *Alienist.* 1994. Random. 1st ed. F/F. M22. $35.00

CARR, Caleb. *Devil Soldier.* 1992. NY. Random. 1st ed. F/F. H11. $65.00

CARR, Charles. *Colonists of Space.* 1954. Ward Lock. VG/VG. P3. $20.00

CARR, Harry. *Vaya Con Dios, Will.* 1935. Angelus Pr. 8vo. intro WS Hart. NF. T10. $500.00

CARR, Harry. *West Is Still Wild.* 1932. Houghton Mifflin. 1st ed. sgn. ils. tan cloth. VG. T10. $35.00

CARR, Jayge. *Ghosts' High Noon.* 1969. Harper Row. 1st ed. xl. dj. P3. $10.00

CARR, Jayge. *It Walks by Night.* 1930. Harper. 4th. VG. P3. $50.00

CARR, Jayge. *Leviathan's Deep.* 1979. Doubleday. F/F. P3. $15.00

CARR, Jayge. *Patrick Butler for the Defense.* nd. BC. VG/VG. P3. $8.00

CARR, Jayge. *Scandal at High Chimneys.* 1959. Hamish Hamilton. 1st ed. NF/NF. P3. $35.00

CARR, Jayge. *Three Coffins.* 1935. Harper. 2nd. VG. P3. $20.00

CARR, Jayge. *Treasure in the Heart of the Maze.* 1985. Doubleday. 1st ed. rem mk. F/F. G10. $15.00

CARR, John Dickson. *Dead Sleep Lightly.* 1983. Doubleday. 1st ed. 8vo. 181p. F/dj. T10. $100.00

CARR, John Dickson. *Gilded Man.* 1942. Morrow. 1st ed. xl. VG. P3. $15.00

CARR, John Dickson. *Problem of the Wire Cage.* 1939. Harper. 1st ed. 296p. orante cloth. VG+. B22. $9.00

CARR, Joseph J. *Old-Time Radios! Restoration & Repair.* 1991. Tab. 4to. ils. 256p. VG. K5. $15.00

CARR, Lucien. *Missouri: A Bone of Contention.* 1888. Boston. xl. VG. O7. $15.00

CARR, Michael H. *Geology of the Terrestrial Planets.* 1984. NASA. 4to. 317p. pict brd. K5. $40.00

CARR, Terry. *Best SF of the Year #6.* 1977. HRW. 1st ed. F/F. P3. $18.00

CARR, Terry. *Infinite Arena.* 1977. Thomas Nelson. 1st ed. VG/VG. P3. $18.00

CARR, Terry. *Universe 17.* 1987. Doubleday. 1st ed. RS. F/F. P3. $18.00

CARR, Winifred. *Hussein's Kingdom.* 1966. London. Frewin. 1st ed. 8vo. ils. 176p. VG/dj. W1. $20.00

CARRASCO, David. *Quetzalcoatl & the Irony of Empire.* 1985. Chicago U. 233p. wrp. F3. $15.00

CARRASCO & MOCTEZUMA. *Moctezuma's Mexico.* 1992. Niwot. CO U. 1st ed. 4to. 188p. F/dj. T10. $50.00

CARRILLO, Leo. *California I Love.* 1961. Englewood Cliffs. 1st ed. 8vo. ils Don Perceval. 280p. F/VG. T10. $35.00

CARRINGTON, Grant. *Time's Fool.* 1981. Doubleday. 1st ed. F/F. P3. $13.00

CARRINGTON, Hereward. *Psychical Phenomena & the War.* 1920. Am U Pub. 2nd. 12mo. 364p. cloth-backed brd. VG. G1. $37.50

CARROLL, Earl. *Body Merchant: Story of Earl Carroll.* 1976. Ward Ritchie. 1st ed. F/VG. D2. $20.00

CARROLL, Gladys Hasty. *Light Here Kindled.* 1967. Little Brn. 1st ed. NF/NF. B35. $30.00

CARROLL, John A. *Reflections of Western Historians.* 1969. Tucson. 1st ed. 314p. AN/dj. P4. $20.00

CARROLL, Jonathan. *After Silence.* 1992. London. MacDonald. 1st ed. F/F. T2. $30.00

CARROLL, Jonathan. *Black Cocktail.* 1990. Legend. 1st ed. F/F. P3. $25.00

CARROLL, Jonathan. *Bones of the Moon.* 1987. Arbor. 1st Am ed. F/F. G10. $15.00

CARROLL, Jonathan. *Child Across the Sky.* 1989. Legend. 1st ed. F/F. P3. $25.00

CARROLL, Jonathan. *Outside the Dog Museum.* 1991. McDonald. 1st ed. F/F. G10. $30.00

CARROLL, Lewis. *Alice in Wonderland.* ca 1920. Ward Lock. VG/VG. M19. $50.00

CARROLL, Lewis. *Alice in Wonderland.* nd. London. Juvenile Prod. ils/8 pl. 190p. VG+. M5. $110.00

CARROLL, Lewis. *Alice in Wonderland.* nd. McKay. ils Lucie Atwell. VG. M5. $275.00

CARROLL, Lewis. *Alice in Wonderland.* 1990. NJ. Unicorn. 4th. unp. laminated brd. F. T5. $15.00

CARROLL, Lewis. *Alice's Adventures in Wonderland & Through Looking Glass.* nd. McKay. rpt. 12mo. G+. B17. $15.00

CARROLL, Lewis. *Alice's Adventures in Wonderland.* before 1908. Toronto. Musson. 1st ed thus. Ils BG Pease. bl cloth. NM/VG. D1. $250.00

CARROLL, Lewis. *Alice's Adventures in Wonderland.* nd. Whittlesey. 2nd. sm 4to. ils Tenniel. VG+/worn. M5. $12.00

CARROLL, Lewis. *Alice's Adventures in Wonderland.* 1922. Dodd Mead. 1st Am ed thus. ils G Hudson. emb gr brd. NF/VG. D1. $375.00

CARROLL, Lewis. *Alice's Adventures in Wonderland.* 1982. Berkeley. 1st trade ed. folio. F/F. B4. $100.00

CARROLL, Lewis. *Alice's Adventures in Wonderland.* 1982. CA U. 1st ed. ils/sgn Barry Moser. red cloth. F/case. D1. $225.00

CARROLL, Lewis. *Alice's Adventures in Wonderland.* 1985. Holt. 2nd. ils Michael Hague. VG/VG. B17. $12.00

CARROLL, Lewis. *Alice's Adventures in Wonderland/Through the Looking Glass.* 1883. Macmillan. new ed/50th thousand. ils Tenniel. bl cloth. G+. M5. $30.00

CARROLL, Lewis. *Alice's Adventures in Wonderland/Through the Looking Glass.* 1946. Random. 2 vol. 8vo. ils Fritz Kredel. F/G case. M5. $25.00

CARROLL, Lewis. *Alice's Adventures Under Ground.* 1886. London. Macmillan. 1st/only ed. facsimile of orig ms book. inscr. aeg. B24. $4,750.00

CARROLL, Lewis. *Complete Alice & Hunting of the Snark.* 1987. Salem House. 1st collected ed. ils Ralph Steadman. 336p. F/dj. S9. $75.00

CARROLL, Lewis. *Hunting of the Snark.* 1981. Los Altos. Centennial ed. 1/1955. ils Henry Holiday. linen. F. A17. $35.00

CARROLL, Lewis. *Rhyme? And Reason?* 1888. Macmillan. ils Frost/Holiday. 214p. red cloth. D1. $150.00

CARROLL, Lewis. *Tangled Tale.* 1885. London. 1st ed. ils AB Frost. VG. A11. $65.00

CARROLL, Lewis. *Through the Looking Glass & What Alice Found There.* 1983. Berkeley. 1st trade ed. ils/sgn Barry Moser. w/poster. B4. $100.00

CARROLL, Lewis. *Through the Looking Glass.* nd. Whittlesey. 1st ed? sm 4to. VG+/G. M5. $16.00

CARROLL, Lewis. *Verses From Alice.* (1944). London. Collins. 1st ed thus. ils. gilt bl cloth. VG/VG. D1. $225.00

CARROLL, Robert S. *Old at Forty; or, Young at Sixty Simplifying Science...* 1920. NY. Macmillan. inscr/dtd 1920. 147p. bl cloth. VG. B14. $45.00

CARROLL, Ruth. *Bounce & the Bunnies.* 1934. Reynal Hitchcock. 1st ed. VG. P2. $30.00

CARROLL, Ruth. *Chessie.* 1936. Messner. 1st ed. ils Ruth Carroll. gr cloth. VG. D1. $50.00

CARROLL & CARROLL. *Luck of the Roll & Go.* 1935. Macmillan. 1st ed. 12mo. 132p. G+. C14. $10.00

CARRUTH, Hayden. *Aura, a Poem.* 1977. W Burke, VT. Janus. 1/50. folio portfolio. AN/linen clamshell box/paper label. B24. $4,250.00

CARRUTH, William Herbert. *Each in His Own Tongue.* 1925. Volland-Wise Parslow. 12mo. ils. VG/dj. M5. $12.00

CARSON, Jane. *Colonial Virginia Cookery.* 1968. Colonial Williamsburg. 1st ed. sgn. 8vo. 212p. VG/wrp. B11. $15.00

CARSON, R. *Sea Around Us.* 1951. Oxford. 22nd. 230p. pict brd. VG. D8. $8.00

CARSON, Rachel. *Sea Around Us.* 1951. NY. Oxford. 1st ed. inscr. NF/NF. C2. $250.00

CARSON, Rachel. *Sea Around Us.* 1980. LEC. 1/2000. sgn. photos Eisenstadt. full cloth. F/NF case. B4. $175.00

CARSON, Rachel. *Silent Spring.* 1962. 1st ed. VG/VG. S13. $30.00

CARSTAIRS, G.M. *This Island Now.* 1963. London. 103p. VG/dj. A13. $25.00

CARTER, Angela. *American Ghosts & Old World Scholars.* 1993. Chatto Windus. 1st ed. F/F. G10. $25.00

CARTER, Angela. *Artificial Fire.* 1988. McClelland Stewart. 1st ed. F/F. P3. $25.00

CARTER, Angela. *Fireworks.* 1981. Harper Row. 1st ed. NF/NF. P3. $30.00

CARTER, Angela. *Wise Children.* 1991. Canada. Little Brn. 1st ed. F/F. P3. $20.00

CARTER, Craig J.M. *Ships Annual, 1958.* 1958. London. Allen. 96p. VG/dj. T7. $30.00

CARTER, G.S. *General Zoology of the Invertebrates.* 1948. Sidgwick Jackson. 3rd. 13 pl/ils. cloth. clip dj. B11. $35.00

CARTER, Helen. *Book of Insect Oddities.* 1938. Jr Literary Guild. 4to. ils. VG. B17. $7.50

CARTER, Hodding. *Angry Scar: Story of Reconstruction.* 1959. Doubleday. 425p. G/G. B10. $20.00

CARTER, Jimmy. *Always a Reckoning.* 1995. 1st ed. sgn. NF/NF. S13. $55.00

CARTER, John. *Books & Book Collectors.* 1956. London. 196p. F/NF. A4. $85.00

CARTER, John. *Taste & Technique in Book Collecting.* 1948. np. 1st Am ed. 226p. NF/VG. A4. $85.00

CARTER, Lin. *Dreams From R'lyeh.* 1975. Arkham. 1st ed. 1/3252. F/F. T2. $35.00

CARTER, Lin. *Kingdoms of Sorcery.* 1976. Doubleday. 1st ed. F/F. P3. $23.00

CARTER, Lin. *Valley Where Time Stood Still.* 1974. Doubleday. 1st ed. NF/NF. P3. $20.00

CARTER, Lin. *Volcano Ogre.* 1976. Delacorte. 1st ed. F/F. P3. $15.00

CARTER, Lin. *Zakron, Lord of the Unknown, in Invisible Death.* 1975. Doubleday. NF/VG+. G10. $4.00

CARTER, Michelle. *On Other Days While Going Home.* 1987. Morrow. 1st ed. F/F. A20. $12.00

CARTER, Nick (a few); see Avallone, Mike.

CARTER, Paul. *Road to Botany Bay.* 1987. London. Faber. 1st ed. 384p. VG/dj. P4. $25.00

CARTER, Polly. *Harriet Tubman.* 1990. Silver Pr. 1st ed. unp. F. C14. $6.00

CARTER & HAMLET. *Land That I Love.* 1980. Tabor City. Atlantic. sgn. 8vo. VG/VG. B11. $20.00

CARTER & HOUGH. *Dream Season.* 1987. HBJ. 1st ed. F/F. P8. $50.00

CARTER & POLLARD. *Enquiry Into the Nature of Certain 19th-Century Pamphlets.* 1971. np. 412p. VG. A4. $95.00

CARTHEW, Thomas. *Reports of Cases Adjudged in Court of King's Bench...* 1728. London. Nutt Gosling. 1st ed. contemporary calf. M11. $250.00

CARTIER, Xam Wilson. *Be-Bop, Re-Bop.* 1987. Ballantine/Available. 1st ed. pbo. author's 1st novel. F/wrp. B4. $85.00

CARTIER, Xam Wilson. *Muse-Echo Blues.* 1991. Harmony. 1st ed. F/F. B4. $45.00

CARUANA, A.A. *Recent Discoveries at Notabile.* 1881. GPO. 1st ed. 11 mtd albumen photos. red cloth. VG. C6. $350.00

CARUSO, John Anthony. *Southern Frontier.* 1963. Bobbs Merrill. 1st ed. maps. 448p. VG. B10. $15.00

CARVER, J.A. *Infinity Link.* 1984. Bluejay. 1st ed. sgn. F/F. P3. $25.00

CARVER, J.A. *Rapture Effect.* 1987. Tor. 1st ed. RS. F/F. P3. $20.00

CARVER, Raymond. *Cathedral.* 1983. Knopf. 1st ed. F/NF. M19. $50.00

CARVER, Raymond. *Fires: Essays, Poems, Stories.* 1983. Santa Barbara. 1st ed. sgn. F. C2. $200.00

CARVER, Raymond. *My Father's Life.* 1986. Derrydale. 1st ed. 1/40. sgn. ils/sgn Schanilec. F/wrp. C2. $225.00

CARVER, Raymond. *Put Yourself in My Shoes.* 1974. Santa Barbara. Capra. 1st ed. inscr/dtd 1992. F/wrp. C2. $250.00

CARVER, Raymond. *Where I'm Calling From.* 1988. Franklin Lib. 1st ed. sgn. red/gilt stp leather. F. S9. $225.00

CARVER, Raymond. *Where I'm Calling From: New & Selected Stories.* 1988. Atlantic Monthly. 1st ed. F/dj. A18. $40.00

CARVIC, Heron. *Odds on Miss Seeton.* 1975. Harper Row. 1st ed. VG/VG. P3. $18.00

CARVIC, Heron. *Picture Miss Seeton.* 1968. Geoffrey Bles. 1st ed. VG/G. P3. $25.00

CARY, Joyce. *African Witch.* 1936. London. 1st ed. sgn. VG/VG. C2. $75.00

CARY, Joyce. *Memoirs of the Bibotes.* 1960. Austin, TX. 1st ed. 154p. VG. W1. $25.00

CARY, Joyce. *Prisoner of Grace.* 1952. Michael Joseph. 1st ed. 398p. VG+/dj. M20. $38.00

CARY, Mary. *Frequently Martha.* 1910. Harper. 167p. VG. B10. $10.00

CARY, Mary. *How It Happened.* 1914. Harper. ils. 164p. G. B10. $8.00

CARY, Mary. *Mary Cary.* 1910. Harper. 1st ed. NF/VG. B4. $85.00

CASE, David. *Third Grave.* 1981. Arkham. 1st ed. 1/4258. F/F. T2. $12.00

CASE, Robert Ormond. *Empire Builders.* 1949. Portland. Binfords Mort. revised ed. 8vo. 352p. map ep. F. T10. $45.00

CASEY, Michael. *Obscenities.* 1972. New Haven. Yale. ARC/1st ed. RS. F/F. B4. $125.00

CASEY, Robert E. *Declaration of Independence. Ils Story of Its Adaption...* ca 1920-30. Fredericksburg, VA. private prt. 192p. bl cloth. VG. B22. $7.00

CASEY, Robert J. *Baghdad & Points East.* 1931. McBride. 300p. G. W1. $12.00

CASEY & HACKLER. *Sensible Cruising.* 1986. Seascape Enterprises. 330p. VG/dj. T7. $20.00

CASO, Alfonso. *Aztecs: People of the Sun.* 1958. Norman, OK. 1st ed. ils Miguel Covarrubias. 125p. F/F. T10. $75.00

CASPAR, Franz. *Tupari.* 1956. London. VG. O7. $30.00

CASPARRI, Petro. *Tractatus Canonicus de Matrimonio. Third Edition.* 1904. Paris. Gabriel Beauchesne. gr cloth. M11. $45.00

CASPARY, Vera. *Weeping & the Laughter.* 1950. Little Brn. 1st ed. VG/VG. P3. $35.00

CASSANDRA, Knye; see Disch, Thomas.

CASSIDAY, Bruce. *Floater.* 1960. Abelard Schuman. VG/VG. P3. $20.00

CASSIDY, Jospeh. *Mexico: Land of Mary's Wonder.* 1958. NY. St Anthony Guild. 1st ed. photos. 192p. dj. F3. $25.00

CASSIDY, Maurice. *Coronary Disease, the Harveian Oration of 1946.* 1946. London. 1st ed. 16p. VG. A13. $20.00

CASTENEDA, Carlos. *Second Ring of Power.* 1977. NY. 1st ed. VG+/dj. H7. $20.00

CASTER, Pere. *Faites Votre Marche.* 1935. Paris. Flammarion. 1st ed. ils Nathalie Parain. VG. P2. $35.00

CASTLE, Dennis. *Pantomime Story of Aladdin.* nd. London. ils Darby Headley. uncut. VG+. M20. $62.00

CASTLEMON, Harry. *Don Gordon's Shooting Box.* 1883. Phil. 12mo. ils 352p. emb cloth. VG. A17. $10.00

CATE, Wirt A. *Lamar Secession & Reunion.* 1935. Chapel Hill. 1/400. VG/VG. M8. $250.00

CATE, Wirt A. *Lucius QC Lamar: Secession & Reunion.* 1935. Chapel Hill. 1st ed. 1/400. sgn. 594p. VG/dj. M8. $250.00

CATERPILLAR TRACTOR. *50 Years on the Tracks.* 1954. Peoria. 1st ed. photos. VG/VG. B5. $75.00

CATHER, Willa. *Death Comes for the Archbishop.* 1927. Knopf. 1st ed. 1/175. sgn. NF. B4. $1,250.00

CATHER, Willa. *December Night: A Scene From Willa Cather's Novel...* 1933. Knopf. 1st ed. ils Schmidt. F/dj. A18. $40.00

CATHER, Willa. *Life of Mary Baker G Eddy & History of Christian Science.* 1909. Doubleday Page. VG/dj. B4. $1,000.00

CATHER, Willa. *Lucy Gayheart.* 1935. Knopf. 1st ed. gr cloth/prt label. F/NF. B24. $125.00

CATHER, Willa. *My Mortal Enemy.* 1926. NY. 1st ed. VG/worn box. B5. $35.00

CATHER, Willa. *Not Under Forty.* 1936. Knopf. 1st ed. 1/333. sgn. bl cloth. F/dj/case. B24. $485.00

CATHER, Willa. *Obscure Destinies.* 1932. NY. 1st ed. VG/VG. B5. $75.00

CATHER, Willa. *Old Beauty & Others.* 1948. Knopf. 1st ed. VG/VG. A18. $30.00

CATHER, Willa. *Professor's House.* 1925. Knopf. 6th/Holiday ed. inscr. cloth/batik brd. NF/case. B4. $750.00

CATHER, Willa. *Sapphira & the Slave Girl.* 1940. Knopf. 1st ed. gr cloth. F/NF. B24. $165.00

CATHER, Willa. *Sapphira & the Slave Girl.* 1940. Knopf. 1st ed. VG/VG-. B10. $35.00

CATICH, Edward. *Origin of the Serif, Brush Writing & Roman Letters.* 1968. np. ltd ed. 4to. inscr. ils. 310p. F/VG. w/sgn letter. A4. $350.00

CATLIN, George. *North American Indians, Being Letters & Notes on Manners...* 19226. Edinburgh. John Grant. 2 vol. 8vo. teg. maroon cloth. xl. NF. T10. $750.00

CATLING, Patrick Skene. *Jazz Jazz Jazz.* 1981. St Martin. 1st ed. F/NF. B2. $25.00

CATLOW, Joseph Peel. *On the Principles of Aesthetic Medicine...* 1867. London /Birmingham. Churchill/Hudson. emb Victorian cloth. NF. G1. $275.00

CATTELL, Ann. *Mind Juggler & Other Ghost Stories.* 1966. Exposition. 1st ed. VG/VG. P3. $15.00

CATTON, Bruce. *Coming Fury.* 1961. Doubleday. 1st ed. 565p. VG/G. B10. $25.00

CATTON, Bruce. *Stillness at Appomattox.* 1953. NY. 8vo. 518p. tan/blk cloth. F/dj/box. T3. $10.00

CAUNITZ, William J. *Black Sand.* 1989. Crown. 1st ed. VG/VG. P3. $19.00

CAUNITZ, William J. *Exceptional Clearance.* 1991. Crown. 1st ed. F/F. N4. $20.00

CAUNITZ, William J. *One Police Plaza.* 1984. Crown. 1st ed. author's 1st book. F/F. H11. $50.00

CAUNITZ, William J. *Suspects.* 1986. Crown. 1st ed. NF/F. H11. $20.00

CAUZ, Louis. *Plate: A Royal Tradition.* 1984. Toronto. Ontario Jockey Club. 4to. VG/VG. O3. $65.00

CAVALCA, Alessandro. *Essamine Militare...* 1620. Venice. Sessa. 4to. 188p. contemporary vellum. K1. $450.00

CAVANAH, Frances. *Children of the White House.* 1936. 1st ed. ils Genevieve Foster. VG+/VG+. S13. $18.00

CAVANAH, Frances. *Louis of New Orleans.* 1941. McKay. ils Leonard Weisgard. pict brd. VG. B17. $6.50

CAVANNA, Betty. *Fancy Free.* 1961. Morrow. 1st ed. F/VG. M5. $28.00

CAVANNA, Betty. *Girl Can Dream.* 1958. Westminster. 189p. VG/G+. P2. $15.00

CAVANNA, Betty. *Passport to Romance.* 1955. Morrow. 1st ed. 249p. VG+/VG. P2. $20.00

CAVANOUGH & DAVIES. *Melbourne Cup.* 1973. Wellington. 4th. VG/VG. O3. $25.00

CAVE, C.J.P. *Structure of the Atmosphere in Clear Weather.* 1912. Cambridge. 144p. cloth. G. K5. $70.00

CAVE, Emma. *Blood Bond.* 1979. Harper Row. 1st ed. F/F. P3. $25.00

CAVE, Hugh B. *Cross on the Drum.* 1960. Werner Laurie. 1st ed. VG/VG. P3. $25.00

CAVE, Hugh B. *Disciples of Dread.* 1988. NY. Tor. 1st ed. sgn. F/F. T2. $25.00

CAVENDISH. *Laws & Principles of Whist.* 1897. Phil. 22nd. 186p. VG. S1. $10.00

CAVENDISH. *Laws of Piquet Adopted by Portland & Turf Club...* 1892. London. 8th. 208p. VG. S1. $8.00

CAVENDISH. *Whist Developments, American Leads & Plain-Suit Echo.* 1885. London. 2nd. 172p. VG. S1. $12.00

CAZORT. *Mr Jackson's Mushrooms.* 1979. Ottowa. National Gallery of Canada. sm folio. ils. 161p. F. A4. $50.00

CECIL, David. *English Poets.* 1942. London. Collins. thin 8vo. 8 pl. NF. T10. $10.00

CECIL, Henry. *Unlawful Occasions.* 1962. London. Michael Joseph. 1st ed. F/NF. M22. $25.00

CELINE, Louis-Ferdinand. *Journey to the End of the Night.* 1949. New Directions. ARC. RS. F/NF. B35. $46.00

CELINE, Louis-Ferdinand. *Rigadoon.* 1974. Delacorte. ARC/1st ed. RS. F/dj. S9. $60.00

CELLI, Rose. *Wild Animals & Their Little Ones.* 1935. Artists/Writers Guild. ils Rojankovsky. VG/stiff wrp. M5. $48.00

CERAM, C.W. *Gods, Graves & Scholars.* 1954. Knopf. 15th. ils. cloth. VG. W1. $16.00

CERF, Bennett. *Anything for a Laugh.* 1946. Grosset Dunlap. ils O'Connro Barrett. VG. P12. $4.00

CERF, Bennett. *Bennett Cerf's Bumper Crop.* 1956. Garden City. ils Paul Galdone. VG/G+. P12. $5.00

CERF, Bennett. *Encyclopedia of Modern Humor.* 1954. Doubleday. VG. P12. $5.00

CERF, Bennett. *Laugh Day.* 1965. Doubleday. 1st ed. inscr. RS. F/NF. T2. $45.00

CERVANTES, Fernando. *Devil in the New World.* 1994. Yale. ils/index. 182p. dj. F3. $25.00

CERWIN, Herbert. *These Are the Mexicans.* 1947. Reynal Hitchcock. ils/index. 384p. dj. F3. $15.00

CESS & SPARROW. *Radiation Heat Transfer.* 1966. Belmont, CA. 1st ed. 322p. VG/dj. P4. $20.00

CHABER, M.E. *Acid Nightmare.* 1967. HRW. 1st ed. VG/VG. P3. $22.00

CHABON, Michael. *Model World & Other Stories.* 1991. Morrow. 1st ed. F/F. H11. $25.00

CHABON, Michael. *Mysteries of Pittsburgh.* 1988. Morrow. 1st ed. author's 1st book. F/F. M23. $25.00

CHACE, Arthur F. *Precision Crusing.* 1987. Norton. 1st ed. ils Brad Dellenbaugh. VG/VG. A16. $10.00

CHADBOURNE, P.A. *Instinct: Its Office in the Animal Kingdom...* 1872. Putnam. 12mo. 307p. beveled-edge ochre cloth. VG. G1. $65.00

CHADWICK, Lester. *Baseball Joe Around the World (#18).* 1918. Cupples Leon. 246p. VG/dj. M20. $42.00

CHADWICK, Mrs. J. *Home Cookery: A Collection of Tried Receipts...* 1984. Birmingham. 2 vol in 1. quarter leather. F. A17. $22.00

CHADWICK. *Celtic Britain.* 1964. Eng. F/VG. D2. $20.00

CHAFF, Sandra. *Women in Medicine: Biography of Literature...* 1977. Metuchen, NJ. 1st ed. 1124p. VG. A13. $200.00

CHAGALL, Marc. *Drawings & Water Colors for the Ballet.* 1969. NY. 1st ed. F/NF dj/case. w/original lithograph. N3. $200.00

CHAGALL, Marc. *Vitraux Pour Jerusalem.* 1961. Paris. Musee Arts Decoratifs. 1st ed. 1/300. sgn. w/orig pl. C6. $900.00

CHAINES, A. *Pets.* 1904. Stokes. 1st ed. lg 4to. ils Louis Rhread. VG. M5. $65.00

CHAITIN, Peter. *James A Michener's USA.* 1981. Crown. 1st ed. F/F. H11. $75.00

CHALEANT, W. *Story of Inyo.* 1922. chicago. 1st ed. map. 358p. ES. VG. B5. $55.00

CHALFONT, W.A. *Dangerous Passage: Santa Fe Trail & the Mexican War.* 1994. OK U. 1st ed. 8vo. 325p. M/M. T10. $35.00

CHALFONT, W.A. *Montgomery of Alamein.* 1976. Atheneum. 1st Am ed. 365p. F/dj. A17. $12.50

CHALFONT, W.A. *Story of Inyo.* 1922. Chicago. 1st ed. VG. B5. $50.00

CHALKER, Jack L. *Messiah Choice.* 1985. Bluejay. 1st ed. F/F. P3. $17.00

CHALMERS, J. Alan. *Atmospheric Electricity.* 1950 (1949). Clarendon. 2nd. 8vo. 175p. G/dj. K5. $48.00

CHALMERS, Stephen. *Affair of the Gallows Tree.* 1930. Crime Club. 1st ed. VG. P3. $30.00

CHALONER, John Armstrong. *Robbery Under Law; or, Battle of the Millionaires.* 1915. Palmetto. 240p. VG. B10. $18.00

CHALONER, John Armstrong. *Swan-Song of Who's Looney Now?* 1914. Palmetto. Hippodrome ed. photos. 371p. VG-. B10. $18.00

CHAMBERLAIN, Alexander F. *Child: Study in the Evolution of Man.* 1900. Scribner. Contemporary Science series. 12mo. 498p. VG. G1. $45.00

CHAMBERLAIN, Austen. *Politics From Inside. An Epistolary Chronicle 1906-1914.* 1937. New Haven. 8vo. 676p. bl cloth. F/worn. P4. $20.00

CHAMBERLAIN, George Agnew. *Overcoat Meeting.* 1949. NY. Barnes. pres. VG/fair. O3. $45.00

CHAMBERLAIN, Hope Summerell. *Old Days in Chapel Hill...* 1926. NC U. 1st ed. 325p. NF. M8. $45.00

CHAMBERLAIN, Samuel. *Beyond New England Thresholds.* 1937. NY. 1st ed. VG/VG. B5. $25.00

CHAMBERLAIN & CHAMBERLAIN. *Hunts of the United States & Canada.* 1908. Boston. Wiles. 1st ed. 1/500. sgns. VG. O3. $125.00

CHAMBERLAIN & SPRUNT. *South Carolina Bird Life.* 1949. Columbia. 1st ed. pl. 585p. VG. B5. $85.00

CHAMBERLAIN. *Beyond New England Thresholds.* 1937. Hastings. cloth. VG/dj. D2. $40.00

CHAMBERLIN, Ethel Glere. *Shoes & Ships & Sealing Wax.* 1928. Saalfield. 8vo. ils Janet Laura Scott. VG/G. B17. $10.00

CHAMBERLIN, Ethel Glere. *Shoes & Ships & Sealing Wax.* 1928. Akron. ils Janet Laura Scott. VG. A17. $7.50

CHAMBERLIN, Harry. *Riding & Schooling Horses.* 1934. WA. 1st ed. O3. $38.00

CHAMBERLIN & SALISBURY. *Geology Vol II: Earth History Genesis-Paleozoic.* 1923. Holt. 2nd. 692p. G. D8. $25.00

CHAMBERS, Peter; see Phillips, Dennis.

CHAMBERS, Robert W. *King in Yellow.* 1895. F Tennyson Neely. VG. P3. $350.00

CHAMBERS, Robert W. *Maker of Moons.* 1896. NY. 1st ed. VG. B5. $75.00

CHAMBERS, Robert W. *Streets of Ascalon.* 1912. Appleton. 1st ed. VG. P3. $25.00

CHAMBERS, Whitman. *Invasion!* 1943. Dutton. 1st ed. VG. P3. $20.00

CHAMPLIN, Charles. *Back There Where the Past Was: A Small Town Boyhood.* 1989. Syracuse. 2nd prt. 8vo. F/NF. T10. $35.00

CHAMPOLLION, Jacques. *World of the Egyptians.* 1971. Geneva. Minerva. 1st ed. 157p. NF/dj. W1. $25.00

CHANCE, M. *Princess Elizabeth & Her Dogs.* 1937. 1st ed. photos. K2. $40.00

CHANDLER, A. Bertram. *Beyond the Galactic Rim.* 1982. Allison Busby. F/F. P3. $20.00

CHANDLER, A. Bertram. *Bring Back Yesterday.* 1981. Allison Busby. 1st ed. F/F. P3. $20.00

CHANDLER, A. Bertram. *Glory Planet.* Avalon. 1964 xl. dj. P3. $8.00

CHANDLER, A. Bertram. *Rim of Space.* 1961. Avalon. 1st ed. F/F. P3. $45.00

CHANDLER, A. Bertram. *When the Dream Dies.* 1981. Allison Busby. F/F. P3. $20.00

CHANDLER, Allison. *Trolley Through the Countryside.* 1963. Denver. 384p. Vg/dj. B18. $35.00

CHANDLER, David G. *Campaigns of Napoleon.* 1966. NY. ils. 1172p. VG/dj. B18. $35.00

CHANDLER, David. *Atlas of Military Strategy.* 1980. NY. 1st ed. 208p. VG/dj. B18. $22.50

CHANDLER, Raymond. *Big Sleep.* 1946. 1st Forum ed. MTI. VG/VG. S13. $25.00

CHANDLER, Raymond. *Big Sleep.* 1947. Stockholm. 1st ed/correct 1st issue. VG. A11. $45.00

CHANDLER, Raymond. *Farewell, My Lovely & the Lady in the Lake.* 1967. NY. 1st combined ed. F/NF clip. A11. $45.00

CHANDLER, Raymond. *Farewell, My Lovely.* 1940. NY. 1st ed. author's 2nd book. NF/VG. C6. $2,000.00

CHANDLER, Raymond. *High Window.* 1942. Knopf. 1st ed. G/VG. xl. P3. $125.00

CHANDLER, Raymond. *Killer in the Rain.* 1964. Boston. 1st Am ed. F/NF. C2. $125.00

CHANDLER, Raymond. *Lady in the Lake.* 1944. Hamish Hamilton. G/VG. P3. $30.00

CHANDLER, Raymond. *Little Sister.* 1949. Houghton Mifflin. 1st ed. NF/VG. M19. $350.00

CHANDLER, Raymond. *Little Sister.* 1949. Houghton Mifflin. 1st ed. xl. dj. P3. $20.00

CHANDLER, Raymond. *Little Sister.* 1949. Houghton Mifflin. 1st ed. 1st issue orange cloth. VG. M22. $50.00

CHANDLER, Raymond. *Long Goodbye.* 1953. Hamish Hamilton. VG. P3. $30.00

CHANDLER, Raymond. *Long Goodbye.* 1954. Houghton Mifflin. 1st Am ed. VG/VG-. M22. $150.00

CHANDLER, Raymond. *Midnight Raymond Chandler.* nd. BC. VG/VG. P3. $10.00

CHANDLER, Raymond. *Mystery Omnibus.* 1945. Forum. 2nd ed. VG. MTI. P3. $18.00

CHANDLER, Raymond. *Playback.* 1958. Thriller. VG/VG. P3. $15.00

CHANDLER, Raymond. *Red Wing.* 1946. Tower. 1st ed. VG. P3. $20.00

CHANDLER, Raymond. *Spanish Blood.* 1946. Tower. VG/VG. P3. $25.00

CHANDLER & PARKER. *Poodle Springs.* 1989. Putnam. 1st ed. F/F. P3. $19.00

CHANT, Joy. *Grey Mane of Morning.* 1977. Allen Unwin. 1st ed. F/F. P3. $25.00

CHAPDELAINE, Perry A. *Laughing Terran.* 1977. London. Hale. 1st ed. sgn. F/VG. B11. $35.00

CHAPEL, Charles Edward. *Finger Printing.* 1941. Coward McCann. 293p. VG/dj. M20. $27.00

CHAPEL, Charles Edward. *Gun Collector's Handbook of Values.* 1951. Coward McCann. photos. G+/fair. P12. $7.50

CHAPELLE, Howard I. *American Sailing Craft.* 1936-1939. NY. 239p. VG. T7. $55.00

CHAPELLE, Howard I. *History of the American Sailing Navy.* nd. Bonanza. rpt. VG/VG. A16. $20.00

CHAPELLE, Howard I. *National Watercraft Collection.* 1960. WA. VG. O7. $125.00

CHAPIN, Carl M. *Three Died Beside the Marble Pool.* 1936. Crime Club. 1st ed. hc. VG. P3. $20.00

CHAPIN, James Henry. *From Japan to Granada.* 1889. NY. Putnam. 1st ed. inscr. 12mo. 325p. xl. G. B11. $25.00

CHAPIN, Lucy Stock. *Teddie's Best Christmas Tree.* 1929. Gibson. 12mo. VG. M5. $28.00

CHAPLIN, Charles. *My Autobiography.* 1964. NY. 1st prt. 512p. F/dj. A17. $12.50

CHAPLIN, Ralph. *Bars & Shadows.* 1922. Leonard. 1st ed. F/NF. B2. $75.00

CHAPMAN, Allen. *Dividing the Circle.* 1990. NY. Horwood. 36 pl. 209p. VG. K5. $45.00

CHAPMAN, Allen. *Fred Fenton, Marathon Runner.* 1915. Cupples Leon. VG-/dj. A17. $5.00

CHAPMAN, Allen. *Radio Boys at Mountain Pass (#4).* 1922. Grosset Dunlap. lists to #5. 218p. VG/dj. M20. $35.00

CHAPMAN, Allen. *Radio Boys Trailing a Voice (#5).* 1922. Grosset Dunlap. 214p. VG/dj. M20. $55.00

CHAPMAN, Carleton. *Physicans, Law & Ethics.* 1948. NY. 192p. wrp. A13. $15.00

CHAPMAN, F. Spencer. *Lightest Africa.* 1955. London. Chatto Windus. 8vo. 288p. VG/dj. P4. $20.00

CHAPMAN, George. *Chapman's Homer: The Whole Works of Homer.* 1903. London. brn full leather. VG. B30. $140.00

CHAPMAN, Lee; see Bradley, Marion Zimmer.

CHAPMAN, Walker. *Golden Dream.* 1967. Indianapolis. 1st ed. maps. 436p. VG. F3/O7. $15.00

CHAPMAN, Walker. *Loneliest Continent.* 1964. Greenwich. VG. O7. $20.00

CHAPMAN, Walker. *Loneliest Continent.* 1964. NYGS. 1st ed. 279p. F/F. T10. $25.00

CHAPMAN, Walker. *Search for El Dorado.* 1967. Bobbs Merrill. 1st ed. 272p. dj. F3. $25.00

CHAPMAN & PRATT. *Methods of Analysis for Soils, Plants & Waters.* 1982 (1961). Berkeley. lg 8vo. 309p. new cloth. NF. B1. $22.50

CHAPPELL, Fred. *Brighten the Corner Where You Are.* 1989. St Martin. 1st ed. inscr. F/F. C2. $50.00

CHAPPELL, Fred. *Gaudy Place.* 1973. Harcourt. 1st ed. sgn. F/F. C2. $100.00

CHAPPELL, Fred. *Midquest: A Poem.* 1981. Baton Rouge. 1st ed. inscr. F/F. C2. $40.00

CHAPPELL, Fred. *Moments of Light.* 1980. Los Angeles. 1st ed. F/F. C2. $75.00

CHAPPELL, Fred. *More Shapes Than One: A Book of Stories.* 1991. St Martin. 1st ed. F/F. G10. $15.00

CHAPUT, W.J. *Dead in the Water.* 1991. St Martin. 1st ed. VG/VG. P3. $16.00

CHARBONNEAU, Louis. *No Place on Earth.* nd. BC. VG/VG. P3. $8.00

CHARBONNEAU, Louis. *Way Out.* 1966. Barrie Rockliff. 1st ed. VG/VG. P3. $25.00

CHARDIN, John. *Sir John Cardin's Travels in Persia.* 1927. London. Argonaut. 1/975. 287p. VG. T7. $150.00

CHARHADI, Driss Ben Hamed. *Life Full of Holes.* 1964. NY. 1st ed. trans/inscr Paul Bowles. F/NF. C6. $150.00

CHARLTON, Keith. *Post-Conquest Developments in Teotihuacan Valley, Mexico.* 1973. Iowa City. 217p. wrp. F3. $20.00

CHARNAS, Suzy McKee. *Bronze King.* 1985. Houghton Mifflin. 1st ed. VG/VG. P3. $18.00

CHARNAS, Suzy McKee. *Dorothea Dreams.* 1986. Arbor. 1st ed. RS. F/F. P3. $20.00

CHARNAS, Suzy McKee. *Vampire Tapestry.* 1980. Simon Schuster. 1st ed. 8vo. F/F. T10. $10.00

CHARNAY, Desire. *Ancient Cities of the New World.* 1887. Harper. 1st ed. 514p. F3. $200.00

CHARRIERE, Henri. *Papillon.* 1970. Morrow. 1st Am ed. NF/NF. M22. $15.00

CHARROUX, Robert. *One Hundred Thousand Years of Man...* nd. Laffont Special Ed. hc. VG. P3. $10.00

CHARTERIS, John. *Field Marshall Earl Haig.* 1929. SCribner. 407p. gilt bl cloth. F. B22. $8.50

CHARTERIS, Leslie. *Ace of Knaves.* nd. Sun Dial. VG. P3. $15.00

CHARTERIS, Leslie. *Ace of Knaves.* 1937. Doubleday Crime Club. 1st ed. VG. M22. $12.00

CHARTERIS, Leslie. *Five Complete Novels.* 1983. Avenel. 2nd. F/F. P3. $15.00

CHARTERIS, Leslie. *Saint & the People Importers.* 1972. Detective BC. VG. P3. $8.00

CHARTERIS, Leslie. *Saint & the Templar Treasure.* 1979. Crime Club. 1st ed. VG/VG. P3. $20.00

CHARTERIS, Leslie. *Saint Errant.* 1953. Hodder Stoughton. 2nd ed. VG/G. P3. $25.00

CHARTERIS, Leslie. *Saint Goes West.* 1942. Musson. 1st ed. VG/G. P3. $25.00

CHARTERIS, Leslie. *Senior Saint.* 1959. Hodder Stoughton. 1st ed. VG/VG. P3. $35.00

CHARTERS, Ann. *Jack Kerouac: A Bibliography.* 1975. Phoenix Bookshop. revised. F/sans. B2. $65.00

CHARTERS, Ann. *Kerouac.* 1973. Straight Arrow. 1st ed. VG/VG. P3. $40.00

CHARTERS, Samuel. *Louisiana Black.* 1987. NY. Marion Boyers. rpt. F/NF. R11. $12.00

CHARYN, Jerome. *Isaac Quartet.* 1984. Zomba. 1st ed. F/F. P3. $30.00

CHARYN, Jerome. *Once Upon a Droshky.* 1964. np. 1st ed. author's 1st book. F/NF. M19. $35.00

CHASE, Glen; see Fox, Gardner F.

CHASE, James Hadley. *Cade.* 1967. Robert Hale. 2nd. VG/VG. P3. $14.00

CHASE, James Hadley. *Figure It Out for Yourself.* 1950. Robert Hale. 1st ed. VG/G. P3. $30.00

CHASE, James Hadley. *I'll Bury My Dead.* 1954. Dutton. 1st ed. VG/VG. P3. $10.00

CHASE, James Hadley. *You Have Yourself a Deal.* 1968. NY. Walker. 1st ed. NF/F. H11. $20.00

CHASE, John. *Frenchmen, Desire, Good Children & Other Street Stories...* 1960. New Orleans. Crager. new ed. sgn. 268p. VG/VG. B11. $25.00

CHASE, Mary Ellen. *Plum Tree.* 1949. Macmillan. 1st ed. sgn. NF/VG. B4. $85.00

CHASE, Richard. *Jack Tales.* 1943. Boston. 7th prt. 202p. dj. A17. $12.50

CHASE & CHASE. *Post Classic Perspective: Excavations at Maya Site...* 1988. San Francisco. Pari. 1st ed. 138p. wrp. F3. $30.00

CHASE-RIBOUND, Barbara. *Sally Hemings.* 1979. Viking. 1st ed. F/NF. B2. $35.00

CHASE-RIBOUND, Barbara. *Sally Hemings.* 1979. Viking. 2nd. 372p. VG/VG. B10. $15.00

CHASTAIN, Thomas. *Case of Too Many Murders.* 1989. Morrow. 1st ed. F/F. P3. $15.00

CHASTAIN, Thomas. *Pandora's Box.* 1974. Mason Lipscomb. 1st ed. VG/VG. P3. $20.00

CHASTEL, Andre. *Chronicle of Italian Renaissance Painting.* 1984. Cornell. 1st ed. 294p. NF/dj. M20. $42.00

CHATEAUBRIAND, F.R. *Chateubriand's Travels in America.* 1969. Lexington. VG. O7. $35.00

CHATHAM, Russell D. *Silent Seasons: 21 Fishing Adventures by 7 American Experts.* 1978. Dutton. 1st ed. sgn contributor Hjortsberg. F/F. C2. $100.00

CHATHAM, Russell D. *Striped Bass on the Fly: Guide to California Waters.* 1977. San Francisco. Examiner. 1st ed. author's 1st book. sgn/dtd 1977. F/wrp. C2. $250.00

CHATTERTON, E. Keble. *Captain John Smith.* 1927. London. VG. O7. $35.00

CHATTERTON, E. Keble. *Ventures & Voyages.* 1928-1935. London/NY. ils. 217p. VG. T7. $35.00

CHATWIN, Bruce. *In Patagonia.* 1977. London. Cape. 1st ed. author's 1st book. F/dj. C2. $650.00

CHATWIN, Bruce. *On the Black Hill.* 1982. London. Cape. 1st ed. F/F. C2. $60.00

CHATWIN, Bruce. *On the Black Hill.* 1983. Viking. 1st ed. F/VG. M23. $15.00

CHATWIN, Bruce. *Songlines.* 1987. Franklin Center. 1st ed. sgn. leather. F. C2. $200.00

CHATWIN, Bruce. *Viceroy of Ouidah.* 1980. Summit. 1st ed. F/F. M19. $35.00

CHATWIN & THEROUX. *Patagonia Revisited.* 1985. Salisbury. Michael Russell. 1st ed. 1/250. sgns. F/glassine. C2. $350.00

CHAUCER, Geoffrey. *Canterbury Tales.* 1934. Covici Friede. 1st trade ed. ils Rockwell Kent. NF/G. M19. $50.00

CHAUCER, Geoffrey. *Complete Works...* 1915. Oxford. marbled ep. aeg. red full leather. F. B30. $68.00

CHAUCER, Geoffrey. *Poetical Works of...* 1861. London. Griffin Bohn. 8 vol. 12mo. teg. gilt bdg. VG. T10. $500.00

CHAUCER, Geoffrey. *Works of Geoffrey Chaucer & Others...* 1905. London. facsimile of 1532 ed. w/orig 1532 ed leaf. VG. C2. $175.00

CHAUNDLER, Christine. *Famous Myths & Legends.* 1986. Bracken. F/F. P3. $20.00

CHAUVIN, Paul. *Canticle of the Three Children in the Fiery Furnace.* ca 1940. London. ils Frances Delehanty. VG. A17. $14.50

CHAVEZ, Denise. *Face of an Angel.* 1994. FSG. 1st ed. F/F. M23. $40.00

CHAVEZ, Fray Angelico. *Eleven Lady Lyrics & Other Poems.* 1956. St Anthony Guild. sgn. 96p. G. B11. $25.00

CHAYEFSKY, Paddy. *Altered States.* 1978. Harper Row. 1st ed. VG/VG. P3. $20.00

CHEESEMAN, H.R. *Bibliography of Malaya.* 1959. London. VG. O7. $35.00

CHEETHAM, Anthony. *Science Agianst Man.* 1971. MacDonald. 1st ed. VG/VG. P3. $28.00

CHEETHAM, Nicholas. *Mexico: A Short History.* 1971. Crowell. 1st Am ed. ils/map. 302p. dj. F3. $15.00

CHEEVER, Benjamin. *Letters of John Cheever.* 1988. Simon Schuster. 1st ed. VG+/VG+. A20. $14.00

CHEEVER, Henry T. *Autobiography & Memorials of Captain Obadiah Congar.* 1861. NY. Harper. 16mo. 266p. T7. $85.00

CHEEVER, John. *Bullet Park.* 1969. NY. 1st ed. NF/NF. A11. $30.00

CHEEVER, John. *Enormous Radio & Other Stories.* 1953. NY. 1st ed. author's 2nd book. VG/VG. C6. $150.00

CHEEVER, John. *Expelled* (1987) Sylvester Orphanos. 1st separate ed. 1/185. sgns contributors. F/case. B24. $350.00

CHEEVER, John. *Falconer.* 1977. NY. 1st ed. sgn. F/F. C6. $95.00

CHEEVER, John. *Homage to Shakespeare.* 1968. Stevenson, CT. 1/150. sgn. F/F. C6. $200.00

CHEEVER, John. *Stories of...* 1978. NY. 1st ed. F/F. A17. $15.00

CHEEVER, John. *Way Some People Live.* 1943. NY. 1st ed. author's 1st book. NF/NF. A15. $500.00

CHEKHOV, Anton. *Moscow Art Theatre Series of Russian Plays.* 1923. NY. 1st ed thus. F/NF. C6. $60.00

CHEKHOV, Anton. *Two Plays by Anton Chekhov: The Cherry Tree & Three Sisters.* 1966. LEC. 1st ed. 1/1500. ils/sgn Szalay. 153p. F/case. C2. $45.00

CHENEY, M. *Coed Killer.* 1976. NY. 1st ed. VG/VG. B5. $30.00

CHENG-WU, Fei. *Brush Drawing in the Chinese Manner.* 1957. London. 1st ed. VG/G. S13. $22.00

CHENOWETH & JENSEN. *Applied Engineering Mechanics.* 1972. NY. McGraw Hill. 3rd. 8vo. 451p. VG. P4. $20.00

CHERMAN, Jay. *Real Book About Horses.* 1952. Garden City. VG/G. O3. $10.00

CHERNIN, Kim. *Obsession.* 1981. Harper. 1st ed. F/F. M19. $22.50

CHERRY, Kelly. *My Life & Dr Joyce Brothers.* 1990. Algonquin. 1st ed. F/F. H11. $25.00

CHERRY, Kelly. *Sick & Full of Burning.* 1974. Viking. 1st ed. F/NF. B4. $45.00

CHERRY, P.P. *Western Reserve & Early Ohio.* 1920. Fouse. 229p. VG. M20. $52.00

CHERRYH, C.J. *Brothers of Earth.* nd. BC. VG/VG. P3. $8.00

CHERRYH, C.J. *Chanur's Legacy.* 1992. DAW. 1st ed. F/F. P3. $20.00

CHERRYH, C.J. *Cyteen.* 1988. Warner. 1st ed. F/F. T2. $65.00

CHERRYH, C.J. *Foreigner.* 1994. DAW. 1st ed. F/F. P3. $20.00

CHERRYH, C.J. *Rusalka.* 1989. Del Rey. 1st ed. hc. NF/NF. P3. $19.00

CHESBRO, George B.; see Cross, David.

CHESBRO, George C. *Dark Chant in a Crimson Key.* 1992. Mysterious. 1st ed. rem mk. F/F. H11. $20.00

CHESBRO, George C. *Fear in Yesterday's Rings.* 1991. Mysterious. 1st ed. F/F. P3. $19.00

CHESBRO, George C. *Jungle of Steel & Stone.* 1988. Mysterious. 1st ed. F/F. H11. $20.00

CHESBRO, George C. *Second Horseman Out of Eden.* 1989. Atheneum. 1st ed. F/F. N4. $35.00

CHESBRO, George C. *Shadow of a Broken Man.* 1977. Simon Schuster. 1st ed. VG/VG. P3. $30.00

CHESBRO, George C. *Shadow of a Broken Man.* 1981. np. 1st ed. author's 1st book. F/NF. M19. $32.50

CHESBRO, George C. *Veil.* 1986. Mysterious. 1st ed. F/F. P3. $20.00

CHESNUTT, Charles W. *Colonel's Dream.* 1905. NY. 1st ed. VG. C6. $300.00

CHESTER, H.W. *Recollections of the War of the Rebellion.* 1996. Wheaton, IL. 1st ed. 257p. AN. B18. $42.50

CHESTER, Himes. *For Love of Imabelle.* 1957. Greenwich. Gold Medal. 1st ed. F. A11. $65.00

CHESTER, Himes. *Sort Panik.* 1947. Copenhagen. Westermann. 1st Danish ed. author's 1st novel. VG+/wrp. A11. $75.00

CHESTER, Peter; see Phillips, Dennis.

CHESTER & WHALLEY. *History of Children's Book Illustration.* 1988. np. 4to. ils. 268p. F/F. A4. $195.00

CHESTERTON, G.K. *Father Brown Book.* 1959. Cassell. 2nd ed. xl. P3. $10.00

CHESTERTON, G.K. *Man Who Was Thursday.* nd. Dodd Mead. VG. P3. $20.00

CHESTERTON, G.K. *Return of Don Quixote.* 1927. Chatto Windus. 1st ed. 1st bdg. F/NF. C2. $150.00

CHESTERTON, G.K. *Thing.* 1957. np. 1st ed. F/VG. M19. $25.00

CHESTNUT, Robert; see Cooper, Clarence.

CHETWIN, Grace. *Atheling.* 1988. Tor. 1st ed. F/F. P3. $19.00

CHETWOOD, William R. *Voyages & Adventures of Captain Robert Boyle...* 1828. Exeter. 2 vol. VG. O7. $100.00

CHEVIGNY, H. *Lord of Alaska.* 1971. Portland. w/sgn 2p letter. VG/VG. B5. $27.50

CHEYNERY, Edward P. *European Background of American History.* 1904. NY. xl. VG. O7. $20.00

CHEYNEY, Peter. *Dames Don't Care!* nd. Coward McCann. 1st Am ed/2nd imp. 250p. VG/dj. M20. $37.00

CHEYNEY, Peter. *Dames Don't Care!* 1936. Coward McCann. 1st ed. VG. P3. $30.00

CHEYNEY, Peter. *Dark Bahama.* 1951. Detective BC. VG/G. P3. $20.00

CHEYNEY, Peter. *Dark Bahama.* 1951. Dodd Mead. 1st Am ed. VG/VG. M22. $20.00

CHEYNEY, Peter. *Lady Beware.* 1950. Walter Black. 1st ed. VG/VG. M22. $15.00

CHEYNEY, Peter. *Tough Spot for Cupid & Other Stories.* 1945. Vallancy. 1st ed. VG/VG. P3. $50.00

CHIDSEY, Donald Barr. *Captain Adam.* 1953. Crown. 1st ed. VG/VG. P3. $20.00

CHIDSEY, Donald Barr. *Panama Passage.* 1946. Doubleday. 1st ed. VG/VG. P3. $20.00

CHILD, C.M. *Physiological Foundations of Behavior.* (1924). Holt. 330p. bl-gr cloth. G1. $50.00

CHILD, Heather. *Decorative Maps.* 1956. London. Studio. F. O7. $45.00

CHILD & PRESTON. *Mount Dragon.* 1966. Forge. 1st ed. VG/G+. P3. $20.00

CHILD & PRESTON. *Relic.* 1995. Forge. 1st ed. AN/AN. N4. $30.00

CHILDERS, James Saxon. *Erskine Ramsay: His Life & Achievements.* 1942. NY. 1st ed. inscr. 552p. VG. B18. $47.50

CHILDERS & RUSSO. *Nighshades & Health.* 1977. Somerville. Horticultural pub. 8vo. photos. cloth. xl. B1. $16.50

CHILDRESS, Alice. *Like One of the Family.* 1956. Brooklyn. Independence Pub. 1st ed. author's 1st book. F/NF. B4. $150.00

CHILDRESS, Alice. *Short Walk.* 1979. Coward McCann. 1st ed. F/NF. B4. $45.00

CHILDRESS, Mark. *Crazy in Alabama.* 1993. Putnam. 1st ed. sgn. F/F. M23. $50.00

CHILDRESS, Mark. *Tender.* 1990. Harmony. 1st ed. sgn. F/F. M23. $55.00

CHILDS, Marilyn. *Men Behind the Morgan Horse.* 1979. Leominster. Traditional Pr. 1/2500. sgn. VG. O3. $495.00

CHILES, Webb. *Ocean Waits.* 1984. NY. Norton. photos. 271p. dj. T7. $22.00

CHILTON, John. *Who's Who of Jazz.* 1979. Time Life. 2nd ed. VG/VG. P3. $20.00

CHILTON & JONES. *Louis: The Louis Armstrong Story.* 1971. Little Brn. 1st Am ed. 256p. VG/dj. M20. $20.00

CHILTON. *Chilton Automobile Directory.* Oct 1918. ils/ads. 770p. VG. B5. $65.00

CHIPMAN, Daniel. *Essay on the Law of Contracts, for Payment...* 1822. Middlebury. Chipman/Copeland. 1st ed. contemporary sheep. M11. $450.00

CHITTENDEN, Hiram Martin. *American Fur Trade of the Far West, a History.* 1954. 2 vol. VG. A4. $95.00

CHITTENDEN, Hiram Martin. *Yellowstone National Park.* 1915. Stewart Kidd. photos/fld map. VG-. P12. $25.00

CHITTY, Joseph. *Treatise on the Game Laws & on Fisheries...* 1812-1816. London. Clarke. contemporary calf. M11. $850.00

CHIZMAR, Richard T. *Thrillers.* 1993. Baltimore. 1st ed. 1/500. sgn edit/ils/contributors. F/F/case. T2. $60.00

CHIZMAR, Richard. *Cold Blood.* 1991. Shingletown. Ziesing. 1st ed. 1/500. sgn edit/ils/all contributors. F/F/case. T2. $75.00

CHOPMAN, Donald E. *Nuno de Guzman & the Province of panuco in New Spain.* 1967. Glendale. VG. O7. $55.00

CHORLTON, William. *American Grape Grower's Guide.* 1856. NY. 1st ed. ils. 172p. brn cloth. B14. $65.00

CHOUINARD, Jeffrey. *Mouths of Stone.* 1955. Carolina Academic Pr. 1st ed. 242p. dj. AN. F3. $40.00

CHOULANT, Ludwig. *History & Bibliography of Anatomic Ils Trans & Annotated...* 1920. Chicago. 1st Eng trans. 435p. VG. A13. $350.00

CHOULES, John Overton. *Cruise of the Steam Yacht North Star...* 1854. Boston. Gould Lincoln. leather. G+/custom case. A16. $200.00

CHRISMAN, Miriam Usher. *Biography of Strasbourg Imprints 1480-1599.* 1982. New Haven. Yale. 1st ed. 8vo. 418p. gilt purple cloth. F/sans. T10. $45.00

CHRISTENSEN. *Early American Wood Carving.* 1952. np. cloth. VG/VG. D2. $20.00

CHRISTENSEN. *Index of American Design.* 1950. np. 1st ed. cloth. VG/VG. D2. $55.00

CHRISTIAN, George L. *Sketch of the Origin & Erection of Confederate Memorial...* nd. The Institute. 2nd. photos. 32p. VG/wrp. B10. $20.00

CHRISTIAN, W. Asbury. *Marah: Story of Old Virginia.* 1903. Jenkins. 1st ed. G-. B10. $12.00

CHRISTIE, Agatha. *ABC Murders.* 1945. Tower. VG/VG. P3. $10.00

CHRISTIE, Agatha. *Agatha Christie: An Autobiography.* 1977. np. 26 photos. 529p. F/VG. A4. $35.00

CHRISTIE, Agatha. *And Then There Were None.* 1945. Grosset Dunlap. photoplay ed. VG/VG. M22. $30.00

CHRISTIE, Agatha. *At Bertram's Hotel.* 1965. Collins Crime Club. 1st ed. VG/VG. P3. $35.00

CHRISTIE, Agatha. *Big Four.* 1927. Dodd Mead. 2nd. 8vo. NF. S9. $25.00

CHRISTIE, Agatha. *By the Prickling of My Thumbs.* 1968. Dodd Mead. 1st ed. VG/G. P3. $25.00

CHRISTIE, Agatha. *Cat Among the Pigeons.* 1960. Dodd Mead. 1st ed. F/NF. H11. $45.00

CHRISTIE, Agatha. *Elephants Can Remember.* 1972. Collins Crime Club. 1st ed. VG/VG. P3. $23.00

CHRISTIE, Agatha. *Endless Night.* 1968. Dodd Mead. 1st ed. VG/F. H11. $20.00

CHRISTIE, Agatha. *Nemesis.* 1971. Collins Crime Club. 1st ed. VG/torn. P3. $18.00

CHRISTIE, Agatha. *Ordeal by Innocence.* 1958. Collins Crime Club. 1st ed. NF/NF. P3. $40.00

CHRISTIE, Agatha. *Pale Horse.* 1961. Collins. 1st ed. F/F. M19. $65.00

CHRISTIE, Agatha. *Postern of Fate.* 1973. Collins Crime Club. 1st ed. VG/VG. P3. $23.00

CHRISTIE, Agatha. *Sad Express.* 1940. Dodd Mead. 1st ed. VG/VG. P3. $45.00

CHRISTIE, Agatha. *Sleeping Murder.* 1976. Collins Crime Club. 1st ed. NF/NF. P3. $20.00

CHRISTIE, Agatha. *Third Girl.* 1966. Collins. 1st ed. F/VG. M19. $35.00

CHRISTIE, Agatha. *Third Girl.* 1967. Dodd Mead. 1st ed. F/NF. H11. $25.00

CHRISTIE, Agatha. *Third Girl.* 1967. Dodd Mead. 1st ed. VG/VG. P3. $20.00

CHRISTISON, Robert. *Treatise on Poisons in Relation to Medical Jurisprudence.* 1845. Phil. 1st Am ed. 756p. VG. B14. $150.00

CHRISTOPHER, Anne. *Monkey Twins.* 1935. Whitman. 1st ed. ils Inez Hogan. VG. M5. $10.00

CHRISTOPHER, John. *No Blade of Grass.* 1956. Simon Schuster. 1st ed. VG/VG. M19. $45.00

CHRISTOPHER, John. *Pendulum.* 1968. Simon Schuster. 1st ed. VG/VG. P3. $15.00

CHRISTOPHER, John. *Prince in Waiting.* 1970. Hamish Hamilton. 1st ed. VG/G. P3. $13.00

CHRISTOPHER, John. *Ragged Edge.* nd. Simon Schuster. VG/VG. P3. $15.00

CHRISTOPHER, John. *Sword of the Spirits.* 1972. Hamish Hamilton. 1st ed. F/F. P3. $15.00

CHRISTY, E.V.A. *Cross-Saddle & Side-Saddle.* nd. Lippincott. 1st Am ed. G+. O3. $65.00

CHRISTY, E.V.A. *If Wishes Were Horses Beggars Could Ride.* 1947. Nicholson Watson. 1st ed. VG. O3. $38.00

CHRISTY, Howard Chandler. *Courtship of Miles Standish.* 1903. Indianapolis. 1st ed. ils. VG/fair. B5. $45.00

CHUA, Cathy. *History of Australian Bridge 1930-1990.* 1993. Australia. 290p. M. S1. $15.00

CHUB & JOHNSON. *Test Your Bids in Contract According to Official System...* 1931. Phil. 44p. VG. S1. $10.00

CHUBIN, Barry. *Feet of a Snake.* 1984. Arbor. 1st ed. VG/VG. P3. $18.00

CHURCH, David Hopkins. *Saved by the Bell.* 1940. Dietz. 29p. G+. B10. $15.00

CHURCH, GOWERS & LATHAN. *Influence of Heredity on Disease...* 1909. London. 4to. 142p. red cloth. NF. B14. $275.00

CHURCH, Peggy Pond. *Wind's Trail: Early Life of Mary Austin.* 1990. Mus NM Pr. 1st ed. photos. F/dj. A18. $20.00

CHURCHILL, David. *It, Us & the Others.* 1979. Harper Row. F/F. P3. $13.00

CHURCHILL, Winston S. *My African Journey.* 1908. Hodder Stoughton. 1st ed. 61 photos. NF. B24. $650.00

CHURCHILL, Winston. *History of the English-Speaking Peoples.* 1956. New World. 1st ed. VG+/VG. w/clip sgn. S13. $35.00

CHURCHILL, Winston. *History of the English-Speaking Peoples.* 1956-1958. London. 4 vol. 1st ed. NF/NF. B30. $400.00

CHURCHILL, Winston. *History of the English-Speaking Peoples.* 1966. Dodd Mead. BOMC. 4 vol. NF/VG. P12. $50.00

CHURCHILL & REYNOLDS. *Story of the Great War.* 1916-20. NY. Collier. 8 vol. half leather. VG. A17. $75.00

CHURCHILL & WEBSTER. *Children's Music Box.* 1945. Morrow. probable 1st ed. 4to. G+. B17. $6.00

CHURCHWARD, James. *Children of Mu.* 1931. Ives Washburn. 1st ed. sgn. VG. H7. $75.00

CHURCHWARD, James. *Lost Continent of Mu.* 1926. Wm Edwin Rudge. 1st ed. VG. P3. $50.00

CHURCHWARD, James. *Lost Continent of Mu.* 1946. Ives Washburn. 14th. 335p. tattered dj. F3. $15.00

CHYET, Stanley F. *Lopez of Newport.* 1970. Detroit. VG. O7. $20.00

CIANFRANI, Theodore. *Short History of Obstetrics & Gynecology.* 1960. Springfield. 1st ed. 449p. xl. A13. $75.00

CIARDI, John. *I Met a Man.* (1961). Houghton Mifflin. 8vo. ils. 74p. VG. C14. $6.00

CIARDI, John. *King Who Saved Himself From Being Saved.* 1965. Lippincott. ils Gorey. unp. VG/dj. M20. $34.00

CIRNI, Jim. *Come On.* 1989. NY. Soho. 1st ed. F/F. H11. $20.00

CLAMPITT, Amy. *Homage to John Keats.* 1984. Sarabande. 1st ed. 1/250. sgn. F/case. C2. $250.00

CLAMPITT, Amy. *Kingfisher.* 1983. Knopf. 1st ed. F/F. C2. $125.00

CLAMPITT, Amy. *What the Light Was Light.* 1985. Knopf. 1st ed. sgn. F/NF. C2. $75.00

CLANCY, Tom. *Cardinal of the Kremlin.* 1988. Putnam. 1st ed. VG/VG. P3. $20.00

CLANCY, Tom. *Clear & Present Danger.* 1989. Putnam. 1st ed. NF/NF. H11/P3. $40.00

CLANCY, Tom. *Debt of Honor.* 1994. Putnam. 1st ed. NF/VG+. N4. $20.00

CLANCY, Tom. *Hunt for Red October.* 1984. Naval Inst. 1st ed. NF/VG. M19. $500.00

CLANCY, Tom. *Patriot Games.* 1987. Putnam. 1st ed. VG/VG. P3. $45.00

CLANCY, Tom. *Red Storm Rising.* 1986. Putnam. 1st ed. author's 2nd book. F/F. H11. $70.00

CLANCY, Tom. *Red Storm Rising.* 1986. Putnam. 1st ed. VG/VG. P3. $45.00

CLANCY, Tom. *Sum of All Fears.* 1991. Putnam. 1st ed. NF/NF. P3. $25.00

CLANCY, Tom. *Sum of All Fears.* 1991. Putnam. 1st ed. w/sgn leaf. F/F. B2. $50.00

CLARESON, Thomas. *Voices for the Future Vol 3.* 1984. Bowling Green. F/F. P3. $15.00

CLARK, Ann Nolan. *In My Mother's House.* 1941. Viking/Jr Literary Guild. 1st ed. ils Velino Herrara. VG/G. P2. $110.00

CLARK, Ann Nolan. *Little Navajo Bluebird.* 1943. Viking. 1st ed. ils Paul Lanz. 143p. VG/VG. P2. $50.00

CLARK, Arthur H. *Travels in the New South: A Bibliography.* 1962. OK U. 2 vol. 1135 entries. F/F. A4. $195.00

CLARK, Arthur H. *Travels in the Old South: A Bibliography.* 1969. OK U. 3 vol. F/VG pub case. A4. $375.00

CLARK, Badger. *Sun & Saddle Leather.* 1922. Boston. Badger. 11th. 8vo. gilt brn cloth. NF. T10. $50.00

CLARK, Curt; see Westlake, Donald E.

CLARK, David Sanders. *Index to Maps of the American Revolution in Books...* 1974. Westport. Greenwood. AN. O7. $75.00

CLARK, Dick. *Murder on Tour.* 1989. Mysterious. 1st ed. rem mk. F/F. N4. $12.50

CLARK, Douglas. *Sick to Death.* 1971. Stein Day. 1st ed. VG/VG. P3. $20.00

CLARK, E. Warren. *Life & Adventure in Japan.* 1878. NY. photos. 247p. gilt cloth. VG. B14. $45.00

CLARK, Eleanor. *Baldur's Gate.* 1970. Pantheon. 1st ed. NF/NF. B35. $25.00

CLARK, Eleanor. *Oysters of Locmariaquer.* 1964. Pantheon. 1st ed. NF/NF. B4. $75.00

CLARK, Eleanor. *Rome & a Villa.* 1952. Doubleday. NF/VG. B4. $45.00

CLARK, Elmer T. *Arthur James Moore, World Evangelist.* 1960. NY. Methodist Church. sgn. 8vo. marbled brd/brn spine. F. B11. $15.00

CLARK, George Henry. *Life-Sketches of Reverend George Henry Clark.* 1852. Boston. 12mo. 160p. emb blk cloth. xl. G. T3. $15.00

CLARK, George L. *Equity, an Analysis & Discussion of Modern Equity Problems.* 1928. Cincinnati. Johnson & Hardin. M11. $35.00

CLARK, George R. *Short History of the United States Navy.* 1927. Lippincott. fair/G. A16. $20.00

CLARK, Gordon L. *Judges & the Cities, Interpreting Local Autonomy.* 1985. Chicago. M11. $25.00

CLARK, Ida Cato. *Rockbridge Rhymes.* 1960. np. VG/stiff wrp. B10. $12.00

CLARK, James. *Shoeing & Balancing the Light Harness Horse.* 1916. Buffalo. Horse World. 1st ed. VG. O3. $185.00

CLARK, Kenneth. *Animals & Men.* 1977. NY. 1st ed. F/F. B5. $45.00

CLARK, Kenneth. *Civilization.* 1969. NY. 1st ed. F/F. B5. $45.00

CLARK, Kenneth. *Drawings of Leonardo da Vinci...* 1968-69. London. Phaidon. 3 vol. cloth. dj. D2. $650.00

CLARK, Kenneth. *Leonardo da Vinci: An Account of His Development...* 1952 (1939). Cambridge. 2nd. 204p. cloth. D2. $65.00

CLARK, Mark W. *Calculated Risk.* 1950. Harper. sgn. 17 pl. 500p. G. B11. $25.00

CLARK, Mark W. *Calculated Risk.* 1950. NY. 1st ed. ils/map. 500p. G. B18. $15.00

CLARK, Mary Higgins. *Anastasia Syndrome & Other Stories.* 1989. Simon Schuster. 1st ed. VG/VG. P3. $20.00

CLARK, Mary Higgins. *Cry in the Night.* 1983. Collins. 1st ed. VG/VG. P3. $20.00

CLARK, Mary Higgins. *I'll Be Seeing You.* 1993. Simon Schuster. 1st ed. NF/NF. N4. $20.00

CLARK, Mary Higgins. *Stranger Is Watching.* nd. BC. VG/VG. P3. $8.00

CLARK, Mary Higgins. *Stranger Is Watching.* 1977. Simon Schuster. 1st ed. sgn. NF/F. H11. $60.00

CLARK, Mary Higgins. *Weep No More, My Lady.* 1987. Simon Schuster. 1st ed. VG/VG. P3. $15.00

CLARK, Mary Higgins. *Where Are the Children?* 1975. Simon Schuster. UP. author's 1st mystery. F/wrp. B4. $450.00

CLARK, Mary Higgins. *While My Pretty One Sleeps.* 1989. Simon Schuster. 1st ed. F/F. H11. $25.00

CLARK, Paul. *Hauhau: Pai Marire Search for Maori Identity.* 1975. Auckland. VG. O7. $20.00

CLARK, Philip. *Flight Into Darkness.* 1948. Simon Schuster. 1st ed. G. P3. $10.00

CLARK, Robert D. *Life of Matthew Simpson.* 1956. Macmillan. 1st ed. 344p. gr cloth. F/dj. B22. $7.00

CLARK, Sterling B.F. *How Many Miles From St Jo?* 1988. Ye Galleon. 1st ed thus. F/sans. A18. $17.50

CLARK, Thomas D. *Southern Country Editor.* 1948. Bobbs Merrill. 1st ed. 365p. VG. B10. $12.00

CLARK, Tom. *Heartbreak Hotel.* 1981. West Branch, IA. Toothpaste Pr. 1/500. sgn/#d. F/sewn wrp. T10. $100.00

CLARK, W.J. *International Language Past, Present & Future.* 1907. London. 205p. gilt cloth. VG. A17. $15.00

CLARK, Walter Von Tilberg. *Ox-Bow Incident.* 1940. Random. ARC/1st prt. F/pict wrp. B24. $500.00

CLARK, Walter. *Histories of the Several Regiments & Battalions From NC...* 1901. Raleigh/Goldsboro, NC. 5 vol. 1st ed. cloth. VG. M8. $750.00

CLARK, Walter. *Vermont: City of Trembling Leaves.* 1945. NY. 1st ed. VG/VG. B5. $40.00

CLARK & KIRWAN. *South Since Appomattox: Century of Regional Change.* 1967. Oxford. ils. 438p. VG. B10. $12.00

CLARK. *Cambridge History of Africa. Volumes 1 Through 5.* 1975-1982.. ils. xl. NF. A4. $185.00

CLARK. *Venture in History, Production, Publicaeion...Bancroft.* 1973. CA U. ils. 190p. F. A4. $40.00

CLARKE, Anna. *Cabin 3033.* 1986. Crime Club. 1st ed. hc. F/F. P3. $13.00

CLARKE, Anna. *Last Voyage.* 1982. St Martin. 1st ed. VG/VG. P3. $18.00

CLARKE, Anna. *Legacy of Evil.* 1976. Collins Crime Club. 1st ed. VG/VG. P3. $20.00

CLARKE, Arthur C. *Earthlight.* 1972. HBJ. 1st ed. VG/VG. P3. $20.00

CLARKE, Arthur C. *Fountains of Paradise.* 1979. HBJ. 1st ed. VG/VG. P3. $25.00

CLARKE, Arthur C. *Ghost From the Grand Banks.* 1990. Bantam. 1st ed. F/F. P3. $20.00

CLARKE, Arthur C. *Glide Path.* 1963. HBJ. 1st ed. VG+/worn. N3. $25.00

CLARKE, Arthur C. *Interplanetary Flight.* 1951. Harper. 1st ed. author's 1st book. F/NF. M19. $100.00

CLARKE, Arthur C. *Islands in the Sky.* 1979. Gregg. 1st ed. F/F. P3. $20.00

CLARKE, Arthur C. *Making of a Moon.* 1958. Harper. hc. VG. P3. $75.00

CLARKE, Arthur C. *Prelude to Space.* 1970. HBW. NF/NF. P3. $15.00

CLARKE, Arthur C. *Reach for Tomorrow.* 1970. HBW. VG/VG. P3. $20.00

CLARKE, Arthur C. *Report on Planet Three.* 1972. Harper Row. 1st ed. VG. P3. $25.00

CLARKE, Arthur C. *Sands of Mars.* 1963. Sidgwick Jackson. 7th ed. xl. dj. P3. $5.00

CLARKE, Arthur C. *Songs of Distant Earth.* 1986. Del Rey. 1st ed. F/F. P3. $18.00

CLARKE, Arthur C. *Tales From the White Hart.* 1970. HBW. 1st ed. NF/NF. P3. $75.00

CLARKE, Arthur C. *View From Serendip.* 1977. Random. 1st ed. VG/VG. P3. $25.00

CLARKE, Arthur C. *1984: Spring, a Choice of Futures.* 1984. Del Rey. 1st ed. VG. P3. $15.00

CLARKE, Arthur C. *2010: Odyssey Two.* 1982. Ballantine. 1st ed. NF/dj. M21. $20.00

CLARKE, Arthur C. *2061: Odyssey Three.* 1988. Del Rey. 1st ed. VG/VG. P3. $18.00

CLARKE, Donald Henderson. *Alabam'.* 1946. Tower. VG/VG. P3. $10.00

CLARKE, Donald Henderson. *Housekeeper's Daughter.* 1940. Triangle. 4th. MTI. G/G. P3. $15.00

CLARKE, Donald Henderson. *That Mrs Renney.* 1937. Vanguard. 1st ed. F/NF. M19. $25.00

CLARKE, Gerald. *Capote: A Biography.* 1988. Simon Schuster. 1st ed. photos. 631p. F/F. B10. $15.00

CLARKE, I.F. *Voices Prophesying War 1763-1984.* 1966. Oxford. 1st ed. NF/NF. P3. $45.00

CLARKE, Thurston. *Equator: A Journey.* 1988. NY. Morrow. 1st ed. 8vo. 464p. AN/dj. P4. $25.00

CLARKE & JACYNA. *Nineteenth-Century Origins of Neuroscientific Concepts.* 1987. Los Angeles. 1st ed. 593p. dj. A13. $70.00

CLARKE & LEE. *Garden of Rama.* 1991. Bantam. 1st ed. F/F. N4. $22.50

CLARKE & LEE. *Ghost From the Grand Banks.* 1990. Bantam. 1st Am ed. F/NF. M21. $14.00

CLARKE & LEE. *Rama II.* 1989. Bantam. 1st Am ed. F/F. G10. $10.00

CLARKSON, Charles Ervine. *Rose of Old Virginia: A Romance...* 1927. Calvert-McBride. VG. B10. $25.00

CLARY, James. *Ladies of the Lake.* nd. np. 2nd. VG/VG. A16. $27.00

CLASSEN, Ewald. *ABC Bilderbuch.* ca 1930s. Zurich. Schweizer Bilderbuchverlag. 8vo. F/stiff pict wrp. B24. $285.00

CLAUDIA, Susan. *Clock & Bell.* 1974. Crime Club. 1st ed. xl. dj. P3. $5.00

CLAUDY, Carl H. *Adventures in the Unknown: Land of No Shadow (#3).* 1933. Grosset Dunlap. 214p. VG/dj. M20. $72.00

CLAUDY, Carl H. *Blue Grotto Terror.* 1934. Grosset Dunlap. VG. P3. $30.00

CLAUDY, Carl H. *Mystery Men of Mars.* 1933. Grosset Dunlap. 1st ed. NF. P3. $30.00

CLAUSS, Ludwig Ferdinand. *Rasse und Seele: Eine Einfuhrung in den Sinn der Leiblichen.* 1937. Munchen. Lehmann. 8th. 189p. xl. G1. $40.00

CLAVELL, James. *King Rat.* 1962. 1st ed. author's 1st book. NF/VG. A4. $200.00

CLAVELL, James. *Thrump-O-Moto.* 1986. 1st ed. F/F. S13. $14.00

CLAVELL, James. *Whirlwind.* 1986. Morrow. 1st ed. NF/NF. P3. $35.00

CLAVELL, James. *Whirlwind.* 1986. Morrow. 1st ed. sgn. F/F. B2. $45.00

CLAY, Beatrice. *Stories From Le Morte d'Arthur...* 1962. Dent. VG. P3. $15.00

CLAY, Enid. *Constant Mistress.* 1934. Golden Cockerel. 1/300. sgn. ils/sgn Eric Gill. 40p. F. B24. $450.00

CLAYMORE, Tod. *Appointment in New Orleans.* 1950. Cassell. 1st ed. hc. VG/G. P3. $30.00

CLAYTON, Helen Helm. *World Weather: Including Discussion of Influence...* 1923. Macmillan. 1st ed. 8vo. 383p. cloth. G. K5. $25.00

CLAYTON, Jo. *Soul Drinker.* nd. Guild America. hc. VG/VG. P3. $10.00

CLAYTON, John Bell. *Walk Toward the Rainbow.* 1954. Macmillan. 1st ed. 308p. G. B10. $15.00

CLAYTON & PRICE. *Seven Wonders of the Ancient World.* 1988. NY. Dorset. 1st ed. ils. 176p. NF/dj. W1. $20.00

CLEAR, R. *Old Magazines Collector's Price Guide.* 1974. np. sm 4to. 68p. G. T3. $10.00

CLEARY, Beverly. *Dear Mr Henshaw.* 1983. Morrow. 1st ed. ils. 134p. NF/clip. C14. $25.00

CLEARY, Beverly. *Girl From Yamhill.* 1988. Morrow. 1st ed. 279p. VG+/dj. M20. $22.00

CLEARY, Beverly. *Ramona Forever.* 1984. Morrow. 1st ed. ils Alan Tiegreen. 182p. VG/dj. M20. $27.00

CLEARY, Beverly. *Socks.* 1973. Morrow. 1st ed. 156p. cloth. VG/dj. M20. $27.00

CLEARY, Jon. *Beaufort Sisters.* 1979. Collins. 1st ed. xl. dj. P3. $5.00

CLEARY, Jon. *Fall of an Eagle.* 1964. Morrow. 1st ed. VG/G. P3. $25.00

CLEARY, Jon. *Faraway Drums.* 1982. Morrow. 1st ed. VG/VG. P3. $20.00

CLEARY, Jon. *Man's Estate.* 1972. Collins. 1st ed. VG/VG. P3. $20.00

CLEARY, Jon. *Ninth Marquess.* 1972. Morrow. 1st ed. VG/VG. P3. $25.00

CLEARY, Jon. *Peter's Pence.* 1974. Morrow. 1st ed. VG/VG. P3. $20.00

CLEARY, Jon. *Sound of Lightning.* 1976. Morrow. 1st ed. VG/VG. P3. $20.00

CLEARY, Joy. *Strike Me Lucky.* 1962. Morrow. 1st ed. xl. dj. P3. $5.00

CLEAVELAND, Agnes Morley. *No Life for a Lady.* 1941. Houghton Mifflin. inscr. ils Edward Borein. VG/dj. T10. $115.00

CLEAVELAND, C.H. *Pronouncing Medical Lexicon.* 1856. Cincinnati. 16mo. 312p. rebound. G. T3. $28.00

CLEAVER & HATTON. *Bibliography of Periodical Works of Charles Dickens.* 1933. London. lg paper ed. 1/250. 31p. 403p. VG. A4. $650.00

CLEEVE, Brian. *Death of a Painted Lady.* 1962. Hammond Hammond. 1st ed. VG. P3. $25.00

CLELAND, R.G. *From Wilderness to Empire.* 1944. NY. Knopf. stated 1st ed. 8vo. gray cloth. NF. P4. $20.00

CLELAND, R.G. *From Wilderness to Empire: History of California.* 1944. Knopf. 1st ed. 8vo. 388p. VG/dj. T10. $45.00

CLELAND, R.G. *History of Phelps Dodge.* 1952. NY. 1st ed. VG/G. B5. $25.00

CLEMENCE, G.M. *Motion of Mercury, 1765-1937.* 1943. WA, DC. 4to. 221p. wrp. K5. $30.00

CLEMENS, Cyril. *Josh Billings: Yankee Humorist.* 1932. Webster Groves. 197p. VG/dj. B5. $25.00

CLEMENS, Samuel L. *Adventures of Huckleberry Finn.* 1885. NY. 1st Am ed/1st state. 174 ils EW Kemble. F/chemise/case. B24. $6,500.00

CLEMENS, Samuel L. *Adventures of Huckleberry Finn.* 1885. NY. Webster. 1st ed. 8vo. mixed states. gilt gr cloth. VG. T10. $1,500.00

CLEMENS, Samuel L. *American Claimant.* 1892. Chas Webster. 1st ed. VG. M19. $125.00

CLEMENS, Samuel L. *Christmas Fireside. The Story of a Bad Little Boy...* 1949. Hillsborough, CA. Allen. 1/75. 12mo. ils. F. B24. $500.00

CLEMENS, Samuel L. *Double-Barrelled Detective Story.* 1902. NY. Harper. 1st ed. ils. VG. B5. $75.00

CLEMENS, Samuel L. *Horse's Tale.* 1907. Harper. 1st ed. 153p. VG. M20. $105.00

CLEMENS, Samuel L. *Jumping Frog, by Mark Twain.* 1984. Northampton, MA. 1/50. 8vo. ils/sgn AJ Robinson. AN/chemise/box. B24. $850.00

CLEMENS, Samuel L. *Letters From Earth.* 1959. edit DeVoto. VG/VG. B5. $40.00

CLEMENS, Samuel L. *Library of Humor.* 1888. NY. 1st ed. ils Kemble. VG. B5. $145.00

CLEMENS, Samuel L. *Life on the Mississippi.* 1944. LEC. 1/1200. ils/sgn TH Benton. quarter morocco. F/VG box. C6. $275.00

CLEMENS, Samuel L. *Mark Twain's Autobiography.* 1924. London/NY. 2 vol. 1st ed. VG. C6. $50.00

CLEMENS, Samuel L. *Mark Twain's Sketches, New & Old.* 1875. Hartford. Am Pub. 1st ed/2nd issue. 320p. gilt bl cloth. F. B24. $675.00

CLEMENS, Samuel L. *Punch, Brothers, Punch! And Other Sketches.* 1878. NY. Slote Woodman. 1st ed/2nd prt. ffe rpr. G. T10. $150.00

CLEMENS, Samuel L. *Roughing It.* 1872. Hartford. Am Pub. subscription issue. 300 ils. 592p. aeg. G-. B35. $300.00

CLEMENS, Samuel L. *Stolen White Elephant, Etc.* 1882. Boston. Osgood. 1st Am ed. 12mo. pict brn cloth. VG. T10. $100.00

CLEMENS, Samuel L. *Stolen White Elephant.* 1882. London. Chatto Windus. 1st ed/1st prt. 8vo. G. T10. $185.00

CLEMENS, Samuel L. *Tom Sawyer, Detective As Told by Huckleberry Finn.* 1897. Chatto Windus. 1st ed (Nov ads). NF. B4. $325.00

CLEMENS, Samuel L. *War Prayer.* 1968. 1st ed thus. ils John Groth. NF/VG. S13. $15.00

CLEMENS, Samuel L. *Washoe Giant in San Francisco.* 1938. George Fields. 1st ed. F/NF. N3. $95.00

CLEMENS, Samuel L. *What Is Man?* 1910. London. Watts. 1st Eng ed. F/case. B4. $300.00

CLEMENS, Samuel L. *1601, Conversation As It Was by the Social Fireside...* nd. np. private prt for Lyle Stuart. rpt of 1939 ed. F/case. A4. $85.00

CLEMENS, Samuel L. *1601.* 1933. Golden Hind. 1st ed thus. VG. B5. $95.00

CLEMENS, Samuel L. *1601: Conversation As It Was by the Social Fireside...* 1939. Chicago. private prt. 1/550. intro/sgn Franklin Meine. VG. A4. $185.00

CLEMENS, Susy. *Papa: Intimate Biography of Mark Twain.* 1985. Garden City. 1st ed. 236p. F/dj. A17. $10.00

CLEMENT, Hal. *Cycle of Fire.* 1964. Gollancz. 2nd ed. VG/VG. P3. $20.00

CLEMENT, Hal. *Needle.* 1950. Doubleday. 1st ed. VG/VG. P3. $60.00

CLEMENTS, Mark A. *Land of Nod.* 1995. Donald Fine. 1st ed. inscr. F/NF. N4. $35.00

CLEMENTS & SHEAR. *Genera of Fungi.* 1954 (1931). NY. 2nd. ils/pl. gr cloth. VG+. B26. $22.50

CLEMENTS & WEAVER. *Plant Ecology.* 1938 (1929). NY. 2nd. ils/map. 601p. VG. B26. $27.50

CLERIHEW, E. *Biography for Beginners.* 1905. London. 1st ed. author's 1st book. ils GK Chesterton. VG+. C6. $175.00

CLERKE, Agnes M. *System of the Stars.* 1905 (1890). London. Blk. 2nd. 8vo. 403p. G. K5. $100.00

CLEVE, John; see Offutt, Andrew.

CLEVELAND, Ray L. *Ancient South Arabian Necropolis.* 1965. John Hopkins. 1st ed. 4to. ils/plans. 188p. VG. W1. $45.00

CLIFFORD, Alexander G. *Conquest of North Africa 1940-43.* 1943. Boston. 1st ed. 450p. VG. A17. $14.50

CLIFFORD, Derek. *Pelargoniums.* 1970 (1958). London. revised 2nd. ils/photos/biblio/index. VG/dj. B26. $38.00

CLIFFORD, Francis. *Amigo, Amigo.* 1973. Coward. 1st ed. F/NF. H11. $25.00

CLIFFORD, Francis. *Drummer in the Dark.* 1976. HBJ. 1st ed. VG/VG. P3. $20.00

CLIFFORD, Francis. *Wild Justice.* 1972. CMG. 1st ed. VG/VG. P3. $25.00

CLIFFORD & ILLINGWORTH. *Voyage of the Golden Lotus.* 1963. Wellington. Reed. ils/charts/diagrams. 222p. VG. T7. $24.00

CLIFTON, Bud; see Stacton, David.

CLIFTON, Lucille. *Amifika.* 1977. Dutton. 1st ed. inscr. VG/G. B17. $8.50

CLIFTON, Lucille. *Everett Anderson's Goodbye.* 1983. Holt. 1st ed. ils Ann Grifalconi. VG/G. B17. $5.00

CLIFTON, Mark. *Eight Keys to Eden.* 1960. Doubleday. 1st ed. VG/VG. P3. $40.00

CLINE, C. Terry. *Attorney Conspiracy.* 1983. Arbor. 1st ed. VG/VG. P3. $15.00

CLINE, C. Terry. *Quarry.* 1987. NAL. 1st ed. VG/VG. P3. $18.00

CLINE, John. *Forever Beat.* 1990. Dutton. 1st ed. VG/VG. P3. $20.00

CLINGEMPEEL, Harry Miller. *Little Twigs of Clover.* 1966. JP Bell. 73p. VG/G. B10. $8.00

CLINTON, Henry. *Narrative of Lt-Gen Sir Henry Clinton.* 1783. London. 4th. VG. O7. $175.00

CLISE, Michelle Durkson. *Ophelia's Voyage to Japan.* 1986. Clarkson Potter. 1st ed. F/VG. M5. $70.00

CLIVE, William. *Tune That They Play.* 1973. Macmillan. 1st ed. VG/VG. P3. $15.00

CLIVE & GILMAN. *Kg 200.* nd. Simon Schuster. 2nd. VG/VG. P3. $13.00

CLOETE, Stuart. *Watch for Dawn.* 1939. Boston. 1st ed. VG/dj. A17. $10.00

CLOKE, Rene. *Heidi.* c 1980. London. Award. 1st ed thus. 4to. ils. unp. NF. C14. $10.00

CLOUD, James. *No One Loves With Solitude.* 1969. UNC. unp. VG. B10. $8.00

CLOWES, Ernest S. *Shipways to the Sea: Our Inland & Costal Waterways.* 1929. Baltimore. William & Wilkins. 1st ed. 196p. G. B18. $25.00

CLOWES, G.S. *Sailing Ships.* 1931. London. VG/wrp. O7. $25.00

CLYDE, Oswald John. *Benjamin Franklin, Printer.* 1927. NY. facsimile ils. 244p. red cloth. VG. B14. $100.00

CLYMER, Eleanor. *Belinda's New Spring Hat.* 1969. Franklin Watts. 1st ed. 8vo. 32p. VG+. C14. $7.00

CLYMER. *Treasury of Early American Automobiles 1877-1925.* 1950. Bonanza. cloth. NF/NF. D2. $40.00

CLYNE, Geraldine. *Jolly Jump-Ups' Vacation Trip.* 1942. McLoughlin. obl 4to. 6 popups. VG. T10. $90.00

CLYNE, Geraldine. *Jolly Jump-Ups See the Circus.* 1944. McLoughlin. mechanical. VG. C8. $125.00

CLYNE, Geraldyne. *Jolly Jump-Ups Favorite Nursery Stories.* 1942. McLoughlin. G+. P2. $55.00

COAD. *New Jersey in Traveler's Accounts 1524-1971...* 1972. np. 633 annotated entries. 221p. F. A4. $75.00

COAST PUBLISHING COMPANY. *21 Black Jack: How To Win the Las Vegas Way.* 1970. Las Vegas. 3rd. 64p. VG/wrp. S1. $3.00

COATES, Harold Wilson. *Stories of Kentucky Feuds.* 1942. Knoxville, TN. Holmes-Darst Coal Corp. 1st ed thus. 280p. M8. $45.00

COATES, Walter John. *Land of Allen & Other Verse.* 1928. North Montpelier. Recluse. inscr assoc copy. 8vo. F. B11. $75.00

COATS, Peter. *House & Garden Book of Garden Decoration.* 1970. NY. 1st Am ed/2nd prt. ils/tissue guards. 89p. B26. $55.00

COATSWORTH, Elizabeth. *Alice-All-By-Herself.* 1937. Macmillan. 1st ed. sgn. ils Marguerite de Angeli. VG/G+. P2. $100.00

COATSWORTH, Elizabeth. *Cat Who Went to Heaven.* 1930. Macmillan. 1st ed. ils Lynd Ward. VG+. P2. $85.00

COATSWORTH, Elizabeth. *Cat Who Went to Heaven.* 1931. Macmillan. 5th. ils Lynd Ward. 57p. VG. C14. $30.00

COATSWORTH, Elizabeth. *Fair American.* 1943. Macmillan. 2nd. 8vo. VG. B17. $5.00

COATSWORTH, Elizabeth. *Grandmother Cat & the Hermit.* 1970. Macmillan. 1st ed. ils Irving Booker. F/VG+. P2. $25.00

COATSWORTH, Elizabeth. *White House.* Sept 1942. Macmillan. 1st prt. ils Helen Sewell. G+. C8. $40.00

COBB, Benjamin. *Yankee Mother Goose.* 1902. Hurst. ils Ella Brison. G. P2. $35.00

COBB, Frank. *Aviator's Luck.* 1927. Saalfield. ils. G. A17. $5.00

COBB, Irvin S. *One Third Off.* 1921. Doran. ils Tony Sarg. G+. P12. $5.00

COBBE, Frances Power. *Darwinism in Morals & Other Essays.* 1872. London. 1st ed. 399p. VG. A13. $100.00

COBBETT, William. *Life of Andrew Jackson, President of the US.* 1834. np. 16mo. 206p. quarter leather/tan brd. VG. T3. $45.00

COBLENTZ, Cate. *Blue & Silver Necklace.* 1937. Boston. Little Brn/Atlantic Monthly. 1st ed. 242p. G+/torn. T5. $35.00

COBLENTZ, Cate. *Scatter, the Chipmunk.* 1946. Children's Pr. 8vo. ils Schwartz. VG. B17. $6.00

COBLENTZ, Stanton A. *Under the Triple Suns.* 1955. Fantasy. 1st ed. VG/G. P3. $35.00

COBURN, Alvin Langdon. *Alvin Langdon Coburn.* 1986. NY. Aperture. 1st ed. 4to. F/dj. S9. $45.00

COBURN, Andrew. *No Way Home.* 1992. Dutton. 1st ed. rem mk. NF/VG. N4. $17.50

COBURN, Andrew. *Sweetheart.* 1985. Secker Warburg. 1st ed. VG/VG. P3. $20.00

COCHRAN & MURPHY. *Temple Dogs.* 1989. NAL. 1st ed. F/F. P3. $20.00

COCHRAN & ODLUM. *Star at Noon.* 1954. Boston. 1st ed. sgn. 274p. VG/dj. B18. $45.00

COCKER. *Loneliness & Time: Story of British Travel Writing...* 1992. np. ils. 312p. F/F. A4. $23.00

COCKRUM, William Monroe. *History of the Underground Railroad...* 1915. Oakland City, IN. Cockrum Prt Co. 1st ed. 336p. NF/VG. M8. $250.00

COCTEAU, Jean. *Difficulty of Being.* 1967. Coward McCann. 1st ed. 8vo. F/NF clip. S9. $25.00

COCTEAU, Jean. *Theatre.* 1957. np. 2 vol. 1st trade ed. 40 orig lithos. 8vo. cloth. NF. C2. $500.00

CODY, Iron Eyes. *Iron Eyes: My Life As a Hollywood Indian.* 1982. Everest. 1st ed. inscr. 290p. w/4 photos. T10. $150.00

CODY, William F. *Buffalo Bill's Life Story: An Autobiography.* 1924. NY. ils NC Wyeth. VG. A15. $25.00

CODY & INMAN. *Great Salt Lake Trail.* 1978. Williamstown. rpt of 1898 ed. 529p. gilt bl cloth. AN. P4. $25.00

COE, Jonathan. *Winshaw Legacy; or, What a Carve Up!* 1995. Knopf. 1st Am ed. F/F clip. B4. $45.00

COE, Michael. *America's First Civilization.* 1968. Smithsonian. 1st ed. 160p. dj. F3. $30.00

COE, Michael. *Breaking the Maya Code.* 1992. Thames Hudson. revised/expaned ed. 224p. F3. $20.00

COE, Tucker. *Murder Among Children.* 1967. Random. 1st ed. VG/G. P3. $20.00

COE, William. *Tikal.* 1973. Phil U Mus. 4th. 123p. wrp. F3. $20.00

COEL, Margaret. *Eagle Catcher.* 1995. CO U. 1st ed. AN/dj. M22. $85.00

COFFEY, Brian; see Koontz, Dean R.

COFFEY, Frank. *Modern Masters of Horror.* 1981. CMG. 1st ed. NF/NF. P3. $20.00

COFFEY, Thomas M. *Imperial Tragedy: Japan in WWII.* 1970. Cleveland. 1st ed. 531p. VG/dj. A17. $15.00

COFFIN, Charles Carleton. *Our New Way Around the World.* 1869. Fields Osgood. 1st ed. 8vo. 524p. VG. T3/W1. $35.00

COFFIN, Charles E. *Gist of Whist, Including American Leads...* 1895. NY. 5th. 110p. VG. S1. $10.00

COFFIN, Geoffrey; see Mason, Van Wyck.

COFFIN & PRUIT. *Energy Resources of the Denver Basin.* 1978. Rocky Mtn Assn Geologists. hc. 272p. F. D8. $30.00

COFFMAN, F.L. *Atlas of Treasure Maps.* 1957. Thomas Nelson. 41 maps. NF. O7. $65.00

COFFMAN, Virginia. *From Satan, With Love.* 1983. Piatkus. hc. F/F. P3. $15.00

COGGER & ZWEIFEL. *Reptiles & Amphibians.* 1992. NY. Smithmark. 1st ed. 4to. F/F. B1. $40.00

COGGINS, Clemency. *Cenote of Sacrifice.* 1984. Austin, TX. 1st ed. 176p. wrp. F3. $25.00

COGGINS, Jack. *Marine Painter's Guide.* 1983. Van Nostrand. 11 pl. 170p. VG/dj. T7. $45.00

COGSWELL, H.L. *Water Birds of California.* 1977. Berkeley. mc pl/ils. 399p. F/F. B11. $30.00

COHEN, Ben. *Cardograms: A Composite Excercise in Bridge, Solo & Whist.* 1960. London. 90p. VG. S1. $8.00

COHEN, Ben. *Change to ACOL.* 1957. London. 2nd imp. 158p. VG. S1. $6.00

COHEN, Daniel. *Masters of Horror.* 1984. Clarion. 1st ed. F/F. T2. $16.00

COHEN, I. Bernard. *Some Early Tools of American Science.* 1950. Cambridge. photos/pl. red cloth. F/dj. B14. $75.00

COHEN, Joel. *Inside Corner: Talks With Tom Seaver.* 1974. Atheneum. 1st ed. F/F. P8. $40.00

COHEN, KATZ & SUNDBY. *Breakthrough in Bridge.* 1974. WI. 186p. VG/wrp. S1. $5.00

COHEN, Leonard. *Beautiful Losers.* 1966. Viking. 1st ed. F/NF. C2. $75.00

COHEN, Miriam. *When Will I Read?* 1977. Greenwillow. 1st ed. ils Lillian Hoban. unp. NF/VG clip. C14. $10.00

COHEN, Octavus Roy. *Crimson Alibi.* 1929. Dodd Mead. VG. P3. $20.00

COHEN, Octavus Roy. *Outer Gate.* 1927. Little Brn. 1st ed. F/VG. M19. $65.00

COHEN, Saul B. *Problems & Trends in American Geography.* 1967. NY. VG. O7. $20.00

COHEN, Stanley. *330 Park.* 1977. Putnam. 1st ed. F/F. P3. $15.00

COHEN & MITCHELL. *Men of Zeal: A Candid Inside Story of Iran-Contra Hearings.* 1988. Viking. 1st ed. ils. NF/dj. W1. $20.00

COHEN & SCHARFF. *Cohen's Complete Book of Gin Rummy.* 1973. NY. 346p. VG/dj. S1. $6.00

COHN. *George Cruikshank: A Catalogue Raisonne of Work...* nd. np. rpt of 1924 ed. 1/150. ils/notes/facsimiles. 422p. F. A4. $75.00

COKE, Edward. *Compleate Copy-Holder...* 1641. London. T Cotes/W Cooke. 1st ed. sm 4to. 180p. modern gilt calf/morocco label. K2. $250.00

COKE, Edward. *First Part of the Institutes of the Laws of England...* 1629. London. 2nd/corrected. contemporary calf. G. M11. $3,500.00

COKE, Edward. *Le Tierce Part des Reportes del Edward Coke Lattorney...* 1602. London. 1st ed of part 3. contemporary calf. M11. $1,250.00

COKE, Edward. *Third Part of the Institutes of Laws of England...* 1671. London. early ed of 3rd part of 4. modern calf. M11. $850.00

COKER, Elizabeth Boatwright. *Bees.* 1968. Dutton. 1st ed. sgn. VG/VG. B11. $40.00

COKER, Elizabeth Boatwright. *India Allan.* 1953. Dutton. 1st ed. VG/G. P3. $15.00

COLACELLO, Bob. *Holy Terror: Andy Warhol Close Up.* 1990. Harper Collins. 1st ed. F/F. P3. $23.00

COLBERG, Nancy. *Wallace Stegner: A Descriptive Bibliography.* 1990. Confluence. 1st ed. photos. AN/sans. A18. $50.00

COLBERT, E.-C.V. *Voyage dans l'Interieur des Etats-Unis et au Canada.* 1935. Baltimore. VG. O7. $45.00

COLBERT, E.H. *Men & Dinosaurs: The Search in Field & Laboratory...* 1968. Dutton. 1st ed. ils/pl. VG/dj. D8. $20.00

COLBERT & COLBERT. *Virginia: Off the Beaten Path, a Guide to Unique Places.* 1986. E Woods. 176p. VG. B10. $5.00

COLBY, Charles. *Morse & Gaston's Diamond Atlas.* 1857. NY. Gaston. sq 12mo. 54 maps. 240p. VG. O7. $375.00

COLDEN, Cadwallader. *History of Five Indian Nations of Canada...* 1755. London. Davis Wren Ward. 3rd. 16mo. 260p. leather. fair. B36. $300.00

COLDHAM. *Complete Book of Emigrants 1607-1660...* 1992. np. 618p. F/F. A4. $35.00

COLE, Adrian. *Place Among the Fallen.* 1987. Arbor. 1st ed. NF/NF. P3. $20.00

COLE, Bill. *Fishheads.* 1991. Louisville, KY. 144p. VG. S1. $6.00

COLE, Burt. *Blue Climate.* 1977. Harper Row. 1st ed. VG/VG. P3. $13.00

COLE, Burt. *Funco File.* nd. BC. VG/VG. P3. $8.00

COLE, Burt. *Quick.* 1989. Morrow. 1st ed. NF/NF. P3. $20.00

COLE, E.B. *Philosophical Corps.* 1961. Gnome. 1st ed. F/F. P3. $30.00

COLE, Ernest. *House of Bondage.* 1967. Ridge/Random. 1st ed. F/F. B2. $45.00

COLE, Ernest. *House of Bondage: South African Black Man Exposes...* 1967. Random. 4to. photos. 179p. F/NF. R11. $35.00

COLE, F.J. *History of Comparative Anatomy From Aristotle...* 1975. NY. 524p. wrp. A13. $20.00

COLE, Franklyn W. *Introduction to Meteorology.* (1970). John Wiley. 4th. 8vo. 388p. VG. K5. $12.00

COLE, George Watson. *Catalogue of Books Relating to Discovery & Early History...* nd. 5 vol. rpt of orig 1907 ed. 1/100. F. A4. $300.00

COLE, Grenville A.J. *Gypsy Road.* 1894. Macmillan. 1st ed. 8vo. ils. 166p. VG. W1. $18.00

COLE, Harriette. *Jumping the Broom: African-American Wedding Planner.* 1993. NY. Holt. 1st ed. 207p. AN/dj. P4. $20.00

COLE, Margaret Rossa. *Grandma Takes a Freighter.* 1950. Exposition. sgn. 104p. VG/G. B11. $15.00

COLE, William. *Oh, What Nonsense!* 1966. Viking. 1st ed. 8vo. 80p. red/orange pict cloth. VG/NF. T5. $30.00

COLE & FRASER. *African Art & Leadership.* 1972. WI U. F/F. D2. $40.00

COLE & ROSS. *Arts of Ghana.* 1977. UCLA. F/stiff wrp. D2. $80.00

COLE. *International Rare Book Prices.* 1987. Modern 1st Eds. 257p. F. A4. $25.00

COLEMAN, J.W. *Molly Maguire Riots.* 1936. Richmond. 1st ed. 189p. VG. B5. $50.00

COLEMAN, John Winston Jr. *Bibliography of Kentucky History.* 1949. KY U. 1st ed. 516p. VG. M8. $150.00

COLEMAN, Mary Haldrane. *Story of a Portrait.* 1935. Dietz. 1st ed. sgn. 40p. VG. B10. $10.00

COLEMAN, Nevils S.J. *Miniatures of Georgetown.* 1934. WA. 1/500. sgn. 496p. VG. B5. $45.00

COLEMAN, Wanda. *Imagoes.* 1983. Santa Barbara. 1/26 lettered. sgn. F. B4. $185.00

COLEMAN, Wanda. *Mad Dog Black Lady.* 1979. Blk Sparrow. 1/26 lettered. sgn. patterned cloth. F/acetate dj. B4. $200.00

COLEMAN, Wanda. *War of the Eyes & Other Stories.* 1987. Blk Sparrow. 1/26 lettered. sgn. F/acetate dj. B4. $185.00

COLEMAN & LINK. *Medical Support of the Army Air Forces in World WWar II.* 1955. WA. 1st ed. 1027p. A13. $100.00

COLEMAN & THORN. *Singing Time: Songs for Nursery & School.* March 1930. John Day. 2nd. 4to. 48p. VG+. C14. $12.00

COLERIDGE, Samuel Taylor. *Poetical Works of...* nd. London. aeg. red full leather. VG. B30. $100.00

COLERIDGE, Samuel Taylor. *Sibylline Leaves: A Collection of Poems.* 1817. London. Rest Fenner. 1st ed. 8vo. 303p. teg. gr cloth case. B24. $1,650.00

COLERIDGE, Samuel Taylor. *Zapolya: A Christmas Tale, in Two Parts...* 1817. London. Fenner. 1st ed. 128p. later tan calf/red morocco label. F. B24. $750.00

COLES, K. Adlard. *Sailing Years.* 1981. London. Granada. 37 pl. 212p. VG/dj. T7. $22.00

COLES, L.B. *Beauties & Deformities of Tobacco-Using...* 1851. Boston. 167p. blk cloth. VG. B14. $125.00

COLES, Manning. *All That Glitters.* 1954. Doubleday Crime Club. 1st ed. 189p. VG/dj. M20. $35.00

COLES, Manning. *Basle Express.* 1956. Crime Club. 1st ed. VG. P3. $15.00

COLES, Manning. *Dangerous by Nature.* 1950. Doubleday. 1st ed. VG/VG. N4/P3. $30.00

COLES, Manning. *Drink to Yesterday.* 1944. Canada. Musson. VG/VG. P3. $30.00

COLES, Manning. *Green Hazard.* 1945. Canada. Musson. ffe removed. VG/VG. P3. $20.00

COLES, Manning. *No Entry.* 1958. Doubleday. 1st ed. VG. P3. $20.00

COLES, Manning. *Not for Export.* 1954. Hodder Stoughton. 1st ed. VG. P3. $25.00

COLES, Manning. *They Tell No Tales.* 1942. Doubleday Crime Club. 1st ed. VG. M22. $10.00

COLES, Manning. *Without Lawful Authority.* 1944. Canada. Musson. 1st ed. VG/VG. P3. $25.00

COLES, Phillips. *Gallery of Girls.* 1911. NY. Century. 1st ed. VG. B5. $200.00

COLES, Phillips. *Young Man's Fancy.* 1912. Bobbs Merrill. 1st ed. VG. B5. $200.00

COLES & RAMSAY. *Mechanical Treatment of Deformities of the Mouth...* 1868. London. ils. 95p. red cloth. VG. B14. $150.00

COLETTI, Luigi. *Tomaso da Modena.* 1963. Venezia. Neri Pozza. ils/pl. 144p. xl. D2. $95.00

COLFER, Enid. *Cucumber: Story of a Siamese Cat.* 1961. Thomas Nelson. 1st ed. ils Victor Dowling. 98p. F/clip. C14. $15.00

COLIN. *Letters of Robert Louis Stevenson to His Family & Friends.* 1905. np. 2 vol. ils. VG. A4. $35.00

COLLIDGE & COOLIDGE. *Navajo Indians.* 1930. Houghton Mifflin. 8vo. 316p. map ep. F/dj. T10. $100.00

COLLIER, John. *His Monkey Wife.* 1931. Appleton. 1st ed. VG. P3. $35.00

COLLIER, Peter. *Fondas: A Hollywood Dynasty.* 1991. Putnam. 1st ed. NF/NF. P3. $23.00

COLLIER, Richard. *House Called Memory.* 1961. Dutton. 1st ed. VG/VG. P3. $15.00

COLLIGNON, Jules. *Les Mille et un Jours.* 1844. Paris. Pourrat Freres. 8vo. 434p. VG. D1. $200.00

COLLINGWOOD, Stuart. *Life & Letters of Lewis Carroll.* 1898. Fisher Unwin. 448p+12 ads. gilt gr cloth. VG. D1. $125.00

COLLINS, G.B. *Wildcats & Shamrocks.* 1977 (1976). Menonnite Pr. 2nd. 90p. F/clip. D8. $10.00

COLLINS, Hunt; see Hunter, Evan.

COLLINS, Joe G. *Last of Steam.* 1960. Howell North. 1st ed. 269p. NF/dj. M20. $42.00

COLLINS, John S. *My Experiences in the West.* 1970. Lakeside. 252p. VG+. M20. $27.00

COLLINS, Larry. *Maze.* 1989. Simon Schuster. 1st ed. VG/VG. P3. $20.00

COLLINS, Leighton. *Air Facts Reader 1939-41.* 1974. NY. ils. 240p. VG. A17. $12.50

COLLINS, Max. *Carnal Hours.* 1994. NY. 1st ed. sgn. F/F. A15. $25.00

COLLINS, Max. *Million-Dollar Wound.* 1986. Tor. 1st ed. VG/VG. P3. $18.00

COLLINS, Max. *Nice Weekend for Murder.* 1986. Walker. 1st ed. VG/VG. P3. $16.00

COLLINS, Max. *No Cure for Death.* 1983. Walker. 1st ed. VG/VG. P3. $15.00

COLLINS, Max. *Spree.* 1987. NY. 1st ed. sgn. F/F. A15. $35.00

COLLINS, Max. *True Detective.* 1983. NY. 1st ed. sgn. F/F. A15. $30.00

COLLINS, Michael; see Lynds, Dennis.

COLLINS, Paul. *Alien Worlds.* 1979. Void. 1st ed. NF/NF. P3. $30.00

COLLINS, Paul. *Envisaged Worlds.* 1978. Void. 1st ed. NF/NF. P3. $30.00

COLLINS, Paul. *Other Worlds.* 1978. Void. 1st ed. NF/NF. P3. $30.00

COLLINS, Sewell. *Rubaiyat of a Scotch Terrier.* 19226. NY. Stokes. ils Sewell Collins. F/rpr. H4. $35.00

COLLINS, Wilkie. *Moonstone.* 1946. Literary Guild. VG/torn. P3. $8.00

COLLINS, Wilkie. *Woman in White.* 1860. NY. 1st ed/2nd issue. VG+. C6. $275.00

COLLINS, Wilkie. *Woman in White.* 1933. Daily Express. VG. P3. $20.00

COLLINS, William. *Poetical Works..., Enriched With Elegant Engravings...* 1798. London. Bensley. 12mo. 165p. fore-edge painting. aeg. full morocco. T10. $450.00

COLLINS & GROSS. *Souvenir Guide to Gettysburg National Military Park.* 1971. self pub. revised. photos/maps. 72p. wrp. B10. $10.00

COLLINS & LAPIERRE. *Fifth Horseman.* 1980. Simon Schuster. 1st ed. NF/NF. M22. $15.00

COLLINS & LAPIERRE. *Mountbatten & the Partition of India.* 1982. Bangladesh. 191p. dj. A17. $10.00

COLLINS & LATHAM. *SF & Fantasy Book Review Annual 1988.* 1988. Meckler. 1st ed. hc. VG. P3. $25.00

COLLINS & SHARP. *Roses Ils & How To Grow Them.* 1951. Portland. ils. 160p. F/VG. B26. $20.00

COLLINS & TIGNOR. *Egypt & the Sudan.* 1967. Englewood Cliffs. 1st ed. 8vo. map. 180p. NF/dj. W1. $16.00

COLLINSON, Frank. *Life in the Saddle.* 1964. Norman. 2nd. 12mo. ils Harold Bugbee. 244p. NF/dj. T10. $35.00

COLLIS, Maurice Henry. *Contributions to Operative Surgery: Operations...* 1867. Dublin. ils/pl. modern wrp. B14. $275.00

COLLIS, Maurice. *Cortes & Montezuma.* 1955. NY. VG. O7. $30.00

COLLIS, Maurice. *Foreign Mud.* 1947. NY. VG. O7. $30.00

COLLISON, Thomas F. *Gin Chow's First Annual Almanac.* 1932. Los Angeles. Wetzel. 3rd. 12mo. ils Elizabeth E Mason. 61p. T10. $25.00

COLLODI, Carlo. *Adventures of Pinocchio.* nd. Macmillan. 3rd. ils Attilio Mussino. trans CD Chiesa. 404p. VG. D1. $225.00

COLLODI, Carlo. *Pinocchio, the Adventures of a Marionette.* 1904. Ginn. sm 8vo. ils Charles Copeland. teg. gilt cloth. VG. M5. $75.00

COLLODI, Carlo. *Pinocchio, the Adventures of a Marionette.* 1937. LEC. 1st ed. 1/1500. ils/sgn Richard Floethe. F/case. C2. $75.00

COLLODI, Carlo. *Pinocchio.* ca 1944. Italgeo. abridged trade ed. ils Vsevolod Nicouline. pict brd. VG. M5. $75.00

COLLODI, Carlo. *Pinocchio.* nd. McKay. ils/8 pl. gilt dk gr cloth/lg pl. VG/worn. M5. $65.00

COLLODI, Carlo. *Pinocchio.* 1920. Lippincott. ils Maria Kirk. 234p. bl cloth/beige spine. VG. D1. $85.00

COLLODI, Carlo. *Pinocchio.* 1933. Bl Ribbon. 1st ed. ils Harold Lentz. 4 popups. 96p. VG+/dj. D1. $675.00

COLLODI, Carlo. *Pinocchio.* 1940. Whitman. ils Disney Studios. VG. P2. $40.00

COLLODI, Carlo. *Story of a Puppet; or, Adventures of Pinocchio.* 1892. NY. Cassell. 1st Am issue of 1st Eng-language ed. 8vo. 232p. NF. B24. $2,000.00

COLLYER & VERPLANCK. *Sloops of the Hudson.* 1908. NY. Morrow. ils. 171p. T7. $65.00

COLMAN, Charles W. *In His Own Country & Other Poems.* 1942. private prt. 194p. VG. B10. $15.00

COLMAN, Samuel. *Nature's Harmonic Unity, a Treatise on Its Relation...* 1912. NY. 4to. ils. 327p. VG. B14. $100.00

COLOMBO, John Robert. *Other Canadas.* 1979. McGraw Hill Ryerson. 1st ed. VG/VG. P3. $20.00

COLQUHOUN, Archibald. *Currier & Ives.* 1950. Cleveland. VG. O7. $35.00

COLQUHOUN, Archibald. *Mastery of the Pacific.* 1902. NY. xl. VG. O7. $55.00

COLTER, Cyrus. *Hippodrome.* 1973. Chicago. 1st ed. sgn. F/NF clip. A11. $60.00

COLTON, G. Woolworth. *Colton's General Atlas.* 1859. NY. JH Colton. 1st ed. lg folio. 170 steel pl. half morocco/gray cloth. VG. C6. $1,200.00

COLTON, Harold S. *Hopi Kachina Dolls, With a Key to Their Identification.* 1964. NM U. revised. 4to. ils. VG. A4. $85.00

COLTON, Harold S. *Hopi Kachina Dolls.* 1970. NM U. revised ed. 4to. 150p. prt cloth. T10. $30.00

COLTON, James; see Hansen, Joseph.

COLTON. *Miracle Men of the Telephone.* 1947. NGS. VG. H7. $20.00

COLUM, Padraic. *Balloon.* 1929. Macmillan. 1st ed. 8vo. NF/chip. T10. $35.00

COLUM, Padraic. *Boy Who Knew What the Birds Said.* 1918. Macmillan. 1st ed. ils. VG+. M20. $28.00

COLUM, Padraic. *Six Who Were Left in a Shoe.* 1923. Chicago. Volland. ils Dugald Stewart Walker. 40p. NF. A4. $65.00

COLVER, Anne. *Bread-And-Butter Journey.* 1970. HRW. 1st ed. sgn. 8vo. 101p. F/VG. T5. $30.00

COLVIN, Thomas E. *Cruising As a Way of Life.* 1979. NY. Seven Seas. 206p. VG/dj. T7. $20.00

COLWIN, Laurie. *Goodbye Without Leaving.* 1990. Poseidon. UP. F/wrp. B4. $75.00

COLWIN, Laurie. *Lone Pilgrim.* 1981. Knopf. 1st ed. sgn. F/F. B4. $75.00

COLWIN, Laurie. *Passion & Affect.* 1974. NY. 1st ed. sgn. NF/F. A11. $55.00

COMBE, Andrew. *Principles of Physiology Applied to Preservation of Health.* 1840. NY. ils. 291p. VG. B14. $55.00

COMBE, George. *Constitution of Man Considered in Relation to External...* 1829. Boston. Carter Hendee. 1st Am ed. 12mo. rebound gr buckram. NF. G1. $85.00

COMFORT, Will Levington. *Son of Power.* nd. Gundy. 1st Canadian ed. VG. P3. $10.00

COMMAGER, Henry Steele. *Second St Nicholas Anthology.* 1950. Random. 1st ed. 8vo. ils. 486p. NF. C14. $12.00

COMPARATO. *Chronicles of Genius & Folly, R Hoe & Company...* 1979. np. ils. 846p. F. A4. $35.00

COMPTON, D.G. *Windows.* 1979. Berkley Putnam. 1st ed. VG/VG. P3. $13.00

COMPTON, R.R. *Manual of Field Geology.* 1962. NY. John Wiley. 378p. G. D8. $15.00

COMRIE, John. *History of Scottish Medicine.* 1932. np. 2 vol. VG. A13. $175.00

COMSTOCK, Enos B. *Out of the Woods, Wild Animal Stories.* 1941. Dodd Mead. 8vo. VG/G. B17. $5.00

COMSTOCK, Enos B. *Tuck-Me-In Stories.* 1918. Moffat Yard. 3rd. 76p. pict cloth. VG. A17. $30.00

COMSTOCK, J.L. *Outlines of Physiology...* 1843. NY. 3rd ils. 322p. F. B14. $75.00

COMSTOCK, Jim. *Pa & Ma & Mister Kennedy.* 1965. Appalachian Pr. inscr. 128p. VG/VG. B10. $10.00

CONAD, Jack Randolph. *Horn & the Sword.* 1957. Dutton. 1st ed. 222p. VG/dj. T10. $30.00

CONANT, Susan. *Bloodlines.* 1993. Doubleday. 1st ed. NF/NF. P3. $17.00

CONDAX, Kate. *Horse Sense.* 1990. NY. Prentice Hall. 1st ed. VG/VG. O3. $15.00

CONDER, Josiah. *Modern Traveller.* 1830. London. Duncan. 18mo. ils. 356p. cloth. VG. W1. $18.00

CONDIT, Ira J. *Fig.* 1947. Waltham, MA. ils/tables. 222p. bl buckram. VG+. B26. $62.50

CONDIT, Ira J. *Fiscus: The Exotic Species.* 1969. Berkeley. ils/pl. VG/wrp. B26. $60.00

CONDON, George E. *Stars in the Water: Story of the Erie Canal.* 1974. NY. 1st ed. sgn. 338p. VG/VG. B5. $35.00

CONDON, George E. *Stars in the Water: Story of the Erie Canal.* 1974. NY. 338p. VG/torn. B18. $15.00

CONDON, Richard. *Abandoned Woman.* 1977. Dial. 1st ed. VG/VG. P3. $20.00

CONDON, Richard. *Bandicoot.* 1978. Dial. 1st ed. NF/NF. H11. $20.00

CONDON, Richard. *Death of a Politician.* 1978. Marek. 1st ed. F/F. B35. $20.00

CONDON, Richard. *Ecstasy Business.* 1967. Dial. 1st ed. NF/NF. H11. $25.00

CONDON, Richard. *Entwining.* 1980. Marek. 1st ed. VG/VG. P3. $20.00

CONDON, Richard. *Infinity of Mirrors.* 1964. NY. Random. 1st ed. F/NF. H11. $40.00

CONDON, Richard. *Prizzi's Family.* 1986. Putnam. 1st ed. VG/VG. P3. $18.00

CONDON, Richard. *Prizzi's Honor.* 1982. Michael Joseph. 1st ed. VG/VG. P3. $25.00

CONDON, Richard. *Prizzi's Money.* 1994. Crown. 1st ed. AN/dj. M22. $15.00

CONDON, Richard. *Trembling Upon Rome.* 1983. Michael Joseph. 1st ed. F/F. P3. $25.00

CONDON, Richard. *Venerable Bead.* 1992. St Martin. VG/VG. P3. $22.00

CONDON, Richard. *Verticle Smile.* 1971. Dial. 1st ed. VG/VG. P3. $25.00

CONDON, Richard. *Whisper of the Axe.* 1976. Dial. 2nd. VG/VG. P3. $15.00

CONDON & SUGRUE. *We Called It Music.* 1947. Holt. 1st ed. NF/torn. B2. $40.00

CONEY, Michael G. *Celestial Steam Locomotive.* nd. Houghton Mifflin. 2nd. VG/VG. P3. $15.00

CONEY, Michael G. *Celestial Steam Locomotive.* 1983. Houghton Mifflin. 1st ed. F/F. G10. $15.00

CONEY, Michael G. *Fang the Gnome.* 1988. NAL. 1st ed/1st prt. 8vo. ils. 345p. F/F. T10. $75.00

CONEY, Michael G. *Gods of the Greataway.* 1984. Houghton Mifflin. 1st ed. VG/VG. P3. $16.00

CONEY, Michael G. *Hello Summer, Goodbye.* 1975. Gollancz. 1st ed. sgn. F/F. P3. $30.00

CONGRAT-BUTLAR, Stefan. *Open Look.* 1969. Funk Wagnall. 1st ed. inscr. VG. w/promo material. S9. $45.00

CONKLIN, Groff. *The Best of SF.* 1946. Crown. 1st ed. G. P3. $15.00

CONKLING, Margaret C. *Memoirs of the Mother & Wife of Washington.* 1851. Auburn. new/revised/enlarged ed. 248p. G+. B18. $37.50

CONNELL, Charles. *Aphrodisiacs in Your Garden.* 1966. NY. ils. VG/dj. B26. $15.00

CONNELL, Evan S. *At the Crossroads.* 1965. Simon Schuster. 1st ed. VG/VG. M19. $75.00

CONNELL, Evan S. *Diary of a Rapist.* 1966. NY. 1st ed. F/F. B5. $50.00

CONNELL, Evan S. *Mrs Bridge.* 1959. Viking. 1st ed. F/F. B4. $400.00

CONNELL, Evan S. *Son of the Morning Star.* 1984. North Point. 1st ed. F/1st issue. C2. $75.00

CONNELL, Evan S. *White Lantern.* 1980. NY. 1st ed. F/F. A17. $9.50

CONNELLEY, William Elsey. *Quantrill & the Border Wars.* 1910. Cedar Rapids. Torch. 1st ed. 542p. cloth. NF. M8. $175.00

CONNELLY, Michael. *Black Echo.* 1992. Little Brn. ARC. F/wrp. M22. $50.00

CONNELLY, Michael. *Black Echo.* 1992. Little Brn. 1st ed. NF/NF. P3. $20.00

CONNELLY, Michael. *Black Echo.* 1992. Little Brn. 1st ed. sgn. F/F/bl promo band. T2. $60.00

CONNELLY, Michael. *Black Ice.* 1993. Little Brn. 1st ed. F/F. H11/M23. $35.00

CONNELLY, Michael. *Black Ice.* 1993. Little Brn. 1st ed. sgn. F/F. T2. $40.00

CONNELLY, Michael. *Black Ice.* 1993. Little Brn. 1st ed. VG/VG. P3. $20.00

CONNELLY, Michael. *Last Coyote.* 1995. Little Brn. 1st ed. sgn. F/F. T2. $30.00

CONNINGTON, J.J. *Grim Vengeance.* 1929. Little Brn. 1st ed. VG. P3. $35.00

CONNINGTON, J.J. *Two Ticket Puzzle.* 1930. Little Brn. 1st ed. VG. P3. $35.00

CONNOLLY. *Children's Modern First Editions: Their Value to Collectors.* 1988. np. 189 photos. 335p. F/F. A4. $165.00

CONNOR, Nellie Victoria. *Essence of Good Perfume.* 1940. Burbank. Ivan Deach. 1st ed. 1/100. inscr twice to Congressman Du Priest. VG. B4. $485.00

CONNOR, Ralph. *Gaspards of Pine Croft: A Romance of the Windemere.* 1923. Doran. 1st ed. F/VG. A18. $15.00

CONNOR, Ralph. *Rock & the River: A Romance of Quebec.* 1931. McClelland Stewart. 1st Canadian ed. inscr/sgn. VG/fox. A18. $20.00

CONNOR, Ralph. *Sky Pilot.* nd. Grosset Dunlap. VG. P3. $10.00

CONNOR, Ralph. *To Him That Hath: A Novel of the West Today.* 1921. Doran. 1st ed. VG+/VG+. A18. $15.00

CONNOR & STANNARD. *Comeback: My Race for the America's Cup.* 1987. St Martin. 1st ed. ils. 239p. NF/VG. P12. $8.00

CONOVER, David. *Finding Marilyn.* 1981. Grosset Dunlap. VG/VG. P3. $20.00

CONOVER, H.S. *Grounds Maintenance Handbook.* 1958 (1953). NY. 2nd. ils/photos/tables. 501p. dj. B26. $17.50

CONQUEST, Pleasonton Jr. *At Large.* 1933. Dietz. inscr. 94p. VG. B10. $10.00

CONRAD, Barnaby. *Tahiti.* 1962. NY. VG. O7. $20.00

CONRAD, D.H. *Memoir of Reverend James Chisholm.* 1856. NY. 1st ed. 12mo. 193p. gr cloth. xl. VG. T3. $28.00

CONRAD, Earl. *Da Vinci Machine.* 1968. Fleet. VG/VG. P3. $13.00

CONRAD, Earl. *Gulf Stream North.* (1980). Sagaponack. Second Chance. reissue. NF/NF. R11. $11.00

CONRAD, H.L. *Uncle Dick Wootton.* 1950. Long. rpt. 1/500. VG+. A15. $75.00

CONRAD, Joseph. *Chance: A Tale in Two Parts.* 1913. London. Methuen. 1st ed/1st issue. 1/50. dk gr cloth. F/pict dj. B24. $7,500.00

CONRAD, Joseph. *Heart of Darkness.* 1969. LEC. 1st ed. 1/1500. ils/sgn Robert Stone. F/NF case. C2. $75.00

CONRAD, Joseph. *Joseph Conrad to Richard Curle.* 1928. NY. Rudge. 1/850. pres. NF. C2. $45.00

CONRAD, Joseph. *Lord Jim.* 1900. Edinburgh/London. Blackwood. gray-gr cloth. VG. P3. $525.00

CONRAD, Joseph. *Lord Jim.* 1900. NY. 1st Am ed. NF. A9. $175.00

CONRAD, Joseph. *Lord Jim.* 1959. NY. LEC. 1/1500. ils/sgn Lynd Ward. quarter leather. NF/case. T10. $90.00

CONRAD, Joseph. *Mirror of the Sea: Memories & Impressions.* 1906. London. Methuen. 1st ed/1st issue (40p ads/untrimmed). VG. C2. $125.00

CONRAD, Joseph. *Nostromo.* 1923. Doubleday Page. VG. P3. $25.00

CONRAD, Joseph. *Outcast of the Islands.* 1896. London. 1st ed. author's 2nd book. VG. C6. $195.00

CONRAD, Joseph. *Personal Record.* 1912. Harper. 220p. VG. A4. $295.00

CONRAD, Joseph. *Tales of Hearsay.* 1928. Doubleday Page. 1st ed. NF/G. M19. $65.00

CONRAD, Joseph. *Typhoon & Other Stories.* 1903. London. 1st ed/1st issue. VG. C6. $250.00

CONRAD, Joseph. *Typhoon.* nd. Readers Lib. VG/torn. P3. $20.00

CONRAD, Joseph. *Under Western Eyes.* 1911. London. Methuen. 1st ed. NF. C2. $200.00

CONRAD, Joseph. *Within the Tides.* 1915. London. Dent. 1st ed. ribbed cloth. F/prt dj. B24. $600.00

CONRAD, Joseph. *Works of...* 1926-27. Doubleday Page. 25 vol. VG. P12. $125.00

CONRAD, Joseph. *Youth, Typhoon & the End of the Tether.* 1972. LEC. 1/1500. ils/sgn Robert Shore. prt/sgn Ward Ritchie. F/case. C2. $75.00

CONROY, Albert; see Albert, Marvin H.

CONROY, Frank. *Body & Soul.* 1993. Houghton Mifflin. 1st ed. F/F. H11. $25.00

CONROY, Frank. *Body & Soul.* 1993. Houghton Mifflin. 1st ed. 8vo. F/dj. w/promo kit. S9. $45.00

CONROY, Frank. *Midair.* 1985. Dutton. 1st ed. F/NF. M19. $17.50

CONROY, Frank. *Stop-Time.* 1967. 1st ed. author's 1st book. VG/VG. C4. $100.00

CONROY, Pat. *Beach Music.* 1995. Doubleday. 1st ed. sgn. F/F. B35. $55.00

CONROY, Pat. *Great Santini.* 1976. Boston. 1st ed. author's 1st novel. NF/NF. C6. $150.00

CONROY, Pat. *Lords of Discipline.* 1980. London. 1st ed. VG/VG. C4. $50.00

CONROY, Pat. *Prince of Tides.* 1986. Houghton Mifflin. 1st ed. NF/NF. B35/P10. $50.00

CONSIGNY, Jean-Marie. *Gardening for Fun in California.* 1940. Hollywood. ils. 249p. dj. B26. $12.50

CONSTANTINE, Albert. *Know Your Woods.* 1975 (1959). NY. revised ed. ils. dj. B26. $36.00

CONSTANTINE, K.C. *Always a Body To Trade.* 1983. Godine. 1st ed. VG/VG. M22. $55.00

CONSTANTINE, K.C. *Fix Like This.* 1975. Saturday Review. 1st ed. author's 4th novel. NF/NF. M22. $55.00

CONSTANTINE, K.C. *Joey's Case.* 1988. Mysterious. 1st ed. AN/dj. M22. $15.00

CONSTANTINE, K.C. *Man Who Liked Slow Tomatoes.* 1982. Godine. 1st ed. author's 5th novel. NF/NF. M22. $75.00

CONSTANTINE, Murray. *Swastika Night.* 1940. London. Left BC. 196p. VG. A17. $7.50

CONTRERAS & ZOLLA. *Plantas Toxicas de Mexico.* 1982. Mexico. 26 pl. 271p. F/dj. B26. $50.00

CONWAY, Hugh. *Called Back.* nd. Detective Club. hc. G/G. P3. $15.00

CONWAY, Moncure Daniel. *Autobiography.* 1904. Boston. 1st ed. 1/100. sgn. 2 vol. G+. B18. $95.00

COOK, Canfield. *Lucky Terrell: Secret Mission (#3).* 1943. Grosset Dunlap. lists 2 titles. 210p. VG+/dj. M20. $16.00

COOK, Charles A. *Among the Pimas; or, Mission to the Pima & Maricopa...* 1893. Albany, NY. Ladies Union Mission School. 1st ed. 12mo. VG. T10. $250.00

COOK, David. *Player's Handbook, 2nd Ed.* 1989. TSR Advanced Dungeons & Dragons. hc. VG. P3. $20.00

COOK, Ferris. *Invitation to the Garden.* 1992. NY. ils/photos. F/dj. B26. $35.00

COOK, George Cram. *Greek Coins. Poems & Memorabilia.* 1925. Doran. 1st ed. F/NF. B2. $125.00

COOK, Gladys Emerson. *American Champions.* 1945. Macmillan. 1st ed. ils. F/G. M5. $35.00

COOK, Jack. *Face of Falsehood: Key to Moby Dick.* 1986. Owego. VG. O7. $45.00

COOK, James. *Explorations of Captain James Cook in the Pacific.* 1957. LEC. 1/1500. ils/sgn Ingleton. designer/sgn Douglas Dunstan. NF/case. C2. $200.00

COOK, James. *James Cook, Surveyor of Newfoundland.* 1965. San Francisco. David Magee. facsimile. 10 charts. F. O7. $495.00

COOK, John R. *Border & the Buffalo.* 1967. Citadel. facsimile of 1907 ed. F/NF. T10. $25.00

COOK, O.F. *Relationships of the Ivory Palms.* 1910. WA, DC. ils. VG/wrp. B26. $15.00

COOK, Robin. *Brain.* 1981. Putnam. 1st ed. VG/VG. P3. $25.00

COOK, Robin. *Coma.* 1977. Little Brn. 1st ed. NF/NF. M19. $65.00

COOK, Robin. *Coma.* 1977. Little Brn. 1st ed. NF/VG clip. M22. $20.00

COOK, Robin. *Godplayer.* 1983. Putnam. 1st ed. VG/VG. P3. $18.00

COOK, Robin. *Harmful Intent.* 1990. Putnam. 1st ed. VG/VG. P3. $19.00

COOK, Robin. *Private Parts in Public Places.* 1969. Atheneum. 1st ed. VG/torn. P3. $40.00

COOK, Robin. *Sphinx.* 1979. Putnam. 1st ed. VG/VG. P3. $23.00

COOK, Theodore A. *History of English Turf.* 1901-1904. London. 3 vol. ils. gr cloth. VG+. H3. $750.00

COOK, Thomas H. *City When It Rains.* 1991. Putnam. 1st ed. VG/VG. P3. $20.00

COOK, Thomas H. *Night Secrets.* 1990. Putnam. 1st ed. F/F. P3. $20.00

COOK, Thomas H. *Sacrificial Ground.* 1988. Putnam. 1st ed. F/VG+. A20. $18.00

COOK, Thomas H. *Streets of Fire.* 1989. Putnam. 1st ed. F/F. A20. $17.00

COOK, Thomas H. *Tabernacle.* 1983. Houghton Mifflin. 1st ed. 8vo. 313p. F/F. T10. $25.00

COOK, Warren L. *Flood Tide of Empire: Spain & the Pacific NW, 1543-1819.* 1973. New Haven. Yale. 1st ed. 4to. 620p. F/dj. T10. $150.00

COOK & DOYLE. *Three New Genera of Stilt Palms...* 1913. WA, DC. ils. unopened wrp. B26. $22.00

COOK & MILLER. *Mystery, Detective & Espionage Fiction...* 1988. Garland. VG. P3. $150.00

COOKE, Alistair. *Christmas Eve.* 1952. 1st ed. VG/VG. K2. $35.00

COOKE, Alistair. *Douglas Fairbanks: Making of a Screen Character.* 1940. MOMA Film Lib. VG. D2. $35.00

COOKE, Carleton S. *Notes on Elementary Equitation.* 1921. Squadron A Cavalry. 104p. VG/wrp. O3. $45.00

COOKE, David C. *Best Detective Stories of Year 1950.* 1950. Dutton. 1st ed. VG/VG. P3. $25.00

COOKE, Donald E. *Firebird.* 1939. Chicago. ils. gilt cloth. F. A17. $10.00

COOKE, Edmund Vance. *Told to the Little Tot.* 1906. Dodge. 1st ed. ils Bessie Collins Pease. G+. M5. $75.00

COOKE, Francis B. *Corinthian Yachtsman's Handbook.* 1913. London. Arnold. 22 fld plans. 312p. VG. T7. $65.00

COOKE, G. Walter. *Death Is the End.* 1965. Geoffrey Bles. 1st ed. VG/VG. P3. $18.00

COOKE, John Esten. *Stories of the Old Dominion: From Settlement to Revolution.* 1879. Harper. ils. 337p. G. B10. $25.00

COOKE & CURY. *Bagdad: How to See It.* 1937. Cairo. World-Wide Pub. 3rd. xl. G. W1. $18.00

COOLEY, F.S. *Sketch of the Development of the Modern Horse.* ca 1900. Old Town. Bickmore Gall Cure Co. 93p. O3. $22.00

COOLIDGE, Calvin. *Have Faith in Massachusetts.* 1919. Cambridge. Riverside. 12mo. 275p. G. T3. $12.00

COOLING, B. Franklin. *Benjamin Franklin Tracy: Father of Modern Am Fighting Navy.* 1973. Achon. VG/VG. A16. $10.00

COOMBES, Lenora. *Let's Go Shopping.* 1948. Simon Schuster. 1st ed. 8vo. 42p. VG. T5. $20.00

COON, Carleton S. *Southern Arabia, a Problem for the Future.* 1944. WA. Smithsonian. removed. 8vo. map. F. P4. $8.50

COONEY, Barbara. *Chanticleer & the Fox.* (1958). TY Crowel. NF/G. C14. $18.00

COONTS, Stephen. *Final Flight.* 1988. Doubleday. 1st ed. NF/F. H11. $20.00

COONTS, Stephen. *Flight of the Intruder.* 1986. Annapolis. 1st ed. author's 1st book. F/F. H11. $40.00

COONTS, Stephen. *Flight of the Intruder.* 1986. Naval Inst. 1st ed. F/F clip. B35. $35.00

COONTZ, Robert E. *From the Mississippi to the Sea.* 1930. Dorrance. 1st ed. sgn pres. 13 pl. 483p. VG. B11. $50.00

COOPER, Alice. *Me, Alice.* 1976. Putnam. 1st ed. ils. F/NF. B4. $50.00

COOPER, Basil. *And Afterward, the Dark.* 1977. Arkham. 1st ed. 1/4259. F/F. T2. $12.00

COOPER, Basil. *Black Death.* 1991. Minneapolis. Fedogan Bremer. 1st ed. F/F. T2. $32.00

COOPER, Basil. *Curse of the Fleers.* 1977. St Martin. 1st ed. VG/VG. P3. $20.00

COOPER, Basil. *From Evil's Pillow.* 1973. Arkham. 1st ed. F/F. M21. $15.00

COOPER, Basil. *Here Be Demons.* 1978. St Martin/Robert Hale. 1st ed. xl. dj. P3. $12.00

COOPER, Basil. *House of the Wolf.* 1983. Arkham. 1st ed. ils/sgn Stephen Fabian. VG. B11. $50.00

COOPER, Craig. *What's Funny About Murder?* 1968. Roy. hc. VG/VG. P3. $15.00

COOPER, Dennis. *Closer.* 1989. Grove. 1st ed. F/F. H11. $25.00

COOPER, Dennis. *Wrong.* 1992. Grove Weidenfeld. 1st ed. F/F. H11. $20.00

COOPER, Edmund. *All Fool's Day.* 1966. Hodder Stoughton. 1st ed. VG/VG. P3. $20.00

COOPER, Edmund. *Kronk.* 1971. Putnam. 1st ed. VG/VG. P3. $20.00

COOPER, Edmund. *Transit.* 1964. Faber. 1st ed. VG/VG. P3. $30.00

COOPER, Frederic Taber. *Argosy of Fables.* 1921. Stokes. apparent 1st ed. cloth. VG. M5. $165.00

COOPER, J. California. *Family.* 1991. Doubleday. 1st ed. sgn. author's 1st novel. F/F. B4. $75.00

COOPER, J. California. *Homemade Love.* 1986. St Martin. 1st ed. inscr. F/NF. B4. $100.00

COOPER, J. California. *Piece of Mine.* 1984. Navarro, CA. Wild Trees. 1st ed. NF/pict wrp. B4. $185.00

COOPER, James Fenimore. *Headsman & Oak Openings.* nd. London. marbled brd/red half leather. VG. B30. $68.00

COOPER, James Fenimore. *Last of the Mohicans.* 1977. Franklin Lib. ils NC Wyeth. aeg. F. A18. $50.00

COOPER, James Fenimore. *Last of the Mohicans.* 1982. Franklin Lib. aeg. leather spine. F. P3. $20.00

COOPER, James Fenimore. *Pathfinder.* 1965. LEC. intro Robert E Spiller. ils Richard Powers. F/dj/case. A18. $60.00

COOPER, Jefferson; see Fox, Gardner F.

COOPER, John R. *Mel Martin & the Southpaw's Secret (#2).* 1947. Cupples Leon. 212p. Vg/dj. M20. $27.00

COOPER, John R. *Southpaw's Secret.* 1952. Garden City. VG. P3. $8.00

COOPER, Susan. *Silver on the Tree.* 1977. Atheneum. 1st ed. VG/VG. P3. $25.00

COOPER, Will. *Death Has a Thousand Doors.* 1976. Bobbs Merrill. 1st ed. VG/VG. P3. $15.00

COOPER & HUMBLE. *World's Greatest Blackjack Book.* 1980. NY. 413p. VG. S1. $8.00

COOPER & TREAT. *Man O'War.* 1950. NY. Messner. 1st ed. VG. O3. $45.00

COOTER. *Phrenology in the British Isles: An Annotated Hist Biblio...* 1989. 431p. F. A4. $50.00

COOVER, John Edgar. *Experiments in Psychical Reasearch at Leland Stanford...* 1917. Stanford. 5 pl. 642p. ES. NF. G1. $100.00

COOVER, Robert. *Gerald's Party.* 1985. Linden. 1st ed. sgn. rem mk. F/F. B2. $40.00

COOVER, Robert. *Hair O' the Chine.* 1979. Bruccoli Clark. 1st ed. 1/450. sgn/#d. F/sans. C2. $50.00

COOVER, Robert. *Pinocchio in Venice.* 1991. Linden. 1st ed. sgn. F/F. B2. $45.00

COOVER, Robert. *Public Burning.* 1977. Viking. 1st ed. F/F. H11. $55.00

COOVER, Robert. *Public Burning.* 1977. Viking. 1st ed. sgn. NF/NF. B2. $45.00

COOVER, Robert. *Water Pourer: Unpublished Chapter From Origin of Brunists.* 1972. Bruccoli Clark. 1st ed. 1/300. sgn/#d. F/NF. C2. $75.00

COPE, Kathleen. *Days in Dixie.* 1991. Black Belt. 1st ed. sgn. 119p. VG/VG. B10. $12.00

COPELAND, Richard. *No Face in the Mirror.* 1980. Macmillan. 1st ed. VG/VG. P3. $15.00

COPELAND, Aaron. *Copeland on Music.* 1960. NY. 1st ed. 8vo. 280p. gilt blk cloth. F/VG clip. H3. $45.00

COPPARD, A.E. *Fearful Pleasures.* 1946. Arkham. 1st ed. VG/VG. M22/T2. $45.00

COPPARD, A.E. *Nixey's Harlequin.* 1931. London. 1st ed. G/dj. V4. $65.00

COPPARD, A.E. *Nixey's Harlequin.* 1932. Knopf. 1st ed. VG. M22. $15.00

COPPEL, Alfred. *Apocalypse Brigade.* 1981. HRW. 1st ed. VG/VG. P3. $15.00

COPPEL, Alfred. *Burning Mountain.* 1983. HBJ. 1st ed. VG/VG. P3. $16.00

COPPEL, Alfred. *Dragon.* 1977. HBJ. 1st ed. VG/VG. P3. $15.00

COPPEL, Alfred. *Gate of Hell.* 1967. HBJ. 1st ed. VG/VG. P3. $13.00

COPPEL, Alfred. *Glory.* 1993. Tor. 1st ed. F/F. G10. $12.00

COPPEL, Alfred. *Hastings Conspiracy.* 1980. HRW. 1st ed. VG/VG. P3. $20.00

COPPEL, Alfred. *Marburg Chronicles.* 1985. Dutton. 1st ed. F/F. H11. $20.00

COPPEL, Alfred. *Night of Fire & Snow.* 1957. Simon Schuster. 1st ed. VG/VG. P3. $25.00

COPPEL, Alfred. *Show Me a Hero.* 1987. HBJ. 1st ed. F/F. P3. $17.00

COPPEL, Alfred. *Thirty-Four East.* 1974. HBJ. 1st ed. VG/VG. P3. $20.00

COPPOLA, Eleanor. *Notes.* 1979. Simon Schuster. 1st ed. NF/clip. B4. $50.00

CORBEN, Richard. *Flights Into Fantasy.* 1981. Thumb Tack. 1st ed. F/F. P3. $30.00

CORBETT, James. *Death Pool.* 1936. Herbert Jenkins. 1st ed. VG/VG. P3. $75.00

CORBETT, Jim. *Jungle Lore.* 1953. Oxford. 1st ed. F/NF. M19. $25.00

CORBETT, Jim. *Man-Eaters of Kumaon.* 1946. Oxford. ils. blk stp gr bdg. G. P12. $6.00

CORBETT, Jim. *Man-Eaters of Kumaon.* 1946. Oxford. photos. xl. VG. P12. $4.00

CORBETT, Jim. *Man-Eating Leopard of Durraprayag.* 1948. NY. 1st ed. VG/VG. B5. $37.50

CORBETT, Jim. *My India.* 1952. Oxford. 2nd. VG/VG. B5. $22.50

CORBETT, Jim. *Temple Tiger & More Man-Eaters of Kumaon.* 1953. NY. 2nd. VG/VG. B5. $30.00

CORBIN, Alain. *Les Filles de Noce: Misere Sexuelle et Prostitution.* 1978. Paris. 1st ed. 571p. VG/wrp. A13. $20.00

CORBITT, Helen. *Helen Corbitt Cooks for Looks.* 1967. Boston. sgn. 115p. VG/G. B11. $8.00

CORBY, Grant W. *Geology & Oil Possibilities of the Philippines.* 1951. Manila. Dept Agriculture & Natural Resources. 87 maps. F/case. O7. $250.00

CORCOS, Lucille. *City Book.* 1972. Western Pub. 1st ed. ils. pict brd. VG+. M5. $14.00

CORDER, Eric. *Murder, My Love.* 1973. Playboy. 1st ed. VG/G. P3. $12.00

CORDINGLY, David. *Under the Black Flag: Romance...Life Among the Pirates.* 1995. Random. 2nd. 320p. M. M20. $25.00

CORDRY & CORDRY. *Mexican Indian Costumes.* 1968. Austin. TX U. 1st ed. 16 pl. 373p. gilt red cloth. F/dj. T10. $300.00

CORE, George. *Southern Fiction Today.* 1969. GA U. 102p. VG. B10. $15.00

CORE, Sue. *Henry Morgan, Knight & Knave.* 1943. North River. inscr. 8vo. 210p. F/F. B11. $55.00

CORE, Sue. *Maid in Panama.* 1938. NY. Clermont. 1st ed. 195p. dj. F3. $30.00

CORE, Sue. *Ravelings From a Panama Tapestry.* 1942. North River. 2nd. inscr. 161p. dj. F3. $30.00

CORELLI, Marie. *Barabbas.* 1896. Phil. 1st ed. decor silver-stp cloth. VG. A17. $10.00

CORELLI, Marie. *Master-Christian.* nd. Briggs. hc. VG. P3. $25.00

CORELLI, Marie. *Wormwood.* nd. Donohue. decor brd. VG. P3. $20.00

COREY, Harry Harmon. *Cory Family.* 1941. Minneapolis. Argus. 2nd. 188p. VG+. M20. $30.00

CORKILL, Louis. *Fish Lane.* 1951. Bobbs Merrill. 1st ed. VG/VG. P3. $10.00

CORKRAN, David H. *Cherokee Frontier: Conflict & Survival.* 1962. Norman, OK. 1st ed. ils/maps. 302p. F/NF. T10. $35.00

CORLE, Edwin. *Desert Country.* 1941. DSP. 1st ed. 8vo. 357p. map ep. red cloth. VG. T10. $35.00

CORLETT & WEE. *City & the Forest.* 1986. Singapore. ils/biblio/index. 186p. sc. B26. $17.50

CORMAN, Cid. *Clocked Stone.* 1959. Ashland. 1/210. sgn Corman/Ohno. F. C2. $450.00

CORMAN, Cid. *In No Time.* 1963. Kyoto. Origin. 1st ed. 12mo. inscr to pub. F/wrp. C2. $175.00

CORMAN, Roger. *How I Made a Hundred Movies in Hollywood.* 1990. Random. 1st ed. VG/VG. P3. $20.00

CORNELL, Julien. *Trail of Ezra Pound.* 1966. London. Faber. M11. $50.00

CORNELL, S.S. *Cornell's Physical Geography.* 1876. Appleton. ils/maps. 104p. quarter leather. G+. A17. $22.50

CORNWELL, Bernard. *Copper Head.* 1994. Harper Collins. 1st ed. F/F. M23. $20.00

CORNWELL, Bernard. *Crackdown.* 1990. Michael Joseph. 1st ed. NF/NF. P3. $20.00

CORNWELL, Bernard. *Killer's Wake.* 1989. Putnam. 1st ed. NF/NF. P3. $20.00

CORNWELL, Bernard. *Rebel.* 1993. Harper Collins. 1st ed. F/F. M23. $25.00

CORNWELL, Patricia D. *All That Remains.* 1992. Scribner. 1st Am ed. sgn. F/F. C2. $60.00

CORNWELL, Patricia D. *All That Remains.* 1992. Scribner. 1st ed. F/F. M23. $25.00

CORNWELL, Patricia D. *Body Farm.* 1994. NY. 1st ed. F/F. V4. $45.00

CORNWELL, Patricia D. *Body Farm.* 1994. Scribner. 1st ed. rem mk. F/F. H11. $20.00

CORNWELL, Patricia D. *Body of Evidence.* 1991. Scribner. 1st ed. F/F. H11. $100.00

CORNWELL, Patricia D. *Cruel & Unusual.* 1993. Scribner. 1st ed. F/F. M23/P3. $20.00

CORNWELL, Patricia D. *From Potter's Field.* 1965. Scribner. 1st ed. F/F. P3. $24.00

CORONADO, Francisco. *Muster Roll & Equipment of the Expedition.* 1939. Ann Arbor. VG/wrp. O7. $45.00

CORRELL, D.S. *Potato & Its Wild Relatives.* 1962. Renner. TX Research. lg 8vo. ils/pl/maps. 606p. cloth. dj. B1. $45.00

CORRIGAN, Douglas. *That's My Story.* 1938. NY. 1st ed. pres. VG/dj. B5. $60.00

CORRIGAN, J.D. *Working With the Microscope.* 1941. McGraw Hill. 418p. F. D8. $15.00

CORRINGTON, Julian D. *Adventures With the Microscope.* 1934. Rochester, NY. Bausch Lomb. 8vo. 455p. VG. K5. $60.00

CORSALE, Lorraine. *Mountain Images: Photographic Essay of Central Appalachia.* 1987. Lancaster, KY. Christian Appalachian Project. sgn. VG/G. B11. $15.00

CORSON & LORRAIN. *Electromagnetic Fields & Waves.* 1962. San Francisco. Freeman. 706p. F. P4. $25.00

CORT, Mary Lovina. *Siam; or, Heart of Father India.* 1886. NY. 398p. gr cloth. VG. B14. $95.00

CORTES DE FIGUEROA, Leslie. *Stuffed Shirt in Taxco.* 1961. Mexico. 1st ed. ils. 164p. F3. $10.00

CORTESAO, Armando. *History of Portuguese Cartography. 2 Volumes.* 1969 & 1971. Lisboa. 2 vol. 1/1000. Eng text. ils. F. O7. $850.00

CORTESAO, Armando. *Nautical Chart of 1424 & the Early Discovery...* 1954. Coimbra. ltd ed. sgn. 22 maps. M/case. O7. $625.00

CORTISSOZ, Royal. *Works of Charles A Platt.* 1925. NY. 2nd. VG/VG. B5. $205.00

CORTRIGHT, Edgar. *Exploring Space With a Camera.* 1968. Washington. 1st ed. 214p. heavy bl cloth. NF. B22. $7.50

CORY, Desmond. *Bennett.* 1977. Crime Club. 1st ed. VG/VG. P3. $15.00

CORY, Desmond. *Feramontov.* 1966. Muller. VG. P3. $8.00

CORY, Desmond. *Pilgrim on the Island.* 1961. Walker. 1st ed. ffe removed. xl. dj. P3. $5.00

COST, March. *Bitter Green of the Willow.* 1967. Chilton. 1st ed. ils Anne Anderson. VG+/worn. M5. $28.00

COSTAIN, Thomas B. *Below the Salt.* 1957. Doubleday. 1st ed. VG/VG. P3. $35.00

COSTAIN, Thomas B. *High Towers.* 1949. Doubleday. 1st ed. VG/G. P3. $15.00

COSTAIN, Thomas B. *Tontine.* 1955. Doubleday. 1st ed. VG/VG. P3. $35.00

COSTELLO, A.E. *Our Firemen: History of NY Fire Depts, Volunteer & Paid.* 1887. NY. 1st ed. ils/index/ads. 1112p. VG. B5. $165.00

COSTELLO, Louisa Stuart. *Rose Garden of Persia.* nd. London. TN Foulis. Rose Garden series. 188p. gilt brd. G. B18. $45.00

COSTIKYAN, Greg. *Another Day, Another Dungeon.* nd. BC. F/F. P3. $8.00

COSTINER, Merle. *Hearse of a Different Color.* 1952. Phoenix. 1st ed. VG/G. P3. $18.00

COTT, Jonathan. *Pipers at the Gate: Wisdom of Children & Literature.* 1985. NY. ils Seuss/Sendak/Steig. 327p. F/wrp. A17. $7.50

COTTER, Clay. *Mystery & Adventure Stories: Hidden Peril (#8).* 1939. Cupples Leon. 204p. VG+/dj. M20. $10.00

COTTER, E.P.C. *Teach Yourself Contract Bridge.* 1969. London. 128p. VG/VG. S1. $6.00

COTTERILL, George F. *Climax of a World Quest.* 1928. Seattle. Olympic. 1st ed. inscr. 226p. gilt gr cloth. w/photo. VG. T10. $50.00

COTTERILL, R.S. *Southern Indians.* 1954. OK U. 1st ed. ils/pl/biblio/index. 255p. NF. T10. $45.00

COTTRELL, Leonard. *Lost Pharaohs: Romance of Egyptian Archaeology.* 1971. London. Evans. 33 pl. 256p. VG. W1. $16.00

COULING, David. *Steam Yachts.* 1980. Naval Inst. VG/VG. A16. $25.00

COULTER, Ellis Merton. *William G Brownlow: Fighting Parson of Southern Highlands.* 1937. Chapel Hill. 1st ed. 432p. NF/VG. M8. $75.00

COULTER, Harris. *Divided Legacy: A History of the Schism in Medical Thought.* 1975-82. WA. 3 vol. VG. A13. $150.00

COULTER, Stephen. *Embassy.* nd. Coward McCann. 2nd. xl. dj. P3. $5.00

COULTER & GERSTENFELD. *Historical Bibliographies.* 1965. NY. xl. VG. O7. $15.00

COUNCIL OF JEWISH WOMEN. *Helpful Hints to Housewives.* 1940s. np. 8vo. mostly recipes. 287p. prt brd/new cloth spine. T10. $75.00

COUNSELMAN, Mary Elizabeth. *Half in Shadow.* 1978. Arkham. 1st ed. 1/4288. F/F. T2. $12.00

COUNSELMAN, Mary Elizabeth. *Half in Shadow.* 1980. London. Wm Kimber. 1st Eng ed. F/F. T2. $25.00

COURLANDER, Harold. *Drum & the Hoe.* 1960. Berkeley. 1st ed. ils. VG/VG. B5. $45.00

COURTENAY, F. Dudley. *Standard Manual on Play.* 1938. London. 96p. sbdg. VG/wrp. S1. $10.00

COURTENAY, F. Dudley. *Standardized Code of Contract Bridge Bidding.* 1937. NY. 108p. sbdg. VG. S1. $8.00

COURTENAY, F. Dudley. *System the Experts Play.* 1936. np. new/revised. 106p. sbdg. S1. $20.00

COURTENAY & WALSHE. *Losing Trick Count.* 1937. London. 5th. 176p. VG. S1. $15.00

COURTIER, S.H. *Ligny's Lake.* 1971. Simon Schuster. 1st ed. xl. dj. P3. $7.00

COURTNEY, Michael. *Play Cards With Tim.* 1995. Australia. Seres. pb. 137p. M. S1. $15.00

COURTRIGHT, G. *Tropicals.* 1988. Portland. Timber Pr. 4to. ils. cloth. dj. B1. $38.00

COURTWRIGHT, David. *Dark Paradise: Opiate Addiction in America Before 1940.* 1982. Cambridge. 1st ed. 270p. VG. A13. $30.00

COUSIN, Victor. *Lectures on the True, the Beautiful & the Good.* 1854. Appleton. 1st Eng-language ed. 391p. rebound lib buckram. VG. G1. $40.00

COUSINS, Norman. *Anatomy of an Illness.* 1979. Norton. 1st ed. F/NF. M23. $12.00

COUTURIER, Marc. *Les Dessins du Troisieme Jour.* 1993. Mars-Avril. ils/pl. brd. D2. $35.00

COVARRUBIAS, Miguel. *All Men Are Brothers.* 1948. LEC. Stratford Pr. 1/1500. sgn. hand-made paper brd. AN/cloth case. B24. $325.00

COVARRUBIAS, Miguel. *Eagle, Jaguar & the Serpent.* 1954. Knopf. 1st ed. 314p. dj. F3. $125.00

COVARRUBIAS, Miguel. *Indian Art of Mexico & Central America.* 1966. Knopf. 2nd. 360p. dj. F3. $95.00

COVENEY & HIGHFIELD. *Frontiers of Complexity: Search for Order...* 1995. Fawcett. 1st ed. F/F. w/pub letter. G10. $15.00

COVERT & ELLSWORTH. *Water Supply Investigations in Yukon-Tanana Region, AL...* 1909. GPO. 8vo. 3 fld maps. 108p. new cloth. F. T10. $75.00

COVILLE, Bruce. *Jenifer Murdley's Toad.* 1992. HBJ. F/F. P3. $17.00

COVINGTON, Vicki. *Bird of Paradise.* 1990. Simon Schuster. 1st ed. sgn. F/F. M23. $40.00

COVVIN, Tristam P. *Old Ball Game: Baseball in Folklore & Fiction.* 1971. Herder. 1st ed. F/VG+. P8. $22.50

COWAN, John F. *New Invasion of the South.* 1881. NY. 1st ed. 12mo. 103p. G. T3. $50.00

COWAN, Robert G. *Ranchos of California.* 1956. Fresno. Am Lib Guild. 1st ed. 151p. map pp. beige cloth. F. T10. $25.00

COWAN, Sam K. *Sergeant York.* nd. Grosset Dunlap. VG/VG. P3. $20.00

COWAN & COWAN. *Bibliography of History of California 1510-1930.* 1933. San Francisco. John Nash. 4 vol. 4to. VG. T10. $600.00

COWARD, Noel. *Noel Coward Diaries.* 1982. Little Brn. 1st ed. VG+/VG+. A20. $23.00

COWARD, Noel. *Pretty Polly & Other Stories.* 1965. Doubleday. 1st Am ed. 8vo. NF/clip. T10. $40.00

COWARD, Noel. *Spangled Unicorn.* 1982. Frisch. 1st ed thus. 101p. dj. A17. $10.00

COWARD, Noel. *Suite in Three Keys.* 1967. Garden City. 1st Am ed. inscr. NF/NF. C6. $125.00

COWARD, Noel. *This Happy Breed.* 1947. Doubleday. 1st Am ed. F/F. B4. $85.00

COWDERY, James F. *Cowdery's Forms...Adapted To Use in Alaska, Arizona...* 1943. San Francisco. Bancroft Whitney. M11. $35.00

COWDERY, Mae V. *We Lift Up Our Voices.* 1936. Phil. Alpress. 1st ed. 1/350. VG. B4. $250.00

COWDRY, E.V. *Problems of Aging: Biological & Medical Aspects.* 1939. Baltimore. 1st ed. 758p. VG. A13. $75.00

COWLEY, John D. *Bibliography of Abridgments, Digest, Dictionaries...* 1932. London. Selden Soc. M11. $50.00

COWLEY, Malcolm. *Blue Juniata Collected Poems.* 1968. 1st ed. NF/VG+. S13. $20.00

COWLEY, Malcolm. *Exile's Return.* 1981. NY. 1/2000. 8vo. photos. 2281p. F/case. T10. $350.00

COWLEY, Malcolm. *Faulkner-Cowley File: Letters & Memories 1944-1962.* nd. np. 1st ed. VG/VG. M17. $35.00

COWLEY, Stewart. *Spacecraft 2000 to 2100 AD.* nd. Chartwell. 1st ed. NF/NF. G10. $15.00

COWLEY, Stewart. *Spacecraft 2000 to 2100 AD.* 1978. Chartwell. hc. F/F. P3. $7.00

COWLEY, Stewart. *Spacewreck.* 1979. Exeter. 1st Am ed. F/F. G10. $20.00

COWPER, Richard. *Clone.* 1973. Doubleday. 1st ed. F/F. P3. $20.00

COWPER, Richard. *Custodians & Other Stories.* 1976. Gollancz. 1st ed. author's 1st SF short story collection. AN/dj. M21. $35.00

COWPER, Richard. *Tithonian Factor.* 1984. Gollancz. 1st ed. F/F. P3. $25.00

COWPER, William. *Diverting History of John Gilpin...* 1925. Stokes. 1st ed thus. 12mo. 79p. red cloth. G+. T5. $30.00

COWPER. *Cowper's Poetical Works.* nd. London. red full leather. VG. D30. $40.00

COX, C.B. *Biogeography: An Ecological & Evolutionary Approach.* 1977. Oxford. Blackwell Scientific. 2nd/2nd prt. ils. VG/wrp. B11. $18.50

COX, Elizabeth. *Familiar Ground.* 1984. Atheneum. 1st ed. F/F. M23. $20.00

COX, Isaac. *Annals of Trinity Country.* 1940. Eugene, OR. rpt of 1858 ed. 1/350. 265p. NF/NF case. T10. $45.00

COX, Joseph A. *Recluse of Herald Square...* 1964. Macmillan. pres. worn dj. M11. $35.00

COX, Palmer. *Juvenile Budget.* ca 1900. Donohue. ils Palmer Cox. VG. D1. $75.00

COX, Richard T. *Many Seasons.* 1976. private prt. 58p. G. B10. $8.00

COX, Warren E. *Chinese Ivory Sculputre.* 1966. Bonanza. photos/index. 118p. dj. A17. $20.00

COX & GILBERT. *Oxford Book of English Ghost Stories.* 1986. Oxford. F/F. P3. $20.00

COX & GILBERT. *Victorian Ghost Stories.* 1991. Oxford. F/F. P3. $20.00

COX & GILBERT. *Victorian Ghost Stories.* 1991. Oxford. 1st ed. NF/dj. M21. $15.00

COX & TERMAN. *Genetic Studies of Genius. Vol 2: Early Mental Traits...* 1926. Stanford. thick 8vo. 842p. xl. VG/dj. G1. $75.00

COXE, Daniel. *Description of the English Province of Carolina.* 1976. Gainesville. VG. O7. $25.00

COXE, George Harmon. *Barotique Mystery.* 1936. Knopf. 1st ed. ffe removed. VG. P3. $30.00

COXE, George Harmon. *Butcher, Baker, Murder-Maker.* 1954. Knopf. 1st ed. VG. P3. $25.00

COXE, George Harmon. *Dangerous Legacy.* 1946. Knopf. VG/VG. P3. $15.00

COXE, George Harmon. *Fenner.* 1971. Knopf. 1st ed. NF/NF. P3. $15.00

COXE, George Harmon. *Glass Triangle.* 1944. Triangle. VG/VG. P3. $12.00

COXE, George Harmon. *Groom Lay Dead.* 1947. Triangle. VG/VG. P3. $10.00

COXE, George Harmon. *Murder in Havana.* 1943. Knopf. 1st ed. VG. P3. $20.00

COXE, George Harmon. *Never Bet Your Life.* 1952. Knopf. 1st ed. VG. P3. $22.00

COXE, George Harmon. *Silent Witness.* 1973. Knopf. 1st ed. VG/VG. P3. $20.00

COXERE, Edward. *Adventures by Sea of Edward Coxere.* 1946. NY. VG. O7. $20.00

COYLE, Daniel. *Hardball: Season in the Projects.* 1993. Putnam. 1st ed. F/F. P8. $17.50

COYLE, Harold. *Bright Star.* 1990. Simon Schuster. 1st ed. F/F. P3. $20.00

COYNE, John. *Child of Shadows.* nd. Quality BC. VG/VG. P3. $10.00

COZZENS, James Gould. *Last Adam.* 1933. HBJ. 1st ed. xl. VG. P3. $10.00

COZZENS, Samuel. *Marvelous Country.* 1967. Minneapolis. Ross Haines. rpt. 1/1500. 540p. AN/dj. P4. $25.00

CRABTREE, Helen. *Suddle Seat Equitation.* (1982). Doubleday. later prt. VG/VG. O3. $35.00

CRACE, Jim. *Continent.* 1986. Harper Row. 1st ed. F/F. A20/M23. $22.00

CRADOCK, Mrs. H.C. *Josephine Keeps House.* nd. England. Blackie. sm 4to. 8 pl. 64p. VG/VG. T5. $130.00

CRAFT, David. *Negro Leagues.* 1993. Crescent. 1st ed. F/F. P8. $20.00

CRAFT, Ruth. *Winter Bear.* 1976. Atheneum. 2nd. unp. cloth. F/G. C14. $12.00

CRAIG, David. *Contact Lost.* 1970. Stein Day. ffe removed. VG/VG. P3. $12.00

CRAIG, David. *Double Take.* 1972. Stein Day. 1st ed. VG/VG. P3. $15.00

CRAIG, Edward. *Gordon Craig: Story of His Life.* 1968. NY. Knopf. cloth. F/VG. D2. $15.00

CRAIG, Gordon. *Germany 1866-1945.* 1978. Oxford. 825p. VG. A17. $15.00

CRAIG, John D. *Danger Is My Business.* 1938. Simon Schuster. photos. 309p. gilt red bdg. G+. P12. $12.00

CRAIG, Patricia. *Oxford Book of English Detective Stories.* 1990. Oxford. 1st ed. F/F. P3. $25.00

CRAIG. *Room at the Top; or, How To Reach Success, Happiness...* ca 1900. Augusta, ME. 12mo. ils. 400p. brn cloth. VG. T3. $20.00

CRAINE & REINDORP. *Chronicles of Michigan.* 1970. OK U. 1st ed. 254p. dj. F3. $35.00

CRAINE & REINDORP. *Codex Perez & the Book of the Chilam Balm of Mani.* 1979. OK U. 1st ed. 209p. dj. F3. $35.00

CRAIS, Robert. *Monkey's Raincoat.* 1993. Doubleday. 1st Am hc ed. F/F. M23. $35.00

CRAIS, Robert. *Monkey's Raincoat.* 1993. Doubleday. 1st ed. rem mk. F/F. H11. $20.00

CRAIS, Robert. *Stalking the Angel.* 1989. Bantam. 1st ed. NF/NF. M22/M23. $30.00

CRAIS, Robert. *Stalking the Angel.* 1989. Bantam. 1st ed. VG/VG. P3. $20.00

CRAM, Mildred. *Promise.* 1949. Knopf. 1st ed. VG/VG. P3. $30.00

CRAMER, John. *Twister.* 1989. Morrow. 1st ed. F/F. P3. $19.00

CRAMER, Kathryn. *Walls of Fear.* 1990. Morrow. 1st ed. F/F. P3. $20.00

CRAMER, Stuart. *Secrets of Karl Germain.* 1962. Cleveland Hts. inscr. 70p. stiff wrp. B18. $22.50

CRAMPTON, C. Gregory. *Zunis of Cibola.* 1979. UT U. 2nd. 4to. ils. 201p. F/dj. T10. $125.00

CRAMPTON, Gertrude. *Further Pottlebly Adventures.* 1951. Aladdin. 1st ed. ils Anne Merriman. 93p. VG. T5. $15.00

CRAMPTON, Gertrude. *Golden Christmas Book.* 1947. Simon Schuster. 2nd. NF. C8. $125.00

CRANE, Clinton H. *Clinton Crane's Yachting Memories.* 1952. Van Nostrand. 1st ed. sgn. 8vo. 216p. F/VG. B11. $45.00

CRANE, Frances. *Cinnamon Murder.* 1946. Random. 1st ed. NF/VG. H11. $30.00

CRANE, Frances. *Horror on the Ruby X.* 1956. Detective BC. VG. P3. $10.00

CRANE, Hart. *Bridge.* 1930. Paris. Blk Sun. 1/200 on Holland paper. VG/VG. C6. $1,400.00

CRANE, J. *Fiddler Crabs of the World.* 1975. Princeton. 4to. 50 pl/drawings. 736p. cloth. dj. B1. $75.00

CRANE, Joan. *Willa Cather: A Bibliography.* 1982. Lincoln, NE. 1st ed. F/F. B2. $40.00

CRANE, Leo. *Desert Drums.* 1928. Little Brn. 1st ed. 8vo. photos/fld map. bl cloth. NF. T10. $125.00

CRANE, Leo. *Indians of the Enchanted Desert.* 1925. Little Brn. 1st ed. 8vo. 364p. pict bl cloth. VG. T10. $75.00

CRANE, Robert. *Hero's Walk.* 1954. Ballantine. F/F. P3. $35.00

CRANE, Stephen. *George's Mother.* 1896. NY/London. 1st ed. author's 4th book. VG. C6. $95.00

CRANE, Stephen. *Monster & Other Stories.* 1899. NY. 1st ed. NF. A9. $200.00

CRANE, Stephen. *Monster & Other Stories.* 1899. NY/London. 1st ed. VG. A20/C6. $150.00

CRANE, Walter. *Chattering Jack.* ca 1880. London. Routledge. mtd on linen. VG. D1. $75.00

CRANE, Walter. *Flora's Feast, a Masque of Flowers.* 1889. London. Cassell. 1st ed. thin 4to. pict brd/cloth spine. T10. $175.00

CRANE, Walter. *Flower Wedding.* 1905. London. Cassell. ils. 40p. VG. D1. $250.00

CRANE, Walter. *Queen's Summer; or, Journey of the Lily & the Rose.* 1891. London. 1st ed. VG. M17. $125.00

CRANE & MOSES. *Politics, an Intro to Study of Comparative...Law.* 1884. NY. Putnam. russet cloth. G. M11. $75.00

CRATON, Michael. *History of the Bahamas.* 1969. London. VG. O7. $20.00

CRAVEN, Roy. *Ceremonial Centers of the Maya.* 1974. Gainsville, FL. 1st ed. 152p. dj. F3. $45.00

CRAWFORD, F. Marion. *Little City of Hope.* 1907. Macmillan. hc. VG. P3. $10.00

CRAWFORD, F. Marion. *To Leeward.* 1911. Ward Lock. VG. P3. $13.00

CRAWFORD, J. Marshall. *Mosby & His Men: A Record of the Adventures...* 1867. NY. Carleton. 1st ed. 375p. VG. M8. $275.00

CRAWFORD, Ned. *Naming the Animals.* 1980. Faber. 1st ed. F/NF. G10. $20.00

CRAWFORD, Phillis. *Hello the Boat.* 1938. Holt. 1st ed. ils Edward Laning. 227p. VG/G. P2. $35.00

CRAWFURD, Oswald. *Portugal: Old & New.* 1880. NY. VG. O7. $75.00

CRAWLEY, Rawdon. *Whist: Its Theory & Practice..* 1859. London. 7th. VG. S1. $20.00

CRAWLEY, Rayburn. *Valley of Creeping Men.* 1930. Harper. 1st ed. VG. P3. $35.00

CRAWSHAY-WILLIAMS, Rupert. *Methods & Criteria of Reasoning...* (1957). Routledge/Kegan Paul. 296p. w/8p catalog. F/dj. G1. $37.50

CREASEY, John. *Alibi.* 1971. Scribner. 1st ed. VG/VG. P3. $15.00

CREASEY, John. *As Empty As Hate.* 1972. World. 1st ed. hc. VG/VG. P3. $15.00

CREASEY, John. *As Merry As Hell.* 1973. Hodder Stoughton. 1st ed. VG/VG. P3. $18.00

CREASEY, John. *Baron & the Chinese Puzzle.* 1966. Scribner. 1st ed. VG/VG. P3. $20.00

CREASEY, John. *Baron on Board.* 1988. Walker. 1st ed. F/F. P3. $15.00

CREASEY, John. *Blight Mystery.* 1968. Walker. 1st ed. F/F. P3. $15.00

CREASEY, John. *Call for the Baron.* 1976. Walker. 1st ed. VG/G. P3. $15.00

CREASEY, John. *Clutch of Coppers.* 1969. HRW. 2nd. VG/VG. P3. $13.00

CREASEY, John. *Crime-Haters.* nd. BC. VG/VG. P3. $8.00

CREASEY, John. *Day of Fear.* 1978. HRW. 1st ed. VG/VG. P3. $15.00

CREASEY, John. *Double for Death.* 1969. HRW. 1st ed. F/F. P3. $18.00

CREASEY, John. *Executioners.* 1967. Scribner. 1st ed. NF/NF. N4. $20.00

CREASEY, John. *Famine Mystery.* 1968. Walker. 1st ed. F/F. P3. $15.00

CREASEY, John. *Follow the Toff.* 1967. Walker. 1st ed. VG/VG. P3. $15.00

CREASEY, John. *Gallows Are Waiting.* 1973. McKay. 1st ed. VG/VG. P3. $20.00

CREASEY, John. *Gideon's Badge.* 1966. Hodder Stoughton. 1st ed. NF/NF. P3. $25.00

CREASEY, John. *Gideon's Drive*. 1976. Harper Row. 1st ed. VG/VG. P3. $25.00

CREASEY, John. *Gideon's Men*. 1972. Harper. 1st ed. VG/VG. M22. $20.00

CREASEY, John. *Gideon's Press*. 1973. Detective BC. VG. P3. $6.00

CREASEY, John. *Gideon's Sport*. 1970. Harper Row. 1st ed. VG/VG. P3. $20.00

CREASEY, John. *Go Ahead With Murder*. 1960. Hodder Stoughton. 1st Eng ed. F/VG. M19. $35.00

CREASEY, John. *Hang the Little Man*. 1963. Hodder Stoughton. 1st ed. NF/NF. P3. $25.00

CREASEY, John. *I Am the Withered Man*. 1973. McKay-Washburn. 1st ed. NF/NF. P3. $15.00

CREASEY, John. *Inferno*. 1966. Walker. 1st ed. VG/VG. P3. $15.00

CREASEY, John. *Inspector West Alone*. 1975. Scribner. 1st ed. VG/VG. P3. $15.00

CREASEY, John. *Inspector West at Home*. 1973. Scribner. 1st ed. VG/VG. P3. $15.00

CREASEY, John. *Kidnaped Child*. 1971. HRW. 1st ed. VG/VG. P3. $18.00

CREASEY, John. *Killing Strike*. 1961. Scribner. 1st ed. VG/VG. P3. $15.00

CREASEY, John. *Kind of Prisoner*. 1981. Ian Henry. VG/VG. P3. $15.00

CREASEY, John. *Life for a Death*. 1973. HRW. 1st ed. NF/NF. P3. $15.00

CREASEY, John. *Man Who Was Not Himself*. 1976. Stein Day. 1st ed. VG/G. P3. $15.00

CREASEY, John. *Masters of Bow Street*. 1974. Simon Schuster. 1st ed. VG/VG. P3. $25.00

CREASEY, John. *Most Deadly Hate*. 1974. Dutton. 1st ed. VG/VG. P3. $18.00

CREASEY, John. *Murder, London-New York*. 1973. Hodder Stoughton. VG/VG. P3. $15.00

CREASEY, John. *Murder With Mushrooms*. 1974. NY. 1st ed. VG/VG. B5. $20.00

CREASEY, John. *Out of the Shadows*. 1971. World. VG/VG. P3. $16.00

CREASEY, John. *Perilous Country*. 1973. Walker. VG/VG. P3. $13.00

CREASEY, John. *Rocket for the Toff*. 1960. Hodder Stoughton. 1st ed. VG/VG. P3. $25.00

CREASEY, John. *Smog*. 1971. Thriller BC. VG/VG. P3. $8.00

CREASEY, John. *So Young To Burn*. 1968. Scribner. 1st ed. VG/VG. P3. $15.00

CREASEY, John. *Splinter of Glass*. 1972. Detective BC. VG. P3. $8.00

CREASEY, John. *Take a Body*. 1972. Cleveland. World. 1st ed. F/F. H11. $25.00

CREASEY, John. *Taste of Treasure*. 1966. HRW. 1st ed. VG/VG. P3. $15.00

CREASEY, John. *Theft of Magna Carta*. 1973. Scribner. 1st ed. VG/VG. P3. $15.00

CREASEY, John. *This Man Did I Kill?* 1974. Stein Day. 1st ed. NF/VG. M22. $10.00

CREASEY, John. *Toff & the Toughs*. 1968. Walker. 1st ed. VG/VG. P3. $15.00

CREASEY, John. *Toff Proceeds*. 1968. Walker. 1st ed. F/F. P3. $15.00

CREELEY, Robert. *Charm*. 1971. Calder Boyars. 1st Eng ed. NF/VG. M19. $17.50

CREELEY, Robert. *Electronic Life*. 1983. Knopf. 1st ed. NF/NF. M19. $25.00

CREELEY, Robert. *Island*. 1963. Scribner. 1st ed. poet's 1st novel. sgn. F/F. C2. $60.00

CREELEY, Robert. *Le Fou: Poems*. 1952. Columbia. 1st ed. author's 1st book. sgn. F/decor wrp. C2. $150.00

CREELEY, Robert. *Rising Sun*. 1992. Knopf. 1st ed. F/F. M19. $17.50

CREMER, R. *Lugosi: Man Behind the Cape*. 1976. Chicago. 1st ed. VG/VG. B5. $40.00

CREOLE, Ellis. *Down, Down the Mountain*. 1934. NY. 1st ed. ils. VG. B5. $32.50

CRESSLER, Alfred M. *Vignettes of Writers & Artists*. 1956. San Francisco. 1/300. NF. N3. $20.00

CREWE, Benjamin J. *Practical Treatise on Petroleum*. 1887. Phil. Baird. 1st ed. 8vo. 70 engravings/2 fld pl. gilt cloth. VG. T10. $250.00

CREWS, Harry. *All We Need of Hell*. 1987. Harper Row. 1st ed. F/F. M23. $50.00

CREWS, Harry. *Blood & Grits*. 1979. Harper Row. 1st ed. F/F. M19. $85.00

CREWS, Harry. *Body*. 1990. Poseidon. 1st ed. sgn. F/F. B11. $75.00

CREWS, Harry. *Childhood: Biography of a Place*. 1995. Athens. GA U. 1st ed. ils Michael McCurdy. F/dj. S9. $45.00

CREWS, Harry. *Feast of Snakes*. 1976. Atheneum. UP. F/wrp. C2. $200.00

CREWS, Harry. *Feast of Snakes*. 1976. NY. 1st ed. sgn. VG/VG. B5. $125.00

CREWS, Harry. *Hawk Is Dying*. 1973. NY. 1st ed. VG/G. B5. $50.00

CREWS, Harry. *Knockout Artist*. 1988. Harper Row. 1st ed. F/F. M23. $25.00

CREWS, Harry. *Mulching of America*. 1995. Simon Schuster. 1st ed. sgn. F/dj. S9. $45.00

CREWS, Harry. *Scarlover*. 1992. Poseidon. 1st ed. F/F. M22/M23. $20.00

CRICHTON, Antoinette. *M, for Madeline, D, for Dick: A Rhythmical Romance...* 1887. Wm Gr. 23p. VG. B10. $20.00

CRICHTON, Kyle S. *Law & Order Ltd: Rousing Life of Elfego Baca of New Mexico*. 1928. Santa Fe. 1st ed. 8vo. 14 pl. VG. T10. $95.00

CRICHTON, Michael. *Andromeda Strain*. 1969. Knopf. 1st ed. F/F clip. H11. $115.00

CRICHTON, Michael. *Andromeda Strain*. 1969. NY. Knopf. 1st ed. NF/VG+. B4. $125.00

CRICHTON, Michael. *Binary*. 1972. Knopf. 1st ed. NF/NF. H11. $65.00

CRICHTON, Michael. *Binary*. 1972. Knopf. 3rd. VG/VG. P3. $15.00

CRICHTON, Michael. *Case of Need*. nd. BC. VG/VG. P3. $8.00

CRICHTON, Michael. *Case of Need*. 1968. NAL. 1st ed. NF/NF. B35. $35.00

CRICHTON, Michael. *Congo*. nd. BC. VG/VG. P3. $10.00

CRICHTON, Michael. *Congo*. 1980. Knopf. 1st ed. F/F. B35. $65.00

CRICHTON, Michael. *Congo*. 1980. Knopf. 1st ed. F/VG. M19. $35.00

CRICHTON, Michael. *Congo*. 1980. Knopf. 1st trade ed. F/NF. M22. $50.00

CRICHTON, Michael. *Disclosure*. 1994. Knopf. 1st ed. F/F. H11. $35.00

CRICHTON, Michael. *Five Patients*. 1970. Knopf. 1st ed. author's 2nd book. VG/F. H11. $45.00

CRICHTON, Michael. *Great Train Robbery*. 1975. Knopf. 1st ed. F/F. H11. $60.00

CRICHTON, Michael. *Great Train Robbery*. 1975. Knopf. 1st ed. NF/NF. M19. $45.00

CRICHTON, Michael. *Great Train Robbery*. 1975. Knopf. 1st ed. VG/VG. P3. $30.00

CRICHTON, Michael. *Jasper Johns.* 1977. Abrams/Whitney Mus. 1st ed. folio. F/F. B4. $100.00

CRICHTON, Michael. *Jurassic Park.* nd. Quality BC. VG/VG. P3. $10.00

CRICHTON, Michael. *Jurassic Park.* 1990. NY. Knopf. 1st ed. F/F. B30/T2. from $55 to $65.00

CRICHTON, Michael. *Jurassic Park.* 1993. Knopf. gift ed. sgn. mc pl. VG/VG. B11. $55.00

CRICHTON, Michael. *Lost World.* 1995. Knopf. 1st ed. F/F. N4. $22.50

CRICHTON, Michael. *Rising Sun.* 1992. Knopf. 1st trade ed. F/dj. M22. $15.00

CRICHTON, Michael. *Sphere.* 1987. Knopf. 1st ed. F/F. M19/P3/T2. from $20 to $25.00

CRICHTON, Michael. *Sphere.* 1987. London. Macmillan. 1st ed. F/F. P3. $25.00

CRICHTON, Michael. *Terminal Man.* 1972. Knopf. 1st ed. F/F. C2. $75.00

CRICHTON, Michael. *Terminal Man.* 1972. Knopf. 1st ed. VG/VG. P3. $60.00

CRICHTON, Michael. *Terminal Man.* 1972. London. Cape. 1st ed. F/F. T2. $45.00

CRICHTON, Robert. *Camerons.* 1972. Knopf. 1st ed. F/F. H11. $30.00

CRIDER, Bill. *Booked for a Hanging.* 1992. NY. 1st ed. F/F. H11. $25.00

CRIDER, Bill. *Murder Most Fowl.* 1994. St Martin. F/F. P3. $19.00

CRIDER, Bill. *My Heart Cries for You.* 1992. Mystery Scene. 1st ed. 1/100. sgn/#d. F/sans. P3. $15.00

CRIDER, Bill. *Ryan Rides Back.* 1988. Evans. 1st ed. 8vo. 181p. F/F. T10. $15.00

CRIDER, Bill. *Time for Hanging.* 1989. Evans. 1st ed. AN/dj. M22. $15.00

CRILE, George W. *Origin & Nature of the Emotion.* 1915. Phil. 1st ed. 8vo. ils. gilt blk cloth. NF. H3. $150.00

CRIPPS, Louise L. *Spanish Caribbean From Columbus to Castro.* 1979. Boston. VG. O7. $30.00

CRISP, N.J. *Brink.* 1982. Viking. F/F. P3. $15.00

CRISP, N.J. *Gotland Deal.* 1976. Viking. 1st ed. F/F. P3. $15.00

CRISP, N.J. *London Deal.* 1979. St Martin. 1st ed. VG/VG. P3. $18.00

CRISP, William. *Compleat Agent.* 1984. Macmillan. 1st ed. F/F. P3. $15.00

CRISPIN, Edmund. *Fen Country.* 1979. Gollancz. 1st ed. F/F. P3. $25.00

CRISPIN, Edmund. *Love Lies Bleeding.* 1981. Walker. VG/VG. P3. $20.00

CRISPIN, Edmund. *Moving Toyshop.* 1946. Lippincott. 1st ed. F/VG. M19. $65.00

CRISPIN & NORTON. *Gryphon's Eyrie.* 1984. Tor. 1st ed. F/F. P3. $18.00

CRISWELL, Grover C. *Confederate & Southern States Bonds.* 1980. 8vo. 374p. gray cloth. VG. T3. $30.00

CRISWELL, Grover C. *Confederate & Southern States Currency.* 1976. np. 8vo. 294p. ils. gray cloth. VG. T3. $30.00

CRITCHFIELD, Howard J. *General Climatology.* 1966 (1960). Englewood Cliffs. 2nd. 4to. 420p. VG/dj. K5. $14.00

CRITCHFIELD & LITTLE. *Geographic Distribution of the Pines of the World.* 1966. USDA. 4to. 97p. wrp. B1. $28.50

CROCKER, W.M. *Mary Ware Doll Book.* 1914. Boston. 1st ed. 48p. NF. D1. $425.00

CROCKETT, S.R. *Adventurer in Spain.* 1903ntur. Isbister. hc. VG. P3. $20.00

CROCKETT, S.R. *Sir Toady Crusoe.* 1905. Stokes. 1st ed. ils. 356p. G. C14. $12.00

CROFTS, Freeman Wills. *Tragedy in the Hollow.* 1939. Dodd Mead. 1st ed. VG. P3. $35.00

CROFTS, Thomas. *History of the Service of the Third Ohio Veteran Volunteer.* 1910. Toledo. Stoneman. 1st ed. 296p. cloth. M8. $275.00

CROLL, James. *Discussions on Climate & Cosmology.* 1889 (1885). London. Stanford. 8vo. fld chart. 327p. cloth. G. K5. $32.00

CROMBIE, Deborah. *All Shall Be Well.* 1994. Scribner. 1st ed. F/F. H11. $25.00

CROMBIE, Deborah. *Share in Death.* 1993. Scribner. 1st ed. author's 1st book. F/F. H11. $35.00

CROMIE, William J. *Exploring the Secrets of the Sea.* 1962. Englewood Cliffs. VG. O7. $15.00

CROMIE, William J. *Exploring the Secrets of the Sea.* 1967. Prentice Hall. ils. 300p. gilt bl cloth. NF/VG. P12. $5.00

CROMPTON & VAN DER MEER. *Victorian Advent Pop-Up Book.* 1993. np. opens to 30-inch street scene. F. A4. $65.00

CRONE, G.R. *Maps & Their Makers: An Intro to History of Cartography.* 1978. Folkestone. Dawson. ils. AN/dj. O7. $75.00

CRONIN, Michael. *Night of the Party.* 1958. Ives Washburn. 1st ed. VG/VG. P3. $13.00

CRONKITE, Walter. *Remembering the Moon.* 1989. W Stockbridge. Thornwillow. 1/1250. 4to. 82p. teg. box. w/prospectus. B24. $750.00

CRONLEY, Jay. *Quick Change.* 1981. Doubleday. 1st ed. VG/VG. M22. $35.00

CRONQUIST, A. *Intermountain Flora.* 1986 (1972). Bronx. NY Botanical Garden. lg 8vo. 270p. cloth. B1. $38.00

CRONQUIST & GLEASON. *Manual of the Vascular Plants of NE US & Adjacent Canada.* 1963. Princeton. ils. 810p. gr cloth. B26. $40.00

CRONQUIST & GLEASON. *Natural Geography of Plants.* 1964. Columbia. 8vo. 420p. cloth. VG. B1. $65.00

CRONYN, George W. *Path of the Rainbow: Anthology of Songs & Chants...* 1918. Boni Liveright. 1st ed/2nd prt. 8vo. 347p. gilt blk cloth. T10. $100.00

CROOKES & DOBBIE. *New Zealand Ferns.* 1952. Auckland. 5th. ils. 406p. VG/worn. B26. $50.00

CROSBY, Ernest. *Captain Jinks, Hero.* 1902. Funk Wagnall. 1st ed. ils Dan Beard. 393p. VG. M20. $20.00

CROSBY, John. *Company of Friends.* 1977. Stein Day. 1st ed. VG/G. P3. $13.00

CROSCUP, G.E. *Syncronic Chart of United States History.* 1910. NY. 4to. ils. 94p. gray cloth. G. T3. $10.00

CROSS, Amanda. *James Joyce Murder.* 1967. Macmillan. 2nd. VG/VG. P3. $10.00

CROSS, Amanda. *No Word From Winifred.* 1986. Dutton. 1st ed. NF/NF. P3. $20.00

CROSS, Amanda. *Players Come Again.* 1990. Random. 1st ed. F/F. P3. $18.00

CROSS, E.A. *Wings for You: A Book About Aviation.* 1943. NY. 4th. 355p. A17. $9.00

CROSS, John Keir. *Best Horror Stories 2.* 1965. Faber. F/F. P3. $35.00

CROSS, Mark. *Perilous Hazard.* 1961. Ward Lock. VG/VG. P3. $15.00

CROSS, Robin. *SF Films.* 1985. Gallery. hc. VG/VG. P3. $12.00

CROSS, SCHIEFELE & SHAW. *Arizona: Its People & Resources.* 1960. Tucson. 75th Anniversary Commemorative Vol. 386p. VG. T10. $35.00

CROSSMAN, C.L. *China Trade.* 1973. Princeton. 2nd. VG/VG. B5. $50.00

CROSSMAN, Edward C. *Military & Sporting Rifle Shooting.* 1932. Sm Arms Technical Pub. 499p. VG/dj. M20. $45.00

CROTTY, D.G. *Four Years Campaigning in the Army of the Potomac.* 1874. MI. 1st ed. 207p. rebound quarter leather. VG+. B18. $195.00

CROTZ, Keith. *Ewaniana: Writing of Joe & Nesta Ewan.* 1989. Chillicothe, IL. Am Botanist. 67p. cloth. dj. A10. $25.00

CROUCH, Tom D. *Eagle Aloft: Two Centuries of the Balloon in America.* 1983. Smithsonian. thick 8vo. 770p. F/dj. T10. $60.00

CROUTIER, Alev. *Taking the Waters; Spirit, Art & Sensuality.* 1992. NY. 224p. VG. A13. $40.00

CROW, John. *Epid of Latin America.* 1946. Doubleday. 756p. dj. F3. $15.00

CROWDER, Herbert. *Weatherhawk.* 1990. Putnam. 1st ed. NF/NF. P3. $20.00

CROWE, Cameron. *Fast Times at Ridgemont High.* 1981. Simon Schuster. 1st ed. VG/VG. P10. $40.00

CROWE, John; see Lynds, Dennis.

CROWE. *With Thackeray in America.* 1893. Scribner. ils. 179p. VG. A4. $25.00

CROWHURST, Eric. *Precision Bidding in ACOL.* 1983. London. 256p. VG/wrp. S1. $8.00

CROWLEY, John. *Beasts.* 1976. Doubleday. 1st ed. VG/VG. P3. $30.00

CROWLEY & DOYLE. *Chaplet of Verse by California Catholic Writers.* 1889. San Francisco. Diepenbrock. inscr. 171p. NF. T10. $45.00

CROWN, Lawrence. *Marilyn at Twentieth Century Fox.* 1987. Planet. hc. F/F. P3. $20.00

CROWNFIELD, Gertrude. *Strong Hearts & Bold.* 1938. Lippincott. ils Marguerite DeAngeli. 307p. VG+/G. P2. $55.00

CRUIKSHANK, George. *Comic Almanack.* 1835-1853. Chatto Windus. 4 vol. Bayntum bdg. F. B14. $350.00

CRUIKSHANK, George. *German Popular Stories, Trans From the Kinder...* 1823. London. Baldwin. 2 vol. 1st Eng trans/1st issue. aeg. F. B24. $6,000.00

CRUIKSHANK, George. *Inundation: A Christmas Story by Mrs Gore.* ca 1840. Boston. 1st Am ed. VG. C6. $85.00

CRUM, H. *Focus on Peatlands & Peat Mosses.* 1988. Ann Arbor. 8vo. 306p. cloth. F. B1. $50.00

CRUM, Laura. *Cutter.* 1994. NY. 1st ed. author's 1st book. F/F. H11. $25.00

CRUM, William Leonard. *Advertising Fluctuations, Seasonal & Cyclical.* 1927. Chicago/NY. AW Shaw Co. ils/index. 308p. F. B14. $45.00

CRUMLEY, James. *Dancing Bear.* 1983. NY. 1st ed. F/F. A11. $50.00

CRUMLEY, James. *Last Good Kiss.* 1978. Random. 1st ed. NF/NF. B2/M22. $50.00

CRUMLEY, James. *Mexican Tree Duck.* 1993. Mysterious. ARC. 8vo. F/wrp. S9. $35.00

CRUMLEY, James. *Mexican Tree Duck.* 1993. Mysterious. 1st ed. F/F. M23. $25.00

CRUMLEY, James. *One to Count Cadence.* 1969. Random. ARC. sgn twice. author's 1st novel. F/NF. M19. $350.00

CRUMLEY, James. *Wrong Case.* 1975. Random. 1st ed. G/VG. M22. $250.00

CRUMP, Irving. *Boy's Book of Mounted Police.* 1917. Dodd Mead. sgn/dtd 1917. 297p. VG. M20. $75.00

CRUMP, William H. *World in a Pocket Book.* 1860. Phil. 12mo. 465p. gray cloth. G. T3. $27.00

CRUTCH & GREENE. *Lewis Carroll Handbook, Being a New Version...* 1970. ils. 323p. xl. VG. A4. $65.00

CRUTCHFIELD, James A. *Tennesseans at War.* 1987. Nashville. 1st ed. 191p. F/dj. A17. $20.00

CSAPODI. *Bibliotheca Coriniana, Biblioteka Krola Macieja Korwina.* 1981. sm folio. Hungarian text. 114 full-p pl. 326p. F/VG. A4. $135.00

CUFF, David J. *Atlas of Pennsylvania.* 1989. Phil. Temple U. 304p. AN/dj. O7. $75.00

CULBERT & RICE. *Precolumbian Population History to Maya Lowlands.* 1990. Albuquerque. 1st ed. 395p. F3. $35.00

CULBERTSON, Ely. *Famous Hands of the Culbertson-Lenz Match.* 1932. NY. 438p. VG. S1. $20.00

CULBERTSON, Jo. *Calypso: Four-Trump Game.* 1955. Phil. 1st ed. 73p. VG/worn. S1. $3.00

CULBERTSON & WEBSTER. *Culbertson-Webster Contract System: Laugh While You Learn...* 1932. NY. ils. 152p. VG/dj. S1. $20.00

CULBRETH, D. *Manual of Materia Medica & Pharmacology.* 1906. Phil. 8vo. ils. 976p. gr cloth. T3. $38.00

CULLEN, Countee. *Black Christ.* 1929. NY. 1st ed. VG/G+. B5. $80.00

CULLEN, Countee. *Caroling Dusk: Anthology of Verse by Negro Poets.* 1927. Harper. 237p. xl. VG. R11. $15.00

CULLEN, Countee. *Color.* 1925. Harper. author's 1st book. 108p. VG+. R11. $40.00

CULLEN, Countee. *Copper Sun.* 1927. NY. 1st ed. VG. A11. $45.00

CULLEN, Countee. *Medea & Some Poems.* 1935. Harper. 1st ed. F/dj. B24. $225.00

CULLEN, Countee. *Medea & Some Poems.* 1935. NY. 1st ed. VG+/G clip. H7. $100.00

CULLEN, Edgar M. *American Liberty in Danger Declares Judge Cullen.* nd. NY. Allied. reissue. 15p. self wrp. M11. $35.00

CULLEN, Joseph P. *Peninsula Campaign 1862...* 1973. NY. Bonanza. 1st ed thus. 192p. NF/NF. M8. $35.00

CULLUM, Grove. *Selection & Training of the Polo Pony.* 1934. NY. Scribner. 1st/A ed. G. O3. $65.00

CULLUM, Ridgwell. *Triumph of John Kars.* 1917. Chapman Hall. G. P3. $10.00

CULPAN, Maurice. *Minister of Injustice.* 1970. Walker. 1st ed. VG/VG. P3. $10.00

CULVER, Alice Ross. *Sunshine & Shadow Forest.* 1919. Altemus Wee Book. 1st ed. 16mo. VG. M5. $65.00

CULVER, Henry B. *Book of Old Ships.* 1935. Garden City. VG/VG. A16. $30.00

CULVER, Timothy J. *Ex Officio.* 1970. Evans. 1st ed. xl. dj. G. P3. $6.00

CUMBERLAND, Marten. *Etched in Violence.* 1953. Hurst Blackett. 1st ed. VG/G. P3. $20.00

CUMMING, Duncan. *Gentleman Savage: Life of Mansfield Perkins.* 1987. London. VG. O7. $20.00

CUMMING, Gordon. *Outdoor Life's Anthology of Hunting Adventures.* 1946. Outdoor Life. photos. VG. P12. $8.00

CUMMING, Primrose. *Mystery Horse.* 1957. Criterion. ils Maurice Tulloch. 8vo. 213p. bl cloth. VG. T5. $15.00

CUMMING, William P. *British Maps of Colonial America.* 1974. Chicago. F/dj. O7. $75.00

CUMMING, William P. *Exploration of North America 1630-1776.* 1974. Putnam. maps/ils. F/dj. O7. $135.00

CUMMINGS, E.E. *Christmas Tree.* 1928. NY. Am Book Bindery. 1st ed. inscr/dtd 1939. B24. $750.00

CUMMINGS, E.E. *Eimi.* 1933. Covici Friede. 1st ed. 1/1381. sgn. VG. B4. $250.00

CUMMINGS, E.E. *I. Six Nonlectures.* 1953. Cambridge. Harvard. 1st ed. 1/350. sgn. F/NF. B24. $350.00

CUMMINGS, E.E. *Miscellany.* 1958. NY. Argophile. 1st ed/1st state. inscr. dk bl cloth. F. B24. $485.00

CUMMINGS, E.E. *Red Front.* 1933. Chapel Hill. Contempo. 1st ed. 1/200. F/wrp. C6. $200.00

CUMMINGS, Jack. *Escape From Yuma.* 1990. Walker. 1st ed. Walker Western series. F/F. A18. $10.00

CUMMINGS, Ray. *Man Who Mastered Time.* nd. AL Burt. hc. VG. P3. $20.00

CUMMINGS, Ray. *Tarrano the Conqueror.* 1930. McClurg. VG+/VG. G10. $100.00

CUMMINGS, Ray. *Tarrano the Conqueror.* 1930. McClurg. 1st ed. VG. P3. $50.00

CUNARD, Nancy. *Parallax.* 1925. London. 1/420. VG. C6. $200.00

CUNARD, Nancy. *Thoughts About Ronald Firbank.* 1971. NY. 1st ed. 1/226. F/sewn wrp/marbled-paper dj. A11. $35.00

CUNNINGHAM, E.V. *Assassin Who Gave Up His Gun.* 1969. Morrow. 1st ed. VG/VG. P3. $15.00

CUNNINGHAM, E.V. *Case of the Poisoned Eclairs.* 1979. HRW. 1st ed. VG/VG. P3. $18.00

CUNNINGHAM, E.V. *Case of the Russian Diplomat.* 1978. HRW. 1st ed. VG/VG. P3. $18.00

CUNNINGHAM, E.V. *Helen.* 1966. Doubleday. 1st ed. VG/VG. P3. $22.00

CUNNINGHAM, E.V. *Wabash Factor.* 1986. Delacorte. 1st ed. VG/VG. P3. $15.00

CUNNINGHAM, Eugene. *Triggernometry: A Gallery of Gunfighters.* 1934. NY. Pr of Pioneers. 1st ed. 8vo. photos. gilt bl cloth. F/NF. T10. $350.00

CUNNINGHAM, Frank. *Sky Master: Story of Donald Douglas & Douglas Aircraft Co.* 1943. Dorrance. 8vo. 321p. gilt bl cloth. VG. T10. $45.00

CUNNINGHAM, J. Morgan; see Westlake, Donald E.

CUNNINGHAM, Jere. *Abyss.* 1981. NY. Wyndham. 1st ed. F/NF. H11. $30.00

CUNNINGHAM, Jere. *Abyss.* 1981. Wyndham. 1st ed. VG/VG. P3. $20.00

CUNNINGHAM, Jere. *Visitor.* 1978. St Martin. NF/NF. P3. $20.00

CUNNINGHAM, Michael. *Home at the End of the World.* 1990. NY. FSG. 1st ed. author's 1st book. NF/F. H11. $40.00

CUNNINGHAM & GRAHAM. *Father Archangel of Scotland & Other Essays.* 1896. London. Blk. 1st ed. 12mo. cloth. NF. T10. $115.00

CURLE, Richard. *Characes of Dostoevsky.* 1950. London. 224p. dj. A17. $9.50

CURLE, Richard. *Collecting American First Editions.* 1930. Bobbs Merrill. 1st ed. 1/1250. sgn. F/case. B24. $85.00

CURNOW, I.J. *World Mapped: Being Short History of Attempts to Map World.* 1930. London. Sifton Praed. 18 maps. F/dj. O7. $45.00

CURRAN, Terrie. *All Booked Up.* 1987. Dodd Mead. 1st ed. NF/NF. P3. $16.00

CURRENT. *Encyclopedia of the Confederacy.* 1993. np. 4 vol. 600 photos/67 maps. 1916p. NF. A4. $275.00

CURREY. *Science Fiction & Fantasy Authors...* 1979. np. 4to. 600p. F. A4. $150.00

CURRIE, Kit. *Mr Drench's Horse; or, Life in the Antiquarian Book Trade.* 1985. Newton, PA. Bird & Bull. 1/300. F/prt wrp. T10. $35.00

CURRINGTON, O.J. *Break-Out.* 1978. Andre Deutsch. 1st ed. VG/VG. P3. $18.00

CURRY, Jabez Lamar Monroe. *Secession & the Civil War.* 1976. Syracuse, NY. Bl & Gray. rpt of 1899 ed. cloth. NF/NF. M8. $20.00

CURRY, Jane Louise. *Magical Cupboard.* 1976. Atheneum. 1st ed. ils. 138p. NF/VG. P2. $20.00

CURRY, Larry. *American West: Painters From Catlin to Russell.* 1972. Viking. 1st ed. 132 pl. F/clip. A16. $40.00

CURTIES, Henry. *Out of the Shadows.* 1911. Greening. decor brd. VG. P3. $35.00

CURTIS, Jack. *Crows' Parliament.* 1987. Dutton. 1st ed. VG/VG. P3. $20.00

CURTIS, Jack. *Glory.* 1988. Dutton. 1st ed. VG/VG. P3. $25.00

CURTIS, Natalie. *Indian's Book.* 1907. NY. 1st ed. F. A9. $350.00

CURTIS, Paul A. *Guns & Gunning.* 1941. Outdoor Life. photos. gilt gr bdg. VG. P12. $15.00

CURTIS, Robert. *Man Who Changed His Name.* nd. Hutchinson. G. P3. $20.00

CURTIS & WHITEHEAD. *W Somerset Maugham: Critical Heritage.* 1987. np. 488p. F/F. A4. $45.00

CURTISS, Frederic H. *Little Book on Travel Books.* 1936. London. VG. O7. $25.00

CURTISS, Ursula. *Noonday Devil.* 1953. Eyre Spottiswoode. 1st ed. VG/VG. P3. $25.00

CURWOOD, James Oliver. *Baree, Son of Kazan.* nd. Grosset Dunlap. VG/VG. P3. $10.00

CURWOOD, James Oliver. *Black Hunter.* 1926. Canada. Copp Clark. 1st ed. VG. P3. $25.00

CURWOOD, James Oliver. *Country Beyond.* 1922. Cosmopolitan. 1st ed. G. P3. $12.00

CURWOOD, James Oliver. *Country Beyond.* 1922. Cosmopolitan. 1st ed. ils Walt Louderback. VG+/dj. A18. $50.00

CURWOOD, James Oliver. *Great Lakes: The Vessels That Plough Them...* 1991. NY. Amereon. rpt of 1967 2nd ed. 1/325. AN. A16. $175.00

CURWOOD, James Oliver. *Plains of Abraham.* 1928. Doubleday Doran. 1st ed. hc. VG. P3. $20.00

CURZON, Clare. *Three-Core Lead.* 1988. Collins Crime Club. 1st ed. F/F. P3. $20.00

CURZON, Robert. *Visits to the Monasteries in the Levant.* 1865. London. Murray. 5th. 12mo. ils. 367p. gilt bl calf. NF. T10. $200.00

CUSHING, Harvey. *Personality of a Hospital.* 1930. Boston. pres. 8vo. red cloth. F. B14. $85.00

CUSHING, Harvey. *Pioneer Medical Schools of New York.* 1934. Syracuse. 36p. VG/gr prt wrp. B14. $125.00

CUSHMAN, D.Q. *History of Ancient Sheepscot & Newcastle.* 1882. Bath. G. M17. $30.00

CUSSLER, Clive. *Cyclops.* 1986. Simon Schuster. 1st ed. NF/NF. P3. $20.00

CUSSLER, Clive. *Dragon.* 1990. Simon Schuster. NF/NF. P3. $22.00

CUSSLER, Clive. *Night Probe!* 1981. McClelland Stewart. 1st ed. F/F. P3. $30.00

CUSSLER, Clive. *Night Probe!* 1981. NY. Bantam. 1st ed. rem mk. NF/NF. H11. $30.00

CUSSLER, Clive. *Sahara.* 1992. Simon Schuster. 1st ed. NF/NF. P3. $20.00

CUSSLER, Clive. *Treasure.* 1988. Simon Schuster. 1st ed. NF/F. H11. $25.00

CUSSLER, Clive. *Treasure.* 1988. Simon Schuster. 1st ed. VG/VG. P3. $20.00

CUSSLER, Clive. *Vixen 03.* 1978. Viking. 1st ed. NF/NF. P3. $35.00

CUST, Robert Needham. *Linguistic & Oriental Essays Written From Year 1840-1901.* 1901. London. Luzac. 1st ed. 8vo. 485p. xl. VG. W1. $18.00

CUSTER, George A. *My Life on the Plains; or, Personal Experience...* 1963. Folio Soc. 1st ed thus. 254p. cloth. VG/box. M20. $47.00

CUTHORN, Peter J. *British Maps of the American Revolution.* 1972. Philip Freneau. 17 maps. 79p. F. O7. $95.00

CUTLER, Carl C. *Greyhounds of the Sea.* 1930. NY. Halcyon House. rpt. 117 ils. 592p. VG. T7. $50.00

CUTLER, Leland. *America Is Good to a Country Boy.* 1954. Stanford. 4to. 271p. wht cloth spine/paper brd. F. T10. $35.00

CUTLER, Manasseh. *First Map & Description of Ohio.* 1918. WA. Lowdermilk. 1/200 on Japan vellum. lg fld map. F. O7. $250.00

CUTLER, Stan. *Best Performance by a Patsy.* 1991. Dutton. 1st ed. VG/G. P3. $15.00

CUTLER, Stan. *Face on the Cutting Room Floor.* 1991. Dutton. 1st ed. rem mk. F/F. H11. $25.00

CUTLER. *Sir James M Barrie: Bibliography With Full Collations...* 1931. np 1/1000. F/VG case. A4. $175.00

CUTTEN, George. *Three Thousand Years of Mental Healing.* 1911. NY. 318p. VG. A13. $100.00

CUTTER, Charles R. *Legal Culture of Northern New Spain, 1700-1810.* 1995. Albuquerque. NM U. M11. $40.00

CWIKLINSKI, Jan. *Captain Leaves His Ship.* 1955. Doubleday. VG/VG. A16. $25.00

D'AMATO, Barbara. *Hard Tack*. 1991. Scribner. 1st ed. NF/NF. P3. $19.00

D'AMATO, Brian. *Beauty*. 1992. Delacorte. 1st ed. F/F. G10/H11. $20.00

D'AMBROSIO, Charles. *Point*. 1995. Little Brn. 1st ed. F/F. M23. $40.00

D'ARBLEY, Madame. *Diary & Letters of Madame D'Arbley, Edited by Her Niece*. 1854. London. Colburn. 7 vol. new ed. 12mo. half maroon calf. NF. T10. $500.00

D'AULAIRE, Madame. *Fortunia*. 1974. NY. Frank Hallman. 1st ed. 1/300. ils/sgn Sendak. trans/sgn Schaubeck. F. D1. $125.00

D'AULAIRE & D'AULAIRE. *Abraham Lincoln*. 1937. Doubleday. later rpt. VG. B17. $6.00

D'AULAIRE & D'AULAIRE. *Magic Meadow*. 1958. Doubleday. 1st ed. ils. 55p. VG/VG. D1. $60.00

D'AULAIRE & D'AULAIRE. *Sidsel Longskirt*. 1935. Winston. 1st ed thus. 124p. VG/VG. P2. $35.00

D'AULAIRE & PARIN. *Animals Everywhere*. 1940. Doubleday. 1st ed. sm 4to. VG. C8. $150.00

D'AULAIRE & PARIN. *Columbus*. 1955. Doubleday. 1st ed. lg 4to. VG/dj. M5. $65.00

D'AULAIRE & PERRAULT. *Fairy Garland*. 1928. London. Cassell. 1st/deluxe/ltd ed. 1/1ils Dulac. gilt vellum. NF. D1. $650.00

D'AULNAN, Louise. *En Dukkes Levnetslob*. ca 1850. Copenhagen. Bing. 12mo. 169p. expertly rebacked. NF. B24. $350.00

DABBS, James McBride. *Southern Heritage*. 1932. UNC. 1st ed. 456p. VG. B10. $20.00

DABNEY, Betty Page. *Ancient Bond*. 1954. Dietz. ils Elizabeth Richmond. 47p. VG/VG. B10. $8.00

DABNEY, Virginius. *Don Miff, As Told by His Friend John Bouche Wacker*. 1890. Lippincott. 492p. VG. B10. $15.00

DACEY, Philip. *Gerald Manlry Hopkins Meets Walt Whitman in Heaven*. 1982. Penmaen. ltd ed. 1/75. sgn/#d. F/sans. V1. $75.00

DADD, George. *American Reformed Horse Book*. 1883. Orange Judd. VG. O3. $45.00

DADSWELL, M.J. *Common Strategies of Andadromous & Catadromous Fishes*. 1987. Am Fisheries Soc. 8vo. ils. 561p. pict brd. VG. B1. $45.00

DAGMAR, Peter. *Alien Skies*. 1967. Arcadia. VG/VG. P3. $15.00

DAHL, Roald. *Charlie & the Great Glass Elevator*. 1972. Knopf. 1st ed. ils Schidelman. 163p. VG/VG. D1. $45.00

DAHL, Roald. *Danny the Champion of the World*. 1975. Knopf. 1st ed. ils Jill Bennett. F/NF. P2. $35.00

DAHL, Roald. *Going Solo*. 1st ed. VG/VG. M17. $22.50

DAHL, Roald. *Kiss Kiss*. 1960. Knopf. 1st ed. VG/VG. M22. $35.00

DAHL, Roald. *Roald Dahl Omnibus*. 1986. Dorset. 11th. F/F. P3. $15.00

DAHL, Roald. *Switch Bitch*. 1974. Knopf. 1st ed. F/F. M21. $35.00

DAHL, Roald. *Switch Bitch*. 1974. Knopf. 1st ed. VG/VG. P3. $20.00

DAHL, Roald. *Two Fables*. 1987. FSG. 1st ed. F/F. P3. $13.00

DAHL & KEHOE. *Young Judy*. 1975. NY. Mason Charter. 1st ed. inscr pres both authors. xl. T10. $50.00

DAIKEN, Leslie. *Children's Games, Throughout the Year*. 1949. Batsford Ltd. 1st ed. 8vo. 216p. red cloth. VG/G+. T5. $85.00

DAIKEN, Leslie. *Children's Toys Throughout the Ages*. 1965 (1963). Spring. revised ed. 8vo. ils. NF/G. M5. $15.00

DAILEY, Abraham H. *Mollie Fancher, the Brooklyn Enigma...* 1894. Brooklyn, NY. 6 pl. 262p. VG. G1. $100.00

DAILEY, Janet. *Glory Game*. 1985. Poseidon. 1st ed. sgn. rem mk. F/F. B35. $35.00

DALBY, Richard. *Horror for Christmas*. 1992. Michael O'Mara. 1st ed. F/F. P3. $28.00

DALBY, Richard. *Mistletoe & Mayhem*. 1993. Castle. F/F. P3. $15.00

DALBY, Richard. *Mystery for Christmas*. 1990. Gallery. VG/VG. P3. $13.00

DALE, Henry. *Harveian Oration on Some Epochs in Medical Research*. 1935. London. 1st ed. 35p. VG. A13. $25.00

DALE, T.F. *Polo Past & Present*. 1905. London. Scribner/Country Life. 1st ed. G+. O3. $85.00

DALE, T.F. *Riding & Polo Ponies*. 1902. London. Lawrence & Bullen. 1st ed. VG. O3. $125.00

DALEY, Arthur. *Inside Baseball*. 1950. Grosset Dunlap. VG/VG. P3. $20.00

DALEY, Brian. *Han Solo at Star's End*. 1979. Del Rey. 1st ed. VG/VG. P3. $15.00

DALEY, Brian. *Han Solo at Stars' End*. 1979. Ballantine. 1st ed. F/NF. M23. $20.00

DALEY, Robert. *Dangerous Edge*. 1983. Simon Schuster. 1st ed. NF/NF. P3. $25.00

DALEY, Robert. *Fast One*. 1978. Crown. 1st ed. VG/VG. P3. $20.00

DALEY, Robert. *Hands of a Stranger*. 1985. Simon Schuster. 1st ed. F/F. H11. $25.00

DALEY, Robert. *Hands of a Stranger*. 1985. Simon Schuster. 1st ed. VG/VG. P3. $20.00

DALEY, Robert. *Man With a Gun*. 1988. Hutchinson. 1st ed. NF/NF. P3. $22.00

DALEY, Robert. *Strong Wind Red As Blood*. 1975. Harper. 1st ed. VG/VG. p3. $18.00

DALEY, Robert. *Target Blue*. 1973. Delacorte. 1st ed. VG. P3. $25.00

DALEY, Robert. *To Kill a Cop*. 1976. Crown. 1st ed. VG/VG. P3. $20.00

DALEY, Robert. *Treasure*. 1977. Random. 1st ed. 341p. dj. F3. $15.00

DALEY, Robert. *Wall of Brass*. 1994. Little Brn. 1st ed. F/F. P3. $23.00

DALEY, Robert. *Year of the Dragon*. 1981. Simon Schuster. 1st ed. F/F. H11. $25.00

DALGLIESH, Alice. *Bears of Hemlock Mountain*. 1952. Scribner. 3rd. ils Helen Sewell. unp. VG+. C14. $8.00

DALGLIESH, Alice. *Courage of Sarah Noble*. 1954. Scribner. 1st ed. ils Leonard Weisgard. 54p. VG/VG. P2. $35.00

DALGLIESH, Alice. *Smiths & Rusty*. 1936. Scribner. 1st ed. sgn. 118p. VG/VG. P2. $40.00

DALI, Salvador. *Jerusalem Bible*. 1970. Doubleday. 32 full-p pl. 1200+p. aeg. leatherette. box. D2. $200.00

DALLAS, Sandra. *Buster Midnight's Cafe*. 1990. Random. 1st ed. F/F. M23. $25.00

DALLIMORE & JACKSON. *Handbook of Coniferae & Ginkgoaceae*. 1967 (1923). NY. 4th. 46 pl/131 ils. 729p. B26. $75.00

DALMAS, Herbert. *Exit Screaming*. 1966. Walker. 1st ed. hc. VG/VG. P3. $18.00

DALRYMPLE, Dyron. *Hunting Across North America.* 1970. Outdoor Life/Harper Row. ils/photos. G. P12. $6.00

DALRYMPLE, James. *Institutions of the Law of Scotland...* 1681. Edinburgh. The Heir of Andrew Anderson. 1st ed. modern calf. M11. $2,500.00

DALTON, John C. *Treatise on Human Physiology.* 1971. Phil. 8vo. 728p. full leather. w/32p catalog. VG. T3. $50.00

DALTON, W. *Bridge Abridged or Practical Bridge.* 1908. London. 8th. 215p. VG. S1. $8.00

DALTON, W. *Bridge at a Glance.* 1904. London. 2nd. 100p. VG. S1. $8.00

DALY, Carroll John. *Hidden Hand.* nd. Grosset Dunlap. hc. VG/VG. P3. $35.00

DALY, Carroll John. *Snarl of the Beast.* 1981. Gregg. 1st ed. F/F. P3. $25.00

DALY, Conor. *Local Knowledge.* 1995. Kensington. 1st ed. F/F. M23. $35.00

DALY, Louise Haskell. *Alexander Cheves Haskell: Portrait of a Man.* 1934. Norwood, MA. Plimpton. 1st ed. 1/300. 224p. VG. M8. $450.00

DAME, William Meade. *From the Rapidan to Richmond & the Spotsylvania Campaign.* 1920. Baltimore. Gr Lucas. 1st ed. 213p. cloth. NF. M8. $150.00

DAMIANI, D. Petri. *Opera Omnia. Primun Quidem Studio et Labore...* 1623. Lugduni. Landri. folio. 784p. VG. W1. $125.00

DAMM & LEHMANN. *Meyers Kleiner Weltatlas.* 1935. Leipzig. Bibliographisches Institut. 34 double-p maps. F. O7. $65.00

DANA, Charles A. *Recollections of the Civil War.* 1898. NY. 1st ed. 296p. VG. B18. $65.00

DANA, James D. *New Text-Book of Geology.* 1883 (1863). NY. Ivison Blakeman Taylor. 4th. 412p. G. K5. $20.00

DANA, Richard Henry. *Two Years Before the Mast.* 1947. NY. Aldus Printers. ils/sgn Mueller. ship's canvas brds. VG/case. T10. $115.00

DANA, Rose; see Ross, W.E.D.

DANA & FORD. *Dana's Textbook of Mineralogy.* 1922. NY. John Wiley. 3rd. 720p. VG. D8. $25.00

DANBY, Mary. *65 Great Tales of the Supernatural.* 1979. octopus. 1st ed. F/F. P3. $20.00

DANCE, Bill. *Bill Dance's Bass 'n Objects.* 1981. Memphis. self pub. 1st ed. sgn. 270p. F/VG. B11. $20.00

DANCER, Rex. *Bad Birl Blues.* 1994. Simon Schuster. 1st ed. author's 1st book. F/F. H11. $25.00

DANDRIDGE, Dorothy. *Everything & Nothing.* 1957. NY. 1st ed. VG/VG. B5. $30.00

DANE, Clemence. *Arrogant History of White Ben.* 1939. Literary Guild. VG/VG. P3. $20.00

DANE, Clemence. *Babyons.* 1934. Doubleday Doran. rpt. VG/G+. M21. $30.00

DANE, Clemence. *Flower Girls.* 1955. Norton. 1st ed. VG. P3. $10.00

DANEON, Emile. *Tides of Time.* 1952. Ballantine. VG/G. P3. $30.00

DANFORTH, Keyes. *Boyhood Reminiscences.* 1895. NY. VG. O7. $35.00

DANFORTH, Susan. *Land of Norumbega: Maine in the Age of Exploration...* 1988. Portland. ME Humanities Council. 4to. ils. F/wrp. O7. $30.00

DANIEL, Rosemary. *Fatal Flowers: On Sin, Sex, and Suicide in Deep South.* 1980. HRW. 1st ed. 294p. VG/VG. B10. $25.00

DANIELS, Dorothy; see Daniels, Norman.

DANIELS, Jan; see Ross, W.E.D.

DANIELS, Jonathan. *Devil's Backbone.* 1962. McGraw Hill. 8vo. 278p. F/dj. B5/T10. $25.00

DANIELS, Jonathan. *New South Creed: Study in Southern Mythmaking.* 1970. Knopf. 1st ed. 298p. VG/VG. B10. $10.00

DANIELS, Les. *Black Castle.* 1978. Scribner. 1st ed. NF/NF. P3. $25.00

DANIELS, Les. *Comix.* 1971. Outerbridge Dientsfrey. VG/VG. P3. $30.00

DANIELS, Les. *Silver Skull.* 1979. Scribner. 1st ed. VG/VG. P3. $30.00

DANIELSEN, Robert J. *Book One: Relay Precision: The One Heart Relay.* 1977. Hackensack. 84p. pb. NF. S1. $10.00

DANIELSSON, B. *Raroia: Happy Island of the South Seas.* 1953. Rand McNally. 55 ils. 304p. T7. $18.00

DANN, Jack. *Immortal: Short Novels of the Transhuman Future.* 1978. Harper Row. AN/wrp. M21. $15.00

DANN, Jack. *Starhiker.* 1977. Harper Row. 1st ed. F/F. P3. $25.00

DANN, Jack. *Timetipping.* 1980. Doubleday. 1st ed. F/F. P3. $18.00

DANSEREAU, Pierre. *Biogeography.* 1957. NY. 128 ils/39 tables/glossary/biblio. 394p. VG/dj. B26. $45.00

DANTE. *La Divina Commedia di Dante.* 1822. Lincolns Inn Fields. Pickering. 2 vol. teg. miniature. NF. T10. $250.00

DANTICAT, Edwidge. *Breath, Eyes, Memory.* 1994. NY. Soho. 1st ed. author's 1st book. F/clip. H11. $35.00

DANTICAT, Edwidge. *Breath, Eyes, Memory.* 1994. Soho. 1st ed. author's 1st book. F/F. M23. $50.00

DARBY, J.N. *Murder in the House With Blue Eyes.* 1939. Bobbs Merrill. 1st ed. VG/VG. P3. $35.00

DARK & UNDERWOOD. *When in Doubt, Fire the Manager.* 1980. Dutton. 1st ed. VG+/VG. P8. $30.00

DARLING, Ester Birdsall. *Baldy of Nome.* 1923. Phil. Penn. 1st ed. ils Hattie Longstreet. sm 4to. 301p. NF. H4. $20.00

DARLING, Jay N. *As Dink Saw Hoover.* 1954. Ames, IA. inscr. 8vo. 139p. F. B11. $50.00

DARLINGTON, W.M. *Gist's Journals.* 1893. Pittsburgh. 1st ed. NF. A15. $225.00

DARLINGTON & HOWGEGO. *Printed Maps of London Circa 1553-1850.* 1964. London. Philip. 1st ed. 20 ils. F/rpr dj. O7. $75.00

DARLOW & MOULE. *Historical Catalogue of Printed Editions of Holy Scripture.* nd. np. 4 vol. rpt of 1903-1911 ed. F. A4. $200.00

DARNELL & LURIA. *Virologia Generale.* 1970. Bologna. 1st Italian ed. 8vo. ils. F/dj. B14. $50.00

DARNTON & DANIEL. *Revolution in Print: Press in France 1775-1800.* 1989s. CA U. 2nd. 351p. F/wrp. A17. $15.00

DARRACOTT, Joseph. *England's Constable: Life & Letters of John Constable.* 1985. London. Folio Soc. 1st ed. 8vo. ils. beige cloth. F/case. T10. $35.00

DARRAH, W.C. *Cartes Des Visite in 19th-Century Photography.* 1981. Gettysburg. 1st ed. F/F. B5. $80.00

DARRAH, W.C. *Cartes des Visite in 19th-Century Photography.* 1981. Gettysburg. 4to. 221p. red cloth. VG/dj. T3. $40.00

DARRAH, W.C. *Stereo Views.* 1964. Gettysburg, PA. 8vo. 255p. bl cloth. VG. T3. $40.00

DARRAH, W.C. *World of Stereographs.* 1977. Gettysburg. 4to. 246p. gr cloth. F/dj. T3. $35.00

DARROW, Clarence S. *Farmington.* 1904. Chicago. 1st ed. VG. B5. $35.00

DARROW, Clarence S. *Persian Pearl & Other Essays.* 1902. Chicago. Ricketts. 2nd. NF. B2. $85.00

DARROW, Clarence S. *Resist Not Evil.* 1903. Charles H Kerr. 1st ed. sgn. NF/sans. B4. $1,250.00

DARROW, George M. *Strawberry.* 1966. HRW. 1st ed. ils. 447p. F/dj. T10. $50.00

DARTON, N.H. *Geology & Underground Waters of South Dakota.* 1909. GPO. 14 pl/7 figures/lg fld map. 156p. new cloth. F. T10. $75.00

DARTON. *Children's Books in England: Five Centuries of Social Life.* 1958. Cambridge. 2nd. ils. 385p. F. A4. $75.00

DARVAS, Robert. *Right Through the Pack.* 1957. London. 2nd. 220p. VG/dj. S1. $15.00

DARVAS & LUKACS. *Spotlight on Card Play.* 1960. NY. 160p. VG. S1. $9.00

DARWIN, Charles. *Descent of Man & Selection in Relation to Sex.* 1971. LEC. 1/1500. ils/sgn Kredel. 362p. F/case. C2. $200.00

DARWIN, Charles. *Expression of Emotions in Man & Animals.* 1872. London. John Murray. apparent variant. ils/pl. 374p. G. G1. $575.00

DARWIN, Charles. *Expression of the Emotions in Man & Animals.* 1872. London. John Murray. 1st ed/1st issue. NF. B2. $500.00

DARWIN, Charles. *Formation of Vegetable Mould.* 1882. NY. 1st Am ed. G+. M17. $50.00

DARWIN, Charles. *Insectivorous Plants.* 1875. Appleton. 1st Am ed. 12mo. VG. G1. $85.00

DARWIN, Charles. *Life & Letters of Charles Darwin...* 1888. London. John Murray. 3 vol. 3rd revised ed/2nd prt. G1. $150.00

DARWIN, Charles. *Monograph on the Subject of Sub-Class Cirripedia...* 1851-1854. London. Ray Soc. 2 vol. 1st ed. 40 pl. bl cloth. NF. C6. $1,200.00

DARWIN, Charles. *On Various Contrivances By Which British & Foreign Orchids.* 1862. London. John Murray. 1st ed/1st issue. 8vo. fld pl. 365p. VG. C6. $1,200.00

DARWIN, Charles. *Origin of Species by Means of Natural Selection.* nd. NY. AL Burt. rpt from 6th London ed. 538p. VG. D8. $10.00

DARWIN, Charles. *Structure & Distribution of Coral Reefs.* 1897. NY. 3rd. 344p. half leather. NF. A13. $45.00

DARWIN, Charles. *Variation of Animals & Plants Under Domestication.* 1868. London. John Murray. 2 vol. 1st ed/2nd issue. ES. gr cloth. NF. C6. $750.00

DARWIN, Erasmus. *Zoomania or the Laws of Organic Life. Vol 1, Part 2.* 1797. Phil. 486p. full leather. VG. B5. $250.00

DARWIN, Francis. *Life & Letters of Charles Darwin.* 1959. NY. 2 vol. fwd GG Simpson. box. B26. $40.00

DARWIN, Francis. *More Letters of Charles Darwin.* 1903. NY. 2 vol. ils. xl. G. V4. $60.00

DASA, Philangi. *Swedenborgianism: Its Secrets & Thibetan Origin.* 1887. Los Angels. Buddhistic Swedenborgian Brotherhood. 322p. ES. NF. B14. $55.00

DASH, Samuel. *Eavesdroppers, the Unknown Story of Wire Tapping Today...* 1959. New Brunswick. Rutgers. M11. $45.00

DASHIELL, Margaret. *Spanish Moss & English Myrtle.* 1930. Stratford. ils. 46p. G+. B10. $15.00

DASKAM, Josephine. *Memoirs of a Baby.* 1904. Harper. 1st ed. ils Fanny Cory. VG+. M5. $65.00

DASTRUP. *Field Artillery History & Sourcebook.* 1994. np. 232p. F. A4. $70.00

DAUBER. *Show Book of Nursery Rhymes.* 1945. Capitol. shaped book. spiral red metal. VG. D1. $50.00

DAUBS, Edwin H. *Monograph of Lemnaceae.* 1965. Urbana. 21 pl/map. 118p. F. B26. $25.00

DAUDET, Alphonse. *Recollections of a Literary Man.* 1889. London. Routledge. ils. 268p. VG. A4. $85.00

DAUGHERTY, James. *Daniel Boone.* 1939. Viking. 1st ed. VG+/partial. C8. $95.00

DAUGHERTY, James. *Of Courage Undaunted: Across the Continent With Lewis...* 1951. NY. 1st ed. ils. 168p. F. A17. $15.00

DAUM & WILLIAMSON. *American Petroleum Industry 1859-1899...* 1959. NW U. 864p. VG/torn. D8. $15.00

DAUMAS, E. *Horses of the Sahara.* 1863. London. Allen. 1st ed. trans James Hutton. VG+. O3. $225.00

DAUMAS, E. *Horses of the Sahara.* 1968. Austin, TX. ils. 256p. VG/VG. B5. $32.50

DAUPHINE, CLAUDE; see Weiss, Joe.

DAVENPORT, Basil. *SF Novel.* 1959. Advent. 1st ed. F/F. P3. $40.00

DAVENPORT, Basil. *13 Ways To Dispose of a Body.* 1966. Dodd Mead. VG/torn. P3. $13.00

DAVENPORT, Basil. *13 Ways To Kill a Man.* 1966. Faber. 1st ed. NF/NF. P3. $18.00

DAVENPORT, C. *Foot & Shoeing.* 1958. London. 1st prt. 55p. O3. $10.00

DAVENPORT, Guy. *Da Vinci's Bicycle. 10 Stories by Guy Davenport.* 1979. Johns Hopkins. 1st ed. cloth. F/NF. B2. $100.00

DAVENPORT, Guy. *Eclogues.* 1981. North Point. 1st ed. F/F. B35. $20.00

DAVENPORT, Horace. *Doctor Dock: Teaching & Learning Medicine...* 1987. New Brunswick, NJ. 1st ed. 342p. dj. A13. $30.00

DAVID, Elizabeth. *French Country Cooking.* (1951). Horizon. 1st Am ed. F/NF clip. B4. $150.00

DAVID, Lavinia R. *Buttonwood Island.* 1943. Doubleday. ils Paul Brown. cloth. VG. M5. $15.00

DAVID & MCKAY. *Blessings of Liberty, an Enduring Constitution...* 1989. Random. VG/dj. M11. $45.00

DAVIDSON, Anstruther. *Catalogue of Plants of Los Angeles County, Part I...* 1896 (1892). Los Angeles. S CA Acad of Sciences. rpt. worn wrp. B26. $25.00

DAVIDSON, Avram. *Best of Avram Davidson...* 1979. Doubleday. 1st ed. VG/VG. P3. $20.00

DAVIDSON, Avram. *Redward Edward Papers.* 1978. Doubleday. 1st ed. VG/VG. P3. $20.00

DAVIDSON, Bill. *Cut Off.* 1972. Stein Day. 1st ed. VG/VG. P3. $15.00

DAVIDSON, Donald. *Lee in the Mountains & Other Poems.* 1938. Houghton Mifflin. 1st ed. 137p. VG/G. B10. $125.00

DAVIDSON, Donald. *Long Street Poems.* 1961. Vanderbilt. 1st ed. 92p. VG/box. B10. $75.00

DAVIDSON, Eugene. *Making of Adolf Hitler.* 1977. NY. 1st prt. 408p. A17. $12.50

DAVIDSON, Eugene. *Trial of the Germans: Account of 22 Defendants...* 1969. NY. 4th. 636p. VG/worn. A17. $18.50

DAVIDSON, Harold G. *Edward Borein, Cowboy Artist: Life & Works of JE Borein...* 1974. Doubleday. 1st trade ed. 4to. 189p. VG/dj. T10. $75.00

DAVIDSON, Joe. *Art of the Cigar Label.* 1989. Longmeadow. 1st ed. 251p. cloth. M20. $37.00

DAVIDSON, John; see Neutzel, Charles.

DAVIDSON, Lionel. *Long Way to Shiloh.* 1966. Gollancz. 2nd. VG/VG. P3. $15.00

DAVIDSON, Lionel. *Sun Chemist.* 1976. Knopf. 1st ed. VG/VG. P3. $25.00

DAVIDSON, Martin. *Stars & the Mind.* 1947. London. Scientific BC. ils/photos. 210p. cloth. G. K5. $12.00

DAVIDSON, William H. *Brooks of Honey & Butter: Plantations & People...* 1971. Outlook. 2nd. photos/fld map. VG/VG. B10. $100.00

DAVIE, Donald. *Poet As Sculptor (Ezra Pound).* 1965. Lodnon. 1st ed. assn copy. F/NF. V1. $45.00

DAVIES, Arthur Ernest. *Moral Life: A Study in Genetic Ethics.* 1909. Baltimore. Review Pub. 187p. bl cloth/paper labels. G1. $40.00

DAVIES, Arthur I. *Death Plays a Duet.* 1977. Exposition. 1st ed. VG/VG. P3. $10.00

DAVIES, David Stuart. *Holmes of the Movies.* 1978. Bramhall. 1st ed. VG/VG. P3. $15.00

DAVIES, Frederick. *Death of a Hit-Man.* 1982. St Martin. 1st ed. xl. dj. P3. $5.00

DAVIES, John. *Phrenology: Fad & Science, a 19th-Century American Crusade.* 1971. Hamden, CT. 1st ed. 203p. VG. A13. $50.00

DAVIES, Kenneth. *Ionospheric Radio Propagation.* 1965. Nat Bureau Standards. Monograph 80. 8vo. 470p. VG. K5. $25.00

DAVIES, L.P. *Land of Leys.* 1979. Doubleday. 1st Am ed. NF/NF. N4. $25.00

DAVIES, L.P. *Shadow Before.* 1970. Doubleday. BC. VG/G. N4. $8.00

DAVIES, Mary Carolyn. *Joy Toy Man of Joy Toy Town.* ca 1930. np ils Queen Holden. unp. VG/dj. M20. $77.00

DAVIES, Nigel. *Aztec Empire.* 1987. OK U. 1st ed. 342p. dj. F3. $35.00

DAVIES, Nigel. *Tolec Heritage.* 1980. OK U. 1st ed. 401p. dj. F3. $30.00

DAVIES, Paul. *Last Three Minutes.* 1994. Harper Collins. 1st ed. F/F. B35. $18.00

DAVIES, Pete. *Dollarville.* 1989. Random. 1st ed. F/F. P3. $18.00

DAVIES, Robertson. *Feast of Stephen.* 1970. Toronto/Montreal. 1st ed. F/VG+. A11. $150.00

DAVIES, Robertson. *Murther & Walking Spirits.* 1991. London. Sinclair Stevenson. 1st ed. 1/150. sgn/#d. F/dj. C2. $175.00

DAVIES, Robertson. *Murther & Walking Spirits.* 1991. London. 1st ed. sgn. F/F. C2. $75.00

DAVIES, Robertson. *What's Bred in the Bone.* 1986. Viking. 5th. F/F. P3. $18.00

DAVIES, Thomas. *Preparation & Mounting of Microscopic Objects...* 1896. London. ils. 214p. red cloth. F. B14. $37.50

DAVIES, William H. *True Travelers.* 1923. Harcourt Brace. 1st probable ed. ils Wm Nicholson. F/VG. C8. $120.00

DAVIS, A.M. *Illustrated Atlas of Berks County.* 1876. 100 maps w/business directory. complete. loose. S13. $375.00

DAVIS, Berrie. *Fourth Day of Fear.* 1973. Putnam. 1st ed. VG/VG. P3. $13.00

DAVIS, Burke. *Billy Mitchell Affair.* 1967. Random. 1st ed. sgn. 8vo. 373p. VG/VG. B11. $50.00

DAVIS, Burke. *Civil War: Strange & Interesting Facts.* 1982. NY. 8vo. ils. 249p. blk cloth. F/dj. T3. $20.00

DAVIS, Burke. *Dwelling Places.* 1980. Scribner. 1st ed. sgn. VG/VG. B11. $25.00

DAVIS, Burke. *Roberta E Lee.* 1956. Winston-Salem, NC. Blair. 1st ed. inscr. ils John Opper. VG/VG. B11. $45.00

DAVIS, C. Henry. *Painless Childbirth Eutocia & Nitrous Oxid-Oxygen Analgesia.* 1916. Chicago. 164p. red cloth. VG. B14. $35.00

DAVIS, C.H. *Narrative of the North Polar Expedition, US Ship Polaris.* 1876. Washington. engravings/photos/maps. G+. B30. $125.00

DAVIS, Charles G. *Ships of the Past.* 1929. Marine Research Soc. 1st ed. ils. 170p. VG. w/sgn letter & brochure. M20. $100.00

DAVIS, Charles J. *California Salt-Water Fishing.* (1949). NY. 1st ed. F/G+. N3. $15.00

DAVIS, Dorothy Salisbury. *Death in the Life.* 1976. Scribner. 1st ed. VG/VG. P3. $18.00

DAVIS, Dorothy Salisbury. *God Speed the Night.* 1968. Scribner. 1st ed. VG/G. P3. $18.00

DAVIS, Dorothy Salisbury. *Shock Wave.* 1974. Arthur Baker. 1st ed. VG/VG. P3. $18.00

DAVIS, Dorothy Salisbury. *Where the Dark Streets Go.* 1969. Scribner. 1st ed. F/F. H11. $25.00

DAVIS, Dorothy Salisbury. *Where the Dark Streets Go.* 1969. Scribner. 2nd. VG/VG. P3. $13.00

DAVIS, E. Adams. *On the Night Wind's Telling.* 1946. Norman, OK. 1st ed. 276p. dj. F3. $30.00

DAVIS, Grania. *Moonbird.* 1986. Doubleday. 1st ed. rem mk. F/NF. G10. $15.00

DAVIS, Grania. *Moonbird.* 1986. Doubleday. 1st ed. RS. F/F. P3. $20.00

DAVIS, H.L. *Honey in the Horn.* 1977. Franklin Lib. ils. full leather. A17. $25.00

DAVIS, H.L. *Kettle of Fire.* 1959. Morrow. 1st ed. M/dj. A18. $20.00

DAVIS, Harriet Eager. *Elmira: Girl Who Loved Edgar Allan Poe.* 1966. Houghton Mifflin. 1st ed. VG/dj. M21/P3. $20.00

DAVIS, J. Madison. *Murder of Frau Shutz.* 1988. NY. Walker. 1st ed. author's 1st book. F/F. H11. $30.00

DAVIS, Janet S. *Completely Cowed.* 1969. Phil. Chilton. 1st ed. author's 1st novel. F. B4. $75.00

DAVIS, Jefferson. *Jefferson Davis: Constitutionalist; His Letters...* 1923. Jackson, MS. MS Dept Archives & Hist. 10 vol. 1st ed. VG. M8. $650.00

DAVIS, Jefferson. *Report of the Secretary of War Communicating Information...* 1857. WA. Nicholson. 1st ed. 8vo. 21 pl/fld pl. VG. I10. $250.00

DAVIS, John Gordon. *Taller Than Trees.* 1975. Doubleday. 1st ed. F/F. P3. $15.00

DAVIS, Kathryn. *Girl Who Trod on a Loaf.* 1993. Knopf. 1st ed. F/F. H11. $25.00

DAVIS, Kathryn. *Labrador.* 1988. FSG. 1st ed. author's 1st book. F/clip. H11. $40.00

DAVIS, Keith. *Desire Charnay.* 1981. NM U. 1st ed. 4to. 212p. dj. F3. $45.00

DAVIS, Kenneth C. *Don't Know Much About Geography.* 1992. NY. VG. O7. $20.00

DAVIS, Lavinia R. *Melody Muttonbone & Sam.* 1947. Doubleday. 1st ed. ils Paul Brown. 244p. F/VG. P2. $25.00

DAVIS, Lavinia R. *Roger & the Fox.* 1947. Doubleday. sgn. ils Hildegard Woodward. VG. P2. $25.00

DAVIS, Lavinia R. *Threat of Dragons.* 1948. Crime Club. G. P3. $7.00

DAVIS, Lindsey. *Silver Pigs.* 1989. Crown. 1st ed. NF/NF. M23. $20.00

DAVIS, Mac. *Lore & Legends of Baseball.* 1953. Lantern. 1st ed. ils. VG/G+. P8. $15.00

DAVIS, Margo. *Antique Black.* 1973. San Francisco. Scrimshaw. 1st ed. photos. F/dj. S9. $125.00

DAVIS, Marguerite. *Told Under the Blue Umbrella: New Stories for New Children.* 1934. Macmillan. 4th. 161p. VG. C14. $5.00

DAVIS, Mary Lee. *Uncle Sam's Attic.* 1930. Boston. WA Wilde. 8vo. 402p. VG. P4. $25.00

DAVIS, Mildred. *Strange Corner.* 1967. Crime Club. 1st ed. VG/VG. P3. $20.00

DAVIS, Mildred. *They Buried a Man.* nd. BC. VG/VG. P3. $8.00

DAVIS, Nicholas A. *Campaign From Texas to Maryland.* 1963. Richmond. Presbyterian Comm of Pub. 3 pl. 168p. wrp. M8. $2,500.00

DAVIS, Richard Beale. *Literature & Society in Early Virginia, 1608-1840.* 1973. LSU. 332p. VG/VG. B10. $35.00

DAVIS, Richard Harding. *Gallagher.* 1906. Scribner. VG. P3. $10.00

DAVIS, Richard Harding. *Rulers of the Mediterranean.* 1894. NY. Harper. 8vo. ils. VG. W1. $24.00

DAVIS, Richard Harding. *West From a Car Window.* 1892. Harper. 1st ed. ils Remington. bl cloth. NF. T10. $150.00

DAVIS, Richard. *Encyclopedia of Horror.* 1981. Octopus. 1st ed. VG. P3. $20.00

DAVIS, Richard. *Space 3.* 1976. Abelard. 1st ed. VG/VG. P3. $22.00

DAVIS, Robertson. *Manticore.* 1972. Viking. 1st Am ed. F/NF. B2. $45.00

DAVIS, Ron; see Kent, Hal.

DAVIS, Thulani. *1959* 1992. Grove Weidenfeld. ARC. author's 1st novel. F/wrp. B4. $45.00

DAVIS, Thulani. *1959.* 1992. Grove Weidenfeld. 1st ed. F/F. M23. $20.00

DAVIS, William C. *Image of War, 1861-1865; Vol II: Guns of '62.* 1982. Garden City. 4to. 460p. F/NF. T3. $30.00

DAVIS, William C. *Image of War: 1861-1865.* 1981. Nat Hist Soc/Doubleday. 6 vol. photos. VG+/dj. M20. $350.00

DAVIS, William C. *Rebels & Yankees: Commanders of the Civil War.* 1990. NY. folio. 256p. F/F. T3. $30.00

DAVIS, William M. *Coral Reef Problem.* 1928. NY. VG. O7. $55.00

DAVIS, William M. *Lesser Antilles.* 1920. NY. VG. O7. $35.00

DAVIS, William M. *Nimrod of the Sea; or, American Whaleman.* 1926. Boston. Lariat. 8vo. 406p. partially unopened. NF. T10. $125.00

DAVIS, William M. *Nimrod of the Sea; or, American Whaleman.* 1972. Quincy, MA. Christopher Pub. rpt. 405p. VG/dj. T7. $35.00

DAVIS, William Stearns. *Short History of the Near East.* 1922. Macmillan. 13 maps. 408p. VG. W1. $18.00

DAVIS & PEDLER. *Dynostar Menace.* 1975. Scribner. 1st ed. F/F. P3. $10.00

DAVIS & PEDLER. *Mutant 59.* nd. BC. VG/VG. P3. $8.00

DAVIS & WATKINS. *Children's Theatre.* 1960. NY. 416p. VG/VG. A17. $5.00

DAVY, Kenneth L. *Let's Learn Bridge.* 1946. London. 47p. stiff brd. VG. S1. $5.00

DAWE, Carlton. *Life Cartridge.* 1937. Ward Lock. 1st ed. xl. VG. P3. $20.00

DAWKINS, Cecil. *Quiet Enemy.* 1963. Atheneum. 1st ed. author's 1st book. NF/NF. B35. $30.00

DAWKINS, W. Boyd. *Early Man in Britain.* 1880. London. Macmillan. 1st ed. ils. 537p. teg. decor cloth. VG. T10. $125.00

DAWS & SHEEHAN. *Hawaiians.* 1970. Sydney. VG. O7. $75.00

DAWSON, Carol. *Body of Knowledge.* 1994. Algonquin. 1st ed. sgn. F/F. M23. $30.00

DAWSON, David Laing. *Last Rights.* 1990. Canada. Macmillan. 1st ed. NF/NF. P3. $20.00

DAWSON, James. *Hell Gate.* 1971. McKay. VG/VG. P3. $10.00

DAWSON, Joseph Martin. *Brooks Takes the Long Look.* 1931. Waco, TX. Baylor. sgn. VG. B11. $20.00

DAWSON, Muriel. *Happy Hours Picture Book.* nd. Raphael Tuck. 8vo. 16 glossy p. VG. M5. $65.00

DAWSON, Muriel. *My Book of Nursery Rhymes.* nd. Raphael Tuck. 4to. 16 glossy p. VG/stiff wrp. M5. $75.00

DAWSON, Muriel. *Nursery Rhymes for Children.* 1940. Lowe. ils Muriel Dawson. 20p. F. M5. $60.00

DAWSON, Percy. *Soviet Samples: Diary of an American Physiologist.* 1938. Ann Arbor. 1st ed. 568p. wrp. A13. $30.00

DAWSON, Raymond. *Chinese Experience.* 1978. NY. VG. O7. $20.00

DAWSON & FOSTER. *Seashore Plants of California.* 1982. Berkeley. 12mo. ils/pl. VG/VG. B1. $26.50

DAY, Alexandra. *Paddy's Pay-Day.* 1989. Viking Kestrel. 1st ed. 4to. F/F. B17. $9.00

DAY, Beth. *Little Professor of Piney Woods.* 1955. Messner. 1st ed. inscr. 192p. VG/VG. B11. $100.00

DAY, Clarence. *Life With Father.* 1947. Sun Dial. MTI. VG/VG. P3. $20.00

DAY, David. *Tolkien Bestiary.* 1979. Ballantine. 1st ed. VG/VG. P3. $25.00

DAY, Dianne. *Strange Files of Fremont Jones.* 1995. Doubleday. 1st ed. F/F. M23. $75.00

DAY, Gene. *Future Day.* 1979. Flying Buttress. 1st ed. decor brd. VG. P3. $15.00

DAY, Gina. *Tell No Tales.* 1967. Hart Davis. 1st ed. F/F. P3. $15.00

DAY, James M. *Maps of Texas 1527-1900: Map Collection TX State Archives.* 1964. Austin. Pemberton. expanded version of 1st ed. 178p. F/wrp. O7. $125.00

DAY & LEE. *Castles.* 1984. Bantam. 1st ed. hc. F/F. P3. $25.00

DAY & MORRISON. *Typographic Book 1450-1935.* 1963. London. 1st ed. 377 pl. 99p. F/dj/case. T10. $300.00

DAY & MOSELEY. *Chan Chan: Andean Desert City.* 1992. Jahrhundert, Germany. ils. 183p. wrp. F3. $45.00

DAYAN, Yael. *Dust.* 1963. World. 12mo. 190p. cloth. VG. W1. $16.00

DAYTON, Fred Erving. *Steamboat Days.* 1925. Stokes. ils John Wolcott Adams. G. B16. $60.00

DAZEY, Charles. *In Old Kentucky.* 1937. Detroit. Blue Ox. 147p. VG/stiff wrp. B10. $35.00

DE ALARCON, Pedro Antonio. *Three-Cornered Hat.* 1959. LEC. 1st ed. 1/1500. ils/sgn Duvoisin. 155p. F/case. C2. $50.00

DE ALMEIDA. *Ocupacao Portuguesa em Africa na Epoca Contemporanea.* 1936. Lisboa. inscr. VG/wrp. O7. $35.00

DE ANDREA, William L. *Killed in the Ratings.* 1978. HBJ. 1st ed. author's 1st book. F/F. H11. $45.00

DE ANGELI, Marguerite. *Black Fox of Lorne.* 1956. Doubleday. 1st ed. 8vo. VG. C14. $15.00

DE ANGELI, Marguerite. *Jared's Island.* 1947. Doubleday. 1st ed. ils. 95p. VG/poor. C14. $15.00

DE ANGELI, Marguerite. *Just Like David. Jack & Jill Magazine Version.* Sept 1951. np. ils. 12p. G. P2. $15.00

DE ANGELI, Marguerite. *Petite Suzanne.* 1937. Doubleday/Jr Literary Guild. ils. VG. M5. $25.00

DE ANGELI, Marguerite. *Turkey for Christmas.* 1949. Westminster. 1st ed. unp. VG/dj. M20/P2. $50.00

DE ANGELI & DE ANGELI. *Empty Barn.* 1946. Westminster. ils. VG/VG. P2. $35.00

DE AYALA, Juan. *Letter to Ferdinand & Isabella.* 1965. NM U. ltd ed. 1/750. 90p. F3. $45.00

DE BALZAC, Honore. *Eugenie Grandet.* 1960. London. 4to. ils Rene bon Sussan. beige cloth/leather decor. F/case. T10. $60.00

DE BEAUVOIR, Simone. *Les Belles Images.* 1968. Collins. 2nd ed. hc. NF/NF. P3. $15.00

DE BENHAM, Frank. *Discovery & Exploration: An Atlas-History...* 1960. np. ils. 272p. VG/VG. A4. $45.00

DE BENOUVILLE, Guillain. *Unknown Warriors.* 1949. Simon Schuster. 1st ed. 372p. VG. A17. $9.50

DE BERG, Jeanne. *Women's Rites.* nd. BC. VG/VG. P3. $8.00

DE BERNIERES, Louis. *Corelli's Mandolin.* 1994. Pantheon. ARC. 8vo. F/wrp. S9. $35.00

DE BERNIERES, Louis. *War of Don Emmanuel's Nether Parts.* 1992. NY. Morrow. 1st ed. author's 1st book. NF/F. M23. $20.00

DE BESAULT, Lawrence. *President Trujillo: His Life & the Dominican Republic.* 1941. Santiago. El Diario. 3rd. inscr to US Ambassador. VG/G. B11. $65.00

DE BOSSCHERE, Jean. *Marthe & the Madmen.* 1928. Covici Friede. 1st ed. author's 1st novel. F/NF. B35. $75.00

DE BOSSHERE, J. *Folk Tales of Flanders.* 1918. Dodd Mead. 1st Am ed. 4to. 179p. teg. gr cloth. VG. D1. $275.00

DE BOUGAINVILLE, Louis. *History of a Voyage to the Malouine Islands.* 1773. London. Goldsmith. 2nd. 10 pl/7 charts. 294p. gilt calf. T7. $900.00

DE BREYNE, P.J.C. *Penseees d'un Croyant Catholique, ou Considerations...* 1840. Paris. Poussielgue-Rusand. 2nd. 496p. VG. G1. $125.00

DE BRUNHOFF, Jean. *Babar the King.* 1935. Smith Haas. 1st Am ed. folio. 47p. VG. D1. $750.00

DE BRUNHOFF, Jean. *Historie de Barbar le Petit Elephant.* 1931. Paris. Jardin de Modes. 1st ed. sm folio. 48p. F. B24. $550.00

DE BRUNHOFF, Jean. *Le Roi Babar.* 1933. Jardin Des Modes. 1st ed. ils. 48p. VG-. P2. $275.00

DE BRUNHOFF, Jean. *Travels of Babar.* 1934. Random. 1st ed thus? 8vo. ils. VG/G. M5. $65.00

DE BRUNHOFF, Laurent. *Babar & That Rascal Arthur.* 1948. Methuen. 1st ed. 48p. VG-. P2. $215.00

DE BRUNHOFF, Laurent. *Babar's Mystery.* 1978. Random. 2nd. unp. NF. C14. $12.00

DE BRUNHOFF, Laurent. *Barbar's Bookmobile.* 1974. Random. 1st Am ed. ils VG/VG box. P2. $35.00

DE BURY, Richard. *Philobibon.* 1888. Kegan Paul Trench. 12mo. 259p. teg. brn buckram. VG. T10. $70.00

DE BUSTAMANTE, Antonio S. *World Court.* 1925. Macmillan. VG/defective. M11. $65.00

DE CALLATAY, Vincent. *Atlas of the Sky.* 1958. Macmillan. trans Harold Spencer Jones. xl. K5. $18.00

DE CAMP, Catherine Crook. *Creatures of the Cosmos.* 1977. Westminster. 1st ed. VG/G. P3. $20.00

DE CAMP, L. Sprague. *Conan Grimoire.* 1972. Mirage. 1st ed. sng. VG/VG. P3. $65.00

DE CAMP, L. Sprague. *Conan Swordbook.* 1969. Mirage. 1st ed. sgn. VG. P3. $65.00

DE CAMP, L. Sprague. *Continent Makers.* 1953. Twayne. VG. P3. $25.00

DE CAMP, L. Sprague. *Energy & Power.* 1962. Golden. hc. NF. P3. $15.00

DE CAMP, L. Sprague. *Golden Wind.* 1969. Doubleday. 1st ed. hc. xl. dj. P3. $20.00

DE CAMP, L. Sprague. *Honorable Barbarian.* 1989. Del Rey. 1st ed. F/F. P3. $17.00

DE CAMP, L. Sprague. *Lest Darkness Fall.* 1949. Phil. Prime. revised/1st ed thus. sgn. F/NF 2nd state dj. T2. $95.00

DE CAMP, L. Sprague. *Lest Darkness Fall.* 1949. Prime. 1st ed. NF/VG. M19. $50.00

DE CAMP, L. Sprague. *Literary Swordsmen & Sorcerers.* 1976. Arkham. 1st ed. F/F. P3. $20.00

DE CAMP, L. Sprague. *Tales Beyond Time.* 1973. GK Hall Lg Prt. xl. dj. G. P3. $10.00

DE CAMP, L. Sprague. *Unbeheaded King.* 1983. Del Rey. 1st ed. F/F. P3. $18.00

DE CAMP, L. Sprague. *Undesired Princess.* 1951. Fpci. 1st ed. VG/VG. P3. $75.00

DE CAMP, L. Sprague. *Wheels of If.* 1948. Shasta. 1st ed. VG/VG. P3. $150.00

DE CAMP & DE CAMP. *Dark Valley.* 1983. Bluejay. 1/1000. sgns/#d. F/F/case. P3. $80.00

DE CAMP & DE CAMP. *Footprints on Sand.* 1981. Advent. 1st ed. F/F. P3. $20.00

DE CAMP & NYBERG. *Return of Conan.* 1957. Gnome. 1st ed. VG/VG. P3. $90.00

DE CAMP & PRATT. *Castle of Iron.* 1950. Gnome. 1st ed. VG/G. P3. $75.00

DE CASTANEDA, Pedro. *Journey of Coronado.* 1990. Golden. VG. O7. $20.00

DE CASTELLANE, Comte. *Souvenirs of Military Life in Algeria.* 1886. Remington. 2 vol. 1st ed. VG. W1. $150.00

DE CASTRO, D. Joao. *Journal of Action Upon the Coast of Spain.* 1968. Amsterdam/NY. VG. O7. $75.00

DE CASTRO, D. Joao. *Le Routier de Dom Joan de Castro...* 1936. Paris. Librairie Orientaliste Paul Geuthner. F/prt wrp. O7. $300.00

DE CERVANTES, Miguel. *History of Don Quixote.* 1923. Doran. 1st Am ed thus. ils Jean DeBosschere. 311p. G+. P2. $75.00

DE CERVANTES, Miguel. *Life & Exploits of the Ingenious Gentleman Don Quixote...* 1766. London. Tonson. 4 vol. 4th. 8vo. 31 pl. full vellum. F. B24. $600.00

DE CHANCIE, John. *Magicnet.* 1993. Baltimore. Borderlands. 1st ed. 1/350. sgn. F/F. T2. $18.00

DE CHANCIE, John. *Magicnet.* 1993. Morrow. 1st ed. RS. F/NF. G10. $9.00

DE CHATELAIN, Madame. *Blind Fisherman & His Three Sons.* ca 1860. Wm Tegg. 4to. 25p. VG. T10. $150.00

DE CHIRICO, Giorgio. *Hebdomeros.* 1966. Four Seasons Book Soc. 1st Eng-language ed. 1/500. F/NF. B2. $100.00

DE COY, Robert H. *Nigger Bible.* 1967. Holloway. 3rd. pb. 299p. VG+. P11. $20.00

DE CREVECOEUR, M.-G. *Journey Into Northern Pennsylvania & State of New York.* 1964. Ann Arbor. 1st ed thus. 570p. VG. B18. $27.50

DE DILLMONT, T.H. *Encyclopedia of Needlework.* ca 1940s. np. 1087 ils/pl. 813p. VG. B5. $55.00

DE FELITTA, Frank. *Entity.* 1978. Putnam. 1st ed. G/G. P3. $13.00

DE FOE, Daniel. *Life & Adventures of Robinson Crusoe.* 1914. Chicago/NY. Rand McNally. ils Milo Winter. 382p. gr pebble cloth. F. H4. $75.00

DE FOE, Daniel. *Life & Surprising Adventures of Robinson Crusoe, Mariner.* 1930. LEC. 1/1500. 8vo. ils/sgn EA Wilson. 385p. gr cloth. F/case. B24. $200.00

DE FOREST, J.W. *Miss Ravenel's Conversion.* 1867. NY. 1st ed. VG. A9. $100.00

DE FRANCESCO, Grete. *Power of the Charlatan.* 1939. New Haven. 1st ed. 288p. VG. A13. $60.00

DE GALBA, Marti Joan. *Tirant Lo Blanc.* 1984. Schocken. UP/1st Eng-language ed. F. B35. $25.00

DE GAMA, Jose Basilio. *Uruguay.* 1982. Berkeley. 1st ed. index/biblio. 264p. dj. F3. $25.00

DE GANS, Raymonde. *Tutankhamen.* 1978. Geneva. Ferni. 1st ed. 4to. ils. quarter morocco. VG. W1. $45.00

DE GAULE, Charles. *Call To Honour 1940-1942.* 1955. London. 1st Eng ed. 2 vol. VG/dj. B18. $25.00

DE GINGINS-LASSARAZ, F. *Natural History of the Lavenders.* 1967. Boston. NE Herb Soc. xl. VG. A10. $50.00

DE GRAZIA, Diane. *Correggio & His Legacy: 16th-Century Italian Drawings.* 1984. Nat Gallery of Art. ils/pl. 415p. D2. $65.00

DE GRAZIA, Edward. *Girls Lean Back Everywhere.* 1992. Random. M11. $27.50

DE GUERIN, Basil C. *Man With Three Eyes.* 1955. Children's Pr. 1st ed. decor brd. VG. P3. $15.00

DE HARSANYI, Zsolt. *Star-Gazer.* 1939. Putnam. 1st ed. 8vo. 572p. dj. K5. $12.00

DE HARTE, William C. *Observations on Military Law & the Constitution...* 1869. NY. Appleton. contemporary sheep. M11. $250.00

DE HEJIA & PAL. *From Merchants to Emperors.* 1986. Corenll/Pierpont Morgan. F. D2. $40.00

DE HOLGUIN, Beatrice. *Tales of Palm Beach.* 1968. NY. Vantage. 1st ed. sgn. 8vo. 181p. VG/G. B11. $40.00

DE JARNETTE, Eva Magruder. *Out on a Scurdgeon & Other Negro Stories in Dialect.* 1928. JW Burke. 52p. VG. B10. $20.00

DE JODE, Gerard. *Speculum Orbis Terrarum.* 1965. Amsterdam. Theatrvm Oribs Terrarvm. facsimile. AN/dj. O7. $325.00

DE JONG, Meindert. *Almost All-White Rabbit Cat.* 1972. Macmillan. 1st ed. ils H Vestal. 113p. VG/VG. P2. $30.00

DE JONG, Meindert. *Bells of the Harbor.* 1941. Harper. 1st ed. ils Kurt Wiese. 289p. NF/VG. P2. $50.00

DE JONG, Meindert. *Dirk's Dog, Bellow.* 1939. Harper. 1st ed. ils Kurt Wiese. VG/G. P2. $45.00

DE JONG, Meindert. *Journey From Peppermint Street.* 1968. Harper Row. ils Emily McCully. 242p. VG+/VG. T5. $25.00

DE JONG, Meindert. *Singing Hill.* 1962. Harper Row. 1st ed. ils Sendak. VG+/G. P2. $85.00

DE KNIGHT, Freda. *Date With a Dish. A Cookbook of American Negro Recipes.* 1948. NY. 1st ed. 426p. VG. B5. $25.00

DE LA FONTAINE. *Fables de la Fontaine.* 1981. Boston. Alphabet Pr. 1st ed. ils Marie Angel. AN/case. D1. $85.00

DE LA MARE, Walter. *At First Sight.* 1928. Crosby Gaige. 1st ed. 1/650. sgn. VG. S9. $45.00

DE LA MARE, Walter. *Ding Dong Bell.* 1924. London. 1st ed. F/F. C2. $65.00

DE LA MARE, Walter. *Down-Adown-Derry.* 1922. London. Constable. 1st ed. ils Dorothy Lathrop. teg. gilt bl cloth. VG. T5. $90.00

DE LA MARE, Walter. *Mr Bumps & His Monkey.* 1942. Chicago. Winston. 1st ed. ils Dorothy Lathrop. 67p. VG/VG. D1. $120.00

DE LA MARE, Walter. *Peacock Pie: Book of Rhymes.* 1913. London. 1st ed. F/dj. C2. $75.00

DE LA MARE, Walter. *Songs of Childhood.* 1916. Longman Gr. 2nd. 16mo. gr cloth. F. C2. $45.00

DE LA MARE, Walter. *Stuff & Nonsense & So On.* 1927. London. 1st ed. ils Bold. VG/dj. C2. $65.00

DE LA MARTINE. *Past, Present & Future of the Republic.* 1850. NY. 12mo. 163p. blk cloth. xl. T3. $12.00

DE LA MOTTE FOUQUE. *Undine.* 1909. Doubleday Page. 1st Am ed. ils Rackham. gr brd. VG. B17. $125.00

DE LA NEZIENE. *Tot au Cirque.* ca 1920. Paris. Hachette. ils. VG. D1. $95.00

DE LA RAME, Louise. *Bimbi.* 1910. Lippincott. 1st ed thus. ils Maria Kirk. teg. gilt red cloth. VG+. M5. $45.00

DE LA REE, Gerry. *Art of the Fantastic.* 1978. De La Ree. 1st ed. NF/NF. P3. $50.00

DE LA REE, Gerry. *Second Book of Virgil Finlay.* 1978. De La Ree. 1st ed. 1/1300. NF/NF. P3. $40.00

DE LA REE, Gerry. *Sixth Book of Virgil Finlay.* 1980. De La Ree. 1/1300. NF/NF. P3. $35.00

DE LA ROCHE, Mazo. *Renny's Daughter.* 1951. Little Brn. 1st ed. VG/G. P3. $18.00

DE LA TORRE, Lillian. *Detections of Dr Sam Johnson.* 1960. Crime Club. 1st ed. VG/VG. P3. $30.00

DE LA TORRE, Lillian. *Dr Sam: Johnson, Detector.* 1946. KNopf. 12mo. 257p. VG/dj. T10. $60.00

DE LANOYE, Ferdinand. *Ramses le Grand ou l'Egypt il y a 3300 Ans.* 1872. Paris. Hachette. 2nd. sm 8vo. ils. 326p. xl. VG. W1. $20.00

DE LARRABEITI, Michael. *Borribles.* 1978. Macmillan. 2nd ed. VG/VG. P3. $18.00

DE LEON, Thomas Cooper. *Four Years in Rebel Capitals: An Inside View...* 1892. Mobile, AL. Author's Authograph ed. sgn. 376p. cloth. VG. M8. $175.00

DE LILLO, Don. *Americana.* 1971. Houghton Mifflin. 1st ed. author's 1st book. F/F. C2. $350.00

DE LILLO, Don. *Great Jones Street.* 1973. Houghton Mifflin. 1st ed. F/VG. H11. $85.00

DE LILLO, Don. *Libra.* 1988. Viking. 1st ed. F/F. P3. $20.00

DE LILLO, Don. *Names.* 1982. Knopf. UP. F/prt wrp. C2. $75.00

DE LILLO, Don. *Ratner's Star.* 1976. NY. 1st ed. F/F. C6. $50.00

DE LILLO, Don. *White Noise.* 1985. Viking. 1st ed. rem mk. F/NF. H11. $40.00

DE LINT, Charles. *Dreams Underfoot.* 1993. Tor. 1st ed. sgn. F/F. P3. $30.00

DE LINT, Charles. *Ghost of Wind & Shadow.* 1991. Axolotl Special Ed. 1st ed. sgn. F/F. P3. $45.00

DE LINT, Charles. *Ivory & the Horn.* 1995. Tor. 1st ed. F/F. P3. $22.00

DE LINT, Charles. *Memory & Dream.* 1994. NY. Tor. 1st ed. sgn. F/F. M23. $45.00

DE LINT, Charles. *Our Lady of the Harbor.* 1991. Axolotl Special Ed. 1st ed. sgn. F/F. P3. $45.00

DE LINT, Charles. *Wild Wood.* 1994. Bantam. 1st ed. F/F. P3. $20.00

DE LONG, George W. *Voyage of the Jeannette.* 1883. Boston. 1st ed. 2 vol. G+. B18. $125.00

DE LONGCHAMPS, Joanne. *Wishing Album.* 1970. Nashville. Vanderbilt. 1st ed. NF/NF. B4. $65.00

DE LORIA, Vine. *God Is Red.* 1973. NY. 1st ed. VG/VG. B5. $30.00

DE MARINIS, Rick. *Lovely Monster.* 1975. NY. 1st ed. author's 1st book. F/F. A11. $40.00

DE MARINIS, Rick. *Scimitar.* 1977. Dutton. 1st ed. VG/VG. P3. $25.00

DE MARINIS, Rick. *Year of the Zinc Penny.* 1989. Norton. 1st ed. VG/VG. P3. $18.00

DE MAUPASSANT, Guy. *Dark Side of Guy DeMaupassant.* 1989. Carroll Graf. 1st ed. F/F. T2. $20.00

DE MAUPASSANT, Guy. *Mont Oriel.* nd. St Dunstan Soc. hc. VG. P3. $15.00

DE MEDINA, Pedro. *Navigator's Universe.* 1972. Chicago. facsimile. 224p. dj. K5. $45.00

DE MILLE, Agnes. *Lizzie Borden: A Dance of Death.* 1968. Atlantic/Little Brn. 1st ed. AN/dj. B4. $100.00

DE MILLE, Nelson. *Charm School.* 1988. Warner. 1st ed. NF/NF. N4. $30.00

DE MONVEL, M. Boutet. *Nos Enfants par Anatole France.* (1900). Paris. Librarie Hachette. early prt. folio. NF. B4. $85.00

DE MORGAN, Augustus. *Essay on Probabilities on Their Application to Life...* 1838. Longman Brn Gr. 1st ed. 12mo. 306p. full bl calf. T10. $300.00

DE MOUSTIER, C.A. *Theatre...CA DeMoustier.* 1803. French text. marbled ep. aeg. full leather. VG. S13. $20.00

DE MUSSET, Paul. *Mr Wind & Madam Rain.* 1864. Harper. 1st Am ed. gilt bl cloth. VG. M5. $125.00

DE ONIS, Harriet. *Golden Land.* 1948. Knopf. 1st ed. 395p. dj. F3. $15.00

DE PAOLA, Tomie. *Songs of the Fog Maiden.* 1979. Holiday House. 1st ed. ils. NF/G+. P2. $28.00

DE PORTOLA, Gaspar. *Diary.* 1909. Berkeley. 1st ed. 8vo. 59p. T10. $50.00

DE PROROK, Byron. *Dead Men Do Tell Tales.* 1942. Creative Age. 1st ed. 8vo. 328p. VG. W1. $18.00

DE QUILLE, Dan. *Big Bonanza.* 1959. Knopf. 5th. 8vo. 440p. F/NF. T10. $35.00

DE RACHEWILTZ, Boris. *Black Eros: Sexual Customs of Africa.* 1964. NY. VG+. N3. $25.00

DE RIAZ, Yvan A. *Book of Knives.* 1981. Crown. 1000+ photos. 170p. cloth. dj. D2. $50.00

DE RICCI. *English Collectors of Books & Manuscripts 1530-1930...* 1960. IN U. ils. 212p. NF/VG. A4. $60.00

DE RICO, Ulderico. *Rainbow Goblins.* 1978 (1977). Warner. 1st Am prt. 4to. VG+. C8. $65.00

DE SAINT-EXUPERY, Antoine. *Little Prince.* nd. HBW. rpt. 8vo. VG/VG. B17. $6.50

DE SAINT-EXUPERY, Antoine. *Night Flight.* 1932. NY/London. Century. 1st Am ed. 198p. cloth. G. B18. $20.00

DE SAINT-EXUPERY, Antoine. *Wind, Sand & Stars.* 1939. Reynal Hitchcock. 1st Am trade ed. ils Cosgrave. VG+/dj. B14. $55.00

DE SAINT-EXUPERY, Antoine. *Wind, Sand & Stars.* 1939. Reynal Hitchcock. 1st ed. VG/VG. H4. $20.00

DE SEGONZAC, Andre. *Dunoyer de Segonzac: Dessins 1900-1970.* 1970. Geneva. Pierre Cailler. ils. 455p. cloth. dj. D2. $200.00

DE SEGUR, Madame. *Happy Surprises.* 1929. Whitman. ils Eleanore Mineah Hubbard. trans Julia Olcott. VG. M5. $30.00

DE SEGUR, Madame. *Memoirs of a Donkey.* 1924. Macmillan. 1st Am ed. Little Library. 12mo. 238p. VG. T10. $125.00

DE SEVERSKY, Alexander P. *Victory Through Air Power.* 1942. NY. 354p. dj. A17. $10.00

DE SUZE, J.A. *Little Folks Trinidad.* ca 1930. np. 8th. photos/maps. 170p. VG. A17. $10.00

DE TERRA, Helmut. *Humboldt.* 1955. NY. VG. O7. $35.00

DE TOCQUEVILLE, Alexis. *Democracy in America.* 1945. 2 vol. 1st ed thus. NF/VG. S13. $45.00

DE TROYES, Cretien. *Complete Romances of Chretien DeTroyes.* 1993. IN U. VG/VG. P3. $35.00

DE VAUCOULEURS, Gerald. *Physics of the Planet Mars.* 1954. London. Faber. 365p. G/dj. K5. $100.00

DE VIEL & MICHAELS. *How To Play Canasta.* 1949. NY. 32p. VG/wrp. S1. $3.00

DE VINNE, T.L. *Invention of Printing.* 1878. np. 2nd. 144 ils. 557p. VG. A4. $235.00

DE VOS, L. *Atlas of Sponge Morphology.* 1991. Smithsonian. 4to. ils. 117p. cloth. F. B1. $27.00

DE VOTO, Bernard. *Across the Wide Missouri.* 1947. Houghton Mifflin. later prt. 8vo. ils. 483p. map ep. S13/T10. $45.00

DE VRIES, Hugo. *Intracellular Pangeneis Including a Paper on Fertilization.* 1910. Chicago. 1st Eng trans. 270p. A13. $100.00

DE VRIES, Peter. *But Who Wakes the Bugler?* 1940. Boston. 1st ed. author's 1st book. ils Charles Addams. VG. A17. $35.00

DE WAAL, R. *World Bibliography of Sherlock Holmes & Dr Watson.* 1974. NY. ils. 526p. red br. F/F. H3. $50.00

DE WARVILLE, Brissot. *New Travels in United States of North America.* 1919. Bowling Gr, OH. CS Van Tassel. 544p. cloth. M20. $32.00

DE WITT & ERICKSON. *Littlest Reindeer.* c 1946. Children's Pr. probable 1st ed. 8vo. unp. VG. C14. $8.00

DEADERICK, Barron. *Forrest: Wizard of the Saddle.* 1960. Memphis. SC Tool. pb. F. B30. $45.00

DEAK. *Picturing America 1497-1899: Prints, Maps & Drawings...* 1988. Princeton. 2 vol. 4to. 1029 ils. VG/VG. A4. $335.00

DEAN, Amber. *Dead Man's Float.* 1970. Putnam. 1st ed. VG/VG. P3. $20.00

DEAN, Amber. *Foggy Foggy Dew.* 1947. NY. DDCC. 1st ed. NF/NF. H11. $20.00

DEAN, Amber. *Snipe Hunt.* 1949. Unicorn Mystery BC. VG. P3. $15.00

DEAN, Amber. *Wrap It Up.* 1946. Crime Club. 1st ed. VG/fair. P3. $20.00

DEAN, Bashford. *Helmets & Body Armor in Modern Warfare.* 1977. Tuckahoe. ltd ed. 1/1000. 325p. VG/dj. B18. $125.00

DEAN, Graham M. *Agent Nine Solves His First Case.* 1935. Chicago. 1st ed. VG/dj. A17. $9.50

DEAN, J.S. *ABC of the Electric Car.* 1925. E Pittsburgh. Westinghouse Electric Co. 2nd. ils. 83p. VG. B18. $22.50

DEAN, Robert George. *Affair at Lover's Leap.* 1953. Crime Club. 1st ed. G/G. P3. $18.00

DEAN, Spencer. *Dishonor Among Thieves.* 1958. Detective BC. G/G. P3. $7.00

DEAN, Spencer. *Murder After a Fashion.* 1960. Crime Club. 1st ed. xl. VG/VG. P10. $10.00

DEANDREA, William L. *Five O'Clock Lightning.* 1982. St Martin. 1st ed. F/F. T2. $20.00

DEANDREA, William L. *Killed in the Ratings.* 1978. HBJ. 1st ed. author's 1st novel. F/F. T2. $30.00

DEANDREA, William L. *Killed on the Rocks.* 1990. Mysterious. 1st ed. F/F. P3. $18.00

DEANE, Norman; see Creasey, John.

DEANS, Samuel. *New England Farmer.* 1822. Boston. Wells Lilly. 3rd. 532p. full leather. VG. A10. $135.00

DEARBORN, George V.N. *Moto-Sensory Development: Observations on First 3 Years...* 1920. Baltimore. Warwick. 12mo. 215p. gray cloth. xl. VG. G1. $50.00

DEARMAN, H.B. *Not the Critic: Novel of Psychiatry & the Law.* 1965. Wingate. 1st ed. 400p. VG/G+. B10. $15.00

DEBO, Angie. *Geronimo: The Man, His Time, His Place.* 1977. Norman, OK. 2nd. 8vo. 480p. F/dj. T10. $25.00

DEBUS, Allen. *Science, Medicine & Society in the Renaissance...* 1972. NY. 2 vol. 1st ed. VG. A13. $50.00

DECKER, J.S. *As Orquideas e sue Cultura.* 1956. Sao Paulo. 2nd. ils. 123p. pict brd. B26. $30.00

DECKER, Peter. *Beyond a Big Mountain.* 1959. Hastings. 1st ed. inscr. ils Nick Eggenhofer. F/F. A18. $35.00

DECKER & DECKER. *Volcanoes.* 1981. San Francisco. Freeman. 1st ed. 244p. F. D8. $22.00

DECKER & HAMMOND. *Christian Mother Goose Book.* Feb 1980. Grand Junction, CO. Christian Mother Goose Book Co. 3rd. 111p. VG+. C14. $12.00

DEE, Jonathan. *Liberty Campaign.* 1993. Doubleday. 1st ed. author's 2nd novel. F/F. M22. $30.00

DEEPING, Warwick. *Old Pybus.* 1930. Cassell. 8th. VG. P3. $10.00

DEERING, John Richard. *Lee & His Cause; or, The Why & How of the War...* 1907. NY/WA. Neale. 1st ed. 2 pl. 183p. cloth. VG. M8. $175.00

DEGGE, Simon. *Parson's Counsellor, With the Law of Tithes or Tithing...* 1695. London. Atkins. 5th. modern reverse calf. M11. $450.00

DEIGHTON, Len. *Battle of Britain.* 1980. Clarke Irwin. F/F. P3. $25.00

DEIGHTON, Len. *Berlin Game.* 1983. Hutchinson. 1st ed. F/F. P3. $18.00

DEIGHTON, Len. *Berlin Game.* 1984. Knopf. 1st Am ed. F/NF. N4. $22.50

DEIGHTON, Len. *Billion Dollar Brain.* 1968. London. Cape. 1st ed. NF/NF clip. M22. $65.00

DEIGHTON, Len. *Blitzkrieg.* 1979. Jonathan Cape. 1st ed. VG. P3. $20.00

DEIGHTON, Len. *Catch a Falling Spy.* 1976. Detective BC. VG. P3. $8.00

DEIGHTON, Len. *Close-Up.* 1972. Clarke Irwin. 1st ed. VG/G. P3. $25.00

DEIGHTON, Len. *Expensive Place To Die.* 1967. Jonathan Cape. 1st ed. VG/G. P3. $35.00

DEIGHTON, Len. *Funeral in Berlin.* 1964. Jonathan Cape. 1st ed. VG/VG. P3. $60.00

DEIGHTON, Len. *Funeral in Berlin.* 1965. Putnam. 1st ed. author's 2nd book. F/dj. H11/M19. $45.00

DEIGHTON, Len. *London Match.* 1985. Knopf. 1st ed. F/F. P3. $18.00

DEIGHTON, Len. *Mamista.* 1991. Harper Collins. 1st Am ed. F/F. N4. $25.00

DEIGHTON, Len. *Mamista.* 1991. London. Century. 1st ed. F/F. P3. $25.00

DEIGHTON, Len. *Mamista.* 1991. London. Century. 1st ed. VG+/F. A20. $15.00

DEIGHTON, Len. *Mexico Set.* 1985. Knopf. 1st ed. VG/VG. P3. $17.00

DEIGHTON, Len. *Spy Hook.* 1988. Hutchinson. 1st ed. F/F. P3. $20.00

DEIGHTON, Len. *Spy Hook.* 1988. Knopf. 1st Am ed. F/F. N4. $25.00

DEIGHTON, Len. *Spy Line.* 1989. Knopf. 1st ed. F/F. P3. $20.00

DEIGHTON, Len. *Spy Sinker.* 1990. Harper Collins. 1st Am ed. F/F. N4. $25.00

DEIGHTON, Len. *Spy Sinker.* 1990. Hutchinson. 1st ed. F/F. P3. $25.00

DEIGHTON, Len. *Spy Story.* 1974. HBJ. 1st ed. VG/VG. P3. $20.00

DEIGHTON, Len. *SS-GB.* 1978. Jonathan Cape. 1st ed. VG/VG. P3. $25.00

DEIGHTON, Len. *SS-GB.* 1979. Knopf. 1st Am ed. F/VG. N4. $25.00

DEIGHTON, Len. *SS-GB.* 1979. Knopf. 1st ed. VG/VG. P3. $20.00

DEIGHTON, Len. *Violent Ward.* 1993. Harper Collins. 1st Am ed. F/F. N4. $25.00

DEIGHTON, Len. *Winter.* 1987. Knopf. 1st ed. VG+/VG+. A20. $17.00

DEIGHTON, Len. *Xpd.* 1981. Knopf. 1st ed. F/F. P3. $20.00

DEILITZSCH, Franz. *System der Biblischen Pshychologie.* 1861. Leipzig. Dorffling. 2nd. 500p. VG. G1. $100.00

DEKAN, Jan. *Moravia Magna: The Great Moravian Empire, Its Art & Times.* 1981. Control Data Arts. 1st Am ed. 166p. cloth. VG+/dj. M20. $22.00

DEKKER, Carl. *Woman in Marble.* 1972. Bobbs Merrill. 1st ed. VG/VG. P3. $20.00

DEL MARTIA, Aston; see Fearn, John Russell.

DEL REY, Lester. *Badge of Infamy.* 1976. Dobson. 1st ed. VG/VG. P3. $20.00

DEL REY, Lester. *Best SF Stories of the Year.* 1972. Dutton. 1st ed. VG/VG. P3. $20.00

DEL REY, Lester. *Cave of Spears.* 1957. Knopf. 1st ed. VG. P3. $20.00

DEL REY, Lester. *Moon of Mutiny.* 1961. HRW. 1st ed. xl. dj. G. P3. $15.00

DEL REY, Lester. *Moon of Mutiny.* 1979. Gregg. 1st ed. F/F. P3. $20.00

DEL REY, Lester. *Rocket From Infinity.* 1966. HRW. 1st ed. NF/NF. P3. $30.00

DEL REY, Lester. *Step to the Stars.* 1954. Winston. 1st ed. VG/VG. P3. $25.00

DEL REY, Lester. *Year After Tomorrow.* 1954. Winston. 1st ed. VG. P3. $20.00

DEL VECCHIO, Giorgio. *Man & Nature, Selected Essays.* 1969. Notre Dame. M11. $35.00

DEL VECCHIO, John M. *13th Valley.* 1982. Bantam. 1st ed. author's 1st book. F/F. H11. $45.00

DELACROIX, Eugene. *Album de Croquis.* 1961. Paris. Quatre Chemins. 2 vol. 1/500. ils. quarter leather/cloth. D2. $180.00

DELAFIELD, R. *Report on the Art of War in Europe.* 1861. WA. Geo W Bowman. House ed. 41 pl/fld maps/plans. emb blk cloth. G. T10. $200.00

DELAMBRE, Jean-Baptiste. *Astronomie.* 1814. Paris. Courcier. 1st ed. 3 vol. VG. K5. $600.00

DELANEY & TOBIN. *Dictionary of Catholic Biography.* 1961. 4to. 1259p. VG. A4. $150.00

DELANO, Alonzo. *Life on the Plains & Among the Diggings.* 1966. Ann Arbor. U Microfilms. facsimile of 1854 ed. silvered bl cloth. NF. T10. $35.00

DELANY, Samuel R. *Atlantis: Three Tales.* 1995. Seattle. Incunabula. inscr. F/F. w/sgn typed letter. B2. $85.00

DELANY, Samuel R. *Bridge of Lost Desire.* 1987. Arbor. 1st ed. rem mk. F/NF. G10. $15.00

DELANY, Samuel R. *Nebula Winners Thirteen.* 1980. Harper Row. 1st ed. VG/VG. P3. $25.00

DELANY, Samuel R. *Stars in My Pocket Like Grains of Sand.* 1984. Bantam. 1st ed. NF/NF. P3. $18.00

DELANY & DELANY. *Having Our Say: The Delany Sisters' First 100 Years.* 1993. NY. Kodansha. UP. F/wrp. B4. $45.00

DELAUNAY, Charles. *New Hot Discography.* 1948. NY. Criterion. 1st ed. VG. B2. $75.00

DELEHANTY, Elizabeth. *Arise From Sleep.* 1942. NY. 1st ed. author's 1st novel. F/F. A17. $9.50

DELEHANTY, Elizabeth. *Arise From Sleep.* 1942. Viking. 1st ed. inscr. author's 1st novel. F/NF. B4. $50.00

DELISLE, Guillaume. *Atlante Novissimo Che Contiene Tutte le Parti del Mondo.* 1740-1750. Venice. 2 vol. 1st ed. 78 double-p maps. half vellum. C6. $9,000.00

DELL, Floyd. *Love in the Machine Age.* 1930. NY. Farrar. 1st ed. NF/G. B2. $75.00

DELLBRIDGE, John. *Unfit To Plead.* 1949. Hurst Blackett. 1st ed. VG/G. P3. $18.00

DELMAS, D.M. *Speeches & Addresses.* 1901. San Francisco. Robertson. 8vo. 363p. brn cloth/leather label. T10. $60.00

DELVING, Michael. *China Expert.* 1976. Scribner. 1st ed. NF/NF. P3. $25.00

DELVING, Michael. *Smiling the Boy Fell Dead.* 1967. MacDonald. 1st ed. VG/VG. P3. $30.00

DEMAREST, Arthur. *Archaeology of Santa Leticia...* 1986. Tulane. 4to. 272p. F3. $45.00

DEMAREST, Phyllis Gordon. *Angelic City.* 1961. London. Hutchinson. 1st ed. 8vo. bl cloth. F/VG. T10. $25.00

DEMARIS, Ovid. *Last Mafioso.* 1981. Time. 4th. hc. VG. P3. $15.00

DEMESSE, Lucien. *Quest for the Babingas.* 1958. London. Adventurers Club. 8vo. 187p. VG/VG. P4. $15.00

DEMIJOHN, Thomas; see Disch, Thomas.

DEMILLE, Nelson. *Spencerville.* 1994. Warner. 1st ed. NF/NF. P3. $24.00

DEMING, Richard. *Famous Investigators.* 1963. Whitman. VG. P3. $6.00

DEMING. *James Joyce: Critical Heritage, Vol I & II...1941.* 1986. 2 vol. 821p. F/F. A4. $45.00

DEMOOR, Jean. *Die Anormalen Kinder und Ihre Behandlung in Haus und Schule.* 1901. Oskar Bonde. 292p. modern blk linen. VG. G1. $85.00

DENBY, Edwin. *Mediterranean Cities: Sonnets by Edwin Denby.* 1956. NY. Wittenborn. inscr. photos Rudolph Burckhardt. F/dj. C2. $250.00

DENDY, Walter C. *Philosophy of Mystery.* 1845. Harper. 442p. Victorian cloth. G1. $50.00

DENE, Shafto. *Trail Blazing in the Skies.* 1943. Akron. 1st ed. 34p photo section+78p text. VG/torn. B18. $22.50

DENEVI, D. *Earthquakes.* 1977. Celestial Arts. 1st ed. 230p. F/dj. D8. $15.00

DENEVI, Marco. *Secret Ceremony.* 1961. Time. ltd ed. F/NF case. B35. $30.00

DENHAM, Bertie. *Foxhunt.* 1988. St Martin. 1st Am ed. F/F. O3. $15.00

DENING, Greg. *Mr Bligh's Bad Language.* 1992. Cambridge. 1st Am ed. 8vo. 445p. F/dj. T10. $35.00

DENISON, E.E. *Play of Auction Hands.* 1922. Boston. 284p. VG. S1. $10.00

DENKER, Henry. *Experiment.* 1976. Simon Schuster. 1st ed. F/F. P3. $10.00

DENNIS, Morgan. *Morgan Dennis Dog Book, With Some Special Cats.* 1946. NY. 1st ed. 4to. 68p. NF/G+. C14. $20.00

DENNIS, Patrick. *Around the World With Auntie Mame.* 1958. Harcourt Brace. 1st ed. F/F. B35. $26.00

DENNIS, Patrick. *Little Me.* 1961. Dutton. 3rd. VG/VG. D2. $15.00

DENSLOW, W.W. *Denslow's Picture Book Treasury.* 1990. Arcade. 1st ed. rem mk. F/F. B17. $9.00

DENSLOW, W.W. *Denslow's Three Bears.* 1903. G/wrp. M17. $35.00

DENSLOW, W.W. *Dillingham's Magic Picture Book, Series 1.* 1908. Dillingham. 4to. NF/pict wrp. D1. $200.00

DENT, Lester. *Dead at the Take-Off.* 1946. Detective BC. VG/VG. P3. $18.00

DENTINGER, Jane. *Death Mask.* 1988. Scribner. 1st ed. NF/NF. N4. $20.00

DENTON, Clara J. *Daisy Dells, Rhymes & Verses.* 1927. Whitman. Just Right Book. ils Garnett Cheney. gr cloth. G+. T5. $35.00

DEPERO, Fortunato. *Fortunato Depero.* 1970. Luglio-Sett. ils. 305p. xl. D2. $95.00

DERBYSHIRE, John. *Seeing Calvin Coolidge in a Dream.* 1996. St Martin. 1st ed. author's 1st novel. F/F. M23. $40.00

DERLETH, August. *Beachheads in Space.* 1952. Pelligrini Cudahy. 1st ed. VG. P3. $20.00

DERLETH, August. *Bright Journey.* 1940. Scribner. sgn. 8vo. 424p. map ep. G. B11. $50.00

DERLETH, August. *Casebook of Solar Pons.* 1965. Mycroft Moran. 1st ed. xl. dj. R10. $10.00

DERLETH, August. *Chronicles of Solar Pons.* 1973. Mycroft Moran. 1st ed. 1/4176. F/F. T2. $15.00

DERLETH, August. *Dwellers in Darkness.* 1976. Arkham. 1st ed. 1/3926. F/F. T2. $35.00

DERLETH, August. *Harrigan's File.* 1975. Arkham. 1st ed. F/F. P3. $20.00

DERLETH, August. *Mischief in the Lane.* 1944. Scribner. 1st ed. G/G. N4. $65.00

DERLETH, August. *Mr Fairlie's Final Journey.* 1968. Mycroft Moran. 1st ed. F/F. P3. $40.00

DERLETH, August. *New Poetry Out of Wisconsin.* 1969. Stanton Lee. 1st ed. F/F. P3. $50.00

DERLETH, August. *Night Side.* 1947. Rinehart. 1st ed. VG/VG. P3. $65.00

DERLETH, August. *Outer Side of the Moon.* 1949. Pelligrini Cudahy. 2nd. VG. P3. $18.00

DERLETH, August. *Portals of Tomorrow.* nd. BC. VG/VG. P3. $8.00

DERLETH, August. *Sleep No More.* 1944. Farrar Rinehart. VG/VG. P3. $40.00

DERLETH, August. *Sleep No More.* 1944. Farrar Rinehart. 1st ed. F/VG. M19. $65.00

DERLETH, August. *Solar Pons Omnibus.* 1982. Arkham. 2 vol. 1st ed thus. 1/3031. F/sans/case. T2. $40.00

DERLETH, August. *Thirty Years of Arkham House.* 1970. Arkham. 1st ed. VG/VG. P3. $60.00

DERLETH, August. *Walden West.* 1961. NY. 1st ed. pres. VG/VG. B5. $35.00

DERLETH, August. *When Evil Wakes.* 1963. Souvenir. 1st ed. sgn. VG/VG. P3. $75.00

DERLETH, August. *Wind in the Elms. Poems by August Derleth.* 1941. Phil. Ritten. 1st ed. 1/25. sgn. tan linen. F/clear Lucite dj. B24. $325.00

DERLETH, August. *Writing Fiction.* 1971. Greenwood. rpt of 1946 ed. F. R10. $15.00

DERLETH & SCHORER. *Colonel Markesan & Less Pleasant People.* 1966. Arkham. 1st ed. NF/NF. P3. $40.00

DERRY, Joseph T. *Confederate Military History: Georgia.* 1976. Syracuse, NY. Bl & Gray. rpt of 1899 ed. 460p. F/NF. M8. $20.00

DERSHOWITZ, Alan M. *Advocate's Devil.* 1994. Warner. 1st ed. F/F. N4. $25.00

DERSHOWITZ, Alan M. *Contrary to Popular Opinion.* 1992. 1st ed. F/F. K2. $20.00

DERSHOWITZ, Alan M. *Reversal of Fortune.* 1986. Random. 1st ed. F/F. A20. $10.00

DESAULT, P.J. *Treatise on Fractures, Luxations & Other Affections...* 1805. Phil. pl. 412p. tree calf. VG. B14. $145.00

DESCURET, Jean Baptiste Felix. *La Medecine des Passions...* 1844. Liege. J-G Lardinois. 3rd. 476p. G. G1. $125.00

DESMOND, Adrian. *Archetypes & Ancestors: Palaeontology in Victorian London.* 1982. Chicago. 1st ed. 287p. dj. A13. $25.00

DESMOND, Alice Curtis. *Far Horizons.* 1931. McBride. 1st ed. sgn. 8vo. bl cloth. G. B11. $25.00

DESMOND, Hugh. *Terror Walks by Night.* 1945. Wright Brn. VG/G. P3. $20.00

DESMOND & MOORE. *Darwin.* 1992. Warner. 1st ed. F/F. M23. $35.00

DESSART, Gina. *Cry for the Lost.* 1959. Harper. 1st ed. VG/VG. P3. $10.00

DETTE. *Adventures of Olle.* 1946. NY. 1st ed. ils. F/rpr. A17. $17.50

DEUCHER & WHEELER. *Curtain Calls for Franz Schubert: A Musical Play.* 1941. Dutton. 1st ed. 103p. VG+. C14. $10.00

DEUCHER & WHEELER. *Sebastian Bach: Boy From Thuringia.* 1937. Dutton. 1st ed. 8vo. 126p. VG+. C14. $10.00

DEUEL, Leo. *Conquistadors Without Swords.* 1967. St Martin. 1st ed. 647p. cranberry cloth. NF. B22. $7.00

DEUTSCH, Babette. *Honey Out of the Rock.* 1925. Appleton. 1st ed. inscr to author Leon Feuchtwanger. NF. B4. $85.00

DEUTSCH, H. *Huey Long Murder Case.* 1963. Garden City. 1st ed. VG/VG. B5. $22.50

DEUTSCH, Harold C. *Conspiracy Against Hitler in the Twilight War.* 1968. Minneapolis. 1st ed. 394p. VG. B18. $22.50

DEUTSCH, Otto. *Music Publishers' Numbers: A Selection of 40 Dated Lists...* 1946. 30p. VG/wrp. A4. $45.00

DEUTSCHER, Isaac. *Stalin: A Political Biography.* 1949. NY/London. 1st ed. 600p. silvered red cloth. F/VG. H3. $50.00

DEUTSCHMAN, Deborah. *Signals.* 1978. Seaview. 1st ed. sgn. F/F. B4. $45.00

DEUTSCHMAN, Deborah. *Signals.* 1978. Seaview. 1st ed. VG/VG. P3. $15.00

DEVERDUN, Alfred Louis. *True Mexico: Mexico-Tenochtitlan.* 1938. Winasha, WI. private prt. sgn. 303p. bl brd. B11. $65.00

DEVEREUX, W.B. *Position & Team Play in Polo.* 1914. Brooks Bros. 1st ed. O3. $35.00

DEVLIN, R.M. *Plant Physiology.* 1975. Van Nostrand. 3rd. 8vo. ils. brd. B1. $32.00

DEVON, Gary. *Lost.* 1986. Knopf. 1st ed. VG/VG. P3. $18.00

DEW, Thomas. *Digest of the Laws, Customs, Manners & Institutions...* 1853. Appleton Century. 1st ed. contemporary tree calf. rebacked. M11. $150.00

DEWAR, John. *Dewar Manuscripts, Vol 1: Scottish West Higland Folk Tales.* 1963. Glasgow. 1st ed. ils. 397p. VG/VG. B5. $65.00

DEWDNEY, Selwyn. *Wind Without Rain.* 1946. Copp Clark. hc. VG. P3. $8.00

DEWEESE, Gene. *Adventures of a Two-Minute Werewolf.* 1983. Weekly Reader. VG. P3. $8.00

DEWES, Simon. *Panic in Pursuit.* 1944. Rich Cowan. VG. P3. $20.00

DEWEY, Evelyn. *Behavior Development in Infants...* 1935. Columbia. 321p. thatched red buckram. VG/dj. G1. $50.00

DEWEY, Frank L. *Thomas Jefferson, Lawyer.* 1986. VA U. 1st ed. sgn. 184p. F/F. B10. $20.00

DEWEY, John. *Psychology.* 1896. Am Book Co. 3rd. 427p. pebbled mauve cloth. VG. G1. $50.00

DEWEY, Thomas B. *Case of the Chased & the Unchaste.* nd. BC. VG/VG. P3. $8.00

DEWEY, Thomas B. *How Hard To Kill.* 1962. Simon Schuster. 1st ed. G/G. P3. $20.00

DEWHURST, Eileen. *House That Jack Built.* 1984. Crime Club. 1st ed. VG/VG. P3. $15.00

DEXTER, Colin. *Jewel That Was Ours.* 1992. Crown. 1st ed. F/F. P3. $20.00

DEXTER, Colin. *Wench Is Dead.* 1989. St Martin. 1st ed. F/F. P3. $16.00

DEXTER, Elisha. *Narrative of Wreck & Loss of Whaling Brig Wm & Joseph...* 1988. Ye Galleon. facsimile of 2nd of 1848. ils. T7. $30.00

DEXTER, John (some); see Bradley, Marion Zimmer.

DEXTER, Pete. *Brotherly Love.* 1991. Random. 1st ed. sgn. F/F. H11. $45.00

DEXTER, Pete. *Deadwood.* 1986. Random. 1st ed. F/F. M23. $20.00

DEXTER, Pete. *Paperboy.* 1995. Random. 1st ed. F/F. H11. $25.00

DEXTER, Pete. *Paris Trout.* 1988. Random. 1st ed. F/F. H11. $45.00

DEXTER, Peter. *Paris Trout.* 1988. Random. 1st ed. inscr. NF/F. H11. $60.00

DEXTER, Will. *This Is Magic.* nd. Bell. 2nd. hc. VG. P3. $5.00

DI CHIARA, Robert. *Dick & the Devil.* 1989. NY. Tor. 1st ed. F/F. H11. $20.00

DI CLERICO & PAVELEC. *Jersey Game.* 1991. Rutgers. 1st ed. F/F. P8. $15.00

DI MAGGIO, Dom. *Real Grass, Real Heroes.* 1991. Zebra. 1st ed. photos. F/F. P8. $15.00

DI MAGGIO, Joe. *Di Maggio Album.* 1989. Putnam. 1/700. 2 vol. sgn. 4to. full leather. AN/cloth case/shipping carton. B4. $975.00

DI MONA, Joseph. *Last Man at Arlington.* 1973. Fields. 1st ed. NF/F. H11. $20.00

DI SALVO, Jackie. *War of Titans: Blake's Critique of Milton...* 1983. Pitts. 358p. VG. A17. $10.00

DIAMOND, Edwin. *Behind the Times.* 1993. Villard. 1st ed. sgn. rem mk. F/F. B35. $30.00

DIAZ DEL CASTILLO, Bernal. *Discovery & Conquest of Mexico 1517-1521.* 1933. London. Routledge. 8vo. ils/maps/plans. gilt red cloth. VG. T10. $45.00

DIAZ DEL CASTILLO, Bernal. *Discovery & Conquest of Mexico 1517-1521.* 1953. Mexico. 383p. leather. F3. $35.00

DIBBLE, Sheldon. *Voice From Abroad; or, Thoughts on Missions...* 1844. Lahainaluna. Pr of Mission Seminary. 1st ed. 12mo. 132p. VG. C6. $350.00

DIBDIN, Michael. *Cabal.* 1993. Doubleday. 1st ed. sgn. F/F. T2. $20.00

DIBDIN, Michael. *Dirty Tricks.* 1991. Summit. 1st Am ed. sgn. F/F. T2. $20.00

DIBDIN, Michael. *Dying of the Light.* 1993. London. Faber. 1st ed. sgn. F/F. T2. $20.00

DIBDIN, Michael. *Last Sherlock Holmes Story.* 1978. Pantheon. 1st ed. F/F. P3. $25.00

DIBDIN, Michael. *Ratking.* 1989. Bantam ARC/1st ed. sgn. F/F. w/promo material. T2. $25.00

DIBDIN, Michael. *Vendetta.* 1991. Doubleday. 1st Am ed. AN/F. N4. $27.50

DIBDIN, Thomas F. *Bibliographical, Antiquarian & Picturesque Tour...* 1829. London. Jennings/Major. 3 vol. 2nd. 12 pl/33 facsimile sgns. purple cloth. A4. $395.00

DIBDIN, Thomas F. *Bibliomania.* 1876. London. VG. O7. $175.00

DIBNER, Bern. *Atlantic Cable.* 1959. Norwalk. VG/wrp. O7. $35.00

DIBNER & RETI. *Leonardo da Vinci: Technologist.* 1969. Norwalk. 96p. brd. D2. $45.00

DICE, Lee R. *Natural Communities.* 1952. Ann Arbor. 1st ed. ils. 547p. VG+/dj. B26. $52.50

DICHTER & SHAPIRO. *Handbook of American Sheet Music, 1768-1889.* 1977. 8vo. 76 full-p ils. 297p. G. T3. $10.00

DICK, Philip K. *Beyond Lies the Wub.* 1988. Gollancz. 1st ed. F/F. P3. $25.00

DICK, Philip K. *Broken Bubble.* 1988. Arbor/Morrow. 1st ed. F/F. T2. $25.00

DICK, Philip K. *Broken Bubble.* 1989. Gollancz. 1st ed. F/F. P3. $30.00

DICK, Philip K. *Divine Invasion.* 1981. Timescape. 1st ed. rem mk. F/F. G10. $30.00

DICK, Philip K. *Father-Thing.* 1989. Gollancz. 1st ed. F/F. P3. $25.00

DICK, Philip K. *Galactic Pot-Healer.* 1969. Berkley. 1st ed. F/VG. M19. $75.00

DICK, Philip K. *Golden Man.* 1980. SF BC. 1st hc ed. F/NF. T2. $15.00

DICK, Philip K. *Mary & the Giant.* 1988. Gollancz. 1st ed. F/F. P3. $25.00

DICK, Philip K. *Nick & the Glimmung.* 1988. Gollancz. 1st ed. F/F. P3. $30.00

DICK, Philip K. *Our Friends From Frolix 8.* nd. Ace. BC. NF/G. R10. $4.00

DICK, Philip K. *Radio Free Albemuth.* 1985. Arbor. UP. F/wrp/proof dj. C2. $60.00

DICK, Philip K. *Radio Free Albemuth.* 1985. Arbor. 1st ed. F/F. P3. $20.00

DICK, Philip K. *Transmigration of Timothy Archer.* 1982. Timescape. 1st ed. xl. dj. P3. $10.00

DICK, Steven J. *Plurality of Worlds.* 1982. Cambridge. 1st prt. xl. dj. K5. $25.00

DICK, Trella Lamson. *Tornado's Big Year.* 1956. Follett. 8vo. VG/VG. B17. $7.50

DICK, William B. *Dick's Games of Patience; or, Solitaire With Cards...* 1883. NY. Dick Fitzgerald. 33 full-p tableaux. 143p. brick cloth. VG. T10. $350.00

DICK & JANE READER. *Dick & Jane.* 1936. Scott Foresman. sc. VG+. G6. $250.00

DICK & JANE READER. *Elson Basic Reader. Dick & Jane.* 1936 (1930). Scott Foresman. 12mo. 40p. VG/wrp. D1. $85.00

DICK & JANE READER. *Elson Gray Basic Readers — Pre-Primer.* 1930. Scott Foresman. orig ed. 12mo. VG+/wrp. C8. $125.00

DICK & JANE READER. *Fun Wherever We Are.* 1962. Scott Foresman. sc. VG. G6. $70.00

DICK & JANE READER. *Fun With Dick & Jane.* 1946-47. Scott Foresman. hc. VG. G6. $125.00

DICK & JANE READER. *Fun With Our Family.* 1962. Scott Foresman. sc. VG. G6. $70.00

DICK & JANE READER. *Guess Who.* 1951. New Basic Reader. sc. VG. G6. $70.00

DICK & JANE READER. *Happy Days With Our Friends.* 1948. Scott Foresman. Teacher ed. 95p. cloth. VG. M20. $45.00

DICK & JANE READER. *Little Friends.* 1930. Elson Basic Reader. 4 heavy cutouts in portfolio. uncut. w/primer offer. M20. $200.00

DICK & JANE READER. *More Dick & Jane Stories.* 1934. Scott Foresman. sc. VG+. G6. $250.00

DICK & JANE READER. *New Our New Friends.* 1956. Scott Foresman. 2nd reader for 1st grade. VG+. M5. $42.00

DICK & JANE READER. *New We Come & Go.* 1956. Scott Foresman. sc. VG. G6. $70.00

DICK & JANE READER. *New We Work & Play.* 1956. Scott Foresman. 2nd of 3 pre primers. sc. VG. M5. $42.00

DICK & JANE READER. *Our New Friends.* 1946. Scott Foresman. 2nd reader for 1st grade. VG+. M5. $60.00

DICK & JANE READER. *Sally, Dick & Jane.* 1962. Scott Foresman. sc. VG. G6. $70.00

DICK & JANE READER. *We Come & Go.* 1940. Scott Foresman. 12mo. mk copy sold direct to public. VG/wrp. C8. $60.00

DICK & NELSON. *Ganymede Takeover.* 1988. Severn. 1st hc ed. F/F. G10. $25.00

DICK & ROBINSON. *Golden Age of the Great Passenger Airships...* 1987. WA. 2nd. 226p. VG/dj. B18. $37.50

DICKASON. *Daring Young Men: Story of American Pre-Raphaelites.* 1970. Bloomington. VG. D2. $25.00

DICKENS, Charles. *American Notes for General Circulation.* 1975. LEC. 1/1500. ils/sgn Raymond Houlihan. 272p. F/case. C2. $60.00

DICKENS, Charles. *Annotated Christmas Carol.* 1976. NY. 1st ed. 182p. VG/dj. A17. $25.00

DICKENS, Charles. *Barnaby Rudge.* 1987. Folio Soc. VG. P3. $30.00

DICKENS, Charles. *Bleak House.* 1852-1853. London. Bradbury Evans. 20 monthly parts in 19. 8vo. F/half leather case. T10. $1,850.00

DICKENS, Charles. *Bleak House.* 1853. Harper. 2 vol. 1st Am ed. VG. M19. $250.00

DICKENS, Charles. *Bleak House.* 1853. London. Bradbury Evans. 1st ed. ils Phiz. VG. M19. $350.00

DICKENS, Charles. *Captain Boldheart & Other Stories in a Holiday Romance.* 1927. Macmillan. 1st ed thus. ils Beatrice Pearse. VG. M5. $20.00

DICKENS, Charles. *Charles Dickens 1825-1870: His Portraits & Signatures.* nd. ils. F/wrp. A4. $35.00

DICKENS, Charles. *Chimes.* 1931. LEC. 1/1500. ils/sgn Rackham. 129p. F/case. B24. $475.00

DICKENS, Charles. *Christmas Carol in Four Staves.* 1979. private prt. ils Charles Dougherty. gilt red brd. F. M5. $25.00

DICKENS, Charles. *Christmas Carol.* nd. Lippincott. early ed. 8vo. ils Rackham. gr prt cloth. VG. T10. $25.00

DICKENS, Charles. *Christmas Carol.* 1990. Stewart Tabori & Chang. 1st ed. F/F. P3. $30.00

DICKENS, Charles. *Christmas Carol: A Changing Picture & Lift-the-Flap Book.* 1989. np. 18 flaps/4 changing picture wheels. 30p. F. A4. $40.00

DICKENS, Charles. *Christmas Stories.* nd. Doubleday Jr Classics. hc. VG/VG. P3. $12.00

DICKENS, Charles. *David Copperfield.* 1983. Folio Soc. hc. VG. P3. $30.00

DICKENS, Charles. *Dickens' Children.* 1912. Scribner. 1st ed. ils JW Smith. unp. VG. D1. $125.00

DICKENS, Charles. *Dickens Digest.* 1943. Whittlesey. VG. P3. $23.00

DICKENS, Charles. *Great Expectations.* 1987. Oxford. F/F. P3. $11.00

DICKENS, Charles. *Hard Times.* 1966. LEC. 1st ed. ils/sgn Charles Raymond. 279p. F/case. C2. $75.00

DICKENS, Charles. *Hard Times.* 1987. Oxford. F/F. P3. $11.00

DICKENS, Charles. *Haunted Man & the Ghost's Bargain.* 1848. Bradley Evans. 1st ed. 188p. cloth/rebacked spine. VG. M19. $125.00

DICKENS, Charles. *Life & Adventures of Nicholas Nickleby...* 1838-1839. London. Chapman Hall. 20 8vo parts in 19. 1st issue. morocco box. B24. $3,250.00

DICKENS, Charles. *Little Dorrit.* 1857. London. 1st book ed. contemporary half calf. VG. C6. $200.00

DICKENS, Charles. *Little Dorrit.* 1857. London. Bradbury Evans. 1st book ed/1st issue. modern half calf. NF. T10. $300.00

DICKENS, Charles. *Master Humphrey's Clock.* 1840-1841. Chapman Hall. 1st ed in book form. VG. M19. $275.00

DICKENS, Charles. *Oliver Twist.* 1984. Folio Soc. VG. P3. $30.00

DICKENS, Charles. *Posthumous Papers of the Pickwick Club.* 1887. London. Chapman Hall. 2 vol. 1/8 on Japan vellum. sgn prt/pub/edit. F/box. B24. $3,000.00

DICKENS, Charles. *Posthumous Papers of the Pickwick Club.* 1933. Oxford. 1/1500. ils/sgn John Austen. gilt buckram. F/dj/case. T10. $200.00

DICKENSON, W.H. *Treatise on Albuminuria.* 1881. NY. Wood. 1st Am ed. 11 pl. VG. H7. $50.00

DICKEY, James. *Alnilam.* 1987. Doubleday. 1st ed. F/F. M23. $25.00

DICKEY, James. *Deliverance.* 1970. Houghton Mifflin. 1st prt. VG+/VG+. P10. $55.00

DICKEY, James. *Eye-Beaters, Blood, Victory, Madness, Buckhead & Mercy.* 1970. Doubleday. 1st trade ed. F/NF. B4. $100.00

DICKEY, James. *Tucky the Hunter.* 1978. Crown. 1st ed. ils Marie Angel. unp. AN. D1. $35.00

DICKEY & PENNER. *Soil Survey of Osage County Kansas.* 1985. USDA. 100p+50p maps. VG. D8. $5.00

DICKINSON, Emily. *Brighter Garden.* 1990. Philomel/Putnam. 1st prt. 4to. ils Tash Tudor. F/F. C8. $75.00

DICKINSON, Emily. *Complete Poems of Emily Dickinson.* 1960. Little Brn. 1st ed. F/NF. C2. $75.00

DICKINSON, Emily. *Five Poems.* 1989. London. 1/50. 12mo. 10p. tissue guards. F/emb stiff wrp. B24. $150.00

DICKINSON, Emily. *Poems. Second Series.* 1891. Boston. 1st ed. VG. C6. $1,000.00

DICKINSON, LAIRD & MAXWELL. *Voices From the Southwest.* 1976. Northland. ltd 1st ed. sgn Lawrence Clark Powell. 159p. F/case. B19. $100.00

DICKINSON, LAIRD & MAXWELL. *Voices From the Southwest.* 1976. Northland. 1st trade ed. F/F. B19. $30.00

DICKINSON, Peter. *Annerton Pit.* 1977. Atlantic/Little Brn. 1st ed. F/F. P3. $23.00

DICKINSON, Peter. *Blue Hawk.* 1976. Little Brn. 1st ed. VG/VG. P3. $20.00

DICKINSON, Peter. *City of Gold.* 1980. Pantheon. 1st ed. VG/VG. P3. $18.00

DICKINSON, Peter. *Devil's Children.* 1986. Delacorte. 1st ed. VG/VG. P3. $15.00

DICKINSON, Peter. *Flight of Dragons.* 1979. Harper Row. 1st ed. VG/VG. P3. $25.00

DICKINSON, Peter. *Lizard in the Cup.* 1972. Harper Row. 1st ed. VG/VG. P3. $20.00

DICKINSON, Peter. *Merlin Dreams.* 1988. Delacorte. 1st ed. 4to. F/F. B17. $14.00

DICKINSON, Peter. *Old English Peep Show.* 1969. Harper Row. 1st ed. VG/VG. P3. $20.00

DICKINSON, Peter. *Play Dead.* 1992. Mysterious. 1st Am ed. rem mk. F/F. N4. $15.00

DICKINSON, Peter. *Play Dead.* 1992. Mysterious. 1st ed. NF/NF. P3. $18.00

DICKINSON, Peter. *Poison Oracle.* 1974. Pantheon. VG/VG. P3. $18.00

DICKINSON, Peter. *Sinful Stones.* 1974. Harper Row. 1st Am ed. F/NF. T2. $15.00

DICKMAN, William J. *Around the Potomac: Verses About Places & People I Love.* 1968. Newell-Cole. unp. VG. B10. $12.00

DICKSON, Carter; see Carr, John Dickson.

DICKSON, Gordon R. *Alien Art.* 1973. Dutton. 1st ed. F/F. P3. $25.00

DICKSON, Gordon R. *Dickson!* 1984. Nesfa. F/F. P3. $15.00

DICKSON, Gordon R. *Dragon & the Djinn.* 1996. NY. Ace. 1st ed. 8vo. AN/dj. T10. $25.00

DICKSON, Gordon R. *Dragon at War.* 1992. Ace. 1st ed. F/F. P3. $19.00

DICKSON, Gordon R. *Final Encyclopedia.* 1984. Tor. 1st ed. F/F. P3. $20.00

DICKSON, Gordon R. *Forever Man.* 1986. Ace. 1st ed. NF/NF. P3. $20.00

DICKSON, Gordon R. *In Iron Years.* 1980. Doubleday. 1st ed. rem mk. F/NF. G10. $10.00

DICKSON, Gordon R. *In Iron Years.* 1980. Doubleday. 1st ed. VG/VG. P3. $15.00

DICKSON, Gordon R. *Mutants.* 1970. Macmillan. 1st ed. VG/VG. P3. $20.00

DICKSON, Gordon R. *R-Master.* 1973. Lippincott. 1st ed. VG/VG. P3. $25.00

DICKSON, Gordon R. *Star Road.* 1975. Robert Hale. 1st ed. VG/VG. P3. $15.00

DICKSON, Gordon R. *Three to Dorsai!* nd. BC. VG/VG. P3. $8.00

DICKSON, Gordon R. *Time Storm.* nd. BC. hc. VG/G. P3. $7.00

DICKSON, Gordon R. *Wolf & Iron.* 1990. Tor. 1st ed. F/F. P3. $19.00

DICKSON, Gordon R. *Wolfing.* nd. BC. VG/VG. P3. $8.00

DICKSON, Gordon. *Alien Art.* 1973. Dutton. 1st ed. F/G+. M19. $17.50

DICKSON, Grierson. *Traitors' Market.* 1936. Hutchinson. 1st ed. G. P3. $20.00

DICKSON, Harris. *Old-Fashioned Senator: Story-Biography of John S Williams.* 1925. Stokes. photos. 204p. VG. B10. $35.00

DICKSON & MCALEER. *Unit Pride.* 1981. Doubleday. 1st ed. F/NF. B4. $100.00

DICKSTEIN & DWORETSKY. *Horology Americana.* 1972. NY. private prt. ltd ed. sgns. 212p. F/VG. B11. $65.00

DIDEROT, Denis. *Rameau's Nephew & Other Works.* 1926. London. Chapman Hall 1st ed thus. 1/1000. VG. A17. $15.00

DIDION, Joan. *After Henry.* 1992. Simon Schuster. 1st ed. F/F. B35. $24.00

DIDION, Joan. *Book of Common Prayer.* 1977. Simon Schuster. 1st ed. sgn. F/dj. B4. $125.00

DIDION, Joan. *Democracy.* 1984. Simon Schuster. 1st ed. rem mk. F/NF. G10. $15.00

DIDION, Joan. *Miami.* 1987. Simon Schuster. UP. F/wrp. B4. $45.00

DIDION, Joan. *Play It As It Lays.* 1970. FSG. 1st ed. F/VG+. A20. $17.00

DIDION, Joan. *Salvador.* 1983. Simon Schuster. 1st ed. 108p. dj. F3. $10.00

DIEHL, Charles. *Theodora: Empress of Byzantium.* 1972. NY. Unger. 204p. VG/dj. W1. $18.00

DIEHL, William. *Chameleon.* 1981. Random. 1st ed. F/NF. H11. $30.00

DIEHL, William. *Chameleon.* 1981. Random. 1st ed. NF/VG. M19. $20.00

DIEHL, William. *Sharky's Machine.* 1978. Delacorte. 1st ed. F/F. H11. $70.00

DIEHL, William. *27.* 1990. Villard. 1st ed. NF/NF. P3. $20.00

DIETRICH, Otto. *Hitler.* 1955. Chicago. 277p. VG/tape rpr. A17. $10.00

DIETZ, Lena. *History & Modern Nursing.* 1967. Phil. 2nd. 381p. VG. A13. $35.00

DIEZ, Ernst. *Die Kunst der Islamischen Volker.* ca 1915. Berlin. Athenaion. 199p. VG/dj. W1. $40.00

DIKTY, T.E. *Best SF Stories & Novels Ninth.* nd. BC. VG/VG. P3. $10.00

DILL, Alonzo Thomas. *George Wythe: Teacher of Liberty.* 1979. VA Independence Bicentennial Comm. 101p. VG. B10. $35.00

DILLARD, Annie. *American Childhood.* 1987. Harper Row 1/250. sgn. F/NF case. S9. $150.00

DILLARD, Annie. *American Childhood.* 1987. Harper Row. 1st ed. F/NF. M23. $20.00

DILLARD, Annie. *Living.* 1992. Harper Collins. 1st ed. F/dj. A18. $25.00

DILLARD, Annie. *Living.* 1992. Harper Collins. 1st ed. sgn. F/F. B2. $35.00

DILLARD, Annie. *Living.* 1992. Harper Collins. 1st ltd ed. 1/300. sgn. F/case. A18/S19. from $100 to $125.00

DILLARD, Annie. *Pilgrim at Tinker Creek* 1974. Harper. 1st ed. 271p. VG/dj. M20. $42.00

DILLARD, Annie. *Writing Life.* 1989. Harper Row. 1st ed. F/F. M23. $20.00

DILLARD, J. Hardy. *From News Stand to Cyrano.* 1935. Stratford. 46p. G/G. B10. $6.00

DILLARD, J.M. *Star Trek Generations.* 1994. Pocket. 1st ed. hc. VG/VG. P3. $20.00

DILLARD, R.H.W. *Sounder Few: Essays From the Hollins Critic.* 1971. GA U. VG/VG. B10. $12.00

DILLARD, R.H.W. *1st Man on the Sun.* 1983. LSU. 1st ed. AN/dj. G10. $10.00

DILLEY, Arthur U. *Oriental Rugs & Carpets.* 1959. Phil. 75 pl/7 maps. F/dj. A17. $40.00

DILLON, R. *Siskiyou Trail.* 1975. NY. 1st ed. Am Trail series. VG/VG. B5. $45.00

DILNOT, George. *Scotland Yard.* 1929. Geoffrey Bles. VG. P3. $40.00

DIMAND, M.S. *Handbook of Muhammadan Art.* 1947. NY. Hartsdale. 2nd. ils. VG. W1. $35.00

DIMAND, M.S. *Indian Miniatures.* nd. NY. Crown. 28p. VG/wrp. W1. $20.00

DIMENT, Adam. *Bang Bang Birds.* 1968. Dutton. 1st ed. xl. dj. P3. $6.00

DIMENT, Adam. *Dolly, Dolly Spy.* 1967. Dutton. 1st ed. F/F. P3. $15.00

DIMENT, Adam. *Think Inc.* 1971. Michael Joseph. 1st ed. VG/VG. P3. $18.00

DIMITRY & HARRELL. *Confederate Military History: Louisiana & Arkansas.* 1976. Bl & Gray. rpt of 1899 ed. cloth. F/NF. M8. $20.00

DIMONA, Joseph. *To the Eagle's Nest.* 1980. Morrow. 1st ed. VG/VG. P3. $15.00

DINESEN, Isak. *Anecdotes of Destiny.* 1958. Random. 1st ed. NF/G. M19. $35.00

DINESEN, Isak. *Out of Africa.* 1938. Random. 1st Am ed. F/F. B4. $450.00

DINESEN, Isak. *Seven Gothic Tales.* 1934. Smith Haas. 1st ed. VG/G. P3. $60.00

DINESEN, Isak. *Winter's Tales.* 1942. NY. 1st ed. VG-. A17. $10.00

DINWIDDIE, Emily A. *Songs in the Evening.* 1911. Sherman. 1st ed. 79p. teg. VG. B10. $10.00

DIPPER, Alan. *Golden Virgin.* 1973. Walker. 1st ed. VG/VG. P3. $20.00

DIPPIE, Brian. *Looking at Russell.* 1987. Ft Worth. Amon Carter Mus. 1st ed. 8vo. 144p. beige cloth. F/F. T10. $25.00

DIRINGER & REGENSBURGER. *Alphabet: A Key to the History of Mankind.* 1968. 2 vol. 3rd. 4to. F/VG case. A4. $250.00

DIRLAM, H.K. *John Chapman by Occupation a Gatherer & Planter...* 1965. Mansfield, OH. Richland Co Hist Soc. 79p. VG. A10. $45.00

DISCH, Thomas M. *Bad Moon Rising.* 1973. Harper Row. 1st ed. VG/VG. P3. $28.00

DISCH, Thomas M. *Black Alice.* nd. BC. VG/VG. P3. $10.00

DISCH, Thomas M. *Businessman: Tale of Terror.* 1984. Harper Row. 1st ed. F/NF. G10. $20.00

DISCH, Thomas M. *Getting Into Death.* 1976. Knopf. 1st ed. F/F. M19. $25.00

DISCH, Thomas M. *Getting Into Death.* 1976. NY. 1st Am ed. inscr. F. A11. $35.00

DISCH, Thomas M. *MD: A Horror Story.* 1991. Knopf. 1st ed. rem mk. F/F. G10. $20.00

DISCH, Thomas M. *MD: A Horror Story.* 1991. Knopf. 1st ed. VG/VG. P3. $15.00

DISCH, Thomas M. *On Wings of Song.* 1979. St Martin. 1st ed. xl. dj. P3. $8.00

DISCH, Thomas M. *Torturing Mr Amberwell.* 1985. Cheap Street. 1/124. sgn. ils/sgn Judy King-Rieniets. F/dj/case. S9. $125.00

DISERENS, Charles M. *Influence of Music on Behavior.* 1926. Princeton. 224p. prt beige cloth. VG. G1. $45.00

DISNEY, Doris Miles. *Chandler Policy.* 1971. Putnam. 1st ed. VG/VG. P3. $20.00

DISNEY, Doris Miles. *Departure of Mr Gaudette.* 1964. Crime Club. 1st ed. VG/VG. P3. $30.00

DISNEY, Doris Miles. *Last Straw.* 1954. Crime Club. 1st ed. VG/VG. P3. $25.00

DISNEY, Doris Miles. *Three's a Crowd.* 1971. Crime Club. 1st ed. VG/VG. P3. $20.00

DISNEY, Dorothy Cameron. *Hangman's Tree.* 1949. Random. 1st ed. VG/fair. P3. $10.00

DISNEY STUDIOS. *Adventures of Mickey Mouse, Book 1.* 1931. McKay. ils. G+/wrp. M17. $375.00

DISNEY STUDIOS. *Adventures of Mickey Mouse, Book 1.* 1931. McKay. 1st ed. ils. pict label/cloth. G. A17. $400.00

DISNEY STUDIOS. *Adventures of Mickey Mouse, Book 1.* 1932. McKay. VG/pict wrp. D1. $85.00

DISNEY STUDIOS. *Adventures of Mickey Mouse, Book 2.* 1932. McKay. 8vo. pict brd. VG. D1. $400.00

DISNEY STUDIOS. *Baby Weems.* 1941. Doubleday Doran. 8vo. unp. ils bl cloth. VG. C14. $12.00

DISNEY STUDIOS. *Big Bad Wolf & Little Red Riding Hood.* 1934. Bl Ribbon. 1st ed. ils. VG/dj. D1. $450.00

DISNEY STUDIOS. *Bunty.* 1935. Whitman. popups. 28p. VG. D1. $85.00

DISNEY STUDIOS. *Donald Duck & His Nephews.* 1940. DC Heath. sm 8vo. VG+. C8. $65.00

DISNEY STUDIOS. *Donald Duck & the Hidden Gold.* 1951. Simon Schuster. 12mo. VG. B17. $12.00

DISNEY STUDIOS. *Donald Duck in Bringing Up Father.* 1948. Whitman. ils. VG. M5. $22.00

DISNEY STUDIOS. *Donald Duck in Bringing Up the Boys.* 1948. Whitman. 12mo. pict brd. VG. M5. $10.00

DISNEY STUDIOS. *Elmer Elephant.* 1938. Whitman. unp. VG/pict wrp. M20. $77.00

DISNEY STUDIOS. *Ferdinand the Bull.* 1938. Whitman. 12p. VG. M5. $25.00

DISNEY STUDIOS. *Jolly Jump-Ups See the Circus.* 1944. McLoughlin. 6 popups. VG. D1. $185.00

DISNEY STUDIOS. *Mickey Mouse & the Bat Bandit.* 1935. Whitman. Big Little Book. 427p. VG. B14. $125.00

DISNEY STUDIOS. *Mickey Mouse Goes Fishing.* 1936. Whitman. stand-out Mickey at center. 29p. NF. B24. $300.00

DISNEY STUDIOS. *Mickey Never Fails.* 1939. DC Heath. sm 8vo. VG+. C8. $65.00

DISNEY STUDIOS. *Nutcracker Suite From Walt Disney's Fantasia.* 1940. Little Brn. 1st ed. 4to. ils. 6 piano arrangements. F/dj. T10. $250.00

DISNEY STUDIOS. *Peculiar Penguins.* 1934. McKay. from Silly Symphony. 8vo. 45p. cloth/pict label. F. B24. $485.00

DISNEY STUDIOS. *Pop-Up Mickey Mouse.* 1933. Bl Ribbon. 1st ed. thin 8vo. 3 popups. NF. T10. $650.00

DISNEY STUDIOS. *Pop-Up Minnie Mouse.* 1933. Bl Ribbon. 1st ed. 8vo. 3 popups. pict brd. VG. T10. $700.00

DISNEY STUDIOS. *Sketchbook.* 1993. Old Strubridge, CT. Applewood Books. 1st Am trade ed. 4to. F/dj. T10. $30.00

DISNEY STUDIOS. *Snow White & the Seven Dwarfs.* 1979. ils. VG/VG. M17. $40.00

DISNEY STUDIOS. *Thumper.* 1942. Grosset Dunlap. VG+/VG. P2. $35.00

DISNEY STUDIOS. *Uncle Scrooge McDuck: His Life & Times.* 1981. Millbrae, CA. 1/500. gilt leatherette w/onlay. AN. B24. $275.00

DISNEY STUDIOS. *Walt Disney's Circus.* 1944. Simon Schuster. 1st ed. 8vo. unp. VG+/VG+. D1. $225.00

DISNEY STUDIOS. *Walt Disney's Mickey Mouse Cookbook.* 1975. Golden/Western. sm 4to. VG. C8. $35.00

DISSTON, Harry. *Riding Rhymes for Young Riders.* 1951. NY. Bond Wheelwright. 1st ed. pres. VG. O3. $58.00

DIVER, Maud. *Siege Perilous & Other Stories.* 1924. Houghton Mifflin. 1st ed. F/NF. A17. $10.00

DIXIE, Marmaduke. *Beauties of Bridge.* 1938. London. 64p. VG. S1. $15.00

DIXON, Franklin W. *Castaways of the Stratosphere.* nd. Grosset Dunlap. hc. VG/VG. P3. $30.00

DIXON, Franklin W. *Easton Press Hardy Boys.* 12 vol. leather. AN/swrp/case. M20. $2,000.00

DIXON, Franklin W. *Hardy Boys: Clue of the Broken Blade (#21).* 1942. Grosset Dunlap. 1st ed. 218p. VG/dj. M20. $25.00

DIXON, Franklin W. *Hardy Boys: El Misterio del Junco Chino (#39).* 1963. Editorial Acme. 188p. VG+/dj. M20. $45.00

DIXON, Franklin W. *Hardy Boys: Figure in Hiding (#16).* 1937. Grosset Dunlap. 1st ed. 212p. VG/dj. M20. $110.00

DIXON, Franklin W. *Hardy Boys: Flickering Torch Mystery (#22).* 1943. Grosset Dunlap. 1st ed. 212p. cloth. VG/dj. M20. $130.00

DIXON, Franklin W. *Hardy Boys: Footprints Under the Window (#12).* 1941 (1933). Grosset Dunlap. 218p. VG/dj. M20. $117.00

DIXON, Franklin W. *Hardy Boys: Hooded Hawk Mystery (#34).* 1954. Grosset Dunlap. 1st ed. 212p. VG/dj. M20. $20.00

DIXON, Franklin W. *Hardy Boys: Mystery of Cabin Island (#8).* 1929. Grosset Dunlap. lists 20 titles. 214p. VG/dj. M20. $125.00

DIXON, Franklin W. *Hardy Boys: Mystery of Cabin Island (#8).* 1932 (1929). Grosset Dunlap. 1932B ed. 214p. VG+/dj. M20. $130.00

DIXON, Franklin W. *Hardy Boys: Mystery of the Chinese Junk (#39).* 1960. Grosset Dunlap. 1st ed. 184p. VG+/dj. M20. $40.00

DIXON, Franklin W. *Hardy Boys: Secret of the Caves (#7).* 1929. Grosset Dunlap. lists 20 titles. 210p. brn cloth. VG+/wht spine dj. M20. $150.00

DIXON, Franklin W. *Hardy Boys: Secret of the Lost Tunnel (#29).* 1950. Grosset Dunlap. 1st ed. 210p. VG/dj. M20. $20.00

DIXON, Franklin W. *Hardy Boys: Secret of Wildcat Swamp (#31).* 1952. Grosset Dunlap. 1st ed. 212p. VG/dj. M20. $20.00

DIXON, Franklin W. *Hardy Boys: Short-Wave Mystery (#24).* 1945. Grosset Dunlap. 3rd. 217p. VG/dj. M20. $200.00

DIXON, Franklin W. *Hardy Boys: The Hidden Harbor Mystery (#14).* 1935. Grosset Dunlap. G+. P12. $4.00

DIXON, Franklin W. *Hardy Boys: The Hidden Harbor Mystery (#14).* 1935. Grosset Dunlap. lists 18 titles. 219p. VG/dj. M20. $75.00

DIXON, Franklin W. *Hardy Boys: The House on the Cliff.* 1927. Grosset Dunlap. ils Walter Rogers. G+. P12. $5.00

DIXON, Franklin W. *Hardy Boys: The Twisted Claw (#18).* 1939. Grosset Dunlap. 1st ed. 217p. VG/dj. M20. $40.00

DIXON, Franklin W. *Hardy Boys: What Happened at Mignight (#10).* 1931. Grosset Dunlap. lists to #16. 213p. VG/ragged. M20. $87.00

DIXON, Franklin W. *Hardy Boys: While the Clock Ticked (#11)* 1932. Grosset Dunlap. G+. P12. $4.00

DIXON, Franklin W. *Hardy Boys: While the Clock Ticked (#11).* 1932. Grosset Dunlap. lists 18 titles. 213p. VG/dj. M20. $155.00

DIXON, Franklin W. *Hardy Boys: Yellow Feather Mystery (#33).* 1953. Grosset Dunlap. 1st ed. 216p. VG/dj. M20. $25.00

DIXON, Franklin W. *Ted Scott: Following the Sun Shadow (#15).* 1932. Grosset Dunlap. 1st ed. 215p. VG/dj. M20. $77.00

DIXON, Franklin W. *Ted Scott: South of the Rio Grande.* nd. Grosset Dunlap. hc. VG. P3. $8.00

DIXON, Franklin W. *Ted Scott: South of the Rio Grande.* 1928. Grosset Dunlap. ils Walter Rogers. G+. P12. $5.00

DIXON, Franklin W. *Ted Scott: Through the Air to Alaska.* nd. Grosset Dunlap. G. P3. $6.00

DIXON, Joseph S. *Wildlife Portfolio of the Western National Parks.* 1942. GPO. 1st ed. 4to. 121p. xl. VG. T10. $50.00

DIXON, Norman F. *On the Psychology of Military Incompetence.* (1986). NY. Basic. 1st Am ed. 448p. tan cloth. VG/dj. G1. $50.00

DIXON, Roger. *Noah II.* 1975. Harwood Smart. F/F. P3. $15.00

DIXON, T. *Black Hood.* 1924. Grosset. ils. VG/dj. B5. $25.00

DIXON, T. *Clansman.* 1905. NY. 1st ed. MTI. VG/VG. B5. $45.00

DIXON, T. *Foolish Virgin.* 1915. NY. 1st ed. VG/VG. B5. $40.00

DIXON, Thomas Jr. *Life Worth Living: A Personal Experience.* 1905. Doubleday Page. 1st ed. sgn. 32pl. teg. gr brd. G. B11. $45.00

DIXON, William Hepworth. *Holy Land.* 1869. Lippincott/Chapman Hall. ils. 418p. xl. G. W1. $24.00

DIXON, William Scarth. *Men, Horses & Hunting.* nd. Payson. 1st Am ed. VG/fair. O3. $45.00

DOANE, Francis. *Radio: Devices & Communications.* 1927. Internat Lib of Tech. 200p. gr cloth/red buckram spine. VG. B22. $6.00

DOANE, Michael. *City of Light.* 1992. Knopf. 1st ed. F/F. H11. $20.00

DOANE, Pelagie. *Child's Book of Prayers.* 1947. Catholic Man. 4to. ils. VG/G+. B17. $12.50

DOANE, Pelagie. *Small Child's Bible.* 1946. Oxford. 4to. ils. VG-. B17. $8.50

DOBBINS, Paul H. *Death Trap.* 1951. Phoenix. 1st ed. VG/G. P3. $15.00

DOBBS, Fred C. *Golden Age of BC.* 1976. Gage. 1st ed. VG/VG. P3. $15.00

DOBBS, Rose. *More Once Upon a Time Stories.* 1961. Random. 1st ed. 8vo. ils Flavia Gag. VG+/G. M5. $30.00

DOBIE, J. Frank. *Ben Lilly Legend.* 1952. London. Hammond. 1st ed. 8vo. F/VG. T10. $65.00

DOBIE, J. Frank. *Carl Sandburg & St Peter at the Gate.* 1966. Encino. 1/750. F/NF case. B35. $70.00

DOBIE, J. Frank. *I'll Tell You a Tale.* 1960. Little Brn. 2nd. inscr/dtd 1961. ils Carlton Mead. F/F. T10. $250.00

DOBIE, J. Frank. *Longhorns.* 1949. Little Brn. inscr. 388p. VG. B11. $50.00

DOBIE, J. Frank. *Rattlesnakes.* nd. London. Hammond. 1st ed. 8vo. NF/NF. T10. $50.00

DOBIE, J. Frank. *Some Part of Myself.* 1967. Little Brn. 1st ed. 8vo. F/F. T10. $45.00

DOBIE, J. Frank. *Tales of Old-Time Texas.* 1955. Little Brn. 12th. 8vo. F/F. T10. $25.00

DOBIE, J. Frank. *Texan in England.* 1945. Boston. 1st ed. VG/VG. B5. $35.00

DOBREE, Bonamy. *Unacknowledged Legislator.* 1942. Allen Unwin. 1st ed. hc. VG. P3. $20.00

DOBSON, Austin. *Four French Women.* 1890. London. Chatto Windus. 1st ed/lg paper issue. sgn. 207p. VG. T10. $250.00

DOBSON, Austin. *Old Kennsington Place & Other Papers.* 1910. London. inscr/dtd 1910. NF. C6. $85.00

DOBSON, Mrs. *Life of Petrarch.* 1803. London. 5th ed. 2 vol. 8 copper pl. full leather. VG. B18. $125.00

DOBYNS, Stephen. *Boat Off the Coast.* 1987. Viking. 1st ed. VG/VG. P3. $18.00

DOBYNS, Stephen. *Saratoga Snapper.* 1986. Viking. 1st ed. F/F. P3. $16.00

DOCTOR X; see Nourse, Alan E.

DOCTOROW, E.L. *Book of Daniel.* 1971. Random. 1st ed. rem mk. NF/F. M22. $40.00

DOCTOROW, E.L. *Ragtime.* 1975. Random. 1st ed. NF/NF. M19. $20.00

DOCTOROW, E.L. *Ragtime.* 1976. London. 1st ed. inscr. F/NF. A11. $60.00

DODD, Edward. *Polynesian Seafarring. Volume III: Ring of Fire.* 1972. Dodd Mead. ils/photos/maps. 192p. VG/dj. T7. $40.00

DODGE, Bertha S. *It Started in Eden.* 1979. NY. ils. 288p. VG. B26. $22.00

DODGE, David. *Plunder of the Sun.* 1950. Michael Joseph. G/torn. P3. $10.00

DODGE, David. *20,000 Leagues Behind the 8 Ball.* 1951. Random. 1st ed. VG/G. P3. $25.00

DODGE, Ernest S. *Beyond the Capes.* 1971. Little Brn. 1st ed. sgn. 8vo. 429p. VG/VG. B11. $35.00

DODGE, Jim. *Fup.* 1st ed. author's 1st book. F/F. B30. $20.00

DODGE, Louis. *Sandman's Forest.* 1918. Scribner. 1st ed. ils Paul Branson. 283p. G+. P2. $30.00

DODGE, Louis. *Sandman's Mountain.* 1920. Scribner. 1st ed. ils Paul Bransom. 278p. VG. T5. $45.00

DODGE, Mary Mapes. *Mary Anne.* 1983. Lothrop Lee. 1st thus. 8vo. VG/VG. B17. $6.50

DODWELL, Christina *Traveller on Horseback in Eastern Turkey & Iran.* 1989. NY. Walker. 1st am ed. maps. 191p. NF/dj. W1. $18.00

DOE, John. *Bridge Manual Illustrated.* 1902. London. 4th. 122p. VG. S1. $15.00

DOEBEL, Gunter. *Johannes Kepler.* 1983. Verlag Styria. German text. 256p. dj. K5. $30.00

DOENITZ, Admiral. *Memoirs: Ten Years Twenty Days.* 1959. Cleveland. 1st ed. VG/VG. B5. $35.00

DOERFLINGER, William. *Shanty Men & Shanty Boys.* 1951. NY. 1st ed. ils. 374p. VG/VG. B5. $45.00

DOERNER, Klaus. *Madmen Bourgeois: A Social History of Insanity...* 1981. Oxford. 1st Eng trans. 361p. VG/dj. A13. $45.00

DOERR, Harriet. *Consider This, Senora.* 1993. Harcourt. 1st ed. sgn. F/clip. H11. $40.00

DOHAN, Mary Helen. *Mr Roosevelt's Steamboat.* 1981. Dodd Mead. VG/VG. A16. $17.50

DOHERTY, James L. *Race & Education in Richmond.* ca 1972. self pub. 1st ed. 162p. VG-. B10. $35.00

DOIG, Ivan. *Dancing at the Rascal Fair.* 1987. Atheneum. 1st ed. VG/VG. B5. $40.00

DOIG, Ivan. *Dancing at the Rascal Fair.* 1987. Atheneum. 1st ed. sgn. M/dj. A18. $60.00

DOIG, Ivan. *English Creek.* 1984. Atheneum. 1st ed. sgn. AN/dj. A18. $80.00

DOIG, Ivan. *Heart Earth.* 1993. Atheneum. 1st ed. sgn. F/F. M19. $30.00

DOIG, Ivan. *History of the Pacific Northwest Forest & Range...* 1977. Forest Service. 1st ed. sgn. F/stapled wrp. B4. $250.00

DOIG, Ivan. *Ride With Me, Mariah Montana.* 1990. Atheneum. 1st ed. F/F. A18. $30.00

DOIG, Ivan. *Sea Runners.* 1982. Atheneum. ARC. RS. NF/NF. A18. $30.00

DOIG, Ivan. *Sea Runners.* 1982. Atheneum. 1st ed. sgn. AN/dj. A18. $100.00

DOIG, Ivan. *This House of Sky: Landscapes of a Western Mind.* 1978. HBJ. 1st ed. author's 1st book. sgn. AN/dj. A18. $175.00

DOIG, Ivan. *This House of Sky: Landscapes of a Western Mind.* 1978. HBJ. 1st ed. NF/VG. M19. $125.00

DOIG, Ivan. *Winter Brothers: A Season at the Edge of America.* 1980. HBJ. 1st ed. sgn. AN/dj. A18. $100.00

DOIG, Ivan. *Winter Brothers: A Season at the Edge of America.* 1980. HBJ. 1st ed. VG/VG. B5. $45.00

DOLE & GORDAN. *Maine of the Sea & Pines.* 1928. Boston. 1st ed. 2 fld maps/50 pl. VG. B5. $47.50

DOLINER, Roy. *Sandra Rifkin's Jewels.* 1966. NAL. 1st ed. VG/VG. P3. $20.00

DOLLAR, Robert. *Memoirs of Robert Dollar.* 1925. np. A16. $62.00

DOLLARD, John. *Frustration & Aggression.* 1939. Oxford. 209p. red cloth. G1. $35.00

DOLLARD, John. *Victory Over Fear.* (1942). Reynal Hitchcock. inscr. 12mo. 213p. gray cloth. G1. $75.00

DOLLING, Richard. *Critical Care.* 1991. Morrow. 1st ed. author's 1st book. NF/F. M23. $25.00

DOLMETSCH, Carl R. *Smart Set.* 1966. Dial. 1st ed. sgn. 262p. VG/VG. B11. $75.00

DOMATILLA, John. *Last Crime.* 1981. Atheneum. 1st ed. VG/VG. P3. $20.00

DOMBROWSKI, John. *Area Handbook for Guatemala.* 1970. GPO. 1st ed. 361p. xl. F3. $10.00

DOMINIC, R.B. *Murder, Sunny Side Up.* 1968. Abelard Schuman. 1st ed. VG/VG. P3. $25.00

DOMINIC, R.B. *Unexpected Developments.* 1984. St Martin. 1st ed. VG/VG. P3. $20.00

DOMVILLE & DUNBAR. *Flora of Ulster County, NY.* 1970. New Paltz, NY. map. 136p. sc. B26. $17.50

DONAHEY, William. *Teenie Weenie Neighbors.* 1945. Whittlesey. 2nd. ils. F/VG+. M5. $125.00

DONALD, Henry. *Happy Story of Wallace the Engine.* 1955. Nelson. 1st ed. ils Gilbert Dunlop. 94p. VG/G. P2. $20.00

DONALDSON, Frances. *PG Wodehouse: The Authorized Biography.* 1982. Weidenfeld Nicolson. 1st ed. F/F. P3. $25.00

DONALDSON, Frances. *Yours, Plum. Letters of PG Wodehouse.* 1983. London. 231p. F/F. A4. $25.00

DONALDSON, Henry Herbert. *Growth of the Brain.* 1895. London. Walter Scott/Scribner. 374p. xl. VG. G1. $65.00

DONALDSON, Peter. *Life of Sir William Wallace, Governor General of Scotland...* 1841. Rochester. 132p. G. B18. $22.50

DONALDSON, Stephen R. *Daughter of Regals.* 1984. Del Rey. 1st ed. F/F. P3. $15.00

DONALDSON, Stephen R. *Forbidden Knowledge.* 1991. Bantam. 1st ed. VG/VG. P3. $20.00

DONALDSON, Stephen R. *Gliden-Fire.* 1981. Underwood Miller. 1st ed. xl. dj. P3. $10.00

DONALDSON, Stephen R. *Lord Foul's Bane.* nd. HRW. 4th. VG/VG. P3. $15.00

DONALDSON, Stephen R. *Mirror of Her Dreams.* 1986. Ballantine. 1st ed. F/NF. H11. $35.00

DONALDSON, Stephen R. *Mirror of Her Dreams.* 1986. Del Rey. 1st ed. VG/VG. P3. $25.00

DONALDSON, Stephen R. *One Tree.* 1982. Del Rey. 1st ed. VG/VG. P3. $20.00

DONALDSON, Stephen R. *White Gold Wielder.* 1983. Del Rey. 1st ed. F/F. P3. $20.00

DONALDSON, Thomas. *George Catlin Indian Gallery in the US Museum...* 1885. Smithsonian. 100 pl/maps. VG. A9. $175.00

DONAVAN, John. *Case of the Violet Smoke.* 1940. Mystery House. VG. P3. $20.00

DONEGAN, Jane. *Hydropathic Highway to Health.* 1985. NY. 1st ed. 229p. VG. A13. $40.00

DONER, Mary Frances. *Salvager.* 1958. Minneapolis. Ross Haines. 1st ed. G/poor. A16. $30.00

DONKERSLOOT, Marike. *World on Paper: Cartography in Amsterdam in 17th Century.* 1967. Amsterdam Historisch Mus. ils. F/wrp. O7. $45.00

DONLEAVY, J.P. *Beastly Beatitudes of Balthazar B.* 1968. np. 1st ed. F/VG. M19. $22.50

DONLEAVY, J.P. *Fairy Tales of New York.* 1961. Random. 1st ed. F/NF. M19. $22.50

DONLEAVY, J.P. *Leila.* Franklin Lib. 1st ed. sgn. VG. M17. $30.00

DONLEY, Michael. *Atlas of California.* 1979. Pacific Book Center. folio. maps. 175p. F/dj. O7. $75.00

DONNE, John. *Letters to Several Persons of Honour.* 1868. NY. 12mo. ils. 464p. brn cloth. G. T3. $17.00

DONNEL, C.P. *Murder-Go-Round.* 1945. McKay. VG. P3. $15.00

DONNELLY, Elfie. *Offbeat Friends.* 1982. Crown. 1st Am ed. 8vo. 119p. NF/clip. C14. $12.00

DONNELLY, Ignatius. *Great Cryptogram.* 1988. Chicago. 2nd. ils. 998p. G. B5. $65.00

DONNELLY, Joe. *Stone.* 1990. Barrie Jenkins. 1st ed. F/F. P3. $30.00

DONNISON, T.E. *Old Fairy Tales Told Anew.* ca 1901. London. Tuck. 4to. F/self wrp. B24. $150.00

DONOVAN, Robert J. *Assassins.* 1955. Harper. 1st ed. NF/NF. B35. $25.00

DONOVAN, Robert J. *Eisenhower: The Inside Story.* 1956. Harper. 1st ed. 423p. bl cloth. VG/fair. B22. $5.50

DONY, John G. *Flora of Bedfordshire.* 1953. Lutton. 1st ed. 24 photos/ils. map. 532p. VG/dj. B26. $45.00

DOOLEY, Sallie May. *Dem Good Ole Times.* 1916. Doubleday Page. ils Suzanne Gutherz. 150p. G+. B10. $45.00

DOOLING, Richard. *Critical Care.* 1987. Holt. 1st ed. F/F. M23. $25.00

DOOLITTLE, Hilda. *Hymen, by HD.* 1921. NY. Holt. 1st ed. author's 2nd book. NF/gr prt wrp. B24. $350.00

DOOLITTLE, Hilda. *Palimpsest.* 1926. Houghton Mifflin. 1st Am ed. 1/700 from French sheets. VG/NF. B4. $350.00

DOOLITTLE, Jerome. *Body Scissors.* 1990. Pocket. 1st ed. NF/NF. P3. $18.00

DOOLITTLE, Jerome. *Dali.* 1974. Leon Amiel. 1st ed. VG/VG. P3. $15.00

DOOLITTLE, Jerome. *Half Nelson.* 1994. Pocket. 1st ed. VG/VG. P3. $20.00

DOOLITTLE, Jerome. *Strangle Hold.* 1991. Pocket. hc. F/F. P3. $20.00

DORE, Gustave. *La Fontaine's Fables.* ca 1880. Cassell. NF. M19. $200.00

DORF, Fran. *Flight.* 1992. Dutton. 1st ed. F/NF. H11. $20.00

DORF, P. *Liberty Hyde Bailey.* 1956. Ithaca. 1st ed. VG/VG. B5. $25.00

DORIN, Patrick C. *Lake Superior Iron Ore Railroads.* 1969. Seattle. Superior. 1st ed. G/G. A16. $27.50

DORLING, Taprell. *Sea Escapes & Adventures.* 1927. Stokes. 15 pl/5 maps. 286p. VG. T7. $24.00

DORMAN, John Frederick. *Farish Family of Virginia & Its Forebears.* 1967. private prt. ils. 168p. VG. B10. $45.00

DORN, Robert D. *Manual of the Vascular Plants of WY.* 1977. NY. 2 vol. 2144 species described. F. B26. $145.00

DORNBUSCH, C.E. *Military Bibliography of the Civil War.* 1983. 3 vol. 8vo. maroon cloth. T3. $60.00

DORRIS, Michael. *Native American 500 Years Later.* 1975. Crowell. 1st ed. 4to. 333p. VG/dj. T10. $40.00

DORRIS, Michael. *Yellow Raft in Blue Water.* 1987. Holt. 1st ed. author's 1st book. F/F. A15/M19/M23. $25.00

DORRIS & ERDRICH. *Crown of Columbus.* 1991. Harper Collins. 1st ed. sgns. F/F. M19. $25.00

DORSON, Richard M. *America Begins: Early American Writing.* 1950. Pantheon. 26 pl. 438p. A17. $15.00

DORST, Jean. *Migrations of Birds.* 1963. Houghton Mifflin. 1st Am ed. 476p. F. B22. $16.00

DOS PASSOS, John. *USA. Trilogy.* 1930-1936. NY/London. Harper. 3 vol. 1st ed. 8vo. VG/dj. S9. $950.00

DOS PASSOS & SHAY. *Down Cape Cod.* 1947. Nat Travel Club. ils. VG. P12. $7.00

DOSS, James D. *Shaman Laughs.* 1995. St Martin. 1st ed. F/F. M23. $30.00

DOSS, James D. *Shaman Sings.* 1994. St Martin. 1st ed. author's 1st novel. sgn. F/F. T2. $45.00

DOSS, James D. *Shaman Sings.* 1994. St Martin. 1st ed. F/NF. M23. $40.00

DOSTOEVSKY, Fyodor. *Brothers Karamazov.* 1949. LEC. 2 vol. 1/1500. sgn. silver-stp red cloth. case. K1. $85.00

DOSTOEVSKY, Fyodor. *Brothers Karamazov.* 1990. North Point. 2nd. F/F. P3. $30.00

DOSTOEVSKY, Fyodor. *Crime & Punishment.* 1992. Knopf. 1st ed. F/F. P3. $25.00

DOTEN, Dana. *Art of Bundling.* 1938. Countryman/Farrar Rinehart. 1st ed. 190p. VG/dj. M20. $30.00

DOTEN, Dana. *Art of Bundling.* 1938. Countryman/Farrar Rinehart. 190p. G/torn. B18. $17.50

DOTY, Robert M. *American Folk Art in Ohio Collections.* 1976. Akron Art Inst. unp. cloth. NF/NF. M20. $32.00

DOTY, Robert M. *American Folk Art in Ohio Collections.* 1976. Dodd Mead. VG/dj. D2. $20.00

DOUCETTE, E. *Fisherman's Guide to Maine.* 1951. Random. 1st ed. VG. H7. $20.00

DOUDS, William S. *Thy Kingdom Come — Why Not Now?* 1940. NY. Beaver. sgn. 12mo. 287p. fair/G. B11. $12.50

DOUGHTY, Paul. *Huaylas: An Andrean District in Search of Progress.* 1968. Ithaca. Cornell. 1st ed. 284p. dj. F3. $20.00

DOUGLAS, Arthur. *Last Rights.* 1986. St Martin. 1st ed. F/F. P3. $15.00

DOUGLAS, Carole Nelson. *Pussyfoot.* 1993. Tor. 1st ed. NF/NF. P3. $15.00

DOUGLAS, David C. *Norman Achievement: 1050-1100.* 1969. Berkeley. 1st ed. 271p. NF/dj. M20. $18.00

DOUGLAS, Ellen. *Can't Quit You, Baby.* 1988. Atheneum. 2nd. sgn. F/F. B11. $15.00

DOUGLAS, Jack. *Shams.* 1899. Thompson Thomas. G. P12. $8.00

DOUGLAS, James Postell. *Douglas's Texas Battery, CSA.* 1966. Smith County Hist Soc. 1st ed. 238p. F/NF. M8. $45.00

DOUGLAS, M. *Frozen North.* nd. Boston. De Wolfe Fiske. ils/map. 176p. VG. D1. $35.00

DOUGLAS, Marjorie Stoneman. *Everglades.* 1947. NY. Rivers of Am series. VG/G+. B5. $45.00

DOUGLAS, Marjorie Stoneman. *Everglades.* 1947. NY. Rivers of America series. ltd ed. sgn. VG/VG. B5. $90.00

DOUGLAS, Michael. *Dealing; or, Berkeley-to-Boston Forty-Brick Lost-Bag Blues.* 1970. Knopf. 1st ed. NF/NF. M19. $65.00

DOUGLAS, Norman. *Angel of Manfredonia.* 1929. San Francisco. Windsor. 1/225. sgn. marbled brd/cloth spine. NF. T10. $150.00

DOUGLAS, Norman. *Birds & Beasts of the Greek Anthology.* 1927. Florence. private prt. 1/500. sgn. 219p. VG/dj. T10. $250.00

DOUGLAS, William O. *Democracy's Manifesto.* 1962. Garden City. 1st ed. F/VG. N3. $10.00

DOUGLAS, William O. *My Wilderness, the Pacific West.* 1960. Doubleday. inscr. G/dj. M11. $125.00

DOUGLAS, William O. *Strange Lands & Friendly People.* 1951. Harper. 8vo. half cloth. VG. P4. $15.00

DOUGLASS, Ben. *History of Wayne County, Ohio.* 1878. Indianapolis. 1st ed. 868p. G. B18. $145.00

DOVE, Rita. *Darker Face of the Earth: A Verse Play in Fourteen Scenes.* 1994. Brownsville, OR. Story Line. 1/224. sgn. AN. B4. $85.00

DOVE, Rita. *Fifth Sunday.* 1985. Lexington. 1st ed. F/wrp. B4. $150.00

DOVE, Rita. *Mother Love.* 1995. Norton. 1st ed. sgn. F/F. B35. $65.00

DOVE, Rita. *Selected Poems.* 1993. Pantheon. 1st ed. F/F. B4. $65.00

DOW, George Francis. *Slave Ships & Slaving.* 1927. Marine Research Soc. 1st ed. 349p. VG+/dj. M20. $255.00

DOW. *Anthology & Bibliography of Niagara Falls. Vol II.* 1921. np. ils. VG. A4. $30.00

DOWD, J.H. *Childhood.* 1935. Scribner. 1st ed. ils. VG/partial. M5. $65.00

DOWDEN, Anne Ophelia T. *Look at the Flower.* 1963. NY. ils. F/dj. B26. $17.50

DOWDEN & THOMSON. *Roses.* 1965. NY. ils Dowden. 42p. VG. B26. $11.00

DOWER, William. *Early Annals of Kokstad & Griqualand East.* 1978. Pietermaritzburg. Natal. 8vo. 192p. xl. VG. W1. $20.00

DOWLING, Edith Bannister. *Patchwork of Poems About SC.* 1970. Beaufort. Peacock. sgn. 47p. VG. B10. $8.00

DOWLING, Edward J. *Know Your Lakers of WWI.* 1978. MI. Marine Pub. G/wrp. A16. $12.00

DOWNER, E.R. *Atlas of Uganda.* 1967. Kampala. Dept Lands & Surveys. 37 maps. F. O7. $95.00

DOWNER. *First Christmas: An Advent Calendar to Treasure.* 1992. np. accordion-style unfld to 9-ft ils. F. A4. $35.00

DOWNES, Olin. *Olin Downes on Music. A Selection of His Writings...* 1957. NY. 1st prt. 473p. blk/bl bdg. F/VG clip. H3. $50.00

DOWNEY, Bill. *Tom Bass: Black Horseman.* 1975. St Louis. Saddle & Bridle Inc. 8vo. inscr. red cloth. F/dj. T10. $100.00

DOWNEY, Fairfax. *Cats of Destiny.* 1950. Scribner. 1st ed. 170p. VG/G. P2. $28.00

DOWNEY, Fairfax. *Dog of War.* 1943. Dodd Mead. 1st ed. VG/G. O3. $38.00

DOWNEY, Fairfax. *Guns at Gettysburg.* 1958. NY. 1st ed. VG/VG. B5. $32.50

DOWNEY, Fairfax. *Shining Filly.* 1954. Scribner. 1st/A ed. VG/G. O3. $25.00

DOWNEY, Fairfax. *Storming of the Gateway, Chattanooga, 1863.* 1960. McKay. 1st ed. 303p. cloth. NF/NF. M8. $50.00

DOWNING, A.J. *Fruits & Fruit Trees of America.* 1849. NY. 9th. VG. V4. $175.00

DOWNS & PFINGSTEN. *Salamanders of Ohio.* 1989. Columbus. 8vo. ils/photos/pl. pict wrp. B1. $28.00

DOYLE, Arthur Conan. *Adventures of Sherlock Holmes.* 1892. NY. Harper. 1st Am ed/later state. 8vo. gilt pict cloth. VG. T10. $250.00

DOYLE, Arthur Conan. *Book of Sherlock Holmes.* (1950). World/Rainbow Classics. 8vo. ils. 320p. VG+/G. C14. $6.00

DOYLE, Arthur Conan. *Case-Book of Sherlock Holmes.* 1927. London. John Murray. 1st ed in reddish-pink cloth. VG. C2. $225.00

DOYLE, Arthur Conan. *Croxley Master & Other Tales of the Ring & the Camp.* 1919. NY. 1st ed thus/1st issue. VG/VG. C6. $85.00

DOYLE, Arthur Conan. *Exploits of Brigadier Gerard.* 1896. Appleton. 1st ed. F. M19. $50.00

DOYLE, Arthur Conan. *Hound of the Baskervilles.* 1985. San Francisco. 1/400. photos/sgn Michael Kenna. 204p. AN/case. w/poster. B24. $400.00

DOYLE, Arthur Conan. *Man From Archangel & Other Tales of Adventure.* 1919. NY. 12mo. orange cloth. G. A17. $20.00

DOYLE, Arthur Conan. *Memories & Adventures.* 1924. Boston. 1st Am ed. VG. B5. $50.00

DOYLE, Arthur Conan. *Refugees.* 1893. NY. 2nd. ils Thulstrup. VG. A17. $22.50

DOYLE, Arthur Conan. *Return of Sherlock Holmes.* 1987. Mysterious. 1st ed thus. ils FD Steele. F. A17. $20.00

DOYLE, Arthur Conan. *Rodney Stone.* 1896. NY. 1st Am ed. F/rare dj/case. C2. $500.00

DOYLE, Arthur Conan. *Sir Nigel.* 1906. McClure Phillips. 1st ed. VG. P3. $85.00

DOYLE, Arthur Conan. *Tragedy of the Korosko.* 1898. London. VG. C6. $65.00

DOYLE, Arthur Conan. *Vital Message.* 1919. Doran. 1st ed. VG. P3. $60.00

DOYLE, Arthur Conan. *Vital Message.* 1919. Hodder Stoughton. G. P3. $45.00

DOYLE, Arthur Conan. *White Company.* 1939. John Murray. 65th. VG. P3. $15.00

DOYLE, James E. *Chronicle of England: BC 55...AD 1485.* 1864. London. Longman Gr. 1st ed. ils Edmund Evans. gilt cloth. VG. T10. $450.00

DOYLE, Richard. *Jack the Giant Killer.* 1888. Eyre Spottiswoode. 4to. 48p. w/rare pub leaf. F. B24. $575.00

DOYLE, Roddy. *Paddy Clarke Ha Ha Ha.* 1994. Viking. 1st Am ed. F/F. T2. $45.00

DOYLE & MACDONALD. *Knight's Wyrd.* 1992. HBJ. 1st ed. F/F. P3. $17.00

DOYLE & MCDIARMID. *Baker Street Dozen.* 1987. Congdon Weed. F/F. P3. $20.00

DOZOIS, Gardner. *Goedesic Dreams: Best Short Fiction of Gardner Dozois.* 1991. St Martin. 1st ed. F/F. G10. $25.00

DR. SEUSS; see Geisel, Theodor Seuss.

DRABBLE. *Oxford Companion to English Literature, Fifth Edition.* 1985. np. 1167p. NF/NF. A4. $45.00

DRACO, F. *Devil's Church.* 1961. Rinehart. 1st ed. VG/VG. P3. $30.00

DRAGO, Harry Sinclair. *Canal Days in America.* 1972. Bramhall. 311p. VG/dj. M20. $32.00

DRAGO, Harry Sinclair. *Outlaws on Horseback.* 1964. Dodd Mead. 1st trade ed. 8vo. ils. F/NF. T10. $50.00

DRAKE, Lauren. *Getting the Most Out of a Powerboat.* 1953. Norton. 1st ed. VG/dj. A16. $17.50

DRAKE, Samuel A. *Pine Tree Coast.* 1891. Boston. 1st ed. ils/pl/map. gr cloth. F. H3. $85.00

DRAKE, Stillman. *Telescopes, Tides & Tactics.* 1983. Chicago. VG. O7. $25.00

DRAKE, W. Raymond. *Gods & Spacemen Throughout History.* 1975. Renery. VG. P3. $15.00

DRAYTON & SIZER. *Heads & Faces: How To Study Them...* 1888. NY. Fowler. 199p. Victorial bdg. NF. T10. $150.00

DREADSTONE, Carl; see Campbell, Ramsey.

DREISER, Theodore. *American Tragedy.* 1925. Boni Liveright. 2 vol. F. B2. $75.00

DREISER, Theodore. *American Tragedy.* 1925. Boni Liveright. 2 vol. 1st ed. 1/55 (795 total). sgn pres. w/pub card. F/case. B24. $950.00

DREISER, Theodore. *Bulwark.* 1946. Doubleday. 1st ed. F/F. B35. $30.00

DREISER, Theodore. *Sister Carrie.* 1917. Boni Liveright. 3rd (1st Boni). F/VG+. B4. $650.00

DREISER, Theodore. *Sister Carrie.* 1939. LEC. 1/1500. ils/sgn Reginald Marsh. 387p. F/NF case. C2. $250.00

DREISER, Theodore. *Traveler at Forty.* 1913. NY. 1st ed. 526p. G. A17. $25.00

DREPPARD. *American Pioneer Arts & Artists.* 1942. np. fwd Rockwell Kent. cloth. NF/VG. D2. $45.00

DRESSES, Elia. *Masque of Days.* 1901. London. Cassell. 1st ed. ils Walter Crane. VG. D1. $325.00

DREVER, James. *Instinct in Man: A Contribution to Psychology of Education.* 1917. Cambridge. 281p. ruled russet cloth. G1. $40.00

DREWRY, Carleton. *To Love That Well.* 1975. Barnes. VG/G. B10. $15.00

DREYER & SAXON. *Friends of Joe Gilmore.* 1948. Hastings. ils. VG+/dj. P4. $22.50

DRIESCH, Hans. *Parapsychologie, die Wissenschaft von den Okkulten...* (1932). Munchen. Bruckmann. 150p. prt blk/orange stiff wrp. G1. $37.50

DRIGGS & JACKSON. *Westward America.* 1942. NY. Am Pioneer Trails Assoc. inscr/sgns. 40 mc pl. G. B11. $75.00

DRINKER, Cecil K. *Not So Long Ago: A Chronicle of Medicine & Doctors...* 1937. NY. 183p. bl cloth. dj. B14. $95.00

DRINKWATER, John. *American Vignettes 1860-1865.* 1931. Houghton Mifflin. 1/385. sgn. VG. T10. $125.00

DRUCKER, Bruce. *Bankroll.* 1989. Dutton. 1st ed. rem mk. F/F. H11. $20.00

DRUHOT, George Stanley. *American Topographer: Working Years of GS Druhot...* 1985. Rancho Cordova. Landmark. ils. map ep. F/rpr dj. O7. $45.00

DRUMMOND, D.H. *Montreal in Halftone.* ca 1910. Montreal. Clarke. obl 4to. photos. cloth. VG. T10. $50.00

DRUMMOND, Henry. *Tropical Africa.* 1891. Scribner. 4th ed. 228p. purple cloth. G. B22. $8.00

DRUMMOND, Ivor. *Frog in the Moonflower.* 1972. Macmillan. 1st ed. F/F. P3. $23.00

DRUMMOND, Walter; see Silverberg, Robert.

DRURY, Allen. *Preserve & Protect.* 1968. Doubleday. VG/VG. P3. $13.00

DRURY. *Diaries & Letters of Henry H Spalding & Asa Bowen Smith...* 1958. Arthur H Clark. ils. 379p. VG. A4. $125.00

DRUZHKOV, Yuri. *Adventures of Pencil & Screwbolt.* 1973. Moscow. Progress Pub. 1st ed. 128p. VG. A17. $10.00

DRYBROUGH, T.B. *Polo.* 1898. London. Vinton. 1st ed. VG. O3. $95.00

DRYDEN, John. *Of Dramatic Poetry: An Essay, 1668.* 1928. London. 1/580. 4to. marbled brd/linen spine. VG+. A11. $225.00

DRYDEN, John. *Poetical Works of...* 1855. Edinburgh. James Nichol. 1st standard ed. 2 vol. bl morocco. F. C2. $150.00

DRYER, J.L.E. *Tycho Brahe: Picture of Scientific Life.* 1890. Edinburgh. Blk. 1st ed. rebound. VG. K5. $250.00

DU BOIS, Theodora. *Fowl Play.* 1951. Detective BC. VG. P3. $8.00

DU BOIS, William Pene. *Bear Circus.* nd. Viking/Weekly Reader. possible 1st ed. ils. 48p. G+. C14. $11.00

DU BOIS, William Pene. *Bear Circus.* 1971. Viking. 1st ed. ils. F/VG. P2. $45.00

DU BOIS, William Pene. *Gentleman Bear.* 1985. FSG. 1st ed. 78p. VG+/dj. M20. $15.00

DU BOIS, William Pene. *Otto at Sea.* 1936. Viking. 1st ed. ils. unp. G. D1. $125.00

DU BOIS, William Pene. *Otto in Africa.* c 1961. NY. 1st ed. ils. 39p. VG+. C14. $30.00

DU BOIS, William Pene. *Porko Von Popbutton.* 1969. Harper Row. 1st ed. F/VG. P2. $25.00

DU BOIS, William Pene. *Three Policemen; or, Young Bottsford of Farbe Island.* 1938. Viking. 1st ed. ils. 92p. VG/G. D1/T5. from $85 to $95.00

DU BOIS, William Pene. *21 Balloons.* 1947. Viking BC. VG/VG. B17. $4.00

DU BOSE, John Witherspoon. *General Joseph Wheeler & the Army of Tennessee.* 1912. NY. Neale. 1st ed. 476p. cloth. NF. M8. $450.00

DU HAYS, Charles. *Percheron Horse.* 1886. Baltimore. ltd ed. 4to. trans WT Walters. VG/tissue dj. O3. $695.00

DU MAURIER, Daphne. *Breaking Point.* 1959. Doubleday. 1st ed. VG/VG. P3. $30.00

DU MAURIER, Daphne. *Echoes From the Macabre.* 1977. Doubleday. 1st ed. VG/VG. P3. $18.00

DU MAURIER, Daphne. *My Cousin Rachel.* 1952. Canada. Longman Gr. 1st ed. VG/G. P3. $18.00

DU MAURIER, Daphne. *My Cousin Rachel.* 1952. Doubleday. 1st Am ed. 348p. VG/dj. M20. $22.00

DU MAURIER, Daphne. *Parasites.* 1949. Canada. Ryerson. 1st ed. VG/VG. P3. $20.00

DU MAURIER, Daphne. *Rendezvous & Other Stories.* 1972. Gollancz. 1st ed. VG/VG. P3. $25.00

DU MAURIER, Daphne. *Scapegoat.* 1957. Doubleday. 1st ed. VG/VG. P3. $30.00

DU MAURIER, George. *Martian.* 1897. Harper. hc. VG. P3. $75.00

DU MAURIER, George. *Tribly.* 1894. Harper. G. P3. $35.00

DU PONT, H.A. *Early Generations of the Du Pont & Allied Families.* 1923. np. 2 vol. VG. M17. $40.00

DU PONT, Victor M. *Journey to France & Spain.* 1961. Ithaca. VG. O7. $30.00

DU PUY, William Atherton. *Nation's Forests.* 1938. Macmillan. 1st ed. ils. VG. P12. $20.00

DU VAL, H.C. *Bridge Rules in Rhyme.* 1902. nY. 7p. G. S1. $8.00

DUANE, Diane. *Spider-Man: The Venom Factor.* 1994. Putnam. 1st ed. hc. F/F. P3. $20.00

DUARTE & GASPARINI. *Arte Colonial en Venezuela.* 1974. Caracas. Ed Arte. ils/biblio. 241p. cloth. dj. D2. $115.00

DUBACH & TABER. *Questions About the Oceans.* 1969. WA. VG. O7. $15.00

DUBOIS, Gaylord. *Long Rider & Treasure Vanished Men.* nd. Whitman. VG. P3. $10.00

DUBOIS, Jules. *Operation America.* 1963. Walker. sgn. 8vo. 361p. VG/VG. B11. $25.00

DUBOIS, W.E.B. *Black Folk Then & Now.* 1940. NY. xl. G. B5. $35.00

DUBOSE, John Witherspoon. *Alabama's Tragic Decade: Ten Years of Alabama 1865-1874.* 1940. Webb Book Co. 1st ed. ils/map. 435p. VG. B10. $25.00

DUBUS, Andre. *Bluesman.* 1993. Boston. Faber. 1st ed. F/F. T2. $25.00

DUBUS, Andre. *Finding a Girl in America: Ten Stories & a Novella.* 1980. Boston. Godine. 1st ed. inscr/dtd 1986. F/F. C2. $60.00

DUBUS, Andre. *Land Where My Fathers Died.* 1984. 1/200. sgn. F. C4. $100.00

DUBUS, Andre. *Lieutenant.* 1967. Dial. 1st ed. author's 1st book. inscr. NF/NF. C2. $175.00

DUBUS, Andre. *Selected Stories.* 1988. Boston. Godine. 1st ed. sgn. F/F. C2. $50.00

DUBUS, Andre. *Separate Flights: A Novella & Seven Short Stories.* 1975. Godine. 1st ed. inscr/dtd 1986. F/F. C2. $75.00

DUCKWORTH, C.L.D. *Clyde River & Other Steamers.* 1937. Glasgow. Brn, Son & Ferguson. G. A16. $65.00

DUDA & LUBOS. *Minerals of the World.* 1989. Arch Cape. 4to. 520p. F/F. B1. $65.00

DUDLEY, Carrie. *My Peek-a-Boo Show Book.* 1928. Volland. 1st ed. ils C Dudley. VG. D1. $325.00

DUDLEY & DUDLEY. *Glory & the Grandeur: Teacher's Notes on Richmond...* 1976. private prt. maps. 84p. VG/wrp. B10. $12.00

DUDNIK, Robert M. *Anatomy of a Personal Injury Law Suit...* 1969. Boston. Am Trial Lawyers Assn. bl cloth. M11. $20.00

DUERDEN. *Invisible Present: African Art & Literature.* 1975. Harper Row. F/F. D2. $30.00

DUERRENMATT, Friedrich. *Pledge.* 1959. Knopf. 1st ed. F/F. B35. $45.00

DUFF, Beldon. *Ask No Questions!* nd. Grosset Dunlap. VG/VG. P3. $25.00

DUFFIELD, Anne. *Stamboul Love.* 1934. Knopf. 1st ed. VG. P3. $15.00

DUFFIELD, J.W. *Rapid Boys Under the Sea.* 1923. NY. 1st ed. VG/VG. B5. $20.00

DUFFIELD, Samuel W. *English Hymns: Their Authors & History.* 1888. NY. 3rd. 675p. gilt cloth. A17. $20.00

DUFFY, James. *Murder for Lunch.* 1986. Simon Schuster. 1st ed. F/F. P3. $15.00

DUFFY, James. *Murder Saves Face.* 1991. Simon Schuster. 1st ed. inscr/sgn pen & real names. F/F. M22. $25.00

DUFFY, James. *Murders & Acquisitions.* 1988. Simon Schuster. 1st ed. F/F. P3. $17.00

DUGDALE, William. *Short View of the Late Troubles in England...* 1681. Oxford. Moses Pitt. sm folio. 971p. full calf. T10. $750.00

DUGGAR, Benjamin M. *Plant Physiology.* 1922 (1911). NY. Rural TB series. ils. 516p. B26. $15.00

DUGMORE, A. Radclyffe. *Romance of the Newfoundland Caribou.* 1913. Lippincott. 186p. ils/maps. VG. A10. $50.00

DUGMORE, A. Radclyffe. *Wild Life & the Camera.* 1912. Heinemann. 1st ed. 8vo. 332p. bl cloth. VG. B11. $75.00

DUGUID, Julian. *Green Hell: Adventures in Mysterious Jungles of E Bolivia.* 1931. NY. Century. 1st ed. photos. 339p. F3. $20.00

DUJARDIN-BEAMETZ, **Professor.** *Diseases of the Stomach & Intestines: A Manual...* 1886. NY. Wood. 8vo. 389p. cloth. NF. B14. $75.00

DUKE, Basil Wilson. *History of Morgan's Cavalry.* 1867. Cincinnati. Miami Prt & Pub. 1st ed. 578p. VG. M8. $150.00

DUKE, Basil Wilson. *Reminiscences of General Basil W Duke.* 1911. Doubleday Page. 1st ed. 512p. F. M8. $450.00

DUKE, Donald. *Water Trails West.* 1978. Doubleday. 1st ed. VG/VG. P3. $20.00

DUKE, R.T.W. *In My Library & Other Poems.* 1927. Michie. 64p. G. B10. $15.00

DUKE OF SAINT-SIMON. *Memoirs of Louis XIV, Vol 1.* nd. Collier. VG. P3. $15.00

DULAC, Edmond. *Sinbad the Sailor & Other Stories.* 1914. 1st ed. 23 pl. VG+. S13. $275.00

DULAC, Edmund. *Edmund Dulac's Fairy Book.* nd (1916). Hodder Stoughton. 1st ed. 170p. VG. P2. $250.00

DULAC, Edmund. *Picture-Book for the French Red Cross.* 1915. Hodder Stoughton. 1st ed. 20 pl. VG/VG-. P2. $350.00

DULAC, Edmund. *Poetical Works of Edgar Allan Poe.* nd. Doran. early ed. 8vo. G. B17. $75.00

DULAC, Edmund. *Stories From the Arabian Nights.* 1911. Hodder Stoughton. 8vo. 24 mc pl. VG. B17. $50.00

DULL, Paul S. *Battle History of Imperial Japanese Navy.* 1978. Naval Inst. 433p. VG. A17. $10.00

DULLES, Allen. *Great Spy Stories.* 1948. Castle. 2nd. VG/VG. P3. $15.00

DULLES, Foster. *American Red Cross, a History.* 1950. NY. 1st ed. 544p. VG. A13. $35.00

DULLES, Foster. *Eastward Ho!* 1931. London. VG. O7. $35.00

DULLES, Foster. *Lowered Boats.* 1933. NY. 1st ed. ils. 292p. VG. B5. $40.00

DUMAS, Alexandre. *Black Tulip.* nd. Collins. hc. VG/G. P3. $15.00

DUMAS, Alexandre. *Camille.* 1937. LEC. 1/1500. ils/sgn Laurencin. 214p. NF. C2. $450.00

DUMAS, Alexandre. *Camille.* 1955. NY. 1/1500. ils/sgn Bernard Lamotte. F/case. T10. $75.00

DUMAS, Alexandre. *Chevalier d'Harmental.* 1899. Little Brn. VG. P3. $20.00

DUMAS, Alexandre. *Chicot the Jester.* 1956. Collins Classics. hc. VG/G. P3. $15.00

DUMAS, Alexandre. *Count of Monte-Cristo.* 1846. London. Chapman Hall. 2 vol. 1st Eng-language ed. engravings. aeg. F. H3. $425.00

DUMAS, Alexandre. *Count of Monte-Cristo.* 1901. NY. 2 vol. 12mo. teg. half red leather. VG. H3. $50.00

DUMAS, Alexandre. *Edmund Dantes.* 1911. Leslie-Judge. VG. P3. $30.00

DUMAS, Alexandre. *Queen's Necklace.* nd. Collins. hc. leather. F. P3. $20.00

DUMAS, Alexandre. *Works of...* 1893-1895. Boston. Estes Lauriat. 10 vol. deluxe ltd ed. 1/1000. teg. red morocco. F. H3. $625.00

DUMAS, Claudine; see Malzberg, Barry.

DUMAYNE, Frederick. *Reminiscences of Frederick Dumayne.* 1945. Aberdeen. private prt. 52p. VG. M8. $85.00

DUMBAULD, Edward. *Life & Legal Writings of Hugo Grotius.* 1968. Norman, OK. G/dj. M11. $35.00

DUNBAR, Alexander. *Treatise on the Diseases Incident to the Horse...* 1871. Wilmington. James Webb. 1st ed. G. O3. $75.00

DUNBAR, C.O. *Earth.* 1967. World. 252p. cloth. VG/dj. D8. $25.00

DUNBAR, C.O. *Historical Geology.* 1949. NY. John Wiley. 567p. G. D8. $15.00

DUNBAR, Paul Laurence. *Candle-Lightin' Time.* 1901. Dodd Mead. 1st ed. photos. gilt cloth. F/dj. B24. $750.00

DUNBAR, Paul Laurence. *Joggin' Erlong.* 1906. Dodd Mead. photos. orig red calico/photo label. F. C6. $300.00

DUNBAR, Paul Laurence. *Joggin' Erlong.* 1906. Dodd Mead. 1st ed. sepia photos. 119p. VG. B10. $250.00

DUNBAR, Paul Laurence. *Poems of Cabin & Field.* 1900. Dodd Mead. ils Alice Morse. NF. M19. $150.00

DUNBAR, Paul Laurence. *Poems of Cabin & Field.* 1902. Dodd Mead. 125p. VG-. B10. $125.00

DUNBAR, Paul Laurence. *Uncalled.* 1898. Dodd Mead. 1st ed. author's 1st novel. 255p. B bdg. fair. B10. $75.00

DUNBAR, Sophie. *Behind Eclaire's Doors.* 1993. NY. 1st ed. author's 1st book. F/F. H11. $25.00

DUNBAR, Tony. *Crooked Man.* 1994. Putnam. 1st ed. F/F. P3. $22.00

DUNBAR & RODGERS. *Principles of Stratigraphy.* 1957. NY. John Wiley. 356p. VG. D8. $20.00

DUNCAN, Dave. *Cursed.* 1995. Ballantine. 1st ed. RS. F/NF. G10. $12.00

DUNCAN, Dave. *Upland Outlaws.* 1993. Ballantine. 1st ed. F/F. G10. $12.00

DUNCAN, David. *Another Tree in Eden.* 1956. Heinemann. 1st ed. NF/NF. P3. $40.00

DUNCAN, Francis. *Dangerous Mr X.* 1939. Herbert Jenkins. 1st ed. VG. P3. $35.00

DUNCAN, Kunigunde. *Tether: Una Gray's Story.* 1953. Boston. Page. 1st imp. 394p. F/dj. A17. $10.00

DUNCAN, Louis. *Medical Men in the American Revolution.* 1970. NY. 414p. VG. A13. $100.00

DUNCAN, Peter; see Blassingame, Lurton.

DUNCAN, Robert L. *China Dawn.* 1988. Delacorte. 1st ed. VG/VG. P3. $20.00

DUNCAN, Robert L. *Temple Dogs.* 1977. Morrow. 1st ed. VG/VG. P3. $18.00

DUNCAN, Shirley. *Two Wheels to Adventure.* 1957. London. 1st ed. sgn. 8vo. 222p. gr cloth. VG. B11. $25.00

DUNCAN, T. Bentley. *Atlantic Islands.* 1972. Chicago. VG. O7. $25.00

DUNCAN, William J. *RMS Queen Mary: Queen of Queens.* 1969. Grosset Dunlap. 1st ed. sgn. 287p. VG/worn. B11. $25.00

DUNHILL, Alfred. *Gentle Art of Smoking.* 1954. Putnam. 1st ed. VG/VG. N4. $60.00

DUNKIN, Edwin. *Midnight Sky.* ca 1869. Religious Tract Soc. ils/charts. 326p. K5. $150.00

DUNLAP, Knight. *Religion: Its Function in Human Life...* 1946. McGraw Hill. 362p. emb red cloth. NF. G1. $65.00

DUNLAP, Orrin E. *Advertising by Radio.* 1929. NBC. ARC/1st ed. 186p. bl cloth. F. B14. $55.00

DUNLAP, Susan. *Death & Taxes.* 1992. Delacorte. 2nd. F/F. P3. $18.00

DUNLAP, Susan. *Karma.* nd. Severn. 1st Eng hc ed. F/F. M19. $45.00

DUNLAP. *Gunsmithing: A Manual of Firearms Design, Construction...* 1963. Harrisburg. Stackpole. 2nd. 742p. VG/worn. A4. $55.00

DUNLOP, Richard. *Great Trails of the West.* 1971. Abingdon. 1st ed. sgn. 320p. F/dj. A17. $15.00

DUNN, Ballard S. *Brazil: Home for Southerners; or, Practical Account...* 1866. NY/New Orleans. 300p. gilt gr cloth. G. B14. $220.00

DUNN, Dorothy. *Murder's Web.* 1950. Harper. sgn. VG/VG. P3. $30.00

DUNN, J. Allan. *Boru: The Story of an Irish Wolfhound.* nd. Grosset Dunlap. VG/G. P3. $12.00

DUNN, Katherine. *Attic.* 1970. Harper. 1st ed. author's 1st book. F/F. B4. $275.00

DUNN, L.C. *Genetics in the 20th Century: Essays...* 1951. NY. 1st ed. 634p. NF. B14. $45.00

DUNNE, John Gregory. *Dutch Shea, Jr.* 1982. NY. Linden. 1st ed. rem mk. F/F. H11. $20.00

DUNNE, John Gregory. *Harp.* 1989. Simon Schuster. F/F. A20. $12.00

DUNNE, John Gregory. *Playland.* Franklin Lib. 1st ed thus. sgn. VG. M17. $30.00

DUNNE, Peter Masten. *Juan Antonio Balthasar, Padre Visador to Sonora Frontier...* 1957. Tucson. AZ Pioneers' Hist Soc. 1/600. 8vo. F/dj. T10. $100.00

DUNNE, Peter Masten. *Pioneer Black Robes on the West Coast.* 1940. Berkeley. 1st ed. 8vo. 286p. gilt red cloth. F. T10. $100.00

DUNNETT, Dorothy. *Dolly & the Nanny Bird.* 1982. Knopf. 1st ed. VG/VG. P3. $18.00

DUNNETT, Dorothy. *King Hereafter.* 1982. Michael Joseph. 1st ed. NF/NF. P3. $27.00

DUNNETT, Dorothy. *Photogenic Soprano.* 1968. Houghton Mifflin. 1st ed. VG/VG. P3. $30.00

DUNNING, H.W. *Today on the Nile.* 1905. Pott. 1st ed. 17 pl/1 fld map. 270p. VG. W1. $12.00

DUNNING, John. *Booked To Die.* 1992. Scribner. 1st ed. sgn. xl. VG/F. A20. $85.00

DUNNING, John. *Bookman's Wake.* 1995. NY. 1st ed. sgn. F/F. B5. $75.00

DUNNING, John. *Tune in Yesterday.* 1976. Hall. 1st ed. VG/VG. B5. $100.00

DUNNINGTON, G. Waldo. *Carl Friedrich Gauss: Titan of Science.* 1955. NY. Hafner. 1st ed. 8vo. 479p. xl. K5. $35.00

DUNPHY, Jack. *Dear Genius: A Memoir of My Life With Truman Capote.* 1987. NY. 1st ed. F/F. A11. $20.00

DUNSANY, Lord. *Alexander & Three Small Plays.* 1926. Putnam. 1st ed. VG. P3. $40.00

DUNSANY, Lord. *Ghosts of the Heaviside.* 1980. Owlswick. F/F. P3. $20.00

DUNSANY, Lord. *Mr Jorkens Remembers Africa.* 1934. Heinemann. 1st ed. VG. P3. $125.00

DUNSANY, Lord. *Sword of the Welleran & Other Stories.* 1907. London. Allen. 1st ed. contemporary gr coarse-grained morocco. F. C2. $125.00

DUNSANY, Lord. *Sword of Welleran.* nd. Boston. Luce. ils. VG. B5. $55.00

DUNTHORNE, Gordon. *Flower & Fruit Prints of the 18th & Early 19th Centuries.* nd. rpt of 1938 ed. 1/250. 80 full-p pl. 289p. F. A4. $125.00

DUPLAIX, Georges. *Gaston & Josephine.* 1936. Harper. 1st ed. ils. 48p. G. D1. $85.00

DUPLAIX, Georges. *Gaston & Josephine.* 1948. Simon Schuster. 1st ed thus. ils Rojankovsky. VG. D1. $37.50

DUPLAIX, Georges. *Merry Shipwreck.* 1942. Harper. 1st ed. ils Tibor Gergeley. VG+. P2. $42.00

DUPLAIX, Georges. *Pee-Gloo.* 1935. Harper. 1st ed. ils Duplaix. VG. D1. $200.00

DUPREY, Jacques. *Voyage aux Origines Francaises de L'Uruguay.* 1952. Montevideo. VG/wrp. O7. $75.00

DUPREY, Kenneth. *Old Houses on Nantucket.* 1965. NY. Architectural Pub. 2nd. VG/VG. B5. $55.00

DURAND, Loup. *Daddy.* 1988. Villard. 1st ed. F/F. H11. $30.00

DURAND, Loup. *Jaguar.* 1990. Villard. 1st ed. F/F. H11. $25.00

DURANT & DURANT. *Pictorial History of American Ships.* 1953. NY. Barnes. G/dj. A16. $38.00

DURBIN. *Observations in Europe, Principally in France...* 1844. NY. vol 2 only. 12mo. 312p. xl. G. T3. $15.00

DURDEN, Charles. *Fifth Law of Hawkins.* 1990. St Martin. 1st ed. NF/NF. P3. $20.00

DURGIN. *Hand Papermaking.* 1986 1992. Minneapolis. 4to. VG+/wrp. A4. $145.00

DURHAM, Victor G. *Submarine Boys, for the Flag.* 1910. Altemus. ils. G+. P12. $5.00

DURHAM, Victor G. *Submarine Boys on Duty.* 1909. Saafield. 1st ed. ils. G+/G+. P12. $10.00

DURIE, Alistair. *Weird Tales.* 1979. Jupiter. 1st ed. NF/worn. R10. $20.00

DURRELL, Gerald. *Talking Parcel.* 1974. London. Collins. 1st ed. 8vo. 190p. F/F. T5. $30.00

DURRELL, Lawrence. *Clea.* 1960. London. Faber. 1st ed. red cloth. F/F. B24. $100.00

DURRELL, Lawrence. *Dark Labyrinth.* 1962. Dutton. 1st ed. F/F. M19. $45.00

DURRELL, Lawrence. *Nunquam.* 1970. London. 1st ed. sgn. F/F. C6. $100.00

DURRELL, Lawrence. *Quinx.* 1985. Viking. 1st ed. F/F. A20. $14.00

DURRELL, Lawrence. *Red Limbo Lingo. A Poetry Notebook.* 1971. NY. Dutton. 1st ed. 1/200. sgn. gilt red cloth. F/blk case. B24. $175.00

DURRELL, Lawrence. *Tunc.* 1968. London. 1st ed. F/NF. C6. $40.00

DURSO, Joseph. *Amazing.* 1970. Houghton Mifflin. 1st ed. VG/G. P8. $15.00

DURSO, Joseph. *Casey.* 1967. Prentice Hall. 1st ed. VG/VG. P8. $25.00

DURST, Paul. *Florentine Table.* 1980. Scribner. 1st ed. F/F. P3. $20.00

DUTHIE, Eric. *Mystery & Adventure Stories for Girls.* 1962. Odhams. 1st ed. hc. VG/VG. P3. $25.00

DUTOURD, Jean. *Dog's Head.* 1951. John Lehmann. 1st ed. VG/VG. P3. $40.00

DUTTON, Benjamin. *Navigation & Nautical Astronomy.* 1942. US Naval Inst. ils/graphs. gilt bl bdg. VG. P12. $8.00

DUTTON, Fred W. *Life on the Great Lakes: A Wheelman's Story.* 1981. Detroit. Wayne State. AN. A16. $25.00

DUTTON, June. *Peanuts Cook Book.* 1969. Determined. ils Schulz. F/VG+. C8. $20.00

DUVAL. *Entwicklung und Lehren des Krieges in Spanien.* 1938. Berlin. fld map/ils. 190p. G+. B18. $45.00

DUVEEN. *Bibliotheca Alchemica et Chemica, an Annotated Catalogue...* nd. rpt of 1949 Weil ed. 1/150. 16 pl. 691p. F. A4. $150.00

DUVOISIN, Roger. *And There Was America.* 1938. Knopf. 1st ed. 75p. gray cloth. G+. T5. $25.00

DUVOISIN, Roger. *Donkey-Donkey.* 1933. Whitman. 1st ed. 8vo. VG. M5. $45.00

DUVOISIN, Roger. *Lonely Veronica.* nd. Knopf. sm 4to. unp. NF. C14. $10.00

DUYCKINCK, E.A. *History of the War for the Union: Civil, Military & Naval.* 1861. NY. 3 vol. steel engravings. marbled ep. brn half leather. B30. $275.00

DUYCKINCK & DUYCKINCK. *Cyclopaedia of American Literature.* 1855. NY. 2 vol. VG. O7. $125.00

DWIGHT, Allan. *To the Walls of Cartagena.* 1967. Colonial Williamsburg. ils Leonard Vosburgh. 161p. VG. B10. $12.00

DWIGHT, Theodore. *History of Connecticut From First Settlement to Present...* 1859. NY. 450p. VG. B14. $75.00

DWIGHT, Timothy. *Travels in New England & New York.* 1969. Harvard. 4 vol. VG/VG case. M17. $50.00

DWIGHT, Timothy. *Travels; In New England & New York.* 1821-1822. New Haven. 4 vol. 1st ed. 3 fld maps. orig brd. VG. C6. $500.00

DWYER, Deanna; see Koontz, Dean R.

DWYER, K.R.; see Koontz, Dean R.

DWYER, MASON & MURDOCH. *New Perspectives on Politics...of Early Modern Scotland.* nd. Edinburgh. John Donald. 8vo. 329p. F/NF. P4. $20.00

DYER. *Pompeii: Its History, Buildings & Antiquities...* 1871. np. ils/fld maps. VG. A4. $35.00

DYERS, William E. *Dyers Story.* 1944. NY. 1st ed. VG/VG. B5. $22.50

DYJAK & WILKINS. *Bertha's Garden.* 1995. Houghton Mifflin. 1st ed. 12mo. unp. F/F. C14. $12.00

DYKES, Jeff C. *Western High Spots: Reading & Collecting Guides.* 1977. Northland. 1st ed. inscr. F/F. A18. $75.00

DYKES, Jeff. *Fifty Great Western Illustrators.* 1975. Northland. 1st collector's ed. 1/200. sgn. M/case. A18. $200.00

DYKES, Robert. *Amateur Cinematographer's Handbook on Movie Making.* 1931. Boston. 111p. red cloth. VG. B5. $100.00

DYKSTRA, Lenny. *Nails.* 1987. Garden City. 1st ed. VG/VG. B5. $25.00

DYLAN, Thomas. *Adventures in the Skin Trade & Other Stories.* 1955. New Directions. 1st ed. 275p. VG/dj. M20. $62.00

DYLAN, Thomas. *Quite Early One Morning.* 1954. New Directions. 1st ed. 239p. VG/dj. M20. $42.00

DYSON, Freeman. *Infinite in All Directions.* 1988. Harper Row. 8vo. 321p. F/F. K5. $15.00

DYSON, John. *South Sea Dream: Adventure in Paradise.* 1982. Little Brn. photos. 243p. VG/dj. T7. $22.00

DYSON. *Pictures to Print: The 19th-Century Engraving Trade.* 1984. 4to. ils. 234p. VG/VG. A4. $65.00

DZIEMIANOWICZ & WEINBERG. *Famous Fantastic Mysteries.* 1991. Gramercy. 1st ed. F/F. P3. $20.00

DZIEMIANOWICZ & WEINBERG. *Hard-Boiled Detectives.* 1992. Gramercy. 1st ed. F/F. P3. $20.00

DZIEMIANOWICZ & WEINBERG. *Tough Guys & Dangerous Dames.* 1993. Barnes Noble. F/F. P3. $15.00

EAGAN, Pierce. *Life of an Actor.* 1825. London. 27 full-p ils by Cruikshank. gilt full calf. F. B14. $400.00

EAGER, Edward. *Mouse Manor.* 1952. Ariel. 1st ed. ils Beryl Bailey-Jones. VG. P2. $20.00

EAGLETON, D.F. *Writers & Writings in Texas.* 1913. Broadway. 1st ed. teg. VG. H7. $25.00

EALAND, C.A. *Insects & Man: An Account of the Most Important Harmful...* 1915. NY. 16 pl. 341p. gr cloth. VG. B14. $100.00

EAMES, Genevieve Torrey. *Horse To Remember.* 1947. Messner. 1st ed. 146p. tan cloth. VG/G. T5. $30.00

EAMES & MACDANIELS. *Introduction to Plant Anatomy.* 1925. McGraw Hill. 1st ed/6th imp. 8vo. 364p. cloth. B1. $35.00

EARL, Guy Chaffee. *Enchanted Valley & Other Sketches.* 1976. Glendale. Arthur Clark. 8vo. 160p. gilt gray cloth. T10. $50.00

EARLE, Peter. *Prophet in the Wilderness.* 1971. Austin, TX. 1st ed. 254p. dj. F3. $20.00

EARLE, Peter. *Sack of Panama.* 1981. London. VG. O7. $15.00

EARLE, Peter. *Wreck of the Almiranta.* 1979. Macmillan. 1st ed. photos. 260p. NF/VG. P12. $22.00

EARLE. *Two Centuries of Costume in America: MDCXX-MDCCCXX.* 1903. np. 2 vol. 96 pl. 824p. NF. A4. $145.00

EARLEY, Tony. *Here We Are in Paradise.* 1994. Boston/NY. Little Brn. 1st ed. author's 1st book. sgn. F/F. M23. $40.00

EARLEY, Tony. *Here We Are in Paradise.* 1994. Little Brn. 1st ed. author's 1st book. F/F. M23. $35.00

EARLEY, Tony. *Here We Are in Paradise.* 1994. Little Brn. 1st ed. rem mk. F/F. H11. $30.00

EARLY, Jack; see Scoppetone, Sandra.

EARNSHAW, Brian. *Starclipper & Song Wars.* 1985. Methuen. decor brd. VG. P3. $13.00

EASSON & ESSICK. *William Blake: Book Illustrator: A Bibliography...* 1972. np. 4to. 66 pl. 72p. VG. A4. $95.00

EASTLAKE, Martha. *Rattlesnake Under Glass: A Roundup of Authentic Western...* 1965. Simon Schuster. 1st ed. VG+/dj. B4. $75.00

EASTON, Carol. *Straight Ahead.* 1973. NY. 1st ed. VG/VG. B5. $30.00

EASTON, Nat. *Bill for Damages.* 1958. Roy. 1st ed. VG/VG. P3. $18.00

EASTON, Robert. *Lord of the Beasts: Saga of Buffalo Jones...* 1961. Tucson. 2nd. 8vo. ils. 287p. F/NF. T10. $25.00

EASTWOOD, James. *Diamonds Are Deadly.* 1969. McKay. 1st ed. NF/NF. H11. $20.00

EASTWOOD, T. *Stanford's Geological Atlas of Great Britain.* 1964. London. Edward Stanford. redrawn/rewritten ed. 288p. NF/dj. D8. $15.00

EATON, Charles Edward. *Countermoves.* 1962. NY. 32p. dj. A17. $7.50

EATON, Clement. *History of the Southern Confederacy.* 1954. Macmillan. 1st ed. 351p. cloth. NF/VG. M8. $45.00

EATON, John P. *Falling Star.* 1991. Norton. VG/dj. A16. $30.00

EATON, Seymour. *Robert Burns' Rare Print Collection.* 1900. Phil. Kennedy. Connoisseur ed. 8 fld w/31 pl. G. A17. $45.00

EATON, Seymour. *Roosevelt Bears: Their Travel & Adventure.* 1906. Phil. 1st ed. ils VF Campbell. 180p. VG+. D1. $325.00

EBBINGHAUS, Hermann. *Uber das Gedachtnis: Untersuchungen...* 1885. Leipzig. Duncker Humblot. 167p. VG. G1. $1,650.00

EBERHARD, Wolfram. *Early Chinese Cultures & Their Development: A New Working...* 1938. GPO. revised. trans. VG. P4. $9.50

EBERHART, Mignon G. *Alpine Condo Crossfire.* 1984. Random. 1st ed. NF/NF. P3. $15.00

EBERHART, Mignon G. *Another Man's Murder.* 1957. Random. 1st ed. NF/NF. H11. $25.00

EBERHART, Mignon G. *Bayou Road.* 1979. Random. 1st ed. F/F. H11. $20.00

EBERHART, Mignon G. *Bayou Road.* 1979. Random. 1st ed. VG/VG. P3. $15.00

EBERHART, Mignon G. *Casa Madrone.* 1980. Random. 1st ed. VG/VG. P3. $15.00

EBERHART, Mignon G. *Family Affair.* 1981. Random. 1st ed. F/F. H11. $20.00

EBERHART, Mignon G. *Family Affair.* 1981. Random. 1st ed. VG/VG. P3. $15.00

EBERHART, Mignon G. *Hand in Glove.* 1937. Crime Club. 1st Eng ed. VG/VG. M19. $85.00

EBERHART, Mignon G. *Hangman's Whip.* 1942. Triangle. VG. P3. $10.00

EBERHART, Mignon G. *Hunt With the Hounds.* 1950. Detective BC. 247p. VG/G. B10. $10.00

EBERHART, Mignon G. *Pattern.* 1937. Doubleday Doran. 1st ed. G. P3. $20.00

EBERHART, Mignon G. *Postmark Murder.* 1956. Random. 1st ed. VG/NF. H11. $25.00

EBERHART, Mignon G. *White Cockatoo.* 1933. Crime Club. 1st ed. VG. P3. $40.00

EBERHART, Mignon G. *Witness at Large.* 1966. Random. 1st ed. F/F. P3. $20.00

EBERHART, Richard. *Bravery of Earth.* 1930. NY. 1st Am ed. sgn. F/NF. C6. $150.00

EBON, Martin. *They Knew the Unknown.* 1971. World. 1st ed. VG. P3. $15.00

EBY & FLEMING. *Case of the Malevolent Twin.* 1946. Dutton. 1st ed. G. P3. $12.00

ECCLES, Audrey. *Obstetrics...in Tudor & Stuart England.* 1982. Kent. 1st ed. 145p. VG/dj. A13. $40.00

ECHOLS, Samuel Anthony. *Proceedings of the State Agricultural Society...* 1869. Atlanta. Economical Job Prt Office. 1st ed. 70p. VG/wrp. M8. $250.00

ECKERT, Allan W. *Conquerors.* 1970. Little Brn. 1st ed. 720p. cloth. VG+/dj. M20. $40.00

ECKERT, Allan W. *Crossbreed.* 1968. Boston. 1st ed. F/F. B5. $35.00

ECKERT, Allan W. *Frontiersmen.* 1967. Little Brn. 1st ed. 626p. VG+/dj. M20. $60.00

ECKERT, Allan W. *Great Auk.* 1963. Little Brn. 1st ed. sgn. 202p. VG/dj. M20. $77.00

ECKERT, Allan W. *Wilderness War.* 1978. Little Brn. 1st ed. 496p. VG+/dj. M20. $25.00

ECKHOFF & MAURO. *List of Foreign Service Post Records in National Archives.* 1967. WA. VG/wrp. O7. $10.00

ECKLEY & PERRET. *Young French Chef...a First Cookbook.* 1969. Platt Munk. ils Catherine Cambier. F/VG. M5. $40.00

ECKSTEIN, Gustav. *Pet Shop.* 1944. Harper. 1st ed. sgn. VG/dj. M20. $27.00

ECKSTROM, Fannie Hardy. *Penobscot Man.* 1972. Somerworth. facsimile of 1924 ed. 351p. VG/dj. B5. $40.00

ECO, Umberto. *Foucault's Pendulum.* 1988. HBJ. 1st Am ed. F/F. N4. $30.00

ECO, Umberto. *Foucault's Pendulum.* 1988. HBJ. 1st ed. sgn. rem mk. F/F. B35. $55.00

ECO, Umberto. *Name of the Rose*. 1983. HBJ. 1st Am ed. F/F. B4. $150.00

ECO, Umberto. *Postscript to the Name of the Rose*. 1983. HBJ. 1st ed. F/F. A20. $21.00

EDDINGS, David. *Demon Lord of Karanda*. 1988. Del Rey. 1st ed. NF/NF. P3. $20.00

EDDINGS, David. *Domes of Fire*. 1993. Del Rey. 1st ed. F/F. P3. $22.00

EDDINGS, David. *Sorceress of Darshiva*. 1989. Del Rey. 1st ed. VG/VG. P3. $20.00

EDDINGTON, A.S. *Nature of the Physical World*. 1929. NY. 361p. VG. A13. $15.00

EDDINGTON, A.S. *Stars & Adams*. 1927. Clarendon. 2nd. 127p. cloth. G. K5. $20.00

EDEL, Leon. *Psychological Novel 1900-1950*. 1961. London. 1st revised ed. inscr. NF/NF. A11. $40.00

EDEL & LAURENCE. *Bibliography of Henry James*. 1961. np. 2nd. ils. 438p. VG. A4. $125.00

EDEN, Dorothy. *Important Family*. 1982. Morrow. 1st ed. F/F. P3. $14.00

EDEN, Dorothy. *Time of the Dragon*. 1975. Hodder Stoughton. 1st ed. VG/VG. P3. $18.00

EDEN, Dorothy. *Whistle for the Crows*. 1962. Hodder Stoughton. 1st ed. VG/VG. P3. $25.00

EDERS, Bruno. *Full-Length Animated Feature Films*. 1977. Hastings. cloth. NF/VG. D2. $30.00

EDEY & JOHANSON. *Lucy: The Beginnings of Humankind*. 1981. Simon Schuster. 1st ed. sgns. F/F. B2. $50.00

EDGERTON, Clyde. *Floatplane Notebooks*. 1988. Algonquin. 1st ed. sgn. F/F. M23. $30.00

EDGERTON, Clyde. *Killer Diller*. 1991. Algonquin. 1st ed. NF/F. N4. $22.50

EDGERTON, Clyde. *Raney*. 1985. Chapel Hill. AP. author's 1st book. F/wrp. w/pub letter. C2. $550.00

EDGERTON, Clyde. *Raney*. 1985. Chapel Hill. Algonquin. 1st ed. author's 1st book. inscr/dtd 1992. F/NF. C2. $275.00

EDGERTON, Clyde. *Understanding the Floatplane*. 1987. Chapel Hill. 1st ed. 1/500. sgn. F/wrp. C2. $65.00

EDGLEY, Leslie. *Fear No More*. 1946. Simon Schuster. 1st ed. G/G. P3. $18.00

EDINGTON, May. *Dance of Youth*. 1932. Macauley. 1st ed. NF/VG+. B4. $65.00

EDMAN, Irwin. *Candle in the Dark*. 1939. Viking. 1st ed. F/NF. B35. $22.00

EDMINSTER, F. *Ruffed Grouse*. 1947. Macmillan. 1st ed. VG. H7. $35.00

EDMONDS, Harry. *Secret Voyage*. 1946. MacDonald. VG. P3. $10.00

EDMONDS, I.G. *Magic Brothers*. 1979. Elsevier/Nelson. 1st ed. hc. VG/VG. P3. $15.00

EDMONDS, Walter D. *Musket & the Cross*. 1968. Boston. 1st ed. VG/VG. B5. $30.00

EDMONSON, Munro. *Heaven Born Merida & Its Destiny*. 1986. Austin, TX. 1st ed. 309p. dj. F3. $40.00

EDMUNDS, Abe Craddock. *Ulysses & Other Poems*. 1923. RB De Vine. 62p. G. B10. $12.00

EDMUNDS, Murrell. *Earthenware: A Group of Stories*. 1930. Lynchburg. Little Book Shop. author's 2nd novel. G. B10. $12.00

EDMUNDS, Murrell. *Moon of My Delight: A Play in 3 Acts*. 1960. Yoseleff. 1/1000. sgn. VG/box. B10. $15.00

EDMUNDS, Murrell. *Not Many — But Free!* 1943. self pub. inscr. VG. B10. $12.00

EDMUNDS, Murrell. *Shadow of a Great Rock*. 1969. Barnes. inscr. 180p. VG/G. B10. $20.00

EDMUNDS, Murrell. *They Don't Cost You a Thin Dime; or, Songs for Nothing*. 1961. np. inscr. VG. B10. $10.00

EDMUNDS, Pocahantas Wright. *Tales of the Virginia Coast*. 1950. np. sgn. VG/G. B10. $15.00

EDMUNDS, Pocohantas Wright. *Land of Sand: Legends of the NC Coast*. 1941. Garrett Massie. sgn. ils MM Junkin. VG. B10. $20.00

EDRIDGE-GREEN, Frederick W. *Memory: Its Logical Relations & Cultivation*. 1888. London. Bailliere Tindall Cox. 12mo. maroon cloth. G. G1. $60.00

EDSALL, F.S. *World of Psychic Phenomena*. 1958. McKay. 1st ed. VG. P3. $20.00

EDWARDS, Anne. *Road to Tara: Life of Margaret Mitchell*. 1983. Ticknor Fields. 1st ed. 369p. VG/VG. B10. $25.00

EDWARDS, Eleanor. *World Famous Great Mystery Stories*. 1960. Hart. hc. VG. P3. $15.00

EDWARDS, Florence Dunn. *Menino*. 1940. Grosset Dunlap. sm 4to. NF/partial. M5. $25.00

EDWARDS, George C. *Treatise on the Poers & Duties of Justice of the Peace...* 1836. Ithaca. G. V4. $60.00

EDWARDS, George Wharton. *Forest of Arden With Some of Its Legends*. 1914. NY. Stokes. 1st ed. sgn. 8vo. 216p. VG. B11. $65.00

EDWARDS, Harry Stillwell. *Eneas Africanus*. 1920. JW Burke. 47p. VG/stiff wrp. B10. $15.00

EDWARDS, Harry Stillwell. *His Defense & Other Stories*. 1899. NY. 1st ed. VG. B5. $40.00

EDWARDS, Harry Stillwell. *Sons & Fathers*. 1937. Atlanta. Little Brn. ltd ed. sgn. G. B11. $20.00

EDWARDS, Leo. *Andy Blake (#1)*. 1928 (1921). Grosset Dunlap. lists 2 titles. 280p. cloth. VG/dj. M20. $40.00

EDWARDS, Leo. *Andy Blake's Comet Coaster (#2)*. 1928. Grosset Dunlap. lists 2 titles. 247p. VG/VG. M20. $60.00

EDWARDS, Leo. *Jerry Todd & the Bob-Tailed Elephant (#9)*. 1929. Grosset Dunlap. lists 13 titles. 235p. VG/VG. M20. $50.00

EDWARDS, Leo. *Jerry Todd & the Oak Island Treasure*. 1925. Grosset Dunlap. ils Bert Salg. 233p. VG/dj. M20. $57.00

EDWARDS, Leo. *Jerry Todd & the Waltzing Hen*. 1925. Grosset Dunlap. ils BN Salg. G. P12. $5.00

EDWARDS, Leo. *Jerry Todd in the Whispering Cave*. 1927. Grosset Dunlap. G+. P12. $6.00

EDWARDS, Leo. *Poppy Ott & the Freckled Goldfish (#5)*. 1928. Grosste Dunlap. 269p. VG/dj. M20. $47.00

EDWARDS, Lionel. *Thy Servant the Horse*. 1925. London. Country Life. 1st ed. ils. VG/VG. O3. $85.00

EDWARDS, Peter. *Blood Brothers*. 1990. Key Porter. 1st ed. VG. P3. $25.00

EDWARDS & LORT. *Bibliography of British Columbia, Years of Growth...* 1975. U of Victoria. 4to. 446p. F. A4. $95.00

EDWIN, Maribel. *Sound Alibi*. 1938. Hillman Curl. 1st ed. VG. P3. $30.00

EELLS & O'DAY. *High Times Hard Times*. 1981. Putnam. 1st ed. rem mk. F/NF. B2. $45.00

EFFINGER, George Alec. *Death in Florence*. 1978. Doubleday. 1st ed. xl. VG. P3. $5.00

EFFINGER, George Alec. *Fire in the Sun*. 1989. Doubleday. 1st ed. inscr. F/F. B11. $35.00

EFFINGER, George Alec. *Heroics*. 1979. Doubleday. 1st ed. VG/VG. P3. $20.00

EFFINGER, George Alec. *Look Away.* 1990. Eugene. Axolotl. sgn Effinger/Benford. F/wrp. B11. $20.00

EFFINGER, George Alec. *Mixed Feelings.* 1974. Harper Row. 1st ed. F/F. P3. $20.00

EFFINGER, George Alec. *Shadow Money.* 1988. Tor. 1st ed. inscr. F/F. B11. $35.00

EFFINGER, George Alec. *What Entropy Means to Me.* 1972. Doubleday. 1st ed. NF/NF. P3. $15.00

EFFINGER, George Alec. *When Gravity Falls.* 1987. Arbor. 1st ed. F/F. P3. $17.00

EFFINGER, George Alec. *When Gravity Falls.* 1987. Arbor. 1st ed. inscr. F/F. B11. $50.00

EGAN, Lesley. *Blind Search.* 1977. Crime Club. 1st ed. VG/VG. P3. $20.00

EGAN, Lesley. *Scenes of Crime.* 1976. Crime Club. 1st ed. VG/VG. P3. $20.00

EGON, Nicholas. *Paintings of Jordan.* 1986. London. Scorpion. 48 pl. cloth. NF/dj. W1. $45.00

EHLE, John. *Land Breakers.* 1964. Harper Row. 1st ed. VG/VG. B35. $23.00

EHLE, John. *Move Over, Mountain.* 1957. Morrow. 1st ed. author's 1st book. inscr/dtd 1957. RS. NF/NF. C2. $200.00

EHRLICH, Amy. *Annie, The Storybook Based on the Movie.* 1982. Random. 1st ed. MTI. red brd. F. T5. $25.00

EHRLICH, Gretel. *Heart Mountain.* 1988. Viking. 1st ed. sgn. F/clip. B4. $65.00

EHRLICH, Max. *Deep Is the Blue.* 1964. Doubleday. 1st ed. VG/VG. P3. $18.00

EHRLICH, Max. *Reincarnation in Venice.* 1979. Simon Schuster. 1st ed. VG/VG. P3. $15.00

EICHLER, Alfred. *Death of an Ad Man.* 1954. Abelard Schuman. hc. VG/VG. P3. $15.00

EINARSEN, A.S. *Pronghorn Angelope & Its Management.* 1948. Wildlife Inst. photos. VG. M17. $30.00

EINSTEIN, Albert. *Out of My Later Years.* 1950. Philosophical Lib. 1st ed. NF. B35. $42.00

EINSTINE & INFIELD. *Evolution of Physics.* (1938). Simon Schuster. 15th. 3 pl/drawings. 319p. G/dj. K5. $35.00

EINTIN & YAAKOV. *Public Library Catalog, Ninth Edition.* 1989. HW Wilson. 1338p. VG. A4. $35.00

EISENBERG, Deborah. *Under the 82nd Airborne.* 1992. FSG. 1st ed. F/F. A20. $20.00

EISENBERG, Harvey. *Tom & Jerry & Their Friends.* 1950. Golden Story Book. hc. MTI. VG. P3. $15.00

EISENBERG, Larry. *Best Laid Schemes.* 1971. Macmillan. 1st ed. hc. F/F. P3. $20.00

EISENBERG, Philip. *Won Kim's Ox.* 1956. Follett. 4to. VG/VG. B17. $8.50

EISENHOWER, David. *Eisenhower at War 1943-45.* 1986. NY. 5th prt. 977p. F/dj. A17. $17.50

EISENHOWER, Dwight D. *Pictures I've Kept.* 1969. Doubleday. 1st ed. 237p. gilt blk cloth. NF/dj. B22. $5.50

EISENHOWER, Dwight D. *White House Years.* 1963 & 1965. Garden City. 2 vol. 1st ed. 1/1500. sgn. 8vo. F/pub case. C6. $850.00

EISENHOWER, Julie. *Mystery & Suspense.* 1976. Curtis. hc. VG/VG. P3. $18.00

EISENHOWER & EINENHOWER. *Five-Star Favorites: Recipes From Friends of Mamie & Ike.* 1974. NY. inscr/dtd. 272p. taped dj. A17. $25.00

EISENSTEIN, Phyllis. *Born to Exile.* 1978. Arkham. 1st ed. 1/4148. F/F. T2. $30.00

EISENSTEIN, Phyllis. *Crystal Palace.* 1991. London. Grafton. 1st ed. sgn. F/F. T2. $35.00

EISLER, Steven. *Alien World: Complete Ils Guide.* 1980. Crescent. hc. F/F. P3. $13.00

EISMANN & JANSON. *Far Right.* 1963. McGraw Hill. 1st ed. inscr Eismann. F/NF. B2. $40.00

EISNER, Simon; see Kornbluth, Cyril.

EISNER, Will. *Signal From Space.* 1983. Kitchen Sink. decor brd. VG. P3. $20.00

EITEL, W. *Structural Conversations in Crystalline Systems...* 1958. Geological Soc of Am. 183p. cloth. F. D8. $24.00

EKLUND, Gordon. *Grayspace Beast.* 1976. Doubleday. 1st ed. F/F. P3. $20.00

EKMAN, L.C. *Secenic Geology of the Pacific Northwest.* 1970. Binford Mort. 2nd. 310p. F. D8. $12.00

EKSTROM, Kjell. *Essays & Studies on American Language & Literature.* 1950. Upsala. 197p. VG. B10. $25.00

ELAM, Richard M. *Young Visitor to Mars.* nd. Grosset Dunlap. G/G. P3. $15.00

ELBERT & ELBERT. *Miracle Houseplants.* 1984. Crown. updated ed. lg 8vo. 272p. half cloth. dj. B1. $25.00

ELDBRIDGE, Roger. *Shadow of the Gloom-World.* 1977. Gollancz. 1st ed. F/F. P3. $15.00

ELDER, Michael. *Oil-Seeker.* 1977. Readers Union BC. VG/VG. P3. $8.00

ELDREDGE, Laurence H. *Trials of a Philadelphia Lawyer.* 1968. Phil. Lippincott. G/worn. M11. $25.00

ELDREDGE, N. *Fossils.* 1991. Abrams. 1st ed. 160 photos by Murray Alcosser. M/dj. D8. $30.00

ELDREDGE, Zoeth Skinner. *History of California.* ca 1914. NY. Century History Co. 5 vol. 8vo. emb pigskin. F. T10. $500.00

ELDRIDGE, Charlotte. *Godey Lady Doll.* 1953. Hastings. 1st ed. 209p. VG/dj. M20. $32.00

ELGIN, Suzette Haden. *Gentle Art of Verbal Self-Defense.* nd. Dorset. 22nd. VG. P3. $13.00

ELGIN, Suzette Haden. *Grand Jubilee.* 1981. Doubleday. 1st ed. VG/VG. P3. $15.00

ELIAS & ELIAS. *Elias' Modern Dictionary of Arabic-English.* 1986. Beirut. Dar al-Jil. 912p. VG. W1. $25.00

ELIOT, George. *Daniel Deronda.* 1876. Edinburgh/London. 4 vol. VG. C6. $200.00

ELIOT, George. *Felix Holt the Radical. In Three Volumes.* 1866. Edinburgh/London. Blackwood. 3 vol. 1st ed. 8vo. Carter's D bdg. F. B24. $600.00

ELIOT, George. *George Eliot's Life As Related in Letters & Journals.* 1885-1886. Edinburgh/London. 3 vol. VG. C6. $180.00

ELIOT, Simon. *Some Patterns & Trends in British Publishing 1800-1919.* 1994. London. Bibliographical Soc. 179p. wrp. M11. $20.00

ELIOT, Sonny. *Eliot's Art.* 1972. Wayne St. 1st ed. ils Herzog. VG/VG. A17. $15.00

ELIOT, T.S. *Confidential Clerk.* 1954. Harcourt Brace. 1st ed. NF/NF. B35. $50.00

ELIOT, T.S. *Confidential Clerk.* 1954. London. 1st ed/1st state. NF/NF. C6. $65.00

ELIOT, T.S. *Cultivation of Christmas Trees.* 1956. FSC. 1st ed. F. B35. $70.00

ELIOT, T.S. *Elder Statesman.* 1959. FSC. 1st ed. F/F. M19. $25.00

ELIOT, T.S. *For Lancelot Andrews.* 1929. Doubleday Doran. 1st ed. VG/fair. M19. $85.00

ELIOT, T.S. *From Poe to Valery.* 1948. NY. 1st ed. 1/1500. F/sans. A11. $75.00

ELIOT, T.S. *Notes Towards the Definition of Culture.* 1949. Harcourt Brace. 1st ed. VG/VG. M19. $35.00

ELIOT, T.S. *Old Possum's Book of Practical Cats.* 1939. Harcourt Brace. 1st ed. F/VG. M19. $200.00

ELIOT, T.S. *Old Possum's Book of Practical Cats.* 1982. HBJ. 1st ed thus. ils Gorey. F/F. M19. $25.00

ELIOT, T.S. *Poetry & Drama.* 1951. Cambridge. 1st ed. 8vo. 44p. gilt blk cloth. F/VG. T10. $100.00

ELIOT, T.S. *Three Voices of Poetry.* 1954. Cambridge. 1st ed. NF/NF. M19. $35.00

ELIOTT, E.C. *Kemlo & the Martian Ghosts.* 1954. Thomas Nelson. VG/VG. P3. $18.00

ELIOTT, E.C. *Kemlo & the Sky Horse.* 1954. Thomas Nelson. 1st ed. VG/VG. P3. $20.00

ELIOTT, E.C. *Kemlo & the Zombie Men.* 1958. Thomas Nelson. 1st ed. VG/VG. P3. $20.00

ELKIN, Stanley. *Bad Man.* 1967. Random. 1st ed. F/NF. B2. $60.00

ELKIN, Stanley. *Bad Man.* 1967. Random. 1st ed. NF/NF. M23. $45.00

ELKIN, Stanley. *Boswell.* 1964. Random. 1st ed. author's 1st book. NF/NF. B2. $125.00

ELKIN, Stanley. *Franchiser.* 1976. FSG. 1st ed. F/F. B35. $35.00

ELKIN, Stanley. *George Mills.* 1982. Dutton. 1st ed. NF/NF. B35. $20.00

ELKIN, Stanley. *George Mills.* 1982. Dutton. 1st ed. rem mk. F/F. M23. $25.00

ELKIN, Stanley. *MacGuffin.* 1991. NY. Linden. 1st ed. F/F. M23. $20.00

ELKIN, Stanley. *Mr Ted Bliss.* ARC/ltd ed. 1/1500. sgn/#d. AN/sans. B30. $35.00

ELKINS, Aaron J. *Curses!* 1989. Mysterious. 2nd. F/F. P3. $15.00

ELKINS, Aaron J. *Fellowship of Fear.* 1982. Walker. 1st ed. xl. VG. N4. $40.00

ELKINS, Aaron J. *Icy Clutches.* 1990. Mysterious. 1st ed. F/F. H11/N4. $25.00

ELKINS, Aaron J. *Old Scores.* 1993. Scribner. 1st ed. AN/dj. N4. $25.00

ELKINS & ELKINS. *Rotten Lies.* 1995. Mysterious. 1st ed. rem mk. AN. N4. $17.50

ELLENBERGER, Henri. *Discovery of the Unconscious: History of Evolution...* 1970. NY. 932p. VG. A13. $60.00

ELLER, E.M. *Houses of Peace...Acount of the Moravians...in NC.* 1937. Revell. ils. 287p. VG/VG-. B10. $65.00

ELLER, John. *Charlie & the Ice Man.* 1981. St Martin. 1st ed. VG/VG. P3. $13.00

ELLET, Mrs. *Queens of American Society.* 1868. NY. 12mo. ils. 464p. brn cloth. G. T3. $20.00

ELLIN, Stanley. *Dark Fantasitc.* 1983. Andre Deutsch. 1st ed. F/F. P3. $20.00

ELLIN, Stanley. *House of Cards.* 1967. MacDonald. 1st ed. VG/torn. P3. $15.00

ELLIN, Stanley. *Luxembourg Run.* 1977. Random. 1st ed. NF/NF. P3. $30.00

ELLIN, Stanley. *Star Light, Star Bright.* 1979. Random. 1st ed. NF/NF. P3. $20.00

ELLIN, Stanley. *Stronghold.* 1974. Random. 1st ed. VG/VG. P3. $20.00

ELLIN, Stanley. *Winter After This Summer.* 1960. Random. 1st ed. VG/VG. P3. $35.00

ELLIOT, Bob. *Eastern Brook Trout.* 1950. NY. 1st ed. VG. B5. $25.00

ELLIOT, Elizabeth. *Savage My Kinsman.* 1961. Harper. 1st ed. 4to. 160p. dj. F3. $20.00

ELLIOT, Elizabeth. *Through Gates of Splendor.* 1957. Harper. 1st ed. ils. 256p. F3. $10.00

ELLIOT, James L. *Red Stacks Over the Horizon.* 1967. Grand Rapids. Eerdmans. VG/VG. A16. $65.00

ELLIOT, Jonathan. *Debates in the Several State Conventions on Adoption...* 1996. Buffalo. Wm S Hein. facsimile of 1891 Phil ed. M11. $425.00

ELLIOT, T.J. *Medieval Bestiary.* 1971. Boston. Godine. 1st ed. ils Gillian Tyler. F/dj/case. D1. $65.00

ELLIOT & THACKER. *Beasts & Men.* 1912. London. ils/pl. 299p. gilt red cloth. VG. H3. $30.00

ELLIOTT, Charles. *Turkey Hunting With Charles Elliott.* 1979. McKay. 1st ed. photos. VG/VG. P12. $18.00

ELLIOTT, Don (some); see Silverberg, Robert.

ELLIOTT, H. Chandler. *Reprieve From Paradise.* 1955. Knome. 1st ed. NF/NF. P3. $35.00

ELLIOTT, James W. *Secrets of a Country Doctor.* 1992. Overmountain. photos. 100p. VG/VG. B10. $10.00

ELLIOTT, James. *Black Dahlia.* 1987. Mysterious. 1st ed. B stp on bottom edges. NF/F. H11. $40.00

ELLIOTT, James. *Cold Cold Heart.* 1994. Delacorte. 1st ed. F/F. H11. $30.00

ELLIOTT, Mabel A. *Conflicting Penal Theories in Statutory Criminal Law.* 1931. Chicago. worn. M11. $50.00

ELLIOTT & RICHARDS. *Julia Ward Howe, 1819-1910.* 1915. Boston/NY. 2 vol. 1/450. w/orig ms leaf on despotic rulers. VG+. C6. $200.00

ELLIS, Albert. *Comparison of Use of Direct & Indirect Phrasing...* 1947. Am Psychologial Assn. 41p. prt brn wrp. G1. $35.00

ELLIS, Bret Easton. *Less Than Zero.* 1985. Simon Schuster. 1st ed. NF/NF. P3. $20.00

ELLIS, Bret Easton. *Rules of Attraction.* 1987. Simon Schuster. 1st ed. NF/NF. P3. $18.00

ELLIS, Bruce. *Bishop Lamy's Santa Fe Cathedral.* 1985. NM U. 8vo. ils/plans/photos. 208p. AN/wrp. T10. $10.00

ELLIS, Edward S. *Life of Kit Carson.* 1899. Phil. Wanamaker. 8vo. 260p. gr cloth. NF. T10. $75.00

ELLIS, Edward S. *Shod With Silence.* 1896. Henry Coates. 1st ed. ils. G+. P12. $10.00

ELLIS, John B. *Sights & Secrets of the National Capital.* 1869. US Pub. 512p. VG. B10. $25.00

ELLIS, John. *Sharp End: Fighting Man in WWII.* 1980. NY. BC. F/dj. A17. $7.00

ELLIS, Mel. *No Man for Murder.* 1973. HRW. F/F. P3. $8.00

ELLIS, Ray. *South by Southeast.* 1983. Birmingham. Oxmoor. 1st ed. pl. 122p. cloth. dj. D2. $100.00

ELLIS, William Donohue. *Bounty Lands.* 1952. World. 1st ed. sgn. 492p. VG. B11. $25.00

ELLIS, William Donohue. *Bounty Lands.* 1952. World. 1st ed. sgn. 492p. VG/dj. M20. $42.00

ELLIS & WEST. *Whole World Stamp Catalog.* 1981. NY. Crescent. 1st Am ed. 160p. VG/dj. P4. $25.00

ELLIS. *Home With Books: How Booklovers Live & Care for Their Lib.* 1995. np. 4to. ils. 248p. F/F. A4. $50.00

ELLISON, Harlan. *Again, Dangerous Visions.* nd. BC. VG/VG. P3. $12.00

ELLISON, Harlan. *Approaching Oblivion.* 1974. Walker. sgn. F/F. P3. $100.00

ELLISON, Harlan. *Harlan Ellison's Chocolate Alphabet.* 1978. Last Gasp. 1st ed. F. R10. $15.00

ELLISON, Harlan. *Shatterday.* 1980. Houghton Mifflin. 1st ed. NF/NF. P3. $50.00

ELLISON, Harlan. *Strange Wine*. 1978. Harper Row. 1st ed. sgn. F/NF. M21. $60.00

ELLISON, Ralph. *Shadow & Act*. 1964. NY. 1st ed. sgn. F/F. C6. $275.00

ELLMAN, Richard. *Letters of James Joyce: Vol 2*. 1966. NY. 472p. F/clip. A17. $15.00

ELLROY, James. *Big Nowhere*. 1988. Mysterious. 2nd ed. F/F. P3. $18.00

ELLROY, James. *Black Dahlia*. 1987. Mysterious. 1st ed. NF/NF. P3. $25.00

ELLROY, James. *Blood on the Moon*. 1984. Mysterious. 1st ed. F/NF. B2. $35.00

ELLROY, James. *Blood on the Moon*. 1984. Mysterious. 1st ed. sgn. F/NF. B2. $65.00

ELLROY, James. *Blood on the Moon*. 1985. np. 1st Eng ed. F/F. M19. $50.00

ELLROY, James. *LA Confidential*. 1990. Mysterious. 1st ed. F/F. M19. $25.00

ELLROY, James. *LA Confidential*. 1990. Mysterious. 1st ed. VG/VG. P3. $20.00

ELLROY, James. *White Jazz*. 1992. Knopf. 1st ed. F/F. P3. $22.00

ELLSBERG, Edward. *Captain Paul*. 1941. Literary Guild. G. A16. $15.00

ELLSBERG, Edward. *Hell on Ice: Saga of the Jeannette*. 1938. Dodd Mead. 1st ed. G. A16. $20.00

ELLSBERG, Edward. *On the Bottom*. 1929. Literary Guild. ils. 324p. G+. P12. $12.50

ELLSWORTH, Huntington. *Palestine & Its Transformation*. 1911. Houghton Mifflin. 1st ed. 8vo. 443p. xl. VG. W1. $28.00

ELMAN & PEPER. *Hunting America's Game Animals & Birds*. 1975. Winchester. ils. gilt red bdg. G+/G. P12. $10.00

ELON, Amos. *Timetable*. 1980. Doubleday. VG/VG. P3. $15.00

ELTON, Charles. *Pattern of Animal Communities*. 1966. NY. Wiley. 432p. VG/dj. A10. $22.00

ELWELL, Edward. *Portland & Vicinity*. 1876. Portland. 1st ed. lacks ffe. B5. $70.00

ELWES, H.J. *Elwes Genus Lilium, a Monograph*. 1880. London. 30 color pl/supplement. very scarce. A10. $13,000.00

ELWOOD, Roger. *And Walk Now Gently Through the Fire*. 1972. Chilton. 1st ed. VG/VG. P3. $20.00

ELWOOD, Roger. *Continuum 4*. 1975. Putnam. 1st ed. VG/VG. P3. $20.00

ELWOOD, Roger. *Dystopian Visions*. 1975. Prentice Hall. 1st ed. VG/VG. P3. $20.00

ELWOOD, Roger. *Far Side of Time*. 1974. Dodd Mead. 1st ed. VG/VG. P3. $15.00

ELWOOD, Roger. *Future Kin*. 1974. Doubleday. 1st ed. F/F. P3. $15.00

ELWOOD, Roger. *Monster Tales*. 1974. Rand McNally. 2nd ed. decor brd. VG. P3. $12.00

ELWOOD, Roger. *Other Side of Tomorrow*. 1973. Random. 1st ed. VG/VG. P3. $15.00

ELWOOD, Roger. *Tomorrow's Alternatives*. 1973. Macmillan. 2nd ed. VG/VG. P3. $13.00

ELWOOD, Roger. *Way Out*. 1973. Whitman. hc. decor brd. VG. P3. $8.00

ELWOOD & SILVERBERG. *Epoch*. nd. BC. VG/VG. P3. $10.00

ELY, Ben-Ezra Stile. *There She Blows: Narrative of a Whaling Voyage...* 1971. Wesleyan U. 1st ed thus. 208p. cloth. NF/dj. M20. $25.00

ELY, David. *Trot*. nd. Pantheon. 2nd. VG/VG. P3. $18.00

EMANUEL, Walter. *Dog Day*. 1902. Dutton. 1st Am ed. 16mo. O3. $35.00

EMBLETON & KING. *Glacial & Periglacial Geomorphology*. 1969. Edward Arnold. 2nd. 608p. F/torn. D8. $32.00

EMERSON, Earl W. *Deviant Behavior*. 1988. Morrow. 1st ed. F/F. P3. $18.00

EMERSON, Earl W. *Fat Tuesday*. 1987. Morrow. 1st ed. F/F. P3. $17.00

EMERSON, Earl W. *Help Wanted: Orphans Preferred*. 1990. Morrow. 1st ed. VG/VG. P3. $18.00

EMERSON, F. *North American Arithmetic. Part Third*. 1838. Boston. 12mo. 288p. leather. xl. T3. $12.00

EMERSON, Harry. *Is Your Cosmic Radio Working*. 1972. Coral Gables. Your Cosmic Radio. sgn. 12mo. 192p. VG/VG. B11. $35.00

EMERSON, Jill; see Block, Lawrence.

EMERSON, Ralph Waldo. *Essays of...* 1962. Heritage. 4to. boxed. A17. $15.00

EMERSON, Ralph Waldo. *Miscellanies*. 1884 (1883). Houghton Mifflin. 1st Am ed. 425p. gilt bl cloth. VG. B22. $30.00

EMERSON, Ralph Waldo. *Nature*. 1929. Munich. Bremer. 1/250 (of 530 total). 4to. 88p. xl. F. B24. $300.00

EMERSON, Thomas I. *System of Freedom of Expression*. 1970. Random. VG/dj. M11. $65.00

EMERSON, Thomas I. *Toward a General Theory of First Amendment*. 1966. Random. M11. $45.00

EMERY, Carlyle. *Twinkle Town Tales Book No 4*. 1929. St Louis. Hamilton-Brown Shoe Co. 8vo. VG. M5. $25.00

EMERY, K.O. *Sea Off Southern California*. 1960. NY. VG. O7. $25.00

EMMERMANN, Curt. *Leica-Technick. 30-35*. 1938. Tausend. German text. ils. 344p. F. N3. $35.00

EMMERSON, John C. *Steamboat Comes to Norfolk Harbor*. 1947. Portsmouth, VA. ils. 455p. VG. T7. $30.00

EMMERSON, John C. *Steamboat Comes to Norfolk Harbor...1815-1825...* 1949. np. inscr pres. 453p. VG. B10. $75.00

EMMONS, Della G. *Leschi of the Nisquallies*. 1965. TS Denison. inscr. 8vo. 416p. map ep. G. B11. $45.00

EMMONS, Della G. *Sacajawea of the Shoshones*. 1943. Portland. VG. O7. $30.00

EMMONS, Frederick. *Atlantic Liners 1925-1970*. 1972. Bonanza. VG/VG. A16. $17.50

EMMONS, W.H. *Geology of Petroleum*. 1921. McGraw Hill. 1st ed/3rd imp. 610p. G. D8. $20.00

EMRSON, Nathaniel B. *Unwritten Literature of Hawaii...* 1909. WA. ils. 288p. VG. B18. $55.00

ENDE, Michael. *Mirror in the Mirror*. 1986. Viking. 1st ed. F/NF. G10. $10.00

ENDSLEY, John Darrel. *Endsley Family in the New World*. 1976. Paulding, OH. 206p. NF. M20. $22.00

ENGDAHL, Sylvia Louise. *Doors of the Universe*. 1981. Atheneum. 1st ed. 8vo. 262p. tan cloth. F/NF. T5. $30.00

ENGDAHL, Sylvia Louise. *Enchantress From the Stars*. 1970. Atheneum. 1st ed. xl. dj. P3. $8.00

ENGEL, David H. *Japanese Gardens for Today*. 1959. Rutland. Tuttle. 2nd. 270p. emb cloth. F/dj. A17. $45.00

ENGEL, Howard. *City Called July*. 1986. Viking. 1st ed. VG/VG. P3. $20.00

ENGEL, Howard. *Dead & Buried*. 1990. Canada. Viking. 1st ed. VG/VG. P3. $25.00

ENGEL, Howard. *Murder Sees the Light*. 1984. Viking. 1st ed. NF/NF. P3. $18.00

ENGEL, Howard. *Ransom Game.* 1981. Clarke Irwin. 1st ed. sgn. F/F. P3. $30.00

ENGEL, Howard. *Victim Must Be Found.* 1988. Viking. 1st ed. F/F. P3. $20.00

ENGELBERG. *Making of the Shelley Myth: An Annotated Bibliography...* 1988. np. 492p. VG. A4. $75.00

ENGELL, John. *Sea Surveys: Britain's Contribution to Hydrography.* 1965. London. HMSO. 2nd. ils. M/wrp. O7. $20.00

ENGELS, V. *Adirondack Fishing in the 1930s.* 1978. Syracuse. 1st ed. VG/VG. B5. $25.00

ENGERMAN & FOGEL. *Time on the Cross: Economics of American Negro Slavery.* 1974. Little Brn. 2nd prt. 8vo. 286p. F/NF. T10. $20.00

ENGH, M.J. *Rainbow Man.* 1993. Tor. 1st ed. hc. F/F. P3. $18.00

ENGLEMANN, B. *In Hitler's Germany: Daily Life in the Third Reich.* 1986. NY. 335p. VG/dj. A17. $10.00

ENGLERT, Sebastian. *Island at the Center of the World.* 1970. NY. VG. O7. $20.00

ENGLISH, Charles; see Nuetzel, Charles.

ENGLISH, G.L. *Getting Aquainted With Minerals.* 1934. McGraw Hill. 1st ed/14th imp. ils. 324p. VG. D8. $20.00

ENGSTROM, Elizabeth. *Nightmare Flower.* 1992. Tor. 1st ed. F/F. P3. $20.00

ENGSTROM, Robert. *Encounter Program.* 1977. Doubleday. F/F. P3. $15.00

ENRIGHT, Elizabeth. *Doublefields: Memories & Stories.* 1966. HBW. 1st ed. inscr/dtd 1967. VG/VG. B4. $55.00

ENRIGHT, Elizabeth. *Four-Story Mistake.* (1942). EM Hale. rpt. 177p. gr cloth. xl. G+. T5. $18.00

ENTERLINE, James R. *Viking America.* 1972. Garden City. VG. O7. $35.00

EPEL, Naomi. *Writers Dreaming.* 1993. Crown. ARC. RS. F/F. B35. $16.00

EPHRON, Nora. *Heartburn.* 1983. Knopf. 1st ed. F/F clip. M23. $20.00

EPHRON, Nora. *Wallflower at the Orgy.* 1970. NY. 1st hc ed. inscr. F/F. A11. $50.00

EPPENSTEIN, Louise. *Sally Goes Shopping Alone.* 1940. Platt Munk. ils Esther Friend. 44p. bl cloth. T5. $22.00

EPPERSON, Aloise B. *Hills of Yesterday & Other Poems.* 1943. self pub. 74p. VG. B10. $35.00

EPPES, Garrett. *Floating Island: A Tale of Washington.* 1985. Houghton Mifflin. 1st ed. 286p. F/VG. B10. $10.00

EPSTEIN, Sam. *Game of Baseball.* 1965. Garrard. 1st ed. xl. G. P8. $10.00

ERASMUS. *Erasmi Colloquin Selecta; or, Selected Colloquies...* 1806. Trenton. James Oram. inscr/dtd 1829, calf. VG. B14. $75.00

ERDMAN, Loula Grace. *Edge of Time.* 1951. Hodder Stoughton. 1st Eng ed. VG/VG. A18. $10.00

ERDMAN, Loula Grace. *Save Weeping for the Night.* 1975. Dodd Mead. 1st ed. F/F. A18. $20.00

ERDMAN, Paul. *Last Days of America.* 1981. Simon Schuster. 1st ed. VG/VG. P3. $15.00

ERDMAN, Paul. *Panic of '89.* 1986. Andre Deutsch. 1st ed. F/F. P3. $20.00

ERDNASE, S.W. *Artifice, Ruse & Subterfuge at the Card Table.* 1902. Chicago. 205p. VG. S1. $10.00

ERDOES, Richard. *Sun Dance People.* 1972. Knopf. 1st ed. 8vo. ils. 218p. VG/dj. T10. $35.00

ERDRICH, Louise. *Beet Queen.* 1986. Holt. 1st ed. F/F. H11/M23. $30.00

ERDRICH, Louise. *Beet Queen.* 1986. Holt. 1st ed. sgn. F/F. A18. $60.00

ERDRICH, Louise. *Jacklight.* 1984. HRW. 1st ed. inscr. NF/wrp. B4. $250.00

ERDRICH, Louise. *Tracks.* 1988. Holt. 1st ed. F/F. M23. $20.00

ERDRICH, Louise. *Tracks.* 1988. Holt. 1st ed. VG+/VG+. A20. $12.00

ERDSTEIN, Erich. *Inside the Fourth Reich.* 1977. St Martin. 1st ed. VG/VG. P3. $15.00

ERICKSON, Steve. *Days Between Stations.* 1985. NY. Poseidon. 1st ed. author's 1st book. rem mk. F/dj. S9. $50.00

ERICKSON, Steve. *Tours of the Black Clock.* 1989. Poseidon. 1st ed. F/F. M23. $20.00

ERNEST, Edward. *Animated Circus Book.* 1943. Grosset Dunlap. 4 moveables. sbdg. VG/torn. D1. $300.00

ERNSBERGER, George. *Mountain King.* 1978. Morrow. 1st ed. NF/NF. P3. $25.00

ERSKINE, John. *Adam & Eve.* 1927. Bobbs Merrill. VG. P3. $13.00

ERSKINE, John. *Institute of the Law of Scotland, in Four Books...* 1773. Edinburgh. John Bell. 1st ed. contemporary speckled calf. M11. $650.00

ERSKINE, John. *Private Life of Helen of Troy.* 1925. Bobbs Merrill. VG. P3. $18.00

ERSKINE, Margaret. *Fatal Relations.* 1955. Hammond Hammond. 1st ed. VG. P3. $30.00

ERSKINE, Margaret. *House in Belmont Square.* 1963. Hodder Stoughton. 1st ed. VG/VG. P3. $35.00

ERSKINE, Thomas. *Report of Cause Between Joseph Foster & Miss Esther Mellish.* 1802. London. J Ridgway. only ed. 106p. modern buckram. M11. $450.00

ERTE. *Erte. With an Extract From Erte's Memoirs.* 1972. Parma. Franco Maria Ricci. 1/200. 70 pl. 181p. F/box. B24. $450.00

ERVINE. *Bernard Shaw: His Live, Work & Friends.* 1956. np. 20 photos. 628p. VG/worn. A4. $25.00

ERWITT, Elliot. *Photographs & Antiphotographs.* 1972. NYGS. 1st ed. obl 4to. NF/dj. S9. $150.00

ESAU, K. *Plant Anatomy.* 1965. Wiley. 2nd. 8vo. 96 pl. 767p. cloth. NF. B1. $50.00

ESCHER, M.C. *World of...* 1971. Abrams. 1st ed. VG/VG. B5. $35.00

ESDAILE, James. *Hypnosis in Medicine & Surgery...* 1957. NY. facsimile of 1846 ed. 259p. VG. A13. $50.00

ESHBACH, Lloyd Arthur. *Downriver.* 1988. Houghton Mifflin. 1st ed. RS. F/F. P3. $20.00

ESHBACH, Lloyd Arthur. *Dr Jekyll & Mr Holmes.* 1979. Doubleday. 1st ed. VG/VG. P3. $35.00

ESHBACH, Lloyd Arthur. *Kill Zone.* 1984. Mysterious. 1st ed. VG/VG. P3. $18.00

ESHBACH, Lloyd Arthur. *King of the Corner.* 1992. Bantam. 1st ed. F/F. P3. $20.00

ESHBACH, Lloyd Arthur. *Lady Yesterday.* 1987. Houghton Mifflin. 1st ed. F/F. P3. $25.00

ESHBACH, Lloyd Arthur. *Motown.* 1991. Bantam. 1st ed. hc. VG/VG. P3. $20.00

ESHBACH, Lloyd Arthur. *Of Worlds Beyond: Science of SF Writing.* 1947. Fantasy. 1st ed. 1/1262. F/NF. T2. $50.00

ESHBACH, Lloyd Arthur. *Over My Shoulder: Reflections on a SF Era.* 1983. Oswald Train. 1st ed. F/F. T2. $25.00

ESHBACH, Lloyd Arthur. *Peeper.* 1989. Bantam. 1st ed. hc. F/F. P3. $17.00

ESHBACH, Lloyd Arthur. *Silent Thunder.* 1989. Houghton Mifflin. 1st ed. F/F. P3. $17.00

ESHBACH, Lloyd Arthur. *Tyrant of Time.* 1955. Fantasy. 1st ed. hc. Donald Grand bdg. F/F. P3. $20.00

ESHBACH, Lloyd Arthur. *Tyrant of Time.* 1955. Fantasy. 1st ed. variant bdg. F/F. T2. $20.00

ESIN, Emel. *Mecca the Blessed, Madinah the Radiant.* 1963. NY. Crown. ils. 222p. NF/dj. W1. $55.00

ESKEW, G.L. *Pageant of the Packets.* 1929. NY. 1st ed. VG/G. B5. $50.00

ESKRIDGE, Robert Lee. *Umi, the Hawaiian Boy Who Became King.* 1937 (1936). Jr Literary Guild. ils. 105p. brn cloth. VG/G. T5. $30.00

ESQUEMELING, John. *Buccaneers of America.* 1911. London/NY. Allen/Macmillan. ils/maps. 508p. VG. B14. $150.00

ESQUIVEL, Laura. *Like Water for Chocolate.* 1992. Doubleday. ARC. 8vo. F/wrp. S9. $85.00

ESQUIVEL, Laura. *Like Water for Chocolate.* 1992. Doubleday. 1st ed. F/F. B35. $60.00

ESSER, Josef. *Grundsatz und Norm in der Richterlichen Fortbildung...* 1956. Tubingen. xl. worn. M11. $20.00

ESSLING & GERARD. *Les Livres a Figures Venitiens de la Fin du XV Siecle...* nd. Venice. 6 vol. rpt of 1907-1914 ed. 1/350. F. A4. $495.00

ESTES, Clarissa. *Women Who Run With the Wolves.* 1992. 1st ed. NF/NF. S13. $20.00

ESTES, Eleanor. *Ginger Pye.* 1951. Harcourt Brace. 1st ed. 250p. VG/VG. P2. $150.00

ESTES, Eleanor. *Hundred Dresses.* 1944. Harcourt Brace. 1st ed. ils Louis Slobodkin. 80p. F/VG. P2. $75.00

ESTLEMAN, Loren D. *Downriver.* 1988. Houghton Mifflin. 1st ed. F/F. A20. $16.00

ESTLEMAN, Loren D. *Every Brilliant Eye.* 1986. Houghton Mifflin. 1st ed. F/F. A20. $20.00

ESTLEMAN, Loren D. *General Murders.* 1988. Houghton Mifflin. 1st ed. F/F. A20/H11. $20.00

ESTLEMAN, Loren D. *Kill Zone.* 1984. Mysterious. 1st ed. F/NF. N4. $40.00

ESTLEMAN, Loren D. *Sugartown.* 1984. Houghton Mifflin. 1st ed. sgn/dtd. F/VG+. A20. $25.00

ESTLEMAN, Loren D. *Sweet Women Lie.* 1990. Houghton Mifflin. 1st ed. F/F. H11/P3. $20.00

ESTLEMAN, Loren D. *Whiskey River.* 1990. Bantam. 1st ed. NF/NF. P3. $18.00

ESTRIN, Mary Lloyd. *To the Manor Born.* 1979. NYGS. 1st ed. F/F. B4. $100.00

ETCHISON, Dennis. *California Gothic.* 1995. Dreamhaven. 1st ed. sgn. F/F. P3. $28.00

ETCHISON, Dennis. *Dark Country.* 1982. Scream. 1st ed. VG/VG. P3. $100.00

ETIEMBLE. *Yun Yu: An Essay on Eroticism & Love in Ancient China.* 1970. Geneva. Nagel. 172p. cloth. NF/dj/case. M20. $105.00

ETS, Marie Hall. *Mister Penny.* 1935. Viking. 1st ed. ils. VG/G. P2. $125.00

ETTINGHAUSEN, Maurice. *Rare Books & Royal Collectors...* 1966. np. 222p. F/NF. A4. $50.00

EUBANK, Keith. *Munich.* 1963. OK U. 1st ed. 322p. VG/tape rpr. A17. $15.00

EUBERHORST, Karl. *Das Wirklich-Komische: Ein Beitrag zur Psychologie.* 1896. Leipzig. Georg Wigand. 562p. VG. G1. $125.00

EUCLID. *Tacquet...Elementa Euclidea GEometriae Planae...* 1722. Cambridge. Cornfield/Knapton. 6 fld pl/diagrams. 330p. calf. K1. $185.00

EULALIE. *Mother Goose Rhymes.* 1933. Platt Munk. ils. VG. M5. $35.00

EUSTIS, Helen. *Fool Killer.* 1954. Doubleday. 1st ed. VG/G. P3. $20.00

EUWER, Anthony H. *Christopher Cricket on Cats.* 1909. NY. Little Book Concern. 2nd. ils Anthony Euwer. unp. VG. D1. $95.00

EVANOFF, Vlad. *Fresh-Waters Fisherman's Bible.* 1964. Doubleday. sc. G+. P12. $4.00

EVANOFF, Vlad. *Hunting Secrets of the Experts.* 1964. Doubleday. 1st ed. ils. VG/G+. P12. $12.00

EVANOVICH, Janet. *One for the Money.* 1994. Scribner. 1st ed. author's 1st book. rem mk. F/F. H11. $30.00

EVANOVICH, Janet. *One for the Money.* 1994. Scribner. 1st ed. F/F. M23. $50.00

EVANS, Adelaide Bee. *Easy Steps on the Bible Story.* 1911. Review Herald. ils. 616p. G. W1. $12.00

EVANS, Bergen. *Spoor of Spooks & Other Nonsense.* 1954. Knopf. 1st ed. VG/VG. P3. $18.00

EVANS, Billy. *What's What in Baseball.* ca 1940s. np. self pub. G+. P8. $70.00

EVANS, David S. *Frontiers of Astronomy.* 1946. London. Sigma. 1st ed. 175p. G/dj. K5. $6.00

EVANS, Donald. *Hanover.* 1976. Barnes. 1st ed. VG/G. O3. $35.00

EVANS, Elizabeth. *Anne Tyler.* 1993. NY. 1st ed. 1/100. F/F. w/sgn leaf. $75.00

EVANS, Eva Knox. *Jerome Anthony.* 1936. Putnam. 1st ed. sgn. ils Eric Berry. VG+/VG. C8. $75.00

EVANS, George Bird. *Upland Shooting Life.* 1971. Knopf. 1st ed. photos. NF/VG. P12. $15.00

EVANS, Hiram. *Is the Ku Klux Klan Constructive or Destructive?* 1924. Girard, KS. Haldeman Julius. 1st ed thus. 64p. VG. M8. $45.00

EVANS, Humphrey. *Mystery of the Pyramids.* 1979. NY. Crowell. 1st ed. ils. 184p. VG/dj. W1. $22.00

EVANS, Katherine. *Little Tree, a Mexican Tale.* 1956. Bruce. 8vo. pict brd. VG. B17. $4.00

EVANS, Larry. *Fighting Heart.* 1914. Grosset Dunlap. 4 pl. F/dj. A17. $9.50

EVANS, Mari. *JD.* 1973. Doubleday. trade ed. ils Jerry Pinkney. ES. F/F. B4. $100.00

EVANS, Max. *One Eyed Sky.* 1974. Nash. 1st separately-pub ed. ils. F/F. A18. $25.00

EVANS, Nicholas. *Horse Whisperer.* 1995. Delacorte. 1st ed. F/F. H11. $35.00

EVANS, Pauline Rush. *Good Housekeeping's Best Book of Fun & Nonsense.* nd. Good Housekeeping. ils Oscar Wilde. VG/G+. P12. $4.00

EVANS, Walker. *Walker Evans: American Photograhs.* nd. NY. MOMA. 1st ed. 4to. VG/dj. S9. $100.00

EVANS & GAINEY. *Lodger: Arrest & Escape of Jack the Ripper.* 1995. London. Century. 1st ed. F/F. T2. $45.00

EVANS & ROWLANDS. *Cambrian Bibliography.* 1869. Llanidloes. John Pryse. 776p. NF. A4. $185.00

EVANS. *English Art 1307-1461.* 1981 (1949). Hacker. reissue. F. D2. $45.00

EVANS. *Life & Art of George Cruikshank.* 1978. np. 4to. ils. 192p. F/F. A4. $40.00

EVANS. *List of Publications of Bureau of American Ethnology...* 1971. Smithsonian. 140p. F/wrp. A4. $75.00

EVASHEVSKI, Forest. *Scoring Power With the Winged T.* 1957. Dubuque, IA. 1st ed. VG/G. B5. $22.50

EVAT, Harriet. *Secret of the Singing Tower.* 1953. Indianapolis. 1st ed. ils. 243p. VG/VG. A17. $7.50

EVERETT, Edward. *Importance of Education & Useful Knowledge.* 1844. Boston. 12mo. 396p. gilt brn cloth. T3. $25.00

EVERETT, Fred. *Fun With Trout.* 1952. Harrisburg. 1st ed. NF/VG. N3. $25.00

EVERS & EVERS. *More About Copy-Kitten.* 1946. Rand McNally. 12mo. VG. B17. $6.00

EVERSON, Dave. *Suicide Squeeze.* 1991. NY. 1st ed. F/NF. H11. $25.00

EVERSON, William. *Blowing of the Seed.* 1966. New Haven. Wenning. 1st ed. 1/218. sgn pres. F. B24. $300.00

EVERSON, William. *Man-Fate: Swan Song of Brother Antoninus.* 1974. New Directions. 1st ed. NF/NF. M19. $35.00

EVERSON, William. *Pictorial History of the Western Film.* 1969. 244p. F/dj. M13. $30.00

EVERSON, William. *Triptych for the Living. Poems.* 1951. Seraphim. 1st ed. 1/100. 8vo. 26p. goat vellum/red cloth ties. F. B24. $2,850.00

EVERSON & POWELL. *Take Hold Upon the Future.* 1994. Scarecrow. 1st ed. edit WR Eshelman. M/sans. B19. $70.00

EVERTON, Macduff. *Modern Maya.* 1991. NM U. 1st ed. 4to. 260p. wrp. F3. $30.00

EWEN, Robert B. *Contract Bridge: How To Improve Your Technique.* 1975. NY. 63p. VG. S1. $6.00

EWEN, Robert B. *Defensive Bidding Quiz Book.* 1980. NY. 105p. VG/wrp. S1. $5.00

EWES, Basil. *Empire.* 1906. Copp Clarke. 3rd. hc. VG. P3. $10.00

EWING, Frederick R.; see Sturgeon, Theodore.

WING, Juliana Horatia. *Brownies.* 1946. 1st ed. dj. K2. $35.00

EWING, Juliana Horatia. *Three Christmas Trees.* 1930. Macmillan. 1st ed thus. ils Pamela Bianco. VG. M5. $25.00

EXLEY, Fred. *Fan's Notes.* 1968. NY. 1st ed. author's 1st book. NF/dj. A15. $60.00

EXUM, Wallace Louis. *Battlewagon.* 1974. Vantage. 1st ed. 12mo. 179p. map ep. F/F. B11. $40.00

EYESTER, Warren. *Goblins of Eros.* 1957. Random. 1st ed. F/NF. B4. $45.00

EYO & WILLETT. *Treasures of Ancient Nigeria.* 1980. Detroit Inst/Knopf. F/stiff wrp. D2. $35.00

FA & SOUTHWICK. *Ecology & Behavior of Food-Enhanced Primate Groups.* 1988. NY. Alan R Liss. 8vo. ils/photos. 355p. F/F. B1. $52.00

FABER, Harold. *Discoverers of America.* 1992. NY. VG. O7. $20.00

FABIAN, Robert. *Fabian of the Yard.* 1950. Naldrett. 2nd. hc. VG. P3. $10.00

FABIAN, Stephen. *Fantasy by Fabian.* 1978. De La Ree. 1st ed. NF/NF. P3. $35.00

FABIAN, Stephen. *More Fantasy by Fabian.* 1979. De La Ree. 1st ed. NF/NF. P3. $35.00

FABJANCE, John. *101 Professional Card Tricks.* 1976. Wheeling, IL. 32p. VG/wrp. S1. $5.00

FABRICANT & WERNER. *Treasury of Doctor Stories by World's Great Authors.* 1946. NY. 1st ed. 493p. VG. A13. $30.00

FADIMAN, Clifton. *Story of Young King Arthur.* 1961. Random. G. P3. $8.00

FADIMAN, Clifton. *Wally the Wordworm.* 1964. Macmillan. 1st ed. 12mo. pict brd. VG. M5. $20.00

FAHY, Everett. *Legacy of Leonardo: Italian Renaissance Paintings...* 1979. Nat Gallery Art/Knoedler. ils. 118p. stiff wrp. D2. $40.00

FAIBISOFF & TRIPP. *Bibliography of Newspapers in Fourteen New York Counties.* 1978. np. ils. 316p. VG. A4. $85.00

FAIN, Sara Pett. *Fiddle & the Bow.* 1952. Christopher. 201p. VG/G. B10. $15.00

FAIR, A.A.; see Gardner, Erle Stanley.

FAIRBAIRN, Ann. *Five Smooth Stones.* 1966. NY. 1st ed. VG/G. B5. $25.00

FAIRBAIRN, Roger; see Carr, John Dickson.

FAIRBRIDGE, Rhodes W. *Encyclopedia of Oceanography.* 1966. NY. VG. O7. $45.00

FAIRCHILD, David. *World Was My Garden.* 1938. Scribner. 1st ed. 8vo. gr cloth. VG. T10. $75.00

FAIRLEIGH, Runa. *Old-Fashioned Mystery.* 1983. Lester & Orpen Denys. 1st ed. VG/VG. P3. $20.00

FAIRLEY, James. *Irish Whales & Whaling.* 1981. Belfast. xl. VG. O7. $40.00

FAIRLIE, Gerard. *Suspect.* nd. Detective Story Club. hc. VG. P3. $20.00

FALCONER, Sovereign. *To Make Death Love Us.* 1987. Doubleday. RS. F/F. P3. $18.00

FALK, Allan. *Team Trial.* 1991. Lansing, MI. 156p. F. S1. $8.00

FALK, Edwin A. *USS Mayflower.* nd (1946). NY. sgn. 8vo. 41p. VG. B11. $50.00

FALK, I.S. *Security Against Sickness, a Study of Health Insurance.* 1936. NY. 1st ed. 423p. VG. A13. $60.00

FALK, Toby. *Treasures of Islam.* 1985. London. Sotheby's/Philip Wilson. 1st ed. ils. 400p. NF/dj. W1. $125.00

FALK. *Print Price Index '93.* 1992. Sound View Pr. 4to. 1470p. F. A4. $175.00

FALKNER, J. Meade. *Moonfleet.* 1962. Tempo. hc. lib pb bdg. VG. P3. $7.00

FALL, Bernard B. *Hell in a Very Small Place: Seige of Dien Bien Phu.* 1967. Lippincott. 1st ed. F/NF. B4. $225.00

FALLIS, Gregory S. *Lightning in the Blood.* 1993. NY. 1st ed. F/F. H11. $25.00

FALLOWELL, Duncan. *Drug Tales.* 1979. Hamish Hamilton. 1st ed. F/F. P3. $20.00

FANNIN, Cole. *Roy Rogers in River of Peril.* 1957. Whitman. hc. G. P3. $15.00

FANNING, Edmund. *Voyages & Discoveries in South Seas, 1792-1832.* 1924. Salem. ils. 335p. VG. T7. $120.00

FANNING, L.M. *Our Oil Resources.* 1945. McGraw Hill. 331p. NF. D8. $10.00

FANTE, John. *Dago Red.* 1940. Viking. 1st ed. author's 3rd book. VG/dj. S9. $400.00

FANTHORPE, R. Lionel. *Hand of Doom.* 1968. Arcadia. hc. VG/VG. P3. $20.00

FARADAY, Cornelia Bateman. *European & American Carpets & Rugs.* 1929. Grand Rapids. 1st ed. ils. 382p. xl. VG. B18. $75.00

FARAH, Cynthia. *Literature & Landscape.* 1980. TX Western Pr. 1st ed. 137p. F/F. B19. $50.00

FARB, Peter. *Face of North America: The Natural History of a Continent.* 1963. np. 1st ed. 316p. cloth. VG/torn. D8. $15.00

FARB, Peter. *Man's Rise to Civilization As Shown by Indians of N Am...* 1968. Dutton. 8vo. 332p. blk cloth. VG. T10. $35.00

FARBER, Norma. *Did You Know It Was a Narwhale?* 1967. Atheneum. 1st ed. ils. unp. xl. NF/NF. C14. $8.00

FARBER, Norma. *Up the Down Elevator.* 1979. Addison Wesley. 1st ed. 12mo. unp. F/VG. C14. $10.00

FARCY, Charles. *Etudes Politiques De L'Aristocratie Anglaise...* 1843. Paris. quarter morocco. G. M11. $125.00

FARIES, Belmont. *Christmas Stamps From Around the World.* 1982. Dallas. Somesuch. 1/800. prt/sgn DG Kelley & Susan Acker. F/case. B24. $150.00

FARINA, Richard. *Been Down So Long It Looks Like Up To Me.* 1st ed. author's 1st novel. VG/poor. B30. $50.00

FARINI, M. *Baby's Own Book.* ca 1920s. NY. 8vo. F/glassine/box. M5. $48.00

FARIS, John T. *Seeing the Sunny South.* 1921. Lippincott. 1st ed. ils. VG. P12. $25.00

FARIS, John. *Fury.* 1976. Playboy. 1st ed. VG+/VG. M21. $25.00

FARIS, John. *Old Roads Out of Philadelphia.* 1917. Lippincott. 1st ed. VG. O3. $58.00

FARIS, Lillie A. *Old Testament Stories Retold for Children.* 1938. Platt Munk. ils W Fletcher White. VG/G. B17. $15.00

FARIS & HUSAYN. *Crescent in Crisis: An Interpretive Study...* 1955. KS. 191p. map ep. cloth. VG/dj. W1. $20.00

FARJEON, Eleanor. *Kaleidoscope.* 1963. NY. Walck. 1st ed thus. ils Ardizzone. 158p. G+. T5. $35.00

FARJEON, Eleanor. *Martin Pippin in the Apple Orchard.* 1928 (1922). Stokes. 6th. 270p. VG. P2. $20.00

FARJEON, Eleanor. *Martin Pippin in the Apple Orchard.* 1952 (1921). 1st UK ed thus. ils Richard Kennedy. NF/NF clip. C8. $40.00

FARJEON, Eleanor. *Prayer for Little Things.* 1945. Houghton Mifflin. ils Elizabeth Orton Jones. VG/dj. M5. $18.00

FARJEON, Eleanor. *Silver Curlew.* 1953. Oxford. 1st ed. ils Ernest Shepard. 182p. VG/G. P2. $50.00

FARJEON, J. Jefferson. *Peril in Pyrenees.* 1946. Collins Crime Club. 1st ed. VG/VG. P3. $30.00

FARJEON & SALE. *Cherrystones.* nd. Lippincott. 1st Am ed. 8vo. 61p. VG+. C14. $30.00

FARLEIGH, John. *Graven Image: An Autobiographical Textbook.* 1940. ils. 388p. RS. VG. A4. $125.00

FARLEY, Jim. *Roosevelt Years.* 1948. McGraw. 3rd. inscr. VG/fair. B22. $5.50

FARLEY, Walter. *Black Stallion & Satan.* 1949. Random. 1st ed. 208p. F/NF. P2. $30.00

FARLEY, Walter. *Black Stallion Revolts.* 1953. NY. 1st ed. VG/VG. B5. $25.00

FARLEY, Walter. *Black Stallion Revolts.* 1953. Random. 1st ed. F/NF. M19. $45.00

FARLEY, Walter. *Black Stallion's Sulky Colt.* 1954. Random. 1st ed. VG/VG. B5. $25.00

FARLEY, Walter. *Black Stallion's Sulky Colt.* 1954. Random. 1st ed. 248p. F/F. P2. $30.00

FARLEY, Walter. *Blood Bay Colt.* 1950. NY. 1st ed. VG/VG. B5. $25.00

FARLEY, Walter. *Island Stallion Races.* 1955. Random. 1st ed. F/VG. M19. $35.00

FARMER, Fannie. *Chafing Dish Possibilities.* 1918. Boston. Little Brn. VG. H7. $15.00

FARMER, Philip Jose. *Blood of Philip Jose Farmer.* 1973. Elmfield. 1st ed. sgn. F/F. M10. $35.00

FARMER, Philip Jose. *Dark Design.* 1977. Berkley Putnam. 1st ed. NF/NF. P3. $20.00

FARMER, Philip Jose. *Dark Is the Sun.* 1979. Del Rey. 1st ed. F/F. P3. $20.00

FARMER, Philip Jose. *Dayworld Breakup.* 1990. NY. Tor. 1st ed. F/dj. H11/P3. $20.00

FARMER, Philip Jose. *Dayworld.* 1985. Putnam. 1st ed. F/F. H11. $25.00

FARMER, Philip Jose. *Dayworld.* 1985. Putnam. 1st ed. NF/NF. P3. $17.00

FARMER, Philip Jose. *Doc Savage: His Apocalyptic Life.* 1973. Doubleday. 1st ed. NF/NF. P3. $35.00

FARMER, Philip Jose. *Gods of Riverworld.* 1983. Phantasia. 1st ed. 1/650. sgn/#d. F/F/case. P3. $50.00

FARMER, Philip Jose. *Gods of Riverworld.* 1983. Putnam. 1st ed. F/F. P3. $25.00

FARMER, Philip Jose. *Love Song.* 1983. Macmillan. 1st ed. 1/500. sgn. F/F. P3. $85.00

FARMER, Philip Jose. *Magic Labyrinth.* 1980. Berkley Putnam. 1st ed. F/F. P3. $18.00

FARMER, Philip Jose. *Mother Was a Lovely Beast.* 1974. Chilton. 1st ed. VG/VG. P3. $35.00

FARMER, Philip Jose. *Red Orc's Rage.* 1991. Tor. F/F. P3. $19.00

FARMER, Philip Jose. *Unreasoning Mask.* 1981. Putnam. 1st ed. sgn. F/F. M10. $25.00

FARMER, Philip Jose. *Unreasoning Mask.* 1981. Putnam. 1st ed. VG/VG. P3. $20.00

FARNOL, Jeffery. *Broad Highway.* 1912. Little Brn. ils. VG. p3. $25.00

FARNOL, Jeffery. *Heritage Perilous.* 1947. Ryerson. 1st Canadian ed. VG. P3. $25.00

FARNOL, Jeffery. *My Lady Caprice.* 1907. Dodd Mead. 1st ed. decor brd. G. P3. $20.00

FARNOL, Jeffery. *My Lord of Wrybourne.* 1948. Ryerson. 1st Canadian ed. VG/chip. P3. $15.00

FARQUHAR, Francis P. *Ralston-Fry Wedding.* 1961. Berkeley. 4to. 24p. F/wrp. T10. $35.00

FARR, Finis. *Margaret Mitchell of Atlanta.* 1965. Morrow. 1st ed. 244p. cloth. VG/dj. M20. $50.00

FARR, Grahame E. *Chepstow Ships.* 1954. Chepstow Soc. ils. 215p. worn dj. T7. $40.00

FARR, John; see Webb, Jack.

FARR, Robert. *Electronic Criminals.* 1975. McGraw Hill. 1st ed. VG. P3. $15.00

FARRAR, Emmie Ferguson. *Old Virginia Houses Along the James.* nd. Bonanza. rpt of 1957 ed. photos. 231p. VG/fair. B10. $15.00

FARRAR, Stewart. *Omega.* 1980. Times Books. 1st ed. VG/VG. P3. $18.00

FARRAR & FARRAR. *Book of the Roycrofters.* 1907. Roycroft. photos. VG. C6. $75.00

FARRELL, Gillian B. *Alibi for an Actress.* 1992. Pocket. 1st ed. author's 1st book. F/F. H11. $25.00

FARRELL, James T. *Bernard Clare.* 1946. NY. 1st ed. F/VG. H7. $30.00

FARRERE, Claude. *Useless Hands.* 1926. Dutton. 1st ed. VG. P3. $45.00

FARRINGTON, E. *Ernest H Wilson: Plant Hunter.* 1931. Boston. 1st ed. VG/VG. B5. $25.00

FARRINGTON, S. Kip Jr. *Ships of the US Merchant Marine.* 1947. Dutton. G/dj. A16. $22.50

FARRINGTON, S. Kip. Jr. *Atlantic Game Fishing.* 1937. NY. Kennedy. 1st ed. inscr. F/F. B11. $285.00

FARRINGTON, S. Kip. Jr. *Pacific Game Fishing.* 1942. Coward McCann. 1st ed. inscr. lg 8vo. 290p. gilt bl brd. F. B11. $85.00

FARRINGTON, S. Kip. Jr. *Sport Fishing Boats.* 1949. NY. 1st ed. ils. VG/VG. B5. $22.50

FARRIS, John. *Catacombs.* nd. BC. VG/VG. P3. $8.00

FARRIS, John. *Fury.* 1976. Playboy. 1st ed. VG/fair. P3. $20.00

FARRIS, John. *Sacrifice.* nd (1994). Forge. UP. sgn. F/prt wrp. M22. $65.00

FARRIS, John. *Scare Tactics.* 1988. Tor. 1st ed. VG/VG. P3. $18.00

FARRUKH, Omar A. *Qur'anic Arabic: Elementary Course in Arabic...* 1964. Beirut. Khayats. 8vo. 92p. VG/wrp. W1. $12.00

FARSON, Daniel. *Hamlyn Book of Ghosts in Fact & Fiction.* 1980. Hamlyn. 3rd. hc. VG/VG. P3. $12.00

FARWELL, Byron. *Armies of the Raj.* 1989. Norton. 1st ed. sgn. 399p. F/F. B11. $25.00

FARWELL, Byron. *Gurkhas.* 1984. Norton. 1st ed. F/VG. B11. $35.00

FARWELL, Byron. *Man Who Presumed. A Biography of Stanley.* 1957. Holt. 1st ed. sgn. author's 1st book. 8vo. 334p. F/VG. B11. $85.00

FASH, William. *Scribes, Warriors & Kings.* 1991. Thames Hudson. 1st ed. 4to. 192p. dj. F3. $45.00

FASSETT, Norman C. *Leguminous Plants of Wisconsin.* 1939. Madison. ils. 157p. gr cloth. B26. $22.50

FAST, Howard. *Goethals & the Panama Canal.* 1942. Jr Literary Guild/Messner. 230p. dj. F3. $15.00

FAST, Howard. *Hunter & the Trap.* 1968. Dial. 3rd. VG/VG. P3. $10.00

FAST, Jonathan. *Inner Circle.* nd. BC. VG/VG. P3. $8.00

FAST, Jonathan. *Mortal Gods.* 1978. Harper Row. 1st ed. F/F. P3. $15.00

FAST, Julius. *Beatles: The Real Story.* 1968. Putnam. 1st ed. F/NF. B2. $40.00

FATES, Gil. *What's My Line?* 1978. Prentice Hall. 1st ed. inscr. NF/NF. B4. $150.00

FATIO, Louis. *Happy Lion & the Bear.* 1964. Whittlesey. 1st ed. ils Roger Duvoisin. VG+/VG. P2. $25.00

FATIO, Louis. *Happy Lion.* 1954. Whittlesey. 1st ed. ils Roger Duvoisin. F/VG. P2. $50.00

FATOUT, Paul. *Ambrose Bierce: Devil's Lexicographer.* 1951. Norman. 1st ed. VG/VG. B5. $27.50

FAUDEL-PHILLIPS, H. *Driving Book.* 1943. Waltham Cross. Temple House. 47p. VG. O3. $25.00

FAULK, Odie B. *Destiny Road: Gila Trail & the Opening of the Southwest.* 1973. Oxford. 1st ed. 232p. VG+/dj. M20. $27.00

FAULKNER, Charles H. *Prehistoric Native American Art of Mud Glyph Cave.* 1986. Knoxville, TN. 1st ed. 29 pl/4 tables. 124p. AN/dj. T10. $35.00

FAULKNER, Georgene. *Road to Enchantment: Fairy Tales From the World Over.* 1929. NY. 1st ed. ils Frederick Richardson. VG. M5. $65.00

FAULKNER, Nancy. *Rebel Drums.* 1952. Doubleday. 1st ed. ils Lee Ames. 218p. G+/fair. B10. $12.00

FAULKNER, Nancy. *Secret of the Simple Code.* 1965. Doubleday. 1st ed. F/NF. N4. $25.00

FAULKNER, William. *As I Lay Dying.* 1930. NY. Cape Smith. 1st ed/1st issue (I on p 11 unaligned). tan cloth. F/F. B24. $1,250.00

FAULKNER, William. *Big Woods.* 1955. NY. 1st ed. F/VG clip. C6. $200.00

FAULKNER, William. *Big Woods.* 1955. NY. 1st ed. VG. B5. $60.00

FAULKNER, William. *Collected Stories of William Faulkner.* 1950. Random. 1st ed/1st issue (title p/top edge in bl). NF/clip. C2. $400.00

FAULKNER, William. *Doctor Martino & Other Stories.* 1934. Smith Haas. 1st ed. gilt bl cloth. F/closed tear. B24. $500.00

FAULKNER, William. *Doctor Martino & Other Stories.* 1934. Smith Haas. 1st ed. 371p. VG/dj. M20. $205.00

FAULKNER, William. *Fable.* 1954 (1950). Random. 427p. VG/G+. B10. $50.00

FAULKNER, William. *Go Down Moses & Other Stories.* 1942. NY. 1st ed. blk cloth. F/NF. A9. $650.00

FAULKNER, William. *Go Down Moses & Other Stories.* 1942. Random. 1st ed/1st issue. red top edge. blk cloth. NF/clip. C2. $450.00

FAULKNER, William. *Idyl in the Desert.* 1931. Random. 1st ed. 1/400. sgn. F/glassine dj. B24. $1,250.00

FAULKNER, William. *Intruder in the Dust.* 1948. Random. 1st ed. VG/VG. B30. $175.00

FAULKNER, William. *Light in August.* 1932. Smith Haas. 1st ed. VG. A11. $115.00

FAULKNER, William. *Light in August.* 1932. Smith Haas. 1st ed. 1st bdg. F/NF. B24. $650.00

FAULKNER, William. *Light in August.* 1932. Smith Haas. 1st prt. 480p. VG/dj/glassine. M20. $750.00

FAULKNER, William. *Light in August.* 1959. Modern Lib. 444p. gr cloth. NF/VG. B22. $3.00

FAULKNER, William. *Lion in the Garden: Interviews With William Faulkner...1962.* nd. np. 1st ed. edit Meriwether/Milgate. VG/VG. M17. $40.00

FAULKNER, William. *Mayday.* 1976. South Bend. Notre Dame. 1st ed. 1/225. F/case. C2. $300.00

FAULKNER, William. *New Orleans Sketches.* 1955. Tokyo. 1st ed. NF/tan mottled wrp. A11. $155.00

FAULKNER, William. *Notes on a Horse Thief.* 1950. Greenville. Levee. 1st ed. 1/975. sgn. F/sans. C2. $750.00

FAULKNER, William. *Portable Faulkner.* April 1946. Viking. 1st ed. ils ep. F. B14. $55.00

FAULKNER, William. *Pylon.* Feb 1935. Smith Haas. 1st ed. 1st issue dj. T14. $175.00

FAULKNER, William. *Pylon.* 1935. Smith Haas. 1st ed. 1/300. sgn. special bdg. F/NF case. C2. $1,250.00

FAULKNER, William. *Salmagundi.* 1932. Casanova. 1st ed. 1/500. F/decor wrp/orig unprt case. C2. $750.00

FAULKNER, William. *Sanctuary.* 1931. NY. 1st ed. NF. C2. $375.00

FAULKNER, William. *Sanctuary.* 1931. NY. 1st ed. NF/NF. C6. $3,000.00

FAULKNER, William. *Unvanquished.* 1938. Random. 1st ed. ils Edward Shenton. F/dj. B24. $525.00

FAULKNER, William. *White Rose of Memphis.* 1935. Coley Taylor. 542p. G/G. B10. $35.00

FAULKNER, William. *Wild Palms.* 1939. Random. 1st ed. 1/250. sgn. F. C2. $1,500.00

FAULKNER, William. *Wishing Tree.* 1967. Random. 1st trade ed. F/dj. C2. $75.00

FAUST, Joe Clifford. *Desperate Measures.* nd. BC. VG/VG. P3. $8.00

FAUST, Ron. *Tombs of Blue Ice.* 1974. Bobbs Merrill. 1st ed. VG/VG. P3. $20.00

FAWCETT, Claire Hallard. *We Fell in Love With the Circus.* 1949. NY. Lindquist. 1st ed. sgn. 8vo. 198p. VG/fair. B11. $50.00

FAWCETT, E. Douglas. *Hartmann the Anarchist.* 1893. Arnold. 1st ed. scarce title. VG. P3. $200.00

FAWCETT, Edgar. *Buntling Ball: A Gaeco-American Play.* 1885. Funk Wagnall. 8vo. ils CD Weldon. gilt blk cloth. VG. T10. $75.00

FAWCETT, P.H. *Lost Trails, Lost Cities.* 1953. NY. VG. O7. $25.00

FAWCETT, Rosamond A. *Flora of Riverside & Vicinity.* 1939. Riverside. 172p. VG. B26. $50.00

FAY, Charles Edey. *Mary Celeste: Odyssey of an Abandoned Ship.* 1942. Peabody Mus. 1/150. sgn. lg 8vo. 261p. VG/case. B11. $150.00

FAY, Edwin Hedge. *This Infernal War: The Confederate Letters of...* 1958. Austin, TX. 1st ed. 474p. cloth. F/NF. M8. $85.00

FAYLE, E. *Seaborne Trade: A History of the Great War...* 1920. London. Murray. 2 text vol+1 case of 9 fld maps. VG. T7. $160.00

FEARS, Wayne J. *Hunting Whitetails Successfully.* 1986. N Am Hunting Club. 1st ed. photos. VG. P12. $10.00

FEATHER, Leonard. *Encyclopedia of Jazz in the Sixties.* 1966. Horizon. 1st ed. F/NF. B2. $50.00

FEATHER, Leonard. *Passion for Jazz.* 1980. Horizon. 1st ed. F/F. B2. $30.00

FECHHEIMER, Hedwig. *De Plastic der Agypter.* 1922. Berlin. Cassirer. 158 pl. G. W1. $25.00

FECHNER, Gustav Theodor. *Die Drei Motive und Grunde des Glaubens.* 1863. Leipzig. Breitkopf und Hartel. 256p. gr cloth. VG. G1. $275.00

FEDDEN, Robin. *Egypt; Land of the Valley.* 1977. Travel BC. 32 pl. NF/dj. W1. $12.00

FEDER, Lillian. *Crowell's Handbook of Classical Literature.* 1980. NY. 6th. 448p. F/dj. A17. $15.00

FEDO, Michael. *Man From Lake Wobegon.* 1987. St Martin. 1st ed. F/VG+. A20. $16.00

FEDOSEYEV, Grigori. *Pashka of Bear Ravine.* 1967. Pantheon. 1st ed. 8vo. F/VG. B17. $4.50

FEE, Sylvia H. *Means Landscape Estimating.* 1987. Kingston, MA. checklists/tables/worksheets, 279p. F/dj. B26. $30.00

FEELEY, Pat. *Best Friend.* 1977. Dutton. 1st ed. F/F. P3. $20.00

FEHRENBACH, T.R. *Comanches: The Destruction of a People.* 1974. Knopf. 1st ed. 8vo. 557p. NF/dj. T10. $45.00

FEHRENBACH. *This Kind of War.* 1963. NY. 1st ed. F/F. A9. $35.00

FEIBLEMAN, Peter S. *Charlie Boy.* 1980. Little Brn. 1st ed. VG/VG. P3. $15.00

FEIBLEMAN, Peter S. *Tiger, Tiger Burning Bright.* 1963. World. 1st ed. photos. G/G. B10. $12.00

FEIFER, George. *Tennozan: Battle of Okinawa & the Atomic Bomb.* 1992. NY. 1st ed. 622p. M/dj. A17. $15.00

FEIFER, J. *Great Comic Book Heroes.* 1965. 1st ed. 189p. F. M13. $37.00

FEIGL, H. *Readings in the Philosophy of Science.* 1953. Appleton Century Crofts. 811p. cloth. VG. D8. $12.50

FEIKEMA, Feike; see Manfred, Frederick.

FEIST, Raymond. *Prince of the Blood.* 1989. Doubleday. 1st ed. F/F. M19. $17.50

FEIST & WURTS. *Mistress of the Empire.* 1992. Doubleday. 1st ed. F/F. P3. $20.00

FEJES, Claire. *Villagers.* 1981. Random. 1st ed. inscr/dtd 1985. F/dj. S9. $30.00

FELCONE. *Printing in Princeton, NJ 1786-1864.* 1989. np. 1/1000. 800p. F. A4. $60.00

FELDHAUS, Franz. *Geschichte des Technischen Zeichens.* 1959. Wilhelmshaven. 2nd. 121p. VG. A13. $25.00

FELDMAN, Annette. *Handmade Lace & Patterns.* 1975. Harper. 1st ed. 208p. VG/dj. M20. $24.00

FELICE, Cynthia. *Downtime.* 1985. Bluejay. 1st ed. F/F. P3. $20.00

FELL, Egbert W. *Flora of Winneago County, IL.* 1955. WA, DC. ils. 207p. VG. B26. $30.00

FELLER & GILBERT. *Now Pitching Bob Feller.* 1990. Birch Lane. 1st ed. sgn. photos. F/VG+. P8. $45.00

FELLER & HURWITZ. *How To Operate Under the Wage-Hour Law.* 1938. NY. Alexander. M11. $45.00

FELSKO, Elsa M. *Blumen-Fibel.* 1956. Berlin. Grunewald. 300 pl. 282p. gilt gr leather spine/brd. B26. $40.00

FELT, Ephraim P. *Manual of Tree & Shrub Insects.* 1926 (1924). NY. Rural Manuals series. ils. 382p. B26. $25.00

FELT, Sue. *Hello-Goodbye.* 1960. Doubleday. 1st ed. 8vo. unp. VG+/VG. T5. $20.00

FENGER, Frederic A. *Cruise of the Diablesse.* 1926. NY. Yachting. 1st ed. inscr. 8vo. 315p. VG. B11. $75.00

FENN, Eleanor F. *Grandfather Lovechild's Valentine & Orson.* ca 1870. Phil. Simpson. ils FO Darley. F/ils wrp. B24. $175.00

FENTON, Carroll. *World of Fossils.* 1933. Appleton. 1st ed. edit Watson Davis. F. B14. $45.00

FENTON, Eugenie. *Sher, Lord of the Jungle.* 1962. London. Ernest Benn. 1st ed. ils Joan Kiddell-Monroe. 96p. VG/G. P2. $20.00

FENTON, Robert W. *Big Swingers.* 1967. Englewood Cliffs. 1st ed. 8vo. 238p. F/F. T10. $75.00

FENTON, Robert W. *Big Swingers.* 1967. Prentice Hall. VG/VG. P3. $50.00

FENTON & FENTON. *Fossil Book: Exciting Story of Plants, Animals...* 1958. Doubleday. 1st ed. ils. xl. D8. $7.50

FERBER, Edna. *Cimarron.* 1930. Doubleday Doran. 1st ed. 8vo. VG/dj. S9. $45.00

FERBER, Edna. *Cimarron.* 1930. Doubleday. ARC. sgn. NF/cloth clamshell case. B4. $275.00

FERBER, Edna. *Giant.* 1952. Doubleday. 1st ed. VG/VG. M10. $17.50

FERBER, Edna. *Giant.* 1952. Garden City. 1st ed. F/NF. H11. $50.00

FERBER, Edna. *Ice Palace.* 1958. Doubleday. 1st ed. F/NF. M19. $17.50

FERBER, Edna. *Saratoga Trunk.* 1941. Doubleday. 1st ed. F/NF. H11. $55.00

FERBER & KAUFMAN. *Royal Family.* 1928. Doubleday Doran. 1st ed. F/clip. B4. $350.00

FERBUSH, Bliss. *Sheppard & Enoch Pratt Hospital.* 1971. Phil. 1st ed. sgn. 266p. VG/dj. A13. $20.00

FERE, C. *Epilepsies et les Epileptiques.* 1890. Paris. ils/pl/mtd photos. 636p. VG. B14. $750.00

FERE, C. *La Pathologie des Emotions...* 1892. Paris. Ancienne Librairie Germer Bailliere et Cie. VG. G1. $250.00

FERGUSON, E. *Mexico Revisited.* 1955. Knopf. 1st ed. 346p. dj. F3. $25.00

FERGUSON, Helen. *Julia & the Bazooka.* 1970. Knopf. 1st ed. F/F. B35. $25.00

FERGUSON, William. *Maya Ruins of Mecixo in Color.* 1977. Norman, OK. 1st ed. 4to. 246p. dj. F3. $45.00

FERGUSON, Wynne. *Practical Auction Bridge.* 1926. NY. 222p. VG. S1. $5.00

FERGUSON & MULLER. *Evolutionary Significance of the Exine.* 1976. np. Linnean Soc Symposium #1. F. B26. $35.00

FERGUSON & ROYCE. *Maya Ruins in Central America in Color.* 1984. NM U. 1st ed. 4to. 387p. dj. F3. $60.00

FERGUSSON, Bruce. *Mace of Souls.* 1989. Morrow. 1st ed. F/F. P3. $21.00

FERGUSSON, Bruce. *Shadow of His Wings.* 1987. Arbor. 1st ed. F/F. P3. $17.00

FERGUSSON, Erna. *Dancing Gods: Indian Ceremonials of New Mexico & Arizona.* 1931. Knopf. 1st ed. sgn. 8vo. 276p. G. B11. $45.00

FERGUSSON, Harvey. *Wolf Song.* 1927. Knopf. 1/100. sgn/#d. F/glassine dj. A18. $300.00

FERGUSSON, Harvey. *Wolf Song.* 1978. Gregg. 1st ed thus. ils Wm T Pilkington. F/F. A18. $17.50

FERLATTE, William J. *Flora of the Trinity Alps of Northern California.* 1974. Berkeley. 8vo. 206p. bl cloth. F. T10. $25.00

FERLINGHETTI, Lawrence. *Her.* 1966. MacGibbon Kee. 1st Eng ed. NF/NF. M19. $65.00

FERLINGHETTI, Lawrence. *Love in the Days of Rage.* 1988. Bodley Head. 1st ed. F/F. R10. $15.00

FERLINGHETTI, Lawrence. *Love in the Days of Rage.* 1988. Bodley Head. 1st ed. sgn. VG. M17. $32.50

FERLINGHETTI, Lawrence. *Secret Meaning of Things.* 1968. New Directions. 1st ed. pres. VG+/VG+. H4. $100.00

FERLINGHETTI & PETERS. *Literary San Francisco: A Pictorial History...* 1980. Harper. 1st ed. photos. F/dj. A18. $35.00

FERMAN, Edward L. *Best Fantasy Stories From Fantasy & SF.* 1985. Octopus. F/F. P3. $15.00

FERMI, Laura. *Illustrious Immigrants.* 1968. Chicago. sgn. ils. 440p. VG/dj. K5. $25.00

FERNALD, Edward A. *Atlas of Florida.* 1981. Tallahassee. 800+ ils. F. O7. $55.00

FERNALD, M.L. *Two Summers of Botanizing in Newfoundland.* 1926. np. photos. wrp. B26. $15.00

FERNALD & PATTON. *Water Resources Atlas of Florida.* 1984. FL State. ils. 291p. VG. D8. $35.00

FERRARS, Elizabeth X. *Alibi for a Witch.* 1952. Crime Club. 1st ed. hc. VG. P3. $20.00

FERRARS, Elizabeth X. *Alive & Dead.* 1974. Collins Crime Club. 1st ed. VG/VG. P3. $25.00

FERRARS, Elizabeth X. *Answer Came There None.* 1992. Collins Crime Club. 1st ed. F/F. P3. $22.00

FERRARS, Elizabeth X. *Depart This Life.* 1958. Crime Club. 1st ed. VG/VG. P3. $25.00

FERRARS, Elizabeth X. *Hanged Man's House.* 1974. Collins Crime Club. 1st ed. xl. dj. P3. $8.00

FERRARS, Elizabeth X. *Last Will & Testament.* 1978. Crime Club. hc. VG/VG. P3. $16.00

FERRARS, Elizabeth X. *Thinner Than Water.* 1982. Doubleday. 1st ed. VG/VG. P3. $15.00

FERRIAR, John. *Essay Towards a Theory of Apparitions.* 1813. London. 1st ed. 8vo. 139p. contemporary morocco/gray brd. VG. C6. $200.00

FERRIER, David. *Functions of the Brain.* 1886. Putnam. 2nd. 498p. emb Victorian cloth. VG. G1. $475.00

FERRIER, R.W. *Arts of Persia.* 1989. Yale. ils. 334p. NF/dj. W1. $75.00

FERRIGNO, Robert. *Cheshire Moon.* 1994. Avon. hc. VG. P3. $5.00

FERRIGNO, Robert. *Dead Man's Dance.* 1995. Putnam. ARC. F/wrp. M22. $20.00

FERRIGNO, Robert. *Horse Latitudes.* 1990. Morrow. 1st ed. F/F. M22. $50.00

FERRIGNO, Robert. *Horse Latitudes.* 1990. Morrow. 1st ed. NF/NF. P3. $20.00

FERRIS, James Cody. *X-Bar-X Boys at Copperhead Gulch.* 1933. Grosset Dunlap. 219p. VG/dj. M20. $42.00

FERRIS, James Cody. *X-Bar-X Boys on Big Bison Trail (#4).* 1927. Grosset Dunlap. ils Walter Rogers. 216p. VG/dj. M20. $42.00

FERRIS, James Cody. *X-Bar-X Boys on Big Bison Trail (#4).* 1927. Grosset Dunlap. 216p. NF/VG. M20. $40.00

FERRIS, James Cody. *X-Bar-X Boys Seeking the Lost Troopers (#20).* 1941. Grosset Dunlap. 1st ed. 213p. VG/dj. M20. $37.00

FERRIS, James Cody. *X-Bar-X Boys: Branding the Wild Herd (#13).* 1934. Grosset Dunlap. lists to this title. 215p. VG+/G. M20. $40.00

FERRIS, Paul. *High Places.* 1977. CMG. 1st ed. VG/VG. P3. $15.00

FERRIS, Timothy. *Red Limit.* 1977. Morrow. ils. 287p. xl. dj. K5. $8.00

FERRY, W. Hawkins. *Buildings of Detroit: A History.* 1969 (1968). Wayne State. 2nd. 479p. dj. A17. $75.00

FEST, Joachim C. *Hitler.* 1974. NY. photos. 875p. VG. A17. $12.50

FETZER, Leland. *Pre-Revolutionary Russian SF: An Anthology.* 1982. Ardis. 1st ed. F. G10. $30.00

FEUCHTWANGER, Lion. *Proud Destiny.* 1947. Viking. 1st ed. VG/VG. P3. $18.00

FEVAL, Paul; see Bedford-Jones, H.

FICHTENBAUM, Paul. *World of Major League Baseball.* 1987. Coombe. VG/VG. P3. $10.00

FIEDLER, Leslie A. *Olaf Stapledon: A Man Divided.* 1983. Oxford. 1st ed. hc. F/F. P3. $20.00

FIEDLER, Maggi. *Corky's Pet Parade.* 1946. NY. ils. 32p. VG. A17. $15.00

FIELD, Edward Salisbury. *Twin Beds.* nd. Grosset Dunlap. MTI. hc. VG. P3. $20.00

FIELD, Eugene. *Christmas Tales & Christmas Verse.* 1912. Scribner. 1st ed thus. 8vo. VG+. M5. $70.00

FIELD, Eugene. *Favorite Poems.* 1940. Grosset Dunlap. 8vo. VG/fair. M5. $12.00

FIELD, Eugene. *House.* 1896. NY. 1st ed. VG. A17. $9.50

FIELD, Eugene. *Little Willie.* 1901. WA. private prt. 1/100. VG+/wrp. P2. $45.00

FIELD, Eugene. *Poems of Childhood.* 1904. Scribner. 1st ed thus. ils Parrish. NF. C2. $150.00

FIELD, Eugene. *Works of...* 1900. Scribner. 12 vol. gilt cloth. F. A17. $50.00

FIELD, Eugene. *Wynken Blynken & Nod, & Other Verses.* 1925. Newark, NJ. lg 4to. VG. C8. $75.00

FIELD, Eugene. *Wynken Blynken & Nod, & Other Verses.* 1937. Akron. Saalfield. ils Fern B Peat. 10p. VG/stiff wrp. T10. $50.00

FIELD, Evan. *What Nigel Knew.* 1981. Potter. 1st ed. hc. F/F. P3. $13.00

FIELD, Louise. *Peter Rabbit & His Ma.* 1917. Saalfield. ils FB Peat. unp. VG. M20. $18.00

FIELD, Louise. *Peter Rabbit & His Pa.* 1916. Saalfield. isl Fern B Peat. unp. VG. M20. $12.00

FIELD, Maria Antonia. *Chimes of Mission Bells.* 1914. San Francisco. 1st ed. inscr. 79p. VG. P4. $20.00

FIELD, Rachel. *All This & Heaven Too.* 1938. Macmillan. 1st ed. F/NF. B4. $85.00

FIELD, Rachel. *All This & Heaven Too.* 1938. NY. 1st ed. inscr. VG. O7. $60.00

FIELD, Rachel. *American Folk & Fairy Tales.* 1929. Scribner/Jr Literary Guild. ils. VG+/worn. M5. $60.00

FIELD, Rachel. *And Now Tomorrow.* 1942. NY. 1st ed. VG. O7. $20.00

FIELD, Rachel. *Calico Bush.* 1931. NY. 1st ed. woodcuts. VG/G. B5. $35.00

FIELD, Rachel. *Hepatica Hawks.* 1932. Macmillan. 1st ed. 239p. VG. P2. $25.00

FIELD, Rachel. *Hitty, Her First Hundred Years.* 1930 (1929). Macmillan. ils Dorothy Lathrop. VG. M5. $35.00

FIELD, Rachel. *Time Out of Mind.* 1935. NY. 1st ed. VG. O7. $50.00

FIELD, Stephen J. *Personal Reminiscences of Early Days in California...* 1880. np. 1st ed. 8vo. gilt cloth. VG. T10. $750.00

FIELD, Sylvester. *Job Trotter Seeks Health, Finds Negroes' Earthly Paradise...* 1904. Broadway Pub. inscr. 68p. VG. A4. $150.00

FIELD. *Transformation Playing Cards.* 1987. np. 4to. ils. 216p. F. A4. $45.00

FIELDING, Henry. *History of Tom Jones, a Foundling.* 1749. London. Prt for A Miller. 6 vol. 1st ed. 12mo. F/chemise/case. B24. $9,750.00

FIELDING, Henry. *Joseph Andrews.* 1939. Random. VG/VG. P3. $20.00

FIELDING, Henry. *Journey From This World to the Next.* 1930. Golden Cockerel. 1/500. VG. N3. $75.00

FIELDING, Henry. *Works of.../Miscellanies & Poems.* 1871-1872. London. 11 vol. ils Cruikshank. teg. gr morocco. VG. H3. $375.00

FIELDING, Mantle. *Dictionary of American Painters, Sculptors & Engravers.* 1974. np. 461p. VG/VG. A4. $85.00

FIELDS, Wilmer. *My Life in the Negro Leagues.* 1992. Meckler. 1st ed. F/F. P8. $60.00

FIENNES, Gerald. *Sea Power & Freedom.* 1918. Putnam. 1st ed. 374p. VG. P12. $15.00

FIES, Oswald. *Genealogie und Psychologie der Musiker.* 1910. Bergmann. 97p. later red cloth. VG. G1. $40.00

FIEUEROA, Jose. *Manifesto to the Mexican Republic.* 1978. Berkeley. VG. O7. $35.00

FIFIELD, William. *Modigliani.* 1976. Morrow. 1st ed. photos. 317p. cloth. dj. D2. $35.00

FIGUEROA, Jose. *Manifesto to the Mexican Republic.* 1978. Berkeley. 1st ed. 156p. dj. F3. $20.00

FILANYSON, Donald. *Michaelangelo: The Man.* 1935. np. 1st ed. photos. VG/VG. S13. $20.00

FILLEBROWN, R.H.M. *Rhymes of Happy Childhood.* 1908. Winston. 1st ed. ils Edwin John Prittie. teg. VG. M5. $75.00

FILLIS, James. *Breaking & Riding With Military Commentaries.* 1911. London. Hurst Blackett. VG. O3. $95.00

FINCH, C. *Of Muppets & Men.* 1981. NY. 1st ed. VG/VG. B5/S13. $35.00

FINCH, Hilda. *Christmas Time.* nd. np. pop-ups. 20p. sbdg. VG. A4. $30.00

FINCH, Jeremiah S. *Sir Thomas Browne.* 1950. NY. 1st ed. ils. VG. A17. $10.00

FINCH, Roger. *Sailing Craft of the British Isles.* 1975. London. Collins. ils/plans. 160p. dj. T7. $35.00

FINDLAY, James. *Modern Latin American Art.* 1983. Greenwood. 1st ed. 301p. F3. $35.00

FINDLEY, Ferguson. *Waterfront.* 1951. DSP. 1st ed. VG. P3. $15.00

FINDLEY, W. *History of the Insurrection in 4 West.* 1796. Phil. 1st ed. teg. 3-quarter leather/marbled brd. VG. A15. $500.00

FINE, Anne. *Killjoy.* 1987. Mysterious. 2nd. VG/VG. P3. $15.00

FINE, Stephen. *Molly Dear.* 1988. St Martin. 1st ed. F/F. P3. $19.00

FINGER, Charles. *Affair at the Inn.* 1938. Camden, NJ. Haddon Craftsmen. ils Baldridge. inscr Bellows. F/dj. T10. $35.00

FINGER, Charles. *Heroes From Hakluyt.* 1928. Holt. 1st ed. inscr. 8vo. 331p. F. B11. $55.00

FINGER, Charles. *In Lawless Land.* 1924. Mitchell Kennerley. 1st ed. 292p. w/sgn letter. F/VG. P2. $75.00

FINGER, Charles. *Tales From Silver Lands.* 1926 (1924). Doubleday Page. ils Paul Honore. 22p. G+. P2. $25.00

FINGER, Frances L. *Catalogue of the Incunabula in Elmer Belt Lib of Viciana.* 1971. Los Angeles. Ward Ritchie. 1/500. 80p. D2. $85.00

FINKEL, George. *Loyal Virginian.* 1968. Viking. 282p. F/F. B10. $10.00

FINKELSTEIN, Sidney. *Jazz: A People's Music.* 1948. Citadel. 1st ed. F/NF. B2. $50.00

FINKELSTEIN & LONDON. *Greater Nowhere.* 1988. NY. VG. O7. $20.00

FINKELSTEIN. *Copyright Law, Symposium Number Seventeen...* 1969. Columbia. 199p. F. A4. $35.00

FINLAY, Ernest. *Drylake Desperadoes.* 1944. Phoenix. xl. VG. P3. $5.00

FINLAY, Virgil. *Astrology Sketch Book.* 1975. Donald Grant. 1st ed. VG. P3. $25.00

FINLEY, M.I. *Atlas of Classical Archaeology.* 1977. NY. xl. VG. O7. $10.00

FINLEY, Martha. *Elsie Dinsmore: Christmas With Grandma Elsie (#14).* 1888. Dodd Mead. 317p. red cloth. VG. M20. $150.00

FINLEY, Martha. *Elsie Dinsmore: Elsie at Ion (#19).* 1893. Dodd Mead. 291p. red cloth. VG. M20. $12.50

FINLEY, Martha. *Elsie Dinsmore: Elsie at the World's Fair (#20).* 1894. Dodd Mead. 259p. VG. M20. $16.00

FINLEY, Martha. *Elsie Dinsmore: Elsie in the South (#24).* 1898. Dodd Mead. 324p. red cloth. VG. M20. $20.00

FINLEY, Martha. *Elsie Dinsmore: Elsie's Journey on Inland Waters (#21).* 1895. Dodd Mead. 283p. red cloth. VG+. M20. $16.00

FINLEY, Martha. *Elsie Dinsmore: Elsie's Kith & Kin (#12).* 1886. Dodd Mead. 338p. red cloth. VG. M20. $12.50

FINLEY, Martha. *Elsie Dinsmore: Elsie's Young Folks (#25).* 1900. Dodd Mead. 285p. VG+. M20. $20.00

FINLEY, Martha. *Elsie Dinsmore: Grandmother Elsie (#8).* 1910 (1882). Dodd Mead. 298p. red cloth. VG+. M20. $12.50

FINLEY, Ruth. *Old Patchwork Quilts & Women Who Make Them.* 1929. Phil. 1st ed. 100 pl. 202p. VG. B5. $85.00

FINMORE, Rhonda Lee. *Immoral Earnings; or, Mr Martin's Profession.* 1951. London. MH Pub. orig cloth. remnant dj. M11. $65.00

FINNEY, Charles G. *Past the End of the Pavement.* 1939. NY. 1st ed. sgn. VG/VG. C6. $100.00

FINNEY, Jack. *Assault on a Queen.* nd. BC. VG/VG. P3. $8.00

FINNEY, Jack. *Good Neighor Sam.* 1963. Simon Schuster. ARC. VG. M19. $75.00

FINNEY, Jack. *Night People.* 1977. Doubleday. 1st ed. VG/VG. P3. $30.00

FINNEY, Jack. *Time & Again.* 1970. Simon Schuster. BC. VG+/dj. M21. $10.00

FINNEY, Jack. *Time & Again.* 1970. Simon Schuster. stated 1st prt. rem mk. NF/NF. M22. $10.00

FIOR, G. Dalla. *La Nostra Flora.* 1963. Trento. 2nd. 239 pl. 752p. VG/dj. B26. $30.00

FIRBANK, Ronald. *Flower Beneath the Foot.* 1924. Brentano. 1st Am ed. VG-/dj. B2. $40.00

FIRBANK, Ronald. *Princess Zoubaroff.* 1920. London. Grant Richard. 1st ed. F. B2. $125.00

FIRBANK, Ronald. *5 Novels by Ronald Firbank.* 1949. New Directions. 1st Am ed. F/NF. C2. $40.00

FIREBAUGH, Ellen. *Physician's Wife & the Things That Pertain to Her Life.* 1894. Phil. 1st ed. 186p. cracked inner hinge. A13. $100.00

FIREMAN, Bert M. *Talk Honoring Lawrence Clark Powell on Occassion of 70th...* 1977. Platyne. 1/115. NF/wrp. B19. $75.00

FIRESTONE, Harvey S. Jr. *Romance & Drama of the Rubber Industry.* 1933. Firestone Tire & Rubber. 1/650. ils. 127p. VG. B18. $22.50

FIRMIN, Peter. *Basil Brush Goes Flying.* 1977 (1969). Prentice Hall. 1st Am ed. 8vo. 48p. F/fair. C14. $12.00

FIRTH, C.H. *Naval Songs & Ballads.* 1908. London. Navy Record Soc. ils. 387p. VG. T7. $60.00

FIRTH, Raymond. *Tikopia Ritual & Belief.* 1967. Boston. VG. O7. $25.00

FISCHER, Bruno. *Evil Days.* nd. BC. VG/VG. P3. $8.00

FISCHER, Bruno. *Quoth the Raven.* 1944. Crime Club. 1st ed. VG. P3. $25.00

FISCHER, Erwin. *Berlin Indictment.* 1971. World. 1st ed. xl. dj. P3. $5.00

FISCHER, H.F.W.D. *Leges Barbarorum in Usum Studiosorum...* 1951. Leiden. EJ Brill. 48p. prt sewn wrp. M11. $50.00

FISCHER, H.R. *Grosser Weltatlas der Buchergilde.* 1963. Frankfurt am Main. 100 maps. F. O7. $85.00

FISCHER & WIESER. *Oldest Map With the Name America of the Year 1507...* 1968 (1903). Amsterdam. rpt. 26 double-p maps/6 text maps. AN. O7. $150.00

FISCHMAN, Bernard. *Man Who Rode 10-Speed Bicycle to Moo.* 1979. Marek. hc. F/F. P3. $10.00

FISH, Helen Dean. *Animals of American History.* 1939. Stokes. 1st ed. ils Paul Branson. NF/VG. P2. $25.00

FISH, Helen. *Animals of the Bible.* 1937. Stokes. 1st ed/2nd state. ils/sgn Dorothy Lathrop. NF/VG+. P2. $275.00

FISH, Robert L. *Pursuit.* 1978. Doubleday. 1st ed. VG/VG. P3. $20.00

FISHBEIN, Morris. *Doctors at War.* 1945. NY. 1st ed. 418p. G. A17. $8.50

FISHBEIN, Morris. *Frontiers of Medicine.* 1933. Baltimore. 207p. xl. A13. $15.00

FISHER, Aileen. *Cricket in the Thicket.* 1963. Scribner. ils Rojankovsky. 61p. NF/G+. T5. $15.00

FISHER, Aileen. *My Cat Has Eyes of Sapphire Blue.* 1973. NY. 1st ed. juvenile. 24p. VG+/dj. B18. $12.50

FISHER, Aileen. *That's Why.* 1946. Nelson. 1st ed. 96p. VG/VG. P2. $20.00

FISHER, Aileen. *We Went Looking.* 1968. NY. 1st ed. 25p. VG/dj. B18. $12.50

FISHER, Anne. *Oh Glittering Promise!* 1949. Bobbs Merrill. 8vo. gilt bl cloth. G. T10. $25.00

FISHER, Carrie. *Surrender the Pink.* 1990. Simon Schuster. 1st ed. F/F. B35. $20.00

FISHER, Carrie. *Surrender the Pink.* 1990. Simon Schuster. 1st ed. VG/VG. K2. $12.00

FISHER, Clay. *Crossing.* 1958. Houghton Mifflin. 1st ed. VG/VG. B10. $12.00

FISHER, Clay. *Oldest Maiden Lady in New Mexico & Other Stories.* 1962. Macmillan. 1st ed. F/F. A18. $20.00

FISHER, E.T. *Report of a French Protestant Refugee in Boston...* 1868. Brooklyn. 1/125. 42p. cloth/brd. G. B14. $100.00

FISHER, Harrison. *Bachelor Belles.* 1908. Dodd Mead. 1st ed. 22 pl. VG+. B5. $185.00

FISHER, Harrison. *Harrison Fisher Book.* 1908. Scribner. G+. B5. $175.00

FISHER, Harrison. *Hiawatha.* 1906. Indianapolis. 1st ed. VG. B5. $125.00

FISHER, Harrison. *Longfellow's Hiawatha.* 1906. Indianapolis. 1st ed thus. VG. B5. $100.00

FISHER, John. *Midmost Waters.* 1952. London. VG. O7. $25.00

FISHER, Louise B. *Eighteenth-Century Garland: Flower & Fruit Arrangements...* 1951. Colonial Williamsburg. 1st ed. photos. 91p. VG/G. B10. $25.00

FISHER, M.F.K. *Alphabet for Gourmets.* 1949. NY. 1st ed. VG/VG. B5. $50.00

FISHER, M.F.K. *Among Friends.* 1971. NY. 1st ed. F/NF clip. A11. $250.00

FISHER, M.F.K. *Consider the Oyster.* 1941. Duell Sloan. 1st ed. F/NF. C2. $125.00

FISHER, M.F.K. *Cordiall Water.* 1961. Little Brn. 1st ed. F/VG+. M19. $100.00

FISHER, M.F.K. *Cordiall Water: Garland of Odd & Old Receipts...* nd. np. 1st ed. VG/VG. M17. $45.00

FISHER, M.F.K. *Here Let Us Feast: A Book of Banquets.* 1946. Viking. 1st ed. F/F. C2. $100.00

FISHER, M.F.K. *With Bold Knife & Fork.* 1969. Putnam. 1st ed. F/F. C2. $75.00

FISHER, Major. *Through the Saddle & Saddle Room.* 1890. London. Bentley. 1st ed. G+. O3. $48.00

FISHER, Paul R. *Hawks of Fellheath.* 1980. Atheneum. 1st ed. hc. VG/VG. P3. $18.00

FISHER, R.A. *Digest of the Reported Cases...* 1871. San Francisco. Sumner Whitney. contemporary sheep. M11. $125.00

FISHER, Robert Lewis. *Odyssey of Tobacco.* 1939. Prospect. 1st ed. ils. 93p. VG. T10. $45.00

FISHER, Steve. *Hell-Black Night.* 1970. Sherbourne. 1st ed. NF/NF. P3. $25.00

FISHER, Steve. *Saxon's Ghost.* 1969. Sherbourne. 1st ed. NF/NF. P3. $30.00

FISHER, Vardis. *Children of God.* 1939. Harper. 1st ed. VG/VG. P3. $45.00

FISHER, Vardis. *City of Illusion.* 1941. Harper. 1st ed. VG. P3. $45.00

FISHER, Vardis. *Divine Passion.* 1948. NY. 1st ed. VG/VG. B5. $35.00

FISHER, Vardis. *Golden Rooms.* 1944. Vanguard. VG/VG. P3. $23.00

FISHER, Vardis. *Idaho: A Guide in Word & Picture.* 1937. Caxton. 1st ed. F. A18. $200.00

FISHER, Vardis. *No Villain Need Be.* 1936. Caxton. 1st ed. F/chip. A18. $75.00

FISHER, Vardis. *Orphans in Gethsemane: A Novel of the Past in the Present.* 1990. Alan Swallow. 1st ltd ed. 1/200. sgn. w/4 broadsides. VG/dj. A18. $250.00

FISHER, Vardis. *Tale of Valor.* 1958. Doubleday. 1st ed. VG. P3. $25.00

FISHER, Vardis. *Tale of Valor.* 1958. Doubleday. 1st ed. VG/VG. B5. $30.00

FISHER, Vardis. *Tale of Valor.* 1958. Doubleday. 1st ed. 8vo. 456p. map ep. beige cloth. VG+/NF. T10. $35.00

FISHER, Vardis. *Tale of Valor: A Novel of the Lewis & Clark Expedition.* 1958. Doubleday. 1st ed. F/F. A18. $40.00

FISHER, Vardis. *Toilers of the Hills.* 1928. Houghton Mifflin. 1st ed. NF/dj. A18. $80.00

FISHER & HOLMES. *Gold Rushes & Mining Camps of the Early American West.* 1968. Caxton. 1st ed. inscr/sgn Fisher & Holmes. F/dj. A18. $125.00

FISHER. *Invisible Empire: A Bibliography of the Ku Klux Klan.* 1980. 202p. F. A4. $35.00

FISHER. *Trial of the Constitution.* 1862. Phil. 8vo. 391p. brn cloth. G. T3. $22.00

FISHWICK, M. *Lee After the War.* 1963. NY. 1st ed. VG/VG. B5. $25.00

FISK, Nicholas. *Space Hostages.* 1984. Kestrel. decor brd. F. P3. $15.00

FISK, Robert. *Pity the Nation. Abduction of Lebanon.* 1990. Atheneum. 1st ed. 8vo. 3 maps. NF/dj. W1. $22.00

FISKE, Dorsey. *Bound to Murder.* 1987. St Martin. 1st ed. NF/NF. P3. $18.00

FISKE, John. *Myths & Myth-Makers: Old Tales & Superstitions...* 1902. Boston. rpt. 354p. gilt cloth. A17. $15.00

FISTERE & FISTERE. *Jordan: The Holy Land.* 1964. Beirut. Middle East Export. 8vo. ils. 220p. VG/dj. W1. $22.00

FITCH, Florence May. *Book About God.* July 1956. Lee Shepard. 4th. ils Weisgard. F/VG clip. C14. $12.00

FITE & FREEMAN. *Book of Old Maps Delineating American History...* 1926. Harvard. folio. 75 maps. F. O7. $375.00

FITTS, John Nelson. *New Deal Solitaire: 33 New Games All for One Deck.* 1934. NY. 96p. VG. S1. $8.00

FITZENMEYER, Frieda. *Once Upon a Time: Book One.* 1984. Warwick. 1/125. sgn. ils/sgn CJ Blinn. miniature. F. B24. $125.00

FITZGERALD, Edward. *Rubaiyat of Omar Khayyam.* ca 1925. Crowell. ils Pogany. NF. M19. $35.00

FITZGERALD, Edward. *Rubaiyat of Omar Khayyam.* nd. Crowell. early rpt. ils Willy Pogany. G. B17. $10.00

FITZGERALD, Edward. *Rubaiyat of Omar Khayyam.* 1952. Garden City. ils Edmund Dulac. 191p. VG/VG. T5. $25.00

FITZGERALD, F. Scott. *All the Sad Young Men.* 1926. NY. 1st ed. VG. B5. $50.00

FITZGERALD, F. Scott. *Evil Eye.* 1915. Cincinnati/NY/London. 1st ed. 4to. 92p. NF/custom box. C6. $1,650.00

FITZGERALD, F. Scott. *F Scott Fitzgerald's St Paul Plays 1911-1914.* 1978. Princeton. 1st ed. 200-word inscr. F/F. A11. $75.00

FITZGERALD, F. Scott. *Flappers & Philosophers.* 1920. NY. 1st ed. VG. C6. $200.00

FITZGERALD, F. Scott. *Great Gatsby.* 1925. NY. 1st issue. VG. A15. $250.00

FITZGERALD, F. Scott. *Great Gatsby.* 1925. Scribner. 1st ed/1st issue. F. B24. $700.00

FITZGERALD, F. Scott. *Great Gatsby.* 1934. Modern Lib. 1st ed thus. VG. O7. $35.00

FITZGERALD, F. Scott. *Great Gatsby.* 1984. San Francisco. 1/400. ils/sgn Michael Graves. 180p. AN. B24. $400.00

FITZGERALD, F. Scott. *Kultahattu.* 1959. Helsinki. 1st Finnish ed. NF/wrp/integral dj. A11. $6.00

FITZGERALD, F. Scott. *Tales of the Jazz Age.* 1922. NY. 1st ed. VG. B5. $75.00

FITZGERALD, F. Scott. *Tender Is the Night.* 1934. NY. 1st ed. VG. B5. $75.00

FITZGERALD, F. Scott. *Tender Is the Night.* 1953. London. 1st ed thus. F/F. C6. $100.00

FITZGERALD, John D. *Papa Married a Mormon.* 1955. Englewood Cliffs. 1st ed. 8vo. ils. gilt bdg. F/NF. T10. $35.00

FITZGERALD, Kevin. *Quiet Under the Sun.* 1954. Little Brn. 1st ed. VG/VG. P3. $20.00

FITZGERALD, Maurice J. *Handbook of Criminal Investigation.* 1974. Arco. 8th. F/F. P3. $18.00

FITZGERALD, Michael. *Universal Pictures: A Panoramic History in Words...* 1977. New Rochelle. photos/index. 766p. G/dj. A17. $20.00

FITZGERALD, Nigel. *Black Welcome.* 1962. Macmillan. 1st ed. VG/G. P3. $15.00

FITZGERALD, Nigel. *Day of the Adder.* 1973. Collins Crime Club. NF/NF. P3. $15.00

FITZGERALD, Percy. *Bardell Versus Pickwick: Trial for Breach of Promise...* 1902. London. Elliot Stock. gr cloth. M11. $135.00

FITZGERALD, W.N. *Harness Makers' Illustrated Manual.* 1875. NY. 1st ed. O3. $95.00

FITZGIBBON, Constantine. *Life of Dylan Thomas.* 1965. Little Brn. 1st Am ed. F/NF. V1. $20.00

FITZGIBBON, Constantine. *When Kissing Had To Stop.* 1960. Cassell. 3rd ed. VG/G. P3. $18.00

FITZHERBERT, Anthony. *La Novel Natura Breuium...Dernierement Reuieu & Corrigee...* 1916. London. Companie of Stationers. contemporary calf. G. M11. $750.00

FITZHUGH, Percy Keese. *Pee-Wee Harris on the Trail (#2).* 1922. Grosset Dunlap. lists 5 titles. 211p. VG/dj. M20. $30.00

FITZHUGH, Percy Keese. *Pee-Wee Harris: Fixer (#7).* 1924. Grosset Dunlap. lists to this title. 208p. VG/dj. B10. $25.00

FITZHUGH, Percy Keese. *Pee-Wee Harris: Mayor for a Day (#9).* 1926. Grosset Dunlap. 1st ed. 246p. VG/dj. M20. $27.00

FITZHUGH, Percy Keese. *Tom Slade: Parachute Jumper (#19).* 1930. Grosset Dunlap. last title in series. 197p. VG/dj. M20. $150.00

FITZHUGH, Percy Keese. *Westy Martin (#1).* 1924. Grosset Dunlap. 196p. VG/dj. M20. $22.00

FITZSIMMONS, Cortland. *Crimson Ice.* 1935. Stokes. 1st ed. NF/VG. B4. $85.00

FITZSIMMONS, Cortland. *Death on the Diamond.* 1934. Grosset Dunlap. rpt. 332p. VG/dj. M20. $42.00

FITZSIMMONS, Cortland. *Red Rhapsody.* 1933. Stokes. 1st ed. VG. P3. $25.00

FITZWYGRAM, F. *Horses & Stables.* 1894. London. Longman Gr. 4th. VG. O3. $45.00

FIXICO, Donald L. *Termination & Relocation, Federal Indian Policy 1945-60.* 1986. Albuquerque. M11. $35.00

FLACCUS, Quintus Horatius. *Carmina Alcaica & Carmina Sapphica.* 1903. Chelsea. Ashendene. 2 vol. 1/150. gold leaf decor. F/half morocco case. B24. $1,650.00

FLACH, Frederic F. *Fridericus.* 1980. Lippincott Crowell. 1st ed. VG/G. P3. $13.00

FLAMMARION, Camille. *Atmosphere.* 1873. Harper. edit James Glaisher. 8vo. 453p. half leather. G. K5. $125.00

FLANAGAN & FLANAGAN. *American Folklore: A Bibliogaphy 1950-1974.* 1977. Scarecrow. 1st ed. 406p. F3. $20.00

FLANNAGAN, Roy. *County Court.* 1937. Doubleday Doran. 1st ed. 274p. VG/G. B10. $15.00

FLANNER, Janet. *Men & Monuments.* 1957. Harper. w/review photo. F/VG. B1. $25.00

FLAUBERT, Gustave. *Salammbo.* 1886 (1885). London. Saxon. 1st ed. 421p. cloth. VG. M20. $82.00

FLAVIN, Martin. *Red Poppies & White Marble.* 1962. NY. Nelson. 1st ed. 8vo. 314p. VG/dj. W1. $18.00

FLAYDERMAN, Norm. *Flayderman's Guide to Antique American Firearms.* 1983. Northfield, IL. ils. 624p. G. T3. $20.00

FLAYHART & WARWICK. *QE2.* 1985. Norton. 1st ed. sgn. sgns/inscr Flayhart. 176p. F/F/VG case. B11. $55.00

FLECHTNER, Myron. *Gallipolis: Being Account of the French Five Hundred...* 1940. Columbus. ils. 47p. VG/wrp. B18. $45.00

FLECKER, James Elroy. *Hassan: Story of Hassan of Bagdad...* 1924. Knopf. 1st Am ed. 12mo. 169p. VG. W1. $20.00

FLEET, Betsy. *Henry Fleet: Pioneer, Explorer, Trader, Planter...* 1989. Whittet Sheperson. 110p. VG. B10. $20.00

FLEETWOOD, Hugh. *Beast.* 1979. Atheneum. 1st ed. VG/VG. P3. $18.00

FLEETWOOD, Hugh. *Painter of Flowers.* 1972. Viking. 1st ed. hc. VG/VG. P3. $22.00

FLEETWOOD, Hugh. *Redeemer.* 1979. Hamish Hamilton. 1st ed. VG/VG. P3. $13.00

FLEISCHER, Richard. *Just Tell Me When To Cry.* 1993. Carroll Graf. 1st ed. 8vo. inscr. F/F. T10. $50.00

FLEISCHMANN, Melanie. *American Border Gardens.* 1993. NY. photos. 144p. AN/dj. B26. $20.00

FLEMING, Archibald Lang. *Archibald the Arctic.* 1956. Appleton Century Crofts. 1st ed. 8vo. ils/photos/index. 399p. F/NF. T10. $25.00

FLEMING, G.H. *Dizziest Season.* 1984. Morrow. 1st ed. F/VG+. P8. $50.00

FLEMING, Ian. *Bonded Fleming.* 1965. Viking. 1st ed. VG/VG. P3. $40.00

FLEMING, Ian. *Doctor No.* 1958. Jonathan Cape. 1st ed. VG. P3. $60.00

FLEMING, Ian. *Dr No.* 1958. Macmillan. 1st Am ed. NF/VG. M19. $100.00

FLEMING, Ian. *Man With the Golden Gun.* 1965. Jonathan Cape. 1st ed. VG/VG. P3. $50.00

FLEMING, Ian. *Man With the Golden Gun.* 1965. Jonathan Cape. 1st Eng ed. F/VG. M19. $65.00

FLEMING, Ian. *Man With the Golden Gun.* 1965. NAL. 1st Am ed. F/F. B2. $45.00

FLEMING, Ian. *Man With the Golden Gun.* 1965. NAL. 1st ed. F/NF. T2. $40.00

FLEMING, Ian. *Man With the Golden Gun.* 1965. NAL. 1st ed. VG/G. P3. $35.00

FLEMING, Ian. *Octopussy & the Living Daylights.* 1966. Jonathan Cape. 1st ed. F/F. P3. $50.00

FLEMING, Ian. *On Her Majesty's Secret Service.* 1963. NAL. 1st Am ed. F/NF. M22. $60.00

FLEMING, Ian. *Thrilling Cities.* 1964. NAL. 1st ed. VG. M22. $10.00

FLEMING, Ian. *Thunderball.* 1961. Jonathan Cape. 1st ed. VG/VG. P3. $50.00

FLEMING, Ian. *You Only Live Twice.* 1964. London. Cape. true 1st ed. VG/VG. M22. $45.00

FLEMING, Ian. *You Only Live Twice.* 1964. NAL. 1st Am ed. F/NF. B2. $40.00

FLEMING, Ian. *You Only Live Twice.* 1964. NAL. 1st ed. VG/G. P3. $35.00

FLEMING, Joan. *Be a Good Boy.* 1971. Putnam. 1st ed. VG/VG. P3. $20.00

FLEMING, Joan. *Dirty Butter for Servants.* 1972. Hamish Hamilton. 1st ed. VG/VG. P3. $20.00

FLEMING, Joan. *In the Red.* 1961. Ives Washburn. 1st ed. author's 5th novel. VG/VG. M22. $15.00

FLEMING, Joan. *Kill or Cure.* 1968. Ives Washburn. 1st ed. VG/VG. P3. $15.00

FLEMING, Joan. *Malice Matrimonial.* 1959. Ives Washburn. 1st ed. VG. P3. $25.00

FLEMING, Joan. *Midnight Hag.* 1966. Ives Washburn. 1st ed. VG/VG. P3. $20.00

FLEMING, Joan. *Nothing Is the Number When You Die.* 1965. Ives Washburn. 1st ed. VG/VG. P3. $20.00

FLEMING, Joan. *Nothing Is the Number When You Die.* 1965. London. Collins. 1st ed. NF/VG. M22. $15.00

FLEMING, Joan. *Too Late! Too Late! The Maiden Cried.* 1975. Putnam. 1st ed. VG/VG. P3. $20.00

FLEMING, Joan. *You Won't Let Me Finish.* 1973. Collins Crime Club. 1st ed. VG/VG. P3. $20.00

FLEMING, William. *Vocabulary of Philosophy...* 1887. Scribner Welford. 4th. 12mo. 439p. emb brn cloth. G1. $37.50

FLEMING & GORE. *English Garden.* 1980 (1979). London. ils/pl. 256p. VG/dj. B26. $40.00

FLEMING. *Sinclair Lewis: A Reference Guide.* 1980. np. 240p. F. A4. $45.00

FLEROFF, Alexander. *Russlands Vegatationsbilder.* 1907. Petersburg. Erste Serie, Heft 1 & 2. sepia photos. 13p. B26. $20.00

FLETCHER, Colin. *Man From the Cave.* 1981. NY. sgn. VG. O7. $50.00

FLETCHER, David. *Raffles.* 1977. Putnam. 1st ed. hc. F/F. P3. $15.00

FLETCHER, Inglis. *Cormorant's Brood.* 1959. Lippincott. 1st ed. VG/VG. P3. $15.00

FLETCHER, Inglis. *Roanoke Hundred.* 1948. Bobbs Merrill. 1st ed. sgn. VG. B11. $50.00

FLETCHER, Inglis. *Wind in the Forest.* 1957. Bobbs Merrill. 1st ed. VG/G. P3. $15.00

FLETCHER, J.S. *Murder of the Lawyer's Clerk.* 1933. Knopf. 1st ed. G. P3. $20.00

FLETCHER, J.S. *Talleyrand Maxim.* 1930. Ward Lock. 1st ed. VG. P3. $35.00

FLETCHER, Lucille. *...And Presumed Dead.* 1963. Random. 1st ed. VG. P3. $10.00

FLETCHER, S.W. *How To Make a Fruit Garden.* 1906. NY. photos/plans. 283p. VG. B26. $28.00

FLEXNER, James Thomas. *Steamboats Come True: American Inventors in Action.* 1944. Viking. 1st ed. G/poor. A16. $35.00

FLEXNER, S.B. *I Hear America Talking.* 1976. NY. 1st ed. VG/VG. B5. $30.00

FLEXNER. *Wilder Image: Painting of America's Native School...* 1962. Little Brn. cloth. NF/VG. D2. $55.00

FLINT, Harrison L. *Landscape Plants for Eastern North America.* 1983. NY. photos/drawings. F/dj. B26. $60.00

FLINT, Jeremy. *How To Play Bridge.* 1988. London. 62p. VG+. S1. $6.00

FLINT, Timothy. *Recollections of the Last Ten Years in Valley of MS.* 1968. Carbondale, IL. 343p. VG/dj. B18. $35.00

FLINT, Timothy. *Western Monthly Review.* 1828. Cincinnati. 8vo. 756p. xl. T3. $60.00

FLINT & SHARP. *Competetive Bidding.* 1980. London. 202p. VG. S1. $15.00

FLOETHE & FLOETHE. *Fountain of the Friendly Lion.* 1966. Scribner. 1st/A ed. 4to. yel cloth. NG/G+. T5. $30.00

FLORA, Fletcher. *Irrepressible Peccadillo.* 1962. Macmillan. 1st ed. G/G. P3. $20.00

FLORA, Snowden D. *Tornadoes of the United States.* 1953. Norman, OK. ils/figures. 194p. G/tattered. K5. $20.00

FLORENCE, Ronald. *Perfect Machine.* 1994. Harper Collins. 2nd. 451p. F/F. K5. $27.00

FLORESCU, Radu. *In Search of Frankenstein.* 1975. NGS. 1st ed. hc. VG/VG. P3. $20.00

FLOREY, Jane. *Mr Snitzel's Cookies.* 1950. Rand McNally. Elf-Jr Book. 1st ed. 16mo. ils. VG. M5. $12.00

FLORIN, Lambert. *Boot Hill: Historic Graves of the Old West.* nd. Bonanza. ils. 192p. gray cloth. VG/dj. T10. $25.00

FLORY, Clyde. *Centennial Volume: Bucks County Medical Soc of Phil...* 1949. Sellersville. 1st ed. 255p. xl. A13. $30.00

FLOURNOY, Theodor. *Spiritism & Psychology.* 1911. Harper. 1st Eng-language ed. 354p. bl cloth. VG. G1. $50.00

FLOWER, F.A. *History of Republican Party.* 1884. Springfield. 1st ed. ils. VG+. A15. $45.00

FLOWER, Jessie Graham. *Grace Harlow's Return to Overton College.* 1915. Altemus. 256p. VG/dj. M20. $27.00

FLOWER, Jessie Graham. *Grace Harlowe's Golden Summer.* 1917. Altemus. 256p. VG/dj. M20. $27.00

FLOWER, Jessie Graham. *Grace Harlowe's Overland Riders & the Kentucky Mountaineers.* 1921. Altemus. 253p. VG/dj. M20. $27.00

FLOWER, Jessie Graham. *Grace Harlowe's Overland Riders in the High Sierras (#22).* 1923. Altemus. 251p. VG/dj. M20. $27.00

FLOWER, Jessie Graham. *Grace Harlowe's Problem.* 1916. Altemus. 256p. VG/dj. M20. $22.00

FLOWER, Pat. *Crisscross.* 1976. Collins Crime Club. 1st ed. F/F. P3. $13.00

FLOWER, Pat. *Vanishing Point.* 1977. Stein Day. VG/VG. P3. $10.00

FLOWERS, Charles. *It Never Rains in Los Angeles.* 1970. Coward McCann. 1st ed. F/F. B2. $35.00

FLOWERS, Seville. *Some Ferns of Montana.* nd. Missoula. ils. 37p. stapled wrp. B26. $16.00

FLUKINGER. *Windows of Light: A Bibliography of Serial Literature...* 1994. np. 4to. ils. 418p. VG/wrp. A4. $85.00

FLYEMAN, Rose. *Adventures With Benghazi.* 1946. Eyre Spottiswoode. 1st ed. 8vo. ils. F/VG. M5. $65.00

FLYEMAN, Rose. *Fairies & Chimneys.* 1929 (1920). Doubleday. 12mo. ils. VG. M5. $35.00

FLYEMAN, Rose. *Frou the Hare.* nd. London. Allen Unwin. 2nd. Wild Animal Book 4. VG+/VG. C8. $75.00

FLYEMAN, Rose. *Martin the Kingfisher.* nd. Allen Unwin. 3rd. Wild Animal Book 7. VG+/VG. C8. $75.00

FLYNN, George L. *Great Moments in Baseball.* 1987. Bison. F/F. P3. $10.00

FOCK, H. *Fast Fighting Boats 1870-1945...* 1978. US Naval Inst. 304p. F/dj. A17. $45.00

FOCK, V. *Theory of Space, Time & Gravitation.* 1976. Oxford. Pergamon. 2nd. 448p. K5. $30.00

FOCKEMA & VAN THOFF. *Geschiedenis der Kartografie van Nederland...* 1947. Martinus Nijhoff. 23 maps/2 pl. F. O7. $75.00

FODOR, Nandor. *Between Two Worlds.* nd. BC. hc. VG. P3. $7.00

FOGAZZARO, Antonio. *Saint.* 1907. Copp Clarke. hc. decor brd. VG. P3. $10.00

FOGGITT, Bill. *Weatherwise: Facts, Fictions & Predictions.* 1992. Phil. Running Pr. ils Walter VanLotringen. F/F. K5. $6.00

FOGLE, James. *Drugstore Cowboy.* nd. NY. Delta Fiction. AP. 8vo. NF/wrp. w/edit sgn letter. S9. $45.00

FOHLMEISTER, Jurgen. *Polar Flight.* 1992. NY. ARC/1st ed. 188p. F/dj. B18. $12.50

FOLEY, J.W. *Sons of School Days.* 1906. Doubleday. 1st ed. silhouettes by Katherine Buffum. cloth. VG+. M5. $45.00

FOLEY, Martha. *Best American Short Stories 3.* 1965. MacGibbon Kee. 1st ed. VG/VG. P3. $20.00

FOLEY, Rae. *Last Gamble.* 1956. Dodd Mead. 1st ed. VG/VG. P3. $29.00

FOLEY, Rae. *Suffer a Witch.* 1965. Dodd Mead. 1st ed. VG/VG. P3. $20.00

FOLEY, Rae. *Trust a Woman?* 1973. Dodd Mead. 1st ed. VG/VG. P3. $15.00

FOLEY & LORD. *Folk Arts & Crafts of New England.* 1970. Chilton. Anniversary ed. 282p. F/dj. A17. $25.00

FOLI, P.R.S. *Fortune Telling by Cards at a Glance.* 1956. Baltimore. 122p. VG/worn. S1. $6.00

FOLLETT, Helen. *Magic Portholes.* 1932. NY. ils Armstrong Sperry. 321p. VG. A17. $10.00

FOLLETT, Ken. *Dangerous Fortune.* 1993. Delacorte. 1st ed. F/F. H11. $30.00

FOLLETT, Ken. *Eye of the Needle.* 1978. Arbor. 1st ed. author's 1st book. NF/NF. H11. $40.00

FOLLETT, Ken. *Key to Rebecca.* 1980. Morrow. 1st ed. F/F. H11. $40.00

FOLLETT, Ken. *Key to Rebecca.* 1980. Morrow. 1st ed. F/VG clip. N4. $25.00

FOLLETT, Ken. *Lie Down With Lions.* 1986. Morrow. F/F. P3. $19.00

FOLLETT, Ken. *Night Over Water.* 1991. Morrow. 1st ed. NF/NF. N4. $20.00

FOLLETT, Ken. *Pillars of the Earth.* 1989. Morrow. 1st ed. sgn. F/F. B2. $45.00

FOLLETT, Ken. *Power Twins.* 1990. Morrow. 1st Am ed. F/F. G10. $10.00

FOLLETT, Ken. *Triple.* 1979. Arbor. 1st ed. F/F. H11. $45.00

FOLMSBEE, Beulah. *Little History of the Horn Book.* 1942. Horn Book Inc. 12mo. 6 mtd pl. 57p. VG. T10. $250.00

FOLSOM, Allan. *Day After Tomorrow.* 1994. Little Brn. ARC. F/NF. G10. $30.00

FOLSOM, Franklin. *Explorations of America.* 1958. Grosset Dunlap. 1st ed. 149p. VG/dj. A17. $8.50

FONER, P. *Paul Robeson Speaks: Writings, Speeches, Interviews.* 1978. NY. 1st ed. 623p. VG/VG. B5. $20.00

FONSTAD, Karen Wynn. *Atlas of the Land.* nd. BC. VG/VG. P3. $13.00

FONTES, Montserrat. *First Confession.* 1991. Norton. 1st ed. author's 1st novel. NF/NF. M22. $30.00

FOOTE, H.W. *Annals of King's Chapel, From the Puritan Age of New Eng...* 1882. Boston. 2 vol. ils. VG. M17. $50.00

FOOTE, Shelby. *Love in a Dry Season.* 1951. NY. 1st ed. VG/VG. B5. $70.00

FOOTE, Shelby. *Novelist's View of History.* 1981. Palaemon. 1/140. sgn. F/stiff wrp. B10. $35.00

FOOTE, Shelby. *September, September.* 1st ed. NF/F. B30. $100.00

FOOTNER, Hulbert. *Doctor Who Held Hands.* 1929. Crime Club. 1st ed. VG. P3. $35.00

FORBES, Colin. *Stockholm Syndicate.* 1982. Dutton. 1st ed. VG/VG. P3. $18.00

FORBES, Colin. *Target Five.* 1973. Collins. 1st ed. VG/VG. P3. $18.00

FORBES, Edgar Allen. *Leslie's Photographic Review of The Great War.* 1920. Leslie-Judge. hc. G. p3. $40.00

FORBES, Esther. *America's Paul Revere.* 1946. Houghton Mifflin. 1st ed. 4to. 46p. VG. C14. $12.00

FORBES, Graham B. *In Track Athletics.* 1913. Grosset Dunlap. ils. VG. P12. $6.00

FORBES, John D. *Death Warmed Over.* 1971. Pagent. 1st ed. inscr. 151p. pb. VG. B10. $12.00

FORBES, Stanton. *But I Wouldn't Want To Die.* 1972. Crime Club. 1st ed. VG/VG. P3. $20.00

FORBES, William Cameron. *As to Polo.* 1911. np. 1st ed. G. O3. $40.00

FORBUSH, E.H. *Birds of Massachusetts & Other New England States. Vol 1.* 19225. MA Dept Agriculture. 8to. ils LA Fuertes. 481p. cloth. VG. B1. $75.00

FORBUSH, William Byron. *Manual of Play.* 1914. Phil. ils. 3353p. xl. VG. A17. $7.50

FORD, Clara A. *Tipi Sings: A Dog Story.* 1941. Stokes. inscr/dtd 1946. ils D Thorne. 110p. bl cloth. VG/torn. T5. $15.00

FORD, Corey. *Best of Corey Ford.* 1975. NY. 1st ed. VG/VG. B5. $25.00

FORD, Douglas. *Admiral Vernon & the Navy. Memoir & Vindication.* 1907. London. Fisher Unwin. ils. 322p. VG. T7. $60.00

FORD, Florence. *Shadow on the House.* 1958. Collins Crime Club. 1st ed. VG/VG. P3. $25.00

FORD, Ford Madox. *Brown Owl: A Fairy Story.* 1892. London. Unwin. 1st ed. author's 1st book. 165p. F. B24. $1,000.00

FORD, G.M. *Who in Hell Is Wanda Fuca?* 1995. Walker. 1st ed. F/F. M23. $40.00

FORD, Gerald. *Time To Heal.* 1979. Harper. 1st ed. NF/NF. w/sgn 1st day cover of White House. S13. $45.00

FORD, Hilary; see Silverberg, Robert.

FORD, James Allan. *Judge of Men.* 1968. Hodder Stoughton. NF/NF. P3. $7.00

FORD, Jesse Hill. *Liberation of Lord Byron Jones.* 1965. Boston. 1st ed. F/F. A17. $10.00

FORD, Julia Ellsworth. *Imagina.* 1914. Duffield. 1st ed. 178p. gilt cloth. F. B24. $650.00

FORD, Kathleen. *Jeffrey County.* 1986. St Martin. 1st ed. 197p. VG/VG. B10. $12.00

FORD, Leslie. *Bahamas Murder Case.* 1951. Detective BC. VG. P3. $8.00

FORD, Marcia; see Radford, R.L.

FORD, Paul Leicester. *Great K&A Train Robbery.* 1897. NY. 1st book ed. NF. C6. $75.00

FORD, Richard. *Independence Day.* 1995. Knopf. 1st ed. NF/NF. G10. $10.00

FORD, Richard. *Independence Day.* 1995. Knopf. 1st ed. sgn. F/F. M23. $60.00

FORD, Richard. *Independence Day.* 1995. Knopf. 1st ed. 1/150. sgn/#d. F/case. C2. $150.00

FORD, Richard. *Piece of My Heart.* 1976. Harper Row. 1st ed. author's 1st book. sgn. F/F. M23. $375.00

FORD, Richard. *Piece of My Heart.* 1976. Harper. ARC. sgn. author's 1st book. NF/pict wrp. B4. $450.00

FORD, Richard. *Rock Springs.* 1987. Atlantic Monthly. 1st ed. sgn. F/NF. M23. $45.00

FORD, Richard. *Sportswriter.* 1996. Knopf. 1st Am hc ed. sgn. F/F. B4. $50.00

FORD, Richard. *Ultimate Good Luck.* 1981. Houghton Mifflin. 1st ed. sgn. author's 2nd book. F/F. B4. $250.00

FORD, Richard. *Wildlife.* 1990. Atlantic Monthly. 1st ed. sgn. F/F. M23. $35.00

FORD, Richard. *Wildlife.* 1990. London. Collins Harvill. 1st ed. 1/600. F/dj. S9. $100.00

FORD, Worthington C. *United States & Spain in 1790.* 1890. Brooklyn. VG. O7. $55.00

FORD & PEPE. *Slick.* 1987. Morrow 1st ed. sgn. F/F. P8. $45.00

FORDER, Archibald. *Ventures Among the Arabs.* 1905. Boston. Hartshorn. sgn. 8vo. fld map/pl. 292p. VG. B11. $85.00

FORDHAM, Herbert George. *Studies in Carto-Bibliography, British & French...* 1969. London. Dawsons. rpt of 1914 ed. AN. O7. $65.00

FORDHAM, Mary Weston. *Magnolia Leaves.* 1897. Walker Evans Cogswell. 1st ed. intro Brooker T Washington. NF. B4. $450.00

FOREMAN, Michael. *Arabian Nights.* 1992. Gollancz. 1/200. sgn ils/trans. aeg. AN/case. P2. $150.00

FORESTER, C.S. *Captain From Connecticut.* 1942. Clipper. VG/VG. P3. $30.00

FORESTER, C.S. *Captain Hornblower RN.* 1955. Michael Joseph. 14th. VG. P3. $10.00

FORESTER, C.S. *Commodore Hornblower.* 1945. Boston. 1st Am ed. 384p. VG/dj. B18. $22.50

FORESTER, C.S. *General.* 1936. Little Brn. 1st ed. VG. P3. $35.00

FORESTER, C.S. *Gold From Crete.* 1971. Michael Joseph. 1st ed. NF/NF. P3. $25.00

FORESTER, C.S. *Hornblower & Atropos.* 1953. London. 1st ed. VG/VG. B5. $50.00

FORESTER, C.S. *Hornblower Companion.* 1964. Boston. 1st ed. VG/VG. B5. $90.00

FORESTER, C.S. *Last Nine Days of Bismarck.* 1959. Boston. 1st ed. VG/VG. B5. $45.00

FORESTER, C.S. *Lieutenant Hornblower.* 1952. Michael Joseph. 1st ed. G. P3. $17.00

FORESTER, C.S. *Lord Hornblower.* 1946. Little Brn. 1st ed. hc. VG. P3. $25.00

FORESTER, C.S. *Man in the Yellow Raft.* 1962. Boston. 1st ed. VG/VG. B5. $35.00

FORESTER, C.S. *Nightmare.* 1954. Michael Joseph. 1st ed. VG/VG. P3. $35.00

FORESTER, C.S. *Ship.* 1943. Canada. Saunders. 1st ed. hc. VG. P3. $25.00

FORESTER, C.S. *Sky & the Forest.* 1948. Michael Joseph. 1st ed. VG/VG P3. $20.00

FORESTER, C.S. *To the Indies.* 1940. Canada. Saunders. 1st ed. VG. P3. $30.00

FORGY, H. *And Pass the Ammunition.* 1944. NY. 1st ed. ils. 242p. VG/VG. B5. $22.50

FORMAN, Michael. *Michael Foremen's World of Fairy Tales.* 1991. Little Brn/Arcade. 1st Am ed. 142p. F/F. C14. $22.00

FORNEY, Matthias N. *Catechism of the Locomotive.* 1891. NY. 6 fld maps. 709p. pict cloth. G. B18. $95.00

FORQUET & GAROZZO. *Italian Blue Team Bridge Book.* 1969. NY. 274p. VG. S1. $20.00

FORREST, Mary; see Freeman, Julia Dean.

FORREST, Richard. *Death at Yew Corner.* 1981. HRW. 1st ed. VG/VG. P3. $15.00

FORREST, Richard. *Death in the Willows.* 1979. Rinehart. 1st ed. VG/VG. P3. $15.00

FORSTER, E.M. *Albergo Empedocle & Other Writings.* 1968. Liveright. 1st ed. hc. VG/VG. P3. $35.00

FORSTER, E.M. *Maurice.* 1971. Norton. 1st ed. F/NF. B2. $45.00

FORSTER, Frederick J. *On the Road to Make-Believe.* 1924. Rand McNally. 1st ed. lg 4to. ils Uldene Trippe. VG. M5. $60.00

FORSTER, Margaret. *Daphne Du Maurier: Life of Renowned Storyteller.* 1993. NY. 1st Am ed. 457p. F/dj. A17. $12.00

FORSYTE, Charles. *Murder With Minarets.* 1968. Cassell. 1st ed. VG/VG. P3. $18.00

FORSYTH, Frederick. *Day of the Jackal.* 1971. Viking. 1st ed. author's 1st book. F/NF. H11. $60.00

FORSYTH, Frederick. *Day of the Jackal.* 1971. Viking. 1st ed. VG/G. P3. $35.00

FORSYTH, Frederick. *Devil's Alternative.* 1979. Hutchinson. 1st ed. F/F. P3. $30.00

FORSYTH, Frederick. *Dogs of War.* 1974. Viking. 1st ed. VG/VG. P3. $45.00

FORSYTH, Frederick. *Fist of God.* 1994. Bantam. 1st ed. F/F. H11. $25.00

FORSYTH, Frederick. *Fourth Protocol.* 1984. Viking. 1st Am ed. NF/VG+. N4. $22.50

FORSYTH, Frederick. *Negotiator.* 1989. Bantam. 1st Am ed. NF/VG+. N4. $22.50

FORSYTH, Frederick. *Negotiator.* 1989. Bantam. 1st ed. NF/NF. P3. $25.00

FORSYTH, Frederick. *No Comebacks.* 1982. Viking. hc. VG/VG. P3. $25.00

FORSYTH, Frederick. *Odessa File.* 1972. Viking. 1st ed. author's 2nd novel. NF/NF. H11/M22. $30.00

FORSYTH, Frederick. *Shepherd.* 1976. Viking. 1st ed. NF/NF. P3. $45.00

FORT, Charles. *Complete Books of...* nd. Dover. hc. F/F. P3. $30.00

FORT, Paul. *Livre des Ballades.* 1920. Paris. Piazza L'Edition d'Art. ils Rackham. contemporary bdg. T10. $1,500.00

FORTLAGE, Karl. *Acht Psychologischen Vortrage.* 1869. Jena. Mauke's Verlag. 348p. contemporary brd. G1. $85.00

FORWARD, Robert L. *Dragon's Egg.* 1980. Del Rey. 1st ed. F/F. P3. $20.00

FORWARD, Robert L. *Martian Rainbow.* 1991. Ballantine. 1st ed. F/F. G10. $10.00

FORWARD, Robert L. *Timemaster.* 1992. Tor. 1st ed. F/F. P3. $20.00

FORWOOD, W. Stump. *Historical & Descriptive Narrative of Mammoth Cave of KY...* 1870. Phil. 225p. brn cloth. VG. B14. $100.00

FOSHAY, Ella M. *Reflections of Nature.* 1984. NY. ils. 4to. 202p. F/dj. B26. $25.00

FOSS, Michael. *Undreamed Shores.* 1974. London. VG. O7. $20.00

FOSTER, Alan Dean. *Cachalot.* 1994. Severn. F/F. G10. $20.00

FOSTER, Alan Dean. *Day of the Dissonance.* 1984. Phantasia. 1st ed. 1/375. sgn/#d. F/F/case. P3. $40.00

FOSTER, Alan Dean. *Empire Strikes Back Storybook.* 1980. Random. MTI. G. P3. $10.00

FOSTER, Alan Dean. *Into the Out Of.* 1986. Warner. 1st ed. F/F. P3. $16.00

FOSTER, Alan Dean. *Moment of the Magician.* 1984. Phantasia. 1st ed. 1/375. sgn/#d. F/F/case. P3. $40.00

FOSTER, Alan Dean. *Spoils of War.* 1993. Del Rey. 1st ed. F/F. P3. $20.00

FOSTER, Alan Dean. *Star Wars.* 1977. Del Rey. 1st ed. F/F. P3. $30.00

FOSTER, Alan Dean. *To the Vanishing Point.* 1988. Warner. 1st ed. NF/NF. P3. $16.00

FOSTER, Alan Dean. *To the Vanishing Point.* 1990. Severn. 1st ed. F/F. G10. $20.00

FOSTER, Genevieve. *Abraham Lincoln's World.* 1944. Scribner. 1st ed. 4to. VG+/G. M5. $70.00

FOSTER, Genevieve. *George Washington's World.* 1946. Scribner. sgn. 344p. VG/dj. M20. $27.00

FOSTER, Hal. *Prince Valiant in the New World.* 1956. Hastings. VG/VG. P3. $35.00

FOSTER, Hal. *Prince Valiant's Perilous Voyage.* 1954. Hastings. VG/VG. P3. $35.00

FOSTER, Harry. *Tropical Tramp With the Tourists.* 1925. Dodd Mead. 1st ed. ils. 335p. F3. $20.00

FOSTER, Iris; see Posner, Richard.

FOSTER, J.W. *Pre-Historic Races of the United States of America.* 1887. Chicago. Griggs. 6th. 8vo. ils. 415p. VG. T10. $150.00

FOSTER, M.S. *Causes of Spatial & Temporal Patterns In Rocky...* 1988. San Francisco. CA Academy of Sciences. 4to. 45p. pict wrp. B1. $15.00

FOSTER, Maximilian. *Crooked.* 1928. Phil. 1st ed. F/NF. B4. $150.00

FOSTER, R.F. *Auction Bridge.* 1909. NY. 128p. VG. S1. $5.00

FOSTER, R.F. *Foster's Whist Manual.* 1891. Chicago. 3rd. 214p. VG. S1. $6.00

FOSTER, R.F. *Moat House Mystery.* 1930. MacAulay. G. P3. $20.00

FOSTER, R.F. *Royal Auction Bridge With Full Treatment of New Count...* 1912. NY. 2nd. 346p. VG. S1. $15.00

FOSTER, R.F. *Whist Tactics.* 1895. London. 141p. VG. S1. $15.00

FOSTER, R.J. *General Geology.* 1973. Merrill. 2nd. 721p. F. D8. $15.00

FOSTER & FOSTER. *Forbidden Journey: Life of Alexandra David-Neel.* 1987. San Francisco. 1st ed. 8vo. 363p. AN/dj. P4. $22.00

FOSTER & STODDARD. *Pops Foster, New Orleans Jazz Man.* 1971. Berkeley. 1st ed. F/NF. B2. $30.00

FOTHERGILL, Philip. *Historical Aspects of Organic Evolution.* 1953. London. 427p. VG. A13. $25.00

FOUDE, James A. *English Seamen in the Sixteenth Century.* 1930. London. 309p. half morocco. F. A17. $30.00

FOUGASSE. *School of Purposes: A Selection of Fougasse Posters...* 1946. Methuen. 1st ed. 8vo. VG/G. B17. $8.50

FOWLER, Christopher. *Red Bride.* 1993. Roc. 1st ed. hc. F/F. P3. $20.00

FOWLER, Christopher. *Rune.* 1991. Ballantine. 1st ed. author's 2nd novel. AN/dj. M22. $30.00

FOWLER, Connie May. *Sugar Cage.* 1992. Putnam. 1st ed. author's 1st book. sgn. F/F. M23. $40.00

FOWLER, Earlene. *Fool's Puzzle.* 1994. Berkley. 1st ed. F/F. M23. $40.00

FOWLER, Earlene. *Irish Chain.* 1995. Berkley. 1st ed. F/F. M23. $30.00

FOWLER, Gene. *Beau James.* 1949. Viking. 1st ed. sgn Fowler. 8vo. F/NF. T10. $150.00

FOWLER, Ila Earle. *Captain John Fowler of Virginia & Kentucky...* 1942. Hobson. 1st prt. photos. 166p. VG. B10. $35.00

FOWLER, Jacob. *Journal of Jacob Fowler.* 1965. Minneapolis. Ross Haines. 183p. AN/dj. P4. $25.00

FOWLER, Karen Joy. *Sarah Canary.* 1991. Holt. 1st ed. F/F. H11. $25.00

FOWLES, John. *Cinderella.* 1974. Little Brn. 1st Am ed. ils Sheilah Beckett. 32p. VG+/torn. T5. $24.00

FOWLES, John. *Cinderella.* 1974. London. Cape. 1st ed. thin 4to. F/clip. C2. $60.00

FOWLES, John. *Collector.* 1963. Little Brn. 1st ed. F/F. P3. $75.00

FOWLES, John. *Daniel Martin.* 1977. London. 1st ed. sgn. F/F. C2. $50.00

FOWLES, John. *French Lieutenant's Woman.* 1969. Little Brn. 1st ed. VG/VG. H11. $35.00

FOWLES, John. *French Lieutenant's Woman.* 1969. London. 1st ed. ils. F/F. C2. $125.00

FOWLES, John. *Maggot.* 1985. Little Brn. 1st ed. F/NF. H11. $30.00

FOWLES, John. *Maggot.* 1985. London. 1st ed. 1/500. sgn. F/NF tissue dj. C6. $100.00

FOWLES, John. *Maggot.* 1985. London. 1st trade ed. sgn. F/F. C2. $50.00

FOWLES, John. *Mantissa.* 1982. Little Brn. 1st ed. F/F. P3. $20.00

FOWLES, John. *Poems.* 1973. Ecco. 1st ed. F/dj. C2. $45.00

FOWLES, John. *Shipwreck.* 1974. London. 1st ed. sgn. F/F clip. C2. $150.00

FOWLES & HORVAT. *Tree.* 1979. Little Brn. 1st Am ed. photos. cloth. dj. D2. $65.00

FOWLES & HORVAT. *Tree.* 1979. London. 1st ed. sgns. F/F 1st issue. C2. $175.00

FOWLIE, Wallace. *Dante Today: A Personal Essay.* 1995. French Broad Pr. 1st ed. 1/26 lettered. sgn. F/wrp. C2. $35.00

FOX, Charles. *Frisky, Try Again...An Easy To Read Photo Story Book...* 1959. Reilly Lee. 4to. F/G. M5. $20.00

FOX, Ebenezer. *Revolutionary Adventures of Ebenezer Fox.* 1838. Boston. VG. A9. $150.00

FOX, Frances Margaret. *Little Bear's Laughing Times.* 1939 (1924). Rand McNally. ils Frances Beem. 64p. G+. T5. $15.00

FOX, George. *Amok.* 1978. Simon Schuster. 1st ed. VG/VG. P3. $15.00

FOX, George. *Warlord's Hill.* 1982. Times Books. 1st ed. VG/VG. N4. $17.50

FOX, J.M. *Operation Dancing Dog.* 1974. Walker. 1st ed. hc. VG/torn. P3. $15.00

FOX, J.M. *Shroud for Mr Bundy.* 1952. Little Brn. 1st ed. VG/VG. P3. $15.00

FOX, John. *Little Shepherd of Kingdom Come.* 1931. Scribner. 1st ed. ils NC Wyeth. 322p. VG. D1. $200.00

FOX, John. *Quiche Conquest.* 1978. Albuquerque. 1st ed. index/biblio/maps. 322p. dj. F3. $25.00

FOX, Luke. *Fox From the North-West Passage.* 1965. SR Pub. facsimile of 1635 ed. 2 maps. T10. $50.00

FOX, Richard. *So Far Disordered in Mind: Insanity in California...* 1978. Berkeley. 1st ed. 204p. VG/dj. A13. $35.00

FOX, Smith C. *Sea Songs & Ballads, 1917-1922.* 1923-24. London. Methuen. ils. 136p. VG. T7. $25.00

FOX, William Price. *Doctor Golf.* 1963. Phil. 1st ed. VG/VG. B5. $25.00

FOX, William. *New York at Gettysburg.* 1902. Albany. 3 vol. 1st ed. 5 pocket maps. VG. H3. $150.00

FOX & FROBENIUS. *African Genesis.* 1937. NY. VG. O7. $55.00

FOXON, David. *Libertine Literature in England 1660-1745.* 1965. University Books. 70p. F. A17. $17.50

FOXX, Jack; see Pronzini, Bill.

FOY-VAILLANT, Jean. *Numismata Aerea Imperatorum.* 1697. Paris. Danielem Horthemels. 2 vol in 1. contemporary bdg. K1. $400.00

FOYLE, Kathleen. *Little Good People, Folk Tales of Ireland.* 1949. Warne. 1st ed. 8vo. gr cloth. VG. M5. $35.00

FRAN, Edgar B. *Old French Ironwork.* 1950. Cambridge. 1st ed. ils. 221p. gr/gray cloth. F/VG. H3. $65.00

FRANCE, Anatole. *At the Sign of the Reine Pedauque.* 1923. NY. 1st ed. ils Frank C Pape. 275p. VG/dj. B18. $22.50

FRANCE, Anatole. *Penguin Island.* 1925. Dodd Mead. 1st ed. ils. F/VG. M19. $75.00

FRANCE, Anatole. *Penguin Island.* 1947. NY. Aldus. ils/sgn Malcolm Cameron. gilt bl silk brd. F/F case. T10. $100.00

FRANCE, Anatole. *Revolt of the Angels.* 1924. NY. 1st ed thus. 357p. VG/torn. B18. $22.50

FRANCHERE, Gabriel. *Adventure at Astoria, 1810-1814.* 1967. Norman, OK. 1st ed thus. 8vo. 190p. F/NF. T10. $45.00

FRANCIS, Dick. *Banker.* 1983. Putnam. 1st ed. VG/VG. P3. $20.00

FRANCIS, Dick. *Break In.* 1986. Putnam. 1st ed. VG/VG. P3. $18.00

FRANCIS, Dick. *Comeback.* 1991. Putnam. 1st Am ed. rem mk. VG/VG. M22. $10.00

FRANCIS, Dick. *Danger.* 1983. Michael Joseph. 1st ed. VG/VG. P3. $22.00

FRANCIS, Dick. *Driving Force.* 1992. London. Michael Joseph. 1st ed. NF/NF. M22. $25.00

FRANCIS, Dick. *Edge.* 1989. Putnam. 1st ed. F/F. P3. $18.00

FRANCIS, Dick. *Four Complete Novels.* nd. Avenel. 6th. VG/VG. P3. $13.00

FRANCIS, Dick. *High Stakes.* 1975. Harper. 1st Am ed. VG/VG. M22. $30.00

FRANCIS, Dick. *In the Frame.* 1976. Harper Row. 1st Am ed. 8vo. F/NF. T10. $45.00

FRANCIS, Dick. *Knockdown.* 1975. Harper Row. 1st ed. NF/NF. P3. $35.00

FRANCIS, Dick. *Lester: The Official Biography.* 1986. Michael Joseph. 1st ed. F/F. P3. $20.00

FRANCIS, Dick. *Longshot.* 1990. Michael Joseph. 1st ed. F/F. P3. $20.00

FRANCIS, Dick. *Longshot.* 1990. Putnam. 1st Am ed. F/NF. N4. $20.00

FRANCIS, Dick. *Proof.* 1984. Michael Joseph. 1st ed. VG/VG. P3. $20.00

FRANCIS, Dick. *Rat Race.* 1971. Harper Row. 1st ed. VG/clip. A20. $27.00

FRANCIS, Dick. *Slay-Ride.* 1973. London. 1st ed. F/F. A11. $55.00

FRANCIS, Dick. *Smokescreen.* 1973. Harper Row. 1st ed. VG/VG. P3. $35.00

FRANCIS, Dick. *Sports of Queens. Autobiography of Dick Francis.* 1957. London. 1st ed. 8vo. 238p. F/G. H3. $200.00

FRANCIS, Dick. *Trial Run.* 1978. Michael Joseph. 1st ed. NF/NF. P3. $25.00

FRANCIS, Rene. *Egyptian Esthetics.* 1912. Open Court. 1st ed. 8vo. VG. W1. $20.00

FRANCIS, Richard H. *Whispering Gallery.* 1984. Norton. 1st ed. VG/VG. P3. $15.00

FRANCK, Harry. *Trailing Cortes Through Mexico.* nd. Grosset Dunlap. ils. 373p. dj. F3. $15.00

FRANCOICE. *Jeanne-Marie at the Fair.* 1959. Scribner. early ed. 4to. VG/VG. B17. $15.00

FRANCOIS, Yves Regis. *Ctz Paradigm.* 1975. Doubleday. 1st ed. F/F. P3. $15.00

FRANCON, M. *Progress in Microscopy.* 1961. Evanston, IL. Row Peterson. xl. K5. $30.00

FRANK, Alan. *Galactic Aliens.* 1979. Chartwell. hc. VG/VG. P3. $10.00

FRANK, Alan. *Horror Movies.* 1974. Octopus. 1st ed. VG/VG. P3. $20.00

FRANK, Pat. *Forbidden Area.* 1956. Lippincott. 1st ed. inscr. VG/VG. B11. $75.00

FRANK, Robert. *Americans.* 1978. NY. Aperture. 1st ed thus. sgn/Peter Bogdanovich's copy. NF/dj. S9. $200.00

FRANKENSTEIN, Victor. *Frankenstein Diaries, by Rev Hubert Venables.* 1980. Viking. 1st ed. F/F. R10. $25.00

FRANKFURTER, Felix. *Of Laws & Life & Other Things That Matter...1956-1963.* 1965. Harvard. ils. 8vo. 257p. F/dj. B14. $45.00

FRANKFURTER & GREENE. *Labor Injunction.* 1930. Macmillan. pres. cloth. w/sgn card. M11. $350.00

FRANKLIN, Albert. *Eucador: Portrait of a People.* 1944. Doubleday. 326p. F3. $10.00

FRANKLIN, Benjamin. *Poor Richard: The Almanacks.* 1964. LEC. 1st ed thus. 1/1500. ils/sgn Norman Rockwell. F/NF case. C6. $200.00

FRANKLIN, K.J. *Short History of Physiology.* 1949. NY. 2nd. 147p. VG. A13. $60.00

FRANKLIN, Wayne. *Discoverers, Explorers, Settlers: The Diligent Writers...* 1979. Chicago. 1st prt. 8vo. 252p. gr cloth. AN/dj. P4. $25.00

FRANKS, LAMBERT & TYSON. *Early Oklahoma Oil: A Photographic History 1859-1936.* 1981. TX A&M. 1st ed. 4to. 245p. blk cloth. NF/VG. T10. $50.00

FRANTZ, J. *Gail Borden: Dairyman to the Nation.* 1951. Norman. 1st ed. ils/index. 310p. VG/VG. B5. $30.00

FRANTZ, Joe B. *Essays on Walter Prescott Webb.* 1976. Austin. VG. O7. $50.00

FRANZEN, Jonathan. *Strong Motion.* 1992. FSG. 1st ed. F/F. M23. $20.00

FRANZEN, Jonathan. *Twenty-Seventh City.* 1988. FSG. ARC. author's 1st book. NF/wrp. M23. $25.00

FRASCA, John. *Con Man or Saint?* 1969. Anderson, SC. Droke. 1st ed. sgn. 223p. VG/VG. B11. $20.00

FRASER, Antonia. *Jemima Shore at the Sunny Grave.* 1993. Bantam. 1st ed. F/F. P3. $20.00

FRASER, Antonia. *Jemima Shore's First Case.* 1987. Norton. 1st ed. F/F. P3. $15.00

FRASER, Antonia. *Quiet As a Nun.* 1977. Viking. 1st ed. VG/VG. P3. $18.00

FRASER, Antonia. *Your Royal Hostage.* 1987. Weidenfeld Nicolson. 1st ed. VG/VG. P3. $19.00

FRASER, George MacDonald. *Flash for Freedom!* 1972. Knopf. 1st ed. NF/NF. P3. $45.00

FRASER, George MacDonald. *Flashman & the Dragon.* 1986 (1985). Knopf. 1st Am ed. 320p. NF/NF. M20. $55.00

FRASER, George MacDonald. *Flashman & the Mountain of Light.* 1990. Knopf. 1st ed. VG/VG. P3. $25.00

FRASER, George MacDonald. *Flashman & the Redskins.* 1982. Collins. 1st ed. VG/VG. P3. $22.00

FRASER, George MacDonald. *Flashman's Lady.* 1977. Barrie Jenkins. 1st ed. VG/VG. P3. $40.00

FRASER, George MacDonald. *Pyrates.* 1984. Knopf. 1st ed. F/F. P3. $30.00

FRASER, George MacDonald. *Royal Flash.* 1970. Knopf. 1st ed. NF/NF. P3. $60.00

FRASER, George MacDonald. *Steel Bonnets.* 1972. NY. 1st Am ed. F/NF. N3. $20.00

FRASER, Sylvia. *Pandora.* 1973. Little Brn. VG/VG. P3. $15.00

FRASER & FRASER. *Seven Years on the Pacific Slope.* 1914. NY. 1st ed. 391p. VG. B5. $45.00

FRASSANITO, W. *America's Bloodiest Day: Battle of Antietam 1862.* 1978. 8vo. ils. 304p. red cloth. VG/dj. T3. $20.00

FRASSANITO, W. *Gettysburg: A Journey in Time.* 1975. NY. 8vo. 248p. G. T3. $20.00

FRAYN, Michael. *Landing on the Sun.* 1991. Viking. 1st ed. RS. F/F. P3. $21.00

FRAZEE, Steve. *Best Western Stories of Steve Frazee.* 1984. S IL U. 1st ed. edit Bill Pronzini/Martin Greenberg. M/M. A18. $20.00

FRAZEE, Steve. *Swiss Family Robinson.* 1960. Whitman. hc. MTI. VG. P3. $10.00

FRAZEN, Jonathan. *Twenty-Seventh City.* 1988. FSG. ARC. author's 1st book. NF/wrp. M23. $25.00

FRAZER, James George. *Golden Bough: Studies in Magic & Religion.* 1970. Bloomfield, CT. Sign of Stone Book. 2 vol. ils/sgn Lewicki. F/NF case. T10. $175.00

FRAZETTA, Frank. *Fantastic Art of Frank Frazetta.* 1976. Scribner. 2nd. hc. VG/VG. P3. $30.00

FRAZIER, Adrian. *Behind the Scenes.* 1990. Berkeley. 1st ed. 8vo. 258p. T10. $35.00

FRAZIER, Robert Caine; see Creasey, John.

FREAR & MCLEAN. *Flowers of Hawaii.* 1938. np. ils. VG. M17. $40.00

FREDE, Richard. *Secret Circus.* 1967. Random. 1st ed. VG/VG. P3. $25.00

FREDERICK II OF HOHENSTAUFEN. *Art of Falconry.* 1943. Stanford, CA. trans CA Wood/FM Fyfe. 4to 617p. gr cloth. VG. B14. $200.00

FREDMAN, John. *Epitaph to a Bad Cop.* 1973. David McKay. NF/NF. P3. $15.00

FREDMAN, John. *False Joanna.* 1970. Bobbs Merrill. F/F. P3. $15.00

FREE & HOKE. *Weather: Practical, Dramatic & Spectacular Facts...* 1928. NY Nat Travel Club. 8vo. 337p. cloth. G. K5. $16.00

FREEBORN, Brian. *Good Luck Mister Cain.* 1976. St Martin. 1st ed. VG/G. P3. $12.00

FREEDMAN, J.F. *Against the Wind.* 1991. Viking. 1st ed. F/F. H11. $25.00

FREELING, Nicolas. *Because of the Cats.* 1964. Harper. 1st ed. F/VG. M19. $17.50

FREELING, Nicolas. *Gadget.* 1977. CMG. 1st ed. VG/VG. P3. $23.00

FREELING, Nicolas. *Long Silence.* 1972. Hamish Hamilton. 1st ed. VG/VG. P3. $20.00

FREELING, Nicolas. *Tsing-Boum.* 1969. Harper Row. 1st ed. hc. VG/VG. P3. $20.00

FREELING, Nicolas. *Wolfnight.* 1982. Pantheon. 1st ed. F/F. P3. $15.00

FREEMAN, Andrew. *Father Smith...Account of a Seventeenth-Century Organ Maker.* 1926. London. ils HT Lilley. 80p. bl cloth. VG. T10. $125.00

FREEMAN, D.S. *George Washington/Young Washington.* 1948. NY. 2 vol. 1st ed. map ep. gilt blk cloth. F/VG case. H3. $75.00

FREEMAN, D.S. *Lee's Lieutenants: A Study in Command.* 1972. NY. 3 vol. ils/map. F/dj. B18. $95.00

FREEMAN, D.S. *RE Lee: A Biography.* 1934-1935. np. 4 vol. 1st ed. w/sgn letter & unused Lee & Jackson postage stp. G/box. B5. $395.00

FREEMAN, D.S. *RE Lee: A Biography.* 1945. Scribner. 4 vol. early issue. cloth. VG. M8. $150.00

FREEMAN, D.S. *South to Posterity.* 1939. NY. Scribner. 1st/A ed. VG/VG. B5. $95.00

FREEMAN, Julia Dean. *Women of the South Distinguished in Literature.* 1861 (1860). Derby Jackson. ils. 511p. rebound modern cloth/leather label. B10. $45.00

FREEMAN, Mary E. Wilkins. *Collected Ghost Stories.* 1974. Arkham. 1st ed. 1/4155. F/F. T2. $12.00

FREEMAN, Otis W. *Geography of the Pacific.* 1963. NY. VG. O7. $25.00

FREEMAN, R. Austin. *As a Thief in the Night.* 1928. Burt. G. N4. $12.50

FREEMAN, R. Austin. *Dr Thorndyke Intervenes.* 1934. Dodd Mead. later prt. VG. N4. $15.00

FREEMAN, R. Austin. *Dr Thorndyke's Crime File.* 1941. Dodd Mead. 1st ed. G. N4. $45.00

FREEMAN, R. Austin. *Mr Pottermack's Oversight.* 1930. Dodd Mead. 1st ed. VG/torn. P3. $45.00

FREEMAN, R. Austin. *Penrose Mystery.* 1936. Hodder Stoughton. 1st ed. G. P3. $35.00

FREEMAN, R. Austin. *Silent Witness.* 1915. Winston. 1st ed. VG. M22. $65.00

FREEMAN, R. Austin. *Stoneware Monkey.* 1938. Hodder Stoughton. 1st ed. G. P3. $35.00

FREEMAN, Robert. *Land I Live in & Other Verse.* 1928. Pasadena. Vroman. 1st ed. 12mo. 214p. yel prt coth. VG. T10. $25.00

FREEMAN, T.W. *Hundred Years of Geography.* 1963. Chicago. VG. O7. $20.00

FREEMAN & FREEMAN. *Fun With Science.* 1943. Random. 1st ed. ils. 60p. G/dj. K5. $10.00

FREEMAN. *Undergrowth of Literature.* 1968. np. 27 photos. 222p. VG. A4. $45.00

FREEMANTLE, Brian. *Fix.* 1986. Tor. 1st ed. VG. P3. $18.00

FREEMANTLE, Brian. *Man Who Wanted Tomorrow.* 1975. Jonathan Cape. 1st ed. xl. dj. P3. $8.00

FREEMANTLE, Brian. *O'Farrell's Law.* 1990. Tor. 1st ed. NF/NF. P3. $18.00

FREEMANTLE, Brian. *Rules of Engagement.* 1984. Century. NF/NF. P3. $20.00

FREEMANTLE, Brian. *Run Around.* 1988. Century. 1st ed. F/F. P3. $18.00

FREES, Harry. *Four Little Puppies.* 1939 (1935). Rand McNally. ils. VG. M5. $28.00

FREES, Harry. *Snuggles.* 1958. Rand McNally. ils. glazed brd. VG. M5. $10.00

FREETH, Zahra. *Kuwait Was My Home.* 1956. London. Allen Unwin. 8vo. 164p. VG. W1. $40.00

FREGOSI, Claudia. *Gift.* 1976. Prentice Hall. ils. unp. VG/torn. T5. $15.00

FREMANTLE, Arthur James Lyon. *Three Months in the Southern States: April-June 1863.* 1864. Mobile, AL. SH Goetzel. 1st Confederate ed. 158p. VG. M8. $650.00

FREMONT, Jessie B. *Year of American Travel.* 1960. San Francisco. VG. O7. $125.00

FREMONT, John C. *Geographical Memoir Upon Upper California...* 1964. BC of CA. rpt of 1848 ed. 1/425. map. M. O7. $195.00

FRENCH, Albert. *Billy.* 1993. Viking. 1st ed. author's 1st novel. F/F. T2. $35.00

FRENCH, George. *About Book Making.* 1904. Cleveland. Imperial pr. decor cloth. VG. B18. $35.00

FRENCH, Giles. *Cattle Country of Peter French.* 1964. Portland, OR. 1st ed. 8vo. ils. 167p. map ep. VG/dj. T10. $35.00

FRENCH, Joseph Lewis. *Ghost Story Omnibus.* 1941. Tudor. hc. VG/VG. P3. $35.00

FRENCH, L.H. *Seward's Land of Gold: Five Season's Experience...* nd. NY. Montross Clarke Emmons. 1st ed. 101p. xl. G. A17. $75.00

FRENCH, S. Bassett. *Review of the Protective Tariff & the Farmer.* 1887? np. 40p. sewed. G+. B10. $35.00

FRESHNEY, R.I. *Animal Cell Culture.* 1986. IRL Pr. 8vo. ils/photos. 248p. pict brd. F. B1. $35.00

FREUD, Sigmund. *Das Unbehagen in der Kultur.* 1930. Wien/Leipzig. 12mo. 136p. prt wrp. G1. $175.00

FREUD, Sigmund. *Group Psychology & the Analysis of the Ego.* nd. Boni Liveright. 1st English-language ed/Am issue. gray cloth. G1. $45.00

FREUD, Sigmund. *Massenpsychologie und Ich-Analyse.* (1923). Leipzig/Wien/Zurich. 2nd. prt wrp. G1. $35.00

FREUD, Sigmund. *Origins of Psycho-Analysis.* 1954. London. 1st Eng trans. 486p. VG/dj. A13. $50.00

FREUNDLICH, August L. *Richard Florsheim, the Artist & His Art.* 1976. AS Barnes. sgn. VG/fair. B11. $20.00

FREY, Jame N. *Winter of the Wolves.* nd. BC. F/F. P3. $10.00

FREYER, Frederic. *Black Black Hearse.* 1955. St Martin. 1st ed. VG/G. P3. $25.00

FRICERO, Kate J. *Little French People, Picture Book for Little Folk.* nd. Blackie. lg 4to. ils. VG. M5. $80.00

FRICKE. *Wizard of Oz: Official 50th-Anniversary Pictorial History.* 1989. np. 400 photos. 255p. F/F. A4. $50.00

FRIDDELL, Guy. *Jackstraws.* 1961. Dietz. 1st ed. 172p. VG. B10. $10.00

FRIEDENBERG, Robert V. *Hear O Israel.* 1989. Tuscaloosa. AL U. 1st ed. 177p. F/dj. T10. $35.00

FRIEDENWALD, Harry. *Jewish Luminaries in Medical History...* 1967. NY. facsimile of 1944 ed. 199p. A13. $30.00

FRIEDENWALD, Harry. *Jews & Medicine, Essays.* 1944-46. Baltimore. 2 vol. 1st ed. F. A13. $250.00

FRIEDJUNG, M. *Novae & Related Stars.* 1977. Dordrecht, Holland. Reidel. 228p. VG. K5. $30.00

FRIEDLI, Franz. *Das Uhrenbuch.* 1941. Bern. Francke. 4to. F. B24. $250.00

FRIEDMAN, Bruce Jay. *Current Climate.* 1989. Atlantic Monthly. 1st ed. F/F. A20. $15.00

FRIEDMAN, Bruce Jay. *Let's Hear It for a Beautiful Guy.* 1984. Donald Fine. 1st ed. F/F. A20/P3. $21.00

FRIEDMAN, Bruce Jay. *Stern: A Novel.* 1962. Simon Schuster. 1st ed. author's 1st book. VG/dj. B24. $75.00

FRIEDMAN, H. *Sun & Earth.* 1986. Scientific Am Books. 251p. F/dj. D8. $12.00

FRIEDMAN, Herbert. *Astronomer's Universe.* 1990. Norton. 359p. cloth. VG. K5. $18.00

FRIEDMAN, I.K. *Radical.* 1907. Appleton. 1st ed. F. B2. $150.00

FRIEDMAN, Kinky. *Armadillos & Old Lace.* nd. Simon Schuster. 2nd. F/F. P3. $21.00

FRIEDMAN, Kinky. *Case of Lone Star.* 1987. Morrow. 1st ed. author's 2nd novel. NF/NF. M22. $15.00

FRIEDMAN, Kinky. *Elvis, Jesus & Coca-Cola.* 1993. Simon Schuster. 1st ed. F/F. A20. $15.00

FRIEDMAN, Kinky. *Frequent Flyer.* 1989. Morrow. 1st ed. AN/dj. N4. $30.00

FRIEDMAN, Kinky. *Frequent Flyer.* 1989. Morrow. 1st ed. F/F. H11. $25.00

FRIEDMAN, Kinky. *God Bless John Wayne.* 1995. Simon Schuster. 1st ed. F/F. P3. $22.00

FRIEDMAN, Kinky. *Greenwich Killing Time.* 1986. Morrow. 1st ed. author's 1st book. F/F. H11. $50.00

FRIEDMAN, Kinky. *Musical Charles.* 1991. Morrow. 1st ed. sgn. NF/NF. A20. $25.00

FRIEDMAN, Kinky. *When the Cat's Away.* 1988. Beach Tree. 1st ed. F/F. N4. $35.00

FRIEDMAN, Mickey. *Temporary Ghost.* 1989. Viking. 1st ed. VG/VG. P3. $18.00

FRIEDMAN, Milton. *There's No Such Thing As a Free Lunch.* 1975. LaSalle, IL. 1st ed. F/F. B5. $25.00

FRIEDMAN, Stuart. *Free Are the Dead.* 1954. Abelard-Schuman. VG. P3. $12.00

FRIEDRICH, Otto. *Going Crazy.* 1976. Simon Schuster. 1st ed. F/F. B35. $19.00

FRIEDRICH & FRIEDRICH. *Easter Bunny Overslept.* 1957. Lee Shepard. 1st ed. ils Adrienne Adams. F/NF. P2. $40.00

FRIEL, Arthur O. *Mountains of Mystery.* 1925. Harper. 1st ed. G. P3. $50.00

FRIEND, Oscar J. *Star Men.* 1963. Avalon. 1st ed. xl. dj. P3. $7.00

FRIESNER, Esther. *Spells of Mortal Weaving.* 1986. Avon. hc. VG. P3. $4.00

FRIMMER, Steven. *Neverland.* 1976. NY. xl. VG. O7. $15.00

FRISBIE, Robert D. *Book of Puka-Puka.* 1929. NY. VG. O7. $45.00

FRITZ, Henry E. *Movement for Indian Assimilation, 1860-1890.* 1963. Phil. PA U. 1st ed. ils. 244p. F/dj. T10. $35.00

FRITZ, Jean. *World in 1492.* 1992. NY. VG. O7. $20.00

FRITZSCH, H. *Quarks, the Stuff of Matter.* 1983. NY. Basic Books. 1st Eng ed. F/dj. D8. $15.00

FROBES, Joseph. *Lehrbuch der Experimentellen Psychologie...* 1923. Herder. 2 vol. 3rd. cloth. xl. G1. $35.00

FROELICH, L. *Alphabet de Mademoiselle Lili.* ca 1870-80. Paris. Hetzel. 8vo. 40p. gilt brn cloth. NF. B24. $300.00

FROISSART. *Chronicles of...* 1930. London. marbled brd/red half leather. VG. B30. $125.00

FROLICH, L. *Tony & Puss.* 1870. np. 24p. G+. P2. $65.00

FROLOV, Y.P. *Pavlov & His School: Theory of Conditioned Reflexes.* 1937. NY. 1st ed. 291p. VG. A13. $50.00

FROME, David. *Homicide House.* 1950. Detective BC. VG. P3. $10.00

FROME, David. *Strange Death of Martin Green.* 1931. Crime Club. 1st ed. VG. P3. $40.00

FROMENTIN, Eugene. *Dominique.* 1948. London. Cressent. 1st ed thus. gilt cloth. F. A17. $10.00

FROMM, Erich. *To Have or To Be.* 1976. NY. Harper Row. 1st ed. 216p. NF. B14. $35.00

FRONIUS, Hans. *Die Welt des Theaters. 100 Zeichnungen.* 1964. Vienna. Hans Deutsche. NF. D2. $25.00

FROOM, Le Roy Edwin. *Prophetic Faith of Our Fathers.* 1950. Review Herald. 4 vol. 1st ed? gilt leatherette. F. A17. $75.00

FROST, Frances. *Little Whistler.* 1949. Whittlesey. 1st ed. ils Roger Duvoisin. VG/G. P2. $18.00

FROST, John. *Great Cities of the World.* 1854. Auburn. 12mo. 544p. brn cloth. G. T3. $30.00

FROST, Mark. *List of Seven.* 1993. London. Hutchinson. 1st ed. F/F. H11/N4. $40.00

FROST, Robert. *Aquainted With the Night.* 1993. Madison, WI. Quercus. 1/25. sq 12mo. fld panorama/6p orig aquatints. box. B24. $300.00

FROST, Robert. *Collected Poems.* 1939. NY. 1st ed. sgn. VG/G. B5. $200.00

FROST, Robert. *Further Range.* 1936. NY. ltd ed. 1/803. sgn. VG/VG box. B5. $175.00

FROST, Robert. *In the Clearing.* 1962. NY. HRW. 1st ed. inscr/dtd 1962. F/NF. B24. $475.00

FROST, Robert. *Interviews With Robert Frost.* 1966. Holt. 1st ed. F/NF. C2. $50.00

FROST, Robert. *Lovely Shall Be Choosers.* 1929. NY. 1/475. F/wrp. A11. $50.00

FROST, Robert. *Masque of Reason.* 1945. Holt. stated 1st ed. VG/worn. H4. $40.00

FROST, Robert. *My Objection To Being Stepped On.* 1957. NY. Spiral. 1st ed. 1/650. ils Leonard Baskin. F/wrp. B24. $65.00

FROST, Robert. *North of Boston.* 1977. Dodd Mead. 1st ed thus. F/NF. C2. $35.00

FROST, Robert. *Selected Prose.* sgn. VG/VG. M17. $27.50

FROST, Robert. *Sportswriter.* 1996. Knopf. 1st Am ed. sgn. F/F. B4. $75.00

FROST, Robert. *Stopping by the Woods on a Snowy Evening.* 1978. Dutton. 1st ed. ils Susan Jeffers. VG/G+. P2. $35.00

FROST, Robert. *Way Wout. A One Act Play.* 1929. NY. Harbor. 1st ed. 1/485. inscr/sgn. blk cloth. F. B24. $525.00

FROST, Robert. *West-Running Brook.* 1928. Holt. 1st ed/1st state. sgn. assoc copy. VG. B11. $500.00

FROST, Robert. *Wood-Pile.* 1961. Spiral. 1st ed. 32mo. NF/wrp. C2. $30.00

FROST, Robert. *You Come Too.* 1959. NY. ARC. w/photo. F/NF clip. A11. $45.00

FROST & FROST. *Magic Power of Witchcraft.* 1976. Parker. VG. P3. $13.00

FROST & JENKINS. *I'm Frank Hamer.* 1968. Austin, TX. 1st ed. F/F. E1. $90.00

FROUD & LEE. *Faeries.* 1979. Abrams. 4to. 185 ils. F/dj. T10. $50.00

FRUCHT, Abby. *Licorice.* 1990. St Paul. Graywolf. 1st ed. F/F. H11. $20.00

FRUCHT, Abby. *Snap.* 1988. Ticknor. 1st ed. F/F. H11. $25.00

FRY, C. Luther. *American Villagers.* 1926. Doran. sgn. 8vo. 201p. B11. $25.00

FRY, Henry. *History of North Atlantic Steam Navigation.* 1969. London. Cornmarket. facsimile of 1896 ed. ils/fld map. 324p. VG. T7. $75.00

FRY, Rosalie K. *Adventure Downstream.* ca 1950. London. Hutchinson. lg 8vo. 4 pl. VG. M5. $40.00

FRY, Rosalie K. *Ladybug! Ladybug!* 1940. Dutton. 1st ed. ils. G+. P2. $15.00

FRY, Rosalie K. *Ladybug! Ladybug!* 1940. Dutton. 1st ed. 8vo. ils. F/VG+. M5. $75.00

FRY, Rosalie K. *Pipkin Sees the World.* 1951. Dutton. 1st ed. 8vo. ils. VG+. M5. $38.00

FRY, Rosalie K. *Wind Call.* 1955. London. Dent. 1st ed. 12mo. 115p. gr cloth. T5. $35.00

FRYE & WALTERS. *Subsurface Reconnaissance of Glacial Deposits...* 1950. Lawrence, KS. KS Geological Survey Bulletin #86. VG/wrp. D8. $5.00

FRYER, Donald S. *Songs & Sonnets Atlantean.* 1971. Arkham. 1st ed. 1/2045. F/F. T2. $40.00

FRYER, Jane Earye. *Mary Frances Sewing Book.* 1913. John Winston. all patterns present. VG+. M20. $150.00

FRYER, Jane Eayre. *Mary Frances Cook Book.* 1912. Winston. ils M Hays/JA Boyer. 175p. bl cloth. VG. D1. $160.00

FRYER, Jane Eayre. *Mary Frances First Aid Book.* 1916. Phil. Winston. ils JA Boyer. 144p. bl cloth. VG. D1. $150.00

FRYER. *Secrets of the British Museum.* 1968. np. 160p. F/F. A4. $45.00

FRYMAN, John Felix. *From the Mountains to the Valley.* 1971. private prt. sgn. 115p. VG/VG. B11. $10.00

FUCHS, Samuel. *Metoposcopia & Ophthalmoscopia.* 1615. Argentinae. 26 copperplate portraits. 140p. G. G1. $385.00

FUENTES, Carlos. *Christopher Unborn.* 1989. FSG. 1st ed. F/F. A20. $22.00

FUESS, Claude M. *Calvin Coolidge: Man From Vermont.* 1940. Boston. 1st ed. ils. 522p. VG/dj. B18. $32.50

FUESS, Claude M. *Life of Caleb Cushing.* 1923. Harcourt Brace. 2 vol. cloth. VG. A10. $50.00

FUGGER. *Fugger News-Letters.* 1925. London/NY. VG. O7. $25.00

FUJIKAWA, Gyo. *Surprise! Surprise!* (1978). Grosset Dunlap. ils. NF. C14. $10.00

FULD. *Patriotic Civil War Tokens.* 1965. 12mo. 77p. VG. T3. $12.00

FULGHUM, Robert. *Uh-Oh.* nd. Quality BC. F/F. P3. $10.00

FULLER, Buckminster. *Nine Chains to the Moon.* 1938. Phil. 1st ed. inscr. F/NF. C2. $225.00

FULLER, C. *Breech Loader in the Service 1816-1917.* 1965. New Milford. 1st trade ed. 381p. VG/VG. B5. $65.00

FULLER, George W. *History of the Pacific Northwest.* 1931. NY. VG. O7. $25.00

FULLER, Roger; see Tracy, Don.

FULLER, Samuel. *144 Piccadilly.* 1971. Baron. 1st ed. hc. VG/VG. P3. $35.00

FULLER, Timothy. *Harvard Has a Homicide.* 1942. Triangle. VG/VG. P3. $13.00

FULLER, Timothy. *This Is Murder, Mr Jones.* 1943. Little Brn. 1st ed. G. P3. $30.00

FULLERTON, Alexander. *Bury the Past.* 1954. Peter Davies. VG/VG. P3. $15.00

FULLERTON, Hugh S. *Jimmy Kirkland of the Cascade College Team.* 1915. Winston. ils Charles Paxson Gray. 265p. VG/dj. M20. $87.00

FULTON, John. *Great Medical Bibliographers: A Study in Humanism.* 1951. Phil. 1st ed. 37 pl. 106p. VG. A13. $80.00

FULTON, John. *Humanism in an Age of Science.* 1950. NY. 1st ed. pres. 26p. wrp. A13. $20.00

FULTON, John. *Selected Readings in the History of Physiology.* 1930. Springfield. 1st ed. 317p. VG. A13. $100.00

FULTON & HOFF. *Bibliography of Aviation Medicine.* 1942. Springfield. 1st ed. 237p. dj. A13. $50.00

FULTON & KELLER. *Sign of Babinski: Study of Evolution of Cortical Dominance.* 1932. Springfield/Baltimore. tall 8vo. 165p. panelled bl cloth. G1. $125.00

FULTON & KELLER. *Sign of Babinski: Study of Evolution of...Primates.* 1932. Springfield. ils. 165p. bl cloth. VG. w/pres slip. B14. $300.00

FULVES, Karl. *Self-Working Card Tricks: 72 Foolproof Card Miracles...* 1976. NY. ils. VG/wrp. S1. $3.00

FUNK, Joseph. *Compilation of Genuine Church Music...* 1835. Winchester, VA. 2nd. G. M8. $450.00

FUNKHOUSER, William Delbert. *Wild Life in Kentucky.* 1925. Frankfort, KY. 1st ed. 385p. VG. M20. $47.00

FUNNELL, Charles. *By the Beautiful Sea: Atlantic City.* nd. photos. VG/VG. S13. $20.00

FURMAN, Laura. *Glass House.* 1980. NY. Viking. 1st ed. F/F. M23. $20.00

FURNAS, J.C. *My Life in Writing.* 1989. Morrow. 1st ed. F/F. A20. $20.00

FURNEAUX, Robin. *Amazon.* 1970. NY. VG. O7. $20.00

FUSSELL, Paul. *Norton Book of Travel.* 1987. NY. VG. O7. $20.00

FUSSELL, Paul. *Wartime.* 1989. NY. 1st ed. index/notes. 330p. VG/dj. B18. $15.00

FUTRELL, Robert F. *United States Air Force in Korea 1950-1953.* 1961. NY. 1st ed. ils/maps. 774p. VG/dj. B18. $42.50

FUTRELLE, Jacques. *Diamond Master.* nd. AL Burt. hc. VG/VG. P3. $20.00

FYFE, Thomas Alexander. *Who's Who in Dickens.* 1971. Haskell. VG. P3. $75.00

FYFIELD, Frances. *Deep Sleep.* 1991. Pocket. 1st Am ed. AN/dj. M22. $15.00

FYLEMAN, Rose. *Fairies & Chimneys.* 1930. Doubleday Doran. 8vo. ils. 62p. fair. C14. $5.00

FYSH, Hudson. *Qantas Rising.* 1965. Angus Robertson. 1st ed. sgn. 8vo. 296p. VG. B11. $40.00

G.W.P.; see Pettes, G.W.

GABLER. *Wine Into Words, a History & Bibliography of Wine...* 1985. np. 4to. 416p. F/NF. A4. $45.00

GABORIAU, Emile. *Champdoce Mystery.* 1913. Scribner. hc. VG. P3. $15.00

GABORIAU, Emile. *Count's Millions.* 1913. Scribner. VG. P3. $20.00

GABRIELI, Francesco. *Arabs: A Compact History.* 1963. Hawthorn. 1st ed. 8vo. ils. 216p. VG/dj. W1. $12.00

GADD & PHILIP. *Dickens Dictionary.* 1989. Crescent. F/dj. P3. $10.00

GADDIS, Thomas. *Birdman of Alcatraz.* 1955. 1st ed. MTI. VG/VG. S13. $45.00

GADDIS, Vincent. *Native American Myths & Mysteries.* 1991. Borderland Sciences. revised ed. 183p. wrp. F3. $10.00

GADDIS, William. *Carpenter's Gothic.* 1985. Viking. 1st ed. F/F. H11. $35.00

GADDIS, William. *Frolic of His Own.* 1994. Poseidon. 1st ed. F/F. M23. $50.00

GADDIS, William. *Frolic of His Own.* 1994. Poseidon. 1st ed. rem mk. F/F. H11. $30.00

GADSTON, Iago. *Progress in Medicine: Critical Review of Last Hundred Years.* 1940. NY. 1st ed. 347p. VG. A13. $35.00

GAFDI. *Indigenous African Architecture.* 1974. Van Nostrand Reinhold. F/VG. D2. $75.00

GAG, Wanda. *Growing Pains.* 1940. Coward McCann. 1st ed. ils. 179p. beige cloth. VG/VG. D1. $150.00

GAG, Wanda. *Growing Pains.* 1946. NY. 1st ed. VG/VG. B5. $75.00

GAGE, Nicholas. *Mafia, USA.* 1972. Playboy. 1st ed. NF/G. R10. $10.00

GAGE, Simon Henry. *Microscope.* 1947 (1908). NY. Comstock. 17th. ils. 617p. xl. K5. $30.00

GAGE, Thomas. *English-American.* 1946. Guatemala City. VG. O7. $45.00

GAGE, W.L. *Studies in Bible Lands.* 1869. Boston. 8vo. 12 maps. gilt red cloth. VG. B14. $65.00

GAGE, Wilson. *Big Blue Island.* 1966. World. 3rd. ils Glen Rounds. 121p. NF/VG clip. C14. $6.00

GAGNON, Maurice. *Inner Ring.* 1985. Collins Crime Club. 1st ed. VG/VG. P3. $18.00

GAIGE, Crosby. *Footlights & Highlights.* 1948. Dutton. 1st ed. sgn. VG/dj. D2. $20.00

GAIMAN & PRATCHETT. *Good Omens.* 1990. Workman. 1st Am ed. rem mk. F/F. G10. $12.00

GAINES, Charles. *Stay Hungry.* 1972. Doubleday. 1st ed. author's 1st book. F/VG. M19. $35.00

GAINES, G.T. *Fighting Tennesseans.* 1931. Kingsport. private prt. 1st ed. 127p. VG/VG. B5. $30.00

GAINHAM, Sarah. *Appointment in Vienna.* 1958. Dutton. 1st ed. VG/VG. P3. $15.00

GAINHAM, Sarah. *Cold Dark night.* 1961. Walker. VG/VG. P3. $15.00

GAINHAM, Sarah. *Private Worlds.* 1971. HRW. 1st ed. VG/VG. P3. $15.00

GALBRAITH, John S. *Crown & Charter.* 1974. Berkeley. VG. O7. $35.00

GALDONE, Paul. *Cat Goes Fiddle-i-fee.* 1985. Clarion. 2nd. ils. unp. F/NF. C14. $10.00

GALE, Gloria. *Calendar Model.* 1957. NY. 1st ed. photos. 254p. NF/VG. N3. $45.00

GALE, Zona. *Birth.* 1937. Appleton Century. 1st ed. sgn. F/F. B4. $75.00

GALE, Zona. *Frank Miller of Mission Inn.* 1938. NY. 1st ed. VG/VG. B5. $25.00

GALEWITZ & WINSLOW. *Fontaine Fox's Toonerville Trolley.* 1972. Scribner. ils. VG/G. P12. $8.00

GALILEO. *Dialogue on the Great World Systems.* 1957 (1953). Chicago. 2nd. sm 4to. 506p. VG. K5. $35.00

GALILEO. *Dialogues Concerning Two New Sciences.* 1914. NY. 300p. cloth/brd. VG. B14. $200.00

GALLAGHER, C.H. *Nutritional Factors & Enzymological Disturbances...* 1964. Phil. Lippincott. 8vo. 181p. hc. F. B1. $28.50

GALLAGHER, Stephen. *Boat House.* 1991. NEL. 1st ed. F/F. P3. $28.00

GALLAGHER, Stephen. *Chimera.* 1982. NY. 1st ed. author's 1st book. F/F. H11. $200.00

GALLAGHER, Stephen. *Down River.* 1989. NEL. 1st ed. sgn. F/F. P3. $30.00

GALLAGHER, Stephen. *Follower.* 1991. NEL. 2nd. F/F. P3. $20.00

GALLAGHER, Stephen. *Nightmare, With Angel.* 1993. Ballantine. 1st Am ed. F/F. T2. $15.00

GALLAGHER, Stephen. *Oktober.* 1988. London. NEL. 1st ed. sgn. F/F. T2. $65.00

GALLAGHER, Stephen. *Oktober.* 1989. Tor. 1st ed. NF/F. H11. $25.00

GALLAGHER, Stephen. *Valley of Lights.* 1987. London. NEL. 1st ed. sgn. F/F. T2. $50.00

GALLAGHER. *Jules Verne: A Primary & Secondary Bibliography.* 1980. np. 387p. NF. A4. $65.00

GALLAND, Adolf. *First & the Last: Rise & Fall of German Fighter Forces...* 1954. NY. 1st ed. ils. 368p. G. B18. $50.00

GALLANT, Marvis. *Other Paris.* 1956. Boston. 1st ed. author's 1st book. F/NF. C2. $60.00

GALLANT, Mavis. *Overhead in a Balloon: Twelve Stories of Paris.* 1985. Random. 1st ed. F/F. B4. $65.00

GALLANT, Roy A. *Fires in the Sky.* 1978. NY. 4 Winds. 1st ed. xl. dj. K5. $6.00

GALLENKAMP, Charles. *Maya: The Riddle & Rediscovery of a Lost Civilization.* 1985. NY. Viking. 3rd. 235p. AN/dj. P4. $23.00

GALLICO, Paul. *Abandoned.* 1950. Knopf. 1st ed. VG/VG. P3. $25.00

GALLICO, Paul. *Further Confessions of a Storywriter.* 1961. NY. 1st ed. VG/VG. B5. $30.00

GALLICO, Paul. *Golf Is a Friendly Game.* 1942. NY. 1st ed. VG. B5. $35.00

GALLICO, Paul. *Hand of Mary Constable.* 1954. Heinemann. 1st ed. VG/VG. P3. $20.00

GALLICO, Paul. *Hand of Mary Constable.* 1964. Doubleday. 1st ed. VG/VG. P3. $25.00

GALLICO, Paul. *Hurricane Story.* 1960. Doubleday. 1st ed. 165p. VG/dj. B18. $25.00

GALLICO, Paul. *Lou Gehrig: Pride of the Yankees.* 1942. Grosset Dunlap. VG/G+. P8. $35.00

GALLICO, Paul. *Love, Let Me Not Hunter.* 1963. Doubleday. 1st ed. VG/G. P3. $15.00

GALLICO, Paul. *Ludmila: Story of Liechtenstein.* 1960. Liechtenstein. Vaduz. 4th. ils. 53p. F/VG. C14. $8.00

GALLICO, Paul. *Man Who Was Magic.* 1966. Doubleday. 1st ed. NF/NF. P3. $20.00

GALLICO, Paul. *Man Who Was Magic.* 1966. NY. 1st ed. VG/VG. A17. $7.50

GALLICO, Paul. *Mrs 'Arris Goes to Moscow.* (1974). Delacorte. 1st Am ed. 214p. F/VG. C14. $7.00

GALLICO, Paul. *Mrs 'Arris Goes to Paris.* 1958. Doubleday. VG/G. P3. $15.00

GALLICO, Paul. *Poseidon Adventure.* 1969. Coward. 1st ed. F/NF. H11. $50.00

GALLICO, Paul. *Snow Goose.* 1948. Michael Joseph. 4th. ils Peter Scott. G+. B17. $5.00

GALLISON, Kate. *Death Tape.* 1987. Little Brn. 1st ed. VG/VG. P3. $15.00

GALLIX. *Letters to a Friend: Correspondence...TH White & LJ Potts.* 1982. np. 280p. NF/NF. A4. $55.00

GALLUP, Joseph A. *Sketches of Epidemic Diseases in State of Vermont...* 1815. Boston. 419p. modern bdg. VG. B14. $200.00

GALSWORTHY, John. *Memories.* 1914. Scribner. 1st ils ed. ils Maud Earl. G+. B17. $16.50

GALSWORTHY, John. *Modern Comedy.* 1929. Scribner. 1st ed. VG. P3. $30.00

GALSWORTHY, John. *On Forsythe Change.* 1930. Scribner. 1st ed. 285p. lavender cloth. xl. VG. B22. $5.00

GALT, Alexander S. *Cassell's Popular Science.* 1903 & 1904. London. Cassell. 2 vol. ils. VG. K5. $100.00

GALTON, Francis. *Hereditary Genius: An Inquiry Into Its Laws...* 1892. London. 2nd. 379p. VG. A13. $100.00

GALTON, Francis. *Inquiries Into Human Faculty & Its Development.* 1883. Macmillan. 1st Am ed. ils/pl. 388p. G. G1. $200.00

GAMOW, George. *Atomic Energy in Cosmic & Human Life.* 1946. NY. Macmillan. 1st ed. inscr. 8vo. 3 pl. red cloth. VG. T10. $75.00

GAMOW, George. *One, Two, Three...Infinity.* 1947. Viking. 1st ed. 8vo. 340p. G/dj. K5. $60.00

GANDHI, M.K. *Delhi Diary.* 1948. Ahmedabad. Navajivan. 1st ed. 406p. dj. A17. $25.00

GANDOLFI, Simon. *France-Security.* 1981. Blond Briggs. 1st ed. F/F. P3. $15.00

GANN, Ernest K. *Aviator.* nd. Arbor. 2nd. VG/VG. P3. $13.00

GANN, Ernest K. *Flying Circus.* 1974. NY. 1st ed. 224p. VG/dj. B18. $12.50

GANN, Thomas. *Ancient Cities & Modern Tribes.* 1926. Scribner. 1st ed. 256p. F3. $45.00

GANN, Thomas. *Discoveries & Adventures in Central America.* 1929. Scribner. 1st ed. 261p. NF. F3. $60.00

GANN, Thomas. *Glories of the Maya.* 1938. London. Duckworth. 1st ed. ils/index. 279p. VG. F3. $40.00

GANN, Thomas. *In an Unknown Land.* 1924. Scribner. 1st ed. 263p. F3. $45.00

GANN, W.D. *Tunnel Thru the Air.* 1927. Financial Guardian. 1st ed. VG. P3. $40.00

GANN & THOMPSON. *History of the Maya.* 1931. Scribner. 1st ed. 264p. VG+. F3. $45.00

GANNETT, Samuel S. *Geographic Tables & Formulas.* 1918. WA. 4th. VG. O7. $40.00

GANSBERG & GANSBERG. *Direct Encounters.* 1980. NY. Walker. 2nd. sgns. 8vo. 179p. VG/VG. B11. $25.00

GANTHER, MARTIN & SPALLHOLZ. *Selenium in Biology & Medicine.* 1981. Westport. AVI Pub. 8vo. 573p. cloth. F. B1. $68.00

GARCEAU, J. *Dear Mr G.* 1961. Boston. 1st ed. VG/VG. B5. $40.00

GARCIA, Christina. *Dreaming in Cuban.* 1992. Knopf. 1st ed. F/NF. B2. $65.00

GARCIA, Elise. *Guatemala in Six Tours.* 1978. Guatemala. 1st ed. 12mo. 102p. wrp. F3. $10.00

GARCIA, L. Pericot. *Balearic Islands.* 1973. WA, DC. Praeger. 1st Am ed. 184p. VG/dj. W1. $20.00

GARDINER, Dorothy. *Great Betrayal.* 1949. Doubleday. 1st ed. VG/VG. P3. $20.00

GARDINER, W. *Music of Nature.* 1837. Boston. 8vo. 505p. blk cloth. VG. T3. $30.00

GARDNER, Alexander. *Photographic Sketch Book of the Civil War.* nd. Dover. facsimile of 1866 ed. 224p. VG. T3. $12.00

GARDNER, Asa Bird. *Battles of Gravelly Run, Dinwiddle Courthouse & Five Forks.* 1881. Chicago. 1st ed. 126p. prt wrp bdg into cloth. M8. $85.00

GARDNER, Brian. *Allenby.* 1965. London. 1st ed. 314p. xl. VG. W1. $20.00

GARDNER, Craig Shaw. *Dragon Walking.* 1995. Ace. 1st ed. F/F. G10. $10.00

GARDNER, Eldon. *History of Biology.* 1965. Minneapolis. 2nd. 376p. VG. A13. $17.50

GARDNER, Elsie B. *Maxie at Brinksome Hall.* 1934. Cupples Leon. VG. P3. $15.00

GARDNER, Erle Stanley. *Case of the Amorous Aunt.* 1963. Morrow. 1st ed. NF/VG. B4. $35.00

GARDNER, Erle Stanley. *Case of the Borrowed Brunette.* 1946. Morrow. 1st ed. F/NF. H11. $65.00

GARDNER, Erle Stanley. *Case of the Counterfeit Eye.* 1947. Triangle. hc. VG/VG. P3. $15.00

GARDNER, Erle Stanley. *Case of the Curious Bride.* 1946. Triangle. VG/VG. P3. $15.00

GARDNER, Erle Stanley. *Case of the Dubious Bridegroom.* 1949. NY. 1st ed. F/NF. A15. $60.00

GARDNER, Erle Stanley. *Case of the Fabulous Fake.* 1969. Morrow. 1st ed. NF/dj. H11. $25.00

GARDNER, Erle Stanley. *Case of the Grinning Gorilla.* 1952. Morrow. 1st ed. F/NF. H11. $45.00

GARDNER, Erle Stanley. *Case of the Lucky Loser.* 1957. Morrow. 1st ed. VG/VG. H11. $20.00

GARDNER, Erle Stanley. *Case of the One-Eyed Witness.* 1950. Morrow. 1st ed. VG/fair. H11. $25.00

GARDNER, Erle Stanley. *Case of the Shoplifter's Shoe.* 1938. Morrow. 1st ed. G1. M22. $15.00

GARDNER, Erle Stanley. *Case of the Shoplifter's Shoe.* 1945. Tower. 2nd. VG/VG. P3. $15.00

GARDNER, Erle Stanley. *Case of the Stuttering Bishop.* 1946. Tower. hc. VG/VG. P3. $20.00

GARDNER, Erle Stanley. *Case of the Troubled Trustee.* nd. Black. VG/VG. P3. $10.00

GARDNER, Erle Stanley. *Case of the Vagabond Virgin.* 1948. Morrow. 1st ed. F/VG clip. H11. $50.00

GARDNER, Erle Stanley. *Case of the Velvet Claws.* 1945. Triangle. 4th. VG/VG. P3. $18.00

GARDNER, Erle Stanley. *Court of Last Resort.* 1952. Wm Sloane. 1st ed. NF/G. M19. $35.00

GARDNER, Erle Stanley. *Cut Thin To Win.* 1965. Morrow. 1st ed. NF/F. H11. $35.00

GARDNER, Erle Stanley. *DA Breaks a Seal.* 1946. Morrow. 1st ed. F/F. H11. $70.00

GARDNER, Erle Stanley. *DA Tries a Case.* 1940. Morrow. 1st ed. VG. M22. $20.00

GARDNER, Erle Stanley. *Kept Women Can't Quit.* 1960. Morrow. 1st ed. VG/VG. P3. $30.00

GARDNER, Ethel. *Soarings.* 1990. Cherokee. 1st ed. sgn. 8vo. 120p. F/wrp. B11. $8.50

GARDNER, Jeffrey; see Fox, Gardner F.

GARDNER, John. *Amber Nine.* 1966. Viking. 1st ed. F/NF. M19. $45.00

GARDNER, John. *Corner Men.* 1974. Michael Joseph. 1st ed. F/F. P3. $25.00

GARDNER, John. *Every Night's a Bullfight.* 1971. Michael Joseph. 1st ed. NF/VG. M19. $17.50

GARDNER, John. *For Special Services.* 1982. Coward McCann. 1st ed. F/F. P3. $18.00

GARDNER, John. *For Special Services.* 1982. Jonathan Cape. 1st ed. VG/VG. P3. $25.00

GARDNER, John. *Icebreaker.* 1983. Jonathan Cape. 1st ed. F/F. P3. $25.00

GARDNER, John. *Icebreaker.* 1983. Putnam. 1st ed. F/F. P3. $18.00

GARDNER, John. *Icebreaker.* 1983. Putnam. 1st ed. NF/NF. M19. $15.00

GARDNER, John. *King of the Hummingbirds.* 1977. Knopf. decor brd. NF. P3. $18.00

GARDNER, John. *King's Indian.* 1974. Knopf. 1st ed. rem mk. F/F. H4. $30.00

GARDNER, John. *King's Indian. Stories & Tales.* 1974. Knopf. 1st ed. ils HL Fink. rem mk. NF/clip. S9. $25.00

GARDNER, John. *King's Indian: Stories & Tales.* 1974. Knopf. 1st ed. G/G. P3. $15.00

GARDNER, John. *Last Trump.* 1980. McGraw Hill. 1st ed. VG/VG. P3. $15.00

GARDNER, John. *License Renewed.* 1981. Jonathan Cape. 1st ed. VG/VG. P3. $18.00

GARDNER, John. *Liquidator.* 1965. Viking. 1st ed. hc. VG/VG. P3. $20.00

GARDNER, John. *Madrigal.* 1968. Viking. 1st ed. VG/VG. P3. $23.00

GARDNER, John. *Maestro.* 1993. Otto Penzler. 1st ed. F/F. P3. $23.00

GARDNER, John. *Micklesson's Ghosts.* 1982. Knopf. 1st ed. VG/VG. A20. $12.00

GARDNER, John. *Nickel Mountain.* 1973. Knopf. 1st ed. VG/VG. P3. $30.00

GARDNER, John. *No Deals, Mr Bond.* 1987. Putnam. 1st ed. VG/VG. P3. $14.00

GARDNER, John. *Nobody Lives Forever.* 1986. London. Cape. 1st ed. F/NF. M19. $45.00

GARDNER, John. *Nobody Lives Forever.* 1986. Putnam. 1st ed. VG/VG. P3. $14.00

GARDNER, John. *Nostradamus Traitor.* 1979. Doubleday. UP/1st Am ed. NF/tall wrp. B4. $75.00

GARDNER, John. *October Light.* 1976. Knopf. 1st ed. VG/G. P3. $20.00

GARDNER, John. *Quiet Dogs.* 1982. Hodder Stoughton. 1st ed. NF/NF. P3. $20.00

GARDNER, John. *Role of Honour.* 1984. Jonathan Cape. 1st ed. F/F. P3. $25.00

GARDNER, John. *Scorpius.* 1988. Putnam. 1st ed. VG/VG. P3. $13.00

GARDNER, John. *Secret Houses.* 1987. Putnam. 1st ed. VG/VG. P3. $19.00

GARDNER, John. *Stillness & Shadows.* 1986. NY. 1st ed. F/F. A17. $12.50

GARDNER, John. *Win, Lose or Die.* 1989. Putnam. 1st ed. VG/VG. P3. $14.00

GARDNER, John. *Wreckage of Agathon.* 1970. NY. 1st ed. author's 2nd book. F/dj. B5/C6. $75.00

GARDNER, Leonard. *Fat City.* 1969. FSG. 1st ed. author's 1st novel. VG/VG. M22. $50.00

GARDNER, Martin. *Logic Machines & Diagrams.* 1958. McGraw Hill. 8vo. 157p. VG. K5. $25.00

GARDNER, Martin. *Scientific American Book of Mathematical Puzzles...* 1959. NY. Simon Schuster. ils. 178p. G/dj. K5. $15.00

GARDNER, Matt; see Fox, Gardner F.

GARDNER, Miriam; see Bradley, Marion Zimmer.

GARDNER, Robert E. *Small Arms Makers.* 1863. NY. 4to. 378p. gray cloth. VG. T3. $24.00

GARFIELD, Brian. *Crime of My Life.* nd. Walker. 1st ed. xl. dj. P3. $7.00

GARFIELD, Brian. *Death Sentence.* 1975. Evans. 1st ed. VG/VG. P3. $30.00

GARFIELD, Brian. *Deep Cover.* 1971. Delacorte. 1st ed. G/G. P3. $15.00

GARFIELD, Brian. *Kolchak's Gold.* 1973. McKay. 1st ed. F/F. H11. $30.00

GARFIELD, Brian. *Lawbringers.* 1962. Macmillan. 1st ed. NF/NF. P3. $40.00

GARFIELD, Brian. *Paladin.* 1980. Macmillan. 1st ed. NF/NF. P3. $20.00

GARFIELD, Brian. *Recoil.* 1977. Morrow. 1st ed. VG/VG. P3. $40.00

GARFIELD, Brian. *What of Terry Conniston?* 1971. World. 1st ed. VG/VG. P3. $20.00

GARFIELD, Brian. *Wild Times.* 1978. Simon Schuster. 1st ed. VG/VG. P3. $15.00

GARFIELD, Leon. *Fair's Fair.* 1983. Doubleday. stated 1st ed. ils. unp. NF/VG+. C14. $22.00

GARIEPY, Louis. *Saw-Ge-Mah: Medicine Man.* 1950. Northland. 1st ed. sgn. 12mo. 326p. G/worn. B11. $35.00

GARIS, Cleo F. *Arden Blake & the Orchard Secret (#1).* 1934. AL Burt. 250p. VG/dj. M20. $24.00

GARIS, Howard R. *Buddy & His Chums.* 1930. NY. VG. A17. $6.00

GARIS, Howard R. *Rick & Ruddy Afloat.* 1922. Springfield. 1st ed. ils King. 262p. VG. A17. $7.50

GARIS, Howard R. *Rick & Ruddy in Camp.* 1921. Springfield. 1st ed. ils Milo Winter. 254p. G. A17. $7.00

GARIS, Howard R. *Tom Cardiff in the Big Top (#2).* 1927. Milton Bradley. ils WB King. 256p. VG/dj. M20. $62.00

GARIS, Howard R. *Uncle Wiggily & the Barber.* 1939. Platt Munk. ils George Carlson. 12p. VG+. M5. $10.00

GARIS, Howard R. *Uncle Wiggily's Story Book.* 1939. Platt Munk. lg 8vo. ils Lang Campbell. red brd. VG/worn. M5. $45.00

GARIS, Lilian. *Dragon of the Hills.* nd. Grosset Dunlap. VG. P3. $15.00

GARIS, Roger. *My Father Was Uncle Wiggly.* 1966. McGraw Hill. 1st ed. 217p. VG/dj. M20. $27.00

GARLAKE. *Great Zimbabwe.* 1973. Stein Day. F/VG. D2. $50.00

GARLAND, Hamlin. *Back-Trailers From the Middle Border.* 1928. NY. 1st ed. ils Constance Garland. gilt cloth. VG. A17. $15.00

GARLAND, Hamlin. *Mystery of Buried Crosses.* 1939. NY. 1st ed. photos. 352p. VG/VG. B5. $90.00

GARLAND, Joseph E. *Experiment in Medicine. The 1st 20 Years of Pratt Clinic...* 1960. Riverside. 107p. inscr John F Sullivan. bl cloth. VG. B14. $55.00

GARLAND, Phyl. *Sound of Soul.* 1969. Regnery. 1st ed. inscr. NF/NF. B2. $50.00

GARLAND. *Bibliography of Writings of Sir James Matthew Barrie.* 1928. London. 1/520. ils. 146p. NF. A4. $135.00

GARLAND. *Boy Life on the Prairie.* 1899. Macmillan. 1st ed. F. A18. $75.00

GARLICK, T. *Treatise on Artifical Propagation of Fish.* 1857. Cleveland. ils/maps. 142p. xl. G. B5. $40.00

GARNER, Alan. *Bag of Moonshine.* 1986. Delacorte. 1st Am ed. 8vo. ils. F/F. T10. $50.00

GARNER, Alan. *Red Shift.* 1973. Macmillan. 1st ed. VG/fair. p3. $13.00

GARNER, Elvira. *Ezekiel Travels.* 1938. Holt. 1st ed. unp. VG. M20. $60.00

GARNER, Elvira. *Ezekiel Travels.* 1938. Holt. 1st ed. 8vo. unp. pict brd. VG/VG. D1. $150.00

GARNER, Elvira. *Ezekiel.* 1937. Holt. 1st ed. unp. NF. C14. $25.00

GARNER, Elvira. *Way Down in Tennessee.* 1941. Messner. 1st ed. ils. VG/VG. P2. $50.00

GARNER, William. *Ditto, Brother Rat!* 1972. Collins. 1st ed. hc. VG/VG. P3. $20.00

GARNER, William. *Think Big, Think Dirty.* 1983. St Martin. 1st ed. VG/VG. P3. $16.00

GARNER. *World of Edwardiana.* 1974. Hamlyn. F/F. D2. $40.00

GARNETT. *Letters From John Galsworthy 1900-1932.* 1934. np. 1/3000. pres. 255p. VG. A4. $60.00

GAROZZO & YALLOUZE. *Blue Club.* 1971 (1970). London. VG. S1. $20.00

GARRETT, George. *Evening Performance.* 1985. Doubleday. 1st ed. 518p. VG/VG. B10. $20.00

GARRETT, George. *Luck's Shining Child: Miscellany of Poems & Verses.* 1981. Palaemon. 1st ed. 1/300. sgn. blk cloth. VG. B10. $75.00

GARRETT, George. *Magic Striptease.* 1973. Doubleday. 1st ed. sgn. 272p. VG/VG. B10. $45.00

GARRETT, George. *Welcome to the Medicine Show: Postcards/Flashcards...* 1978. Palaemon. 1/300. sgn. 27p. VG. B10. $75.00

GARRETT, Pat F. *Authentic Life of Billy, the Kid.* 1954. Norman. 3rd. 12mo. 156p. VG/dj. T10. $25.00

GARRIGUE, Francois. *Enchanted Morocco.* 1967. France. Arthaud. ils. 238p. VG/dj. W1. $35.00

GARRISON, Jim. *Star Spangled Contract.* 1976. McGraw Hill. 1st ed. F/F. P3. $18.00

GARRISON, Karl C. *Psychology of Adolescence.* 1934. Prentice Hall. pub copy. panelled dk gr cloth. G1. $35.00

GARRISON, Webb. *Strange Facts About Death.* 1978. Abingdon. 1st ed. VG/VG. P3. $13.00

GARROTT, Hal. *Snythergen.* 1923. NY. 1st ed. ils Dugald Walker. VG+. M5. $50.00

GARTON, Ray. *Crucifax Autumn.* 1988. Dark Havest. 1st ed. pub copy. sgn Garton/ils Bob Eggleton. F/F/case. T2. $65.00

GARTON, Ray. *Live Girls.* 1987. London. Macdonald. 1st Eng/1st hc ed. AN/dj. B4. $250.00

GARTON, Ray. *Lot Lizards.* 1991. Shingletown. Zeising. 1st ed. F/F. T2. $22.00

GARTRAM, John. *Travels in Pennsylvania & Canada.* 1966. Ann Arbor. VG. O7. $20.00

GARVE, Andrew. *Ascent of D-13.* 1969. Thriller BC. VG/VG. P3. $8.00

GARVE, Andrew. *Cuckoo Line Affair.* 1953. Collins Crime Club. 1st ed. VG/VG. P3. $40.00

GARVE, Andrew. *Hide & Go Seek.* 1966. Harper Row. 1st ed. VG/VG. P3. $25.00

GARVEY, Ruth. *Who Dealt? 100 Guideposts to Bridge Bidding.* nd. St Louis. lg format. 24p. VG. S1. $10.00

GARY, Jim. *King of the Royal Mounted.* 1940s. France. Jim Gary dailies. French text. 240p. M13. $35.00

GASCOIGNE, Bamber. *World Theatre.* 1968. Boston. Little Brn. xl. F/VG. D2. $40.00

GASH, Joe. *Newspaper Murders.* 1985. HRW. 1st ed. VG/VG. P3. $15.00

GASH, Joe. *Priestly Murders.* 1984. HRW. 1st ed. F/F. P3. $15.00

GASH, Jonathan. *Firefly Gadroon.* 1982. St Martin. 1st ed. F/F. P3. $35.00

GASH, Jonathan. *Grail Tree.* 1979. Harper. 1st Am ed. 3rd in Lovejoy series. VG/VG. M22. $20.00

GASH, Jonathan. *Great California Game.* 1991. St Martin. 1st ed. VG/G. P3. $15.00

GASH, Jonathan. *Jade Woman.* 1989. St Martin. 1st ed. F/F. P3. $18.00

GASH, Jonathan. *Sleepers of Erin.* 1983. Dutton. 1st ed. F/F. P3. $35.00

GASH, Jonathan. *Spend Game.* 1981. Ticknor Fields. 1st ed. F/F. P3. $60.00

GASH, Jonathan. *Tartan Sell.* 1986. St Martin. 1st ed. F/F. P3. $25.00

GASH & LINGENFELTER. *Newspapers of Nevada: A History & Bibliography 1854-1979.* nd. NV U. 4to. 13 vintage photos. 337p. F/F. A4. $45.00

GASK, Arthur. *Crime Upon Crime.* nd. Roy. hc. VG/G. P3. $18.00

GASK, Arthur. *Silent Dead.* 1950. Herbert Jenkins. 1st ed. VG. P3. $25.00

GASKELL. *New Introduction to Bibliography.* 1978. np. 141 ils. 438p. VG/VG. A4. $85.00

GASS, William H. *In the Heart of the Country AOS.* 1968. NY. 1st ed. author's 2nd book. inscr. F/F. A11. $75.00

GASS, William H. *Omensetter's Luck.* 1966. NAL. 1st ed. author's 1st book. NF/NF. B2. $150.00

GASS, William H. *Willie Masters' Lonesome Wife.* 1968. Evanston. TriQuarterly. inscr. NF/wrp. B2. $75.00

GATENBY, Rosemary. *Deadly Relations.* nd. BC. VG/VG. P3. $8.00

GATENBY, Rosemary. *Fugitive Affair.* 1976. Dodd Mead. 1st ed. VG/VG. P3. $15.00

GATES, Doris. *Blue Willow.* 1956 (1940). Viking. 11th. 8vo. 172p. bl cloth. VG/G. T5. $28.00

GATES, Josephine S. *Live Dolls' Busy Days.* Sept 1907. Bobbs Merrill. 1st ed. ils Virginia Keep. 105p. VG+. P2. $110.00

GATES, Josephine S. *More About Live Dolls.* 1903. Franklin. 1st ed. ils V Keep. VG. D1. $100.00

GATES, Josephine S. *Sunshine Annie.* 1910. Bobbs Merrill. ils Fanny Cory. 148p. red cloth. VG. D1. $135.00

GATES, Susa Young. *Life Story of Brigham Young. By One of His Daughters.* 1930. NY. 1st ed. 388p. gilt blk cloth. VG. H3. $50.00

GATTY & POST. *Around the World in 8 Days.* 1931. NY. 1st ed. sgns. G. V4. $250.00

GAUBA, K.L. *Battles at the Bar.* 1956. Bombay. Tirpathi Ltd. M11. $65.00

GAUCH, Frederick Augustus. *Psychology ...Applied for Use of Colleges.* 1853 (1846). Dodd/Crocker Brewster. 4th. emb Victorian cloth. G1. $75.00

GAUCH, Frederick Augustus. *Psychology; or, View of the Human Soul.* 1841. Dodd/Crocker Brewster. 2nd. 401p. emb Victorian cloth. G1. $200.00

GAUGUIN, Paul. *Noa Noa.* 1924. Paris. ils. VG/wrp. O7. $95.00

GAULT, W.P. *Ohio at Vicksburg.* 1906. Columbus. 1st ed. ils/map. 374p. VG. B18. $75.00

GAULT, William Campbell. *Cat & Mouse.* 1988. St Martin. 1st ed. NF/NF. P3. $15.00

GAULT, William Campbell. *Come Die With Me.* 1959. Random. 1st ed. VG. P3. $20.00

GAULT, William Campbell. *Death in Donegal Bay.* 1984. Walker. 1st ed. NF/NF. P3. $15.00

GAULT, William Campbell. *Ring Around Rosa.* 1955. Dutton. 1st ed. VG/VG. P3. $30.00

GAUNT. *Pre-Raphaelite Tragedy.* 1942. Harcourt. G. D2. $20.00

GAUSSEN, L. *World's Birthday.* 1865. London. Nelson. 270p. gilt cloth. K5. $26.00

GAVIT, Bernard C. *Intro to the Study of Law.* 1951. Brooklyn. Foundation. M11. $35.00

GAWRON, Jean Mark. *Apology for Rain.* 1974. Doubleday. 1st ed. F/F. P3. $15.00

GAY, Romney. *Romney Gay's Big Picture Book.* 1947. Grosset Dunlap. 4to. ils. F/VG+. M5. $65.00

GAY, Romney. *Romney Gay's Box of Books.* 1941. Grosset Dunlap. 8vo. G+/box. M5. $30.00

GAY, Romney. *Tommy Grows Wise.* 1939. Grosset Dunlap. 1st ed. 12mo. unp. pict brd. VG. T5. $30.00

GEDGE, Pauline. *Stargate.* 1982. Macmillan. 1st ed. NF/NF. P3. $20.00

GEIGER, Maynard J. *Palou's Life of Fray Junipero Serra.* 1955. WA. Am Franciscan Hist. 1st ed. sgn. 547p. map ep. gilt bl cloth. NF. T10. $150.00

GEIKIE, A. *Landscape in History.* 1905. Macmillan. 352p. cloth. G. D8. $12.00

GEIS, Darlene. *Colorslide Tour of Mexico.* 1961. Colombia Record. photo. unp. laminated brd. F3. $15.00

GEISEL, Theodor. *And To Think That I Saw It on Mulberry Street.* 1937. NY. 9th. pict brd. VG. M5. $45.00

GEISEL, Theodor. *Cat & the Hat Song Book.* 1967. Random. 1st ed. ils. VG. P2. $200.00

GEISEL, Theodor. *Happy Birthday to You!* 1959. Random. 1st ed. ils. VG/dj. D1. $385.00

GEISEL, Theodor. *If I Ran the Zoo.* 1950. Random. early ed. ils. VG/$2.50 price. D1. $225.00

GEISEL, Theodor. *McElligot's Pool.* 1947. Random. later prt. ils. VG+/torn. M5. $30.00

GEISEL, Theodor. *Seven Lady Godivas.* 1939. Random. 1st ed. 4to. ils. F/dj. B24. $475.00

GEISEL, Theodor. *Yertle the Turtle & Other Stories.* 1958. Random. 1st ed. 8vo. NF/dj. B24. $395.00

GEISEL, Theodor. *You're Only Old Once! A Book for Obsolete Children.* 1986. Random. 1st ed. F/clip. B17. $15.00

GEISEL, Theodor. *500 Hats of Bartholomew Cubbins.* 1938. Vanguard. early ed. ils. NF/clip. D1. $250.00

GELATT, R. *Fabulous Phonograph.* 1955. Lippincott. 1st ed. 320p. VG/VG. B5. $50.00

GEMELLI, Agostino. *La Lotta Contro Lourdes.* 1911. Firenze. Libreria Editirice Fiorentina. 352p. prt wrp. G1. $45.00

GENEROIX, Maurice. *Rrou.* 1932. Minton Balch. 1st Am ed. ils Diana Thorne. VG+/G+. P2. $30.00

GENESTOUX, Magdeleine. *Les Adventures de Passepartout.* 1925. Librairie Hachette. ils Cecil Aldin. VG. P2. $95.00

GENET & HAYES. *Robotic Observatories.* 1989. Mesa, AZ. 8vo. 292p. laminated brd. AN. K5. $15.00

GENTILCORE, R. Louis. *Animals & Maps.* 1969. Berkeley. ils. F/rpr. O7. $65.00

GENTLE, Mary. *Architecture of Desire.* 1993. Roc. 1st ed. F/F. P3. $20.00

GEORGE, David Lloyd. *War Memoirs of...,* *1914-17.* 1933. Boston. 1st ed. 4 vol. F/dj. A17. $50.00

GEORGE, Elizabeth. *For the Sake of Elena.* 1992. Bantam. 1st ed. F/F. H11. $25.00

GEORGE, Elizabeth. *Great Deliverance.* 1988. Bantam. 1st ed. author's 1st novel. sgn. F/F. T2. $60.00

GEORGE, Elizabeth. *Payment in Blood.* nd. BOMC. VG/VG. P3. $10.00

GEORGE, Leopold. *Lehrbuch der Psychologie.* 1854. Berlin. Druck/Georg Reimer. 588p. VG. G1. $125.00

GEORGE, Peter. *Commander-1.* 1965. Delacorte. 1st ed. VG/VG. P3. $20.00

GERARD, Francis. *Secret Sceptre.* 1971. Tom Stacey. VG/VG. P3. $15.00

GERARD, John. *Herbal; or, General History of Plants.* 1975. NY. Dover. rpt of 1633 ed. 1677p. AN/dj. A10. $130.00

GERARD, Max. *Dali.* 1968. NY. Abrams. 1st ed. VG/VG. B5. $75.00

GERARD, Philip. *Hatteras Light.* 1986. Scribner. 1st ed. author's 1st novel. F/F. M23. $35.00

GERASIMOV, I. *Short History of Geographical Science in the Soviet Union.* 1976. Moscow. VG. O7. $20.00

GERBI, Antonello. *Dispute of the New World.* 1973. Pittsburgh. VG. O7. $35.00

GERBI, Antonello. *Nature in the New World.* 1986. Pittsburgh. VG. O7. $25.00

GERDTS, William H. *American Impressionism.* 1984. Abbeville. 1st ed. ils/pl. cloth. dj. D2. $85.00

GERHARD, Frederick. *Illinois As It Is.* 1857. Chicago/Phil. 1st ed. 3 fld maps. 451p. gilt blk cloth. VG. H3. $100.00

GERHARD, Peter. *Guide to the Historical Geography of New Spain.* 1972. Cambridge. VG. O7. $65.00

GERHHARD & GULICK. *Lower California Guidebook.* 1964. Arthur H Clark. 3rd ed/2nd prt. 8vo. 243p. F/dj. T10. $30.00

GERLACH, Arch C. *National Atlas of the United States of America.* 1990. US Geol Survey. lg folio. 417p. F. O7. $795.00

GERLACH, Larry. *Men in Blue.* 1980. Viking. 1st ed. F/VG. P8. $45.00

GERNSHEIM, Helmut. *History of Photography From the Earliest Use of the Camera.* 1955. Oxford. 359 photos mtd on coated stock. 395p. xl. VG. A4. $195.00

GERNSHEIM, Helmut. *Incunabula of British Photographic Literature...* 1984. np. 4to. ils. 159p. F/F. A4. $95.00

GERNSHEIM, Helmut. *Origins of Photography.* 1982. np. sq 4to. 191 photos. 280p. F/F/VG case. A4. $250.00

GERROLD, David. *Chess With a Dragon.* 1987. Walker. 1st ed. RS. F/F. P3. $20.00

GERROLD, David. *Day for Damnation.* 1984. Timescape. 1st ed. F/F. P3. $17.00

GERSHAM, Douglas H. *Lenton Lands.* 1988. Macmillan. 1st ed. F/F. M23. $25.00

GERT ZUR HEIDE, Karl. *Deep South Piano: Story of Little Brother Montgomery.* 1970. London. Studio Vista. 1st ed. F/wrp. B2. $25.00

GESELL, Arnold. *First Five Years of Life.* 1940. NY. 393p. VG/VG. A17. $7.50

GESELL & THOMPSON. *Infant Behavior: Its Genesis & Growth.* 1934. McGraw Hill. ils. panelled prt red cloth. VG. G1. $50.00

GESS, Denise. *Red Whiskey Blues.* 1987. Crown. 1st ed. author's 1st novel. F/F. B35. $20.00

GESSLER, Clifford. *Pattern of Mexico.* 1941. Appleton. 1st ed. 442p. dj. F3. $20.00

GESTON, Mark S. *Mirror to the Sky.* 1992. Morrow. UP of 1st ed. F/wrp. G10. $25.00

GEVITZ, Norman. *DO's: Osteopathic Medicine in America.* 1982. Baltimore. 1st ed. 183p. VG. A13. $30.00

GHEERBRANT, Alain. *Journey to the Far Amazon.* 1954. Simon Schuster. 2nd. 353p. dj. F3. $15.00

GIBB, G. *Saco Lowell Shops.* 1950. Cambridge, MA. 1st ed. sgn. ils/index. 835p. VG/VG. B5. $40.00

GIBBON, Edward. *Decline & Fall of the Roman Empire.* nd. AL Burt. 5 vol. VG. P12. $40.00

GIBBON & HERNDON. *Exploration of the Valley of the Amazon.* 1853. WA. 2 vol. pl. 3-quarter leather. VG. B5. $300.00

GIBBONS, Euell. *Stalking the Blue-Eyed Scallop.* 1965. David McKay. sgn. 8vo. 332p. G/fair. B11. $15.00

GIBBONS, Kaye. *Cure for Dreams.* 1991. Algonquin. ARC. F/wrp. C6. $75.00

GIBBONS, Kaye. *Cure for Dreams.* 1991. Algonquin. 1st ed. sgn. F/F. B35. $50.00

GIBBONS, Kaye. *Ellen Foster.* 1987. Algonquin. 1st ed. F/F. M23. $175.00

GIBBONS, Kaye. *Ellen Foster.* 1987. Chapel Hill. UP. author's 1st book. NF/wrp. B4. $200.00

GIBBONS, Kaye. *Family Life.* 1990. NC Wesleyan College. 1/500. sgn. F/wrp. C6. $55.00

GIBBONS, Kaye. *Frost & Flower: My Life With Manic Depression So Far.* 1995. Atlantic. 1st ed. 1/250. sgn. F. C2. $100.00

GIBBONS, Kaye. *Sights Unseen.* ARC. sgn. VG+/wrp. B30. $30.00

GIBBONS, Kaye. *Virtuous Woman.* 1989. Algonquin. 1st ed. F/F. M23. $40.00

GIBBONS, Kaye. *Virtuous Woman.* 1989. Chapel Hill. Algonquin. 1st state proof. VG/pk wrp. C6. $275.00

GIBBS, James W. *Buckeye Horology.* 1971. Columbia, PA. ils. 128p. xl. G. B18. $25.00

GIBBS, Jim. *Disaster Log of Ships.* 1971. Bonanza. VG/VG. A16. $25.00

GIBSON, Edmund. *Codex Juris Ecclesiastic Anglicani...* 1713. London. 2nd vol only. contemporary calf. M11. $75.00

GIBSON, Edward. *Reach.* 1989. Doubleday. 1st ed. F/NF. G10. $10.00

GIBSON, Eva Katherine. *Zauberlinda the Wise Witch.* 1901. Robert Smith. 1st ed. 8vo. ils. VG. M5. $60.00

GIBSON, Hugh. *Rio.* 1938. Doubleday. sgn. 263p. VG/dj. F3. $15.00

GIBSON, James. *Dr Bodo Otto & Medical Background of American Revolution.* 1937. Springfield. 1st ed. 345p. NF. A13. $100.00

GIBSON, Walter. *Crime Over Casco & Mother Goose Murder.* 1979. Crime Club. 1st ed. F/F. P3. $50.00

GIBSON, Walter. *Norgil: More Tales of Prestidigitatio.* 1979. Mysterious. 1/250. sgn/#d. sgn also as Maxwell Grant. F/NF/box. P3. $125.00

GIBSON, William. *Count Zero.* 1986. Arbor. 1st ed. F/F. P3. $35.00

GIBSON, William. *Mona Lisa Overdrive.* 1988. London. Gollancz. 1st ed. sgn. F/F. T2. $65.00

GIBSON, William. *Neuromancer.* 1984. London. 1st Eng/1st hc ed. author's 1st book. sgn. F/F. A11. $275.00

GIBSON, William. *Virtual Light.* 1993. Bantam. 1st ed. F/F. M23. $30.00

GIBSON & STERLING. *Difference Engine.* 1991. Bantam. 1st ed. hc. F/F. P3. $20.00

GIDE, Andre. *Madeleine.* 1952. NY. 1st Am ed. F/F. A11. $55.00

GIDE, Andre. *Secret Drama of My Life.* 1951. Paris. 1st Eng-language ed. NF/wrp/glassine dj. A11. $85.00

GIDWANI. *Comparative Librarianship, Essays in Honour of DN Marshall.* 1973. Delhi. ils. 245p. F/VG. A4. $95.00

GIELGUD, Val. *Goggle-Box.* 1963. Collins Crime Club. 1st ed. VG. P3. $22.00

GIESY, J.U. *Jason, Son of Jason.* 1966. Avalon. NF/NF. P3. $20.00

GIESY, J.U. *Mystery Woman.* 1929. Whitman. hc. VG/VG. P3. $60.00

GIFFEN, J. Kelly. *Egyptian Sudan.* 1905. Chicago. Revell. 10 pl/1 map. 252p. xl. VG. W1. $25.00

GIFFORD, Barry. *Neighborhood of Baseball.* 1981. NY. 1st ed. sgn. F/NF. A11. $60.00

GIFFORD, Barry. *Quinzaine in Return for a Portrait of Mary Sun.* 1977. Berkeley. 1st ed. sgn. F/wht wrp. A11. $50.00

GIFFORD, Barry. *Wild at Heart.* 1990. Grove Weidenfield. 1st ed. AN/dj. M22. $30.00

GIFFORD, Thomas. *Man From Lisbon.* 1977. McGraw Hill. 1st ed. VG/VG. P3. $25.00

GILB, Dagoberto. *Last Known Residence of Mickey Acuna.* 1994. Grove. 1st ed. F/F. A20. $30.00

GILBERT, A.W. *Potato.* 1917. NY. Macmillan. Rural Science series. 12mo. 16 pl. cloth. B1. $45.00

GILBERT, Anthony. *And Death Came Too.* 1977. Hamish Hamilton. VG/VG. P3. $15.00

GILBERT, Anthony. *Murder Anonymous.* 1968. Random. 1st ed. VG/VG. P3. $20.00

GILBERT, B. *Westering Man: The Life of Joseph Walker.* 1983. Atheneum. 1st ed. 8vo. 339p. F/dj. T10. $35.00

GILBERT, Bentley. *British Social Policy, 1914-1939.* 1970. Ithaca. 343p. dj. A13. $35.00

GILBERT, Geoffrey. *Law of Tenures; Including Theory & Practice of Copyholds...* 1796. London. Strahan. contemporary calf/rebacked. M11. $650.00

GILBERT, Henry. *King Arthur.* nd. Saalfield. hc. G. P3. $12.00

GILBERT, Michael. *Body of a Girl.* 1972. Harper Row. 1st ed. VG/VG. P3. $13.00

GILBERT, Michael. *Flash Point.* 1974. Harper Row. 1st ed. VG/VG. P3. $18.00

GILBERT, Michael. *Petrella at Q.* 1977. Harper Row. 1st ed. VG/tape rpr. P3. $13.00

GILBERT, Michael. *Queen Against Karl Mullen.* 1991. Carroll & Graf. 1st ed. F/F. P3. $19.00

GILBERT, Nan. *Sir Gruss, the Wooly Dog.* 1947. Whitman. 4to. VG+/G. M5. $25.00

GILBERT, Sarah. *Dixie Riggs.* 1991. Warner. 1st ed. rem mk. F/F. B35. $20.00

GILBERT, Sarah. *Hairdo.* 1989. Warner. UP. sgn. F. B35. $55.00

GILBERT, W.S. *Fifty Bab Ballads, Much Sound & Little Sense.* 1887. London. 317p. VG. A4. $20.00

GILBERT, Walter. *George Morland.* 1907. London. Blk. 1st ed. 50 pl. G+. B5. $55.00

GILBERT & GREGG. *Love, a Diptych.* 1994. Captain's Bookshelf. 1/30 hors commerce. sgns. F/wrp. C2. $150.00

GILBERT & JEFFERYS. *Crossties Through Carolina: Story of North Carolina...* 1969. Raleigh. 1st ed. 88p. VG/dj. A17. $30.00

GILBEY, Walter. *Harness Horse.* 1898. London. Vinton. G+. O3. $45.00

GILBOY, Bernard. *Voyage of Pleasure.* 1956. Cambridge. VG. O7. $25.00

GILCHRIST, Ellen. *Land Surveyor's Daughter.* 1979. Fayetteville. Lost Roads. 1st ed. sgn. author's 1st book. F/wrp. B4. $600.00

GILCHRIST, Ellen. *Light Can Be Both Wave & Particle.* 1989. Little Brn. 1st ed. 8vo. F/dj. w/pub letter. S9. $60.00

GILCHRIST, Ellen. *Net of Jewels.* 1992. Little Brn. 1st ed. F/VG+. A20. $20.00

GILCHRIST, Marie E. *Story of the Great Lakes.* 1942. Harper. G. A16. $50.00

GILDEN, Mel. *Harry Newberry & the Raiders...* 1989. Holt. 1st ed. F/F. P3. $15.00

GILES, Baxter; see Offutt, Andrew.

GILES, Elizabeth; see Holt, John Robert.

GILES, Kenneth. *Death Among the Stars.* 1969. Walker. 1st ed. F/F. P3. $10.00

GILES, Leonidus Blanton. *Terry's Texas Rangers.* 1911. Austin. Von Boeckmann-Jones Co. 1st ed. 105p. NF/case. M8. $1,750.00

GILES, Nicki. *Fifth Rapunzel.* 1991. Hodder Stoughton. 1st ed. VG/VG. P3. $20.00

GILES, Nicki. *Marilyn Album.* 1991. Bison Group. hc. F/F. P3. $20.00

GILES, Raymond; see Holt, John Robert.

GILES, Valarius Cincinnatus. *Rags & Hope: the Recollections of Val C Giles...* 1961. Coward McCann. 1st ed. 280p. F/NF. M8. $45.00

GILES, W.E. *Cruise in a Queensland Labour Vessel to the South Seas.* 1968. Canberra/Honolulu. VG. O7. $20.00

GILES & PALMER. *Horseshoe Bend.* 1962. NY. 1st ed. VG/VG. B5. $35.00

GILES & YIESLA. *Shade Trees for Central & Northern United States...* 1992. Champaign. 296p. sc. M. B26. $30.00

GILKES, Lillian. *Cora Crane: Biography of Mrs Stephen Crane.* 1960. IN U. 1st ed. 416p. VG+/dj. M20. $25.00

GILL, Bartholomew. *McGarr & the Method of Descartes.* 1984. Viking. 1st ed. F/F. P3. $15.00

GILL, Bartholomew. *McGarr at the Dublin Horse Show.* 1979. Scribner. 1st ed. VG/VG. P3. $15.00

GILL, Elizabeth. *Crime Coast.* 1931. Crime Club. 1st ed. hc. VG. P3. $20.00

GILL, Eric. *Art & Love.* 1927. Bristol. Cleverdon. 1/35 (of 260). 8vo. sgn. F. w/extra suite of 6 pl. B24. $2,000.00

GILL, Eric. *Canticum Canticorum Salomonis Quod Hebraice Dicitur...* 1931. Weimar. Cranach. 1/268. tall 8vo. 31p. teg. fore-edge painting. dj. case. B24 $2,850.00

GILL, Eric. *Passion of Our Lord Jesus Christ...* 1934. London. Faber. 1/300. 5 engravings. 59p. bl cloth. NF/dj. B24. $350.00

GILL, Eric. *Procreant Hymn, by E Powys Mathers.* 1926. Golden Cockerel. 1/175. 8vo. 20p. wht buckram. F/dj. B24. $1,000.00

GILL, Eric. *Wood Engravings.* 1924. Ditchling. St Dominic. 1/150. 1 woodcut/34 engravings. linen brd. F. B24. $2,750.00

GILL, Graeme. *Rules of the Communist Party of the Soviet Union.* 1988. Armonk. ME Sharpe. M11. $35.00

GILL, Patrick; see Creasey, John.

GILL, Richard. *White Water & Black Magic.* 1940. Holt. 1st ed. 369p. cloth. F3. $25.00

GILLEN, Mollie. *Assasination of the Prime Minister.* 1972. NY. St Martin. M11. $45.00

GILLES, Helen Trybulowski. *Nigeria: From the Bight to Benin to Africa's Desert Sands.* 1944. NGS. photos. F/stiff wrp. P4. $8.50

GILLESPIE, John W. *New Plants from Fiji.* 1930-32. Honolulu. 3 parts. total 140 pl/2 photos. wrp. B26. $45.00

GILLESPIE, Robert B. *Hell's Kitchen.* 1987. Detective BC. VG. P3. $8.00

GILLESPIE, W.M. *Treatise on Land-Surveying.* 1855. Appleton. 6th. 84p tables. 424p. G. A17. $45.00

GILLETT, John M. *Gentians of Canada & Greenland.* 1963. Ottawa. 38 pl. 99p. F. B26. $26.00

GILLETT, Mary. *Army Medical Dept: 1775-1818.* 1981. WA. 299p. VG. A13. $40.00

GILLHAM, Skip. *Seaway Era Shipwrecks.* 1994. Ontario. Riverbank Traders. M. A16. $17.00

GILLHAM, Skip. *Ships Along the Seaway Vol 4.* 1986. Stonehouse. VG/wrp. A16. $7.00

GILLIAM, Dorothy. *Paul Robeson: All-American.* 1976. New Republic Book. 1st ed. 8vo. ils. F/dj. T10. $30.00

GILLIGAN, Edmund. *Gaunt Woman.* 1943. Scribner. 1st ed. VG/G. P3. $20.00

GILLMOR, Donald M. *Free Press & Fair Trial.* 1966. WA. Public Affairs. M11. $45.00

GILLMORE, Rufus. *Ebony Bed Murder.* 1932. Mystery League. 1st ed. xl. VG. P3. $12.00

GILMAN, Caroline. *Oracles From the Poets.* 1845. London/NY. 2nd. gilt bl cloth. NF. C6. $75.00

GILMAN, Charlotte Perkins. *Herland.* 1979. Pantheon. 1st ed. xl. dj. P3. $7.00

GILMAN, Dorothy. *Mrs Polifax & the Golden Triangle.* 1988. Doubleday. 1st ed. VG/VG. P3. $16.00

GILMAN, Robert Cham. *Starkahn of Rhada.* 1970. HBW. 1st ed. VG/VG. P3. $25.00

GILMER, John Harmer. *Letter Addressed to Hon Wm C Rives, by John H Gilmer...* 1864. Richmond? 1st ed. self wrp bdg in cloth. VG. M8. $250.00

GILMOR, Frances. *Windsinger.* 1930. Milton Balch. 1st ed. inscr. 218p. G. B11. $30.00

GILMOR, Harry. *Four Years in the Saddle.* 1866. London. Longman Gr. 1st Eng ed. 310p. cloth/rebacked. M8. $150.00

GILMORE, R. *Ebony Bed Murder.* 1932. NY. 1st ed. VG/VG. B5. $20.00

GILMOUR, John. *British Botanists.* 1946 (1944). London. ils. 48p. VG/dj. B26. $15.00

GILMOUR, Margaret. *Ameliaranne at the Circus.* 1931. McKay. 1st ed. ils SB Pearse. unp. VG/dj. D1. $80.00

GILMOUR & WALTERS. *Wild Flowers: Botanising in Britain.* 1954. London. ils. 242p. dj. B26. $15.00

GILPATRICK, Guy. *Flying Stories.* 1946. Dutton. 1st ed. 8vo. 287p. gray cloth. NF. T10. $35.00

GILPATRICK, Guy. *Half Seas Over.* 1932. NY. 1st ed. VG/VG. B5. $42.50

GILPATRICK, Guy. *Last Glencannon Omnibus.* 1953. NY. 1st ed. VG/VG. B5. $40.00

GILPATRICK, Noreen. *Piano Man.* 1991. St Martin. 1st ed. 8vo. F/F. T10. $100.00

GILPIN, Laura. *Enduring Navaho.* 1971. Austin. 2nd. 4to. 264p. gr cloth. F/NF. T10. $60.00

GILPIN, Laura. *Pueblos: A Camera Chronicle.* 1941. Hastings. thin 8vo. ils. bl cloth. VG/dj. T10. $125.00

GILPIN, Laura. *Temples in Yucatan: A Camera Chronicle of Chichen Itza.* 1948. Hastings. 1st ed. 8vo. 124p. gilt gr cloth. NF/dj. T10. $100.00

GILSON, Charles. *Robin of Sherwood.* nd. Children's Pr. hc. VG. P3. $10.00

GILSTRAP, John. *Nathan's Run.* 1996. Harper Collins. 1st ed. sgn. F/F. M23. $35.00

GIMBEL, Richard. *Thomas Paine: A Bibliographical Check List of Common Sense.* 1956. Yale. 124p. F. A4. $125.00

GINGRICH, Arnold. *Joys of Trout.* 1973. NY. 1st ed. sgn. VG/VG. w/2 letters & ephemera. B5. $40.00

GINGRICH, Arnold. *Well-Tempered Angler.* 1965. NY. 1st ed. VG/VG. B5. $30.00

GINSBERG, Allen. *Collected Poems, 1947-1980.* 1984. Harper. 1st ed. F/NF. B2. $40.00

GINSBERG, Allen. *Howl. Original Draft Facsimile, Transcript & Variant...* 1986. Harper. edit Barry Miles. F/NF. B2. $25.00

GINSBERG, Allen. *Kaddisch.* 1962. Wiesbaden. 1st German ed. inscr Anselm Hollo. NF/wrp/dj. A11. $65.00

GINSBURG, Mirra. *Last Door to Aiya.* 1968. SG Phillips. 1st ed. F/F. P3. $23.00

GINSBURG, Mirra. *Ultimate Threshold.* 1979. HRW. 1st ed. VG/VG. P3. $20.00

GINSBURG, Ralph. *Unhurried View of Erotica.* 1958. np. 4to. 128p. VG. A4. $35.00

GINTHER, Pemberton. *Thirteenth Spoon.* 1932. Cupples Leon. VG. P3. $20.00

GIOVANNI, Nikki. *Gemini.* 1971. Bobbs Merrill. 1st ed. VG/VG. B4. $35.00

GIOVANNI, Nikki. *My House.* 1972. Morrow. 1st ed. F/NF. B4. $45.00

GIOVANNI, Nikki. *Racism 101.* 1994. Morrow. 1st ed. F/F. M23. $35.00

GIOVANNI, Nikki. *Racism 101.* 1994. Morrow. 1st ed. sgn. F/F. M23. $40.00

GIOVANNI, Nikki. *Women & the Men: Poems.* 1975. Morrow. 1st ed. 8vo. F/dj. S9. $35.00

GIOVINAZZO, Buddy. *Life Is Hot in Cracktown.* 1993. NY. Thunder. 1st ed. author's 1st book. F/F. H11. $30.00

GIRARD, James. *Late Man.* 1993. Atheneum. 1st ed. author's 1st novel. F/F. M22/M23. $50.00

GIRARDI, Robert. *Madeleine's Ghost.* 1995. Delacorte. ARC. VG/wrp. M22. $40.00

GIRAUD, S. Louis. *Bookano Stories No 6.* ca 1936. London. Strand. 5 double-p popups. VG. D1. $340.00

GIRAUD, S. Louis. *Daily Express Children's Annual, No 2.* 1930s. London. Lane Pub. 5 popups. pict brd. NF. T10. $200.00

GIRAUD, S. Louis. *Daily Express Children's Annual, No 3.* 1930s. London. Lane Pub. ils. 7 popups. F. T10. $350.00

GISSING, George. *Books & the Quiet Life.* 1922. Portland. 2nd. VG. O7. $20.00

GITTINGS, Robert. *Peach Blossom Forest & Other Chinese...* 1951. Oxford. 1st ed. hc. VG/VG. P3. $20.00

GIVENS, Charles G. *Jig-Time Murders.* 1936. Bobbs Merrill. 1st ed. VG. P3. $25.00

GLADWIN, Harold Sterling. *History of the Ancient Southwest.* 1957. Portland, ME. Bond Wheelwright. 1st ed. sgn. ils. 383p. cloth. F/NF. B24. $125.00

GLAESSNER, Verina. *Kung Fu Cinema of Vengeance.* nd. Bounty. hc. VG. P3. $10.00

GLAISTER, Lesley. *Honour Thy Father.* 1991. Atheneum. 1st ed. F/F. M23. $20.00

GLANZ. *German Jew in America, an Annotated Bibliography.* 1969. np. 4to. 2527 entries. 208p. VG. A4. $35.00

GLASCOW, Ellen. *Deliverance.* 1904. Doubleday Page. 1st ed. sgn/dtd 1931. VG. B4. $100.00

GLASCOW, Ellen. *Deliverance.* 1904. Doubleday Page. 1st ed. VG. B10. $45.00

GLASCOW, Ellen. *Old Dominion Edition.* 1929. Doubleday Doran. VG. B10. $12.00

GLASCOW, Ellen. *Phases of an Inferior Planet.* 1898. NY. Harper. 1st ed. author's 2nd book. F. B4. $85.00

GLASGOW, Joseph A. *Some Memories: Christmas Stories of Virginia Circuit Judge.* 1935. McClure. ils. 90p. VG. B10. $35.00

GLASPELL, Susan. *Norma Ashe.* 1942. Lippincott. 1st ed. F/NF. B4. $50.00

GLASS, Francis. *Life of George Washington in Latin Prose.* 1835. Harper. 233p. full leather. xl. B10. $175.00

GLASSCHEIB, H.S. *March of Medicine: Aberrations & Triumphs of Healing Art.* 1963. London. 1st Eng trans. 360p. VG. A13. $25.00

GLASSCOCK, C.B. *Big Bonanza: Story of the Comstock Lode.* 1931. Portland. Binfords Mort. 8vo. 7 pl. 368p. map ep. F/NF. T10. $35.00

GLAUBKE, Robert. *Lost Treasure Trails.* 1954. Grosset Dunlap. 4to. VG/G. B17. $10.00

GLAZE, A.T. *Business History of Fond DuLac, Wisconsin.* 1905. Fond DuLac. 1st ed. ils/photos/index. 368p. G+. B5. $55.00

GLAZIER, Willard. *Down the Great River (Mississippi).* 1887. Phil. VG. O7. $55.00

GLAZIER, Willard. *Down the Great River.* 1889. Phil. 12mo. 443p. G. T3. $40.00

GLAZIER, Willard. *Headwaters of the Mississippi.* 1894. np. 12mo. ils. 537p. gilt dk gr pict cloth. xl. G. T3. $30.00

GLAZIER, Willard. *Ocean To Ocean on Horseback.* 1903. Phil. 12mo. 544p. G. T3. $25.00

GLAZUNOV, Ilya. *Ilya Glazunov.* 1978. Moscow. ils. 267p. brd. D2. $80.00

GLEASON, O. *Gleason's Horse Book.* (1892). Hubbard. VG. O3. $68.00

GLEASON, O. *Gleason's Veterinary Hand-Book & System of Horse Taming.* 1890. Phil. 2 parts. 8vo. ils. 520p. F. B14. $75.00

GLEASON, Robert. *Wrath of God.* 1994. Harper Prism. UP. NF/wrp. M22. $15.00

GLENN, Lois. *Charles WS Williams: A Checklist.* 1975. Kent State. 128p. VG. A17. $12.50

GLENN, Rewa. *Botanical Explorers of New Zealand.* 1950. Wellington. 1st ed. ils. dj. B26. $48.00

GLENNAN, T. Keith. *Birth of NASA.* 1993. WA, DC. 1st ed. inscr. 389p. VG/dj. B18. $22.50

GLICK & SIMORA. *Bowker Annual of Library & Book Trade Information, 24th Ed.* 1979. 635p. NF. A4. $25.00

GLOBE, Alexander. *Peter Stent, London Printseller, Circa 1642-1665.* 1985. Vancouver. British Columbia U. 4to. 64p. F/dj. T10. $80.00

GLOERSEN, P. *Arctic & Antarctic Sea Ice, 1978-1987...* 1992. WA. NASA. F. O7. $45.00

GLOVER, John H. *Voyage of the Dayspring.* 1926. London. VG. O7. $40.00

GLUBB, John Bagot. *Soldier With the Arabs.* 1957. Hodder Stoughton. 1st ed. 8vo. ils/maps. 460p. F/dj. T10. $75.00

GLUCK, Louise. *Proofs & Theories: Essays on Poetry.* 1994. Ecco. 1st ed. F/F. M23. $35.00

GLUCK, Sinclair. *Green Blot.* nd. AL Burt. VG/VG. P3. $25.00

GLUECK, Nelson. *Rivers in the Desert*. 1959. FSG. 1st ed. ils. 302p. VG/dj. W1. $22.00

GLUSKER & MORRIS. *Southern Album*. 1975. Oxmoor. ltd ed. sgns. 4to. VG/G. B11. $30.00

GLUT, Donald F. *Empire Strikes Back*. nd. BC. MTI. VG/VG. P3. $10.00

GLUT, Donald F. *Vampires of History*. 1972. Mirage. 1st ed. VG/VG. P3. $45.00

GOBLE, Paul. *Star Boy*. 1983. NY. 1st ed. ils. VG+. M5. $12.00

GOBOLD, E. Stanley. *Ellen Glasgow & the Woman Within*. 1972. LSU. photos. 322p. VG/VG. B10. $15.00

GOCHER, W.H. *Fasig's Tales of the Turf & Memoir/Tales of the Turf*. 1903. Hartford. 2 vol. VG. O3. $85.00

GODDARD, Anthea. *Vienna Pursuit*. 1976. Walker. NF/NF. P3. $8.00

GODDARD, Kenneth. *Balefire*. 1983. Bantam. 1st ed. author's 1st book. F/dj. N4/T2. $20.00

GODDEN, Rummer. *Impunity Jane*. 1954. Viking. 1st ed. ils Adrienne Adams. 48p. VG/VG. P2. $50.00

GODDEN, Rummer. *In Noah's Ark*. 1949. Viking. 1st ed. ils. 62p. NF/G+. P2. $30.00

GODDEN, Rummer. *Story of Holly & Ivy*. 1958. Viking. 1st ed. ils Adrienne Adams. 64p. VG/VG. P2. $45.00

GODEY, John. *Fatal Beauty*. 1984. Irwin. 1st ed. G/G. P3. $15.00

GODEY, John. *Nella*. 1981. Delacorte. 1st ed. G+/dj. N4. $17.50

GODEY, John. *Never Put Off 'Til Tomorrow What You Can Kill Today*. 1970. Random. 1st ed. VG/VG. P3. $25.00

GODEY, John. *Talisman*. 1976. Putnam. 1st ed. VG/VG. P3. $20.00

GODEY & HALE. *Lady's Book*. 1869. Phil. Godey. 3 fld pl. 522p. blk leather spine raised band. G. D1. $150.00

GODWIN, Frank. *King Arthur & His Nights...* 1927. Winston. 8vo. VG. B17. $5.00

GODWIN, Gail. *Dream Children*. 1976. Knopf. 1st ed. F/F. M19. $15.00

GODWIN, Gail. *Finishing School*. 1982. Viking. 1st ed. F/F. B4. $35.00

GODWIN, Gail. *Finishing School*. 1984. Franklin Lib. 1st ed. sgn. leather. F. B35. $45.00

GODWIN, Gail. *Perfectionists*. 1970. Harper Row. 1st ed. author's 1st novel. F/F. B4. $275.00

GODWIN, Parke. *Sherwood*. 1991. Morrow. 1st ed. NF/F. M23. $20.00

GODWIN, Parke. *Truce With Time*. 1988. Bantam. 1st ed. NF/NF. M23. $15.00

GODWIN, Parke. *Waiting for the Galactic Bus*. 1988. Doubleday. 1st ed. F/F. P3. $20.00

GODWIN, Tom. *Survivors*. 1958. Gnome. 1st ed. xl. dj. P3. $10.00

GODWIN & KAYE. *Masters of Solitude*. nd. BC. VG/VG. P3. $8.00

GOEBBELS, Joseph. *Vom Kaiserhof Zur Reich Kanzler*. 1934. Berlin. 1st German ed. 308p. VG/VG. B5. $85.00

GOELET, Frances. *Extracts From the Journal of...* 1870. Boston. xl. VG. O7. $20.00

GOELET, Frances. *Voyages & Travels of...* 1970. NY. VG. O7. $55.00

GOERKE, Heinz. *Linnaeus*. 1973 (1966). NY. ils. VG+/dj. B26. $30.00

GOETHE, Ann. *Midnight Lemonade*. 1993. Delacorte. 1st ed. author's 1st book. F/F. H11/M23. $25.00

GOETHE. *Renard the Fox*. nd. np. no pub. obl 32mo. 12 chromolitho pl. F/wrp. H3. $450.00

GOETZMANN, William H. *New Lands, New Man. America & the Second Great Age...* 1986. Viking. 1st ed. 8vo. 528p. half cloth. AN/dj. P4. $25.00

GOETZMANN & GOETZMANN. *West of the Imagination*. 1986. NY. VG. O7. $35.00

GOETZMANN & WILLIAMS. *Atlas of North American Exploration From Norse Voyages...* 1992. np. 4to. 100 maps/90 portraits. 224p. F/F. A4. $35.00

GOFF, Frederick R. *Early Printed Book of Low Countries*. 1958. WA. VG. O7. $15.00

GOFFIN, Robert. *Jazz From the Congo to the Metropolitan*. 1944. Doubleday. 1st ed. NF/NF. B2. $60.00

GOGOL, Nikolai. *Chickikov's Journeys; or, Home Life in Old Russia*. 1994. NY. 2 vol. 1/1200. ils/sgn Lucille Corcos. F/case. T10. $90.00

GOHM, Douglas. *Antique Maps of Europe, the Americas, West Indies...* 1972. London. Octopus. 167 maps. F/dj. O7. $45.00

GOINES, Donald. *Dopefiend. Story of a Black Junkie*. 1971. Los Angeles. true 1st prt (no banner blurb). NF/wrp. A11. $115.00

GOLD, Don. *Intermediate Two-Bids in Bridge: A Modern Alternative...* 1982. NY. 1st ed. 128p. VG/VG. S1. $8.00

GOLD, Eddie. *Golden Era Cubs*. 1985. Bonus Books. 1st ed. F/VG. P8. $20.00

GOLD, H. *Birth of a Hero*. 1951. NY. 1st ed. author's 1st book. F/F. A15. $50.00

GOLD, H.L. *Bodyguard*. nd. BC. VG/VG. P3. $8.00

GOLD, H.L. *Fifth Galaxy Reader*. 1961. BC. VG/VG. P3. $30.00

GOLD, H.L. *Galaxy Reader of SF*. 1952. Crown. 1st ed. hc. VG. P3. $35.00

GOLD, H.L. *Weird Ones*. 1965. Dobson. 1st ed. F/F. P3. $30.00

GOLD, Herbert. *Great American Jackport*. 1969. Random. 1st ed. F/NF. M19. $15.00

GOLD, Michael. *120 Million*. 1929. Internat. 1st ed. inscr. NF. B2. $150.00

GOLDBERG, Marshall. *Anatomy Lesson*. 1974. Putnam. 1st ed. NF/NF. H11. $30.00

GOLDBERG, Marshall. *Karamanov Equations*. 1972. Cleveland. World. 1st ed. author's 1st book. NF/NF clip. H11. $40.00

GOLDBERG, Martha. *Twirly Skirt*. 1954. Holiday. 1st ed. ils Helen Stone. 47p. VG/G. P2. $30.00

GOLDEN, Richard M. *Godly Rebellion: Parisian Cures & the Religious Fronde...* 1981. Chapel Hill. 8vo. 221p. red cloth/wht spine. M. P4. $20.00

GOLDENBERG, J. *Shipbuilding in Colonial America*. 1976. Charlottesville. VG. O7. $35.00

GOLDENWEISER, Alexander. *History, Psychology & Culture*. 1933. Knopf. 476p. maroon cloth. xl. VG. G1. $35.00

GOLDIN, Stephen. *Assault on the Gods*. 1977. Doubleday. F/F. P3. $15.00

GOLDIN, Stephen. *World Called Solitude*. 1981. Doubleday. 1st ed. F/F. P3. $15.00

GOLDING, William. *Close Quarters*. 1987. FSG. 1st ed. F/NF. M23. $15.00

GOLDING, William. *Darkness Visible*. 1979. FSG. 1st ed. F/F. B35. $18.00

GOLDING, William. *Paper Men*. 1984. FSG. 1st ed. F/F. P3. $15.00

GOLDING, William. *Pyramid*. 1967. London. 1st ed. F/F. C6. $65.00

GOLDING, William. *Rites of Passage*. 1980. FSG. 1st ed. F/NF. M23. $20.00

GOLDING, William. *Spire.* 1964. London. 1st ed. F/F. C6. $75.00

GOLDMAN, Francisco. *Long Night of White Chickens.* 1992. Atlantic. 1st ed. F/F. M23. $35.00

GOLDMAN, James. *Man From Greek & Roman..* 1974. Random. 1st ed. NF/NF. P3. $20.00

GOLDMAN, Judith. *James Rosenquist.* 1985. Viking. ils. cloth. dj. D2. $100.00

GOLDMAN, Laurel. *Sounding the Territory.* 1982. Knopf. 1st ed. author's 1st book. F/F. B4. $45.00

GOLDMAN, Lawrence Louis. *Tiger by the Tail.* 1946. David McKay. hc. VG/G. P3. $15.00

GOLDMAN, William. *Brothers.* 1987. Warner. 1st ed. F/F. H11. $25.00

GOLDMAN, William. *Color of Light.* 1984. Granada. 1st ed. VG/VG. P3. $23.00

GOLDMAN, William. *Control.* 1982. Delacorte. 1st ed. rem mk. F/F. H11. $25.00

GOLDMAN, William. *Control.* 1982. Delacorte. 1st ed. VG/VG. P3. $25.00

GOLDMAN, William. *Edged Weapons.* 1985. Granada. F/F. P3. $20.00

GOLDMAN, William. *Father's Day.* 1971. HBJ. 2nd. VG/VG. P3. $13.00

GOLDMAN, William. *Heat.* 1985. Warner. 1st ed. F/F. H11. $25.00

GOLDMAN, William. *Heat.* 1985. Warner. 1st ed. VG/VG. P3. $15.00

GOLDMAN, William. *Hype & Glory.* 1990. Villard. 1st ed. VG. P3. $20.00

GOLDMAN, William. *Marathon Man.* 1974. Delacorte. 1st ed. F/NF. H11. $40.00

GOLDMAN, William. *Marathon Man.* 1974. Delacorte. 1st ed. VG/VG. P3. $30.00

GOLDMAN, William. *Tinsel.* 1979. Delacorte. 1st ed. VG/VG. P3. $25.00

GOLDSBOROUGH, Robert. *Death on Deadline.* 1987. Bantam. 1st ed. F/F. H11. $40.00

GOLDSBOROUGH, Robert. *Last Coincidence.* 1989. Bantam. 1st ed. F/F. H11. $35.00

GOLDSBOROUGH, Robert. *Murder in E Minor.* 1986. Bantam. 1st ed. F/F. P3. $15.00

GOLDSCHEIDER, Ludwig. *Leonardo: Paintings & Drawings.* 1975. London. Phaidon. 8th. ils. cloth. dj. D2. $65.00

GOLDSCHMIDT, E. *Gothic & Renaissance Bookbindings.* 1928. London. Benn. 2 vol. 1st ed. 110 pl. taupe buckram. NF. C6. $500.00

GOLDSCHMIDT, Walter. *Sebei Law.* 1967. Berkeley. CA U. M11. $35.00

GOLDSMITH, Oliver. *Deserted Village.* 1865. Boston. JE Tilton. Keepsake ed. ils. 12mo. cloth. AN. B36. $35.00

GOLDSMITH, Oliver. *She Stoops To Conquer.* 1912. Hodder Stoughton. 1st Am ed. ils Hugh Thomson. F. T10. $150.00

GOLDSMITH, Oliver. *Vicar of Wakefield.* nd. Phil. McKay. 1st Am ed. ils Rackham. NF. A15. $75.00

GOLDSMITH, Oliver. *Vicar of Wakefield.* nd. Phil. McKay. 1st Am ed. ils Rackham. 231p. gilt bl cloth. NF/dj. M20. $175.00

GOLDSMITH, Oliver. *Vicar of Wakefield.* 1843. London. Van Voorst. ils Mulready. teg. modern bl morocco/raised bands. F. T10. $900.00

GOLDSMITH, Oliver. *Vicar of Wakefield.* 1929. London. Harrap. 1/575 (775 total). ils/sgn Rackham. full vellum. T10. $2,250.00

GOLDSMITH, Oliver. *Vicar of Wakefield.* 1929. London. Harrap. 1st ed. ils Rackham. 232p. gilt bdg. VG. M20. $165.00

GOLDSMITH, V F. *Short Title Catalogue of Spanish & Portuguese Books...* 1974. 4to. 256p. F/NF. A4. $45.00

GOLDSTEIN, Kurt. *Die Lokalisation in der Grosshirnrinde Nach den Erfahrungen.* (1925?). Berlin. Julius Springer. 1st separate ed. 842p. lacks rear wrp. rare. G1. $125.00

GOLDSTEIN, Lisa. *Dream Years.* 1985. Bantam. 1st ed. F/F. G10/P3. $15.00

GOLDSTEIN, Lisa. *Red Magician.* 1993. Tor. 1st hc ed. F/F. G10. $15.00

GOLDSTEIN, Lisa. *Strange Devices of Sun & Moon.* 1993. NY. Tor. 1st ed. F/dj. M23/P3. $20.00

GOLDSTEIN, Lisa. *Summer King, Winter Fool.* 1994. Tor. 1st ed. F/F. G10. $15.00

GOLDSTEIN, Richard. *Superstars & Screwballs.* 1991. Dutton. 1st ed. F/F. P8. $15.00

GOLDSTONE & PAYNE. *John Steinbeck: A Bibliographical Catalogue...* 1974. Austin, TX. 1/1200. 240p. VG. A4. $350.00

GOLDTHORPE. *From Queen to Empress: Victorian Dress 1837-1877.* Dec 1988-April 1989. Costume Inst. ils. cloth. F/F. D2. $25.00

GOLDWAITHE, Eaton K. *Cat & Mouse.* 1946. DSP. 1st ed. VG/VG. P3. $25.00

GOLDWAITHE, Eaton K. *Once You Stop, You're Dead.* 1968. Morrow. 1st ed. VG/VG. P3. $18.00

GOLDWAITHE, Eaton K. *Scarecrow.* 1946. Books Inc. VG/G. P3. $10.00

GOLDWATER, Barry. *Conscience of a Conservative.* 1960. Shepardsville. 1st ed. inscr. F. N3. $45.00

GOLDWATER & RATHER. *According to Hoyle, 1742-1850.* 1983. 26p. VG/wrp. A4. $35.00

GOLDWATER. *Radical Periodicals in America 1890-1950...* 1964. Yale. 4to. 321 annotated entries. F. A4. $85.00

GOLENDOCK, P. *NY Yankees 1949-1964.* 1975. Englewood Cliffs. 1st ed. VG/VG. B5. $25.00

GOLLANCZ, Victor. *My Dear Timothy: An Autobiographical Letter...* 1953. NY. 1st ed. F/dj. A17. $15.00

GOLLER, Nicholas. *Tomorrow's Silence.* 1979. Macmillan. 1st ed. VG/VG. P3. $15.00

GONCHAROV, Ivan. *Voyage of the Frigate Pallada.* 1965. London. VG. O7. $55.00

GONDOR, Emery J. *You Are...A Puzzle Book for Children.* 1937. Modern Age. 1st ed. ils. VG/VG. D1. $135.00

GONNE, C.M. *Hints on Horses: How To Judge Them...* 1905. Dutton. 1st Am ed. O3. $35.00

GONZALEZ, Julio. *Catalogo de Mapas y Planos de Venezuela.* 1968. Madrid. 273 entries+8 indices. M/wrp. O7. $65.00

GOOCH, Brad. *City Poet: Life & Times of Frank O'Hara.* 1993. Knopf. 1st ed. rem mk. F/NF. B2. $25.00

GOOD, Howard E. *Black Swamp Farm.* 1967. OH State. 1st ed. ils BO Sutherland. 304p. VG/dj. B18. $15.00

GOOD, Kenneth. *Into the Heart.* 1991. Simon Schuster. 1st ed. 349p. F3. $20.00

GOOD, Ronald. *Geography of the Flowering Plants.* 1964 (1947). London. 3rd. ils/9 maps. torn dj. B26. $45.00

GOOD & PRATT. *World Geography of Petroleum.* 1950. Am Geographic Soc. fld map/photos. 464p. VG/torn. D8. $30.00

GOODALL, John S. *Paddy's Evening Out.* 1973. Atheneum. 1st ed. unp. NF/NF. M20. $25.00

GOODCHILD, George. *Colorado Jim.* nd. Collins Wild West Club. VG. P3. $10.00

GOODE, James. *Story of the Misfits.* 1963. Indianapolis. 1st ed. VG/VG. B5. $35.00

GOODE, Paul. *United States Soldiers' Home.* 1957. private prt. 1st ed. sgn. 8vo. 289p. VG. B11. $75.00

GOODING, E.G.B. *Flora of the Barbados.* 1965. London. ils. VG/dj. B26. $55.00

GOODING, John D. *Durango South Project.* 1980. Tucson, AZ. 4to. 200p. F/wrp. T10. $25.00

GOODIS, David. *Le Casse.* 1954. Paris. Gallimard. 1st French ed. blk/yel brd. VG. A11. $60.00

GOODKIND, Terry. *Wizard's First Rule.* 1994. NY. Tor. 1st ed. F/F. H11. $30.00

GOODMAN, Allegra. *Total Immersion.* 1989. Harper Row. 1st ed. F/F. M23. $20.00

GOODMAN, David Michael. *Western Panorama 1849-1875.* 1966. Glendale. Arthur Clark. 8vo. ils. 328p. gilt red cloth. F. T10. $100.00

GOODMAN, John Bartlett III. *Key to the Goodman Encyclopedia of the CA Gold Rush Fleet.* 1992. Los Angeles. Zamorano Club. only ed. 8vo. 31 fld charts. F/case. T10. $100.00

GOODNOW, Minnie. *Nursing History in Brief.* 1941. Phil. 325p. VG. A13. $20.00

GOODRICH, Charles. *Universal Traveler.* 1836. Hartford. fair. V4. $55.00

GOODRICH, L. *Graphic Art of Winslow Homer.* 1968. Smithsonian. 132 full-p ils. 136p. xl. VG/dj. T3. $20.00

GOODRUM, Charles A. *Best Cellar.* 1987. St Martin. 1st ed. VG/VG. P3. $15.00

GOODWIN, K.L. *Influence of Ezra Pound.* 1966. Oxford. 1st ed. assn copy. F/NF. V1. $35.00

GOODWIN, Maud Wilder. *White Aprons: Romance of Bacon's Rebellion.* 1901. Little Brn. 338p. G. B10. $12.00

GOOLD-ADAMS, Deenagh. *Cook Greenhouse Today.* 1969. London. ils/photos. VG. B26. $15.00

GORDAN. *Fifteenth-Century Books in Library of Howard L Goodhart...* 1955. Overbrook. 1/250. 4to. 160p. F. A4. $175.00

GORDIMER, Nadine. *Sport of Nature.* 1987. Knopf. ARC/1st Am ed. sgn. RS. F/dj. C2. $75.00

GORDON, Albert I. *Intermarriage Interfaith Interracial Interethnic.* 1964. Boston. Beacon. 1st ed. inscr/dtd. 420p. F/dj. B14. $60.00

GORDON, Armistead C. *Gay Gordons: Ballads of Ancient Scottish Clan.* 1902. Staunton. Shultx. 1/250. unp. VG. B10. $15.00

GORDON, Armistead C. *Memories & Memorials of William Gordon McCabe.* 1925. Richmond, VA. Old Dominion. 2 vol. 1st ed. cloth. VG. M8. $250.00

GORDON, Bernard L. *Man & the Sea.* 1970. Garden City. VG. O7. $20.00

GORDON, Caroline. *Aleck Maury Sportsman.* 1934. NY. 1st ed. VG/VG. B5. $145.00

GORDON, Caroline. *Glory of Hera.* 1972. Doubleday. 1st ed. F/NF. B4. $85.00

GORDON, Caroline. *Malefactors.* 1956. Harcourt Brace. 1st ed. 312p. G/G. B10. $25.00

GORDON, Caroline. *None Shall Look Back.* 1937. Scribner. 1st ed. 378p. VG. B10. $15.00

GORDON, Caroline. *Old Red & Other Stories.* 1963. NY. 1st ed. NF/NF. B4. $100.00

GORDON, Cyrus H. *Before the Bible: The Common Background of Greek & Hebrew...* 1962. NY. 1st ed. 4-line inscr. 319p. F/dj. B14. $55.00

GORDON, David; see Garrett, Randall.

GORDON, Donald. *Star-Raker.* 1962. Hodder Stoughton. 1st ed. VG/VG. P3. $20.00

GORDON, Elizabeth. *Bird Children.* 1912. Volland. 2nd. ils MT Ross. F. M5. $150.00

GORDON, Elizabeth. *Four-Footed Folk; or, The Children of the Farm & Forest.* 1914. Whitman. 8vo. ils. VG. M5. $55.00

GORDON, Elizabeth. *Happy Home Children.* 1924. Volland. ils Marion Foster. unp. VG. T5. $45.00

GORDON, Elizabeth. *I Wonder Why?* 1937 (1916). Rand McNally. 12mo. ils. VG. M5. $15.00

GORDON, Elizabeth. *Loraine & the Little People of Spring.* 1918. Rand McNally. 1st ed. ils Ella Lee. 64p. VG. P2. $40.00

GORDON, Elizabeth. *Really-So Stories.* 1924. Volland. 15th. 8vo. 96p. VG. T5. $40.00

GORDON, Elizabeth. *Taming of Giants.* 1950. Viking. 1st ed. ils Garry MacKensie. 57p. VG/G. P2. $20.00

GORDON, Elizabeth. *Witch of Scapefaggot Green.* 1948. Viking. 1st ed. ils William Pene DuBois. 76p. VG+/VG. P2. $75.00

GORDON, Harold J. Jr. *Hitler & the Beer Hall Putsch.* 1972. Princeton. 1st ed. 666p. VG/dj. A17. $20.00

GORDON, Lesley. *Pageant of Dolls* nd. ca 1950? Ward. 16 pl. NF/G. M5. $30.00

GORDON, Max. *Live at the Village Vanguard.* 1980. St Martin. 1st ed. F/F. B2. $25.00

GORDON, Richard. *Captain's Table.* 1954. Michael Joseph. 1st ed. VG/VG. P3. $30.00

GORDON, Richard. *Doctor & Son.* 1959. Michael Joseph. 1st ed. VG/VG. P3. $30.00

GORDON, Richard. *Doctor at Sea.* 1954. Michael Joseph. 13th. VG/VG. P3. $15.00

GORDON, Richard. *Doctor in Love.* 1957. Michael Joseph. 1st ed. VG/VG. P3. $30.00

GORDON, Richard. *Doctor in Swim.* 1962. Michael Joseph. 1st ed. VG/VG. P3. $20.00

GORDON, Richard. *Nuts in May.* 1964. Heinemann. 1st ed. NF/NF. P3. $18.00

GORDON, Ruth. *My Side: The Autobiography of...* 1976. NY. 1st ed. 502p. F/dj. A17. $10.00

GORDON, Stuart. *Two-Eyes.* 1975. Sidgwick Jackson. 1st ed. VG/VG. P3. $20.00

GORDON & GORDON. *Informant.* 1973. Doubleday. 1st ed. hc. VG/G. P3. $15.00

GORDON & GORDON. *Operation Terror.* 1961. Crime Club. VG/VG. P3. $20.00

GORDON. *Gordon's Print Price Annual 1994.* 1994. 4to. NF. A4. $225.00

GOREN, Charles. *Charles Goren's Shortcut to Expert Bridge.* nd. NY. VG. S1. $3.00

GOREN, Charles. *Goren Point Count Bidding Wheel.* 1957. np. VG. S1. $3.00

GORES, Joe. *Come Morning.* 1986. Mysterious. 1st ed. RS. F/F. P3. $20.00

GORES, Joe. *Dead Man.* 1993. Mysterious. 1st ed. F/F. N4. $30.00

GORES, Joe. *Dead Man.* 1993. Mysterious. 1st ed. sgn. F/F. T2. $35.00

GORES, Joe. *Mostly Murder.* 1992. Mystery Scene. deluxe ed. 1/50. sgn/#d. leather. F/sans. P3. $50.00

GORES, Joe. *Wolf Time.* 1989. Putnam. 1st ed. sgn. F/F. T2. $35.00

GOREY, Edward. *Amphigorey.* 1972. Putnam. 1st ed. VG/VG. P3. $30.00

GOREY, Edward. *Amphigorey Too.* 1975. Putnam. 1st ed. unp. F/NF clip. T10. $100.00

GOREY, Edward. *Betrayed Confidence: Seven Series of Dogear Wryde Postcards.* 1992. Orleans, MA. 1st ed. 1/250. sgn/#d. AN/stiff wrp/case. w/sgn prt. B24. $150.00

GOREY, Edward. *Broken Spoke.* 1976. Dodd Mead. 1st ed. 1/250. sgn. F/dj/case. B24. $225.00

GOREY, Edward. *Broken Spoke.* 1979 (1976). London. Benn. 1st ed. ils. VG/VG. P2. $50.00

GOREY, Edward. *Case-Record From a Sonnetorium, by Merrill Moore.* 1951. Twayne. 1st ed. 8vo. F/dj. B24. $350.00

GOREY, Edward. *Curious Sofa, a Pornographic Work by Ogdred Weary.* 1961. NY. Obolensky. 1st ed. 12mo. unp. VG/wrp. T10. $115.00

GOREY, Edward. *Doubtful Guest.* 1957. Doubleday. 1st ed. sgn. prt brd. F/NF. B24. $350.00

GOREY, Edward. *Dracula: A Toy Theatre.* 1979. Scribner. 1st ed. folio. prt on cb. NF/sbdg wrp. B24. $110.00

GOREY, Edward. *Dwindling Party.* 1982. Random. 1st ed. unp. VG+. M20. $105.00

GOREY, Edward. *Eclectic Abecedarium.* 1983. Boston. Bromer. 1st ed. 1/300. sgn. author's 1st miniature book. F. B24. $175.00

GOREY, Edward. *Epiplectic Bicycle.* 1969. Dodd Mead. 1st ed. sgn. F/NF. B24. $95.00

GOREY, Edward. *Fatal Lozenge: An Alphabet.* 1960. NY. 1st ed. inscr. F/wrp. C2. $100.00

GOREY, Edward. *Figbash Acrobate.* 1994. Fantod. 1/500. sgn. F/pict wrp. B24. $45.00

GOREY, Edward. *FMRA.* 1980. NY. Andrew Alpern. 1st ed. 1/426. sgn. AN/clamshell box. B24. $225.00

GOREY, Edward. *Hapless Child.* 1961. NY. 1st ed. inscr. NF/wrp. C2. $125.00

GOREY, Edward. *Haunted Looking Glass.* 1959. Looking Glass Lib. VG/VG. P3. $45.00

GOREY, Edward. *Improvable Landscape: A Piermont Book.* 1986. Albondocani. 1/326. sgn. F/gr pict wrp. B24. $150.00

GOREY, Edward. *Insect God.* 1986. Beaufort. 1st ed thus. 16mo. F/VG. B17. $10.00

GOREY, Edward. *Leaves From a Mislaid Album.* 1972. Gotham Book Mart. 1st ed. 1/550. sgn. F/unbound as issued/gr prt wrp. B24. $375.00

GOREY, Edward. *Light Metres, by Felicia Lamports. Drawings by Edward Gorey.* 1982. Everest House. 1/376. sgn. AN/case. B24. $185.00

GOREY, Edward. *Limerick.* 1973. Salt-Works Pr. 1st ed. sgn. F/prt brn wrp. B24. $185.00

GOREY, Edward. *Other Statue.* 1968. NY. 1st ed. sgn. F/dj. B24. $110.00

GOREY, Edward. *Passementeries Horribles.* 1976. Albondocani. 1st ed. 1/326. sgn. AN/ils wrp. B24. $150.00

GOREY, Edward. *QRV.* 1989. Boston. 1/85 deluxe. sgn. miniature. F/case. B24. $350.00

GOREY, Edward. *Remembered Visit: A Story Taken From Life.* 1965. Simon Schuster. 1st ed. sgn. F/dj. B24. $110.00

GOREY, Edward. *Unstrung Harp; or, Mr Earbrass Writes a Novel.* 1953. DSP. 1st ed. author's 1st book. sgn. NF/NF. B24. $325.00

GOREY, Edward. *Utter Zoo. An Alphabet.* 1967. Meredith. 1st ed. sgn. F/NF. B24. $110.00

GOREY, Edward. *Water Flowers.* 1982. NY. Cogdon Weed. stated 1st ed. F/VG+. H4. $25.00

GOREY, Edward. *Wuggly Ump.* 1963. Lippincott. 8vo. AN/dj. B24. $110.00

GORGAS, Josiah. *Civil War Diary of General Josiah Gorgas...* 1947. AL U. 1st ed. 208p. cloth. NF/VG. M8. $250.00

GORHAM, Bob. *Churchill Downs 100th Kentucky Derby.* 1973. Churchhill Downs. 4to. 247p. VG. O3. $45.00

GORKY, Maxim. *Foma Gordyeeff.* 1901. NY. 1st ed. VG. B5. $30.00

GORMAN, Ed. *Modern Treasury of Great Detective...* 1984. Carroll Graf. 1st ed. sgn. F/F. P3. $27.00

GORMAN, Ed. *Murder Straight Up.* 1986. NY. 1st ed. F/F. H11. $30.00

GORMAN, Ed. *New, Improved Murder.* nd. St Martin. 2nd ed. VG/VG. P3. $13.00

GORMAN, Ed. *Reason Why.* 1992. Mystery Scene. 1st ed. 1/100. sgn/#d. F/sans. P3. $20.00

GORMAN, Ed. *Stalkers.* 1989. Dark Harvest. 1st ed. 1/750. sgn all contributors. F/F/case. P3. $90.00

GORMAN & GREENBERG. *Stalkers.* 1991. Severn. 1st Eng/1st hc ed. F/F. G10. $20.00

GORMAN & GREENBERG. *Stalkers: All New Tales of Terror & Suspense.* 1989. Dark Harvest. 1st ed. 1/750. sgns. F/F/case. P3/T2. $100.00

GORMAN & HORNER. *Digging Dinosaurs: Search That Unraveled the Mystery...* 1988. Workman. 210p. NF/wrp. D8. $12.00

GOSLING, Paula. *Hoodwink.* 1988. Macmillan. 1st ed. F/F. P3. $25.00

GOSLING, Paula. *Loser's Blues.* 1980. Macmillan. 1st ed. VG/VG. P3. $20.00

GOSNELL & SNOW. *On the Decks of Old Ironsides.* 1932. Macmillan. ils. 304p. VG. T7. $55.00

GOSS, Alice Dillon. *New Mother Goose.* 1912. Dodge. ils. VG. M5. $35.00

GOSS, Warren. *Jed, a Boy's Adventures in the Army of '61-'65...* 1889. NY. Crowell. 1st ed. 404p. gr cloth. F. B14. $75.00

GOSSE, P.H. *Wonders of the Great Deep.* 1874. Quaker City Pub. ils. 385p. G+. P12. $15.00

GOSSEN, Gary. *Symbol & Meaning Beyond the Closed Community.* 1986. Inst Mesoamerican Studies. 1st ed. 267p. wrp. F3. $20.00

GOTLIEB, Phyllis. *Heart of Red Iron.* 1989. St Martin. 1st ed. VG/VG. P3. $16.00

GOTLIEB, Phyllis. *O Master Caliban!* 1976. Harper Row. 1st ed. F/F. P3. $20.00

GOTLIEB, Phyllis. *Why Should I Have All the Grief?* 1969. Macmillan. 1st ed. VG/VG. P3. $30.00

GOTTLIEB, Samuel Hirsch. *Overbooked in Arizona.* 1994. Scottsdale. Camelback Gallery. 1st hc ed. 1/501. sgn. F/F/case. T2. $50.00

GOUDY, Alice. *Jupiter & the Cats.* 1953. Scribner. 1st ed. ils Paul Brown. 90p. VG/G+. P2. $40.00

GOUGH, Laurence. *Accidental Deaths.* 1991. Viking. 1st ed. F/F. P3. $25.00

GOUGH, Laurence. *Death on a No 8 Hook.* 1988. Gollancz. 1st ed. NF/NF. P3. $22.00

GOUGH, Laurence. *Hot Shots.* 1989. Viking. 1st ed. rem mk. F/F. N4. $15.00

GOUGH, Laurence. *Serious Crimes.* 1990. Viking. 1st ed. F/F. P3. $25.00

GOULART, Ron. *Broken Down Engine.* 1971. Macmillan. 1st ed. VG/VG. P3. $30.00

GOULART, Ron. *Death in Silver.* 1975. Golden. F. P3. $8.00

GOULART, Ron. *Even the Butler Was Poor.* 1990. Walker. 1st ed. F/F. H11. $20.00

GOULART, Ron. *Odd Job #101.* 1975. Scribner. 1st ed. F/F. P3. $20.00

GOULD, Chester. *Dick Tracy, Ace Detective.* 1943. Whitman. hc. VG. P3. $20.00

GOULD, Frank W. *Grasses of SW United States.* 1981 (1951). Tucson. 4th. 343p. F/wrp. B26. $15.00

GOULD, Heywood. *Glitterburn*. 1981. St Martin. 1st ed. xl. dj. P3. $6.00

GOULD, Lois. *Medusa's Gift*. 1991. Knopf. 1st ed. rem mk. F/F. B35. $20.00

GOULD, S.J. *Bully for Brontasaurus: Reflections in Natural History*. 1991. Norton. 1st ed. 540p. F/dj. D8. $22.00

GOULD, S.J. *Ever Since Darwin: Reflections in Natural History*. 1977. NY. 1st ed. 285p. dj. A13. $30.00

GOULD, S.J. *Mismeasure of Man*. 1981. NY. 1st ed. 352p. VG/dj. A13. $30.00

GOULD, S.J. *Wonderful Life: The Burgess Shale & Nature of History*. 1989. Norton. 1st ed. F/dj. D8. $25.00

GOULDER, G. *John D Rockefeller: The Cleveland Years*. 1972. Cleveland. 1st ed. sgn. ils. 271p. VG/VG. B5. $25.00

GOULDING, M. *Fishes & the Forest*. 1980. Berkeley. 8vo. 279p. cloth. dj. B11. $20.00

GOULDSBOROUGH, John. *Reports...in All the Courts of Westminster...* 1653. London. Adams. 1st ed. contemporary sheep. M11. $250.00

GOURKE, John G. *MacKenzie's Last Fight With the Cheyennes*. 1966. NY. Argonaut. 8vo. ils. 56p. NF. T10. $45.00

GOVER, Paula K. *White Boys & River Girls*. 1995. Algonquin. 1st ed. rem mk. F/F. H11. $20.00

GOVERNMENT PRINTING OFFICE. *Album of American Battle Art 1755-1918*. 1947. Washington. 1st ed. 150 pl. 319p. VG. A17. $50.00

GOVERNMENT PRINTING OFFICE. *Navigation Laws of the United States*. 1927. 536p. VG. P12. $8.00

GOVERNMENT PRINTING OFFICE. *Poisonous Snakes of the World*. 1965. Washington, DC. lg 8vo. 212p. hc. G. B1. $25.00

GOW, Gordon. *Suspense in the Cinema*. 1968. NY. Castle. F/F. D2. $20.00

GOYTISOLO, Juan. *Party's Over*. 1966. Grove. 1st ed. F/F. M19. $20.00

GRABAR, Oleg. *Formation of Islamic Art*. 1973. Yale. 1st ed. ils. 233p. NF/dj. W1. $55.00

GRABAU, A.W. *Textbook of Geology, Part I, General Geology*. 1921. NY. DC Heath. 1st ed. VG. D8. $20.00

GRACE, Peter. *Polo*. 1991. NY. Howell. 1st ed. F/F. O3. $45.00

GRACY, Leonard R. *Duplicate Contract Bridge in the Home & Simple Tournament...* 1933. Phil. 68p. VG. S1. $8.00

GRADY, James. *Hard Bargains*. 1985. Macmillan. 1st ed. NF/NF. P3. $20.00

GRADY, James. *Six Days of the Condor*. 1974. Norton. 1st ed. VG/NF. M22. $40.00

GRADY, James. *Steeltown*. 1989. Bantam. 1st ed. F/F. P3. $19.00

GRAEME, David. *Monsieur Blackshirt*. 1935. Harrap. VG. P3. $25.00

GRAEME, David. *Sword of Monsieur Blackshirt*. 1936. Lippincott. 1st ed. 314p. VG+/dj. M20. $25.00

GRAF, Albert B. *Exotica 3*. 1963. Rutherford. 1828p. VG. B26. $145.00

GRAFTON, C.W. *Rope Began To Hang the Butcher*. 1944. Farrar Rinehart. 1st ed. VG. P3. $30.00

GRAFTON, Sue. *A Is for Alibi*. 1982. HRW. 1st ed. F/3 sm closed tears. P3. $700.00

GRAFTON, Sue. *B Is for Burglar*. 1985. HRW. 1st ed. F/F. P3. $475.00

GRAFTON, Sue. *C Is for Corpse*. 1986. Holt. ARC. inscr twice/sgn/dtd. VG/wrp. M22. $225.00

GRAFTON, Sue. *C Is for Corpse*. 1986. Holt. 1st ed. F/F. P3. $300.00

GRAFTON, Sue. *D Is for Deadbeat*. nd. BC. VG/VG. P3. $8.00

GRAFTON, Sue. *D Is for Deadbeat*. 1987. Holt. 1st ed. inscr/dtd 1987. F/dj. S9. $175.00

GRAFTON, Sue. *F Is for Fugitive*. 1989. Holt. 1st ed. F/F. A9/P3. $35.00

GRAFTON, Sue. *F Is for Fugitive*. 1989. Holt. 1st ed. 261p. VG+/dj. M20. $28.00

GRAFTON, Sue. *G Is for Gumshoe*. 1990. Holt. 1st ed. F/F. B2. $35.00

GRAFTON, Sue. *H Is for Homicide*. 1991. NY. Holt. 1st ed. F/F. H11. $35.00

GRAFTON, Sue. *I Is for Innocent*. 1992. Holt. 1st ed. F/F. H11. $30.00

GRAFTON, Sue. *J Is for Judgement*. 1993. NY. Holt. 1st ed. sgn. F/F. B11. $55.00

GRAFTON, Sue. *J Is for Judgement*. 1993. 1st ed. w/sgn card. F/F. M19. $45.00

GRAFTON, Sue. *J Is for Judgement*. 1993. Holt. 1st ed. VG/VG. P3. $25.00

GRAFTON, Sue. *K Is for Killer*. 1994. Holt. 1st ed. F/F. N4/P3. $22.50

GRAFTON, Sue. *Keziah Dane*. 1967. Macmillan. 1st ed. author's 1st book. F/F. H11. $650.00

GRAFTON, Sue. *Keziah Dane*. 1968. Peter Owen. 1st ed. author's 1st book. F/VG. M19. $450.00

GRAHAM, Don. *No Name on the Bullet*. 1989. NY. 1st ed. VG/VG. B5. $25.00

GRAHAM, Frank. *Casey Stengel*. 1958. John Day. later prt. G+/G+. P8. $15.00

GRAHAM, Frank. *Great Hitters of Major Leagues*. 1969. Random. VG. P3. $10.00

GRAHAM, Frank. *Lou Gehrig, a Quiet Hero*. nd. Putnam. 26th. xl. P3. $8.00

GRAHAM, Henry H. *Quarterback*. ca 1920. Book Concern. 12mo. 63p. VG. A17. $7.00

GRAHAM, James; see Patterson, Henry.

GRAHAM, John Alexander. *Aldeburg*. nd. BC. F/F. P3. $8.00

GRAHAM, John D. *System & Dialectics of Art*. 1937. Delphic Studios. orig ed. 155p. xl. D2. $175.00

GRAHAM, Joseph A. *Sporting Dog*. 1924 (1904). Macmillan. 327p. gr cloth. VG. M20. $17.00

GRAHAM, Margaret. *Swing Shift*. 1951. Citadel. 1st ed. F/VG. B4. $50.00

GRAHAM, Mark Miller. *Reinterpreting Prehistory of Central America*. 1993. Niwot, CO. 1st ed. 336p. dj. F3. $40.00

GRAHAM, Sheilah. *Garden of Allah*. 1970. NY. Crown. 1st ed. F/NF. H11. $40.00

GRAHAM, T. *Elements of Chemistry*. 1843. Phil. royal 8vo. 749p. full leather. xl. T3. $28.00

GRAHAM, W.A. *Story of the Little Big Horn, Custer's Battle*. nd. Bonanza. rpt. F/laminated. E1. $35.00

GRAHAM, Whidden. *Crimson Hairs: An Erotic Mystery*. 1970. Grove. 1st ed. F/F. P3. $20.00

GRAHAM, Winston. *After the Act*. 1966. Doubleday. 1st ed. VG/VG. P3. $15.00

GRAHAM, Winston. *Angel, Pearl & Little God*. 1970. Literary Guild. VG/fair. $10.00

GRAHAM, Winston. *Merciless Ladies*. 1979. Bodley Head. 1st ed. VG/VG. P3. $20.00

GRAHAM, Winston. *Miller's Dance*. 1983. Doubleday. 1st ed. VG/VG. P3. $18.00

GRAHAM, Winston. *Spanish Armadas.* 1972. Collins. VG/VG. P3. $20.00

GRAHAM, Winston. *Woman in the Mirror.* 1975. Bodley Head. 1st ed. VG/VG. P3. $18.00

GRAHAM & TELEK. *Leaf Protein Concentrates.* 1983. Westport. AVI Pub. 8vo. ils. 844p. cloth. F. B1. $125.00

GRAHAME, Kenneth. *Dream Days.* 1899. NY/London. Lane. 1st ed. VG. C6. $75.00

GRAHAME, Kenneth. *Fun O' the Fair.* 1929. London. Dent. 30p. VG. M20. $52.00

GRAHAME, Kenneth. *Golden Age.* 1895. London. Lane. 1st ed. author's 2nd book. VG. C6. $120.00

GRAHAME, Kenneth. *Pagan Papers.* 1894. London. Mathews/Lane. 1/450. VG. C6. $150.00

GRAHAME, Kenneth. *Wind in the Willows.* ca 1908. np. 1st Am ed. G+. w/pub catalog. M17. $85.00

GRAHAME, Kenneth. *Wind in the Willows.* 1933. Scribner. ils EH Shepard. VG/VG. B17. $10.00

GRAHAME, Kenneth. *Wind in the Willows.* 1940. Heritage. 1st prt thus. ils Rackham. 190p. VG+. C14. $20.00

GRAHAME, Kenneth. *Wind in the Willows.* 1966. World. 1st ed. ils Tasha Tudor. 255p. gilt gr cloth. T10. $125.00

GRAHAME, Robert; see Haldeman, Joe.

GRAMATKY, Hardie. *Little Toot.* 1939. NY. Putnam. 1st ed. 12mo. unp. G+. C14. $25.00

GRANDLEY, Richard R.; see Jacks, Oliver.

GRANFIELD, Robert. *Making Elite Lawyers, Visions of Law at Harvard & Beyond.* 1992. NY. UP. M11. $20.00

GRANGER, Bill. *British Cross.* 1983. Crown. 1st ed. F/F. H11. $35.00

GRANGER, Bill. *British Cross.* 1983. Crown. 1st ed. VG/VG. P3. $20.00

GRANGER, Bill. *Burning the Apostle.* 1993. Warner. 1st ed. sgn. AN/dj. N4. $35.00

GRANGER, Bill. *El Murders.* 1987. Holt. 1st ed. F/F. P3. $17.00

GRANGER, Bill. *Hemingway's Notebook.* 1986. NY. Crown. 1st ed. F/F. H11. $25.00

GRANGER, Bill. *Last Good German.* 1991. Warner. 1st ed. VG/VG. P3. $19.00

GRANGER, Bill. *League of Terror.* 1990. Warner. 1st ed. VG/VG. P3. $20.00

GRANGER, Bill. *Man Who Heard Too Much.* 1989. Warner. 1st ed. F/F. P3. $19.00

GRANGER, Bill. *Schism.* 1981. Crown. 1st ed. F/F. A20. $25.00

GRANGER, Bill. *Shattered Eye.* 1982. Crown. 1st ed. F/dj. A20/H11. $25.00

GRANGER, Bill. *There Are No Spies.* 1986. Warner. 1st ed. VG/VG. P3. $17.00

GRANIT, Ragnar. *Receptors & Sensory Perception...* 1955. Yale. 370p. bl-gray cloth. VG/dj. G1. $65.00

GRANLUND, Nils T. *Blondes, Brunettes & Bullets.* 1957. McKay. 1st ed. NF/NF. H11. $40.00

GRANOVETTER, Matthew. *Murder at the Bridge Table.* 1988. NY. 310p. VG/wrp. S1. $8.00

GRANOVETTER & GRANOVETTER. *Tops & Bottoms.* 1982. NY. 182p. F/wrp. S1. $8.00

GRANT, Adele L. *Monograph of Genus Mimulus.* 1924. St Louis. rpt from Annuals of MO Botanical Garden 11. wrp. B26. $35.00

GRANT, Ambrose. *More Deadly Than the Male.* 1946. Eyre Spottiswoode. hc. VG. P3. $30.00

GRANT, Anne. *Memoirs of an American Lady.* 1901. NY. 2 vol. 1/350. 8vo. tog half vellum. VG. T10. $250.00

GRANT, Audrey. *ACBL Introduction to Bridge Bidding, Club Series.* 1990. Memphis, TN. revised. pb. VG. S1. $8.00

GRANT, Bruce. *Concise Encyclopedia of the American Indian.* 1989. NY. Wings Books. 8vo. ils Bjorklund. 352p. F/dj. T10. $25.00

GRANT, Charles L. *Dark Cry of the Moon.* 1985. Donald Grant. 1st ed. sgn. F/F. T2. $35.00

GRANT, Charles L. *Final Shadows.* 1991. Doubleday. 1st ed. hc. F/F. P3. $20.00

GRANT, Charles L. *For Fear of the Night.* 1988. Tor. 1st ed. F/F. P3. $18.00

GRANT, Charles L. *Last Call of Mourning.* 1979. Doubleday. 1st ed. NF/NF. P3. $80.00

GRANT, Charles L. *Long Night of the Grave.* 1986. Donald Grant. 1st ed. sgn. F/F. T2. $35.00

GRANT, Charles L. *Night Visions 2: All Original Stories.* 1985. Dark Harvest. 1st ed. F/F. G10. $75.00

GRANT, Charles L. *Nightmare Seasons.* 1982. Doubleday. 1st ed. F/F. P3. $50.00

GRANT, Charles L. *Pet.* 1986. NY. Tor. 1st ed. sgn. F/F. T2. $32.00

GRANT, Charles L. *Ravens of the Moon.* 1978. Doubleday. 1st ed. VG/VG. P3. $20.00

GRANT, Charles L. *Shadows 3.* 1980. Doubleday. 1st ed. F/F. P3. $30.00

GRANT, Charles L. *Soft Whisper of the Dead.* 1982. Donald Grant. 1st ed. sgn. F/F. T2. $30.00

GRANT, Charles L. *Something Stirs.* 1991. NY. Tor. 1st ed. sgn. F/F. T2. $22.00

GRANT, Charles L. *Something Stirs.* 1991. Tor. 1st ed. F/F. P3. $19.00

GRANT, Charles L. *Tales From the Nightside.* 1981. Arkham. 1st ed. 1/4121. sgn. F/F. T2. $45.00

GRANT, Cyril Fletcher. *Studies in North Africa.* 1923. Dutton. 1st Am ed. ils. 304p. VG. W1. $16.00

GRANT, Edward. *Planets, Stars & Orbs...* 1994. Cambridge. 1st ed. 8vo. 816p. F/F. K5. $40.00

GRANT, James. *Mace's Luck.* 1985. Piatkus. hc. NF/NF. P3. $20.00

GRANT, Joan. *Lord of the Horizon.* 1944. Methuen. 3rd ed. VG. P3. $12.00

GRANT, Landon. *Marshal of Mustang.* nd. MacDonald. hc. VG/VG. P3. $15.00

GRANT, Linda. *Blind Trust.* 1990. Scribner. 1st ed. F/F. H11. $30.00

GRANT, Linda. *Love Nor Money.* nd. BC. F/F. P3. $8.00

GRANT, Madison. *Knife in Homespun America.* 1984. York, PA. 1st ed. pres. VG/VG. B5. $50.00

GRANT, Maxwell (house name); see Davis, Robert Hart; Dent, Lester; Gibson, Walter; Lynds, Dennis.

GRANT, Michael. *Classical Greeks.* 1989. Scribner. F/F. P3. $27.00

GRANT, Michael. *Founders of the Western World.* 1991. Scribner. 1st ed. F/F. P3. $28.00

GRANT, Michael. *Line of Duty.* 1991. Doubleday. 1st ed. F/F. H11. $30.00

GRANT, Michael. *Rise of the Greeks.* 1988. Scribner. 1st ed. VG. P3. $28.00

GRANT, Robert. *Fourscore, an Autobiography.* 1934. Houghton Mifflin. G/worn. M11. $65.00

GRANT, Roderick. *Private Vendetta.* 1978. Scribner. 1st ed. F/F. P3. $15.00

GRANT, Ulysses S. *Personal Memoirs of...* *Two Volumes in One.* 1894. NY. Webster. 1st ed thus. 666p. cloth. NF. M8. $45.00

GRANT, Ulysses S. *Personal Memoirs.* 1885. NY. 2 vol. 1st ed. ils/maps. marbled edges. full calf. VG. H3. $125.00

GRANT, Verne. *Organismic Evolution.* 1977. San Francisco. ils/tables. 418p. F. B26. $28.00

GRANT, Verne. *Plant Speciation.* 1981 (1971). NY. 2nd. ils. sc. VG. B26. $40.00

GRANT, Vernon. *Tinker Tim the Toy Maker.* 1934. Whitman. ils. rebacked spine o/w VG. M5. $55.00

GRANT, Vernon. *Tinker Tim the Toy Maker.* 1934. Whitman. 1st ed. ils. 29p. pict brd. VG/VG. D1. $200.00

GRANTLAND, Keith; see Beaumont, Charles.

GRASS, Gunther. *Dog Years.* 1963. HBW. 1st ed. NF/NF. B35. $25.00

GRASS, Gunther. *Flounder.* 1977. HBJ. 1st ed. NF/NF. B35. $20.00

GRASS, Gunther. *Flounder.* 1977. NY. 1st Am ed. sgn. NF/NF. C2. $75.00

GRASS, Gunther. *Local Anaesthetic.* 1970. HBW. 1st ed. F/F. B35. $32.00

GRASS, Gunther. *Rat.* 1986. HBJ. 1st ed. F/F. B35. $18.00

GRASS, Gunther. *Tin Drum.* 1962. Pantheon. 1st ed. F/NF. B2. $45.00

GRASSET, Joseph. *Semi-Insane & the Semi-Responsible.* 1907. NY. Funk Wagnall. gilt gr cloth. G. M11. $125.00

GRATTAN, C. Hartley. *Southeast Pacific Since 1900.* 1963. Ann Arbor. xl. VG. O7. $10.00

GRATTON, L. *Non-Solar X- & Gamma-Ray Astronomy.* 1970. Dordrecht, Holland. Reidel. ils. 425p. dj. K5. $28.00

GRAU, Shirley Ann. *Black Prince AOS.* 1955. NY. 1st ed/1st issue. sgn. NF/NF. A11. $85.00

GRAVER, Elizabeth. *Have You Seen Me?* 1991. Pittsburgh U. 1st ed. author's 1st book. F/F. B4. $50.00

GRAVES, Anna Melissa. *Far East Is Not Very Far.* 1942. private prt. 1st ed. sgn. 8vo. 317p. VG. B11. $40.00

GRAVES, John. *Goodbye to a River.* 1960. NY. 1st ed. VG/VG. B5. $45.00

GRAVES, Robert. *But It Still Goes On.* 1930. London. Cape. 1st ed/2nd state. 8vo. gilt gr cloth. F/NF. T10. $200.00

GRAVES, Robert. *Claudius the God.* 1935. Smith Haas. 1st ed. G. P3. $25.00

GRAVES, Robert. *Collected Poems.* 1961. Doubleday. 1st ed. F/F. B35. $32.00

GRAVES, Robert. *Greek Myths.* 1988. Moyer Bell. hc. F/F. P3. $25.00

GRAVES, Robert. *Hercules My Shipmate.* 1945. Creative Age. 1st ed. 464p. VG/dj. M20. $47.00

GRAVES, Robert. *Isles of Unwisdom.* 1950. Cassell. 1st ed. VG/VG. P3. $20.00

GRAVES, Robert. *Lars Porsena.* 1927. Dutton. 1st Am ed. red cloth. F. B2. $40.00

GRAVES, Robert. *Love Respelt Again.* 1969. NY. 1st Am ed. 1/1000. sgn. NF/VG. C6. $80.00

GRAVES, Robert. *More Deserving Cases.* 1962. Marlborough College. 1/750. sgn. orig full morocco. F. C6. $125.00

GRAVES, Robert. *Original Rubaiyat of Omar Khayamm.* 1968. Garden City. 1st ed. 1/500. F/case. C2. $125.00

GRAVES, Robert. *Penny Fiddle.* 1960. Doubleday. 1st ed. ils Ardizzone. 63p. VG/dj. M20. $22.00

GRAVES, Robert. *Poems 1926-1930.* 1931. London. 1st ed. 1/1000. VG/VG. C6. $100.00

GRAVES, Robert. *Poems 1970-1972.* 1973. Doubleday. 1st Am ed. F/F. B4. $45.00

GRAVES, Robert. *Shout.* 1929. London. Mathews Marrot. 1/530. sgn. NF/VG. C6. $175.00

GRAVES, Valerie; see Bradley, Marion Zimmer.

GRAVES & PINCHOT. *White Pine: A Study.* 1896. NY. 1st ed. ils. 102p. VG. B5. $32.50

GRAY, A.W. *Bino's Blues.* 1995. Simon Schuster. 1st ed. author's 2nd book. rem mk. F/F. H11. $20.00

GRAY, A.W. *Man Offside.* 1991. Dutton. 1st ed. VG/VG. P3. $20.00

GRAY, Alasdair. *Poor Things.* 1992. HBJ. 1st Am ed. F/F. G10. $25.00

GRAY, Alasdair. *Ten Tales Tall & True.* 1993. Harcourt Brace. 1st Am ed. ils. F/F. G10. $20.00

GRAY, Asa. *How Plants Grow: A Simple Intro to Structural Botany...* 1867 (1858). Invison Phinney Blakeman. 8vo. 500 wood engravings. VG. M5. $40.00

GRAY, Basil. *Persian Painting.* 1930. London. Benn. 2nd. 8vo. VG/torn. W1. $12.00

GRAY, Carole. *Christmas Diorama.* 1992. np. 4 popups w/ties. F. A4. $25.00

GRAY, Charles. *Off at Sunrise: Overland Journal of Charles Glass Gray.* 1976. Huntington Lib. 1st ed. 8vo. ils. bl cloth. F/dj. T10. $45.00

GRAY, Colin S. *Leverage of Sea Power.* 1992. Macmillan. VG/VG. A16. $15.00

GRAY, David. *Gallops & Gallops 2.* 1898 & 1903. Century. 12mo. G. O3. $45.00

GRAY, Edward F. *Leif Eriksson: Discoverer of America.* 1930. NY. sgn. VG. O7. $75.00

GRAY, F. Griswold. *Horse & Buggy Days.* 1936. private prt. pres. O3. $85.00

GRAY, Harold. *Little Orphan Annie & the Gila Monster Gang.* nd. Whitman. hc. VG. P3. $10.00

GRAY, Harold. *Little Orphan Annie Bucking the World.* 1929. Cupples Leon. 8vo. VG. B17. $30.00

GRAY, Harold. *Little Orphan Annie in the Circus.* 1927. Cupples Leon. 8vo. F/VG. B17. $55.00

GRAY, Harold. *Pop-Up Little Orphan Annie & Jumbo the Circus Elephant.* 1935. Bl Ribbon. Pleasure Books. unp. VG. M20. $225.00

GRAY, Harold. *Pop-Up Little Orphan Annie.* 1935. Chicago. Bl Ribbon. 3 popups. VG. B5. $125.00

GRAY, J.A.C. *Amerika Samoa.* 1960. Annapolis. VG. O7. $20.00

GRAY, James Kendricks; see Fox, Gardner F.

GRAY, John Chipman. *Nature & Sources of the Law. Second Edition.* 1985. Birmingham. Legal Classics Lib. facsimile of 1927 ed. M11. $65.00

GRAY, John. *Near Eastern Mythology.* 1969. Hamlyn. 1st ed. ils. 141p. NF/dj. W1. $24.00

GRAY, Lewis H. *Ill Wind: Naval Airship Shenandoah in Novel County, OH.* 1989. Baltimore, MD. 1st ed. sgn. 154p. VG/wrp. B18. $15.00

GRAY, Martin. *For Those I Loved.* 1972. Boston. photos. 351p. VG. A17. $9.50

GRAY, Richard. *System of English Ecclesiastical Law.* 1743. London. J Stagg. last ed. contemporary mottled calf. worn. M11. $150.00

GRAY, Roland Palmer. *Songs & Ballads of the Maine Lumberjacks...* 1924. Cambridge. Harvard. 1st ed. sgn. 8vo. 181p. VG. B11. $50.00

GRAY, Thomas. *Elegy Written in a Country Church Yard.* 1776. London. Dodsley. new ed. 8vo. ils. contemporary (?) half calf. VG. T10. $500.00

GRAY, Thomas. *Elegy Written in a Country Church Yard.* 1938. London. LEC. 1st ed thus. intro H Walpole. ils AM Parker. F/case. C2. $200.00

GRAY, Westmoreland. *Hell's Stomping Grounds.* 1935. Lippincott. 1st ed. F/NF double djs. B4. $85.00

GRAY, Wood. *Hidden Civil War, Story of the Copperheads.* 1942. Viking. 8vo. 314p. T10. $35.00

GRAYDON, William. *Justices & Constables Assistant. Being General Collection...* 1805. Harrisburgh. John Wyeth. working copy. M11. $150.00

GRAYSMITH, Robert. *Sleeping Lady.* 1990. Dutton. 1st ed. VG/VG. P3. $20.00

GRAYSON, C.J. *Decisions Under Uncertainty: Drilling Decisions...* 1960. Harbard. 402p. cloth. F/chip. D8. $10.00

GRAYSON, Richard. *Death En Voyage.* 1986. Gollancz. 1st ed. NF/NF. P3. $20.00

GREAVES, Margaret. *Lucky Coin.* 1989. Steward Tabori Chang. ils Liz Underhill. ils. VG. B17. $9.00

GREELEY, Andrew M. *Cardinal Sins.* 1981. Warner. xl. dj. P3. $5.00

GREELEY, Andrew M. *Final Planet.* 1987. Warner. F/F. P3. $17.00

GREELEY, Andrew M. *God Game.* 1986. Warner. 1st ed. F/F. P3. $17.00

GREELEY, Horace. *Hints Toward Reforms.* 1850. NY. 1st ed. 400p. cloth. G. A17. $25.00

GREELY, Adolpus W. *Three Years of Arctic Service.* 1886. London. 2 vol. ils/fld map. G. M17. $110.00

GREEN, B.A. *Bibliography of the Tennessee Walking Horse.* 1960. Nashville. 1st ed. pres. VG. O3. $125.00

GREEN, Ben K. *More Horse Tradin'.* 1972. NY. 1st ed. VG/VG. B5. $30.00

GREEN, Ben K. *Village Horse Doctor West of the Pecos.* 1980. Knopf. 12th. 8vo. ils Bjorklund. F/dj. T10. $25.00

GREEN, Ben K. *Village Horse Doctor.* 1971. NY. 1st ed. VG/G. B5. $30.00

GREEN, Donald E. *Panhandle Pioneer: Henry C Hitch, His Ranch & His Family.* 1980. Norman. 1st ed/2nd prt. 294p. AN/dj. P4. $25.00

GREEN, Edith Pinero. *Rotten Apples.* 1977. Dutton. 1st ed. VG/VG. P3. $15.00

GREEN, George Dawes. *Caveman's Valentine.* 1994. Warner. 1st ed. F/F. H11/M23. $50.00

GREEN, George Dawes. *Juror.* 1995. Warner. 1st ed. NF/F. H11. $25.00

GREEN, Gerald. *Last Angry Man.* 1956. Scribner. 1st ed. NF/NF. H11. $45.00

GREEN, Henry. *Doting.* 1952. London. 1st ed. VG+/VG. A11. $55.00

GREEN, Henry. *Nothing.* 1950. London. 1st ed. NF/NF. A11. $95.00

GREEN, J.R. *Short History of the English Peoples.* 1894. NY. 4 vol. xl. G. O7. $50.00

GREEN, John. *Priviledges of the Lord Mayor & Aldermen of the City...* 1722. London. James Roberts. contemporary panelled sheep. M11. $350.00

GREEN, Joseph. *Conscience Interplanetary.* 1972. Doubleday. 1st ed. F/F. P3. $15.00

GREEN, Kate. *Shooting Star.* 1992. Harper Collins. 1st ed. AN/dj. M22. $7.00

GREEN, Mason A. *Springfield Memories.* 1876. Springfield, MA. Whitney Adams. 8vo. 110p. gilt gr cloth. F. K1. $30.00

GREEN, N.W. *Mormonism Rise & Progress.* 1874. Hartford. 1st ed. 3-quarter leather. VG. B5. $50.00

GREEN, Paul. *Common Glory...* 1948. UNC. inscr. ils. VG/G. B10. $35.00

GREEN, Paul. *Lonesome Road: Six Plays for the Negro Theatre.* 1926. NY. McBride. 1st ed. 217p. VG. M8. $150.00

GREEN, Roger Lancelyn. *Ten Tales of Detection.* 1968. Dent Dutton. 2nd. VG/VG. P3. $20.00

GREEN, Terence M. *Barking Dogs.* 1988. St Martin. 1st ed. author's 1st novel. F/NF. G10. $12.00

GREEN, Tim. *Outlaws.* 1995. Turner. ARC. F/pict wrp. G10. $20.00

GREEN, William M. *Salisbury Manuscript.* 1973. Bobbs Merrill. 1st ed. F/F. p3. $15.00

GREENAWAY, Kate. *Almanack for 1884.* 1883. London. Routledge. 16mo. NF. B24. $140.00

GREENAWAY, Kate. *Almanack for 1885.* 1884. London. Routledge. 16mo. aeg. wht imitation morocco. F. B24. $175.00

GREENAWAY, Kate. *Almanack for 1888.* 1887. London. Routledge. 16mo. 12 half-p ils. aeg. gitl brn cloth. F. B24. $200.00

GREENAWAY, Kate. *Almanack for 1890.* 1889. London. Routledge. 16mo. 12 half-p ils. bl ep. aeg. gilt gr cloth. F. B24. $200.00

GREENAWAY, Kate. *Almanack for 1894.* 1893. London. Routledge. 16mo. 16 full-p ils. aeg. cream imitation morocco. F. B24. $175.00

GREENAWAY, Kate. *Day in a Child's Life.* nd. Routledge. 1st ed. 4to. VG. M5. $150.00

GREENAWAY, Kate. *Greenaway's Babies.* 1907. Saalfield Muslin Book. G+. M5. $40.00

GREENAWAY, Kate. *Kate Greenaway Pictures.* 1921. London. Warne. 1st ed. ils. VG/torn. D1. $300.00

GREENAWAY, Kate. *Kate Greenaway's Alphabet.* ca 1885. London. Routledge. pict brd. B24. $140.00

GREENAWAY, Kate. *Kate Greenaway's Book of Games.* 1889. London. Routledge. 1st ed. 8vo. 64p. NF. B24. $475.00

GREENAWAY, Kate. *Language of Flowers.* nd. Routledge. 1st ed/1st state. cloth spine/pict brd. VG. M5. $100.00

GREENAWAY, Kate. *Marigold Garden.* nd. Warne. early prt. VG+. S13. $45.00

GREENAWAY, Kate. *Pied Piper of Hamelin.* 1993. Derrydale. 8vo. rem mk. F. B17. $7.50

GREENBAUM, Florence. *Jewish Cook Book. 1,600 Recipes According to Jewish Dietary.* 1925. NY. 5th. 8vo. 438p. gray cloth. NF. B14. $55.00

GREENBERG, Martin. *Coming Attractions.* 1957. Gnome. 1st ed. VG/VG. P3. $25.00

GREENBERG, Martin. *Five SF Novels.* 1952. Gnome. 1st ed. VG/VG. P3. $45.00

GREENBERG, Martin. *International Relations Through SF.* 1978. Franklin Watts. 1st ed. VG/VG. P3. $15.00

GREENBERG, Martin. *Journey to Infinity.* 1951. Gnome. 1st ed. NF/NF. P3. $45.00

GREENBERG, Martin. *New Adventures in Sherlock Holmes.* 1987. Carroll Graf. 1st ed. F/F. P3. $25.00

GREENBERG, Martin. *Robot & the Man.* 1953. Gnome. 1st ed. VG. P3. $25.00

GREENBERG, Martin. *Tony Hillerman Companion: A Comprehensive Guide...* 1994. Harper Collins. AP/1st ed. sgn. F/wrp. T2. $35.00

GREENBERG & GORMAN. *Cat Crimes II.* nd. Quality BC. VG/VG. P3. $10.00

GREENBERG & GREENBERG. *Guide to Corals & Fishes of Florida, Bahamas & Carribean.* 1986. Miami. Seahawk. ils. G. D8. $5.00

GREENBERG & NOLAN. *Bradbury Chronicles.* 1991. Roc. 1st ed. F/F. P3. $20.00

GREENBERG & PRONZINI. *Arbor House Treasury of Mystery...* 1981. BOMC. VG. P3. $18.00

GREENBERG & PRONZINI. *Cloak & Dagger.* 1988. Avenel. 2nd. F/F. P3. $15.00

GREENE, A.C. *Christmas Tree.* 1978. Nonesuch. 1/300. prt/sgn Ferguson. gilt orange cloth. miniature. B24. $100.00

GREENE, A.C. *900 Miles on the Butterfield Trail.* 1994. Denton. 1st ed. 293p. map ep. F/F. T10. $35.00

GREENE, Graham. *Bear Fell Free.* 1935. London. Grayson. 1/250. sgn. NF/NF. C2. $1,000.00

GREENE, Graham. *Brighton Rock & End of the Affair.* 1987. Peerage. F/F. P3. $15.00

GREENE, Graham. *Burnt-Out Case.* 1961. NY. 1st Am ed. F/NF. A11. $25.00

GREENE, Graham. *Comedians.* 1966. London. 1st ed. NF/NF. C6. $50.00

GREENE, Graham. *Doctor Fischer of Geneva.* 1980. Simon Schuster. 1st ed. NF/NF. M22/P3. $15.00

GREENE, Graham. *End of the Affair.* 1951. London. 1st ed. NF/VG+. C6. $95.00

GREENE, Graham. *End of the Affair.* 1951. Viking. 1st ed. NF/NF. P3. $100.00

GREENE, Graham. *Getting To Know the General.* 1984. NY. 1st ed. 4to. 249p. dj. F3. $15.00

GREENE, Graham. *Heart of the Matter.* 1948. Canada. Viking. 1st ed. VG. P3. $50.00

GREENE, Graham. *Heart of the Matter.* 1948. London. 1st ed. NF/VG. C6. $85.00

GREENE, Graham. *Honorary Consul.* 1973. London. Bodley Head. 1st ed. inscr. F/NF. B24. $750.00

GREENE, Graham. *Honorary Consul.* 1973. Simon Schuster. 1st ed. F/NF. M22. $40.00

GREENE, Graham. *Human Factor.* 1978. Bodley Head/Clarke Irwin. 1st ed. VG/VG. P3. $25.00

GREENE, Graham. *Human Factor.* 1978. Simon Schuster. 1st ed. F/NF. M19. $17.50

GREENE, Graham. *In Search of a Character.* 1961. Bodley Head. 1st ed. VG. P3. $25.00

GREENE, Graham. *In Search of a Character: Two African Journals.* 1962. NY. 1st Am ed. F/F. N3. $15.00

GREENE, Graham. *Journey Without Maps.* 1936. London. Heinemann. 1st ed. ils. NF/dj. C2. $2,000.00

GREENE, Graham. *Monsignor Quixote.* 1982. Lester & Orpen Denys. 1st ed. G/G. P3. $15.00

GREENE, Graham. *Our Man in Havana.* 1958. Heinemann. 1st ed. VG. P3. $40.00

GREENE, Graham. *Our Man in Havana.* 1958. Viking. 1st Am ed. F/VG. M22. $75.00

GREENE, Graham. *Our Man in Havana.* 1958. Viking. 1st ed. VG/VG. M19. $65.00

GREENE, Graham. *Reflections.* 1990. London. 1st ed. VG/VG. C4. $35.00

GREENE, Graham. *Shades of Greene.* 1975. Bodley Head/Heinemann. 1st ed. NF. P3. $20.00

GREENE, Graham. *Shipwrecked.* 1953. Viking. 1st ed. NF/VG. M22. $35.00

GREENE, Graham. *Tenth Man.* 1985. Simon Schuster. 1st ed. F/F. P3. $20.00

GREENE, Graham. *This Gun for Hire.* 1944. Triangle. MTI. NF/NF. M19. $35.00

GREENE, Graham. *This Gun for Hire.* 1982. Viking. F/F. P3. $18.00

GREENE, Graham. *19 Stories.* 1947. London. 1st ed. sgn. VG/VG. C2. $300.00

GREENE, Jerome. *Battles & Skirmishes of the Great Sioux War 1876-1877.* 1993. Norman, OK. 1st ed. 8vo. 228p. T10. $25.00

GREENE, Jerome. *Lakota & Cheyenne: Indian Views of Great Sioux War...* 1994. Norman, OK. 1st ed. 8vo. 164p. M/M. T10. $30.00

GREENE, Julia. *Flash Back.* 1983. Severn House. VG/VG. P3. $20.00

GREENE, Merle. *Ancient Maya Relief Sculpture.* 1967. Mus Primitive Art. 1st ed. 1/4000. 60p. VG. F3. $30.00

GREENE, William B. *Mutual Banking: A Simple Plan to Abolish Interest of Money.* 1895? Columbus Junction, IA. Fulton. VG+/wrp. B2. $85.00

GREENER, Leslie. *Discovery of Egypt.* 1989. Dorset. 32 pl. 216p. NF/dj. W1. $16.00

GREENEWALT, Crawford H. *Hummingbirds.* 1960. Doubleday. 4to. portfolio. NF. T10. $100.00

GREENFIELD, Eloise. *Daydreamers.* 1981. Dial. 1st prt. ils Tom Feelings. AN/dj. C8. $75.00

GREENFIELD, Eloise. *Grandmamma's Joy.* 1980. NY. Collins. 1st ed. ils. AN/dj. C8. $55.00

GREENFIELD, Eloise. *Rosa Parks.* 1973. Crowell. 1st ed. ils Eric Marlow. VG/VG. B4. $35.00

GREENFIELD, Eloise. *Sister.* 1974. Crowell. 1st ed. inscr. ils Moneta Barnett. F/NF. B4. $85.00

GREENFIELD, Howard. *Marc Chagall.* 1967. 1st ed. VG/VG. S13. $18.00

GREENHAW, Wayne. *Elephants in the Corn Field: Ronald Reagan...* 1982. Macmillan. 1st ed. 288p. VG. B10. $10.00

GREENLEAF, Simon. *Treatise on the Law of Evidence. Vol III.* 1853. Little Brn. 1st ed. contemporary sheep. M11. $150.00

GREENLEAF, Stephen. *Beyond Blame.* 1986. Villard. 1st ed. VG/VG. P3. $25.00

GREENLEAF, Stephen. *Blood Type.* 1992. Morrow. 1st ed. F/F. H11. $20.00

GREENLEAF, Stephen. *Fatal Obsession.* 1983. Dial. 1st ed. NF/VG. N4. $30.00

GREENLEAF, Stephen. *Grave Error.* 1979. Dial. 1st ed. VG/VG. P3. $18.00

GREENLEAF, Stephen. *Toll Call.* 1987. Villard. 1st ed. VG/VG. P3. $20.00

GREENLEAVES, Winifred. *Trout Inn Mystery.* 1929. Lincoln MacVeagh. 1st ed. NF. P3. $35.00

GREENSMITH, J.T. *Petrology of the Sedimentary Rocks.* 1978. Allen Unwin. 6th. 241p. VG/wrp. D8. $8.00

GREENWELL, Rose Agnes. *Flora of Nelson County, KY.* 1935. WA, DC. 204p. wrp. B26. $20.00

GREENWOOD, Frederick. *Imagination in Dreams & Their Study.* 1894. London. John Lane. 198p. w/16p catalog. gr cloth. G1. $75.00

GREENWOOD, Grace. *New Life in New Lands: Notes of Travel.* 1873. NY. JB Ford. 1st ed. 8vo. F. T10. $100.00

GREENWOOD, John. *Fleet Histories Series Vol II.* 1992. Freshwater. M. A16. $25.00

GREENWOOD, John. *Missing Mr Mosley.* 1985. Walker. F/F. P3. $15.00

GREENWOOD, John. *Namesakes II.* 1973. Cleveland. Freshwater. VG/dj. A16. $70.00

GREENWOOD, John. *Namesakes of the '80s, Vol I.* 1980. Cleveland. Freshwater. VG/dj. A16. $60.00

GREENWOOD, John. *Namesakes 1930-1955.* 1978. Freshwater. AN/dj. A16. $23.00

GREENWOOD, John. *New Namesakes of the Lakes.* 1975. Cleveland. Freshwater. G/fair. A16. $65.00

GREENWOOD, L.B. *Sherlock Holmes & the Case of Sabina Hall.* 1988. Simon Schuster. 1st ed. VG/VG. P3. $20.00

GREENWOOD, Major. *Authority of Medicine: Old & New.* 1943. Cambridge. 1st ed. 32p. stiff wrp. A13. $20.00

GREENWOOD. *Researchers's Guide to American Genealogy, 2nd Edition.* 1990. np. 52 charts/reproductions. 623p. F/F. A4. $25.00

GREER, Carl Richard. *What a Buckeye Cover Man Saw in Europe.* 1923. Hamilton, OH. Becket Paper Co. sgn. 8vo. 190p. VG. B11. $25.00

GREER. *Kissing the Rod. 17th-Century Women's Verse.* 1989. NY. 477p. F/wrp. A17. $10.00

GREGG, Alexander. *History of the Old Cheraws.* 1925. SC. gr cloth. VG. B30. $125.00

GREGG, Cecil Freeman. *Inspector Higgins Goes Fishing.* 1951. Methuen. 1st ed. VG. P3. $20.00

GREGG, Josiah. *Commerce of the Prairies.* 1958. OK U. ils/fld map. 469p. VG. A4. $45.00

GREGG, Linda. *Chosen by the Lion.* 1994. Graywolf. 1st ed. sgn. F/F. C2. $25.00

GREGG, Linda. *Sacraments of Desire, Poems.* 1991. Graywolf. 1st ed. sgn. F/F. C2. $30.00

GREGORY, Dick. *Dick Gregory's Bible Tales.* 1974. Stein Day. 1st ed. 187p. dj. R11. $30.00

GREGORY, Dick. *Nigger.* 1965. Allen Unwin. 1st ed. VG/VG. M19. $45.00

GREGORY, Dick. *Shadow That Scares Me.* 1968. Doubleday. 1st ed. VG. R11. $10.00

GREGORY, Franklin L. *Valley of Adventure.* 1940. Triangle. ffe removed. VG. P3. $10.00

GREGORY, J.C. *Nature of Laughter.* 1924. Harcourt Brace. 241p. gr cloth. G1. $45.00

GREGORY, Jackson. *Case for Mr Paul Savoy.* 1933. Scribner. 1st ed. VG. P3. $20.00

GREGORY, John. *Comparative View of State & Faculties of Man...* 1785. London. Dodsley. new ed. 286p. contemporary calf. NF. G1. $150.00

GREGORY, Robert. *Diz.* 1992. Viking. 1st ed. F/F. P8. $17.50

GREGORY, W. *American Newspapers 1821-1936.* 1967. Kraus Rpt Corp. brn cloth. T3. $140.00

GREGORY. *Gregory's Dictionary: New & Complete Dictionary...* 1822. NY. 3 vol. 140 pl. brn full leather. VG. B30. $350.00

GREIG, Francis. *Heads You Lose.* 1982. Crown. RS. F/F. P3. $15.00

GREIG, J.Y.T. *Psychology of Laughter & Comedy.* 1923. Dodd Mead. 1st Am ed. 304p. panelled maroon cloth. VG. G1. $35.00

GRENDON, Stephen; see Derleth, August.

GRENFELL, Wilfred. *Romance of Labrador.* 1934. NY. 1st ed. ils/pl. pict bl cloth. VG. H3. $40.00

GRENSER, Wodeman Ludwig. *Ueber Aether-Einathmungen Wahrend der Geburt.* 1847. Leipzig. 68p. prt yel wrp. B14. $1,000.00

GRESHAM, Elizabeth. *Puzzle In Porcelain.* 1945. Curtis. VG/wrp. B10. $7.00

GRESHAM, Grits. *Complete Book of Bass Fishing.* 1971. Outdoor Life/Harper Row. photos. G. P12. $7.50

GRESHAM, William Lindsay. *Houdini.* nd. HRW. 11th. VG/VG. P3. $15.00

GRESSITT, J. Linsley. *California Academy-Lingman Dawn-Redwood Expedition.* 1953. San Francisco. ils. 34p. F/wrp. B26. $27.50

GRETT, Willis Ray. *Aeronautical Meteorology.* 1925. NY. Ronald. ils/figures. 144p. G. K5. $14.00

GREW, Joseph C. *Report From Tokyo.* 1942. NY. 88p. dj. A17. $8.50

GREY, Daria. *God Loves a Dumbbell.* ca 1930s. NY. Pegasus. 1st ed. ils. F/VG. B4. $100.00

GREY, Richard. *Memoria Technica; or, New Method of Artificial Memory...* 1796. Dublin. Graisberry Campbell. 12mo. contemporary calf. G1. $75.00

GREY, Zane. *Border Legion.* nd. Black. VG. P3. $8.00

GREY, Zane. *Call of the Canyon.* nd. Grosset Dunlap. hc. VG. P3. $20.00

GREY, Zane. *Call of the Canyon.* 1924. Musson. 1st Canadian ed. F/G. A18. $30.00

GREY, Zane. *Captives of the Desert.* 1953. London. Hodder Stoughton. 1st Eng ed. VG/chip. A18. $20.00

GREY, Zane. *Desert Gold.* nd. Grosset Dunlap. VG/VG. P3. $20.00

GREY, Zane. *Hash Knife Outfit.* 1933. Harper. 1st ed. inscr. F/F case. M19. $1,500.00

GREY, Zane. *Ken Ward in the Jungle.* nd. Grosset Dunlap. VG. P3. $8.00

GREY, Zane. *Last of the Plainsmen.* nd. Grosset Dunlap. VG/G. P3. $15.00

GREY, Zane. *Last Trail.* nd. Triangle. hc. NF/NF. P3. $13.00

GREY, Zane. *Light of Western Stars.* nd. Grosset Dunlap. VG/VG. P3. $20.00

GREY, Zane. *Majesty's Rancho.* nd. Grosset Dunlap. VG/VG. P3. $20.00

GREY, Zane. *Majesty's Rancho.* 1944. Musson. 1st ed. VG. P3. $20.00

GREY, Zane. *Mysterious Rider.* Jan 1921. London/NY. Harper. 1st ed (I-U on c p). VG. H4. $100.00

GREY, Zane. *Nevada.* 1928. Harper. 1st ed. VG. P3. $40.00

GREY, Zane. *Rainbow Trail.* 1915. Grosset Dunlap. 1 pl. 272p. VG. M13. $30.00

GREY, Zane. *Rainbow Trail.* 1981. Ian Henry. F/F. P3. $10.00

GREY, Zane. *Reef Girl.* 1977. Harper Row. 1st ed. NF/NF. A18. $30.00

GREY, Zane. *Riders of the Purple Sage.* nd. Black. VG. P3. $8.00

GREY, Zane. *Shepherd of Guadaloupe.* nd. Grosset Dunlap. VG/VG. P3. $13.00

GREY, Zane. *Spirit of the Border.* 1943. Triangle. 18th. VG/VG. P3. $13.00

GREY, Zane. *Stairs of Sand.* 1945. Musson. VG. P3. $12.00

GREY, Zane. *Thunder Mountain.* 1936. NY. 1st ed. pres. NF/G+. C6. $110.00

GREY, Zane. *To the Last Man.* 1922. Harper. G. P3. $20.00

GREY, Zane. *Vanishing American.* 1925. Musson. 1st ed. VG/G. P3. $35.00

GREY, Zane. *Wanderer of the Wasteland.* 1923. Toronto. Musson. 1st Canadian ed. F/VG. A18. $30.00

GREY, Zane. *West of the Pecos*. nd. Grosset Dunlap. VG/VG. P3. $20.00

GREY, Zane. *Wild Horse Mesa*. 1928. Musson. hc. G. P3. $7.00

GREY, Zane. *Wilderness Trek*. nd. Grosset Dunlap. VG/VG. P3. $20.00

GREY, Zane. *Young Lion Hunter*. nd. Grosset Dunlap. VG/VG. P3. $20.00

GREY, Zane. *Young Lion Hunter*. nd. Thomas Nelson. 1st Eng ed. ils Joseph Cummings Chase. VG. M19. $75.00

GREY, Zane. *Young Pitcher*. 1911. Harper. 248p. VG+. M20. $92.00

GREY, Zane. *Zane Grey Fishing Library*. 1990-91. Derrydale. 1st ltd ed. 1/2500. 10 vol. sgn/#d Loren Grey. M. A18. $750.00

GRIBBIN & ORGILL. *Sixth Winter*. 1979. Simon Schuster. 1st ed. VG/VG. P3. $15.00

GRIBBLE, Leonard. *Case of the Marsden Rubies*. 1932. Harrap. 2nd. VG/VG. P3. $25.00

GRIDLEY, Marion. *Indians of Yesterday*. 1940. Donohue. folio. ils Lone Wolf. VG/VG. B17. $15.00

GRIERSON, Francis D. *Lady of Despair*. 1933. Collins Crime Club. 6th. G. P3. $10.00

GRIERSON, Francis D. *Murder in the Garden*. nd. Grosset Dunlap. decor brd. VG. P3. $15.00

GRIEVOUS, Peter. *Pretty Story Written in Year of Our Lord 1774*. 1971. Williamsburg. facsimile. 4to. 16p. self wrp/string ties. A17. $7.50

GRIFFIN, Appleton P.C. *Discovery of the Mississippi: Bibliographical Account...* 1883. NY. Barnes. rpt. 20p. xl. partially unopened. O7. $65.00

GRIFFIN, Charles. *Skull-Collectors of Formosa*. 1931. Ottawa. Canadian Geog Soc. removed. F. P4. $22.50

GRIFFIN, Gwyn. *Operational Necessity*. nd. BOMC. VG/VG. P3. $10.00

GRIFFIN, John Howard. *John Howard Griffin Reader*. 1968. Houghton Mifflin. 488p. VG+/VG. R11. $15.00

GRIFFIN, Martin. *Frank R Stockton: A Critical Biography*. 1965. Kennikat. rpt of 1939 ed. 178p. A17. $15.00

GRIFFIS, William E. *Sir William Johnson & the Six Nations*. 1891. NY. 1st ed. 12mo. 227p. gilt bl cloth. VG. H3. $125.00

GRIFFIS, William Elliot. *Mikado's Empire...* 1976. NY. 1st ed. 645p. gr cloth. VG. B14. $85.00

GRIFFITH, Fuller. *Lithographs of Childe Hassam: A Catalog*. 1962. Smithsonian. photos/pl. 66p. D2. $60.00

GRIFFITH, Linda. *Thumbelina*. 1977. CA. Intervisual Communications. probable 1st ed. 16mo. NF. T5. $45.00

GRIFFITH, NORTON & SCHAUB. *Flight of Vengeance*. 1992. Tor. 1st ed. F/F. P3. $22.00

GRIFFITH. *Marlene Dietrich: Image & Legend*. 1959. MOMA Film Lib. NF. D2. $20.00

GRIFFITHS, Ella. *Murder on Page Three*. 1984. Quartet Crime. NF/NF. P3. $18.00

GRIFFITHS, J.N.R. *Golden Years of Bridge: Classic Hands From the Past*. 1981. London. 127p. M. S1. $12.00

GRIFFITHS, John. *Loyal & Dedicated Servant*. 1981. Playboy. 1st ed. VG/VG. P3. $18.00

GRIFFON, T. Wynne. *History of the Occult*. 1991. Mallard. hc. VG. P3. $15.00

GRIFFTH, David Wark. *Rise & Fall of Free Speech in America*. 1916. Los Angeles. unp. G/wrp. B18. $15.00

GRIGSON, Geoffrey. *Englishman's Flora*. 1955. London. Phoenix House. 1st ed. 1/50. sgn. 478p. F/case. C2. $750.00

GRIMBLE, Arthur. *Return to the Islands*. 1957. London. Murray. 1st ed. 8vo. ils/map. F/NF. T10. $50.00

GRIMES, Martha. *Deer Leap*. 1985. Little Brn. 1st ed. F/F. P3. $16.00

GRIMES, Martha. *Five Bells & Bladebone*. 1987. Little Brn. 1st ed. VG/VG. P3. $16.00

GRIMES, Martha. *I Am the Only Running Footman*. nd. Little Brn. 2nd ed. VG/VG. P3. $15.00

GRIMES, Martha. *I Am the Only Running Footman*. 1986. Boston. Little Brn. 1st ed. F/NF. B4. $45.00

GRIMES, Martha. *Old Contemptibles*. 1991. Little Brn. 1st ed. rem mk. F/F. H11. $35.00

GRIMES, Martha. *Old Contemptibles*. 1991. Little Brn. 1st ed. VG/VG. P3. $20.00

GRIMES, Martha. *Old Silent*. 1989. Little Brn. 1st ed. F/F. P3. $19.00

GRIMES, Martha. *Send Bygraves*. 1989. Putnam. 1st ed. decor brd. VG. P3. $15.00

GRIMM, Wilhelm. *Dear Mili*. 1988. FSG. 1st ed. ils Sendak. F/F. B17. $10.00

GRIMM & GRIMM. *Dornroschen*. 1948. Zurich. Schiele Globi. ils Herbert Leupin. VG. D1. $85.00

GRIMM & GRIMM. *Fairy Tales by the Brothers Grimm*. 1931. LEC. 1/1500. ils/sgn Kredel. designed/sgn Koch. F/case. B24. $250.00

GRIMM & GRIMM. *Grimm Fairy Tales*. 1962. NY. LEC. 4 vol. 8vo. ils/sgn Lucille Corcos. F/case. T10. $250.00

GRIMM & GRIMM. *Grimm's Fairy Tales*. 1909. London. 1st ed thus. ils Rackham. 325p. gilt red cloth. VG. D1. $1,150.00

GRIMM & GRIMM. *Grimm's Fairy Tales*. 1920. Ward Lock. decor brd. VG. P3. $10.00

GRIMM & GRIMM. *Hansel & Gretel*. 1946. Grosset Dunlap. ils Julian Wehr. sbdg. VG. D1. $150.00

GRIMM & GRIMM. *Little Brother & Little Sister*. 1917. Dodd Mead. 1st ed. ils Rackham. 251p. VG. D1. $275.00

GRIMM & GRIMM. *One Hundred Fairy Tales*. 1980. Franklin Lib. aeg. leather spine. NF. P3. $20.00

GRIMM & GRIMM. *Snow White & the Seven Dwarfs*. 1972. FSG. 1st ed. ils NE Burkert. F/VG+. B4. $100.00

GRIMM & GRIMM. *Tales From Grim*. 1936. Coward McCann. 4th. ils Wanda Gag. VG/VG. D1. $60.00

GRIMM & GRIMM. *Tischlein Deck Dich*. 1948. Zurich. Schiele Globi. ils Herbert Leupin. unp. pict brd. VG. D1. $85.00

GRIMM & ROY. *Human Interest Stories of...Gettysburg*. 1927. Times & News Pub. photos. 60p. G+. B10. $65.00

GRIMSHAW, James A. *Robert Penn Warren: A Descriptive Bibliography 1922-1979*. 1981. VA U. 1st ed. F/F. B10. $35.00

GRIMSLEY, Daniel Amon. *Battles in Culpeper County, VA, 1861-1865*. 1900. Culpeper, VA. private prt. 1st ed. 56p. NF/prt wrp. M8. $375.00

GRIMSLEY, Jim. *Winter Birds*. 1994. Algonquin. 1st ed. F/F. M23. $30.00

GRIMWOOD, Ken. *Into the Deep*. 1995. Morrow. 1st ed. F/F. H11. $25.00

GRIMWOOD, Ken. *Replay*. 1986. Arbor. 1st ed. F/NF. G10. $30.00

GRIMWOOD, Ken. *Replay*. 1986. Arbor. 1st ed. VG/VG. P3. $20.00

GRINNELL, Charles E. *Law of Deceit & Incidents in Its Practice...* 1886. Boston. Little Brn. gr cloth. G. M11. $125.00

GRINNELL, David; see Wollheim, Don.

GRIS, Henry. *New Soviet Psychic Discoveries.* 1979. Souvenir. 1st ed. VG. P3. $20.00

GRISANTI, Mary Lee. *Art of the Vatican.* 1983. NY. Excalibur. 1st Am ed. 143p. F/F. T10. $20.00

GRISCOM, George L. *Fighting With Ross' Texas Cavalry Brigade...* 1976. Hill Jr College. 1st ed. 255p. cloth. NF/NF. M8. $95.00

GRISEWOOD, R. Norman. *Zarlah the Martian.* 1909. Fenno. hc. copyright p removed. G. P3. $50.00

GRISHAM, John. *Chamber.* 1994. Doubleday. 1st ed. inscr. F/F. B30. $35.00

GRISHAM, John. *Client.* 1994. Doubleday. 1st ed. F/F. P3. $25.00

GRISHAM, John. *Client.* 1994. Doubleday. 1st ed. inscr. F/F. B30. $50.00

GRISHAM, John. *Firm.* nd. BC. VG/VG. P3. $10.00

GRISHAM, John. *Firm.* 1991. Doubleday. ARC. inscr. NF/wrp. B30. $400.00

GRISHAM, John. *Firm.* 1991. Doubleday. 1st ed. F/F. M19. $175.00

GRISHAM, John. *Pelican Brief.* 1992. Doubleday. ARC. inscr. F/wrp. B30. $125.00

GRISHAM, John. *Pelican Brief.* 1992. Doubleday. 1st ed. F/F. N4. $65.00

GRISHAM, John. *Pelican Brief.* 1992. Doubleday. 1st ed. F/NF. H11. $50.00

GRISMER, Karl H. *Story of Sarasota.* 1946. Tampa. FL Grower. sgn. lg 8vo. VG. B11. $100.00

GRIST, Brooks D. *Echoes of Yesterday.* 1979. Tulare. 1st ed. 8vo. ils. 138p. F/dj. T10. $25.00

GRIST, Brooks D. *Tales by the Campfire.* 1974. Tulare, CA. 8vo. 175p. bl cloth. F/dj. T10. $25.00

GRISTEIN. *Women in Chemistry & Physics...* 1993. 721p. F. A4. $95.00

GROB, Gerald. *Inner World of American Psychiatry, 1890-1940.* 1985. New Brunswick. 1st ed. 310p. dj. A13. $35.00

GROBANI. *Guide to Football Literature.* 1975. np. 334p. F. A4. $55.00

GROOM, Arthur. *Boy's Book of Heroes.* ca 1950. London. Birn Bros. ils F Stocks May. 124p. G. A17. $10.00

GROOM, Winston. *Forrest Gump.* 1985. Garden City. 1st ed. author's 5th book. sgn. F/F. A11. $375.00

GROOM, Winston. *Gone the Sun.* 1988. Doubleday. 1st ed. F/F. H11. $30.00

GROOM, Winston. *Gone the Sun.* 1988. Doubleday. 1st ed. F/NF. M23. $20.00

GROOM, Winston. *Gump & Co.* 1995. NY. Pocket. 1st ed. sgn. 2nd Gump book. F/dj. S9. $35.00

GROOMS, Red. *Red Grooms' Ruckus Rodeo.* 1987. Abrams. probable 1st ed. 4to. F. B17. $10.00

GROOS, Karl. *Die Spiele der Menschen.* 1899. Jena. Gustav Fischer. 538p. later brn buckram. G1. $75.00

GROPIUS, Walter. *Town Plan for the Development of Selb.* 1969. np. 1st am ed. ils/charts/plans. VG. M17. $80.00

GROSE, Francis. *Military Antiquities Respecting a History of English Army...* 1812. London. 2 vol. 3rd. folio. pl. full diced calf. VG. C6. $750.00

GROSS, Al. *Progress Report of Wisconsin Prairie Chicken Investigations.* 1930. Madison, WI. Conservation Dept. 112p. VG/wrp. A10. $30.00

GROSS, Anthony. *Etching, Engraving & Intaglio Printing.* 1970. Oxford. ils. 184p. F/NF. A4. $45.00

GROSS, Louis S. *Redefining the American Gothic.* 1989. Umi Research. 1st ed. hc. F/F. P3. $35.00

GROSS, Milt. *Dun't Esk!!* 1927. Doran. 1st ed. MTI. VG. P3. $30.00

GROSS, Milt. *Nize Baby.* 1926. Doran. 1st ed. VG. P3. $30.00

GROSSINGER, Jennie. *Art of Jewish Cooking.* 1958. NY. 1st ed. F/dj. B14. $75.00

GROSSMAN, Mordecai. *Philosophy of Helvetius With Special Emphasis...* 1937. Columbia. 181p. prt bl cloth. G1. $375.00

GROSSMAN & HAMLET. *Birds of Prey of the World.* 1964. NY. 1st ed. ils. VG/VG. B5. $55.00

GROSZ, George. *Little Yes & a Big No.* 1946. Dial. 1st ed. NF/NF. B2. $85.00

GROTH, John. *Studio: Asia.* 1952. Cleveland. ARC/1st ed. ils. 208p. VG/dj. B18. $25.00

GROTH, John. *Studio: Europe.* 1945. NY. 283p. cloth. VG. A17. $12.50

GROTIUS, Hugo. *Law of War & Peace...* 1925. Bobbs Merrill. gr cloth. M11. $125.00

GROTIUS, Hugo. *Rights of War & Peace...* 1738. London. Innys Manby. contemporary calf. worn. M11. $1,500.00

GROTTA-KURSKA, Daniel. *Biography of JRR Tolkien: Architect of Middle Earth.* 1978. Running Pr. expanded 1st ed. F/NF. G10. $15.00

GROUT, Donald J. *Short History of Opera.* 1947. NY. 2 vol. 1st ed. ils/musical scores. gilt blk cloth. F/G case. H3. $85.00

GROVE. *Of Brooks & Books.* 1945. np. 1/1500. 94p. NF/NF. A4. $55.00

GROVER, Eulalie Osgood. *Overall Boys: First Reader.* 1905. Chicago. 1st ed. ils Bertha Corbett. 120p. G. A17. $20.00

GROVER, Paula K. *White Boys & River Girls.* 1995. Chapel Hill. Algonquin. AP. author's 1st book. NF/wrp. S9. $30.00

GROVER, Robert. *Here Goes Kitten.* 1964. Grove. 1st ed. sgn. F/F. B11. $65.00

GROVER, Robert. *Maniac Responsible.* 1963. Grove. 1st ed. author's 2nd novel. F/F. T10. $100.00

GROVER, Robert. *Maniac Responsible.* 1963. Grove. 1st ed. 222p. VG/dj. M20. $20.00

GRUBB, Davis. *Fools' Parade.* 1969. NAL/World. 1st ed. sgn. VG/VG. P3. $40.00

GRUBB, Davis. *Night of the Hunter.* 1953. NY. 1st ed. VG/G. B5. $45.00

GRUBB, Davis. *Shadow of My Brother.* 1966. Hutchinson. 1st ed. NF/NF. P3. $25.00

GRUBB, Davis. *Watchman.* 1961. NY. 1st ed. VG/VG. B5. $30.00

GRUBER, Frank. *Bridge of Sand.* 1963. Dutton. 1st ed. VG/VG. P3. $25.00

GRUBER, Frank. *Laughing Fox.* 1943. Tower. VG/VG. P3. $20.00

GRUBER, Frank. *Run, Fool, Run.* 1966. Dutton. 1st ed. VG/VG. P3. $30.00

GRUDGE, Elizabeth. *Dean's Watch.* 1964. Hodder Stoughton. 3rd ed. VG/VG. P3. $10.00

GRUDGE, Elizabeth. *Pilgrim's Inn.* nd. BC. VG/VG. P3. $8.00

GRUDGE, Elizabeth. *White Witch.* 1958. Coward McCann. 1st ed. NF/NF. P3. $25.00

GRUELLE, Johnny. *Johnny Gruelle's Golden Book.* 1925. Donohue. 4to. ils. 95p. VG. D1. $75.00

GRUELLE, Johnny. *Magical Land of Noom.* (1922). Donohue. 4to. ils. 157p. bl-gr cloth/pict label. VG. D1. $300.00

GRUELLE, Johnny. *Man in the Moon Stories*. 1922. Cupples Leon. ils/8 pl. VG. M5. $195.00

GRUELLE, Johnny. *Marcella*. 1929. Volland. 1st ed. 94p. VG. M20. $45.00

GRUELLE, Johnny. *Marcella: A Raggedy Ann Story*. 1929. Donohue. 8vo. unp. VG/dj. D1. $150.00

GRUELLE, Johnny. *Original Raggedy Ann Stories*. 1930s. Donohue. rpt. 95p. VG+/dj. M20. $50.00

GRUELLE, Johnny. *Raggedy Ann & Andy & the Nice Fat Policeman*. 1942. Gruelle. 1st ed. 95p. VG/dj. M20. $115.00

GRUELLE, Johnny. *Raggedy Ann in Cookie Land*. 1931. Volland. 1st ed. ils Gruelle. 95p. VG. M20. $105.00

GRUELLE, Johnny. *Raggedy Ann's Alphabet Book*. 1925. Chicago. Donohue. 12mo. ils. VG. C8. $75.00

GRUELLE, Johnny. *Raggedy Ann's Magical Wishes*. 1930s. Donahue. 94p. VG+/dj. M20. $65.00

GRUELLE, Johnny. *Raggedy Ann's Picture Book*. 1940. McLoughlin. 16p. NF. M5. $95.00

GRUELLE, Johnny. *Raggedy Ann's Wishing Pebble*. 1925. Volland. 14th. 8vo. ils. VG. M5. $75.00

GRUELLE, Johnny. *Raggedy Ann Stories*. 1920. Volland. 1st ed. unp. VG. M20. $62.00

GRUELLE, Johnny. *Raggedy Ann Stories*. 1961. Bobbs Merrill. ils. yel cloth/pl. VG+/dj. M5. $25.00

GRUELLE, Johnny. *Wooden Willie*. 1927. Donohue. 95p. VG. D1. $125.00

GRUENBERG, Sidonie M. *Wonderful Story of How You Were Born*. nd. Doubleday. revised ed. 8vo. ils. 39p. F/VG. C14. $10.00

GRUENFELD, Lee. *All Fall Down*. 1994. NY. Warner. 1st ed. F/NF. H11. $20.00

GRUENFELD, Lee. *Irreparable Harm*. 1993. Warner. 1st ed. author's 1st book. F/F. H11. $25.00

GRUENTHER, Alfred M. *Duplicate Contract Complete: A Guide to Playing...* 1933. NY. 1st prt. 328p. VG. S1. $20.00

GRUMBACH, Doris. *Chamber Music*. 1979. London. 1st ed. inscr. F/F. A11. $40.00

GRUMBACH, Doris. *Company She Kept: A Revealing Portrait of Mary McCarthy*. 1967. Coward McCann. 1st ed. author's 3rd book. VG/VG. S13. $20.00

GRUMBACH, Doris. *Company She Kept: A Revealing Portrait of Mary McCarthy*. 1967. Coward McCann. 1st ed. F/VG. B4. $45.00

GRUMBACH, Doris. *Ladies*. 1984. Dutton. 1st ed. rem mk. F/dj. S9. $25.00

GRUNFELD, Frederic V. *Hitler File: Social History of Germany...1918-45*. 1974. NY. 1st Am ed. 374p. VG/dj. A17. $27.50

GRZIMEK, H.C.B. *Grimek's Animal Life Encyclopedia, Vol 3*. 1972. Van Nostrand. 8vo. ils. 541p. F/F. B1. $60.00

GUENTHER, Konrad. *Naturalist in Brazil*. 1931. Houghton Mifflin. 400p. VG. A10. $37.50

GUERBER, H.A. *Norsemen*. 1986. Avenel. 2nd ed. VG/VG. P3. $10.00

GUERIN, Daniel. *Negroes on the March*. 1956. NY. Weissman. 1st ed. 190p. wrp. R11. $20.00

GUERIN, Marcel. *L'Oeuvre Grave de Manet*. 1969 (1944). Da Capo. ils. cloth. dj. D2. $175.00

GUEST, C.Z. *First Garden*. 1976. Putnam. 1st ed. sgn. ils Cecil Beaton. F/NF. B4. $85.00

GUEST, Edgar A. *Path to Home When Day Is Done*. 1919. Reilly Lee. hc. VG. P3. $20.00

GUEST, Judith. *Ordinary People*. 1976. Viking. 1st ed. author's 1st book. F/F. H11. $40.00

GUILD, Nicholas. *Chain Reaction*. 1983. St Martin. 1st ed. VG/VG. P3. $15.00

GUILES, Fred Lawrence. *Norman Jean: The Life of Marilyn Monroe*. 1969. McGraw Hill. VG. P3. $20.00

GUILEY, Rosemary Ellen. *Moonscapes*. 1991. Prentic Hall. 192p. VG/VG. K5. $13.00

GUILLEMIN, Amadee. *Heavens: Ils Handbook of Popular Astronomy*. 1878. London. Bentley. 7th. 436p. VG. K5. $100.00

GUILLEN, Michael. *Five Equations That Changed the World*. 1995. Hyperion. 1st ed. F/F. M23. $30.00

GUINNESS & SADLER. *Mr Jefferson, Architect*. 1973. NY. 1st ed. 177p. F. B14. $55.00

GUINTHER & TAYLOR. *Positive Flying*. 1978. NY. 1st ed. 229p. G/dj. B18. $12.50

GULICK, Paul. *Strings of Steel*. nd. Grosset Dunlap. MTI. VG. P3. $20.00

GULLETT, D.W. *History of Dentistry in Canada*. 1971. Toronto. 308p. dj. A13. $35.00

GULLIVER, Lemuel. *Travels Into Several Remote Nations of the World*. 1927. London. Benjamin Motte. 2nd. 8vo. 4 parts in 1. gilt calf. VG. T10. $1,000.00

GUMUCHIAN. *Les Livres de l'EnFrance*. 1985. 2 vol. 4to. ils. F/F. A4. $325.00

GUNN, James E. *Alternate Worlds*. 1975. Prentice Hall. VG/VG. P3. $35.00

GUNN, James E. *Dreamers*. 1980. Simon Schuster. 1st ed. VG/VG. N4. $17.50

GUNN, James E. *End of the Dreams*. 1975. Scribner. 1st ed. F/F. P3. $15.00

GUNN, James E. *Joy Makers*. 1984. Crown. F/F. P3. $13.00

GUNN, James E. *Some Dreams Are Nightmares*. 1974. Scribner. 1st ed. F/F. P3. $15.00

GUNN, Victor. *Death's Doorway*. 1973. Collins. VG/VG. P3. $15.00

GUNTHER, Max. *Doom Wind*. 1986. Contemporary. 1st ed. VG/VG. P3. $18.00

GUNTON, George. *Wealth & Progress: A Critical Examination of Wages...* 1897. NY. Appleton. 7th. inscr to Geo Westinghouse. 385p. gilt maroon cloth. VG. T10. $50.00

GUNZ, D. *Maryland Germans: A History*. 1948. Princeton. 1st ed. ils. 476p. VG/VG. B5. $45.00

GUPTA, Yogi. *Yoga & Long Life*. 1969. NY. Yogi Gupta NY Center. sgn. 8vo. VG/G. B11. $15.00

GUPTILL, Arthur L. *Norman Rockwell: Illustrator*. 1975. NY. 4to. 208p. F/dj. T3. $25.00

GUPTILL, Arthur L. *Oil Painting Step-by-Step*. 1953. Watson Guptill. 1st ed. sgn. VG. D2. $40.00

GURGANUS, Allan. *Oldest Living Confederate Widow Tells All*. 1989. Knopf. 1st ed. author's 1st book. F/NF. H11. $40.00

GURGANUS, Allan. *White People*. 1991. Knopf. 1st ed. sgn. F/NF. B2. $50.00

GURGANUS, Allan. *White People*. 1991. NY. 1st ed. 252p. AN/dj. A17. $17.50

GURNEY, A.R. *Gospel According to Joe*. 1974. Harper Row. 1st ed. NF/VG. M23. $15.00

GURNEY, David. *F Certificate*. 1968. Bernard Beis. 1st ed. hc. F. P3. $10.00

GUTHORN, Peter J. *American Maps & Mapmakers of the Revolution*. 1966. Monmouth Beach, NJ. Philip Freneau. 18 maps. F. O7. $100.00

GUTHRIE, A.B. Jr. *Arfive.* 1971. Houghton Mifflin. 1st ed. F/F. A18. $30.00

GUTHRIE, A.B. Jr. *Big It.* 1960. Boston. 1st ed. VG/VG. B5. $40.00

GUTHRIE, A.B. Jr. *Big Sky, Fair Land: Environmental Essays.* 1988. Northland. 1st ed. sgn. F/F. A18. $100.00

GUTHRIE, A.B. Jr. *Big Sky.* 1947. Wm Sloane. 1st ed. 1/500. sgn/#d. F/dj. A18. $250.00

GUTHRIE, A.B. Jr. *Blue Hen's Chick.* 1965. NY. 1st ed. VG/VG. B5. $30.00

GUTHRIE, A.B. Jr. *Fair Land, Fair Land.* 1982. Houghton Mifflin. 1st ed. sgn. F/F. A18. $100.00

GUTHRIE, A.B. Jr. *Genuine Article.* 1977. Houghton Mifflin. 1st ed. F/F. A18. $40.00

GUTHRIE, A.B. Jr. *Last Valley.* 1975. Houghton Mifflin. 1st ed. F/F. A18. $40.00

GUTHRIE, A.B. Jr. *Playing Catch-Up.* 1985. Houghton Mifflin. 1st ed. sgn. F/F. A18. $100.00

GUTHRIE, A.B. Jr. *These Thousand Hills.* 1956. Boston. 1st ed. VG/VG. B5. $20.00

GUTHRIE, A.B. Jr. *These Thousand Hills.* 1956. Houghton Mifflin. inscr. F/VG clip. A18. $100.00

GUTHRIE, Woody. *Bound for Glory.* 1943. NY. 1st ed. G/dj. B5. $65.00

GUTMANN, Joseph. *Hebrew Manuscript Painting.* 1978. Braziller. 1st ed. ils. 119p. F/dj. W1 $30.00

GUTTERSON, David. *Country Ahead of Us, the Country Behind. Stories.* 1989. Harper. 1st ed. author's 1st book. AN/dj. C2. $150.00

GUTTERSON, David. *Snow Falling on Cedars.* 1994. Harcourt. 1st ed. sgn. F/F. C2. $100.00

GUTTERSON, David. *Snow Falling on Cedars.* 1994. Harcourt. 1st ed. AN/dj. M22. $85.00

GUY, Rosa. *Bird at My Window.* 1966. Phil/NY. 1st ed. inscr. F/VG. C6. $150.00

GUY, Rosa. *Children of Longing.* 1970. HRW. 1st hc ed. intro Julius Lester. F/F. B4. $75.00

GUY, Rosa. *Measure of Time.* 1983. HRW. 1st ed. F/F. B4. $55.00

GUY, Rosa. *Ups & Downs of Carl Davis III.* 1989. Delacorte. 1st ed. AN/dj. B4. $45.00

GWALTNEY, John Langston. *Dissenters.* 1986. Random. 1st ed. NF/VG+. R11. $12.00

HAACK, Hermann. *Stielers Hand-Atlas.* 1938. Gotha. Justus Perthes. 108 double-p hinged maps. F. O7. $125.00

HAAG, Earl C. *Pennsylvania German Anthology.* 1988. Susquehanna. 1st ed. 352p. F/dj. A17. $12.50

HAAK, Bob. *Rembrandt: His Life, His Work, His Time.* 1969. Abrams. ils/109 tipped-in pl. 348p. cloth. dj. D2. $125.00

HAAS, Ernst. *Creation.* 1971. London. Michael Joseph. 1st ed. VG/dj. S9. $85.00

HAAS, I. *Bibliography of Material Relating to Private Presses.* 1937. Chicago. Blk Cat. 1/250. F. A15. $85.00

HAAS, Irvin. *America's Historic Houses & Restorations.* 1966. NY. 1st ed. 271p. F/VG. E1. $30.00

HAAS, Irvin. *Citadels, Ramparts & Stockades: America's Historic Forts.* 1979. NY. 1st ed. 211p. F/F. E1. $35.00

HAASE, John. *Seasons & Moments.* 1971. Simon Schuster. 1st ed. inscr. F/F. B11. $30.00

HABERLY, Loyd. *American Bookbuilder in England & Wales...* 1979. London. Bertram Rota. 1/300. ils. 133p. F. A4. $165.00

HABIG, Marion A. *Alamo Chain of Missions.* 1968. Franciscan Herald. 1st ed. 8vo. 304p. gilt bl leatherette. F. T10. $50.00

HACHIYA, Michihiko. *Hiroshima Diary: Journal of a Japanese Physician...* 1955. Chapel Hill. 1st Eng trans. 238p. VG. A13. $100.00

HACK, Inge. *Danish Fairy Tales.* 1964. Follett. 1st ed. 8vo. VG/G. B17. $5.00

HACKER, Margaret Schmidt. *Cynthia Ann Parker: Life & Legend.* 1991. El Paso, TX. 2nd. photo/map. F/stiff wrp. E1. $18.00

HACKER, Marilyn. *Taking Notice.* 1980. Knopf. 1st ed. F/F. B2. $30.00

HACKETT. *Fifty Years of Best Sellers 1895-1945.* 1945. np. 148p. F/F. A4. $30.00

HACKFORTH, Henry L. *Infared Radiation.* 1960. NY. McGraw Hill. 230p. F. P4. $20.00

HADAMARD, Jacques. *Essay on the Psychology of Invention in Mathematical Field.* 1945. Princeton. 12mo. 143p. crimson cloth/paper label. G1. $37.50

HADDIX, Margaret Peterson. *Running Out of Time.* 1995. Simon Schuster. 1st ed. RS. F/F. G10. $10.00

HADER & HADER. *Berta & Elmer Hader's Picture Book of Mother Goose.* 1944 (1930). Coward McCann. 5th. 8vo. VG. M5. $35.00

HADER & HADER. *Billy Butter.* 1936. Macmillan. 1st ed. 12mo. 90p. VG/dj. D1. $85.00

HADER & HADER. *Jamaica Johnny.* 1935. Macmillan. 1st ed. 12mo. VG/torn. D1. $90.00

HADER & HADER. *Squirrely of Willow Hill.* 1950. Macmillan. 1st ed. ils. VG/G+. P2. $35.00

HADER & HADER. *Wish on the Moon.* 1954. Macmillan. 40p. VG/VG. P2. $40.00

HAFEN, Leroy R. *Overland Mail, 1849-1869.* 1926. Cleveland. 1st ed. 361p. VG. E1. $250.00

HAFEN & HAFEN. *Fort Laramie & the Pageant of the West, 1834-1890.* 1984. Lincoln, NE. Bison. 1st ed. 427p. F/stiff wrp. E1. $15.00

HAFFNER, Sebastian. *Meaning of Hitler.* 1979. NY. 1st Am ed. 165p. VG/dj. A17. $9.50

HAFNER, German. *Art of Crete, Mycenae & Greece.* 1968. Abrams. 1st ed. ils. 264p. VG/dj. W1. $35.00

HAGAN, William T. *Sac & Fox Indians.* 1958. Norman. 1st ed. 287p. F/VG. E1. $45.00

HAGEDORN, H. *Boys' Life of Theodore Roosevelt.* 1918. NY. 1st ed. 375p. F/VG. E1. $35.00

HAGEDORN, H. *Roosevelt in Badlands.* 1921. Boston. 1st ed. VG. B5. $40.00

HAGNER, Lillie May. *Alluring San Antonio.* 1947. San Antonio. 3rd. sgn. 142p. VG+/dj. B18. $15.00

HAGUE, Arnold. *Atlas To Accompany Monograph XXXII on Geology...* 1904. US Geol Survey. 24 hinged maps. F. O7. $995.00

HAGUE, Kathleen. *Bear Hugs.* 1989. Holt. 1st ed. F/F. B17. $15.00

HAGUE, Kathleen. *Legend of the Veery Bird.* 1985. HBJ. 1st ed. ils Michael Hague. F/F. B17. $20.00

HAGUE, Michael. *Cinderella & Other Tales From Perrault.* 1989. Holt. 1st ed thus. 78p. T10. $25.00

HAGUE, Michael. *Deck the Halls.* 1991. Holt. 1st ed. rem mk. F/F. B17. $8.00

HAGUE, Michael. *Jingle Bells.* 1990. Holt. 1st ed. ils. rem mk. F/F. B17. $8.00

HAGUE & HAGUE. *Alphabears, an ABC Book.* c 1984. NY. HRW. 2nd. unp. NF. C14. $8.00

HAIG, M.R. *Indus Delta Country.* 1972. Karachi. rpt. VG. O7. $45.00

HAIG-BROWN, Roderick. *Return to the River.* 1946. Toronto. McClelland Stewart. 1st Canadian ed. F/VG+. A18. $80.00

HAIGH & TURN. *Not for Glory: A Personal History of the 1914-18 War.* 1969. London. 1st ed. 113p. NF/NF. E1. $30.00

HAIL, Marshall. *Knight in the Sun.* 1962. Boston. 1st ed. 234p. F/VG. E1. $35.00

HAILEY, Arthur. *Strong Medicine.* 1984. Doubleday. 1st ed. NF/NF. N4. $20.00

HAILMAN, William Nicholas. *Twelve Lectures on History of Pedagogy...* 1874. Cincinnati Teachers Assn. 130p. NF. A4. $95.00

HAINES, Aubrey L. *Yellowstone National Park, Its Exploration...* 1974. Washington, DC. 218p. F/stiff wrp. E1. $15.00

HAINES, F. *Nez Perces, Tribesmen of the Columbia Plateau.* 1955. Norman. 1st ed. photos/maps. 329p. F/VG. E1. $75.00

HAINES, F. *Snake Country Expedition of 1830-31.* 1971. Norman. 1st ed. 172p. F/F. E1. $45.00

HAINES, T. Jenkins. *Richard Judkin's Wooing: A Tale of Virginia in Revolution.* 1898. Tennyson Neely. 1st ed. G+. B10. $50.00

HAINING, Peter. *Werewolf! Horror Stories of the Man-Beast.* 1987. Severn House. 1st ed. AN/dj. M21. $20.00

HAIR, P.E.H. *Atlantic Slave Trade & Black Africa.* 1978. London. VG/wrp. O7. $15.00

HAIRE, Frances. *American Costume Book.* 1934. Barnes. 16 pl. 164p. xl. A10. $80.00

HAIZLIP, Shirlee Taylor. *Sweeter the Juice: A Family Memoir in Black & White...* 1994. Simon Schuster. 1st ed. F/F. R11. $14.00

HAKLUYT. *First Colonists: Hakluyt's Voyages to North America.* 1986. Folio Soc. 1st ed thus. 16 pl. 142p. F/case. T10. $75.00

HALBERSTAM, David. *Breaks of the Game.* 1981. Knopf. 1st ed. rem mk. NF/NF. B4. $45.00

HALBERT, Henry S. *Creek War of 1813 & 1814.* 1895. Chicago. 4 pl/fld map. VG. M8. $350.00

HALBROOK, Stephen P. *That Every Man Be Armed.* 1984. Albuquerque. 1st ed. 274p. F/F. E1. $30.00

HALBURTON, Richard. *Glorious Adventure.* 1927. Bobbs Merrill. 1st ed. sgn. 354p. red cloth. VG. B11. $25.00

HALDEMAN, Joe. *All My Sins Remembered.* 1977. St Martin. 1st ed. F/F. P3. $23.00

HALDEMAN, Joe. *Buying Time.* 1989. Easton. ltd ed. sgn. full leather. unopened. sans/swrp. P3. $65.00

HALDEMAN, Joe. *Dealing in Futures.* 1985. Viking. 1st ed. F/F. P3. $17.00

HALDEMAN, Joe. *Mindbridge.* 1976. St Martin. 1st ed. sgn. F/F. B11. $45.00

HALDEMAN, Joe. *Worlds.* 1981. Viking. 1st ed. NF/NF. P3. $15.00

HALE, Edward Everett. *Man Without a Country & Its History.* 1897. np. 79p. NF. A4. $45.00

HALE, Edward Everett. *Queen of California: Origin of Name of California...* 1945. San Francisco. Colt. 1/500. F. O7. $125.00

HALE, George Ellery. *Signals From the Stars.* 1931. Scribner. 8vo. 138p. cloth. G. K5. $25.00

HALE, Hilary. *Winter's Crimes 16.* 1984. Macmillan. 1st ed. F/F. P3. $15.00

HALE, Janet Campbell. *Bloodlines.* 1993. Random. ARC. w/promo material. F/F. B35. $22.00

HALE, John. *Paradise Man.* 1969. Bobbs Merrill. VG/VG. P3. $10.00

HALE, Kathleen. *Manda.* 1952. Coward McCann. ils Hale. 30p. VG/G. T5. $30.00

HALE, Lucretia. *Peterkin Papers.* 1924. Houghton Mifflin. later prt. F/G. B17. $6.50

HALE, M. *Human Science & Social Order: Hugo Munsterberg...* 1980. Phil. 1st ed. 239p. VG/dj. A13. $30.00

HALE, Matthew. *Primitive Origination of Mankind...* 1677. London. contemporary calf. G. M11. $450.00

HALE, Nancy. *Black Summer.* 1963. Little Brn. 1st ed. sgn. 312p. VG/G+. B10. $15.00

HALE, Nancy. *Dear Beast.* 1959. Little Brn. 1st ed. inscr/dtd 1959. NF. B4. $65.00

HALE, T.J. *Great French Detective Stories.* 1983. Bodley Head. 1st ed. VG/VG. P3. $20.00

HALE & HALE. *Man Without a Country.* (1960). Franlin Watts. 8vo. 53p. VG/VG. C14. $8.00

HALEY, Alex. *Roots.* 1974. 1st ed. VG+/VG. w/clip sgn. S13. $50.00

HALEY, Gail. *Go Away, Stay Away.* 1977. London. Bodley Head. 1st ed. sgn/dtd 1979. 8vo. unp. NF. T5. $45.00

HALEY, Gail. *Story, a Story.* 1971 (1970). Atheneum. 2nd. sgn. F/VG+. P2. $25.00

HALEY, J. Evetts. *Charles Goodnight, Cowman & Plainsman.* 1949. Norman. ils Harold Bugbee. 485p. F/F. E1. $85.00

HALEY, J. Evetts. *Charles Schreiner, General Merchandise.* 1969. np. rpt of 1944 1st ed. F/VG. E1. $40.00

HALEY, J. Evetts. *Flamboyant Judge: Story of Amarillo...* 1972. Canyon, TX. 1st ed. 312p. F/VG. E1. $50.00

HALEY, J. Evetts. *Fort Concho & the Texas Frontier.* 1952. San Angelo Standard-Times. 1st ed. ils Bugbee. F/F. E1. $230.00

HALEY, J. Evetts. *XIT Ranch of Texas & the Early Days of Llano Estacado.* 1929. Chicago. 1st ed. 258p. rpr hinges/case. E1. $425.00

HALEY, J. Evetts. *XIT Ranch of Texas.* 1967. Norman, OK. Western Frontier Lib 2nd. 258p. F/scuff. E1. $25.00

HALFORD, Francis. *9 Doctors & God.* 1955. Honolulu. 306p. dj. A13. $30.00

HALIFAX, Lord. *Lord Halifax's Complete Ghost Book.* 1986. Castle. NF/NF. P3. $15.00

HALIFAX, Lord. *Lord Halifax's Ghost Book.* nd. Didier. 3rd ed. VG. P3. $15.00

HALKETT & LAING. *Dictionary of Anonymous & Pseudonymous Literature...* 1882-1888 4 vol. 3276p. VG. A4. $350.00

HALL, Adam. *Mandarin Cypher.* 1975. Collins. 1st ed. VG/VG. P3. $25.00

HALL, Adam. *Peking Target.* 1982. Playboy. 1st ed. VG. P3. $10.00

HALL, Adam. *Quiller Memorandum.* 1965. Simon Schuster. 1st Am ed. xl. VG/VG. N4. $30.00

HALL, Adam. *Scorpion Signal.* 1979. Collins. 1st ed. NF/NF. P3. $30.00

HALL, Adam. *Sinkiang Executive.* 1978. Doubleday. 1st ed. VG/VG. P3. $20.00

HALL, Adam. *9th Directive.* 1966. Heinemann. 1st ed. VG/VG. P3. $30.00

HALL, Alvin. *Cooperstown.* 1991. Meckler. 1st ed. F/F. P8. $10.00

HALL, Angus. *Signs of Things To Come.* 1975. Danbury. F. P3. $10.00

HALL, Austin. *People of the Comet.* 1948. Griffin. 1st ed. VG/VG. P3. $35.00

HALL, C. *Introduction to Electron Microscopy.* 1983. Malabar. rpt 2nd. 8vo. ils. 397p. F. B1. $35.00

HALL, David C. *Return Trip Ticket.* 1992. NY. 1st ed. F/F. H11. $30.00

HALL, Donald. *Alligator Bride: Poems New & Selected.* 1969. Harper. 1st ed. inscr. NF/NF. C2. $75.00

HALL, Donald. *Here at Eagle Pond.* 1990. Ticknor Fields. 1st ed. sgn. 8vo. 141p. F/VG case. B11. $20.00

HALL, Donald. *Playing Around.* 1974. Little Brn. 1st ed. F/VG+. P8. $30.00

HALL, Donald. *When Willard Met Babe Ruth.* 1st ed. ils/sgn Barry Moser. VG/VG. C4. $30.00

HALL, Elizabeth. *Away in a Cloud.* 1964. Vantage. 1st ed. sgn. 12mo. ils Dean Holt. 123p. F. T10. $20.00

HALL, Ester Greenacre. *Up Creek & Down Creek.* 1936. Random. ils Anna parker Braune. 236p. F/VG. P2. $15.00

HALL, Gordon Langley. *Sawdust Trail: Story of American Evangelism.* 1964. Phil. later prt. 249p. F/VG. E1. $25.00

HALL, Granville, Stanley. *Adolescence: Its Psychology & Its Relations to Physiology...* 1904. Appleton. 2 vol. ruled red cloth. VG. G1. $125.00

HALL, Granville, Stanley. *Founders of Modern Psychology.* 1912. Appleton. 470p. emb panelled red cloth. VG. G1. $50.00

HALL, James B. *Not By the Door.* 1954. Random. 1st ed. F/NF. B4. $75.00

HALL, James Norman. *Far Lands.* 1950. Boston. VG. O7. $25.00

HALL, James Norman. *High Adventure.* 1918. Boston. 236p. G. B18. $25.00

HALL, James W. *Bones of Coral.* 1991. Knopf. ARC. F. M19. $17.50

HALL, James W. *Bones of Coral.* 1991. Knopf. 1st ed. F/F. A20/P3. $20.00

HALL, James W. *Gone Wild.* 1995. Delacorte. 1st ed. NF/NF. P3. $22.00

HALL, James W. *Mean High Tide.* 1994. Delacorte. 1st ed. F/NF. H11. $25.00

HALL, James W. *Mean High Tide.* 1994. Delacorte. 1st ed. NF/NF. P3. $22.00

HALL, James W. *Tropical Freeze.* 1989. Norton. 1st ed. F/F. M23. $20.00

HALL, James W. *Tropical Freeze.* 1989. Norton. 1st ed. sgn. F/F. M19. $25.00

HALL, James W. *Tropical Freeze.* 1989. Norton. 1st ed. VG/F. A20. $15.00

HALL, James W. *Under Cover of Daylight.* 1987. Norton. 1st ed. author's 1st novel. F/NF clip. H11. $50.00

HALL, Martin H. *Confederate Army of New Mexico.* 1978. Austin. 1/35. 1st ed. sgn/#d. 422p. leather. F/case. E1. $350.00

HALL, Martin H. *Sibley's New Mexico Campaign.* 1960. Austin, TX. 1st ed. 366p. NF/NF. M8. $250.00

HALL, Mary Ann Taylor. *Come & Go, Molly Snow.* 1995. Norton. 1st ed. author's 1st book. F/F. M23. $45.00

HALL, Mary Bowen. *Emma Chizzit & Queen Anne Killer.* 1989. NY. Walker. 1st ed. F/F clip. H11. $35.00

HALL, Mary Bowen. *Emma Chizzit & the Sacramento Stalker.* 1991. Walker. 1st ed. F/F. H11. $25.00

HALL, O.M.; see Hall, Oakley.

HALL, Oakley. *Apaches.* 1986. NY. Simon Schuster. 1st ed. 8vo. NF/dj. T10. $25.00

HALL, Oakley. *Bad Lands.* 1978. Atheneum. 1st ed. 8vo. F/dj. T10. $35.00

HALL, Oakley. *Warlock.* 1958. Viking. 1st ed. VG/G. P3. $25.00

HALL, Parnell. *Movie.* 1995. Mysterious. 1st ed. NF/NF. P3. $20.00

HALL, R.H. *Civilization of Greece in the Bronze Age.* 1928. London. Methuen. ils. 302p. VG. W1. $65.00

HALL, Ralph J. *Main Trail.* 1971. San Antonio, TX. photos. F/scuff. E1. $25.00

HALL, Richard. *Lovers on the Nile.* 1980. NY. 1st ed. 254p. F/F. E1. $25.00

HALL, Richard. *Vanishing America.* 1986. Macmillan. 1st ed. photos. VG/VG. P12. $5.00

HALL, Roger. *19.* nd. Norton. 2nd ed. VG/VG. P3. $8.00

HALL, Sam S. *Big Foot Wallace.* 1965. Austin, TX. facsimile. 32p. VG. E1. $25.00

HALL, Thomas. *Sourcebook in Animal Biology.* 1951. NY. 1st ed. 716p. VG. A13. $50.00

HALL, Trevor. *Last Case of Sherlock Holmes, Ivy Johnson Bull of Borley.* 1986. np. ARC. 1/500. pub inscr. F. A4. $125.00

HALL, Winchester. *Self-Development; or, The Unfolding of the Faculties...* 1904. NY. Broadway. 1st ed. 146p. cloth. NF. M11. $35.00

HALL & NORDHOFF. *Bounty Trilogy.* 1936. Little Brn. 903p. silver stp bl cloth. G+. P12. $20.00

HALL & NORDHOFF. *Hurricane.* 1936. Boston. Little Brn. 1st ed. NF/dj. B24. $200.00

HALL & NORDHOFF. *Mutiny on the Bounty.* 1933. Little Brn. 396p. G+. P12. $8.00

HALL & NORDHOFF. *Pitcairn's Island.* 1934. Boston. Little Brn. 1st ed. silver/wht-stp red-brn cloth. F/NF. B24. $250.00

HALL. *Mapping the Next Millennium: Discovery of New Geographies...* 1992. np. 16 pl. 477p. F/F. A4. $30.00

HALLAHAN, William H. *Catch Me: Kill Me.* 1977. Bobbs Merrill. 1st ed. NF/F. H11. $45.00

HALLAHAN, William H. *Search for Joseph Tully.* nd. BC. VG/VG. P3. $6.00

HALLAM, A. *Revolution in the Earth Sciences From Continental Drift...* 1974. Oxford. 127p. hc. NF/dj. D8. $12.00

HALLDORSSON, Haukur. *Trolls in Icelandic Folklore.* 1982. Bokaugafan orn Og Orlygur. P3. $15.00

HALLENBECK, Cleve. *Alvarnunez Cabeza de Vaca.* 1940. Glendale. 1st ed. fld maps. 326p. F. E1. $200.00

HALLER. *Book Collector's Fact Book.* 1976. np. 272p. F/VG. A4. $65.00

HALLER. *Collecting Old Photographs.* 1978. np. ils. 264p. F/F. A4. $145.00

HALLER. *Victorian & Edwardian Photographs.* 1982. np. revised. 70 ils. 80p. F/VG. A4. $35.00

HALLET, Jean-Pierre. *Animal Kitabu.* 1968. Random. 2nd. sgn. F/F. T10. $25.00

HALLIBURTON, Richard. *Glorious Adventure.* 1927. Garden City. rpt. inscr/dtd. VG. E1. $25.00

HALLIBURTON, Richard. *Royal Road to Romance.* 1925. Bobbs Merrill. 399p. gr cloth. VG. B22. $5.50

HALLIDAY, Brett. *Blood on Biscayne Bay.* 1946. Ziff Davis. 1st ed. xl. dj. P3. $8.00

HALLIDAY, Brett. *Dividend on Death.* 1942. Sun Dial. VG. P3. $10.00

HALLIDAY, Brett. *Dolls Are Deadly.* 1960. Dodd Mead. 1st ed. F/NF. H11. $30.00

HALLIDAY, Brett. *Fit To Kill.* 1958. Dodd Mead. 1st ed. xl. ffe removed. dj. P3. $10.00

HALLIDAY, Brett. *Homicidal Virgin.* 1960. Torquil. 1st ed. VG/VG. P3. $25.00

HALLIDAY, Brett. *Murder & the Married Virgin.* 1948. Triangle. 1st. VG/VG. P3. $12.00

HALLIDAY, Brett. *Private Practice of Michael Shayne.* 1940. Holt. 1st ed. VG. P3. $20.00

HALLIDAY, Brett. *She Woke to Darkness.* 1954. Torquil. 1st ed. NF/NF. P3. $20.00

HALLIDAY, Brett. *Target: Mike Shayne.* 1959. Dodd Mead. 1st ed. VG/VG. P3. $15.00

HALLIDAY, Brett. *Too Friendly, Too Dead.* 1963. Dodd Mead. 1st ed. VG/VG. P3. $25.00

HALLIDAY, Fred. *Ambler.* 1983. Simon Schuster. 1st ed. VG/VG. P3. $14.00

HALLIWELL, Leslie. *Dead That Walk.* 1988. Continuum. 1st ed. NF/NF. P3. $25.00

HALLIWELL, Leslie. *Mountain of Dreams, Paramount Picture.* 1976. Stonehill. 1st ed. VG/VG. P3. $25.00

HALLOCK, Charles. *Camp Life in Florida.* 1876. Forest & Stream. fair. V4. $45.00

HALLOCK, Grace T. *Around the World With Hob.* 1931. Quaker Oats. ils Elektra Papadopoulos. 44p. VG. A17. $5.00

HALPER, Albert. *Chicago Crime Book.* 1967. World. 1st ed. VG/VG. P3. $20.00

HALPERN, Frank M. *Directory of Dealers in Science Fiction & Fantas.* 1975. Haddonfield. VG/VG. P3. $20.00

HALPERN, Jay. *Jade Unicorn.* 1979. Macmillan. 1st ed. F/F. P3. $28.00

HALSELL, Grace. *Los Viegos: Secrets of Long Life...* 1976. Rodale. ils. 186p. dj. F3. $10.00

HALSELL, H.H. *Ranger.* 1942. Santa Fe. 1st ed. map ep. 97p. w/sgn letter. F. E1. $65.00

HALSEY. *Forgotten Books of the American Nursery.* 1911. Boston. Goodspeed. 1/700. 255p. xl. VG. A4. $75.00

HALSTEAD, M. *Life...Admiral Dewey From Montpelier to Manila.* 1899. Chicago. 8vo. 452p. G. T3. $25.00

HALSTEAD, Ward C. *Brain & Intelligence: A Quantitative Study of Frontal Lobes.* 1947. Chicago. 206p. gr cloth. VG/dj. G1. $50.00

HALTER. *Collecting First Editions of Franklin Roosevelt...* 1949. np. 1/77. 214p. VG. A4. $350.00

HAMADY, Walter. *Plumfoot Poems.* 1967. Perishable Pr. 1/200. inscr to w/xl label of Robert Duncan. F/box. V1. $150.00

HAMBLETON, James P. *Biographical Sketch of Henry A Wise...* 1856. JW Randolph. 509p. fair. B10. $125.00

HAMBLY, Barbara. *Dark Hand of Magic.* nd. BC. F/F. P3. $8.00

HAMBLY, Barbara. *Those Who Hunt the Night.* 1988. Del Rey. 1st ed. F/F. P3. $20.00

HAMBURG-AMERICAN LINE. *Guide Through Europe.* 1900. Berlin. J Hermann Herz. G. A16. $70.00

HAMER, S.H. *Little Folks Picture Album in Color.* 1904. Cassell. 48 pl. pict red cloth. VG. M5. $175.00

HAMILL, Peter. *Flesh & Blood.* 1977. Random. 1st ed. F/F. H11. $35.00

HAMILTON, C.D.P. *Modern Scientific Whist.* 1984. NY. 599p. VG. S1. $8.00

HAMILTON, Charles. *Cry of the Thunderbird, the American Indian's Own Story.* 1972. Norman. 1st rpt of 1950 1st ed. F/F. E1. $35.00

HAMILTON, Charles. *Early Day Oil Tales of Mexico.* 1966. Houston. Gulf Pub. 1st ed. 246p. dj. F3. $20.00

HAMILTON, David. *Healers, a History of Medicine in Scotland.* 1981. Edinburgh. 1st ed. 318p. dj. A13. $45.00

HAMILTON, Edith. *Mythology.* 1942. Little Brn. 1st ed. F/NF. C2. $75.00

HAMILTON, Edmond. *Battle for the Stars.* nd. BC. VG/VG. P3. $10.00

HAMILTON, Franklin; see Silverberg, Robert.

HAMILTON, Henry W. *Aftermath of War: Experiences of a Quaker Relief Officer...* 1982. Morningside. 1st ed. 257p. cloth. A17. $20.00

HAMILTON, James. *Arthur Rackham: A Biography.* 1990. Arcade. 1st Am ed. folio. F/F. B17. $37.50

HAMILTON, Jane. *Book of Ruth.* 1988. Ticknor Fields. ARC/1st ed. F/F. B4. $350.00

HAMILTON, Jane. *Map of the World.* 1994. Doubleday. 1st ed. F/F. M23. $40.00

HAMILTON, Nan. *Shape of Fear.* 1986. Dodd Mead. 1st ed. VG/VG. P3. $15.00

HAMILTON, Virginia. *All Jahdu Story Book.* 1991. Harcourt Brace. 1st ed. ils Moser. AN/dj. C8. $25.00

HAMILTON, Virginia. *Drylongso.* 1992. Harcourt Brace. 1st ed. AN/dj. C8. $35.00

HAMILTON, Virginia. *Gathering.* 1981. Greenwillow. 1st ed. F/F. B4. $65.00

HAMILTON, W.C. *Statistics in Physical Science.* 1964. Ronald. 1st ed. 230p. F. D8. $20.00

HAMILTON & ROBBE-GRILLET. *Dreams of a Young Girl.* 1971. Morrow. 1st ed. 51 photos. NF/dj. S9. $150.00

HAMILTON. *Arthur Rackham: A Biography.* 1990. ils. 199p. F/F. A4. $35.00

HAMLIN, Percy Gatling. *Old Bald Head (General RS Ewell): Portrait of a Soldier.* 1940. Strasburg, VA. 1st ed. 216p. cloth. NF. M8. $250.00

HAMLIN, William Lee. *True Story of Billy the Kid.* 1959. Caldwell. 1st ed. ils/pl/glossary. 380p. NF. E1. $60.00

HAMMERSTEIN & RODGERS. *South Pacific.* 1949. Random. 1st ed. F/VG. B4. $150.00

HAMMERTON. *George Meredith: His Life & Art...* 1971. np. revised. 55 ils. VG. A4. $25.00

HAMMETT, Dashiell. *Adventures of Sam Spade.* 1945. World. 1st ed. VG/VG. M22. $45.00

HAMMETT, Dashiell. *Big Knockover.* nd. BOMC. VG/fair. P3. $10.00

HAMMETT, Dashiell. *Blood Money.* 1943. Tower. VG. P3. $25.00

HAMMETT, Dashiell. *Creeps by Night.* 1931. John Day. 1st ed. VG. P3. $250.00

HAMMETT, Dashiell. *Creeps by Night.* 1944. Forum. VG. P3. $25.00

HAMMETT, Dashiell. *Dashiell Hammett Omnibus.* nd. Grosset Dunlap. G. P3. $12.00

HAMMETT, Dashiell. *Dashiell Hammett Story Omnibus.* 1966. London. 1st ed. F/NF. A11. $50.00

HAMMETT, Dashiell. *Five Complete Novels.* 1980. Avenel. VG. P3. $13.00

HAMMETT, Dashiell. *Glass Key.* 1945. Knopf. 2nd ed. VG/VG. P3. $25.00

HAMMETT, Dashiell. *Maltese Falcon.* 1934. Modern Lib. 1st ed. NF. M22. $30.00

HAMMETT, Dashiell. *Maltese Falcon.* 1983. San Francisco. Arion. 1/400. silver emb leather. F/mailer. w/prospectus. A11. $400.00

HAMMETT, Dashiell. *Novels of Dashiell Hammett.* nd. BC. VG/VG. P3. $10.00

HAMMETT, Dashiell. *Red Harvest.* 1929. Knopf. 1st ed. author's 1st book. NF. C2. $400.00

HAMMETT, Dashiell. *Thin Man.* 1934. Knopf. 1st ed. G. P3. $75.00

HAMMETT, Dashiell. *Woman in the Dark.* 1988. Knopf. F/F. P3. $16.00

HAMMETT, Dashiell. *Woman in the Dark.* 1988. London. Headline. 1st hc/1st Eng ed. intro RB Parker. F/F. M22. $20.00

HAMMETT, Ralph Warner. *Romanesque Architecture of Western Europe.* 1927. np. photos. VG-. M17. $50.00

HAMMIL, Joel. *Limbo.* 1980. Arbor. 1st ed. VG/VG. P3. $13.00

HAMMOND, Gerald. *Dog in the Dark.* 1989. St Martin. 1st ed. F/F. P3. $15.00

HAMMOND, Gerald. *Home To Roost.* 1991. St Martin. 1st ed. F/F. P3. $17.00

HAMMOND, Gerald. *Stray Shot.* 1988. St Martin. 1st ed. NF/NF. P3. $15.00

HAMMOND, Lawrence. *Movie Treasury Thriller Movies.* 1974. Octopus. VG/VG. P3. $15.00

HAMMOND, Michael. *Among the Hunted.* nd. BC. VG/VG. P3. $5.00

HAMMOND, Michael. *Gathering of Wolves.* 1975. Doubleday. 1st ed. VG/VG. P3. $12.00

HAMMOND, S.H. *Hunting Adventures in the Northern Wilds.* 1856. Derby Jackson. 4 hand-colored pl. gilt bl bdg. fair. P12. $60.00

HAMMOND & HAMMOND. *Dodge City Story.* 1964. Indianapolis. 1st ed. ils. juvenile. 51p. F/chip. E1. $20.00

HAMNER, Earl Jr. *Fifty Roads to Town.* 1953. NY. 1st ed. NF/VG. A11. $65.00

HAMNER, Laura. *Night 'n Hitch.* 1958. Dallas. 1/1000. sgn. ils/maps/index/tables. 350p. F. E1. $90.00

HAMNER, Laura. *Short Grass & Longhorns.* 1943. Norman. 1st ed. VG/G. B5. $30.00

HAMSON, Marie. *Norwegian Family.* 1934. Atlantic Monthly. ils Elsa Jemne. 343p. G+. P2. $15.00

HANAFORD, Phebe. *Abraham Lincoln: His Life & Public Service.* 1904. np. 12mo. 277p. G. T3. $15.00

HANAUER, Elsie. *Old West: People & Places.* 1969. Cranbury, NJ. 1st ed. ils. 169p. F/VG. E1. $30.00

HANCE, Robert A. *Destination Earth II.* 1977. Vantage. VG/VG. P3. $10.00

HANCER. *Paperback Price Guide.* 1982. np. revised. 390p. F/wrp. A4. $25.00

HAND, Learned. *Spirit of Liberty.* 1964. np. Bahr. 6p. gr prt wrp. M11. $45.00

HANDLER, Hans. *Spanish Riding School.* 1972. McGraw Hill. 1st Am ed. VG/VG. O3. $195.00

HANDLER, Jerome S. *Guide to Source Materials for the Study of Barbados History.* 1971. Carbondale. VG. O7. $20.00

HANDY, E.S.C. *Marquesan Legends.* 1930. Honolulu. VG/wrp. O7. $65.00

HANDY, W.C. *Father of the Blues.* 1941. NY. pres. G. B5. $150.00

HANES, Bailey C. *Bill Doolin, Outlaw.* 1968. Norman. 1st ed. sgn. intro Ramon F Adams. photos. F/F. E1. $40.00

HANES, Leigh. *Songs of the New Hercules & Other Poems.* 1930. Humphries. sgn. VG/VG. B10. $12.00

HANF, Walter. *Mexico.* 1967. Rand McNally. 4to. 50 pl. 136p. F. T10. $25.00

HANFF, Helen. *Duchess of Bloomsbury Street.* 1973. Phil. 1st ed. VG. B5. $25.00

HANIGHEN, Frank C. *Santa Anna: The Napoleon of the West.* 1934. NY. 1st ed. 326p. F/chip. E1. $40.00

HANKE, Louis. *Bartolome Arzans de Orsua y Vela's History of Potosi.* 1965. Providence. VG. O7. $65.00

HANKINS, Marie Louise. *Women of New York.* 1861. NY. self pub. 1st ed. 8vo. 354p. cloth. VG. T10. $150.00

HANKINS, Samuel W. *Simple Story of a Soldier.* 1912. Nashville, TN. 1st ed. 63p. VG/prt wrp/clamshell case. M8. $950.00

HANKS, Keith. *Falk.* 1972. Cassell. 1st ed. NF/NF. P3. $20.00

HANKS, O.T. *History of Captain BF Benton's Company...* 1984. Austin, TX. 1st ed. 1/300. F/prt wrp. M8. $45.00

HANLEY, James. *Boy.* 1932. Knopf. 1st Am ed. VG/clip. H4. $75.00

HANLEY, James. *Men in Darkness: Five Stories.* 1932. Knopf. 1st ed. author's 1st book. NF/NF. C2. $200.00

HANNA, A.J. *Prince in Their Midst: Adventurous Life of Achille Murat...* 1946. OK U. 2nd. 275p. cloth. VG/dj. M20. $15.00

HANNA, Melvin W. *Quantum Mechanics in Chemistry.* 1969 (1965). NY. WA Benjamin. 2nd. 8vo. 260p. VG. K5. $22.00

HANNA & HANNA. *Florida's Golden Sands.* 1950. Bobbs Merrill. sgns. 8vo. 5 maps. 429p. G. B11. $35.00

HANNAH, Barry. *Airships.* 1978. Knopf. 1st ed. author's 3rd novel. F/F. B4. $125.00

HANNAH, Barry. *Bats Out of Hell.* 1993. Boston. 1st ed. F/F. V4. $40.00

HANNAU, H.W. *In the Coral Reefs of the Caribbean, Bahamas, Florida...* 1974. Miami. Argos. ils. NF/G. D8. $12.00

HANNEMAN. *Ernest Hemingway: A Comprehensive Bibliography.* 1969. ils. 582p. F. A4. $95.00

HANNON, Ezra; see Hunter, Evan.

HANNUM, Alberta. *Paint the Wind.* 1958. Viking. 1st ed. 8vo. 206p. F/dj. T10. $40.00

HANRAHAN. *Works of Maurice Sendak, 1947-1994.* 1995. np. ils. 105p. ES. F/F. A4. $85.00

HANSBERRY, Lorraine. *Sign in Sidney Brustein's Window.* 1965. Random. 1st ed. NF/dj. B4. $225.00

HANSEN, Harry. *Chicago.* 1942. NY. 1st ed. Rivers of Am series.. 342p. NF. E1. $25.00

HANSEN, Joseph. *Gravedigger.* 1982. HRW. 1st ed. F/F. P3. $20.00

HANSEN, Joseph. *Obedience.* 1988. Mysterious. 1st ed. VG/VG. P3. $20.00

HANSEN, Joseph. *Skinflick.* 1979. HRW. 1st ed. F/F. P3. $15.00

HANSEN, Joseph. *Troublemaker.* 1975. Harper. 1st ed. VG/VG. P3. $25.00

HANSEN, Oskar J.W. *Chien-Mi-Lo: A Satirical Prose Fantasy...* 1927. Chicago. Nordic. 1/700. photos. 41p. VG. B10. $20.00

HANSEN, Robert P. *Back to the Wall.* 1957. Mill Morrow. 1st ed. VG/torn. P3. $15.00

HANSEN, Robert P. *Deadly Purpose.* 1958. Mill Morrow. 1st ed. VG/VG. P3. $20.00

HANSEN, Robert P. *There's Always a Payoff.* 1959. Mill Morrow. VG. P3. $15.00

HANSEN, Robert P. *Trouble Comes Double.* 1954. Mill Morrow. 1st ed. VG/G. P3. $20.00

HANSEN, Ron. *Assassination of Jesse James by the Coward Robert Ford.* 1983. Knopf. 1st ed. 8vo. 304p. F/dj. T10. $35.00

HANSEN, Ron. *Desperadoes.* 1979. Knopf. 1st ed. sgn. NF/F. B4. $100.00

HANSFORD, Charles. *Poems of...* 1961. UNC. edit Servies/Dolmetsch. VG. B10. $12.00

HANSHEW, Thomas W. *Riddle of the Purple Emperor.* nd. McKinlay Stone MacKenzie. VG. P3. $12.00

HANSON, Charles. *Plains Rifle.* 1960. NY. rpt. ils. F/scuff. E1. $40.00

HANSON, Earl. *New Worlds Emerging.* 1949. DSP. 1st ed. inscr. 8vo. 385p. map ep. F/VG. B11. $45.00

HANSON, Earl. *South From the Spanish Main.* 1967. Delacorte. 1st ed. 463p. dj. F3. $25.00

HANSON, Joseph Mills. *Conquest of the Missouri...* 1909. Chicago. 1st ed. ils/map. 458p. F. E1. $100.00

HANSON, Raus McDill. *Virginia Place Names, Derivations, Historical Uses.* 1969. McClure. 1st ed. 253p. F/F. B10. $20.00

HANSON, Rick. *Spare Parts.* 1994. Kensington. 1st ed. author's 1st book. NF/F. H11. $20.00

HANSON & HANSON. *Verlaine: Fool of God.* 1957. NY. 1st ed. 394p. F/F. A17. $15.00

HANSON. *Peter Pan Chronicles: Nearly 100-Year History...* 1993. np. 4to. photos. 288p. F/F. A4. $35.00

HANTZCHEL-CLAIRMONT, W. *Die Praxis des Moderen Maschinebaus.* nd. Berlin. CA Weller. 2 vol. folio. ils/pl. VG. T10. $900.00

HANWAY, J. Edwin. *Memoirs of J Edwin Hanway.* 1942. Douglas, WY. inscr/dtd. photos. 246p. F. E1. $85.00

HANWAY, Jonas. *Historical Account of the British Trade Over Caspian...* 1753. London. 4 vol in 3. ils/fld maps. full leather (rpr). B5. $400.00

HAPGOOD, Charles H. *Maps of the Ancient Sea Kings.* 1966. Chilton. 1st ed. ils. 315p. VG/dj. W1. $45.00

HAPGOOD, Hutchins. *Spirit of the Ghetto: Studies of the Jewish Quarter in NY.* 1902. Funk Wagnall. 1st ed. ils Jacob Epstein. NF. B4. $200.00

HARASZTHY, A. *Grape Culture, Wines & Wine-Making.* 1862. NY. ils. VG. M17. $600.00

HARBINSON, W.A. *Dream Maker.* 1992. NY. Walker. 1st ed. F/F. H11. $25.00

HARBISON, POTTERTON & SHEEHY. *Irish Art & Architecture.* 1978. Thames Hudson. 1st ed. ils. 272p. F/dj. T10. $75.00

HARBORD, J.B. *Glossary of Navigation.* 1938. Glasgow. Brn Ferguson. 4th. 451p. VG. T7. $40.00

HARBORD, James G. *Leaves From a War Diary.* 1925. NY. 2nd. 407p. VG. E1. $35.00

HARDEN, Henry. *Capture of Jefferson Davis: A Narrative...* 1898. Madison, WI. Tracy Gibbs. 1st ed. 105p. cloth. M8. $250.00

HARDEN, Maximilian. *World Portraits: Character Sketches of Famous Men...* 1911. Edinburgh. 1st ed. 425p. gilt cloth. VG. A17. $12.50

HARDEN, Victoria. *Inventing the Nih: Federal Biomedical Research Policy...* 1986. Baltimore. 1st ed. 274p. dj. A13. $30.00

HARDIE, Martin. *English-Coloured Books.* 1906. Putnam. 1st ed. 27 pl. 340p. VG. T10. $200.00

HARDIE. *British School of Etching.* 1921. Prt Collector Club. VG. D2. $40.00

HARDIN, John Wesley. *Life of John Wesley Hardin As Written by Himself.* 1961. Norman, OK. 1st WFL ed. 12mo. ils. F/F. T10. $35.00

HARDIN, John Wesley. *Life of...* 1896. Seguin, TX. 1st ed. 144p. F/wrp case. E1. $250.00

HARDIN & HEDDEN. *Light But Efficient.* 1973. Dallas. 1st ed. 104p. F/F. E1. $45.00

HARDING, Addie Clark. *America Rides the Liners.* 1956. Coward McCann. xl. G. A16. $17.50

HARDING, Addie Clark. *America Rides the Liners.* 1956. NY. Coward McCann. 1st ed. inscr. 8vo. 271p. VG/VG. B11. $50.00

HARDING, Bertita. *Phantom Crown.* 1934. Bobbs Merrill. 1st ed. sgn. 8vo. 381p. gilt bl cloth. VG. B11. $25.00

HARDING, George L. *Published Writings of Carl Irving Wheat.* 1960. San Francisco. 1/350. AN/wrp. O7. $85.00

HARDING, Paul. *Nightingale Gallery.* 1991. Morrow. 1st ed. F/F. P3. $20.00

HARDING, Todd; see Reynolds, Mack.

HARDINGE, George. *Winter's Crimes II.* 1980. St Martin. 1st ed. F/F. P3. $15.00

HARDWICK, Elizabeth. *Ghostly Lover.* 1945. Harcourt Brace. 1st ed. inscr. author's 1st book. fair. B4. $100.00

HARDWICK, Michael. *Prisoner of the Devil.* 1980. Proteus. 3rd ed. VG/VG. P3. $15.00

HARDWICK, Michael. *Private Life of Dr. Watson.* 1983. Dutton. 1st ed. F/F. P3. $25.00

HARDWICK, Michael. *Revenge of the Hound.* 1987. Villard. 1st ed. F/F. H11. $25.00

HARDWICK, Mollie. *Dreaming Damozel.* 1991. St Martin. 1st ed. F/F. P3. $16.00

HARDWICK, Mollie. *Malice Domestic.* 1986. Century. 1st ed. F/F. P3. $20.00

HARDWICK, Mollie. *Uneaseful Death.* 1988. St Martin. 1st ed. F/F. P3. $15.00

HARDWICK & HARDWICK. *Sherlock Holmes Companion.* 1962. John Murray. 1st ed. VG/VG. P3. $40.00

HARDY, Adam; see Bulmer, Kenneth.

HARDY, Allison. *Kate, Bender, Kansas Murderess.* 1944. Girard, KS. 24p. G/wrp. E1. $30.00

HARDY, Frederic. *Parlour Magic.* ca 1884. London. Warne. 24mo. 94p. aeg. cloth. F. B24. $150.00

HARDY, Lindsay. *Nightshade Ring.* 1954. Appleton Century Crofts. VG/VG. P3. $10.00

HARDY, Phil. *Encyclopedia of Western Movies.* 1983. Woodbury. 1st ed. VG/VG. P3. $45.00

HARDY, Robin. *Wicker Man.* 1978. Crown. 1st ed. F/F. P3. $20.00

HARDY, Thomas. *Jude the Obscure.* 1896. NY. 1st Am ed. F. C6. $150.00

HARDY, Thomas. *Wessex Poems.* 1899. NY. 1st Am ed. NF. A15. $100.00

HARDY, Thomas. *Wessex Tales: Strange, Lively & Commonplace.* 1888. London. Macmillan. 1st ed. 2 vol. 8vo. 1st bdg. NF. B24. $1,500.00

HARDY, William P. *Chronology of the Old West.* 1988. NY. 1st ed. sgn. photos/biblio/index, 225p. F/F. E1. $45.00

HARDY & PINION. *One Rare Fair Woman: Thomas Hardy's Letters...* 1972. Miami U. ils. 221p. F/VG. A4. $55.00

HARE, Augustus J.C. *Life & Letters of Frances Baroness Bunsen.* nd. Routledge. 2 vol in 1. ils. gilt blk cloth. VG. T10. $50.00

HARE, Rosalie. *Voyage of the Caroline.* 1927. Longman Gr. ils. 308p. VG. T7. $65.00

HARGRAVE. *History of Playing Cards & Bibliography of Cards & Gaming.* 1930. 4to. ils/pl. 468p. VG. A4. $350.00

HARGREAVES, H.A. *North by 2000.* 1975. Peter Martin. 1st ed. F/F. P3. $25.00

HARGREAVES, Reginald. *Narrow Seas.* 1959. London. Sidgwick Jackson. 1st ed. G/tattered. A16. $25.00

HARGREAVES. *Anne Inez McCaffrey: 40 Years of Publishing...* 1992. np. 1/500. sgns. ils. 346p. F. A4. $200.00

HARIBURTON, R. *New Worlds To Conquer.* 1929. Indianapolis. 1st ed. sgn. VG/VG. B5. $25.00

HARING, C.H. *Spanish Empire in America.* 1947. NY. 1st ed. VG. O7. $75.00

HARING, J.V. *Hand of Hauptman: Handwriting Expert Tells Story...* 1937. Plainfield, NJ. 1st ed. ils. 362p. VG/VG. B5. $45.00

HARINGTON, Donald. *Cockroaches of Stay More.* 1989. HBJ. 1st ed. F/F. P3. $20.00

HARK, Ann. *Story of the Pennsylvania Dutch.* 1943. Harper. 1st ed. 4to. VG. M5. $30.00

HARKER, A. *Metamorphism: A Study of Transformations of Rock Masses.* 1939. Dutton. 2nd. 185 diagrams. 362p. F. D8. $20.00

HARKINS, John E. *Metropolis of the American Nile.* 1982. Woodland Hills, CA. 1st ed. 4to. 224p. F/dj. T10. $35.00

HARKNESS & MOODY. *Ils Encyclopedia of Roses.* 1992. Portland. 304p. AN/dj. B26. $40.00

HARLAN, Caleb. *Ida Randolph of Virginia: A Historical Novel in Verse.* 1890. Phil. Ferris. 2nd. 101p. G+. B10. $25.00

HARLAN, George H. *San Francisco Bay Ferryboats.* 1967. Howell-North. VG/dj. A16. $17.50

HARLEY, J.B. *Mapping the American Revolutionary War.* 1978. Chicago. ils. AN/dj. O7. $55.00

HARLEY, John. *Old Vegetable Neurotics: Hamlock, Opium, Belladonna...* 1869. London. 355p. red cloth. G. B14. $195.00

HARLOW, Alvin F. *Old Waybills.* 1934. NY. 1st ed. ils/photos/biblio/index. 503p. F. E1. $125.00

HARLOW, Neal. *California Conquered: War & Peace on the Pacific...* 1982. Berkeley. ils/maps. VG+/dj. O7. $55.00

HARLOW, Neal. *Maps of Pueblo Lands of San Diego 1602-1874.* 1987. Dawson. 1/375. sgn. 25 maps. F. O7. $300.00

HARLOW, Neal. *Maps of San Francisco Bay From Spanish Discovery...* 1950. San Francisco. BC of CA. 1/375. 21 maps. F. O7. $1,050.00

HARMAN, Henry E. *Idle Dreams of an Idle Day.* 1917. Columbia, SC. sgn. 8vo. VG. B11. $85.00

HARMAN, S.W. *Cherokee Bill, the Oklahoma Outlaw.* 1954. Houston, TX. photos, 63p. VG/wrp. E1. $35.00

HARMER, Michael. *Forgotten Hospital: An Essay.* 1982. Chichester, Eng. 170p. VG. A13. $25.00

HARMON, Nolan B. *Famous Case of Myra Clark Gaines.* 1946. LSU. 1st ed. ils. 481p. VG/dj. B18. $20.00

HARNESS, Charles L. *Krono.* 1988. Watts. 1st ed. F/F. P3. $20.00

HARPENDING, Asbury. *Great Diamond Hoax & Other Stirring Incidents...* 1958. Norman. new ed/1st prt. 211p. F/VG. E1. $20.00

HARPENDING, Asbury. *Great Diamond Hoax.* 1958. OK U. 1st ed thus. 211p. VG/dj. M20. $15.00

HARPER, Charles G. *Smugglers: Picturesque Chapters in Story of Ancient Craft.* 1909. London. Chapman Hall. 1st ed. ils. 252p. teg. T7. $110.00

HARPER, Frank C. *Pittsburgh: Forge of the Universe.* 1957. NY. 1st ed. 320p. VG+/dj. B18. $22.50

HARPER, George W. *Gypsy Earth.* 1982. Doubleday. F/F. P3. $15.00

HARPER, R.G. *Observations on Dispute Between the United States & France.* 1798. Phil. 8vo. 110p. leather. G. T3. $52.00

HARPER, Virginia Jones. *Time Steals Softly.* 1974. Vantage. 1st ed. 250p. VG/dj. B18. $15.00

HARPER, W. *Uncle Sam's Story Book.* 1944. McKay. 1st ed thus. ils Grace Paull. VG+/VG. P2. $20.00

HARRINGTON, Alan. *Revelations of Dr Modesto.* 1955. Knopf. 1st ed. author's 1st novel. NF/dj. B24. $100.00

HARRINGTON, E. Burke. *Reports of Cases Determined in the Court of Chancery...* 1882. Chicago. Callaghan. 2nd. contemporary sheep. M11. $125.00

HARRINGTON, Fred H. *Hanging Judge.* 1951. Caldwell. 1st ed. ils/photos/notes/maps/index. 204p. F/NF. E1. $70.00

HARRINGTON, James. *Oceana & Other Works.* 1747. London. Millar. 3rd. folio. modern quarter calf. F. T10. $450.00

HARRINGTON, William. *Cromwell File.* 1986. St Martin. 1st ed. NF/VG. N4. $17.50

HARRINGTON, William. *Virus.* 1991. Morrow. 1st ed. F/F. M22. $15.00

HARRIS, Albert W. *Blood of the Arab: The World's Greatest War Horse.* 1941. Chicago. 1st ed. 4to. O3. $95.00

HARRIS, Alfred. *Baroni.* 1975. Putnam. 1st ed. VG/VG. P3. $15.00

HARRIS, Benjamin Butler. *Gila Trail.* 1960. Norman. 1st ed. photos. 175p. F/F. E1. $35.00

HARRIS, Brayton. *Age of the Battleship: 1890-1922.* 1965. NY. 2nd. 212p. NF/VG. E1. $25.00

HARRIS, Chauncy D. *Bibliography of Geography. Part I.* 1976. Chicago. VG/wrp. O7. $15.00

HARRIS, Chauncy D. *Geographical Bibliography for American Libraries.* 1985. WA. VG. O7. $25.00

HARRIS, Chauncy D. *Soviet Geography.* 1962. NY. VG. O7. $65.00

HARRIS, Corra. *Happy Pilgrimage.* 1927. Houghton Mifflin. 310p. G+. B10. $12.00

HARRIS, Frank. *Bernard Shaw.* 1931. Gollancz. 2nd ed. VG. P3. $18.00

HARRIS, Frank. *Contemporary Portraits, Fourth Series.* 1923. NY. 1st ed. VG. A17. $15.00

HARRIS, Frank. *My Life & Loves.* 1922. Frank Harris. G. P3. $25.00

HARRIS, Geraldine. *Children of the Wind.* 1982. Greenwillow. 1st ed. VG/G. P3. $13.00

HARRIS, Geraldine. *Prince of the Godborn.* 1982. Greenwillow. 1st ed. VG/G. P3. $13.00

HARRIS, Henry. *Morel Soldiers: Pleasures & Treasures.* 1959. NY. 1st ed. 122p. VG/box. B5. $30.00

HARRIS, Herbert. *John Creasey's Crime Collection, 1983.* 1983. St Martin. 1st ed. xl. dj. P3. $8.00

HARRIS, Herbert. *John Creasey's Mystery Bedside Book.* 1967. Hodder Stoughton. 1st ed. VG/VG. P3. $25.00

HARRIS, Joel Chandler. *Aaron in the Wildwoods.* 1897. 1st ed. ils Oliver Herford. VG+. S13. $50.00

HARRIS, Joel Chandler. *Balaam & His Master.* 1891. Houghton Mifflin. 1st ed. 293p. VG. B10. $100.00

HARRIS, Joel Chandler. *Chronicles of Aunt Minervy Ann.* 1899. Scribner. 1st ed. 210p. G. B10. $50.00

HARRIS, Joel Chandler. *Daddy Jake the Runaway & Other Stories Told After Dark.* 1889. Century. 1st ed. ils. 145p. G. D1. $185.00

HARRIS, Joel Chandler. *Daddy Jake the Runaway & Short Stories Told After Dark.* 1896 (1889). Century. ils Kemble. 198p. VG. B10. $50.00

HARRIS, Joel Chandler. *Free Joe & Other Georgian Sketches.* 1887. Scribner. 1st ed. 236p. B5/B10. $75.00

HARRIS, Joel Chandler. *Gabriel Tolliver: A Story of Reconstruction.* 1902. McClure Phillips. 1st ed/2nd imp. 448p. B10/S13. $65.00

HARRIS, Joel Chandler. *Jump!* 1986. HBJ. 1st ed. ils Barry Moser. 40p. cream brd/beige spine. F/F. T5. $48.00

HARRIS, Joel Chandler. *Making of a Statesman.* 1902. McClure Phillips. 1st ed. 247p. VG. B10. $50.00

HARRIS, Joel Chandler. *Mr Rabbit at Home.* 1895. 1st ed. ils Oliver Herford. VG+. S13. $50.00

HARRIS, Joel Chandler. *On the Wing of Occasions.* 1900. Doubleday Page. 1st ed/A bdg. 310p. VG. B10. $65.00

HARRIS, Joel Chandler. *Plantation Pageants.* 1900 (1899). Houghton Mifflin. ils E Boyd Smith. 247p. G+. B10. $50.00

HARRIS, Joel Chandler. *Shadow Between His Shoulder Blades.* 1907. 1st ed. ils George Harding. VG+. S13. $40.00

HARRIS, Joel Chandler. *Sister Jane: Her Friends & Acquaintances.* 1896. Houghton Mifflin. 1st ed. 363p. G+. B10. $35.00

HARRIS, Joel Chandler. *Stories of Georgia.* 1896. 1st ed. VG. S13. $40.00

HARRIS, Joel Chandler. *Story of Aaron.* 1896. 1st state. ils Oliver Herford. NF. S13. $85.00

HARRIS, Joel Chandler. *Tar-Baby & Other Rhymes of Uncle Remus.* 1905 (1904). Appleton. 4th. ils AB Frost/EW Kemble. G. B10. $45.00

HARRIS, Joel Chandler. *Told by Uncle Remus: New Stories of the Old Plantation.* 1905 (1904). McClure Phillips. 2nd. ils Frost/Conde/Verbeck. 295p. VG-. B10. $85.00

HARRIS, Joel Chandler. *Uncle Remus & His Friends.* 1892. Houghton Mifflin. ils AB Frost. 357p. VG. B10. $75.00

HARRIS, Joel Chandler. *Uncle Remus & His Friends.* 1899. Houghton Mifflin. 12mo. ils AB Frost. VG. B17. $45.00

HARRIS, Joel Chandler. *Uncle Remus Returns.* 1918. Houghton Mifflin. early prt. 174p. VG. B10. $75.00

HARRIS, Joel Chandler. *Uncle Remus; or, Mr Fox, Mr Rabbit & Mr Terrapin.* nd. Routledge. ils AT Elwes. gilt gr cloth. VG/partial. M5. $48.00

HARRIS, Joel Chandler. *Uncle Remus: His Songs & His Sayings.* 1957. LEC. 1/1500. ils/sgn Seong Moy. F/NF case. T10. $90.00

HARRIS, Joel Chandler. *Uncle Remus: His Songs & Sayings/Folklore of Old Plantation.* 1881. Appleton. 1st ed/3rd state. NF. C2. $300.00

HARRIS, John. *Little Grammarian; or, Easy Guide to the Parts of Speech...* 1828. London. John Harris. 1st ed. 12mo. 175p. NF. B24. $350.00

HARRIS, Laura. *Away We Go.* 1945. Garden City. 1st ed. sm 4to. unp. G. T5. $12.00

HARRIS, Lucien Jr. *Butterflies of Georgia.* 1974. Norman. 1st ed. inscr. 8vo. 326p. F/VG. B11. $50.00

HARRIS, MacDonald. *Hemingway's Suitcase.* 1990. Simon Schuster. 1st ed. F/F. M23. $20.00

HARRIS, Marilyn. *Portent.* 1980. Putnam. 1st ed. F/F. P3. $20.00

HARRIS, Mark. *Goy.* 1970. Dial. 1st ed. F/NF. B35. $50.00

HARRIS, Robert. *Fatherland.* 1992. Random. ARC. author's 1st novel. F. B35. $70.00

HARRIS, Steven Michael. *This Is My Trunk.* 1985. Atheneum. 1st ed. 4to. unp. F/F. C14. $12.00

HARRIS, Thomas. *Black Sunday.* nd. Putnam. VG/VG. P3. $18.00

HARRIS, Thomas. *Black Sunday.* 1975. Hodder Stoughton. 1st ed. VG/G. M22. $15.00

HARRIS, Thomas. *I'm OK — Your'e OK.* 1969. Harper Row. 1st ed. NF/NF. B35. $30.00

HARRIS, Thomas. *Red Dragon.* 1981. Putnam. 1st ed. F/NF. M23. $35.00

HARRIS, Thomas. *Red Dragon.* 1981. Putnam. 1st ed. NF/NF. M19. $25.00

HARRIS, Thomas. *Red Dragon.* 1981. Putnam. 1st ed. VG/NF. M22. $20.00

HARRIS, Thomas. *Silence of the Lambs.* 1988. St Martin. 1st ed. F/F. C2. $75.00

HARRIS, Thomas. *Silence of the Lambs.* 1988. St Martin. 1st ed. VG/G. P3. $20.00

HARRIS, Virgil M. *Ancient, Curious & Famous Wills.* 1911. Boston. Little Brn. gilt bl cloth. M11. $75.00

HARRIS, Walter. *Clovis.* 1970. Putnam. 1st ed. VG/VG. P3. $20.00

HARRIS, Wilson. *Guyana Quartet.* 1985. London. Faber. 1st ed. F/dj. C2. $50.00

HARRIS & KENT. *X-Raying the Pharaohs.* 1973. Scribner. 8vo. ils. 195p. F/dj. T10. $25.00

HARRIS & KURTZ. *Adept.* 1992. Severn. 1st world hc ed. F/F. G10. $15.00

HARRIS & KURTZ. *Dagger Magic.* 1995. Ace. 1st ed. F/F. G10. $10.00

HARRIS & RAINEY. *Cowboy: Six-Shooters, Songs & Sex.* 1976. Norman. new ed/1st prt. photos. 167p. VG/wrp. E1. $25.00

HARRISEE, Henry. *Decouverte et Evolution Cartographique de Terre-Neuve...* 1968. Ridgewood. Gregg. M. O7. $75.00

HARRISON, Bob. *Naked New York.* (1961). Paragon. probable 1st ed. 183p. F/dj. B22. $4.50

HARRISON, C.F. *English Manuscripts of the 14th Century.* 1937. London. The Studio. pl. VG/G+. M17. $37.50

HARRISON, C.H. *Summer's Outing & Old Man's Story.* 1891. Chicago. 1st ed. VG. A15. $75.00

HARRISON, Chip; see Block, Lawrence.

HARRISON, Colin. *Break & Enter.* 1990. Crown. 1st ed. NF/NF. P3. $22.00

HARRISON, Constance Cary. *Bachelor Maid.* 1894. Century. 1st ed. 224p. VG. B10. $75.00

HARRISON, Constance Cary. *Count & the Congressman.* 1908. Cupples Leon. 1st ed. 300p. VG/poor. B10. $50.00

HARRISON, Constance Cary. *Edelweiss of the Sierras, Golden-Rod & Other Tales.* 1892. Harper. 1st ed. 209p. VG. B10. $65.00

HARRISON, Edward. *Masks of the Universe.* 1985. Macmillan. 1st prt. G/VG. K5. $15.00

HARRISON, Florence. *Tennyson's Guinevere & Other Poems.* 1912. Blackie. 1st ed. 4to. ils. gilt cream cloth. NF. M5. $250.00

HARRISON, Fred. *Hell Holes & Hangings.* 1968. Clarendon, TX. 1st ed. photos/biblio. 170p. F/scuff. E1. $38.00

HARRISON, Frederic. *On Jurisprudence & the Conflict of Laws.* 1919. Oxford. Clarendon. orig cloth. M11. $125.00

HARRISON, Gordon A. *Cross-Channel Attack.* 1951. WA. 1st ed. ils. 519p. G. B18. $50.00

HARRISON, H. *Great Balls of Fire!* 1977. ils. 118p. F/F. M13. $28.00

HARRISON, Harry. *Adventures of the Stainless Steel Rat.* nd. BC. VG/VG. P3. $10.00

HARRISON, Harry. *One King's Way.* 1995. Tor. 1st ed. F/F. P3. $24.00

HARRISON, Harry. *Plague From Space.* 1965. Doubleday. 1st ed. VG/VG. P3. $75.00

HARRISON, Harry. *Skyfall.* 1977. Atheneum. 1st ed. NF/NF. M19. $50.00

HARRISON, Harry. *Spacecraft in Fact & Fiction.* 1979. Exeter. 1st ed. NF/NF. P3. $20.00

HARRISON, Harry. *Stainless Steel Rat for President.* 1983. Severn. 1st ed. VG/VG. P3. $20.00

HARRISON, Harry. *Stainless Steel Rat Gets Drafted.* 1987. Bantam. 1st ed. F/F. P3. $15.00

HARRISON, Harry. *Stainless Steel Rat's Revenge.* 1970. Walker. 1st ed. xl. dj. P3. $6.00

HARRISON, Harry. *West of Eden.* 1984. Bantam. hc. VG/VG. P3. $20.00

HARRISON, Harry. *Winter in Eden.* 1986. Bantam. 1st ed. sgn. F/F. P3. $25.00

HARRISON, Henry Sydnor. *Queed.* 1911. Houghton Mifflin. 8th. 430p. G. B10. $10.00

HARRISON, Jack. *Famous Saddle Horses & Distinguished Horsemen.* 1933. Columbia. 1st ed. VG. O3. $350.00

HARRISON, Jim. *Dalva.* 1988. Dutton. 1st ed. F/NF. H11. $25.00

HARRISON, Jim. *Selected & New Poems 1961-1981.* 1982. Delacorte. 1st ed. 1/250. sgn. F/case. C2. $200.00

HARRISON, Jim. *Sundog.* 1984. Dutton. 1st ed. F/F. H11. $55.00

HARRISON, Jim. *Woman Lit by Fireflies.* 1990. Houghton Mifflin. 1st ed. F/clip. H11. $25.00

HARRISON, Kathryn. *Thicker Than Water.* 1991. Random. 1st ed. F/NF. H11. $40.00

HARRISON, M. Clifford. *Old Dominion Echoes.* 1960. Stone. 128p. VG. B10. $10.00

HARRISON, M. John. *Climbers.* 1989. Gollancz. 1st ed. F/F. P3. $18.00

HARRISON, M. John. *In Viriconium.* 1982. Gollancz. 1st ed. sgn. F/F. P3. $30.00

HARRISON, M. John. *Storm of Wings.* 1980. Doubleday. 1st ed. NF/NF. P3. $20.00

HARRISON, M. John. *Viriconium Nights.* 1985. Gollancz. 1st ed. sgn. F/F. P3. $25.00

HARRISON, Payne. *Storming Intrepid.* 1989. Crown. 1st ed. author's 1st book. F/F. H11. $30.00

HARRISON, Payne. *Thunder of Erebus.* 1991. Crown. 1st ed. F/F. H111. $20.00

HARRISON, Ray. *Counterfeit Murder.* 1986. Quartet Crime. 1st ed. VG/VG. P3. $22.00

HARRISON, Richard Edes. *Look at the World: Fortune Atlas for World Strategy.* 1944. Knopf. folio. F. O7. $45.00

HARRISON, Shirley. *Diary of Jack the Ripper.* 1993. Hyperion. hc. VG/VG. P3. $22.00

HARRISON, Stelle. *Gunsmith's Manual.* 1972 (1883). NY. facsimile. F. E1. $30.00

HARRISON, Whit; see Whittington, Harry.

HARRISON, William. *Roller Ball Murder.* 1974. Morrow. 1st ed. NF/NF. P3. $18.00

HARRISON & LOXTON. *Bird: Master of Flight.* 1993. np. ils/photos. 288p. F/F. A4. $50.00

HARRISON & STOVER. *Apeman, Spaceman.* 1968. Doubleday. 1st ed. VG/dj. P3. $20.00

HARRISON & TURNER. *Pre-Hispanic Maya Agriculture.* 1978. NM U. 1st ed. 414p. dj. F3. $35.00

HARRISON. *Books About Books.* 1943. np. ils. 264p. NF. A4. $35.00

HARROD, Harold L. *Mission Among the Blackfeet.* 1971. Nortman. 1st ed. photos. 218p. F/scuff. E1. $40.00

HARROD-EAGLES, Cynthia. *Orchestrated Death.* 1991. Scribner. 1st ed. author's 1st crime novel. F/F. H11/N4. $30.00

HARSTON, E.F. Buttemer. *Practice, Pleading & Evidence in the Courts...* 1877. San Francisco. Bancroft. contemporary sheep. M11. $125.00

HARSTON, J. Emmor. *Comanche Land.* 1963. San Antonio. 1st ed. 206p. F/F. E1. $25.00

HART, Alan. *Arafat: Terrorist or Peacemaker.* 1984. London. Sidgwick Jackson. 1st ed. pres. ils. 401p. NF/dj. W1. $20.00

HART, Frances Noyes. *Bellamy Trial.* 1940. Triangle. hc. VG. P3. $15.00

HART, Helen. *Mary Lee at Washington.* 1918. Whitman. 1st ed. 219p. VG/VG. A17. $9.50

HART, Henry H. *Venetian Adventurer.* 1947. Stanford. 3rd. VG. O7. $35.00

HART, Herbert M. *Old Forts of the Far West.* 1965. Seattle. 1st ed. inscr/dtd. 192p. F/worn. E1. $60.00

HART, Herbert M. *Pioneer Forts of the West.* 1967. Seattle. 1st ed. inscr/dtd. 192p. NF/dj. E1. $60.00

HART, Jerome. *In Our Second Country.* 1931. Pioneer. 1st ed. 454p. G. A17. $20.00

HART, John S. *Brief Exposition of the Constitution of the United States...* 1845. Phil. Butler Williams. 1st ed. M11. $150.00

HART, Josephine. *Damage.* 1991. Knopf. 1st Am ed. author's 1st novel. rem mk. F/NF. G10. $30.00

HART, Rhonda M. *Trellising. How To Grow Climbing Vegetables.* 1992. Pownal, VT. ils. AN/dj. B26. $16.00

HART, William S. *My Life East & West.* 1929. Houghton Mifflin. 1st ed. 8vo. NF. T10. $250.00

HART, William S. *My Life East & West.* 1929. NY. probable 2nd. inscr. photos. 363p. NF. E1. $350.00

HART, William S. *Order of Chanta Sutas, a Ritual.* 1925. Hollywood. 1st ed. 98p. leather. NF. E1. $150.00

HART & RICE. *National Portrait Gallery of Distinguished Americans.* 1859. Phil. 3 of 4 vol. brn full leather. VG. B30. $150.00

HART & TOLLERIS. *Big-Time Baseball.* 1950. Hart. photos. 192p. VG. A17. $20.00

HARTE, Bret. *Excelsior.* 1877. NY. Enoch Morgan's Sons. 1st ed/1st prt. 12mo. w/ad for Sapolio soap. F/wrp. B24. $450.00

HARTE, Bret. *Lost Galleon.* 1953. Grabhorn. VG. O7. $45.00

HARTE, Bret. *Pliocene Skull.* 1871. WA. 1st separate ed. ils/inscr EM Schaeffer. 20p. VG. C6. $325.00

HARTE, Bret. *Queen of the Pirate Isle.* 1886. Chatto Windus. 1st ed. ils. beige cloth. VG. D1. $300.00

HARTE, Bret. *Tales of the Gold Rush.* 1944. NY. LEC. ils/stn Fletcher Martin. full brn linen. NF/VG box. T10. $150.00

HARTFIELD, George. *Horse Brasses.* 1965. London. Schuman. 61p. G. O3. $25.00

HARTFORD PEACH SOCIETY. *First Annual Address Delivered Before...* 1829. Hartford. 24p. NF. M8. $250.00

HARTING, Emilie. *Literary Tour Guide to the United States.* 1978. Morrow. 1st ed. 218p. F. B22. $4.00

HARTLAUB, G.F. *Der Genius im Kinde: Zeichnungen und Malversuche Begabter...* 1922. Breslau. Ferdinand Hirt. 187p. prt yel cloth. G1. $37.50

HARTLEY, L.P. *Go-Between.* 1953. London. 1st ed. F/NF. C2. $100.00

HARTLEY, L.P. *Hireling.* 1957. Hamish Hamilton. 2nd ed. VG/VG. P3. $18.00

HARTLEY, Norman. *Earthjacket.* 1970. Walker. 1st ed. VG/G. P3. $15.00

HARTLEY, Norman. *Quicksilver.* 1979. Atheneum. 1st ed. VG/VG. P3. $15.00

HARTLEY. *History & Bibliography of Boxing Books...* nd. np. ils. 359p. F/F. A4. $65.00

HARTMANN, Walter L. *Introduction to the Cultivation of Orchids.* 1971. Mexico. photos/chart. 106p. F/dj. B26. $28.00

HARTNEY, Harold E. *Up & at 'Em.* 1940. Harrisburg, PA. 1st ed. ils. 333p. VG/worn. B18. $150.00

HARTSHORNE, Richard. *Nature of Geography.* 1939. Lancaster. VG. O7. $20.00

HARTWELL, DAvid G. *Foundations of Fear.* 1992. Tor. 1st ed. F/F. G10. $35.00

HARTWIG, G. *Subterranean World.* 1881. Longman Gr. new ed. 8vo. 3 maps. 522p. xl. T10. $75.00

HARVARD UNIVERSITIES PRESS. *Publications of Harvard University Press, Complete...* 1951. 4to. 149p. VG/wrp. A4. $45.00

HARVESTER, Simon. *Bamboo Screen.* 1968. Walker. 1st ed. NF/NF. P3. $15.00

HARVESTER, Simon. *Shadows in a Hidden Land.* 1966. Walker. 1st ed. VG/VG. P3. $20.00

HARVESTER, Simon. *Zion Road.* 1968. Walker. 1st ed. VG/G. P3. $10.00

HARVEY, Gideon. *Vanities of Philosophy & Physick.* 1702. London. 3rd. 318p. modern bdg. B14. $200.00

HARVEY, John. *Ghosts of a Chance.* 1992. Huddersfield. Smith/Doorstop. 1st ed. pb. sgn. F/wrp. T2. $15.00

HARVEY, John. *Lonely Hearts.* 1989. Holt. 1st Am ed. F/F. T2. $30.00

HARVEY, M. Elayn. *Warhaven.* 1987. Franklin Watts. 1st ed. F/F. P3. $16.00

HARVEY, N.P. *Rose in Britain.* 1951. London. photos/diagrams/glossary. VG/dj. B26. $22.00

HARVEY, William. *Circulation of the Blood & Other Writings...* 1977. London. trans Kenneth Franklin. 236p. xl. A13. $35.00

HARVEY. *Scottish Chapbook Literature.* 1971. rpt of 1903 ed. ils. 153p. F. A4. $45.00

HASFORD, Gustav. *Short Timers.* 1979. Harper Row. 1st ed. inscr/dtd 1979. NF/dj. S9. $500.00

HASKELL, Barbara. *Arthur Dove.* 1947-75.. San Francisco Mus Art. ils. 136p. cloth. dj. D2. $65.00

HASKELL, Barbara. *Marsden Hartley.* 1980. Whitney Mus. ils/photo. D2. $75.00

HASKELL, Daniel C. *American Historical Prints.* 1927. NY. VG. O7. $55.00

HASKELL, John. *Haskell Memoirs.* 1960. Putnam. 1st ed. 8vo. 176p. NF/dj. T10. $25.00

HASKELL & LATMORE. *Arthur Rackham: A Bibliography.* 1987. np. 117p. F/F. A4. $45.00

HASKINS, Francine. *I Remember 121.* 1991. San Francisco. Children's Book Pr. 1st ed. sgn. F/sans. B4. $65.00

HASKINS, Jim. *Voodoo & Hoodoo.* 1978. Stein Day. 1st ed. VG/VG. P3. $15.00

HASLAM, John. *Observations on Madness & Melancholy...* 1809. London. 2nd. 345p. half blk sheep/marbled brd. VG. B14. $600.00

HASLIP, Joan. *Crown of Mexico.* 1971. NY. 1st ed. 531p. F/F. E1. $25.00

HASPELS, C.H. Emilie. *Highlands of Phrygia. Sites & Monuments. Vol 1.* 1971. Princeton. 1st ed. 421p. VG. W1. $40.00

HASS, Hans. *Manta: Under the Red Sea With Spear & Camera.* 1953. Chicago. Rand McNally. 8vo. xl. VG/dj. W1. $12.00

HASSALL, John. *Dodge's Red Picture Book, Fairy Tales for Little Folk.* nd. Dodge. inscr. pict red brd. VG. M5. $95.00

HASSAUAREK, F. *Four Years Among Spanish-Americans.* 1868. Hurd Houghton. 401p. gilt spine. E3. $65.00

HASSELL, M.P. *Dynamics of Arthopod Predator-Prey Systems.* 1978. Princeton. 8vo. 237p. F/wrp. B1. $20.00

HASSIN, George B. *Histopathology of the Peripheral & Central Nervous Systems.* June 1933. Baltimore. Wood. 1st ed. ils. 491p. bl cloth. VG. B14. $55.00

HASSLER, Kenneth W. *Dream Squad.* 1970. Lenox Hill. 1st ed. VG/VG. P3. $13.00

HASSLER, William Woods. *AP Hill: Lee's Forgotten General.* 1962. Richmond. Garrett Massie. 2nd. 249p. cloth. NF/NF. M8. $45.00

HASSRICK, Peter. *Charles M Russell.* 1989. NY. 1st ed. 531p. F/F. E1. $50.00

HASSRICK, Peter. *Frederick Remington.* 1973. Abrams. 1st ed. 196p. linen spine/gilt paper brd. F/dj. T10. $125.00

HASSRICK, Peter. *Frederick Remington: Paintings, Drawings & Sculpture...* 1975. Abrams. Concise NAL ed. 4to. 157p. NF/wrp. T10. $25.00

HASSRICK, Peter. *Treasures of the Old West.* 1984. NY. 1st ed. 127p. F/F. E1. $60.00

HASSRICK, Royal B. *Colorful Story of North American Indians.* 1974. London. 1st ed. 144p. F/F. E1. $30.00

HASTINGS, Brook. *Demon Within.* 1953. Crime Club. VG/VG. P3. $15.00

HASTINGS, Macdonald. *Search for the Little Yellow Men.* 1956. Knopf. VG. P3. $10.00

HASTINGS, William T. *Conrad Webb of Hampstead.* 1958. Brown U. ils. 102p. VG. B10. $25.00

HASTY, John Eugene. *Man Without a Face.* 1958. Dodd Mead. VG/VG. P3. $10.00

HATCH, A. *Remington Arms in American History.* 1956. NY. 1st ed. ils/index. 359p. VG/VG. B5. $27.50

HATCH, Alden. *Byrds of Virginia.* 1969. HRW. 1st ed. inscr. 8vo. VG/VG. B11. $40.00

HATCH, Olivia S. *Olivia's African Diary.* 1980. WA. VG. O7. $20.00

HATCH, William H.P. *Greek & Syrian Miniatures in Jerusalem.* 1931. Cambridge. 72 pl. 135p. bl cloth. VG. B14. $100.00

HATCHER, Harlan. *Great Lakes.* 1944. London/NY. Oxford. 1st ed. sgn. 8vo. 384p. VG/VG. B11. $25.00

HATCHER, Harlan. *Lake Erie.* 1945. Bobbs Merrill. 1st ed. sgn. 416p. VG/dj. M20. $32.00

HATCHER, Harlan. *Pictorial History of the Great Lakes.* 1963. Bonanza. VG/VG. A16. $25.00

HATCHER, Julian. *Book of the Garand.* 1948. WA. 1st ed. VG/VG. B5. $65.00

HATCHER, Mattie Austin. *Letters of an Early American Traveller...* 1933. Dallas. ils/maps/index. 216p. F/worn. E1. $100.00

HATHCOCK, Louise. *True Stories of Little Dixie.* 1962. San Antonio. 1st ed. 281p. F/F. E1. $20.00

HATHEWAY, Mary E.N. *Johnny's Vacation & Other Stories.* 1878. Boston. 250p. gilt cloth. VG. A17. $7.50

HATTERAS, Owen; see Menken, H.L.

HATTIN, D.E. *Stratigraphy & Depositional Environment of Green Horn...* 1975. KS Geological Survey. rpt. 182p. F/prt wrp. D8. $8.00

HAUCK, Richard Boyd. *Crockett: A Bio-Bibliography.* 1982. Westport, CT. 1st ed. 169p. F/sans. E1. $25.00

HAUGAARD, Erik Christian. *Chase Me, Catch Nobody!* 1980. Houghton Mifflin. 1st ed. 209p. red cloth. NF/VG. T5. $30.00

HAUPT, A.W. *Introduction to Botany.* 1946. McGraw Hill. 2nd. 8vo. 425p. cloth. B1. $30.00

HAUPTMAN, William. *Storm Season.* 1992. Bantam. 1st ed. F/F. M23. $20.00

HAUSMAN, Gerald. *Sitting on the Blue-Eyed Bear: Navajo Myths & Legends.* 1975. Westport. Lawrence Hill. 1st ed. ils. 8vo. 130p. F/dj. T10. $50.00

HAUSMAN, Patricia. *Right Dose.* 1987. Rodale. 1st ed. VG/VG. P3. $25.00

HAUSNER, Gideon. *Justice in Jerusalem.* 1966. Harper Row. 1st ed. 8vo. VG/dj. W1. $20.00

HAUTMAN, Pete. *Drawing Dead.* 1993. Simon Schuster. 1st ed. author's 1st book. F/F. H11. $45.00

HAVEN, Joseph. *Mental Philosophy...* 1857. Boston. Gould Lincoln. 12mo. 590p. emb Victorian cloth. G. G1. $50.00

HAVIGHURST, Walter. *Long Ships Passing.* 1942. Macmillan. G. A16. $12.50

HAVIGHURST, Walter. *Masters of the Modern Short Story.* 1959. WJ Gage. 1st ed. VG. P3. $15.00

HAVIGHURST, Walter. *Pier 17.* 1935. Macmillan. G/G. A16. $40.00

HAVIGHURST, Walter. *Voices on the River: Story of Mississippi Waterways.* 1966. NY. 1st ed. 309p. F/chip. E1. $40.00

HAWES, Charles Boardman. *Whaling: Wherein Are Discussed the First Whalemen...* 1924. Doubleday. ils Neyland/Ashley. 358p. VG. T7. $65.00

HAWES, Charles. *Dark Frigate.* 1923. Atlantic Monthly. 1st ed. 247p. VG. P2. $40.00

HAWES, Harry. *Philippines' Uncertainty, American Problem.* 1932. NY. 1st ed. ils/photos. 360p. VG/VG. B5. $25.00

HAWES, Herbert Bouldin. *Daughter of the Blood.* 1930. Four Seas. 1st ed. ils. 427p. G. B10. $12.00

HAWGOOD, John A. *America's Western Frontiers.* 1976. NY. 2nd. 450p. F/F. E1. $30.00

HAWK, Dave. *100 Years on Bass.* 1970. San Antonio. 1st ed. 134p. F/F. E1. $25.00

HAWKE, David Freeman. *Those Tremendous Mountains.* 1980. Norton. 1st ed. 8vo. 273p. map ep. NF/dj. T10. $25.00

HAWKEN, Paul. *Magic of Findhorn.* 1975. NY. 1st ed. VG/VG. B5. $25.00

HAWKES, John. *Adventures in the Alaskan Skin Trade.* 1985. Simon Schuster. 1st ed. F/F. M19. $17.50

HAWKES, John. *Death, Sleep & the Traveller.* 1974. New Directions. ARC/1st ed. F/F. w/promo letter. B4. $175.00

HAWKES, John. *Passion Artist.* 1979. Harper Row. 1st ed. F/F. B35. $30.00

HAWKES, John. *Sweet William.* 1993. Simon Schuster. 1st ed. F/F. A20. $16.00

HAWKESWORTH, J. *Relation des Voyages. Volume I.* 1774. Paris. fld pl/maps. G. B5. $450.00

HAWKEYE, Harry. *Dalton Brothers & Their Gang.* 1908. Baltimore. ils. 187p. NF. E1. $75.00

HAWKING, S.W. *Brief History of Time From the Big Bang to Black Holes.* 1988. Bantam. 1st ed. 198p. F/dj. D8. $10.00

HAWKING, Stephen. *Black Holes & Baby Universes & Other Essays.* 1993. Bantam. 1st ed. VG/VG. K5. $15.00

HAWKINS, Daisy Waterhouse. *Old Point Lace & How To Copy It.* 1878. Chatto Windus. 12mo. 17 fld charts. gilt cloth spine. VG. T10. $175.00

HAWKINS, Gerald S. *Beyond Stonehenge.* 1973. Harper Row. BC. 60 photos. VG/dj. T10. $15.00

HAWKINS, Hugh. *History of Johns Hopkins.* 1960. Ithaca. 1st ed. 368p. VG/dj. A13. $40.00

HAWKINS, Wallace. *Case of John C Watrous, US Judge for Texas...* 1950. Dallas. 1st ed. 1/1200. ils. 109p. F/F. E1. $75.00

HAWKINS. *Stonehenge Decoded.* 1965. VG. D2. $20.00

HAWKS, Frank. *Once to Every Pilot.* 1936. NY. 144p. G. B18. $27.50

HAWLEY & ROSSI. *Bertie: The Life After Death of HG Wells.* 1973. NEL. VG/VG. P3. $15.00

HAWTHORNE, Hildegarde. *California's Missions.* 1942. Appleton Century. 1st ed. VG. P3. $35.00

HAWTHORNE, Julian. *Hawthorne Reading, an Essay.* 1902. Cleveland. Rowfant Club. 1/140. 133p. NF/VG case. A4. $325.00

HAWTHORNE, Nathaniel. *Grandfather's Chair With Famous Old People.* 1841. Boston. VG/custom box. C6. $550.00

HAWTHORNE, Nathaniel. *Marble Faun.* 1860. Ticknor Fields. 2 vol. 1st ed/2nd state. VG. M19. $175.00

HAWTHORNE, Nathaniel. *Mosses From an Old Manse.* 1846. Wiley Putnam. 1st ed. 2 vol. 8vo. NF/chemise/case. B24. $3,850.00

HAWTHORNE, Nathaniel. *Our Old Home: A Series of English Sketches.* 1863. Boston. 1st ed. VG. C6. $95.00

HAWTHORNE, Nathaniel. *Rappaccini's Daughter.* 1991. Greenbrae, CA. Allen. 1/115. 8vo. 90p. F. w/prospectus. B24. $350.00

HAWTHORNE, Nathaniel. *Scarlet Letter.* 1984. Pennyroyal. 1st ed thus. ils Barry Moser. cloth. F/case. B4. $125.00

HAWTHORNE, Nathaniel. *Scarlet Letter: A Romance.* March 1850. Boston. Ticknor Reed Fields. 1st ed. 1/2500. B24. $3,850.00

HAWTHORNE, Nathaniel. *Tanglewood Tales.* 1897. Thomas Crowell. VG. P3. $30.00

HAWTHORNE, Nathaniel. *Tanglewood Tales.* 1921. Penn. 1st ed thus. ils Starrett. gilt bl cloth. VG. D1. $285.00

HAWTHORNE, Nathaniel. *Twice-Told Tales.* 1865. Tichnor Fields. 2 vol. new ed. aeg. F. T10. $150.00

HAWTHORNE, Nathaniel. *Wonder Book for Boys & Girls.* 1896. Crowell. 12mo. gilt bl cloth. VG. M5. $25.00

HAWTHORNE, Nathaniel. *Wonder Book for Girls & Boys.* 1893. Riverside. ltd ed. ils Walter Crane. 210p. teg. VG/VG. D1. $700.00

HAY, Henry. *Amateur Magician's Handbook.* nd. Crowell. 3rd ed. VG/VG. P3. $12.00

HAY, James. *Bibliography of Biomechanics Literature.* 1974. Iowa City. 2nd. VG/wrp. A13. $20.00

HAY, John. *Pike Country Ballads.* 1912. Houghton Mifflin. 1st ed thus. F. C2. $100.00

HAY & SYNGE. *Dictionary of Garden Plants.* 1971 (1969). np. ils. 373p. VG/dj. B26. $28.00

HAYAT, M.A. *Principles & Techniques of Electron Microscopy.* 1978. Van Nostrand. 8vo. 318p. F/F. B1. $40.00

HAYCOX, Ernest. *Earthbreakers.* 1942. Little Brn. 1st ed. VG/VG. P3. $35.00

HAYCRAFT & KUNITZ. *Junior Book of Authors.* 1956. Wilson. 2nd revised/3rd prt. 309p. xl. G. C14. $10.00

HAYES, Clair W. *Boy Allies at Liege.* 1915. AL Burt. ils. G+. P12. $5.00

HAYES, Helen. *Gathering of Hope.* 1983. Phil. Fortress. sgn. VG/VG. B11. $15.00

HAYES, Jess G. *Boots & Bullets.* 1968. Tucson. 2nd. index. 139p. F/F. E1. $25.00

HAYES, Jess G. *Sheriff Thompson's Day.* 1968. Tucson. 1st ed. ils/photos/index. 190p. F/F. E1. $35.00

HAYES, Joseph. *Deep End.* 1967. Viking. 1st ed. F/F. B4. $85.00

HAYES, Joseph. *Winner's Circle.* 1980. Delacorte. 1st ed. F/F. H11. $25.00

HAYES, Louis V. *Clinical Diagnosis of Diseases of the Mouth...* 1935. Brooklyn. 8vo. 12 pl/ils/index. VG. B14. $50.00

HAYES, M.H. *Among Horses in Russia.* 1900. London. Everett. 1st ed. VG. O3. $65.00

HAYES, M.H. *Stable Management & Excercise.* 1909. London. Hurst Blackett. 2nd. O3. $20.00

HAYES, Mrs. *Horsewoman: A Practical Guide...* 1910. London. 3rd. VG. O3. $85.00

HAYES, Roland. *My Songs. Afro-American Religious Folk Songs.* 1948. Boston. 1st ed. 128p. VG/G. B5. $40.00

HAYES & HAYES. *Complete History of Guiteau: Assassin of President Garfield.* 1882. Phi/Boston. Hibbard. ils. 523p. gilt gr cloth. VG. B14. $150.00

HAYES & LOOS. *Twice Over Lightly: New York Then & Now.* 1972. HBJ. 1st ed. sgns. F/F. H11. $85.00

HAYES & YOUNG. *Norman & the Nursery School.* ca 1955. Platt Munk. 4to. NF/VG. C14. $18.00

HAYMON, S.T. *Very Particular Murder.* 1989. Constable. 1st ed. F/F. P3. $20.00

HAYNE, Paul H. *Legend & Lyrics.* 1872. Lippincott. 1st ed. 183p. G+. B10. $35.00

HAYNES, B.C. *Techniques of Observing the Weather.* 1947. John Wiley. 8vo. 272p. G. K5. $18.00

HAYNES, David. *Somebody Else's Mama.* 1995. Minneapolis. Milkweed. 1st ed. F/F. M23. $40.00

HAYNES, Fred E. *Criminology.* 1930. McGraw Hill. worn. M11. $25.00

HAYNES, Louise Marshall. *Over the Rainbow Bridge.* 1920. Volland. 21st. A Sunny Book. 8vo. VG. M5. $40.00

HAYS, Wilma Pitchford. *French Are Coming.* 1965. Colonial Williamsburg/HRW. lib ed. F/F. B10. $10.00

HAYSER, Arnold. *Social History of Art.* 1951. NY. 2 vol. 1st Am ed. ils/pl. AN/dj/case. H3. $85.00

HAYTER, Sparkle. *What's a Girl Gotta Do?* 1994. Soho. 1st ed. rem mk. F/F. H11. $30.00

HAYTHORNTHWAITE, Philip. *Uniforms of the French Revolutionary Wars 1789-1802.* 1981. Poole, UK. 1st ed. 147p. NF/G. E1. $30.00

HAYTHORNTHWAITE, Philip. *Weapons & Equipment of the Napoleonic Wars.* 1979. Poole. 1st ed. photos. 190p. F/F. E1. $45.00

HAZARD, Caroline. *From College Gates.* 1928. Boston. 1st ed. sgn. 326p. bl cloth. NF. w/sgn card. B14. $75.00

HAZARD, Lucy Lockwood. *Frontier in American Literature.* 1967. NY. 2nd. 308p. F/NF. E1. $25.00

HAZARD, Rowland G. *Language: Its Connection With the Present Condition...* 1836. Marshall Brn. 12mo. 153p. ochre cloth. G1. $125.00

HAZARD & MITTON. *Active Galactic Nuclei.* 1979. Cambridge. 317p. VG/dj. K5. $30.00

HAZARD & SHAPIRO. *Soviet Legal System.* 1962. Dobbs Ferry. Oceana. M11. $25.00

HAZEL, Paul. *Yearwood.* 1980. Atlantic/Little Brn. 1st ed. F/F. P3. $20.00

HAZEL, Robert. *Poems, 1951-1961.* 1961. Morehead, KY. 1st ed. 62p. VG. B10. $10.00

HAZEN, Barbara Shook. *Animal Daddies & My Daddy.* 1968. Golden. 1st/A ed. 8vo. unp. VG. T5. $15.00

HAZEN, Barbara Shook. *It Isn't Fair! A Book About Sibling Rivalry.* 1986. Golden. 1st ed. 8vo. unp. NF. C14. $5.00

HAZLITT. *Free Man's Library: A Biography of Outstanding Books...* 1956. np. 182p. VG/dj. A4. $55.00

HAZZARD, Shirley. *Evening of the Holiday.* 1966. NY. Knopf. 1st ed. NF/VG. B4. $50.00

HEAD, Edmund. *Report on the Law of Bastardy...* 1840. London. Wm Clownes. 31p. lacks orig wrp. M11. $150.00

HEAD, Francis B. *Journey Across the Pampas & Among the Andes.* 1967. Carbondale. 1st ed thus. 196p. dj. F3. $15.00

HEAD, Francis B. *Narrative.* 1839. London. 1st ed. 488p. cloth/new leather spine. A17. $85.00

HEAD, Henry. *Aphasia & Kindred Disorders of Speech.* 1926. Macmillan. 2 vol. 1st Am ed. 4to. gr cloth. G1. $485.00

HEADLEY, J.G. *Sacred Plains; or, Land of Promise.* 1858. Boston. Higgins Bradley Dayton. 8vo. 239p. G. W1. $25.00

HEADLEY, T.J. *Washington & His General.* 1847. Baker/Scribner. 2 vol. ils. xl. poor. B10. $50.00

HEADLEY, Victor. *Yardie.* 1992. Atlantic. 1st ed. F/F. H11. $30.00

HEAL & O'DAY. *Princes & Paupers in English Church 1500-1800.* 1981. np. Leicester U. 1st ed. 283p. ES. F/F. P4. $25.00

HEALD, Jean. *Picturesque Panama.* 1928. Chicago. Curt Teich. 1st ed. is. gilt bdg. VG. F3. $20.00

HEALD, Tim. *Blue Blood Will Out.* 1974. Stein Day. 1st ed. NF/NF. P3. $25.00

HEALD, Tim. *Brought to Book.* 1988. NY. 1st ed. F/NF. H11. $25.00

HEALD, Tim. *Murder at Moose Jaw.* 1981. Crime Club. 1st ed. VG/VG. P3. $20.00

HEALD, Tim. *Unbecoming Habits.* 1973. Stein Day. 1st ed. VG/VG. P3. $15.00

HEALEY, Ben. *Terrible Pictures.* 1967. Harper Row. 1st ed. VG/VG. P3. $13.00

HEALEY, Ben. *Vespucci Papers.* 1972. Lippincott. 1st ed. VG/VG. P3. $15.00

HEALEY, Tim. *Strange But True.* 1983. Octopus. decor brd. VG. P3. $10.00

HEALY, Jeremiah. *Foursome.* 1993. Pocket 1st ed. F/F. T2. $20.00

HEALY, Jeremiah. *Right To Die.* 1991. Pocket. 1st ed. F/F. P3. $20.00

HEALY, Jeremiah. *So Like Sleep.* 1987. Harper Row. 1st ed. NF/NF. P3. $25.00

HEALY, Jeremiah. *Stacked Goat.* 1986. Harper Row. 1st ed. F/F. A20/P3. $25.00

HEALY, Jeremiah. *Stacked Goat.* 1986. Harper Row. 1st ed. sgn. F/F. T2. $40.00

HEALY, Jeremiah. *Swan Dive.* 1988. Harper Row. 1st ed. F/F. P3. $22.00

HEALY, Jeremiah. *Swan Dive.* 1988. Harper Row. 1st ed. sgn. F/F. T2. $35.00

HEALY, Jeremiah. *Yesterday's News.* 1989. Harper Row. 1st ed. sgn. F/F. T2. $30.00

HEALY & MCCOMAS. *Adventures of Time & Space.* nd. BC. F/F. P3. $15.00

HEALY & MCCOMAS. *Famous Science Fiction Stories.* 1957. Modern Lib. hc. VG. P3. $20.00

HEANEY, Seamus. *Seamus Heaney: Poems & a Memoir.* 1982. LEC. 1/2000. sgn Heaney-/Pearson/Flanagan. F/case. C2. $300.00

HEAPS, Leo. *Log of the Centurion.* 1974. Macmillan. 1st ed. 264p. cloth. VG/dj. M20. $20.00

HEAPS & PORTER. *Singing Sixties.* 1960. Norman. 1st ed. 423p. F/F. E1. $45.00

HEARD, H.F. *Taste of Honey.* 1941. Vanguard. 1st ed. xl. P3. $20.00

HEARD, H.F. *Weird Tales of Terror & Detection.* 1946. Sun Dial. NF/NF. P3. $35.00

HEARD & HEARD. *Bookman's Guide to Americana.* 1977. 8vo. 403p. gr cloth. G. T3. $12.00

HEARN, Lafcadio. *Chin Chin Kobakama.* 1905. Tokyo. Hasegawa. 1st ed. trans Kate James. F/glassine wrp. D1. $300.00

HEARN, Lafcadio. *Leaves From the Diary of an Impressionist.* 1911. Boston/NY. ltd ed. 1/575. NF. C6. $120.00

HEARN, Lafcadio. *Stray Leaves From Strange Literature.* 1884. Boston. Osgood. 1st ed. author's 1st book. 225p. NF. B24. $850.00

HEARN, Lafcadio. *Writings of Lafcadio Hearn.* 1923. Riverside. Koizumi ed. 16 vol. teg. NF. B18. $500.00

HEARN, Michael Patrick. *Myth, Magic & Mystery: 100 Years of Am Children's Book Ils.* 1st ed. 1/500. folio. 240 ils. VG/VG. C4. $60.00

HEARON, Shelby. *Five Hundred Scorpions.* 1987. Atheneum. ARC. F/F. w/promo material. B4. $50.00

HEARON, Shelby. *Painted Dresses.* 1981. Atheneum. 1st ed. sgn. F/F. B4. $75.00

HEARON, Shelby. *Prince of a Fellow.* 1978. Doubleday. 1st ed. NF/VG. B4. $45.00

HEARST, William Randolph. *We Cannot Cure Murder by Murder.* 1926. NY. Am Inc. 14p. G/prt wrp. M11. $25.00

HEAT-MOON, William Least. *Blue Highways.* 1982. Little Brn. 1st ed. 8vo. NF/dj. T10. $100.00

HEATH, Royton E. *Alpine Plants Under Glass.* 1951. London. photos. 171p. B26. $15.00

HEATH & PREISS. *Regulation of Carbon Partitioning in Photosynthetic Tissue.* 1985. Rockville, MD. ils. 374p. flexible leatherette. B26. $15.00

HEBARD, Gil. *Gil Hebard Guns.* 1974. Knoxville. 1st ed. 97p. F/wrp. E1. $25.00

HEBARD, Grace R. *Pathbreakers From River to Ocean.* 1912. Chicago. 2nd. ils/maps/biblio/index. 263p. F. E1. $40.00

HEBDEN, Mark. *Death Set to Music.* 1983. Walker. 1st ed. NF/NF. P3. $18.00

HEBDEN, Mark. *Pel & the Promised Land.* 1993. St Martin. 1st ed. F/F. P3. $18.00

HEBDEN, Mark. *Pel & the Prowler.* 1986. Walker. 1st ed. F/F. P3. $16.00

HEBER, Helmut. *Goebbels.* 1972. NY. 387p. VG/dj. A17. $12.00

HEBERDEN, M.V. *Sleeping Witness.* 1951. Unicorn Mystery BC. VG. P3. $20.00

HEBERT, Anne. *Children of the Black Sabbath.* 1977. Musson. 1st ed. hc. VG/VG. P3. $20.00

HEBERT, Anne. *Kamouraska.* 1973. Musson. 1st ed. VG/VG. P3. $15.00

HEBERT, Anne. *Silent Rooms.* 1974. Musson. 1st ed. F/F. P3. $20.00

HEBWYND & RYTOV. *Living Universe.* 1963. Scientific BC. 128p. VG/dj. K5. $10.00

HECHT, Anthony. *Seven Deadly Sins.* 1958. Gehenna. 1/300. sgn. ils/sgn Leonard Baskin. F/bl wrp. B24. $250.00

HECHT, Ben. *Cat That Jumped Out of the Story.* 1947. Phil. Winston. 1st ed. 8vo. unp. NF/VG+ clip. C14. $45.00

HECHT, Ben. *Gaily, Gaily.* 1963. Garden City. 1st ed. 227p. VG/dj. B18. $22.50

HECHT. *Nativity.* 1981. np. ils unfold to 3 ft. F. A4. $45.00

HECHTLINGER, Aelaide. *American Quilts, Quilting & Patchwork.* 1974. Galahad. 4to. 358p. VG+/clip. H4. $18.00

HECKLE, A. *Bowles' Drawing Book for Ladies; or, Complete Florist...* ca 1765. London. Boweles. 24 engravings. clamshell box w/morocco label. B24. $3,500.00

HECKLEMANN, Charles N. *With Guidons Flying.* 1970. Garden City. 1st ed. 197p. VG/worn. E1. $30.00

HECKSTALL-SMITH, Anthony. *Murder on the Brain.* 1958. Roy. 1st ed. VG/VG. P3. $18.00

HECKSTALL-SMITH, B. *Yachts & Yachting in Contemporary Art.* 1925. London. The Studio. 1/1000. 103 pl. NF. T7. $200.00

HECTOR, L.C. *Handwriting of English Documents.* 1966. London. Edward Arnold. M11. $45.00

HEDGE, Levi. *Elements of Logick; or, Summary of General Principles...* 1818. Cummings Hilliard. 2nd Am. 12mo. VG. G1. $50.00

HEDGERS, Isaac A. *Sugar Canes & Their Products, Culture & Manufacture...* 1879. St Louis. fld pl/ils. brn stp cloth. F. B14. $45.00

HEDGES, Doris. *Dumb Spirit, a Novel of Montreal.* 1952. Arthur Baker. 1st ed. VG/G. P3. $40.00

HEDGES, James B. *Browns of Providence Plantations.* 1968. Providence. VG. O7. $35.00

HEDGES, Joseph; see Harknett, Terry.

HEDGES, Peter. *What's Eating Gilbert Grape?* 1991. Poseidon. ARC. NF. M19. $15.00

HEDGES, Peter. *What's Eating Gilbert Grape?* 1991. Poseidon. 1st ed. F/F. A20. $12.00

HEDGES, W.H. *Pike's Peak or Busted.* 1954. Evanston. 1st ed. 1/750. 141p. VG. B5. $45.00

HEDREN, Paul L. *First Scalp for Custer: Skirmish at Warbonnet Creek...* 1980. Glendale, CA. 1/350. 1st ed. 107p. F. E1. $125.00

HEER, Friedrich. *Der Glaube des Adolf Hitler: Anatomie Einer Politischen...* 1968. Munchen. Bechtle. 752p. VG/dj. A17. $20.00

HEFFER, William. *Saved!* 1979. Summit. BC. VG/G+. P12. $5.00

HEFFERNAN, William. *Ritual.* 1989. NAL. 1st ed. sgn. rem mk. VG+/NF. N4. $22.50

HEFLEY & HEFLEY. *Arabs, Christians, Jews: They Want Peace Now!* 1978. Logos Internat. 1st ed. 245p. NF/dj. W1. $20.00

HEGAN, Alice Caldwell. *Mrs Wiggs of the Cabbage Patch.* 1901. Century. 1st ed. 1st issue bdg. NF. B4. $200.00

HEGEN, Edmund. *Highways Into the Upper Amazon Basin.* 1966. Gainesville, FL. 1st ed. 168p. wrp. F3. $15.00

HEIDNER, F.W. *Laborer's Friend & Employer's Counsel.* 1895. Naperville. self pub. 1st ed. 388p. gilt blk cloth. NF. B2. $50.00

HEIFERMAN, Ronald. *US Navy in World War II.* 1979. Secaucus, NJ. 2nd. 192p. F/F. E1. $35.00

HEIMAN. *When the Cheering Stops.* 1990.. 1st ed. VG/VG. K2. $20.00

HEIMER, Mel. *Empty Man.* 1971. McCall. hc. VG/VG. P3. $15.00

HEINE, Heinrich. *Poems & Ballads of Heinrich Heine.* nd. Hurst. hc. VG. P3. $15.00

HEINE, Heinrich. *Samtliche Werke.* 1911. Leipzig. 10 vol. VG. A17. $85.00

HEINE, Heinrich. *Travel-Pictures Including the Tour in the Harz.* 1887. London. VG. O7. $40.00

HEINECCIUS, J.G. *Elementa Juris Civilis Romani Secundum Ordienem..* 1827. Neapoli. Ex Tipographia Januarii Palma. rare ed. G. M11. $150.00

HEINEMANN, Larry. *Paco's Story.* 1986. FSG. 1st ed. F/F. H11. $40.00

HEINEMANN, Larry. *Paco's Story.* 1987. London. Faber. ARC. 8vo. RS. F/dj. S9. $40.00

HEINLEIN, Robert A. *Cat Who Walks Through Walls.* 1985. Putnam. 1st ed. NF/NF. P3. $20.00

HEINLEIN, Robert A. *Friday.* 1982. HRW. 1st ed. F/F. M23. $40.00

HEINLEIN, Robert A. *Friday.* 1982. HRW. 1st ed. NF/NF. P3. $25.00

HEINLEIN, Robert A. *Grumbles From the Grave.* 1990. Del Rey. 1st ed. F/F. P3. $20.00

HEINLEIN, Robert A. *Job: A Comedy of Justice.* 1984. Del Rey. F/F. P3. $17.00

HEINLEIN, Robert A. *Past Through Tomorrow Book Two.* 1977. NEL. 1st ed. NF/NF. P3. $35.00

HEINLEIN, Robert A. *Stranger in a Strange Land Uncut.* nd. Ace Putnam. 3rd ed. VG/VG. P3. $23.00

HEINLEIN, Robert A. *To Sail Beyond the Sunset.* 1987. Ace Putnam. 1st ed. F/dj. M23/P3. $20.00

HEINLEIN, Robert A. *Tramp Royale.* 1992. Ace Putnam. 1st ed. F/F. P3. $20.00

HEINZERLING, Sarah A. *Call.* 1936. Statesville. Brady. 45p. VG. B10. $8.00

HEISE & HEISE. *Clarence Darrow in Hell, a Play in Two Acts.* 1993. Chicago. Historical Bookworks. 64p. wrp. M11. $8.00

HEISENFELT, Kathryn. *About Customs.* 1939. Grosset Dunlap. lg 4to. VG/fair. M5. $35.00

HEISENFELT, Kathryn. *Jane Withers & the Swamp Wizard.* 1944. Whitman. VG/torn. P3. $12.00

HEISENFELT, Kathryn. *Shirley Temple & Spirit of Dragonwoo.* 1945. Whitman. hc. VG. P3. $13.00

HEITMAN, Ernestine Beckwith. *Rosy the Skunk.* 1952. Pageant. 1st ed. ils Al Kilgore. VG/G. B17. $5.00

HEIZER, Robert F. *Indians of Los Angeles County.* 1968. Los Angeles. rpt. 142p. NF. E1. $30.00

HEIZER & WHIPPLE. *California Indians: A Source Book.* 1971. Berkeley. 2nd. ils/photos/biblio/index. 619p. F/stiff wrp. E1/P4. $15.00

HELD, Julius S. *Rembrandt's Aristotle & Other Rembrandt Studies.* 1969. Princeton. ils. 155p. dj. D2. $85.00

HELD, Peter; see Vance, Jack.

HELD. *Mail Art: An Annotated Bibliography.* 1991. np. 2199 annotated entries. 534p. F. A4. $55.00

HELFAND, William. *Medicine & Pharmacy in American Political Prints...* 1978. Madison. 1st ed. 84p. wrp. A13. $35.00

HELLE, Andre. *Droles de Betes, Texte et Dessins de Andre Helle.* ca 1920. Paris. Tolmer. 22 tipped-in ils. 46p. NF. B24. $800.00

HELLER, Joseph. *Catch-22*. 1961. Simon Schuster. 1st ed. NF/NF. B35. $25.00

HELLER, Joseph. *Catch-22*. 1966. Modern Lib. VG/VG. P3. $18.00

HELLER, Joseph. *Good As Gold*. 1979. NY. 1/500. sgn. special bdg. VG. O7. $65.00

HELLER, Joseph. *Picture This*. 1988. Putnam. 1st ed. F/F. B35. $25.00

HELLER, Joseph. *We Bombed in New Haven*. 1968. Knopf. 1st ed. F/F. M19. $25.00

HELLER, Robert. *Supermarketers*. 1987. Dutton BC. 384p. AN/dj. P4. $16.50

HELLMAN, Lillian. *Days To Come: A Drama in Three Acts*. nd. np. 1st ed. F/NF. C2. $125.00

HELLMAN, Lillian. *Lark*. 1956. Random. 1st ed. inscr. F. B4. $375.00

HELLMAN, Lillian. *Maybe*. 1980. Little Brn. 1st ed. VG+/VG+. A20. $26.00

HELLMAN, Lillian *Moniserrat*. 1950. NY. Dramatists Play Service. inscr/dtd 1950. VG/VG. B4. $400.00

HELLMAN, Lillian. *Scoundrel Time*. 1976. Little Brn. 1st ed. F/F. B35. $30.00

HELLMUTH, Nicholas. *Maya Archaelogy & Ethnography*. 1970. FLAAR. sq 4to. 27p. wrp. F3. $20.00

HELM, MacKinley. *Journeying Through Mexico*. 1948. Little Brn. 1st ed. 297p. F/NF. T10. $45.00

HELM, Thomas Monroe. *Desert Ghost*. 1977. Doubleday. 1st ed. VG/VG. P3. $12.00

HELMERS, Dow. *Historic Alpine Tunnel*. 1963. Sage. sgn. 200p. cloth. NF/dj. M20. $47.00

HELMHOLTZ, H. *Popular Lectures on Scientific Subjects*. 1873. Appleton. trans E Atkinson. 397p. xl. K5. $35.00

HELMS, Randel. *Tolkien's World*. 1974. Houghton Mifflin. 1st ed. VG/torn. P3. $25.00

HELMS, S.W. *Jawa: Lost City of the Black Desert*. 1981. Cornell. 1st ed. 270p. NF/dj. W1. $22.00

HELMS & LOVELAND. *Frontier Adaptations in Lower Central America*. 1976. Phil. ISHI. 1st ed. index/biblio. 178p. dj. F3. $25.00

HELPRIN, Mark. *Ellis Island & Other Stories*. 1981. Delacorte. 1st ed. sgn. F/F. B4. $250.00

HELPRIN, Mark. *Memoir From Antproof Case*. 1995. Harcourt Brace. 1st ed. NF/NF. G10. $12.00

HELPRIN, Mark. *Soldier of the Great War*. 1991. HBJ. 1st ed. F/F. B4. $45.00

HELPRIN, Mark. *Swan Lake*. 1989. Houghton Mifflin. 1st ed. ils Chris Van Allsburg. F/F. B17. $12.50

HELPS, Arthur. *Spanish Conquest in America*. 1865. NY. 2 vol. G. O7. $65.00

HEMINGWAY, Ernest. *Across the River & Into the Trees*. 1950. NY. 1st ed. VG/VG. B5. $60.00

HEMINGWAY, Ernest. *Across the River & Into the Trees*. 1950. Scribner. 1st ed. NF/NF. B35. $95.00

HEMINGWAY, Ernest. *By-Line: Ernest Hemingway*. 1967. NY. 1st ed. 489p. F/F. E1. $30.00

HEMINGWAY, Ernest. *Complete Short Stories of Ernest Hemingway*. 1987. Scribner. ARC/1st ed. RS. F/NF. C2. $75.00

HEMINGWAY, Ernest. *Complete Short Stories*. 1978. NY. Finca Vigia ed. AP. F/wrp. C2. $60.00

HEMINGWAY, Ernest. *Death in the Afternoon*. 1932. Scribner. VG/G. M19. $650.00

HEMINGWAY, Ernest. *Farewell to Arms*. 1929. NY. ltd ed. 1/510. sgn. F/VG dj/case. C6. $5,500.00

HEMINGWAY, Ernest. *For Whom the Bell Tolls*. 1940. Scribner. 1st ed/1st issue. beige cloth. NF. B24. $450.00

HEMINGWAY, Ernest. *Garden of Eden*. 1986. Scribner. 1st ed. F/F. M19. $25.00

HEMINGWAY, Ernest. *In Our Time*. 1925. Boni Liveright. 1st Am ed. author's 1st book. F. B4. $1,000.00

HEMINGWAY, Ernest. *In Our Time. Stories*. 1930. NY. 1st ed thus. intro Edmund Wilson. VG/VG. C2. $500.00

HEMINGWAY, Ernest. *Islands in the Stream*. 1970. Scribner. 1st ed. F/NF. B2. $50.00

HEMINGWAY, Ernest. *Marlin!* 1992. Big Fish Books. 1st book ed. 12mo. F/F. C2. $60.00

HEMINGWAY, Ernest. *Moveable Feast*. 1964. NY. 1st ed. VG/VG. B5. $50.00

HEMINGWAY, Ernest. *Nick Adam Stories*. 1972. Scribner. 1st ed. F/NF. C2. $100.00

HEMINGWAY, Ernest. *Old Man & the Sea*. 1952. Scribner. 1st ed. F/NF. B4. $650.00

HEMINGWAY, Ernest. *Selected Letters 1917-1961*. 1981. NY. 1st ed. 1/500. edit/sgn Carlos Baker. F/case. C2. $100.00

HEMINGWAY, Ernest. *Torrents of Spring*. 1926. NY. 1st ed. VG. B5. $350.00

HEMINGWAY, Ernest. *Two Christmas Tales*. 1959. Berkeley. 1/150. ils Victor Anderson. F/prt wrp. B24. $1,650.00

HEMINGWAY, Ernest. *Winner Take Nothing*. 1933. NY. 1st ed. F. A9. $150.00

HEMINGWAY, Ernest. *Winner Take Nothing*. 1933. NY. 1st ed. NF/VG. C6. $550.00

HEMINGWAY, Ernest. *Winner Take Nothing*. 1933. NY. 1st ed. VG. B5. $95.00

HEMMING, John. *Red Gold*. 1978. Harvard. 1st ed. ils/maps. 677p. dj. F3. $15.00

HEMMING, Robert J. *Gales of November*. 1981. Chicago. Contemporary Books. 1st ed. VG/dj. A16. $25.00

HEMPEL, Amy. *Reasons To Live*. 1985. 1st ed. author's 1st book. F/F. S13. $25.00

HEMPELMANN, Friedrich. *Tierpsychologie vom Standpunkte des Biologen*. 1926. Leipzig. Akademische Verlagsgesellschaft. 676p. gr linen. VG. G1. $37.50

HEMPHILL, Elva Murrell. *Early Days in Dallas County*. 1954. np. 1st ed. 115p. NF. E1. $40.00

HEMPHILL, William Edwin. *Cavalier Commonwealth: History & Government of Virginia*. 1957. McGraw Hill. 606p. VG. B10. $10.00

HEMYNG, Bracebridge. *Jack Harkaway in the Toils*. ca 1910. NY. 308p. VG/wrp. E1. $35.00

HENBEST & MARTEN. *New Astronomy*. 1983. Cambridge. VG. O7. $25.00

HENCKEN, Hugh. *Tarquinia & Etruscan Origins*. 1968. Praeger. 1st ed. ils. 248p. VG/dj. W1. $22.00

HENDERSON, Alice Corbin. *Brothers of Light: Penitentes of the Southwest*. 1937. NY. 1st ed. 126p. F/NF. E1. $95.00

HENDERSON, Daniel. *Hidden Coasts*. 1953. Wm Sloan. 1st ed. sgn. 8vo. F/VG. B11. $25.00

HENDERSON, G.J.R. *Stonewall Jackson & the American Civil War*. nd. NJ. 2 vol. VG+/dj/box. B18. $45.00

HENDERSON, James. *History of Brazil: Comprising Its Geography, Commerce...* 1821. London. Longman. 1st ed. 4to. 28 full-p pl/2 maps. early 20th-C bdg. C6. $950.00

HENDERSON, John. *World of the Ancient Maya*. 1981. Ithaca. 1st ed. 277p. dj. F3. $30.00

HENDERSON, L.F. *Early Flowering of Plants in Lane County, OR in 1934*. 1936. Eugene. monograph. cloth/orig wrp bdg in. F. B26. $15.00

HENDERSON, Lois T. *Hagar.* 1978. Christian Herald. 1st ed. F/F. P3. $10.00

HENDERSON, Louis. *Airplanes, Stories & Pictures.* 1936. Chicago. juvenile. 40p. VG. B18. $15.00

HENDERSON, M.R. *If I Should Die.* 1985. Doubleday. 1st ed. VG/VG. P3. $15.00

HENDERSON, Marjorie Buell. *Laughs With Little Lulu.* 1942. McKay. 1st ed. unp. VG/dj. M20. $67.00

HENDERSON, Marjorie Buell. *Little Lulu.* 1937. Rand McNally. unp. glossy brd. VG. M20. $20.00

HENDERSON, Marjorie Buell. *Little Lulu & Her Pals.* 1938. torn spine. K2. $45.00

HENDERSON, Marjorie Buell. *Little Lulu on Parade.* 1941. 1st ed. VG/VG. S13. $45.00

HENDERSON, Marjorie Buell. *Oh, Little Lulu!* 1943. McKay. 8vo. F/VG. B17. $50.00

HENDERSON, Mary F. *Practical Cooking & Dinner Giving.* 1883. Harper. 12mo. 376p. gilt gr cloth. VG. T10. $75.00

HENDERSON, Mrs. L.R. *Magic Aeorplane.* 1911. Reilly Britton. ils Emile Nelson. G/torn. D1. $185.00

HENDERSON, Peter. *Felix Diaz, the Porfirians & Mexican Revolution.* 1981. Lincoln, NE. 1st ed. 239p. F3. $15.00

HENDERSON, Peter. *Henderson's Handbook of Plants & General Horticulture.* 1890 (1881). NY. new ed. dictionary format. newer buckram. VG. B26. $30.00

HENDERSON, Peter. *Practical Floriculture.* 1869. NY. 12mo. 249p. VG. T3. $30.00

HENDERSON, Richard. *Singlehanded Sailing.* 1976. Internat Marine. ils. 304p. VG/dj. T7. $25.00

HENDERSON, W.J. *Elements of Navigation.* 1901. Harper. G. A16. $10.00

HENDERSON, Zenna. *Ingathering: The Complete People Stories.* 1995. Nesfa. 1st ed. M/M. P3. $25.00

HENDERSON & JONES. *Wonder Tales of Ancient Wales.* nd. Small Maynard. 8vo. 166p. xl. VG+. M5. $60.00

HENDERSON. *DW Griffith: His Life & Work.* 1972. Oxford. F/VG. D2. $25.00

HENDRICK, Ellwood. *Lewis Miller: A Biographical Essay.* 1925. NY. 208p. teg. xl. VG. B18. $45.00

HENDRIE, Laura. *Stygo.* 1994. MacMurray Beck. 1st ed. F/F. M23. $20.00

HENDRIX, John. *If I Can Do It Horseback.* 1964. Austin. 1st ed. 355p. F/G. E1. $40.00

HENDRON, J.W. *Story of Billy the Kid, New Mexico's Number One Desperado.* 1948. Santa Fe. 1st ed. photo. 31p. F/wrp. E1. $40.00

HENDRY, Maurice D. *Cadillac: Standard of the World, the Complete History.* 1977. NY. Automobile Quarterly. 448p. F/NF. A17. $35.00

HENDRYX, James B. *Blood on the Yukon Trail.* 1930. Doubleday Doran Gundy. 1st ed. VG. P3. $25.00

HENDRYX, James B. *Corporal Downey Takes the Trail.* nd. Jarrolds. hc. VG. P3. $15.00

HENDRYX, James B. *Ray Gold.* 1933. Doubleday Doran. 1st ed. 307p. VG/dj. M20. $20.00

HENERY, Thomas R. *White Continent.* 1950. NY. Sloane BC. 257p. VG. P4. $10.00

HENIE & STRAIT. *Queen of Ice, Queen of Shadows (Sonja Henie).* 1985. NY. 1st ed. VG/VG. B5. $35.00

HENIG, Martin. *Handbook of Roman Art.* 1983. Ithaca. Cornell. 1st ed. 8vo. ils. VG/stiff wrp. W1. $12.00

HENIGHAN, Tom. *Well of Time.* 1988. Collins. 1st ed. sgn. F/F. P3. $25.00

HENING, H.B. *George Curry, 1861-1947: An Autobiography.* 1958. NM U. 1st ed. ils/photos. 336p. F/F. E1. $60.00

HENISCH & HENISCH. *Painted Photograph 1839-1914.* 1996. Penn State. 90 pl/11 duotones/28 halftones. 240p. AN. M20. $75.00

HENISSART, Paul. *Winter Spy.* 1976. Simon Schuster. 1st ed. VG/VG. P3. $15.00

HENKEL, F.W. *Weather Science: Elementary Introduction...* 1911. Fisher Unwin. 8vo. 336p. gilt cloth. G. K5. $18.00

HENRY, Alice. *Women & the Labor Movement.* 1923. Doran. 1st ed. VG/wrp. B2. $65.00

HENRY, George W. *All the Sexes: A Study of Masculinity & Femininity.* nd. Rinehart. hc. VG/VG. P3. $12.00

HENRY, Marguerite. *Album of Horses.* 1951. Rand McNally. 1st ed. lg 4to. ils Wesley Dennis. rpr tear. NF. M5. $10.00

HENRY, Marguerite. *Always, Reddy.* 1947. Whittlesey. 1st ed. ils Wesley Dennis. 79p. VG/VG. P2. $30.00

HENRY, Marguerite. *Birds at Home.* 1942. Donohue. ils Jacob Abbott. NF. A17. $20.00

HENRY, Marguerite. *Brighty of the Grand Canyon.* 1953. Rand McNally. 1st/A ed. lg 8vo. VG+/G. M5. $52.00

HENRY, Marguerite. *Dilly Dally Sally.* 1940. Saalfield. ils Gladys Rourke Blackwood. sc. VG. M5. $45.00

HENRY, Marguerite. *Justin Morgan Had a Horse.* 1945. Chicago. Willcox Follett. 1st ed. VG. O3. $45.00

HENRY, Marguerite. *Justin Morgan Had a Horse.* 1945. Wilcox Follett. 1st ed. ils Wesley Dennis. VG/VG. P2. $85.00

HENRY, Marguerite. *Justin Morgan Had a Horse.* 1948. Chicago. Follett. 4th. ils Wesley Dennis. 89p. VG. C14. $12.00

HENRY, Marguerite. *Little Fellow.* 1945. Winston. 1st ed. ils Diana Thorne. F/VG. P2. $35.00

HENRY, Marguerite. *Misty's Twilight.* 1992. NY. Macmillan. 1st prt. VG/G. O3. $25.00

HENRY, Marguerite. *Mustang: Wild Spirit of the West.* 1966. Chicago. 1st ed. inscr w/sketch. 223p. F/VG. E1. $100.00

HENRY, Marguerite. *Mustang: Wild Spirit of the West.* 1966. Rand McNally. 1st ed. pres. VG+/dj. O3. $65.00

HENRY, Marguerite. *Mustang: Wild Spirit of the West.* 1966. Rand McNally. 1st ed. 8vo. 208p. NF. C14. $10.00

HENRY, Marguerite. *Stormy: Misty's Foal.* 1963. Rand McNally. 1st ed. ils Wesley Dennis. VG. O3. $25.00

HENRY, Marguerite. *Stormy: Misty's Foal.* 1963. Rand McNally. 1st ed. 224p. NF. C14. $15.00

HENRY, Marguerite. *Wagging Tails: An Album of Dogs.* 1955. Rand McNally. sm 4to. ils Wesley Dennis. NF/VG. C8. $85.00

HENRY, O.; see O Henry.

HENRY, Robert Selph. *This Fascinating Railroad Business.* 1942. Bobbs Merrill. 1st ed. inscr. 8vo. 520p. maroon brd. VG. B11. $30.00

HENRY. *Irish Art in the Romanesque Periods.* 1970. Cornell. F/F. D2. $35.00

HENSEN, Josiah. *Uncle Tom's Story of His Life.* 1876. London. 16th thousand. VG-. M17. $35.00

HENSLEY, Joe L. *Color Him Guilty.* 1987. Walker. 1st ed. NF/NF. M22. $10.00

HENSLEY, Joe L. *Minor Murders.* 1979. Crime Club. 1st ed. xl. dj. P3. $8.00

HENTY, G.A. *Bravest of the Brave*. nd. Foulsham. VG/VG. P3. $13.00

HENTY, G.A. *By Right of Conquest*. nd. Hurst. decor brd. VG. P3. $18.00

HENTY, G.A. *With the Wolfe in Canada*. 1890. NY. fair. O7. $15.00

HENTY, G.A. *With Wolfe in Canada*. nd. Blackie. VG/VG. P3. $13.00

HEPWORTH, Cathi. *Antics! An Alphabetical Anthology*. ca 1993. NY. Putnam. 2nd. sgn w/sketch. NF/VG+ clip. C14. $15.00

HERBERT, A.P. *Codd's Last Case & Other Misleading...* 1952. Methuen. hc. VG. P3. $18.00

HERBERT, Brian. *Garbage Chronicles*. 1985. WH Allen. 1st ed. VG/VG. P3. $20.00

HERBERT, Brian. *Prisoners of Arionn*. 1987. Arbor. 1st ed. RS. F/F. P3. $20.00

HERBERT, Brian. *Sudanna, Sudanna*. 1985. Putnam. 1st ed. F/F. P3. $16.00

HERBERT, Frank. *Chapterhouse: Dune*. 1985. Putnam. 1st ed. NF/NF. P3. $25.00

HERBERT, Frank. *Dosadi Experiment*. 1977. Berkley Putnam. 1st ed. VG/VG. P3. $30.00

HERBERT, Frank. *Dragon in the Sea*. nd. BC. VG/VG. P3. $10.00

HERBERT, Frank. *Dragon in the Sea*. 1956. Doubleday. 1st ed. VG/G. P3. $175.00

HERBERT, Frank. *Dune Messiah*. 1969. Putnam. 1st ed. xl. dj. P3. $30.00

HERBERT, Frank. *Dune*. 1974. Chilton. 6th ed. VG. P3. $15.00

HERBERT, Frank. *God Emperor of Dune*. 1981. Putnam. 1st ed. VG/VG. P3. $25.00

HERBERT, Frank. *God Makers*. 1972. Putnam. 1st ed. VG/VG. P3. $35.00

HERBERT, Frank. *Green Brain*. 1979. NEL. xl. dj. P3. $6.00

HERBERT, Frank. *Heretics of Dune*. 1984. Putnam. 1st ed. G/dj. P3. $15.00

HERBERT, Frank. *Nebula Winners Fifteen*. 1981. Harper Row. 1st ed. VG/VG. P3. $30.00

HERBERT, Frank. *Saratoga Barrier*. 1970. Rapp Whiting. 1st ed. NF/NF. P3. $35.00

HERBERT, Frank. *White Plague*. 1982. Putnam. 1st ed. VG/VG. P3. $18.00

HERBERT, Frank. *Without Me You're Nothing*. nd. BC. VG/VG. P3. $10.00

HERBERT, H.W. *Cromwell: An Historical Novel*. 1838. NY. 2 vol. author's 2nd book. 3-quarter red morocco. C6. $120.00

HERBERT, H.W. *Frank Forester's Horse & Horsemanship of the United States*. 1857. NY. Stringer Townsend. 2 vol. 1st ed. engravings. gilt brn buckram. T10. $400.00

HERBERT, Ivor. *Arkle: Story of a Champion*. (1968). London. 1st ed. ils. 187p. F/VG. H3. $65.00

HERBERT, James. *Gardens of Allah*. nd. Grosset Dunlap. VG/dj. M21. $15.00

HERBERT, James. *Haunted*. 1988. Hodder Stoughton. 2nd ed. VG/VG. P3. $20.00

HERBERT, James. *Magic Cottage*. 1987. NAL. 1st Am ed. NF/dj. M21. $12.00

HERBERT, James. *Magic Cottage*. 1987. NAL. 1st ed. F/F. P3. $18.00

HERBERT, James. *Moon*. 1986. Crown. 1st ed. VG/VG. P3. $20.00

HERBERT, James. *Sepulchre*. 1987. Hodder Stoughton. 1st ed. F/F. P3. $25.00

HERBERT, Sandra. *Red Notebook of Charles Darwin*. 1980. Ithaca. ils. VG/dj. B26. $25.00

HERBERT, Wally. *Noose of Laurels, Robert E Peary & Race to North Pole*. 1989. np. ils/maps/photos. 395p. F/F. A4. $25.00

HERBERT, Walter H. *Fighting Joe Hooker*. 1944. Bobbs Merrill. 1st ed. 366p. VG. M8. $65.00

HERBERT, William. *Antiquities of the Inns of Court & Chancery*. 1804. London. Vernor & Hood. 2 vol. 24 pl. ornate tooled calf. M11. $1,250.00

HERBERT & HERBERT. *Man of Two Worlds*. 1986. Putnam. 1st ed. F/F. P3. $19.00

HERBERT & RANSOM. *Ascension Factor*. 1989. Ace Putnam. 1st ed. NF/VG+. M21. $15.00

HERBERT & RANSOM. *Lazarus Effect*. 1983. Putnam. 1st ed. VG/dj. M21. $5.00

HERBST, Judith. *Sky Above & Below*. 1983. Atheneum. sl. G. K5. $12.00

HERCULES, Frank. *I Want a Black Doll*. 1967. Simon Schuster. 1st ed. F/NF. B2. $30.00

HEREFORD, Robert. *Old Man River: Memories of Captain Louis Rosche...* 1943. Caldwell. 2nd. 301p. F/chip. E1. $35.00

HERGESHEIMER, Joseph. *Linda Condon*. 1919. NY. 1st ed. 1/50. sgn/#d. VG. V4. $100.00

HERGESHEIMER & WALLACE. *Colonial Houses of Pre-Revolutionary Period of Philadelphia*. 1931. NY. Bonanza. ils. 248p. VG/VG. B5. $35.00

HERLEY, Richard. *Penal Colony*. 1988. Morrow. 1st ed. F/F. H11. $30.00

HERLIHY, James Leo. *All Fall Down*. 1960. NY. 1st ed. F/dj. A17. $17.50

HERLIHY, James Leo. *Midnight Cowboy*. 1965. 1st ed. MTI. VG/VG. S13. $30.00

HERMAN, Pauline. *Family Horse*. 1959. Princeton. Van Nostrant. VG/VG. O3. $20.00

HERMAN, Richard. *Warbirds*. 1989. Donald Fine. 1st ed. VG/VG. P3. $15.00

HERNANDEZ, Keith. *Pure Baseball*. 1994. Harper Collins. 1st ed. F/F. P8. $12.50

HERNANDEZ, Xavier. *San Rafael*. 1992. Houghton Mifflin. 1st Am ed. 4to. dj. F3. $15.00

HERNDON, Brodie. *Chrysalid*. 1976. McClure. 42p. VG. B10. $7.00

HERNDON, Brodie. *Time Clocks*. 1973. McClure. 1st collected ed. 54p. VG/VG. B10. $10.00

HERNDON & WEIKS. *Herndon's Life of Lincoln*. 1942. np. 8vo. 511p. G. T3. $12.00

HERODOTUS. *History*. 1880. London. Murray. 4 vol in 8. 4th. 8vo. ils/maps. NF. T10. $750.00

HERR & WALLACE. *Story of the US Calvary: 1775-1942*. 1953. Bonanza. rpt. 275p. F/F. E1. $30.00

HERR & WELLS. *Bodies & Souls*. 1961. Crime Club. 1st ed. VG/VG. P3. $25.00

HERRICK, C. Judson. *Brains of Rats & Men: A Survey of Origin...* 1926. Chicago. 382p. F/dj. G1. $75.00

HERRICK, C. Judson. *Thinking Machine*. 1932. Chicago. 2nd. 12mo. 374p. VG/dj. G1. $37.50

HERRICK, James. *Short History of Cardiology*. 1942. Springfield. 1st ed. 258p. xl. A13. $100.00

HERRIMAN, George. *Krazy Kat: The Comic Art of George Herriman*. ils. 223p. F. M13. $29.00

HERRIOT, James. *James Herriot's Yorkshire*. 1979. St Martin. 1st ed. VG/VG. P3. $15.00

HERRIOT, James. *Vets Might Fly*. 1976. Michael Joseph. 1st ed. VG/VG. p3. $20.00

HERRON, Shaun. *Bird in Last Year's Nest*. 1974. Evans. 1st ed. VG/VG. P3. $20.00

HERRON, Shaun. *Hound & the Fox & the Harper.* 1970. Random. 1st ed. VG/VG. P3. $20.00

HERRON, Shaun. *Miro.* 1969. Random. 1st ed. MTI. sgn. VG/VG. P3. $30.00

HERRON, Shaun. *Through the Dark & Hairy Wood.* 1972. Random. 1st ed. NF/NF. P3. $20.00

HERRON, Shaun. *Whore-Mother.* 1973. Evans. 1st ed. VG/VG. P3. $23.00

HERRON. *Dark Barbarian: Writings of Robert E Howard.* 1984. np. ils. 261p. F. A4. $45.00

HERSEY, Jean. *Halfway to Heaven: A Guatemala Holiday.* 1947. Prentice Hall. 1st ed. sgn. 8vo. 259p. VG/VG. B11. $35.00

HERSEY, John. *Hiroshima.* 1983. LEC. 1st ed. sgn Hersey/Warren/Lawrence. blk leather. F/case. B4. $1,250.00

HERSEY, John. *War Lover.* 1959. Knopf. 1st ed. G/VG. B35. $18.00

HERSHISER, Orel. *Out of the Blue.* 1989. Wolgemuth Hyatt. 1st ed. F/F. P8. $20.00

HERTRICH, William. *Huntington Botanical Gardens 1905-1949.* 1949. San Marino. Huntington Lib. 1st ed. 1/1000. 167p. NF. T10. $100.00

HERTZBERG, Robert. *Modern Handgun.* 1965. NY. 1st ed. photos. 112p. F/F. E1. $35.00

HERVEY, Harry. *Barracoon.* 1950. Putnam. 1st ed. F/F. B35. $25.00

HERVEY, John. *American Trotter.* 1947. Coward McCann. 1st ed. VG. O3. $95.00

HERZBERG, Alexander. *Zur Psychologie der Philosophie und der Philosophen.* 1926. Leipzig. Felix Meiner. 1st German ed. 248p. orange line. G1. $40.00

HERZOG, Arthur. *IQ 83.* 1978. Simon Schuster. 1st ed. F/F. P3. $15.00

HERZOG, Arthur. *Make Us Happy.* 1978. Crowell. 1st ed. NF/F. B35. $23.00

HERZOG, Arthur. *Make Us Happy.* 1978. Crowell. 1st ed. VG/VG. P3. $15.00

HERZSTEIN, Robert Edwin. *War That Hitler Won: Most Infamous Propaganda Campaign...* 1978. NY. photos. 491p. G. A17. $10.00

HESKY, Olga. *Sequin Syndicate.* 1969. Dodd Mead. 1st ed. VG. P3. $6.00

HESS, Joan. *Malice in Maggody.* 1987. St Martin. 1st ed. inscr. F/NF. T2. $30.00

HESS, Joan. *Mischief in Maggody.* 1988. St Martin. 1st ed. sgn. F/F. T2. $30.00

HESS, Joan. *Much Ado in Maggody.* 1989. St Martin. 1st ed. sgn. F/F. T2. $25.00

HESS, Joan. *Really Cute Corpse.* nd. BC. VG/VG. P3. $8.00

HESSE, Herman. *Beneath the Wheel.* 1968. FSG. 1st ed. NF/VG. B35. $38.00

HESSE, Herman. *Herman Hesse: Autobiographical Writings.* 1972. FSG. 1st ed. 8vo. F/dj. S9. $35.00

HESSE, Herman. *Steppenwolf.* 1946. Holt. VG/VG. P3. $25.00

HESSE, Herman. *Strange News From Another Star.* 1973. GK Hall Large-Print. xl. dj. P3. $7.00

HESSE & MASON. *Pamphlets, Periodicals & Songs of French Revolutionary Era.* 1989. 4to. 563p. NF. A4. $195.00

HESSELBERG, Erik. *Kon-Tiki & I.* 1950. 1st ed. VG+/chip. S13. $15.00

HESSELTINE, William B. *Three Against Lincoln: Murat Halstead Reports of Caucuses...* 1960. LSU. 1st ed. 8vo. 321p. T10. $25.00

HETRICH, William. *Camellias in the Huntington Gardens.* 1954-59. San Marino, CA. 3 vol. gilt bl cloth. VG/dj. B26. $90.00

HEUSER, Ken. *Whitetail Deer Guide.* 1972. HRW. 1st ed. ils. gilt tan bdg. VG/VG. P12. $8.00

HEUSSER, Albert. *Forgotten General, Robert Erskine, FRS, Geographer...* 1928. np. 4to. 228p. VG. A4. $125.00

HEUSSER, Calvin J. *Pollen & Spores of Chile.* 1971. Tucson. photos. tan cloth. F. B26. $50.00

HEWENS, Frank E. *Murder of the Dainty-Footed Model.* 1968. Macmillan. 1st ed. F/F. P3. $18.00

HEWETT, Edgar L. *Ancient Life in the American Southwest.* 1948. NY. Tudor. 8vo. 392p. tan prt cloth. F/NF. T10. $125.00

HEWETT, Edgar L. *Campfire & Trail.* 1943. Albuquerque. 1st ed. 165p. F/chip. E1. $35.00

HEWITT, E.R. *Better Trout Streams.* 1931. NY. VG. B5. $35.00

HEWITT, Oliver. *Wild Turkey & Its Management.* 1967. WA. 1st ed. ils. 589p. VG/VG. B5. $70.00

HEWLETT, Maurice. *Forest Lovers.* 1898. London. 1st ed. w/sgn note. teg. rebound leather. G. B18. $75.00

HEWSON, Maurice. *Escape From the French.* 1981. London. VG. O7. $25.00

HEY, J.S. *Evolution of Radio Astronomy.* 1973. Science Hist Pub. 1st Am ed. VG. K5. $15.00

HEYEN, William. *Swastika Poems.* nd. Vanguard. UP. 90p. VG/wrp. M20. $20.00

HEYER, Georgette. *Black Moth.* 1961. Heinemann. 18th ed. VG/VG. P3. $18.00

HEYER, Georgette. *Cousin Kate.* 1968. Dutton. 1st Am ed. 318p. VG+/dj. M20. $25.00

HEYER, Georgette. *Death in the Stocks.* 1970. Dutton. 1st ed. 263p. VG/dj. M20. $27.00

HEYER, Georgette. *Lady of Quality.* 1972. Bodley Head. 1st ed. F/F. P3. $20.00

HEYER, Georgette. *My Lord John.* 1975. Dutton. 1st ed. VG/VG. P3. $20.00

HEYER, Georgette. *Simon the Coldheart.* 1979. Dutton. 1st ed. VG/VG. P3. $20.00

HEYER, Georgette. *Why Shoot a Butler?* 1973. Dutton. VG/VG. P3. $20.00

HEYERDAHL, Thor. *Aku-Aku: The Secret of Easter Island.* 1958. Chicago. 1st ed. 384p. F/VG. E1. $50.00

HEYERDAHL, Thor. *Fatu-Hiva Back to Nature.* 1974. Garden City. BC. 276p. F/F. E1. $15.00

HEYERDAHL, Thor. *Kon-Tiki Across the Pacific by Raft.* 1950. Chicago. 1st ed. photos. 304p. F. E1. $40.00

HEYERDAHL, Thor. *Ra Expeditions.* 1971. Garden City. VG. O7. $10.00

HEYERDAHL, Thor. *Ra Expeditions.* 1971. Garden City. 1st Am ed. 341p. F/F. E1. $30.00

HEYERDAHL, Thor. *Tigris Expedition: In Search of Our Beginnings.* 1981. Doubleday. 1st ed. 8vo. ils. 349p. VG. W1. $20.00

HEYLIGER, William. *Detectives Inc.* nd. Goldsmith. hc. VG/VG. P3. $15.00

HEYLIGER, William. *Fighting Blood.* 1943. Goldsmith. G+. P12. $6.00

HEYLIGER, William. *Loser's End.* 1937. Goldsmith. VG/VG. $20.00

HEYMAN, G. *Die Psychologie der Frauen.* 1910. Heidelberg. Carl Winter. sm 8vo. 308p. G. G1. $45.00

HEYMAN, Max L. *Prudent Soldier: Biography of Major General...* 1959. Glendale. photos/index. 418p. F. E1. $125.00

HEYWOOD, Thomas. *Life of Merlin, Surnamed Ambrosius; His Prophesies...* 1812. Carmarthen. J Evens. 8vo. list of subscribers. xl. VG. T10. $500.00

HEYWOOD, V.H. *Popular Encyclopedia of Plants.* 1982. Cambridge. ils. VG/dj. B26. $40.00

HIAASEN, Carl. *Double Whammy.* 1987. Putnam. 1st ed. author's 2nd novel. F/F. M22. $70.00

HIAASEN, Carl. *Double Whammy.* 1987. Putnam. 1st ed. sgn. F/F. T2. $100.00

HIAASEN, Carl. *Double Whammy.* 1987. Putnam. 1st ed. sgn. VG/VG. B11. $85.00

HIAASEN, Carl. *Finally...I'm a Doctor.* 1976. Scribner. 1st ed. NF/F. H11. $90.00

HIAASEN, Carl. *Native Tongue.* 1991. Knopf. 1st ed. sgn. F/F. H11. $60.00

HIAASEN, Carl. *Native Tongue.* 1991. Knopf. 1st ed. sgn. NF/NF. N4. $50.00

HIAASEN, Carl. *Native Tongue.* 1991. Knopf. 1st ed. VG+/F. A20. $26.00

HIAASEN, Carl. *Skin Tight.* 1989. Putnam. 1st ed. P stp on top edges. NF/F. H11. $50.00

HIAASEN, Carl. *Skin Tight.* 1989. Putnam. 1st ed. sgn. F/F. T2. $55.00

HIAASEN, Carl. *Stormy Weather.* 1995. Knopf. 1st ed. sgn. F/F. B35. $55.00

HIAASEN, Carl. *Strip Tease.* 1993. Knopf. ARC. F/pict wrp. B35. $75.00

HIAASEN, Carl. *Strip Tease.* 1993. Knopf. 1st ed. F/F. N4. $30.00

HIAASEN, Carl. *Strip Tease.* 1993. Knopf. 1st ed. sgn. F/dj. B11/B35. $45.00

HIAASEN, Carl. *Tourist Season.* 1986. Putnam. 1st ed. author's 1st solo book. rem mk. NF/NF. M23. $25.00

HIAASEN & MONTALBANO. *Trapline.* 1982. Atheneum. 1st ed. F/F. B4. $350.00

HIATT, Ben. *Fish Poems.* 1968. Runcible Spoon. 10p. wrp. A17. $17.50

HIBBEN, Frank C. *Kiva Art of the Anasazi at Pottery Mound.* 1975. Las Vegas. 1st ed. obl 4to. 145p. NF/dj. T10. $100.00

HIBBERD, Shirley. *Familiar Garden Flowers.* nd. Cassell. 3rd series. 12mo. ils FE Hulme. VG+. T10. $45.00

HIBBERT, Christopher. *Personal History of Samuel Johnson.* 1971. Harper. BC. 364p. cloth. AN/dj. B22. $3.50

HICHENS, Robert. *Dweller on the Threshold.* 1911. Century. 1st ed. VG. P3. $40.00

HICKERSON, Thomas Felix. *Happy Valley History & Genealogy.* 1940. Chapel Hill. self pub. 1st ed. 244p. NF/dj. M8. $450.00

HICKEY, T. Earl. *Time Chariot.* 1966. Avalon. 1st ed. VG/VG. P3. $20.00

HICKMAN, James C. *Jepson Manual: Higher Plants of California.* 1993. Berkeley. 240 pl/color map/ils. 1400p. M/dj. B26. $70.00

HICKMAN & WEIS. *Dragon Lance Chronicles.* 1988. TSR. 1st hc ed. F/F. G10. $30.00

HICKOK, Lorena A. *Eleanor Roosevelt: Reluctant First Lady.* 1980. Dodd Mead. 1st ed thus. F/F. M23. $20.00

HICKS, Edwin P. *Belle Starr & Her Pearl.* 1963. Little Rock. 1st ed. photos. 183p. NF/chip. E1. $65.00

HICKS, Granville. *Proletarian Literature in the United States.* 1935. NY. Internat. 1st ed. VG. B2. $45.00

HICKS, James E. *Notes on US Ordnance Vol II 1776-1941.* 1971. Greens Farms, CT. rpt of 1941 ed. ils. 252p. F/VG. E1. $40.00

HICKS, James E. *US Military Firearms.* 1962. Alhambra. 1st ed. ils. 216p. F/F. E1. $40.00

HICKS, Jimmie. *WW Robinson: A Biography & a Bibliography.* 1970. Zamorano Club. 1/825. fwd Lawrence Clark Powell. 83p. F/sans. B19. $35.00

HICKS, John Edward. *Adventures of a Tramp Printer, 1880-1890.* 1950. Kansas City, MO. 1st ed. inscr. 285p. F/F. E1. $45.00

HIGGINBOTHAM, Don. *Daniel Morgan: Revolutionary Rifleman.* 1961. Chapel Hill. 239p. F/VG. E1. $35.00

HIGGINS, Alice. *Babies.* 1933. Whitman. ils Maud Tousey Fangelm. VG+/stiff wrp. M5. $60.00

HIGGINS, Alice. *Runaway Rhymes.* 1931. Rainbow Ed. rpt. 14 pl. gilt bl cloth. G+. T5. $45.00

HIGGINS, George V. *Choice of Enemies.* 1984. Knopf. 1st ed. VG/VG. P3. $18.00

HIGGINS, George V. *City on a Hill.* 1975. Knopf. 1st ed. VG/VG. P3. $35.00

HIGGINS, George V. *Digger's Game.* 1973. Knopf. 1st ed. author's 2nd book. F/NF. H11/M23. $30.00

HIGGINS, George V. *Friends of Eddie Coyle.* 1972. Knopf. 1st ed. author's 1st book. F/F. H11. $50.00

HIGGINS, George V. *Friends of Eddie Coyle.* 1972. Knopf. 1st ed. VG/VG. P3. $30.00

HIGGINS, George V. *Imposters.* 1986. Holt. 1st ed. VG/VG. P3. $17.00

HIGGINS, George V. *Judgment of Deke Hunter.* 1976. Little Brn. 1st ed. VG/VG. P3. $20.00

HIGGINS, George V. *Kennedy for the Defense.* 1980. Knopf. 1st ed. VG/VG. P3. $20.00

HIGGINS, George V. *Outlaws.* 1987. Holt. 1st ed. VG/VG. P3. $19.00

HIGGINS, George V. *Patriot Game.* 1982. Knopf. 1st ed. VG/VG. P3. $20.00

HIGGINS, George V. *Victories.* 1990. Holt. 1st ed. VG/VG. P3. $20.00

HIGGINS, George V. *Wonderful Years, Wonderful Years.* 1988. Holt. 1st ed. VG/VG. P3. $20.00

HIGGINS, George V. *Year or So With Edgar.* 1979. Harper Row. 1st ed. F/F. H11. $35.00

HIGGINS, Jack. *Confessional.* 1985. Stein Day. 1st ed. AN/VG. N4. $15.00

HIGGINS, Jack. *Day of Judgment.* 1978. Collins. 1st ed. VG/VG. P3. $20.00

HIGGINS, Jack. *Eye of the Storm.* 1992. Putnam. 1st ed. F/F. P3. $20.00

HIGGINS, Jack. *Luciano's Luck.* 1981. Collins. 1st ed. VG/VG. P3. $15.00

HIGGINS, Jack. *Night of the Fox.* 1986. Simon Schuster. 1st ed. VG/VG. P3. $18.00

HIGGINS, Jack. *On Dangerous Ground.* 1994. Putnam. 1st ed. VG/VG. P3. $23.00

HIGGINS, Jack. *Season in Hell.* 1989. Simon Schuster. 1st ed. NF/NF. P3. $20.00

HIGGINS, Jack. *Solo.* 1980. Collins. 1st ed. VG/VG. P3. $15.00

HIGGINS, Jack. *Solo.* 1980. Stein Day. 1st ed. VG/VG. P3. $15.00

HIGGINS, Jack. *Storm Warning.* 1976. HRW. 1st ed. VG/VG. P3. $20.00

HIGGINS, Jack. *Storm Warning.* 1986. Collins. 1st ed. VG/VG. P3. $25.00

HIGGINS, Nathan Irvin. *Black Odyssey.* 1977. Pantheon. 1st ed. F/F. M23. $25.00

HIGGINSON, A.H. *Letters From an Old Sportsman to a Young One.* 1929. Doubleday. 1st trade ed. VG. O3. $48.00

HIGGINSON, Thomas Wentworth. *Cheerful Yesterdays.* 1898. Houghton Mifflin. 1st ed. 374p. NF. M8. $85.00

HIGH, Philip E. *These Savage Futurians.* 1969. Dobson. F/F. P3. $25.00

HIGH, Philip E. *Twin Planets.* 1968. Dobson. 1st ed. NF/NF. P3. $25.00

HIGHAM, Charles. *Adventures of Conan Doyle.* 1976. Norton. 1st ed. VG/VG. P3. $25.00

HIGHAM, Charles. *Charles Laughton: An Intimate Biography.* 1976. Doubleday. 1st ed. sgn. 239p. F/NF. T10. $50.00

HIGHSMITH, Patricia. *Black House.* nd. BC. VG/VG. P3. $10.00

HIGHSMITH, Patricia. *Boy Who Followed Ripley.* 1980. Lippincott Crowell. 1st Am ed. sgn. RS. w/author photo. F/F. A11. $100.00

HIGHSMITH, Patricia. *Strangers on a Train.* 1950. NY. 1st ed. author's 1st book. VG/rpr. C2. $75.00

HIGHSMITH, Patricia. *Tales of Natural & Unnatural Catastrophes.* 1989. NY. 1st Am ed. F/F. A17. $9.50

HIGHTOWER, Lynn S. *Flashpoint.* 1995. Harper Collins. F/F. P3. $22.00

HIGHWATER, Jamake. *Sun, He Dies.* 1980. Lippincott Crowell. 1st ed. F/F. M19. $17.50

HIJUELOS, Oscar. *Fourteen Sisters of Emilio Montez O'Brien.* 1993. FSG. 1st ed. NF/F. H11. $35.00

HIJUELOS, Oscar. *Mambo Kings Play Songs of Love.* 1989. FSG. 1st ed. F. B35. $35.00

HILDEBRANDT & HILDEBRANDT. *Art of the Brothers Hildebrandt.* nd. BC. VG/VG. P3. $15.00

HILDEBRANDT & HILDEBRANDT. *Pop-Up Action Circus Book.* nd. NY. Questor/Child Guidance ed. obl 4to. F. T10. $25.00

HILDRETH, P. *White Slave; or, Memoirs of a Fugitive.* 1852. Boston. 1st ed. ils. 408p. VG. B5. $75.00

HILGARTNER, Beth. *Necklace of Fallen Stars.* 1979. Little Brn. 1st ed. F/F. P3. $13.00

HILL, Alfred J. *History of Company E of the Sixth Minnesota Regiment...* 1899. St Paul. 45p. later cloth. M8. $650.00

HILL, Clara C. *Spring Flowers of the Lower Columbia Valley.* 1958. Seattle. ils. VG/dj. B26. $16.00

HILL, Douglas. *Colsec Rebellion.* 1985. Atheneum. 1st ed. VG/VG. P3. $15.00

HILL, Douglas. *Deathwing Over Veynaa.* 1980. Atheneum. 1st Am ed. NF/NF. G10. $5.00

HILL, Douglas. *Exiles of Colsec.* 1984. Gollancz. 1st ed. F/F. P3. $18.00

HILL, Douglas. *Galactic Warlord.* 1979. Gollancz. 1st ed. F/F. P3. $25.00

HILL, Douglas. *Planet of the Warlord.* 1981. Atheneum. 1st Am ed. NF/NF. G10. $5.00

HILL, Grace Livingston. *April Gold.* 1936. Phil. 1st ed. NF/VG. H7. $20.00

HILL, Grace Livingston. *Blue Run.* 1928. Phil. 1st ed. VG/G. H7. $20.00

HILL, Grace Livingston. *Girl in the Woods.* 1942. Lippincott. 303p. VG/dj. M20. $25.00

HILL, Grace Livingston. *Mystery Flowers.* 1936. Phil. 1st ed. VG/G. H7. $20.00

HILL, Grace Livingtston. *Duskin.* 1929. Lippincott. 1st ed. NF/NF. B4. $85.00

HILL, Grace Livingtston. *Unwilling Guest.* 1902. Phil. Judson. 1st ed. F. B4. $100.00

HILL, J.L. *End of the Cattle Trail.* nd. Long Beach. photos. 120p. VG/wrp. E1. $75.00

HILL, John; see Koontz, Dean R.

HILL, Kate Adele. *Home Demonstration Work in Texas.* 1958. San Antonio. Sgn/#d Professional ed. 208p. F/F. E1. $25.00

HILL, Lewis. *Fruits & Berries for the Home Garden.* 1977. NY. ils/photos/drawings. VG+/dj. B26. $17.50

HILL, Mabel B. *Most Popular Mother Goose Songs Illustrated.* 1915. Hinds Hayden Eldredge. sm 4to. VG. C8. $125.00

HILL, Mildred Martin. *Traipsin' Heart.* 1942. NY. Wendell Malliet. 1st ed. inscr. F/NF. B4. $385.00

HILL, Pamela. *Green Salamander.* 1977. St Martin. 1st Am ed. 8vo. F/F. T10. $25.00

HILL, Philip G. *Power Generation.* 1980. MIT. 403p. F/dj. P4. $20.00

HILL, Reginald. *Clubbable Woman.* 1984. Foul Play. VG/VG. P3. $20.00

HILL, Reginald. *Ruling Passion.* 1977. Harper Row. 1st ed. VG/G. P3. $18.00

HILL, Reginald. *Underworld.* 1988. Collins Crime Club. 1st ed. VG/G. P3. $15.00

HILL, Ruth Beebe. *Hanta Yo.* 1979. Garden City. 1st ed. VG/G. B5. $30.00

HILL & HILL. *Indian Petroglyphs of the Pacific Northwest.* 1974. WA U. 1st ed. 320p. cloth. VG/dj. M20. $32.00

HILLEARY, William M. *Webfoot Volunteer, Diary of William M Hilleary 1864-66.* 1965. Corvallis. OR State. 8vo. 240p. T10. $25.00

HILLERMAN, Tony. *Coyote Waits.* 1990. Harper Row. 1st ed. F/F. H11. $35.00

HILLERMAN, Tony. *Coyote Waits.* 1990. Harper Row. 1st ed. NF/NF. P3. $20.00

HILLERMAN, Tony. *Coyote Waits.* 1990. Harper Row. 1st ed. sgn. F/F. T2. $45.00

HILLERMAN, Tony. *Dance Hall of the Dead.* 1991. Armchair Detective. 1st trade ed. M/dj. A18. $25.00

HILLERMAN, Tony. *Dark Wind.* 1983. Gollancz. 1st Eng ed. sgn bookplate. F/F. M19. $75.00

HILLERMAN, Tony. *Finding Moon.* 1995. Harper Collins. 1st ed. 1/300. sgn/#d. F/sans pict case. T2. $150.00

HILLERMAN, Tony. *Hillerman Country.* 1991. NY. 1st ed. F/F. E1. $75.00

HILLERMAN, Tony. *Listening Woman.* 1994. Armchair Detective. ltd ed. 1/26. sgn/lettered. F/sans/case. T2. $55.00

HILLERMAN, Tony. *Mysterious West.* 1994. Harper Collins. 1st ed. sgn Hillerman/JA Jance. F/F. T2. $35.00

HILLERMAN, Tony. *New Mexico, Rio Grande, & Other Essays.* 1992. Graphic Arts Center. 1st ed. photos. M/dj. A18. $35.00

HILLERMAN, Tony. *Sacred Clowns.* 1993. Harper Collins. ARC. F/wrp. B2. $45.00

HILLERMAN, Tony. *Sacred Clowns.* 1993. Harper Collins. later prt. NF/NF. N4. $12.50

HILLERMAN, Tony. *Sacred Clowns.* 1993. Harper Collins. 1st ltd ed. 1/500. sgn/#d. M/case. A18. $100.00

HILLERMAN, Tony. *Sacred Clowns.* 1993. Harper Collins. 1st trade ed. M/dj. A18. $25.00

HILLERMAN, Tony. *Skinwalkers.* 1986. Harper Row. ARC/1st ed. RS. F/F. T2. $50.00

HILLERMAN, Tony. *Talking God.* 1989. Harper Row. 1st ed. F/F. P3. $20.00

HILLERMAN, Tony. *Talking God.* 1989. Harper Row. 1st ed. M/M. A18. $25.00

HILLERMAN, Tony. *Thief of Time.* 1988. Harper Row. 1st ed. M/M. A18. $35.00

HILLIARD, John Northern. *Great Magic: A Practical Treatise on Modern Magic.* 1938. Minneapolis. 3rd. 1004p. buckram. G+. B18. $35.00

HILLIER & SHINE. *Walt Disney's Mickey Mouse Memorabilia...1938.* 1986. Abrams. 4to. 180p. F/F. A4. $60.00

HILLYARD, M.B. *New South: Its Resources & Attractions.* 1887. Baltimore. Mfg Record Co. 413p. aeg. emb leather. VG. B10. $75.00

HILLYER, Robert. *Gates of the Compass.* 1930. Viking. 1st ed. sgn. 83p. bl cloth/cream spine. B11. $40.00

HILLYER, V.M. *Child Training.* 1915. Century. 1st ed. VG. P2. $45.00

HILLYER, V.M. *Kindergarten at Home.* 1951. Baltimore. Calvert School. 1st ed. VG. B5. $35.00

HILTON, George. *Great Lakes Car Ferries.* 1962. Howell-North. 1st ed. VG/dj. A16. $65.00

HILTON, George. *Night Boat.* 1968. Howell-North. 1st ed. sgn. G/fair. A16. $90.00

HILTON, James. *Good-bye, Mr Chips.* 1935. Little Brn. 1st ils ed. 1/600. sgn. ils/sgn HM Brock. F/#d case. B24. $350.00

HILTON, James. *Nothing So Strange.* 1947. Little Brn. 1st ed. VG/VG. P3. $23.00

HILTON, James. *To You, Mr. Chips!* 1938. Hodder Stoughton. 1st ed. VG/G. P3. $30.00

HILTON, John Buxton. *Death of an Alderman.* 1968. Cassell. 1st ed. VG/VG. P3. $30.00

HILTON, John Buxton. *Green Frontier.* 1990. Collins Crime Club. VG/VG. P3. $18.00

HILTON, Ronald. *Bibliography of Latin America & the Caribbean.* 1980. Scarecrow. 1st ed. 675p. F3. $45.00

HILTON. *Pre-Raphaelites.* 1979. Abrams. cloth. F/F. D2. $40.00

HIMES, Chester. *Cotton Comes to Harlem.* 1965. NY. 1st ed. VG/G. B5. $55.00

HIMES, Chester. *Pinktoes.* 1965. Putnam/Stein Day. 1st ed. VG/VG. P3. $40.00

HIMES, Chester. *Pinktoes.* 1965. Putnam/Stein Day. 1st ed thus. NF/NF. M22. $75.00

HIMMEL, Richard. *23rd Web.* 1977. Random. 1st ed. F/F. P3. $15.00

HINCKLEY, F.L. *Directory of Antique Furniture.* 1953. NY. 1st ed. VG/VG. B5. $45.00

HIND, Arthur M. *History of Engraving & Etching From 15th Century to 1914.* 1963. np. rpt. ils. 505p. VG/wrp. A4. $35.00

HIND, Arthur M. *Introduction to History of Woodcut.* 1935. Houghton Mifflin. 2 vol. 1st Am ed. ils. red leather labels. F. T10. $250.00

HIND, Arthur M. *Rembrandt's Etchings: An Essay & a Catalogue.* 1912. London. Methuen. 2 vol. teg. cloth. D2. $115.00

HINDLEY, Geoffrey. *Great Buildings of the World.* 1968. Feltham, Middlesex. 1st ed. 189p. F/F. E1. $25.00

HINDS, N.E.A. *Geomorphology: The Evolution of Landscape.* 1943. Prentice Hall. 1st ed. ils 894p. VG. D8. $20.00

HINDS. *How To Make Money Buying & Selling Old Books.* 1974. ils. 334p. VG/pict wrp. A4. $65.00

HINE, Robert V. *Community on the American Frontier.* 1980. Norman. 1st ed. 292p. F/F. E1. $20.00

HINGSTON. *Genial Showman, Being Reminiscences of Artemus Ward.* 1870. London. JC Hotten. 2 vol. 1st ed. VG. A9. $150.00

HINKEMEYER, Michael T. *Fourth Down, Death.* 1985. St Martin. 1st ed. VG/VG. P3. $14.00

HINKLE, Fred. *Saddle & the Statue.* 1961. Wichita. photos 132p pict cloth. F. E1. $30.00

HINMAN, Russell. *Eclectic Physical Geography.* 1888. Cincinnati. Van Antwerp Bragg. 8vo. 382p. gilt cloth. G. K5. $16.00

HINOJOSA, Gilberto Miguel. *Borderlands Town in Transition. Loredo: 1755-1870.* 1983. College Station. 1st ed. photos. F/F. E1. $25.00

HINSDALE, B A *President Garfield & Education.* 1882. Hiram College Memorial. 433p. decor cloth. G. B18. $17.50

HINSDALE, Wilbert B. *Archaeological Atlas of Michigan.* 1931. Ann Arbor. 21 maps. F. O7. $625.00

HINTON, Harwood P. *Arizona & the West, a Quarterly Journal of History.* Winter 1969. Tucson, AZ. Vol 11, No 4. ils/photos/index. F/wrp. E1. $20.00

HINTON, John Howard. *History of Topography of the United States.* 1830. London. 2 vol. steel engravings/fld maps. VG. B5. $800.00

HINTON, S.E. *Tex.* 1979. Delacorte. ARC. RS. F/F. B4. $100.00

HINTON, S.E. *That Was Then, This Is Now.* 1971. Viking. 1st ed. F/clip. B4. $125.00

HINTON, Ted. *Ambush, the Real Story of Bonnie & Clyde.* 1979. Austin, TX. 1st ed. photos/index. 211p. F/F. E1. $45.00

HINTZE, Naomi A. *You'll Like My Mother.* nd. Putnam. 2nd ed. VG/VG. P3. $10.00

HINXMAN, Margaret. *Night They Murdered Chelsea.* 1984. Collins Crime Club. 1st ed. VG/VG. P3. $13.00

HINZ, Christopher. *Anachronisms.* 1988. St Martin. 1st ed. F/F. P3. $18.00

HIROOKA, Kosaku. *Latest Guide for Travellers to Japan...* 1915. Tokyo. 2nd. ils/fld map. 270p. VG+. B14. $100.00

HIRSCH, Joseph. *First Hundred Years of Mt Sinai Hospital of NY.* 1952. NY. 1st ed. 364p. VG. A13. $30.00

HIRSCH, Nathaniel D.M. *Dynamic Causes of Juvenile Crime.* (1937). Cambridge. Sci-Art Pub. 250p. prt ruled bl cloth. VG. G1. $35.00

HIRSCH, Nathaniel D.M. *Genius & Creative Intelligence.* 1931. Cambridge. Sci-Art Pub. 339p. prt red cloth. G1. $40.00

HIRSH & LOUBERT. *Great Canadian Comic Books.* hc. ils. 264p. F. M13. $125.00

HIRSIMAKI, Eric. *Lakers 1950-1959.* 1991. Mileposts. AN/dj. A16. $40.00

HIRST, Stephen. *Life in a Narrow Place.* 1976. McKay. 2nd. 8vo. 302p. NF/NF. T10. $35.00

HISCOCK, Eric. *Two Yachts, Two Voyages.* 1984. Norton. ils/? maps. VG/dj. T7. $20.00

HISCOX, Gardner D. *Gas, Gasoline & Oil Vapor Engines.* 1898. NY. Henley. 2nd. 8vo. ils/diagrams/photos. VG. T10. $75.00

HISLOP, Herbert R. *Englishman's Arizona: The Ranching Letters of...* 1965. Tucson. 1/510. ils. 74p. F. E1. $100.00

HISLOP, John. *Steeplechasing.* 1951. Graycaines. 1st ed. ils. 256p. gilt gr cloth. VG/dj. H3. $50.00

HISSEY, Jane. *Little Bear Lost.* nd. Hutchinson. 1st ed. 4to. ils. unp. VG. C14. $12.00

HITCHCOCK, Alfred. *Alfred Hitchcock's Fireside Book of Suspense.* 1947. Simon Schuster. 1st ed. VG. M22. $15.00

HITCHCOCK, Alfred. *Best of Mystery.* nd. Galahad. 2nd ed. hc. VG/VG. P3. $10.00

HITCHCOCK, Alfred. *Brief Darkness.* 1988. Castle. hc. VG/VG. P3. $13.00

HITCHCOCK, Alfred. *Daring Detectives.* 1969. Random. VG/VG. P3. $20.00

HITCHCOCK, Alfred. *Haunted Houseful.* 1961. Random. 1st ed. decor brd. VG. P3. $15.00

HITCHCOCK, Alfred. *Solve-Them-Yourself Mysteries.* 1963. Random. decor brd. NF. P3. $15.00

HITCHCOCK, Alfred. *Spellbinders in Suspense.* 1967. Random. VG/VG. P3. $20.00

HITCHCOCK, Alfred. *Stories Not for the Nervous.* 1966. Reinhardt. 1st ed. VG/VG. P3. $25.00

HITCHCOCK, Alfred. *Stories That Go Bump in the Night.* 1977. Random. 1st ed. VG/VG. P3. $18.00

HITCHCOCK, Alfred. *Stories To Be Read With Door Locked.* 1975. Random. 1st ed. VG/VG. P3. $20.00

HITCHCOCK, Alfred. *Supernatural Tales of Terror & Suspense.* 1973. Random. decor brd. VG. P3. $15.00

HITCHCOCK, Alfred. *Tales of Terror.* 1986. Galahad. VG/VG. P3. $15.00

HITCHCOCK, Alfred. *Tales To Send Chills Down Your Spine.* 1979. Dial. 1st ed. VG/VG. P3. $20.00

HITCHCOCK, Alfred. *Tales To Take Your Breath Away.* 1982. Reinhardt. 1st ed. VG/VG. P3. $20.00

HITCHCOCK, Alfred. *Witch's Brew.* 1977. Random. 1st ed. decor brd. VG. P3. $15.00

HITCHCOCK, E.A. *Fifty Years in Camp & Field...* 1909. NY. 1st ed. 514p. gilt bdg. F. E1. $175.00

HITCHCOCK, Edward. *Religious Truth, Illustrated From Science.* 1862. Glasgow. VG. V4. $50.00

HITCHENS, Dolores. *Bank With the Bamboo Door.* 1965. Simon Schuster. 1st ed. xl. dj. P3. $5.00

HITCHENS, Dolores. *Baxter Letters.* 1968. Michael Joseph. 1st ed. VG/G. P3. $20.00

HITCHENS & HITCHENS. *One-Way Ticket.* 1956. Crime Club. 1st ed. VG/VG. P3. $40.00

HITLER, Adolf. *Mein Kampf.* 1939. Stackpole. 1st unexpurgated ed. VG. M19. $100.00

HITLER, Adolph. *Der Grobdeutsche Freiheitskampf. Vol II.* 1941. Muunchen. Zentralverlag der NDSAP. sgn Himmler. VG. B4. $1,600.00

HITTELL, John S. *Discovery of Gold in California.* 1968. Palo Alto. VG. O7. $65.00

HITTELL, Theodore H. *El Triunfo de la Cruz.* 1963. San Francisco. VG. O7. $15.00

HITTI, Philip K. *Arabs: A Short History.* 1953. Macmillan. rpt of 2nd w/corrections. 12mo. VG/dj. W1. $16.00

HJORTSBERG, William. *Falling Angel.* 1978. HBJ. 1st ed. F/NF. H11. $75.00

HJORTSBERG, William. *Gray Matters.* 1971. Simon Schuster. 1st ed. author's 3rd novel. NF/NF. M22. $40.00

HJORTSBERG, William. *Nevermore.* 1994. Atlantic Monthly. 1st ed. F/NF. M22. $25.00

HOBAN, Inez. *Nicodemus & the Goose.* 1945. Dutton. 1st ed. ils. NF. C8. $95.00

HOBAN, Russell. *Harvey's Hideout.* 1969. NY. Parents Magazine. ils Lillian Hoban. unp. G. T5. $10.00

HOBAN, Russell. *Medusa Frequency.* 1987. Atlantic Monthly. 1st ed. F/F. P3. $20.00

HOBAN, Russell. *Mouse & His Child.* nd. Harper Collins. VG/VG. P3. $15.00

HOBAN, Russell. *Mouse & His Child.* 1967. Harper Row. ils Lillian Hoban. 182p. VG/VG. P2. $30.00

HOBAN, Russell. *Pilgermann.* 1983. Jonathan Cape. 1st ed. VG/VG. P3. $25.00

HOBAN, Tana. *AB See.* c 1982. NY. Greenwillow. stated 1st ed. unp. VG+/VG. C14. $12.00

HOBAN, Tana. *Is It Rough? Is It Smooth? Is It Shiny?* 1984. Greenwillow. 1st ed. ils. F/NF. C8. $35.00

HOBAN, Tana. *Red, Blue, Yellow Shoe.* 1986. Greenwillow. 1st ed. 16mo. VG. C14. $8.00

HOBART, Henry. *Reports of That Reverend & Learned Judged...* 1678. London. contemporary calf. M11. $350.00

HOBBS, William Herbert. *Glacial Anticyclones.* 1926. Macmillan. ils/pl/figures. 198p. cloth. G. K5. $36.00

HOBHOUSE, L.T. *Development & Purpose: An Essay Towards a Philosophy...* 1913. Macmillan. thick 8vo. ruled crimson cloth. G1. $65.00

HOBSON, Anthony. *Great Libraries.* 1970. np. 4to. 320p. F/VG. A4. $135.00

HOBSON, Charles E. *Papers of John Marshall, Correspondence, Papers...* 1990. Chapel Hill. 6th vol of Marshall Papers. M11. $50.00

HOBSON, Richard. *Grass Beyond the Mountains.* 1951. NY. 1st ed. VG/VG. B5. $40.00

HOBSON. *Walker Percy: A Comprehensive, Descriptive Bibliography.* 1988. 47 photos. 133p. F. A4. $35.00

HOCH, Edward D. *All But Impossible!* 1981. Ticknor Fields. 1st ed. VG/VG. P3. $20.00

HOCH, Edward D. *Best Detective Stories.* 1980. Dutton. 1st ed. VG/VG. P3. $18.00

HOCH, Edward D. *People of the Peacock.* 1991. Mystery Scene Short Story. 1st ed. 1/100. sgn. hc. sans. P3. $20.00

HOCHBAUM, H.A. *To Ride the Wind.* 1973. Toronto. 1st ed. VG/G. B5. $50.00

HOCHEGGER, Rudolf. *Die Geschichtliche Entwickelung...* 1884. Innsbruck. Wagner'schen Universitats-Buchhandlung. 134p. prt wrp. G1. $50.00

HOCKING, ANNE. *Death Disturbs Mr Jefferson.* 1951. Geoffrey Bles. 1st ed. VG/VG. P3. $25.00

HOCKING, ANNE. *Vultures Gather.* 1946. Geoffrey Bles. 2nd ed. VG/G. P3. $20.00

HOCKING, D. *Trees for Drylands.* 1993. NY. Internat Science Pub. 8vo. 370p. NF/dj. B1. $60.00

HODDER-WILLIAMS, Christopher. *Chain Reaction.* 1959. Hodder Stoughton. 1st ed. VG/VG. P3. $20.00

HODDER-WILLIAMS, Christopher. *Prayer Machine.* 1976. St Martin. 1st ed. VG/VG. P3. $18.00

HODGE, Frederick Webb. *Handbook of American Indians North of Mexico.* 1907. GPO. 2 vol. 8vo. xl. gr buckram. VG. T10. $150.00

HODGE, Paul W. *Concepts of the Universe.* 1969. McGraw Hill. 1st prt. VG. K5. $18.00

HODGE & WRIGHT. *Small Magellanic Cloud.* 1977. Seattle. WA U. ils/charts. VG. K5. $125.00

HODGELL, P.C. *Dark of the Moon.* 1985. Atheneum. 1st ed. RS. F/F. w/promo material. G10. $25.00

HODGES, Russ. *Baseball Complete.* 1952. Rudolph Field. ARC/1st ed. inscr. RS. VG/VG. P8. $60.00

HODGES, Russ. *My Giants.* 1963. Doubleday. 1st ed. VG+/VG. P8. $27.50

HODGKISS, A.G. *Understanding Maps: A Systematic History of Their Use...* 1981. Folkestone. Dawson. 126 maps/ils. AN/dj. O7. $45.00

HODGSON, Barbara. *Tattooed Man.* 1995. Chronicle Books. 1st ed. F/F. M23. $40.00

HODGSON, J.H. *Earthquakes & Earth Structure.* 1964. Prentice Hall. 166p. VG/wrp. D8. $7.50

HOEG, Peter. *Borderliners.* 1994. Toronto. Doubleday. 1st Eng-language ed. author's 2nd novel. F/F. T2. $20.00

HOEG, Peter. *Smilla's Sense of Snow.* 1993. FSG. 1st ed. VG/VG+. N4. $30.00

HOEG, Peter. *Smilla's Sense of Snow.* 1993. FSG. 1st Eng-language ed. author's 1st novel. F/F. M23/T2. $45.00

HOEHLING, A.A. *Great War at Sea: History of Naval Action 1914-1918.* 1965. NY. 1st ed. ils/photos/maps. 336p. VG/VG. E1. $35.00

HOETINK & SLIVE. *Jacob Van Ruesdael.* 1982. Abbeville. ils. 271p. stiff wrp. D2. $50.00

HOFF, Ebbe C. *Bibliographical Sourcebook of Compressed Air, Diving...* 1948. WA. 1st ed. 382p. VG. A13. $60.00

HOFF. *American Watercolor Painting.* 1977. np. cloth. F/F. D2. $75.00

HOFF. *It's Fun Learning Cartooning.* 1952. Stravon. cloth. VG/VG. D2. $50.00

HOFFDING, Harald. *Philosophy of Religion.* 1906. London. Macmillan. trans BE Meyer. 410p. ES. VG. G1. $50.00

HOFFDING, Harald. *Psychologie in Umrissen auf Grundlage der Erfahrung.* 1887. Leipzig. 1st German ed. 463p. leather. G1. $65.00

HOFFENBERG & SOUTHERN. *Candy.* 1964. Putnam. 1st ed. F/F. M19. $85.00

HOFFMAN, Alice. *Drowning Season.* 1979. Dutton. 1st ed. author's 2nd novel. F/F. B4. $65.00

HOFFMAN, Alice. *Illumination Night.* 1987. Putnam. 1st ed. author's 5th book. F/F. B4. $45.00

HOFFMAN, Alice. *Property Of.* 1978. np. 1st Eng ed. F/NF. M19. $32.50

HOFFMAN, Alice. *Second Nature.* 1989. Putnam. ARC. sgn. F/F. w/pub letter. B4. $50.00

HOFFMAN, Blair. *Murder for the Prosecution.* 1993. Carroll Graf. 1st ed. F/NF. H11. $20.00

HOFFMAN, E.T. *Nutcracker.* 1984. Crown. ltd ed. ils Sendak. 102p. M/case. D1. $1,200.00

HOFFMAN, G.W. *Geography of Europe Including Asiatic USSR.* 1969. Ronald Pr. ils. 669p. cloth. VG. D8. $10.00

HOFFMAN, Heinrich. *Slovenly Peter.* nd. Winston. 4to. gilt red cloth. VG. M5. $95.00

HOFFMAN, Heinrich. *Slovenly Peter.* 1920s. Phil. Winston. ils. unp. gilt red cloth. G. D1. $50.00

HOFFMAN, Heinrich. *Der Strewwelpeter.* nd. Frankfort. Rutten Loening. 24p. G+. M20. $60.00

HOFFMAN, Lee. *Loco.* 1969. Doubleday. 1st ed. VG/VG. P3. $18.00

HOFFMAN, Robert L. *More Than a Trial, the Struggle Over Captain Dreyfus.* 1980. NY. Free Pr. M11. $45.00

HOFFMAN, Robert V. *Revolutionary Scene in NJ.* 1942. Am Hist Co. sgn. 8vo. 303p. tan cloth. VG. B11. $75.00

HOFFMAN, Rosekrans. *Sister Sweet Ella.* 1982. Morrow. 1st ed. ils. unp. NF/VG. T5. $25.00

HOFFMAN, William. *Godfires.* 1985. Viking. 304p. F/VG. B10. $10.00

HOFFMANN, E.T.A. *Contes Fantastiques.* (1883). Paris. 2 vol. Librairie des Bibliophiles. quarter leather. VG. T10. $150.00

HOFFMANN, Professor. *More Magic.* nd. McKay. decor brd. NF. P3. $30.00

HOFFMANN, Professor. *Robert-Houdin: Secrets of Conjuring & Magic.* nd. London. ils. VG. M17. $300.00

HOFFMANN. *Tales of Hoffmann.* nd. Dodd Mead. 10 full-p ils. G+. C14. $28.00

HOFLAND, Barbara. *Little Manuel, the Captive Boy.* 1979. Dallas. Somesuch. facsimile of 1831 ed. designed/sgn Carl Hertzog. F. B24. $95.00

HOGAN, James P. *Code of the Lifemaker.* 1983. Del Rey. 1st ed. F/F. P3. $20.00

HOGAN, James P. *Endgame Enigma.* 1987. Bantam. 1st ed. F/F. H11/P3. $20.00

HOGAN, James P. *Entoverse.* 1991. Del Rey. 1st ed. F/F. P3. $20.00

HOGAN, James P. *Proteus Operation.* 1985. Bantam. 1st ed. NF/NF. P3. $20.00

HOGAN, Ray. *Johnny Ringo, Gentleman Outlaw.* 1964. London. 1st ed. 192p. F/G. E1. $40.00

HOGAN, Ray. *Yesterday Rider.* 1976. Doubleday. 1st ed. xl. dj. P3. $5.00

HOGARTH, Burne. *Dynamic Anatomy.* 1984. Watson Guptill. 11th. F/F. P3. $20.00

HOGARTH, Burne. *Tarzan of the Apes.* 1972. Watson Guptill. 1st ed. VG/VG. P3. $30.00

HOGARTH, William. *Hogarth's Peregrination.* 1952. Oxford. VG. O7. $50.00

HOGARTH. *Hogarth Marriage a la Mode & Other Engravings.* 1947. NY. Lear. 1st ed. ils. 90p. F/G. E1. $30.00

HOGG, Ian V. *Armies of the American Revolution.* 1975. Englewood Cliffs. 1st Am ed. ils/photos. 157p. F/F. E1. $45.00

HOGG, Ian V. *Complete Handgun 1300 to Present.* 1979. NY. 1st ed. ils/photos. 128p. F/F. E1. $40.00

HOGG, Ian V. *German Pistols & Revolvers 1871-1945.* 1971. Harrisburg. 1st ed. 160p. F/F. E1. $45.00

HOGG, Ian V. *History of Artillery.* 1974. London. 1st ed. ils/photos. 240p. F/VG. E1. $50.00

HOGG, Ian. *History of Forts & Castles.* 1985. NY. rpt. 256p. F/F. E1. $40.00

HOGG, O.F.G. *Clubs to Cannon: Warfare & Weapons...* 1968. London. 1st ed. 264p. NF/NF. E1. $30.00

HOGNER, Dorothy C. *South to Padre.* 1936h t. NY. 1st ed. 232p. F/VG. E1. $25.00

HOIG, Stan. *Humor of the American Cowboy.* 1970 (1958). Lincoln, NE. Bison. 193p. F/wrp. E1. $10.00

HOKE, Helen. *Terrors, Torments & Traumas.* 1978. Thomas Nelson. 1st ed. VG/VG. P3. $25.00

HOKE, Helen. *Thrillers, Chillers & Killers.* 1979. Elsevier/Nelson. 1st ed. VG/VG. P3. $20.00

HOLABIRD, Katherine. *Angelina & the Princess.* 1984. Potter. 1st Am ed. obl 4to. F/NF. C8. $40.00

HOLBEIN, Hans. *Dance of Death.* 1804. London. Whittingham. 12mo. contemporary half sheep/marbled brd. VG. C6. $150.00

HOLBROOK, Stewart H. *Burning an Empire: Story of American Forest Fires.* 1960. NY. 7th. photos/map. cloth. NF. E1. $25.00

HOLBROOK, Stewart H. *Columbia.* 1956. NY. Lewis & Clark ed. 1/2500. sgn/#d. F/F. E1. $50.00

HOLBROOK, Stewart H. *Little Annie Oakley & Other Rugged People.* 1948. NY. 1st ed. 238p. F/worn. E1. $30.00

HOLBROOK, Stewart H. *Old Post Road...Story of the Boston Post Road.* 1962. NY. 1st ed. Am Trail series. ils/map. F/dj. A17. $25.00

HOLBROOK, Stewart H. *Yankee Loggers.* 1961. np. 123p. NF/wrp. E1. $45.00

HOLDEN, Adele V. *Figurine & Other Poems.* 1961. Dorrance. 1st ed. F/F. B4. $75.00

HOLDEN, Craig. *River Sorrow.* 1994. Delacorte. 1st ed. sgn. F/F. H11. $45.00

HOLDEN, Henrietta Anderson. *Story of the Lone Star State.* 1948. San Antonio. 1/500. 1st ed. sgns. F. E1. $30.00

HOLDEN, Max. *Latest of the World's Best Magic.* nd. NY. 238p. VG. S1. $20.00

HOLDEN, Queen. *Our Baby's Record.* 1927. Boston. Pinkham. 12mo. VG/wrp. M5. $14.00

HOLDING, Elisabeth Sanxay. *Innocent Mrs Duff.* 1946. Dectective BC. VG/VG. P3. $10.00

HOLDING, Elisabeth Sanxay. *Too Many Bottles.* 1951. Simon Schuster. 1st ed. ffe removed. VG. P3. $13.00

HOLDREDGE, H. *Mammy Pleasant.* 1953. NY. 1st ed. VG/VG. B5. $30.00

HOLDSTOCK, Robert. *Encyclopedia of SF.* 1978. Octopus. hc. F/F. P3. $25.00

HOLDSTOCK, Robert. *Where Time Winds Blow.* nd. BC. VG/VG. P3. $8.00

HOLE, Christina. *Witchcraft in England.* nd. BC. hc. VG. P3. $8.00

HOLFORD, Ingrid. *Guinness Book of Weather Facts & Feats.* 1977. Enfield, UK. Guinness Superlatives. xl. K5. $10.00

HOLLAND, C. *Bear Flag.* 1990. 1st ed. VG/VG. K2. $20.00

HOLLAND, C. *Earl.* 1971. Knopf. 1st ed. VG/VG. P3. $20.00

HOLLAND, C. *Lords of Vaumartin.* 1988. Houghton Mifflin. 1st ed. NF/NF. P3. $19.00

HOLLAND, C. *Moncrieff.* 1975. Weybright Talley. 1st ed. VG/VG. P3. $20.00

HOLLAND, C. *Two Ravens.* 1977. Knopf. 1st ed. VG/VG. P3. $20.00

HOLLAND, Dan. *Trout Fisherman's Bible.* 1962. Doubleday. photos. VG. P12. $5.00

HOLLAND, Dan. *Upland Hunter's Bible.* 1961. Doubleday. sc. ils. G+. P12. $3.50

HOLLAND, Ellen Bowie. *Gas As a Grig.* 1963. Austin. sgn. w/sgn card. F/G. E1. $30.00

HOLLAND, Hjalmar R. *America, 1355-1364.* 1946. NY. VG. O7. $35.00

HOLLAND, Hjalmar R. *Old Peninsula Days: Making of an American Community.* 1946. Ephraim, WI. Pioneer Pub. 7th. sgn. ils/maps. gilt blk cloth. NF. T10. $35.00

HOLLAND, HOLLAND & HOLLAND. *Good Shot! A Book of Rod, Gun & Camera.* 1946. Knopf. 1st ltd ed. sgns. VG. B11. $95.00

HOLLAND, Marion. *No Children, No Pets.* 1957 (1956). Weekly Reader BC. 1st ed. 8vo. 182p. G+/G. T5. $12.00

HOLLAND, Ray. *Shotgunning in the Lowlands.* 1945. NY. Barnes. 1st ed. 1/3500. F/VG. H7. $50.00

HOLLAND, Rupert Sargent. *Historic Airships.* 1928. Phil. Macrae Smith. 343p. pict cloth. G+. B18. $45.00

HOLLAND, W. Bob. *Perma Book of Ghost Stories.* 1950. Perma. hc. F. P3. $25.00

HOLLAND & SHADWELL. *Select Titles from the Digest of Justinian.* 1881. Oxford. contemporary morocco. xl. M11. $150.00

HOLLANDER, Bernard. *Brain, Mind & the External Signs of Intelligence.* 1931. Allen Unwin. 288p. navy cloth. VG. G1. $45.00

HOLLANDER, E. *Die Medizin in der Klassischen Malerel.* 1923. Stuttgart. 3rd. 4to. 488p. VG. A13. $250.00

HOLLIDAY, J.S. *World Rushed In: The California Gold Rush Experience.* 1981. NY. 1st ed. 559p. F/F. E1. $35.00

HOLLIDAY, Joe. *Dale of the Mounted Atomic Plot.* 1959. Allen. hc. VG/VG. P3. $18.00

HOLLIDAY, Joe. *Dale of the Mounted in the Arctic.* 1953. Allen. decor brd. VG. P3. $15.00

HOLLIDAY, Michael; see Creasey, John.

HOLLING, Holling C. *Book of Cowboys.* 1936. VG/dj. K2. $48.00

HOLLING, Holling C. *Book of Indians.* 1935. Platt Munk. ils. VG+/G. M5. $28.00

HOLLING, Holling C. *Little Big Bye & Bye.* 1926. Volland. 12th. Sunny Book series. G. M5. $28.00

HOLLING, Holling C. *Minn of the Mississippi.* 1951. Houghton Mifflin. 1st ed. ils. 87p. F/VG. P2. $60.00

HOLLING, Holling C. *Minn of the Mississippi.* 1951. Houghton Mifflin. 1st ed. 87p. yel cloth. VG. T5. $55.00

HOLLING, Holling C. *Paddle to the Sea.* 1941. Houghton Mifflin. 17th. Caldecott honor. VG/VG. B17. $10.00

HOLLING, Holling C. *Tree in the Trail.* 1942. VG/chip. S13. $18.00

HOLLING, Holling C. *Tum Tum Tummy.* 1936. Saalfield. ils. VG-. P2. $45.00

HOLLINGHURST, Alan. *Swimming Pool Library.* 1st ed. author's 1st novel. F/NF. B30. $35.00

HOLLINGWORTH, Leta. *Psychology of Subnormal Children.* 1920. Macmillan. 1st ed. ils. 288p. VG. B14. $55.00

HOLLIS, Jim. *Teach You a Lesson.* 1955. Harper. 1st ed. VG/VG. P3. $18.00

HOLLISTER, Hartman. *Ozzie.* 1974. Vantage. 1st ed. inscr/drawing. 232p. VG/G. B10. $15.00

HOLLISTER, Ovando J. *Mines of Colorado.* 1974. NY. rpt of 1867 ed. 450p. F/F. E1. $30.00

HOLLISTER, Paul M. *Famous Colonial Houses.* 1821. Phil. 1st ed. 170p. teg. decor cloth. G+. B18. $25.00

HOLLISTER, W. *Dinner in the Diner. Great Railroad Recipes.* 1973. Los Angeles. VG/VG. B5. $25.00

HOLLON, W. Eugene. *Lost Pathfinder, Zebulon Montegomery Pike.* 1949. Norman. 1st ed. inscr/dtd. F/NF. E1. $60.00

HOLLOWAY, Carroll C. *Texas Gun Lore.* 1951. San Antonio. ils/biblio/index. 238p. NF/worn. E1. $75.00

HOLMAN, Hugh. *Slay the Murderer.* nd. Grosset Dunlap. VG/VG. P3. $15.00

HOLMAN, Hugh. *Trout in the Milk.* 1945. MS Mill. 1st ed. VG/VG. P3. $30.00

HOLMAN, Louis A. *Old Maps & Their Makers.* 1925. Goodspeed. sgn pres. F/wrp. O7. $50.00

HOLME, Bryan. *Kate Greenaway Book: A Collection of Illustration...* 1983 (1976). NY. Gallery. ils Kate Greenaway. 144p. orange brd. F/VG. T5. $45.00

HOLME, C. Geoffrey. *Children's Toys of Yesterday.* 1932. London. Studio. ils/photos. 128p. beige cloth. VG/VG. D1. $135.00

HOLME, Timothy. *Devil & the Dolce Vita.* 1988. Walker. VG/VG. P3. $17.00

HOLMES, A. *Principles of Physical Geology.* 1965. Ronald Pr. 2nd. 1288p. cloth. VG. D8. $15.00

HOLMES, A. Campbell. *Practical Shipbuilding.* 1916. Longman Gr. 2 vol. 9th. obl 4to. 130 pl/fld plans. VG.T7. $200.00

HOLMES, Charles. *Principles & Practice of Horse-Shoeing.* 1949. Leeds. Farrier's Journal. VG. O3. $35.00

HOLMES, Donald B. *Air Mail: An Ils History 1793-1981.* 1981. NY. 1st ed. 226p. VG/dj. B18. $17.50

HOLMES, Efner Tudor. *Christmas Cat.* 1976. Harper Collins. 4th. ils Tasha Tudor. F/F. B17. $20.00

HOLMES, Jack E. *Politics in New Mexico.* 1967. Albuquerque. 1st ed. 335p. F/VG. E1. $35.00

HOLMES, John Clellon. *Nothing More To Declare.* nd. Dutton. 1st ed. F/NF. M19. $38.00

HOLMES, John Haynes. *Palestine To-Day & To-Morrow.* 1929. Macmillan. 1st ed. 271p. VG. W1. $25.00

HOLMES, Kenneth. *Covered Wagon Women, Diaries & Letters From Western Trails.* 1983-1993. Arthur H Clarke. 11 vol. fld maps/portraits. F. A4. $395.00

HOLMES, Louis A. *Fort McPherson, Nebraska: Guardian of Tracks & Trails.* 1963. Lincoln, NE. 108p. F. E1. $100.00

HOLMES, Oliver Wendell. *Autocrat of the Breakfast Table/Every Man His Own Boswell.* 1858. Boston. 1st ed. 373p. VG. A13. $150.00

HOLMES, Oliver Wendell. *Border Lines of Knowledge in Some Provinces...* 1862. Boston. 1st ed. pub inscr to author. 80p. gr emb cloth. F. B14. $600.00

HOLMES, Oliver Wendell. *Claims of Dentistry. An Address Delivered at Commencement...* 1872. Boston. 35p. modern brd. D14. $150.00

HOLMES, Oliver Wendell. *Common Law.* 1881. Boston. Little Brn. 1st ed. orig cloth. M11. $2,500.00

HOLMES, Oliver Wendell. *Currents & Counter-Currents in Medical Science.* 1861. Ticknor Fields. 1st ed. variant C bdg. VG+. H7. $125.00

HOLMES, Oliver Wendell. *One Hoss Shay.* 1905. Houghton Mifflin. 1st ed thus. teg. F. M5. $85.00

HOLMES, Oliver Wendell. *Our Hundred Days in Europe.* 1887. Boston. 1st ed. 329p. gilt-stp urn on back cover. VG. A4. $45.00

HOLMES, Oliver Wendell. *Over the Teacups.* 1893. Houghton Mifflin. sgn. gilt red cloth. w/sgn note on ffe. T10. $150.00

HOLMES, Oliver Wendell. *Pictures & Problems From London Police Courts.* 1900. London. Thomas Nelson. bl cloth. M11. $50.00

HOLMES, Oliver Wendell. *Poet at the Breakfast Table.* 1872. Boston. 1st ed. 418p. VG. A13. $100.00

HOLMES, Oliver Wendell. *Speeches.* 1891. Little Brn. 1st ed. pres. buff brd. M11. $1,250.00

HOLMES, Prescott. *Battles of the War for the Union.* 1897. Young People's Lib. 16mo. 338p. tan pict cloth. G. T3. $17.00

HOLMES, Samuel Jackson. *Negro's Struggle for Survival: A Study in Human Ecology.* 1937. Berkeley, CA. 1st ed. 296p. cloth. xl. VG. M8. $85.00

HOLMSTROM, J.G. *Drake's Modern Blacksmithing & Horseshoeing.* 1972. NY. Drake. rpt. VG. O3. $25.00

HOLT, A.J. *Pioneering in the Southwest.* 1923. Nashville. 1st ed. 304p. NF. E1. $90.00

HOLT, Edwin Bissell. *Animal Drive & the Learning Process: An Essay...* (1931). Holt. 308p. ruled pebbled bl cloth. xl. VG. G1. $45.00

HOLT, Hazel. *Cruelest Month.* 1991. NY. 1st ed. F/F. H11. $25.00

HOLT, Robert Lawrence. *Good Friday. A Novel.* 1987. Bl Ridge Summit, PA. Aero. 211p. map ep. NF/dj. W1. $18.00

HOLT, Samuel; see Westlake, Donald E.

HOLT, Tom. *Flying Dutch.* 1991. Orbit. 1st ed. F/F. P3. $26.00

HOLT, Tom. *Flying Dutch.* 1992. St Martin. 1st Am ed. F/NF. G10. $15.00

HOLT, Tom. *Goatsong.* 1990. St Martin. 1st ed. VG/VG. P3. $18.00

HOLT, Tom. *Here Comes the Sun.* 1993. Orbit. 1st ed. F/F. P3. $26.00

HOLT, Tom. *Who's Afraid of Beowulf?* nd. BC. VG/VG. P3. $8.00

HOLTBY, Winifred. *South Riding.* 1936. London. Collins. 1st ed. author's last novel. NF/dj. B24. $75.00

HOLTON, Isaac F. *New Granada: 20 Months in the Andes.* 1967. Carbondale. 723p. gilt bl cloth. NF/dj. P4. $18.50

HOLTON, Leonard. *Out of the Depths.* nd. BC. VG/VG. P3. $8.00

HOLTON, Leonard. *Touch of Jonah.* 1968. Dodd Mead. 1st ed. VG/VG. P3. $15.00

HOLUB, Leo. *Leo Holub.* 1982. Stanford Alumni. 1st ed. 125 photos. NF/dj. S9. $150.00

HOLYOAKE, George Jacob. *History of the Last Trial by Jury for Atheism in England.* 1851. London. James Watson. gilt emb bl-gr cloth. M11. $250.00

HOLZER, Erika. *Eye for an Eye.* 1993. Tor. 1st ed. F/F. H11. $30.00

HOLZER, Hans. *Beyond Medicine.* 1973. Henry Regnery. hc. VG. P3. $15.00

HOLZER, Hans. *Haunted Hollywood.* nd. Bobbs Merrill. 2nd ed. VG/VG. P3. $13.00

HOLZER, Hans. *Life After Death.* 1969. Bobbs Merrill. 1st ed. VG. P3. $13.00

HOLZER, Hans. *New Pagans.* nd. BC. VG/VG. P3. $8.00

HOLZMAN, Robert S. *Stormy Ben Butler.* 1954. NY. 1st ed. photo/biblio/index. 207p. F/VG. E1. $45.00

HOLZWORTH, John. *Wild Grizzlies of Alaska.* 1930. NY. 1st ed. VG/G. B5. $60.00

HOME, William Scott. *Strain of Moonlight.* 1985. Strange Company. 1st ed. 1/200. F/pict wrp. G10. $15.00

HOMER. *Iliad.* nd. BOMC. hc. VG/VG. P3. $10.00

HOMER. *Iliad.* 1976. Franklin Lib. leather. F. P3. $35.00

HOMER. *Odyssey of Homer.* 1981. LEC. 1/2000. sgn Moser/Wilson. 300p. F/case. C2. $200.00

HOMER. *Odyssey of Homer.* 1990. CA U. 1st ed. F/F. P3. $25.00

HOMER. *Odyssey.* 1976. Franklin Lib. leather. F. P3. $30.00

HOMES, Geoffrey. *Man Who Didn't Exist* 1938. Triangle. VG. P3. $15.00

HOMES, Geoffrey. *Then There Were Three.* 1944. Books Inc. hc. VG. P3. $10.00

HONIG, Donald. *American League.* 1983. Crown. 1st ed. F/VG+. P8. $75.00

HONIG, Donald. *Boston Red Sox: Illustrated Tribute.* 1984. St Martin. 1st ed. F/VG. P8. $65.00

HONNESS, Elizabeth. *Flight of Fancy.* 1941. Oxford. 1st ed. 8vo. unp. VG. C14. $8.00

HONOUR, Hugh. *New Golden Land.* 1975. NY. ils/photos. 299p. F/VG. E1. $30.00

HOOD, Ann. *Places To Stay the Night.* 1993. Doubleday. 1st ed. sgn. F/F. M19. $20.00

HOOD, C.T. *Manual of Electro Therapeutics.* 1895. Chicago. 1st ed. ils/ads. 181p. VG. B5. $50.00

HOOD, Mary. *And Venus Is Blue.* 1986. Ticknor Fields. 1st ed. F/NF. M23. $25.00

HOOD, Sinclair. *Home of the Heroes.* 1967. McGraw Hill. 1st ed. ils. 144p. xl. G. W1. $12.00

HOOK, Donald D. *Madmen of History.* 1976. Jonathan David. hc. VG/VG. P3. $18.00

HOOK, Thom. *Sky Ship: The Akron Era.* 1976. Annapolis. inscr. 148p. VG/wrp. B18. $22.50

HOOKER, Richard. *M*A*S*H Goes to Maine.* 1972. Morrow. VG/VG. P3. $15.00

HOOKER, Worthington. *Lessons From the History of Medical Delusions.* 1850. NY. Baker Scribner. 105p. cloth. VG. B14. $55.00

HOOKER, Worthington. *Natural History; For Use of Schools & Families.* 1864. NY. ils. 382p. emb cloth. G. A17. $15.00

HOOPER, Frederick. *Military Horse: Equestrian Warrior Through the Ages.* 1976. Cranbury, NJ. 1st Am ed. photos. 105p. F/F. E1. $35.00

HOOVER, F. *Fabulous Dustpan.* 1955. Cleveland. 1st ed. sgn. VG/VG. B5. $25.00

HOOVER, J. Edgar. *Masters of Deceit: Story of Communism in America...* June 1958. Holt. 4-line inscr/dtd 1959. red cloth. VG. B14. $250.00

HOOVER & ZIMMERMAN. *Sioux & Other Native American Cultures of the Dakotas.* 1993. np. 1503 annotated entries. 265p. F. A4. $85.00

HOOVER & ZIMMERMAN. *South Dakota History: An Annotated Bibliography.* 1993. np. 3180 entries. 545p. F. A4. $75.00

HOPE, Andree. *Chronicles of an Old Inn; or, A Few Words About Gray's Inn.* 1887. London. Chapman Hall. xl. M11. $85.00

HOPE, Bob. *Five Women I Love.* 1966. Doubleday. 1st ed. F/clip. B35. $20.00

HOPE, Bob. *I Owe Russia $1,200.* 1963. Doubleday. ils. NF/VG. P12. $4.00

HOPE, Brian; see Creasey, John.

HOPE, Camilla. *Long Shadows.* nd. Internat Fiction Lib. hc. VG/VG. P3. $20.00

HOPE, James Barron. *Wreath of Virginia Bay Leaves.* 1895. West. Johnston. 159p. VG. B10. $25.00

HOPE, Laura Lee. *Bobbsey Twins & Baby May (#17).* 1924. Grosset Dunlap. lists 32 titles. 242p. VG/dj. M20. $27.00

HOPE, Laura Lee. *Bobbsey Twins at the Circus.* 1932. Grosset Dunlap. ils. gr stp gr bdg. G+. P12. $4.00

HOPE, Laura Lee. *Bobbsey Twins at the County Fair (#15).* 1922. Grosset Dunlap. 1st ed. 216p. VG/dj. M20. $52.00

HOPE, Laura Lee. *Bobbsey Twins on Blueberry Island (#10).* 1917. Grosset Dunlap. lists 10 titles. 244p. VG/worn. M20. $37.00

HOPE, Laura Lee. *Outdoor Girls at Cedar Ridge (#21).* 1930. Grosset Dunlap. 1st ed. 214p. G/worn. M20. $37.00

HOPE, Laura Lee. *Outdoor Girls at Spring Hill Farm (#17).* 1927. Grosset Dunlap. lists to #22. 210p. VG/dj. M20. $37.00

HOPE, Laura Lee. *Outdoor Girls in the Air (#22).* 1932. Grosset Dunlap. 1st ed. 213p. VG/dj. M20. $47.00

HOPE, Laura Lee. *Outdoor Girls on a Canoe Trip (#20).* 1930. Grosset Dunlap. lists 21 titles. VG/dj. M20. $47.00

HOPE, Laura Lee. *Outdoor Girls on a Hike (#19).* 1929. Grosset Dunlap. lists to #21. 236p. VG/dj. M20. $42.00

HOPE, Thomas. *Costumes of the Ancients.* 1809. London. Bulmer. 2 vol. 1st ed. 4to. 200 full-p pl. gr pebbled morocco. C6. $350.00

HOPKINS, Kenneth. *Dead Against My Principles.* 1960. HRW. 1st ed. VG/VG. P3. $22.00

HOPKINS, Luther Wesley. *From Bull Run to Appomattox.* 1915. Baltimore. Fleet McGinley. 3rd. 311p. cloth. VG. M8. $85.00

HOPKINS, Sara Winnemucca. *Life Among the Piutes: Their Wrongs & Claims.* 1883. Boston. self pub. inscr. 268p. bl cloth. VG. w/obituary. B14. $350.00

HOPLEY, George; see Woolrich, Cornell.

HOPPE, J.I. *Erklarung der Sinnestauschungen...* 1888. Wurzburg. Adalbert Stuber. 4th. 306p. prt gray wrp. G1. $85.00

HORACE. *Carmina Sapphica.* 1983. Boston. Bromer. Ashendene. 1st prt. 1/150. full brn morocco. AN/box. B24. $275.00

HORAN, Calvin. *Union Army Operations in the Southwest.* 1961. Albuquerque. fld map. 152p. F/NF. E1. $60.00

HORAN, James D. *Across the Cimarron.* 1956. Crown. 1st ed. 301p. VG/dj. M20. $32.00

HORAN, James D. *Authentic Wild West, the Lawmen.* 1980. NY. 1st ed. ils/photos/biblio/index. 309p. F/F. E1. $55.00

HORAN, James D. *Desperate Men: Revelations From Sealed Pinkerton Files.* 1949. NY. 1st ed. ils/index. 296p. NF. E1. $40.00

HORAN, James D. *Desperate Women.* 1952. NY. 1st ed. VG/VG. B5. $20.00

HORAN, James D. *Great American West: Pictorial History...* 1959. NY. 1st ed. ils. 288p. F/F. E1. $50.00

HORAN, James D. *Gunfighters: The Authentic Wild West.* 1976. Crown. 312p. NF/NF. T10. $45.00

HORAN, James D. *King's Rebel.* 1953. NY. 2nd. inscr/dtd. 375p. NF/VG. E1. $25.00

HORAN, James D. *Mathew Brady: Historian With a Camera.* 1955. Bonanza. photos/biblio/index. 244p. NF/NF. E1. $35.00

HORAN, James D. *Mathew Brady: Historian With a Camera.* 1955. NY. 4to. ils. 244p. VG/dj. T3. $30.00

HORAN, James D. *New Vigilantes.* 1975. Crown. 1st ed. VG/VG. P3. $20.00

HORAN, James D. *Pinkertons: Detective Dynasty That Made History.* 1967. NY. 2nd prt. ils. 565p. F/VG. E1. $55.00

HORAN, James D. *Timothy O'Sullivan: America's Forgotten Photographer.* 1966. NY. Bonanza. 400 photos. 334p. F/VG. E1. $40.00

HORANSKY, Ruby. *Dead Ahead.* 1990. Scribner. 1st ed. F/VG+. A20. $12.00

HORGAN, Paul. *Centuries in Santa Fe.* 1957. Macmillan. 8vo. 8 pl/map. VG/dj. T10. $25.00

HORGAN, Paul. *Centuries of Santa Fe.* 1956. Dutton. 1st ed. 363p. F/VG. E1. $50.00

HORGAN, Paul. *Centuries of Santa Fe.* 1956. Dutton. 1st ed. 8vo. 363p. map ep. gilt gr cloth. VG/dj. T10. $35.00

HORGAN, Paul. *Conquistadors in North American History.* 1963. NY. VG. O7. $25.00

HORGAN, Paul. *Devil in the Desert.* 1952. Longman Gr. 1st ed. F/chip. A18. $30.00

HORGAN, Paul. *Distant Trumpet.* 1960. FSC. 1st ed. F/VG+. A18. $40.00

HORGAN, Paul. *Great River: Rio Grande in North American History: 2 Vol.* 1954. BOMC. 1020p. worn case. A17. $30.00

HORGAN, Paul. *Josiah Gregg & His Vision of the Early West.* 1979. FSG. 1st ed. F/NF. M23. $20.00

HORGAN, Paul. *Lamy of Santa Fe.* 1975. NY. 1st ed. sgn. VG/dj. A15. $50.00

HORGAN, Paul. *One Rose for Christmas.* 1952. Longman Gr. 1st ed. VG+/VG. A18. $30.00

HORGAN, Paul. *Peach Stone: Stories From Four Decades.* 1967. FSG. 1st ed. F/VG. A18. $20.00

HORIZON BOOKS. *Horizon Book of the Elizabethan World.* (1967). apparent 1st ed thus? 416p. F/dj. B22. $12.00

HORIZON MAGAZINE EDITORS. *Spanish Armada.* 1966. Am Heritage. 1st ed. 153p. VG. P12. $7.00

HORLER, Sydney. *Curse of Doone.* 1930. Mystery League. 1st ed. VG/VG. P3. $20.00

HORLER, Sydney. *Evil Chateau.* nd. Grosset Dunlap. VG/VG. P3. $25.00

HORLER, Sydney. *False Face.* 1926. Doran. 1st ed. hc. VG. P3. $20.00

HORLER, Sydney. *False Purple.* 1932. Mystery League. 1st ed. VG/VG. P3. $30.00

HORLER, Sydney. *Lady of the Night.* 1941. Herbert Jenkins. 1st ed. VG/G. P3. $30.00

HORLER, Sydney. *My Lady Dangerous.* 1933. Harper. 1st Am ed. VG/NF. B4. $75.00

HORLER, Sydney. *Peril.* 1930. Mystery League. 1st ed. VG. P3. $25.00

HORLER, Sydney. *Tiger Standish Comes Back.* 1970. John Long. NF/NF. P3. $18.00

HORLER, Sydney. *Tiger Standish.* 1933. Crime Club. 1st ed. VG. P3. $15.00

HORN, Calvin. *University in Turmoil & Transition.* 1981. Rocky Mtn Pub. 1st ed. sgn. VG/G. B11. $15.00

HORN, Holloway. *Murder at Linpara.* 1931. Collins. 1st ed. hc. VG. P3. $25.00

HORN, Madeline D. *Farm on the Hill.* 1936. NY. Scribner. 1st ed. ils Grant Wood. VG/dj. D1. $200.00

HORN, Maurice. *Women in the Comics.* 1977. Chelsea. 1st ed. VG/VG. P3. $15.00

HORN, Richard. *Memphis: Objects, Furniture & Patterns.* 1985. Phil. Running Pr. ils/pl. 126p. brd. dj. D2. $25.00

HORN, Stanley F. *Decisive Battle of Nashville.* 1956. Baton Rouge. 1st ed. 181p. F/worn. E1. $45.00

HORN, Tom. *Life of Tom Horn by Himself.* 1904. Denver. 1st ed. 317p. NF/wrp. E1. $135.00

HORNELL, James. *British Coracles & Irish Curaghs.* 1938. London. Soc for Nautical Research. ils/23 pl. 159p. VG/dj. T7. $60.00

HORNER, Francis J. *Case History of Japan.* 1948. NY. 1st ed. 260p. NF. E1. $20.00

HORNER, Harlan Hoyt. *Lincoln & Greeley.* 1953. IL U. 1st ed. 432p. VG/dj. B18. $22.50

HORNIG, Doug. *Deep Dive.* 1988. Mysterious. 1st ed. 264p. F/F. B10. $15.00

HORNIG, Doug. *Foul Shout.* 1984. Scribner. 1st ed. 231p. AN. B10. $15.00

HORNSEY, Pat. *Ships of the Twentieth Century.* 1977. Chartwell. VG/VG. A16. $20.00

HORNUNG, E.W. *Mr Justice Raffles.* 1909. NY. 1st Am ed. gilt cloth. G. A17. $20.00

HORNUNG, E.W. *Raffles.* nd. Readers Lib. VG/tape. P3. $18.00

HORNUNG, E.W. *Raffles: The Amateur Cracksman.* 1991. Isis Lg Prt. decor brd. P3. $20.00

HORNUNG, E.W. *Thief in the Night.* 1905. Scribner. 1st Am ed. 3rd in Raffles series. VG. M22. $20.00

HORST, Claude William. *Model Sail & Power Boats.* 1939. Bruce. revised/enlarged ed. VG/dj. A16. $50.00

HORSTING & VAN HISE. *Midnight Graffiti.* nd. BC. F/F. P3. $10.00

HORTON, Lydiard H. *Dream Problem & the Mechanism of Thought...* 1926. Phil. Cartesian Research Soc. 2 vol. 3rd. 8vo. bl cloth. NF. G1. $100.00

HORTON, R.G. *Youth's History of the Great Civil War in the US.* 1868. NY. 12mo. ils. 384p. gilt gr cloth. G. T3. $42.00

HORWILL. *Dictionary of Modern American Usage.* 1935. Oxford. 360p. VG. A4. $75.00

HORWITZ, Julius. *Inhabitants.* 1960. Cleveland. 1st ed. F/F. A17. $9.50

HORWOOD, William. *Dunction Wood.* 1980. McGraw Hill. 1st ed. VG/VG. P3. $20.00

HORWOOD, William. *Dunction Wood.* 1980. McGraw. 1st ed. F/F. H11. $30.00

HORWOOD, William. *Stonor Eagles.* 1982. Watts. 1st ed. NF/NF. P3. $30.00

HOSKINS, Robert. *Tomorrow's Son.* 1977. Doubleday. 1st ed. VG/VG. P3. $16.00

HOSSENT, Harry. *Movie Treasury: Gangster Movies.* 1974. Octopus. VG/VG. P3. $18.00

HOTCHKISS, Bill. *Ammahabas.* 1983. Norton. 1st ed. sgn. F/F. A18. $20.00

HOTCHKISS, Bill. *Medicine Calf.* 1981. Norton. 1st ed. F/clip VG. A18. $15.00

HOUGH, Emerson. *Covered Wagon.* 1922. Appleton. 1st ed. 8vo. map ep. red cloth. VG. T10. $125.00

HOUGH, Emerson. *54-40 or Fight.* 1909. Bobbs Merrill. 1st ed. 8vo. ils AI Keller. 402p. VG. T10. $60.00

HOUGH, Lynn Harold. *Great Evangel.* 1936. Nashville. Cokesbury. sgn. 12mo. 168p. F/VG. B11. $12.50

HOUGH, Richard. *Bronze Pereus.* 1962. Walker. VG/VG. P3. $10.00

HOUGH, Richard. *Dear Daughter Dead.* 1966. Walker. 1st ed. G/G. P3. $10.00

HOUGH, Richard. *Dreadnought: A History of the Modern Battleship.* 1964. NY. 4th. 268p. F/F. E1. $40.00

HOUGH, Richard. *Fighting Ships.* 1969. London. 1st ed. 304p. NF/tape rpr. E1. $40.00

HOUGH, Richard. *Fleet That Had To Die.* 1958. NY. 1st ed. VG/VG. B5. $25.00

HOUGH, Richard. *Frontier Incident.* 1951. Crowell. NF/NF. P3. $20.00

HOUGH, Richard. *Wings of Victory.* 1980. Morrow. 1st ed. F/F. P3. $13.00

HOUGHTON, Claude. *This Was Ivor Trent.* 1935. Heinemann. 1st ed. hc. VG. P3. $12.00

HOUK, R. *Eastern Wildflowers.* 1989. San Francisco. Chronicle Books. 108p. F/F. B1. $28.00

HOUNSELL, Bernard. *Coach Drives From London.* 1892. Season. 122p. VG. O3. $195.00

HOUSE, Homer D. *Wild Flowers.* 1936. Albany. 3rd. ils. VG. B30. $75.00

HOUSE, Tom. *Jock's Itch.* 1989. Contemporary. 1st ed. F/F. P8. $15.00

HOUSE. *Military Intelligence 1870-1991, a Research Guide.* 1993. np. 882 annotated entries. 165p. F. A4. $60.00

HOUSEHOLD, Geoffrey. *Arabesque.* 1948. Atlantic/Little Brn. 3rd ed. VG/VG. P3. $15.00

HOUSEHOLD, Geoffrey. *Arrows of Desire.* 1985. Atlantic Monthly. 1st ed. VG/VG. P3. $18.00

HOUSEHOLD, Geoffrey. *Courtesy of Death.* 1967. Little Brn. 1st ed. VG/VG. P3. $35.00

HOUSEHOLD, Geoffrey. *Last Two Weeks of Georges Rivac.* 1978. Atlantic/Little Brn. 1st Am ed. F/F. T2. $18.00

HOUSEHOLD, Geoffrey. *Rogue Justice.* nd. Atlantic/Little Brn. 2nd ed. VG/VG. P3. $13.00

HOUSEHOLD, Geoffrey. *Sending.* 1980. Little Brn. 1st Am ed. F/F. T2. $35.00

HOUSEHOLD, Geoffrey. *Summon the Bright Water.* 1981. Atlantic/Little Brn. 1st ed. VG/VG. P3. $18.00

HOUSEHOLD, Geoffrey. *Three Sentinels.* 1972. Little Brn. 1st ed. xl. dj. P3. $6.00

HOUSEHOLD, Geoffrey. *Watcher in the Shadows.* 1962. McClelland Stewart. hc. ffe removed. G. P3. $10.00

HOUSEMAN, A.E. *Introductory Lecture.* 1937. Macmillan. 1st ed. VG/VG. M19. $17.50

HOUSEMAN, A.E. *Name & Nature of Poetry.* 1933. Macmillan. 1st ed. F/NF. H4. $20.00

HOUSEMAN, A.E. *Shropshire Lad.* 1908. London. Grant Richards. ils Wm Hyde. VG. M19. $75.00

HOUSEMAN, A.E. *Shropshire Lad.* 1935. NY. Heritage. ils EA Wilson. 74p. full leather. T10. $250.00

HOUSEWRIGHT, David. *Penance.* 1995. Woodstock. Foul Play. 1st ed. F/F. M23. $40.00

HOUSMAN, L. *Arabian Nights.* 1921. Phil. Penn. ils Virginia Sterrett. 308p. VG. D1. $385.00

HOUSTON, James. *Eagle Song: An Indian Saga Based on True Events.* 1983. HBJ. 8vo. ils. F/NF. T10. $25.00

HOUSTON, James. *Spirit Wrestler.* 1980. HBJ. 1st ed. F/F. A18. $10.00

HOUSTON, Robert. *Fourth Codex.* 1988. Houghton Mifflin. 1st ed. VG/VG. P3. $18.00

HOUTS, Marshall. *From Gun to Gavel. Courtroom Recollections of James Mathers.* 1054. NY 1st ed. 246p. F/NF. E1. $30.00

HOWARD, Alice Woodbury. *Sokar & the Crocodile.* 1959. Macmillan. 14th. 8vo. VG. B17. $4.50

HOWARD, Clark. *American Saturday.* 1981. NY. Marek. 319p. rem mk. VG+/dj. R11. $15.00

HOWARD, Clark. *Arm.* 1967. Los Angeles. Sherbourne. 1st ed. F/F. H11. $50.00

HOWARD, Clark. *Doomsday Squad.* 1970. Weybright Talley. 1st ed. VG/VG. P3. $15.00

HOWARD, Clark. *Mark the Sparrow.* 1975. Dial. 1st ed. VG/VG. P3. $20.00

HOWARD, Elizabeth. *Adventure for Alison.* 1942. Lee Shepard. 8vo. 216p. maroon cloth. G+/worn. T5. $25.00

HOWARD, George Bronson. *Slaves of the Lamp; Being Adventures of Yorke Norroy...* 1917. NY. Watt. 1st ed. ils Arthur Becher. VG. B4. $150.00

HOWARD, Hartley. *Treble Cross.* 1975. Collins Crime Club. 1st ed. VG/VG. P3. $15.00

HOWARD, Helen Addison. *Saga of Chief Joseph.* 1965. Caxton. revised ed. 8vo. ils George D McGrath. F/VG. T10. $40.00

HOWARD, Helen Addison. *War Chief Joseph.* 1941. Caldwell. 2nd. photos/map. 368p. F/worn. E1. $35.00

HOWARD, James. *Murder Takes a Wife.* 1958. Dutton. 1st ed. VG/VG. P3. $20.00

HOWARD, John Galen. *Brunelleschi: A Poem.* 1913. Howell. 1st ed. 1/480. F/case. T10. $125.00

HOWARD, John Kinsey. *Strange Empire: A Narrative of the Northwest.* 1952. NY. 1st ed. 11 maps. F/dj. A17. $30.00

HOWARD, Joseph K. *Strange Empire.* 1952. NY. VG. O7. $45.00

HOWARD, Maureen. *Not a Word About Nightingales.* 1962. Atheneum. 1st ed. author's 1st book. F/NF. B4. $65.00

HOWARD, Mrs. B.C. *Fifty Years in a Maryland Kitchen.* 1944. Barrows. 1st ed. 234p. VG/G. B10. $15.00

HOWARD, Robert E. *Adventures of Dennis Dorgan.* 1974. Fax Collectors. VG/VG. P3. $25.00

HOWARD, Robert E. *Conan the Conqueror.* 1950. Gnome. VG/VG. P3. $75.00

HOWARD, Robert E. *Devil in Iron.* 1976. Donald Grant. F/F. P3. $35.00

HOWARD, Robert E. *Lost Valley of Iskander.* 1974. Fax Collectors. 1st ed. F/F. P3. $25.00

HOWARD, Robert E. *Marchers of Valhalla.* 1972. Donald Grant. 1st ed. NF/NF. P3. $25.00

HOWARD, Robert E. *People of the Black Circle.* 1978. Berkley Putnam. 1st ed. NF/NF. P3. $25.00

HOWARD, Robert E. *Return of Skull-Face.* 1977. Fax Collectors. 1st ed. F/F. T2. $25.00

HOWARD, Robert E. *Road of Azrael.* 1979. Donald Grant. 1st ed. NF/NF. P3. $20.00

HOWARD, Robert E. *Singers in the Shadows.* 1977. SF Graphics. NF/NF. P3. $45.00

HOWARD, Robert E. *Skull-Face Omnibus.* 1974. Neville Spearman. NF/NF. P3. $45.00

HOWARD, Robert E. *Son of the White Wolf.* 1976. Fax Collectors. 1st ed. F/F. P3/T2. $25.00

HOWARD, Robert E. *Swords of Shahrazar.* 1976. Fax Collectors. 1st ed. hc. F/F. P3. $25.00

HOWARD, Robert E. *Tigers of the Sea.* 1974. Donald Grant. 1st ed. F/F. P3. $20.00

HOWARD, Robert E. *Vultures.* 1973. Fictioneer. 1st ed. F/F. P3. $35.00

HOWARD, Robert E. *Worms of the Earth.* 1974. Donald Grant. 1st ed. F/F. P3. $25.00

HOWARD, Robert West. *Horse in America.* 1965. Follett. 1st ed. VG/G. O3. $25.00

HOWARD, Robert West. *Horse in America.* 1965. NY. 2nd. 298p. F/F. E1. $30.00

HOWARD, Robert West. *This Is the West.* 1957. Rand McNally. 1st hc ed. 8vo. ils. 247p. NF/dj. T10. $65.00

HOWARD, Robert West. *Thundergate: The Forts of Niagara.* 1968. Englewood Cliffs. 1st ed. F/VG. E1. $35.00

HOWARTH, David. *Voyage of the Armada.* 1981. NY. VG. O7. $15.00

HOWARTH & HOWARTH. *Story of P&O.* 1986. London. Weidenfeld Nicholson. ils. 224p. dj. T7. $40.00

HOWAT. *Hudson River & Its Painters.* 1972. Viking. VG/VG. D2. $45.00

HOWATSON, M.C. *Oxford Companion to Classical Literature.* 1989. Oxford. 2nd ed. F/F. P3. $45.00

HOWE, James. *Celery Stalks at Midnight.* 1983. Atheneum. 1st ed. 111p. NF/worn. M20. $32.00

HOWE, Julia Ward. *Is Polite Society Polite.* 1900. Houghton Mifflin. 1st ed. inscr/dtd 1904. VG. B4. $500.00

HOWE, Lucien. *Bibliography of Hereditary Eye Defects.* 1928. Cambridge. 58p. wrp. A13. $40.00

HOWE, Octavius T. *Argonauts of '49.* 1923. Cambridge. VG. O7. $95.00

HOWE, Walter. *Professional Gunsmithing.* 1946. Harrisburg. 3rd. ils. 518p. VG/VG. E1. $45.00

HOWELL, Edgar M. *United States Army Headgear 1855-1902.* 1976. Washington, DC. 2nd. cloth. F. E1. $35.00

HOWELL, George Rogers. *Early History of Southampton.* 1887. Albany. 2nd. VG. V4. $75.00

HOWELL, J.V. *Structure of Typical American Oil Fields...* 1948. Tulsa. AAPG Pub. Alexander Watts McCoy Memorial ed. 513p. F. D8. $30.00

HOWELLS, J.M. *Architectural Heritage of Piscataqua.* 1965. NY. Architectural Pub. VG/VG. B5. $37.50

HOWELLS, W.D. *Leatherwood God.* 1916. Century. 1st ed. ils. VG+. A17. $50.00

HOWELLS, W.D. *Rise of Silas Lapham.* 1885. Ticknor. 1st ed/1st state. 8vo. 515p. NF. B24. $250.00

HOWELLS, W.D. *Rise of Silas Lapham.* 1951. Modern Lib. VG/VG. P3. $10.00

HOWELLS, W.D. *Stops of Various Quills.* 1895. Harper. 1st ed. ils Howard Pyle. teg. morocco. F. B24. $650.00

HOWELLS, W.D. *Suburban Sketches.* 1871. NY. VG. C6. $95.00

HOWES, P.G. *Giant Cactus Forest & Its World.* 1954. Boston. 1st ed. pres. 358p. VG/VG. B5. $35.00

HOWES. *USiana, 1650-1950: A Selective Bibliography...* 1962. np. 2nd/1st prt. 652p. F. A4. $250.00

HOWITT. *Spider & the Fly.* 1939. Nonesuch. 1/250. 4to. 12p. A4. $275.00

HOWLAND, Mrs. *American Economical Housekeeper & Family Receipt Book.* 1845. Cincinnati. Derby. fair. H7. $75.00

HOWLETT, Grayle. *Tulsa Oilers All-Time Texas League Record Book.* 1952. Tulsa Sports Corp. revised ed. photos. VG. P8. $50.00

HOWLEY, John. *Psychology & Mystical Experience.* 1920. Kegan Paul/Herder. 275p. gr-gray cloth. G. G1. $50.00

HOWSE & SANDERSON. *Sea Chart: Historical Survey Based on Collections...* 1973. Newton Abbot. 60 fld charts/ils. F/dj. O7. $135.00

HOWSE & SANDERSON. *Sea Chart: Historical Survey...* 1973. McGraw Hill. ils. 4to. VG/dj. T7. $35.00

HOXIE & MARKOWITZ. *Native Americans: An Annotated Bibliography.* 1991. np. 325p. VG. A4. $75.00

HOY, Ken. *Land Life Nature Pop-Up.* 1990. Ideals. 1st ed. 4to. F. B17. $11.00

HOYLAND, John. *Brief History of Civilization.* 1925. London. 1st ed. 288p. VG. A13. $10.00

HOYLE, Fred. *Black Cloud.* nd. BC. VG/VG. P3. $8.00

HOYLE, Fred. *Element 79.* 1967. NAL. 1st ed. VG/VG. P3. $20.00

HOYLE, John T. *Roycroft Anthology.* 1917. Roycroft. VG. C6. $75.00

HOYLE, Trevor. *Last Gasp.* 1983. Crown. 1st ed. VG/VG. P3. $18.00

HOYLE & HOYLE. *Into Deepest Space.* nd. BC. NF/NF. P3. $5.00

HOYLE & HOYLE. *Molecule Man.* nd. BC. NF/NF. P3. $8.00

HOYLE & HOYLE. *Westminster Disaster.* 1978. Harper Row. 1st ed. NF/NF. P3. $15.00

HOYLE & WICKRAMASINGHE. *Lifecloud.* 1978. Harper Row. 1st ed. 8vo. 189p. VG. K5. $15.00

HOYT, Edwin Jonathan. *Buckskin Joe.* 1966. NE U. 1st ed. VG+/dj. M20. $47.00

HOYT, Edwin Jr. *Germans Who Never Lost: Story of the Konigsberg.* 1968. NY. 1st ed. 247p. F/F. E1. $30.00

HOYT, F. *That Wonderful A&P.* 1969. NY. 1st ed. 279p. F/F. B5. $20.00

HOYT, Richard. *Cool Runnings.* 1984. Viking. 1st ed. VG/VG. P3. $18.00

HOYT, Richard. *Darwin's Secret.* 1989. Doubleday. 1st ed. NF/NF. P3. $19.00

HOYT, Richard. *Dragon Portfolio.* 1986. Tor. 1st ed. xl. VG/NF. N4. $12.50

HOYT, Richard. *Head of State.* 1985. Tor. 1st ed. F/F. P3. $15.00

HOYT, Richard. *Marimba.* 1992. Tor. 1st ed. F/F. P3. $20.00

HOYT, Richard. *Marimba.* 1992. Tor. 1st ed. NF/NF. N4. $15.00

HRUSKA, Alan. *Borrowed Time.* 1984. Dial. 1st ed. hc. VG/VG. P3. $22.00

HU, S.T. *Forage Rescources of China.* 1992. Wageningen. ils/maps. 337p. AN. B26. $30.00

HUARTE, Juan. *Essame de gli Ingegni de Gl'huomini...* 1586. Venetia. Presso Aldo. 367p. 19th-C quarter sheep. G1. $385.00

HUBBARD, Jeremiah. *Forty Years Among the Indians.* 1913. Miami, OK. 1st ed. photos. 200p. G. E1. $250.00

HUDDARD, Kin. *Abe Martin's Brown County Folks.* 1910. Indianapolis. 1st ed. VG. B5. $42.50

HUBBARD, Kin. *Back Country Folks.* 1913. Indianapolis. 1st ed. VG. B5. $42.50

HUBBARD, L. Ron. *Alien Affair.* 1986. Bridge. 1st ed. F/F. P3. $25.00

HUBBARD, L. Ron. *Black Genesis.* 1986. Bridge. 1st ed. F/F. P3. $25.00

HUBBARD, L. Ron. *Buckskin Brigades.* 1977. Theta. hc. F/F. P3. $100.00

HUBBARD, L. Ron. *Buckskin Brigades.* 1987. Jameson Books. 1st ed. F/F. P3. $20.00

HUBBARD, L. Ron. *Death Quest.* 1986. Bridge. 1st ed. F/F. P3. $25.00

HUBBARD, L. Ron. *Dianetics.* 1953. Hermitage. 8th. VG. P3. $25.00

HUBBARD, L. Ron. *Dianetics in the Evolution of a Science.* 1974. Am Saint Hill. 10th. VG/VG. P3. $12.00

HUBBARD, L. Ron. *Disaster.* 1987. Bridge. 1st ed. F/F. P3. $25.00

HUBBARD, L. Ron. *Doomed Planet.* 1987. Bridge. 1st ed. F/F. P3. $25.00

HUBBARD, L. Ron. *Dynamics of Life.* 1988. Bridge. VG/VG. P3. $10.00

HUBBARD, L. Ron. *Enemy Within.* 1986. Bridge. 1st ed. F/F. P3. $25.00

HUBBARD, L. Ron. *Fear.* 1991. Bridge. 1st ed. F/F. P3. $17.00

HUBBARD, L. Ron. *Final Blackout.* 1975. Garland. F. P3. $60.00

HUBBARD, L. Ron. *Fortune of Fear.* 1986. Bridge. 1st ed. F/F. P3. $25.00

HUBBARD, L. Ron. *Invaders Plan.* 1985. Bridge. 1st ed. F/F. P3. $25.00

HUBBARD, L. Ron. *Mission Earth.* Bridge. ltd ed. 10 vol set. 1/1000. F/F. P3. $250.00

HUBBARD, L. Ron. *Problems of Work.* 1983. Bridge. VG/VG. P3. $15.00

HUBBARD, L. Ron. *Return to Tomorrow.* 1975. Garland. F. P3. $60.00

HUBBARD, L. Ron. *Scientology: Fundamentals of Thought.* 1988. Bridge. VG/VG. P3. $15.00

HUBBARD, L. Ron. *Self Analysis.* 1972. Am St Hill Organization. 5th. hc. VG/VG. P3. $12.00

HUBBARD, L. Ron. *Typewriter in the Sky & Fear.* 1951. Gnome. 1st ed. VG/VG. P3. $250.00

HUBBARD, L. Ron. *Typewriter in the Sky.* 1994. Authors Services. 1 of set. leather. F. P3. $40.00

HUBBARD, L. Ron. *Villainy Victorious.* 1987. Bridge. 1st ed. F/F. P3. $25.00

HUBBARD, L. Ron. *Voyage of Vengeance.* 1987. Bridge. 1st ed. F/F. P3. $25.00

HUBBARD, Margaret Ann. *Murder at St Dennis.* 1952. Bruce. 1st ed. VG/VG. P3. $20.00

HUBBARD, Margaret Ann. *Murder Takes the Veil.* 1950. Bruce. 2nd ed. VG/VG. P3. $15.00

HUBBARD, Margaret Ann. *Sister Simon's Murder Case.* 1959. Bruce. NF/NF. P3. $15.00

HUBBARD, Margaret Ann. *Step Softly on My Grave.* 1966. Bruce. 1st ed. hc. NF/NF. P3. $18.00

HUBBARD, P.M. *Whisper in the Glen.* 1972. Atheneum. 2nd. VG/VG. P3. $12.00

HUBBLE, Edwin. *Nature of Science & Other Lectures.* 1954. Huntington Lib. 8vo. 83p. VG/dj. K5. $45.00

HUBER, Ernst. *Evolution of Facial Musculature & Facial Expression.* 1931. Baltimore. Johns Hopkins. 8vo. 184p. VG. G1. $50.00

HUBER, Peter. *Galileo's Revenge: Junk Science in the Courtroom.* 1991. Basic. 1st ed. F/F. N4. $25.00

HUBIN, Allen J. *Best of the Detective Stories.* 1977. Dutton. 2nd. VG/VG. P3. $18.00

HUBIN, Allen J. *Bibliography of Crime Fiction 1749-1975...* 1979. 4to. 712p. F. A4. $135.00

HUBLER & REAGAN. *Where's the Rest of Me?* 1965. NY. 2nd. inscr Ronald Reagan. F/NF. A15. $100.00

HUCKEL, J.F. *American Indians First Families of the Southwest.* 1926. Kansas City. 33 full-p pl. VG. B14. $125.00

HUDSON, J. Paul. *Voyage & Search for a Settlement Site.* 1957. Garrett Massie. ils Sidney King. VG. B17. $12.50

HUDSON, Jan; see Smith, George H.

HUDSON, Jeffrey; see Crichton, Michael.

HUDSON, Louise Hubbard. *Folded Wings.* 1947. McClure. inscr. 55p. VG. B10. $8.00

HUDSON, W.H. *Birds in a Village.* 1893. London. 1st ed. VG+. C6. $150.00

HUDSON, W.H. *Birds in Town Village.* 1920. NY. 1st ed. ils. VG/poor. B5. $50.00

HUDSON, W.H. *Far Away & Long Ago: A History of My Early Life.* 1943. Buenos Aires. 1/1500. ils Raul Rosarivo. 307p. suede ep. F/dj/box. B24. $450.00

HUDSON, W.H. *Little Lost Boy.* 1929. Knopf. 3rd. ils Dorothy Lathrop. gr cloth. VG. D1. $95.00

HUDSON, William M. *Andy Adams & His Life & Writings.* 1964. Dallas, TX. 1st ed. photos. F/NF. E1. $35.00

HUDSON, Wilson M. *Diamond Bessie & The Sheperds.* 1972. Austin. 1st ed. 158p. F/F. E1. $30.00

HUET. *Les Hommes de la Danse.* 1954. Lausanne. Guilde du Livre. VG. D2. $50.00

HUFBAUER, Karl. *Exploring the Sun.* 1991. Johns Hopkins. 1st ed. VG/VG. K5. $30.00

HUFFAKER, Clair. *Cowboy & the Cossack.* 1973. NY. 1st ed. VG. B5. $40.00

HUFFMAN, Laton Alton. *Huffman Pictures: Photographs of the Old West.* 1975. Miles City, MT. 24p. F/stiff wrp. E1. $20.00

HUGGINS, Nathan Irvin. *Black Odyssey.* 1977. Pantheon. 1st ed. F/F. M23. $25.00

HUGHART, Barry. *Bridge of Birds: Novel of Ancient China That Never Was.* 1984. St Martin. 1st ed. F/F. T2. $35.00

HUGHEL, Avvon Chew. *Chew Bunch in Browns Park.* 1970. San Francisco. 1st ed. 103p. F. E1. $35.00

HUGHES, Adella Prentiss. *Music Is My Life.* 1947. Cleveland. 1st ed. 319p. G+/dj. B18. $17.50

HUGHES, B.P. *British Smooth-Bore Artillery.* 1969. Harrisburg. 1st ed. 144p. F/reinforced. E1. $45.00

HUGHES, Boyd R. *New Amateur Director's Guide.* 1975. SC. 2nd. 32p. VG/wrp. S1. $5.00

HUGHES, Cledwyn. *He Dared Not Look Behind.* 1947. AA Wyn. VG/VG. P3. $15.00

HUGHES, Colin; see Creasey, John.

HUGHES, Dorothy B. *Blackbirder.* 1943. DSP. 1st ed. VG. P3. $15.00

HUGHES, Dorothy B. *Davidian Report.* nd. BC. VG/VG. P3. $8.00

HUGHES, Dorothy B. *Delicate Ape.* 1945. Tower. VG/VG. P3. $15.00

HUGHES, Dorothy B. *Dread Journey.* 1946. Tower. VG/VG. P3. $15.00

HUGHES, Dorothy B. *Ride the Pink Horse.* nd. Collier. VG. P3. $10.00

HUGHES, Ken. *High Wray.* 1952. John Gifford. 1st ed. VG/VG. P3. $20.00

HUGHES, Langston. *Fields of Wonder.* 1947. Knopf. ARC. RS. NF/red dj. B24. $350.00

HUGHES, Langston. *Fight for Freedom: Story of the NAACP.* 1962. Berkeley. 1st pb issue. 224p. VG+. R11. $10.00

HUGHES, Langston. *Jim Crow's Last Stand.* 1943. Negro Pub Soc of Am. 1st ed. Race & Culture series. F/wht wrp. B24. $235.00

HUGHES, Langston. *Shakespeare in Harlem.* 1942. Knopf. 1st ed. inscr. ils E McKnight Kauffer. NF/NF. B24. $650.00

HUGHES, Langston. *Shakespeare in Harlem.* 1942. NY. 1st ed. inscr/dtd 1942. F/VG. C6. $750.00

HUGHES, Langston. *Weary Blues.* 1926. Knopf. 1st ed. author's 1st book. NF. B24. $500.00

HUGHES, Robert. *Fatal Shore.* 1987. NY. Knopf. 4th. 8vo. 688p. gray cloth. AN/dj. P4. $25.00

HUGHES, Rupert. *She Goes To War.* nd. Grosset Dunlap. MTI. VG. P3. $20.00

HUGHES, Rupert. *Triumphant Clay.* 1951. Hollywood. House-Warven. 1st ed. pres. VG/dj. S9. $45.00

HUGHES, Spike. *Art of Coarse Bridge.* 1976. London. 3rd imp. 118p. VG/VG. S1. $15.00

HUGHES, Tom. *Blue Riband of the Atlantic.* 1973. Scribner. VG/VG. A16. $25.00

HUGHES, W.J. *Rebellious Ranger: Rip Ford & the Old Southwest.* 1964. Norman. 1st ed. 300p. NF/VG. E1. $75.00

HUGHES, William. *Philips' Select Atlas of Modern Geography...* ca 1900. London. Philip. 36 maps. F. O7. $175.00

HUGNER, Charles W. *War Poets of the South & Confederate Camp-Fire Songs.* ca 1895. Atlanta, GA. Byr. NF. M23. $200.00

HUGO, Victor. *Battle of Waterloo.* 1977. LEC. 1/1600. ils/sgn Edouard Detaille. 99p. F/case. C2. $50.00

HUGO, Victor. *Hunchback of Notre Dame.* nd. AL Burt. MTI. VG. P3. $30.00

HUGO, Victor. *Toilers of the Sea.* 1960. LEC. 1/1500. sgn Marangoni/Mardersteig. 579p. F/NF/case. C2. $150.00

HUIE, William Bradford. *Americanization of Emily.* 1959. NY. 1st ed. VG/VG. M19/N3. $35.00

HUIE, William Bradford. *He Slew the Dreamer.* 1970. Delacorte. 2nd. sgn. NF/NF. B35. $40.00

HUIE, William Bradford. *Klansman.* 1967. Delacorte. 1st ed. 303p. VG/VG. R11. $15.00

HUIE, William Bradford. *Revolt of Mamie Stover.* 1951. DSP. 1st ed. F/VG. M19. $35.00

HUIE, William Bradford. *Ruby McCollum.* 1956. NY. 1st ed. VG/VG. B5. $100.00

HULBERT, Archer Butler. *Forty-Niners.* 1931. Boston. 1st ed. ils. 340p. VG. E1. $45.00

HULBERT, Archer Butler. *Future of Road-Making in America.* 1905. Cleveland. Clark. ils. 211p. G. B18. $22.50

HULBERT, Archer Butler. *Niagara River.* 1908. NY. 1st ed. VG. B5. $75.00

HULBERT, Archer Butler. *Records of the Original Proceedings of the Ohio Company...* 1917. Ohio Co series. 3 vol. bl cloth. VG. B30. $65.00

HULL, Clark L. *Aptitude Testing.* (1928). NY. World. 12mo. VG. G1. $65.00

HULL, Clark L. *Hypnosis & Suggestibility: An Experimental Approach.* 1933. Appleton. 416p. emb blk cloth. G. G1. $50.00

HULL, David Stewart. *Film in the Third Reich: A Study...1933-45.* 1969. CA U. 1st ed. 291p. G. A17. $12.00

HULL, Denison. *Thoughts on American Foxhunting.* 1958. NY. McKay. 1/1500. sgn. VG. O3. $65.00

HULL, Edward. *Monograph on the Sub-Oceanic Physiography of North Atlantic.* 1912. London. Stanford. lg folio. 11 maps. F. O7. $225.00

HULL, F.M. *Bee Flies of the World.* 1973. Smithsonian. 4to. 687p. cloth. dj. B1. $50.00

HULL, Richard. *Murderers of Monty.* 1937. London. Faber. 1st ed. NF/VG+. B4. $85.00

HULME, Keri. *Te Kaihua: The Windeater.* 1987. Braziller. 1st ed. sgn. F/F. B11. $40.00

HULME, Peter. *Colonial Encounters.* 1986. London. VG. O7. $35.00

HULME & WHITEHEARD. *Wild Majesty.* 1992. Oxford. VG. O7. $45.00

HULST, Roger A. *Jordaens' Drawings.* 1974. London/NY. Phaidon. 4 vol. cloth. djs. xl. D2. $450.00

HULTEN, Eric. *Flora of Alaska & Neighboring Territories.* 1990 (1968). Stanford. 4to. VG/torn. B26. $70.00

HULTEN, Eric. *Flora of the Aleutian Islands.* 1960. Weinheim/Bergstr. 2nd. sgn. photos. 418p. VG+. B26. $80.00

HULTMAN, Helen Joan. *Murder in the French Room.* 1931. Mystery League. 1st ed. G. P3. $20.00

HULTON, Paul. *America, 1585.* 1984. Chapel Hill. VG. O7. $45.00

HULTON & QUINN. *American Drawings of John White 1577-1590.* 1964. London/Chapel Hill. 2 vol. 1st ed. 1/600. folio. 160 pl. gilt red cloth. C6. $800.00

HULTON & SMITH. *Flowers in Art From East & West.* 1979. London. ils. 150p. sc. AN. B26. $15.00

HUME, David. *You'll Catch Your Death.* 1940. Collins. VG/VG. P3. $35.00

HUME, Edgar. *Medical Work of the Knights Hospitals of St John...* 1940. Baltimore. 1st ed. 371p. VG. A13. $75.00

HUME, H. Harold. *Camellias: Kinds & Culture.* 1951. NY. 1st ed. 271p. B26. $16.00

HUMPHREY, Harry B. *Makers of North American Botany.* 1961. NY. ils. 265p. F/dj. B26. $45.00

HUMPHREY, Lillie Muse. *Aggie.* 1955. Vantage. 1st ed. sm bookstore stp. NF/NF. B4. $150.00

HUMPHREY, William. *My Moby Dick.* 1978. Garden City. 1st ed. VG/VG. B5. $25.00

HUMPHREYS, Arthur L. *Old Decorative Maps & Charts.* 1926. NY/London. Halton Smith Balch. 1/100. ils/pl. F. O7. $550.00

HUMPHREYS, Josephine. *Dreams of Sleep.* 1984. NY. ARC/1st ed. author's 1st book. sgn. RS. C2. $100.00

HUMPHREYS, Josephine. *Fireman's Fair.* 1991. Viking. 1st ed. F/F. M23. $25.00

HUMPHREYS, Josephine. *Rich in Love.* 1987. Viking. 1st ed. F/F. M23. $30.00

HUMPHREYS, Robin A. *Evolution of Modern Latin America.* 1973. Cooper Sq Pub. 8vo. 196p. VG. P4. $17.50

HUMPHREYS, W.J. *Physics of the Air.* 1920. Lippincott. 4to. 665p. G. K5. $45.00

HUMPHREYS, W.J. *Rain Making & Other Weather Vagaries.* 1926. Baltimore. Williams Wilkins. xl. K5. $20.00

HUMPHRIES, Patrick. *Films of Alfred Hitchcock.* 1987. Bison. 2nd. VG/VG. P3. $15.00

HUNCKER, James Gibbons. *Stepplejack.* 1922. NY. ils/index. gilt cloth. VG. A17. $10.00

HUNGERFORD, Edward. *Wells Fargo: Advancing the American Frontier.* 1949. Random. 1st ed. 8vo. ils. 274p. F/VG. T10. $45.00

HUNGRY WOLF, Adolf & B. *Shadows of the Buffalo: A Family Odyssey Among the Indians.* 1983. NY. 1st ed. photos. 288p. F/F. E1. $35.00

HUNNICUTT, Benjamin. *Brazil: World Frontier.* 1949. Nostrand. 1st ed. 387p. dj. F3. $15.00

HUNNICUTT, Ellen. *In the Music Library.* 1987. Puttsburgh. 1st ed. F/F. B4. $45.00

HUNSBERGER. *Clarence Darrow, a Bibliography.* 1981. 215p. F. A4. $30.00

HUNT, A. Lowell. *Florida Today.* 1950. Scribner. 1st ed. sgn. VG/fair. B11. $18.00

HUNT, Aurora. *Kirby Benedict, Frontier Federal Judge.* 1961. Glendale. Arthur H Clark. 8ov. ils/map. F. T10. $150.00

HUNT, Aurora. *Kirby Benedict: Frontier Judge.* 1961. Glendale. VG. O7. $45.00

HUNT, Blanche Seale. *Little Brown Koko.* 1951. VG/dj. K2. $70.00

HUNT, Blanche Seale. *Little Brown Koko.* 1953. Am Colortype. 96p. VG. M20. $40.00

HUNT, Blanche Seale. *Little Brown Koko Has Fun.* nd. Am Colortype. ils Dorothy Wagstaff. 96p. VG. M20. $35.00

HUNT, Blanche Seale. *Stories of Little Brown Koko...Little Brown Koko Has Fun.* 1945. American Colortype. 4to. ils Dorothy Wagstaff. pict brd. VG. M5. $55.00

HUNT, C.B. *Natural Regions of the United States & Canada.* 1974. San Francisco. Freeman. 725p. pict brd. VG. D8. $20.00

HUNT, C.B. *Physiography of the United States.* 1967. Freeman. 1st ed. 480p. F/dj. D8. $20.00

HUNT, Douglas. *Handbook on the Occult.* 1967. Arthur Baker. VG. P3. $20.00

HUNT, E. Howard. *Gaza Intercept.* 1981. Stein Day. 1st ed. 8vo. 302p. VG/dj. W1. $18.00

HUNT, Frazier. *Frazier Hunt's Story of General Custer.* 1979. Monroe Co, MI. Monograph #5. 1/300. F/stiff wrp. E1. $30.00

HUNT, Frazier. *Tragic Days of Billy the Kid.* 1956. NY. 1st ed. sgn. map ep. 316p. pict cloth. F/VG. E1. $75.00

HUNT, Howard. *Murder in State.* 1990. St Martin. 1st ed. hc. VG/VG. P3. $18.00

HUNT, Irene. *Up a Road Slowly.* 1966. Follett. 1st ed. F/VG+. P2. $75.00

HUNT, Kyle; see Creasey, John.

HUNT, Thomas. *Argument for the Bishops Righ in Judging in Capital Causes.* 1682. London. contemporary calf. M11. $150.00

HUNT, William E. *Historical Collections of Coshocton County, Ohio.* 1876. Cincinnati. Robert Clarke. 1st ed. 264p. scarce. B18. $85.00

HUNT & HUNT. *Horses & Heroes: Story of the Horse in America...* 1949. NY. 1st ed. 306p. F/chip. E1. $50.00

HUNTER, Alan. *Death on the Broadlands.* 1984. Walker. 1st ed. F/F. P3. $15.00

HUNTER, Alan. *Gently Between Tides.* 1983. Walker. 2nd. F/F. P3. $12.00

HUNTER, Alan. *Gently Scandalous.* 1990. Constable. 1st ed. NF/NF. P3. $20.00

HUNTER, Alan. *Landed Gently.* 1957. Cassell. 1st ed. VG/torn. P3. $20.00

HUNTER, Charles N. *Galahad.* 1963. San Antonio. 1st ed. F/F. E1. $30.00

HUNTER, Cyrus Lee. *Sketches of Western North Carolina.* 1877. Raleigh, NC. Raleigh News Steam Job Print. 1st ed. VG. M8. $250.00

HUNTER, D'Allard; see Ballard, W.T.

HUNTER, Dard. *Papermaking: History & Technique.* 1943. NY. 1st ed. F/NF. A15. $125.00

HUNTER, Diana. *Jack Ruby's Girls.* 1970. 1st ed. NF/VG clip. S13. $35.00

HUNTER, Donald. *Diseases of Occupations.* 1955. Boston. ils. 1046p. VG. B14. $150.00

HUNTER, Ed. *Another Part of the City.* 1986. Mysterious. 1st ed. NF/NF. M22. $15.00

HUNTER, Ed. *Cinderella.* 1986. Holt. 1st ed. F/F. H11. $35.00

HUNTER, Ed. *Ghosts.* 1980. Viking. 1st ed. F/NF. B4. $125.00

HUNTER, Ed. *House That Jack Built.* 1988. Holt. 1st ed. F/F. N4. $35.00

HUNTER, Ed. *Ice.* 1983. Arbor. 1st ed. F/F. H11. $40.00

HUNTER, Ed. *Mischief.* 1993. Morrow. 1st ed. sgn. F/F. B11. $25.00

HUNTER, Ed. *Pusher.* 1991. Armchair Detective. 1st hc ed. AN/dj. N4. $30.00

HUNTER, Ed. *Rumpelstiltskin.* 1981. Viking. 1st ed. F/F. N4. $45.00

HUNTER, Ed. *There Was a Little Girl.* 1994. Warner. 1st ed. AN. M22. $20.00

HUNTER, Ed. *Widows.* 1992. Morrow. 1st ed. F/F. M22. $20.00

HUNTER, Evan. *Another Part of the City.* 1986. Mysterious. 1st ed. VG/VG. P3. $16.00

HUNTER, Evan. *Blood Relatives.* nd. BC. VG/VG. P3. $8.00

HUNTER, Evan. *Cinderella.* 1986. Holt. 1st ed. VG/VG. P3. $20.00

HUNTER, Evan. *Come Winter.* nd. BC. VG/VG. P3. $8.00

HUNTER, Evan. *Eight-Seven.* nd. BC. VG/VG. P3. $12.00

HUNTER, Evan. *Eighty Million Eyes.* nd. BC. VG/VG. P3. $8.00

HUNTER, Evan. *Every Little Crook & Nanny.* 1972. Doubleday. 1st ed. inscr. VG/VG. M22. $35.00

HUNTER, Evan. *Every Little Crook & Nanny.* 1972. Doubleday. 1st ed. xl. dj. P3. $5.00

HUNTER, Evan. *Far From the Sea.* 1983. Atheneum. 1st ed. F/F. H11. $35.00

HUNTER, Evan. *Far From the Sea.* 1983. Atheneum. 1st ed. VG/VG. P3. $30.00

HUNTER, Evan. *Find the Feathered Serpent.* 1977. Gregg. rpt of 1952 Winston ed. sgn. F/NF. G10. $40.00

HUNTER, Evan. *Find the Feathered Serpent.* 1979. Gregg. 1st ed. F/F. P3. $30.00

HUNTER, Evan. *Ghosts.* 1980. Viking. 1st ed. VG/VG. P3. $22.00

HUNTER, Evan. *Goldilocks.* nd. Arbor. 2nd. VG/VG. P3. $12.00

HUNTER, Evan. *Hail to the Chief.* 1973. Random. 1st ed. VG/VG. P3. $35.00

HUNTER, Evan. *Happy New Year, Herbie.* 1963. Simon Schuster. 1st ed. VG/VG. P3. $75.00

HUNTER, Evan. *Heat.* nd. BC. VG/VG. P3. $8.00

HUNTER, Evan. *Horse's Head.* 1967. Delacorte. 1st ed. VG/VG. P3. $35.00

HUNTER, Evan. *House That Jack Built.* 1988. Holt. 1st ed. NF/NF. P3. $20.00

HUNTER, Evan. *Ice.* nd. BC. VG/VG. P3. $8.00

HUNTER, Evan. *Jack & the Beanstalk.* nd. BC. VG/VG. P3. $8.00

HUNTER, Evan. *Kiss.* 1992. Morrow. 1st ed. VG/VG. P3. $17.00

HUNTER, Evan. *Last Summer.* nd. BC. VG/VG. P3. $8.00

HUNTER, Evan. *Let's Hear It for the Deaf Man.* 1973. Doubleday. 1st ed. VG/VG. P3. $25.00

HUNTER, Evan. *Lightning.* nd. BC. VG/VG. P3. $8.00

HUNTER, Evan. *Love, Dad.* 1981. Crown. 1st ed. VG/VG. P3. $20.00

HUNTER, Evan. *Lullaby.* 1989. Morrow. 1st ed. VG/VG. P3. $20.00

HUNTER, Evan. *Mischief.* 1993. Morrow. 1st ed. NF/NF. P3. $20.00

HUNTER, Evan. *Nobody Knew They Were There.* 1971. Doubleday. 1st ed. VG/VG. P3. $23.00

HUNTER, Evan. *Puss in Boots.* 1987. Holt. 1st ed. VG/VG. P3. $15.00

HUNTER, Evan. *Second Ending.* 1956. Simon Schuster. 1st ed. NF/NF. P3. $75.00

HUNTER, Evan. *Snow White & Rose Red.* 1985. HRW. 1st ed. VG/VG. P3. $20.00

HUNTER, Evan. *Streets of Gold.* nd. BC. VG/VG. P3. $8.00

HUNTER, Evan. *Tricks.* nd. BC. VG/VG. P3. $8.00

HUNTER, Evan. *Vespers.* 1990. Morrow. 1st ed. F/F. P3. $20.00

HUNTER, Evan. *Widows.* 1991. Morrow. 1st ed. F/F. A20. $15.00

HUNTER, Henry C. *How England Got Its Merchant Marine.* 1935. NY. Nat Council of Am Shipbuilders. 369p. VG/dj. M20. $37.00

HUNTER, J. Marvin. *Story of Lottie Deno: Her Life & Times.* 1959. Bandera, TX. 1st ed. 199p. VG. E1. $50.00

HUNTER, J. Marvin. *Trail Drivers of Texas.* 1963. NY. rpt. 2 vol set. sgn. F/case. E1. $350.00

HUNTER, Jack D. *Expendable Spy.* 1965. Dutton. 1st ed. VG/VG. P3. $18.00

HUNTER, Jane Edna. *Nickel & a Prayer.* 1940. Cleveland. Pantheon/Elli Kani. 1st ed. inscr. VG+/VG. B4. $450.00

HUNTER, John D. *Memoirs of a Captivity Among the Indians of North America...* 1823. London. 2nd Eng. 447p. contemporary half calf. VG. C6. $325.00

HUNTER, Milton R. *Utah: Story of Her People 1540-1947, Centennial Hist...* nd. np. 1st ed. ils. VG. B18. $27.50

HUNTER, Stephen. *Day Before Midnight.* 1989. Bantam. 1st ed. hc. VG/VG. P3. $25.00

HUNTER, Stephen. *Dirty White Boys.* 1994. Random. 1st ed. NF/NF. M22. $15.00

HUNTER, Stephen. *Master Sniper.* 1980. Morrow. 1st ed. inscr/dtd 1980. F/F. B4. $225.00

HUNTER, Stephen. *Point of Impact.* 1993. Bantam. 1st ed. F/F. H11. $40.00

HUNTER, Stephen. *Second Saladin.* 1982. Morrow. 1st ed. author's 2nd book. F/F. H11. $35.00

HUNTER, Stephen. *Second Saladin.* 1982. Morrow. 1st ed. author's 2nd book. VG/VG clip. H11. $30.00

HUNTER, Stephen. *Spanish Gambit.* 1985. Crown. 1st ed. VG/VG. P3. $20.00

HUNTER, Thomas Lomax. *Forbidden Fruit & Other Ballads.* 1923. Roycroft. sgn. 88p. VG. B10. $15.00

HUNTER, Thomas Lomax. *Poems of...* 1946. Dietz. inscr. VG. B10. $15.00

HUNTER & ROSE. *Album of Gunfighters.* 1951. Mountain Home, TX. YO Pr. later prt. sgn. 236p. F/case. E1. $300.00

HUNTFORD, Roland. *Amundsen Photographs.* 1987. NY. ils. 199p. F/dj. A17. $30.00

HUNTING, Gardner. *Vicarion.* 1927. Unity. VG. P3. $8.00

HUNTINGTON, E.C. *Fifty Years of Colgate Football: 1890-1940.* 1940. Colgate. 1st ed. photos. 269p. VG+. scarce. B22. $12.00

HUNTINGTON, George. *Robber & Hero: Story of the Raid on First National Bank...* 1962. Minneapolis. 1/1500. rpt of 1895 ed. F/F. E1. $60.00

HUNTLEY, Chet. *Generous Years.* 1968. NY. 215p. F/NF. E1. $15.00

HURD, Michael. *Soldiers' Songs & Marches.* 1966. NY. 1st Am ed. ils. 54p. F/VG. E1. $25.00

HURLEY, P.J. *In Search of Australia.* 1943. Sidney. Dymocks Books Arcade. 134p. VG/dj. P4. $25.00

HURLIMANN, Bettina. *Seven Houses: My Life With Books.* 1976. London. 16p of photos. 216p. NF/NF clip. A4. $65.00

HURLIMANN, Bettina. *Three Centuries of Children's Books in Europe.* 1968. World. 1st Am ed. 297p. VG/dj. M20. $47.00

HURLIMANN, Bettina. *Three Centuries of Children's Books in Europe.* 1968. World. 1st ed thus. 8vo. F/dj. M5. $58.00

HURRELL, F.G. *John Lillibud.* 1935. Kendall Sharp. 1st ed. VG. P3. $10.00

HURST, Fannie. *Family!* 1960. Doubleday. stated 1st ed. pres. F/VG-. H4. $75.00

HURST, Fannie. *Lummox.* 1923. Harper. 1st ed. F/NF. B4. $200.00

HURST, Fannie. *Mannequin.* 1926. Knopf. 1st ed. NF/NF. B4. $150.00

HURST, George Leopold. *Outline of the History of Christian Literature.* 1926. Macmillan. 1st ed. 8vo. 547p. VG. W1. $20.00

HURSTON, Zora Neale. *Dust Tracks on a Road: An Autobiography.* 1942. Lippincott. 1st ed. inscr. NF/VG. B4. $3,500.00

HURSTON, Zora Neale. *Moses: Man of the Mountain.* 1939. Lippincott. 1st ed. F/VG. B4. $750.00

HURSTON, Zora Neale. *Mules & Men.* 1935. Lippincott. 1st ed. ils Miguel Covarrubias. F. B4. $400.00

HURSTON, Zora Neale. *Mules & Men.* 1935. Phil. 1st ed. author's 2nd book. F/VG. C6. $1,200.00

HURSTON, Zora Neale. *Seraph on the Suwanee.* 1948. Scribner. 1st ed. F/VG+. B4. $950.00

HURSTON, Zora Neale. *Tell My Horse.* 1938. Lippincott. 1st ed. sgn. F/F clip. B4. $2,500.00

HURSTON, Zora Neale. *Zora in Florida.* 1991. Orlando. Central FL U. 1st ed. edit Steve Glassman/KL Seidel. AN/dj. B4. $55.00

HURT, Wesley. *Interrelationships Between the Natural Environment...* 1974. Bloomington. 1st ed. 4to. 42p. wrp. F3. $10.00

HURWOOD, Bernhardt J. *Passport to the Supernatural.* nd. BC. VG. P3. $5.00

HUSS, Roy. *Focus on the Horror Film.* 1972. Prentice Hall. 1st ed. F/F. P3. $25.00

HUSSAIN, M. Hadi. *Syed Ahmed Khan: Pioneer of Muslim Resurgence.* 1970. Lahore. Inst Islamic Culture. 259p. VG/torn. W1. $16.00

HUSSEY, Christopher. *English Gardens & Landscapes 1700-1750.* 1967. NY. ils/pl. F/dj. B26. $125.00

HUSSEY, Mark. *Singing of the Real World: Philosophy of Virginia Woolf...* 1986. OSU. 1st ed. 185p. F/dj. A17. $10.00

HUSTON, Cleburne. *Deaf Smith: Incredible Texas Spy.* 1973. Waco. 1st ed. 141p. F/NF. E1. $45.00

HUTCHENS, John K. *One Man's Montana.* 1964. NY. 1st ed. 221p. F/F. E1. $30.00

HUTCHINS, Arthur. *Mozart the Man - The Musician.* 1976. Schrimer. hc. decor brd. F. P3. $25.00

HUTCHINS, James S. *Boots & Saddles at the Little Bighorn.* 1976. Ft Collins. 1st ed. 81p. VG. E1. $40.00

HUTCHINS, Jere C. *Jere C Hutchins, a Personal Story.* 1938. Detroit. private prt. sgn. 8vo. 372p. G/G. B11. $45.00

HUTCHINS, John Abram. *Famous Command: The Richmond Light Infantry Blues.* 1934. Richmond, VA. Garrett Massie. 1st ed. 399p. NF/dj. M8. $175.00

HUTCHINS, Wells A. *Water Rights Laws in the Nineteen Western States.* 1971. UDSA. 3 vol. maroon buckram. M11. $350.00

HUTCHINSON, A.S.M. *Book of Simon.* 1930. Little Brn. 1st ed. ils AH Watson. F/worn. M5. $35.00

HUTCHINSON, Bruce. *Incredible Canadian: Candid Portrait of Mackensie King...* 1953. Longmans. 1st ed. 454p. red cloth. VG+. B22. $5.50

HUTCHINSON, John. *British Flowering Plants: Evolution & Classification...* 1948. London. ils/fld diagram. VG/dj. B26. $22.00

HUTCHINSON, Tom. *Horror & Fantasy in the Movies.* 1974. Crescent. hc. VG. P3. $15.00

HUTCHINSON, Tom. *Horros: A History of Horror Movies.* 1983. Royce. VG/VG. P3. $20.00

HUTCHINSON, W. *Religion of Satan, or Antichrist, Delineated.* 1749. London. 392p. T3. $25.00

HUTCHINSON, W.H. *Gene Autry & the Big Valley Grab.* 1952. Whitman. VG/VG. P3. $18.00

HUTCHINSON, W.H. *Life & Personal Writings of Eugene Manlove Rhodes...* 1956. Norman. 1st ed. photos. 432p. F/chip. E1. $60.00

HUTCHINSON & MULLIN. *Whiskey Jim & a Kid Named Billie.* 1967. Clarendon. 1st ed. ils HD Bugbee. 41p. F/sans. E1. $50.00

HUTCHINSON & STEBBINS. *Flora of the Wright's Lake Area.* 1986. Pollock Pines, CA. sgns. ils. 237p. VG. B26. $22.50

HUTCHISON, E.R. *Tropic of Cancer on Trial, a Case History of Censorship.* 1968. Grove. M11. $35.00

HUTIN, Serge. *History of Alchemy.* 1962. Walker Sun. decor brd. F. P3. $18.00

HUTSON, Shaun. *Breeding Ground.* 1991. MacDonald. VG/VG. P3. $25.00

HUTSON, Shaun. *Deadhead.* 1993. Little Brn. F/F. P3. $30.00

HUTTON, C.A. *Greek Terra Cotta Statuettes.* 1899. London. Seeley. 1st ed. 4to. 75p. maroon Victorian cloth. T10. $125.00

HUTTON, Clarke. *Country ABC.* 1940. Oxford. 52p. VG. A17. $30.00

HUTTON, Harold. *Doc Middleton: Life & Legends...* 1974. Chicago. 1st ed. photos. 290p. F/VG. E1. $50.00

HUTTON, John. *Accidental Crimes.* 1984. Bodley Head. 4th. VG/VG. P3. $15.00

HUXLEY, Aldous. *After Many a Summer Dies the Swan.* 1939. Macmillan. 1st Canadian ed. VG. P3. $60.00

HUXLEY, Aldous. *Along the Road: Notes & Essays of a Tourist.* 1925. London. 1st ed. F/NF. C6. $135.00

HUXLEY, Aldous. *Ape & Essence.* 1948. Harper. 1st Am ed. NF/VG. M19. $25.00

HUXLEY, Aldous. *Apennine.* 1930. Slide Mtn. 1st ed. 1/91. sgn. F/glassine wrp. B24. $650.00

HUXLEY, Aldous. *Art of Seeing.* 1943. Macmillan. 1st Canadian ed. VG/fair. P3. $30.00

HUXLEY, Aldous. *Brave New World.* 1932. Chatto Windus. 1st ed. F/clip. B24. $950.00

HUXLEY, Aldous. *Brave New World.* 1932. Doubleday Doran. 1st Am ed. 1/250. sgn. teg. F/matching case. B24. $1,250.00

HUXLEY, Aldous. *Brave New World Revisited.* 1959. Chatto Windus. 2nd. VG/VG. P3. $25.00

HUXLEY, Aldous. *Brief Candles.* 1930. Chatto Windus. 1st ed. F/NF. M19. $75.00

HUXLEY, Aldous. *Burning Wheel.* 1916. Blackwell. 1st ed. author's 1st book. inscr/dtd 1926. F/wrp/chemise. B24. $1,500.00

HUXLEY, Aldous. *Chrome Yellow.* 1921. Chatto Windus. 1st ed. 325p. VG. M20. $87.00

HUXLEY, Aldous. *Cicadas & Other Poems.* 1931. London. F/VG. C6. $50.00

HUXLEY, Aldous. *Crows of Pearblossom.* 1967. BC. ils Barbara Cooney. VG. B17. $5.00

HUXLEY, Aldous. *Devils of Loudun.* 1952. Harper. 1st ed. hc. VG. P3. $40.00

HUXLEY, Aldous. *Do What You Will.* 1929. London. 1st ed. NF/VG. C6. $100.00

HUXLEY, Aldous. *Eyeless in Gaza.* 1936. Harper. 7th. hc. VG. P3. $15.00

HUXLEY, Aldous. *Limbo.* 1920. Chatto Windus. 1st ed. 292p. VG. M20. $52.00

HUXLEY, Aldous. *Mortal Coils.* 1922. London. 1st ed. VG+/VG. C6. $150.00

HUXLEY, Aldous. *Music at Night.* 1931. np. ltd ed. sgn. F. M19. $100.00

HUXLEY, Aldous. *Music at Night.* 1931. NY. Fountain. 1/842. sgn. VG. B5. $75.00

HUXLEY, Aldous. *Music at Night & Other Essays.* 1931. NY/London. 1st ed. 1/842. sgn. NF. C6. $95.00

HUXLEY, Aldous. *Those Barren Leaves.* 1925. Chatto Windus. 1st ed. 379p. VG/dj. M20. $77.00

HUXLEY, Aldous. *Time Must Have a Stop.* 1944. Harper. 1st ed. NF/VG. M22. $25.00

HUXLEY, Aldous. *Vulgarity in Literature.* 1930. London. 1/260. sgn. NF. C6. $95.00

HUXLEY, Aldous. *World of Light.* 1931. London. 1/160. sgn. NF. C6. $100.00

HUXLEY, Anthony. *Ils History of Gardening.* 1979. BC. 352p. VG+/dj. B26. $35.00

HUXLEY, Elspeth. *African Poison Murders.* nd. BOMC. VG/VG. P3. $10.00

HUXLEY, Elspeth. *Man From Nowhere.* 1965. Morrow. 1st ed. VG/VG. P3. $20.00

HUXLEY, Elspeth. *Merry Hippo.* 1963. Chatto Windus. 2nd. hc. VG/VG. P3. $20.00

HUXLEY, Elspeth. *Murder at Government House.* nd. BOMC. VG/VG. P3. $10.00

HUXLEY, Elspeth. *New Earth: An Experiment in Coloniali.* 1960. Chatto Windus. 1st ed. VG. P3. $20.00

HUXLEY, Elspeth. *Scott of the Antarctic.* 1977. London. Weidenfeld Nicholson. 303p. VG/dj. T7. $40.00

HUXLEY, J. *TH Huxley's Diary of Voyage of HMS Rattlesnake.* 1935. London. 1st ed. VG+. A15. $45.00

HUXLEY, Thomas. *Lay Sermons, Addresses, & Reviews.* 1871. NY. 1st Am ed. 378p. rebound buckram. VG. A13. $30.00

HUXLEY & VAN LAWICK. *Last Days in Eden.* 1984. NY. Amaryllis. 192p. M/dj. P4. $25.00

HUYGEN, W. *Book of the Sandman & Alphabet of Sleep.* 1989. Abrams. 1st ed. ils Poortvliet. 121p. AN/dj. T5. $30.00

HUYGEN, Will. *Gnomes.* 1977. Abrams. VG/VG. P3. $30.00

HUYSMANS, J.K. *Down There.* 1958. University. xl. VG. P3. $10.00

HUYSSEN, Guilielmus Jacobus. *Dissertatio Juridica Inauguralis...* 1778. Lugduni Batavorum. Apud Cornelium Heyligert. 37p. orig self wrp. M11. $125.00

HYDE, Albert E. *Billy, the Kid & the Old Regime in the Southwest.* 1960. Ruidoso, NM. 1/500. 31p. F/wrp. E1. $50.00

HYDE, Charles L. *Pioneer Days: Story of Adventurous & Active Life.* 1939. NY. photos. 286p. G/chip. E1. $50.00

HYDE, Christopher. *Wave.* 1979. McClelland Stewart. 1st ed. VG/VG. P3. $15.00

HYDE, E. Belcher. *Miniature Atlas of the Borough of Manhattan in One Volume.* 1912. NY. Hyde. 8vo. 472p. F. O7. $495.00

HYDE, E. Belcher. *Printed Maps of Victorian London 1851-1900.* 1975. Folkestone. Dawson. 24 maps/ils. M. O7. $95.00

HYDE, Francis. *Far Eastern Trade 1860-1914.* 1973. NY. VG. O7. $25.00

HYDE, George E. *Red Cloud's Folk: A History of the Oglala Sioux Indians.* 1937. Norman. 2nd/revised. 331p. F/F. E1. $55.00

HYDE, George E. *Sioux Chronicle.* 1956. Norman. 1st ed. photos/map. 334p. F/VG. E1. $95.00

HYDE, George E. *Spotted Tail's Folk: A History of the Brule Sioux.* 1961. Norman. 1st ed. 361p. F/VG. E1. $60.00

HYDE, H. Montgomery. *History of Pornography.* 1965. FSG. G/worn. M11. $50.00

HYDE, H. Montgomery. *Other Love, an Historical & Contemporary Survey...* 1970. Heinemann. M11. $75.00

HYDE, Harris; see Harris, Timothy.

HYDE & STODDARD. *History of the Great Northwest.* 1901. Minneapolis. 1st ed. 592p. professional rpr. E1. $200.00

HYER, Julien. *Land of Beginning Again.* 1952. Atheneum. 1st ed. 8vo. 394p. brick cloth. F/NF. T10. $25.00

HYMAN, Jackie. *Eyes of a Stranger.* 1987. St Martin. 1st ed. VG/VG. P3. $18.00

HYMAN, Jane. *Gumby Book of Shapes.* 1986. Doubleday. hc. decor brd. VG. P3. $4.00

HYMAN, Stanley E. *Darwin for Today.* 1963. NY. VG/dj. B26. $17.50

HYMAN, Trina Schart. *How Six Found Christmas.* 1969. Little Brn. 1st ed. ils. cloth. VG. M5. $18.00

HYMANS, Barry. *Hirshhorn: Medici From Brooklyn, a Biography.* 1979. Dutton. 1st ed. ils/index. 206p. dj. D2. $35.00

HYNE, C.J. Cutliffe. *Lost Continent.* 1974. Oswald Train. F/F. P3. $20.00

IBARS. *Bibliografia Paleografica.* 1974. Barcelona. ils. 932p. VG/wrp. A4. $135.00

IBSEN, Henrik. *Et Dukkehjem.* 1879-1882. Copenhagen. 3 vol in 1. 1st ed. contemporary half morocco. VG. C6. $200.00

ICEBERG SLIM; see Beck, Robert.

IDELL, Albert. *Doorway in Antiqua.* 1949. Wm Sloan. 2nd. 210p. dj. F3. $20.00

IEFFETAYO, Femi Funmi. *We the Black Woman.* 1971. Detroit. Blk Arts Pub. 2nd. NF/stapled wrp. B4. $50.00

IKEDA & INOUE. *Letters of Four Seasons.* 1980. Tokyo. 1st ed. 123p. F/dj. A17. $10.00

ILES, Greg. *Black Cross.* 1995. Dutton. 1st ed. sgn. F/NF. N4. $35.00

ILES, Greg. *Spandau Phoenix.* 1993. Dutton. 1st ed. sgn. F/F. M23. $40.00

IMES, Barney. *Juke Joint: Photographs.* 1990. np. 1st ed. 1/100. sgn. photos/sgn Richard Ford. F/case. C2. $200.00

IMLAY, Gilbert. *Topographical Description of the Western Territory...* 1792. London. 1st ed. 8vo. 247p. contemporary calf. C6. $700.00

IMMERGUT, Debra Jo. *Private Property.* 1992. Turtle Bay Books. 1st ed. author's 1st book. F/dj. B4. $35.00

INDICK, Ben P. *George Alec Effinger From Entropy to Budayeen.* 1993. San Bernandino. Borgo. 1st ed. sgn. F/wrp. B11. $20.00

INFIELD, Glen B. *Hitler's Secret Life: Mystery of the Eagle's Nest.* 1979. NY. photos. 317p. VG/wrp. A17. $5.00

INFIELD, Glen B. *Leni Riefenstahl: The Fallen Film Goddess.* 1976. NY. 1st ed. ils. 278p. VG/dj. A17. $20.00

ING, Dean. *Big Lifters.* 1988. Tor. 1st ed. rem mk. F/F. G10. $5.00

ING, Dean. *Nemesis Mission.* 1991. Tor. 1st ed. F/F. P3. $20.00

ING, Dean. *Ransom of Black Stealth One.* 1989. St Martin. 1st ed. F/F. P3. $19.00

INGALLS, Albert G. *Amateur Telescope Making.* 1928 (1926). Scientific Am Pub. 2nd. 285p. cloth. G. K5. $50.00

INGALLS, Eleazar Stillman. *Journal of a Trip to California by Overland Route...* 1979. Ye Galleon. 1st ed thus. F/sans. A18. $17.50

INGE, W.R. *Diary of a Dean.* 1950. Macmillan. 1st ed. 228p. blk cloth. F. B22. $8.00

INGELOW, Jean. *Mopsa the Fairy.* 1927. Macmillan. 1st ed. ils Dugald Walker. 258p. G+. P2. $50.00

INGERSOL, Jared. *Diamond Fingers.* 1970. Robert Hale. 1st ed. hc. xl. dj. P3. $5.00

INGERSOLL, Chester. *Overland to California in 1847...* 1970. Ye Galleon. 1st ed thus. 1/314. M/sans. A18. $17.50

INGHAM, Bruce. *North East Arabian Dialects.* 1982. London. Kegan Paul. 1st ed. 8vo. ils. NF/dj. W1. $25.00

INGHAM, H. Lloyd. *Bury Me Deep.* 1963. Hammond. VG. P3. $8.00

INGLIS, William. *George F Johnson & His Industrial Democracy.* 1935. Huntington. 1st ed. 306p. gilt gr cloth. F/dj. B22. $5.50

INGOLDSBY, Thomas. *Ingoldsby Legends.* 1907. 1st ed. 24 Rackham pl. teg. gilt gr brd. VG+. S13. $250.00

INGPEN, Robert. *Encyclopedia of Mysterious Places.* 1990. Dragons World. 1st ed. F/F. P3. $25.00

INGRAHAM, J.H. *Pillar of Fire; or, Israel in Bondage.* 1899. Cook. 1st ed thus. 96p. marbled brd/gr cloth spine. VG. B22. $5.00

INGRAHAM, Joseph. *Journal of the Brigantine Hope.* 1971. Barre. VG. O7. $95.00

INGRAM & PATTIE. *Jasbo.* 1959. San Antonio. photos. 89p. F/worn. E1. $30.00

INGRAMS, Harold. *Arabia & the Isles.* 1943. London. Murrray. 3rd. ils/2 fld maps. 367p. VG. W1. $45.00

INHELDER, Barbel. *Diagnosis of Reasoning in the Mentally Retarded.* 1968. John Day. 1st Eng-language ed. blk cloth. VG/torn. G1. $40.00

INMAN, Henry. *Buffalo Jones' Forty Years of Adventure.* 1899. Topeka. 1st ed. 469p. F/case. E1. $225.00

INMAN, Henry. *Old Santa Fe Trail: Story of a Great Highway.* 1897. NY. 1st ed. 493p. F. E1. $175.00

INN & LEE. *Chinese Houses & Gardens.* 1950. Bonanza. 2nd. 4to. photos/drawings. 148p. dj. B1. $115.00

INNES, Brian. *Book of Spies.* 1966. Grosset Dunlap. hc. VG. P3. $20.00

INNES, Hammond. *Angry Mountain.* 1950. Collins. 1st ed. VG/G. P3. $18.00

INNES, Hammond. *Big Footprints.* 1977. Collins. 1st ed. NF/NF. P3. $25.00

INNES, Hammond. *Doomed Oasis.* 1960. Collins. 1st ed. VG/VG. P3. $20.00

INNES, Hammond. *Golden Soak.* 1973. Collins. 1st ed. NF/NF. P3. $23.00

INNES, Hammond. *Lekas Man.* 1971. Collins. 1st ed. F/F. P3. $30.00

INNES, Hammond. *Mary Deare.* 1956. Collins. 2nd. VG/VG. P3. $18.00

INNES, Hammond. *Medusa.* 1988. Collins. 1st ed. F/F. P3. $22.00

INNES, Hammond. *North Star.* 1974. Collins. 1st ed. VG/VG. P3. $22.00

INNES, Hammond. *Solomons Seal.* 1980. Collins. 1st ed. VG/VG. P3. $18.00

INNES, Hammond. *Strode Venturer.* 1965. Collins. 1st ed. VG/VG. P3. $25.00

INNES, Luna. *Our Little Danis Cousin.* 1912. Boston. Page. 1st ed. ils. 154p. NF. B14. $35.00

INNES, Michael. *Ampersand Papers.* 1978. Gollancz. 1st ed. F/F. P3. $20.00

INNES, Michael. *Appleby & Honeybath.* 1983. Dodd Mead. 1st ed. F/F. H11. $20.00

INNES, Michael. *Appleby & Honeybath.* 1983. Gollancz. 1st ed. F/F. P3. $18.00

INNES, Michael. *Appleby's Answer.* 1973. Gollancz. 1st ed. F/F. P3. $20.00

INNES, Michael. *Awkward Lie.* 1971. Dodd Mead. 1st ed. xl. dj. P3. $8.00

INNES, Michael. *Carson's Conspiracy.* 1984. Dodd Mead. 1st ed. hc. NF/NF. P3. $18.00

INNES, Michael. *Carson's Conspiracy.* 1984. Gollancz. 1st ed. F/F. P3. $18.00

INNES, Michael. *Death at the Chase.* 1970. Gollancz. 1st ed. xl. dj. P3. $6.00

INNES, Michael. *Death by Water.* 1968. Dodd Mead. 1st ed. VG/VG. P3. $15.00

INNES, Michael. *From London Far.* 1973. Gollancz. 3rd. F/F. P3. $20.00

INNES, Michael. *Gay Phoenix.* 1976. Gollancz. 1st ed. F/F. P3. $20.00

INNES, Michael. *Honeybath's Haven.* 1977. Gollancz. 1st ed. F/F. P3. $20.00

INNES, Michael. *Long Farewell.* 1958. Dodd Mead. 1st ed. NF/NF. M22. $30.00

INNES, Michael. *Michael Innes Treasury.* nd. BC. VG/VG. P3. $10.00

INNES, Michael. *Money From Home.* 1964. Gollancz. 1st ed. VG/VG. P3. $45.00

INNES, Michael. *One-Man Show.* nd. BC. VG/VG. P3. $8.00

INNES, Michael. *Operation Pax.* 1974. Gollancz. 1st ed. F/F. P3. $20.00

INNES, Michael. *Secret Vanguard.* 1972. Gollancz. F/F. P3. $20.00

INNES, Michael. *Sheiks & Adders.* 1982. Dodd Mead. 1st ed. F/F. P3. $15.00

INSH, George P. *Company of Scotland Trading to Africa & the Indies.* 1932. London. xl. VG. O7. $55.00

IONESCO, Eugene. *Hugoliad.* 1987. NY. 1st ed thus. F.dj. A17. $7.50

IONESCO & MIRO. *Quelques Fleurs Pour Des Amis.* 1964. Paris. 1/150. sgn Miro. loose portfolio/wrp/clamshell box. C6. $3,500.00

IONICUS. *Ali Baba & the Forty Thieves.* 1940s. Boston. Houghton Mifflin. 12mo. full panorama. VG. D1. $70.00

IPCAR, Dahlov. *Dark Horn Blowing.* 1978. Viking. 1st ed. VG/VG. P3. $15.00

IRESON, Barbara. *April Witch & Other Strange Tales.* 1978. Scribner. 1st ed. VG/VG. P3. $20.00

IRISH, William; see Hoppley-Woolrich, Cornell.

IRONS, Ernest. *Story of Rush Medical College.* 1953. Chicago. 1st ed. 82p. VG. A13. $20.00

IRONS, Peter. *Justice Delayed, the Record of the Japanese Am Internment...* 1989. Middletown. Wesleyan U. M11. $35.00

IRONS, Peter. *New Deal Lawyers.* 1982. Princeton. M11. $35.00

IRVINE. *How To Make Super Pop-Ups.* 1992. np. 4to. ils. 96p. F/F. A4. $65.00

IRVING, David. *German Atomic Bomb.* 1967. NY. 1st ed. VG/VG. B5. $40.00

IRVING, David. *Hitler's War.* 1977. NY. 1st ed. VG/dj. A17. $17.50

IRVING, David. *War Path: Hitler's Germany 1933-39.* 1978. NY. 301p. VG/dj. A17. $15.00

IRVING, John Treat Jr. *Indian Sketches.* 1955. Norman. 1st ed. 275p. F/VG. E1. $75.00

IRVING, John. *Cider House Rules.* 1985. Morrow. 1st ed. F/F. H11. $40.00

IRVING, John. *Cider House Rules.* 1985. NY. 1st ed. sgn. F/VG tissue dj. C6. $95.00

IRVING, John. *Hotel New Hampshire.* 1981. Dutton. 1st ed. F/NF. N4. $45.00

IRVING, John. *Hotel New Hampshire.* 1981. Dutton. 1st ed. VG/VG. P3. $25.00

IRVING, John. *Prayer for Owen Meany.* 1989. Franklin Lib. ltd ed. sgn. full leather. F. B4. $125.00

IRVING, John. *Prayer for Owen Meany.* 1989. Morrow. 1st ed. F/F. B4. $50.00

IRVING, John. *Prayer for Owen Meany.* 1989. Toronto. Dennys. 1st ed. NF/F. H11. $35.00

IRVING, John. *Smoke Screen of Jutland.* 1966. NY. 1st Am ed. ils/maps. 256p. F/F. E1. $35.00

IRVING, John. *World According to Garp.* 1978. NY. ARC. VG/wrp. C6. $50.00

IRVING, Washington. *Abbotsford & Newstrad Abbey, by Author of the Sketch Book.* 1835. Phil. Carey Lea Blanchard. 1st ed. 12mo. VG. T10. $500.00

IRVING, Washington. *Bracebridge Hall; or, The Humorists.* 1896. Putnam. 2 vol. Holly ed. 8vo. ils. gilt maroon cloth. NF. T10. $45.00

IRVING, Washington. *Crayon Miscellany.* (1895). Putnam. 2 vol. Holly ed. 8vo. ils. teg. gilt maroon cloth. NF. T10. $45.00

IRVING, Washington. *Knickerbocker's History of New York.* 1894. Putnam. 2 vol. Stuyvesant ed. 1/281 on linen. proofs. teg. T10. $500.00

IRVING, Washington. *Legend of Sleepy Hollow.* 1928. London. 1/250. ils/sgn Rackham. teg. full vellum. F/case. T10. $2,000.00

IRVING, Washington. *Legend of Sleepy Hollow.* 1928. London. 1/375. ils/sgn Rackham. full vellum. F. T10. $1,800.00

IRVING, Washington. *Legends of the Alhambra.* 1909. Lippincott. 1st ed thus. ils George Hood. 230p. bl cloth. VG. M20. $52.00

IRVING, Washington. *Life & Voyages of Christopher Columbus.* (1892). Putnam. 5 vol. Holly ed. ils. teg. gilt maroon cloth. NF. T10. $100.00

IRVING, Washington. *Life of George Washington.* 1855-1859. Putnam. 5 vol. marbled brd/leather spine. xl. fair. B10. $95.00

IRVING, Washington. *Rip Van Winkle.* 1905. London. Heinemann. 1st ed. ils Rackham. gilt gr cloth. T10. $400.00

IRVING, Washington. *Rip Van Winkle.* 1969. Abingdon. ils Frank Aloise. 40p. dj. A17. $10.00

IRVING, Washington. *Rip Van Winkle.* 1987. Utrecht. 1/15 deluxe (of 150). miniature. F/case. w/extra suite. B24. $300.00

IRVING, Washington. *Rip Van Winkle: Posthumous Writing of Diedrich...* 1930. LEC. 1/1500. 1st ed. design/prt/sgn Frederic Goudy. leather. F/case. C2. $100.00

IRVING, Washington. *Sketch Book.* nd. Merrill Baker. hc. VG. P3. $15.00

IRVING, Washington. *Sketch Book.* 1882. Putnam. hc. VG. P3. $75.00

IRVING, Washington. *Works of...* 1900. AL Burt. 8 vol. VG. P12. $35.00

IRWIN, David. *Alone Across the Top of the World.* 1935. Phil. Winston. 1st ed. sgn. 15 pl. 254p. VG. B11. $40.00

IRWIN, Eyles. *Series of Adventures in Course of a Voyage of Red Sea...* 1780. London. Dodsley. 1st ed. 3 fld maps. 400p. VG. W1. $390.00

IRWIN, Howard S. *Roadside Flowers of Texas.* 1969 (1961). Austin. 3rd. ils. 295p. F/dj. B26. $14.00

IRWIN, Will. *House That Shadows Built.* 1928. Doubleday Doran. 1st ed. VG. D2. $60.00

IRWIN. *English Neoclassical Art: Studies in Inspiration & Taste.* 1966. NYGS. F/VG. D2. $50.00

ISAACS, Susan Sutherland. *Intellectual Growth in Young Children.* (1930). London. Routledge. 370p. bl cloth. G1. $40.00

ISAACS, Susan Sutherland. *Social Development in Young Children.* 1933. Harcourt Brace. 1st Am ed. 480p. bl cloth. VG/dj. G1. $35.00

ISAACS, Susan. *Shining Through.* 1988. Harper Row. 1st ed. F/F. B35. $25.00

ISADORA, Rachel. *Willaby.* 1977. Macmillan. 1st ed. unp. VG/G. T5. $22.00

ISCHLONDSKY, Naum Efimovich. *Brain & Behavior: Induction As a Fundamental Mechanism...* 1949. St Louis. Mosby. 1st Am ed. 182p. prt bl cloth. NF. G1. $45.00

ISELY, Reymoure Keith. *Strange Code of Justice.* 1974. Bobbs Merrill. 1st ed. VG/VG. P3. $15.00

ISERN, Thomas. *Custom Combining on the Great Plains.* 1981. Norman. 1st ed. 248p. F/F. E1. $35.00

ISHERWOOD, Christopher. *Single Man.* 1964. Simon Schuster. 1st ed. F/NF. B2. $35.00

ISHIGURO, Kazuo. *Remains of the Day.* 1989. NY. 1st Am ed. F/F. C6. $50.00

ISHLONDSKY, N.E. *Artificial Rejuvenation & Voluntary Change of Sex...* 1926. Lawrence. Todd-Wood. 1st ed. photos. 172p. tan cloth. VG. B14. $125.00

ISIRESCU, Peter. *Tales & Stories.* nd. Murray. decor brd. VG. P3. $10.00

ISMAY, General Lord. *Memoirs of...* 1960. Viking. 1st ed. 488p. bl cloth. F/VG. B22. $12.00

ISNARD, H. *Algeria.* 1955. Paris/Grenoble. Arthaud/Nicholas Kaye. 1st ed. 8vo. ils. VG/dj. W1. $20.00

ISRAEL, Nico. *Catalogue Twenty-Five: 250 Fine & Interesting Old Books...* 1989. Amsterdam. ils. cloth. F. O7. $55.00

ISRAEL, Peter. *French Kiss.* 1976. Crowell. 1st ed. VG/VG. P3. $15.00

ISRAEL, Peter. *I'll Cry When I Kill You.* 1988. Mysterious. 1st ed. VG/VG. P3. $18.00

ISRAEL, Peter. *If I Should Die Before I Die.* 1989. Mysterious. 1st ed. VG/VG. P3. $18.00

ISRAEL, Peter. *Stiff Upper Lip.* 1978. Crowell. 1st ed. F/F. P3. $20.00

ISSAVERDENZ, J. *Island of San Lazzaro or the Armenian Monastery Near Venice.* 1879. Venice. Armenian Typography San Lazzaro. photos. aeg. gilt bdg. K1. $125.00

ITO & STEMLER. *Roses of Yesterday.* 1967. Kansas City. ARC. fwd James Cozzens. 54p. dj. B26. $15.00

IVANOFF & ZAMPETTI. *Giacomo Negretti Detto Palma Il Giovane.* 1980. Bergamo. Poligrafiche Bolis. 3 vol. ils/pl. brd. D2. $150.00

IVENS, Dorothy. *Upside-Down Boy.* 1958. Viking. 1st ed. 40p. VG/dj. T5. $15.00

IVES, Morgan; see Bradley, Marion Zimmer.

IVORY & VAN DER MEER. *Little Angels.* 1991. Knopf. 1st ed. F. B17. $7.50

VRINE. *Apes, Angels & Victorians: Story of Darwin, Huxley...* 1955. np. ils. 399p. F/VG. A4. $25.00

IZZEDDIN, Nejla. *Arab World, Past, Present & Future.* 1953. Chicago. Regenry. 1st ed. 8vo. ils. 412p. VG. W1. $25.00

IZZI, Eugene. *Bad Guys.* 1988. NY. 1st ed. F/NF. H11. $35.00

IZZI, Eugene. *Invasions.* 1990. Bantam. 1st ed. F/F. A20/H11. $20.00

IZZI, Eugene. *Take.* 1987. NY. 1st ed. author's 1st book. F/NF. H11. $55.00

IZZI, Eugene. *Tribal Secrets.* 1992. Bantam. 1st ed. NF/NF. M22. $10.00

JABLOKOV, Alexander. *Carve the Sky.* 1991. Morrow. 1st ed. author's 1st novel. F/F. T2. $22.00

JABLOKOV, Alexander. *Deeper Sea.* 1992. Morrow. 1st ed. F/F. G10/P3. $22.00

JACCACI, A.F. *Saharan Caravan.* 1893. Scribner. ils. VG. P4. $15.00

JACKH, Ernest. *Rising Crescent: Turkey, Yesterday, Today & Tomorrow.* 1944. Farrar Rhinehart. 1st ed. ils. 278p. xl. VG. W1. $24.00

JACKMAN, Stuart. *Davidson Affair.* 1966. Eerdmans. VG/VG. P3. $13.00

JACKOBS, Harvey. *Egg of the Glak & Other Stories.* 1969. NY. 1st ed. F/F. A17. $10.00

JACKS, L.P. *Last Legend of Smokeover.* 1939. Hodder Stoughton. VG/VG. P3. $30.00

JACKSON, A.J. *De Havilland Aircraft Since 1915.* 1962. London. ils. 491p. VG/torn. B18. $47.50

JACKSON, Andrew W. *Sure Foundation & Sketch of Negro Life in Texas.* 1939. Houston. private prt. 750+ biographical sketches. photos. 960p. VG. M8. $650.00

JACKSON, Arlina Janette. *If You're Not Sure Where I'm Coming From...* 1987. NY. Vantage. 1st ed. F/VG. B4. $45.00

JACKSON, Aurilda. *Untangled.* 1956. Vantage. 1st ed. F/VG. B4. $100.00

JACKSON, Basil. *Epicenter.* 1971. Norton. 2nd. NF/NF. P3. $10.00

JACKSON, Bruce. *Thief's Primer.* 1969. Macmillan. 1st ed. F/F. H11. $45.00

JACKSON, C.S. *Picturemaker of the Old West: William H Jackson.* 1947. Scribner. NF/G. D2. $60.00

JACKSON, Charles. *Outer Edges.* 1948. NY. 1st ed. 240p. F/dj. A17. $15.00

JACKSON, Donald Dale. *Gold Dust.* 1980. NY. 1st ed. 361p. F/F. E1. $40.00

JACKSON, Donald. *Voyages of the Steamboat Yellow Stone.* 1985. Ticknor Fields. dj. A16. $15.00

JACKSON, G. *Peggy Stewart at School.* 1918. Goldsmith. ils Norman Rockwell. VG/VG. B17. $10.00

JACKSON, G. Gibbard. *World's Aeroplanes & Airships.* 1929. London. Sampson Low. probable 1st ed. 244p. fair. B18. $65.00

JACKSON, Gordon. *History & Archaeology of Ports.* 1983. London. Windmill. 25 ils. VG/dj. T7. $35.00

JACKSON, H. *Black Ivory; or, Story of El Zubeir Pasha, Slaver & Sultan.* 1970. NY. Negro U/Greenwood. rpt of 1913 ed. 118p. F/sans. P4. $18.50

JACKSON, Helen Hunt. *Ramona.* 1884. Roberts. 1st ed. F. A18. $500.00

JACKSON, Holbrook. *Anatomy of Bibliomania.* 1930-1931. London. Soncino. 2 vol. 1/1000. VG. A4. $200.00

JACKSON, J. Hughlings. *Selected Writings of JH Jackson.* 1958. NY. Basic. 2 vol. 1st Am ed. gr cloth. VG/dj. G1. $275.00

JACKSON, James. *Memoir of James Jackson Jr, MD, With Extracts of Letters...* 1835. Boston. 444p. brn cloth. VG. B14. $125.00

JACKSON, John W. *Pennsylvania Navy, 1775-1781.* 1974. Rutgers. 1st ed. 514p. VG/dj. B18. $22.50

JACKSON, John. *Hit on the House.* 1994. Atlantic Monthly. 1st ed. F/F. M22. $10.00

JACKSON, Jon A. *Blind Pig.* 1978. Random. 1st ed. rem mk. F/F. B4. $100.00

JACKSON, Jon. *Ridin' With Ray.* 1995. Santa Barbara. 1st ed. 1/300. sgn. AN. C2. $60.00

JACKSON, Joseph Henry. *Bad Company.* 1939. NY. 1st ed. ils/photos. 346p. F/VG. E1. $40.00

JACKSON, Joseph Henry. *Tintypes in Gold, Four Studies...* 1939. NY. 1st ed. 191p. F/G. E1. $45.00

JACKSON, K.C. *Textbook of Lithology.* 1970. McGraw Hill. 522p. cloth. VG. D8. $20.00

JACKSON, Leroy. *Peter Patter Book.* 1918. Rand McNally. 1st ed. ils Blanche Fisher Wright. VG. P2. $85.00

JACKSON, Mae. *Can I Poet With You.* 1969. NY. Blk Dialogue Pub. 1st ed. tall 8vo. NF/stapled wrp. B4. $75.00

JACKSON, Mary E. *Life of Nellie C Bailey; or, Romance of the West.* 1885. Topeka, KS. ils. 399p. professional rpr/case. E1. $325.00

JACKSON, Richard. *Black Literature & Humanism in Latin America.* 1988. Athens, GA. 1st ed. 166p. dj. F3. $15.00

JACKSON, Sheila. *Ballet in England, a Book of Lithographs.* 1945. Transatlantic Arts. 10 full-p lithographs/line drawings. gilt cloth. F. B24. $375.00

JACKSON, Shirley. *Hangsaman.* 1951. Farrar Strauss. 1st ed. F/VG. B4. $125.00

JACKSON, Shirley. *Lottery.* 1949. Farrar Strauss. 1st ed. VG/G. M22. $95.00

JACKSON, Shirley. *Magic of Shirley Jackson.* 1966. FSG. 1st ed. F/NF clip. B4. $50.00

JACKSON, Shirley. *We Have Always Lived in the Castle.* 1962. Viking. 1st ed. F/NF clip. B4. $150.00

JACKSON, W.T. *Wagon Roads West.* 1952. Berkeley. 1st ed. 422p. VG/fair. B5. $25.00

JACKSON. *Norman Rockwell Identification & Value Guide.* 1980. np. 12mo. 16p. G/wrp. T3. $5.00

JACOB, Edmond. *Ras Shamra et l'Ancien Testament.* 1960. Neuchatel, Switzerland. Delachaux Niestle. 1st ed. ils. 132p. VG/wrp. W1. $18.00

JACOB, Francois. *Logic of Life, a History of Heredity.* 1973. NY. 1st Eng trans. 348p. dj. A13. $40.00

JACOB, OBST & RICHTER. *Completely Ils Atlas of Reptiles & Amphibians...* 1988. Neptune City. TFH Pub. 4to. pict brd. NF. B1. $125.00

JACOBI, Carl. *Disclosures in Scarlet.* 1972. Arkham. 1st ed. 1/3127. F/F. T2. $30.00

JACOBI, Carl. *Revelations in Black.* 1974. Neville Spearman. F/F. P3. $25.00

JACOBS, Flora Gill. *Dollhouse Mystery.* (1958). Coward McCann. 11th. inscr. ils. 96p. NF/NF. C14. $15.00

JACOBS, James Ripley. *Beginning of the US Army 1783-1812.* 1947. Princeton, NJ. 1st ed. 419p. NF. E1. $35.00

JACOBS, Joseph. *Buried Moon.* nd. Bradbury. stated 1st prt. 4to. 13 double-p ils. NF. C14. $14.00

JACOBS, Joseph. *Indian Fairy Tales.* 1892. London. David Nutt. 1st ed. 8vo. VG. M5. $110.00

JACOBS, Joseph. *Master of All Masters.* 1972. Thistle Book. ils Anne Rockwell. unp. VG. T5. $15.00

JACOBS, T.C.H. *Appointment With the Hangman.* 1936. MacAulay. 1st ed. VG. P3. $30.00

JACOBS, T.C.H. *Documents of Murder.* 1933. MacAulay. hc. VG. P3. $25.00

JACOBS, T.C.H. *Red Eyes of Kali.* nd. Stanley paul. hc. xl. dj. P3. $12.00

JACOBS, W.W. *Night Watches.* 1914. Scribner. 1st ed. decor brd. VG. P3. $45.00

JACOBS, Wilbur. *Turner, Bolton & Webb.* 1965. Seattle. VG. O7. $35.00

JACOBS & REIT. *Canvas Confidential.* 1963. Dial. 1st ed. G. P3. $30.00

JACOBSEN, Jerome V. *Educational Foundations of the Jesuits in 16th-C New Spain.* 1938. Berkeley. 1st ed. 8vo. 292p. gilt maroon cloth. F. T10. $50.00

JACOBSEN, Johan A. *Alaskan Voyage 1881-1883.* 1977. Chicago. VG. O7. $65.00

JACOBSON, Mark. *Gojiro.* 1991. Atlantic. 1st ed. F/F. H11. $30.00

JACOBSON, Timothy. *Making Medical Doctors: Science & Medicine...* 1987. Tuscaloosa, AL. 1st ed. 349p. dj. A13. $30.00

JACOBY, Arnold. *Senor Kon-Tiki: Life & Adventure of Thor Heyerdahl.* 1967. NY. 1st ed. F/F. B4. $50.00

JACOBY, Arnold. *Senor Kon-Tiki: Life & Adventure of Thor Heyerdahl.* 1967. NY. 1st prt. 424p. VG/dj. E1. $30.00

JACOBY & JACOBY. *Jacoby on Card Games.* 1986. NY. 239p. F/dj. S1. $6.00

JACQUEMARD, Simonne. *Night Watchman.* 1964. HRW. 1st ed. hc. VG. P3. $13.00

JACQUES, Brian. *Bellmaker.* 1994. NY. Philomel. 1st ed. sgn. ils Allan Curless. F/dj. T10. $50.00

JACQUES, Florence. *Francis Lee Jaques. Artist of the Wilderness World.* 1973. NY. 1st ed. F/F. B5. $125.00

JACQUIER, Henry. *Piracy in the Pacific.* 1976. NY. VG. O7. $20.00

JAEGER, Gustav. *Entdeckund der Seele.* 1884. Leipzig. Ernst Gunthers. 410p. xl. VG. G1. $50.00

JAENSCH, E.R. *Uber die Wahrnehmung des Raumes...* 1911. Leipzig. Johann Ambrosius Barth. 488p. prt brn wrp. VG. G1. $85.00

JAFEK, Bev. *Man Who Took a Bite Out of His Wife.* 1993. Overlook/Penguin. UP. F. B35. $30.00

JAFFE, Rona. *After the Reunion.* nd. BC. hc. VG/VG. P3. $5.00

JAFFE, Rona. *Best of Everything.* 1958. Simon Schuster. 2nd. NF/NF. B35. $30.00

JAFFE, Rona. *Mazes & Monsters.* 1981. Delacorte. 1st ed. VG/VG. P3. $20.00

JAFFE, Susanne. *Other Anne Fletcher.* 1980. NAL. hc. VG/VG. P3. $15.00

JAGENDORF, M. *In the Days of Han.* 1936. Suttonhouse. 1st ed. ils Erwin Neumann. 168p. red cloth. VG. D1. $45.00

JAGO, William. *Science & Art of Bread-Making.* 1895. London. fair. V4. $80.00

JAGO, Willie. *Team Tactics at Bridge.* 1996. Australia. pb. 190p. M. S1. $12.00

JAGODA, Robert. *Friend in Deed.* 1977. Norton. 1st ed. sgn. F/F. B35. $30.00

JAHN, Michael. *Murder at the Museum of Natural History.* 1994. St Martin. 1st ed. F/NF. N4. $20.00

JAKES, John. *Furies.* nd. BC. hc. VG/VG. P3. $8.00

JAKUBOWSKI, Maxim. *New Crimes 3.* 1991. Carrol Graf. F/F. P3. $19.00

JAKUBOWSKI, Maxim. *100 Great Detectives.* 1991. Carroll Graf. 1st Am ed. F/F clip. M22. $25.00

JAMES, Alice. *Catering For Two: Comfort & Economy for Small Households.* 1906. Putnam. VG. I17. $20.00

JAMES, Arthur W. *Commonwealth Vs the Buck Boys.* 1930. Garrett Massie. G. B10. $35.00

JAMES, Bill C. *Jim Miller, the Untold Story of a Texas Badman.* 1989. Wolfe City, TX. 1/300. sgn. F. E1. $40.00

JAMES, Bill C. *Mysterious Killer, James Brown Miller 1861-1909.* 1976. Carrollton, TX. 1/250. sgn/#d. F/stiff wrp. E1. $10.00

JAMES, Bill. *Great American Baseball Stat Book.* 1987. Ballantine. 1st ed. VG+. P8. $15.00

JAMES, Cary. *King & Raven.* 1995. Tor. 1st ed. F/F. P3. $24.00

JAMES, Edward T. *American Plutarch.* 1964. NY. 1st ed. 408p. VG. E1. $20.00

JAMES, George Wharton. *California Romantic & Beautiful.* 1914. Page. 2nd. ils/map. VG. P12. $50.00

JAMES, George Wharton. *In & Around the Grand Canyon.* 1901. Boston. photos. VG. M17. $50.00

JAMES, George Wharton. *Indian Blankets & Their Makers.* 1937. Tudor. new ed. 4to. 213p. cloth. F/dj. T10. $150.00

JAMES, George Wharton. *Indians of the Painted Desert Region.* 1907. Little Brn. later ed. inscr. 8vo. photos. NF. T10. $225.00

JAMES, George Wharton. *Our American Wonderlands.* 1915. Chicago. 1st ed. inscr. 8vo. 297p. bl cloth. F. T10. $150.00

JAMES, George Wharton. *Story of Scraggles.* 1919. Pasadena. Radiant Life. 1st ed. inscr. 8vo. prt cloth. VG. T10. $75.00

JAMES, George Wharton. *Through Ramona's Country.* 1909. Little Brn. VG+. B5. $37.50

JAMES, Grace. *Green Willow & Other Japanese Fairy Tales.* 1910. Macmillan. 1st ed. ils Warwick Goble. 281p. VG. D1. $450.00

JAMES, Grace. *Green Willow.* 1923. London. Macmillan. 3rd ils ed/1st medium 8vo ed. 16 mc pl. NF. A20. $85.00

JAMES, Henry. *English Hours.* nd. Houghton Mifflin. 1st ed. ils Pennell. teg. leather/marbled brd. VG. A20. $75.00

JAMES, Henry. *In the Cage.* 1898. Chicago. Herbert Stone. 1st Am ed. 229p. F. A4. $235.00

JAMES, Henry. *Outcry.* 1911. NY. Scribner. 1st Am ed. NF. A4. $115.00

JAMES, Henry. *Tragic Muse.* 1890. London. Macmillan. 1st Eng ed. 3 vol. 1/500. pub cloth. NF. B24. $2,500.00

JAMES, Henry. *Travelling Companions.* 1919. Boni Liveright. 1st ed. 309p. VG. M20. $32.00

JAMES, Jamie. *Music of the Spheres.* 1993. Grove. 1st ed. rem mk. F/F. B35. $18.00

JAMES, Jesse Jr. *Jesse James, My Father...* 1906 (1899). Cleveland. rpt. F/wrp. E1. $95.00

JAMES, M.R. *Best Ghost Stories of MR James.* 1946. Tower. 5th. hc. F/F. P3. $20.00

JAMES, M.R. *Wailing Well.* 1928. Mill House. 1/157. VG. C6. $300.00

JAMES, Mrs. T.D. *Matsuyama Mirror (Kagami) #10.* nd. London. Griffith Farran. ils. 22p. crepe paper. VG. D1. $110.00

JAMES, P.D. *Children of Men.* 1993. Knopf. 1st ed. F/F. H11. $30.00

JAMES, P.D. *Devices & Desires.* 1990. Knopf. 1st Am ed. w/sgn leaf. F/F. B2. $40.00

JAMES, P.D. *Devices & Desires.* 1990. Knopf. 1st Am trade ed. VG/VG. M22. $10.00

JAMES, P.D. *Innocent Blood.* nd. BOMC. hc. VG/VG. P3. $10.00

JAMES, P.D. *Innocent Blood.* 1980. Scribner. 1st ed. VG/VG. M22. $15.00

JAMES, P.D. *Maul & the Pear Tree.* 1986. Mysterious. 1st ed. hc. VG. P3. $18.00

JAMES, P.D. *Skull Beneath the Skin.* 1982. Lester Orpen Denys. 1st ed. VG/VG. P3. $17.00

JAMES, P.D. *Skull Beneath the Skin.* 1982. Scribner. 1st ed. F/F clip. H11. $30.00

JAMES, P.D. *Taste for Death.* 1986. Knopf. 1st ed. F/F. P3. $19.00

JAMES, P.D. *Unsuitable Job for a Woman.* nd. BC. VG/VG. P3. $8.00

JAMES, Peggy Seitz. *Stow, Ohio: Shadows of Its Past.* 1972. Ann Arbor. ils/notes/index. 307p. VG. B18. $22.50

JAMES, Peter. *Possession.* 1988. Doubleday. 1st ed. NF/NF. P3. $18.00

JAMES, Peter. *Prophecy.* 1994. St Martin. 1st Am ed. F/F. G10. $10.00

JAMES, Philip. *Children's Books of Yesterday.* 1933. London. The Studio. ils. 128p. gr cloth. VG. D1. $75.00

JAMES, Will. *Big Enough.* 1931. NY. 1st ed. G+. B5. $65.00

JAMES, Will. *Cow Country.* 1927. NY. 1st ed. VG-. B5. $80.00

JAMES, Will. *Cowboy in the Making.* 1937. NY. 1st ed. VG. B5. $45.00

JAMES, Will. *Cowboys North & South.* 1924. Scribner. 1st ed. ils. F/VG. A18. $500.00

JAMES, Will. *Lone Cowboy: My Life Story.* 1937. Scribner. ils Will James. 431p. VG+. M20. $67.00

JAMES, Will. *Smoky.* 1929. Scribner. 1st ed thus. ils Will James. 263p. VG+. M20. $87.00

JAMES, Will. *Three Mustangers.* 1933. NY. 1st/A ed. ils. 338p. pict gr cloth. VG. H3. $100.00

JAMES, Will. *Young Cowboy.* 1935. Scribner. later prt. xl. VG/G. M5. $16.00

JAMES, William. *Psychology.* 1892. Holt. 1st ed/3rd prt. 12mo. gr cloth. VG. G1. $85.00

JAMES & SHANNON. *Sheriff AJ Royal, Fort Stockton, Texas.* 1984. np. 1/300. 1st ed. sgn/#d. photos. F. E1. $50.00

JAMES. *Dictionary of American Bibliography, Supplement 3, 1941-45.* 1973. np. 879p. xl. VG. A4. $75.00

JAMES. *Notable American Women 1607-1950.* 1974. Harvard. 3 vol. 2125p. VG/case. A4. $85.00

JAMIESON, John. *Etymological Dictionary of the Scottish Language.* 1879-1882. Paisley. 4 vol. revised. lg 4to. morocco/cloth. VG+. B14. $125.00

JAMIESON. *Infared Physics & Engineering.* 1963. McGraw Hill. 673p. F. P4. $25.00

JANCE, J.A. *Desert Heat.* 1993. Avon. 1st ed. pb. sgn. F/wrp. T2. $10.00

JANCE, J.A. *Failure to Appear.* 1993. Morrow. 1st ed. NF/F. H11. $20.00

JANCE, J.A. *Failure to Appear.* 1993. Morrow. 1st ed. sgn. F/F. T2. $30.00

JANCE, J.A. *Hour of the Hunter.* 1991. Morrow. 1st ed. sgn. F/F. T2. $40.00

JANCE, J.A. *Tombstone Courage.* 1994. Morrow. 1st ed. RS. F/F. P3. $20.00

JANCE, J.A. *Without Due Process.* 1992. Morrow. 1st ed. F/F. P3. $20.00

JANCE, J.A. *Without Due Process.* 1992. Morrow. 1st ed. sgn. F/F. T2. $35.00

JANE, Fred T. *Jane's Fighting Ships 1906-1907.* 1970. NY. rpt. 300p. F/F. E1. $50.00

JANE, Mary C. *Mystery in Old Quebec.* nd. Weekly Reader. VG/VG. P3. $8.00

JANES, E.C. *Story of Knives.* 1968. NY. 1st ed. 127p. NF/NF. E1. $30.00

JANICK, J. *Horticultural Science.* 1963. San Francisco. WH Freeman. 8vo. 472p. cloth. dj. B1. $35.00

JANIFER, Laurence. *Reel.* 1983. Doubleday. 1st ed. RS. F/F. P3. $20.00

JANKOVICH, Miklos. *They Rode Into Europe.* 1971. London. Harrap. 1st ed. VG/VG. O3. $48.00

JANNERSTEN, Eric. *Card Reading: The Art of Guesssing Right at Bridge Table.* 1972. NY. 207p. VG/wrp. S1. $5.00

JANNERSTEN, Eric. *Find the Mistakes: A Bridge Quiz.* 1982. London. 160p. F/dj. S1. $15.00

JANNERSTEN & KELSEY. *Only Chance.* 1980. London. 171p. VG. S1. $10.00

JANNEY, Russell. *Miracle of the Bells.* 1946. McLeod. G/G. P3. $8.00

JANOVY, John Jr. *Vermilion Sea: Naturalist's Journey in Baja, CA.* 1992. Houghton Mifflin. 1st ed. 8vo. 226p. F/dj. B24. $20.00

JANOWITZ, Tama. *American Dad.* 1981. Putnam. 1st ed. F/F. H11. $65.00

JANOWITZ, Tama. *Cannibal in Manhattan.* 1987. Crown. 1st ed. F/F. B35/H11. $20.00

JANOWITZ, Tama. *Slaves of New York.* 1986. Crown. 1st ed. F/F. M19. $25.00

JANOWITZ, Tama. *Slaves of New York.* 1986. Crown. 1st ed. F/NF. B35. $22.00

JANSON, H.W. *History of Art, 4th Ed.* 1991. Abrams. F/F. P3. $50.00

JANSSON, Tove. *Moominsummer Maddness.* 1961. Walck. ils T Warburton. VG+/VG. P2. $30.00

JANVIER, Thomas J. *Legends of the City of Mexico.* 1936 (1910). NY. rpt. ils/photos. 164p. VG. E1. $20.00

JAPRISOT, Sebastien; see Rossi, Jean-Baptiste.

JAQUES, Florence Page. *Canoe Country.* 1958. MN U. 5th. VG. B17. $5.00

JARDIN, Rex. *Devil's Mansion.* 1931. Fiction League. G. P3. $10.00

JARDINE, David. *Criminal Trials. Two Volumes.* 1832-35. London. Chas Knight. 1st complete ed. 3-quarter morocco. G. M11. $350.00

JARES, Joe. *Whatever Happened to Gorgeous George.* 1974. Englewood Cliffs. 1st ed. VG/VG. B5. $20.00

JARRELL, Randall. *Animal Family.* 1965. Pantheon. 12mo. VG/G. B17. $7.50

JARRELL, Randall. *Blood for a Stranger.* 1942. Harcourt Brace. 1st ed. author's 1st book. NF/dj. B24. $300.00

JARRELL, Randall. *Pictures From an Institution.* 1974 (1954). Faber. 290p. F/F. B10. $12.00

JARRELL, Randall. *Seven-League Crutches.* 1951. Harcourt Brace. ARC/1st ed. RS. F/NF. B4. $250.00

JARVIS, George O. *Surgical Adjuster, for Reducing Dislocations...* 1846. Derby, CT. 80p. VG/prt wrp (lacks back). B14. $175.00

JASIENICA, P. *Commonwealth of Both Nations: The Silver Age.* 1987. NY/Miami. Am Inst Polish Culture/Hippocrene. 1st ed. 338p. AN/dj. P4. $20.00

JASON, Jerry; see Smith, George H.

JASON, Leon. *Heckle & Jeckle.* 1957. Wonder. TVTI. VG. P3. $8.00

JASPERS, Karl. *Psychologie der Weltanschauungen.* 1925. Berlin. Julius Springer. 3rd. 486p. buff wrp. G1. $50.00

JASSAU, J.J. *Textbook of Practical Astronomy.* 1932 (1932). McGraw Hill. 3rd. 8vo. 226p. cloth. G. K5. $18.00

JASTROW, Morris. *Gentle Cynic: Being a Translation of Book of Koheleth...* 1927. BC of CA. 1/250. ils from Valenti Angelo. vellum/ties. B24. $250.00

JASTROW, Morris. *War & the Bagdad Railway.* 1917. Phil. VG. O7. $45.00

JASTROW, Robert. *Journey to the Stars.* 1989. Bantam. 1st ed. hc. VG. P3. $20.00

JAY, Charlotte. *Arms for Adonis.* 1960. Collins Crime Club. 1st ed. VG/VG. P3. $25.00

JAY, Charlotte. *Man Who Walked Away.* 1958. Collins Crime Club. hc. VG/torn. P3. $20.00

JAYNE, Walter. *Healing Gods of Ancient Civilizations.* 1925. New Haven. 1st ed. 569p. VG. A13. $150.00

JAYNE, William. *Abraham Lincoln.* 1908. Chicago. 16mo. 58p. quarter leather/blk brd. xl. G. T3. $20.00

JEANS, James. *Astronomy & Cosmogony.* 1961 (1928). Philosophical Lib. rpt of 1929 2nd ed. 428p. G. K5. $10.00

JEFFARES, Norman. *Man & Poet (WB Yeats).* 1949. London. 1st ed. assn copy. VG. V1. $20.00

JEFFERIES, Roderic. *Deadly Petard.* 1983. St Martin. 1st ed. VG/VG. P3. $15.00

JEFFERIES, Roderic. *Two-Faced Death.* 1976. Collins Crime Club. 1st ed. F/F. P3. $35.00

JEFFERS, Alex. *Safe As Houses.* 1995. Boston. Faber. AP. sgn. author's 1st novel. F/wrp. S9. $30.00

JEFFERS, Robinson. *Californians.* 1916. Macmillan. 1st ed. author's 1st commercial book. 217p. NF. T10. $350.00

JEFFERS, Robinson. *Cawdor.* 1983. Yolla Bolly. 1/240 sgns. F/case. S9. $275.00

JEFFERS, Robinson. *Dear Judas & Other Poems.* 1929. NY. 1st ed. F/NF. C6. $120.00

JEFFERS, Robinson. *Medea.* 1946. Random. 1st ed. F/F. B35. $60.00

JEFFERS, Robinson. *Solstice+.* 1935. NY. 1st ed. 1/320. sgn. F/NF. C2. $300.00

JEFFERS, Robinson. *Themes in My Poems.* 1956. San Francisco. 1st ed. 1/350. 6 wood cuts. w/prospectus. F. B24. $275.00

JEFFERSON, Thomas. *Notes on the State of Virginia.* 1787. London. Stockdale. 1st Eng ed. 8vo. lg fld map. 382p. VG/clamshell box. C6. $10,000.00

JEFFERSON, Thomas. *Notes on the State of Virginia.* 1801. Newark. Pennington Gould. 3rd Am. 8vo. 392p. full calf/morocco spine label. C6. $700.00

JEFFEYS, J.G. *Wilful Lady.* 1975. Walker. 1st ed. hc. F/F. P3. $15.00

JEFFRIES, Ewel. *Short Biography of John Leeth.* 1904. Cleveland. 1/267. #d. 70p. F. E1. $165.00

JEFFRIES, Richard. *Story of My Heart, My Autobiography.* 1883. Boston. Roberts Bros. 144p. NF. A4. $195.00

JEKEL, Pamela. *Columbia.* 1986. St Martin. 1st ed. 8vo. 428p. map ep. F/F. T10. $30.00

JEKYLL, Gertrude. *Some English Gardens.* 1905. London. 3rd. 50 full-p pl. teg. gilt stp cloth. B26. $210.00

JEKYLL, Gertrude. *Wall & Water Gardens.* 1901. Scribner. 1st Am ed. 8vo. contemporary half leather. T10. $100.00

JELLICOE, G.A. *Motopia: Study in Evolution of Urban Landscape.* 1961. VG/VG. M17. $45.00

JEN, Gish. *Typical American.* 1991. Houghton Mifflin. 1st ed. author's 1st book. F/F. B35. $35.00

JENKINS, Cecil. *Message From Sirius.* 1961. Collins Crime Club. 1st ed. F/F. P3. $35.00

JENKINS, Dan. *Saturday America.* 1970. Boston. 1st ed. VG/VG. B5. $20.00

JENKINS, David. *Jenkinsius Redivivus; or, The Works of...Judge Jenkins...* 1681. London. Hindmarsh. contemporary calf. M11. $450.00

JENKINS, Dorothy H. *Children Make a Garden.* 1936. Doubleday. 1st ed. 8vo. VG. M5. $28.00

JENKINS, Elizabeth. *Mystery of King Arthur.* 1975. CMG. 1st ed. VG/VG. P3. $20.00

JENKINS, Geoffrey. *Grue of Ice.* 1962. Collins. 1st ed. F/F. P3. $30.00

JENKINS, Geoffrey. *Southtrap.* 1979. Collins. 1st ed. NF/NF. P3. $25.00

JENKINS, Geoffrey. *Twist of Sand.* 1959. Collins. 1st ed. hc. VG/G. P3. $20.00

JENKINS, Herbert. *Malcolm Sage Detective.* nd. Roy. hc. G/G. P3. $15.00

JENKINS, John H. *Basic Texas Books.* 1983. Austin. 1st ed. 648p. F/F. E1. $95.00

JENKINS, John H. *I'm Frank Hamer.* 1968. Austin, TX. 1st ed. sgn. 305p. F/F. E1. $110.00

JENKINS, Peter. *Walk Across America.* 1979. NY. 1st ed. photos. F/F. A17. $10.00

JENKINS, Rolland. *Mediterranean Cruise.* 1924. Knickerbocker. 2nd. 8vo. 40 pl. 279p. cloth. VG. W1. $18.00

JENKINS, Will F. *Forgotten Planet.* 1984. Crown. 1st ed. F/F. P3. $13.00

JENKINS, Will F. *Four From Planet 5.* 1974. Wht Lion. 1st ed. VG/VG. P3. $25.00

JENKINS, Will F. *Murder of the USA.* 1946. Crown. 1st ed. hc. VG/G. P3. $45.00

JENKINS, Will F. *Space Platform.* 1953. Shasta. 1st ed. sgn. NF/NF. B35. $125.00

JENKINS & REES. *Bibliography of History of Wales.* 1931. Cardiff. 218p. VG. A4. $145.00

JENKINSON, Michael. *Ghost Towns of New Mexico, Playthings of the Wind.* 1967. Albuquerque. 1st ed. 156p. F. E1. $35.00

JENKS, Almet. *Huntsman at the Gate.* 1952. Lippincott. 1st ed. VG/G. O3. $45.00

JENKS, George F. *Studies in Cartography: A Festschrift in Honor of GF Jenks.* 1987. Monograph 37. edit PP Gilmartin. brn cloth. M. O7. $35.00

JENNEY & SHELLEY. *Fortunes of Heaven by Percy Bysshe Shelley.* nd. London. Arthur Stockwell. sgn pres. 98p. silver/gray cloth. VG/G. B11. $45.00

JENNINGS, Dean; see Fox, Gardner F.

JENNINGS, Gary. *Killer Storms.* 1970. Lippincott. 8vo. 207p. xl. dj. K5. $11.00

JENNINGS, Herbert Spencer. *Suggestions of Modern Science Concerning Education.* 1918. Macmillan. 12mo. bl buckram. G1. $37.00

JENNINGS, James R. *Freight Rolled.* 1969. San Antonio. 1st ed. photos. 99p. F/F. E1. $15.00

JENNINGS, John J. *Theatrical & Circus Life; or, Secrets of the Stage...* 1882. St Louis. 1st ed. 608p. fair. B18. $75.00

JENNINGS, John. *Banners Against the Wind.* 1954. Little Brn. 1st ed. VG/VG. P3. $15.00

JENNINGS, John. *Chronicle of the Calypso, Clipper.* 1955. Little Brn. 1st ed. VG/VG. P3. $15.00

JENNINGS, John. *Pepper Tree.* 1950. Little Brn. 1st ed. VG/VG. P3. $15.00

JENNINGS, N.A. *Texas Ranger.* 1972. Dallas. revised. fwd J Frank Dobie. hc. F. E1. $35.00

JENNINGS & NORBECK. *Prehistoric Man in the New World.* 1964. Chicago. 1st ed. 633p. dj. F3. $30.00

JENNISON, Christopher. *Wait 'Til Next Year.* 1974. Norton. 1st ed. F/VG+. P8. $35.00

JENSEN, Amy. *Guatemala.* 1955. Exposition. 1st ed. 263p. dj. F3. $15.00

JENSEN, Jen. *Life & Works of...* 1964. Chicago. 1st ed. VG/VG. B5. $145.00

JENSEN, Paul M. *Boris Karloff & His Films.* 1974. AS Barnes. 1st ed. VG/VG. P3. $25.00

JENSEN. *America's Yesterdays: Images in Photographic Archives...* 1978. cloth. F/VG. D2. $65.00

JEPSON, Selwyn. *Golden Dart.* 1949. Crime Club. 1st ed. VG. p3. $15.00

JEPSON, Selwyn. *Keep Murder Quiet.* 1940. Michael Joseph. 1st ed. xl. VG. P3. $12.00

JEPSON, Selwyn. *Man Dead.* 1951. Doubleday. VG. P3. $18.00

JEPSON, Selwyn. *Rogues & Diamonds.* 1925. Lincoln McVeagh/Dial. 1st ed. VG. P3. $35.00

JERKINS, Karen A. *Tender Moments.* 1988. Vantage. 1st ed. F/VG. B4. $45.00

JERNIGAN, Muriel Molland. *Forbidden City.* nd. BC. VG/VG. P3. $8.00

JERNINGHAM, Arthur W. *Remarks on the Means of Directing Fire of Ship's Broadsides.* 1851. London. Parker Furnivall. 10 fld pl/1 map. rebacked/new ep. T7. $225.00

JEROME, V.J.A. *Lantern for Jeremy.* 1952. Masses Mainstream. 1st ed. NF/NF. B2. $30.00

JESSETT, Thomas E. *Reports & Letters of Herbert Beaver 1836-1838.* 1959. Portland. 1/750. F. E1. $60.00

JESSUP, M.K. *Case for the UFO.* 1955. NY. 1st ed. NF/G. N3. $20.00

JESSUP, Richard. *Cincinnati Kid.* 1963. Boston. 1st ed. author's 1st novel. NF/NF. C2. $30.00

JESSUP, Richard. *Foxway.* 1971. Little Brn. 1st ed. VG/VG. P3. $15.00

JETER, K.W. *Death Arms.* 1987. Morrigan. 1st ed. F/F. P3/T2. $30.00

JETER, K.W. *Farewell Horizontal.* 1989. St Martin. 1st ed. F/F. P3. $17.00

JETER, K.W. *In the Land of the Dead.* 1989. Morrigan. 1st ed. F/F. P3/T2. $30.00

JETER, K.W. *Infernal Devices.* 1987. St Martin. 1st ed. F/F. P3. $25.00

JETER, K.W. *Madlands.* 1991. St Martin. 1st ed. F/F. P3. $19.00

JETER, K.W. *Wolf Flow.* 1992. St Martin. 1st ed. F/F. P3. $19.00

JEVONS, Marshall. *Murder at the Margin.* 1978. Horton. 1st ed. 168p. VG/VG. B10. $15.00

JEWERY, Mary. *Warne's Model Cookery & Housekeeping Book.* 1868. London. Warne. People's ed. 12mo. sgn Mrs Geo Westinghouse. VG. T10. $100.00

JEWETT, Sarah Orne. *Queen's Twin & Other Stories.* 1899. Houghton Mifflin. 1st ed. inscr/dtd 1899. silver-stp gr cloth. NF. B24. $650.00

JHABVALA, Ruth Prawer. *Heat & Dust.* 1976. Harper Row. 1st ed. F/F. M23. $20.00

JOBE, Joseph. *Extended Travels in Romantic America...* 1966. Lausanne. 223p. F/case. A17. $45.00

JOBE, Joseph. *Guns: An Illustrated History of Artillery.* 1971. Greenwich. 1st ed. ils/photos. 217p. VG. E1. $45.00

JOBSON, Hamilton. *Shadow That Caught Fire.* 1972. Scribner. 1st ed. F/F. P3. $15.00

JOBSON, Hamilton. *Waiting for Thursday.* 1977. Collins Crime Club. 1st ed. VG/VG. P3. $20.00

JODL, Friedrich. *Lehrbuch der Psychologie.* 1915. Stuttgart. JG Cotta'schen. 2 vol. 4th. G. G1. $50.00

JOE, Yolanda. *He Say She Say.* 1996. Doubleday. ARC. F/wrp. B4. $35.00

JOGUES, Isaac. *Narrative of the Captivity.* 1857. Appleton. 8vo. 358p. VG. T10. $150.00

JOHN, Augustus. *Chiaroscuro: Fragments of Autobiography.* 1952. London. Cape. 1st ed. inscr/dtd 1952. NF. w/sgn postcard. B4. $450.00

JOHN, Augustus. *Chiaroscuro: Fragments of Autobiography.* 1952. NY. 1st ed. 285p. F/dj. A17. $17.50

JOHN, Laurie. *Cosmology Now.* 1976. NY. Taplinger. 8vo. VG/dj. K5. $17.00

JOHNS, A. Wesley. *Man Who Shot McKinley.* 1970. S Brunswick/NY. 1st ed. 293p. VG/dj. B18. $22.50

JOHNS, Anne page. *Fur Tree & Other Poems.* 1943. Dietz. VG/VG. B10. $12.00

JOHNS, E.B. *Camp Travis & Its Part in the World War.* 1919. NY. 1st ed. photos. 337p. G. E1. $110.00

JOHNS, Foster. *Victory Murders.* nd. Economy Book League. VG. P3. $13.00

JOHNS, Francis A. *Bibliography of Arthur Waley.* 1968. Rutgers. 1st ed. photo portfolio. 187p. VG. A17. $15.00

JOHNS, John Edwin. *Florida During the Civil War.* 1963. Gainesville. 1st ed. 265p. NF/NF. M8. $85.00

JOHNS, Masterton. *Beyond Time.* 1966. Arcadia. hc. VG/VG. P3. $15.00

JOHNS, W.E. *Biggles, Pioneer Air Fighter.* nd. Dean. hc. VG/VG. P3. $15.00

JOHNS, W.E. *Biggles & the Pirate Treasure.* 1954. Brock. 1st ed. VG. P3. $15.00

JOHNS, W.E. *Biggles Flies Again.* nd. Dean. hc. VG/VG. P3. $12.00

JOHNS, W.E. *Biggles Flies North.* 1947. Oxford. 3rd. G. P3. $10.00

JOHNS, W.E. *Biggles in the Blue.* 1953. Brock. 1st ed. VG/G. P3. $15.00

JOHNS, W.E. *To Outer Space.* 1957. Hodder Stoughton. 1st ed. VG/G. P3. $20.00

JOHNS, William Allen. *Willie Tolbert: A Memoir.* 1971. Dietz. photos. 61p. VG/G. B10. $15.00

JOHNSON, Adrian. *America Explored: Cartographical History of Exploration...* 1974. NY. Viking. 350 maps/ils. F/dj. O7. $100.00

JOHNSON, Alvin. *Touch of Color & Other Tales.* 1963. NY. 1st ed. F/F. A17. $9.50

JOHNSON, Brita Elizabeth. *Maher-Shalal-hash-Baz; or, Rural Life in Old Virginia.* 1923. Claremont, VA. Sigfried Olson. 328p. VG/G. B10. $20.00

JOHNSON, Clifton. *Highways & Byways of the Great Lakes.* 1911. NY. 12mo. 382p. gilt stp gr cloth. VG. T3. $30.00

JOHNSON, Clifton. *Highways & Byways of the Mississipi Valley.* 1906. Macmillan. 1st ed. photos. VG. P12. $50.00

JOHNSON, Crockett. *Barnaby.* 1943. Holt. 1st ed. 361p. VG/G. P2. $45.00

JOHNSON, Curt. *Artillery: The Big Guns Go to War.* 1975. London. 1st ed. 144p. F/F. E1. $35.00

JOHNSON, Curt. *Best Little Magazine Fiction, 1970.* 1970. NYU. 1st ed. hc. F/F. B35. $85.00

JOHNSON, Denis. *Angels.* 1983. Knopf. 1st ed. author's 1st novel. F/F. M19. $45.00

JOHNSON, Denis. *Resuscitation of a Hanged Man.* 1991. Faber. 1st ed. F/VG+. A20. $15.00

JOHNSON, Diane. *Loving Hands at Home.* 1968. HBW. 1st ed. NF/VG. B4. $50.00

JOHNSON, Diane. *Lying Low.* 1978. Knopf. 1st ed. F/F. M19. $17.50

JOHNSON, Dorothea. *Dorothea Johnson's Entertaining & Etiquette.* 1979. Washington, DC. Acropolis. 2nd. sgn 8vo. VG/VG. B11. $10.00

JOHNSON, Dorothy M. *All the Buffalo Returning.* 1979. Dodd Mead. 1st ed. F/F. A18. $35.00

JOHNSON, E. Richard. *Case Load — Maximum.* 1971. Harper Row. 1st ed. VG/VG. P3. $20.00

JOHNSON, E. Richard. *Mongo's Back in Town.* 1970. Macmillan. 1st ed. F/F. P3. $20.00

JOHNSON, Frederick. *Radiocarbon Dating: A Report on Program to Aid Development.* 1951. Salt Lake City. Soc Am Archeology. 65p. VG. P4. $25.00

JOHNSON, Fridolf. *Rockwell Kent, an Anthology of His Works.* 1982. np. folio. 400 ils. 359p. F/F. A4. $135.00

JOHNSON, Gerald W. *Incredible Tale.* 1950. NY. BC. F/worn. E1. $5.00

JOHNSON, Grace. *Roman Collar Detective.* 1956. Bruce. 2nd. hc. VG/VG. P3. $13.00

JOHNSON, Hildegard Binder. *Carta Marina: World Geography in Strassburg, 1525.* 1963. Minneapolis. 1st ed. map. 159p. F. O7. $55.00

JOHNSON, J. *Typography; or, Printers Instructor.* 1824. London. 2 vol. rebound. VG. B5. $195.00

JOHNSON, Jack. *Jack Johnson: In the Ring & Out.* 1927. Chicago. 1st ed. VG+. A15. $65.00

JOHNSON, John. *Defense of Charleston Harbor Including Ft Sumter...* 1890. Walker Evans Cogswell. 1st ed. fld maps. cloth. VG. M8. $350.00

JOHNSON, L.F. *Famous Kentucky Tragedies & Trials...* 1916. Louisville, KY. Baldwin Law Book Co. gilt bl cloth. M11. $85.00

JOHNSON, Lady Bird. *Beauty for America. Proceedings of White House Conference...* 1965. WA, DC. inscr. gilt cloth. F. B4. $150.00

JOHNSON, Lady Bird. *White House Diary.* 1970. NY. 1st ed. sgn. F. E1. $95.00

JOHNSON, Lee. *Heads for Death.* 1966. John Gifford. 1st ed. VG/G. P3. $15.00

JOHNSON, Lyndon Baines. *Vantage Point.* 1971. HRW. 1st ed. 8vo. ils. 636p. F/dj. T10. $30.00

JOHNSON, Lyndon Baines. *Vantage Point.* 1971. NY. 1st ed. sgn. 636p. F/F. E1. $200.00

JOHNSON, M.L.; see Malzberg, Barry.

JOHNSON, Margaret S. *Red Jocker.* 1950. Morrow. 1st ed. 8vo. 95p. G. C14. $6.00

JOHNSON, Martin. *Congorilla.* 1932. Brewer Warren Putnam. 3rd. sgn Osa/Martin Johnson. 41 pl. 318p. G. B11. $50.00

JOHNSON, Mel; see Malzberg, Barry.

JOHNSON, Milton. *Price of Discontent.* 1929. Gordonsville. Johnson Pub. 319p. VG/G. B10. $10.00

JOHNSON, Owen. *Stover at Yale.* 1940. Grosset Dunlap. VG/G. P12. $8.00

JOHNSON, Peter H. *Parker: America's Finest Shotgun.* 1985. Harrisburg. Hardcover Classic. 3rd. 260p. F/F. E1. $45.00

JOHNSON, Robert Lee. *Contract Bridge Bidding: The Latest Point Count Bidding...* 1952. Hollywood, CA. 36p. VG. S1. $3.00

JOHNSON, Ronald. *American Table.* 1984. Morrow. 1st ed. F/NF. C2. $35.00

JOHNSON, Rossiter. *Campfires & Battlefields: A Pictorial Narrative...* 1967. NY. Civil War Pr. 6th. VG/dj. T10. $40.00

JOHNSON, Samuel. *Elementa Philosophica: Containing Chiefly, Noetica...* 1752. Phil. Franklin Hall. 1st ed. 1/500. rebound full calf. C6. $2,000.00

JOHNSON, Samuel. *Letters of Samuel Johnson 1731-1784.* 1992-1994. Princeton. 5 vol. ils. F/F. A4. $125.00

JOHNSON, SCOTT & SICKELS. *Anthology of Children's Literature.* 1948. Houghton Mifflin. ils NC Wyeth. VG/torn. B17. $45.00

JOHNSON, Stanley. *Doomsday Deposit.* 1980. Dutton. hc. F/F. P3. $13.00

JOHNSON, Stephen. *History of Cardiac Surgery 1896-1955.* 1970. Baltimore. 1st ed. 201p. dj. A13. $100.00

JOHNSON, Thomas M. *Wearing the Edged Weapons of the 3rd Reich.* 1977. Columbia. 1st ed. 63p. F/pict wrp. E1. $40.00

JOHNSON, V.W. *Catskill Fairies.* 1876 (1875). Harper. ils Alfred Fredricks. 163p. aeg. pict bdg. G+. P2. $60.00

JOHNSON, Warren. *Muddling Toward Frugality.* 1978. Sierra Club. 1st ed. 252p. F/dj. A17. $14.50

JOHNSON, William. *Focus on the SF Film.* 1972. Prentice Hall. 1st ed. F/F. P3. $25.00

JOHNSON & LEONARD. *Railroad to the Sea.* 1939. Iowa City. 1st ed. ils. 277p. VG/VG. B5. $45.00

JOHNSON & MALONE. *Dictionary of American Biography.* 1929-1944.. 21 (of 22) vol. 1st prt. 4to. xl. VG. A4. $795.00

JOHNSON & MASTERS. *Human Sexual Response.* 1966. Little Brn. 1st ed. F/NF. B35. $40.00

JOHNSON & WHITE. *Confederate Military History: Maryland & West Virginia.* 1976. Bl & Gray. rpt of 1899 ed. cloth. F/dj. M8. $20.00

JOHNSON & WINTER. *Route Across the Rocky Mountains...* 1982. Ye Galleon. 1st ed thus. ils. M/sans. A18. $17.50

JOHNSON. *Bibliography of Works of Mark Twain, Samuel L Clemens.* 1935 (1910). revised/enlarged. 1/500. 287p. VG. A4. $350.00

JOHNSON. *Civil War Battles.* 1981. NY. 4to. 160p. VG/dj. T3. $20.00

JOHNSON. *Thoreau's Complex Weave...* 1986. VA U. F/F. A4. $45.00

JOHNSTON, Annie Fellows. *Land of the Little Colonel.* 1929. LC Page. 2nd. 133p. purple cloth. VG+. M20. $50.00

JOHNSTON, Annie Fellows. *Little Colonel, Shirley Temple Edition.* Jan 1935. NY. 8vo. 10 full-p photos. 145p. bl cloth. F. B14. $50.00

JOHNSTON, Annie Fellows. *Little Colonel Doll Book.* 1910. Boston. Page. 1st ed. ils MG Johnston. worn. D1. $375.00

JOHNSTON, Annie Fellows. *Little Colonel's Christmas Vacation.* 1931 (1905). Page. 8vo. tan pict cloth. VG. M5. $20.00

JOHNSTON, Annie Fellows. *Little Colonel's House Party.* 1930 (1900). Page. 8vo. tan pict cloth. VG. M5. $20.00

JOHNSTON, Annie Fellows. *Little Colonel Stories.* 1930 (1902). Page. 8vo. ils. tan pict cloth. VG. M5. $20.00

JOHNSTON, Annie Fellows. *Little Colonel.* 1908 (1904). Page. 5th/Ils Holiday Ed. 8vo. gilt cloth. VG. M5. $40.00

JOHNSTON, Charles. *Brink of Jordan.* 1972. Hamilton. 1st ed. 8vo. map. 179p. VG/dj. W1. $16.00

JOHNSTON, Hank. *Death Valley Scotty, Fastest Con in the West.* 1974. Corona del Mar, CA. 1st ed. photos. 160p. F/F. E1. $40.00

JOHNSTON, Harry. *Gay-Dombeys.* 1920. Chatto Windus. 6th. hc. VG. P3. $13.00

JOHNSTON, J.F. *Hillforts of the Iron Age in England & Wales.* 1976. Liverpool. 1st ed. VG/VG. B5. $40.00

JOHNSTON, Jill. *Lesbian Nation: Feminist Solution.* 1973. Simon Schuster. 1st ed. rem mk. VG/VG clip. B4. $75.00

JOHNSTON, Joe. *Adventures of Teebo: A Tale of Magic & Suspense.* 1984. Random. 1st ed. 8vo. unp. C14/P3. $10.00

JOHNSTON, Joseph Eggleston. *Narrative of Military Operations, Directed During War...* 1874. Appleton. 1st ed. 602p. full sheep. VG. M8. $250.00

JOHNSTON, Leah C. *San Antonio: St Anthony's Town.* 1947. San Antonio. 1st ed. photos. F/chip. E1. $30.00

JOHNSTON, Mary. *Aubrey.* 1902. Boston. 1st ed. ils Yohn. gilt cloth. NF. A17. $12.50

JOHNSTON, Mary. *Exile.* 1927. Little Brn. 1st ed. VG/VG. B4. $75.00

JOHNSTON, Mary. *Fortunes of Garin.* 1915. Houghton Mifflin. 1st ed. 375p. G+. B10. $12.00

JOHNSTON, Mary. *Lewis Rand.* 1908. Houghton Mifflin. 1st ed. 8vo. ils FC Yohn. T10. $50.00

JOHNSTON, Mary. *To Have & To Hold.* 1900. Houghton Mifflin. 1st ed. VG. H4. $40.00

JOHNSTON, Paul. *Biblio-Typographica, a Survey of Contemporary Fine Print...* 1930. 1/1050. 4to. ils. 303p. F/F case. A4. $295.00

JOHNSTON, S. Paul. *Horizons Unlimited.* 1941. NY. 1st ed. 354p. G. B18. $15.00

JOHNSTON, Swift P. *Notes on Astronomy: A Complete Elementary Handbook...* 1892. London. Heywood. 2nd. 86p. G. K5. $28.00

JOHNSTON, Terry C. *Borderlords.* 1985. Jameson. 1st ed. F/F. A18. $35.00

JOHNSTON, Velda. *Etruscan Smile.* nc. BC. VG/VG. $8.00

JOHNSTON, Velda. *Flight to Yesterday.* nd. Quality BC. F/F. P3. $10.00

JOHNSTON, Velda. *I Came to a Castle.* 1969. Dodd Mead. 1st ed. VG/VG. P3. $20.00

JOHNSTON, Velda. *Late Mrs. Fonsell.* nd. BC. hc. VG/VG. P3. $8.00

JOHNSTON, Velda. *Man at Windemere.* nd. BC. hc. VG/VG. P3. $8.00

JOHNSTON, Velda. *People on the Hill.* 1971. Dodd Mead. 2nd. VG/torn. P3. $8.00

JOHNSTON, Velda. *Room With Dark Mirrors.* 1975. Dodd Mead. 1st ed. VG/VG. P3. $15.00

JOHNSTON, Velda. *Shadow Behind the Curtain.* nd. BC. VG/VG. P3. $8.00

JOHNSTON, Velda. *Stone Maiden.* nd. BC. VG/VG. P3. $8.00

JOHNSTON, William. *Barney.* 1970. Random. 1st ed. VG/VG. P3. $13.00

JOHNSTON, William. *Dr. Kildare: The Magic Key.* 1964. Whitman. TVTI. VG. P3. $8.00

JOHNSTON, William. *Great Indian Uprising.* 1967. Whitman. TVTI. VG. P3. $10.00

JOHNSTON, William. *Munsters & the Great Camera Caper.* 1965. Whitman. TVTI. NF. P3. $20.00

JOHNSTON, William. *Picture Frame Frame-Up.* 1969. Whitman. TVTI. VG. P3. $10.00

JOHNSTON, William. *Who's Got the Button?* 1968. Whitman. TVTI. VG. P3. $13.00

JOHNSTONE, William. *Creative Art in Britain.* 1950. London. Macmillan. 1st revised ed. 291p. tan cloth. NF/dj. B22. $10.00

JOLIVET, P. *Insects & Plants.* 1986. Brill/Flora & Fauna Pub. 8vo. ils. VG/wrp. B1. $22.50

JOLLY, David C. *Antique Maps, Sea Charts, City Views...* 1984. Boorkline. O7. $45.00

JOLY, Henri. *L'Homme et l'Animal.* 1886. Paris. Hachette. 2nd. inscr. 12mo. 312p. G1. $40.00

JONES, Bill. *Wallace Story.* (1966). AM S Pub. probable 1st ed. 471p. gilt bl cloth. F/NF. B22. $15.00

JONES, Billy M. *Health-Seekers in the Southwest, 1817-1900.* 1967. Norman. 1st ed. ils/photos. 254p. F/VG. E1. $30.00

JONES, Bobby. *Bobby Jones on Golf.* 1966. Garden City. 1st ed. VG/VG. B5. $50.00

JONES, Bobby. *Down the Fairway.* 1927. NY. 1/300. sgn twice. G. B5. $1,500.00

JONES, Bobby. *Golf Is My Game.* 1960. Garden City. 1st ed. VG/VG. B5. $50.00

JONES, Courtway. *Witch of the North.* 1992. Pocket. 1st ed. 8vo. F/dj. T10. $35.00

JONES, D.F. *Fall of Colossus.* nd. BC. VG/VG. P3. $8.00

JONES, D.F. *Fall of Colossus.* 1974. Putnam. 1st ed. NF/VG. M22. $12.00

JONES, D.F. *Xeno.* 1979. British SF BC. VG/VG. P3. $10.00

JONES, D.J. *Introduction to Microfossils.* 1956. Harper. ils. 406p. cloth. F. D8. $25.00

JONES, Dave. *Making & Repairing Western Saddles.* 1982. NY. Aero. 4to. VG/VG. O3. $25.00

JONES, Diana Wynne. *Eight Days of Luke.* 1988. Greenwillow. 1st Am ed. F/F. G10. $15.00

JONES, Diana Wynne. *Everad's Ride.* 1995. Framingham. NESFA. 1st ed. 1/175. sgns. F/F/case. T2. $30.00

JONES, Diana Wynne. *Magicians of Caprona.* 1982. Macmillan. 2nd. NF/NF. P3. $15.00

JONES, Diana Wynne. *Ogre Downstairs.* 1990. Greenwillow. rpt of Macmillan UK ed. F/F. G10. $15.00

JONES, Douglas C. *Arrest Sitting Bull.* 1977. Scribner. 1st ed. NF/F. M23/T10. $25.00

JONES, Douglas C. *Come Winter.* 1989. Holt. 1st ed. 8vo. F/dj. T10. $25.00

JONES, Douglas C. *Courtmartial of George Armstrong Custer.* 1976. NY. 1st ed. 291p. F/VG. E1. $80.00

JONES, Douglas C. *Creek Called Wounded Knee: A Novel.* 1978. NY. 1st ed. 236p. VG/VG. E1. $60.00

JONES, Douglas C. *Elkhorn Tavern.* 1980. HRW. 1st ed. F/NF. M23. $25.00

JONES, Douglas C. *Hickory Cured.* 1987. Holt. 1st ed. F/F. M23. $12.00

JONES, Douglas C. *Winding Stair.* 1979. HRW. 1st ed. F/NF. M23. $15.00

JONES, E. Morse. *Roll of the British Settlers in South Africa.* 1971. Cape Town. Balkema. 2nd. 4to. 174p. VG/dj. W1. $18.00

JONES, Edward. *Musical & Poetical Relicks of Welsh Bards; Bardic Museum.* 1802 & 1808. London. 2 vol. ils. half morocco. T10. $2,500.00

JONES, Elwyn. *Barlow Comes To Judgement.* nd. BC. hc. VG/VG. P3. $5.00

JONES, Fred. *Farm Gas Engines & Tractors.* 1963. McGraw Hill. 4th. 518p. VG+. A10. $35.00

JONES, Gayl. *Eva's Man.* 1976. Random. 1st ed. author's 2nd book. NF/NF. B4. $85.00

JONES, Gayl. *White Rat.* 1977. Random. 1st ed. F/F. B4. $75.00

JONES, Guy. *There Was a Little Man.* 1948. Random. 1st ed. VG/VG. P3. $30.00

JONES, H. Spencer. *Life on Other Worlds.* 1940. Macmillan. 299p. cloth. G. K5. $12.00

JONES, Harold. *100th Anniversary of the Army Medical Library, WA.* 1936. WA. 1st ed. VG. A13. $40.00

JONES, Harry E. *Luger Variations.* 1967. Los Angeles. sgn. 307p. VG/VG. B11. $35.00

JONES, Helen L. *Robert Lawson, Illustrator.* 1972. Boston. Little Brn. 1st ed. ils Robert Lawson. 121p. VG/G+. T5. $55.00

JONES, Howard M. *Major American Writers.* 1948. Harcourt. 1828p. cream cloth. VG. B22. $7.00

JONES, Hugh. *Present State of Virginia From Whence Is Inferred...* 1956. NC U. edit/inscr Richard Morton. 8vo. 295p. F/F. B11. $75.00

JONES, James. *From Here to Eternity.* 1951. Scribner. 1st ed. NF/NF. M19. $150.00

JONES, James. *From Here to Eternity.* 1951. Scribner. 1st ed. 1/1500. sgn pres. F/F. B24. $500.00

JONES, James. *Go To the Widowmaker.* 1967. Delacorte. 1st ed. F/NF. H11. $50.00

JONES, James. *Viet Journal.* 1974. Delacorte. 1st ed. F/F. M19. $20.00

JONES, Jessie Orton. *Secrets.* 1956 (1945). Viking. 4th. ils EO Jones. unp. VG. T5. $25.00

JONES, John William. *Personal Reminiscences, Anecdotes & Letters of RE Lee.* 1876. Appleton. 2nd. 509p. VG. M8. $85.00

JONES, Kenneth Glyn. *Search for the Nebulae.* 1975. Chalfont St Giles, UK. Alpha Academic. 84p. cloth. VG. K5. $26.00

JONES, LeRoi. *Home.* 1968. MacGibbon Kee. 1st ed. NF/NF. M19. $50.00

JONES, LeRoi. *System of Dante's Hell.* 1965. Grove. 1st ed. author's 1st novel. F/NF. M19. $65.00

JONES, Louis Thomas. *Highlights of Pueblo Land.* 1968. San Antonio. 1st ed. photos. 106p. F/F. E1. $20.00

JONES, Louis Thomas. *Indians at Work & Play.* 1971. San Antonio. 1st ed. biblio/index/notes. 156p. F/F. E1. $20.00

JONES, N.E. *Squirrel Hunters of Ohio.* 1898 (1897). Robert Clarke. 363p. gilt gr cloth. VG+. M10. $185.00

JONES, Nettie. *Fish Tales.* 1983. Random. 1st ed. F/NF. B4. $45.00

JONES, Nettie. *Mischief Makers.* 1989. Weidenfeld Nicholson. 1st ed. F/F. B4. $35.00

JONES, O.S. *Disposition of Oil Field Brines.* 1945. Lawrence, KS. 192p. F. D8. $8.00

JONES, O.S. *Fresh-Water Protection From Polution Arising in Oil Fields.* 1950. Lawrence, KS. 132p. F. D8. $10.00

JONES, P. Mansell. *French Introspectives From Montaigne to Andre Gide.* 1970. Kennikat. 115p. A17. $8.50

JONES, R.W. *Cop Out.* 1987. St Martin. 1st ed. VG/VG. P3. $17.00

JONES, Raymond F. *Cybernetic Brains.* 1962. Avalon. 1st ed. F/VG. M19. $45.00

JONES, Raymond F. *Cybernetic Brains.* 1962. Avalon. 1st ed. xl. dj. P3. $7.00

JONES, Raymond F. *Renaissance.* 1951. Gnome. 1st ed. VG/VG. P3. $60.00

JONES, Raymond F. *Secret People.* 1956. Avalon. 1st ed. F/F. P3. $40.00

JONES, Raymond F. *Son of the Stars.* 1952. Avalon. 1st ed. VG/fair. P3. $20.00

JONES, Raymond F. *Stories of Great Physicians.* 1963. Whitman. hc. VG. P3. $8.00

JONES, Raymond F. *Voyage to the Bottom of the Sea.* 1965. Whitman. TVTI. VG. P3. $10.00

JONES, Raymond F. *World of Weather.* 1961. Whitman Badger. hc. NF. P3. $12.00

JONES, Richard Glyn. *Solved!* 1987. BOMC. VG/VG. P3. $10.00

JONES, Richard Glyn. *Unsolved!* nd. BOMC. VG/VG. P3. $10.00

JONES, Robert H. *Asbestos: Its Properties, Occurrence & Uses...* 1890. London. 8vo. 236p. gr cloth. B14. $150.00

JONES, Robert Kenneth. *Shudder Pulps.* 1975. Fax. 1st ed. hc. NF/NF. P3. $35.00

JONES, Shirley. *Impressions.* 1984. S Croyden. Red Hen. 1/40. sm volio. sgns. 8 aquatints on handmade. F/box. B24. $2,000.00

JONES, Stephen. *Best Horror From Fantasy Tales.* 1990. Carroll Graf. 1st ed. F/F. P3. $18.00

JONES, Thomas Goode. *Last Days of the Army of Northern Virginia.* 1893. np. 1st ed. 46p. VG/wrp. M8. $350.00

JONES, Thomas. *Hoyle's Games Improved.* 1779. London. 216p. VG. S1. $250.00

JONES, Thomas. *Pugilist at Rest.* 1993. Little Brn. 1st ed. sgn. F/F. B35. $75.00

JONES, Tristan. *Heart of Oak.* 1984. St Martin. 282p. VG/dj. T7. $18.00

JONES, Tristan. *Steady Trade: A Boyhood at Sea.* 1982. St Martin. 1st ed. F/F. M23. $20.00

JONES, U.J. *History of Early Settlement of the Juniata Valley...* 1856. Phil. Ashmead. 1st ed. 8vo. 380p. brn Victorian cloth. NF. T10. $275.00

JONES, V.S. Vernon. *Aesop's Fables.* 1926. Doubleday. early rpt. 12mo. pict label. VG. B17. $65.00

JONES, Virgil Carrington. *Roosevelt's Rough Riders.* 1971. NY. 1st ed. ils. 354p. VG/G. E1. $35.00

JONES, Wilfred. *Epic of Kings: Hero Tales of Ancient Persia.* 1926. Macmillan. 1st ed. 9 pl. 333p. NF. A17. $20.00

JONES, William. *Grammar of the Persian Language.* 1823. London. Harding Mavor. 8th. ils. 212p. xl. VG. W1. $175.00

JONES & JONES. *Ithaca Sojourners.* 1980. Old Mariner's Pr. sgn. 8vo. 70p. VG. B11. $15.00

JONES & JONES. *Small Rain: Verses From the Bible.* 1953. Viking. 9th. obl 8vo. unp. VG+. C14. $10.00

JONG, Erica. *Fanny.* 1980. NAL. 1st ed. NF/NF. B35. $30.00

JONG, Erica. *Fruits & Vegetables.* 1971. HRW. ARC/1st ed. inscr. author's 1st book. RS. F/dj. w/promo material. B4. $300.00

JONG, Erica. *Witches.* nd. BC. hc. VG/VG. P3. $10.00

JONSON, Ben. *Works of...* 1756. London. Prt for Midwinter. 7 vol. orig calf. G. A17. $100.00

JORDAN, Anne Devereaux. *Fires of the Past.* 1991. St Martin. 1st ed. F/NF. G10. $10.00

JORDAN, Bill. *No Second Place Winner.* 1977. Shreveport, LA. sgn. 8vo. 114p. F/F. B11. $45.00

JORDAN, Cathleen. *Tales From Alfred Hitchcock.* 1988. Morrow. 1st ed. hc. NF/NF. P3. $15.00

JORDAN, David. *Food & Game Fishers.* 1902. 1st ed. teg. VG+. S13. $55.00

JORDAN, David. *Nile Green.* 1973. John Day. 1st ed. VG/VG. P3. $13.00

JORDAN, George. *From Major Jordan's Diaries.* 1961. NY. rpt of 1952 ed. 284p. stiff wrp. A17. $8.50

JORDAN, Gilbert J. *Yesterday in the Texas Hill Country.* 1979. College Station. 1st ed. 171p. leather. F. E1. $40.00

JORDAN, Joe. *Bluegrass Horse Country.* 1940. Lexington. 1st trade ed. sgn. VG. O3. $65.00

JORDAN, June. *Civil Wars.* 1981. Boston. Beacon. 1st ed. NF/VG. R11. $13.00

JORDAN, June. *Passion: New Poems 1977-1980.* 1980. Boston. Beacon. 1st ed. F/NF clip. B4. $50.00

JORDAN, June. *Some Changes.* 1971. Dutton. ARC. inscr. author's 2nd book. RS. F/VG+. B4. $250.00

JORDAN, Nina. *Puzzle & Riddle Book.* 1935. Racine. ils. 86p. VG. A17. $7.50

JORDAN, Pat. *Black Coach.* 1971. Dodd Mead. 248p. VG+/VG+. R11. $15.00

JORDAN, Robert. *Dragon Reborn.* 1991. Tor. 1st ed. F/F. P3. $23.00

JORDAN, Robert. *Shadow Rising.* 1992. NY. Tor. 1st ed. F/F. H11. $50.00

JORDAN, W.K. *Philanthrophy in England, 1480-1660: A Study...* 1959. London. 1st ed. 410p. VG. A13. $25.00

JORDAN & PRICE. *Animal Structures.* 1903. Appleton. 1st ed. 99p. gr cloth. F. B14. $45.00

JORDANOFF, A. *Illustrated Aviation Dictionary.* 1942. NY. 1st ed. ils. 415p. bl cloth. VG/dj. B14. $95.00

JORGENSEN, H.R. *Red Laquer Case.* 1933. World Syndicate. hc. VG. P3. $20.00

JOSCELYN, Archie. *Golden Bowl.* 1931. Internat Fiction Lib. hc. VG/fair. P3. $25.00

JOSCELYN, Archie. *Golden Bowl.* 1931. Internat Fiction Lib. 246p. VG/VG. M20. $32.00

JOSEFOVICI, U. *Die Psychische Vererbung.* 1912. Leipzig. Englemann. 156p. red cloth. VG. G1. $40.00

JOSEPH, Franz. *Star Fleet Technical Manual.* 1975. Ballantine. 1st ed. TVTI. F. P3. $40.00

JOSEPH, Meryl. *Who Won Second Place at Omaha.* 1975. Random. 1st ed. photos. NF/dj. S9. $125.00

JOSEPH & LIPPINCOTT. *Point to the Stars.* 1972 (1963). McGraw Hill. 2nd ed. xl. K5. $7.00

JOSHI, G.N. *Constitution of India.* 1952. Macmillan. 2nd. G/worn. M11. $45.00

JOSHI, S.T. *HP Lovecraft Annotated Bibliography.* 1981. Kent State. hc. VG. P3. $30.00

JOSLIN, Sesyle. *Baby Elephant's Baby Book.* 1964. HBW. 1st ed. 12mo. unp. NF/VG. C14. $15.00

JOURDAN, Catherine R. *ABC of Duplicate Bridge Direction.* 1967. Waltham, MA. 96p. sbdg. VG. S1. $5.00

JOWETT, Benjamin. *Thucydides.* 1930. Chelsea. Ashendene. 1/260. folio. prt on handmade. gilt wht pigskin. F. B24. $3,000.00

JOYCE, James. *Dubliners.* 1969. Modern Lib. VG/VG. P3. $13.00

JOYCE, James. *Exiles: A Play in Three Acts.* 1921. London. Egoist. 2nd. 8vo. gilt blk cloth. VG. T10. $50.00

JOYCE, James. *Finnegan's Wake.* 1939. Viking. 1st ed. 8vo. gilt blk cloth. VG. H3. $200.00

JOYCE, James. *Finnigan's Wake.* 1939. NY. 1st Am ed. NF/VG. C6. $275.00

JOYCE, James. *Haveth Childers Everywhere.* 1930. Paris. 1/500 on Vidalon paper. F/F/VG case. C6. $700.00

JOYCE, James. *James Joyce Miscellany. Second Series.* 1959. Carbondale. 1st ed. 8vo. NF/prt wrp. S9. $25.00

JOYCE, James. *Shorter Finnegan's Wake.* 1967. Viking. ARC/1st Am ed. RS. VG/VG. B4. $85.00

JOYCE, John A. *Jewels of Memory.* 1896. WA, DC. 2nd. ffe missing. VG. B18. $35.00

JOYCE, William. *Day With Wilbur Robinson.* 1990. Harper Row. 1st ed. rem mk. VG/dj. M20. $20.00

JOYCE, William. *Mother Goose.* 1984. Random. 1st ed. 4to. ils. NF. C14. $12.00

JUDA, L. *Wise Old Man: Turkish Tales of Nasreddin Hodja.* (1963). Edinburgh. Thomas Nelson. probable 1st ed. 112p. NF/VG. C14. $12.00

JUDD, B.I. *Handbook of Tropical Forage Grasses.* 1979. Garland. 12mo. photos/drawings. 116p. F. B1. $20.00

JUDD, Frances K. *In the Sunken Garden.* nd. Books Inc. decor brd. VG. P3. $10.00

JUDD, Frances K. *Kay Tracey: Mansion of Secrets (#17).* 1942. Cupples Leon. 208p. VG/dj. M20. $37.00

JUDD, Frances K. *Kay Tracy: Murmuring Portrait (#10).* 1938. Cupples Leon. 204p. cloth. VG+/dj. M20. $25.00

JUDD, Frances K. *Message in the Sand Dunes.* 1938. Cupples Leon. VG. P3. $15.00

JUDD, Frances K. *Strange Echo.* nd. Grosset Dunlap. decor brd. VG. $5.00

JUDD, Frances K. *When the Key Turned.* nd. Books Inc. hc. VG/VG. P3. $12.00

JUDD, Naomi. *Love Can Build a Bridge.* 1993. NY. 1st ed. sgn. F. B5. $25.00

JUDSON, Clara Ingram. *George Washington.* 1952. Follett. 2nd. ils Frankberg. VG/VG. B17. $4.50

JUDSON, Clara Ingram. *Mighty Soo.* 1955. Follett. ils Robert Frankenberg. VG/VG. A16. $16.00

JUNDD, Henry P. *Intro to the Hawaiian Language.* 1962. Honolulu. VG. O7. $10.00

JUPP, Ursula. *Home Port Victoria.* 1967. Victoria, Canada. private prt. sgn. 8vo. 168p. gr cloth. F/F. B11. $40.00

JUPTNER, Joseph P. *US Civil Aircraft.* 1962. Los Angeles. Aero Pub. 2 vol. ils. VG/dj. B18. $125.00

JUST, Ward. *In the City of Fear.* 1982. Viking. 1st ed. F/VG+. A20. $17.00

JUSTER, Norton. *Dot & the Line.* 1963. Random. 1st ed. ils. NF/VG. P2. $25.00

JUSTUS, May. *Gabby Gaffer.* 1975. Minneapolis. Dillon. rpt. 8vo. 106p. VG+/VG. T5. $25.00

JUSTUS, May. *Jumping Johnny & Skedaddle.* 1958. Row Peterson. ils Henneberger. 96p. VG. T5. $20.00

K

KABERRY, Charles. *Book of Baby Dogs.* (1914). Houghton. ils EJ Detmold. 120p. VG. D1. $365.00

KABOTIE, Fred. *Hopi Indian Artist.* 1977. Flagstaff. Mus of AZ. 1st ed. 149p. gilt cloth. F/dj. T10. $75.00

KAESE & LYNCH. *Milwaukee Braves.* 1954. Putnam. 1st ed. VG/G+. P8. $225.00

KAFALLO, Ivan Demitrius. *Profane Chronicles.* 1994. Wexford Barrow. UP. F/pict wrp. B35. $25.00

KAFKA, Franz. *Castle.* 1969. Modern Lib. VG/VG. P3. $15.00

KAFKA, Franz. *Dearest Father.* 1954. Schocken. 1st ed. F/NF. B2. $50.00

KAFKA, Paul. *Love Enter.* 1993. Houghton Mifflin. 1st ed. sgn. AN/dj. B4. $50.00

KAGAN, Solomon. *Contributions of Early Jews to American Medicine.* 1934. Boston. 1st ed. 63p. VG. A13. $65.00

KAIIL, Virginia. *Maxie.* 1956. Scribner. 1st ed. ils. cloth. VG/worn. M5. $30.00

KAHN, David. *Codebreakers.* 1967. NY. 1st ed. VG/VG. B5. $50.00

KAHN, David. *Codebreakers.* 1968. Macmillan. later prt. NF/dj. N4. $30.00

KAHN, E.J. *Big Drink.* 1960. NY. 1st ed. VG/VG. B5. $25.00

KAHN, Fritz. *Design of the Universe.* 1954. NY. Crown. ils/diagrams. 373p. cloth. VG. K5. $8.00

KAHN, James. *Timefall.* 1987. St Martin. 1st ed. RS. F/F. P3. $20.00

KAHN, Joan. *Chilling & Killing.* 1978. Houghton Mifflin. 1st ed. VG/VG. P3. $18.00

KAHN, Joan. *Edge of the Chair.* nd. BOMC. VG/VG. P3. $10.00

KAHN, Joan. *Hanging by a Thread.* 1969. Houghton Mifflin. 1st ed. VG/VG. P3. $15.00

KAHN, Joan. *Some Things Strange & Sinister.* nd. Ellery Queen Mystery Club. hc. VG. P3. $5.00

KAHN, Joan. *Some Things Weird & Wicked.* 1976. Pantheon. 1st ed. F/F. G10. $15.00

KAHN, Joan. *Trial & Terror.* nd. BOMC. VG/VG. P3. $15.00

KAHN, Peggy. *Christmastime at Santa's Workshop.* 1990s. Random. 8vo. F. B17. $7.00

KAHN, Roger. *But Not To Keep.* 1979. Harper Row. 1st ed. VG/VG. A20. $12.00

KAHN, Roger. *Season in the Sun.* 1977. Harper Row. 1st ed. F/VG+. P8. $50.00

KAHN, Roger. *Seventh Game.* 1982. NAL. 1st ed. VG+/VG+. A20. $10.00

KAHRL, William J. *California Water Atlas.* 1979. Sacramento. State of CA. folio. 118p. ES. M. O7. $575.00

KAI-SHEK, Chiang. *Soviet Russia in China.* 1957. FSC. 1st ed. F/NF. B35. $22.00

KAIL, Aubrey. *Medicial Mind of Shakespeare.* 1986. Balgowlah, NSW. 1st ed. 320p. dj. A13. $50.00

KAINS, Josephine; see Goulart, Ron.

KAKONIS, Tom. *Criss Cross.* 1990. NY. 1st ed. F/NF. H11. $30.00

KAKONIS, Tom. *Criss Cross.* 1990. St Martin. 1st ed. VG/VG. P3. $20.00

KAKONIS, Tom. *Double Down.* 1991. Dutton. 1st ed. F/dj. N4. $27.50

KAKONIS, Tom. *Michigan Roll.* 1988. NY. 1st ed. author' 1st book. NF/F. H11. $40.00

KAKONIS, Tom. *Shadow Counter.* 1993. Dutton. 1st ed. AN/F. N4. $17.50

KALLEN, Lucille. *No Lady in the House.* nd. BC. VG/VG. P3. $8.00

KALLEN, Lucille. *Piano Bird.* nd. BC. VG/VG. P3. $8.00

KALLEN, Lucille. *Tanglewood Murder.* 1980. Wyndham. 1st ed. F/F. P3. $15.00

KALMAR & RUBY. *Snoops the Lawyer.* 1919. NY. Waterson Berlin. musical score. 5p. pict wrp. M11. $50.00

KALOGRIDIS, Jeanne. *Covenant With the Vampire.* 1994. Delacorte. 1st ed. F/F. P3. $20.00

KALPAKIAN, Laura. *Graceland.* 1992. Grove Weidenfeld. ARC. 8vo. F/pict wrp. S9. $25.00

KALS, W.S. *How To Read the Night Sky.* (1974). Doubleday. 4th. 155p. VG/VG. K5. $12.00

KALTENBORN, H.V. *Kaltenborn Edits the News.* 1937. Modern Age. 1st ed. NF/stiff pict wrp. B4. $150.00

KALWAJTYS, R.S. *Baby's Treasures...Early Days.* 1943. np. 4to. VG. M5. $25.00

KAMEN, Gloria. *Ringdoves — From the Fables of Bidpai.* 1988. Atheneum. 1st ed. 8vo. 32p. F/NF. C14. $25.00

KAMES, Henry Home. *Elements of Criticism...With Analyses...* 1851. NY. Huntington Mason. contemporary sheep. M11. $125.00

KAMINSKY, Stuart M. *Blood & Rubbles.* 1996. Ballantine. 1st ed. sgn. F/F. T2. $25.00

KAMINSKY, Stuart M. *Blood & Rubbles.* 1996. Fawcett Columbine. 1st ed. F/F. P3. $21.00

KAMINSKY, Stuart M. *Bullet for a Star.* nd. BC. VG/VG. P3. $8.00

KAMINSKY, Stuart M. *Buried Caesars.* 1989. Mysterious. 1st ed. F/F. A20/P3. $18.00

KAMINSKY, Stuart M. *Catch a Falling Clown.* 1981. St Martin. 1st ed. F/F. P3. $40.00

KAMINSKY, Stuart M. *Down for the Count.* 1985. St Martin. 1st ed. F/F. P3. $25.00

KAMINSKY, Stuart M. *Fala Factor.* 1984. St Martin. 1st ed. F/F. P3. $30.00

KAMINSKY, Stuart M. *He Done Her Wrong.* 1983. St Martin. 1st ed. F/F. B2/P3. $35.00

KAMINSKY, Stuart M. *High Midnight.* 1981. St Martin. 1st ed. F/F. P3. $40.00

KAMINSKY, Stuart M. *Howard Hughes.* nd. BC. VG/VG. P3. $8.00

KAMINSKY, Stuart M. *Man Who Walked Like a Bear.* 1990. Scribner. 1st ed. F/F. A20/T2. $20.00

KAMINSKY, Stuart M. *Never Cross a Vampire.* 1980. St Martin. 1st ed. F/NF. T2. $50.00

KAMINSKY, Stuart M. *Opening Shots.* 1991. Mystery Scene. ltd deluxe 1st ed. 1/50. sgn/#d. leather. sans. F. P3. $50.00

KAMINSKY, Stuart M. *Rostrikov's Vacation.* 1991. Scribner. 1st ed. F/F. T2. $25.00

KAMINSKY, Stuart M. *When the Dark Man Calls.* 1983. St Martin. 1st ed. F/F. P3/T2. $30.00

KAMPEN, M.E. *Religion of the Maya.* 1981. Netherlands. EJ Brill. 1st ed. 36p. wrp. F3. $35.00

KANAVEL, Allen B. *Infections of the Hand: A Guide to Surgical Treatment...* 1943. Phil. 7th. 229 ils. 503p. buckram. VG. B14. $60.00

KANDEL, Aben. *Black Sun.* 1929. Harper. 1st ed. NF/NF. B35. $150.00

KANDEL, Lenore. *Love Book.* 1966. San Francisco. Stolen Paper. NF/wrp. B2. $35.00

KANE, Frank. *Bullet Proof.* 1951. Washburn. 1st ed. VG/VG. M22. $55.00

KANE, Frank. *Grave Danger.* 1954. Washburn. VG/torn. P3. $13.00

KANE, Frank. *Red Hot Ice.* 1955. Ives Washburn. hc. VG. P3. $25.00

KANE, Harnett T. *Amazing Mrs Bonaparte.* 1963. Doubleday. 1st ed. sgn. 310p. VG/dj. M20. $27.00

KANE, Harnett T. *Gentlemen, Swords & Pistols.* 1951. Morrow. 1st ed. VG/VG. P3. $20.00

KANE, Harnett T. *Gold Coast.* 1959. Doubleday. 1st ed. pres. photos James Ricau. 212p. VG. B10. $12.00

KANE, Harnett T. *Gold Coast.* 1959. Doubleday. 1st ed. sgn. 8vo. 212p. F/VG. B11. $25.00

KANE, Harnett T. *Louisiana Hayride.* 1941. Morrow. 4th. 471p. cloth. VG/ragged. M20. $30.00

KANE, Harnett T. *Natchez on the Mississippi.* 1947. Morrow. photos. 373p. G/poor. B10. $15.00

KANE, Harnett T. *New Orleans Woman.* 1946. Doubleday. sgn. 8vo. 344p. VG/G. B11. $20.00

KANE, Harnett T. *Plantation Parade.* 1946. Morrow. 3rd. sgn. G/G. P3. $25.00

KANE, Harnett T. *Romantic South.* 1961. Coward McCann. America Vista series. photos. 385p. B10. $15.00

KANE, Harnett T. *Scandalous Mrs Blackford.* 1951. Messner. 1st ed. VG/VG. P3. $15.00

KANE, Henry. *Conceal & Disguise.* 1966. Macmillan. 1st ed. NF/NF. P3. $20.00

KANE, Henry. *Hang by Your Neck.* 1949. Simon Schuster. 1st ed. VG/VG. P3. $20.00

KANE, Henry. *Little Red Phone.* 1982. Arbor House. 1st ed. VG/VG. P3. $18.00

KANE, Henry. *Operation Delta.* 1967. Michael Joseph. 1st ed. VG/VG. P3. $25.00

KANE, Henry. *Report for a Corpse.* 1948. Simon Schuster. 1st ed. VG/torn. P3. $15.00

KANE, Henry. *Virility Factor.* 1971. McKay. 1st ed. VG/VG. P3. $20.00

KANER, H. *Sun Queen.* 1946. Kaner. VG/VG. P3. $30.00

KANFER, Stefan. *International Garage Sale.* 1985. Norton. 1st ed. NF/NF. H11. $20.00

KANIN, Garson. *Do Re Me.* 1955. Little Brn. 1st ed. F/NF. B4. $100.00

KANIN, Garson. *One Hell of an Actor.* 1977. Doubleday. 1st ed. VG+/VG+. A20. $15.00

KANIN & KANIN. *Rashomon.* 1959. Random. 1st ed. F/F. B4. $150.00

KANT, Immanuel. *Philosophy of Law, an Exposition of Fundamental Principles.* 1974. Clifton. Kelley. facsimile of 1887 Eng ed. M11. $65.00

KANTAR, Edwin B. *Defensive Bridge Play Complete.* 1974. N Hollywood. lg format. 528p. VG/wrp. S1. $15.00

KANTOR, Alfred J. *Book of Alfred J Kantor.* 1971. McGraw Hill. 1st ed. F/F. B35. $49.00

KANTOR, MacKinlay. *Andersonville.* 1955. 1st/special Cival War BC ed. sgn. VG/rubbed. S13. $65.00

KANTOR, MacKinlay. *Gettysburg.* 1952. Random. 189p. VG/G. B10. $25.00

KANTOR, MacKinlay. *Lee & Grant at Appomattox.* 1950. Random. 9th. 175p. VG. B10. $12.00

KANTOR, MacKinlay. *Signal 32.* 1950. Random. 1st ed. NF/VG. M22. $20.00

KANTOR, MacKinlay. *Story Teller.* 1967. Doubleday. 1st ed. sgn. F/F. B11. $20.00

KANUSS, William H. *Story of Camp Chase: A History of the Prison...* 1906. Nashville. ME Church. 1st ed. 407p. cloth. NF. M8. $250.00

KAPLAN, E.H. *Field Guide to Coral Reefs of the Caribbean & Florida.* 1982. Houghton Mifflin. 289p. cloth. VG. D8. $18.00

KAPLAN, Fred. *Dickens: A Biography.* nd. Morrow. 4th. hc. F/F. P3. $25.00

KAPLAN, Moise N. *Big Game Fishermen's Paradise.* 1936. Tallahasee. Rose. 1st ed. inscr. 8vo. 324p. gilt bl brd. VG. B11. $175.00

KAPP, Kit S. *Central America Early Maps Up to 1860.* 1974. Kapp. 1st ed. 23 maps. 106p. wrp. F3. $30.00

KARAKE, Dosabhai Framji. *History of the Parsis...* 1977. NY. AMS. 2 vol. rpt of 1884 ed. VG. W1. $65.00

KARDINER, Abram. *Individual & His Society.* 1939. Columbia. 503p. panelled ochre cloth. VG. G1. $50.00

KARIG, Walter. *Zotz!* 1947. Rinehart. VG/torn. P3. $10.00

KARL, Frederick R. *William Faulkner: American Writer.* 1989. NY. 1st ed. 1131p. F/dj. A17. $17.50

KARPEL. *Arts in America, a Bibliography.* 1979. Smithsonian. 4 vol. folio. 2800p. F. A4. $300.00

KARPIN, Fred L. *Contract Bridge: The Play of the Cards.* 1958. MA. 506p. VG. S1. $10.00

KARPINSKI. *Bibliography of Mathematical Works Printed in America...* 1940. MI U. 4to. ils. 697p. F/VG. A4. $350.00

KARPINSKI. *Italian Chiaroscuro Woodcuts...Volume XII.* 1971. Penn State. 4to. ils. 209p. VG. A4. $95.00

KARROW, P.F. *Pleistocene Geology of the Scarborough Area.* 1967. Ontario Dept Mines. 108p. prt brd. VG. D8. $12.00

KARSH, Yousuf. *Karsh.* 1983. NYGS. 1st ed. sgn. F/dj. S9. $175.00

KARSH, Yousuf. *Yousuf Karsh & John Fisher See Canada.* 1960. Rand McNally. 1st ed. ils. NF/dj. S9. $30.00

KARSNER, David. *Debs: His Authorized Life & Letters From Woodstock Prison...* 1919. Boni Liveright. 12mo. inscr to EG Robinson. w/clip Debs sgn. VG. T10. $250.00

KARSTEN, Rafae. *Toba Indians of the Bolivian Grand Chaco.* 1970. Netherlands. Anthropological Pub. 126p. wrp. F3. $25.00

KART, Lawrence. *Motetti. The Motets of Eugenio Montale...* 1973. Graborn Hoyem. 1/300. sgn. trans/sgn trans. w/prospectus. F. B24. $250.00

KASER, David. *Book for a Sixpence: Circulating Lib of America.* 1980. Beta Phi Mu. 194p. quarter cloth. A17. $17.50

KASPAROV, Garry. *Unlimited Challenge: The Autobiography of Garry Kasparov.* 1990. np. ils. F/F. A4. $20.00

KASSABIAN, Mihran Krikor. *Roentgen Rays & Electro-Therapeutics...* 1907. Phil. ils. 545p. gr cloth. VG. B14. $350.00

KASTENBAUM, Robert. *Is There Life After Death?* 1984. Methuen. VG. P3. $18.00

KASTLE, Herbert. *Cross-Country.* 1975. WH Allen. 1st ed. VG/VG. P3. $20.00

KASTLE, Herbert. *Millionaires.* 1972. WH Allen. 1st ed. VG/VG. P3. $15.00

KATO, Ken. *Yamato: Rage in Heaven.* 1990. Warner. 1st ed. rem mk. NF/NF. G10. $5.00

KATZ, Bobbi. *Upside Down & Inside Out: Poems From Your Pockets.* 1973. Franklin Watts. 1st ed. 12mo. ils cloth. F/VG. C14. $15.00

KATZ, David. *Der Vibrationsinn.* 1923. Hierosolymis. German/Hebrew text. prt buff wrp. G1. $50.00

KATZ, Michael J. *Big Freeze.* 1991. Putnam. 1st ed. F/F. P3. $22.00

KATZ, Richard. *Von Hund Zu Hund.* 1956. Zurich. Albert Muller. 1st ed. German text. gilt cloth. F/worn. A17. $12.50

KATZ, Robert. *Ziggurat.* 1977. Houghton Mifflin. 1st ed. VG/VG. P3. $15.00

KATZ, Sali Barnett. *Hispanic Furniture: An American Collection From the SW.* 1986. Architectural Book Pub. ils. 224p. AN/dj. T10. $35.00

KATZ, William. *Facemaker.* 1988. McGraw Hill. 1st ed. NF/NF. P3. $17.00

KATZ, William. *Open House.* nd. BC. VG/VG. P3. $8.00

KATZ. *Choreography by George Balanchine, a Catalogue of Works.* 1983. 1/2000. 4to. 410p. F. A4. $295.00

KATZEFF, Paul. *Full Moons: Fact & Fantasy...* 1981. Citadel. 1st ed. xl. dj. K5. $20.00

KATZENBACH, John. *In the Heat of the Summer.* 1982. NY. 1st ed. author's 1st book. NF/NF. H11. $20.00

KATZENBACH & KATZENBACH. *Practical Book of American Wallpaper.* 1951. Phil. 1st ed. inscr. 142p. w/samples. NF/G. N3. $55.00

KAUFMAN, Frederick. *Forty-Two Days & Nights on the Iberian Peninsula.* 1987. HBJ. 1st ed. F/F. H11. $40.00

KAUFMAN, Sue. *Diary of a Mad Housewife.* 1967. NY. Random. 1st ed. red H stp on front fly. NF/VG+. B4. $85.00

KAUFMANN, David. *Geschichte der Attributenlehre in der Judischen...* 1967. Amsterdam. Philo. 2 books in 1. rpt of 1877-80 ed. VG. W1. $45.00

KAUFMANN DOIG, Federico. *El Peru Arqueologico.* 1976. Lima. 1st ed. 12mo. 288p. F3. $10.00

KAULBACH, William. *Female Characters of Goethe.* 1868. Munich. Frederick Bruckmann. 22 mtd albumens. aeg. NF. T10. $250.00

KAVAN, Anna; see Ferguson, Helen.

KAVANAGH, Dan. *Flaubert's Parrot.* 1985. Knopf. 1st ed. F/F. H11. $65.00

KAVANAGH, Dan. *History of the World in 10-1/2 Chapters.* 1989. Knopf. 1st ed. clip. F/F. H11. $35.00

KAVANAGH, Dan. *Talking It Over.* 1991. Knopf. 1st ed. F/F. H11. $30.00

KAVANAGH, Dan. *Talking It Over.* 1991. NY. 1st Am ed. sgn. NF/NF. A15. $25.00

KAVENEY, Roz. *Tales From the Forbidden Planet.* 1987. Titan. 1st ed. F/F. P3. $25.00

KAY, Gertrude Alice. *Us Kids & the Circus.* 1928. Saalfield. unp. VG. M20. $72.00

KAY, Gertrude Alice. *When the Sandman Comes.* nd. Chicago. Stanton VanVliet. 8vo. 183p. G+. T5. $30.00

KAY, Guy Gavriel. *Song for Arbonne.* 1992. Canada. Viking. 1st ed. F/F. P3. $25.00

KAY, Guy Gavriel. *Summer Tree.* 1984. McClelland Stewart. 1st ed. VG/VG. P3. $25.00

KAY, Guy Gavriel. *Summer Tree.* 1985. Arbor. 1st ed. NF/NF. P3. $25.00

KAY, Guy Gavriel. *Tigana.* 1990. Roc. 1st ed. F/F. P3. $20.00

KAY, Guy Gavriel. *Wandering Fire.* nd. BC. VG/VG. P3. $8.00

KAY, Ross. *Go Ahead Boys & the Mysterious Old House (#3).* 1916. Barse Hopkins. 232p. VG+/dj. M20. $40.00

KAY, Terry. *Year the Lights Came On.* 1976. Houghton Mifflin. 1st ed. VG. M23. $20.00

KAYE, M.M. *Death in Cyprus.* 1984. Allen Lane. VG/VG. P3. $20.00

KAYE, M.M. *Death in Kenya.* 1983. Allen Lane. VG/VG. P3. $17.00

KAYE, M.M. *Death in Zanzibar.* 1983. St Martin. 1st ed. hc. VG/VG. P3. $15.00

KAYE, M.M. *Fair Pavilions.* 1978. Allen Lane. 1st ed. VG/VG. P3. $25.00

KAYE, M.M. *Fair Pavilions.* 1978. St Martin. 1st Am ed. F/F. B4. $85.00

KAYE, M.M. *Shadow of the Moon.* 1957. Longman. 1st ed. VG/VG. P3. $30.00

KAYE, Marvin. *Devils & Demons.* nd. BC. VG/VG. P3. $10.00

KAYE, Marvin. *Ghosts.* 1981. Doubleday. 1st ed. VG/VG. P3. $25.00

KAYE, Marvin. *Laurel & Hardy Murders.* 1977. Dutton. 1st ed. VG/VG. P3. $20.00

KAYE, Marvin. *Lively Game of Death.* 1974. Arthur Barker. VG/VG. P3. $20.00

KAYE, Marvin. *Masterpieces of Terror & Supernatural.* 1985. Doubleday. 2nd. VG/VG. P3. $16.00

KAYE, Marvin. *Possession of Immanuel Wolf.* 1981. Doubleday. 1st ed. VG/G. P3. $13.00

KAYE, Marvin. *Stein & Day Handbook of Magic.* nd. BOMC. VG/VG. P3. $10.00

KAYE, Marvin. *Wintermind.* 1982. Doubleday. 1st ed. F/F. P3. $15.00

KAYE, Marvin. *Witches & Warlocks.* nd. BC. VG/VG. P3. $10.00

KAYE, Mollie. *Black Bramble Wood.* 1938. Collins. 1st ed. ils Margaret Tempest. VG. M5. $45.00

KAYTOR, Marilyn. *21: Life & Times of New York's Favorite Club.* 1975. Viking. 1st ed. 191p. blk cloth. B22. $5.00

KAZANTZAKIS, Nikos. *Report to Greco.* 1965. Simon Schuster. 1st ed. F/F. M19. $20.00

KAZANTZAKIS, Nikos. *Symposium.* 1974. Crowell. 1st ed. F/F. B35. $25.00

KEANE, John B. *Bodhran Makers.* 1992. NY. 4 Walls 8 Windows. 1st ed. F/F. M23. $20.00

KEARNEY, Patrick. *History of Erotic Literature.* 1982. np. 4to. 192p. F/F. A4. $45.00

KEARNEY & KUTLER. *Super Soaps.* 1977. Grosset Dunlap. 1st ed. F/F. P3. $20.00

KEARY, C.F. *Dawn of History: An Introduction to Pre-Historic Study.* 1904. Scribner. new ed. 367p. VG. W1. $12.00

KEATES, J.S. *Cartographic Design & Production.* 1973. London. Longman. 1st ed. ils. F/dj. O7. $30.00

KEATING, Bern. *Alaska.* 1969. WA. NGS. 1st ed. 208p. bl cloth. NF/dj. P4. $10.00

KEATING, H.R.E. *Bedside Companion to Crime.* 1989. Mysterious. 1st ed. F/F. P3. $20.00

KEATING, H.R.E. *Body in the Billiard Room.* 1987. Hutchinson. 1st ed. F/F. P3. $20.00

KEATING, H.R.E. *Death & the Visiting Firemen.* 1973. Crime Club. 1st ed. VG/VG. P3. $20.00

KEATING, H.R.E. *Inspector Ghote Hunts the Peacock.* 1968. Dutton. 1st ed. F/F. P3. $20.00

KEATING, H.R.E. *Under a Monsoon Cloud.* 1986. Viking. 1st ed. NF/NF. P3. $16.00

KEATING, H.R.E. *Whodunit?* 1982. Van Nostrand Reinhold. 1st ed. VG/VG. P3. $25.00

KEATING, J.M. *History of the Yellow Fever: Yellow Fever Epidemic of 1878.* 1879. Memphis. gr cloth. VG. B3. $200.00

KEATS, Ezra Jack. *Peter's Chair.* 1967. Harper Row. 8vo. pict brd. VG. B17. $6.50

KEATS, Ezra Jack. *Snowy Day.* 1962. NY. Viking. 1st ed. 8vo. VG+/VG. C8. $100.00

KEDDIE, Niccki R. *Roots of Revolution: An Interpretive History of Modern Iran.* 1981. Yale. 1st ed. ils. 321p. VG. W1. $12.00

KEDOURIE, Elie. *Islam in the Modern World & Other Stories.* 1981. HRW. 1st Am ed. 332p. NF/dj. W1. $22.00

KEEBLE, John. *Broken Ground.* 1987. Harper Row. 1st ed. VG/VG. P3. $18.00

KEEBLE, John. *Yellowfish.* 1980. Harper Row. 1st ed. F/F. A18. $20.00

KEEBLE, John. *Yellowfish.* 1980. Harper Row. 1st ed. VG/VG. A20. $16.00

KEEGAN, John. *Churchill's Generals.* 1991. NY. 1st Am ed. 368p. M/dj. A17. $12.50

KEEGAN, John. *Six Armies in Normandy: From D-Day to Liberation...* 1982. NY. 3rd. 365p. dj. A17. $10.00

KEEL, John A. *Jadoo.* 1957. Messner. 1st ed. VG. P3. $20.00

KEELE & POYNTER. *Short History of Medicine.* 1961. London. 1st ed. 160p. dj. A13. $40.00

KEENAN, Brian. *Evil Cradling: The Five-Year Ordeal of a Hostage.* 1992. Viking. 1st Am ed. 297p. VG/dj. W1. $18.00

KEENANA, Henry F. *Iron Gate.* 1891. Appleton. 1st ed. VG. B10. $45.00

KEENE, Carolyn. *Dana Girls in the Shadow of the Tower.* 1934. Grosset Dunlap. G+/fair. P12. $7.00

KEENE, Carolyn. *Dana Girls: By the Light of the Study Lamp.* nd. Grosset Dunlap. VG. P3. $8.00

KEENE, Carolyn. *Dana Girls: Circle of Footprints.* nd. Grosset Dunlap. VG. P3. $8.00

KEENE, Carolyn. *Dana Girls: Clue in the Cobweb.* nd. Grosset Dunlap. VG. P3. $8.00

KEENE, Carolyn. *Dana Girls: Curious Coronation.* nd. Grosset Dunlap. VG. P3. $8.00

KEENE, Carolyn. *Dana Girls: Haunted Lagoon (#21).* 1959. Grosset Dunlap. lists to #22. 182p. VG+/dj. M20. $25.00

KEENE, Carolyn. *Dana Girls: Mystery at the Crossroads.* 1954. Grosset Dunlap. gr bdg. VG. P3. $8.00

KEENE, Carolyn. *Dana Girls: Mystery of the Bamboo Bird.* nd. Grosset Dunlap. VG. P3. $8.00

KEENE, Carolyn. *Dana Girls: Portrait in the Sand (#12).* 1943. Grosset Dunlap. 1st ed. 216p. VG/dj. M20. $40.00

KEENE, Carolyn. *Dana Girls: Secret at Lone Tree Cottage.* 1943. Grosset Dunlap. bl bdg. VG. P3. $12.00

KEENE, Carolyn. *Dana Girls: Secret at the Hermitage (#5).* 1936. Grosset Dunlap. 1st ed. 218p. purple cloth. VG/dj. M20. $255.00

KEENE, Carolyn. *Dana Girls: Three-Cornered Mystery (#4).* 1935. Grosset Dunlap. lists to #6. 217p. VG/dj. M20. $180.00

KEENE, Carolyn. *Dana Girls: Winking Ruby Mystery.* 1957. Grosset Dunlap. VG. P3. $8.00

KEENE, Carolyn. *Nancy Drew Cookbook.* 1975 (1973). Grosset Dunlap. inscr. 159p. VG. M20. $100.00

KEENE, Carolyn. *Nancy Drew: Broken Anchor.* 1983. Wanderer Books. blk stp orange cloth. VG/G+. P12. $5.00

KEENE, Carolyn. *Nancy Drew: Bungalow Mystery (#3).* (1930). Grosset Dunlap. 1937B prt. 204p. VG/dj. M20. $155.00

KEENE, Carolyn. *Nancy Drew: Bungalow Mystery.* nd. Grosset Dunlap. VG. P3. $4.00

KEENE, Carolyn. *Nancy Drew: Clue in the Crossword Cipher.* nd. Grosset Dunlap. VG. P3. $4.00

KEENE, Carolyn. *Nancy Drew: Clue in the Diary.* 1932. Grosset Dunlap. VG. P3. $15.00

KEENE, Carolyn. *Nancy Drew: Clue in the Jewel Box.* nd. Grosset Dunlap. VG. P3. $4.00

KEENE, Carolyn. *Nancy Drew: Clue of the Black Keys (#28).* 1960 (1951). Grosset Dunlap. Cameo ed. 181p. VG+/dj. M20. $45.00

KEENE, Carolyn. *Nancy Drew: Clue of the Tapping Heels (#16).* (1939). Grosset Dunlap. 1939C prt. 214p. VG/dj. M20. $87.00

KEENE, Carolyn. *Nancy Drew: Hidden Staircase.* 1980. Grosset Dunlap. G+. P12. $4.00

KEENE, Carolyn. *Nancy Drew: Mystery of the Brass-Bound Trunk (#17).* (1940). Grosset Dunlap. 1940B prt. 220p. VG/dj. M20. $87.00

KEENE, Carolyn. *Nancy Drew: Mystery of the Glowing Eye.* 1974. Grosset Dunlap. NF. P12. $4.00

KEENE, Carolyn. *Nancy Drew: Mystery of the Ivory Charm (#13).* 1937A (1936). Grosset Dunlap. 3rd. 216p. VG+/dj. M20. $250.00

KEENE, Carolyn. *Nancy Drew: Mystery of the Lost Dogs.* 1977. Grosset Dunlap. VG. B17. $15.00

KEENE, Carolyn. *Nancy Drew: Nancy's Mysterious Letter (#7).* (1932). Grosset Dunlap. 1932C prt. lists to #8. VG/dj. M20. $280.00

KEENE, Carolyn. *Nancy Drew: Nancy's Mysterious Letter (#7).* 1933A. Grosset Dunlap. 5th. 209p. VG/ragged edged dj. M20. $225.00

KEENE, Carolyn. *Nancy Drew: Password to Larkspur Lane (#10).* 1934B. Grosset Dunlap. 5th. 220p. VG+/dj. M20. $225.00

KEENE, Carolyn. *Nancy Drew: Ringmaster's Secret.* 1953. Grosset Dunlap. bl stp bl cloth. G. P12. $4.00

KEENE, Carolyn. *Nancy Drew: Secret of Red Gate Farm (#6).* (1931). Grosset Dunlap. 1937B prt. 208p. VG/dj. M20. $155.00

KEENE, Carolyn. *Nancy Drew: Secret of the Twin Puppets.* 1977. Grosset Dunlap. VG. B17. $15.00

KEENE, Carolyn. *Nancy Drew: Sign of the Twisted Candles (#9).* (1933). Grosset Dunlap. 1937D prt. 217p. VG/dj. M20. $87.00

KEEP, Josiah. *West Coast Shells.* 1891. San Francisco. Carson. 12mo. gilt brn cloth. G. T10. $25.00

KEEPING, Charles. *Tinker Tailor Folk Song Tales.* 1969. World. 1st Am ed. ils. F/dj. P2. $30.00

KEEPING, Charles. *Tinker Tailor Folk Song Tales.* 1969. World. 1st Am ed. 4to. unp. F/clip. C14. $25.00

KEES, Hermann. *Ancient Egypt.* 1977. Chicago. 25 pl/11 maps. 392p. VG. W1. $12.00

KEES, Weldon. *State of the Nation: 11 Interpretations by Saroyan...* 1940. Cincinnati. 1st ed. 1/99. sgn all 7 contributors. F/wrp. C2. $200.00

KEESHAN, Robert. *She Loves Me, She Loves Me Not.* 1963. Harper. probable 1st ed. ils Sendak. NF/VG+. C8. $65.00

KEIL, Charles. *Urban Blues.* 1966. Chicago. 1st ed. F/NF. B2. $35.00

KEILLOR, Garrison. *Lake Wobegon Days.* 1985. Viking. 1st ed. F/F. M23. $20.00

KEILLOR, Garrison. *WLT: A Radio Romance.* 1991. Viking. 1st ed. F/VG+. A20. $10.00

KEIM, Randolph. *Sherman.* 1904. WA. 1/12000. VG. V4. $75.00

KEITH, Agnes Newton. *Children of Allah Between the Sea & Sahara.* 1966. Little Brn. 1st Am ed. 467p. VG/dj. W1. $12.00

KEITH, Arthur Berriedale. *Sovereignty of the British Dominions.* 1929. London. Macmillan. G/worn. M11. $85.00

KEITH, Arthur. *Darwinism & What It Implys.* 1928. London. 1st ed. 56p. VG. A13. $45.00

KEITH, Brandon. *Affair of the Gentle Saboteur.* 1966. Whitman. TVTI. VG. P3. $13.00

KEITH, Brandon. *Affair of the Gunrunner's Gold.* 1967. Whitman. TVTI. G. P3. $7.00

KEITH, Brandon. *Message From Moscow.* 1966. Whitman. TVTI. VG. P3. $10.00

KEITH, David. *Matter of Accent.* 1943. Dodd Mead. VG. P3. $25.00

KEITH, Thomas. *New Treatise on the Use of the Globes...* 1826. NY. Wood. 4th Am from last London ed. scuffed leather. K5. $120.00

KELEMEN, Pal. *Medieval American Art.* 1956. Macmillan. 2 vol. 1st ed. 306 pl. gilt red cloth. NF. T10. $150.00

KELEMEN, Pal. *Medieval American Art.* 1956. NY. Macmillan. 1st 1-vol ed. 308p. map ep. NF/NF. T10. $65.00

KELL, John McIntosh. *Recollections of a Naval Life...* 1900. Neale. 1st ed. 307p. cloth. VG. M8. $350.00

KELLAND, Clarence Budington. *Mark Tidd, Editor.* 1917. Harper. ils. F. M5. $15.00

KELLAND, Clarence Budington. *Mark Tidd's Citadel (#6).* 1916. Grosset Dunlap. 279p. VG+/dj. M20. $20.00

KELLEAM, Joseph E. *Hunters of Space.* 1960. Avalon. 1st ed. hc. F/F. P3. $20.00

KELLEAM, Joseph E. *Little Men.* 1960. Avalon. 1st ed. F/F. P3. $20.00

KELLEAM, Joseph E. *When the Red King Woke.* 1966. Avalon. 1st ed. F/F. P3. $20.00

KELLER, Frances Ruth. *Contented Little Pussy Cat.* 1949. Platt Munk. ils Adele Werber/Doris Laslo. VG. B17. $12.50

KELLER, Harry. *Official Detective Omnibus.* 1948. DSP. 1st ed. hc. VG. P3. $20.00

KELLER, Helen. *Song of the Stone Wall.* 1910. NY. 1st ed. VG. B5. $55.00

KELLER, Helen. *World I Live In.* 1908. Century. 12mo. 4 pl. 196p. prt gr cloth. G1. $50.00

KELLER, John. *Game of Draw Poker.* 1887. NY. 84p. VG. S1. $25.00

KELLER & SCHOENFELD. *Principles of Psychology: A Systematic Text...* 1950. Appleton Century. 431p. olive cloth/painted labels. G1. $35.00

KELLERMAN, Jonathan. *Butcher's Theater.* 1986. Bantam. 1st ed. F/NF. N4. $35.00

KELLERMAN, Jonathan. *Devil's Waltz.* 1993. Bantam. 1st ed. sgn. NF/NF. M22. $35.00

KELLERMAN, Jonathan. *Private Eyes.* 1992. Bantam. 1st ed. NF/NF. P3. $22.00

KELLERMAN, Jonathan. *Time Bomb.* 1990. Bantam. 1st ed. F/F. A20. $20.00

KELLEY, David. *Astronomical Identities of Mesoamerican Gods.* 1980. Miami. 1st ed. 54p. F3. $20.00

KELLEY, Donald R. *Historians & the Law in Postrevolutionary France.* 1984. Princeton. M11. $27.50

KELLEY, F.C. *Life & Times of Kin Hubbard.* 1952. NY. 1st ed. dj. A17. $10.00

KELLEY, Leo P. *Luke Sutton: Outrider.* 1984. Doubleday. 1st ed. F/F. P3. $13.00

KELLEY, Leo P. *Time 110100.* 1972. Walker. 1st ed. F/F. P3. $15.00

KELLEY, Robert. *Racing in America 1937-1959.* 1960. NY. Jockey Club. 1/1000. VG. O3. $150.00

KELLEY, Susan. *Summertime Soldiers.* 1986. Walker. 1st ed author's 2nd book. F/F. H11. $40.00

KELLEY, William Melvin. *Dancers on the Shore.* 1964. Doubleday. 1st ed. F/F. B2. $50.00

KELLNER, Bruce. *Bibliography of the Work of Carl Van Vechten.* 1980. Westport. 258p. VG. A17. $15.00

KELLOGG, M. Bradley. *Wave & the Flame.* 1987. Gollancz. 1st ed. VG/VG. P3. $20.00

KELLOGG, Marjorie. *Tell Me That You Love Me, Junie Moon.* 1968. FSG. 1st ed. F/F clip. B4. $100.00

KELLOGG, Robert H. *Life & Death in Rebel Prisons: Andersonville, Florence...* 1868. Hartford. ils. 424p. gilt cloth. VG. B14. $75.00

KELLOGG, W.K. *Kellogg's Funny Jungleland.* 1909. Kellogg. moveables. cereal giveaway. VG. D1. $40.00

KELLY, J. Frederick. *Early Domestic Architecture of Connecticut.* 1924. New Haven. Yale. 4to. 48 pl/242 text ils. tan buckram. VG. T10. $175.00

KELLY, J.B. *Arabia, the Gulf & the West.* 1980. NY. Basic. 1st Am ed. 8vo. 5 maps. F/dj. W1. $35.00

KELLY, Mary Ann. *My Old Kentucky Home, Good Night.* 1978. Exposition. 1st ed. sgn. 8vo. 32 pl. VG/G. B11. $25.00

KELLY, Mary. *Dead Man's Riddle.* 1967. Walker. VG/VG. P3. $18.00

KELLY, Mary. *Girl in the Alley.* 1974. Walker. 1st ed. VG/VG. P3. $15.00

KELLY, Pat. *River of Lost Dreams: Navigation on the Rio Grande.* 1986. Lincoln, NE. 8vo. ils/index. 149p. F/dj. T10. $25.00

KELLY, S.J. *History of St Paul's Protestant Episcopal Church...* 1945. E Cleveland. 160p. VG. B18. $9.50

KELLY, Susan. *Hope Against Hope.* 1991. Scribner. 1st Am ed. author's 1st novel. AN/dj. M22. $15.00

KELLY, Susan. *Summertime Soldiers.* 1986. Walker. 1st ed. author's 2nd novel. F/F. T2. $20.00

KELLY, Susan. *Trail of the Dragon.* 1988. Walker. 1st ed. F/F. T2. $15.00

KELLY, Vince. *Achieving a Vision: Life Story of PW Tewksbury.* (1941). Australia. George M Dash. sgn pres ed. 8vo. 220p. VG/worn. B11. $50.00

KELLY, W.K. *Decameron of Boccaccio.* 1869. London. marbled brd/brn half leather. VG. B30. $68.00

KELLY, Walt. *At the Mercy of the Elephants.* 1990. Eclipse. 1st ed. F. P3. $20.00

KELLY, Walt. *Diggin' Fo' Square Roots.* 1990. Eclipse. 1st ed. F. P3. $20.00

KELLY, Walt. *Pogo & Albert.* 1989. Eclipse. 1st ed. F. P3. $20.00

KELLY & KELLY. *Dancing Diplomats.* 1950. NM U. 1st ed. ils Gustave Baumann. 254p. dj. F3. $25.00

KELSEY, H.W. (Hugh) *Bridge: The Mind of the Expert.* 1981. London. NF/NF. S1. $12.00

KELSEY, H.W. (Hugh). *Countdown to Better Bridge.* 1986. Louisville. 184p. VG/wrp. S1. $7.00

KELSEY, H.W. (Hugh). *Instant Bridge.* 1975. Toronto. 70p. VG/wrp. S1. $5.00

KELSEY, H.W. (Hugh). *Simple Squeezes.* 1985. England. 120p. F/dj. S1. $15.00

KELSEY, H.W. (Hugh). *Simple Squeezes.* 1985. London. 120p. VG/wrp. S1. $8.00

KELSEY, H.W. (Hugh). *Test Your Pairs Play.* 1985. London. 80p. F/wrp. S1. $4.00

KELSEY, Vera. *Satan Has Six Fingers.* 1943. Crime Club. VG. P3. $15.00

KELSEY, Vera. *Whisper Murder!* nd. Collier. hc. VG. P3. $15.00

KELTON, Elmer. *Good Old Boys.* 1985. TX Christian U. 1st ed thus. M/M. A18. $10.00

KEMELMAN, Harry. *Day the Rabbi Resigned.* 1992. Fawcett Columbine. 1st ed. F/F. P3. $20.00

KEMELMAN, Harry. *Monday the Rabbi Took Off.* 1972. Hutchinson. 1st ed. VG/VG. P3. $25.00

KEMELMAN, Harry. *Sunday the Rabbi Went Hungry.* 1966. Crown. 1st ed. VG/VG. P3. $40.00

KEMELMAN, Harry. *Thursday the Rabbi Walked Out.* 1978. Morrow. 1st ed. NF/NF. P3. $25.00

KEMELMAN, Harry. *Wednesday the Rabbi Got Wet.* 1976. Morrow. 3rd ed. VG/VG. P3. $12.00

KEMELMAN, Harry. *Weekend With the Rabbi.* nd. BC. VG/VG. P3. $10.00

KEMP, Harry. *Chanteys & Ballads.* 1920. Brentano. 1st ed. sgn. 12mo. 173p. bl cloth. VG. B11. $50.00

KEMP, Oliver. *Wilderness Homes.* 1908. NY. Outing. 1st ed. 163p. VG. B5. $60.00

KEMP, Sarah. *Over the Edge.* 1979. Crime Club. 1st ed. VG/VG. P3. $18.00

KEMPSON, Ewart. *Contract Bridge: How To Play It.* ca 1952. London. 160p. VG. S1. $8.00

KEMPSON, Ewart. *First Pocket Book of Bridge Problems.* 1961. NY. 79p. VG. S1. $6.00

KEMPSON, Ewart. *Quintessence of CAB: CAB System of Bidding.* 1959. London. 160p. VG/dj. S1. $12.00

KEMPSON, Ewart. *Second Book of Bridge Problems.* 1962. NY. 80p. VG/dj. S1. $7.00

KEMPTON, Murray. *Part of Our Time.* 1955. NY. 1st ed. dj. A17. $10.00

KENDALL, Aubyn. *Art & Archaeology of Pre-Columbian Middle America.* 1977. Boston. Hall. 1st ed. 324p. F3. $60.00

KENDEIGH, S. Charles. *Parental Car & Its Evolution in Birds.* 1952. IL Biological Monographs. 356p. prt bl wrp. G1. $40.00

KENDRAKE, Carleton; see Gardner, Erle Stanley.

KENDREW, James. *Cries of York, for Amusement of Young Children.* ca 1811-20. York. 32mo. 28 woodcuts. 32p. F/tan self wrp/paper fld. B24. $225.00

KENDRICK, Baynard. *Flames of Time.* 1948. Scribner. 1st ed. VG/G. P3. $35.00

KENDRICK, Tony. *Neon Tough.* 1988. Putnam. 1st ed. NF/NF. P3. $20.00

KENDRICK, Tony. *81st Site.* 1980. NAL. 1st ed. VG/VG. P3. $18.00

KENDRICK. *Early Reading of Thomas Wentworth Higginson.* 1939. np. 4to. 218p. cloth. A4. $195.00

KENEALLY, Thomas. *Confederates.* 1980. Harper Row. 1st ed. F/F clip. M23. $30.00

KENEALLY, Thomas. *Place at Whitton.* 1965. Walker. 1st ed. VG/VG. P3. $18.00

KENEALLY, Thomas. *Playmaker.* 1987. Simon Schuster. 1st ed. VG/VG. P3. $20.00

KENEALLY, Thomas. *Schindler's List.* 1982. 1st ed. sgn. F/VG. M19. $250.00

KENNEDY, Adam. *Just Like Humphrey Bogart.* 1978. Viking. 1st ed. VG/VG. P3. $15.00

KENNEDY, John Fitzgerald. *Profiles in Courage.* 1956. NY. 1st ed. ils. F/NF. B14. $150.00

KENNEDY, Joseph. *Preliminary Report: Eighth Census 1860.* 1862. WA. 8vo. 294p. gr cloth. xl. VG. T3. $35.00

KENNEDY, Leigh. *Journal of Nicholas the American.* 1987. London. Cape. 1st ed. xl. VG/VG. M21. $65.00

KENNEDY, Margaret. *Constant Nymph.* 1925. Doubleday Page. G. P3. $7.00

KENNEDY, Margaret. *Fool of the Family.* 1930. Doubleday Doran. 1st ed. NF/VG. B4. $65.00

KENNEDY, Robert F. *To Seek a Newer World.* 1967. Doubleday. 1st ed. F/NF. M23. $30.00

KENNEDY, Roger G. *Mission: History & Architecture of Missions of North Am.* 1993. Houghton Mifflin. 1st ed. photos. 240p. F/dj. A17. $30.00

KENNEDY, William. *Billy Phelan's Greatest Game.* 1978. NY. 1st ed. F/NF. C6. $60.00

KENNEDY, William. *Billy Phelan's Greatest Game.* 1978. NY. 1st ed. VG/VG. B5. $42.50

KENNEDY, William. *Hurrah for the Life of a Sailor!* 1900. Edinburgh. Blackwood. 47 pl/maps. 356p. VG. T7. $75.00

KENNEDY, William. *Legs.* 1974. Coward McCAnn. 1st ed. author's 2nd novel. VG/G. M22. $50.00

KENNEDY, William. *Quinn's Book.* 1988. Viking. 1st ed. F/F. H11. $30.00

KENNEDY, William. *Riding the Yellow Trolley Car.* 1993. Viking. 1st trade ed. F/F. B35. $22.00

KENNEDY & KENNEDY. *Charlie Malarky & the Belly-Button Machine.* 1986. Atlantic Monthly. 1st ed. sgns. ils Glen Baxter. F/F. B4. $100.00

KENNEDY & ROSS. *Bibliography of Negro Migration.* 1934. Columbia. 1st ed. 251p. cloth. VG+. M8. $75.00

KENNEY, Charles. *Hammurabi's Code.* 1995. Simon Schuster. 1st ed. F/F. M23. $25.00

KENNEY. *Catalogue of Rare Astronomical Books in San Diego State...* 1988. 1/1000. ils. 336p. F/F cloth case. A4. $125.00

KENT, Charles W. *Revival of Interest in Southern Letters.* 1900. BF Johnson. 27p. wrp. B10. $25.00

KENT, James. *Lectures on Homoepathic Philosophy.* 1900. Lancaster. 1st ed. 290p. VG. A13. $100.00

KENT, Louise Andre. *He Went With Magellan.* 1943. Houghton Mifflin. 1st ed. inscr. 200p. cloth. VG+/dj. B22. $5.00

KENT, Rockwell. *Beowulf.* 1932. Random. 1/950. sgn w/thumbprint. VG. T10. $425.00

KENT, Rockwell. *Birthday Book.* 1931. 1/1850. sgn. silk brd. VG+. S13. $250.00

KENT, Rockwell. *Canterbury Tales.* 1934. NY. 1st ed. VG/G. B5. $40.00

KENT, Rockwell. *It's Me Oh Lord.* 1955. NY. 1st ed. VG. B5. $70.00

KENT, Rockwell. *N by E.* 1930. Brewer Warren. 1st trade ed. 1/100. inscr. w/extra leaf. F/case. B24. $850.00

KENT, Rockwell. *N by E.* 1930. Random. 1/900. sgn. 8 full-p pl. 245p. silver bl cloth. F/case. B24. $375.00

KENT, Rockwell. *Northern Christmas.* 1941. NY. 1st ed. VG/VG. B5. $37.50

KENT, Rockwell. *Rockwell Kent's Greenland Journal.* 1962. NY. 1/1000. NF/case. w/suite of 6 orig lithos (1 sgn). C6. $225.00

KENT, Rockwell. *Rockwellkentiana.* 1933. Harcourt Brace. 1st ed. inscr pres/dtd. 90+ pl. w/photo. NF/dj. B24. $850.00

KENT, Rockwell. *Salamina.* nd. Harcourt Brace. 8vo. 336p. xl. dj. B11. $30.00

KENT, Rockwell. *Salamina.* 1934. Harcourt. 1st ed. sgn. F/partial dj. w/obituary. B14. $125.00

KENT, Rockwell. *Voyaging Southward From the Strait of Magellan.* 1924. Putnam. 1st trade ed. ils. teg. F/bl dj. B24. $475.00

KENT, Rockwell. *Wilderness: A Journal of Quiet Adventure in Alaska.* 1937. Halcyon. rpt. 65 woodcuts. 217p. VG. T7. $65.00

KENT, Rockwell. *1938 International Exhibition of Paintings.* nd. Carnegie Inst. 12mo. ils. VG/wrp. T10. $25.00

KENYON, Michael. *May You Die in Ireland.* 1965. Morrow. 2nd ed. hc. F/F. P3. $12.00

KENYON, Michael. *Whole Hog.* 1967. Collins Crime Club. 1st ed. VG/G. P3. $15.00

KER, N.R. *Medieval Manuscripts in British Libraries.* 1969. London. Clarendon. 10 pl. 437p. xl. A17. $20.00

KERENYI, C. *Greece in Colour.* 1957. McGraw Hill. 1st ed. atlas folio. 32 tipped-in pl. VG. W1. $45.00

KERN, Gregory; see Tubb, E.C.

KERN. *Tale of a Cat As Told by Himself.* 1902. np. ils. 92p. VG. A4. $85.00

KEROUAC, Jack. *Scripture of the Golden Eternity.* 1960. Totem. 1st ed/3rd state. VG/wrp. M19. $45.00

KEROUAC, Jan. *Baby Driver.* 1981. NY. 1st ed. VG/VG. B5. $20.00

KERR, Archibald William. *Shadow of Drumcarnett.* 1929. Alexander-Ouseley. VG. P3. $30.00

KERR, Ben; see Ard, William (Thames).

KERR, E. *Yoknapatawph: Faulkner's Little Postage Stamp of Native...* 1969. NY. 1st ed. VG/VG. B5. $42.50

KERR, James. *Clinic.* nd. BC. VG/VG. P3. $8.00

KERR, P.F. *Optical Mineralogy.* 1959. McGraw Hill. 3rd. 442p. VG. D8. $20.00

KERR, Philip. *March Violets.* 1989. Viking. 1st ed. NF/NF. P3. $18.00

KERR, Robert Nolan. *Tunes for Little Players: A Piano Book.* 1947. Phil. ils. 35p. G/wrp. A17. $6.50

KERR & RIVKIN. *Hello, Hollywood.* 1962. Doubleday. 1st ed. sgns. VG+. D2. $25.00

KERSH, Gerald. *Fowlers End.* 1957. Simon Schuster. 1st ed. NF/NF. P3. $50.00

KERSH, Gerald. *Night & the City.* 1948. World Forum. 2nd. VG. P3. $10.00

KERSH, Gerald. *Prelude to a Certain Midnight.* 1947. Heinemann. 1st ed. VG. P3. $30.00

KERSH, Gerald. *Sergeant Nelson of the Guards.* 1945. Winston. VG. P3. $20.00

KERSH, Gerald. *Weak & the Strong.* 1946. Simon Schuster. 1st ed. F/NF. B35. $25.00

KESEY, Ken. *Further Inquiry.* 1990. Viking. 1st ed. F/F. B35. $25.00

KESEY, Ken. *Sailor Song.* 1992. Viking. 1st ed. sgn. F/F. A18. $50.00

KESSEL, John. *Meeting in Infinity: Allegories & Extrapolations.* 1992. Arkham. 1st ed. F/F. T2. $22.00

KESSLER, Ronald. *Richest Man in the World: Study of Adnan Khashoggi.* 1986. Warner. 1st ed. xl. dj. W1. $20.00

KESTERTON, David. *Darkling.* 1982. Arkham. 1st ed. 1/3126. author's 1st novel. F/F. P3/T2. $13.00

KETCHAM, Hank. *I Wanna Go Home!* 1965. 1st ed. NF/VG. S13. $20.00

KETCHUM, Philip. *Death in the Night.* 1939. Phoenix. ffe removed. G. P3. $10.00

KETCHUM, Philip. *Wyatt Earp.* 1956. Whitman. VG. P3. $15.00

KETCHUM, Richard. *Winter Soldiers.* 1973. London. MacDonald. 1st ed. F/clip. M23. $20.00

KETTELL, T.P. *Southern Wealth & Northern Profits.* 1860. NY. royal 8vo. 173p. brn cloth. G. T3. $55.00

KETTERER, Bernadine. *Manderley Mystery.* 1937. Eldon. 1st ed. VG. P3. $20.00

KEUNING, J. *Willem Jansz Blaeu: A Biography & History of His Work.* 1973. Amsterdam. Theatrvm Orbis Terrarvm. 8vo. 23 maps. AN/dj. O7. $45.00

KEVERNE, Richard. *More Crook Stuff.* 1938. Constable. 1st ed. VG. P3. $60.00

KEVORKIAN, Jack. *Story of Dissection.* 1959. NY. 1st ed. 80p. dj. A13. $50.00

KEYES, Daniel. *Minds of Billy Milligan.* 1981. Random. 2nd. VG/VG. P3. $15.00

KEYES, Frances Parkinson. *All This Is Louisiana.* 1950. Harper. inscr to Taylor Caldwell. 317p. VG/dj. M20. $75.00

KEYES, Francis Parkinson. *Once on Esplanade.* 1947. Dodd Mead. 1st ed. sgn. ils Addison Burbank. VG/dj. M20. $125.00

KEYES, T. *Battle of Disneyland.* 1974. WH Allen. 1st ed. VG/VG. P3. $20.00

KEYHOE, Donald. *Aliens From Space.* nd. BC. VG. P3. $8.00

KEYHOE, Donald. *Flying Saucers From Outer Space.* 1953. Holt. 1st ed. VG/G. P3. $18.00

KEYNES, Geoffrey. *Letters of Sir Thomas Browne.* 1946. London. 440p. dj. A13. $50.00

KEYSTONE, Oliver. *Arsenic for the Teacher.* 1950. Phoenix. VG. P3. $10.00

KHAN, K.S. Khaja. *Studies in Tasawwuf.* 1977. Lahore. rpt of 2nd revised ed. 8vo. 260p. VG/dj. W1. $14.00

KHAYYAM, Omar. *Rubaiyat.* nd. Crowell. ils Willy Pogany. teg. full leather. VG. T10. $125.00

KHAYYAM, Omar. *Rubaiyat.* nd. NY. Crowell. ils Willy Pogany. teg. F/dj/box. T10. $150.00

KHAYYAM, Omar. *Rubaiyat.* 1909. Hodder Stoughton. ils Edmund Dulac. gilt cloth. VG. T10. $350.00

KHAYYAM, Omar. *Rubaiyat.* 1940. NY. ils Szyk. padded leather. G. V4. $45.00

KHAYYAM, Omar. *Rubiayat of Omar Khayyam; & Salaman & Absal of Jami.* 1879. London. Bernard Quaritch. 8vo. 112p. quarter gr morocco/burgandy cloth. K1. $375.00

KHEIRALLAH, George. *Arabia Reborn.* 1952. Albuquerque. 1st ed. ils. 307p. VG/dj. W1. $45.00

KHORANA. *Africa in Literature for Children & Young Adults.* 1994. 363p. F. A4. $65.00

KIBLER, James E. *Poetry of William Gilmore Simms.* 1979. Rpt Co. ARC. 478p. VG. D10. $35.00

KIBLER, James E. *Pseudonymous Publications of William Gillmore Simms.* 1976. GA U. ARC. 102p. VG. B10. $25.00

KIDD, John. *On the Adaptation of External Nature to Physical Condition.* 1833. London. Pickering. 375p. contemporary bl cloth. G1. $135.00

KIDDER, D.P. *Ancient Egypt: Its Monuments & History.* 1854. NY. Carlton Phillips. 12mo. map ftspc. 214p. VG. T10. $50.00

KIDDER, T. *Road to Yuba City.* 1974. NY. ARC/1st ed. RS. F/NF. A15. $75.00

KIDDER, Tracy. *Among Schoolchildren.* 1989. Houghton Mifflin. 1st ed. F/F. A20. $18.00

KIDWELL, Claudia B. *Cutting a Fashionable Fit.* 1979. Smithsonian. sgn. F. D2. $35.00

KIENZLE, William X. *Assault With Intent.* nd. BC. VG/VG. P3. $8.00

KIENZLE, William X. *Rosary Murders.* 1979. Hodder Stoughton. 1st ed. VG/VG. P3. $22.00

KIENZLE, William X. *Shadow of Death.* 1983. Andrews McMeel. 1st ed. VG/VG. P3. $15.00

KIEREIN, John. *Kamikaze No Trump.* 1977. Boulder. 45p. VG/wrp. S1. $8.00

KIERNAN, Thomas. *Miracle at Coogans Bluff.* 1975. Crowell. 1st ed. VG+/VG+. P8. $35.00

KIES. *Occult in the Western World, an Annotated Bibliography.* 1986. np. 244p. F. A4. $45.00

KIG, Charles. *Campaigning With Crook.* 1967. Norman. 2nd. 12mo. 166p. F/dj. T10. $25.00

KIJEWSKI, Karen. *Copy Kat.* 1992. Doubleday. 1st ed. F/F. H11. $35.00

KIJEWSKI, Karen. *Copy Kat.* 1992. Doubleday. 1st ed. VG/VG. P3. $18.00

KIJEWSKI, Karen. *Kat's Cradle.* 1992. Doubleday. 1st ed. AN/dj. N4. $40.00

KIJEWSKI, Karen. *Wild Kat.* 1994. Doubleday. 1st ed. F/F. A20. $12.00

KILBOURN, William. *Pipeline.* 1970. Clarke Irwin. VG/VG. P3. $15.00

KILBURN, Richard. *Choice Presidents Upon All Acts of Parliament...* 1694. London. 5th. contemporary panelled sheep. worn. M11. $450.00

KILEY. *Hemingway: Old Friend Remembers.* 1965. np. 19 photos. 198p. F/VG. A4. $75.00

KILIAN, Crawford. *Icequake.* 1979. Douglas McIntyre. 1st ed. NF/NF. P3. $30.00

KILIAN, Crawford. *Tsunami.* 1983. Douglas McIntyre. 1st ed. F/F. P3. $20.00

KILLION, C.E. *Honey in the Comb.* 1951. Killion. 8vo. photos. 114p. cloth. NF. B1. $25.00

KILMER, Joyce. *Trees & Other Poems.* 1917. 1st ed. VG+. S13. $25.00

KILPATRICK, Franklin P. *Human Behavior From the Transactional Point of View.* 1952. Hanover, NH. 4to. 259p. prt gray cloth. G1. $35.00

KILPATRICK, James Jackson. *Southern Case for School Segregation.* 1962. Crowell Collier. 1st ed. 220p. VG/VG. B10. $15.00

KILUPAILA. *Bibliography of Hydrometry.* 1961. Notre Dame. 998p. xl. VG. A4. $185.00

KILWORTH, Gary. *Angel.* 1993. Gollancz. 1st ed. F/F. G10. $25.00

KILWORTH, Gary. *Downers.* 1991. Methuen. 1st ed. F/F. P3. $20.00

KILWORTH, Gary. *Hunter's Moon.* 1989. Unwin Hyman. 1st ed. F/F. P3. $22.00

KILWORTH, Gary. *In Solitary.* 1977. Faber. 1st ed. F/F. P3. $20.00

KIMBLE, George H.T. *Our American Weather.* (1955). McGraw Hill. 3rd. 322p. G/dj. K5. $12.00

KIMBROUGH, Emily. *Floating Island.* 1968. Harper Row. 1st ed. sgn. ils Vasiliu. F/dj. B14. $45.00

KIMMEL, S. *Mad Booths of Maryland.* 1940. Indianapolis. 1st ed. VG/VG. B5. $40.00

KINCAID, Jamaica. *Lucy.* 1990. FSC. ARC. sgn. F/wrp. B4. $50.00

KINCAID, Jamaica. *Lucy.* 1990. FSC. 1st ed. sgn. F/F. B4. $85.00

KINCAID, Nanci. *Crossing Blood.* 1992. Putnam. 1st ed. author's 1st novel. F/F. M23. $25.00

KINDER, Gary. *Light Years.* 1987. Atlantic Monthly. 1st ed. VG. P3. $19.00

KINER, Ralph W. *Kiner's Korner.* 1987. Arbor. 1st ed. F/VG+. P8. $25.00

KINERT, Reed. *Little Helicopter.* 1947. Macmillan. possible 1st ed. 8vo. unp. VG/VG clip. C14. $15.00

KING, Alfred Castner. *Mountain Idylls & Other Poems.* 1901. NY. 120p. G. A17. $25.00

KING, Ben. *Southland Melodies.* 1911. Forbes. 128p. VG. B10. $125.00

KING, Charles. *Campaigning With Crook.* 1967. Norman. 2nd. 12mo. 166p. F/dj. T10. $25.00

KING, Charles. *Mama's Boy.* 1992. NY. Pocket. 1st ed. author's 1st book. F/F. H11. $25.00

KING, Dick. *Ghost Towns of Texas.* 1953. Naylor. 1st ed. cloth. VG/dj. M20. $25.00

KING, Dorothy N. *Santa's Cuckoo Clock.* 1954. Polygraphic Co of Am. 4to. popups. sbdg. NF/box. T10. $150.00

KING, Dorothy N. *Take the Children.* 1945. Morrow. 1st ed. 16mo. pres. 6 moveable internat dolls. VG. D1. $120.00

KING, Evan. *Children of the Black-Haired People.* 1955. NY. 1st ed. dj. A17. $15.00

KING, Florence. *Southern Ladies & Gentlemen.* 1975. Stein Day. 1st ed. 216p. reading copy. B10. $12.00

KING, Florence. *When Sisterhood Was in Flower.* 1982. Viking. 1st ed. 190p. VG/VG. B10. $25.00

KING, Francis. *Voices in an Empty Room.* 1984. Hutchinson. 1st ed. VG/VG. P3. $19.00

KING, Frank. *Case of the Painted Girl.* 1949. Nimmo. VG. P3. $20.00

KING, Grace. *Memories of a Southern Woman of Letters.* 1932. NY. 1st ed. 398p. VG-/torn. B18. $22.50

KING, Henry C. *Background of Astronomy.* 1957. London. Watts. 1st ed. G/dj. K5. $12.00

KING, Henry C. *Pictorial Guide to the Stars.* 1967. Crowell. 1st ed. 4to. 167p. cloth. G. K5. $15.00

KING, J.C.H. *Artifical Curiosities From the Northwest Coast of America.* 1981. London. 1st ed. 87 pl. 119p. NF/dj. T10. $100.00

KING, Jaime. *Ancient Mexico.* 1987. Albquerque. 2nd. 134p. wrp. F3. $10.00

KING, Joe. *San Francisco Giants.* 1958. Prentice Hall. 1st ed. VG. P8. $12.50

KING, Larry L. *Of Outlaws, Con Men, Whores, Politicians & Other Artists.* 1980. NY. Viking. 1st ed. 8vo. 274p. F/dj. T10. $25.00

KING, Laurie. *Monstrous Regiment of Women.* 1995. Scribner. 1st ed. sgn. F/F. T2. $35.00

KING, Laurie. *To Play the Fool.* 1995. St Martin. 1st ed. sgn. F/F. T2. $35.00

KING, Laurie. *With Child.* 1996. St Martin. 1st ed. sgn. F/F. T2. $25.00

KING, Lester. *Medical World of the 18th Century.* 1958. Chicago. 1st ed. 346p. VG. A13. $65.00

KING, Martha Bennett. *Bean Blossom Hill.* 1957. Container Corp of Am. 1st ed. 36p. VG/G. T5. $40.00

KING, Martin Luther. *Strength To Love.* 1963. NY. 1st ed. VG/VG. B5. $35.00

KING, Martin Luther. *Why We Can't Wait.* 1964. Harper Row. 1st ed. photos. NF/NF. R11. $60.00

KING, P.B. *Evolution of North America.* 1977. Princeton. fld map. NF/dj. D8. $30.00

KING, Rufus. *Lethal Lady.* 1948. Detective BC. VG. P3. $20.00

KING, Rufus. *Murder in the Wilett Family.* 1931. Crime Club. VG. P3. $20.00

KING, Rufus. *Valcour Meets Murder.* 1932. Crime Club. 1st ed. VG. P3. $30.00

KING, Stephen. *Bare Bones: Conversations on Terror With Stephen King.* 1988. McGraw Hill. 1st ed. F/F. T2. $20.00

KING, Stephen. *Carrie.* 1974. Doubleday. 1st ed. xl. poor. P3. $75.00

KING, Stephen. *Christine.* 1983. Viking. 1st ed. VG/VG. P3. $60.00

KING, Stephen. *Cujo.* 1981. Viking. 1st ed. F/F. B4. $125.00

KING, Stephen. *Cujo.* 1981. Viking. 1st ed. VG/VG. P3. $65.00

KING, Stephen. *Cujo.* 1981. Viking. 1st ed. 319p. VG. B18. $45.00

KING, Stephen. *Cycle of the Werewolf.* 1983. Land of Enchantment. hc. NF/NF. P3. $125.00

KING, Stephen. *Cycle of the Werewolf.* 1983. Land of Enchantment. 1st trade ed. ils Bernie Wrightson. F/F. B4. $150.00

KING, Stephen. *Danse Macabre.* 1981. Everest. 1st ed. F/F. P3. $100.00

KING, Stephen. *Danse Macabre.* 1981. Everest. 1st ed. VG/G. P3. $60.00

KING, Stephen. *Dark Half.* 1989. Viking. 1st ed. F/F. P3. $30.00

KING, Stephen. *Dark Tower II: The Drawing of the Three.* 1987. Donald Grant. ltd ed. 1/800. sgn. ils/sgn Phil Hale. AN/AN. B24. $475.00

KING, Stephen. *Dark Tower II: The Drawing of the Three.* 1987. Donald Grant. 1st ed. F/F. P3. $100.00

KING, Stephen. *Dark Tower III: Waste Lands.* 1991. Donald Grant. ltd ed. 1/1250. sgn. ils/sgn Ned Dameron. AN/dj/case. B24. $350.00

KING, Stephen. *Dark Tower III: Waste Lands.* 1991. Donald Grant. 1st ed. F/F. P3. $45.00

KING, Stephen. *Dark Tower: Gunslinger.* 1982. Donald Grant. ltd ed. F/NF. B4. $575.00

KING, Stephen. *Dark Tower: Gunslinger.* 1982. Donald Grant. ltd ed. VG/VG. P3. $450.00

KING, Stephen. *Dead Zone.* 1979. Viking. 1st ed. F/F. B4. $150.00

KING, Stephen. *Different Seasons.* 1982. Viking. 1st ed. VG/VG. P3. $75.00

KING, Stephen. *Different Seasons.* 1982. Viking. 1st ed. inscr/dtd 1983. F/F. B24. $285.00

KING, Stephen. *Dolan's Cadillac.* 1989. Lord John. 1st ed. 1/1000. sgn. F. B24. $275.00

KING, Stephen. *Dolores Claiborne.* 1993. Viking. 1st ed. F/F. N4/P3. $25.00

KING, Stephen. *Eyes of the Dragon.* 1984. Bangor. Philtrum. 1/1000. sgn. F/case. B4. $750.00

KING, Stephen. *Eyes of the Dragon.* 1987. Viking. 1st ed. F/NF. H11. $40.00

KING, Stephen. *Eyes of the Dragon.* 1987. Viking. 1st trade ed. VG+/VG+. M21. $25.00

KING, Stephen. *Firestarter.* nd. Viking. 4th ed. NF/NF. P3. $20.00

KING, Stephen. *Firestarter.* 1980. Phantasia. 1st ed. 1/725. sgn/dtd. cover ils/sgn Michael Whelan. F/dj/case. B24. $550.00

KING, Stephen. *Four Past Midnight.* 1990. Viking. 1st ed. F/F. P3. $23.00

KING, Stephen. *Gerald's Game.* 1992. Viking. 1st ed. F/F. P3. $23.00

KING, Stephen. *It.* 1986. Viking. 1st ed. NF/NF. P3. $45.00

KING, Stephen. *Misery.* 1987. London. Hodder Stoughton. 1st ed. F/NF. T2. $25.00

KING, Stephen. *Misery.* 1987. NY. Viking. 1st ed. F/F. H11. $50.00

KING, Stephen. *Misery.* 1987. Viking. 1st ed. NF/NF clip. N4. $30.00

KING, Stephen. *Misery.* 1987. Viking. 1st ed. NF/NF. P3. $40.00

KING, Stephen. *My Pretty Pony.* 1989. Vernona, Italy. Stamperia Valonega. 1st trade ed. AN/case. M21. $65.00

KING, Stephen. *Needful Things.* 1991. Viking. 1st ed. F/F. P3. $25.00

KING, Stephen. *Night Shift.* 1978. Doubleday BC. NF/VG. M21. $15.00

KING, Stephen. *Pet Sematary.* 1983. Doubleday. 1st ed. F/F. P3. $50.00

KING, Stephen. *Pet Sematary.* 1983. Doubleday. 1st ed. F/NF. H11. $45.00

KING, Stephen. *Pet Sematary.* 1983. Doubleday. 1st ed. NF/VG. N4. $35.00

KING, Stephen. *Pet Sematary.* 1983. Hodder Stoughton. 1st ed. VG/VG. P3. $75.00

KING, Stephen. *Shining.* 1977. Doubleday. 1st ed. author's 3rd book. F/F. A4. $250.00

KING, Stephen. *Skeleton Crew.* 1985. Putnam. 1st ed. F/F. P3. $60.00

KING, Stephen. *Skeleton Crew.* 1985. Scream. 1/1000. sgn. ils/sgn JK Potter. F/F. B4. $400.00

KING, Stephen. *Stand.* 1978. Doubleday. 1st ed. NF/NF. M19/P3. $175.00

KING, Stephen. *Stand.* 1990. Doubleday. 8th. F/F. P3. $23.00

KING, Stephen. *Thinner.* 1984. NAL. 1st ed. F/F. T2. $70.00

KING, Stephen. *Thinner.* 1984. NAL. 1st ed. VG/VG. M22. $35.00

KING, Stephen. *Tommyknockers.* 1987. Putnam. 1st ed. F/NF. N4. $35.00

KING, Stephen. *Tommyknockers.* 1987. Putnam. 1st ed. VG/VG. P3. $25.00

KING, Tabitha. *Caretakers.* 1984. Methuen. 1st ed. F/F. P3. $50.00

KING, Thomas Butler. *War Steamers. Report No 681.* 29th Congresss, 1st session. disbound. VG. A16. $250.00

KING, W.J. Harding. *Mysteries of the Libyan Desert.* 1925. London. Seeley. 8vo. ils/map. xl. VG. W1. $65.00

KING & POLIKARPUS. *Down Town.* 1985. Arbor. 1st ed. F/F. P3. $20.00

KING & SHERATON. *Is Salami Better Than Sex?* sgn. VG/VG. K2. $30.00

KING & STRAUB. *Talisman.* 1984. Viking. 1st ed. NF/NF. H11/P3. $40.00

KINGSBURY, Donald. *Moon Goddess & the Son.* 1986. Baen. 1st ed. hc. F/F. P3. $20.00

KINGSBURY. *Records of the Virginia Company of London, Court Book...* 1906. GPO. 635p. VG. A4. $245.00

KINGSLEY, Charles. *Heroes or Greek Fairy Tales.* nd. SB Gundy. decor brd. VG. P3. $45.00

KINGSLEY, Charles. *Saint's Tragedy; or, True Story of Elizabeth of Hungary.* 1848. London. JW Parker. 1st ed. author's 1st book. 271p. Victorian cloth. VG. T10. $200.00

KINGSLEY, Charles. *Water Babies.* nd. London. Sunshine series. ils Harry Theaker. VG. M5. $65.00

KINGSLEY, Charles. *Water Babies.* 1916. Dodd Mead. 1st ed thus. ils JW Smith. 362p. VG+. D1. $150.00

KINGSMILL, Hugh. *Return of William Shakespeare.* 1929. Indianapolis. VG/G. B5. $20.00

KINGSOLVER, Barbara. *Animal Dreams.* 1990. Harper Collins. 1st ed. F/F. H11. $55.00

KINGSOLVER, Barbara. *Bean Trees.* 1988. Harper Row. 1st ed. author's 1st book. F/F. H11. $200.00

KINGSOLVER, Barbara. *Bean Trees.* 1988. London. Virago. 1st ed. author's 1st book. F/dj. S9. $65.00

KINGSOLVER, Barbara. *Pigs in Heaven.* 1993. Harper Collins. 1st ed. F/F. M23. $25.00

KINGSTON, Maxine Hong. *China Men.* 1980. Knopf. 1st ed. sgn. F/F. B4. $85.00

KINGSTON, William H.G. *Mark Seaworth: Tale of the Indian Ocean...* 1855. NY. Francis. 3 steel engravings. 401p. VG. T7. $40.00

KINNAIRD, Clark. *This Must Not Happen Again!* 1945. Pilot. VG/VG. P3. $20.00

KINNELL, Galway. *Three Poems.* 1976. NY. 1st ed. 1/100. sgn. wrp. C2. $75.00

KINNEY, Charles; see Gardner, Erle Stanley.

KINNEY, Richard. *Harp of Silence.* 1962. Pantheon. sgn. 8vo. 64p. gilt bl brd. VG. B11. $8.00

KINNEY, Thomas. *Devil Take the Foremost.* 1947. Crime Club. 1st ed. VG. P3. $10.00

KINSCELLA, Hazel G. *Music on the Air.* 1934. Viking. possible 1st ed. 438p. bl cloth. F. B22. $6.00

KINSELLA, W.P. *Iowa Baseball Confederacy.* 1986. Boston. 1st ed. VG/VG. B5. $20.00

KINSLEY, Peter. *Three Cheers for Nothing.* 1964. Dutton. 1st ed. author's 1st novel. NF/VG. M22. $10.00

KINTNER, Elvan. *Letters of Robert Browning & Elizabeth Barrett Browning...* 1969. Cambridge. 2 vol. VG/G. V4. $45.00

KIPLING, Rudyard. *Animal Stories.* 1953. Macmillan. VG. P3. $20.00

KIPLING, Rudyard. *Captain's Courageous.* 1897. NY. 1st Am ed. VG. C6. $95.00

KIPLING, Rudyard. *Choice of Kipling's Verse Made by TS Eliot...* 1943. Scribner. 1st Am ed. F/VG. B4. $65.00

KIPLING, Rudyard. *Debits & Credits.* 1926. Macmillan. 1st ed. 8vo. gilt red cloth. NF/dj. T10. $100.00

KIPLING, Rudyard. *Diversity of Creatures.* 1917. London. Macmillan. 1st ed. teg. F/VG. T10. $150.00

KIPLING, Rudyard. *Five Nations.* 1903. London. 1st ed. VG. M19. $50.00

KIPLING, Rudyard. *Independence.* 1923. London. Macmillan. 1st ed. 8vo. 32p. F/stiff gray prt wrp. T10. $100.00

KIPLING, Rudyard. *Jungle Book.* 1894. Century. 1st Am ed. 303p. VG+. P2. $100.00

KIPLING, Rudyard. *Jungle Book.* 1928. Doubleday Doran. hc. decor brd. G. P3. $20.00

KIPLING, Rudyard. *Jungle Book/Second Jungle Book.* 1894-1895. Macmillan. 2 vol. 1st ed. ils JL Kipling. aeg. VG/case. D1. $1,450.00

KIPLING, Rudyard. *Jungle Books, Vol I & II.* 1948. Doubleday. 2 vol. ils Aldren Watson. VG/G. M21. $30.00

KIPLING, Rudyard. *Kipling's Fantasy Stories.* 1992. Tor. 1st ed. F/F. P3. $18.00

KIPLING, Rudyard. *Kipling's SF.* 1992. Tor. 1st ed. hc. F/F. P3. $18.00

KIPLING, Rudyard. *Light That Failed.* 1891. London. 1st ed. VG. C6. $95.00

KIPLING, Rudyard. *Light That Failed.* 1924. Doubleday Page. G. P3. $15.00

KIPLING, Rudyard. *Puck of Pook's Hill.* 1906. Doubleday. 1st ed. ils Rackham. VG+. M5. $28.00

KIPLING, Rudyard. *Second Jungle Book.* 1895. London. Macmillan. 1st ed. ils J Lockwood. aeg. gilt bdg. VG. P2. $200.00

KIPLING, Rudyard. *Second Jungle Book.* 1906. Macmillan. 9th. VG. P3. $25.00

KIPLING, Rudyard. *Selected Prose & Poetry of...* 1937. NY. 1030p. gilt cloth. NF. A17. $15.00

KIPLING, Rudyard. *Tour of Inspection.* 1928. Anthoensen. 1st book ed. 1/93. sm 8vo. 51p. NF. B24. $185.00

KIRCK. *Neale Books: An Annotated Bibliography.* 1977. np. ils. 254p. F. A4. $85.00

KIRK, George E. *Short History of the Middle East...* 1955. London. Methuen/Praeger. 3rd. 8vo. 14 maps. 292p. G. W1. $12.00

KIRK, Michael. *Cut in Diamonds.* 1986. Doubleday Crime Club. 1st ed. NF/NF. P3. $13.00

KIRK, Michael. *Mayday From Jalaga.* 1983. Crime Club. 1st ed. VG/VG. P3. $15.00

KIRK, Russell. *Creature of the Twilight.* 1966. Fleet. 1st ed. VG/VG. P3. $35.00

KIRK, Russell. *Lord of the Hollow Dark.* 1979. St Martin. 1st ed. NF/NF. P3. $25.00

KIRK, Russell. *Princess of All Lands.* 1979. Arkham. 1st ed. 1/4220. F/F. T2. $45.00

KIRK, Russell. *Watchers at the Strait Gate: Mystical Tales.* 1984. Arkham. 1st ed. 1/3459. F/F. T2. $15.00

KIRKBRIDE, Thomas S. *On the Construction, Organization & General Arrangements...* 1880. Phil. 2nd. 320p. red cloth. VG. B14. $100.00

KIRKBRIDGE, Ronald. *Winds, Blow Gently.* 1945. Frederick Fell. 1st ed. VG/VG. P3. $20.00

KIRKLAND, Charles P. *Liability of Government of Great Britain...* 1863. NY. Randolph. 1st ed thus. VG. M8. $45.00

KIRN, Walter. *My Hard Bargain.* 1990. Knopf. 1st ed. F/F. B35. $30.00

KIRSCHNER, Edwin J. *Zeppelin in the Atomic Age.* 1957. Urbana. 1st ed. ils. 80p. VG/dj. B18. $47.50

KIRST, Hans Hellmut. *Heroes for Sale.* 1982. Collins. 1st ed. F/F. P3. $20.00

KIRST, Hans Hellmut. *Night of the Generals.* 1963. Collins. 1st ed. VG/VG. P3. $20.00

KIRST, Hans Hellmut. *Time for Truth.* 1974. Coward McCann. 1st ed. F/NF. H11. $25.00

KIRST, Hans Hellmut. *Wolves.* 1968. Coward McCann. 1st ed. VG/VG. P3. $25.00

KIRSTEIN, Lincoln. *Portrait of Mr B: Photographs of George Balanchine.* 1984. Ballet Soc. 1st ed. 154p. cloth. dj. M20. $32.00

KIRT, Russell. *Princess of All Lands.* 1979. Arkham. 1st ed. F/dj. M21. $45.00

KISER, Ellis. *Atlas of the City of Yonkers, Westchester County, New York.* 1907. Phil. Mueller. lg folio. 25 double-p maps. O7. $165.00

KISHON, Ephraim. *Look Back, Mrs Lot!* 1961. Atheneum. 1st Am ed. F/clip. B4. $50.00

KISTER. *Best Encyclopedias: A Guide to General & Specialized...* 1986. np. 356p. xl. VG. A4. $25.00

KITCHIN, John. *Le Court Leete et Court Baron Collect per John Kitchin...* 1598. London. Thomae Wight/Bonhami Norton. modern sheep. M11. $1,250.00

KITTO, John. *Palestine From the Patriarchal Age to the Present Time.* 1900. NY. Collier. 8vo. ils. 426p. teg. VG. W1. $12.00

KITTREDGE, Mary. *Cadaver.* 1992. St Martin. 1st ed. 3rd in Edwina Crusoe series. F/NF. M22. $15.00

KITZINGER, Ernest. *Portraits of Christ.* 1940. King Penguin. hc. VG. P3. $25.00

KIVELSON, Margaret. *Solar System.* 1986. Englewood Cliffs. 1st prt. 4to. 436p. K5. $20.00

KJELGAARD, Jim. *Coming of the Mormons.* 1963. NY. Random. Landmark ed. 8vo. 183p. NF/dj. T10. $25.00

KJERSMEIER. *Afrikanske Negerskulptuere.* nd. Wittenborn Schultz. VG/VG. D2. $120.00

KLAMKIN, Charles. *Weathervanes: History, Manufacture & Design...* 1975. Hawthorn. 1st ed. 4to. VG/G. O3. $45.00

KLAUS & STEINHAUS. *Bamboo Organ in the Catholic Paris Church of St Joseph...* 1977. Delaware, OH. 4to. ils. 283p. F/NF. T10. $125.00

KLAVAN, Andrew. *Darling Clementine.* 1988. Permanent Pr. ltd prt. 1/2000. author's 2nd novel. AN/dj. M22. $50.00

KLAVAN, Andrew. *Don't Say a Word.* 1991. Pocket. 1st ed. F/F. H11. $25.00

KLAVAN, Andrew. *Don't Say a Word.* 1991. Pocket. 1st ed. VG/VG. P3. $20.00

KLAVAN, Andrew. *Face of the Earth.* 1980. Viking. 1st ed. F/F. H11. $40.00

KLAVAN, Andrew. *Face of the Earth.* 1980. Viking. 1st ed. VG/VG. P3. $20.00

KLAVAN, Andrew. *Scarred Man.* 1990. Doubleday. 1st ed. F/F. M22. $30.00

KLEBER, L.O. *Suffrage Cookbook.* 1915. Pittsburgh. 1st ed. 243p. G. B5. $55.00

KLEIN, Dave. *Great Infielders of the Major League.* 1972. Random. VG. P3. $8.00

KLEIN, Emil. *Enjoy Your Bridge.* 1947. London. 191p. VG. S1. $5.00

KLEIN, Gerard. *Overlords of War.* nd. BC. NF/NF. P3. $5.00

KLEIN, Herman. *Herman Klein & the Gramophone.* 1990. Amadeus. photos/notes/index. 618p. F/dj. A17. $25.00

KLEIN, Joe. *Payback.* 1984. Knopf. 1st ed. inscr. F/F. B4. $350.00

KLEIN, T.E.D. *Ceremonies.* 1984. Viking. 1st ed. VG+/dj. M21. $25.00

KLEIN, T.E.D. *Dark Gods.* 1985. Viking. 1st ed. VG+/dj. M21. $30.00

KLEIN, Zachary. *Still Among the Living.* 1990. Harper Row. 1st ed. F/F. P3. $19.00

KLEIN & PELLET. *That Pellet Woman.* 1965. NY. Stein Day. 1st ed. 8vo. 379p. VG/dj. T10. $45.00

KLEINFIELD, S. *Biggest Company on Earth (AT&T).* 1981. NY. 1st ed. VG/VG. B5. $20.00

KLEINPELL, R.M. *Miocene Stratigraphy of California.* 1938. Am Assn Petroleum Geol. 1st ed. 450p. VG. D8. $25.00

KLETT & MUYBRIDGE. *One City: Two Visions, San Francsico Panoramas 1878-1990.* 1990. np. 11p text. 2 10-ft accordian-fld photos. VG. A4. $125.00

KLIMT, Gustav. *Twenty-Five Drawings Selected & Interpreted by Alice Strobl.* 1964. Vienna. 1st ed. 25 pl. loose portfolio/pub case. F. C6. $400.00

KLINCK, Carl. *Robert Service: A Biography.* 1976. NY. 1st ed. VG/VG. B5. $22.50

KLINE, Fred. *I, Dodo.* 1968. San Francisco. 1st ed. 16mo. 1/200. wrp. A17. $7.50

KLINE, Otis Adelbert. *Maza of the Moon.* 1930. McClurg. 1st ed. VG/dj. M21. $60.00

KLINE, Otis Adelbert. *Outlaws of Mars.* 1961. Avalon. 1st ed. VG/VG. P3. $30.00

KLINE, Otis Adelbert. *Planet of Peril.* nd. Grosset Dunlap. VG. P3. $30.00

KLINE, Otis Adelbert. *Port of Peril.* 1949. Grandon. VG/VG. P3. $35.00

KLINE, Otis Adelbert. *Swordsman of Mars.* 1960. Avalon. 1st ed. VG/VG. P3. $30.00

KLINEFELTER, Walter. *Third Display of Old Maps & Plans...* 1973. LaCrosse. Sumac. 1/300. ils. F/dj. O7. $55.00

KLINGER, Ron. *Improve Your Bridge Memory.* 1964. London. 93p. VG/wrp. S1. $5.00

KLINGER, Ron. *Playing To Win at Bridge: Practical Problems...* 1976. London. 125p. VG/wrp. S1. $6.00

KLINGER, Ron. *World Championship Pairs Play.* 1983. London. 167p. F/dj. S1. $12.00

KLINGER, Ron. *100 Winning Bridge Tips.* 1987. London. 128p. VG/wrp. S1. $6.00

KLOMAN & TULLY. *It's a Great Relief.* 1934. Vanguard. ARC/1st ed. rebound half leather. w/promo material. B4. $85.00

KLUCKHOHN, Clyde. *To the Foot of the Rainbow.* 1927. Century. 1st ed. 8vo. ils. 276p. stp gr cloth. F/dj. T10. $85.00

KLUDAS, Arnold. *Great Passenger Ships of the World Vol 3, 1924-1935.* 1986. Wellingborough. Patrick Stephens. VG/dj. A16. $25.00

KLUDAS, Arnold. *Great Passenger Ships of the World.* 1986. Wellingborough. Patrick Stephens. 6 vol. VG/VG. A16. $240.00

KLUGE, Alexander. *Battle.* 1967. NY. 1st ed. trans from German. F/dj. A17. $8.50

KLUGE, P.F. *Eddie & the Cruisers.* 1980. Viking. 1st ed. author's 2nd book. rem mk. NF/F. H11. $25.00

KLUGER, Richard. *Sheriff of Nottingham.* 1992. Viking. 1st ed. VG/VG. P3. $23.00

KNAPP, Arthur Jr. *Race Your Boat Right.* 1952. Van Nostrand. 1st ed. sgn. 8vo. 296p. B11. $35.00

KNAUSEL, Hans G. *Zeppelin & the United States of America.* 1981. Germany. Friedrichshafen. 256p. F/dj. B18. $20.00

KNEALE, Nigel. *Year of the Sex Olympics.* 1976. Ferret Fantasy. 1st ed. F/F. P3. $20.00

KNEBEL, Fletcher. *Bottom Line.* 1974. Doubleday. 1st ed. G/dj. N4. $17.50

KNEBEL, Fletcher. *Night of Camp David.* 1965. Harper Row. 1st ed. F/NF. H11. $35.00

KNEBEL, Fletcher. *Trespass.* 1969. Doubleday. 1st ed. VG/VG. P3. $20.00

KNEBEL, Fletcher. *Vanished.* 1968. Doubleday. 1st ed. F/NF. H11. $40.00

KNEBEL, Fletcher. *Vanished.* 1968. Doubleday. 1st ed. VG/VG. P3. $20.00

KNEEBONE, John T. *Southern Liberal Journalists & Issue of Race 1920-1944.* 1985. UNC. pub pres. 312p. F/F. B10. $25.00

KNEIPP, Marianne. *Reflections & Observations, Essays of Denton A Cooley, MD.* 1984. Austin, TX. 1st ed. 240p. dj. A13. $25.00

KNERR, M.E.; see Smith, George H.

KNIGHT, Austin M. *Modern Seamanship.* 1917. NY. 8vo. ils. 712p. cloth. G-. T3. $14.00

KNIGHT, Austin M. *Modern Seamanship.* 1943. Van Nostrand. 10th. 847p. VG. P12. $10.00

KNIGHT, C. Morley. *Hints on Driving.* 1895. London. Bell. 2nd. 212p. cloth. VG. A10. $20.00

KNIGHT, Charles. *William Caxton, the First English Printer.* 1844. London. Knight. 1st ed. 12mo. 240p. contemporary half leather. T10. $150.00

KNIGHT, Clayton. *Lifeline in the Sky.* 1957. NY. 1st ed. inscr. 268p. cloth. VG/dj. B18. $125.00

KNIGHT, Clifford. *Affair of the Corpse Escort.* 1946. David McKay. 1st ed. VG/fair. P3. $20.00

KNIGHT, Clifford. *Affair of the Scarlet Crab.* 1937. Dodd Mead. 1st ed. VG. P3. $20.00

KNIGHT, Clifford. *Affair of the Sixth Button.* 1947. McKay. 1st ed. VG/G. P3. $18.00

KNIGHT, Clifford. *Death & Little Brother.* 1952. Dutton. 1st ed. VG. P3. $15.00

KNIGHT, Damon. *Best From Orbit.* 1975. Berkley Putnam. 1st ed. VG/VG. P3. $18.00

KNIGHT, Damon. *Best of Damon Knight.* 1978. Taplinger. VG/VG. P3. $20.00

KNIGHT, Damon. *Beyond Tomorrow.* 1965. Harper Row. 1st ed. VG/VG. P3. $20.00

KNIGHT, Damon. *Century of SF.* 1962. Simon Schuster. 1st ed. VG/VG. P3. $30.00

KNIGHT, Damon. *Cv.* 1985. Tor. 1st ed. NF/NF. P3. $18.00

KNIGHT, Damon. *Dark Side.* nd. BC. VG/VG. P3. $8.00

KNIGHT, Damon. *Dimension X.* 1970. Simon Schuster. 1st ed. VG/G. P3. $20.00

KNIGHT, Damon. *Nebula Award Stories.* nd. BC. VG/VG. P3. $8.00

KNIGHT, Damon. *One Side Laughing.* 1991. St Martin. 1st ed. F/F. P3. $17.00

KNIGHT, Damon. *Orbit 7.* 1970. Putnam. 1st ed. xl. dj. P3. $8.00

KNIGHT, Damon. *SF Argosy.* 1972. Simon Schuster. 1st ed. VG/VG. P3. $25.00

KNIGHT, Damon. *Tomorrow & Tomorrow.* nd. Simon Schuster. 2nd ed. VG. P3. $10.00

KNIGHT, Damon. *Tomorrow & Tomorrow.* 1974. Gollancz. 1st ed. F/F. M19. $17.50

KNIGHT, Damon. *World & Thorinn.* 1980. Berkley Putnam. 1st ed. xl. dj. P3. $5.00

KNIGHT, David; see Prather, Richard.

KNIGHT, Edgar W. *Henry Harrisse on Collegiate Education.* 1947. Chapel Hill. VG/wrp. O7. $45.00

KNIGHT, Eric. *Flying Yorkshireman.* 1938. Harper. 1st ed. VG/dj. M21/P3. $15.00

KNIGHT, Eric. *Sam Small Flies Again.* 1942. Harper. 1st ed. VG. P3. $15.00

KNIGHT, Kathleen Moore. *Death Blew Out the Match.* 1935. Crime Club. 1st ed. G. P3. $20.00

KNIGHT, Kathleen Moore. *High Rendezvous.* 1954. Crime Club. 1st ed. ffe removed. VG/VG. P3. $18.00

KNIGHT, Kathleen Moore. *Intrigue for Empire.* 1944. Crime Club. 1st ed. VG. P3. $15.00

KNIGHT, Kathleen Moore. *Port of Seven Strangers.* 1945. Detective BC. VG. P3. $10.00

KNIGHT, Kathleen Moore. *Stream Sinister.* 1945. Detective BC. VG. P3. $10.00

KNIGHT, Kathryn Lasky. *Dark Swan.* 1994. NY. 1st ed. F/F. H11. $20.00

KNIGHT, Kathryn Lasky. *Mumbo Jumbo.* 1991. Summit. 1st ed. F/F. H11. $25.00

KNIGHT, Marjorie. *Alexander's Birthday.* 1940. Dutton. 1st ed. ils Howard Simon. 120p. VG/G. T5. $30.00

KNIGHT, Marjorie. *Land of Lost Hankerchiefs.* 1954. Dutton. 1st ed. 8vo. ils. VG+/G. M5. $35.00

KNIGHT, R.P. *Landscape: A Didactic Poem.* 1972. Westmead. Gregg. 104p. VG. A17. $9.50

KNIPPEL, Dolores. *Poems for the Very Young Child.* 1932. Racine. ils Ellsworth. 125p. VG. A17. $7.50

KNOBLOCH, Irving W. *Preliminary Verified List of Plant Collectors in Mexico.* 1983. Plainfield, NJ. 179p. VG/orange wrp. w/sgn letter. B26. $30.00

KNOCK, Florence. *Passiflorals for Your Garden.* 1965. Kansas City. photos/line drawings. 100p. xl. B26. $20.00

KNOLLES, Richard. *Generall Historie of the Turkes, From the First Beginning...* 1638. London. Adam Islip. 5th. ils. contemporary tooled calf. VG. C6. $950.00

KNOTTS, Raymond. *And the Deep Blue Sea.* 1944. Farrar Rinehart. 1st ed. VG/VG. P3. $30.00

KNOWLAND, Helen. *Madame Baltimore.* 1949. Dodd Mead. 1st ed. VG. P3. $10.00

KNOWLES, John. *Doing Better & Feeling Worse: Health in the United States.* 1977. NY. 1st ed. 287p. VG. A13. $30.00

KNOX, Bill. *Draw Batons!* 1973. Doubleday Crime Club. 1st ed. NF/NF. P3. $15.00

KNOX, Calvin; see Silverberg, Robert.

KNOX, George William. *Development of Religion in Japan.* 1907. NY. 204p. red cloth. NF. B14. $75.00

KNOX & SWEET. *On a Mexican Mustang, Through TX, From Gulf to Rio Grande.* 1883. Hartford, CT. ils. 672p. professional rpr. E1. $200.00

KNUDSON, Albert C. *Doctrine of God.* 1930. NY. Abingdon Cokesbury. 1st ed. sgn. 8vo. 434p. VG/G. B11. $40.00

KNYSTAUTAS, A. *Natural History of the USSR.* 1987. McGraw Hill. 4to. 224p. F/F. B1. $38.50

KOBOTIE, Fred. *Hopi Indian Artist.* 1977. Flagstaff. Mus of N AZ. 1st ed. ils. 2-tone cloth. F/dj. T10. $75.00

KOCH, H.W. *Hitler Youth: Origins & Development 1922-1945.* 1975. NY. 348p. VG/dj. A17. $20.00

KOCH, Rudolf. *Die Bergpredigt Jesu Christi in der Lutherschen Ubersetzung.* ca 1915. Leipzig. Xenien. 4to. mottled vellum. F. B24. $285.00

KOCH, Rudolf. *Die Geschichte vom Weihnachtsstern.* 1920. Leipzig. Seemann. 1/100. lg oblong 4to. sgn. NF. B24. $385.00

KOCH, Rudolf. *Die Weihnachtsgeschichte von der Geburt Jesu Christi...* 1921. Offenbach. Drucke. 1/5 on Japan (of 150). 9 woodcuts. portfolio. B24. $1,250.00

KOCH, Vivienne. *William Carlos Williams.* 1950. New Directions. 1st ed. assn copy. NF/VG. V1. $35.00

KOCHER, Theodore. *Text-Book of Operative Surgery.* 1895. London. Blk. VG. H7. $125.00

KOEBEL, W.H. *In the Maoriland Bush.* ca 1911. London. 8vo. 316p. VG. N3. $25.00

KOEHLER, S.R. *American Art Review.* 1880. Boston. Estes Lauriat. 4 vol. 1/500. sgn/#d. 92 Japan proof etchings. aeg. F. T10. $5,000.00

KOEMAN, C. *Handleiding Voor die Studie van de Topografische Kaarten...* 1963. Groningen. Wolters. Dutch/Eng text. 34 maps/fld index. F. O7. $75.00

KOEMAN, I.C. *Joan Blaeu & His Grand Atlas.* 1970. Amsterdam. 28 maps. M/stiff wrp. O7. $30.00

KOERS, Albert W. *International Regulation of Marine Fisheries...* 1973. West Byfleet. Fishing News Ltd. M11. $50.00

KOFFKA, Kurt. *Die Grundlagen der Psychischen Entwicklung...* 1921. Osterwieck am Harz. AW Zickfeldt. 278p. cloth. G1. $100.00

KOFFKA, Kurt. *Principles of Gestalt Psychology.* 1935. Harcourt Brace. 720p. bl-gr cloth. ES. G1. $50.00

KOFOED, Jack. *Moon Over Miami.* 1955. Random. 1st ed. sgn pres. 8vo. 272p. VG/VG. B11. $65.00

KOGAN & WENDT. *Bet a Million.* 1948. Indianapolis. 1st ed. VG/VG. B5. $22.50

KOGER, Lisa. *Farlanburg Stories.* 1990. Norton. 1st ed. F/F. M23. $20.00

KOGOS, Fred. *Dictionary of Yiddish Slang & Idioms.* 1967. NY. Citadel. 1st ed. F/F. H11. $25.00

KOHLER, Wolfgang. *Dynamics in Psychology.* 1940. Liveright. sm 8vo. 158p. panelled bl cloth. G. G1. $35.00

KOHLER, Wolfgang. *Gestalt Psychology: Intro to New Concepts...* 1929. Liveright. 404p. bl cloth. VG. G1. $50.00

KOIE & RECHINGER. *Symbolae Afganicae V.* 1963. Copenhagen. ils. 267p. wrp. B26. $30.00

KOJA, Kathe. *Skin.* 1993. Delacorte. 1st ed. F/F. G10. $20.00

KOLAGA, Walter A. *All About Rock Gardens & Plants.* 1966. NY. ils. 385p. VG/dj. B26. $15.00

KOLB, E.L. *Through the Grand Canyon From WY to Mexico.* 1958. Macmillan. new ed. sgn. 8vo. 344p. VG. B11. $45.00

KOLLER, Larry. *Salt-Water Fishing.* 1954. Bobbs Merrill. photos. VG/G. P12. $12.00

KOLUPAEV, Victor. *Hermit's Swing.* 1980. Macmillan. 1st ed. VG/VG. P3. $15.00

KOMIE, Lowell B. *Judge's Chambers & Other Stories.* 1987. Chicago. Academy Chicago Pub. M11. $45.00

KONEFSKY, Samuel J. *Constitutional World of Mr Justice Frankfurter.* 1949. Macmillan. M11. $45.00

KOOCK, Mary Faulk. *Cuisine of the Americas.* 1967. Austin. sgn. 8vo. VG/VG. B11. $10.00

KOONTZ, Dean R. *Bad Place.* 1990. Putnam. 1st ed. NF/NF. N4. $22.50

KOONTZ, Dean R. *Blood Risk.* 1973. Bobbs Merrill. 1st ed. F/G+. M19. $175.00

KOONTZ, Dean R. *Blood Risk.* 1973. Bobbs Merrill. 1st ed. rem mk. NF/NF. B4. $200.00

KOONTZ, Dean R. *Chase.* 1972. Random. 1st ed. as by KR Dwyer. F/F. H11. $240.00

KOONTZ, Dean R. *Cold Fire.* 1991. Putnam. 1st ed. F/F. P3. $23.00

KOONTZ, Dean R. *Dark Rivers of the Heart.* 1994. Knopf. ARC of 1st trade ed. F/pict wrp. G10. $60.00

KOONTZ, Dean R. *Door to December.* 1988. London. 1st hc ed. F/F. T2. $50.00

KOONTZ, Dean R. *Dragon Tears.* 1993. London. Headline. 1st ed. F/F. T2. $50.00

KOONTZ, Dean R. *Dragon Tears.* 1993. Putnam. 1st ed. VG/VG. P3. $23.00

KOONTZ, Dean R. *Dragonfly.* 1975. Random. 1st ed. as by KR Dwyer. F/NF. H11. $165.00

KOONTZ, Dean R. *Dragonfly.* 1975. Random. 1st ed. NF/NF. H11. $135.00

KOONTZ, Dean R. *Eyes of Darkness.* 1989. Dark Harvest. 1st hc ed. F/F. T2. $35.00

KOONTZ, Dean R. *Face of Fear.* 1977. Bobbs Merrill. 2nd. xl. dj. P3. $30.00

KOONTZ, Dean R. *Face of Fear.* 1989. London. Headline. 1st hc ed. F/F. T2. $45.00

KOONTZ, Dean R. *Funhouse.* nd. Doubleday. BC. VG/dj. M21. $15.00

KOONTZ, Dean R. *Hidaway.* 1992. Putnam. 1st ed. VG/VG. P3. $23.00

KOONTZ, Dean R. *House of Thunder.* 1988. Dark Harvest. 1st ed. F/NF. M19. $75.00

KOONTZ, Dean R. *House of Thunder.* 1988. Dark Harvest. 1st hc ed. 1/550. sgn. ils/sgn Phil Parks. F/F/case. T2. $125.00

KOONTZ, Dean R. *How To Write Best-Selling Fiction.* 1981. 1st ed. NF/NF. S13. $50.00

KOONTZ, Dean R. *How To Write Best-Selling Fiction.* 1981. Writer's Digest. 1st ed. w/sgn bookplate. F/F. T2. $150.00

KOONTZ, Dean R. *Key to Midnight.* 1989. Dark Harvest. 1st ed. F/F. T2. $35.00

KOONTZ, Dean R. *Mask.* 1989. London. Headline. 1st hc ed. F/F. T2. $65.00

KOONTZ, Dean R. *Midnight.* 1989. London. Headline. 1st ed. F/F. T2. $45.00

KOONTZ, Dean R. *Midnight.* 1989. Putnam. 1st ed. F/F. H11. $40.00

KOONTZ, Dean R. *Midnight.* 1989. Putnam. 1st ed. VG/VG. P3. $25.00

KOONTZ, Dean R. *Mr Murder.* 1993. London. Headline. 1st ed (precedes Am). F/F. T2. $70.00

KOONTZ, Dean R. *Mr Murder.* 1993. Putnam. 1st ed. VG/VG. P3. $24.00

KOONTZ, Dean R. *Night Chills.* 1976. Atheneum. 1st ed. F/F. P3. $300.00

KOONTZ, Dean R. *Oddkins.* 1988. Warner. 1st ed. F/F. P3. $50.00

KOONTZ, Dean R. *Oddkins: A Fable for All Ages.* 1988. London. Headline. 1st ed. F/pict wrp. T2. $20.00

KOONTZ, Dean R. *Servants of Twilight.* nd. Quality BC. VG/VG. P3. $15.00

KOONTZ, Dean R. *Shadowfires.* nd. BC. F/F. P3. $10.00

KOONTZ, Dean R. *Shadowfires.* 1990. Dark Harvest. F/F. P3. $45.00

KOONTZ, Dean R. *Shattered.* 1973. Random. 1st ed. xl. dj. VG. P3. $30.00

KOONTZ, Dean R. *Strange Highways.* 1995. Warner. ARC of 1st Am trade ed. F/pict wrp. G10. $60.00

KOONTZ, Dean R. *Surrounded.* 1974. Bobbs Merrill. 1st ed. G/G. P3. $200.00

KOONTZ, Dean R. *Trapped.* 1993. Eclipse. 1st ed. ils Anthony Bilau. F/NF. G10. $10.00

KOONTZ, Dean R. *Twilight Eyes.* 1985. Land of Enchantment. 1st ed. NF/NF. G10. $35.00

KOONTZ, Dean R. *Twilight Eyes.* 1985. Plymouth. Land of Enchantment. 1st ed. sgn. F/F. T2. $65.00

KOONTZ, Dean R. *Voice of the Night.* 1980. Doubleday. 1st ed. xl. dj. P3. $35.00

KOONTZ, Dean R. *Wall of Masks.* 1975. Bobbs Merrill. 1st ed. as by Brian Coffey. F/NF. H11. $240.00

KOONTZ, Dean R. *Watchers.* 1987. Putnam. 1st ed. F/F. T2. $50.00

KOONTZ, Dean R. *Winter Moon.* 1994. Headline. 1st ed. F/F. P3. $40.00

KOOP & ROSA. *Rowdy Joe Lowe: Gambler With a Gun.* 1989. Norman, OK. 1st ed. 188p. F/F. E1. $30.00

KOPAL, Zdenek. *Astronomical Centers of the World.* 1988. Cambridge. 1st prt. VG/VG. K5. $30.00

KOPAL, Zdenek. *Man & His Universe.* 1972. NY. Morrow. 31 pl. 313p. VG/VG. K5. $17.00

KORMAN, Justine. *Who Framed Roger Rabbit Storybook.* 1988. Golden. 2nd. MTI. VG. P3. $8.00

KORN, Bertram. *Early Jews of New Orleans.* 1969. 1st ed. ltd. sgn. VG/VG. S13. $45.00

KORNBLUTH, C.M. *Best of...* 1977. Taplinger. 1st ed. hc. F/F. P3. $15.00

KORNBLUTH, C.M. *Mile Beyond the Moon.* nd. BC. VG/VG. P3. $10.00

KORNBLUTH, C.M. *Mindworm.* 1955. Michael Joseph. 1st ed. VG/VG. P3. $75.00

KORNBLUTH, C.M. *Not This August.* nd. BC. VG/VG. P3. $10.00

KORNBLUTH, C.M. *Syndic.* 1953. BC. VG/VG. P3. $10.00

KORNBLUTH, C.M. *Syndic.* 1953. Doubleday. 1st ed. NF/NF. P3. $75.00

KORNBLUTH, C.M. *Takeoff.* 1952. Doubleday. 1st ed. VG/G. P3. $60.00

KORNBLUTH & POHL. *Space Merchants.* 1953. Ballantine. 1st ed. NF/VG+. G10. $150.00

KOROWICZ, Marek Stanislaw. *Some Present Aspects of Sovereigny in International Law.* 1961. Leyden. AW Sythoff. 120p. wrp. M11. $25.00

KORSTEN, Frans. *Catalogue of the Library of Thomas Baker.* 1990. Cambridge. M11. $85.00

KOSINSKI, Jerzy. *Being There.* 1970. HBJ. 1st ed. F/F. H11. $60.00

KOSINSKI, Jerzy. *Passion Play*. 1979. St Martin. VG/VG. P3. $30.00

KOSINSKI, Jerzy. *Passion Play*. 1979. St Martin. 1st ed. inscr. NF/NF. M19. $100.00

KOSINSKI, Jerzy. *Steps*. 1968. Random. 1st ed. F/F. M19. $85.00

KOSTER, Henry. *Travels in Brazil*. 1968. Carbondale. rpt of 1816 ed. 182p. dj. F3. $15.00

KOSTER, R.M. *Mandragon*. 1979. Morrow. 1st ed. VG/VG. P3. $18.00

KOTKER, Norman. *Earthly Jerusalem*. 1969. Scribner. 1st ed. 8vo. 307p. map ep. VG/dj. W1. $12.00

KOTZWINKLE, William. *Christmas at Fontaine's*. 1982. Putnam. 1st ed. ils Joe Servello. F/F. T2. $15.00

KOTZWINKLE, William. *Fata Morgana*. nd. BOMC. hc. VG/VG. P3. $10.00

KOTZWINKLE, William. *Game of Thirty*. 1994. Houghton Mifflin/Seymour Lawrence. 1st ed. F/NF. G10. $12.00

KOTZWINKLE, William. *Hot Jazz Trio*. 1989. Houghton Mifflin/Seymour Lawrence. 1st ed. F/F. T2. $25.00

KOTZWINKLE, William. *Jack in the Box*. 1980. Putnam. 1st ed. VG/VG. P3. $18.00

KOTZWINKLE, William. *Midnight Examiner*. 1989. Houghton Mifflin. 1st ed. F/F. P3. $18.00

KOVAR, Edith. *Fairy Gold & Other Stories*. 1931. Whitman. lg 4to. ils. VG. M5. $60.00

KOZAKIEWICZOWIE, Helena. *Renaissance in Poland*. 1976. Warsaw. Arkady. ils/pl/map. 330p. cloth. dj. D2. $80.00

KRABBE, Tim. *Vanishing*. 1993. Random. 1st Am ed. AN/dj. M22. $25.00

KRAFT, James L. *Like Unto: A Philosophical Review of Vacation Journey...* 1939. private prt. 12mo. 56p. VG. P4. $15.00

KRAMER, Jane. *Off Washington Square: Reporter Looks at Greenwich Village*. 1963. DSP. ARC. author's 1st book. F/NF. B4. $85.00

KRAMISH, Arnold. *Griffin: Greatest Untold Espinage Story of WWII*. 1986. Boston. 1st ed. 294p. F/dj. A17. $9.50

KRANTZ, John. *Portrait of Medical History & Current Medical Problems*. 1962. Baltimore. 1st ed. 156p. VG. A13. $20.00

KRANTZ, Judith. *Scruples*. 1978. Crown. 1st ed. F/NF. B4. $85.00

KRANZ, Jacqueline. *American Nautical Art & Antiques*. 1975. Crown. rem mk. G. A16. $40.00

KRASILOVSKY, Phyllis. *Cow Who Fell in the Canal*. 1957. Doubleday. 1st ed. ils Peter Spier. pict brd. G+. T5. $30.00

KRASNER, William. *Stag Party*. 1957. Harper. 1st ed. VG/VG. P3. $20.00

KRAUS, Rene. *Europe in Revolt*. 1942. NY. 1st prt. 563p. dj. A17. $10.00

KRAUS & KRAUS. *Gothic Choirstalls of Spain*. 1986. London. Kegan Paul. 1st ed. photos. 218p. F/F. T10. $35.00

KRAUS. *History of Way & Williams...1895-1898*. 1984. KNA Pr. 1/500. F. A4. $125.00

KRAUSE, Herbert. *Oxcart Trail*. 1954. Bobbs Merrill. 1st ltd Minnesota ed. inscr/sgn twice. F/F. A18. $35.00

KRAUSE, Herbert. *Wind Without Rain*. 1939. Bobbs Merrill. 1st ed. inscr. NF/NF. A18. $35.00

KRAUSE & LEMKE. *United States Paper Money*. 1981. Iola, WI. 4to. 204p. VG. T3. $8.00

KRAUSKOPF, K.B. *Introduction to Geochemistry*. 1967. McGraw Hill. 721p. cloth. VG. D8. $30.00

KRAUSS, Bob. *Exceptional View of Life: Easter Seal Story*. 1977. Honolulu. 1st ed. ils. 64p. dj. A17. $10.00

KRAUSS, Ruth. *Bundle Book*. 1951. Harper. early ed. ils Helen Stone. unp. G+. T5. $30.00

KRAUSS, Ruth. *Bundle Book*. 1951. NY. Harper. 1st ed. ils Helen Stone. unp. VG/torn. D1. $60.00

KRAUSS, Ruth. *Hole Is To Dig*. 1952. Harper. 1st ed. ils Maurice Sendak. 48p. VG/worn. D1. $200.00

KRAUSS, Ruth. *How To Make an Earthquake*. nd. NY. Harper. 8vo. 28p. G+. C14. $5.00

KRAUSS, Ruth. *Open House for Butterflies*. 1960. Harper. 1st ed. ils Maurice Sendak. unp. VG/torn. D1. $200.00

KRAUSS, Ruth. *Open House for Butterflies*. 1960. Harper. 1st ed. ils Sendak. F/F. P2. $275.00

KREIDOLF, Ernst. *Lenzgekind*. 1926. Zurich. ils Ernst Kriedolf. unp. VG. D1. $120.00

KREISLER, Fritz. *Four Weeks in the Trenches: War Story of a Violinist*. 1915. Boston. Houghton Mifflin. 1st ed. inscr/dtd July 1915. silvered cloth. F. B14. $250.00

KREITH, Frank. *Radiation Heat Transfer*. 1962. Scranton. Internat TB Co. 236p. VG+. P4. $25.00

KREMENTZ, Jill. *Very Young Gardener*. 1991. Dial. 1st ed. sm 4to. F/F. C8. $35.00

KRENKEL, Roy G. *Cities & Scenes From the Ancient World*. 1974. Owlswick. 1st ed. F/F. T2. $35.00

KRENSKY, Stephen. *Witching Hour*. 1981. Atheneum. 1st ed. 8vo. 155p. F/NF. C14. $15.00

KRESS, Nancy. *Beggars and Choosers*. 1994. Tor. 1st ed. F/F. P3. $23.00

KRESS, Nancy. *Beggars in Spain*. 1993. Easton. 1st ed. sgn. leather. F. M23. $100.00

KRESS, Nancy. *Beggars in Spain*. 1993. Morrow. 1st trade ed. F/NF. G10. $15.00

KRESS, Nancy. *Brain Rose*. nd. Quality BC. hc. VG/VG. P3. $10.00

KRESS, Nancy. *Golden Grove*. 1984. Bluejay. 1st ed. hc. NF/NF. P3. $20.00

KRESS, Nancy. *White Pipes*. 1985. Bluejay. 1st ed. F/F. T2. $25.00

KRETSCHMER, Konrad. *Die Italienis Chen Portolane des Mittelalters...* 1962 (1909). Hildescheim. G Olms. ils. F. O7. $75.00

KREUTZER, W. *Notes & Observations Made During 4 Years' Service...* 1872. Phil. 1st ed. ils/map. 368p. G+. B5. $135.00

KREYMBORG, Al. *Plays for Merry Andrews*. 1920. NY. 1st ed. 1/50. VG. A15. $40.00

KRIEGER, L.C.C. *Mushroom Handbook*. 1967. Dover. 12mo. 32 mc pl/126 ils. 560p. VG/wrp. B1. $20.00

KROCH, Adolph. *Great Bookstore in Action*. 1940. Chicago. inscr. cloth. VG. A4. $35.00

KROEBER, Theodora. *Inland Whale*. 1959. Bloomington. IU. 1st ed. 8vo. ils. 205p. F/VG clip. T10. $45.00

KROEBER, Theodora. *Ishi in Two Worlds: Biography of the Last Wild Indian...* 1969. Berkeley. 9th. 8vo. 258p. F/NF. T10. $25.00

KROLL, Harry Harrison. *Darker Grows the Valley*. 1947. Bobbs Merrill. 1st ed. VG/G. P3. $10.00

KROLL, Harry Harrison. *Their Ancient Grudge*. 1946. Bobbs Merrill. 1st ed. 8vo. gilt bl cloth. VG/VG. T10. $25.00

KROLL, Steven. *Hand-Me-Down Doll*. 1983. Holiday House. possible 1st ed. 8vo. unp. VG+. T5. $20.00

KROMBEIN, K.V. *Catalog of the Hymenoptera in America North of Mexico*. 1979. Smithsonian. 3 vol. 4to. VG. B1. $200.00

KRONHAUSEN. *Erotic Book of Plates.* 1970. 185 pl. 213p. F/NF. A4. $125.00

KRONHEIM. *Aunt Friendly's Nursery Book.* nd. Warne. 12mo. gilt brn cloth. VG. M5. $125.00

KRONKE, Horst. *Die Welt der Schiffahrt en Miniature.* 1992. Herford. Koehlers Verlagsgesellschaft. AN. A16. $34.00

KRUCKEBERG, Arthur R. *Gardening With Native Plants of the Pacific Northwest.* 1982. Seattle. ils. VG/dj. B26. $50.00

KRUGER, Mary. *Death on the Cliff Walk.* 1994. Kensington. 1st ed. author's 1st book. F/F. H11. $30.00

KRUGER, Paul. *Finish Line.* 1968. Simon Schuster. 1st ed. VG/VG. P3. $20.00

KRUGER, Paul. *If the Shroud Fits.* 1969. Simon Schuster. 1st ed. VG/VG. P3. $20.00

KRUM, Charlotte. *Jingling ABC's.* 1929. Row Peterson. 1st ed. 8vo. ils. rpr p. VG. M5. $60.00

KRUMBEIN & SLOSS. *Stratigraphy & Sedimentation.* 1951. San Francisco. WH Freeman. 1st ed. 497p. G. D8. $14.00

KRUMGOLD, Joseph. *...And Now Miguel.* (1953). TY Crowell. 2nd. 245p. NF. C14. $12.00

KRUMMEL & SADIE. *Music Printing & Publishing.* 1990. np. ils. 629p. F/F. A4. $35.00

KRYNINE, D.P. *Soil Mechanics.* 1941. McGraw Hill. 1st ed/4th imp. 451p. G. D8. $15.00

KRYZHANOVSHII, O.L. *Lepidopterous Fauna of the USSR & Adjacent Countries.* 1988. Smithsonian. 8vo. trans from Russian. 405p. F/dj. B1. $48.00

KUBASTA. *Circus Life.* 1960. London. Bancroft. 1st ed. folio. popup. NF. T10. $250.00

KUBASTA. *Der Fliegende Koffer.* 1962. Prague. Artia. obl 4to. 8 double-p popups. cloth spine. VG. T10. $175.00

KUBASTA. *Sleeping Beauty.* 1961. London. Bancroft. moveables. G+. P2. $110.00

KUBASTA. *Tip+Top on the Farm.* 1961. London. Bancroft. 6 double-p popups. NF. T10. $200.00

KUBE-MCDOWELL, Michael P. *Alternities.* nd. BC. hc. VG. P3. $8.00

KUBE-MCDOWELL, Michael P. *Quiet Pools.* 1990. Ace. hc. F/F. P3. $18.00

KUBIENA, W.L. *Micromorphological Features of Soil Geography.* 1970. Rutgers. 254p. F/dj. D8. $15.00

KUCHLER, A.W. *Portenial Natural Vegetation of the Conterminous US.* 1964. NY. 117 photos. VG/case. B26. $58.00

KUHLKEN, Ken. *Loud Adios.* 1991. NY. 1st ed. F/F. H11. $40.00

KUHLMAN, Charles. *Legend Into History: The Custer Mystery.* 1977. Ft Collins. new ed. 249p. NF. E1. $55.00

KUHN, Alfred. *Das Alte Spanien: Landscaft, Geschichte, Kunst.* 1925. Berlin. Neufeld Henius. 267 ils. 336p. VG. W1. $45.00

KUHN, Herbert. *On the Track of Prehistoric Man.* 1955. Random. 1st ed. 211p. dj. F3. $15.00

KUHN, Thomas. *Sources for History of Quantum Physics: An Inventory...* 1967. Phil. 1st ed. 176p. VG. A13. $25.00

KUHNS, William T. *Memories of Old Canton.* 1937. np. 1st ed. 64p. xl. G. B18. $27.50

KUIPER, Gerald P. *Earth As a Planet.* 1964 (1954). Chicago. 4th. 4to. 751p. VG/dj. K5. $40.00

KUKLICK, Bruce. *To Everything a Season.* 1991. Princeton. later prt. F/F. P8. $20.00

KULPE, Oswald. *Introduction to Philosphy: Handbook for Students...* 1897. London. Sonnenschein. 1st Eng-language ed. 12mo. brn cloth. VG. G1. $50.00

KUMMEL & TEICHERT. *Stratigraphic Boundary Problems: Permian & Traissic...* 1970. Lawrence, KS. 474p. cloth. AN/dj. D8. $30.00

KUMMER, Frederic Arnold. *Courage Over the Andes.* (1940). Winston/Jr Literary Guild. 8vo. 251p. NF. C14. $6.00

KUMMER, Frederic Arnold. *First Days of Knowledge.* 1923. Doran. 1st ed. VG. P3. $20.00

KUMMER, Frederic Arnold. *Song of Sixpence.* 1913. Watt. 1st ed. VG. P3. $15.00

KUNDERA, Milan. *Immortality.* 1991. Grove Weidenfield. 1st ed. F/F. A20. $10.00

KUNDERA, Milan. *Joke.* 1969. NY. 1st Am ed. author's 1st book. F/NF. C2. $100.00

KUNETKA & STRIEBER. *War Day.* 1984. HRW. 1st ed. NF/NF. N4. $30.00

KUNHARDT, C.P. *Steam Yachts & Launches: Their Machinery & Management.* 1887. Forest & Stream. 1st ed. 97 ils. 239p. G. A17. $45.00

KUNHARDT, Dorothy. *Brave Mr Buckingham.* 1935. Harcourt Brace. 1st ed. ils. unp. beige cloth. VG/dj. D1. $120.00

KUNHARDT, Philip. *Life in Camelot: The Kennedy Years.* nd. Little Brn. BC. 319p. blk brd/spine. NF/VG. B22. $7.50

KUNICZAK, W.S. *Sempinski Affair.* 1969. Doubleday. 1st ed. RS. VG/VG. P3. $20.00

KUNKEL & GARDNER. *What Do You Advise? Guide to the Art of Counseling.* 1946. Ives Washburn. 314p. prt gr cloth. VG/dj. G1. $35.00

KUNTSLER, James Howard. *Embarrassment of Riches.* 1985. NY. Dial. 1st ed. rem mk. F/NF. B4. $50.00

KUNZ, George Frederick. *Gems & Precious Stones of North America.* 1892. NY. Scientific Pub Co. 2nd. ils Louis Prang. gilt cloth. F. B14. $350.00

KUNZ, George Frederick. *Rings for the Finger.* 1917. Lippincott. 1st ed. ils/pl. 381p. F. B14. $400.00

KUNZOG, John C. *One-Horse Show. Chronicle of Early Circus Days.* 1942. Jamestown, NY. self pub. 1st ed. sgn. gilt gr cloth. F/VG. H3. $125.00

KURAN, Aptullah. *Sinan: Grand Old Master of Ottoman Architecture.* 1987. Int Turkist Study/Ada. 1st ed. pres. photos. 319p. NF/dj. W1. $70.00

KURATA, Shigeo. *Nepenthes of Mount Kinabulu.* 1976. Sabah, Malaysia. ils/photos. 80p. sc. VG/dj. B26. $20.00

KUREISHI, Hanif. *Buddha of Suburbia.* 1990. Viking. 1st ed. author's 1st novel. F/F. M23. $30.00

KURELEK, William. *Prairie Boy's Summer.* 1975. Montreal. Tundra. 1st ed. sm 4to. F/F. C8. $35.00

KURTEN, Bjorn. *How To Deep-Freeze a Mammoth.* nd. Columbia. 2nd. VG/VG. P3. $17.00

KURTZ, Katherine. *Bastard Prince.* 1994. Ballantine. 1st ed. F/F. G10. $10.00

KURTZ, Katherine. *Bishop's Heir.* nc. BC. VG/VG. P3. $8.00

KURTZ, Katherine. *Harrowing of Gwynedd.* 1989. Del Rey. 1st ed. hc. F/F. P3. $18.00

KURTZ, Katherine. *Quest for Saint Camber.* nd. Del Rey. 6th. VG/VG. P3. $15.00

KURYLO, Friedrich. *Ferdinand Braun: A Life of the Nobel Prizewinner...* 1981. Cambridge. 289p. dj. A13. $25.00

KURZWEIL, Allen. *Case of Curiosities.* 1992. HBJ. 1st ed. rem mk. F/F. H11. $30.00

KUSCHE, Lawrence David. *Bermuda Triangle Mystery — Solved.* 1975. Harper Row. 1st ed. VG/VG. P3. $18.00

KUSHNER, Ellen. *Thomas, the Rhymer.* 1990. Morrow. 1st ed. F/F. G10. $45.00

KUSKIN, Karla. *Philharmonic Gets Dressed.* nd. Harper Row. 8vo. unp. F/VG clip. C14. $6.00

KUTTNER, Henry. *Best of...* nd. BC. VG/VG. P3. $10.00

KUTTNER, Henry. *Fury.* 1950. Grosset Dunlap. VG/VG. P3. $45.00

KUTTRUFF, Karl. *Ships of the Great Lakes, a Pictorial History.* 1976. Detroit. Wayne State. VG. A16. $40.00

KVAMME, Torstein O. *Christmas Caroler's Book in Song & Story.* 1935. Chicago. ils. 80p. G/wrp. A17. $5.00

KWITNY, Jonathan. *Shakedown.* 1977. Putnam. 1st ed. VG/VG. P3. $15.00

KYD, Thomas. *Blood of Vintage.* 1947. Lippincott. 1st ed. VG. P3. $20.00

KYLE, David A. *Book of SF Ideas & Dreams.* 1977. Hamlyn. VG/VG. P3. $20.00

KYLE, David A. *Pictorial History of SF.* 1977. Hamlyn. 2nd. hc. VG/VG. P3. $20.00

KYLE, Duncan. *Black Camelot.* 1978. Collins. 1st ed. F/F. P3. $15.00

KYLE, Duncan. *Dancing Men.* 1986. Holt. 1st ed. F/F. P3. $20.00

KYLE, Duncan. *Stalking Point.* 1981. St Martin. 1st ed. F/F. P3. $16.00

KYLE, Elisabeth. *On Lennox Moor.* 1954. Jr Literary Guild. BC. 8vo. 188p. VG/G. T5. $15.00

KYLE & SHAMPO. *Medicine & Stamps.* 1970. Chicago. 1st ed. 216p. VG. A13. $40.00

KYNE, P.G. *Go Getter.* 1921. NY. 1st ed. G+/dj. B5. $35.00

KYNE, Peter B. *Enchanted Hill.* 1924. Cosmopolitan. 1st ed. ils Dean Cornwell. F/VG. A18. $40.00

KYNE, Peter B. *Kindred of the Dust.* 1922. Copp Clark. hc. VG. P3. $20.00

KYNE, Peter B. *Never the Twain Shall Meet.* 1923. Cosmopolitan. 1st ed. ils Dean Cornwell. F/F. A18. $35.00

KYNE, Peter B. *Pride of Palomar.* 1921. Cosmopolitan. 1st ed. sgn. ils Ballinger/Cornwell. VG/VG. A18. $50.00

KYNE, Peter B. *They Also Serve.* 1927. Cosmopolitan. 1st ed. ils Baldridge/Brown. F/F. A18. $25.00

KYNE, Peter B. *Tide of Empire.* 1928. Cosmopolitan. 1st ed. ils WS Broadhead. F/VG. A18. $40.00

KYSOR, Harley D. *Aircraft in Distress.* 1956. Phil. 1st ed. sgn. 432p. G. B18. $22.50

L'AMOUR, Louis. *Bendigo Shafter.* nd. Bantam Louis L'Amour Collection. 2nd. VG. P3. $12.00

L'AMOUR, Louis. *Daybreakers.* nd. Bantam Louis L'Amour Collection. 11th. VG. P3. $12.00

L'AMOUR, Louis. *Education of a Wandering Man.* 1989. Bantam. VG/VG. P3. $17.00

L'AMOUR, Louis. *Hills of Homicide.* 1984. Bantam Louis L'Amour Collection. 1st ed. VG. P3. $20.00

L'AMOUR, Louis. *Jubal Sackett.* 1985. Bantam. 1st ed. hc. VG/VG. P3. $20.00

L'AMOUR, Louis. *Last of the Breed.* 1986. Bantam. 1st ed. hc. VG/VG. P3. $20.00

L'AMOUR, Louis. *Lonesome Gods.* nd. Bantam Louis L'Amour Collection. 2nd. hc. VG. P3. $12.00

L'AMOUR, Louis. *Outlaws of Mesquite.* 1990. Bantam. 1st ed. hc. VG/VG. P3. $17.00

L'AMOUR, Louis. *Rider of the Ruby Hills.* nd. Bantam Louis L'Amour Collection. 2nd. VG. P3. $12.00

L'AMOUR, Louis. *Rustlers of West Fork.* 1991. Bantam. 1st ed. VG/VG. P3. $20.00

L'AMOUR, Louis. *Sackett Companion.* 1988. Bantam. 1st ed. hc. VG/VG. P3. $20.00

L'AMOUR, Louis. *Shamelady.* 1966. Heinemann. 1st ed. VG. P3. $10.00

L'AMOUR, Louis. *Smoke From This Altar.* 1991. Bantam Louis L'Amour Collection. 1st ed. VG. P3. $20.00

L'AMOUR, Louis. *Trail to Seven Pines.* 1992. Bantam. 1st ed. NF/NF. P3. $20.00

L'AMOUR, Louis. *Utah Blaine.* nd. Bantam Louis L'Amour Collection. 2nd. hc. VG. P3. $12.00

L'ENGLE, Madeleine. *Camilla Dickinson.* 1951. Simon Schuster. 1st ed. inscr. F/VG. B4. $275.00

L'ENGLE, Madeleine. *Circle of Quiet.* 1972. 1st ed. VG/VG. S13. $15.00

L'ENGLE, Madeleine. *Lines Scribbled on an Envelope & Other Poems.* 1969. FSG 1st ed. F/NF. B4. $65.00

L'ENGLE, Madeleine. *Summer of the Great-Grandmother.* 1974. FSG. 4th. rem mk. F/F. B17. $10.00

L'ENGLE, Madeleine. *Walking on Water: Reflections on Faith & Art.* 1980. Wheaton, IL. Harold Shaw. 1st ed. F/F. B4. $45.00

L'ENGLE, Madeleine. *Wind in the Door.* 1973. FSG. 1st ed. 211p. gr cloth. VG/G. D1. $35.00

L'HOMMEDIEU, Dorothy. *Tinker, the Little Fox Terrier.* 1942. Lippincott. 1st ed. ils Marguerite Kirmse. VG. M5. $20.00

LA CHAPELLE, Edward R. *Field Guide to Snow Crystals.* 1969. Seattle. ils. 101p. wrp. K5. $12.00

LA FARGE, Oliver. *Enemy Gods.* 1937. Boston. Houghton Mifflin. 1st ed. 8vo. VG/dj. S9. $30.00

LA FONTAINE. *Fables of La Fontaine.* 1940. Harper. 1st ed. ils Andre Helle. trans MW Brown. 39p. VG. D1. $100.00

LA MONT, Violet. *Child's Book of Ballet.* 1953. Maxton. ils. glazed brd. VG. M5. $15.00

LA PLANTE, Lynda. *Bella Mafia.* 1991. Morrow. 1st ed. AN/dj. M22. $35.00

LA PLANTE, Lynda. *Cold Shoulder.* 1994. Macmillan. 1st ed. VG/VG. P3. $22.00

LA PLANTE, Richard. *Hog Fever.* 1995. NY. Forge. 1st ed. F/F. H11. $20.00

LA PLANTE, Richard. *Leopard.* 1994. NY. Forge. 1st ed. F/F. H11. $20.00

LA PLANTE, Richard. *Mantis.* 1993. Tor. 1st ed. F/F. H11. $25.00

LA PRADE, Ernest. *Alice in Orchestralia.* 1946. Doubleday. xl. G. P3. $12.00

LA ROCHEFOUCAULD. *Maxims of...* 1931. Haworth. 1/1075. leg. Sangorski/Sutcliffe bdg. F. T10. $250.00

LA RUE, Mabel. *Cats for the Tooseys.* 1939. Nelson. 1st ed. ils Kurt Wiese. VG/G+. P2. $75.00

LABAREE & WHITFIELD. *Mr Franklin: A Selection From His Personal Letters.* 1956. New Haven. Yale. 1/250. sgn/#d. 8vo. 61p. F/VG case. B11. $120.00

LABATT, Henry J. *Reports of Cases Determined in District Courts...* 2 Vol. nd. np. later facsimile of orig 1857-58 ed. M11. $75.00

LABE, Louize. *Les Vingtquatre Sonnets.* 1937. Grundslee, Austria. Stamperia Santuccio. 1/24. Brugalla bdg. chemise/case. B24. $4,850.00

LACEY, Robert. *Kingdom.* 1981. HBJ. 1st Am ed. 8vo. ils/maps/charts. 631p. NF/dj. W1. $20.00

LACKEY, Louana. *Pottery of Acatlan.* 1982. OK U. 1st ed. 164p. dj. F3. $30.00

LACKEY, Mercedes. *Winds of Change.* 1992. DAW. 1st ed. F/F. P3. $20.00

LACKINGTON, J. *Confessions of J Lackington...* 1808. NY. Wilson Hitt. 16mo. 189p. F. T10. $250.00

LACKINGTON, J. *Confessions of..., Late Bookseller, at the Temple of Muses.* 1808. NY. Wilson Hitt. 12mo. 189p. F. T10. $250.00

LACY, Charles DeLacy. *History of the Spur.* nd. London. Connoisseur. 1st ed. O3. $395.00

LACY, Ed. *Lead With Your Left.* 1957. Harper. 1st ed. VG/G. P3. $25.00

LADD, George T. *Outlines of Physiological Psychology.* 1898. Scribner. 1st ed/7th prt. 505p. pannelled pebbled olive cloth. G1. $35.00

LADD & WOODWORTH. *Elements of Physiological Psychology: A Treatise...* 1911 (1877). Scribner. revised ed. thick 8vo. xl. G1. $40.00

LAENNEC, R.T.H. *Treatise on the Diseases of the Chest...* 1823. Phil. 1st Am ed. 8 pl. 319p. morocco/brd. VG. B14. $475.00

LAFFERTY, Perry. *Jabonski of LA.* 1991. Donald Fine. F/F. P3. $19.00

LAFFERTY, R.A. *Archipelago.* nd. Manuscript. F/F. P3. $35.00

LAFFERTY, R.A. *Arrive at Easterwine.* nd. Scribner. VG/VG. P3. $15.00

LAFFERTY, R.A. *Does Anyone Else Have Something To Add?* 1974. Scribner. 1st ed. F/F. P3. $20.00

LAFFERTY, R.A. *East of Laughter.* 1988. Morrigan. 1st ed. F/F. P3. $30.00

LAFFERTY, R.A. *Flame Is Green.* 1971. Walker. 1st ed. NF/NF. P3. $30.00

LAFFERTY, R.A. *Not To Mention Camels.* 1976. Bobbs Merrill. 1st ed. F/F. P3. $20.00

LAFFERTY, R.A. *Okla Hannali.* 1972. Doubleday. xl. dj. P3. $15.00

LAFFERTY, R.A. *Serpent's Egg.* 1987. Morrigan. 1st ed. F/F. P3. $30.00

LAFFERTY, R.A. *Space Chantey.* 1976. Dobson. 1st ed. F/F. P3. $40.00

LAFFONT, Robert. *Ancient Art of Warfare.* 1966. Greenwich. 2 vol. ils/maps. VG/case. B18. $195.00

LAFRANCHIS, Jean. *Marcoussis. Sa Vie, Son Oeuvre.* 1961. Paris. photos/pl. 342p. D2. $250.00

LAGERLOF, Selma. *Jerusalem. Trans From Swedish by Jessie Brochner.* 1903. London. Heinemann. 396p. gr cloth. VG. B14. $75.00

LAGRON, E.M. *Defensive Bridge.* 1933. Indianapolis. 1st ed. 162p. VG. S1. $8.00

LAIDLAW, Marc. *Kalifornia.* 1993. St Martin. 1st ed. F/F. G10. $25.00

LAIDLAW, Marc. *Orchid Eater.* 1994. NY. 1st ed. F/F. H11. $25.00

LAIKEN, Deidre S. *Killing Time in Buffalo.* 1990. Little Brn. 1st ed. rem mk. F/F. H11. $25.00

LAING, Alexander. *American Sail: Pictorial history.* 1961. NY. Dutton. 1st ed. ils. VG/dj. T7. $40.00

LAING, Alexander. *End of Roaming.* 1930. Farrar Rinehart. 1st ed. VG. P3. $20.00

LAING, Alexander. *Great Ghost Stories of the World.* 1939. Garden City. hc. G. P3. $20.00

LAING, Janet. *Honeycombers.* nd. Hodder Stoughton. hc. VG. P3. $8.00

LAIRD. *Hopi Bibliography, Comprehensive & Annotated.* 1977. AZ U. 753p. F. A4. $35.00

LAIT, Jack. *Big House.* nd. Grosset Dunlap. MTI. VG. P3. $25.00

LAKE, Paul. *Among the Mortals.* 1994. Story Line. UP. F. B35. $20.00

LALLY, Dick. *Pinstriped Summers.* 1985. Arbor. 1st ed. F/VG+. P8. $25.00

LAMAR, Howard R. *Far Southwest 1846-1912: A Territorial History.* 1966. New Haven. 1st ed. 8vo. 560p. fld pocket map. F/NF. T10. $50.00

LAMAR, Howard R. *Reader's Encyclopedia of the American West.* 1977. NY. 1st ed. 1306p. VG/laminated. E1. $40.00

LAMB, D.S. *History of the Medical Society of the District of Columbia.* 1909. WA. 1st ed. 501p. xl. A13. $40.00

LAMB, Dana. *Enchanted Vagabonds.* 1938. Harper. 1st ed. 415p. F3. $20.00

LAMB, Frank. *Indian Baskets of North America.* 1972. Riverside. 1st ed. 155p. map ep. F/dj. T10. $50.00

LAMB, Harold. *Alexander of Macedon.* 1946. Doubleday. 1st ed. VG/fair. P3. $20.00

LAMB, Harold. *Crusades. Iron Men & Saints.* 1930. Doubleday Doran. 1st ed. 8vo. 368p. VG. W1. $18.00

LAMB, Harold. *Durandal.* 1981. Donald Grant. 1st hc ed. ils Austin/Barr. F/F. T2. $20.00

LAMB, Harold. *Nur Mahal.* 1935. Doubleday Doran. VG. P3. $25.00

LAMB, Harold. *Sea of the Ravens.* 1983. Donald Grant. 1st hc ed. ils Austin/Barr. F/F. T2. $20.00

LAMB, Harold. *Three Palladins.* 1977. Donald Grant. 1st ed. VG/G. P3. $15.00

LAMB, Hugh. *Taste of Fear.* 1976. Taplinger. 1st ed. F/F. P3. $25.00

LAMB, Hugh. *Tide of Terror.* 1972. WH Allen. 1st ed. ffe removed. xl. dj. P3. $15.00

LAMB, Hugh. *Victorian Nightmares.* 1977. Taplinger. 1st ed. F/F. P3. $25.00

LAMB, Wally. *She's Come Undone.* 1992. NY. Pocket. 1st ed. F/F. H11. $40.00

LAMB & LAMB. *Tales From Shakespeare.* ca 1900. Nister Dutton. ils W Paget. VG+. M5. $135.00

LAMB & LAMB. *Tales From Shakespeare.* 1909. London. Dent. 1/750. ils/sgn Rackham. 304p. gilt wht buckram/ties. F. B24. $1,150.00

LAMB & LAMB. *Tales From Shakespeare.* 1924. 1st ed. ils Frank Godwin. VG. S13. $20.00

LAMBE, T.W. *Soil Testing for Engineers.* 1951. John Wiley. 1st ed. 165p. VG. D8. $10.00

LAMBERMONT & PIRIE. *Helicopters & Autogyros of the World.* 1970. Caranbury, NJ. revised/enlarged ed. 446p. VG. B18. $22.50

LAMBERT, Derek. *Golden Express.* 1984. Stein Day. 1st ed. VG/VG. P3. $15.00

LAMBERT, Derek. *Red Dove.* 1983. Stein Day. 1st ed. VG/VG. P3. $15.00

LAMBERT, Derek. *Red House.* 1972. Michael Joseph. 1st ed. VG/VG. P3. $20.00

LAMBERT, Jacques. *Latin America.* 1967. Berkeley. 1st ed. 413p. dj. F3. $10.00

LAMBERT, Janet. *Summer for Seven.* 1952. Dutton. 1st ed. 190p. VG/G+. P2. $25.00

LAMONT & WATKINS. *Horticulture of Australian Plants.* 1985. S Perth, WA. photos. 112p. sc. F. B26. $25.00

LAMOTT, Anne. *Joe Jones.* 1985. Northpoint. 1st ed. author's 3rd novel. F/F. B4. $45.00

LAMPELL, Millard. *Pig With One Nostril.* 1975. Doubleday. 1st ed. 48p. VG/G+. P2. $20.00

LAMPORT, Felicia. *Cultural Slag.* 1966. Houghton Mifflin. 1st ed. ils Edward Gorey. 136p. VG+/dj. M20. $34.00

LAMSON, Zachery G. *Autobiography of Capt Zachary G Lamson, 1797-1814.* 1908. Boston. Clarke. ils. 279p. VG. T7. $55.00

LANAHAN, Eleanor. *Scottie: the Daughter of...* 1995. Harper Collins. ARC. F/NF. w/promo material. B4. $45.00

LANCASTER, Bruce. *American Revolution.* 1957. Doubleday. ils Lee F Ames. VG/G. B17. $5.00

LANCASTER, Graham. *Nuclear Letters.* 1979. Atheneum. 1st ed. VG/VG. P3. $15.00

LANCASTER, Roy. *Trees for Your Garden.* 1974. NY. ils/photos. 145p. VG/dj. B26. $15.00

LANCOUR, Gene. *Globes of Llarum.* 1980. Doubleday. 1st ed. VG/VG. P3. $15.00

LANCOUR, Gene. *War Machines of Kalinth.* 1977. Doubleday. 1st ed. F/F. P3. $18.00

LANDER, David. *History of the Lander Family of Virginia & Kentucky.* 1926. Regan. 12msgn. 12mo. 213p. G. B11. $50.00

LANDGRAF, John L. *Land-Use in the Ramah Area of New Mexico.* 1954. cambridge, MA. 8vo. 17 maps/plans. 97p. F/wrp. T10. $35.00

LANDING, W. Frank. *War Cry of the South.* 1958. Exposition. 1st ed. 119p. VG/G. B10. $12.00

LANDIS, Dorothy. *My Flower Book.* 1961. Rand McNally. 1st ed. 8vo. VG. M5. $8.00

LANDOLT, Elias. *Unsere Alphenflora.* 1960. Zurich. inscr. 316 photos. 218p. VG/torn. B26. $20.00

LANDON, Christopher. *Unseen Enemy.* nd. BC. VG/VG. P3. $8.00

LANDON, Fred. *Lake Huron.* 1944. Bobbs Merrill. 1st ed. sgn. Am Lake series. 8vo. 398p. gr brd. B11. $35.00

LANDON, Herman. *Gray Magic.* nd. AL Burt. hc. VG/VG. P3. $25.00

LANDRETH, Marsha. *Clinic for Murder.* 1993. Walker. 1st ed. AN/dj. N4. $25.00

LANDSDALE, Joe R. *Mucho Mojo.* 1994. Warner. 1st ed. rem mk. F/F. G10. $20.00

LANDSTROM. *Columbus: Story of Don Critobal Colon, Admiral...* 1967. F/VG. D2. $25.00

LANDY, Eugene E. *Underground Dictionary.* 1971. Simon Schuster. 1st ed. F/NF. B2. $40.00

LANE, E.W. *Thousand & One Nights.* 1889. London. 3 vol. ils. VG. M17. $50.00

LANE, Jeremy. *Yellow Men Sleep.* 1983. Donald Grant. 1st ed thus. ils Alan McLucky. F/F. T2. $20.00

LANE, Maggie. *Needlepoint by Design.* 1970. Scribner. 1st ed. sgn. VG+/dj. M20. $18.00

LANE, Mark. *People of Georgia: An Illustrated Social History.* 1975. Beehive. 350p. VG/box. B10. $55.00

LANE, Sheldon. *For Bond Lovers Only.* 1965. NY. 1st Am ed. VG+/wrp. A11. $45.00

LANE & RUPP. *Nazi Ideology Before 1933: A Documentation.* 1978. TX U. 180p. dj. A17. $17.50

LANES, Selma G. *Art of Maurice Sendak.* 1980. Abrams. 1st ed. ils Sendak. 278p. VG. D1. $150.00

LANFRANCO, Guido G. *Guide to the Flora of Malta.* 1955. Valetta. ils/line drawings. wrp. B26. $25.00

LANG, Andrew. *Aucassin & Nicolete.* 1931. LEC. 1/1500. ils/sgn Vojtech Preissig. gilt cloth. VG. B11. $55.00

LANG, Andrew. *Blue Fairy Book.* 1889. London. 1st ed. ils Ford/Hood. gilt bl cloth. VG. M5. $600.00

LANG, Andrew. *Chronicles of Pantouflia.* 1981. Godine. 1st ed. VG/VG. P3. $15.00

LANG, Andrew. *Cock Lane & Common-Sense.* 1894. Longman Gr. 8vo. 357p+24p ads. gilt red cloth. VG. D1. $125.00

LANG, Andrew. *Green Fairy Book.* 1899. London. 5th. ils HJ Ford. aeg. F. M5. $75.00

LANG, Andrew. *In Fairyland.* 1979. Derrydale. 1st thus. ils Richard Doyle. VG/VG. B17. $12.50

LANG, Andrew. *My Own Fairy Book.* 1895. Longman Gr. 1st Am ed. ils Browne/Scott/Lemin. aeg. NF. D1. $175.00

LANG, Andrew. *Red Book of Animal Stories.* 1983. Franklin Lib. leather spine. NF. P3. $20.00

LANG, Andrew. *Red Fairy Book.* 1924. McKay. 1st ed thus. ils Gustaf Tenggren. 285p. red cloth. VG+. D1. $285.00

LANG, Daniel. *Casualties of War.* 1969. McGraw. 1st ed. F/F. H11. $40.00

LANG, Daniel. *From Hiroshima to the Moon.* 1959. NY. 1st ed. 496p. G/torn. B18. $15.00

LANG, Jean. *Book of Myths.* ca 1920. Nelson. 16 pl. gilt bl cloth. VG. M5. $60.00

LANG, Paul H. *Music in Western Civilization.* 1941. NY. 1st ed. ils. red/gilt-stp blk cloth. VG. H3. $45.00

LANGE, Algot. *In the Amazon Jungle.* 1912. Putnam. 1st ed. inscr. 8vo. 405p. VG. B11. $65.00

LANGE, C.G. *Ueber Gemuthsbewegungen.* 1887 (1885). Leipzig. Theodor Thomas. 1st German ed. 92p. modern blk linen/wrp. G1. $125.00

LANGE, John; see Crichton, Michael.

LANGE, Karl. *Uber Apperzeption: Eine Psychologisch-Padagogische...* 1879. Plauen. FE Neupert. thin 8vo. 112p. G1. $125.00

LANGE, O.L. *Physiological Plant Ecology IV.* 1983. Berlin. 644p. VG. B26. $25.00

LANGE, Oliver. *Incident at La Junta.* 1974. Peter Davis. 1st ed. hc. VG/VG. P3. $30.00

LANGE, Oliver. *Vandenberg.* 1971. Stein Day. VG/VG. P3. $15.00

LANGENHEIM & THIMANN. *Botany: Plant Biology & Its Relation to Human Affairs.* 1982. NY. ils. 624p. B26. $22.50

LANGER, Walter C. *Mind of Adolf Hitler: Secret Wartime Report.* 1972. NY. Basic. 269p. VG/dj. A17. $12.50

LANGFORD, Gerald. *Destination.* 1981. Stonehenge. 166p. w/sgn letter. F/VG. B10. $15.00

LANGHORNE, Dr. *Fables of Flora.* 1804. Langworth. 9 full-p engravings. 70p. full leather. A10. $75.00

LANGLEY, Noel. *Tale of the Land of the Green Ginger.* 1937. Morrow. 1st ed. 4to. 143p. gr cloth. VG/VG. D1. $135.00

LANGLEY, Noel. *There's a Porpoise Close Behind Us.* 1953. Arthur Barker. 12th. G/G. P3. $12.00

LANGLOIS & SEIGNOBOS. *Introduction to Study of History.* 1912. London. Duckworth. 2nd. 12mo. 350p. VG. T10. $25.00

LANGSTAFF, John. *St George & the Dragon: A Mummer's Play.* 1973. Atheneum. 1st ed. 8vo. 48p. NF/clip. C14. $30.00

LANGSTAFF & LANGSTAFF. *Jim Along Josie: A Collection of Folk Songs & Singing Games.* 1970. Harcourt Brace. 1st ed. ils. VG+/dj. C8. $35.00

LANGTON, Jane. *Memorial Hall Murder.* 1978. Harper Row. 1st ed. NF/F. H11. $45.00

LANHAM, Edwin. *Clock at 8:16.* 1970. Doubleday. 1st ed. VG/VG. P3. $15.00

LANHAM, Edwin. *Death of a Corinthian.* 1953. Harcourt Brace. 1st ed. VG/VG. P3. $15.00

LANHAM, Edwin. *Iron Maiden.* 1954. Harcourt Brace. 1st ed. VG/VG. P3. $18.00

LANHAM, Edwin. *Six Black Camels.* 1961. Harcourt Brace. 1st ed. xl. VG/VG. P10. $10.00

LANHAM, Fritz G. *Putting Troy in a Sack.* 1916. Austin. 1st ed. sgn. 8vo. 141p. teg. bl cloth/wht spine. VG. B11. $70.00

LANIA, Leo. *Hemingway: A Pictorial Biography.* 1961. NY. Studio/Viking. 1st ed. F/NF. B2. $35.00

LANIER, Charles. *More Foxhunting in England.* 1927. private prt. 1st ed. VG. O3. $35.00

LANIER, Charles. *We Go Foxhunting Abroad.* 1924. private prt. 1st ed. VG. O3. $35.00

LANIER, Sidney. *Bob: the Story of Our Mockingbird.* 1899. NY. 1st ed. ils. G. B5. $45.00

LANIER, Sidney. *English Novel: A Study in Development of Personality.* 1900 (1897). Scribner. 302p. VG. B10. $25.00

LANIER, Sidney. *King Arthur & His Knights of the Round Table.* nd. MacDonald. hc. ils Junior Li. VG/VG. P3. $20.00

LANIER, Sidney. *Poems of...* 1929. Scribner. new ed. 262p. teg. VG/VG. B10. $25.00

LANIER, Sterling E. *Unforsaken Hero.* 1983. Ballantine. 1st ed. sgn. F/NF. T2. $25.00

LANMAN, Charles. *Haw-Ho-Noo; or, Records of a Tourist.* 1850. Lippincott Gambo. 1st ed. 8vo. 266p. blk T-grain cloth. F. T10. $300.00

LANSDALE, Joe R. *Act of Love.* 1989. London. Kinnell. 1st Eng/1st hc ed. sgn. AN/dj. M22. $75.00

LANSDALE, Joe R. *Act of Love.* 1989. London. Kinnell. 1st hc ed. author's 1st novel. F/F. T2. $35.00

LANSDALE, Joe R. *Act of Love.* 1992. Baltimore. CD Pub. 1st ed thus. 1/750. sgn. ils/sgn MA Nelson. AN/dj/case. M22. $75.00

LANSDALE, Joe R. *Cold in July.* 1989. Mark V Ziesing. 1st ed. NF/NF. P3. $25.00

LANSDALE, Joe R. *Jonah Hex: Tow-Gun Mojo.* 1994. DC Comics. 1st ed thus. sc. M22. $15.00

LANSDALE, Joe R. *Mucho Mojo.* 1994. Mysterious. 1st ed. AN/dj. M22. $35.00

LANSDALE, Joe R. *New Frontier.* 1989. Doubleday. 1st ed. sgn. VG/VG. P3. $30.00

LANSDALE, Joe R. *Nightrunners.* 1987. Dark Harvest. 1st ed. NF/NF. P3. $35.00

LANSDALE, Joe R. *Razored Saddles.* 1989. Dark Harvest. 1st trade ed. sgn. AN/dj. M21. $40.00

LANSDALE, Joe R. *Savage Season.* 1990. Ziesing. 1st hc ed. AN/dj. M22. $50.00

LANSDALE, Joe R. *Two-Bear Mambo.* 1995. Mysteious. 1st ed. NF/NF. P3. $20.00

LANSFORD, William. *Pancho Villa.* 1965. Herbourne. 1st ed. 283p. dj. F3. $20.00

LANSING, Alfred. *Endurance.* 1959. McGraw Hill. 1st ed. ils. 282p. VG/dj. T7. $20.00

LANTZ, Sherlee. *Pageant of Pattern for Needlepoint Canvas.* 1973. Atheneum. 1st ed. ils/pl/photos. 509p. F/dj. T10. $125.00

LANTZ, Sherlee. *Trianglepoint: From Persian Pavilions to Op Art...* 1976. Viking/The Studio. 1st ed. 8vo. ils. F/F. T10. $50.00

LAPIDE, Cornelius A. *Commentaria in Duodecim Prophetas Minores.* 1628. Anwerp. Martinum Nutium. 1st ed. folio. pigskin/brass clasps. K1. $300.00

LAPORTE MOLINA, Juan Pedro. *Bibliografia de la Arqueologia Guatemalteca. A-I. Tomo 1.* 1981. Guatemala. 1st ed. 271p. wrp. F3. $20.00

LAQUEUR, Walter. *Road to Jerusalem.* 1968. Macmillan. 1st Am ed. 8vo. 368p. VG/dj. W1. $18.00

LARDNER, Ring. *Say It With Oil.* 1923. NY. 1st ed. NF/VG clip. C6. $200.00

LARIAR, Lawrence. *Day I Died.* 1952. Appleton Century Crofts. xl. VG. P3. $8.00

LARIAR, Lawrence. *Death Paints a Picture.* 1943. Phoenix. xl. G. P3. $10.00

LARIAR, Lawrence. *Girl With the Frightened Eyes.* 1945. Detective BC. VG. P3. $7.00

LARIAR, Lawrence. *He Died Laughing.* 19432. Phoenix. 1st ed. xl. dj. P3. $12.00

LARKE & PATTON. *Life of General US Grant: His Early Life & Military Career.* 1885. NY. 8vo. 572p. gilt red pict cloth. VG. T3. $42.00

LARKIN, David. *Faeries Pop-Up Book.* 1980. Abrams. ils Brian Froud/Alan Lee. NF. T5. $60.00

LARKIN, David. *Giants.* 1979. Abrams. VG/VG. P3. $30.00

LARKIN, Margaret. *Singing Cowboy: Book of Western Songs.* 1963. NY. Oak Pub. later prt. 8vo. 176p. F/wrp. T10. $25.00

LARMOTH, Jeanine. *Murder on the Menu.* 1972. Scribner. 1st ed. VG/VG. P3. $25.00

LARNED, J.N. *Literature of American History: A Bibliographical Guide.* 1953. np. 4145 entries. 597p. F. A4. $125.00

LARNED, J.N. *Literature of American History: A Bibliographical Guide.* 1966. 4145 entries. 597p. VG/VG. A4. $115.00

LAROM, Henry. *Ride Like an Indian!* 1958. Wesley Dennis. BC. VG/VG. O3. $15.00

LARRICK, Nancy. *Junior Science Book of Rain, Hail, Sleet & Snow.* 1961. Champaign, IL. Garrard. 8vo. 63p. xl. K5. $6.00

LARRIMORE, Lida. *Blossoming of Patricia-the-Less.* 1924. Phil. Penn. 1st ed. ils Hattie L Price. bl cloth. VG. M20. $32.00

LARSEN, William. *Montague of Virginia: Making of a Southern Progressive.* 1965. LSU. G/G. B10. $25.00

LARSON, Andrew Karl. *I Was Called to Dixie.* 1961. Salt Lake City. 1st ed. pres. ils. 681p. F/VG. T10. $50.00

LARSON, T.A. *History of Wyoming.* 1967. Lincoln, NE. 8vo. ils Jack Brodie. 619p. NF/dj. T10. $25.00

LASANSKY, Mauricio. *Nazi Drawings.* 1976. IA U. revised ed. 4to. G. A17. $27.50

LASKEY, Muriel. *Aunt Mathilda & the Lost Cheese.* 1946. Pied Piper. ils Doris Stolberg. VG/VG. B17. $7.50

LASKEY, Muriel. *Teddy Bear.* 1946. NY. ils. pict brd. VG. M5. $20.00

LASSWELL, Harold D. *World Politics & Personal Insecurity.* 1935. Whittlesey. 308p. blk cloth. G1. $45.00

LASSWELL, M. *Mrs Rasmusson's One Arm Cookery.* 1946. Boston. 1st ed. VG/VG. B5. $37.50

LATANE, A.D. *Vagaries & Memories.* 1937. Michie. sgn. 42p. VG. B10. $12.00

LATCH, Jean. *Plusieurs Tres-bons Cases, Come ils Estoyent Adjudgees...* 1662? London. 1st ed. contemporary sheep. M11. $250.00

LATHAM, Jean Lee. *Young Man in a Hurry: Story of Cyrus W Field.* 1958. Harper Row. ils Victor Mays. 238p. xl. VG. T5. $15.00

LATHEM, Emma. *Ashes to Ashes.* 1971. Simon Schuster. 1st ed. VG/VG. P3. $15.00

LATHEM, Emma. *By Hook or by Crook.* nd. BC. VG/VG. P3. $8.00

LATHEM, Emma. *Double, Double, Oil & Trouble.* nd. BC. VG/VG. P3. $8.00

LATHEM, Emma. *Going for the Gold.* nd. Simon Schuster. 2nd. VG/VG. P3. $10.00

LATHEM, Emma. *Green Grow the Dollars.* nd. BC. VG/VG. P3. $8.00

LATHEM, Emma. *Longer the Thread.* 1971. Simon Schuster. 1st ed. VG/VG. P3. $15.00

LATHEM, Emma. *Pick Up Sticks.* nd. BC. VG/VG. P3. $8.00

LATHEM, Emma. *Stich in Time.* nd. BC. VG/VG. P3. $8.00

LATHROP, Dorothy. *Angel in the Woods.* 1947. Macmillan. 1st ed. ils. F/G. M5. $60.00

LATHROP, Dorothy. *Animals of the Bible.* nd. Lippincott. 13th. rem mk. F/F. B17. $10.00

LATHROP, Dorothy. *Fairy Circus.* 1942 (1931). Macmillan. ils/6 pl. VG. M5. $80.00

LATHROP, Dorothy. *Puppies for Keeps.* 1943. Macmillan. 1st ed. ils. VG/G+. P2. $75.00

LATHROP, Sallie B. Comer. *Comer Family Grows Up.* 1945. Birmingham. photos. 211p. G. B10. $25.00

LATIMER, Jonathan. *Lady in the Morgue.* nd. BC. VG/VG. P3. $8.00

LATOUR, Bruno. *Les Microbes Guerre et Paix Suivi de Irreductiones.* 1984. Paris. 1st ed. 281p. wrp. A13. $20.00

LATTIMORE, Deborah Nourse. *Flame of Peace.* 1987. Harper Row. 1st ed. 4to. VG/VG. B17. $6.00

LATTIMORE, Richard. *Some Odes of Pindar.* 1942. Norfolk. 1st ed. 30p. VG/wrp. A17. $15.00

LAUFER, Berthold. *Introduction of Tobacco Into Europe.* 1924. Chicago. Field Mus. 45p. wrp. F3. $20.00

LAUGHLIN, Clarence John. *Ghosts Along the Mississippi.* nd. Bonanza. rpt of 1961 ed. 100 photos. unp. G/G. B10. $25.00

LAUGHLIN, David. *Gringo Cop.* 1975. Carlton. 1st ed. sgn. 8vo. 127p. tan cloth. VG/G. B11. $15.00

LAUGHLIN, James. *Ezra.* 1994. Dim Gray Bar. 1/100. sgn, ils/sgn Guy Davenport. F/wrp. V1. $75.00

LAUGHLIN, Ruth. *Caballeros.* 1947 (1946). Caxton. 2nd. 418p. cloth. VG/dj. M20. $22.00

LAUMER, Frank. *Massacre!* 1968. Gainesville. 1st ed. sgn. 8 pl. 188p. F/VG. B11. $50.00

LAUMER, Keith. *Earthblood.* nd. BC. VG/VG. P3. $8.00

LAUMER, Keith. *Glory Game.* 1973. Doubleday. 1st ed. VG/VG. P3. $20.00

LAUMER, Keith. *Infinite Cage.* 1976. Dobson. F/F. P3. $20.00

LAUMER, Keith. *Night of Delusions.* 1972. Putnam. 1st ed. VG/VG. P3. $25.00

LAUMER, Keith. *Other Side of Time.* 1971. Walker. 1st ed. xl. dj. P3. $8.00

LAUMER, Keith. *Retief's Ransom.* 1975. Dobson. 1st ed. F/F. P3. $20.00

LAUMER, Keith. *Shape Changer.* 1972. Putnam. 1st ed. VG/VG. P3. $20.00

LAUMER, Keith. *World Shuffler.* 1970. Putnam. 1st ed. VG/VG. P3. $20.00

LAURAT, Lucien. *Marxism & Democracy.* 1940. London. Left BC. 254p. VG. A17. $9.50

LAURENCE, William L. *Men & Atoms.* 1959. Simon Schuster. 1st ed. sgn. 8vo. 302p. VG/G. B11. $50.00

LAURIAT, Charles. *Lusitania's Last Voyage.* 1915. Boston. 1st ed. VG. B5. $45.00

LAUT, Agnes C. *Blazed Trail of the Old Frontier.* 1926. NY. McBride. 1st ed. ils Charles M Russell. 8vo. 271p. pict buckram. T10. $150.00

LAUTREAMONT, Isidore Ducasse. *Maldoror (Les Chants de Maldoror).* 1943. Guy Wernham. 1/1000. 303p. F/case. T10. $100.00

LAVEILE, E. *Life of Father De Smet, SJ.* 1981. Loyola. facsimile of 1915 ed. 398p. gilt gr cloth. F. T10. $25.00

LAVELL, Edith. *Linda Carlton's Ocean Flight (#2).* 1931. AL Burt. lists 3 titles. 283p. VG+/dj. M20. $85.00

LAVENDER, David. *Red Mountain.* 1963. Doubleday. 1st ed. 8vo. map ep. VG/dj. T10. $45.00

LAVENDER, David. *Southwest.* 1980. Harper Row. 1st ed. 8vo. 352p. F/dj. T10. $45.00

LAVENDER, David. *Westward Vision: The Oregon Trail.* 1963. NY. 1st ed. Am Trail series. F/dj. A17. $25.00

LAVER, James. *Macrocosmos, a Poem.* 1930. Knopf. ltd ed. sgn. 32p. G/stiff wrp. B11. $50.00

LAVINTHAL, Hy. *Defence Tricks.* 1963. Waltham, MA. 192p. VG/dj. S1. $8.00

LAW, Alexander. *To an Easy Grave.* 1986. St Martin. 1st ed. VG/VG. P3. $15.00

LAWLISS, Chuck. *Civil War Sourcebook: A Traveler's Guide.* 1991. Harmony. 1st ed. 308p. stiff prt wrp. M8. $18.00

LAWRENCE, Cynthia. *Barbie's New York Summer (#2).* 1962. Random. 178p. VG-. M20. $10.00

LAWRENCE, D.H. *Aaron's Rod.* 1922. Secker. 1st Eng ed. NF/G. M19. $175.00

LAWRENCE, D.H. *Fantasia of the Unconscious.* 1922. Seltzer. 1st ed. F/G+. M19. $250.00

LAWRENCE, D.H. *Letters of...* 1932. London /NY. 1/525. full vellum. NF. C6. $150.00

LAWRENCE, D.H. *Modern Lover.* 1934. Viking. 1st ed. NF/G. M19. $100.00

LAWRENCE, D.H. *Pansies.* 1929. London. private prt. 1/500. sgn. F/prt wrp/glassine/case. B24. $650.00

LAWRENCE, D.H. *Plumed Serpent.* 1926. London. Secker. 1st ed. brn cloth. F/beige dj. B24. $475.00

LAWRENCE, D.H. *Prussian Officer.* 1914. London. Duckworth. 1st ed/1st issue. gilt bl cloth. NF. B24. $250.00

LAWRENCE, D.H. *Sons & Lovers.* 1975. Avon. LEC. 1/2000. ils/sgn Sheila Robinson. 443p. F/case. C2. $100.00

LAWRENCE, D.H. *Studies in Classic American Literature.* 1923. NY. 1st ed. VG/VG. C2. $150.00

LAWRENCE, Elizabeth. *His Very Silence Speaks.* 1989. Detroit. Wayne State. 1st ed. F/F. O3. $28.00

LAWRENCE, Elizabeth. *Little Bulbs: Tale of Two Gardens.* 1957. NY. 1st ed. 248p. VG/dj. B26. $20.00

LAWRENCE, G.H.M. *B-P-H: Botanico-Periodicum-Huntianum.* 1968. Pittsburgh. Hunt Botanical Lib. 4to. 1063p. cloth. NF. B1. $35.00

LAWRENCE, G.H.M. *Intro to Plant Taxonomy.* (1955). NY. later prt. ils MR Sheeham. 179p. F. B26. $22.50

LAWRENCE, George Alfred. *Border & Bastille.* nd (1879). NY. Pooley. 291p. fair. B10. $35.00

LAWRENCE, Hilda. *Blood Upon the Snow.* 1944. Detective BC. VG. P3. $10.00

LAWRENCE, Louise. *Moonwind.* 1986. Harper Row. 1st ed. F/F. P3. $15.00

LAWRENCE, Louise. *Warriors of Taan.* 1988. Harper Row. 1st ed. F/F. P3. $15.00

LAWRENCE, Margery. *Daughter of the Nile.* 1956. Robert hale. 1st ed. VG/G. P3. $20.00

LAWRENCE, Mike. *Major Suit Raises.* 1983. TX. 86p. VG. S1. $4.00

LAWRENCE, Robert. *Gounod's Faust.* (1943). NY. Grosset Dunlap/Metropolitan Opera Guild. G+. C14. $12.00

LAWRENCE, Robert. *Hansel & Gretel: Story of Humperdinck's Opera.* (1938). NY. Grosset Dunlap/Metropolitan Opera Guild. VG/G. C14. $15.00

LAWRENCE, T.E. *Diary of TE Lawrence MCMXI.* 1937. London. 1/40 on Medway paper. photos. full vellum. F/case. C6. $4,200.00

LAWRENCE, T.E. *Diary.* 1937. London. Corvinus. 1st ed. 1/130 on parchment. 13 full-p pl. F. B24. $3,750.00

LAWRENCE, T.E. *Odyssey of Homer.* 1932. London. Rudge. 1/530. pub Bruce Rogers. full blk morocco. F/case. B24. $2,850.00

LAWRENCE, T.E. *Revolt in the Desert.* nd. Garden City. xl. poor. P3. $10.00

LAWRENCE, T.E. *Revolt in the Desert.* 1927. Doran. 1st Am ed. 8vo. fld map. 335p. VG/dj. T10. $200.00

LAWRENCE, T.E. *Seven Pillars of Wisdom: A Triumph.* 1935. Doubleday Doran. 1st Am ed. ils. xl. VG. W1. $22.00

LAWRENCE, T.E. *TE Lawrence to His Biographers, Robert Graves & Liddel Hart.* 1938. NY. 2 vol. 1st ed. 1/500. sgns. F/VG/case. C6. $450.00

LAWRENCE, Vera Brosky. *Music for Patriots, Politicians & Presidents.* 1975. NY. 4to. ils. 480p. F/dj. T3. $30.00

LAWRENCE, W.J. *Elizabethan Playhouse & Other Studies.* 1912. Stratford-on-Avon. 2 vol. 1st ed. 1/760. VG. C2. $75.00

LAWS, Stephen. *Ghost Train.* 1985. Beaufort. 1st ed. VG/VG. P3. $20.00

LAWSON, A.C. *Atlas of Maps & Seismograms...CA Earthquake of April 1906.* 1970 (1908). Carnegie Inst. rpt. 25 maps/15 seismographs. obdg. NF. B1. $45.00

LAWSON, Robert. *Astonishing Life of Benjamin Franklin, by His Good Mouse...* 1944. Little Brn. later prt. VG/VG. B35. $30.00

LAWSON, Robert. *Country Colic, the Weeder's Digest.* 1943. Little Brn. 2nd. 8vo. VG/VG. B17. $17.00

LAWSON, Robert. *Rabbit Hill.* (1944). Viking. 6th prt. 8vo. F/G. B17. $22.50

LAWSON, Robert. *Rabbit Hill.* 1944. Viking. 1st ed. 8vo. ils/sgn Lawson. VG. M5. $75.00

LAWSON, Robert. *Rabbit Hill.* 1963. Viking. 10th. 128p. NF/VG clip. C14. $8.00

LAWSON, Robert. *Robbut: A Tale of Tails.* 1948. Viking. 1st ed. 8vo. 94p. ils ep. VG/VG. D1. $120.00

LAWSON, Robert. *Tough Winter.* 1954. Viking. 1st ed. 128p. VG/VG. M20. $45.00

LAWSON, Ted W. *Thirty Seconds Over Tokyo.* 1943. NY. 1st ed. 221p. tan pict cloth. NF. B5. $75.00

LAWSON, William. *Countrie Housewife's Garden.* 1948. Ferrin, IL. Trovillion Private Pr. ltd ed. pub sgns. 12mo. VG. B11. $25.00

LAWTON, Charles. *Winning Forward Pass.* 1940. Cupples Leon. 1st ed. ils. G+. P12. $5.00

LAWTON, Wilbur. *Boy Aviators in Africa.* 1910. Hurst. ils. VG. P12. $7.00

LAXTON, Paul. *A to Z of Regency London.* 1985. Lympne Castle. Harry Margary/Guildhall Lib. 4to. ils/maps. F/dj. O7. $75.00

LAYCOCK, Thomas. *Mind & Brain; or Correlations of Consciousness...* 1860. Edinburgh. Sutherland Knox/Simpkin Marshall. 2 vol. VG. G1. $450.00

LAYET, Alexandre. *Hygiene des Professions et des Industries.* 1875. Paris. 1st ed. sgn. 560p. quarter vellum. A13. $100.00

LAYHEW, Jane. *Rx for Murder.* 1946. Lippincott. 1st ed. VG/VG. P3. $20.00

LAZIUS, Wolfgang. *Austria.* 1972. Amsterdam. facsimile. lg folio. 12 double-p maps. M. O7. $135.00

LE CARRE, John. *Call for the Dead.* nd. BOMC. NF/NF. P3. $10.00

LE CARRE, John. *Call for the Dead.* 1962. Walker. pirated ed. F/F. B35. $200.00

LE CARRE, John. *Le Carre Omnibus.* 1964. Gollancz. 2nd. VG. P3. $20.00

LE CARRE, John. *Little Drummer Girl.* 1964. Hodder Stoughton. 1st ed. NF/NF. P3. $25.00

LE CARRE, John. *Little Drummer Girl.* 1983. Knopf. 1st ed. F/F. H11. $50.00

LE CARRE, John. *Little Drummer Girl.* 1983. Knopf. 1st ed. w/sgn leaf. F/NF. B2. $75.00

LE CARRE, John. *Looking-Glass War.* 1965. Heinemann. 1st ed. VG/VG. P3. $75.00

LE CARRE, John. *Looking-Glass War.* 1987. Octopus. VG/VG. P3. $10.00

LE CARRE, John. *Naive & Sentimental Lover.* 1972. Knopf. 1st ed. VG/VG. P3. $75.00

LE CARRE, John. *Night Manager.* 1993. Knopf. 1st ed. F/F. A20. $15.00

LE CARRE, John. *Perfect Spy.* 1985. Knopf. 1st ed. VG/VG. P3. $25.00

LE CARRE, John. *Perfect Spy.* 1986. Knopf. 1st ed. w/sgn leaf. F/F. B2. $125.00

LE CARRE, John. *Russia House.* 1989. Knopf. 1st ed. F/F. B35. $25.00

LE CARRE, John. *Secret Pilgrim.* 1991. Knopf. 1st ed. F/F. P3. $22.00

LE CARRE, John. *Secret Pilgrim.* 1991. Knopf. 1st ed. w/sgn leaf. F/F. B2. $85.00

LE CARRE, John. *Small Town in Germany.* 1968. Coward McCann. 1st Am ed. 1/500. pres. sgn. gilt bdg. NF. B4. $500.00

LE CARRE, John. *Small Town in Germany.* 1968. Coward McCann. 1st ed. NF/clip. H11. $55.00

LE CARRE, John. *Small Town in Germany.* 1968. Coward McCann. 1st ed. VG/VG. P3. $50.00

LE CARRE, John. *Smiley's People.* 1980. Hodder Stoughton. 1st ed. VG/VG. P3. $25.00

LE CARRE, John. *Smiley's People.* 1980. Knopf. 1st ed. w/sgn leaf. F/F. B2. $150.00

LE CARRE, John. *Smiley's People.* 1980. Knopf. 2nd. VG/VG. P3. $20.00

LE CARRE, John. *Spy Who Came in From the Cold.* 1964. Gollancz. 17th. VG/VG. P3. $10.00

LE CARRE, John. *Three Complete Novels.* nd. Avenel. 2nd. F/F. P3. $15.00

LE CARRE, John. *Tinker, Tailor, Soldier, Spy.* 1974. Hodder Stoughton. 1st ed. VG/VG. P3. $75.00

LE CARRE, John. *Tinker, Tailor, Soldier, Spy.* 1974. Knopf. 1st ed. NF/NF. B35. $35.00

LE DENTU, Jose. *Bridge Facile.* 1970. np. French text. pb. 446p. VG. S1. $5.00

LE FANU, J. Sheridan. *Catalogue of Portraits & Other Paintings...* nd. F/dj. D2. $60.00

LE FANU, J. Sheridan. *Flying Dragon.* nd. Detective Club. G. P3. $25.00

LE FANU, J. Sheridan. *Hours After Midnight.* 1975. Leslie Frewin of London. 1st ed. ils Geoffrey Bourne-Taylor. F/F. R10. $20.00

LE FANU, J. Sheridan. *Purcell Papers.* 1975. Arkham. 1st ed. 1/4288. F/F. T2. $12.00

LE FANU, J. Sheridan. *Uncle Silas.* 1947. Cresset. VG. P3. $40.00

LE FANU, William. *Bio-Bibliography of Edward Jenner.* 1985. Winchester. 2nd. 160p. dj. A13. $60.00

LE FANU, William. *English Books Printed Before 1701...* 1963. Edinburgh. 1st ed. 28p. VG. A13. $30.00

LE FANU, William. *List of Original Writings of Joseph Lord Lister.* 1965. Edinburgh. 1st ed. 20p. VG. A13. $35.00

LE FEVRE, Felicity. *Cock, the Mouse & Little Red Hen.* nd. Jacobs. probable 1st ed. 12mo. ils Tony Sarg. VG. M5. $60.00

LE FREE, Betty. *Santa Clara Pottery Today.* 1975. Albuquerque. 1st paper ed. 8vo. 114p. F/wrp. T10. $15.00

LE GRAND. *Augustus & the Desert.* 1948. Bobbs Merrill. 1st ed. ils. NF/VG. P2. $40.00

LE GRAND. *Augustus & the River.* 1939. Bobbs Merrill. sgn. ils. 128p. VG/G+. P2. $35.00

LE GUIN, Ursula K. *Buffalo Gals & Other Animal Presences.* 1990. Gollancz. 1st ed. F/F. P3. $28.00

LE GUIN, Ursula K. *Compass Rose.* 1982. Harper Row. 1st ed. NF/NF. P3. $30.00

LE GUIN, Ursula K. *Eye of the Heron.* 1983. Harper Row. 1st ed. NF/NF. P3. $25.00

LE GUIN, Ursula K. *Fisherman of the Inland Sea.* 1994. Harper Prism. 1st ed. 1/1500. pub pres. sans. F. P3. $25.00

LE GUIN, Ursula K. *Left Hand of Darkness.* nd. Harper Row. 1st ed thus. VG/G. M21. $5.00

LE GUIN, Ursula K. *Searoad.* 1991. Harper Collins. 1st ed. F/F. P3. $20.00

LE GUIN, Ursula K. *Three Hainish Novels.* nd. BC. hc. VG/VG. P3. $10.00

LE GUIN, Ursula K. *Very Far Away From Anywhere Else.* 1976. Atheneum. 1st ed. F/NF. B4. $85.00

LE GUIN, Ursula K. *Wind's Twelve Quarters.* 1978. Harper Row. 2nd. VG/VG. P3. $15.00

LE MAIR, H. Willebeek. *Our Old Nursery Rhymes.* 1911. Augener. ils. gilt bl cloth. VG. M5. $95.00

LE MAOUT, Emmanuel. *Botanique Organographie et Taxonomie.* 1854. Paris. L Curmer. ils/20 pl. 388p. aeg. tan morocco. case. K1. $175.00

LE MARCHAND, Elizabeth. *Affacombe Affair.* 1985. Walker. F/F. P3. $20.00

LE MARCHAND, Elizabeth. *Unhappy Returns.* 1977. Hart Davis/MacGibbon. 1st ed. hc. VG. P3. $20.00

LE MAY, Alan. *One of Us Is a Murderer.* 1930. Crime Club. VG. P3. $20.00

LE MAY, Alan. *Smoky Years.* 1938. Triangle. G. P3. $10.00

LE MOEL & ROCHAT. *Catalogue General des Cartes, Plans et Dessins...* 1972. Paris. 18 multi-p fld ils. F. O7. $45.00

LE MOYNE, Pierre. *La Gallerie des Femmes Fortes.* 1665. Paris. La Companie des Marchands Libraires du Palais. 12mo. K1. $450.00

LE PRINCE, Joseph. *Mosquito Control in Panama.* 1916. Putnam. 1st ed. sgn. 335p. F3. $25.00

LE QUEUX, William. *Behind the Bronze Door.* nd. Goldsmith. hc. G. P3. $10.00

LE QUEUX, William. *Broken Thread.* 1916. Ward Lock. G. P3. $30.00

LE QUEUX, William. *Golden Three.* 1931. Fiction League. VG. P3. $20.00

LEA, Robert H. *Bridge Is Easy With the Lea System.* 1965. CO. 1st ed. 144p. VG. S1. $8.00

LEA, Tom. *King Ranch.* 1957. Little Brn. 2 vol. ils. VG. A4. $125.00

LEA, Tom. *King Ranch.* 1957. Little Brn. 2 vol. inscr pres. ils/maps. beige/red cloth. K1. $200.00

LEA, Tom. *Primal Yoke.* 1960. Little Brn. 1st ed. ils. F/F. A18. $35.00

LEA, Tom. *Selection of Paintings & Drawings From the 1960s.* 1969. Encino. 1st ltd Rio Bravo ed. 1/200. sgns. F/case. A18. $175.00

LEA, Tom. *Wonderful Country.* 1952. Boston. Little Brn. 1st ed. 8vo. 387p. VG. P4. $25.00

LEACH, D.G. *Rhododendrons of the World.* 1961. Scribner. 1st ed. 4to. 544p. cloth. dj. B1. $100.00

LEACOCK, Stephen. *Iron Man & the Tin Woman.* 1929. Dodd Mead. 1st ed. VG. P3. $60.00

LEAF, Munro. *Ferdinand the Bull.* 1936. Viking. 1st ed. ils Robert Lawson. VG. M5. $145.00

LEAF, Munro. *Ferdinand the Bull.* 1938. Whitman. ils Walt Disney Studios. VG. D1. $85.00

LEAF, Munro. *Wee Gillis.* 1938. 1st ed. ils Robert Lawson. VG+. S13. $45.00

LEAF, Munro. *Wee Gillis.* 1938. Viking. 1st ed. ils Robert Lawson. F/VG. P2. $120.00

LEAF, Paul. *Comrades.* 1985. NY. NAL. 1st ed. F/F. H11. $25.00

LEAHY, John Martin. *Drome.* 1952. Fantasy. 1st ed. F/NF. M19. $75.00

LEAKEY, Richard. *Origins.* (1977). Dutton. 1st Am ed? 264p. gilt brn cloth. F/dj. B22. $6.50

LEAR, Edward. *Book of Nonsense.* 1980. Viking. Metro Mus Art. 4to. 53p. unp. F. C14. $15.00

LEAR, Edward. *Le Hibou et la Poussiquette.* 1961. Little Brn. 1st ed. ils Barbara Cooney. 31p. NF/VG clip. C14. $20.00

LEAR, Edward. *Nutcracker & the Sugar-Tongs.* 1978. Little Brn. 1st ed. unp. NF. C14. $7.00

LEAR, Peter; see Lovesey, Peter.

LEARY, Lewis. *Book-Peddling Parson.* 1984. Algonquin. 1st ed. ils. 158p. F/dj. T10. $35.00

LEARY, Lewis. *Literary Career of Nathaniel Tucker 1750-1807.* 1951. Duke. 1st ed. 108p. VG. B10. $35.00

LEASOR, James. *Green Beach.* 1975. Heinemann. 1st ed. F/F. P3. $25.00

LEASOR, James. *Jade Gate.* 1976. Heinemann. 1st ed. F/F. P3. $25.00

LEASOR, James. *Millionth Chance: Story of the R 101.* 1957. NY. ils. 244p. VG/dj. B18. $45.00

LEASOR, James. *Passport to Peril.* 1966. Heinemann. 1st ed. VG/G. P3. $20.00

LEASOR, James. *Sergeant-Major.* 1955. Harrap. 2nd. VG/G. P3. $20.00

LEASOR, James. *Tank of Serpents.* 1986. Collins. 1st ed. VG/VG. P3. $20.00

LEASOR, James. *They Don't Make Them Like That Any More.* 1970. Doubleday. 1st ed. VG/VG. P3. $18.00

LEAST HEAT MOON, William. *Blue Highways: A Journey Into America.* 1982. Boston. 1st ed. F/NF. C6. $55.00

LEATHER, Edwin. *Duveen Letter.* 1980. Macmillan. 1st ed. VG/VG. P3. $15.00

LEATHER, Edwin. *Mozard Score.* 1979. Crime Club. 1st ed. VG/VG. P3. $20.00

LEATHER & SMITH. *Panorama of Gaff Rig.* 1977. Annapolis. Naval Inst. ils. 112p. VG/dj. T7. $25.00

LEAVITT, Nancy. *Road Alphabet.* 1993. Stillwater, ME. 1/26. opens into panorama. chemise. B24. $175.00

LEBOWITZ, Fran. *Social Studies.* 1981. Random. 1st ed. F/F. B4. $35.00

LECKIE, R. *Strong Men Armed: Marines in WWII.* 1962. NY. 1st ed. VG/VG. B5. $25.00

LECOUVREUR, Frank. *From East Prussia to the Golden Gate.* 1906. NY/Los Angeles. Angelina Book Concern. 1st ed. ils. cloth. T10. $500.00

LEDERER, William J. *Sarkhan.* 1965. McGraw Hill. 1st ed. F/F. B4. $85.00

LEDFORD, Preston Lafayette. *Reminiscences of the Civil War 1861-1865.* 1909. Thomasville, NC. News Prt. 1st ed. 104p. VG/wrp/clamshell box. M8. $1,200.00

LEDYARD, Bill. *Winter in Florida.* 1869. NY. 2nd. ils/ads/railroad routes. 222p. B5. $50.00

LEE, Andrea. *Sarah Phillips.* 1984. Random. 1st ed. author's 1st book. F/F. B4. $40.00

LEE, Audrey. *Clarion People.* 1968. McGraw Hill. 1st ed. sgn. F/F. B4. $95.00

LEE, Austin. *Miss Hogg & the Squash Club Murder.* 1957. Jonathan Cape. 1st ed. VG/VG. P3. $25.00

LEE, Chang-Rae. *Native Speaker.* 1995. Riverhead. 1st ed. F/F. M23. $35.00

LEE, Fitzhugh. *Chancellorsville: Address of General Fitzhugh Lee...1879.* 1879. Richmond. GW Gary. 1st ed. 44p. VG. M8. $175.00

LEE, Fred J. *Casey Jones.* 1939. 1st ed. VG/G. S13. $35.00

LEE, Gus. *China Boy.* 1991. Dutton. ARC. 8vo. NF/prt wrp. S9. $40.00

LEE, Gypsy Rose. *G-String Murders.* 1942. Tower. 2nd. VG. P3. $10.00

LEE, Gypsy Rose. *Mother Finds a Body.* 1944. Tower. 2nd. VG. P3. $10.00

LEE, Harper. *To Kill a Mockingbird.* 1960. London. UK AP. VG+/brn wrp. S9. $450.00

LEE, Jack H. *Stampede & Tales of the Far West.* ca 1938. Greensburg. private prt. 8vo. 154p. G. P4. $25.00

LEE, Jay M. *Artilleryman.* 1920. Kansas City, MO. 1st ed. sgn pres. ils/fld maps/fld pl. G. B18. $195.00

LEE, Jennette. *Tase of Apples.* 1913. Dodd Mead. 1st ed. ils FW Taylor. F/NF. B4. $85.00

LEE, John. *Ninth Man.* 1976. Doubleday. VG/VG. P3. $15.00

LEE, Lawrence. *Cockcrow at Night: Heroic Journey & 18 Other Stories.* 1973. Boxwood. inscr. 216p. VG. B10. $45.00

LEE, Lawrence. *Mountain.* 1936. Fielding. Ivy. 1/50. inscr. VG. B10. $75.00

LEE, Lawrence. *Summer Goes On.* 1933. Scribner. 1st ed. 64p. VG/VG. B10. $75.00

LEE, Lilian. *Farewell to My Concubine.* 1993. Morrow. 1st ed. F/F. H11. $25.00

LEE, R. Brown. *Gray Ghosts of Confederacy.* 1958. Baton Rouge. 1st ed. VG/G. B5. $30.00

LEE, R.W. *Antique Fakes & Reproductions.* 1950. Northborough, MA. 2nd. VG/G. B5. $45.00

LEE, Raymond E. *London Journal of General Raymond E Lee, 1940-41.* 1971. Boston. 1st ed. 489p. map ep. VG/dj. B18. $20.00

LEE, Robert E. *Recollections & Letters of Robert E Lee.* 1926 (1924). Garden City. 471p. VG-. B10. $25.00

LEE, Ruth Webb. *Early American Pressed Glass.* 1933. photos. VG/VG. S13. $20.00

LEE, Stan. *Bring on the Bad Guys.* 1976. ils. 253p. F. M13. $15.00

LEE, Stan. *Captain America.* 1981. Marvel/Grandreams. hc. NF. P3. $10.00

LEE, Stan. *Dunn's Conundrum.* 1984. Harper Row. 1st ed. F/F. P3. $15.00

LEE, Stephen D. *Confederate Military History: South After the War...* 1976. Bl & Gray. rpt of 1899 ed. cloth. F/NF. M8. $20.00

LEE, Tanith. *Book of the Beast: Secret Books of Paradys II.* 1991. Woodstock. Overlook. 1st ed. F/F. T2. $20.00

LEE, Tanith. *Book of the Damned: Secret Books of Paradys I.* 1990. Woodstock. Overlook. 1st hc ed. F/F. T2. $25.00

LEE, Tanith. *Electric Forest.* nd. BC. VG/VG. P3. $10.00

LEE, Tanith. *Elephantasm.* 1993. Headline. 1st ed. F/F. P3. $30.00

LEE, Tanith. *Silver Metal Lover.* nd. BC. NF/NF. P3. $8.00

LEE, Tanith. *Wars of Vis.* nd. BC. NF/NF. P3. $10.00

LEE, W. Storrs. *California: Literary Chronicle.* ca 1968. Funk Wagnall. 3rd. 8vo. 537p. NF/VG. T10. $25.00

LEE, W. Storrs. *Great California Deserts.* c 1963. Putnam. 1st ed. 8vo. 306p. F/clip. T10. $25.00

LEE, Wayne C. *Bat Masterson.* 1960. Whitman. TVTI. VG. P3. $15.00

LEE, William; see Burroughs, W.S.

LEE & STEPHEN. *Dictionary of National Biography From Earlist Times...* 1964. Oxford. 22 vol. xl. VG. A4. $1,250.00

LEE & VAN HECKE. *Gangsters & Hoodlums.* nd. Castle. hc. G/G. P3. $12.00

LEE. *Concise Dictionary of National Biography From Beginnings...* nd. Oxford. 1606p. VG. A4. $125.00

LEECH, D.D.T. *List of Post Offices in the United States...* 1857. WA. John C Rives. index. G. A17. $30.00

LEEDALE, G.F. *Euglenoid Flagellates.* 1967. Prentice Hall. 8vo. 242p. ils. VG/dj. B1. $32.00

LEEK, Sybil. *Diary of a Witch.* nd. BC. VG/VG. P3. $8.00

LEEK & SUGAR. *Assassination Chain.* 1976. Corwin. VG/VG. P3. $18.00

LEEMAN, Wayne A. *Price of Middle East Oil: An Essay in Political Economy.* 1962. Cornell. 1st ed. 8vo. 274p. cloth. NF/dj. W1. $20.00

LEETE, Frederick DeLand. *Palestine: Land of the Light.* 1932. Houghton Mifflin. 1st ed. 279p. VG. W1. $12.00

LEFCOURT, Peter. *Deal.* 1991. Random. 1st ed. AN/dj. M22. $20.00

LEFEBURE, Molly. *Murder With a Difference.* 1958. Heinemann. 1st ed. VG. P3. $20.00

LEGARET, Jean. *Tightrope.* 1968. Little Brn. 1st ed. xl. dj. P3. $5.00

LEGG, Wickham. *Dictionary of National Biography 1931-1940.* 1950. Oxford. 984p. VG. A4. $95.00

LEGMAN, G. *Horn Book.* 1964. University Books. VG/VG. P3. $25.00

LEGMAN, G. *Limerick.* 1979. NY. Bell. 1/1700. F/VG. H4. $25.00

LEHANE, Brendan. *Wizards & Witches.* 1985. Time Life. 4th. hc. VG. P3. $15.00

LEHANE, Dennis. *Drink Before the War.* 1994. Harcourt Brace. 1st ed. F/F. H11/M23. $50.00

LEHANE, Ernest. *French Atlantic Affair.* 1977. Atheneum. 1st ed. F/F. P3. $15.00

LEHMANN, Arthur-Heinz. *Noble Stallion.* 1955. Holt. 1st Am ed. VG/G. O3. $25.00

LEHMANN, Henri. *Pre-Columbian Ceramics.* 1962. London. Elek. 1st ed. 128p. dj. F3. $30.00

LEHMANN, Valgene. *Atwater's Prairie Chickens.* 1941. GPO. 65p. VG/wrp. A10. $30.00

LEHRER, Jim. *Kick the Can.* 1988. Putnam. 1st ed. F/NF. M23. $20.00

LEIBER, Fritz. *Bazaar of the Bizarre.* 1978. Donald Grant. 1st ed. sgn. ils/sgn Stephan Pergrine. F/NF. T2. $45.00

LEIBER, Fritz. *Best of...* nd. BC. VG/VG. P3. $10.00

LEIBER, Fritz. *Big Time.* 1976. Severn. 1st ed. F/F. P3. $25.00

LEIBER, Fritz. *Gather, Darkness!* nd. Grosset Dunlap. VG/VG. P3. $25.00

LEIBER, Fritz. *Green Millenium.* 1977. Severn. 1st ed. NF/NF. P3. $25.00

LEIBER, Fritz. *Heroes & Horrors.* 1978. Whispers. 1st ed. pub/sgn Stuart Schiff. F/F. T2. $20.00

LEIBER, Fritz. *Knight & Knave of Swords.* 1988. Morrow. 1st ed. F/F. P3. $18.00

LEIBER, Fritz. *Night's Black Agents.* 1980. Gregg. 1st ed. sgn. VG/sans. P3. $45.00

LEIBER, Fritz. *Specter Is Haunting Texas.* nd. BC. VG/VG. P3. $8.00

LEIBOVITZ, Annie. *Photographs 1970-1990.* 1991. Harper Collins. 1st ed. 1/326. sgn. F/NF case. S9. $250.00

LEICESTER, Paul. *Federalist.* (1898). NY. 2 vol in 1. 793p. gilt brn cloth. F. H3. $125.00

LEIDER, Philip. *Stella Since 1970.* 1978. Ft Worth Art Mus. ils/pl. 136p. wrp. D2. $65.00

LEIGH, James. *Ludi Victor.* 1980. Coward. 1st ed. NF/F. H11. $15.00

LEIGH, Janet. *There Really Was a Hollywood.* 1984. Doubleday. 1st ed. sgn. F/NF. B2. $50.00

LEIGH, Robert. *Girl With the Bright Head.* 1982. Macmillan. 1st ed. VG/VG. P3. $18.00

LEIGH, Stephen. *Crystal Memory.* nd. BC. VG/VG. P3. $8.00

LEIGHLY, John. *California As an Island: An Illustrated Essay.* 1972. San Francisco. BC of CA. folio. ils/maps. M. O7. $1,750.00

LEIGHTON, Clare. *Four Hedges: A Gardners Chronicle.* 1935. Macmillan. 166p. gr cloth. F. B22. $6.00

LEINSTER, Murray. *Great Stories of SF.* 1951. Random. 1st ed. G. P3. $15.00

LEINSTER, Murry; see Jenkins, Will F.

LEIRIS, Michael. *Brisees: Broken Branches.* 1989. North Point. 1st Am ed. 266p. AN/dj. A17. $9.50

LEISER, Erwin. *Nazi Cinema.* 1975. NY. 1st Am ed. 179p. dj. A17. $15.00

LEITCH, Mary Sinton. *Lyric Virginia Today.* 1932. Dial. 251p. VG/G. B10. $25.00

LEITHAUSER, Brad. *Hence.* 1989. Knopf. 1st ed. F/F. P3. $19.00

LEITHAUSER, Joachim G. *Mappae Mundi: Die Geistige Eroberung der Welt.* 1958. Berlin. Safari. 131 maps. F/dj. O7. $65.00

LEJARD, Andre. *Art of the French Book.* nd. London. ils. VG/G. M17. $32.50

LEJEUNE, Anthony. *Strange & Private War.* 1987. Crime Club. 1st ed. VG/VG. P3. $15.00

LELAND, John Adams. *Othneil Jones.* 1956. Lippincott. 1st ed. 253p. VG/VG. B10. $12.00

LEM, Stanislaw. *Invincible.* 1973. Seabury. 1st ed. VG/VG. P3. $22.00

LEM, Stanislaw. *Memoirs of Space Traveler.* 1982. Harcourt. 1st ed. F/F. P3. $15.00

LEM, Stanislaw. *More Tales of Pirx the Pilot.* 1982. HBJ. 1st ed. F/F. P3. $15.00

LEM, Stanislaw. *Return From the Stars.* 1980. HBJ. UP. F. B35. $25.00

LEM, Stanislaw. *Return From the Stars.* 1980. HBJ. 1st ed. F/F. P3. $15.00

LEM, Stanislaw. *Tales of Pirx the Pilot.* 1979. HBJ. F/F. P3. $15.00

LEMAN, A.D. *Diseases of Swine.* 1986. Ames, IA. 6th. 8vo. 930p. cloth. F. B1. $60.00

LEMMING, David Abrams. *World of Myth.* 1990. Oxford. 1st ed. F/F. P3. $25.00

LENARD, Alexander. *Valley of the Latin Bear.* 1965. Dutton. 1st ed. 219p. dj. F3. $20.00

LENGYAL, O. *Five Chimneys.* 1947. Chicago. VG/worn. B5. $30.00

LENOIR, John Monte. *Famous Thoroughbreds I Have Known.* 1953. Borden. 1st ed. VG/G. O3. $58.00

LENSKI, Lois. *Arabella & Her Aunts.* 1932. 1st ed. VG+/worn. S13. $20.00

LENSKI, Lois. *Big Book of Mr Small.* 1985. Derrydale. 1st ed thus. VG+. C8. $50.00

LENSKI, Lois. *Chimney Corner Fairy Tales.* 1928. NY. Minton Balch. 1st ed. 183p. VG/VG. D1. $140.00

LENSKI, Lois. *Ice Cream Is Good.* 1948. Nat Dairy Council. 1st ed. F/wrp. P2. $25.00

LENSKI, Lois. *Little Train.* (1940). Oxford. 3rd. VG/G. P2. $35.00

LENSKI, Lois. *Now It's Fall.* 1948. Oxford. presumed 1st ed. gr brd. VG. M5. $40.00

LENSKI, Lois. *Read-To-Me Storybook.* 1947. Crowell. 1st or early ed. 8vo. VG+/dj. M5. $65.00

LENSKI, Lois. *Read-To-Me.* 1947. Crowell. 11th. 8vo. VG. B17. $7.50

LENSKI, Lois. *San Francisco Boy.* 1955. Lippincott. 1st ed. 8vo. VG+/G. M5. $75.00

LENSKI, Lois. *Songs of Mr Small.* 1954. Oxford. 1st ed. 4to. xl. VG. M5. $45.00

LENSKI, Lois. *Strawberry Girl.* 1945. Lippincott. 1st ed. 194p. G+. P2. $75.00

LENSKI, Lois. *Texas Tomboy.* 1950. Lippincott. 1st ed. VG/G+. P2. $75.00

LENTZ, Harold. *Jack the Giant Killer.* 1932. Bl Ribbon. 8vo. 4 popups. VG. T10. $400.00

LENTZ, Harold. *Pop-Up Mother Goose.* 1934. Bl Ribbon. 8vo. 3 double-p popups. VG. T10. $200.00

LENTZ, Harold. *Puss in Boots.* 1934. Bl Ribbon. 3 double-p popups, pict brd. F. T10. $350.00

LENTZ, Harris M. *SF Horror & Fantasy... Vol 1.* 1983. McFarland. 1st ed. F. P3. $45.00

LENZ, Sidney S. *Lenz on Bridge: Vol 2.* 1927. NY. 456p. VG. S1. $10.00

LENZEN, G. *History of Diamond Production & Diamond Trade.* 1970. Barrie Jenkins. trans from German. 230p. VG. D8. $20.00

LENZNER, Robert. *Great Getty: Life & Loves of J Paul Getty...* 1985. Crown. 1st ed. 283p. AN/dj. B22. $5.50

LEON, Donna. *Death at La Fenice.* 1992. Harper Collins. 1st ed. author's 1st book. F/F. H11. $35.00

LEON, Donna. *Death in a Strange Country.* 1993. Harper Collins. 1st ed. F/F. H11. $25.00

LEON-PORTILLA, Miguel. *Aztec Thought & Culture.* 1971. Norman, OK. 3rd. 8vo. ils/map/biblio. 237p. NF. T10. $25.00

LEONARD, Charles L. *Secret of the Spa.* nd. BC. VG/VG. P3. $10.00

LEONARD, Elmore. *Bandits.* 1987. Arbor. 1st ed. NF/NF. N4. $27.50

LEONARD, Elmore. *Bandits.* 1987. Arbor. 1st ed. VG/VG. P3. $18.00

LEONARD, Elmore. *Cat Chaser.* nd. BOMC. F/F. P3. $10.00

LEONARD, Elmore. *Cat Chaser.* 1982. Arbor. 1st ed. F/F. H11. $50.00

LEONARD, Elmore. *Dutch Treat.* Arbor. 1st ed. VG/VG. A20. $20.00

LEONARD, Elmore. *Dutch Treat.* NY. Arbor. 1st ed. NF/NF. H11. $25.00

LEONARD, Elmore. *Freaky Deaky.* 1988. Arbor/Morrow. 1st ed. F/F. M23. $20.00

LEONARD, Elmore. *Freaky Deaky.* 1988. Arbor/Morrow. 1st ed. xl. dj. P3. $8.00

LEONARD, Elmore. *Get Shorty.* 1990. Delacorte. 1st ed. F/F. H11/M22. $25.00

LEONARD, Elmore. *Glitz.* nd. Arbor. 5th. VG/VG. P3. $10.00

LEONARD, Elmore. *Glitz.* 1985. Arbor. 1st ed. NF/NF. M22. $15.00

LEONARD, Elmore. *Hombre.* 1989. Armchair Detective. 1st ed this. M/dj. A18. $20.00

LEONARD, Elmore. *Killshot.* 1989. Arbor. 1st ed. F/F. P3. $20.00

LEONARD, Elmore. *La Brava.* 1983. Arbor 1st ed. F/F. H11. $40.00

LEONARD, Elmore. *Maximum Bob.* 1991. Delacorte. 1st ed. F/F. B35. $25.00

LEONARD, Elmore. *Maximum Bob.* 1991. Delacorte. 1st ed. M/dj. N4. $30.00

LEONARD, Elmore. *Pronto.* 1993. Delacorte. 1st ed. F/F. P3. $22.00

LEONARD, Elmore. *Rum Punch.* 1992. Delacorte. UP. F. B35. $30.00

LEONARD, Elmore. *Rum Punch.* 1992. Delacorte. 1st ed. F/F. B35. $25.00

LEONARD, Elmore. *Rum Punch.* 1992. Delacorte. 1st ed. M/dj. N4. $27.50

LEONARD, Elmore. *Split Images.* 1981. Arbor. 1st ed. F/F. H11. $55.00

LEONARD, Elmore. *Split Images.* 1986. GK Hall Lg Prt. VG/VG. P3. $17.00

LEONARD, Elmore. *Stick.* 1983. Arbor. 1st ed. F/F. H11. $35.00

LEONARD, Elmore. *Touch.* 1987. Arbor. 1st ed. F/F. M22/P3. $20.00

LEONARD, Fred. *Guide to the History of Physical Education.* 1949. Phil. 3rd. 480p. VG. A13. $60.00

LEONARD, Irving. *Barque Times in Old Mexico.* 1959. Ann Arbor. 1st ed. 260p. dj. F3. $35.00

LEONARD, William Ellery. *Beowulf.* 1939 (1923). Heritage Club. ils Lynd Ward. 120p. tan textured linen. VG. T5. $45.00

LEPPER. *Bibliographical Introduction to 75 Modern American Authors.* 1976. np. 443p. NF/VG. A4. $125.00

LEPROHON, Pierre. *Michelangelo Antonioni: An Introduction.* 1963. Simon Schuster. VG. D2. $12.00

LERANGIS, Peter. *Star Trek IV: The Voyage Home.* 1986. Just For Boys BC. VG. P3. $6.00

LERMAN, Rhoda. *Call Me, Ishtar.* 1973. HRW. ARC/1st ed. inscr. author's 2nd novel. RS. F/F. B4. $65.00

LERNER, Eric. *Big Bang Never Happened.* 1991. Times Books. 2nd prt. VG/VG. K5. $18.00

LERNER, Frederik Andrew. *Modern SF & the American Literary Community.* 1985. Scarecrow. 1st ed. NF/sans. G10. $15.00

LERNER, J. *Review of Amino Acid Transport Processes...* 1978. Orono. 8vo. 234p. cloth. NF. B1. $35.00

LEROUX, Gaston. *Burgled Heart.* 1925. John Long. 1st ed. G. P3. $35.00

LEROUX, Gaston. *Man of a Hundred Faces.* 1930. MacAulay. 1st ed. VG. P3. $35.00

LEROUX, Gaston. *Mystery of the Yellow Room.* 1908. Brentano. 1st ed. VG. P3. $40.00

LEROUX, Gaston. *New Terror.* 1926. MacAulay. 1st ed. VG. P3. $35.00

LEROUX, Gaston. *Nomads of the Night.* 1925. MacAulay. VG. P3. $30.00

LEROUX, Gaston. *Phantom of the Opera.* nd. Grosset Dunlap. G. P3. $20.00

LEROUX, Gaston. *Phantom of the Opera.* 1911. Grosset Dunlap. photoplay ed. 357p. VG/dj. M20. $100.00

LEROY, L.W. *Biostratigraphy of the Maqfi Section, Egypt.* 1953. GSA Memoir #54. 73p. cloth. F. D8. $16.00

LEROY & LOW. *Graphic Problems in Petroleum Geology.* 1954. Harper. 238p. G/prt wrp. D8. $20.00

LESCROART, John T. *13th Juror.* 1994. Donald Fine. 1st ed. F/F. M22. $40.00

LESENSEN, Thomas Petigru. *Landmarks of Charlston Including Description...* 1939. Garrett Massie. 112p. map ep. xl. reading copy. B10. $15.00

LESHER, Phyllis A. *The Ah-Ness of Things! Haiku & Senryu.* 1970. Homestead, FL. Olivant. unp. VG. B10. $12.00

LESLEY, Craig. *River Song.* 1989. Houghton Mifflin. 1st ed. F/F. A18. $35.00

LESLEY, Craig. *River Song.* 1989. Houghton Mifflin. 1st ed. sgn. M/dj. A18. $50.00

LESLIE, Lawrence J. *Camp Fire & Trail: Lost in the Great Dismal Swamp (#4).* 1913. NY Book Co. lists 6 titles. 184p. VG/dj. M20. $10.00

LESLIE, Lawrence J. *Rivals of the Trail.* 1913. NY Book Co. ils. G+. P12. $8.00

LESLIE, Madelaine. *Minnie's Pet Horse.* 1864. Lee Shepard. inscr. gilt gr cloth. F. B4. $125.00

LESLIE, Madelaine. *Minnie's Pet Monkey.* 1864. Lee Shepard. inscr. gr cloth. NF. B4. $125.00

LESLIE, Vernon. *Faces in Clay.* 1973. Middleton, NY. 1st ed. sgn. 67 pl. map ep. gr brd. F/VG. B11. $60.00

LESQUEREUX, Leo. *Contributions to the Fossil Flora of Western Territories...* 1878. GPO. Part II. 366p. VG. A10. $125.00

LESSER, Friedrich C. *Theologie des Insectes ou Demonstration des Perfections...* 1742. La Haye. 2 vol. 2 pl. contemporary sheep. B14. $450.00

LESSER, Maurice A. *Common Sense in Medicine.* 1976. Boston. inscr. red cloth. F. B14. $35.00

LESSER, Milton. *Man With No Shadow.* 1974. Prentice Hall. 1st ed. VG/VG. P3. $15.00

LESSER, Milton. *Search for Bruno Heidler.* 1967. Boardman. 1st ed. NF/NF. P3. $20.00

LESSER, Milton. *Stadium Beyond the Stars.* 1960. Winston. 1st ed. xl. VG. P3. $12.00

LESSER, Milton. *Summit.* 1970. Geis. 1st ed. sgn. VG/VG. P3. $30.00

LESSER, Milton. *Translation.* 1976. Prentice Hall. 1st ed. VG/VG. P3. $20.00

LESSER, Milton. *1956.* 1981. Arbor. 1st ed. VG/VG. P3. $15.00

LESSING, Doris. *Golden Notebook.* 1962. Simon Schuster. 1st Am ed. F/NF. B2. $65.00

LESSING, Doris. *Good Terrorist.* 1985. Jonathan Cape. 1st ed. NF/NF. P3. $20.00

LESSING, Doris. *Good Terrorist.* 1985. London. 1/250. sgn. F/F tissue. C6. $95.00

LESSING, Doris. *Grass Is Singing.* 1950. ARC. 1st Am ed. author's 1st book. NF. C2. $100.00

LESSING, Doris. *Making of the Representative...* 1982. Jonathan Cape. 1st ed. VG/VG. P3. $25.00

LESSING, Doris. *Sentimental Agents in Volyen Empire.* 1983. Jonathan Cape. 1st ed. VG/VG. P3. $25.00

LESSING, Doris. *Sirian Experiments.* 1981. Jonathan Cape. 1st ed. F/F. P3. $25.00

LESSING, Doris. *Summer Before Dark.* nd. BC. VG/VG. P3. $8.00

LESSTRANG, Jacques. *Great Lakes St Lawrence System.* 1984. Harbor House. G/wrp. A16. $12.50

LESTER & SLEEMAN. *America's Cup, 1851-1987.* 1986. Sydney. Lester-Townsend. ils. 239p. Vg/dj. T7. $50.00

LETHEM, Jonathan. *Gun With Occasional Music.* 1994. Harcourt Brace. 1st ed. F/F. M23. $50.00

LEUBA, James H. *Psychological Study of Religion: Its Origin, Function...* 1912. Macmillan. 371p. panelled bl cloth. VG. G1. $35.00

LEUCI, Bob. *Odessa Beach.* 1985. Freundlich. 1st ed. F/F. H11. $20.00

LEVACHEZ, Charles Francois. *Bound-Up Collecton of 58 Engraved Broadsides.* ca 1795-1800. folio. teg. full tan morocco. K1. $750.00

LEVENE, Malcolm. *Carder's Paradise.* 1969. Walker. 1st ed. F/F. P3. $15.00

LEVENSON, Sam. *In One Era & Out the Other.* 1973. Simon Schuster. VG/G+. P12. $5.00

LEVERENZ & LEVINE. *Mindful Pleasures. Essays on Thomas Pynchon.* 1976. Little Brn. 1st ed. sgn by 5 contributors. F/F. B2. $75.00

LEVI, Peter. *Grave Witness.* 1985. St Martin. 1st ed. F/F. P3. $13.00

LEVI, Primo. *Moments of Reprieve.* 1985. Summit. 1st ed. F/F. B35. $16.00

LEVI, Primo. *Truce: Survivor's Journey Home From Auschwitz.* 1965. London. Bodley Head. 1st ed. F/dj. B14. $75.00

LEVI & REGGE. *Dialogo.* 1989. Princeton. 1st ed. F/clip. B35. $20.00

LEVIN, Betty. *Sword of Culann.* 1973. Macmillan. 1st ed. VG/VG. P3. $18.00

LEVIN, Ira. *Boys From Brazil.* 1976. Random. 1st ed. NF/NF. M22. $50.00

LEVIN, Ira. *This Perfect Day.* 1970. Random. 1st ed. F/NF. H11. $40.00

LEVINE, Isaac Don. *Mitchell.* 1943. NY. 1st ed. ils. 420p. F/dj. B18. $20.00

LEVINE, Phil. *Walk With Thomas Jefferson.* 1988. NY. 1st ed. sgn. NF/dj. A15. $60.00

LEVINE, Philip. *Simple Truth.* 1994. Knopf. 1st ed. F/F. M23. $30.00

LEVINE. *Spanish Women Writers, a Bio-Bibliographical Source Book.* 1993. 596p. F. A4. $95.00

LEVINREW, Will. *For Sale — Murder.* 1932. Mystery League. 1st ed. VG. P3. $20.00

LEVINREW, Will. *Murder From the Grave.* 1932. Tudor. VG. P3. $20.00

LEVINSON, Saul. *Red Hot Murder.* 1949. Phoenix. 1st ed. hc. VG. P3. $15.00

LEVITAN. *Collection of References Pertaining to Miniature Books.* 1985. np. 1/500. 459 references. F. A4. $85.00

LEVITT, I.M. *Space Traveler's Guide to Mars.* 1958 (1956). Holt. 2nd. VG/dj. K5. $14.00

LEVITT, R. *World of Tennessee Williams.* 1978. NY. 1st ed. VG/G. B5. $35.00

LEVORSEN, A. *Geology of Petroleum.* 1967. Freeman. 2nd. 724p. F/dj. D8. $25.00

LEVOY, Myron. *Penny Tunes & Princesses.* 1972. Harper Row. 1st ed. ils Ezra Jack Keats. pict brd/cloth spine. NF/VG. T5. $35.00

LEVY, David. *Clyde Tombaugh: Discoverer of Planet Pluto.* 1991. Tucson. 8vo. 211p. sc. VG. K5. $14.00

LEVY, Elizabeth. *Dracula Is a Pain in the Neck.* 1983. Weekly Reader. VG. P3. $8.00

LEVY, J.M. *Experiments on Attention & Memory...* 1916. Berkeley. prt gray wrp. G1. $37.50

LEVY, Lewis. *Pinochle Primer.* 1912. NY. sm format. 24p. VG/wrp. S1. $5.00

LEVY, Sara G. *Mother Goose Rhymes for Jewish Children.* 1945. Bloch. 1st ed. 4to. ils Jessie B Robinson. VG. M5. $75.00

LEWELLEN, T.C. *Billiken Courier.* 1968. Random. 2nd. F/F. P3. $8.00

LEWES, George Henry. *Studies in Animal Life.* 1860. Harper. 1st Am ed. 12mo. 146p. G. G1. $45.00

LEWIN, Kurt. *Die Entwicklung der Experimentellen Willenpsychologie...* 1929. Leipzig. Hirzel. 8vo. 28p. prt gray wrp. G1. $40.00

LEWIN, Michael Z. *Called by a Panther.* 1991. Mysterious. F/F. P3. $18.00

LEWIN, Michael Z. *Hard Line.* nd. BC. VG/VG. P3. $8.00

LEWIN, Michael Z. *Missing Woman.* 1981. Knopf. 1st ed. VG/VG. P3. $15.00

LEWIN, Michael Z. *Silent Salesman.* nd. BC. VG/VG. P3. $8.00

LEWINS, Robert. *Life & Mind on the Basis of Modern Medicine.* 1877. London. 1st ed. 66p. VG. A13. $75.00

LEWIS, A. *Raider's Dawn & Other Poems.* 1942. NY. 1st Am ed. author's 1st book. F/F. C2. $50.00

LEWIS, Alfred Allen. *Man of the World: Herbert Bayard Swope.* 1978. Bobbs Merrill. 1st ed. 307p. NF/dj. B22. $5.50

LEWIS, Arthur H. *Children's Party.* 1972. Trident. 1st ed. VG/VG. P3. $25.00

LEWIS, Arthur H. *Copper Beeches.* 1971. Trident. 1st ed. xl. dj. P3. $20.00

LEWIS, Bernard. *Arabs in History.* 1964. Hutchinson. 2nd. 4 maps. 200p. VG. W1. $16.00

LEWIS, C.S. *Christian Behavior: A Further Series of Broadcast Talks.* 1943. Geoffrey Bles. 1st ed. F/VG. A18. $50.00

LEWIS, C.S. *English Literature in the 16th Century Excluding Drama.* 1954. Oxford. 1st ed. F/chip. A18. $75.00

LEWIS, C.S. *English Literature in the 16th Century Excluding Drama.* 1965. Oxford. Clarendon. later prt. 8vo. xl. F/dj. T10. $25.00

LEWIS, C.S. *Experiment in Criticism.* 1961. Cambridge. 1st ed. 8vo. F/dj. T10. $75.00

LEWIS, C.S. *Four Loves.* 1960. Harcourt. 1st Am ed. RS. F/NF. B2. $45.00

LEWIS, C.S. *Hideous Strength.* 1945. Bodley Head. 1st ed. VG. P3. $50.00

LEWIS, C.S. *Horse & His Boy.* 1954. Macmillan. 12th. 8vo. 191p. orange cloth. VG/VG. T5. $25.00

LEWIS, C.S. *Letters to an American Lady.* 1967. Arbor/Morrow. 1st ed. F/F. T2. $60.00

LEWIS, C.S. *Letters to an American Lady.* 1967. Eerdmans. 1st Am ed. F/clip. A18. $35.00

LEWIS, C.S. *Letters to Malcolm: Chiefly on Prayer.* 1964. Bles. 1st ed. F/clip. A18. $35.00

LEWIS, C.S. *Lion, Witch & the Wardrobe.* 1983. Macmillan. 1st ed. 8vo. VG/VG. B17. $20.00

LEWIS, C.S. *Prince Caspian: Return to Narnia.* 1951. Bles. 1st ed. ils Pauline Baynes. VG. A18. $150.00

LEWIS, C.S. *Prince Caspian: Return to Narnia.* 1960 (1951). London. Bles. 3rd. ils Pauline Baynes. 195p. bl brd. VG/VG. T5. $30.00

LEWIS, C.S. *Problem of Pain.* 1945. NY. 1st Am ed. F/VG. N3. $10.00

LEWIS, C.S. *Reflections on the Psalms.* 1958. London. Bles. 1st ed. 8vo. 141p. F/dj. A18/T10. $65.00

LEWIS, C.S. *Screwtape Letters.* 1945. Saunders. Canadian 1st ed. VG. P3. $18.00

LEWIS, C.S. *Surprised by Joy: Shape of My Early Life.* 1955. Bles. 1st ed. F/clip. A18. $125.00

LEWIS, C.S. *Til We Have Faces.* 1957. Harcourt Brace. 1st Am ed. 8vo. 313p. F/NF. T10. $200.00

LEWIS, Cecil Day. *Beechen Virgil & Other Poems.* 1925. London. 1st ed. author's 1st book. 32p. F/stiff wrp. C6. $350.00

LEWIS, Charles. *Cain Factor.* 1975. Harwood Smart. 1st ed. F/F. P3. $13.00

LEWIS, Clara J. *I Love Spring.* 1965. Little Brn. 1st ed. 8vo. 28p. VG. C14. $5.00

LEWIS, Deborah; see Grant, Charles L.

LEWIS, Dio. *Talks About People's Stomachs.* 1870. Boston. Fields Osgood. cloth. G. B14. $75.00

LEWIS, Florence Jay. *Climax.* 1944. Books Inc. VG. P3. $15.00

LEWIS, G.G. *Practical Book of Oriental Rugs.* 1920. Phil. 6th. fld map/124 pl. 375p. VG. B5. $95.00

LEWIS, George. *Luminous Night.* 1970. Dial. 263p. VG/VG. B10. $10.00

LEWIS, Janet. *Earth-Bound, 1924-1944.* 1946. Aurora, NY. Wells College. 1st ed. 1/300. w/prospectus. F. B24. $200.00

LEWIS, Janet. *Wife of Martin Guerre.* 1941. San Francisco. Colt. 1st trade ed. NF/VG. B4. $250.00

LEWIS, Lloyd. *Sherman, Fighting Prophet.* 1932. NY. 1st ed. VG/G. B5. $32.50

LEWIS, Oscar. *Death in the Sanchez Family.* 1969. NY. Random. 1st ed. 8vo. F/NF. T10. $35.00

LEWIS, Oscar. *Hearn & His Biographers: Record of Literary Controversy.* 1930. Grabhorn. 1/350. NF. w/facsimile letters. M19. $125.00

LEWIS, Oscar. *Lost Years: Biographical Fantasy.* 1951. Knopf. 1st ed. 12mo. 121p. F/NF. T10. $45.00

LEWIS, Oscar. *Sutter's Fort: Gateway to the Golden Fields.* 1966. Prentice Hall. 1st ed. 224p. F/F. T10. $35.00

LEWIS, R.S. *Elements of Mining.* 1941. John Wiley. 2nd. 579p. G. D8. $18.00

LEWIS, Richard. *There Are Two Lives: Poems of Children in Japan.* 1970. Simon Schuster. 1st ed. 8vo. 96p. F/NF clip. C14. $12.00

LEWIS, Roy Harley. *Fine Bookbinding in the Twentieth Century.* 1984. NY. Arco. 1st ed. ils. 151p. NF/dj. T10. $35.00

LEWIS, Roy. *Error of Judgment.* 1971. Collins Crime Club. 1st ed. NF/NF. P3. $20.00

LEWIS, Roy. *Once Dying, Twice Dead.* 1984. St Martin. 1st ed. VG/VG. P3. $15.00

LEWIS, Roy. *Premium on Death.* 1987. Detective BC. VG. P3. $8.00

LEWIS, Roy. *Salamander Chill.* 1988. Collins Crime Club. 1st ed. NF/NF. P3. $18.00

LEWIS, Roy. *Uncertain Sound.* 1987. St Martin. 1st ed. F/F. P3. $15.00

LEWIS, Sinclair. *Ann Vickers.* 1933. NY. 1st ed. VG/VG. B5. $65.00

LEWIS, Sinclair. *Arrowsmith.* 1925. Harcourt Brace. sgn. 448p. VG. M20. $82.00

LEWIS, Sinclair. *Babbitt* (#22). 1946. Bantam. 1st pb ed. 408p. VG/pict wrp/dj. M20. $40.00

LEWIS, Sinclair. *Babbitt.* 1922. Harcourt Brace. 1st ed. NF/G. M19. $250.00

LEWIS, Sinclair. *Babbitt.* 1922. McLeod. Canadian 1st ed. VG. P3. $30.00

LEWIS, Sinclair. *Bethel Merriday.* 1940. NY. 1st ed. VG/VG. B5. $45.00

LEWIS, Sinclair. *Elmer Gantry.* 1927. Harcourt Brace. 1st ed/1st prt. 432p. VG/dj. M20. $155.00

LEWIS, Sinclair. *It Can't Happen Here.* nd. Sun Dial. VG. P3. $25.00

LEWIS, Sinclair. *Main Street.* 1937. Chicago. Lakeside/LEC. 1/1500. ils/sgn Grant Wood. 367p. F/case. B24. $600.00

LEWIS, Sinclair. *Main Street.* 1937. LEC. 1/1500. ils/sgn Grant Wood. 367p. NF. C2. $375.00

LEWIS, Sinclair. *Main Street.* 1966. Harbrace Modern Classic. hc. xl. VG. P3. $8.00

LEWIS, Sinclair. *Our Mr Wrenn: The Romantic Adventures of a Gentle Man.* 1914. Harper. ARC/1st ed. NF. B24. $250.00

LEWIS, Sinclair. *World So Wide.* 1951. Random. 1st ed. NF/NF. B35. $30.00

LEWIS, Thomas. *Clinical Electrocardiography.* 1913. London. ils. 120p. gr cloth. G. B14. $175.00

LEWIS, Thomas. *Rules & Direction for Employment of Injections...* 1856. Boston. 54p. VG/prt wrp. B14. $85.00

LEWIS, Wilmarth. *Collector's Progress.* 1951. np. ils Wilmarth Lewis. 266p. NF/VG. A4. $35.00

LEWIS, Wyndham. *Apes of God.* 1930. London. Arthur. 1/750. VG/VG. M19. $650.00

LEWIS, Wyndham. *Filibusters in Barbary.* 1932. Nat Travel Club. 1st ed. pl/maps. 308p. cloth. VG. W1. $16.00

LEWIS, Wyndham. *Moliere the Comic Mask.* 1959. 1st ed. VG/VG. S13. $12.00

LEWIS, Wyndham. *Sea-Mists of the Winter.* 1981. Blk Sparrow. 1st ed. chapbook. F. B35. $6.00

LEWIS & LEWIS. *Laugharne & Dylan Thomas.* 1967. London. 1st ed. F/VG+. N3. $15.00

LEWIS & WILLIAMS. *Arthurian Torso.* 1948. London. Oxford. 1st ed. 8vo. 199p. F/dj. T10. $400.00

LEWIS. *Heath Robinson: Artist & Comic Genius.* 1973. London. ils. 223p. F/F. A4. $125.00

LEWIS. *Storied New Mexico: An Annotated Bibliography...* 1991. np. 238p. F/F. A4. $45.00

LEWISOHN, L. *Case of Mr Crump.* 1926. Paris. 1st ed. 1/500 for US. sgn. leather/brd. NF. A15. $100.00

LEWITT, Shariann N. *Memento Mori.* 1995. Tor. 1st ed. F/F. P3. $22.00

LEY, James. *Reports of Divers Resolutions in Law...* 1659. London. contemporary calf. M11. $650.00

LEY, Willy. *Worlds of the Past.* 1971. Golden. VG. P3. $15.00

LEYBOURNE. *Collector's Guide to Old Fruit Jars.* 1993. 7th. sgn. 302p. NF/wrp. A4. $45.00

LEYLAND & SCOTT-CHARD. *Smugglers of the Skies.* 1958. Edmund Ward. hc. VG/G. P3. $15.00

LEYNER, Mark. *Et Tu, Babe.* 1992. Harmony. 1st ed. rem mk. F/F. B35. $22.00

LI, H.-L. *Trees of Pennsylvania.* 1972. Phil. 8vo. ils. 276p. F/wrp. B1. $20.00

LIAUTARD, A. *Animal Castration.* 1885. NY. Jenkins. 1st ed. VG. O3. $95.00

LIBBY, Bill. *Heroes of the Hot Corner.* 1972. Watts. 1st ed. sgn. VG+/VG. P8. $75.00

LIBBY, Bill. *Vida, His Own Story.* 1972. Prentice Hall. 1st ed. VG/VG. P8. $75.00

LICHTENBERG, Jacqueline. *Dushau.* 1985. Warner. UP. NF/wrp. G10. $10.00

LICHTENBERG, Jacqueline. *Rensime.* 1984. Doubleday. 1st ed. VG/VG. P3. $18.00

LICHTENBERG & LORRAH. *Channel's Destiny.* 1982. Doubleday. 1st ed. sgn. F/F. G10. $25.00

LIDA. *La Ferme du Pere Castor.* 1937. Pere Castor. ils Helene Overtik. G+. P2. $40.00

LIDA. *Plouf the Little Wild Duck.* 1936. Harper. ils Feodor Rojankovsky. VG/G. P2. $35.00

LIDDELL, Viola Goode. *With a Southern Accent.* 1948. OK U. 1st ed. inscr. map ep. 261p. VG/VG-. B10. $25.00

LIEBER, Francis. *Character of the Gentleman.* 1864. Lippincott. 3rd. brn cloth. M11. $225.00

LIEBERMAN, Herbert. *Brilliant Kids.* 1975. Macmillan. 1st ed. NF/NF. H11. $30.00

LIEBERMAN, Herbert. *City of the Dead.* 1976. Simon Schuster. 1st ed. F/F. P3. $16.00

LIEBERMAN, Herbert. *Climate of Hell.* 1978. Simon Schuster. 1st ed. rem mk. NF/NF. H11. $20.00

LIEBERMAN, Herbert. *Night Call From a Distant Time Zone.* 1982. Crown. 1st ed. F/F. H11. $35.00

LIEBERMAN, Herbert. *Night Call From a Distant Time Zone.* 1982. Crown. 1st ed. VG/VG. P3. $25.00

LIEBERMAN, Herbert. *Sandman, Sleep.* 1993. NY. 1st ed. F/F. H11. $20.00

LIEBLING, A.J. *Honest Rainmaker.* 1953. Garden City. 1st ed. VG/G. B5. $35.00

LIEBLING, A.J. *Wayward Pressman.* 1947. NY. 1st ed. VG/G. B5. $40.00

LIEF, Alfred. *Firestone Story.* 1951. NY. ils. teg. 437p. leather. VG/case. B18. $20.00

LIEF, Alfred. *It Floats (Proctor & Gamble).* 1958. NY. 1st ed. VG/VG. B5. $30.00

LIFTON, Robert Jay. *Nazi Doctors: Medical Killing & Psychology of Genocide.* 1986. NY. Basic. 8vo. 561p. VG/wrp. A17. $15.00

LIGGETT, Winifield. *Easy Road to Contract Bridge.* 1932. Cleveland. 189p. VG. S1. $20.00

LIGHTFOOT, Beryl H. *Jolly Jack Horner.* 1916. Whitman. ils Eliz Rosenkrans. 64p. lacks backstrip o/w G. A17. $15.00

LIGHTMAN, Alan. *Einstein's Dreams.* 1993. Pantheon. 1st ed. sgn. F/F. H11. $65.00

LIGHTNER, A.M. *Space Olympics.* 1967. Norton. 1st ed. VG. P3. $15.00

LIGHTNER, A.M. *Space Plague.* 1966. Norton. 1st/lib ed. F/VG+ clip. G10. $20.00

LIGOTTI, Thomas. *Grimscribe.* 1991. Carroll Graf. 1st Am ed. F/F. G10. $15.00

LIGOTTI, Thomas. *Noctuary.* 1994. Carroll Graf. 1st Am ed. F/F. G10. $20.00

LIGOTTI, Thomas. *Songs of a Dead Dreamer.* 1990. Carroll Graf. preceded by ltd ed. F/F. R10. $20.00

LILJENCRANTZ, Ottilie A. *Thrall of Leif the Lucky.* 1902. Chicago. 1st ed. ils Kinneys. 354p. gilt cloth. G. A17. $7.00

LILLARD, Richard. *Desert Challenge.* 1942. Knopf. 1st ed. 8vo. fld map. 388p. rpl ffe. VG. T10. $75.00

LINAKIS, Steven. *Killing Ground.* 1970. McKay. 1st ed. VG/VG. P3. $20.00 ·

LINAWEAVER, Brad. *Moon of Ice.* 1988. Arbor/Morrow. 1st ed. rem mk. F/NF. G10. $10.00

LINCOLN, Abraham. *Literary Works of Abraham Lincoln.* 1942. LEC. 1/1500. ils/sgn John Steuart Curry. 294p. F/NF case. C2. $150.00

LINCOLN, Joseph. *Cape Cod Ballads.* 1902. Trenton, NJ. Brandt. 1st ed. author's 1st book. gilt yel cloth. F. B24. $135.00

LINCOLN, Joseph. *Cape Cod Ballads.* 1902. Trenton. 1st ed. VG. B5. $85.00

LINCOLN, Joseph. *Head Tide.* 1932. Appleton. 1st ed. 8vo. F/NF. T10. $50.00

LINCOLN, Joseph. *New Hope.* 1941. NY. 1st ed. VG/VG. B5. $25.00

LINCOLN, Joseph. *Our Village.* 1909. NY. 1st ed. VG. B5. $85.00

LINCOLN, Joseph. *Out of the Fog.* 1940. NY. 1st ed. sgn. VG/VG. B5. $50.00

LINDBERGH, Anne Morrow. *Bring Me a Unicorn: Diaries & Letters, 1922-1928.* 1972. HBJ. 1st ed. F/F. B35. $30.00

LINDBERGH, Anne Morrow. *Earth Shine.* 1969. Harcourt Brace. 1st ed. F/F clip. B35. $35.00

LINDBERGH, Anne Morrow. *Gifts From the Sea.* 1955. Pantheon. 1st ed. F/NF case. B35. $50.00

LINDBERGH, Anne Morrow. *Hour of Gold, Hour of Lead: Diaries & Letters, 1929-1932.* 1973. HBJ. 1st ed. F/F. B35. $30.00

LINDBERGH, Charles. *We.* 1927. Putnam. 1st ed. NF. M19. $75.00

LINDBURG, D.G. *Macaques.* 1980. Van Nostrand. 8vo. 384p. F/F. B1. $25.00

LINDGREN, Astrid. *Brothers Lionheart.* 1984. Hodder Stoughton. 4th ed. NF. P3. $15.00

LINDGREN, Astrid. *Six Bullerby Children.* 1963. London. Methuen. 1st ed. 12mo. 92p. G+/G+. T5. $20.00

LINDHORST, Will L. *Tricks & Magic by the Famous Magician Will L Lindhorst.* 1934. Reilly Lee. 12mo. VG/dj. B17. $15.00

LINDMAN, M. *Flicka, Ricka, Dicka & the Girl Next Door.* 1945 (1940). Whitman. 6th. ils Maj Lindman. lib bdg. VG. D1. $85.00

LINDMAN, M. *Snipp, Snapp, Snurr & the Gingerbread.* 1932. Chicago. Whitman. 1st ed. 4to. VG/torn. D1. $130.00

LINDMAN, M. *Snipp, Snapp, Snurr & the Reindeer.* 1957. Whitman. ils. unp. gr cloth. xl. G+. T5. $25.00

LINDNER, Gustav Adolf. *Manual of Empirical Psychology.* 1889. Boston. Heath. 1st Eng-language ed. 8vo. 274p. russet cloth. VG. G1. $65.00

LINDNER, Leslie. *Journal of Beatrix Potter.* 1966. London. Warne. photos. 448p. gilt gr cloth. VG/VG. D1. $60.00

LINDQUIST, Jennie D. *Crystal Tree.* 1966. Harper Row. ils Mary Chalmers. 8vo. 297p. xl. G+. T5. $22.00

LINDQUIST, Jennie D. *Little Silver House.* 1959. Harper. ils Garth Williams. 213p. gr cloth. VG/G. T5. $22.00

LINDSAY, David M. *Campfire Reminiscences. Tales of Hunting & Fishing...* 1912. Boston. 1st ed. ils. 233p. VG. P3. $75.00

LINDSAY, James H. *Greenhorn in Europe.* 1929. Dorrance. 125p. VG/G. B10. $10.00

LINDSAY, Maud. *Little Missy.* 1922. Lothrop. 1st ed. ils Florence Young. VG. M5. $75.00

LINDSAY, Maud. *More Mother Stories.* 1922 (1905). Milton Bradley. 8vo. ils FC Sanborn/Fanny Railton. G. M5. $22.00

LINDSAY, Vachel. *Johnny Appleseed.* 1960. Macmillan. 16th. ils George Richards. VG/VG. B17. $7.50

LINDSAY, Vachel. *Litany of Washington Street.* 1929. NY. 1st ed. VG/G. B5. $30.00

LINDSAY, W. Lauder. *Mind in the Lower Animals in Health & Disease.* 1880. Appleton. 2 vol. 1st Am ed. 543p. brn cloth. G1. $100.00

LINDSAY & NEU. *French Political Pamphlets 1547-1648.* 1969. np. describes 6742 pamphlets. 522p. F/F. A4. $65.00

LINDSEY, David L. *Cold Mind.* 1983. Harper Row. 1st ed. F/NF. H11. $35.00

LINDSEY, David L. *Heat From Another Sun.* 1984. Harper Row. 1st ed. F/F. N4. $30.00

LINDSEY, David L. *In the Lake of the Moon.* nd. Atheneum. 3rd ed. VG/VG. P3. $15.00

LINDSEY, Maud. *Story-Teller.* 1915. Lee Shepard. 1st ed. ils Florence Lily Young. 117p. VG. P2. $45.00

LINDSEY, Robert. *Gathering of Saints.* 1988. Simon Schuster. 1st ed. F/F. M23. $20.00

LINEBARGER, Paul. *Instrumentality of Mankind.* 1989. London. Gollancz. 1st hc ed. F/F. T2. $25.00

LINEBARGER, Paul. *Norstrilia.* 1989. London. Gollancz. 1st hc ed. F/F. T2. $30.00

LINEBARGER, Paul. *Quest of the Three Worlds.* 1989. London. Gollancz. 1st hc ed. F/F. T2. $25.00

LINEBARGER, Paul. *Rediscovery of Man.* 1988. London. Gollancz. 1st Eng hc ed. F/F. T2. $25.00

LINEN, James. *Poetical & Prose Writings.* 1865. NY. Widdleton. 1st ed. 8vo. 423p. ribbon cloth. VG. T10. $75.00

LININGTON, Elizabeth. *Anglophile.* nd. BC. F/F. P3. $8.00

LININGTON, Elizabeth. *Consequence of Crime.* nd. BC. VG/VG. P3. $8.00

LININGTON, Elizabeth. *Date With Death.* 1966. Harper Row. 1st ed. xl. dj. P3. $8.00

LININGTON, Elizabeth. *Greenmask!* nd. BC. VG/VG. P3. $8.00

LININGTON, Elizabeth. *No Evil Angel.* nd. BC. VG/VG. P3. $10.00

LININGTON, Elizabeth. *Practice To Deceive.* 1971. Harper Row. 1st ed. VG/VG. P3. $20.00

LININGTON, Elizabeth. *Proud Man.* 1955. Viking. 1st ed. VG/torn. P3. $30.00

LININGTON, Elizabeth. *Strange Felony.* 1987. Doubleday Lg Prt. 1st ed. VG/VG. P3. $17.00

LINK, P.K. *Basic Petroleum Geology.* 1987. OGCI Pub. 493 ils. 425p. F/dj. D8. $30.00

LINKLATER, Eric. *Private Angelo.* 1957. London. McCorquodale. 1/2000. 12mo. VG. A17. $9.50

LINKLATER, Eric. *Voyage of the Challenger.* 1972. Doubleday. ils/32 pl. 288p. T7. $25.00

LINZEE, David. *Belgravia.* 1979. Seaview. 1st ed. VG/VG. P3. $18.00

LIPMAN, Michael. *Chatterlings in Wordland.* 1935 (1928). Wise Parslow. revised. 4to. 112p. VG. T5. $35.00

LIPMAN. *American Primitive Painting.* 1942. Oxford. NF/G. D2. $50.00

LIPPINCOTT, Bertram. *Indians, Privateers & High Society.* 1961. Lippincott. 1st ed. inscr. 301p. G/G. B11. $35.00

LIPPINCOTT, David. *Salt Mine.* 1979. Viking. 1st ed. VG/VG. P3. $15.00

LIPPINCOTT, David. *Savage Ransom.* 1978. Rawson Assoc. 1st ed. VG/VG. P3. $20.00

LIPPINCOTT, David. *Voice of Armageddon.* 1974. Putnam. 1st ed. VG/VG. P3. $13.00

LIPPINCOTT, Joseph W. *Chiseltooth the Beaver.* 1936. London. Harrap. 1st ed. ils Ernest Aris. 159p. VG. A17. $10.00

LIPPINCOTT, Norman. *Murder at Glen Athol.* 1935. Canada. Doubleday Doran. VG. P3. $20.00

LIPPS, Theodor. *Das Selbstbewusstsein...* 1901. Wiesbaden. Bergmann. 42p. contemporary gr cloth. G1. $40.00

LIPTON, Lawrence. *Holy Barbarians.* 1959. Messner. 1st ed. F/NF. B2. $50.00

LISH, Gordan. *Dear Mr Capote.* 1983. HRW. 1st ed. author's 1st novel. F/F. B35. $30.00

LISH, Gordan. *Mourner at the Door.* 1988. Viking. 1st ed. F/F. B35. $25.00

LISS, Howard. *Willie Mays Album.* 1966. Hawthorn. 1st ed. VG+. P8. $75.00

LISSNER, Ivar. *Man, God & Magic.* 1961. Putnam. 1st ed. VG. P3. $25.00

LISTER, Joseph. *Third Huxley Lecture.* 1907. London. 1st ed. 58p. VG. A13. $80.00

LISTER, Raymond. *Craftsman in Metal.* 1968. Barnes. 1st Am ed. 208p. VG+. M20. $15.00

LISTER & LISTER. *In Search of Maya Glyphs.* 1970. NM U. 1st ed. 170p. dj. F3. $45.00

LITCHFIELD, Edward H. *Governing Postwar Germany.* 1972. Kennikat. 661p. F. A17. $17.50

LITTAUER, Vladimir. *Be a Better Horseman.* 1941. Derrydale. ltd ed. 1/1500. VG. O3. $58.00

LITTAUER, Vladimir. *Horseman's Progress.* 1962. Princeton. Van Nostrand. 1st ed. VG/G. O3. $45.00

LITTAUER, Vladimir. *Modern Horsemanship for Beginners.* 1946. Garden City. rpt. VG/G. O3. $18.00

LITTAUER, Vladimir. *Riding Forward.* 1934. Morrow. 1/350. sgn. VG. O3. $48.00

LITTAUER, Vladimir. *Schooling Your Horse.* 1966. Princeton. Van Nostrand. VG/G. O3. $30.00

LITTEL & ROBINS. *Images & Realities.* 1971. Praeger. F/VG. D2. $55.00

LITTELL, Robert. *Debriefing.* 1979. Harper Row. 1st ed. VG/VG. P3. $20.00

LITTELL, Robert. *Defection of AJ Lewinter.* 1973. Houghton Mifflin. 1st ed. author's 1st novel. F/NF. H11. $35.00

LITTELL, Robert. *Defection of AJ Lewinter.* 1973. Houghton Mifflin. 1st ed. VG/VG. P3. $30.00

LITTLE, Frances. *House of the Misty Star.* 1915. McClelland Goodchild. VG. P3. $20.00

LITTLE, George. *American Cruiser's Own Book.* 1846. NY. Marsh. 11 engravings. 384p. VG. T7. $70.00

LITTLE, Tom. *Egypt.* 1958. London. Benn. 1st ed. fld map. 334p. VG/torn. W1. $18.00

LITTLE & LITTLE. *Black Shrouds.* 1942. Triangle. hc. VG. P3. $15.00

LITTLE & WADSWORTH. *Common Trees of Puerto Rico & the Virgin Islands.* 1964. Washington. USDA. lg 8vo. maps. cloth. VG. B1. $68.00

LITTLE. *Abby Aldrich Rockefeller Folk Art Collection.* 1957. NF/case. D2. $125.00

LITTLEFIELD, Bill. *Baseball Days.* 1993. Little Brn. 1st ed. AN/dj. P8. $12.50

LITTLEHOLES, L. *Pablo Casals: A Life.* 1948. NY. 1st revised ed. VG/VG. B5. $22.50

LITTLETON, Thomas. *Littleton's Tenures in English, Lately Perused...* 1612. London. Companie of Stationers. contemporary calf. M11. $650.00

LITVINOV, Ivy. *His Master's Voice.* 1973. Gollancz. xl. dj. P3. $5.00

LITWHILER, Danny. *Baseball Coach's Guide to Drills & Skills.* 1963. Prentice Hall. 1st ed. VG+/G+. P8. $20.00

LIU. *Americans & Chinese: Historical Essay & Bibliography.* 1963. Harvard. 223p. VG/VG. A4. $45.00

LIVELY, Penelope. *Moon Tiger.* 1988. Grove. 1st ed. F/F. M23. $20.00

LIVERMORE, A.A. *War With Mexico Reviewed.* 1850. Boston. 12mo. 310p. VG. T3. $30.00

LIVINGSTON, A.D. *Dealing With Cheats.* 1973. Phil. 1st ed. sgn. 320p. VG/dj. S1. $15.00

LIVINGSTON, Armstrong. *Doublecross.* 1929. Internat Fiction Lib. VG/VG. P3. $35.00

LIVINGSTON, Armstrong. *On the Right Wrists.* nd. AL Burt. VG/VG. P3. $30.00

LIVINGSTON, Jack. *Hell-Bent for Election.* 1988. St Martin. 1st ed. NF/NF. P3. $17.00

LIVINGSTON, Jack. *Nightmare File.* 1986. St Martin. 1st ed. F/F. P3. $18.00

LIVINGSTON, Nancy. *Fatality at Bath & Wells.* nd. BC. VG/VG. P3. $8.00

LIVINGSTON, Nancy. *Mayhem in Parva.* 1991. St Martin. VG/VG. P3. $17.00

LIVINGSTON-LITTLE, D.E. *Economic History of North Idaho 1800-1900.* 1965. Los Angeles. Morrison. 8vo. 25 pl/6 maps. 133p. NF. T10. $35.00

LIVY. *History of Early Rome.* 1970. LEC. 1/1500. sgn Mardesteig/Scorzelli. 500p. F/case. C2. $150.00

LJONE, Oddm. *Green Light for Adventure.* 1957. London. Allen. 1st ed. 252p. dj. F3. $20.00

LLEWELLYN, Richard. *Few Flowers for Shiner.* 1950. Macmillan. 1st ed. hc. VG/VG. P3. $18.00

LLEWELLYN, Richard. *Flame for Doubting Thomas.* 1953. Macmillan. 1st ed. VG/VG. P3. $25.00

LLOYD, Alan. *Great Prize Fight.* 1977. CMG. 1st Am ed. 188p. VG/dj. M20. $17.00

LLOYD, Ann. *Good Guys, Bad Guys.* 1983. Orbis Great Movies. 1st ed. VG. P3. $15.00

LLOYD, Ann. *There's Something Going on Out There.* 1982. Orbis Great Movies. VG. P3. $15.00

LLOYD, Christopher. *Atlas of Maritime History.* 1975. NY. Arco. 70+ maps. F/dj. O7. $45.00

LLOYD, Christopher. *Ships & Seamen.* 1961. World. ils. 223p. gilt gr bdg. VG/G. P12. $15.00

LLOYD, Eyre. *Succession Laws of Christian Countries...* 1877. London. Stevens Haynes. gilt crimson cloth. M11. $225.00

LLOYD, Hugh. *Bronc Burnett: Grand-Slam Homer (#7).* 1951. Putnam. 1st ed. 183p. VG/clip. M20. $40.00

LLOYD, Hugh. *Hal Keen & the Mysterious Arab (#5).* 1931. Grosset Dunlap. lists 7 titles. 237p. VG/dj. M20. $62.00

LLOYD, Hugh. *Hal Keen: Copperhead Trail Mystery (#3).* 1931. Grosset Dunlap. lists 6 titles. 218p. VG/dj. M20. $60.00

LLOYD, J.W. *Muskmelon Production.* 1928. Orange Judd. 12mo. 126p. cloth. B1. $14.00

LLOYD, John Uri. *Red Head.* 1903. NY. 1st ed. 9 pl. VG. B5. $30.00

LLOYD, Lodowick. *Brief Conference of Divers Lawes: Divided...* 1602. London. Thomas Creede. modern speckled calf. M11. $75.00

LLOYD & PALMER. *Obstinate Ghost.* 1968. Odhams. 1st ed. VG/VG. P3. $25.00

LLOYD. *Lloyd's Register of British & Foreign Shipping, 1894-95.* 1895. London. fair. A16. $100.00

LOADER, Jayne. *Between Pictures.* 1987. Grove. 1st ed. F/F. B35. $18.00

LOBAGOLA. *African Savage's Own Story.* 1970. NY. Negro U. rpt. 8vo 402p 8vo M/sans. P4. $22.00

LOBBAN & HARRISON. *Seaweed Ecology & Physiology.* 1994. Cambridge. lg 8vo. ils. pict brd. NF. B1. $45.00

LOBECK, A.K. *Geomorphology: Introduction to Study of Landscapes.* 1939. McGraw Hill. 1st ed/7th imp. 731p. VG. D8. $40.00

LOBECK, A.K. *Things Maps Don't Tell Us.* 1957. Macmillan. 2nd. 72 ils. VG/dj. D8. $26.00

LOBECK & TELLINGTON. *Military Maps & Air Photographs: Their Use...* 1944. McGraw Hill. 4to. 2 maps. F. O7. $55.00

LOBEL, Anita. *Potatoes, Potatoes.* 1967. Harper Row. ils. unp. NF/VG. T5. $25.00

LOBEL, Arnold. *Frog & the Toad Together.* 1973 (1972). NY. 2nd. 8vo. 64p. F/NF. C14. $12.00

LOBEL, Arnold. *Mouse Soup.* (1977). Harper Row. ne. ils. 64p. VG+/G clip. C14. $6.00

LOBEL, Arnold. *Mouse Soup.* 1977. Harper Row. 1st ed. 8vo. VG/VG. B17. $20.00

LOBLEY, Douglas. *Ships Through the Ages.* 1972. London. Octopus. VG/VG. A16. $15.00

LOCHNER, Wolfgang. *Weltgeschichte der Luftfahrt.* 1970. Wurtzburg. 1st ed. ils/photos. 415p. F/F. B18. $25.00

LOCHRIDGE, Richard. *Death on the Hour.* 1974. Lippincott. 1st ed. VG/VG. P3. $20.00

LOCHRIDGE, Richard. *Something Up a Sleeve.* 1972. Lippincott. 1st ed. F/F. P3. $15.00

LOCHRIDGE & LOCKRIDGE. *Client Is Cancelled.* nd. BC. VG/VG. P3. $10.00

LOCHRIDGE & LOCKRIDGE. *Death on the Hour.* 1974. Lippincott. 1st ed. VG/VG. P3. $20.00

LOCHRIDGE & LOCKRIDGE. *Death Takes a Bow.* 1943. Detective BC. VG. P3. $7.00

LOCHTE, Dick. *Blue Bayou.* 1992. NY. Simon Schuster. 1st ed. F/F. H11. $20.00

LOCHTE, Dick. *Laughing Dog.* 1988. Arbor. 1st ed. F/F. T2. $20.00

LOCHTE, Dick. *Laughing Dog.* 1988. Arbor/Morrow. 1st ed. VG/VG. P3. $18.00

LOCHTE, Dick. *Sleeping Dog.* 1985. Arbor 1st ed. sgn. author's 1st novel. F/F. T2. $35.00

LOCKE, David R.; see Nasby, Petroleum.

LOCKE, E.W. *Three Years in Camp & Hospital.* 1870. Boston. Russell. 8vo. 408p. G. T10. $100.00

LOCKE, John. *Locke's Versuch uber den Menschlicen Verstand.* 1795-1797. Leseinstituts. 3 vol. 1st ed this trans. 12mo. lib bookplates. G1. $225.00

LOCKER, Frederick. *Patchwork, Second Series.* 1927. Cleveland. Rowfant Club. 1/200. 135p. VG/cloth dj/VG case. A4. $285.00

LOCKHART, Robert Bruce. *Scotch, the Whiskey of Scotland in Fact & Story.* 1952. London. rpt of 1st ed. 184p. tan cloth. VG. D14. $50.00

LOCKRIDGE & LOCKRIDGE. *Norths Meet Murder.* 1946. World/Tower. 1st ed thus. VG/VG. M22. $30.00

LOCKWOOD, Hazel. *Golden Boof of Birds.* 1945 (1943). Simon Schuster. 3rd. ils Rojankovsky. unp. VG/VG. T5. $20.00

LOCKWOOD & SALO. *Gypsies & Travelers in North America.* 1994. 196p. VG/wrp. A4. $65.00

LODGE, Edith. *Song of the Hill: Selected Poems.* 1964. np. F/VG. B10. $8.00

LODGE, Oliver. *Pioneers of Science.* 1904 (1893). London. Macmillan. 2nd. 8vo. 404p. gilt cloth. K5. $40.00

LOEB, Jacques. *Comparative Physiology of Brain & Comparative Psychology.* 1803. Putnam. John Murray. later prt. 309p. pebbled gr cloth. xl. G1. $35.00

LOEB, Jacques. *Mechanistic Conception of Life: Biological Essays.* 1912. Chicago. 232p. brn cloth. VG. G1. $150.00

LOEB, Jacques. *Organism As a Whole...* 1916. Putnam/Knickerbocker. 379p. gr cloth. VG. G1. $65.00

LOENING, Grover. *Takeoff Into Greatness.* 1968. NY. 1st ed. inscr. VG/dj. B18. $35.00

LOEWENSTEIN, Andrea Freud. *This Place.* 1984. Pandora. UP. VG. B35. $20.00

LOEWINSOHN, Ron. *Magnetic Field(s).* 1983. Knopf. 1st ed. F/NF. H11. $25.00

LOFTING, Hugh. *Doctor Dolittle's Caravan.* 1926. Stokes. 1st ed. hc. G. P3. $35.00

LOFTING, Hugh. *Doctor Dolittle.* 1967. Lippincott. set of 6. VG/box. P3. $75.00

LOFTING, Hugh. *Dr Dolittle & the Secret Lake.* 1948. Lippincott. 1st ed. 8vo. 366p. ils cloth. VG. C14. $25.00

LOFTING, Hugh. *Voyages of Doctor Dolittle.* 1922. Stokes. 1st ed. hc. G. P3. $35.00

LOFTS, Norah. *Emma Hamilton.* 1978. CMG. 1st Am ed. 192p. VG/dj. M20. $15.00

LOFTS, Norah. *Gad's Hall.* 1978. Doubleday. 1st ed. VG/VG. P3. $25.00

LOFTS, Norah. *Haunting of Gad's Hall.* 1979. Doubleday. 1st ed. VG/VG. P3. $22.00

LOFTS, Norah. *Queens of England.* 1977. Doubleday. 1st Am ed. 192p. cloth. NF/dj. M20. $20.00

LOGUE, Christopher. *Husbands.* 1995. FSG. 1st ed. F/F. B35. $17.00

LOGUE, John. *Follow the Leader.* 1979. Crown. 1st ed. VG/VG. P3. $20.00

LOHR, J.A.C. *Kunst en Vernuft. Blijkbaar in de Vershillende...* 1820. Groningen. Van Groenenbergh. 12mo. 25 pl. 100p. NF/wrp/box. B24. $1,850.00

LOKVIG, Tor. *Star Trek, The Motion Picture Pop-Up.* 1980. Wanderer. 1st ed. MTI. VG. P3. $15.00

LOMAX, Alan. *Mister Jelly Roll.* 1950. DSP. 1st ed. F/NF. B2. $60.00

LOMAX, Louise. *San Antonio's River.* 1948. Naylor. 1st ed. 95p. brd. VG/dj. B18. $22.50

LONDON, Darryl. *Man of Respect.* 1986. Lyle Stuart. VG/fair. P3. $10.00

LONDON, Jack. *Abysmal Brute.* 1913. Century. 1st ed/1st issue. yel/blk-stp olive cloth. NF/dj. B24. $1,500.00

LONDON, Jack. *Before Adam.* 1907. Macmillan. 1st ed. decor brd. VG. P3. $80.00

LONDON, Jack. *Before Adam.* 1907. Macmillan. 1st ed. NF. M19. $125.00

LONDON, Jack. *Essays of Revolt.* 1926. Vanguard. 1st ed. NF. M19. $75.00

LONDON, Jack. *Jerry of the Islands.* 1917. Macmillan. 1st ed. NF. M19. $125.00

LONDON, Jack. *Little Lady of the Big House.* 1916. Macmillan. 1st ed. decor brd. G. P3. $75.00

LONDON, Jack. *Michael, Brother of Jerry.* 1917. Macmillan. 1st ed. NF. M19. $125.00

LONDON, Jack. *Moon-Face: And Other Stories.* 1906. Macmillan. 1st ed. bl cloth. NF. B24. $285.00

LONDON, Jack. *Night-Born.* nd. Grosset Dunlap. VG. P3. $15.00

LONDON, Jack. *On the Makaloa Mat.* 1919. Macmillan. 1st ed. bl/yel-stp teal cloth. NF. B24. $250.00

LONDON, Jack. *Scarlet Plague.* 1915. NY. 1st ed. VG/VG. B5. $135.00

LONDON, Jack. *Son of the Sun.* nd. Newnes. hc. VG. P3. $15.00

LONDON, Jack. *Sun-Dog Trail.* 1951. World. hc. VG. P3. $25.00

LONDON, Jack. *Unabridged Jack London.* nd. Courage. 11th. VG/VG. P3. $22.00

LONDON, Jack. *White Fang.* 1906. NY. 1st ed. VG. B5. $95.00

LONDON, Rose. *Cinema of Mystery.* nd. Bounty. hc. VG/VG. P3. $10.00

LONDON & WITKIN. *Photography Collector's Guide.* 1980. np. 4to. ils. 438p. F/F. A4. $195.00

LONG, Charles R. *Infinite Brain.* 1957. Avalon. 1st ed. hc. NF/NF. P3. $20.00

LONG, Constance E. *Collected Papers on the Psychology of Phantasy.* 1920. London. Bailliere Tindall Cox. 216p. bl cloth. G1. $40.00

LONG, Frank Belknap. *Howard Phillips Lovecraft: Dreamer on the Nightside.* 1975. Arkham. 1st ed. 1/5000. F/F. R10. $25.00

LONG, Frank Belknap. *In Mayan Splendor.* 1977. Arkham. 1st ed. 1/2947. F/F. T2. $10.00

LONG, Frank Belknap. *It Was the Day of the Robot.* 1964. Dobson. 1st ed. VG/VG. P3. $30.00

LONG, Frank Belknap. *Rim of the Unknown.* 1972. Arkham. 1st ed. 1/3640. F/F. T2. $55.00

LONG, Harmon. *Silverface.* nd. Rich Cowan. VG/G. P3. $20.00

LONG, Huey P. *Every Man a King.* 1933. National Book. 1st ed. VG. M19. $75.00

LONG, Julius. *Keep the Coffins.* 1947. Julian Messner. 1st ed. VG/VG. P3. $25.00

LONG, Lydia Belknap; see Long, Frank Belknap.

LONG, Margaret. *Affair of the Heart.* 1953. Random. 1st ed. F/F. B4. $50.00

LONG, William J. *School of the Woods.* 1902. Ginn. 361p. gilt gr cloth. VG. M20. $37.00

LONG, William J. *Wilderness Ways.* 1900. Ginn. ils Copeland. 155p. pict cloth. G. A17. $12.50

LONGFELLOW, Henry Wadsworth. *Aftermath.* 1873. Boston. Osgood. 1st ed. 8vo. 144p. gilt gr cloth. NF. B24. $100.00

LONGFELLOW, Henry Wadsworth. *Children's Longfellow.* 1910s?. Hodder Stoughton. ils ES Farmer. VG. B17. $15.00

LONGFELLOW, Henry Wadsworth. *Courtship of Miles Standish & Other Poems.* 1858. Ticknor Fields. 1st Am ed/1st issue. 8vo. 215p. aeg. tan cloth. F/case. B24. $850.00

LONGFELLOW, Henry Wadsworth. *Courtship of Miles Standish.* nd. NY. Hurst. ftspc Grosch. 16mo. 279p. hc. G. B36. $35.00

LONGFELLOW, Henry Wadsworth. *Paul Revere's Ride.* 1963. Franklin Watts. 1st ed. 8vo. unp. NF. C14. $8.00

LONGFELLOW, Henry Wadsworth. *Seaside & the Fireside.* ca 1850. Liverpool. 2nd Eng ed/1st hc ed. sgn. gr cloth. VG. C6. $350.00

LONGFELLOW, Henry Wadsworth. *Song of Hiawatha.* 1855. Boston. 1st Am ed/1st prt. VG. C6. $160.00

LONGFELLOW, Henry Wadsworth. *Song of Hiawatha.* 1855. Boston. 1st ed/1st prt. NF. A9. $250.00

LONGLEY, Pearl Dorr. *Rebirth of Venkata Reddi.* 1946. Judson. 2nd ed. VG. P3. $8.00

LONGSTREET, Stephen. *Century on Wheels: Story of Studebaker.* 1952. Holt. VG. O3. $65.00

LONGYEAR, Barry B. *City of Baraboo.* 1980. Berkley Putnam. 1st ed. sgn. F/F. P3. $25.00

LONGYEAR, Barry B. *Sea of Glass.* 1987. St Martin. 1st ed. sgn. F/F. P3. $25.00

LOOMIS, Alfred. *Fair Winds in the Far Baltic.* 1928. NY/London. ils. 265p. VG. T7. $24.00

LOOMIS, Alfred. *Yachts Under Sail.* 1933. 1st ed. photos. VG+/chip. S13. $28.00

LOOMIS, Charles F. *Flowers of Lost Romance.* 1929. Houghton Mifflin. 1st ed. 288p. gold cloth. xl. VG. B22. $10.00

LOOMIS, Elias. *Treatise on Astonomy.* 1879 (1865). Harper. 8vo. 346p. modern bdg. G. K5. $55.00

LOOMIS, Noel M. *Wells Fargo.* 1968. NY. Clarkson Potter. 1st ed. ils. 344p. VG/dj. T10. $50.00

LOOS, Anita. *Kiss Hollywood Good-By.* 1974. Viking. 4th. NF/NF. B35. $25.00

LOOSE, G. *Guide to American Bird Names, Origins...* 1989. Virginia Beach. Grunwald Radcliff. 8vo. F/wrp. B1. $14.00

LOPATE, Carol. *Women in Medicine.* 1968. Baltimore. 1st ed. 204p. dj. A13. $25.00

LOPEZ, Barry. *Arctic Dreams.* 1986. Scribner. 1st ed. sgn. F/F. A18. $60.00

LOPEZ, Barry. *Crossing Open Ground.* 1988. Scribner. 1st ed. sgn. M/dj. A18. $40.00

LOPEZ, Barry. *Crow & Weasel.* 1990. North Point. 1st ed. 4to. rem mk. VG/dj. B17. $45.00

LOPEZ, Barry. *Crow & Weasel.* 1990. North Point. 1st state (gold stp cover & spine). sgn. M/dj. A18. $100.00

LOPEZ, Barry. *Field Notes: Grace Note of the Canyon Wren.* 1994. Knopf. 1st ed. sgn. M/M. A18. $35.00

LOPEZ, Barry. *Of Wolves & Men.* 1978. Scribner. 1st ed. F/F. A18. $125.00

LOPEZ, Barry. *River Notes: Dance of Herons.* 1979. Andrews McMeel. 1st ed. sgn. F/dj. A18. $100.00

LOPEZ, Barry. *Winter Count.* 1981. Scribner. 1st ed. F/F. A18. $80.00

LOPEZ & RAYMOND. *Medieval Trade in the Mediterranean World.* 1990. Columbia. 8vo. 458p. VG. W1. $28.00

LOPEZ. *Alexander Pope: An Annotated Bibliography 1945-1967.* 1970. FL U. 154p. F. A4. $45.00

LORAC, E.C.R. *Shroud of Darkness.* nd. BC. VG/VG. P3. $8.00

LORAIN, Peter. *Clandestine Operations.* 1983. NY. 1st ed. ils/maps. F/dj. A17. $15.00

LORAINE, Philip. *Photographs Have Been Sent to Your Wife.* 1971. Collins Crime Club. VG/VG. P3. $15.00

LORAINE, Philip. *WIL, One to Curtis.* 1967. Collins. 1st ed. VG/VG. P3. $20.00

LORANT, Stefan. *Lincoln: A Picture Story of His Life.* 1969. NY. ils. 336p. orange cloth. VG. T3. $15.00

LORANT, Stefan. *Lincoln: His Life in Photographs.* 1941. NY. 4to. 160p. ils. brn cloth. VG/dj. T3. $20.00

LORANT, Stefan. *New World: First Pictures of America.* 1946. NY. 1st ed. ils. 292p. VG/dj. B18. $65.00

LORD, Francis A. *Civil War Collector's Encyclopedia.* 1979. np. 4to. ils. 360p. bl cloth. VG/dj. T3. $22.00

LORD, Glenn. *Last Celt.* 1976. Donald Grant. 1st ed. VG/VG. P3. $30.00

LORD, Graham. *Who Killed the Pie Man?* 1975. Saturday Review/Dutton. 1st ed. VG/VG. P3. $20.00

LORD, Sheldon; see Block, Lawrence.

LORD, Walter. *Night To Remember.* 1955. NY. Holt. sgn. 8vo. 209p. VG/VG. B11. $50.00

LORD & GAMAGE. *Marblehead: The Spirit of '76 Lives Here.* 1972. Chilton. photos/line drawings. 395p. VG/dj. T7. $30.00

LORD. *Last Celt: Bio Bibliography of Robert Ervin Howard.* 1976. Donald Grant. 4to. ils. 416p. NF/NF. A4. $65.00

LORDE, Audre. *Black Unicorn.* 1978. Norton. 1st ed. F/F. B4. $75.00

LORDE, Audre. *From a Land Where Other People Life.* 1973. Detroit. Broadside Pr. ARC. RS. F/stapled wrp. B4. $100.00

LORENZEN. *20 Years of Analog/Astounding SF.* 1971. Locomotive Workshop. 40p. VG/wrp. A4. $45.00

LORIMER, George Horace. *Letters From Self-Made Merchant to His Son.* 1927. NY. 1st ed. sgn. VG/VG. B5. $40.00

LORMEL, L. *Convalescence de Bebe.* ca 1885. Paris. ils H Lemar. VG. D1. $325.00

LORRAINE, Paul. *Two Worlds.* 1952. Curtis Warren. VG/VG. P3. $45.00

LORTZ, Richard. *Lovers, Living Lovers.* 1977. Putnam. 1st ed. NF/NF. P3. $25.00

LORWIN, M. *Dining With William Shakespeare.* 1976. NY. 1st ed. VG/VG. B5. $40.00

LOSSING, Benson J. *Seventeen Hundred & Seventy-Six; or, War of Independence.* 1847. NY. ils. 510p. G. B18. $47.50

LOTH, David. *Chief Justice John Marshall & Growth of the Republic.* 1949. Norton. 1st ed. 395p. VG/poor. B10. $35.00

LOTI, Pierre. *Into Morocco.* 1892. Rand McNally. 1st ed. 343p. xl. VG. W1. $16.00

LOTT, Milton. *Last Hunt.* 1955. London. Collins. 1st ed. F/VG+. A18. $20.00

LOTTMAN, Herbert R. *Petain, Hero or Traitor?* 1985. NY. 1st ed. 444p. F/dj. A17. $10.00

LOTZE, Rudolf Hermann. *Medizinishe Psychologie oder Physiologie der Seele.* 1896. Berlin. Dannenberg. 632p. VG. G1. $85.00

LOTZE, Rudolf Hermann. *Outline of Psychology Dictated Portions of Lectures...* 1886. Boston. Ginn. 1st Eng-language ed. 12mo. 200p. pebbled gr cloth. G1. $45.00

LOUAGE, A. *Course of Philosophy.* 1883 (1873). Baltimore. 2nd. 12mo. 290p. G. G1. $32.50

LOUEY, Chisolm. *Snow Queen & Other Stories for the Five-Year-Old.* nd. London. Jack. ils Katherine Cameron. 60p. VG. M20. $77.00

LOUGHBOROUGH, Mary Ann. *My Cave Life in Vicksburg With Letters of Trial & Travel.* 1864. NY. Appleton. 1st ed. 196p. cloth. NF. M8. $250.00

LOUGHERY, John. *Alias SS Van Dine.* 1992. Scribner. 1st ed. AN/dj. N4. $20.00

LOUIS, P.C.A. *Pathological Researches on Phthisis.* 1836. Boston. trans Charles Cowan. 550p. blk cloth. G. B14. $125.00

LOUTTIT, C.M. *Bibliography of Bibliographies of Psychology 1900-1927.* 1970. NY. facsimile of 1928 ed. 108p. VG. A13. $20.00

LOUV'A. *Les Betes Que J'Aime.* 1950s. Paris. Flammarion. 8vo. unp. VG/stiff wrp. C14. $15.00

LOVE, Christopher. *Mr Love's Case: Wherein Is Published, First, His Petitions.* 1651. London. Cole. only ed. 3-quarter marbled brd. xl. M11. $450.00

LOVE, Deborah. *Annaghkeen.* 1970. Random. 1st ed. NF/dj. B4. $75.00

LOVE, Edmund G. *Hourglass: History of 7th Infantry Division in WWII.* 1950. Infantry Journal Pr. 1st ed. 496p. VG. A17. $30.00

LOVE, Edmund G. *Set-Up.* 1980. Doubleday. 1st ed. sgn. F/F clip. H11. $30.00

LOVE, Edwin M. *Rocking Island.* 1927. Nelson. 1st ed. 182p. bl cloth. VG. M20. $47.00

LOVECRAFT, H.P. *At the Mountains of Madness.* 1975. Arkham. 4th. NF/NF. P3. $25.00

LOVECRAFT, H.P. *Best Supernatural Stories of HP Lovecraft.* 1945. Tower. 2nd. VG/VG. P3. $35.00

LOVECRAFT, H.P. *Beyond the Wall of Sleep.* 1943. Arkham. 1st ed. 1/1217. NF/dj. B24. $1,600.00

LOVECRAFT, H.P. *Dagon & Other Macabre Tales.* 1969. Arkham. 2nd. NF/NF. P3. $30.00

LOVECRAFT, H.P. *Dark Brotherhood.* 1966. Arkham. 1st ed. 1/3460. F/F. M21. $125.00

LOVECRAFT, H.P. *Dunwich Horror & Other...* 1970. Arkham. 3rd. F/F. P3. $30.00

LOVECRAFT, H.P. *Illustrated Fungi From Yuggoth.* 1983. Dream House. 1st ed thus. 1/250. ils/sgn Robert Kellough. F. G10. $20.00

LOVECRAFT, H.P. *Shuttered Room.* 1959. Sauk City. 1st ed. VG/G. B5. $90.00

LOVECRAFT, H.P. *Something About Cats & Other Pieces.* 1949. Arkham. 1st ed. F/NF. B24. $225.00

LOVEL. *Cape Cod Story of Thornton W Burgess.* 1974. 1/500. sgn. ils. 111p. ES. VG. A4. $185.00

LOVELACE, Delos W. *Ils King Kong.* 1971. Crime Club. 1st ed. VG/VG. P3. $15.00

LOVELACE, Maud Hart. *Betsy-Tacy & Tib.* 1946 (1941). Crowell. 5th. ils Lenski. VG/G. M5. $55.00

LOVELAND, Seymour. *Ils Bible Story Book.* 1923. RAnd McNally. ils Milo Winter. VG. B17. $12.50

LOVESEY, Peter. *Bertie & the Seven Bodies.* 1990. Mysterious. 1st ed. VG/VG. P3. $23.00

LOVESEY, Peter. *Bertie & the Tinman.* 1987. Dudley Head. 1st ed. F/F. P3. $20.00

LOVESEY, Peter. *Bertie & the Tinman.* 1988. Mysterious. 1st Am ed. F/NF. N4. $17.50

LOVESEY, Peter. *Butchers & Other Stories of Crime.* 1985. Mysterious. 1st ed. F/F. P3. $18.00

LOVESEY, Peter. *Case of Spirits.* 1975. Dodd Mead. 1st Am ed. F/NF. T2. $25.00

LOVESEY, Peter. *Keystone.* 1983. Pantheon. 1st ed. F/F. P3. $15.00

LOVESEY, Peter. *Last Detective.* 1991. Doubleday. 1st ed. F/F. P3. $18.00

LOVESEY, Peter. *Spider Girl.* 1980. Viking. 1st ed. VG/VG. P3. $15.00

LOVETT, Robert L. *Lateral Curvature of the Spine & Rounded Shoulders.* 1907. Phil. 1st ed. 188p. cloth. VG. w/author's card. B14. $200.00

LOVETT, Sarah. *Dangerous Attachments.* 1995. Villard. UP. F/wht wrp. M22. $30.00

LOW, A.M. *Adrift in the Stratosphere.* nd. Peal. hc. G/G. P3. $18.00

LOW, A.P. *Report on the Dominion Government Expedition to Hudson Bay.* 1906. Ottawa. 1st ed. fld geological survey. 355p. brn cloth. VG. C6. $125.00

LOW, Alice. *Macmillan Book of Greek Gods...* 1985. Macmillan. 2nd. VG. P3. $25.00

LOWE, Alice. *Witch Who Was Afraid of Witches.* nd. Pantheon. stated 1st ed. 8vo. ils. NF/VG clip. C14. $12.00

LOWE, E.J. *Ferns: British & Exotic.* 1872. London. Bell. 8 vol. 2nd. 479 pl. red cloth. VG. A10. $675.00

LOWE, Frank. *I Beg To Differ: A Collection.* 1973. Montreal. Inforcor. apparant 1st ed. 224p. F/VG. B22. $4.50

LOWE, Kenneth. *Haze of Evil.* 1953. Crime Club. 1st ed. VG. P3. $12.00

LOWE, Kenneth. *No Tears for Shirley Minton.* 1956. Detective BC. VG. P3. $8.00

LOWE, Samuel. *New Story of Peter Rabbit.* 1926. Whitman. ils Wright/Vetsch. VG. D1. $75.00

LOWE, Viola Ruth. *Beautiful Story of Joan of Arc, Martyr Maid of France.* 1933. Whitman. ils ODV Guillonnet. VG. B17. $15.00

LOWELL, Amy. *John Keats.* 1925. Houghton Mifflin. 2 vol. ils. F/VG. C2. $75.00

LOWELL, James Russell. *Bigelow Papers.* 1859. London. 1st ed thus. NF. C6. $75.00

LOWELL, James Russell. *Under the Willows & Other Poems.* 1869. London. 1st ed. VG. C6. $65.00

LOWELL, Robert. *Life Studies.* 1959. NY. 1st Am ed. VG/VG. C6. $85.00

LOWELL, Robert. *Lord Weary's Castle.* 1946. Harcourt Brace. 1st ed. F/dj. T10. $300.00

LOWELL, Robert. *Lord Weary's Castle.* 1946. NY. 1st trade ed. VG/VG. C6. $95.00

LOWELL, Robert. *Voyage & Other Versions of Poems by Baudelaire.* 1968. London. 1st ed. 1/200. sgn. ils/sgn Nolan. F/NF case. C2. $300.00

LOWENSTAM, H.A. *Biostratigraphic Studies in Niagaran Inter-Reef Formations.* 1948. Springfield, IL. IL State. 146p. sc. D8. $12.00

LOWERY, Lawrence F. *Sounds Are High, Sounds Are Low.* 1969. HRW. 1st ed. 8vo. unp. VG+/VG. C14. $6.00

LOWERY. *Collectors Guide to Big Little Books & Similar Books.* F. M13. $55.00

LOWIE, Robert H. *Indians of the Plains.* 1954. NY. Am Mus Natural Hist. 1st ed. 8vo. 222p. bl cloth. NF. T10. $50.00

LOWMAN, Al. *Printing Arts in Texas.* 1975. np. 1st ed. 1/395. ils Barbara Holman. 107p. F. C2. $100.00

LOWNDES, Marie Belloc. *Lodger.* 1969. Hamish Hamilton. VG/VG. P3. $25.00

LOWNSBERY, Eloise. *Boy Knight of Reims.* 1927. Houghton Mifflin. 1st ed. inscr. 8vo. gilt bl cloth. G. B11. $35.00

LOWNSBERY, Eloise. *Marta the Doll.* 1946. Longman Gr. 1st ed. 118p. G. C14. $10.00

LOWREY, Grosvenor P. *English Neutrality: Is the Alabama a British Pirate?* 1863. NY. Randolph. 1st ed. 36p. VG. M8. $45.00

LOWRY, Beverly. *Come Back, Lolly Ray.* 1977. Doubleday. 1st ed. author's 1st book. F/NF. B4. $125.00

LOWRY, Beverly. *Daddy's Girl.* 1981. Viking. 1st ed. F/NF. M23. $20.00

LOWRY, Beverly. *Emma Blue.* 1978. Doubleday. 1st ed. F/NF. M23. $25.00

LOWRY, Malcolm. *October Ferry to Gabriola.* 1970. NY. 1st ed. F/NF. A17. $20.00

LOWTHER, George. *Superman.* 1942. Random. ils. 215p. VG. M13. $100.00

LOWTHER. *Bibliography of British Columbia, Laying the Foundations...* 1968. U of Victoria. 4to. 2173 annotated entries. F. A4. $125.00

LOWY, Samuel. *Psychological & Biological Foundations of Dream...* (1942). Kegan Paul. 1st prt. 260p. blk cloth. VG. G1. $35.00

LOY, William G. *Atlas of Oregon.* 1976. OR U. 1st ed. ES. F. O7. $100.00

LUARD, Nicholas. *Gondar.* 1988. Simon Schuster. 1st ed. NF/NF. P3. $20.00

LUARD, Nicholas. *Shadow Spy.* 1979. HBJ. 1st ed. VG/VG. P3. $20.00

LUBBOCK, Basil. *Colonial Clippers.* 1955. Glasgow. rpt. NF. N3. $20.00

LUBBOCK, Basil. *Log of the Cutty Sark.* 1925. Boston. Chas Lauriat. 422p. cloth. VG. M20. $82.00

LUBBOCK, Basil. *Sail: The Romance of Clipper Ships.* 1972. G&D Madison Sq Pr. 85 full-p pl. 150p text. gilt cloth case. A17. $150.00

LUBBOCK, John. *Pre-Historic Times, As Illustrated by Ancient Remains...* 1972. Appleton. 1st Am ed. 8vo. ils. 640p. VG. T10. $100.00

LUBBOCK, Percy. *Portrait of Edith Wharton.* 1947. Appleton Century. 1st ed. NF/VG+. B4. $45.00

LUCAS, Cary. *Unfinished Business.* 1947. Simon Schuster. 1st ed. VG. P3. $10.00

LUCAS, Charles. *Pitcairn Island Register Book.* 1929. London. Soc for Promoting Christian Knowledge. 181p. VG. T7. $160.00

LUCAS, E.V. *Another Book of Verses for Children.* 1925. Macmillan. 2nd. ils. NF. M5. $75.00

LUCAS, E.V. *Playtime & Company.* 1925. London. Meuthen. ltd 1st ed. 1/100. ils Shepard. 95p. VG/orig glassine. D1. $775.00

LUCAS, E.V. *Playtime & Company: A Book for Children.* nd. London. Methuen. 1st ed. ils Lucas/Shepard. 95p. VG/VG. D1. $175.00

LUCAS, George; see Foster, Alan Dean.

LUCAS, John W. *Thermal Characteristics of the Moon.* 1972. Cambridge. 8vo. 340p. cloth/dj. K5. $15.00

LUCAS. *Art Books: A Basic Bibliography on the Fine Arts.* 1968. np. 255p. VG. A4. $85.00

LUCE, Helen. *In the Midst of Death.* 1980. Macmillan. 1st ed. NF/NF. P3. $15.00

LUCE, J.V. *Lost Atlantis: New Light on an Old Legend.* 1970. McGraw Hill. 3rd. 224p. NF/dj. W1. $30.00

LUCRETIUS. *De Rerum Natura (Of the Nature of Things).* 1957. Los Angeles. LEC. 1st ed. 1/1500. ils/sgn Paul Landacre. F/case. C2. $75.00

LUDLAM, Harry. *Biography of Bram Stoker.* 1962. Foulsham. 1st ed. hc. VG/VG. P3. $45.00

LUDLUM, Robert. *Aquitaine Progression.* 1984. Random. 1st ed. VG/VG. P3. $35.00

LUDLUM, Robert. *Bourne Identity.* nd. Marek. 6th ed. VG/VG. P3. $15.00

LUDLUM, Robert. *Bourne Identity.* 1980. Marek. 1st ed. F/F. H11. $30.00

LUDLUM, Robert. *Bourne Supremacy.* 1986. Random. 1st ed. F/F. H11/P3. $25.00

LUDLUM, Robert. *Bourne Ultimatum.* 1990. Random. 1st ed. VG/VG. P3. $22.00

LUDLUM, Robert. *Chancellor Manuscript.* 1977. Dial. 1st ed. F/F. B35. $30.00

LUDLUM, Robert. *Cry of the Halidon.* 1974. Delacorte. 1st ed. as Jonathan Ryder. F/NF. H11. $70.00

LUDLUM, Robert. *Gemini Contenders.* 1976. Dial. 1st ed. F/NF. H11. $45.00

LUDLUM, Robert. *Holcroft Covenant.* 1978. Marek. 1st ed. F/NF. H11. $30.00

LUDLUM, Robert. *Icarus Agenda.* 1988. Random. 1st ed. F/F. H11. $25.00

LUDLUM, Robert. *Icarus Agenda.* 1988. Random. 1st ed. NF/NF. B35/N4/P3. $20.00

LUDLUM, Robert. *Matarese Circle.* 1979. Marek. 1st ed. F/F. H11/P3. $35.00

LUDLUM, Robert. *Matlock Paper.* 1973. Dial. 1st ed. NF/NF. N4. $95.00

LUDLUM, Robert. *Osterman Weekend.* 1972. World. 1st ed. F/F. M19. $65.00

LUDLUM, Robert. *Parsifal Mosaic.* 1982. Random. 1st ed. F/F. H11. $30.00

LUDLUM, Robert. *Rhinemann Exchange.* 1974. Dial. 2nd. VG/VG. P3. $15.00

LUDLUM, Robert. *Rhinemann Exchange.* 1974. NY. Dial. 1st ed. rem mk. F/NF. H11. $40.00

LUDLUM, Robert. *Road to Gandolfo.* 1975. NY. Dial. 1st ed. 8vo. VG/dj. S9. $30.00

LUDLUM, Robert. *Road to Omaha.* 1992. Random. 1st ed. F/F. P3. $24.00

LUDLUM, Robert. *Robert Ludlum.* 1986. Peerage. VG/VG. P3. $15.00

LUDLUM, Robert. *Scarlatti Inheritance.* 1971. World. 1st ed. author's 1st book. VG+/fair. N4. $125.00

LUDLUM, Robert. *Trevayne.* 1973. Delacorte. 1st ed. as by Jonathan Ryder. NF/NF. H11. $110.00

LUDWIG, Emil. *Mediterranean Shores.* 1931. NY. McBride. 2nd. 8vo. 268p. ils ep. cloth. xl. VG. W1. $16.00

LUDWIG, Emil. *Nile: Life Story of a River.* 1938. Allen Unwin. 1st 1-vol ed. 687p. VG. W1. $12.00

LUKAS, Jan. *Greece. Griechenland. La Grece.* ca 1950. Prague. Artia. 1st ed. 4to. 78 pl. 22p. cloth. VG/dj. W1. $25.00

LUKE, Peter. *Hadrian VII.* 1969. Knopf. 1st ed. 124p. VG/dj. M20. $47.00

LUKE, Thomas; see Masterton, Graham.

LUKEMAN, Tim. *Rajan.* 1979. Doubleday. 1st ed. hc. F/F. P3. $15.00

LUKENS, Adam. *Conquest of Life.* 1960. Avalon. 1st ed. NF/NF. P3. $25.00

LUKENS, Adam. *Eevalu.* 1963. Avalon. 1st ed. NF/NF. P3. $20.00

LUKENS, John. *Adders Abounding.* 1954. Hodder Stoughton. 1st ed. VG. P3. $20.00

LULFING. *Handschriften und Alte Drucke, Kostbarkeiten Bibliotheken...* 1981. Leipzig. German text. pl. 275p. F/VG. A4. $135.00

LUMLEY, Brian. *Beneath the Moors.* 1974. Arkham. 1st ed. 1/3842. F/F. T2. $45.00

LUMLEY, Brian. *Burrowers Beneath.* 1988. Ganley. F/F. P3. $23.00

LUMLEY, Brian. *Caller of the Black.* 1971. Arkham. 1st ed. author's 1st book. NF/VG+. R10. $35.00

LUMLEY, Brian. *Fruiting Bodies & Other Fungi.* 1993. Tor. 1st ed. F/F. G10. $15.00

LUMLEY, Brian. *Horror at Oakdeene & Others.* 1977. Arkham. 1st ed. F/NF. R10. $30.00

LUMLEY, Brian. *Mad Moon of Dreams.* 1987. Ganley. 1st ed. F/F. P3. $21.00

LUMLEY, Brian. *Necroscope IV: Deadspeak.* 1990. Kinnell. 1st ed. sgn. F/F. P3. $40.00

LUMLEY, Brian. *Ship of Dreams.* 1986. Ganley. 1st ed. F/F. P3. $21.00

LUMMIS, Charles F. *Gold Fish of Gran Chimu.* 1911. Chicago. McClurg. 1st ed. 12mo. 126p. VG. T10. $50.00

LUMMIS, Charles F. *Man Who Married the Moon & Other Pueblo Indian Folk-Stories.* 1894. Century. 1st ed. 32 stories. w/sgn. VG+. A18. $125.00

LUMMIS, Charles F. *Some Strange Corners of Our Country.* 1892. Century. 1st ed. VG. A18. $50.00

LUNAN, Duncan. *Interstellar Contact: Communication With Other Intelligence.* 1975. Chicago. Regnery. 8vo. 324p. VG/VG. K5. $22.00

LUNDGEN & YEAGER. *Across High-Frontier: Story of a Test Pilot.* 1985. NY. 1st ed. ils. 288p. VG/VG. B5. $45.00

LUNDMARK, Knut. *Studies of Anagalactic Nebulae: First Paper.* 1927. Uppsala. Almqvist/Wiksells Boktryckeri. 4to. 124p. wrp. K5. $50.00

LUNNY. *Early Maps of North America.* 1961. NJ Hist Soc. 26 full-p facsimilies. hc. NF. A4. $65.00

LUNT, Dudley Cammett. *Road to the Law. Second Printing.* 1932. Whittlesey. brn cloth. M11. $45.00

LUNT, James. *Hussein of Jordan.* 1989. Morrow. 1st ed. 8vo. 5 maps. NF/dj. W1. $20.00

LUPER, Albert. *Music of Brazil.* 1943. Pan American Union. Music series. 4to. 40p. mimeographed. F3. $10.00

LUPICA, Mike. *Dead Air.* nd. BC. VG/VG. P3. $8.00

LUPOFF, Richard A. *Circumpolar!* 1984. Timescape. 1st ed. F/F. P3. $20.00

LUPOFF, Richard A. *Countersolar!* 1987. Arbor. 1st ed. F/F. P3. $17.00

LUPOFF, Richard A. *Forever City.* 1987. Walker. 1st ed. F/F. P3. $25.00

LUPOFF, Richard A. *Lovecraft's Book.* 1985. Arkham. 1st ed. 1/3544. F/F. T2. $16.00

LUPOFF, Richard A. *Space War Blues.* 1980. Gregg. sans. P3. $15.00

LUPOFF, Richard A. *Sword of the Demon.* 1976. Harper Row. 1st ed. sgn. F/F. M19. $35.00

LUPOFF, Richard A. *Sword of the Demon.* 1977. Harper Row. 1st ed. F/F. P3. $18.00

LURIE, Alison. *Foreign Affairs.* 1984. Franklin Lib. 1st ed. sgn. leather. F. B35. $40.00

LURIE, Alison. *Foreign Affairs.* 1985. Random. AP. F/wrp. M19. $85.00

LURIE, Alison. *Nowhere City.* 1965. Heinemann. 1st Eng (precedes Am) ed. NF/VG. M19. $75.00

LURIE, Alison. *Truth About Lorin Jones.* 1988. Little Brn. 1st ed. AN/dj. B4. $45.00

LURIE, Alison. *War Between the Tates.* 1974. Random. 1st ed. F/VG. M19. $45.00

LUSIS. *Chess: An Annotated Bibliography 1969-1988.* 1991. 4to. 320p. F. A4. $75.00

LUST, R. *Stellar & Solar Magnetic Fields.* 1965. Amsterdam. 8vo. photos/diagrams. 460p. VG. K5. $40.00

LUSTBADER, Eric Van; see Van Lustbader, Eric.

LUTHER, Tal. *Collecting Taos Authors.* 1993. np. Collector ed. 1/100. ils. 101p. cloth. F. A4. $45.00

LUTZ, John. *Bloodfire.* 1991. Henry Holt. 1st ed. NF/NF. P3. $18.00

LUTZ, John. *Dancing With the Dead.* 1992. St Martin. 1st ed. AN/dj. M22. $15.00

LUTZ, John. *Kiss.* 1988. Henry Holt. 1st ed. VG/VG. P3. $18.00

LUTZ, John. *Lazarus Man.* 1979. Morrow. 1st ed. NF/NF. H11. $15.00

LUTZ, John. *Ride the Lightning.* 1991. Mystery Short Story. ltd ed. 1/100. sgn. F/sans. P3. $20.00

LUTZ, John. *Scorcher.* 1987. Holt. 1st ed. F/F. A20. $10.00

LUTZ, John. *SWF Seeks Same.* 1990. St Martin. 1st ed. F/F. M22. $15.00

LVEY, Mervyn. *Moons of Paradise: Reflections of the Breast in Art.* 1965. 1st ed. ils. VG/VG. S13. $25.00

LYALL, Alfred C. *Asiatic Studies: Religious & Social.* 1882. Murray. 1st ed. 8vo. 332p. VG. W1. $35.00

LYALL, Gavin. *Crocus List.* 1986. Viking. 1st ed. VG/VG. P3. $16.00

LYALL, Gavin. *Midnight Plus One.* 1965. Scribner. 4th. VG/VG. P3. $15.00

LYALL, Gavin. *Shooting Script.* 1966. Scribner. 1st ed. VG/VG. P3. $35.00

LYDE, Marilyn Jones. *Edith Wharton: Convention & Morality in Work of a Novelist.* 1959. OK U. 1st ed. NF/VG+. B4. $45.00

LYDENS, Z.Z. *Story of Grand Rapids.* 1966. Kregel. ils. VG/G. P12. $20.00

LYLE, Sparky. *Bronx Zoo.* 1979. Crown. 1st ed. sgn. F/VG+. P8. $35.00

LYLES. *Dell Paperbacks 1942 to Mid-1962...* 1983. np. 2168 titles. 472p. F. A4. $65.00

LYLES. *Putting Dell on the Map, a History of Dell Paperbacks.* 1983. np. ils. 180p. VG. A4. $45.00

LYMAN, George D. *Ralston's Ring: California Plunders the Comstock Lode.* 1944. Scribner. 8vo. 368p. NF/dj. T10. $35.00

LYMAN, George D. *Saga of the Comstock Lode.* 1934. Scribner. 1st ed. 8vo. ils. ribbed bl cloth. NF. T10. $125.00

LYMINGTON, John. *Froomb!* nd. BC. hc. VG/VG. P3. $8.00

LYMINGTON, John. *Giant Stumbles.* 1960. Hodder Stoughton. 1st ed. NF/VG+. G10. $15.00

LYNAM, Edward. *British Maps & Map-Makers.* 1947. London. Collins. 3rd. ils/maps. F/dj. O7. $35.00

LYNCH, W.F. *Narrative of the United States' Expedition to River Jordan.* 1849. Phil. ils/fld maps. G. M17. $125.00

LYND, Leslie. *Tender Melody.* 1948. Arcadia. xl. dj. P3. $5.00

LYNDS, Dennis. *Blue Death.* nd. BC. VG/VG. P3. $8.00

LYNDS, Dennis. *Castrato.* 1986. Donald Fine. 1st ed. VG/VG. P3. $15.00

LYNDS, Dennis. *Nightrunners.* 1978. Dodd Mead. 1st ed. xl. dj. P3. $5.00

LYNDS, Dennis. *Silent Scream.* 1973. Dodd Mead. 1st ed. VG/VG. P3. $25.00

LYNES, Russell. *Cadwallader: A Diversion.* 1959. Harper. NF/NF. P3. $10.00

LYNN, Elizabeth A. *Silver Horse.* 1984. Bluejay. 1st ed. F/F. P3. $18.00

LYNN, NIELSEN & RALPHS. *Ecology & Economic Impact of Poisonous Plants...* 1988. Boulder. Westview. 8vo. 428p. cloth. B1. $27.00

LYON, Bentley. *Summer Stalk.* 1992. NY. 1st ed. F/F. H11. $20.00

LYON, Jane D. *Clipper Ships & Captains.* 1962. Am Heritage Jr Lib. 1st ed. 153p. VG. P12. $12.00

LYON, Patricia. *Native South Americas.* 1974. Little Brn. 1st ed. 433p. F3. $20.00

LYONS, Arthur. *At the Hands of Another.* 1983. HRW. 1st ed. VG/VG. P3. $20.00

LYONS, Arthur. *Dead Are Discreet.* 1974. Mason Lipscomb. 1st ed. 8vo. F/NF. T10. $100.00

LYONS, Dorothy. *Dark Sunshine.* 1951. Harcourt Brace. 1st ed. VG/fair. O3. $35.00

LYONS, Dorothy. *Harlequin Hullabaloo.* 1949. Harcourt Brace. 1st ed. ils Wesley Dennis. 264p. VG/G. T5. $30.00

LYONS, Dorothy. *Silver Birch.* 1939. Harcourt Brace. VG. O3. $25.00

LYONS, M.C. *Arabic Translation of Themistius Commentary on Aristoteles.* 1973. Columbia. 1st ed. 390p. NF/dj. W1. $45.00

LYONS, Paul. *Going for Broke.* 1991. Algonquin. 1st ed. rem mk. F/F. H11. $25.00

LYONS, Ruth. *Remember With Me.* 1969. Doubleday. sgn. 8vo. 272p. VG. B11. $15.00

LYONS, T.A. *Magnetism of Iron & Steel Ships.* 1884. GPO. 20 pl/tables/figures. 123p. gilt bl cloth. NF. T10. $125.00

LYONS & TRUZZI. *Blue Sense.* 1991. Mysterious. 1st ed. F/F. P3. $20.00

LYTLE, Andrew. *Bedford Forrest & Critter Company.* 1931. NY. 1st ed. VG. B5. $75.00

LYTLE, Horace. *No Hunting?* 1928. Field Sports. 1st ed. VG/VG. P3. $30.00

LYTLE, William. *Merchant Steam Vessels of the United States 1807-1868.* 1952. CT. Steamship Hist Soc of Am. 1/1000. w/supplements. G. A16. $75.00

LYTTON, Bulwer. *Last Days of Pompeii.* 1926. Scribner. 1st ed. ils FC Yohn. 425p. VG/dj. M20. $105.00

LYTTON, E.B. *Eugene Aram.* 1842. Exeter. 2 vol. VG. M19. $75.00

LYTTON, Edward G. *Pilgrims of the Rhine.* 1834. London. 1st ed. ils/11 Indian proof engravings. 341p. aeg. F. H3. $125.00

M'MAHON, Bernard. *American Gardener's Calendar.* 1806. Phil. Graves. fld pl. 666p. rebacked. A10. $375.00

MAAS, Peter. *Made in America.* 1979. Viking. 1st ed. F/F. H11. $30.00

MAAS, Peter. *Serpico.* 1973. Viking. 1st ed. VG. P3. $12.00

MAASS, Edgar. *World & Paradise.* 1950. Scribner. 1st ed. VG/VG. P3. $20.00

MABBOTT, Thomas Ollive. *Politican: Unfinished Tragedy of Edgar A Poe.* 1923. EA Poe Shrine. 89p. VG. B10. $75.00

MABIE, Peter. *A to Z Book.* 1929. Whitman. 4to. unp. NF/pict wrp. D1. $60.00

MABRY, William Alexander. *Disfranchisement of the Negro in Mississippi.* 1933. np. sgn. gilt navy bl brd. VG. B11. $75.00

MACARTNEY, Clarence Edward. *Grant & His Generals.* 1953. NY. ils/map ep. 352p. G+. B18. $22.50

MACASKILL, Wallace R. *Out of Halifax.* 1937. Derrydale. 1st ed. sgn. 98 pl. bl/gray cloth. F. B11. $250.00

MACASKILL, Wallace R. *WR Macaskill: Seascapes & Sailing Ships.* 1989. Halifax. Nimbus. 113 ils. 128p. VG/dj. T7. $40.00

MACAULAY, David. *Castle.* 1977. Houghton Mifflin. VG/VG. P3. $18.00

MACAULAY, Rose. *Pleasure of Ruins.* 1964. Thames Hudson. 286p. VG/dj. B18. $47.50

MACAULAY, Thomas Babington. *History of England From the Accession of James II.* 1849-1850. Boston. 2 vol. VG. A4. $100.00

MACAVOY, R.A. *King of the Dead.* 1991. Morrow. 1st ed. VG. P3. $19.00

MACAVOY, R.A. *Third Eagle.* 1989. Doubleday. 1st ed. F/F. P3. $19.00

MACAVOY, R.A. *Trio for Lute.* nd. BC. VG/VG. P3. $10.00

MACBETH, George. *Poems From Oby.* 1983. Atheneum. 1/750. F/F. B35. $60.00

MACBETH, George. *Seven Witches.* 1978. HBJ. F/F. P3. $15.00

MACBETH, Norman. *Darwin Retired: An Appeal to Reason.* 1971. Boston. 178p. VG/dj. B26. $17.50

MACBRIDE, Thomas H. *Lessons in Elementary Botany for Secondary Schools.* 1900 (1895). Boston. new ed. 241p. decor cloth. NF. B26. $20.00

MACBRIDE & MARTIN. *Myxomycetes: A Descriptive List of Known Species...* 1934. NY. ils. 339p. VG/torn. B26. $40.00

MACCAIG, Norman. *Rings on a Tree.* 1968. Chatto Windus. 1st ed. F/NF. V1. $20.00

MACCATHMHAOIL. *Mountain Singer.* nd. NY. AMS Pr. rpt of Mansel/Dublin 1909 ed. F/sans. V1. $15.00

MACCHI, Giulio. *Cartes et Figures de la Terre.* 1980. Paris. Centre Georges Pompidou. F/wrp. O7. $75.00

MACCORKLE, William Alexander. *White Sulphur Springs: Traditions, History & Social Life...* 1924 (1916). Neale. photos. 410p. VG/poor. B10. $50.00

MACCURDY, George Grant. *Recent Discoveries Bearing on Antiquity of Man in Europe.* 1910. GPO. removed. 8vo. VG. P4. $15.00

MACCURDY, John T. *Common Principles in Psychology & Physiology.* 1928. Cambridge. 284p. ruled brn cloth. NF/dj. G1. $65.00

MACDIARMID, Hugh. *Lap of Honour.* 1967. London. Macgibbon Kee. 1st ed. RS. V1. $25.00

MACDONALD, Betty. *Nancy & Plum.* 1952. Lippincott. 1st ed. 12mo. G+. C8. $30.00

MACDONALD, C. *Ochiltree: The Coal & Iron Industries of Nova Scotia.* 1909. Halifax. fld pl/maps/plans. 267p. brn cloth. F. B14. $45.00

MACDONALD, Cynthia. *Wholes.* 1980. Knopf. 1st ed. F/NF. V1. $15.00

MACDONALD, George. *At the Back of the North Wind.* 1919. Phil. McKay. 1st ed. ils JW Smith. 342p. gray cloth. VG. D1. $125.00

MACDONALD, George. *At the Back of the North Wind.* 1924. Macmillan. 1st ed thus. ils FD Bedford. VG. M5. $75.00

MACDONALD, George. *At the Back of the North Wind.* 1959. JM Dent. 2nd. VG/VG. P3. $18.00

MACDONALD, George. *Princess & Curdie.* nd. Collins. VG/VG. P3. $20.00

MACDONALD, George. *Princess & Curdie.* nd. Lippincott. 1st Am ed. 8vo. ils. gilt lettered ils cloth. VG. M5. $125.00

MACDONALD, George. *Princess & Curdie.* 1927. Macmillan. 1st ed. ils Dorothy Lathrop. VG. P2. $75.00

MACDONALD, George. *Princess & the Goblin.* 1907. Lippincott. ils Marie Kirk. 305p. stp red cloth. VG. D1. $165.00

MACDONALD, George. *Princess & the Goblin.* 1927. Saalfield. decor brd. G. P3. $20.00

MACDONALD, George. *Princess & the Goblin.* 1935 (1907). Lippincott. 10th. 8vo. ils Maria Kirk. VG/G. M5. $35.00

MACDONALD, Golden; see Brown, Margaret Wise.

MACDONALD, John D. *Barrier Island.* 1986. Knopf. 1st ed. VG/VG. P3. $18.00

MACDONALD, John D. *Cinnamon Skin.* 1982. Harper Row. 1st ed. F/F. P3/T2. $20.00

MACDONALD, John D. *Condominium.* nd. BOMC. VG/VG. P3. $10.00

MACDONALD, John D. *Crossroads.* 1959. Simon Schuster. 1st ed. VG/G. P3. $125.00

MACDONALD, John D. *Deep Blue Good-By.* 1975. Detective BC. VG. P3. $8.00

MACDONALD, John D. *Empty Copper Sea.* 1978. Lippincott. 1st ed. F/NF. H11. $55.00

MACDONALD, John D. *Empty Copper Sea.* 1978. Lippincott. 1st ed. VG/G. P3. $30.00

MACDONALD, John D. *Empty Copper Sea.* 1978. Lippincott. 1st ed. VG/VG. M22. $35.00

MACDONALD, John D. *Executioners.* 1958. Simon Schuster. 1st ed. VG. P3. $45.00

MACDONALD, John D. *Five Complete Travis McGee Novels.* nd. Avenel. 7th. hc. F/F. P3. $15.00

MACDONALD, John D. *Free Fall in Crimson.* 1981. Harper Row. 1st ed. VG/VG. P3. $30.00

MACDONALD, John D. *Free Fall in Crimson.* 1981. Harper Row. 1st ed. 8vo. F/F. T10. $45.00

MACDONALD, John D. *Good Old Stuff.* 1984. Knopf. 1st ed. F/NF clip. A11. $195.00

MACDONALD, John D. *Green Ripper.* 1979. Lippincott. 1st ed. F/F. P3. $25.00

MACDONALD, John D. *Lonely Silver Rain.* 1985. Knopf. 1st ed. F/F. H11. $30.00

MACDONALD, John D. *Lonely Silver Rain.* 1985. Knopf. 1st ed. VG/VG. P3. $18.00

MACDONALD, John D. *More Good Old Stuff.* 1984. Knopf. 1st ed. F/F. P3. $25.00

MACDONALD, John D. *Murder for Money.* 1982. Harper Row. AP. 8vo. NF/prt gr wrp. S9. $40.00

MACDONALD, John D. *Murder for Money.* 1982. Harper Row. UP/1st separate ed. 48p. F/wrp. A11. $45.00

MACDONALD, John D. *One Fearful Yellow Eye.* 1977. Lippincott. 1st hc ed. F/NF. T2. $165.00

MACDONALD, John D. *One More Sunday.* 1984. Hodder Stoughton. 1st ed. NF/NF. P3. $30.00

MACDONALD, John D. *Quick Red Fox.* nd. np. 1st hc ed. F/VG+. N3. $95.00

MACDONALD, John D. *Scarlet Ruse.* 1980. Lippincott Crowell. 1st Am hc ed. F/F. T2. $100.00

MACDONALD, John D. *Slam the Big Door.* 1987. Mysterious. 2nd. F/F. P3. $17.00

MACDONALD, John D. *Time & Tomorrow.* nd. BC. VG/VG. P3. $10.00

MACDONALD, John Ross; see Millar, Kenneth.

MACDONALD, Kate. *Anne of Green Gables Cookbook.* 1985. Toronto. Oxford. 1st ed. ils Barbara Dilella. 48p. F. T5. $35.00

MACDONALD, Patricia J. *Little Sister.* nd. BC. VG/VG. P3. $8.00

MACDONALD, Philip. *Death & Chicanery.* 1963. Herbert Jenkins. VG/VG. P3. $30.00

MACDONALD, Philip. *List of Adrian Messenger.* 1959. Doubleday. 2nd? VG/VG. P3. $18.00

MACDONALD, Philip. *Polferry Mystery.* nd. Literary Pr. VG/VG. P3. $40.00

MACDONALD, Philip. *Warrant for X.* 1941. Triangle. 2nd. VG. P3. $13.00

MACDONALD, Philip. *X V. Rex.* 1973. Collins Crime Club. VG/VG. P3. $20.00

MACDONALD, Ross; see Millar, Kenneth.

MACDONALD, William Colt. *Punchers of Phantom Pass.* 1973. Collins. VG/VG. P3. $12.00

MACDOUGAL, D.T. *Mutations, Variations & Relationships of Oenotheras.* 1907. WA, DC. ils. 92p. VG+. B26. $30.00

MACE, Elisabeth. *Out There.* 1977. Greenwillow. VG/VG. P3. $13.00

MACFADDEN, H.A. *Rambles in the Far West.* 1906. Hollidayburg, PA. 1st ed. 42 pl. VG+. H7. $50.00

MACFARLANE, James. *Coal Regions of America: Their Topography, Geology...* 1875. NY. Appleton. 3rd. 8vo. 29 maps. purple cloth. F. B14. $125.00

MACGILLIVRAY, W. *Travels & Research of Alexander Von Humboldt: Journeys...* 1840. NY. ils. 367p. blk cloth. F. B14. $75.00

MACGOWAN & NEWBERRY. *Mystery Woman.* nd. Grosset Dunlap. VG/G. P3. $20.00

MACGRATH, Harold. *Blue Rajah Murder.* 1930. Crime Club. VG. P3. $20.00

MACGREGOR, A.J. *Green Umbrella.* 1950. Wills Hepworth. 1st ed. 24 pl. F/fair. M5. $35.00

MACGREGOR, Angusine. *Mrs Bunny's Refugee.* nd. Dodge. ils. cloth spine/paper brd. G. M5. $75.00

MACGREGOR, David R. *China Bird.* 1961. London. Chatto Windus. G. A16. $30.00

MACH, Ernst. *Erkenntnis und Irrtum: Skizzen zur Psychologie Forschung.* 1905. Leipzig. Johann Ambrosius Barth. 8vo. 461p. G. G1. $350.00

MACHAM, Standish. *Life Apart: The English Working Class 1890-1914.* 1977. Cambridge. 1st ed. 272p. dj. A13. $30.00

MACHEN, Arthur. *Caerleon Edition of the Works of Arthur Machen.* 1923. London. Martin Secker. 9 vol. 1/1000. sgn. teg. gray cloth. NF. T10. $750.00

MACHEN, Arthur. *Chronicle of Clemendy.* 1923. Soc Pantagruelists. ltd ed. sgn. 8vo. 331p. VG. B11. $85.00

MACHEN, Arthur. *Tales of Horror & the Supernatural.* 1948. Knopf. 1st ed. xl. dj. P3. $25.00

MACHEN, Arthur. *Terror.* 1917. McBride. 1st ed. VG. P3. $45.00

MACHETANZ & MACHETANZ. *Where Else But Alaska.* 1954. NY. 1st ed. VG/VG. B5. $30.00

MACINNES, Helen. *Above Suspicion.* 1941. Triangle. VG/VG. P3. $18.00

MACINNES, Helen. *Cloak of Darkness.* 1982. Harcourt Brace. 1st ed. VG/VG. P3. $12.00

MACINNES, Helen. *Horizon.* 1946. Little Brn. 1st ed. VG/G. P3. $25.00

MACINNES, Helen. *Message From Malaga.* nd. BC. xl. dj. P3. $5.00

MACINNES, Helen. *Prelude to Terror.* 1978. HBJ. VG/VG. P3. $15.00

MACINNES, Helen. *Ride a Pale Horse.* 1984. HBJ. 1st ed. VG/VG. P3. $20.00

MACISAAC, Fred. *Vanishing Professor.* 1927. Waterson. 1st ed. hc. VG. P3. $35.00

MACK, Gerstle. *Land Divided: History of the Panama Canal...* 1944. Knopf. 1st ed. sgn. 8vo. 650p. F/G. B11. $60.00

MACK, Nila. *Let's Pretend.* 1948. Whitman. ils Catherine Barnes. NF/VG+. C8. $85.00

MACKAY, Charles. *Life & Liberty in America; or, Sketches of a Tour...* 1859. NY. 1st Am ed. 12mo. 10 full-p pl. 413p. rebound. G. T3. $65.00

MACKAY-SMITH, Alexander. *American Foxhound, 1747-1967.* 1968. Millwood. Am Foxhound Club. 1st/only ed. 1/1000. sgn. O3. $425.00

MACKAY-SMITH, Alexander. *American Foxhunting.* 1970. Millwood. 1/2500. sgn/#d. VG. w/sgn edit letter. O3. $48.00

MACKENZIE, D.R. *Movement & Dispersal of Agriculturally Important Biotic...* 1985. Baton Rouge. lg 8vo. 611p. F. B1. $45.00

MACKENZIE, Donald. *Cool Sleeps Balaban.* 1964. Houghton Mifflin. 1st ed. xl. dj. P3. $4.00

MACKENZIE, Donald. *Genial Stranger.* nd. Houghton Mifflin. 2nd. VG/VG. P3. $13.00

MACKENZIE, Donald. *Night Boat From Puerto Verda.* 1970. Houghton Mifflin. xl. dj. P3. $5.00

MACKENZIE, Donald. *Postscript to a Dead Letter.* 1973. Houghton Mifflin. 1st ed. VG/VG. P3. $20.00

MACKENZIE, Donald. *Raven & the Paperhangers.* 1980. Macmillan. 1st ed. F/F. P3. $15.00

MACKENZIE, Donald. *Raven After Dark.* 1979. Houghton Mifflin. 1st ed. F/F. P3. $8.00

MACKENZIE, Donald. *Raven's Shadow.* 1985. Crime Club. 1st ed. F/F. P3. $15.00

MACKENZIE, Donald. *Sleep Is for the Rich.* 1971. Macmillan. 1st ed. VG/VG. P3. $18.00

MACKENZIE, George. *Institutions of the Law of Scotland.* 1688. Edinburgh. John Reid. 2nd/corrected/enlarged. 12mo. 408p. modern calf. K1. $300.00

MACKENZIE, Jean Kenyon. *African Clearings.* 1924. Houghton Mifflin. 1st ed. pres. 8vo. 270p. cloth. G. W1. $18.00

MACKENZIE, Kenneth K. *North American Cariceae.* 1940. NY Botanical Garden. 2 vol. folio. F. B26. $345.00

MACKENZIE, W. Roy. *Ballads & Sea Songs From Nova Scotia.* 1928. Harvard. lacks ffe. VG-. M17. $40.00

MACKENZIE, William H. *Evolution of United States Policy on Foreign Fishing Fees.* 1982. Charlottesville. VA U. 97p. prt wrp. M11. $20.00

MACKEY & SOOY. *Early California Costumes 1769-1847.* 1932. Stanford/Oxford. cloth. VG. D2. $40.00

MACKINNON, A. *Plants of Northern British Columbia.* 1992. Edmonton. 578p. 351p. sc. AN. B26. $17.50

MACKINNON, Allan. *Man Overboard.* nd. BC. VG/VG. P3. $8.00

MACKINSTRY, Elizabeth. *Aladdin & the Wonderful Lamp.* 1935. Macmillan. 1st ed. ils. gr cloth. F/G. M5. $60.00

MACKINSTRY, Elizabeth. *Aladdin & the Wonderful Lamp.* 1935. Macmillan. 1st ed. 4to. unp. VG+ C14 $35.00

MACKINSTRY, Elizabeth. *Puck in Pasture.* 1925. Doubleday. 1st ed. 8vo. ils. VG. M5. $32.00

MACKLIN, Elizabeth. *Woman Kneeling in the Big City.* 1992. Norton. 1st ed. poet's 1st book. sgn. RS. F/F. w/promo sheet. V1. $45.00

MACLACHLAN, David. *Treatise on Law of Merchant Shipping.* 1932. London. Sweet Maxwell. 7th. 936p. G. A16. $60.00

MACLAFFERTY, James Henry. *My Soul's Cathedral & Other Poems.* 1919. Paul Elder. thin 8vo. 22p. gilt brd. F/F. T10. $35.00

MACLAREN, Ian. *Beside the Bonnie Brier Bush.* 1895. NY. Dodd. pres from Andrew Carnegie. gr cloth. VG. T10. $400.00

MACLAY, John. *Other Engagements.* 1987. Dream House. 1st ed. 1/1000. NF/sans. R10. $5.00

MACLEAN, A.D. *Winter's Tales 26.* 1980. Macmillan. 1st ed. NF/NF. P3. $18.00

MACLEAN, Alistair. *Athabasca.* 1980. Collins. 1st ed. F/F. P3. $20.00

MACLEAN, Alistair. *Athabasca.* 1980. Doubleday. 1st Am ed. F/NF. N4. $30.00

MACLEAN, Alistair. *Bear Island.* 1971. Collins. 1st ed. VG/VG. P3. $25.00

MACLEAN, Alistair. *Caravan to Vaccares.* 1970. Collins. 1st ed. VG/VG. P3. $25.00

MACLEAN, Alistair. *Circus.* 1975. Doubleday. 1st Am ed. VG/G. N4. $20.00

MACLEAN, Alistair. *Floodgate.* 1983. Collins. 1st ed. F/F. P3. $20.00

MACLEAN, Alistair. *Force 10 From Navarone.* 1968. Doubleday. 1st Am ed. VG+/VG. N4. $27.50

MACLEAN, Alistair. *Goodbye California.* 1977. Collins. 1st ed. VG/VG. P3. $20.00

MACLEAN, Alistair. *Goodbye California.* 1978. Doubleday. 1st ed. NF/NF. H11. $15.00

MACLEAN, Alistair. *Partisans.* 1982. Collins. 1st ed. F/F. P3. $20.00

MACLEAN, Alistair. *Puppet on a Chain.* 1969. Collins. hc. VG/VG. P3. $25.00

MACLEAN, Alistair. *River of Death.* 1981. Collins. 1st ed. F/F. P3. $20.00

MACLEAN, Alistair. *San Andreas.* 1984. Collins. 1st ed. F/F. P3. $20.00

MACLEAN, Alistair. *Santorini.* 1986. Collins. 1st ed. F/F. P3. $20.00

MACLEAN, Alistair. *Seawitch.* 1977. Doubleday. 1st Am ed. F/NF. N4. $25.00

MACLEAN, Alistair. *Way to Dusty Death.* 1973. Collins. 1st ed. VG/VG. P3. $25.00

MACLEAN, Alistair. *Way to Dusty Death.* 1973. Doubleday. 1st ed. NF/NF. H11. $20.00

MACLEAN, Alistair. *Where Eagles Dare.* 1967. Doubleday. 1st ed. NF/NF. H11. $20.00

MACLEAN, Katherine. *Missing Man.* 1975. Berkley Putnam. 1st ed. VG/VG. P3. $15.00

MACLEAN, Norman. *River Runs Through It.* 1976. Chicago. ARC/1st ed. 8vo. RS. F/dj. w/promo material. S9. $1,750.00

MACLEAN, Norman. *River Runs Through It.* 1976. Chicago. 1st ils ed. VG/VG. B5. $35.00

MACLEAN, Norman. *River Runs Through It.* 1989. Pennyroyal. 1/200. sgn Maclean/Moser/Redford. marbled brd/red leather. AN. C2. $1,000.00

MACLEISH, Archibald. *Eleanor Roosevelt Story.* (1965). Boston. ils. 101p. gilt bl cloth. F/VG. H3. $45.00

MACLEISH, Archibald. *Fall of the City: A Verse Play for Radio.* 1937. Farrar Rinehart. 8vo. 33p. orange brd. NF/torn glassine. T10. $45.00

MACLEISH, Archibald. *Human Season, Selected Poems 1926-1972.* 1972. Houghton Mifflin. 1st ed. assn copy. F/NF. V1. $20.00

MACLEISH, Archibald. *Poems.* 1943. London. rpt. F/sans. V1. $15.00

MACLEISH, Archibald. *Poetry & Journalism: A Lecture.* 1958. MN U. 1st ed. RS. NF/prt wrp. V1. $15.00

MACLEISH, Archibald. *Riders on the Earth.* 1978. Houghton Mifflin. 1st ed. assn copy. F/NF. V1. $25.00

MACLEISH, Roderick. *Prince Ombra.* 1982. Congdon. 1st ed. F/F. H11. $20.00

MACLEISH & VAN DOREN. *Dialogues.* 1964. Dutton. 1st ed. F/F. B35. $35.00

MACLEOD, Barbara. *Children's Twilight Tales.* 1942. NY. Harrison. 1st ed. inscr/dtd 1942. ils John Morgan. NF. C14. $25.00

MACLEOD, Charlotte. *Astrology for Skeptics.* 1972. Macmillan. 1st ed. VG. P3. $20.00

MACLEOD, Charlotte. *Christmas Stockings.* 1991. Mysterious. 2nd ed. F/F. P3. $20.00

MACLEOD, Charlotte. *Mistletoe Mysteries.* nd. BC. hc. F/F. P3. $10.00

MACLEOD, Mary. *King Arthur & His Knights.* 1950. Rainbow Classics. hc. F/F. P3. $20.00

MACMANUS, Seumas. *Hibernian Nights.* 1966. Macmillan. 5th. VG/VG. P3. $18.00

MACMANUS, Seumas. *Well O' the World's End.* 1939. Macmillan. 1st ed. 8vo. ils Richard Bennett. xl. T10. $25.00

MACMICHAEL, William. *Gold-Headed Cane.* 1993. NY. facsimile of 1915. quarter leather. VG. A13. $30.00

MACMILLAN, Cyrus. *Canadian Wonder Tales.* nd. ils George Sheringham. VG. M17. $27.50

MACMILLAN, Miriam. *Green Seas & White Ice: Far North With Captain Mac.* 1948. Dodd Mead. 9th. sgn. 8vo. F/F. B11. $40.00

MACNALTY, Arthur. *Princess in the Tower & Other Royal Mysteries.* 1955. np. 1st ed. 212p. dj. A13. $10.00

MACNEICE, Louis. *Eighty-Five Poems.* 1959. London. Faber. 1st ed. assn copy. F/NF. V1. $30.00

MACNEICE, Louis. *Poems.* 1937. Random. assn copy. F/G. V1. $75.00

MACNEIL, Neil; see Ballard. W.T.

MACNEISH, Richard. *First Annual Report of Tehuacan Archaeological Botanical...* 1961. Andover, MA. 4to. 32p. wrp. F3. $20.00

MACPHAIL, Elizabeth C. *Kate Sessions: Pioneer Horticulturist.* 1976. San Diego. photos. 153p. sc. VG. B26. $30.00

MACQUITTY, William. *Abu Simbel.* 1965. Putnam. 1st ed. ils. VG/tattered. W1. $28.00

MACTYRE, Paul. *Fish on a Hook.* 1963. Hodder Stoughton. NF/NF. P3. $8.00

MACVEAGH, Wayne. *Law & Democracy. An Address Delivered...* 1886. New Haven. 33p. prt wrp. M11. $50.00

MACVICAR, Angus. *Atom Chasers.* 1960. Burke. VG/VG. P3. $12.00

MACVICAR, Angus. *Secret of the Lost Planet.* 1961. Burke. VG/VG. P3. $13.00

MACY, Juliette. *Duex Enfants a la Mer.* 1937. Macmillan. 1st ed. ils L Brooke McNamara. NF/VG. M5. $30.00

MADAN, Falconer. *Books in Manuscript.* 1893. London. 1st ed. VG. S13. $15.00

MADAN, Martin. *Thelyphthora; or, Treatise on Female Ruin...* 1780. London. Dodsley. 1st ed. contemporary calf. K1. $350.00

MADDEN. *Art, Crafts & Architecture in Early Illinois.* 1974. F/F. D2. $40.00

MADDEROM, Gary. *Four-Chambered Villain.* 1971. Macmillan. 1st ed. F/F. P3. $13.00

MADDOCK, Reginald. *Time Maze.* 1960. Thomas Nelson. 1st ed. G/G. P3. $15.00

MADDOCKS, Melvin. *Great Liners.* 1978. Time Life. VG. A16. $20.00

MADISON, Lucy Foster. *Washington.* 1925. Penn. 1st ed. ils. 399p. G+. C14. $18.00

MADSEN, Axel. *Borderlines.* 1975. Macmillan. 1st ed. VG/VG. P3. $15.00

MAEDER. *Dick Tracy: Official Biography.* 1990. ils/photos. 218p. F. M13. $14.00

MAETERLINCK, Maurice. *Life & Flowers.* 1907. London. 312p. VG. B26. $20.00

MAETERLINCK, Maurice. *Our Friend the Dog.* 1913. NY. 1st ed. gilt bl cloth. NF. M5. $110.00

MAFFEI, Paolo. *Monsters in the Sky.* 1980. MIT. 8vo. ils/photos. 342p. VG/torn. K5. $15.00

MAGEE, David. *Course in Correct Cataloging.* 1958. San Francisco. 1/175. 8vo. 16p. F/stiff wrp. T10. $50.00

MAGILL, Mary Tucker. *Magill's First Book in Virginia History.* 1908. JP Bell. ils. 217p. G. B10. $12.00

MAGILL. *Great Women Writers: Lives & Works of 135...* 1994. np. 4to. 611p. VG/VG. A4. $40.00

MAGINI, Giovanni Antonio. *Italia.* 1974. Amsterdam. facsimile. 61 double-p maps. AN/dj. O7. $175.00

MAGINNIS, A.J. *Atlantic Ferry.* 1983. London. Whittaker. 1st popular ed. ils. 208p. worn. T7. $110.00

MAGNER, D. *Magner's ABC Guide to Sensible Horse-Shoeing.* 1899. Werner. 1st ed. ils. O3. $95.00

MAGNER, D. *New System of Educating Horses.* 1876. Lovell. 11th. VG. O3. $65.00

MAGNER, D. *Taming & Educating Horses.* 1888. Battle Creek. 1112p. binding copy. O3. $65.00

MAGOUN, F. Alexander. *Frigate Constitution & Other Historic Ships.* 1928. Marine Research Soc. 154p. VG. M20. $200.00

MAGRIEL, Paul. *Backgammon.* 1979. NY. 4th. sgn. VG/dj. S1. $20.00

MAHAN, A.T. *Influence of Sea Power Upon History 1660-1783.* 1896. Little Brn. 12th. 8vo. 4 maps. 557p. teg. VG. W1. $45.00

MAHARAJAH OF COOCH BEHAR. *Thirty-Seven Years of Big Game Shooting in Cooch Behar...* 1993. Prescott. Wolfe. ltd facsimile of 1908 ed. 471p. aeg. F. A17. $45.00

MAHON, Denis. *Il Guercino...* 1968. Bologna. Alfa Ott. 2nd. ils/pl. 235p. stiff wrp. D2. $75.00

MAHONEY & WHITNEY. *Realms of Gold.* 1929. Doubleday Doran. 5th. 796p. VG. P2. $50.00

MAHY, Margaret. *Man Whose Mother Was a Pirate.* 1985. Viking Kestral. 1st ed thus. ils Margaret Chamberlain. F/F. T5. $20.00

MAILER, Norman. *Advertisements for Myself.* 1959. Putnam. 1st ed. F/F. B35. $65.00

MAILER, Norman. *Advertisements for Myself.* 1959. Putnam. 1st ed. VG/VG. w/tipped-in sgn. S13. $40.00

MAILER, Norman. *American Dream.* 1965. Andre Deutsch. 1st ed. VG/VG. P3. $30.00

MAILER, Norman. *Ancient Evenings.* 1983. Little Brn. 1st ed. F/F. B35. $34.00

MAILER, Norman. *Ancient Evenings.* 1983. Little Brn. 1st ed. sgn. F/F. B2. $85.00

MAILER, Norman. *Barbary Shore.* 1951. NY. 1st ed. author's 2nd book. VG/VG. w/sgn. S13. $110.00

MAILER, Norman. *Barbary Shore.* 1951. NY. 1st ed. F/VG+. N3. $60.00

MAILER, Norman. *Deer Park.* 1955. 1st ed. NF/VG. w/sgn. S13. $85.00

MAILER, Norman. *Deer Park.* 1955. Putnam. 1st ed. NF/VG. M19. $65.00

MAILER, Norman. *Executioner's Song.* 1979. Little Brn. 1st ed. NF/NF. M19. $25.00

MAILER, Norman. *Fight.* 1975. Little Brn. 1st ed. F/VG+. A20. $28.00

MAILER, Norman. *Harlot's Ghost.* 1991. Random. 1st ed. AN/dj. M22. $25.00

MAILER, Norman. *Marilyn.* 1974. Grosset Dunlap. stated 1st prt. tan cloth/brn letters. F/NF. H4. $35.00

MAILER, Norman. *Marilyn.* 1974. Grosset Dunlap. VG/VG. P3. $20.00

MAILER, Norman. *Prisoner of Sex.* 1971. Boston. 1st ed. F/clip. A17. $25.00

MAILER, Norman. *Tough Guys Don't Dance.* 1984. Random. 1st ed. F/F. B35. $30.00

MAILS, Thomas E. *Dog Soldiers, Bear Men & Buffalo Women.* 1973. Englewood Cliffs. Prentice Hall. 1st ed. ils. 384p. F/VG. T10. $100.00

MAIMONIDES, Moses. *Treatise on Hemorrhoids.* 1969. Phil. 79p. VG. A13. $50.00

MAINE, Charles Eric. *Count-Down.* 1959. Hodder Stoughton. VG/VG. P3. $30.00

MAINE, Charles Eric. *Isotope Man.* nd. BC. VG/VG. P3. $8.00

MAINE, Charles Eric. *Timeliner.* 1955. Hodder Stoughton. 1st ed. NF/NF. P3. $20.00

MAINE, Floyd Shuster. *Lone Eagle..White Sioux.* 1956. NM U. 1st ed. sgn. 8vo. VG/VG. B11. $100.00

MAINE, Henry Sumner. *Ancient Law, Its Connection With the Early History...* 1864. Scribner. 1st Am ed. 3-quarter calf. M11. $450.00

MAINE, Henry Sumner. *Village-Communities in the East & West...* 1876. NY. Holt. 3rd. quarter morocco. M11. $250.00

MAIR, George B. *Miss Turquoise.* 1965. Random. 1st ed. VG/VG. P3. $15.00

MAIRE, R. *Etudes sur la Flore et la Vegetation du Sahara Central I-II.* 1933. Algiers. ils. 272p. VG. B26. $35.00

MAITLAND, Frederic W. *Charters of the Borough of Cambridge.* 1901. Cambridge. gilt bl cloth. G. M11. $125.00

MAITLAND, Frederic W. *Essays on the Teaching of History.* 1901. Cambridge. gilt bl cloth. M11. $85.00

MAITLAND, Lester J. *Knights of the Air.* 1929. Garden City. 1st ed. ils. 338p. G+. B18. $95.00

MAJOR, Charles. *When Knighthood Was in Flower.* nd. Grosset Dunlap. MTI. VG. P3. $20.00

MAJOR, A. *Short Whist With Precepts for Tyros by Mrs B.* 1850. London. 11th. 111p. G. S1. $15.00

MAJOR A. & PROFESSOR P. *Short Whist With an Essay...* 1865. London. 18th. 147p. bdg loose. S1. $15.00

MAJORS, Simon; see Fox, Gardner F.

MAKOWSKI. *Quilting, 1915-1983.* 1985. 157p. F. A4. $35.00

MALAMUD, Bernard. *Assistant.* 1957. Farrar. 1st ed. author's 2nd book. NF/NF. H11. $120.00

MALAMUD, Bernard. *Dubin's Lives.* 1979. NY. Farrar. 1st ed. F/NF. H11. $30.00

MALAMUD, Bernard. *God's Grace.* 1982. FSG. 1st ed. NF/NF. B30. $20.00

MALAN, A.H. *Famous Homes of Great Britain; Other Famous Homes; More...* 1900-1902. np. 3 vol. photos. VG. M17. $125.00

MALANGA, Gerard. *Rosebud.* 1975. Penmaen. ltd ed. 1/700. F/wrp over stiff brd. V1. $15.00

MALET, Capt. *Annals of the Road.* 1876. Longman Gr. 1st ed. O3. $135.00

MALGAIGNE, J.F. *Surgery & Ambroise Pare.* 1965. Norman, OK. 1st Eng trans. 435p. VG. A13. $100.00

MALING, Arthur. *Bent Man.* 1975. Detective Book Club. VG. P3. $8.00

MALING, Arthur. *Koberg Link.* 1979. Harper Row. 1st ed. VG/VG. P3. $15.00

MALING, Arthur. *Schroeder's Game.* 1977. Harper Row. 1st ed. xl. dj. P3. $5.00

MALING, Peter Bromley. *Early Charts of New Zealand 1542-1851.* 1969. Wellington. Reed. 59 maps. F/case. O7. $400.00

MALITZ, Jerome. *Personal Landscapes.* 1989. Portland. 132 photos. 272p. F/dj. B26. $22.50

MALLARD, Robert Q. *Plantation Life Before Emancipation.* 1892. Richmond, VA. Whittet Shepperson. 1st ed. 237p. NF. M8. $250.00

MALLOCH, Douglas. *Someone To Care.* 1925. Wise Parslow. 12mo. ils. VG/dj. M5. $12.00

MALLOCK, W.H. *Heart of Life.* 1895. Putnam. VG. P3. $20.00

MALLON, John. *Opening Leads & Signals.* 1964. NY. 159p. VG/dj. S1. $6.00

MALLON, Thomas. *Arts & Sciences.* 1988. NY. 1st ed. F/F. A17. $10.00

MALLOWAN, M.E.L. *Early Mesopotamia & Iran.* 1965. London. Thames Hudson. 1st ed. 8vo. ils. 138p. xl. G. W1. $18.00

MALLOY, William. *Mystery Book of Days.* 1990. Mysterious. decor brd. F. P3. $15.00

MALO, Vincent Gaspard. *And Why Not?* 1958. Arthur Barker. 1st ed. NF/NF. P3. $25.00

MALONE, Bill C. *Southern Music, American Music.* 1979. Lexington. 1st ed. F/NF. B4. $75.00

MALONE, Michael. *Foolscap.* 1991. Little Brn. 1st ed. rem mk. F/F. H11. $25.00

MALONE, Michael. *Handling Sin.* 1986. Little Brn. 1st ed. F/NF. H11. $30.00

MALONE, Michael. *Time's Witness.* 1989. Little Brn. UP. F/wht wrp. M22. $45.00

MALONE, Michael. *Time's Witness.* 1989. Little Brn. 1st ed. VG/NF. M22. $12.00

MALONE, Michael. *Uncivil Seasons.* 1983. Delacorte. 1st ed. F/F. M22. $65.00

MALORY, Thomas. *Chronicles of King Arthur.* 1988. London. Folio Soc. 1st ed thus. ils Edward Bawden. F. T10. $300.00

MALORY, Thomas. *Le Morte d'Arthur.* 1920. London. Warner. 2 vol. 4to. ils W Russell Flint. emb cloth. F. T10. $450.00

MALORY, Thomas. *Le Morte d'Arthur: History of King Arthur...* 1920. London. Medici Soc. 2 vol. 1st trade ed. ils Flint. teg. NF. T10. $350.00

MALORY, Thomas. *Morte d'Arthur.* nd. Appleton Century Crofts. VG. P3. $15.00

MALOT, Hector. *Adventures of Perrine.* 1936. Rand McNally. Windemere Classic. ils Milo Winter. F/chip. M5. $35.00

MALOT, Hector. *Nobody's Boy.* 1916. Cupples Leon. 1st ed. ils JB Gruelle. 372p. VG. M20. $52.00

MALOUF, David. *Johnno.* 1978. Braziller. 1st Am ed. sgn. F/F. B2. $65.00

MALRAUX, Andre. *Days of Wrath.* 1936. Random. 1st ed. VG/VG. A20. $23.00

MALVILLE & PUTNAM. *Prehistoric Astronomy in the Southwest.* 1993. Boulder, CO. Johnson Books. revised. 8vo. 108p. wrp. K5. $9.00

MALZBERG, Barry N. *Beyond Apollo.* 1975. Readers Union. VG/VG. P3. $10.00

MALZBERG & PRONZINI. *Dark Sins, Dark Dreams.* 1978. Doubleday. 1st ed. VG/VG. P3. $18.00

MALZBERG & PRONZINI. *Guernica Night.* 1974. Bobbs Merrill. 1st ed. F/F. P3. $20.00

MALZBERG & PRONZINI. *Herovit's World.* 1973. Random. 1st ed. VG/VG. P3. $20.00

MALZBERG & PRONZINI. *Man Who Loved the Midnight Lady.* 1980. Doubleday. 1st ed. VG/G. P3. $15.00

MAMET, David. *Some Freaks.* 1989. 1st ed. NF/NF. S13. $25.00

MAMMANA, Dennis. *Star Hunters: Quest To Discover Secrets of the Universe.* 1990. Phil. Running Pr. 1st ed. 160p. F/F. K5. $20.00

MAN, John. *Encyclopedia of Space Travel & Astronomy.* 1979. London. Octopus. 4to. 224p. VG/VG. K5. $12.00

MANCHESTER, William. *Death of a President.* 1967. 1st ed. VG/VG. K2. $22.00

MANCHESTER, William. *Goodbye, Darkness: Memoir of the Pacific War.* 1980. Boston. 1st ed. 401p. VG/tape rpr. A17. $10.00

MANCHESTER, William. *World Lit Only by Fire.* 1992. Little Brn. 1st ed. w/sgn leaf. F/F. B2. $40.00

MANDAVA & MORGAN. *CRC Handbook of Natural Pesticides.* 1987. Boca Raton. 198p. AN. B26. $75.00

MANDAVILLE, James P. *Flora of Eastern Saudi Arabia.* 1990. London. ils/photos/maps. 482p. VG/dj. B26. $125.00

MANDEVILLE. *Used Book Price Guide. Retail Prices of Rare, Scarce... 1972-1973.* 2 vol. 5 Year ed. F. A4. $45.00

MANDEVILLE. *Used Book Price Guide. Retail Prices of Rare, Scarce...* 1977. 4to. 479p. F. A4. $40.00

MANER, William. *Deadly Nighshed.* 1986. Doubleday. 1st ed. 181p. VG/VG. B10. $12.00

MANFRED, Frederick. *Brother.* 1950. Doubleday. 1st ed. F/VG. A18. $25.00

MANFRED, Frederick. *Giant.* 1951. Doubleday. 1st ed. F/VG. A18. $25.00

MANFRED, Frederick. *Green Earth.* 1977. Crown. 1st ed. F/F. A18. $25.00

MANFRED, Frederick. *King of Spades.* 1966. Trident. 1st ed. sgn. F/VG. A18. $40.00

MANFRED, Frederick. *Man Who Looked Like the Prince of Wales.* 1965. Trident. 1st ed. inscr. F/F. A18. $20.00

MANFRED, Frederick. *Manly-Hearted Woman.* 1975. Crown. 1st ed. sgn. F/F. A18. $15.00

MANFRED, Frederick. *This Is the Year.* 1947. Doubleday. 1st ed. F/VG. A18. $40.00

MANFRED, Frederick. *Wanderlust: A Trilogy*. 1962. Alan Swallow. 1st ed thus. NF/dj. A18. $50.00

MANGUEL, Alberto. *Dictionary of Imaginary Places*. 1980. Lester Orpen Denys. 1st ed. VG/VG. P3. $35.00

MANKILLER & WALLIS. *Mankiller: A Chief & Her People*. 1993. St Martin. AP. 8vo. NF/prt wrp. w/pub letter. S9. $35.00

MANLY, G.B. *Aircraft Powerplant Manual*. 1942. Chicago. Drake. ils/index. fair. B18. $35.00

MANN, Albert William. *History of the 45th Regiment MA Volunteer Militia...* 1908. Boston. Wallace Spooner. 1st ed. 562p. VG. M8. $150.00

MANN, E.B. *Killer's Range*. 1943. Triangle. VG/VG. P3. $6.00

MANN, E.B. *Stampede*. 1943. Triangle. hc. G. P3. $4.00

MANN, E.B. *Thirsty Range*. 1945. Triangle. hc. VG. P3. $10.00

MANN, Gerhard. *Holstein Horses*. nd. Bayreuth. Schwartz. German text. VG/VG. O3. $25.00

MANN, May. *Elvis & the Colonel*. 1977. Drake. hc. VG/VG. P3. $20.00

MANN, Thomas. *Beloved Returns*. 1940. Knopf. 1st Am ed. 453p. VG/dj. M20. $57.00

MANN, Thomas. *Confessions of Felix Krull, Confidence Man*. 1955. Knopf. stated 1st Am ed. VG+/VG. H4. $20.00

MANN, Thomas. *Doctor Faustus*. 1948. Knopf. 1st ed. NF/VG. M19. $45.00

MANN, Thomas. *Holy Sinner*. 1951. Canada. Knopf. VG. P3. $20.00

MANN, Thomas. *Stories of Three Decades*. 1936. Knopf. VG/VG. P3. $35.00

MANNES, Marya. *Message From a Stranger*. 1948. Viking. 1st ed. author's 1st book. F/F. B4. $45.00

MANNES, Marya. *Message From a Stranger*. 1948. Viking. 1st ed. VG. P3. $10.00

MANNES, Marya. *More in Anger: Some Opinions, Uncensored & Unteleprompted*. 1958. Lippincott. 1st ed. inscr. F/VG. B4. $125.00

MANNES, Marya. *They*. 1968. Doubleday. 1st ed. sgn. F/dj. P3. $30.00

MANNIN, Ethel. *Lovely Land: Hashemite Kingdom of Jordan*. 1965. Hutchinson. 1st ed. 8vo. 203p. NF/dj. W1. $22.00

MANNING, George C. *Basic Design of Ships*. 1945. Nostrand. 1st ed. 212p. VG+. M20. $27.00

MANNING-SANDERS, Ruth. *Book of Magic Animals*. 1974. Methuen. 1st ed. F/F. P3. $20.00

MANNING-SANDERS, Ruth. *Sir Green Hat & the Wizard*. 1974. Methuen. F/F. P3. $15.00

MANNIX, Daniel. *Fox & the Hound*. 1967. Dutton. 1st ed. G+. O3. $18.00

MANOR, Jason. *Too Dead To Run*. 1953. Viking. 1st ed. VG/VG. P3. $18.00

MANSBRIDGE, Michael. *John Nash: Complete Catalogue 1752-1835*. 1991. Rizzoli. ils/drawings. F/dj. A17. $45.00

MANSO, Peter. *Mailer: His Life & Times*. 1985. NY. 1st ed. 718p. F/F. A17. $14.50

MANTEGAZZA, Paolo. *Sexual Relations of Mankind*. 1932. NY. Falstaff. 1st ed. 1/1500. 272p. VG. W1. $25.00

MANTLE, Mickey. *Education of a Baseball Player*. 1967. Simon Schuster. 1st ed. VG/VG. P8. $50.00

MANTLE, Mickey. *My Favorite Summer 1956*. 1991. Doubleday. later prt. F/F. P8. $125.00

MANTLE, Mickey. *Quality of Courage*. 1964. Doubleday. 1st ed. VG/G+. P8. $45.00

MANTLE, Winifred. *Tinker's Castle*. 1963. HRW. 1st ed. 8vo. 222p. VG/G+. T5. $25.00

MANTRAN, Robert. *Turkey*. 1955. Hachette. 1st ed. 8vo. 127p. VG. W1. $30.00

MANUEL, Frank E. *Portrait of Isaac Newton*. 1968. Cambridge. 8vo. 478p. xl. VG/dj. K5. $30.00

MANZER. *Abstract Journal 1790-1920...* 1977. np. 312p. F. A4. $45.00

MANZINI, Gianna. *L'Opera Complete Del Greco*. 1969. Rizzoli. 1st hc ed. Italian text. VG. P3. $15.00

MAPES, Mary A. *Surprise!* 1944. np. Howell Soskin. ils Fredenthal. 18p. sbdg. A17. $10.00

MAPLE, Eric. *Witchcraft*. 1973. Octopus. hc. VG. P3. $15.00

MAPSON, Jo-Ann. *Blue Rodeo*. 1994. Harper Collins. 1st ed. F/F. M23. $25.00

MARA, Bernard; see Moore, Brian.

MARAFIOTI, P. *Caruso's Method of Voice Production...* 1927. Appleton. ils. 300p. F. B14. $37.50

MARAINI, Fosco. *Jerusalem, Rock of Ages*. 1969. Harcourt. 1st ed. 122p. NF/dj. W1. $30.00

MARAMOROSCH, K. *Invertebrate Tissue Culture*. 1976. Academic. 8vo. ils. 393p. cloth. VG. B1. $65.00

MARAN, Rene. *Batouala*. 1922. Thomas Seltzer. 1st ed. VG. B2. $45.00

MARASCO, Robert. *Parlor Games*. nd. BC. VG/VG. P3. $8.00

MARCET, Jane Haldimand. *Conversations on Vegetable Physiology...* 1829. London. Longman. 2 vol. pl. VG. A10. $150.00

MARCH, Harold. *Gide & the Hound of Heaven*. 1952. Phil. 1st ed. dj. A17. $12.50

MARCH, Joseph Moncure. *Wild Party*. 1994. Pantheon. 1st ed. F/F. B35. $40.00

MARCH, William. *Come in at the Door*. 1934. Smith Haas. 1st ed. NF/dj. B2. $65.00

MARCHAJ, C.A. *Seaworthiness: The Forgotten Factor*. 1986. Camden. Internat Marine. 187 ils. 371p. VG/dj. T7. $35.00

MARCHIONE, Margherita. *Philip Mazzei: Jefferson's Zealous Whig*. 1975. Am Inst Italian Studies. 350p. VG/VG. B10. $35.00

MARCUS, J.S. *Art of Cartography*. 1991. Knopf. 1st ed. F/F. M23. $20.00

MARCUS, J.S. *75 Years of Children's Book Week Posters...* 1994. np. 4to. 96p. F/F. A4. $65.00

MARCUS, Stanley. *Quest for the Best*. 1979. Viking. 1/850. ils. 228p. F/dj. w/author's miniature bookplate. B24. $150.00

MARGULIES, Leo. *From Off This World*. 1949. Merlin. 1st hc ed. VG/VG. P3. $50.00

MARGULIES, Leo. *My Best SF Story*. 1949. Merlin. 1st ed. VG. P3. $50.00

MARIAH, Paul. *Apparitions of a Black Pauper's Suit: 13 Eulogies*. 1976. Hoddypoll. 1st ed? 32p. VG/wrp. A17. $15.00

MARIANA. *Miss Flora McFlimsey's Christmas Eve*. 1949. Lee Shepard. 4th. 12mo. ils. NF/VG. M5. $40.00

MARIANA. *Miss Flora McFlimsey's Valentine*. 1962. Lee Shepard. 1st ed. 16mo. F/VG. M5. $60.00

MARIANI, Paul. *Prime Mover*. 1985. Grove. 1st ed. F/clip. V1. $15.00

MARIE, Adrien. *Une Journee d'Enfant*. 1883. Paris. 1st ed. folio. French text. 20 pl. ornate gilt cloth. VG. M5. $475.00

MARIL, Nadja. *Runaway Molly Midnight: The Artist's Cat*. 1980. Owing Mills, MD. Stemmer. 1st ed. 8vo. 25p. gilt brd. F. C14. $6.00

MARILL, Alvin H. *Samuel Goldwyn Presents.* 1967. Barnes. VG/VG. P3. $35.00

MARINONI, Augusto. *I Rebus di Leonardo da Vinci.* 1954. Firenze. Olschki. 1/1500. ils/pl. D2. $75.00

MARION, Pierre. *Afin Que Battle le Coeur: L'Epopee de la Chirurgie...* 1990. Lyon. 1st ed. 248p. wrp. A13. $35.00

MARIUS, Richard. *Coming of Rain.* 1969. Knopf. 1st ed. F/F. H11. $45.00

MARJORIBANKS, Edward. *For the Defense: Life of Sir Edward Marshall Hall.* 1930. Macmillan. 8vo. 471p. brn cloth. VG. T10. $25.00

MARK, Jan. *Ennead.* 1978. Crowell. 1st ed. F/F. P3. $10.00

MARKER, R.J. *Household Brigade Drag Hounds 1893 1894.* 1895. Windsor. Oxley. only ed. 4to. 43p. marbled ep. gilt half leather/cloth. T10. $150.00

MARKHAM, Beryl. *West With the Night.* 1987. North Point. 1st ed thus. F/clip. M23. $20.00

MARKHAM, Edwin. *New Poems: Eighty Songs at 80.* 1931. 1st ed. VG+/chip. S13. $20.00

MARKHAM, Edwin. *Real Romance in America 1455-1910.* 1910. NY. Lakeside. 13 vol. ils/index. gilt cloth. A17. $85.00

MARKHAM, Edwin. *Shoes of Happiness & Other Poems.* 1932. Doubleday Doran. sgn. 12mo. 192p. gr brd. G. B11. $25.00

MARKHAM, Robert. *Colonel Sun.* 1968. Harper Row. 1st ed. VG/VG. P3. $35.00

MARKOV, A.V. *Moon: A Russian View.* 1962. Chicago. 8vo. 391p. 2 fld pocket lunar charts. cloth. G. K5. $35.00

MARKOWITZ & ROSPER. *Deadly Dust: Silicosis & Poltics of Occupational Disease...* 1991. Princeton. 229p. dj. A13. $30.00

MARKS, J.; see Highwater, Jamake.

MARKS-HIGHWATER, J.; see Highwater, Jamake.

MARKSTEIN, George. *Chance Awakening.* 1978. Ballantine. 1st ed. NF/NF. H11/P3. $20.00

MARKSTEIN, George. *Cooler.* 1974. Souvenir. 1st ed. F/F. P3. $20.00

MARKSTEIN, George. *Tara Kane.* 1978. London. Cape. 1st ed. NF/NF. P3. $25.00

MARKUS, Julia. *Uncle.* 1978. Houghton Mifflin. 2nd prt. author's 1st book. F/F. B4. $75.00

MARLETT, Melba. *Frightened Ones.* 1956. Doubleday. 1st ed. VG/VG. P3. $20.00

MARLITT, E. *Old Mam'selle's Secret.* nd. Lovell Coryell. hc. G. P3. $10.00

MARLOWE, Derek. *Do You Remember England?* 1972. Viking. 1st ed. F/F. P3. $25.00

MARLOWE, Derek. *Nightshade.* 1976. Viking. 1st ed. VG/VG. P3. $25.00

MARLOWE, Hugh; see Patterson, Henry.

MARLOWE, Piers. *Knife for Your Heart.* 1966. John Gifford. VG/VG. P3. $13.00

MARLOWE, Piers. *Men in Her Death.* 1964. BC. xl. dj. P3. $8.00

MARLOWE, Stephen; see Lesser, Milton.

MARON, Margaret. *Lieutenant Harald & the Treasure Island Treasure.* 1991. Mystery Scene Short Story. 1/100. sgn/#d. F. P3. $20.00

MARON, Margaret. *Shooting at Loons.* 1994. Mysterious. 1st ed. rem mk. F/F. N4. $20.00

MARON, Margaret. *Shooting at Loons.* 1994. Mysterious. 1st ed. sgn. F/F. T2. $25.00

MARON, Margaret. *Southern Discomfort.* 1993. Mysterious. 1st ed. F/F. T2. $25.00

MARQUAND, John P. *BF's Daughter.* 1946. Little Brn. 1st ed. VG/VG. P3. $30.00

MARQUAND, John P. *HM Pulham, Esquire.* 1941. Little Brn. 1st ed. VG/VG. P3. $30.00

MARQUAND, John P. *Life at Happy Knoll.* 1957. Boston. 1st ed. VG/VG. B5. $22.50

MARQUAND, John P. *Melville Goodwin, USA.* 1951. Little Brn. 1st ed. VG/VG. P3. $25.00

MARQUAND, John P. *Mr Moto: Four Complete Novels.* 1983. Avenel. VG/VG. P3. $15.00

MARQUAND, John P. *Thank You, Mr Moto.* nd. Herbert Jenkins. 3rd. VG/VG. P3. $18.00

MARQUAND, John P. *Thank You, Mr Moto/Mr Moto Is So Sorry.* 1977. Curtis. VG/VG. P3. $15.00

MARQUAND, John P. *Unspeakable Gentleman.* 1922. Scribner. 1st ed. author's 1st novel. 265p. VG/tattered. M20. $52.00

MARQUAND, John P. *Women & Thomas Harrow.* 1958. Little Brn. 1st ed. VG/VG. P3. $30.00

MARQUAND, John P. *Your Turn, Mr Moto.* 1987. Souvenir. VG/VG. P3. $15.00

MARQUEZ, Gabriel Garcia. *Autumn of the Patriarch.* 1976. Harper Row. 5th. VG/VG. P3. $12.00

MARQUEZ, Gabriel Garcia. *Chronicle of a Death Foretold.* nd. BC. VG/VG. P3. $10.00

MARQUEZ, Gabriel Garcia. *Chronicle of a Death Foretold.* 1983. Knopf. 1st ed/1st state. F/F clip. M23. $35.00

MARQUEZ, Gabriel Garcia. *Clandestine in Chile.* 1987. Holt. 1st ed. F/F. B35. $60.00

MARQUEZ, Gabriel Garcia. *Collected Novellas.* 1990. Harper Collins. 1st ed. NF/NF. M23. $20.00

MARQUEZ, Gabriel Garcia. *Cronica de una Muerte Anunciada.* 1981. Bogota. 1st ed. F/F. A11. $40.00

MARQUEZ, Gabriel Garcia. *Doom of Damocles/El Cataclismo de Damocles.* 1986. Bogota. 1st bilingual/Colombian ed. 1/3000. F/wrp. A11. $40.00

MARQUEZ, Gabriel Garcia. *El Amor en Los Tiempos del Colera.* 1985. Bogota. 1st ed. NF/NF. C6. $50.00

MARQUEZ, Gabriel Garcia. *El General en su Laberinto.* 1989. Mexico. 1st ed. 1/100. sgn. F. C2. $350.00

MARQUEZ, Gabriel Garcia. *General in His Labyrinth.* nd. BC. VG/VG. P3. $10.00

MARQUEZ, Gabriel Garcia. *General in His Labyrinth.* 1990. Knopf. 1st ed. F/F. B35/M23. $20.00

MARQUEZ, Gabriel Garcia. *La Adventura de Miguel Littin Clandestino en Chile.* 1986. Bogota. 1st ed. F/F. A11. $45.00

MARQUEZ, Gabriel Garcia. *Love in the Time of Cholera.* 1988. Knopf. ltd ed. 1/350. sgn. F/dj/case. B4. $500.00

MARQUEZ, Gabriel Garcia. *Love in the Time of Cholera.* 1988. Knopf. 1st ed. NF/F. H11. $40.00

MARQUEZ, Gabriel Garcia. *Love in the Time of Cholera.* 1988. London. Cape. 1st ed. F/NF. M23. $25.00

MARQUEZ, Gabriel Garcia. *One Hundred Years of Solidude.* 1982. LEC. 1/2000. sgn Rabassa/Reid/Ferrer. w/orig prt. F/case. C2. $250.00

MARQUIS, Don. *Archy's Life of Mehitabel.* 1933. Garden City. 1st ed. F/F. C2. $100.00

MARQUIS, Don. *Danny's Own Story.* 1912. Garden City. 1st ed. author's 1st book. ils EW Kemble. VG. C2. $40.00

MARQUIS, Don. *Dreams & Dust.* 1915. Harper. 1st ed. 8vo. teg. F. T10. $50.00

MARRANT, John. *Narrative of Lord's Wonderful Dealings With John Marrant.* 1790. Dublin. Dugdale. 6th. 12mo. prt self wrp. C6. $500.00

MARRIC, J.J.; see Creasey, John.

MARRIOTT, Alice. *Mara: The Potter of San Idelfonso.* 1976. OK U. 14th. 8vo. ils Margaret Lefranc. 294p. blk cloth. NF. T10. $25.00

MARRIOTT, Crittenden. *Isle of Dead Ships.* 1925. Lippincott. VG. P3. $25.00

MARRIOTT & RACHLIN. *American Indian Mythology.* 1968. Crowell. 4th. 8vo. 121p. F/VG. T10. $35.00

MARSCHALL. *America's Great Comic-Strip Artists.* 1989. ils. 295p. F/dj. M13. $70.00

MARSH, J.B.T. *Story of the Jubilee Singers With Their Songs.* nd. Houghton Mifflin. 18th thousand/revised. ils. 265p. fair. B10. $100.00

MARSH, Ngaio. *Artists in Crime.* nd. Grosset Dunlap. VG. P3. $12.00

MARSH, Ngaio. *Clutch of Constables.* 1968. Collin Crime Club. 1st ed. VG/VG. P3. $25.00

MARSH, Ngaio. *Colour Scheme.* 1942. Canada. Crime Club. 1st ed. VG/VG. P3. $25.00

MARSH, Ngaio. *Dead Water.* 1963. Little Brn. 1st ed. VG. P3. $15.00

MARSH, Ngaio. *Death of a Peer.* 1940. Little Brn. true 1st ed. NF/VG. M22. $75.00

MARSH, Ngaio. *Five Complete Novels.* 1983. Avenel. 1st ed. VG/torn. P3. $13.00

MARSH, Ngaio. *Grave Mistake.* 1978. Collins Crime Club. 1st ed. VG/VG. P3. $20.00

MARSH, Ngaio. *Hand in Glove.* 1962. Collins Crime Club. 1st ed. VG/VG. P3. $25.00

MARSH, Ngaio. *Killing Dolphin.* 1966. Little Brn. 1st ed. VG/VG. P3. $40.00

MARSH, Ngaio. *Last Ditch.* 1977. Little Brn. 1st ed. F/F. P3. $30.00

MARSH, Ngaio. *Light Thickens.* 1982. Collins Crime Club. 1st ed. VG/VG. P3. $18.00

MARSH, Ngaio. *Night at the Vulcan.* nd. BC. VG/VG. P3. $8.00

MARSH, Ngaio. *Photo Finish.* 1980. Collins Crime Club. 1st ed. VG/VG. P3. $18.00

MARSH, Ngaio. *Scales of Justice.* 1955. Collins Crime Club. 1st ed. VG/VG. P3. $30.00

MARSH, Ngaio. *Singing in the Shrouds.* 1959. Collins Crime Club. VG/VG. P3. $25.00

MARSH, Ngaio. *Spinsters in Jeopardy.* 1954. Collins Crime Club. VG. P3. $25.00

MARSH, Ngaio. *Tied Up in Tinsel.* 1972. Collins Crime Club. 1st ed. VG/dj. P3. $20.00

MARSH, Ngaio. *When in Rome.* 1971. Little Brn. VG/G. P3. $20.00

MARSHALL, Alan; see Westlake, Donald E.

MARSHALL, Charles. *Aide-de-Camp of Lee: Being the Papers of Col Chas Marshall.* 1927. Little Brn. 1st ed. maps/pl. 287p. cloth. NF. M8. $85.00

MARSHALL, Edison. *American Captain.* 1954. Farrar Straus Young. 1st ed. VG/VG. P3. $25.00

MARSHALL, Edison. *Earth Giant.* 1960. Doubleday. 1st ed. VG/VG. P3. $20.00

MARSHALL, Edison. *Pagan King.* 1959. Doubleday. 1st ed. F/F. H11. $30.00

MARSHALL, Edison. *Princess Sophia.* 1958. Doubleday. 1st ed. VG/VG. P3. $25.00

MARSHALL, Edison. *Shikar & Safari.* 1947. NY. 2nd. VG/VG. B5. $25.00

MARSHALL, Francis Ireland. *Magic Inc Yearbook 1967-68.* 1968. Magic Inc. sgn. 4to. 112p. VG/wrp. B11. $25.00

MARSHALL, Henry Rutgers. *Instinct & Reason: An Essay...* 1898. Macmillan. 8vo. 574p. pebbled russet cloth. G1. $50.00

MARSHALL, Henry Rutgers. *Max-Muller, Friedrich.* 1893. London. Longman Gr. thick 12mo. 585p. G. G1. $50.00

MARSHALL, Jack. *Bearings.* 1969. Harper Row. 1st ed. RS. F/NF. V1. $20.00

MARSHALL, James. *Cut-Ups Carry On.* nd. Viking. BOMC. ils. NF. C14. $8.00

MARSHALL, James. *Red Riding Hood.* 1987. Dial. stated 1st ed. ils. F/NF. C14. $18.00

MARSHALL, James. *Santa Fe: The Railroad That Build an Empire.* 1945. Random. ltd ed. sgn. fld map/photos. maroon buckram. F/case. T10. $150.00

MARSHALL, James. *Summer in the South.* 1977. Houghton Mifflin. 1st ed. sgn. F/F. C8. $55.00

MARSHALL, Jim. *Swinging Doors.* 1949. Seattle. McCaffrey. 1st ed. 8vo. 267p. prt cloth. NF. T10. $200.00

MARSHALL, John. *Life of George Washington.* 1804-1807. London. Richard Phillips. 10 vol. 150 extra pl+3 maps. Zaehnadorf bdg. VG. C6. $1,100.00

MARSHALL, John. *Life of Washington. Volume 2.* 1832. Phil. 8vo. 448p. leather. xl. T3. $10.00

MARSHALL, Logan. *Story of the Panama Canal.* 1913. np. 286p. F3. $20.00

MARSHALL, Mel. *Steelhead.* 1973. Winchester. photos. VG/G+. P12. $15.00

MARSHALL, Paule. *Brown Girl, Brownstones.* 1959. Random. 1st ed. author's 1st book. F/F. B4. $750.00

MARSHALL, Paule. *Daughters.* 1991. Atheneum. 1st ed. AN/dj. B4. $45.00

MARSHALL, Paule. *Praisesong for the Widow.* 1983. Putnam. 1st ed. sgn. F/F clip. B4. $175.00

MARSHALL, Paule. *Soul Clap Hands & Sing.* 1961. NY. 1st ed. inscr. author's 2nd book. NF/VG. N3. $55.00

MARSHALL, Raymond. *In a Vain Shadow.* 1951. Jarrolds. 1st ed. VG/VG. P3. $25.00

MARSHALL, Rosamond. *Kitty.* 1945. Forum. 3rd. MTI. VG/VG. P3. $18.00

MARSHALL, William. *Faraway Man.* 1984. HRW. 1st ed. VG/VG. P3. $15.00

MARSHALL, William. *Gelignite.* 1977. HRW. 1st ed. NF/NF. M19. $35.00

MARSHALL, William. *Head First.* 1986. Secker Warburg. 1st ed. VG/VG. P3. $20.00

MARSHALL, William. *Inches.* 1994. Mysterious. 1st ed. F/F. M23/N4. $20.00

MARSHALL, William. *Manila Bay.* 1986. Viking. 1st ed. F/F. M23. $20.00

MARSHALL, William. *Manila Bay.* 1986. Viking. 1st ed. VG/VG. P3. $16.00

MARSHALL, William. *Out of Nowhere.* 1988. Mysterious. 1st ed. F/F. P3. $16.00

MARSHALL, William. *Perfect End.* 1981. HRW. 1st ed. F/F. M19. $35.00

MARSHALL, William. *Roadshow.* 1985. HRW. 1st ed. F/F. P3. $15.00

MARSHALL, William. *Thin Air.* 1978. HRW. 1st ed. F/F. M19. $35.00

MARSHALL, William. *Whisper.* 1988. Viking. 1st ed. F/F. P3. $20.00

MARSHALL & PECKHAM. *Campaigns of the American Revolution: An Atlas...* 1976. Ann Arbor/Maplewood. 58 maps. F/dj. O7. $85.00

MARSON, G.F. *Ghosts, Ghouls & Gallows.* 1946. Rider. 1st ed. VG/torn. P3. $25.00

MARSTEN, Richard; see Hunter, Evan.

MARSTON, Edward. *Nine Giants.* 1991. St Martin. 1st Am ed. xl. VG/NF. N4. $10.00

MARSTON, Paul. *Winning Decisions in Competitive Bidding: Bidding Strategy.* 1995. Australia. 91p. M. S1. $12.00

MARSTON, William Moulton. *Emotions of Normal People.* 1928. Harcourt Brace. 405p. gr cloth. VG/torn. G1. $45.00

MART, Amis. *Rachel Papers.* 1974. NY. 1st Am ed. VG/VG. A15. $60.00

MARTEL, John. *Partners.* 1964. Viking. 1st ed. VG/dj. P3. $20.00

MARTEL, Suzanne. *City Under Ground.* 1964. Viking. 1st ed. G+/dj. P3. $20.00

MARTENS & SISSON. *Fiction of Jack London.* 1972. np. ils. 55p. F. A4. $35.00

MARTENS & SISSON. *Jack London, First Editions, Illustrated...* 1979. np. 1/1000. ils. 167p. NF. A4. $265.00

MARTI, Samuel. *Mundra Manos Simbolicas en Asia y America.* 1971. Mexican. 1st ed. 1/2000. 163p. stiff wrp. F3. $45.00

MARTI-IBANEZ, Felix. *Prelude to Medical History.* 1961. NY. 1st ed. 253p. dj. A13. $35.00

MARTIN, A.E. *Outsiders.* 1945. BC. VG. P3. $8.00

MARTIN, Billy. *Billyball.* 1987. np. 1st ed. inscr. F/NF. M19. $45.00

MARTIN, Charles. *Past Closing Time.* 1995. Barth. ltd ed. 1/200. chapbook w/poem card. F/wrp. V1. $25.00

MARTIN, Daris. *Among the Faithful.* 1937. London. Joseph. 1st ed. pres. 8vo. 288p. xl. VG. W1. $20.00

MARTIN, David. *Crying Heart Tattoo.* 1982. HRW. 1st ed. F/F. P3. $20.00

MARTIN, David. *Hero of the Town.* 1965. Morrow. VG/VG. P3. $15.00

MARTIN, David. *K9 & the Beasts of Vega.* 1982. Rourke. hc. TVTI. VG. P3. $5.00

MARTIN, David. *Tap, Tap.* 1994. Random. 1st ed. F/F. P3. $20.00

MARTIN, E.G. *Sailorman.* 1933. London. Oxford. ils. 90p. VG. T7. $50.00

MARTIN, Edgar. *Books & the Mystery of Unlucky Vas.* 1943. Whitman. VG. P3. $7.00

MARTIN, Edward Sandford. *Luxury of Children.* 1905. Harper. 8vo. ils Stilwell. G. B17. $20.00

MARTIN, Eugene. *Randy Starr Leading the Air Circus.* 1932. Akron. ils. 216p. cloth. VG/dj. A17. $5.00

MARTIN, Franklin. *South America From a Surgeon's Point of View.* 1922. NY. 1st ed. 325p. VG. A13. $50.00

MARTIN, Frederick Townsend. *Passing of the Idle Rich.* 1911. Doubleday Page. 1st ed. 8vo. 264p. NF. T10. $50.00

MARTIN, George R.R. *Armageddon Rag.* 1983. Poseidon. 1st ed. NF/NF. P3. $20.00

MARTIN, George R.R. *Fevre Dream.* nd. BC. NF/NF. P3. $8.00

MARTIN, George R.R. *New Voices in SF.* 1977. Macmillan. 1st ed. xl. dj. P3. $5.00

MARTIN, George R.R. *Sandkings.* nd. BC. VG/VG. P3. $8.00

MARTIN, George R.R. *Windhaven.* 1981. Timescape. 1st ed. sgn. F/F. P3. $40.00

MARTIN, George Victor. *Bells of St Mary's.* 1946. Grosset Dunlap. MTI. VG/VG. P3. $20.00

MARTIN, Graham Dunstan. *Soul Master.* 1984. Unwin. 1st ed. F/NF. G10. $12.00

MARTIN, Jack; see Etchison, Dennis.

MARTIN, John B. *Adlai Stevenson & the World.* 1964. Random. BC. 8vo. 721p. AN/case. B22. $6.00

MARTIN, Lee. *Hacker.* 1992. NY. 1st ed. F/NF. H11. $20.00

MARTIN, Lee. *Mensa Murders.* 1990. NY. 1st ed. F/F. H11. $25.00

MARTIN, Malachi. *King of Kings.* 1980. Simon Schuster. 1st ed. NF/F. H11. $20.00

MARTIN, Pete. *Will Acting Spoil Marilyn Monroe?* 1956. Garden City. 1st ed. VG/VG. B5. $45.00

MARTIN, Stuart. *Fifteen Cells.* 1928. Harper. 3rd. G. P3. $15.00

MARTIN, Valerie. *Mary Reilly.* 1990. Doubleday. ARC. F/wrp. B4. $65.00

MARTIN, Valerie. *Penny Saving.* 1990. London. Michael Joseph. 1st ed. sgn. F/F. T2. $30.00

MARTIN, W. *De Hollandsche Schilderkunst in de Zwventiende...* 1936. Amsterdam. VG. V4. $35.00

MARTIN, William. *Nerve Endings.* 1984. Crown. 1st ed. F/F. B11/H11. $25.00

MARTIN, William. *Rising of the Moon.* 1987. Crown. 1st ed. F/F. H11. $20.00

MARTIN & MARTIN. *Maps of Texas & the Southwest 1513-1900.* 1984. NM U. 59 maps. quarter leather/sailcloth. F/dj. O7. $395.00

MARTIN & NOEL. *Flora of Albany & Bathurst.* 1960. Grahamstown, RSA. map. 128p. sc. VG. B26. $15.00

MARTIN & TARR. *Earthquakes at Ukatat Bay, Alaska...* 1912. USGS. 135p. xl. VG. D8. $45.00

MARTIN & TUTTLE. *Windhaven.* 1981. Timescape. 1st ed. NF/NF. G10. $15.00

MARTINEAU, Harriet. *Faith As Unfolded by Many Prophets: An Essay...* 1833. Boston. 1st ed. pub inscr pres. 177p. VG. B14. $350.00

MARTINEK, Frank V. *Don Winslow & Scorpion's Stronghold.* 1946. Whitman. ils. VG. P3. $8.00

MARTINEZ, Al. *Jigsaw John.* 1975. Tarcher. 1st ed. hc. VG. P3. $15.00

MARTINI, Steve. *Undue Influence.* 1994. Putnam. 1st ed. NF/NF. M22. $12.00

MARTINS, A. *O Bombardeamento da Alexandria.* 1882. Porto/Rio de Janerio. fld map. 126p. marbled brd. VG. O7. $75.00

MARTYN, Wyndham. *Murder Island.* 1928. McBride. 1st ed. VG. P3. $35.00

MARVEL. *Battle Summer.* 1853. NY. 12mo. 289p. half leather. G. T3. $12.00

MARVELL, Andrew. *Complete Works in Verse & Prose of Andrew Marvell.* 1872-1875. London. Prt for Private Circulation. 4 vol. 1/100. VG. C6. $250.00

MARX, Fritz Morstein. *Government in the Third Reich.* 1936. NY. 1st ed. 158p. G. A17. $15.00

MARX, Groucho. *Groucho & Me.* 1959. Random. 1st ed. sgn Groucho. F/NF. D2. $60.00

MARX, Samuel. *Deadly Illusions.* 1990. Random. 1st ed. F/F. A20. $10.00

MARX. *Handbook of Marxism.* 1935. NY. 12mo. 1087p. red cloth. F. H3. $100.00

MASCETTI, Manuela Dunn. *Vampire: Complete Guide to the World...* 1992. Viking Studio. 1st ed. F/F. P3. $25.00

MASEFIELD, John. *Minnie Maylow's Story & Other Tales & Scenes.* 1931. Macmillan. 1st Am ed. 8vo. 194p. VG/dj. T10. $75.00

MASEFIELD, John. *Reynard the Fox.* 1919. London. Heinemann. 1/250. sgn. gilt quarter vellum. VG. T10. $150.00

MASEFIELD, John. *Right Royal.* 1920. London. Heinemann. 1st ed. gr brd. NF. V1. $30.00

MASEFIELD, John. *Selected Poems.* 1923. Macmillan. Autograph ed. 1/400. sgn. 8vo. wht cloth/bl brd. VG. T10. $150.00

MASEFIELD, John. *South & East.* 1929. Medici Soc. 1st ed. 1/260. sgn. ils/sgn Jacynth Parsons. NF. M19. $225.00

MASHA. *Masha's Cats & Kittens.* 1970. Am Heritage. 4to. ils. VG/VG. B17. $10.00

MASO, Carole. *Ava.* 1993. Normal, IL. Dalkey Archive. author's 3rd novel. M/dj. B4. $35.00

MASON, A.E.W. *House in Lordship Lane.* 1946. Dodd Mead. xl. P3. $10.00

MASON, A.E.W. *Prisoner in the Opal.* 1929. Crime Club. G. P3. $18.00

MASON, A.E.W. *Three Gentlemen.* 1932. Hodder Stoughton. G. P3. $10.00

MASON, Arthur. *Wee Men of Ballywooden.* 1930. Doubleday. 1st ed. 8vo. ils Lawson. VG. M5. $60.00

MASON, Bobbie Ann. *Feather Crowns.* 1993. Harper Collins. 1st ed. F/F. H11. $25.00

MASON, Bobbie Ann. *Feather Crowns.* 1993. Harper Collins. 1st ed. rem mk. F/F. G10. $10.00

MASON, Bobbie Ann. *Feather Crowns.* 1993. NY. Harper Collins. 1st ed. sgn. F/F. M23. $40.00

MASON, Bobbie Ann. *In Country.* 1985. Harper Row. 1st ed. F/F. H11. $30.00

MASON, Bobbie Ann. *Love Life.* 1989. Harper Row. 1st ed. sgn. NF/NF. M23. $30.00

MASON, Bobbie Ann. *Shiloh & Other Stories.* 1982. Harper Row. 1st ed. F/NF. B4. $85.00

MASON, Bobbie Ann. *Silence+Lila.* 1988. Harper. 1st ed. sgn. F/F. B4. $65.00

MASON, Douglas R. *Phaeton Condition.* 1973. Putnam. 1st ed. F/F. P3. $15.00

MASON, F. Van Wyck. *Brimstone Club.* 1971. Little Brn. 1st ed. F/F. H11. $35.00

MASON, F. Van Wyck. *Guns for Rebellion.* 1977. Doubleday. 1st ed. F/F. H11. $25.00

MASON, F. Van Wyck. *Roads to Liberty.* 1972. Little Brn. 1st ed. F/F. H11. $20.00

MASON, F. Van Wyck. *Trumpets Sound No More.* 1975. Little Brn. 1st ed. 8vo. 297p. T10. $20.00

MASON, John Monck. *Remarks Upon Poyning's Law...* 1758. Dublin. only ed. new quarter morocco. M11. $450.00

MASON, Lisa. *Arachne.* 1990. Morrow. 1st ed. author's 1st novel. F/F. G10. $20.00

MASON, Miriam E. *Timothy Has Ideas.* 1943. Macmillan. 1st ed. 128p. VG+. C14. $18.00

MASON, Paule. *Man in the Garden.* 1969. McKay Washburn. 1st ed. VG/VG. P3. $15.00

MASON, Steve. *Johnny's Song: Poetry of a Vietnam Veteran.* 1986. Bantam. 1st ed. F/NF. M23. $20.00

MASON, Van Wyck. *Blue Hurricane.* 1955. Jarrolds. 1st ed. VG/rpr. P3. $8.00

MASON, Van Wyck. *Cutlass Empire.* 1949. Doubleday. VG/VG. P3. $20.00

MASON, Van Wyck. *Deadly Orbit Mission.* 1968. Doubleday. 1st ed. VG/VG. P3. $23.00

MASON, Van Wyck. *Hong Kong Airbase Murders.* nd. Grosset Dunlap. VG. P3. $15.00

MASON, Van Wyck. *Manila Galleon.* 1961. Little Brn. 1st ed. VG. P3. $20.00

MASON, Van Wyck. *Saigon Singer.* 1946. Doubleday. 1st ed. G. P3. $7.00

MASON, Van Wyck. *Spider House.* 1932. Mystery League. 1st ed. NF/VG. M22. $75.00

MASON, Van Wyck. *Vesper Service Murders.* 1931. Crime Club. 1st ed. VG. P3. $25.00

MASON, William. *Poems.* 1779. London. 1st ed. marbled ep. full calf. VG+. S13. $30.00

MASON. *Bibliography of Oscar Wilde.* 1914. London. ils. 637p. VG. A4. $135.00

MASPERO, Gaston. *Passing of the Empires 850 BC to 330 BC.* 1900. Appleton. 1st Am ed. 824p. xl. G. W1. $20.00

MASS, Willard. *Poems by...* 1938. Farrar Rinehart. 1st ed. NF/dj. V1. $20.00

MASSA, Aldo. *Phoenicians.* 1977. Minerva. 1st ed. 4to. 144p. NF/dj. W1. $22.00

MASSAD, Stewart. *Doctors & Other Casualties.* 1993. Warner. 1st ed. author's 1st book. NF/NF. H11. $15.00

MASSIE, Allan. *One Night in Winter.* 1984. Bodley Head. 1st ed. F/F. P3.2500 $15.00

MASSIE, Chris. *Green Circle.* 1944. Tower. xl. dj. P3. $10.00

MASSIE, S. *Land of the Firebird.* 1980. NY. 1st ed. F/F. B5. $35.00

MASTER, Edgar Lee. *Lincoln the Man.* 1931. NY. 1st ed. ils. 420p. VG. B18. $17.50

MASTERMAN, Walter S. *Crime of the Reckaviles.* 1943. Methuen. 3rd. VG. P3. $18.00

MASTERMAN, Walter S. *Green Toad.* 1929. Dutton. 1st ed. VG. P3. $25.00

MASTERMAN, Walter S. *2.L.O.* nd. McKinley Stone McKenzie. VG. P3. $15.00

MASTERS, David. *Romance of Excavation.* 1923. Dodd Mead. 1st ed. 8vo. 23 pl. VG. W1. $12.00

MASTERS, Edgar Lee. *Lee: A Dramatic Poem.* 1926. Macmillan. 1st ed. 139p. F/VG. B10. $40.00

MASTERS, Edgar Lee. *Mitch Miller.* nd. Grosset Dunlap. ils John Sloan. VG/VG. S13. $12.00

MASTERS, Edgar Lee. *More People.* 1939. NY. 1st ed. VG/VG. B5. $35.00

MASTERSON, Elsie. *Nothing Whatever To Do.* 1956. NY. 1st ed. VG/VG. B5. $20.00

MASTERSON, Whit. *Evil Come, Evil Go.* nd. BC. VG/VG. P3. $8.00

MASTERSON, Whit. *Gravy Train.* 1971. Dodd Mead. 1st ed. VG/VG. P3. $20.00

MASTERSON, Whit. *Last One Kills.* 1969. Dodd Mead. VG/VG. P3. $20.00

MASTERSON, Whit. *Man on a Nylon String.* 1963. Dodd Mead. 1st ed. xl. dj. P3. $8.00

MASTERSON, Whit. *Officer Needs Help.* 1965. Dodd Mead. 1st ed. xl. dj. P3. $7.00

MASTERSON, Whit. *Why She Cries, I Do Not Know.* 1972. Dodd Mead. VG/VG. P3. $18.00

MASTERTON, Graham. *Maiden Voyage.* 1984. St Martin. 1st Am ed. VG/VG. A16. $20.00

MASTERTON, Graham. *Mirror.* 1988. Tor. 1st ed. F/F. P3. $20.00

MASTERTON, Graham. *Scare Care.* 1989. Tor. 1st ed. F/F. P3. $20.00

MASTERTON, Graham. *Sweetman Curve.* 1990. Severn. 1st hc ed. F/F. G10. $15.00

MASTERTON, Richard. *7 Steps to Midnight.* 1993. Forge. 1st ed. F/F. G10. $25.00

MASTON, Charles T. *Systematic Study of Genus Limnanthes.* 1952. Berkeley. ils. VG+/wrp. B26. $25.00

MATE, Ferenc. *Waterhouses: Romantic Alternative.* 1977. Vancouver. Albatross. VG/VG. A16. $12.00

MATE, Ferenc. *World's Best Sailboats.* 1986. Albatross. 448 photos. 288p. VG/dj. T7. $45.00

MATERA, Lia. *Prior Convictions.* 1991. Simon Schuster. 1st ed. AN/dj. N4. $25.00

MATES, Julian. *American Musical State Before 1800.* 1962. Rutgers. 1st ed. 331p. VG/dj. M20. $28.00

MATETSKY, Amanda. *Adventures of Superman Collecting.* 1988. W Plains, MO. 1/2500. 215p. F/NF case. B18. $75.00

MATHE, Jean. *Leonardo Da Vinci: Anatomical Drawings.* 1978. Barcelona. 1st ed. 122p. VG/dj. A13. $60.00

MATHER, Berkeley. *Achilles Affair.* 1973. Collins. VG/VG. P3. $15.00

MATHER, Berkeley. *Gold of Malabar.* 1967. Scribner. 1st ed. VG/VG. P3. $25.00

MATHER, Berkeley. *Pass Beyond Kashmir.* 1973. Collins. VG/VG. P3. $15.00

MATHES, W. Michael. *From the Gulf to the Pacific: Diary of the Kino Atondo...* 1969. Los Angeles. Dawson. ils/fld map. M. O7. $85.00

MATHES, W. Michael. *Vizcaino & Spanish Expansion in the Pacific Ocean 1580-1630.* 1968. CA Hist Soc. 38 maps. F/dj. O7. $75.00

MATHESON, Elizabeth. *Blithe Air: Photographs From England, Wales & Ireland...* 1995. Jargon Soc. 1st trade ed. sgns. AN/dj. C2. $60.00

MATHESON, Richard. *Created By.* 1993. Bantam. 1st ed. F/F. P3. $22.00

MATHESON, Richard. *Earthbound.* 1994. Tor. 1st Am ed. AN/F. N4. $22.50

MATHESON, Richard. *Hell House.* 1971. Viking. 1st ed. xl. dj. P3. $35.00

MATHESON, Richard. *Robert Bloch: Appreciations of the Master.* 1995. Tor. 1st ed. F/F. P3. $25.00

MATHESON, Richard. *Shadow on the Sun.* 1994. Evans. 1st ed. F/F. P3. $20.00

MATHESON, Richard. *Shrinking Man.* nd. BC. VG/VG. P3. $10.00

MATHESON, Richard. *7 Steps to Midnight.* 1993. Forge. 1st ed. F/F. N4. $25.00

MATHESON, Richard. *7 Steps to Midnight.* 1993. Forge. 1st ed. NF/NF. P3. $22.00

MATHEWS, Alfred. *Ohio & Her Western Reserve.* 1902. Appleton. lacks 1 map. 330p. gilt red cloth. VG. M20. $25.00

MATHEWS, D.L. *Very Welcome Death.* 1961. HRW. 1st ed. VG. P3. $8.00

MATHEWS, Edward B. *Bibliography & Cartography of Maryland...* 1897. Johns Hopkins. VG/wrp. O7. $85.00

MATHEWS, John Joseph. *Wah' Kon-Tah: Osage & the White Man's Road.* 1932. Norman, OK. 1st ed. 357p. VG/dj. B18. $35.00

MATHEWS, John Joseph. *Wah'Kon-Tah.* 1932. Norman, OK. 1st ed. ils. 359p. map ep. orange prt cloth. NF. T10. $50.00

MATHEWS, John Mabry. *American Constitutional System. Second Edition.* 1940. McGraw Hill. xl. G. M11. $35.00

MATHEWS. *Dictionary of Americanisms on Historical Principles.* 1951. Chicago U. 2 vol. 1946p. VG/VG. A4. $135.00

MATHIAS & MATHIAS. *Revision of Asteriscium & Some Related Hydrocotyloid...* 1962. Berleley. ils. 86p. VG+/wrp. B26. $15.00

MATHIESON, Theodore. *Great Detectives.* 1960. Simon Schuster. 1st ed. VG/G. P3. $30.00

MATHIS, Edward. *From a High Place.* nd. BC. VG/VG. P3. $8.00

MATHIS, Edward. *Natural Prey.* 1987. Scribner. 1st ed. F/F. P3. $16.00

MATISSE. *Homage to Henri Matisse.* 1970. np. ils. 126p. F/F. A4. $95.00

MATISSE. *Jazz.* 1983. np. 1/250. folio. ils. 156p. F/F/VG cb case. A4. $300.00

MATLEY, John. *27th Day.* nd. BC. VG/VG. P3. $8.00

MATSCHAT, Cecile Hulse. *American Butterflies & Moths.* 1942. Random. ils. VG. B17. $10.00

MATSCHAT, Cecile Hulse. *Suwanee River.* 1938. Farrar Rinehart. 4th. 8vo. gr cloth. VG/dj. T10. $25.00

MATSELL, George W. *Vocabulum; or, Rogue's Lexicon.* 1859. NY. Matsell. red cloth. M11. $350.00

MATTES. *Platte River Road Narratives, Descriptive Bibliography...* 1988. IL U. maps. 647p. F. A4. $95.00

MATTHEWS, Anthony. *Swinging Murder.* 1969. Walker. 1st ed. VG/VG. P3. $15.00

MATTHEWS, Greg. *Further Adventures of Huckleberry Finn.* 1983. Crown. 1st ed. VG/VG. P3. $16.00

MATTHEWS, Greg. *Little Red Rooster.* 1978. NAL. 1st ed. F/F. H11. $30.00

MATTHEWS, Greg. *One True Thing.* 1989. Grove Weidenfeld. 1st ed. rem mk. F/F. H11. $20.00

MATTHEWS, Greg. *Power in the Blood.* 1993. Harper Collins. 1st ed. F/F. H11. $20.00

MATTHEWS, Greg. *Wisdom of Stones.* 1994. Harper Collins. AP. 8vo. F/prt wrp. S9. $30.00

MATTHEWS, Harry. *Cigarettes.* 1987. Weidenfeld. 1st ed. F/F. H11. $30.00

MATTHEWS, Harry. *Country Cooking & Other Stories.* 1980. Providence. Burning Deck. 1st ed. 1/100. sgn/#d. F/F. B2. $100.00

MATTHEWS, Harry. *Sinking of Odrdek Stadium & Other Novels.* 1975. Harper. 1st ed. F/F. B2. $60.00

MATTHEWS, Jack. *Tales of the Ohio Land.* 1978. Columbus. 1st ed. ils. 187p. VG/dj. B18. $9.50

MATTHEWS, Janet Snyder. *Edge of the Wilderness.* 1983. Tulsa, OK. inscr. 8vo. 464p. F/F. B11. $40.00

MATTHEWS, John V. *Rufus Choate, the Law & Civic Virtue.* 1980. Phil. Temple U. G/dj. M11. $45.00

MATTHEWS, Kevin, see Fox, Gardner F.

MATTHEWS, Leslie. *History of Pharmacy in Britain.* 1962. Edinburgh. 1st ed. 427p. VG. A13. $75.00

MATTHEWS, Patricia. *Unquiet.* 1991. Severn. 1st ed. NF/NF. P3. $20.00

MATTHEWS, Robert E. *Labor Relations & the Law.* 1953. Little Brn. M11. $15.00

MATTHEWS, William. *Forseeable Futures.* 1987. Houghton Mifflin. 1st ed. F/NF. V1. $15.00

MATTHEWS. *How To Paint Signs & Sho' Cards.* 1920. Ogilvie. VG. D2. $35.00

MATTHIAE, Paolo. *Ebla: Empire Rediscovered.* 1980. Hodder Stoughton. 1st ed. ils. 237p. F/dj. W1. $18.00

MATTHIESSEN, Peter. *At Play in the Fields of the Lord.* 1965. NY. 1st ed. sgn. VG/VG. C6. $135.00

MATTHIESSEN, Peter. *Far Tortuga.* 1975. NY. 1st ed. F/F. C6. $95.00

MATTHIESSEN, Peter. *In the Spirit of Crazy Horse.* 1983. Viking. 1st ed. VG/VG. M19. $150.00

MATTHIESSEN, Peter. *Indian Country.* 1984. Viking. 1st ed. 8vo. NF/dj. S9. $75.00

MATTHIESSEN, Peter. *Men's Lives. Surfmen & Baymen of the South Fork.* 1986. NY. 1st trade ed. inscr. NF/NF. C6. $100.00

MATTHIESSEN, Peter. *Oomingmak. Expedition to the Musk Ox Island in Bering Sea.* 1967. NY. 1st ed. w/sgn slip. F/F. C6. $60.00

MATTHIESSEN, Peter. *Sal Si Puedes.* 1969. Random. 1st ed. 8vo. NF/NF. S9. $60.00

MATTHIESSEN, Peter. *Sal Si Puedes: Cesar Chavez & the New Am Revolution.* 1969. NY. 1st ed. F/F. C2. $75.00

MATTHIESSEN, Peter. *Sand Rivers.* 1981. Viking. 1st ed. F/NF. M19. $35.00

MATTHIESSEN, Peter. *Sea Pool.* 1972. Doubleday. 1st ed. ils WP DuBois. 78p. F/VG. P2. $25.00

MATTHIESSEN, Peter. *Shorebirds of North America.* 1967. Viking. 1st ed. folio. NF/VG clip. B4. $250.00

MATTHIESSEN, Peter. *Wildlife in America.* 1959. NY. 1st ed. author's 1st natural history work. F/VG. C6. $125.00

MATTHIESSEN & PORTER. *Tree Where Man Was Born & the African Experience.* 1972. Dutton. 1st ed. 4to. 247p. F/dj. T10. $45.00

MATTINGLY, Harold. *Outlines of Ancient History From Earliest Times...* 1914. Cambridge. 1st ed. ils/maps. 482p. VG. W1. $20.00

MATZYE, Albert. *Beginner's Guide to Buying & Selling Used Books.* 1973. np. 8vo. 52p. VG/wrp. T3. $5.00

MAUCLAIR, Camille. *Auguste Rodin: The Man, His Ideas, His Works.* 1905. London. ils. VG. M17. $40.00

MAUDLIN, Bill. *Sort of a Saga.* 1949. NY. 301p. VG/dj. B18. $25.00

MAUGER, Thierry. *Ark of the Desert.* 1991. Souffles. 1st ed. folio. 57 pl. VG/dj. W1. $45.00

MAUGHAM, Robin. *Barrier.* 1973. McGraw Hill. 1st Am ed. F/F. B4. $100.00

MAUGHAM, Robin. *Conversations With Willie: Recollections of WS Maugham.* 1978. np. 24 photos. 205p. NF/VG. A4. $35.00

MAUGHAM, Robin. *Last Encounter.* 1973. McGraw Hill. 1st Am ed. F/F. B4. $100.00

MAUGHAM, W. Somerset. *Book-Bag.* 1932. Florence. 1st ed. 1/725. sgn. NF/VG. C6. $225.00

MAUGHAM, W. Somerset. *Cakes & Ale.* 1930. London. 1st ed. VG/VG. C6. $125.00

MAUGHAM, W. Somerset. *Catalina.* 1984. Doubleday. 1st ed. VG/VG. P3. $30.00

MAUGHAM, W. Somerset. *Sacred Flame.* 1928. London. 1st ed. NF/NF. C6. $125.00

MAULDIN, Bill. *Sort of a Sage.* 1949. NY. 1st ed. F/F. B5. $20.00

MAULDIN, Bill. *Up Front.* 1945. Holt. 1st ed. F/F. B35. $60.00

MAUND, Benjamin. *Botanic Garden.* 1925-1836. London. Baldwin. 6 vol. gilt 3-quarter leather. A10. $2,500.00

MAUNDEVILE, John. *Voiage & Travaile.* 1839. London. Edward Lumley. rpt from 1725 ed. 8vo. 326p. new cloth. T10. $150.00

MAUROIS, Andre. *Miracle of France.* 1948. Harper. 1st ed. 477p. bl cloth. F/G. B22. $6.00

MAUROIS, Andre. *Voyage to the Island of the Articoles.* 1929. Appleton. 1st ed. F/NF. B2. $75.00

MAURY, Richard. *Saga of Cimba.* 1939. Harcourt. 1st ed. ils. VG. T7. $24.00

MAVITY, Nancy Barr. *Tule Marsh Murder.* 1929. Crime Club. 1st ed. VG. P3. $20.00

MAVRODIN, Valentin. *Fine Arms From Tula. Firearms & Edged Weapons in Hermitage.* 1977. Abrams. ils. cloth. dj. D2. $75.00

MAXWELL, A.E. *Art of Survival.* 1989. Doubleday. 1st ed. VG/VG. P3. $18.00

MAXWELL, Lilian. *'Round New Brunswick Roads.* 1951. Ryerson. VG. P3. $15.00

MAXWELL, Thomas. *Kiss Me Once.* 1986. Mysterious. 1st ed. F/F. P3. $17.00

MAXWELL, William Bulloch. *Mysterious Father: Tragedy in Five Acts.* 1965. GA U. 57p. VG. B10. $10.00

MAXXE, Robert; see Rosenblum, Robert.

MAY, Barbara. *Buckle Horse.* 1956. Holt. 1st ed. ils Paul Brown. NF/VG. C8. $95.00

MAY, Julian. *Diamond Mask.* 1994. Knopf. 1st ed. RS. F/F. G10. $10.00

MAY, Julian. *Intervention.* 1987. Houghton Mifflin. 1st ed. F/NF. G10. $12.00

MAY, Julian. *Jack the Bodiless.* 1991. Knopf. 1st ed. RS. F/F. G10. $10.00

MAY, Julian. *Magnificat.* 1996. Knopf. 1st ed. RS. F/F. P3. $24.00

MAY, Julian. *Many-Colored Land & Golden Torc.* nd. BC. VG/VG. P3. $10.00

MAY, Sophie. *Dottie's Flyaway.* 1897. Lee Shepard. G+. P12. $10.00

MAY, Sophie. *Dotty Dimple at Her Grandmother's.* 1895. Lee Shepard. ils. G+. P12. $10.00

MAY, Sophie. *Dotty Dimple at Play.* 1896. Lee Shepard. G+. P12. $10.00

MAY, Sophie. *Dotty Dimple Out West.* 1910. Lee Shepard. G+. P12. $10.00

MAYBURY, Anne. *Midnight Dancers.* nd. BC. VG/VG. P3. $8.00

MAYBY, J. Cecil. *By Stygian Waters.* 1933. Houghton. 1st ed. hc. VG. P3. $75.00

MAYDON, H.C. *Big Game Shooting in Africa.* 1951. London. Lonsdale Lib #14. 445p. VG/G. B5. $60.00

MAYER, Bernadette. *Poetry By...* 1976. Kulcher. 1st ed. F/sans. V1. $20.00

MAYER, Karl Herbert. *Classic Maya Relief Columns.* 1981. Acoma Books. 1st ed. 4to. 51p. wrp. F3. $35.00

MAYER, Mercer. *East of the Sun & West of the Moon.* 1980. Four Winds. 1st ed. 4to. 47p. gilt burgundy cloth. VG/torn. D1. $40.00

MAYER, Mercer. *Frog on His Own.* 1973. Dial. 1st ed. RS. F/F. C14. $18.00

MAYER, Milton. *They Thought They Were Free: The German 1933-45.* 1967. Chicago. rpt. 8vo. 346p. VG/wrp. A17. $6.00

MAYER & TOKOI. *Der Adler: The Official Nazi Luftwaffe Magazine.* 1977. NY. 200p. dj. A17. $25.00

MAYERSBERG, Paul. *Homme Fatale.* 1992. NY. 1st ed. F/F. H11. $20.00

MAYES, Herbert R. *Editor's Treasury: 2 Vols.* 1968. NY. 1st ed. 2195p. djs. A17. $15.00

MAYHAR, Ardath. *How the Gods Wove in Kyrannon.* 1979. Doubleday. 1st ed. xl. dj. P3. $5.00

MAYHEW, Vic. *Fireball.* 1977. Methuen. 1st ed. VG/VG. P3. $15.00

MAYLE, Peter. *Where Did I Come From?* 1973. Secaucus, NJ. Lyle Stuart. 1st ed. F/NF. B4. $125.00

MAYLE, Peter. *Year in Provence.* 1990. 1st ed. VG/VG. S13. $15.00

MAYNARD, Joyce. *Baby Love.* 1981. Knopf. 1st ed. NF/F. H11. $40.00

MAYNARD, Joyce. *Looking Back: A Chronicle of Growing Up Old in the Sixties.* 1973. Doubleday. 1st ed. F/F. B4. $100.00

MAYNARD, Joyce. *To Die For.* 1992. Dutton. 1st ed. F/dj. M22. $20.00

MAYNE, William. *Max's Dream.* 1977. Greenwillow. 1st Am ed. 88p. VG/G+. P2. $20.00

MAYNE, William. *Year & a Day.* 1976. Dutton. ARC/1st ed. 86p. NF/VG. P2. $25.00

MAYO, Claude Banks. *Your Navy: Organizations, Customs & Traditions...* 1939. Los Angeles. Parker Baird. sgn. 8vo. 372p. gilt bl brd. VG. B11. $40.00

MAYO, Jim; see L'Amour, Louis.

MAYO CLINIC. *Physicians of the Mayo Clinic & Mayo Foundation...* 1927. Phil. 1st ed. 578p. VG. A13. $50.00

MAYOR, Archer. *Fruits of the Poisonous Tree.* 1994. Mysterious. 1st ed. F/F. P3. $20.00

MAYOR, Archer. *Skeleton's Knee.* 1993. Mysterious. 1st ed. F/F. M23. $25.00

MAYS, Willie. *Willie Mays: My Life In & Out of Baseball.* 1966. Dutton. 1st ed. VG/G+. P8. $45.00

MAZ. *Cash on Destruction.* 1962. Neville Spearman. 1st ed. VG/G+. P3. $25.00

MAZAR, Benjamin. *Beth She'Arim.* 1973-76. Rutgers. 1st ed. pl. NF/dj. W1. $125.00

MAZIERE, Francis. *Mysteries of Easter Island.* 1965. Laffont. VG. P3. $10.00

MAZZEI, Philip. *My Life & Wanderings.* 1980. np. ils. 469p. F/VG. A4. $45.00

MAZZOCCO, Robert. *Trader.* 1980. Trader. 1st ed. F/dj. V1. $10.00

MCADAM, Roger William. *Commonwealth: Giantess of the Sound.* 1959. NY. Stephen Daye. 1st ed. VG/dj. A16. $40.00

MCADOO, Eleanor Wilson. *Priceless Gift: Love Letters of Woodrow Wilson...* 1962. McGraw Hill. 1st ed. pres. 324p. F/NF. T10. $35.00

MCAFEE, John P. *Slow Walk in a Sad Rain.* 1993. Warner. 1st ed. F/F. H11. $30.00

MCALISTER, Hugh. *Flight of the Silver Ship.* 1930. Saalfield. VG/VG. P3. $30.00

MCALISTER, Hugh. *Stand By: Story of a Boy's Achievement in Radio.* 1930. Saalfield. VG-/dj. A17. $5.00

MCALLISTER, Jim. *Down Under in the Carolinas.* 1979. Greenville, SC. 1st ed. sgn. 8vo. 186p. F/VG. B11. $20.00

MCALLISTER, Lee. *Squaw Dance.* 1991. Tje. 1st ed. sgn. VG/VG. P3. $20.00

MCALPINE, J.F. *Manual of Nearctic Diptera. Vol 2.* 1987. Canadian Goverment Pub. 4to. 287 pl. cloth. VG. B1. $68.50

MCANDREWS, Anita. *Conquistador's Lady.* 1990. Santa Barbara. Fithian. 1st ed. 226p. wrp. F3. $10.00

MCAULEY, Paul J. *Eternal Light.* 1993. Morrow/AvoNova. 1st ed. F/F. M23. $25.00

MCAULEY, Paul J. *King of the Hill.* 1991. Gollancz. 1st ed. hc. F/F. P3. $35.00

MCAULEY, Paul J. *Pasquale's Angel.* 1995. Morrow. 1st Am ed. F/F. G10. $15.00

MCAULEY, Paul J. *Secret Harmonies.* 1989. Gollancz. 1st ed. F/F. P3. $35.00

MCBAIN, Dean Howard Lee. *Supreme Court & the Constitution.* 1936. NY. Am Book Co. 31p. stapled wrp. M11. $15.00

MCBAIN, Ed; see Hunter, Evan.

MCBRIDE, Mary Margaret. *Story of Dwight W Morrow.* 1930. Farrar Rinehart. orig brn cloth. M11. $45.00

MCCAFFERY, John. *American Dream: Half-Century View From American Magazine.* 1964. Doubleday. 1st ed. 626p. purple cloth. F/dj. B22. $4.00

MCCAFFREY, Anne. *Chronicles of Pern: First Fall.* 1993. Ballantine. 1st Am ed. F/F. G10. $15.00

MCCAFFREY, Anne. *Coelura.* 1987. NY. Tor. 1st ed thus. ils Ned Dameron. F/dj. T10. $25.00

MCCAFFREY, Anne. *Coelura.* 1987. Tor. 1st ed. ils Ned Dameron. NF/NF. M20. $22.00

MCCAFFREY, Anne. *Dolphins of Pern.* 1994. Ballantine. 1st ed. F/NF. w/pub letter. G10. $10.00

MCCAFFREY, Anne. *Dragonlady of Pern.* 1984. Brandywyne. Deluxe Ltd ed. sgn. 286p. F/F case. A4. $50.00

MCCAFFREY, Anne. *Dragonriders of Pern.* nd. BC. VG/VG. P3. $12.00

MCCAFFREY, Anne. *Dragonsdawn.* nd. BC. VG. P3. $8.00

MCCAFFREY, Anne. *Dragonsinger.* 1977. Atheneum. 2nd. VG/VG. P3. $30.00

MCCAFFREY, Anne. *Harper Hall of Pern.* nd. BC. VG/VG. P3. $10.00

MCCAFFREY, Anne. *Killashandra.* 1985. Del Rey. 1st ed. F/F. P3. $17.00

MCCAFFREY, Anne. *Moreta: Dragonlady of Pern.* 1983. Del Rey. 1st ed. VG/VG. P3. $15.00

MCCAFFREY, Anne. *Pegasus in Flight.* 1990. Del Rey. 1st ed. F/F. P3. $20.00

MCCAFFREY, Anne. *Renegades of Pern.* 1989. Del Rey. 1st ed. VG/VG. P3. $20.00

MCCAFFREY, Anne. *Rowman.* 1990. Ace Putnam. 1st ed. F/F. P3. $20.00

MCCAFFREY, Anne. *Stitch in Snow.* 1985. Tor. 1st ed. VG/VG. P3. $18.00

MCCAFFREY, Anne. *Stitch in Snow: An Adult Make-Believe Tale.* 1984. Brandywyne Books. 1st ed. 1/1000. sgn. F/F/case. G10. $45.00

MCCAFFREY, Anne. *Wings of Pegasus.* nd. BC. NF/NF. P3. $10.00

MCCAFFREY, Eugene. *Player's Choice.* 1987. Facts on File. 1st ed. F/VG+. P8. $25.00

MCCAFFREY & NYE. *Dragonlover's Guide to Pern.* nd. Quality BC. NF/NF. P3. $15.00

MCCAFFREY & SCARBOROUGH. *Power Play.* 1995. Del Rey. F/F. P3. $22.00

MCCAFFREY & SCARBOROUGH. *Powers That Be.* 1989. Del Rey. 1st ed. VG/VG. P3. $20.00

MCCAIG, Donald. *Man Who Made the Devil Glad.* 1986. Crown. 1st ed. 214p. F/F. B10. $12.00

MCCAIG, Robert. *Danger Trail.* 1975. Doubleday. 1st ed. VG/VG. P3. $12.00

MCCAIG, Robert. *Toll Mountain.* 1973. Collins. VG/VG. P3. $10.00

MCCALL, Anthony; see Kane, Henry.

MCCALLUM, H.D. *Wire That Fenced the West.* 1965. Norman. 1st ed. ils. 285p. VG/G. B5. $45.00

MCCAMMON, Robert R. *Boy's Life.* 1991. Pocket. 1st ed. F/F. H11/N4. $35.00

MCCAMMON, Robert R. *Gone South.* 1992. Pocket. 1st ed. F/F. N4. $27.50

MCCAMMON, Robert R. *Mine.* 1990. Pocket. 1st ed. NF/F. H11. $25.00

MCCAMMON, Robert R. *Mystery Walk.* 1983. HRW. ARC/1st ed. VG/VG. w/pub card. M23. $40.00

MCCAMMON, Robert R. *Mystery Walk.* 1983. HRW. 1st ed. VG/VG. P3. $35.00

MCCAMMON, Robert R. *Swan Song.* 1989. Dark Harvest. 1st hc ed. F/F. T2. $60.00

MCCAMMON, Robert R. *Usher's Passing.* 1984. Holt Rinehart. 1st ed. NF/NF. M19. $35.00

MCCANN, I.G. *With National Guard on the Border.* 1917. St Louis. 1st ed. VG+. A15. $90.00

MCCANN, Randolph. *Ozark Folklore: An Annotated Bibliography.* 1987. MO U. 2 vol. F/F. A4. $90.00

MCCARRY, Charles. *Last Supper.* 1983. Dutton. 1st ed. F/F. A20. $24.00

MCCARRY, Charles. *Secret Lovers.* 1977. Dutton. 1st ed. VG/VG. P3. $23.00

MCCARRY, Charles. *Tears of Autumn.* 1975. Saturday Review. 1st ed. NF/NF. H11. $30.00

MCCARTHY, Albert. *Jazz on Record: A Critical Guide...* 1968. London. Hanover. 1st ed. VG. B2. $25.00

MCCARTHY, Carlton. *Detailed Minutiae of Soldier Life in Army of Northern VA...* 1888. Richmond, VA. McCarthy. 2nd. 224p. cloth. NF. M8. $150.00

MCCARTHY, Carlton. *Detailed Minutae of Soldier Life in Army of Northern VA...* 1882. Richmond. 1st ed. ils. 224p. G. B5. $100.00

MCCARTHY, Cormac. *All the Pretty Horses.* 1992. Knopf. 1st ed. F/F. H11. $230.00

MCCARTHY, Cormac. *All the Pretty Horses.* 1993. London. Pan. 1st Eng ed. F/F. A18/C2. $100.00

MCCARTHY, Cormac. *Crossing.* 1994. Knopf. 1st ed. F/F. B35. $40.00

MCCARTHY, Cormac. *Crossing. Vol 2 of Border Trilogy.* 1994. Knopf. 1st ed/special issue. 1/1000. sgn. F. C2/C6. $350.00

MCCARTHY, Cormac. *Stonemason.* 1994. Ecco. 1/350. sgn. F/case. M19. $450.00

MCCARTHY, Cormac. *Stonemason: A Play in Five Acts.* 1994. Hopewell. AP. 1/41. F/wrp. C2. $400.00

MCCARTHY, Cormac. *Suttree.* 1979. Random. 1st ed. F/NF. C2. $900.00

MCCARTHY, Gary. *First Sheriff.* 1979. Doubleday. 1st ed. VG/VG. P3. $10.00

MCCARTHY, Justin. *History of Our Time.* 1886. London. Chatto Windus. 4 vol. 8vo. gilt full gr calf. VG. T10. $275.00

MCCARTHY, Mary. *Birds of America.* 1971. HBJ. 1st ed. F/NF. B4. $75.00

MCCARTHY, Mary. *Cannibals & Missionaries.* 1979. HBJ. 1st ed. VG/VG. P3. $15.00

MCCARTHY, Mary. *Group.* 1963. HBW. 1st ed. F/NF. H11. $60.00

MCCARTHY, Mary. *Ideas & the Novel.* 1980. HBJ. 1st ed. F/F. B35. $28.00

MCCARTHY, Mary. *Memories of a Catholic Girlhood.* 1957. Harcourt Brace. 1st ed. NF/NF. B4. $65.00

MCCARTHY, Mary. *Oasis.* 1949. Random. 1st ed. F/VG. B4. $65.00

MCCARTHY, Mary. *Sights & Spectacles: Theatre Chronicles 1937-1958.* 1959. London. Heinemann. 1st Eng ed. F/NF. B4. $55.00

MCCARTHY, Shawna. *Isaac Asimov's Fantasy!* 1985. Dial. ARC. F/dj. P3. $15.00

MCCARTHY & MORRELL. *Some Other Rainbow.* 1993. Bantam. 1st ed. 8vo. ils. 524p. NF/dj. W1. $20.00

MCCARTY, John L. *Maverick Town: Story of Old Tascosa.* 1946. Norman. 1st ed. inscr. 8vo. 277p. VG. B11. $25.00

MCCARTY, John. *Spatter Movies.* 1984. St Martin. 1st ed. F/F. P3. $25.00

MCCAULAY, Fannie Caldwell. *Lady & Sada San.* 1912. Century. 1st ed. F/VG. B4. $85.00

MCCAULEY, Kirby. *Dark Forces.* 1980. Viking. 1st ed. VG/VG. P3. $30.00

MCCAULEY, Kirby. *Frights.* 1976. St Martin. 1st ed. F/F. P3. $45.00

MCCAULEY, Kirby. *Frights.* 1976. St Martin. 1st ed. sgn 7 contributors. F/F. P3. $250.00

MCCAULEY, Michael J. *Jim Thompson: Sleep With the Devil.* 1991. Mysterious. 1st ed. F/F. R10. $20.00

MCCAUSLAND, Hugh. *Old Sporting Characters & Occasions From Sporting...* 1948. Batchworth. 1st ed. 172p. VG/dj. M20. $30.00

MCCINLEY, Phyllis. *Horse Who Lived Upstairs.* 1944. Lippincott. 1st ed. ils Helen Stone. VG+/G. P2. $30.00

MCCLANAHAN, Ed. *Famous People I Have Known.* 1985. FSG. 1st ed. 8vo. F/dj. S9. $25.00

MCCLARY, Thomas Calvert. *Three Thousand Years.* 1954. Fantasy. 1st ed. VG/VG. P3. $40.00

MCCLELLAN, Elisabeth. *Historic Dress in America.* 1904-1910. Phil. GW Jacobs. 2 vol. 1st ed. ils Sophie B Steel. gilt bl cloth. NF. T10. $150.00

MCCLOSKEY, Robert. *Make Way for Ducklings.* 1943 (1941). Viking. 4th. unp. beige pict cloth. VG. T5. $30.00

MCCLOSKEY, Robert. *One Morning in Maine.* 1962 (1952). Viking. 7th. 64p. bl cloth. VG+/VG. T5. $25.00

MCCLOSKY, Marky. *Goodbye But Listen.* 1968. Vanderbilt. 1st ed. F/VG. V1. $20.00

MCCLOY, Helen. *Changeling Conspiracy.* 1976. Dodd Mead. 1st ed. F/F. P3. $23.00

MCCLOY, Helen. *Do Not Disturb.* 1945. Tower. VG. P3. $15.00

MCCLOY, Helen. *Goblin Market.* 1944. Detective BC. VG. P3. $15.00

MCCLOY, Helen. *One That Got Away.* 1946. Detective BC. VG/VG. P3. $13.00

MCCLOY, Helen. *Question of Time.* 1971. Dodd Mead. 1st ed. F/F. P3. $20.00

MCCLOY, Helen. *Smoking Mirror.* 1979. Dodd Mead. 1st ed. VG/VG. P3. $18.00

MCCLOY, Helen. *Through a Glass, Darkly.* 1950. Detective BC. VG. P3. $10.00

MCCLOY, Helen. *Two-Thirds a Ghost.* 1956. Random. 1st ed. VG/G. P3. $35.00

MCCLUNG, John A. *Sketches of Western Adventure: Containing an Account...* 1832. Phil. 1st ed/2nd issue. 8vo. 360p. C6. $600.00

MCCLURE, Alfred J.P. *Steamin' to Bells Around the Middle Sea.* 1900. self pub. 1/350. sgn. 335p. VG. B11. $150.00

MCCLURE, James. *Caterpillar Cop.* 1972. London. 1st ed. F/F. N3. $50.00

MCCLURE, James. *Snake.* 1976. Harper Row. 1st ed. F/F. P3. $20.00

MCCLURE, James. *Steam Pig.* 1971. Harper Row. 1st ed. author's 1st book. F/F. H11. $35.00

MCCLURE, James. *Sunday Hangman.* 1977. Harper Row. 1st ed. VG/VG. P3. $20.00

MCCLURE, Michael. *Josephine: The Mouse Singer.* 1980. New Directions. 1st ed. NF/wrp. V1. $10.00

MCCLURE, Michael. *Selected Poems.* 1986. New Directions. 1st ed. F/wrp. V1. $10.00

MCCLURE. *Heroes, Heavies & Sagebrush.* 1972. ils/photos. 351p. dj. M13. $37.00

MCCOLLUM, Lee. *Our Sons at War.* 1940. Chicago. 216p. VG. A17. $7.50

MCCONNAUGHEY, Gibson J. *Two Centuries of Virginia Cooking.* 1977. Mid-South. 1st ed. sgn. 8vo. 346p. gr cloth. F/VG. B11. $30.00

MCCONNELL, Frank. *Blood Lake.* 1987. Walker. 1st ed. F/F. H11. $20.00

MCCONNELL, Frank. *Liar's Poker.* 1993. Walker. 1st ed. F/F. H11. $20.00

MCCONNELL, Frank. *Murder Among Friends.* nd. BC. VG/VG. P3. $8.00

MCCONNOR, Vincent. *Man Who Knew Hammett.* 1988. NY. Tor. 1st ed. F/F. T2. $14.00

MCCONNOR, Vincent. *Paris Puzzle.* 1981. Macmillan. 1st ed. VG/VG. P3. $18.00

MCCORD, David. *Notes From Four Cities 1927-1953.* 1969. Worcester. Achille J St Onge. 1/1500. aeg. brn leather. miniature. T10. $50.00

MCCORKLE, Jill. *Crash Diet.* 1992. Algonquin. 1st ed. sgn. F/F. M23. $40.00

MCCORKLE, Jill. *Ferris Beach.* 1990. Algonquin. 1st ed. F/F. M23. $25.00

MCCORKLE, Jill. *Tending to Virginia.* 1987. Chapel Hill. Algonquin. 1st ed. sgn. F/F. M23. $45.00

MCCORMACK, Nancy Cox. *Peeps, the Really Truly Sunshine Fairy.* (1918). Volland. 32nd. ils KS Dodge. VG. M20. $25.00

MCCORMACK, Nancy Cox. *Peeps, the Really Truly Sunshine Fairy.* 1919 (1918). Volland. 20th. Sunny Book series. ils. VG. M5. $75.00

MCCORMICK, Cyrus. *Century of the Reaper.* 1931. Boston. 1st ed. ils 307p. VG. B5. $25.00

MCCORMICK, Donald. *Master Book of Spies.* 1973. Hodder Causton. 1st ed. VG. P3. $20.00

MCCORMICK, Virginia Taylor. *Winter Apples.* 1942. Putnam. sgn. 95p. VG/poor. B10. $10.00

MCCORMICK, Wilfred. *Rocky McCune: Proud Champions (#6).* 1959. McKay. 1st ed. 176p. VG/dj. M20. $47.00

MCCORMICK, Wilfred. *Rocky McCune: Too Many Fowards.* 1960. David McKay. 1st ed. 180p. VG+/dj. M20. $40.00

MCCORQUODALE, Robin. *Dansville.* 1986. Harper Row. 1st ed. F/F. H11. $20.00

MCCOWN, Clint. *Member-Guest.* 1995. Doubleday. ARC. F/wrp. B4. $35.00

MCCOY, H. *They Shoot Horses, Don't They?* 1935. NY. 1st ed. author's 1st book. inscr. NF/NF. A15. $750.00

MCCOY, Melvyn H. *Ten Escape From Tojo.* 1944. Farrar Rinehart. 1st ed. F/F. P3. $25.00

MCCOY, Truda Williams. *McCoys: Their Story.* 1976. Pikeville, KY. 1st ed. ils. 338p. VG/VG. B5. $32.50

MCCRACKEN, Elizabeth. *Here's Your Hat What's Your Hurry.* 1993. Random. 1st ed. F/F. M23. $40.00

MCCRACKEN, Harold. *Frederic Remington Book, Pictorial History of the West.* 1966. Doubleday. 1st trade ed. 285p. NF/dj. T10. $145.00

MCCRACKEN, Harold. *Frederic Remington's Own West.* 1960. Dial. 4th. 8vo. ils. NF. T10. $25.00

MCCRACKEN, Harold. *God's Frozen Children.* 1930. Garden City. 1st ed. sgn. VG/VG. B5. $45.00

MCCRACKEN, Harold. *Portrait of the Old West.* 1952. NY. McGraw Hill. 1st ed. folio. ils. 232p. F/NF. T10. $125.00

MCCRACKEN, Russell. *Elegant Elephant.* 1944. Rand McNally. ils. VG/dj. M20. $78.00

MCCRACKEN, Russell. *Mystery of Carmen the Cow.* 1946. Rand McNally. 1st ed. 31p. VG/G+. P2. $45.00

MCCRACKEN. *Gatherings in Honor of Dorothy E Milner.* 1974. Baltimore. Walters Art Gallery. 4to. 353p. VG. A4. $125.00

MCCRAE, John. *In Flanders Fields & Other Poems.* 1919. NY. 1st ed. 141p. VG. A13. $125.00

MCCRAW. *Prophets of Regulation: Charles Francis Adams...* 1984. Harvard. 31 photos. 415p. F/VG. A4. $40.00

MCCRUM, Robert. *In the Secret State.* 1980. Simon Schuster. 1st ed. VG/VG. P3. $15.00

MCCRUMB, Sharyn. *Hangman's Beautiful Daughter.* 1992. Scribner. 1st ed. F/F. H11. $35.00

MCCRUMB, Sharyn. *Hangman's Beautiful Daughter.* 1992. Scribner. 1st ed. sgn. F/F. M23. $40.00

MCCRUMB, Sharyn. *If Ever I Return, Pretty Peggy-O.* 1990. Scribner. 1st ed. F/F. H11. $70.00

MCCRUMB, Sharyn. *She Walks These Hills.* 1994. Scribner. 1st ed. sgn. F/F. M23. $50.00

MCCRUMB, Sharyn. *Windsor Knot.* 1990. Ballantine. UP. NF/red paper wrp. M23. $25.00

MCCRUMB, Sharyn. *Windsor Knot.* 1990. Ballantine. VG/VG. P3. $17.00

MCCULLERS, Carson. *Member of the Wedding.* 1946. Boston. 1st ed. VG/VG. B5. $70.00

MCCULLERS, Carson. *Member of the Wedding.* 1946. Houghton Mifflin. 1st ed. F/F. B24. $350.00

MCCULLERS, Carson. *Sweet As a Pickle & Clean As a Pig.* 1964. Houghton Mifflin. 1st ed. ils Rolf Gerard. F/F. B4. $175.00

MCCULLEY, Johnston. *Rangers' Code.* nd. Grosset Dunlap. G. P3. $12.00

MCCULLEY, Johnston. *Scarlet Scourge.* 1925. Chelsea House. 1st ed. VG. P3. $35.00

MCCULLEY, Johnston. *White Man's Chance.* nd. Grosset Dunlap. VG. P3. $20.00

MCCULLOCH, Warren S. *Embodiments of Mind.* 1965. MIT. fwd JY Lettvin. 402p. bl cloth. VG/dj. G1. $100.00

MCCULLOCH. *Children's Books of the 19th Century.* 1979. ils. 18 photos. 152p. VG. A4. $75.00

MCCULLOUGH, Colleen. *Thorn Birds.* 1977. Harper Row. 1st ed. NF/NF. B35. $40.00

MCCULLOUGH, David Willis. *City Sleuths & Tough Guys.* 1989. Houghton Mifflin. 1st ed. VG/VG. P3. $20.00

MCCULLOUGH, David. *Path Between the Seas.* 1977. Simon Schuster. BC. bl cloth. AN/dj. B22. $5.50

MCCULLOUGH, E. *Good Old Coney Island.* 1957. NY. 1st ed. VG/VG. B5. $22.50

MCCULLY, Walbridge. *Blood on Nassau's Moon.* nd. BC. G+/G+. P3. $5.00

MCCUTCHAN, Philip. *Poulter's Passage.* 1967. Harrap. 1st ed. NF/NF. P3. $18.00

MCCUTCHEON, George Barr. *Brewster's Millions.* nd. Grosset Dunlap. MTI. VG. P3. $13.00

MCCUTCHEON, George Barr. *In of the Hawk & Raven.* nd. AL Burt. VG/VG. P3. $20.00

MCDADE. *Annals of Murder: A Bibliography of Books & Pamphlets...* 1900. OK U. 1126 entries. 400p. NF/NF. A4. $145.00

MCDANIEL, R. *Vinegarroon: Saga of Judge Roy Bean.* 1936. Kingsport, TN. 1st ed. 8vo. 143p. pict cloth. NF. T10. $50.00

MCDERMID, Finlay. *Ghost Wanted.* 1945. Tower. 1st ed. G+/G+. P3. $13.00

MCDERMID, Finlay. *See No Evil.* 1959. Simon Schuster. 1st ed. xl. dj. P3. $6.00

MCDERMID, Val. *Dead Beat.* 1992. NY. 1st ed. F/F. H11. $35.00

MCDERMOTT, Alice. *Bigamist's Daughter.* 1982. Random. 1st ed. author's 1st book. F/F. B4. $125.00

MCDERMOTT, Alice. *Weddings & Wakes.* 1992. FSG. 1st ed. sgn. F/F. B4. $65.00

MCDERMOTT, J.F. *Up the Missouri With Audubon.* 1951. Norman. 1st ed. ils. 222p. VG/VG. B5. $37.50

MCDERMOTT, John. *Russian Journal & Other Selections From...Lewis Carroll.* 1935. NY. 1st ed. VG/G. B5. $45.00

MCDEVITT, Jack. *Engines of God.* 1994. Ace. 1st ed. F/F. P3. $22.00

MCDONALD, Forrest. *Presidency of Thomas Jefferson.* 1976. KSU. 3rd. 201p. VG. B10. $15.00

MCDONALD, Gregory. *Brave.* 1991. Barricade. 1st ed. AN/dj. M22. $30.00

MCDONALD, Gregory. *Exits & Entrances.* 1988. Boston. Hill. sgn. F/F. B11. $12.00

MCDONALD, Gregory. *Fletch, Too.* nd. BC. VG/VG. P3. $8.00

MCDONALD, Gregory. *Fletch, Too.* 1986. Warner. 1st ed. F/F. N4. $25.00

MCDONALD, Gregory. *Fletch Won.* 1985. Warner. 1st ed. VG/VG. P3. $15.00

MCDONALD, Gregory. *Son of Fletch.* 1993. Putnam. 1st ed. AN/dj. M22. $15.00

MCDONALD, Gregory. *Who Took Roby Rinaldi?* 1992. Bantam. 1st ed. F/F. P3. $23.00

MCDONALD, William A. *Progress Into the Past.* 1967. Collier Macmillan. 1st ed. 8vo. ils. 476p. NF/dj. W1. $25.00

MCDONELL, Gordon. *Intruder From the Sea.* nd. BC. VG/VG. P3. $8.00

MCDONELL, J.M. *Half Crazy.* 1995. Little Brn. 1st ed. F/F. H11. $25.00

MCDONNELL, Michael. *Blackwater Volume 1.* nd. BC. VG/G+. P3. $10.00

MCDOUGALL, Alexander. *Autobiography of Capt Alexander McDougall.* 1968. Great Lakes Hist Soc. G. A16. $40.00

MCDOUGALL, William. *Group Mind: Sketch of Principles of Collective Psychology...* 1920. Cambridge. tall 8vo. 304p. ruled ochre cloth. VG. G1. $85.00

MCDOWELL, Charles. *One Thing After Another.* 1960. Dietz. 1st ed. 178p. F/VG. B10. $10.00

MCDOWELL, Charles. *What Did You Have in Mind?* 1963. Morrow. 1st ed. 192p. VG/VG. B10. $12.00

MCDOWELL, Frederick. *Ellen Glasgow & the Ironic Art of Fiction.* 1960. WI U. ARC. 292p. VG/G. B10. $35.00

MCDOWELL, Jack. *Mexico.* 1973. Lane. 1st ed. 4to. 256p. dj. F3. $20.00

MCDOWELL, Michael. *Toplin.* 1985. Scream. 1st ed. sgn. ils/sgn Harry Morris. F/F. G10. $50.00

MCELFRESH, Adeline. *Keep Back the Dark.* 1951. Phoenix. VG/G+. P3. $20.00

MCELLIGOTT, James N. *American Debater.* 1863. Chicago. Griggs. revised. 360p. brn stp cloth. K1. $50.00

MCELROY, David. *Making It Simple.* 1975. Ecco. 1st ed. assn copy. F/NF. V1. $10.00

MCELROY, John. *Red Acorn: Romance of the War.* 1898. National Tribune. 322p. G. B10. $20.00

MCELROY, Joseph. *Plus.* 1976. Knopf. 1st ed. 215p. AN/dj. B22. $9.50

MCEWAN, Ian. *Black Dogs.* 1992. Doubleday. 1st ed. AN/dj. M22. $20.00

MCEWAN, Ian. *Child in Time.* 1987. Houghton Mifflin. 1st ed. F/F. B35. $18.00

MCEWAN, Ian. *First Love, Last Rites.* 1975. Random. 1st Am ed. F/F. T2. $30.00

MCFADDEN, B. *Keeping Fit: Health, How Lose, How Regained.* 1926. NY. photos. 215p. F. B14. $55.00

MCFADDEN, B. *McFadden's New Hair Culture.* 1901. NY. ils. 140p. F. B14. $35.00

MCFALL, Patricia. *Night Butterfly.* 1992. NY. 1st ed. sgn. author's 1st book. F/F. H11. $40.00

MCFARLAND, Dennis. *Music Room.* 1990. Houghton Mifflin. 1st ed. F/F. H11. $55.00

MCFARLAND, Ross A. *Human Factors in Air Transport Design.* 1946. McGraw Hill. 8vo. gray cloth. G1. $60.00

MCFARLAND & NICHOLS. *American Author Series: Norman Maclean.* 1988. Lewiston. Confluence. 1st ed. 1/748. sgns. F/dj. C2. $50.00

MCFERREN, Martha. *Contour for Ritual.* 1988. LSU. 1st ed. F/F. V1. $10.00

MCGARRY, Jean. *Airs of Providence.* 1985. Johns Hopkins. 1st ed. author's 1st book. F/clip. B4. $45.00

MCGAUGHEY, Neil. *Otherwise Known As Murder.* 1994. Scribner. 1st ed. author's 1st book. F/F. M23. $35.00

MCGILL, Jerry. *Red Ryder & the Thunder Trail.* 1956. Whitman. G. P3. $12.00

MCGILL, Ralph. *South & the Southerner.* 1959. Little Brn. 1st ed. 307p. VG/G. B10. $10.00

MCGILLIGAN, Pat. *Backstory: Interviews With Screenwriters of Hollywood's...* 1986. CA U. 1st ed. 8vo. ils. 382p. F/F. T10. $25.00

MCGILLIGAN, Patrick. *Double Life: George Cukor.* 1991. NY. 1st ed. 404p. F/dj. A17. $10.00

MCGINLEY, Patrick. *Bogmail.* 1981. Ticknor. 1st ed. F/NF. H11. $25.00

MCGINLEY, Phyllis. *All Around the Town.* 1948. 1st ed. VG/VG. S13. $25.00

MCGINLEY, Phyllis. *Love Letters of...* 1954. Viking. sgn. VG/VG. B11. $8.00

MCGINLEY, Phyllis. *Saint-Watching.* 1969. Viking. 1st ed. F/F. B4. $45.00

MCGIVERN, William P. *Caper of the Golden Bulls.* 1966. Dodd Mead. 1st ed. VG/VG. P3. $25.00

MCGIVERN, William P. *Night Extra.* nd. BC. VG. P3. $4.00

MCGIVERN, William P. *Rogue Cop.* nd. BC. VG/VG. P3. $8.00

MCGIVERN, William P. *Summitt.* 1982. Arbor. 1st ed. F/F. H11. $25.00

MCGOVERN, William. *Jungle Baths & Inca Ruins.* 1927. Grosset Dunlap. ils. 526p. F3. $15.00

MCGOWAN, Helen. *Motor City Madam.* 1964. Pageant. 1st ed. F/VG. B4. $85.00

MCGOWN, Jill. *Murder at the Old Vicarage.* nd. BC. VG/VG. P3. $8.00

MCGOWN, Jill. *Murder...Now & Then.* 1993. St Martin. 1st Am ed. AN/F. N4. $22.50

MCGOWN, Pearl. *Color in Hooked Rugs.* 1954. 1st ed. photos. VG/worn. S13. $15.00

MCGRATH, Patrick. *Grotesque.* 1989. Poseidon. 1st ed. F/F. M23. $30.00

MCGRATH, Patrick. *Spider.* 1990. Poseidon. 1st ed. F/F. P3. $20.00

MCGRATH, Patrick. *Spider.* 1990. Poseidon. 1st ed. rem mk. NF/F. G10. $15.00

MCGRATH, Thomas. *New & Selected Poems.* 1964. Alan Swallow. 1st ed. NF/sans. V1. $25.00

MCGRAW & WAGNER. *Merry-Go-Round in Oz.* 1963. Reilly Lee. xl. dj. P3. $25.00

MCGRAW & WAGNER. *Merry-Go-Round in Oz.* 1963. Reilly Lee. 1st ed. ils Dick Martin. 303p. ils ep. NF/NF. D1. $675.00

MCGRAW & WAGNER. *Mery-Go-Round in Oz.* 1963. Reilly Lee. 1st ed. ils Dick Martin. pict wht cloth. VG+. B17. $225.00

MCGREW, Fenn. *Taste of Death.* 1953. Rinehart. 1st ed. VG. P3. $10.00

MCGREW, R. Brownell. *R Brownell McGrew.* 1978. Kansas City. Lowell. 1st ed. sgn. 128p. F/dj. T10. $125.00

MCGREW, Roderick. *Encyclopedia of Medical History.* 1985. NY. 400p. VG. A13. $60.00

MCGROATY, John Steven. *Just California & Other Poems.* 1933. Los Angeles. Times Mirror. 1st ed. 12mo. 205p. ribbed bl cloth. T10. $45.00

MCGUANE, Thomas. *Bushwacked Piano.* 1971. NY. 1st ed. author's 2nd book. F/torn. A15. $55.00

MCGUANE, Thomas. *Keep the Change.* 1989. Houghton Mifflin. 1st ed. NF/NF. I111. $20.00

MCGUANE, Thomas. *Sporting Club.* 1968. Simon Schuster. 1st ed. author's 1st book. rem mk. G/clip NF. H11. $85.00

MCGUANE, Thomas. *To Skin a Cat.* 1986. Dutton. 1st ed. F/F. M23. $20.00

MCGUFFEY. *McGuffey's New Third Eclectic Reader for Young Learners.* 1865. Van Antwerp. leather spine/paper brd. M5. $75.00

MCGUFFEY. *McGuffey's Newly Revised Eclectic First Reader.* 1853. Cincinnati. Winthrop Smith. 108p. G-. B18. $27.50

MCGUFFEY. *McGuffey's Thin Eclectic Primer.* 1867. Am Book Co. 12mo. 60p. wrp. M5. $85.00

MCGUIRE, Jerry. *Elijah.* 1973. Northland. 1st ed. ils Joe Beller. F/F. A18. $15.00

MCGUIRE, Patrick O. *Fiesta for Murder.* 1962. Hammond. 1st ed. VG/VG. P3. $20.00

MCHARGUE, Georgess. *Hot & Cold Running Cities.* 1974. Holt. 1st ed. F/F. P3. $15.00

MCHENRY & ROPER. *Smith & Wesson Handguns.* 1945. Huntington, WV. 1st ed. ils. 233p. VG/dj. B5. $45.00

MCHENRY & ROPER. *Smith & Wesson Handguns.* 1945. Huntington. 1st ed. 63 pl. Vg/VG. B5. $125.00

MCHUGH, Heather. *Hinge & Sign Poems 1968-1993.* 1994. Wesleyan. 1st ed. F/F. V1. $35.00

MCILVAINE, Iane. *To Win the Hunt.* 1966. Barre. 1st ed. VG/case. O3. $48.00

MCILVANNEY, William. *Papers of Tony Veitch.* 1983. Hodder Stoughton. 1st ed. VG/VG. P3. $25.00

MCILVOY, Kevin. *Fifth Station.* 1988. Algonquin. 1st ed. F/F. B35. $12.00

MCINERNEY, Jay. *Brightness Falls.* 1992. Knopf. 1st ed. rem mk. F/F. B35. $16.00

MCINERNEY, Jay. *Story of My Life.* 1988. Atlantic Monthly. 1st ed. F/F. B35/P3. $20.00

MCINERNY, Ralph. *Bishop As Pawn.* 1978. Vanguard. 1st ed. VG/VG. P3. $15.00

MCINERNY, Ralph. *Her Death of Cold.* 1977. Vanguard. 1st ed. NF/NF. P3. $20.00

MCINERNY, Ralph. *Judas Priest.* nd. BC. VG/VG. P3. $8.00

MCINERNY, Ralph. *Search Committee.* 1991. Atheneum. 1st ed. NF/NF. P3. $20.00

MCINERNY, Ralph. *Second Vespers.* 1980. Vanguard. 1st ed. NF/NF. P3. $18.00

MCINERNY, Ralph. *Seventh Station.* 1977. Vanguard. 1st ed. author's 2nd book. VG/VG. M22. $30.00

MCINTOSH, David C. *How To Build a Wooden Boat.* 1987. Brooklin, ME. Wooden Boat. ils. 255p. Vg/dj. T7. $40.00

MCINTOSH, J.T. *One in Three Hundred.* nd. BC. VG/VG. P3. $10.00

MCINTOSH, J.T. *World Out of Mind.* nd. BC. VG/VG. P3. $10.00

MCINTOSH, John. *Origin of the North American Indians.* 1043. NY. Nafic Cornish new ed. 12mo. gilt cloth. VG/dj. T10. $150.00

MCINTYRE, Vonda N. *Dreamsnake.* nd. Houghton Mifflin. BC. NF/dj. M21. $7.50

MCINTYRE, Vonda N. *Dreamsnake.* nd. Houghton Mifflin. VG/VG. P3. $18.00

MCINTYRE, Vonda N. *Exile Waiting.* nd. BC. VG/VG. P3. $8.00

MCINTYRE, Vonda N. *Search for Spock.* 1984. Boston. Gregg. 1st ed. sgn. F/F. B11. $40.00

MCINTYRE, Vonda N. *Superluminal.* 1983. Houghton Mifflin. 1st ed. F/F. P3. $25.00

MCKAY, Claude. *Selected Poems.* 1953. NY. 1st ed. ils. 112p. VG/VG. B5. $50.00

MCKAY, Robert. *Skean.* 1976. Nashville. Nelson. 1st ed. F/NF. H11. $20.00

MCKEE, Russell. *Great Lakes Country.* 1966. Crowell. VG/VG. A16. $30.00

MCKEEVER, William A. *Training the Boy.* 1913. NY. 2nd. ils. 368p. VG. A17. $10.00

MCKELVEY, Blake. *Urbanization of America 1860-1915.* 1963. Rutgers. 2nd. 8vo. 370p. VG. T10. $25.00

MCKELVIE, Martha Groves. *Lawman of the West.* 1978. Phil. Franklin. 8vo. ils. F/dj. T10. $35.00

MCKENNEY, John. *Tack Room Tattles.* 1934. Scribner. 1st/A ed. G. O3. $35.00

MCKENNEY, Thomas L. *Sketches of a Tour to the Lakes.* 1972. Boston. Imprint Soc. 1/1950. 413p. F/case. T10. $150.00

MCKENNON, Joe. *Horse Dung Trail. Saga of the American Circus.* 1975. Sarasota. Carnival. 1st ed. sgn. 8vo. 528p. VG/VG. B11. $35.00

MCKERNAN, Victoria. *Osprey Reef.* 1990. Carroll Graf. 1st ed. F/F. P3. $18.00

MCKILLIP, Patricia A. *Fool's Run.* 1987. Warner. 1st ed. hc. F/F. P3. $16.00

MCKILLIP, Patricia A. *Harpist in the Wind.* 1979. Atheneum. 1st ed. hc. xl. dj. P3. $7.00

MCKILLIP, Patricia A. *Heir of the Sea & Fire.* 1977. Atheneum. 2nd. F/F. P3. $13.00

MCKILLIP, Patricia A. *Moon & Face.* 1985. Atheneum. 1st ed. NF/NF. P3. $25.00

MCKILLIP, Patricia A. *Night Gift.* 1976. Atheneum. 1st ed. VG/VG. P3. $30.00

MCKILLIP, Patricia A. *Sorceress & the Cygnet.* 1991. Ace. 1st ed. F/F. P3. $18.00

MCKINLEY, Robin. *Hero & the Crown.* 1985. Greenwillow. 1st ed. VG/VG. P3. $18.00

MCKINLEY, William. *Authentic Life of William McKinley.* 1901. np. 8vo. ils. 503p. cloth. G. T3. $12.00

MCKITTERICK, Molly. *Medium Is Murder.* 1992. NY. 1st ed. author's 1st book. F/F. H11. $30.00

MCKITTERICK, Molly. *Murder in a Mayonnaise Jar.* 1993. NY. 1st ed. F/NF. H11. $20.00

MCKNIGHT, R. *Kind of Light That Shines in Texas.* 1992. Little Brn. 1st ed. F/F. A20. $25.00

MCLACHLAN, Ian. *Seventh Hexagram.* 1976. Macmillan. 1st ed. NF/NF. P3. $15.00

MCLANATHAN, Richard. *Brandywine Heritage: Howard Pyle, NC Wyeth, Andrew Wyeth...* 1971. Brandywine River Mus. 1st ed. ils/pl. 121p. dj. A17. $25.00

MCLAREN, John. *Gardening in California.* 1924. San Francisco. Robertson. 3rd ed. 8vo. 395p. VG. T10. $45.00

MCLAREY, Myra. *Water From the Well.* 1995. Atlantic Monthly. 1st ed. F/F. M23. $20.00

MCLAUGHLIN, Dean. *Hawk Among the Sparrows.* 1976. Scribner. 1st ed. VG/VG. P3. $15.00

MCLAUGHLIN, Robert. *Short Wait Between Trains & Other Stories.* 1945. NY. 1st ed. 206p. G+. B18. $17.50

MCLAURIN, Hamish. *What About North Africa? Travel in Morocco...* 1927. Scribner. 1st ed. pres. 8vo. 362p. VG. W1. $18.00

MCLAURIN, John J. *Sketches in Crude-Oil. Some Accidents & Incidents...* 1898 Harrisburg. 2nd. 452p. G. W1. $35.00

MCLAURIN, Tim. *Cured by Fire.* 1995. NY. Putnam. 1st ed. sgn. F/F. M23. $25.00

MCLAURIN, Tim. *Keeper of the Moon.* 1991. Norton. 1st ed. rem mk. F/NF. M23. $35.00

MCLAURIN, Tim. *Woodrow's Trumpet.* 1989. Norton. 1st ed. F/F. M23. $25.00

MCLEAN, Ruari. *George Cruikshank.* nd. ils. w/list of ils books. VG/VG. S13. $25.00

MCLELLAN, Charles Arthur. *Art of Shoeing & Balancing the Trotter.* 1927. NY. Trotter & Pacer. 1st prt. G+. O3. $125.00

MCLENDON, S.G. *History of the Public Domain of Georgia.* Feb 1924. Atlanta. sm 8vo. 200p. gilt brn cloth. NF. B14. $45.00

MCLENDON & SMITH. *Don't Quote Me!: Washington Newswomen & Power of Society.* 1970. Dutton. 1st ed. sgns. NF/VG+. B4. $125.00

MCLEOD, W. *Geography of Palestine.* 1854. London. 9th. map. G+. M17. $25.00

MCLOUGHLIN, John C. *Toolmaker Koan.* 1987. Baen. 1st ed. F/F. P3. $17.00

MCLOUGHLIN BROTHERS. *ABC Nursery Rhymes.* nd. McLoughlin. lg 4to. VG+/pict wrp. M5. $180.00

MCLOUGHLIN BROTHERS. *Aquarium.* ca 1880. NY. McLoughlin. Little Showman's series. 1st issue. popup. VG. T10. $350.00

MCLOUGHLIN BROTHERS. *Christmas Sunshine.* 1906. McLoughlin. 4to. VG/wrp. M5. $65.00

MCLOUGHLIN BROTHERS. *History of Tom Thumb.* ca 1880s. McLouglin. 6 pl. VG/wrp. M5. $65.00

MCLOUGHLIN BROTHERS. *Lion's Den.* ca 1880. Little Showman's series. 1st issue. pop-ups. lacks 2 bars/others rpr. VG. T10. $250.00

MCLOUGHLIN BROTHERS. *Menagerie & Arab Show.* 1890. McLoughlin. 16p. VG/wrp. M5. $48.00

MCLOUGHLIN BROTHERS. *Mother Goose.* ca 1895. McLoughlin. shaped book. 14p. VG. D1. $225.00

MCLOUGHLIN BROTHERS. *Nursery Rhymes ABC.* ca 1900. McLoughlin. 12p text. NF/stiff wrp. M5. $225.00

MCLOUGHLIN BROTHERS. *Old Woman & Her Pig.* 1890. NY. Little Pig series. ils. unp. G/wrp. D1. $40.00

MCLOUGHLIN BROTHERS. *Our Holidays, Recitations & Excercises for New Year.* 1906. McLoughlin. 12mo. VG. B17. $10.00

MCLOUGHLIN BROTHERS. *Peep at Buffalo Bill's Wild West.* 1887. McLoughlin. 4to. 9 pl. NF/self wrp. B24. $175.00

MCLOUGHLIN BROTHERS. *Pied Piper of Hamelin.* 1931. McLoughlin Jr Color Classic. 12mo. F. M5. $15.00

MCLOUGHLIN BROTHERS. *Rip Van Winkle.* ca 1880. McLoughlin. ils Thomas Nast. VG/pict wrp. D1. $285.00

MCLOUGHLIN BROTHERS. *Simple Simon & Bo-Peep.* 1896. McLouglin. 16p. VG+/wrp. M5. $50.00

MCLOUGHLIN BROTHERS. *Topsy.* ca 1900. McLoughlin. shaped book. NF/stiff pict wrp. D1. $350.00

MCLOUGHLIN BROTHERS. *Wild Beast Show.* ca 1880. Little Showman's series. 1st issue. popup. VG. T10. $350.00

MCLUHAN, T.C. *Touch the Earth: Self-Portrait of Indian Existence.* 1971. NY. Promontory. 1st ed. 8vo. ils. 185p. F/dj. T10. $50.00

MCMAHAN, Anna B. *With Shelly in Italy.* 1905. Chicago. 1/250. G. V4. $40.00

MCMANUS, James. *Great America.* 1993. Harper. 1st ed. F/F. V1. $15.00

MCMICHAEL, John. *Circulation: Proceedings of Harvey Tercentenary Congress.* 1958. Springfield. 1st Am ed. 503p. VG. A13. $100.00

MCMILLAN, R.A. *Calculations for Marine Engineers.* 1912. Griffin. ils. 336p. maroon cloth. G+. P12. $12.00

MCMILLAN, Terry. *Disappearing Acts.* 1989. Viking. 1st ed. author's 2nd book. F/F. B4. $80.00

MCMILLAN, Terry. *Mama.* 1987. Houghton Mifflin. AP. sgn. F/wrp. M19. $250.00

MCMILLAN, Terry. *Waiting to Exhale.* 1992. Viking. ARC. sgn. RS. F/dj. S9. $125.00

MCMILLAN, Terry. *Waiting To Exhale.* 1992. Viking. UP. F/pict wrp. B35. $80.00

MCMILLAN, Terry. *Waiting To Exhale.* 1992. Viking. 1st ed. rem mk. F/F. H11. $55.00

MCMILLIN, Ralph E. *Poems of...* 1919. Boston. self pub. probable 1st/only ed. 86p. teg. VG+/F. B22. $6.50

MCMULLEN, Mary. *Bad-News Man.* nd. Detective BC. VG. P3. $8.00

MCMULLEN, Mary. *But Nellie Was So Nice.* 1979. Crime Club. VG/VG. P3. $15.00

MCMULLEN, Mary. *Gift Horse.* 1985. Crime Club. 1st ed. VG/VG. P3. $15.00

MCMULLEN, Mary. *Man With Fifty Complaints.* 1978. Crime Club. 1st ed. VG/VG. P3. $15.00

MCMULLERS. *Clock Without Hands.* 1961. Boston. 1st ed. inscr. NF/NF clip. C2. $400.00

MCMURRAY, George. *Jose Donoso.* 1979. Boston. Twayne. 1st ed. 178p. xl. A17. $7.50

MCMURTRIE, Douglas. *Alphabets: Manual of Letter Design...* 1926. Pelham. 1st ed. F/NF. C2. $100.00

MCMURTRIE, Douglas. *Fichet Letter.* 1927. NY. Pr of Ars Typographica. 1/200. 4to. 58p. F. T10. $200.00

MCMURTRIE, Douglas. *Two Georgia Printed Acts of 1757 & 1763.* 1933. Blk Cat. 1st ed. 1/120. 11p. VG/orange wrp. C2. $125.00

MCMURTRY, Douglas. *Book: Story of Printing & Bookmaking.* 1989. np. rpt of 1938 ed. ils. 676p. F/F. A4. $25.00

MCMURTRY, Larry. *All My Friends Are Going To Be Strangers.* 1972. Simon Schuster. 1st ed. F/F clip. H11. $135.00

MCMURTRY, Larry. *Anything for Billy.* 1988. Simon Schuster. 1st ed. NF/NF. P3. $22.00

MCMURTRY, Larry. *Buffalo Girls.* 1990. NY. 1st ed. NF/NF. P3. $20.00

MCMURTRY, Larry. *Buffalo Girls.* 1990. NY. 1st ed. sgn. F/NF. C6. $50.00

MCMURTRY, Larry. *Buffalo Girls.* 1990. Simon Schuster. 1st ed. F/F. A18. $25.00

MCMURTRY, Larry. *Buffalo Girls.* 1992. NY. AP. F/wrp. C2. $30.00

MCMURTRY, Larry. *Desert Rose.* 1983. Simon Schuster. 1st ed. F/F. B2. $40.00

MCMURTRY, Larry. *Last Picture Show.* nd. BC. VG/VG. P3. $8.00

MCMURTRY, Larry. *Lonesome Dove.* 1985. NY. 1st ed. VG/VG. B5. $125.00

MCMURTRY, Larry. *Lonesome Dove.* 1985. Simon Schuster. 1st ed. NF/F. H11. $200.00

MCMURTRY, Larry. *Moving On.* 1970. NY. 1st ed. VG/VG. B5. $60.00

MCMURTRY, Larry. *Some Can Whistle.* 1989. Simon Schuster. 1st ed. F/F. A18/H11. $25.00

MCMURTRY, Larry. *Some Can Whistle.* 1989. Simon Schuster. 1st ed. VG/VG. N4. $17.50

MCMURTRY, Larry. *Terms of Endearment.* 1975. Simon Schuster. 1st ed. F/NF. M19. $150.00

MCMURTRY, Larry. *Terms of Endearment.* 1975. Simon Schuster. 1st ed. inscr. F/NF. B24. $400.00

MCMURTRY, Larry. *Terms of Endearment.* 1977. Allen. 1st Eng ed. F/NF. M19. $85.00

MCMURTRY, Larry. *Texasville.* 1987. Simon Schuster. 1st ed. NF/NF. P3. $25.00

MCMURTRY, Larry. *Texasville.* 1987. Simon Schuster. 1st ed. sgn. F/F. B30. $45.00

MCMURTRY, R. Gerald. *Let's Talk of Lincoln.* 1939. Harrogate, TN. 1st ed. sgn. 41p. VG. B18. $17.50

MCMURTRY & OSSANA. *Pretty Boy Floyd.* 1994. Simon Schuster. advance excerpt sgns B4 $125.00

MCNALLY, Raymond T. *Dracula Was a Woman.* 1983. McGraw Hill. 1st ed. F/VG+. M21. $15.00

MCNALLY, T.M. *Until Your Heart Stops.* 1993. Villard. 1st ed. F/F. H11. $30.00

MCNAMARA, Joseph D. *Fatal Command.* 1987. Arbor. 1st ed. F/F. H11. $25.00

MCNAMARA, Joseph D. *Fatal Command.* 1987. Arbor. 1st ed. VG/VG. P3. $18.00

MCNAMEE, Eoin. *Resurrection Man.* 1995. Picador. 1st ed. F/F. M23. $40.00

MCNASPY, C.J. *Lost Cities of Paraguay.* 1982. Chicago. Loyola. 1st ed. 159p. dj. F3. $45.00

MCNAUGHTON, Colin. *There's an Awful Lot of Weirdos in Our Neighborhood...* 1987. Simon Schuster. 1st ed. 93p. F/VG. C14. $10.00

MCNEER, May. *Story of Florida.* 1947. Harper. ils CH DeWitt. VG. B17. $10.00

MCNEER, May. *Story of the Southern Highlands.* nd. Harper. 4to. ils. unp. VG+. C14. $18.00

MCNEIL, Everett. *With Kit Carson in the Rockies.* 1909. Dutton. 8vo. VG. B17. $8.50

MCNEIL, John. *Spy Game.* 1980. CMG. 1st ed. VG/VG. P3. $15.00

MCNEIL & REESE. *Bid Against the Masters: Best of Bidding Forum.* 1993. London. 128p. M. S1. $12.00

MCNEILE, H.C. *Bull-Dog Drummond.* nd. Grosset Dunlap. G. P3. $10.00

MCNICHOLS, Charles L. *Crazy Weather.* 1944. Macmillan. 1st ed. 8vo. 195p. G/dj. T10. $35.00

MCPARTLAND, John. *No Down Payment.* nd. Simon Schuster. 2nd. VG/G+. P3. $15.00

MCPHEDRAN, Marie. *Cargoes on the Great Lakes.* nd. Indianapolis. 226p. VG/dj. B18. $9.50

MCPHEDRAN, Marie. *Cargoes on the Great Lakes.* 1952. Toronto. ils Dorothy Ivens. G/G. A16. $25.00

MCPHEE, John. *Basin & Range.* 1981. FSG. 1st ed. 216p. F. D8. $20.00

MCPHEE, John. *Control of Nature.* 1989. FSG. 1st ed. 272p. VG/prt wrp. D8. $12.00

MCPHEE, John. *Deltoid Pumpkin Seeds.* 1973. FSG. 1st ed. F/F. H11. $45.00

MCPHEE, John. *Giving Good Weight.* 1979. FSG. 1st ed. NF/F. H11. $30.00

MCPHEE, John. *In Suspect Terrain.* 1983. FSG. 1st ed. F/NF clip. H11. $35.00

MCPHEE, John. *Pine Barrens.* 1968. NY. 1st ed. pres. F/F. C2. $225.00

MCPHEE, John. *Pine Barrens.* 1968. NY. 1st ed. VG/G. B5. $45.00

MCPHEE, John. *Place de la Concorde Suisse.* 1984. FSG. 1st ed. 1/200. sgn. F/case. S9. $125.00

MCPHEE, John. *Survival Bark Canoe.* 1975. NY. 1st ed. VG. B5. $45.00

MCPHEE, John. *Wimbledon.* 1972. 1st ed. photos. NF/NF. S13. $25.00

MCPHERSON, Sandra. *Patron Happiness.* 1983. Ecco. 1st ed. F/F. V1. $15.00

MCPHERSON, William. *Testing the Current.* 1984. Simon Schuster. 1st ed. author's 1st book. F/NF. H11. $30.00

MCPHERSON, William. *To the Sargasso Sea.* 1987. NY. 1st ed. rem mk. F/F. A17. $9.50

MCPHERSON, William. *To the Sargasso Sea.* 1987. Simon Schuster. 1st ed. F/F. H11. $20.00

MCPHERSON. *Battle Chronicle of the Civil War.* 1989. 6 vol. 4to. photos. F/F. A4. $85.00

MCQUEEN, Andrew. *Clyde River-Steamers of the Last Fifty Years.* 1923. Glasgow. Gowans Gray. G. A16. $50.00

MCQUEEN, Ian. *Sherlock Holmes Detected.* 1974. David Charles. 1st ed. VG/VG. P3. $30.00

MCQUILLAN, Karin. *Cheetah Chase.* 1994. Ballantine. 1st ed. F/F. M23. $20.00

MCRAVEN, Charles. *Country Blacksmithing.* 1981. Harper Row. VG/G+. O3. $35.00

MCROYD, Allan. *Death in Costume.* 1940. Greystone. 1st ed. VG. P3. $30.00

MCSHANE, Mark. *Lashed But Not Leashed.* 1976. Crime Club. 1st ed. VG/VG. P3. $15.00

MCSHERRY, Frank D. *Detectives to Z.* 1985. Bonanza. 1st ed. VG/VG. P3. $15.00

MCSWEEN, Harry Y. *Stardust to Planets.* 1993. St Martin. 1st ed. 8vo. 241p. VG. K5. $16.00

MCVITTIE, G.C. *General Relativity & Cosmology.* 1956. John Wiley. 1st ed. cloth. xl. K5. $35.00

MEACHEM, Beth. *Terry's Universe.* 1988. Tor. 1st ed. F/F. P3. $17.00

MEAD, G.R.S. *Fragments of the Faith Forgotten.* 1960. NY. 633p. F/dj. A17. $25.00

MEAD, Margaret. *Blackberry Winter. My Earlier Years.* 1972. Morrow. BC. 350p gr cloth. F/torn. B22. $3.50

MEAD, Margaret. *Ruth Benedict.* 1974. NY. Columbia. 2nd. 180p. AN/dj. P4. $17.50

MEAD & WILLIAMS. *Tennessee Williams: An Intimate Biography.* 1983. Arbor. 1st ed. 352p. F/NF. P4. $25.00

MEADE, Everard. *Dragonfly.* 1985. Claycomb. 1st ed. sgn. 179p. VG/VG. B10. $15.00

MEADE, Everard. *Golden Geese.* 1968. Dodd Mead. 274p. VG/G. B10. $10.00

MEADE, Julian. *Teeny & the Tall Man.* 1936. Doubleday Doran. 1st ed. ils Grace Paull. 155p. VG/G. P2. $30.00

MEADE, Richard; see Haas, Ben.

MEADE, Shepherd. *'Er.* 1970. Harrap. 1st ed. VG/VG. P3. $15.00

MEADE, Shepherd. *Carefully Considered Rape of World.* 1965. Simon Schuster. 1st ed. xl. dj. P3. $8.00

MEADOWS, Hank. *Cooking With Hank.* 1970. np. 1st ed. sgn. 8vo. 171p. F/F. B11. $10.00

MEADOWS, Mary Whitlock. *Patrins: The Metaphysical Poetry of...* 1972. Atlanta. G+. B10. $15.00

MEANY, Tom. *Babe Ruth.* nd. Grosset Dunlap. NF/NF. P3. $25.00

MEANY, Tom. *Baseball's Greatest Hitters.* 1950. AS Barnes. later prt. VG+/VG. P8. $35.00

MEANY, Tom. *Yankee Story.* 1960. Dutton. 1st ed. VG. P8. $30.00

MECKIER. *Innocent Abroad: Charles Dickens' American Engagements.* 1990. KY U. 272p. F/F. A4. $35.00

MEE, Charles L. Jr. *Meeting at Potsdam.* 1975. NY. BC. VG/dj. A17. $6.00

MEEKER, Ezra. *70 Years of Progress in Washington.* 1921. Seattle. Meeker. sgn. 8vo. 381p. gilt gr cloth. K1. $45.00

MEETER, George F. *Holloman Story.* 1967. Albuquerque. 1st ed. 203p. VG/dj. B18. $15.00

MEEUSE, A.D.J. *All About Angiosperms.* 1987. Delft. Eburon. 8vo. 212p. F/wrp. B1. $25.00

MEGGENDORFER, Lothar. *All Alive: Movable Toybook.* ca 1890. London. Grevel. 8 moveable pl. paper brd/cloth spine. T10. $1,800.00

MEGGENDORFER, Lothar. *Militarisches Ziehbilderbuch Von L Meggendorfer.* ca 1910. Munchen. Braun Schneider. 4to. NF. w/instruction sheet. T10. $2,500.00

MEGREW, Roi Cooper. *Under Cover.* 1914. Little Brn. 1st ed. G. P3. $20.00

MEHRTENS, J.M. *Living Snakes of the World.* 1987. NY. Sterling. 8vo. photos. 480p. F/F. B1. $50.00

MEIGS, Cornelia. *Crooked Apple Tree.* 1929. Boston. 1st ed. ils Helen Grose. pict cloth. VG. A17. $10.00

MEIGS, Cornelia. *Fair Wind to Virginia.* 1955. Macmillan. 1st ed. ils John C Wonsetler. 198p. VG/VG. B10. $10.00

MEIGS, Cornelia. *Mounted Messenger.* 1943. Macmillan. 1st ed. 187p. F/NF. A17. $10.00

MEIGS, Cornelia. *White Winter.* 1948. Bobbs Merrill. 1st ed. 209p. VG/VG. P2. $25.00

MEIGS, Cornelia. *Willow Whistle.* 1931. Macmillan. 1st ed. 144p. G+. P2. $28.00

MEIGS, Cornelia. *Wind in the Chimney.* 1935. Macmillan. 4th. 8vo. VG. B17. $5.50

MEIGS, Elizabeth. *Silver Quest.* 1949. Bobbs Merrill. 1st ed. VG/G. O3. $15.00

MEIGS. *Critical History of Children's Literature...* 1953. np. ils. 648p. VG/VG. A4. $95.00

MEIK, Vivian. *People of the Leaves.* 1931. Holt. 8vo. 184p. VG. P4. $20.00

MEILACH. *Creating Art From Anything.* 1968. F/VG. D2. $25.00

MEINARDUS, Otto F.A. *Cradles of Faith: Jerusalem-Sinai.* 1966. Cairo. Arab Bookshop. 12mo. ils. G. W1. $14.00

MEINECKE, Conrad. *Your Cabin in the Woods.* 1945. 1st ed. ils. NF/chip. S13. $45.00

MELLAART, James. *Earliest Civilizations of the Near East.* 1965. McGraw Hill. 1st ed. sm 8vo. ils. xl. VG. W1. $30.00

MELLERSH, H.E.L. *Minoan Crete.* 1967. Putnam. 1st ed. ils. NF/dj. W1. $22.00

MELLIN, Jeanne. *Complete Morgan Horse.* 1986. Lexington. Stephen Greene. 1st ed. VG/VG. O3. $45.00

MELLIN, Jeanne. *Morgan Horse Handbook.* (1973). Brattleboro. 2nd. VG. O3. $40.00

MELLIN, Jeanne. *Morgan Horse.* 1961. Brattleboro. Stephen Greene. 1st ed. VG/VG. O3. $45.00

MELLON, Paul. *Painting in England 1700-1850: Collection of...* 1963. VA Mus of Art. 2 vol. VG/G. D2. $65.00

MELLOY, Camille. *Comment Erro Parcourut la Finlande.* ca 1930s. Belgium. Zonnewendes SA-Courtrai. 5 pl. VG. M5. $85.00

MELTON & PURDY. *Bright Wheels Rolling: Story of James Melton, Autorama.* 1954. Phil. McRae Smith. sgn Melton. 189p. NF. B14. $125.00

MELTZER, Milton. *Light in the Dark: Life of Samuel Gridley.* 1964. Crowell. 1st ed. 239p. xl. F. B22. $4.00

MELVILLE, Herman. *Battle-Pieces & Aspects of the War.* 1866. Harper. 1st ed/1st issue. 8vo. 272p. gilt lavender cloth. NF. B24. $1,500.00

MELVILLE, Herman. *Confidence Man.* 1954. Hendricks. VG. P3. $20.00

MELVILLE, Herman. *Encantadas; or, Enchanted Isles.* 1940. Burlingame, CA. 1st separate ed. 1/550. VG. C6. $175.00

MELVILLE, Herman. *John Marr & Other Poems.* 1922. Princeton. 1st trade ed. NF. C6. $120.00

MELVILLE, Herman. *Mardi: And a Voyage Thither.* 1849. NY. 1st Am ed. 2 vol. 8vo. ribbed gr cloth. NF. B24. $2,750.00

MELVILLE, Herman. *Moby Dick.* nd. Grosset Dunlap. MTI. G. P3. $10.00

MELVILLE, Herman. *Moby Dick.* 1930. NY. 1st trade ed. ils Rockwell Kent. VG. B5. $35.00

MELVILLE, Herman. *Moby Dick.* 1930. NY. 1st trade ed. ils Rockwell Kent. VG/G. B5. $90.00

MELVILLE, Herman. *Moby Dick.* 1979. Franklin Lib. hc. gilt leather spine. NF. P3. $20.00

MELVILLE, Herman. *Moby Dick; or, The Whale.* 1930. Chicago. Lakeside. 3 vol. 1/1000. 4to. F/glassine/dj/aluminum case/band. B24. $5,500.00

MELVILLE, Herman. *Moby Dick; or, The Whale.* 1930. Chicago. Lakeside. 3 vol. 1st ed. 1/1000. G+. B5. $600.00

MELVILLE, Herman. *Moby Dick; or, The Whale.* 1975. NY. Artists Ltd Ed. folio. sgn Cousteau/Neiman. gilt brn morocco. F/case. B24. $1,250.00

MELVILLE, Herman. *Omoo: A Narrative of Adventures in the South Seas.* 1847. London. 1st ed (precedes US). author's 2nd book. VG. C6. $425.00

MELVILLE, James. *Imperial Way.* 1986. Deutsch. 1st ed. VG/VG. P3. $25.00

MELVILLE, Jennie. *Making Good Blood.* 1989. St Martin. 1st ed. VG/VG. P3. $18.00

MENAPACE, John. *Letter in a Klein Bottle: Photographs.* 1984. Jargon Soc. 1st ed. sgn Menapace/Williams. An/dj. C2. $45.00

MENARD, H.W. *Geology, Resources & Society...* 1974. Freeman. 1st ed. 621p. F. D8. $10.00

MENASHE, Samuel. *Many Named Beloved.* 1961. London. 1st ed. F/NF. V1. $15.00

MENCKEN, H.L. *Chrestomathy.* 1949. NY. 1st ed. VG. B5. $35.00

MENCKEN, H.L. *Europe After 8:15.* 1914. John Lane. 1st ed. ils Thomas Hart Benton. NF/dj. B24. $525.00

MENCKEN, H.L. *James Branch Cabell.* 1927. McBride. ils. 32p. B10. $50.00

MENCKEN, H.L. *Prejudices, Third Series.* 1922. Knopf. 1st ed. F/dj. B24. $475.00

MENCKEN, H.L. *Prejudices. Fifth Series.* 1926. NY. 1/200. sgn. VG/VG. C6. $250.00

MENDELSOHN, Jane. *I Was Amelia Earhart.* 1996. Knopf. 1st ed. author's 1st novel. F/F. M23. $30.00

MENDELSON, Wallace. *Felix Frankfurter: A Tribute.* 1964. Reynal. M11. $45.00

MENDELSSOHN. *South African Bibliography.* nd. 2 vol. rpt of 1910 London. ed. 1/175. F. A4. $95.00

MENDENHALL, Walter C. *Ground Waters of the Indio Region, California...* 1909. GPO. 8vo. ils/pl/2 lg fld maps. new cloth. F. T10. $75.00

MENDENHALL, Walter C. *Some Desert Watering Places in Southeastern California...* 1909. GPO. photos. 98p. bl cloth/paper label. F. T10. $75.00

MENDOZA, Eduardo. *Truth About Savolta Case.* 1992. Pantheon. 1st ed. F/F. A20. $18.00

MENDOZA & ROCKWELL. *Norman Rockwell's Americana ABC.* c 1975. Dell/Abrams. unp. NF. C14. $8.00

MENEN, Aubrey. *Cities in the Sand.* 1973. Dial. 1st ed. ils. 272p. NF/dj. W1. $30.00

MENEN, Aubrey. *Rama Retold.* 1954. Chatto Windus. xl. dj. P3. $10.00

MENOTTI, Gian Carlo. *Last Savage.* 1964. NYGS. 1st ed. ils Montressor. F/worn. A17. $10.00

MERCER, A.S. *Banditti of the Plains.* 1935. Grabhorn. ltd ed. ils Arvilla Parker. NF. T10. $150.00

MERCER, Henry. *Hill-Caves of Yucatan.* 1975. OK U. 1st ed. 183p. dj. F3. $35.00

MERCHANT, Paul; see Ellison, Harlan.

MERCIER, Charles. *Nervous System & the Mind.* 1888. London. Macmillan. 374p. gilt pebbled mauve cloth. G1. $125.00

MEREDITH, George. *Diana of the Crossways.* nd. Rand McNally. hc. VG. P3. $20.00

MEREDITH, George. *Letters of George Meredith to Alice Meynell...* 1923. Nonesuch. 1st ed. 1/850. 102p. cloth spine/paper brd. NF/VG. M8. $20.00

MEREDITH, Richard. *Vestiges of Time.* 1978. Doubleday. NF/NF. G10. $10.00

MEREDITH, Roy. *Face of Robert E Lee in Life & Legend.* 1947. Scribner. 1st ed. ils. 143p. G/fair. B10. $25.00

MEREDITH, Scott. *Bar 1: Roundup of Best Western Stories.* 1952. London. Andrew Dakers. 1st Eng ed. F/chip. A18. $35.00

MEREDITH, William. *Cheer.* 1980. Knopf. 1st ed. F/F. V1. $25.00

MEREDITH, William. *Hazard the Painter.* 1975. Knopf. 1st ed. F/F. V1. $15.00

MERIAN, Matthieu. *La Danse des Mortes.* 1756. Basel. Ches Jean Rodolphe Imhof. 132p. contemporary calf. K1. $1,250.00

MERIWETHER, Louise. *Daddy Was a Numbers Runner.* 1970. Prentice Hall. 1st ed. F/VG+ clip. B4. $85.00

MERLE, Robert. *Day of the Dolphin.* 1969. Simon Schuster. 1st ed. F/F. H11. $25.00

MERLE, Robert. *Malevil.* 1973. Simon Schuster. 1st ed. rem mk. F/NF. H11. $20.00

MERRIAM, D.F. *Symposium on Cyclic Sedimentation.* 1964. Lawrence, KS. 2 vol. F/wrp. D8. $50.00

MERRIAM, Eve. *Funny Town.* 1963. Crowell Collier. 1st ed. ils Evaline Ness. pict brd. G+. T5. $20.00

MERRICK, Leonard. *Quaint Companions.* nd. Hodder Stoughton. intro HG Wells. VG. P3. $15.00

MERRICK, William. *Packard Cae.* 1961. Random. 1st ed. G+/G+. P3. $10.00

MERRIL, Judith. *Beyond Human Ken.* 1952. Random. 1st ed. VG/VG. P3. $35.00

MERRIL, Judith. *Beyond the Barriers of Space & Time.* nd. BC. VG. P3. $10.00

MERRIL, Judith. *Daughters of Earth.* 1969. Doubleday. 1st ed. xl. dj. P3. $6.00

MERRIL, Judith. *SF 12.* 1968. Delacorte. 1st ed. VG/VG. P3. $20.00

MERRIL, Judith. *SF 57.* 1957. Gnome. 1st ed. F/F. P3. $40.00

MERRIL, Judith. *SF 59.* 1959. Gnome. 1st ed. VG/VG. P3. $30.00

MERRIL, Judith. *Shadow on the Hearth.* 1953. Sidgwick Jackson. 1st ed. RS. G+/dj. P3. $30.00

MERRILL, George Perkins. *Report on Researches on Chemical & Mineralogical...* 1916. Nat Academy Sciences. 4to. fld table. 29p. wrp. K5. $40.00

MERRILL, James M. *William Tecumseh Sherman.* 1971. Chicago. 1st ed. 445p. VG/dj. B18. $37.50

MERRIMAN, Henry Seton. *Return to Peyton Place.* 1959. NY. 1st ed. 256p. G/dj. A17. $8.50

MERRIMAN, Paul R. *Flora of Richmond & Vicinity...* 1930. VA Academy of Science. ils. 353p. VG. B10. $25.00

MERRITT, A. *Dwellers in the Mirage.* 1932. Liveright. 1st ed. NF. P3. $200.00

MERRITT, A. *Face in the Abyss.* 1931. Liveright. 1st ed. hc. G. P3. $90.00

MERRITT, A. *Fox Woman.* 1946. New Collectors Group. hc. VG. P3. $30.00

MERRITT, A. *Seven Footprints to Satan.* nd. Grosset Dunlap. MTI. VG/remnant. P3. $35.00

MERRITT, A. *Ship of Ishtar.* 1973. Tom Stacey. hc. VG. P3. $20.00

MERRY, Thomas. *American Thoroughbred.* 1905. Los Angeles. 1st ed. ES. VG. O3. $195.00

MERTON, Thomas. *Clement of Alexandria: Selections From the Protreptikos.* 1962. New Directions. 1st ed. F/NF. V1. $20.00

MERTON, Thomas. *No Man Is an Island.* 1955. Harcourt Brace. ARC. RS. F/dj. B4. $150.00

MERTON, Thomas. *Seed of Destruction.* 1964. Farrar. 1st ed. F/F. B2. $35.00

MERTON, Thomas. *Seeds of Contemplation.* 1949. New Directions. 1st ed. F/dj. B24. $300.00

MERTON, Thomas. *Seven Story Mountain.* 1948. Harcourt Brace. 1st ed. 1st issue wht cloth. NF/VG. M19. $450.00

MERTON, Thomas. *Thirty Poems.* 1944. New Directions. 1st ed. author's 1st book. NF/wrp. C6. $95.00

MERTON, Thomas. *Tower of Babel.* 1957. James Laughlin. 1st separate ed. folio. 31p. F/NF case. B24. $1,250.00

MERTON, Thomas. *Waters of Siloe.* 1949. Harcourt Brace. 1st ed. photos. NF/VG. M19. $35.00

MERTZ, Barbara Gross. *Ammie, Come Home.* 1968. Meredith. 1st ed. VG/VG. P3. $40.00

MERTZ, Barbara Gross. *Deeds of the Disturber.* nd. BC. VG/VG. P3. $10.00

MERTZ, Barbara Gross. *Die for Love.* 1984. Congdon Weed. 1st ed. VG/VG. P3. $30.00

MERTZ, Barbara Gross. *Into the Darkness.* 1990. Simon Schuster. 1st ed. F/F. P3. $20.00

MERTZ, Barbara Gross. *Jackal's Head.* 1968. Meredith. 1st ed. VG/VG. P3. $40.00

MERTZ, Barbara Gross. *Last Camel Died at Noon.* 1991. Warner. 1st ed. xl. dj. P3. $8.00

MERTZ, Barbara Gross. *Legend in Green Velvet.* 1976. Dodd Mead. 1st ed. NF/NF. P3. $50.00

MERTZ, Barbara Gross. *Lion in the Valley.* 1986. Atheneum. 1st ed. hc. F/F. P3. $20.00

MERTZ, Barbara Gross. *Master of Blacktower.* 1966. Appleton Century. 1st ed. VG/VG. P3. $40.00

MERTZ, Barbara Gross. *Naked Once More.* 1989. Warner. 1st ed. F/F. P3. $18.00

MERTZ, Barbara Gross. *Sea King's Daughter.* 1975. Dodd Mead. 1st ed. VG/VG. P3. $25.00

MERTZ, Barbara Gross. *Shattered Silk.* 1986. Atheneum. 1st ed. F/F. P3. $16.00

MERTZ, Barbara Gross. *Smoke & Mirrors.* 1989. Simon Schuster. 1st ed. F/F. P3. $18.00

MERTZ, Barbara Gross. *Snake, the Crocodile & the Dog.* 1992. Warner. 1st ed. F/F. P3. $20.00

MERWIN, Mrs. George. *Three Years in Chile.* 1966. Carbondale, IL. 1st ed thus. 102p. dj. F3. $15.00

MERWIN, Sam. *Matter of Policy.* 1946. Mystery House. 1st ed. VG/VG. P3. $25.00

MERWIN, W.S. *Finding the Islands.* 1982. North Point. 1st ed. sgn/dtd. F/stiff wrp. V1. $25.00

MERWIN, W.S. *Unframed Originals; Recollections by...* 1982. Atheneum. 1st ed. sgn. F/F. V1. $35.00

MESSICK, Dale. *Brenda Starr, Girl Reporter.* 1943. Whitman. VG/VG. P3. $15.00

METALIOUS, Grace. *Return to Peyton Place.* 1960. London. Frederick Muller. 1st ed. F/NF. B4. $50.00

METCALF, A.R. *Auction Bridge.* 1911. Chicago. 2nd. 91p. VG. S1. $15.00

METCALF, A.R. *Bridge That Wins With Thirty Illustrative Deals.* 1905. Chicago. 131p. VG. S1. $15.00

METCALF, A.R. *Real Auction Bridge.* 1916. Chicago. 3rd. 53p. VG. S1. $10.00

METCALFE, Whitaker. *Two Weeks Before Murder.* 1959. Arcadia. 1st ed. hc. VG/VG. P3. $15.00

METHENY, D. *Harcy Heather Species & Some Related Plants.* 1991. Seaside, OR. ils. 186p. sc. AN. B26. $16.00

METRAS, Gary. *Night Watches.* 1981. Adastra. 1st ed. inscr. F/wrp. V1. $15.00

METZ, Jerred. *Halley's Comet, 1910: Fire in the Sky.* 1985. St Louis. Singing Bone. 8vo. 124p. VG/dj. K5. $12.00

METZ, Leon C. *Pat Garrett: Story of a Western Lawman.* 1977. Norman, OK. 3rd. 8vo. 328p. VG/2nd prt dj. T10. $35.00

METZDORF. *Tinker Library, Bibliographical Catalogue.* 1959. 1st ed. 1/500. NF. A4. $385.00

MEYER, Arthur. *Analysis of de Generatione Animalium of William Harvey.* 1936. Stanford. 1st ed. 167p. VG/dj. A13. $50.00

MEYER, Franklyn. *Me & Caleb.* 1962. Follett. 1st ed. sgn. ils Laurence Smith. 160p. VG/G. P2. $35.00

MEYER, Larry L. *Shadow of a Continent.* 1975. Palo Alto. Am West Pub. 1st ed. ils. F/NF. T10. $35.00

MEYER, Nicholas. *Canary Trainer.* 1993. Norton. 1st ed. AN/dj. N4. $25.00

MEYER, Nicholas. *Seven-Per-Cent Solution.* 1974. Dutton. 1st ed. VG/VG. P3. $35.00

MEYER, Nicholas. *West End Horror.* 1976. Dutton. 1st ed. VG/VG. P3. $25.00

MEYER, Susan. *Treasury of Great Children's Book Illustrators.* 1983. NY. Abrams. 1st ed. ils. 272p. VG/VG. B14. $32.50

MEYERS, Annette. *Big Killing.* 1989. Bantam. 1st ed. author's 1st book. F/F. H11. $30.00

MEYERS, Annette. *Blood on the Street.* 1992. Doubleday. 1st ed. F/F. H11. $25.00

MEYERS, Barlow. *Adventure at Two Rivers.* 1961. Whitman. 1st ed. TVTI. F. P3. $15.00

MEYERS, Barlow. *Have Gun, Will Travel.* 1959. Whitman. TVTI. G. P3. $6.00

MEYERS, Barlow. *Janet Lemon at Camp Calamity.* 1962. Whitman. TVTI. VG. P3. $9.00

MEYERS, Barlow. *Restless Gun.* 1959. Whitman. TVTI. VG. P3. $15.00

MEYERS, Manny. *Last Mystery of Edgar Allan Poe.* 1978. Lippincott. 1st ed. VG/VG. P3. $18.00

MEYNELL, Laurence. *Affair at Barwold.* 1985. Macmillan. 1st ed. NF/NF. P3. $20.00

MEYNELL, Laurence. *Bluefeather.* 1972. Tom Stacey. VG/VG. P3. $15.00

MEYNELL, Laurence. *Death by Arrangement.* 1972. McKay Washburn. VG/VG. P3. $15.00

MEYNELL, Laurence. *Don't Stop for Hooky Hefferman.* 1977. Stein Day. 1st ed. VG/VG. P3. $18.00

MEYNELL, Laurence. *Hooky & the Prancing Horse.* 1980. Macmillan. 1st ed. F/F. P3. $20.00

MEYNELL, Laurence. *Hooky Catches a Tartar.* 1986. Macmillan. 1st ed. F/F. P3. $22.00

MEZEY, Robert. *Lovemaker.* 1961. Cummington. 1st ed. 1/2000. sgn. F/NF. B35. $50.00

MIALE & SELZER. *Nuremberg Mind: Psychology of the Nazi Leaders.* 1975. NY Times. 302p. VG/tape rpr. A17. $15.00

MIAN, Mary. *Take Three Witches.* 1971. Houghton Mifflin. 1st ed. sgn. ils Eric Von Schmidt. F/F. B11. $40.00

MICHAEL, Barbara; see Mertz, Barbara Gross.

MICHAEL, Bryan; see Moore, Brian.

MICHAEL, Paul. *Academy Awards: A Pictorial History.* 1978. Crown. VG/VG. P3. $30.00

MICHAELS & ORDE. *Night They Stole Manhattan.* 1980. Putnam. 1st ed. F/F. P3. $15.00

MICHEL, Emile. *Rembrandt Etchings.* 1972. Leningrad. Aurora Art. 100 facsimile pl. w/36p pamphlet. loose in box. D2. $200.00

MICHEL, Emile. *Rembrandt: His Life, His Work, His Time.* 1903. Heinemann/Scribner. 3rd ed. 77 pl. full tan leather. D2. $120.00

MICHELS, Philip Verrill. *Crystal Sceptre.* 1906. Harper. VG. P3. $20.00

MICHENER, James A. *Alaska.* 1988. Random. 1st ed. NF/NF clip. H11. $20.00

MICHENER, James A. *Bridges at Toko-Ri.* 1953. Random. 1st ed. VG/VG. M19. $150.00

MICHENER, James A. *Caribbean.* 1989. Random. 1st ed. F/F. A20. $16.00

MICHENER, James A. *Centennial.* 1974. Random. 1st ed. F/NF. B2. $65.00

MICHENER, James A. *Chesapeake.* 1978. Random. ltd ed. 1/500. sgn. F/case. B4. $450.00

MICHENER, James A. *Chesapeake.* 1978. Random. 1st ed. F/F. H11. $40.00

MICHENER, James A. *Covenant.* 1980. Random. 1st ed. w/sgn leaf. F/F. B2. $175.00

MICHENER, James A. *Firstfruits.* 1973. Phil. Jewish Pub. 1st ed. F/NF. H11. $55.00

MICHENER, James A. *Iberia.* 1968. Random. 1st ed. B stp on bottom edges. F/F. H11. $60.00

MICHENER, James A. *Japanese Prints.* 1959. Rutland. 1st ed. VG/VG. B5. $105.00

MICHENER, James A. *Kent State.* 1971. Random. 1st ed. F/F. H11. $50.00

MICHENER, James A. *Legacy.* 1987. Random. 1st ed. F/F. N4. $25.00

MICHENER, James A. *Mexico.* 1992. Random. 1st ed. F/NF. H11. $20.00

MICHENER, James A. *Novel.* 1991. Random. 1st ed. F/F. A20. $14.00

MICHENER, James A. *Poland.* 1983. NY. 1/500. sgn. F/case. C6. $120.00

MICHENER, James A. *Presidential Lottery.* 1969. NY. 1st ed. F/F. B5. $55.00

MICHENER, James A. *Sayonara.* 1954. NY. 1st ed. VG/dj. B5/P3. $45.00

MICHENER, James A. *South Pacific.* 1992. HBJ. 1st ed. ils Michael Hague. F/F. B17. $13.50

MICHENER, James A. *Sports in America.* 1976. Random. 1st ed. NF/NF clip. H11. $30.00

MICHENER, James A. *Texas.* 1985. NY. 1st ed. 1/1000. sgn. F/case. C6. $100.00

MICHENER, James A. *Texas.* 1985. Random. 1st ed. F/F. A18. $30.00

MICLEA, Ion. *Sweet Bucovina.* 1977. Bucharest. Editura Sprt-Turism. 500+ pl/photos. ES. cloth. dj. D2. $80.00

MIDDLEBROOK, Deane Wood. *Anne Sexton: A Biography.* 1991. Houghton Mifflin. 1st ed. VG+/NF. V1. $10.00

MIDDLEBROOK, Louis F. *Maritime Connecticut During the American Revolution.* 1925. Essex Inst. 1/1250. teg. VG/dj. T7. $120.00

MIDDLETON, Christopher. *Nonsequences.* 1965. Norton. 1st ed. VG+/VG. V1. $20.00

MIDDLETON, George. *These Things Are Mine: Autobiography...* 1947. np. ils. 448p. VG. A4. $25.00

MIDDLETON, W.E. Knowles. *Catalog of Meteorological Instruments in Mus of Hist...* 1969. Smithsonian. 4to. ils/photos. 128p. G. K5. $75.00

MIDLAM, Charles E. *Sex Etc. Out on a Limerick.* 1977. Freedom. 1st ed. sgn. ffe removed. 8vo. 100p. VG/G. B11. $18.00

MIDLER, Bette. *Saga of Baby Divine.* 1983. Crown. 1st ed. sgn. ils Todd Schorr. F/F. B4. $75.00

MIEROW & SHRESTHA. *Himalayan Flowers & Trees.* 1978. Kathmandu, Nepal. ils. 210p. sc. G. B26. $25.00

MIERS, Earl Schenck. *American Civil War: A Popular Illustrated History...* 1961. NY. Golden. 4to. 324p. T10. $35.00

MIERS, Earl Schenck. *Composing Sticks & Mortar Boards.* 1941. Rutgers. 1st trade ed. 97p. VG. A17. $12.50

MIERS, Earl Schenck. *General Who Marched to Hell.* 1951. NY. 1st ed. VG/VG. B5. $25.00

MIHALAS, D. *Galactic Astronomy.* 1968. Freeman. 1st ed. 257p. VG. D8. $10.00

MILAN, Victor. *Cybernetic Shogun.* 1990. Morrow. 1st ed. F/F. P3. $20.00

MILAREPA. *Hundred Thousand Songs of Milarepa.* 1962. NY. University. 1st ed thus. 2 vol. F/NF case. C2. $60.00

MILBOURNE, Christopher. *Houdini: A Pictorial Life.* 1976. Crowell. 1st ed. ils. F/NF. G10. $25.00

MILECK. *Hermann Hesse: Biography & Bibliography.* 1977. CA U. 2 vol. 1434p. F. A4. $125.00

MILEN, A.A. *Red Birds.* 1987. Viking. 1st ed. NF/NF. P3. $15.00

MILES, Betty. *Cooking Book.* 1959. Knopf. 1st ed. ils Joe Lowrey. cloth. F/VG. M5. $35.00

MILES, John. *Blackmailer.* 1974. Bobbs Merrill. 1st ed. VG/VG. P3. $15.00

MILES, Keith; see Tralins, Bob.

MILES, William. *Horse's Foot & How To Keep It Sound.* 1866. NY. Orange Judd. xl. VG. O3. $35.00

MILET, Jacques. *Toy Boats.* 1979. Cambridge. Patrick Stephens. 1st ed. VG/VG. A16. $65.00

MILL, John Stuart. *On Liberty: Subjection of Women.* 1895. NY. Holt. 2 works in 1 vol. 394p. brn cloth. F. B14. $60.00

MILL, John Stuart. *Subjection of Women.* 1869. Appleton. gilt brn cloth. M11. $450.00

MILLAN, Verna. *Mexico Reborn.* 1939. Houghton Mifflin. 1st ed. 312p. dj. F3. $20.00

MILLAR, George. *Oyster River: One Summer on an Island Sea.* 1964. Knopf. 268p. VG. T7. $18.00

MILLAR, Kenneth. *Archer in Jeopardy.* nd. BC. VG/VG. P3. $10.00

MILLAR, Kenneth. *Blue Hammer.* 1976. Knopf. 1st ed. VG/VG. N4/P3. $35.00

MILLAR, Kenneth. *Goodbye Look.* 1969. Knopf. 5th. VG/VG. P3. $18.00

MILLAR, Kenneth. *Great Stories of Suspense.* nd. BOMC. VG/G. P3. $10.00

MILLAR, Kenneth. *Moving Target.* 1986. Allison Busby. 1st ed. F/F. P3. $23.00

MILLAR, Kenneth. *Sleeping Beauty.* 1973. Knopf. 1st ed. NF/F. H11. $45.00

MILLAR, Kenneth. *Sleeping Beauty.* 1973. Knopf. 1st ed. VG/VG. P3. $35.00

MILLAR, Kenneth. *Three Roads.* 1948. NY. 1st ed. F/NF. C2. $450.00

MILLAR, Margaret. *Banshee.* 1983. Morrow. 1st ed. F/F. M22. $20.00

MILLAR, Margaret. *Iron Gates.* 1945. Random. 1st ed. VG. M22. $12.00

MILLAR. *Tudor, Stuart & Early Georgian Pictures...* 1963. 2 vol. F/F/case. D2. $100.00

MILLARD, Oscar. *Missing Person.* 1972. McKay Washburn. 1st ed. VG/VG. P3. $15.00

MILLAY, Edna St. Vincent. *Conversation at Midnight.* 1937. Harper. 1st ed. NF/NF. B35. $28.00

MILLAY, Edna St. Vincent. *Harp-Weaver & Other Poems.* 1923. Harper. 1st ed. NF/chip. B2. $60.00

MILLAY, Edna St. Vincent. *Huntsman, What Quarry?* 1929. Harper. 1st ed. F/F. B4. $100.00

MILLAY, Edna St. Vincent. *King's Henchman.* 1927. Harper. 1st ed. 1/26 lettered sgn. NF. B4. $350.00

MILLAY, Edna St. Vincent. *Make Bright the Arrows.* 1940. Harper. 1st ed. NF/rpr. V1. $20.00

MILLAY, Edna St. Vincent. *Poems Selected for Young People.* 1951. Harper Row. later rpt. VG/VG. D17. $7.50

MILLAY, Edna St. Vincent. *Renascence & Other Poems.* 1917. NY. 1st ed/2nd issue. VG+. C6. $100.00

MILLAY, Edna St. Vincent. *Wine From These Grapes.* 1934. London/NY. Harper. 1st ed. limb bl morocco. F/marbled case. B24. $100.00

MILLEN, Nina. *Children's Games From Many Lands.* 1943. NY. 2nd. sm 8vo. VG/dj. M5. $18.00

MILLEN & WORTHINGTON. *Photographic Primer: A Manual of Practice.* 1896. Riverton, NJ. private prt. 164p. brn cloth. VG. B14. $100.00

MILLER, Arthur. *Price.* 1968. Viking. 1st ed. F/NF. H11. $40.00

MILLER, Arthur. *Timebends.* 1987. Grove. 1st ed. sgn. F/F. B2. $75.00

MILLER, Arthur. *View From the Ridge.* 1955. Viking. 1st ed. 160p. VG/dj. M20. $32.00

MILLER, Bertha. *Illustrators of Children's Books 1946-1956.* 1958. ils. xl. VG/VG. S13. $20.00

MILLER, Bill. *Ocean Liners.* 1990. Mallard. VG/VG. A16. $40.00

MILLER, Byron. *Sail, Steam & Splendour.* 1977. Time. VG/VG. A16. $75.00

MILLER, Charlotte. *Fifty Drawings by Canaletto From Royal Lib of Windsor...* 1983. HBJ. Johnson rpt. 1/520. 50 facsimile pl. 44p. gilt clamshell case. A17. $350.00

MILLER, Dick. *Triumphant Journey: Saga of Bobby Jones.* 1980. NY. 1st ed. VG/VG. B5. $25.00

MILLER, E.B. *Bataan Uncensored.* 1949. Brainerd, NM. 1st ed. ils. 403p. VG/G. B5. $50.00

MILLER, E.D. *Modern Polo Second Edition Revised & Enlarged.* 1902. London. Hurst Blackett. O3. $65.00

MILLER, Emily Huntington. *Captain Fritz: His Friends & Adventures.* 1878. Dutton. 12mo. ils. gilt/silvered bl cloth. G. B14. $45.00

MILLER, F.T. *General Douglas MacArthur, Fighter for Freedom.* 1942. Phil. U Book & Bible. 3rd. 280p. G. A17. $7.50

MILLER, F.T. *History of WWII.* 1945. Phil. photos/maps. 967p. VG. A17. $17.50

MILLER, F.T. *Photographic History of Civil War.* 1912. NY. 10 vol. 1st ed. VG. B5. $275.00

MILLER, F.T. *Photographic History of the Civil War. Part 7.* 1957. NY. 4to. 352p. G/dj. T3. $15.00

MILLER, Frank. *Complete Frank Miller Batman.* 1987. Longmeadow. 2nd. gilt leather. F. P3. $50.00

MILLER, Genevieve. *Bibliography of the Writings of Henry E Sigerist...* 1966. Montreal. 1st ed. 112p. dj. A13. $25.00

MILLER, George O. *Landscaping With Native Plants of Texas & the Southwest.* 1991. Stillwater, MN. ils. 128p. sc. AN. B26. $17.50

MILLER, Harriet Parks. *Pioneer Colored Christians.* 1911. Clarksville, TN. WP Titus. 1st ed. photos. 8vo. 103p. VG. C6. $175.00

MILLER, Heather Ross. *Wind Southerly.* 1967. Harcourt Brace. 1st ed. assn copy. F/VG+. V1. $10.00

MILLER, Helen Topping. *After the Glory.* 1958. BC. 222p. VG/VG. B10. $10.00

MILLER, Henry. *Book of Friends: A Tribute to Friends of Long Ago.* 1976. Capra. 1st prt. F/F. H4. $30.00

MILLER, Henry. *Books in My Life.* 1952. New Directions. 1st ed. VG/VG. M19. $125.00

MILLER, Henry. *Colossus of Maroussi.* 1941. Colt. 1st ed. G. M19. $125.00

MILLER, Henry. *Cosmological Eye.* 1939. Norfolk. 1st ed. VG/G. B5. $95.00

MILLER, Henry. *Cosmological Eye.* 1945. London. 1st ed. G/G. V4. $60.00

MILLER, Henry. *Smile at the Foot of the Ladder.* 1948. DSP. 1st ed. NF/VG. M19. $125.00

MILLER, Henry. *Tropic of Capricorn.* 1961. Grove. 1st ed. F/VG. M10. $225.00

MILLER, Hugh. *Cruise of the Betsey; or, Summer Ramble...* 1858. Boston. Gould Lincoln. 524p. VG. M20. $40.00

MILLER, J.P. *Skook.* 1985. Hutchinson. NF/NF. P3. $20.00

MILLER, Jane. *August Zero.* 1993. Copper Canyon. UP. F/wrp. V1. $25.00

MILLER, Jimmy. *Big Win.* 1969. Knopf. 1st ed. VG/VG. P3. $20.00

MILLER, Joaquin. *Overland in a Covered Wagon: An Autobiography.* 1930. NY. ils. 130p. new calf. A17. $25.00

MILLER, Joaquin. *True Bear Stories.* 1900. Rand McNally. 3rd. 8vo. 259p. gr cloth. G. T10. $45.00

MILLER, Joaquin. *Unwritten History: Life Among the Modocs.* 1874. Hartford. Am Pub. 1st ed. ils. 445p. gilt half leather. VG. A17. $200.00

MILLER, John A. *Jackson Street & Other Soldier Stories.* 1995. Berkeley. 1st ed. sgn. F/F. M23. $40.00

MILLER, Kenn. *Tiger the Lurp Dog.* 1983. Little Brn. 1st ed. NF/NF. B4. $65.00

MILLER, Madeleine Hemingway. *Ernie.* 1975. 1st ed. 4to. NF/NF. S13. $25.00

MILLER, Marc. *Death Is a Liar.* 1959. Arcadia. 1st ed. VG/VG. P3. $15.00

MILLER, Max. *Cruise of the Cow: Being an Introduction to San Diego...* 1951. Dutton. 1st ed. 8vo. map/photos. 256p. bl cloth. VG/worn. P4. $25.00

MILLER, Maxine Adams. *Bright Blue Beads: American Family in Persia.* 1962. Caxton. 2nd. 8vo. ils RA Hayraptian. VG/dj. W1. $12.00

MILLER, Merle. *What Happened.* 1972. Harper Row. 1st ed. F/NF. H11. $30.00

MILLER, Olive Beaupre. *Little Pictures of Japan.* 1925. Chicago. ils Katherine Sturges. VG+. M5. $45.00

MILLER, Olive Beaupre. *My Bookhouse.* 1920-1925. Chicago. 6 vol. gilt blk bdg. VG. M20. $200.00

MILLER, Olive Beaupre. *My Bookhouse.* 1937. Bookhouse. 12 vol. dk bl bdg. VG. P2. $145.00

MILLER, Olive Beaupre. *My Travelship Prospectus.* 1925-27. Bookhouse for Children. ils Petersham. cloth. M20. $82.00

MILLER, Olive Beaupre. *Nursery Friends From France.* 1927. Chicago. Bookhouse. ils Petersham. 191p. G. A17. $15.00

MILLER, Olive Beaupre. *Tales Told in Holland.* 1952. Bookhouse for Children. 29th. ils Petersham. 192p. VG+. C14. $18.00

MILLER, Olive Beaupre. *Up One Pair of Stairs.* 1928. My Bookhouse. gilt red cloth/pl. VG. M5. $10.00

MILLER, Paul Eduard. *Esquire's 1945 Jazz Book.* 1945. Barnes. 1st ed. NF/NF. B2. $65.00

MILLER, Rand. *Myst: The Book of Atrus.* 1995. Hyperion. F. P3. $23.00

MILLER, Raymond C. *Kilowatts at Work, a History of Detroit Edison Co.* 1957. Detroit. Wayne State. 1st ed. ils. 467p. VG/dj. B18. $35.00

MILLER, Richard A. *Bridge Brilliance & Blunders.* 1974. NJ. 219p. VG/wrp. S1. $4.00

MILLER, Richard Roscoe. *Slavery & Catholicism.* 1957. Durham, NC. 1st ed. pres. 259p. cloth. VG. M8. $45.00

MILLER, Richard. *Snail.* 1984. HRW. 1st ed. F/NF. M23. $20.00

MILLER, Samuel. *Dilemma of Modern Belief.* 1963. NY. Harper. 1st ed. sgn. 113p. F/VG. B11. $12.50

MILLER, Sarah. *Rhodes.* 1969. London. Kraus Rpt. rpt of 1952 Chatto Windus ed. AN/sans. P4. $25.00

MILLER, Snowden. *Roy Rogers & the Riders of the Sawfoot.* 1955. Adprint. VG. P3. $15.00

MILLER, Stewart. *Florida Fishing.* 1931. NY. Watt. 1st ed. inscr. ils/pl. 320p. G/G. B11. $125.00

MILLER, Sue. *Distinguished Guest.* 1995. Harper Collins. ARC. F/wrp. B4. $35.00

MILLER, Sue. *For Love.* 1993. Harper Collins. 1st ed. author's 4th book. AN/dj. B4. $35.00

MILLER, Sue. *Good Mother.* 1986. Harper Row. 1st ed. sgn. NF/NF. M22. $40.00

MILLER, Wade. *Deadly Weapon.* 1946. Farrar Straus. 1st ed. VG. P3. $18.00

MILLER, Walter M. *Canticle for Leibowitz.* 1960. Lippincott. 2nd. VG/VG. P3. $30.00

MILLER, Warren Hastings. *Boy Explorers & the Ape-Man of Sumatra.* 1923. Harper. 1st ed. G. P3. $10.00

MILLER, William D. *Mr Crump of Memphis.* 1964. LSU. VG/G. B30. $40.00

MILLER, William H. *German Ocean Liners of the 20th Century.* 1989. Eng. Patrick Stephens. 1st ed. sgn. 4to. 208p. F/F. B11. $50.00

MILLER, William H. *Last Blue Water Liners.* 1986. St Martin. 1st Am ed. VG/dj. A16. $15.00

MILLER, William H. *Transatlantic Liners at War: Story of the Queens.* 1985. Arco. VG/VG. A16. $25.00

MILLER. *Slavery & Slaving in World History.* 1993. 4to. 573p. F. A4. $125.00

MILLIS, Walter. *Forrestal Diaries.* 1951. Viking. 1st ed. 581p. bl/red cloth. F/dj. B22. $6.00

MILLIS, Walter. *Martial Spirit.* 1931. Literary Guild of Am. 8vo. ils. map ep. NF. T10. $25.00

MILLIS, Walter. *Road to War: American 1914-1917.* 1935. Houghton Mifflin. 1st ed. 466p. cranberry cloth. F. B22. $6.00

MILLMAN, Leonard. *Kayak Full of Ghosts: Eskimo Tales.* 1987. Santa Barbara. Capra. 208p. stiff wrp. A17. $8.50

MILLS, Arthur. *Intrigue Island.* 1930. Dollins. 1st ed. hc. VG/torn. P3. $50.00

MILLS, Clarence A. *Living With the Weather.* 1934. Cincinnati. Caxton. 8vo. 206p. gilt cloth. G. K5. $15.00

MILLS, Enos. *Watched by Animals.* 1922. Doubleday Page. 1st ed. 8vo. 243p. gilt gr cloth. VG. T10. $60.00

MILLS, Enos. *Wild Life on the Rockies.* 1988. Lincoln, NE. 1st NE U ed. 271p. F/sans. T10. $15.00

MILLS, Frank C. *History of American Jacks & Mules.* 1971. Hutchinson. sgn. 255p. VG. O3. $65.00

MILLS, Hobie. *Song Comes Native.* 1981. Countryman. 1st ed. 189p. F/VG. B10. $12.00

MILLS, James. *Report to the Commissioner.* 1972. FSG. 1st ed. VG/tape rpr. P3. $14.00

MILLS, Ralph J. *March Light.* 1983. Sparrow. ltd ed. 1/500. F/wrp. V1. $10.00

MILLS, Robert P. *Best of Fantasy & SF. 10th Series.* 1961. Doubleday. 2nd. VG/VG. P3. $18.00

MILLS, W. *Phantom Scarlet.* 1940. Hodder Stoughton. 1st ed. VG/fair. P3. $25.00

MILLS & NELSON. *Talking Dolls.* 1930. Greenberg. 1st ed. ils Tony Sarg. G+. P2. $45.00

MILLSTEIN, Gilbert. *God & Harvey Grosbeck.* 1983. Doubleday. 1st ed. NF/NF. B35. $30.00

MILNE, A.A. *Birthday Party.* 1948. Dutton. 1st ed. NF/VG. C8. $50.00

MILNE, A.A. *By Way of Introduction.* 1929. Dutton. 1st/lg paper ed. 1/166. sgn. F. T10. $250.00

MILNE, A.A. *Christopher Robin Verses.* 1932. Dutton. 1st Am ed. ils EH Shepard. bl cloth. VG+. T10. $100.00

MILNE, A.A. *Fourteen Songs From Where We Were Very Young.* 1934 (1924). London. Methuen. 14th. music H Fraser-Simson. VG/G+. C8. $85.00

MILNE, A.A. *House at Pooh Corner.* 1928. London. 1st ed. ils Shepard. 180p. teg. gilt salmon cloth. F. B14. $350.00

MILNE, A.A. *House at Pooh Corner.* 1928. Methuen. 1st ed. ils EH Shepard. teg. gilt pink cloth. VG/torn. D1. $425.00

MILNE, A.A. *Ivory Door: A Play.* 1928. NY. 1st ed. VG/G. B5. $40.00

MILNE, A.A. *Now We Are Six. With Decorations by EH Shepard.* 1927. London. Methuen. 1st ed. sgn/dtd Shepard. Bayntun Riviere bdg. F. B24. $1,350.00

MILNE, A.A. *Once Upon a Time.* 1922. Putnam. 1st ed/2nd imp. ils Charles Robinson. 358p. VG. D1. $85.00

MILNE, A.A. *When I Was Very Young.* 1930. Fountain. 1st ed. 1/842. sgn. F/case. T10. $750.00

MILNE, A.A. *Winnie-the-Pooh.* 1926. Dutton. 1st Am ed. ils EH Shepherd. F/worn. C2. $150.00

MILNE, A.A. *Winnie-The-Pooh.* 1926. London. Methuen. 1st ed. ils Shepard. teg. gilt gr cloth. F/dj. w/photo. B14. $1,600.00

MILNE, David. *Essay on Comets.* 1828. Edinburgh. Blk. 4to. 189p. half leather. xl. G. K5. $300.00

MILNE, J. *Earthquakes & Other Earth Movements.* 1939. Kegan Paul. 7th. 244p. F. D8. $20.00

MILNE, John. *Dead Birds.* 1987. Viking. 1st Am ed. F/F. N4. $20.00

MILNER, George. *Leave-Taking.* 1966. Dodd Mead. 1st ed. VG/VG. P3. $13.00

MILTON, George Fort. *Age of Hate: Andrew Johnson & the Radicals.* 1930. Coward McCann. 1st ed. 787p. VG. B10. $30.00

MILTON, J.R. *Notes to a Bald Buffalo.* 1976. Spirit Mound. 1st ed. F/F. A18. $15.00

MILTON, John. *Paradise Lost: A Poem by John Milton.* 1937. Golden Cockerel. 1/200. 379p. Zaehnsdorf half morocco/Cockerell cloth. F. B24. $1,200.00

MIMS & PAYNE. *Southern Prose & Poetry for Schools.* 1910. Scribner. 440p. VG. B10. $12.00

MIN, Anchee. *Katherine.* 1995. NY. Riverhead. 1st ed. author's 2nd book. F/F. H11. $30.00

MINAHAN, John. *Face Behind the Mask.* 1986. Norton. 1st ed. F/F. P3. $15.00

MINARIK, Else Holmelund. *Father Bear Comes Home.* 1959. Harper. 1st ed? 8vo. VG+. M5. $60.00

MINARIK, Else Holmelund. *Little Bear.* (1957). Harper Row. later rpt. ils Sendak. VG. B17. $5.00

MINARIK, Else Holmelund. *Little Bear.* 1957. Harper. probable 1st ed. 8vo. VG. M5. $125.00

MINARIK, Else Holmelund. *No Fighting, No Biting!* 1958. ils/sgn Sendak. VG/G. w/sgn Sendak card. S13. $85.00

MINER, Valerie. *All Good Women.* 1987. Freedom, CA. 1st ed. F/NF. B4. $45.00

MINES, Samuel. *Best From Startling Stories.* 1953. Holt. 1st ed. VG. P3. $25.00

MINES, Samuel. *Startling Stories.* 1954. Cassell. 1st ed. xl. dj. P3. $12.00

MINK, Arthur D. *History of Alliance Newspapers.* 1946. np. 1st ed. 30p. VG. B18. $37.50

MINKS, Benton. *100 Greatest Hitters.* 1988. Boston. 1st ed. F/VG+. P8. $12.50

MINNIGERODE, Meade. *Some Mariners of France.* 1930. Putnam. 1st ed. 320p. gilt bl bdg. VG. P12. $8.50

MINOR, Kate Pleasants. *From Dixie.* 1893. West Johnson. 167p. leather spine. G. B10. $75.00

MINOT, Susan. *Lust & Other Stories.* 1989. Houghton Mifflin. 1st ed. F/F. H11. $25.00

MINTER, John Easter. *Chagres.* 1948. Rinehart. 1st ed. sgn. Rivers of America series. VG/VG. B11. $65.00

MINTY, Leonard. *Legal & Ethical Aspects of Medical Quackery.* 1932. London. 1st ed. 262p. VG. A13. $50.00

MINTZ, James William. *Jesse.* 1984. Overmountain. 1st ed. sgn. F/F. B4. $100.00

MINTZ, L.W. *Historical Geology: Science of a Dynamic Earth.* 1972. Merrill. 2nd. ils. xl. VG. D8. $15.00

MINTZ. *Trail: A Bibliography of Travelers on Overland Trail to CA.* 1987. ils. 226p. F/F. A4. $95.00

MIRBEAU, Ken; see Weiss, Joe.

MIRO, Joan. *Bouquet de Reves Pour Neila, by Yvan Goll.* 1967. Paris. Mourlot. 1/150. sgn. 18 prt. unbound as issued. F/wrp/chemise/case. B24. $3,650.00

MIROV, N.T. *Composition of Gum Turpentines of Pines.* 1961. WA, DC. pres. 158p. VG. B26. $32.50

MIRSKY, Reba Paeff. *Beethoven.* 1957. ils WT Mars. VG/dj. B30. $10.00

MISRACH, Richard. *Telegraph 3 AM.* 1974. Cornucopia. 1st ed. 1/3000. author's 1st book. F/F clip. S9. $125.00

MISS MULOCK; see Mulock, Dinah.

MITCHAM, Gilroy. *Man From Bar Harbour.* 1958. Dobson. 1st ed. NF/NF. P3. $30.00

MITCHAM, Judson. *Somewhere in Ecclesiastes.* 1991. Columbia. MO U. 1st ed. sgn. pb. F/wrp. M23. $25.00

MITCHARD, Jacquelyn. *Deep End of the Ocean.* 1996. Viking. 1st ed. author's 1st book. F/F. M23. $50.00

MITCHELL, Don. *Souls of Lambs.* 1979. Houghton Mifflin. ils Georganne Schroeder. F/VG. B17. $6.50

MITCHELL, Donald. *Wet Days at Edgewood.* 1865. Scribner. 324p. rebacked. A10. $45.00

MITCHELL, Edith. *Betty, Bobbie & Bubbles.* 1921. Volland. 18th. ils. G+. M5. $48.00

MITCHELL, Gladys. *Crozier Pharoahs.* 1984. Michael Joseph. 1st ed. VG/VG. P3. $16.00

MITCHELL, Gladys. *Spotted Hemlock.* 1985. St Martin. 1st ed. NF/NF. P3. $15.00

MITCHELL, Gladys. *Twenty-Third Man.* 1985. Michael Joseph. 1st ed. NF/NF. P3. $20.00

MITCHELL, Gladys. *Uncoffin'd Clay.* 1982. St Martin. 1st ed. NF/NF. P3. $15.00

MITCHELL, Gladys. *When Last I Died.* 1985. Hogarth. VG/VG. P3. $15.00

MITCHELL, Gladys. *Winking at the Brin.* 1977. McKay Washburn. hc. F/F. P3. $15.00

MITCHELL, J. Leslie. *Earth Conquerors.* 1934. Simon Schuster. 1st ed. 8vo. ils/maps. 370p. VG. W1. $12.00

MITCHELL, J.A. *Amos Judd.* 1901. Scribner. ils AJ Keller. 251p. rust cloth. VG+. B22. $6.50

MITCHELL, James Coffield. *Tennessee Justice's Manual & Civil Officer's Guide.* 1934. Nashville. Mitchell Norvell. contemporary sheep. M11. $250.00

MITCHELL, James. *Dead Ernest.* 1987. Holt. 1st ed. F/F. P3. $16.00

MITCHELL, James. *Death & Bright Water.* 1974. Morrow. 1st ed. VG/VG. P3. $25.00

MITCHELL, James. *Red File for Callan.* 1969. Simon Schuster. 1st ed. xl. dj. P3. $6.00

MITCHELL, James. *Woman To Be Loved.* 1990. Sinclair Stevenson. 1st ed. F/F. P3. $25.00

MITCHELL, Jerry. *Sandy Koufax.* 1966. Grosset Dunlap. 1st ed. VG. P8. $20.00

MITCHELL, Joseph. *Decisive Battles of the Civil War.* 1955. Putnam. sgn. 8vo. maps. VG/G. B11. $20.00

MITCHELL, Joseph. *Joe Gould's Secret.* 1965. Viking. 1st ed. F/F. B4. $100.00

MITCHELL, Joseph. *Old Mr Flood.* 1948. NY. stated 1st ed. 111p. F/F. E1. $30.00

MITCHELL, Joseph. *Old Mr Flood.* 1948. NY. 1st ed. sgn. VG/VG. A9. $50.00

MITCHELL, Lucy Sprague. *North America.* 1931. Macmillan. 1st ed. 8vo. 383p. G. C14. $8.00

MITCHELL, Lucy Sprague. *Red, White & Blue Auto.* 1943. Scott. probable 1st ed. 8vo. ils Tibor Gergely. VG. M5. $60.00

MITCHELL, Margaret. *Margaret Mitchell's Gone With the Wind Letters, 1936-49.* 1976. Macmillan. 1st prt. photos. 441p. VG/VG. B10. $40.00

MITCHELL, Minnie Belle. *Hoosier Boy: James Whitcomb Riley.* 1942. 1/500. sgn. Childhood of Famous Am series. VG/VG. B30. $17.50

MITCHELL, Richard M. *Steam Launch.* 1982. Internat Marine Pub. VG/dj. A16. $25.00

MITCHELL, Richard S. *Checklist of NY State Plants.* 1986. NY. ils. 272p. F/F. B26. $17.50

MITCHELL, Ruth. *My Brother Bill: Biography of General Mitchell.* 1953. NY. 1st ed. F/dj. B18. $22.50

MITCHELL, S. Weir. *Pearl.* 1906. Century. 1st ed. gr cloth. VG+. V1. $20.00

MITCHELL, S.A. *Parallaxes of 260 Stars.* nd. Charlottesville. NC U. 4to. photos. 695p. xl. wrp. K5. $30.00

MITCHELL, Samuel. *Solitaire Bridge.* 1928. NY. 3rd. 144p. VG. S1. $8.00

MITCHELL, W.O. *Since Daisy Creek.* 1984. Beaufort. 1st ed. F/F. A18. $10.00

MITCHELL. *Bibliography of 17th-Century German Imprints in Denmark...* 1969. U of KS Libraries. 2 vol. ils. 783p. VG. A4. $195.00

MITFORD, Jessica. *American Way of Birth.* 1992. London. 1st ed. 237p. dj. A13. $35.00

MITFORD, Nancy. *Blessing.* 1951. Canada. Random. 1st ed. VG. P3. $8.00

MITFORD, T.B. *Inscriptions of Kourion.* 1971. Am Philosophical Soc. 1st ed. 422p. VG/dj. W1. $45.00

MITSCHERLICH, Alexander. *Doctors of Infamy: Story of Nazi Medical Crimes.* 1949. NY. photos/index. 172p. cloth. G. A17. $20.00

MITSCHERLICH, Alexander. *Doctors of Infamy: Story of Nazi Medical Crimes.* 1949. NY. 1st Eng trans. 172p. VG. A13. $60.00

MITTELHOLZER, Edgar. *Old Blood.* 1958. Doubleday. 1st ed. VG/VG. P3. $30.00

MITTON, Simon. *Daytime Star: Story of Our Sun.* 1981. Scribner. 8vo. 191p. VG. K5. $12.00

MIX, Paul E. *Life & Legend of Tom Mix.* 1972. Barnes. VG/VG. P3. $23.00

MO, Timothy. *Redundancy of Courage.* 1991. Chatto Windus. 1st ed. VG/G. A20. $30.00

MOATS, Alice. *Thunder in Their Veins.* 1932. Century. 1st ed. 279p. dj. F3. $25.00

MOBERG, V. *Last Letter Home.* 1961. NY. 1st ed. VG/VG. B5. $35.00

MOCK, Elizabeth. *Architecture of Bridges.* 1949. NY. MOMA. 1st ed. 127p. VG. B5. $30.00

MOCTEZUMA, Eduardo. *Obras Maetras del Templo Mayor.* 1988. Mexico City. Banamex. 1st ed. 4to. 180p. gilt bdg. F/VG. T10. $50.00

MODARRESSI & TYLER. *Tumble Tower.* 1993. Orchard Books. 1st ed. sgns. AN/dj. B4. $75.00

MODEL, Lisette. *Lisette Model.* 1979. NY. Aperture. 1st ed. folio. rem mk. VG. S9. $100.00

MODELSKI, Andrew M. *Railroad Maps of North America: First Hundred Years.* 1984. WA. Lib Congress. 92 maps. AN/dj. O7. $125.00

MODESITT, L.E. *Death of Chaos.* 1995. Tor. 1st ed. F/F. P3. $25.00

MODESITT, L.E. *Green Progression.* 1992. Tor. 1st ed. NF/NF. P3. $20.00

MODOC. *Collector's Guide to Antiquarian Bookstores.* 1984. intro Rostenberg/Stern. 529p. F/F. A4. $25.00

MOERY, Robert. *Kevin.* 1970. NJ. Bradbury. 1st ed. unp. gold cloth. VG/torn. T5. $20.00

MOFFAT, Gwen. *Over the Sea to Death.* 1976. Scribner. 1st ed. VG/VG. P3. $15.00

MOFFAT, Stanley M. *Throw in the Guest Towel.* nd. np. sgn. VG. B11. $5.00

MOFFATT. *Norman Rockwell, a Definitive Catalogue.* 1986. 2 vol. 1188p. F/case. A4. $195.00

MOFFETT, Judith. *Time, Like an Ever-Rolling Stream.* 1992. St Martin. F/F. P3. $22.00

MOFFITT, Virginia May. *Pollyanna of Magic Valley.* nd. Grosset Dunlap. VG/VG. P3. $10.00

MOLEN, Sam. *Take 2 & Hit To Right.* 1959. Dorrance. 1st ed. VG/G+. P8. $15.00

MOLESWORTH, Mrs. *Cuckoo Clock & the Tapestry Room.* 1925. Macmillan. 1st ed thus. 8vo. ils. F/dj. M5. $35.00

MOLESWORTH, Mrs. *Cuckoo Clock.* (1916). Lippincott. 11th. 8vo. 283p. G. C14. $6.00

MOLESWORTH, Mrs. *Little Miss Peggy.* 1887. London. 1st ed. ils Walter Crane. red cloth. VG. M5. $48.00

MOLIERE. *Le Malade Imaginaire.* 1921. Paris. Rene Kieffer. 1st ed. 1/450. inscr Helen Hayes. rebound. NF. B4. $500.00

MOLIERE. *Tartuffe.* 1930. LEC. ltd ed. sgn. VG/G case. B11. $55.00

MOLLO, Victor. *Bridge Basics & Beyond.* 1976. NY. 155p. VG/wrp. S1. $4.00

MOLLO, Victor. *Bridge Immortals.* 1968. NY. VG/worn. S1. $10.00

MOLLO, Victor. *Bridge in the Fourth Dimension.* 1974. London. 160p. F/dj. S1. $12.00

MOLLO, Victor. *Bridge in the Menagerie.* 1967. NY. 1st Am ed. 152p. VG. S1. $8.00

MOLLO, Victor. *Bridge Psychology.* 1958. London. 127p. VG/dj. S1. $8.00

MOLLO, Victor. *How Good Is Your Bridge?* 1969. NY. 1st Am ed. 149p. VG. S1. $5.00

MOLLO & GARDENER. *Bridge for Beginners.* 1964. London. 2nd. 189p. VG/wrp. S1. $4.00

MOLLO & NIELSEN. *How Good Is Your Defense?* 1976. NY. 1st Am ed. 256p. VG. S1. $4.00

MOMADAY, N. Scott. *In the Presence of the Sun: Stories & Poems 1961-1991.* 1992. St Martin. 1st ed. F/NF. M23. $40.00

MOMSEN, Richard. *Routes Over Serra Do Mar.* 1964. Rio. ils. 173p. F3. $15.00

MONACHAN, John; see Burnett, W.R.

MONAGHAN, Frank. *French Travelers in the United States 1765-1932.* 1961. np. 1/750. 10 pl. 164p. VG. A4. $125.00

MONAGHAN, Jay. *Book of the American West.* 1963. Messner. 1st ed. 4to. 608p. NF/dj. T10. $95.00

MONAGHAN, Jay. *Book of the American West.* 1969. Simon Schuster. new prt. 608p. dj. A17. $27.50

MONAGHAN, Jay. *Lincoln Bibliography, 1839-1939.* 1945. Springfield. 2 vol. 8vo. bl cloth. G. T3. $30.00

MONAGHAN, Jay. *Overland Trail.* 1947. Indianapolis. Bobbs Merrill. 1st ed. 8vo. map ep. red cloth. NF/dj. T10. $50.00

MONAGHAN, Jay. *Swamp Fox of the Confederacy: Life & Military Service...* 1956. Tuscaloosa, AL. Confederate Pub. 1st ed. 1/450. 123p. stiff prt wrp. M8. $85.00

MONAGHAN. *Common Heritage: Noah Webster's Blue Black Speller.* 1983. np. 304p. F. A4. $35.00

MONCRIEFF, A.R. Hope. *Heart of Scotland.* 1909. London. Blk. 205p. teg. G+. B18. $25.00

MONCRIEFF, A.R. Hope. *Romance & Legend of Chivalry.* 1986. Crescent. 1st ed. F/F. P3. $20.00

MONOT, Stephen. *Chill of Dark.* 1964. Doubleday. 1st ed. F/NF. H11. $35.00

MONOT, Stephen. *Ghost Images.* 1979. Harper Row. 1st ed. F/NF. H11. $20.00

MONROE, Marilyn. *My Story.* 1974. Stein Day. 1st ed. VG/VG. P3. $25.00

MONSARRAT, Nicholas. *Master Mariner Book 2: Darken Ship.* 1980. Cassell. 1st ed. VG/VG. P3. $17.00

MONSARRAT, Nicholas. *Time Before This.* 1962. Cassell. 1st ed. VG/VG. P3. $25.00

MONSARRAT, Nicholas. *White Rajah.* 1961. Cassell. 1st ed. VG/VG. P3. $30.00

MONTAGU, Ewen. *Beyond Top Secret Ultra.* 1978. CMG. 1st ed. F/F. P3. $13.00

MONTAGUE, John. *Chosen Light.* 1967. London. 1st ed. inscr to fellow poet. F/NF. V1. $45.00

MONTALE, Eugenio. *Poet in Our Time.* 1972. Urizen. 1st Am ed. F/VG. V1. $15.00

MONTANUS, Arnoldus. *Die Unbekante Neue Welt, Oder Beschriebung des Welt-Teils...* 1673. Amsterdam. J Von Meurs. 16 maps/32 double-p views/ils. complete. T10. $7,500.00

MONTECINO, Marcel. *Big Time.* 1990. Morrow. 1st ed. F/F. H11. $30.00

MONTECINO, Marcel. *Big Time.* 1990. Morrow. 1st ed. NF/NF. P3. $20.00

MONTEILHET, Hubert. *Perfect Crime or Two.* 1971. Simon Schuster. 1st ed. VG/VG. P3. $16.00

MONTEILHET, Hubert. *Road to Hell.* 1965. Chapman Hall. 1st ed. VG/VG. P3. $25.00

MONTEIRO, Palmyra. *Catalogue of Latin American Flat Maps 1926-1964.* 1969. Austin. TX U. 2 vol. M/rpr. O7. $85.00

MONTEITH, James. *Barness's Elementary Geography.* 1896. Am Book Co. ils/map. 97p. cloth. G. D1. $35.00

MONTELEONE, Thomas F. *Borderlands 2.* 1991. Borderlands Pr. 1st ed. 1/750. sgn. F/F/case. G10. $60.00

MONTELIUS, Oscar. *Age of Bronze in Egypt.* 1891. WA. GPO. removed. 6 pl. VG. P4. $17.50

MONTGOMERY, Frances. *Billy Whisker's Vacation.* 1908. Barse. 1st ed. ils Hugo VonHofsten. VG. M5. $85.00

MONTGOMERY, Frances. *Billy Whiskers' Kids.* 1903. Saalfield. ils W Fry. 134p. VG. P2. $40.00

MONTGOMERY, Frances. *Billy Whiskers in France.* 1919. Saalfield. ils Florence Williams. VG. P2. $40.00

MONTGOMERY, Frances. *Wonderful Electric Elephant.* 1903. Saalfield. 1st ed. ils Collidge. 253p. VG. P2. $110.00

MONTGOMERY, L.M. *Emily Climbs.* 1925. Stokes. ils ML Kirk. NF/dj. C2. $125.00

MONTGOMERY, L.M. *Further Chronicles of Avelea.* 1956. Ryerson. 2nd. xl. dj. P3. $8.00

MONTGOMERY, L.M. *Jane of Lantern Hill.* 1936. McClelland Stewart. 1st ed. G. P3. $25.00

MONTGOMERY, L.M. *Rilla of Ingleside.* 1923 (1921). AL Burt. sm 8vo. NF/dj. M5. $25.00

MONTGOMERY, L.M. *Story Girl.* 1911. Boston. Page. 1st ed. VG/remnant dj. B5. $95.00

MONTGOMERY, Ruth. *Aliens Among Us.* 1985. Putnam. 1st ed. VG. p3. $13.00

MONTGOMERY, Ruth. *Gift of Prophecy.* 1965. Morrow. 8th. sgn Jeane Dixon. VG/VG. P3. $30.00

MONTGOMERY, Ruth. *Search for the Truth.* 1967. Morrow. 1st ed. VG/VG. P3. $13.00

MONTGOMERY, Rutherford. *Capture of the Golden Stallion.* nd. Grosset Dunlap. VG. O3. $10.00

MONTGOMERY, Rutherford. *Hill Ranch.* 1951. Doubleday. 1st ed. 12mo. ils Barbara Cooney. VG/VG. B17. $20.00

MONTGOMERY, Rutherford. *Midnight.* nd. Grosset Dunlap. VG. O3. $10.00

MONTGOMERY, Rutherford. *Tim's Mountain.* 1959. World. 1st ed. 12mo. 219p. F/NF. C14. $15.00

MONTI. *French Revolutionary Pamphlets at the University of Florida.* 1971. 2810 entries. 173p. NF. A4. $65.00

MONTROSS, David. *Traitor's Wife.* 1962. Crime Club. 1st ed. G+/G+. P3. $13.00

MONTUNO MORENTE, Vincente. *Nuestra Senora de la Capilla.* 1950. MAdrid. 1st ed. 424p. wrp. F3. $25.00

MOODIE, Roy. *Antiquity of Disease.* 1923. Chicago. 1st ed. 148p. VG. A13. $50.00

MOODY, Ralph. *Fields of Home.* 1953. Chicago. Peoples BC. 8vo. 335p. F/NF. T5. $22.00

MOODY, Ralph. *Fields of Home.* 1953. NY. 1st ed. VG. B5. $35.00

MOODY, Ralph. *Man of the Family.* 1951. NY. 1st ed. VG. B5. $40.00

MOODY, Ralph. *Stagecoach West.* 1967. Promontory. 8vo. ils/7 maps. 341p. NF/dj. T10. $35.00

MOODY, Susan. *Grand Slam.* 1995. Otto Penzler. 1st ed. F/F. M23. $20.00

MOOG, Vianna. *Bandeirantes & Pioneers.* 1964. Braziller. 1st ed. 316p. dj. F3. $20.00

MOON, Grace. *Magic Trail.* 1929. Doubleday. stated 1st ed. ils Carl Moon. VG. M5. $25.00

MOON, Grace. *Missing Katchina.* 1930. Doubleday Doran. 1st ed. 8vo. VG. M5. $25.00

MOON, Grace. *Nadita (Little Nothing).* 1927. Doubleday. stated 1st ed. ils Carl Moon. VG. M5. $25.00

MOON, Grace. *Wongo & the Wise Old Crow.* 1923. Reilly Lee. ils Carl Moon. 188p. VG/G+. P2. $50.00

MOONEY, C.P.J. *Mid-South & Its Builders.* 1920. Memphis. poor. B30. $150.00

MOORCOCK, Michael. *Before Armageddon.* 1975. Allen. 1st ed. F/F. P3. $20.00

MOORCOCK, Michael. *Breakfast in the Ruins.* 1971. Random. 1st ed. F/F. P3. $23.00

MOORCOCK, Michael. *Byzantium Endures.* 1981. Random. 1st ed. VG/VG. P3. $20.00

MOORCOCK, Michael. *Casablanca.* 1989. Gollancz. 1st ed. F/F. P3. $28.00

MOORCOCK, Michael. *Chinese Agent.* 1971. Macmillan. 1st ed. xl. dj. P3. $10.00

MOORCOCK, Michael. *City in the Autumn Stars.* 1987. Ace. 1st ed. F/F. P3. $17.00

MOORCOCK, Michael. *Elric of Melnibone.* 1977. Blue Star. 1/2000. F/sans/case. P3. $35.00

MOORCOCK, Michael. *Elric Saga: Part II.* nd. BC. VG/G+. P3. $8.00

MOORCOCK, Michael. *End of All Songs.* 1976. Harper. 1st ed. F/F. P3. $15.00

MOORCOCK, Michael. *Etrophy Tango.* 1981. NEL. 1st ed. F/F. P3. $30.00

MOORCOCK, Michael. *Fortress of the Pearl.* 1989. Ace. 1st Am ed. AN/dj. M21. $12.00

MOORCOCK, Michael. *Fortress of the Pearl.* 1989. London. Gollancz. 1st ed. F/F. P3. $25.00

MOORCOCK, Michael. *Hollow Lands.* 1974. Harper Row. 1st ed. F/F. P3. $15.00

MOORCOCK, Michael. *Land Leviathan.* 1974. Doubleday. 1st ed. F/F. P3. $15.00

MOORCOCK, Michael. *Letters From Hollywood.* 1986. Harrap. 1st ed. F/F. P3. $25.00

MOORCOCK, Michael. *Mother London.* nd. BC. F/F. P3. $13.00

MOORCOCK, Michael. *Mother London.* 1989. Harmony. 1st Am ed. NF/dj. M21. $15.00

MOORCOCK, Michael. *Wizardry & Wild Romance.* 1987. Gollancz. 1st ed. F/F. P3. $25.00

MOORE, Alma Chestnut. *Grasses: Earth's Green Wealth.* 1960. NY. ils. 150p. VG/dj. B26. $15.00

MOORE, Anne Carroll. *My Roads to Childhood: Views & Reviews...* 1939. np. 399p. VG/VG. A4. $40.00

MOORE, Brian. *Black Robe.* 1985. Dutton. 1st ed. F/F. H11. $45.00

MOORE, Brian. *Catholics.* 1973. HRW. 1st ed. F/F. B35. $45.00

MOORE, Brian. *Cold Heaven.* 1983. McClelland Stewart. 1st ed. VG/VG. P3. $20.00

MOORE, Brian. *Color of Blood.* 1987. McClelland Stewart. 1st ed. F/F. P3. $20.00

MOORE, Brian. *Emperor of Ice Cream.* 1965. McClelland Stewart. 1st ed. NF/NF. P3. $25.00

MOORE, Brian. *Emperor of Ice Cream.* 1965. Viking. 1st ed. F/F. H11. $50.00

MOORE, Brian. *Feast of Lupercal.* 1957. Little Brn. 1st ed. NF/NF. B35. $50.00

MOORE, Brian. *Fergus.* 1970. Holt. 1st ed. F/F. H11. $40.00

MOORE, Brian. *Fergus.* 1970. HRW. 1st ed. xl. dj. P3. $6.00

MOORE, Brian. *Great Victorian Collection.* 1975. FSG. 1st ed. VG/VG. P3. $30.00

MOORE, Brian. *Lies of Silence.* 1990. Denys. 1st ed. F/F. P3. $23.00

MOORE, C.L. *Best of CL Moore.* nd. BC. VG/VG. P3. $10.00

MOORE, C.L. *Judgment Night.* 1952. Gnome. 1st ed. G+/G+. P3. $75.00

MOORE, C.L. *Scarlet Dream.* 1981. Donald Grant. 1st ed. F/F. T2. $25.00

MOORE, Christopher. *Coyote Blue.* 1994. Simon Schuster. 1st ed. F/F. G10. $15.00

MOORE, Christopher. *Coyote Blue.* 1994. Simon Schuster. 1st ed. sgn. F/F. T2. $35.00

MOORE, Christopher. *Practical Demonkeeping.* 1992. St Martin. 1st ed. author's 1st book. F/F. H11. $30.00

MOORE, Christopher. *Practical Demonkeeping.* 1992. St Martin. 1st ed. author's 1st novel. sgn. F/F. T2. $45.00

MOORE, Clement C. *Account of a Visit From St Nicholas.* 1962. Pasadena. Wm Cheney. 1/200. ils. 11p. miniature. F/box. B24. $225.00

MOORE, Clement C. *Annotated Night Before Christmas.* 1991. Summit. 1st ed. 8vo. F/F. B17. $8.00

MOORE, Clement C. *Night Before Christmas Pop-Up.* 1989. np. 6 popups. F. A4. $30.00

MOORE, Clement C. *Night Before Christmas.* 1942. Everett Shinn Ils ed. 1st ed thus. VG. B30. $35.00

MOORE, Clement C. *Night Before Christmas.* 1946. Akron. Saalfield Jingle Book. ils. 34p. F/box. A17. $75.00

MOORE, Clement C. *Night Before Christmas.* 1981. Holt. 8th. ils Michael Hague. VG. B17. $9.50

MOORE, Clement C. *Night Before Christmas.* 1991. Gramercy. 16mo. ils Rackham. F/F. B17. $5.00

MOORE, Clement C. *Twas the Night Before Christmas.* 1992. Derrydale. 16mo. ils JW Smith. F/sans. B17. $5.00

MOORE, Clement C. *Visit of St Nicholas.* 1900s. NY. McLoughlin. ils Thomas Nast. VG/wrp. D1. $325.00

MOORE, Colleen. *Silent Star.* 1968. Garden City. sgn. VG/VG. B5. $20.00

MOORE, Daphne. *In Nimrod's Footsteps.* 1974. London. Allen. 1st ed. VG/VG. O3. $25.00

MOORE, David M. *Green Plant: Story of Plant Life on Earth.* 1982. Cambridge. 288p. F/dj. B26. $32.00

MOORE, Edith Wyatt. *Natchez Under the Hill.* 1958. S Hist Pub. sgn. 131p. VG/dj. M20. $17.00

MOORE, Edward Alexander. *Story of a Cannoneer Under Stonewall Jackson...* 1910. Lynchburg, VA. JP Bell. 2nd. 331p. cloth F/NF. M8. $250.00

MOORE, Ewell. *War Tax, a Complete Analysis of the War Revenue...* 1917. San Francisco. Bosch. 31p. prt stapled wrp. M11. $20.00

MOORE, Frank. *Women of the War: Their Heroism & Self-Sacrifice.* 1867. Hartford. 1st ed. 596p. VG. A13. $100.00

MOORE, George. *Man & His Motives.* (1850). Harper. 1st Am ed. 302p. emb Victorian cloth. VG. G1. $50.00

MOORE, Geraldine. *Behind the Ebony Mask: What American Negroes Really Think...* 1961. Birmingham. 1st ed. ils. 220p. VG/VG. B5. $30.00

MOORE, H.T. *Novels of John Steinbeck: A First Critical Study...* 1939. Chicago. VG+/G. N3. $25.00

MOORE, Harold E. *Major Groups of Palms & Their Distribution.* 1973. Ithaca. 115p. M/wrp. B26. $40.00

MOORE, Henry. *Sketch Book.* nd. London. 1st ed? sgn/dtd 1940. NF. A15. $75.00

MOORE, Isabel. *Talks in a Library With Laurence Hutton.* 1905. NY. Putnam. 1st ed. 8vo. 458p. bl cloth. w/inscr card. T10. $25.00

MOORE, J. Staunton. *Annals of Henrico Parish...* 1904. Williams Prt. VG-. B10. $75.00

MOORE, John L. *Breaking of Ezra Riley.* 1990. Nashville. Thomas Nelson. 1st ed. 8vo. AN/wrp. T10. $10.00

MOORE, John Monroe. *South Today.* 1916. Missionary Education Movement. 1st ed. 251p. VG. B10. $15.00

MOORE, John Trotwood. *Summer Hymnal: A Romance of Tennessee.* 1925. Nashville. rpt. cloth. G. A17. $7.50

MOORE, John W. *Notes on Raiatean Flowering Plants With Descriptions...* 1963. Honolulu. ils. 36p. F. B26. $15.00

MOORE, Joseph West. *Picturesque Washington: Pen & Pencil Sketches.* 1866. S Bend, IN. 4to ils. 308p. gilt gr cloth. VG. T3. $30.00

MOORE, Lorrie. *Anagrams.* 1986. Knopf. 1st ed. NF/NF. M23. $25.00

MOORE, Lorrie. *Forgotten Helper: Story for Children.* 1987. Kipling. 1st ed. F/F clip. B4. $65.00

MOORE, Lorrie. *Life Like.* 1990. London. Faber. 1st ed. author's 3rd book. F/dj. S9. $45.00

MOORE, Lorrie. *Like Life.* 1990. Knopf. 1st ed. rem mk. F/F. M23. $20.00

MOORE, Lorrie. *Self-Help.* 1985. Knopf. AP. author's 1st book. F/prt wrp. S9. $200.00

MOORE, Lorrie. *Who Will Run the Frog Hospital?* 1994. Knopf. AP. 8vo. F/prt wrp. S9. $85.00

MOORE, Marianne. *Complete Poems.* 1981. Macmillan. F/rpr. V1. $10.00

MOORE, Marianne. *O To Be a Dragon.* 1959. Viking. 1st ed. F/NF. V1. $20.00

MOORE, Marianne. *What Are Years.* 1941. Macmillan. 1st ed. F/NF. B4. $150.00

MOORE, Norman. *History of Study of Medicine in British Isles.* 1908. Oxford. 1st ed. 202p. VG. A13. $100.00

MOORE, Patrick. *Destination Luna.* 1955. Lutterworth. 1st ed. VG/G+. P3. $15.00

MOORE, Patrick. *Guide to Mars.* nd. Norton. 3rd. xl. dj. P3. $5.00

MOORE, Patrick. *Guide to the Moon.* 1953. Norton. 8vo. 255p. xl. G. K5. $14.00

MOORE, Patrick. *How To Make the Most of Your Telescope.* 1985. Harlow, UK. Longman. 1st ed. photos/diagrams. 80p. VG. K5. $15.00

MOORE, Patrick. *Wheel in Space.* 1956. Lutterworth. 1st ed. VG. P3. $15.00

MOORE, R.C. *Orthography As a Factor in Stability...* 1952. KS Geological Survey Bulletin #96. F/prt wrp. D8. $8.00

MOORE, R.C. *Treatise on Invertebrate Paleontology Vol 1 Part C...* 1964. NY. Geological Soc of Am/KS U. ils. 510p. G. D8. $32.00

MOORE, Robin. *Fiedler: The Colorful Mr Pops...* 1968. Boston. Little Brn. 1st ed. 372p. F. B14. $95.00

MOORE, Robin. *Fifth Estate.* 1973. Doubleday. 1st ed. VG/VG. P3. $18.00

MOORE, Robin. *Green Berets.* 1965. Crown. 1st ed. NF/NF. B35. $100.00

MOORE, Ruth. *Earth We Live On: Story of Geological Discovery.* 1956. Knopf. 416p. VG. D8. $17.50

MOORE, Susanna. *Whiteness of Bones.* 1989. Doubleday. 1st ed. AN/dj. B4. $50.00

MOORE, Thomas. *Memoirs of the Life of Rt Hon Richard Brinsley Sheridan.* 1866. NY. Widdleton. 2 vol. 12mo. half gr morocco w/sgn letter. K1. $650.00

MOORE, Virginia. *Rising Wind.* 1928. Dutton. 1st ed. 282p. F/G. B10. $35.00

MOORE, Virginia. *Whole World, Stranger.* 1957. Macmillan. 1st ed. F/NF. B35. $20.00

MOORE, Ward. *Bring the Jubilee.* 1987. Easton. leather. F. P3. $18.00

MOORE, Ward. *Greener Than You Think.* 1947. Sloane. 1st ed. VG/torn. P3. $35.00

MOORE, Warren. *Spurling Sail & Steam.* 1980. Grosset Dunlap. 50 pl/drawings/map. 175p. T7. $110.00

MOORE & SCHLUNDT. *Radioactivity of the Thermal Waters of Yellowstone...* 1909. GPO. ils/pl. VG/wrp. B14. $30.00

MOORE & WELSH. *Utah Plants.* 1973 (1965). Provo. 3rd. ils. orange cloth. B26. $32.00

MOORE. *Reader's Guide to William Gaddis's The Recognitions.* 1982. NE U. 348p. F/sans. A4. $35.00

MOORE. *Unicorn: William Butler Yeats' Search for Reality.* 1954. np. 519p. F/VG. A4. $35.00

MOOREHEAD, Alan. *Eclipse.* 1968. Harper Row. 1st ed thus. 319p. dj. A17. $10.00

MOOREHEAD, Alan. *Fatal Impact: An Account of the Invasion of South Pacific...* 1966. Harper Row. 1st ed. 230p. VG+/dj. M20. $18.00

MOOREHEAD, Alan. *March to Tunis: North African War, 1940-1943.* 1965. NY. 1st Am ed. 592p. F/dj. A17. $10.00

MOOREHEAD, Alan. *White Nile.* 1960. Hamish Hamilton. 1st ed. NF/NF. C2. $100.00

MOOREHEAD, Warren K. *Fort Ancient: Great Prehistoric Earthwork of Warren Co, OH.* 1890. Cincinnati. bl cloth. VG. B30. $60.00

MOORHOUSE, W.W. *Study of Rocks in Thin Section.* 1959. Harper Row. 1st ed. 514p. VG. D8. $25.00

MORA, Gilles. *Walker Evans' Havana 1933.* 1989. Pantheon. 1st Am ed. 80 photos. AN/dj. A17. $20.00

MORAN, Richard. *Dallas Down.* 1988. Collins. 1st ed. F/F. P3. $25.00

MORAN. *Creating a Legend: Descriptive Catalog of Writing...* 1973. 618p. xl. VG. A4. $145.00

MORCOMBE, Michael. *Australia's Western Wildflowers.* 1968. Perth. 1st ed. ils/map. VG/dj. B26. $42.00

MORCOMBE, Michael. *Australia's Wildflowers.* 1970. Melbourne. photos/line drawings, 128p. VG+/dj. B26. $38.00

MORE, Jasper. *Mediterranean.* 1956. London. Batsford. 1st ed. 336p. xl. VG. W1. $20.00

MORE, Thomas. *Utopia.* 1934. LEC. 1st ed. 1/1500. prt/sgn Bruce Rogers. 165p. F/VG case. C2. $125.00

MOREHEAD, A. *Darwin & the Beagle.* 1969. Harper Row. 1st ed/5th imp. 280p. F/dj. D8. $25.00

MOREHEAD, Albert H. *Pocket Book of Games.* 1944. NY. 1st prt. 308p. VG/wrp. S1. $3.00

MORELAND, George L. *Balldom: The Britannica of Baseball. A Complete History...* 1914. NY. 12mo. 304p. pict red cloth. G+. H3. $125.00

MORELAND, John Richard. *Shadow at My Heel.* 1946. Kaleidograph. sgn. 180p. VG/fair. B10. $18.00

MORELEY, Christopher. *Ex Libris Carissimis.* 1932. Phil. PA U. inscr. 133p. NF. T10. $125.00

MORELEY, Christopher. *I Know a Secret.* 1927. Doubleday Page. 1st ed. inscr. VG+/VG. A20. $40.00

MORELEY, Christopher. *Kitty Foyle.* 1939. Lippincott. 1st ed. F/clip. A20. $30.00

MORELEY, Christopher. *Middle Kingdom.* 1944. Harcourt Brace. 1st ed. 8vo. VG/dj. S9. $25.00

MORELEY, Christopher. *Parnassus on Wheels.* 1931. NY. Modern Lib. 1st ed. VG. B5. $25.00

MORELEY, Christopher. *Powder of Sympathy.* 1923. Doubleday Page. 1st ed. inscr. F/VG+. A20. $45.00

MORELL, David. *Covenant of the Flame.* nd. Quality BC. F/F. P3. $10.00

MORELL, David. *League of Night & Fog.* 1987. Dutton. 1st ed. VG/VG. P3. $18.00

MORELLA, Joe. *Those Great Movie Ads.* 1972. 1st ed. ils/photos. VG/VG. S13. $30.00

MORGAN, A.T. *Yazoo; or, On the Picket Line of Freedom in the South.* 1884. WA, DC. self pub. 1st ed. 512p. ES. cloth. VG. M8. $350.00

MORGAN, Al. *Essential Man.* 1977. Playboy. 1st ed. F/F. P3. $15.00

MORGAN, Albert Talmon. *Yazoo; or, On the Picket Line of Freedom in the South.* 1884. WA, DC. self pub. 1st ed. 512p. ES. cloth. VG. M8. $350.00

MORGAN, C. Lloyd. *Animal Life & Intelligence.* 1891. London. Edward Arnold. 40 woodcuts. 412p. panelled bl cloth. VG. G1. $125.00

MORGAN, Dale. *Great Salt Lake.* 1947. Indianapolis. 1st ed. sgn. VG/VG. B5. $65.00

MORGAN, Dan. *Concrete Horizon.* 1976. Millington. 1st ed. F/F. P3. $15.00

MORGAN, Dan. *High Destiny.* 1975. Millington. 1st ed. F/F. P3. $15.00

MORGAN, David. *Revised New System for Educating the Horse.* 1898. Springfield. 232p. O3. $35.00

MORGAN, E. Seidel. *Governor of Desire.* 1993. LSU. 1st ed. F/F. V1. $15.00

MORGAN, F.R. *Teddy Bears on Rollers.* 1908. Chicago. 1st ed. G. B5. $40.00

MORGAN, John Medford; see Fox, Gardner F.

MORGAN, John Tyler. *Address of Hon JT Morgan on the Unveiling of Monuments...* 1879. Globe. 1st ed. 24p. prt wrp. M8. $45.00

MORGAN, L.H. *American Beaver & His Works.* nd. Lippincott. 1st ed. 8vo. 330p. red cloth. VG. B1. $235.00

MORGAN, Lewis H. *Indian Journals 1859-1862.* 1959. Ann Arbor. 1st ed. ils/pl. blk/brn-stp olive cloth. F. T10. $45.00

MORGAN, Lewis H. *Study of the Houses of the American Aborigines...* 1880. Cambridge. 8vo. 14 pl/ils. 163p. F. B14. $125.00

MORGAN, Nina. *Prairie Star.* 1955. Viking. 1st ed. ils Robert Henneberger. 189p. F/VG. P2. $20.00

MORGAN, Robert. *Hinterlands: A Mountain Tale in Three Parts.* 1994. Algonquin. UP. F/wrp. C2. $35.00

MORGAN, Robin. *Monster.* 1972. Random. 1st ed. F/F. V1. $15.00

MORGAN, Rod; see Fox, Gardner F.

MORGAN, William Henry. *Personal Reminiscences of the War of 1861-65...* 1911. Lynchburg, VA. JP Bell. 1st ed. 286p. NF/VG. M8. $275.00

MORGAN & RICHARDS. *Book of Apples.* 1993. London. ils/pl. 304p. AN/dj. B26. $30.00

MORGAN & RICHARDS. *Paradise Out of the Common Field.* 1990. London. ils/pl. F/dj. B26. $25.00

MORGAN & SWARTWOUT. *Fragile Empires: Correspondence of Samuel Swartwout...* 1978. Austin. 1st ed. 384p. E1. $35.00

MORGAN. *Noah Webster.* 1975. np. 223p. F/NF. A4. $35.00

MORGENSTERN, S. *Silent Gondoliers.* 1983. Del Rey. 1st ed. F/F. P3. $18.00

MORI, Haruhide. *Conversation on DH Lawrence.* 1974. UCLA. 1/1250. ils. 46p. F/sans. B19. $20.00

MORICE, Anne. *Death of a Heavenly Twin.* 1974. St Martin. 1st ed. VG/G+. P3. $15.00

MORICE, Anne. *Fatal Charm.* 1988. St Martin. 1st ed. F/F. P3. $18.00

MORICE, Anne. *Murder in Outline.* 1979. St Martin. F/F. P3. $15.00

MORICE, Anne. *Planning for Murder.* 1991. St Martin. 2nd. VG/VG. P3. $15.00

MORICE, Anne. *Publish & Be Killed.* 1985. St Martin. 1st ed. VG/VG. P3. $13.00

MORICE, Anne. *Treble Exposure.* 1987. St Martin. 1st ed. F/F. P3. $18.00

MORIN, Louis. *Vielle Idylle.* 1891. Paris. Lib L Conquet. pub inscr. teg. Gruel bdg/orig wrp bound-in. F. B24. $1,500.00

MORIN, Relman. *Dwight D Eisenhower: A Gauge of Greatness.* (1969). Assoc Pr. probable 1st ed thus. 256p. gr cloth. F. B22. $7.00

MORISON, Samuel Eliot. *John Paul Jones: A Sailor's Biography.* 1959. Little Brn. BC. ils/charts/photos. gilt bl bdg. G+. P12. $6.00

MORISON, Samuel Eliot. *Spring Tides.* 1965. Houghton Mifflin. 1st ed. ils. G+. P12. $8.00

MORISON, Stanley. *Typographic Book 1450-1935: A Study of Fine Typography...* 1963. Chicago. 300 full-p pl. 455p. F/F clip/F case. A4. $300.00

MORKOT, Robert. *Egypt.* 1988. Chartwell. 1st ed. photos. 79p. NF/dj. W1. $20.00

MORLER, J. *Zohrab the Hostage.* 1832. London. 3 vol. 1st ed. lacks spines/worn. A15. $75.00

MORLEY, Sylvanus. *Guide Book to the Ruins of Quirgua.* 1935. DC. 1st ed. 205p. cloth. F3. $85.00

MORPURGO, Ida B. *Die Himmel Skuche (The Cloud Kitchen).* 1933. Munchen. ils Ida Bohatta Morpurgo. VG. D1. $110.00

MORRELL, David. *Brotherhood of the Rose.* 1984. NY. 1st ed. F/F. H11. $60.00

MORRELL, David. *Covenant of the Flame.* 1991. Warner. 1st ed. F/F. H11. $25.00

MORRELL, David. *Desperate Measures.* 1994. Warner. 1st ed. F/F. H11. $20.00

MORRELL, David. *First Blood.* 1972. NY. Evans. 1st ed. author's 1st book. F/F. C2. $100.00

MORRELL, David. *Fraternity of the Stone.* 1985. NY. 1st ed. F/F. H11. $40.00

MORRELL, David. *Totem.* 1992. London. 1st ed. inscr. NF/NF. A15. $25.00

MORRESSY, John. *Frostworld & Dreamfire.* 1977. Doubleday. 1st ed. F/F. P3. $15.00

MORRESSY, John. *Long Communion.* 1974. Walker. 1st ed. xl. dj. P3. $5.00

MORRIS, Ann Axtell. *Digging in the Southwest.* 1934. Doubleday Doran. 8vo. photos. blk-stp orange cloth. VG. T10. $35.00

MORRIS, C.B. *Surrealism & Spain.* 1972. London. Cambridge. 1st ed. F/NF. B2. $25.00

MORRIS, Desmond. *Animal Days.* 1979. Jonathan Cape. 1st ed. F/F. P3. $15.00

MORRIS, F.O. *History of British Birds.* 1851-1857. London. Groombridge. 6 vol. 1st ed. 8vo. 358 pl. 20th-C morocco. NF. C6. $650.00

MORRIS, George Ford. *Portraitures of Horses.* 1952. Shrewbury. 1st ed. 4to. O3. $595.00

MORRIS, Herbert. *Peru.* 1983. Holt Rinehart. 1st ed. F/VG+. V1. $10.00

MORRIS, James. *Islam Inflamed: A Middle East Picture.* 1957. NY. Pantheon. 1st ed. 8vo. 7 maps. 326p. VG/dj. W1. $20.00

MORRIS, James. *Manhattan '45.* 1987. NY. 1st ed. photos. 272p. F/F. E1. $25.00

MORRIS, James. *Places.* 1972. London. 1st ed. F/NF. B4. $50.00

MORRIS, Jan; see Morris, James.

MORRIS, Janet. *Beyond Sanctuary.* 1985. Baen. 1st ed. F/F. P3. $20.00

MORRIS, Janet. *Beyond Wizardwall.* 1986. Baen. 1st ed. F/F. P3. $20.00

MORRIS, Janet. *Threshold.* 1990. Roc. 1st ed. F/F. P3. $17.00

MORRIS, Jim. *Sheriff of Purgatory.* 1979. Doubleday. 1st ed. VG/VG. P3. $15.00

MORRIS, John. *Candywine Development.* 1971. Citadel. 1st ed. VG/VG. P3. $13.00

MORRIS, John. *Checkerboard Caper.* 1975. Citadel. 1st ed. VG/VG. P3. $18.00

MORRIS, Lloyd. *Curtain Time: Story of the American Theater.* 1953. Random. VG/VG. D2. $22.00

MORRIS, Lloyd. *Incredible New York: High Life & Low Life...* 1951. NY. 1st ed. photos. 370p. NF/G. E1. $40.00

MORRIS, Norval. *Brothel Boy & Other Parables of the Law.* 1992. Oxford. M11. $20.00

MORRIS, Paul C. *American Sailing Coasters of the North Atlantic.* 1973. Chardon, OH. Block Osborn. 1st ed. ils. 224p. VG. T7. $65.00

MORRIS, Rosamund. *Great Suspense Stories.* 1962. Hart. VG/VG. P3. $20.00

MORRIS, William. *Art & Its Producers: Arts & Crafts of Today.* 1901. London. 1st ed. inscr/dtd 1901. NF. C6. $225.00

MORRIS, William. *Masters in This Hall.* 1859. Berkeley. 1/100. sgn. leather. miniature. F/chemise/ribbon ties. B24. $265.00

MORRIS, William. *News From Nowhere.* 1941. Nelson. VG/VG. P3. $25.00

MORRIS, William. *Selections From William Morris.* 1959. Foreign Languages Pub. VG. P3. $30.00

MORRIS, Willie. *James Jones: A Friendship.* 1978. Doubleday. 1st ed. VG+/VG+. A20. $25.00

MORRIS, Willie. *Last of the Southern Girls.* 1973. Knopf. ARC. author's 1st work of fiction. F/wrp. w/promo material. S9. $30.00

MORRIS, Willie. *Yazoo: Integration in the Deep-Southern Town.* 1971. Harper Magazine. 1st ed. F/F. B4. $85.00

MORRIS, Wright. *Collected Stories: 1948-1986.* 1986. Harper Row. 1st ed. M/M. A18. $12.50

MORRIS, Wright. *Love Among the Cannibals.* 1957. Harcourt Brace. 1st ed. F/NF. B24. $100.00

MORRIS & MORRIS. *Trust Territory.* 1992. Roc. 1st ed. F/F. P3. $20.00

MORRISON, Arthur. *Red Triangle.* 1903. LC Page. 1st ed. VG+. N4. $65.00

MORRISON, G. James. *Maps: Their Uses & Construction...* 1911. London. Stanford. xl. VG+. O7. $65.00

MORRISON, Lillian. *Yours Till Niagra Falls: A Collection...* (1950). Crowell. 18th. 24mo. 182p. gold brd. xl. G+/VG. T5. $20.00

MORRISON, Theodore. *Notes of Death & Life.* 1935. Crowell. 1st ed. assn copy. F/G. V1. $20.00

MORRISON, Toni. *Beloved.* 1987. Knopf. 1st ed. F/F. C2/H11. $75.00

MORRISON, Toni. *Bluest Eye.* 1970. HRW. 1st ed. author's 1st book. F/VG+ clip. B4. $1,750.00

MORRISON, Toni. *Bluest Eye.* 1979. Chatto Windus. 1st ed thus. F/F. B4. $350.00

MORRISON, Toni. *Jazz.* 1992. Knopf. 1st ed. F/F. B4. $45.00

MORRISON, Toni. *Jazz.* 1992. Knopf. 1st ed. sgn. F/F. C2. $125.00

MORRISON, Toni. *Playing in the Dark: Whiteness & Literary Imagination.* 1992. Harvard. 1st ed. F/F. B4. $65.00

MORRISON, Toni. *Song of Solomon.* 1977. Knopf. 1st ed. author's 3rd novel. NF/NF. B4. $100.00

MORRISON, Toni. *Song of Solomon.* 1977. Knopf. 1st ed. F/F. M19. $125.00

MORRISON, Toni. *Song of Solomon.* 1978. Chatto Windus. 1st ed. F/F. B4. $200.00

MORRISON, Toni. *Sula.* 1974. Knopf. 1st ed. sgn. author's 2nd book. F/NF. B4. $1,250.00

MORRISON, Toni. *Tar Baby.* 1981. Knopf. 1st ed. F/NF. M19. $75.00

MORRISON, Toni. *Tar Baby.* 1981. NY. 1st trade ed. inscr. F/NF. C6. $120.00

MORROW, Anne. *Hour of Lead, Hour of Gold: Diaries & Letters 1929-1932.* 1973. Harcourt. 1st ed. 340p. cloth. F/dj. B22. $7.50

MORROW, Bradford. *Bibliography of Writings of Wyndham Lewis.* 1978. Blk Sparrow. 1st ed. sgn. F/F. B2. $65.00

MORROW, Honore Willsie. *With Malice Toward None.* 1928. Morrow. 1st ed. 342p. VG/G. B10. $10.00

MORROW, James. *City of Truth.* 1990. Legend. 1st ed. F/F. P3. $25.00

MORROW, James. *City of Truth.* 1992. St Martin. 1st Am ed. F/NF. G10. $18.00

MORROW, James. *Continent of Lies.* 1984. HRW. 1st ed. author's 2nd novel. F/F. T2. $25.00

MORROW, James. *Only Begotten Daughter.* nd. BC. VG/VG. P3. $8.00

MORROW, James. *Only Begotten Daughter.* 1990. Morrow. 1st ed. F/F. G10/T2. $45.00

MORROW, James. *This Is the Way the World Ends.* 1986. Holt. 1st ed. F/F. M23. $20.00

MORROW, James. *Towing Jehovah.* 1994. Harcourt Brace. 1st ed. F/F. M23. $40.00

MORSE, A. Reynolds. *Works of MP Shiel: A Study in Bibliography.* 1948. Fpci. 1st ed. F/F. P3. $35.00

MORSE, Benjamin, M.D.; see Block, Lawrence.

MORSE, Evangeline. *Brown Rabbit: Her Story.* 1967. Chicago. Follett. 1st ed. ils David Stone Martin. F/NF clip. B4. $75.00

MORSE, Samuel French. *Life As Poetry.* 1970. Pegasus. 1st ed. assn copy. F/NF. V1. $25.00

MORSE, Samuel French. *Time of Year, a First Book of Poems.* 1943. Cummington, MA. 1st ed. 1/275. intro Wallace Stevens. F. B24. $300.00

MORTENSEN, William. *Monsters & Madonnas.* 1936. San Francisco. Camera Craft Pub. 1st ed. photos. sbdg. F/tissue dj. S9. $450.00

MORTIMER, John. *Charade.* 1986. Viking. F/F. P3. $20.00

MORTIMER, John. *Dunster.* 1993. Viking. 1st ed. NF/NF. P3. $21.00

MORTIMER, John. *Like Men Betrayed.* 1987. Viking. 1st ed. F/F. P3. $20.00

MORTIMER, John. *Narrowing Stream.* 1988. Viking. VG/VG. P3. $20.00

MORTIMER, John. *Oxford Book of Villains.* 1992. Oxford. NF/NF. P3. $25.00

MORTIMER, John. *Summer's Lease.* 1988. Franklin Lib. 1st ed. aeg. bl leather. F. B11. $45.00

MORTIMER, Roger. *Jockey Club.* 1958. London. 1st ed. ils. 184p. gr cloth. F/VG. H3. $65.00

MORTON, Anthony. *Case for the Baron.* 1949. DSP. 1st ed. VG/VG. P3. $35.00

MORTON, Anthony. *Double Frame.* nd. BC. VG/VG. P3. $8.00

MORTON, H.V. *Through Lands of the Bible.* 1938. Dodd Mead. 1st ed. ils. 452p. VG. W1. $18.00

MORTON, Robert. *Southern Antiques & Folk Art.* 1976. Oxmoor. 1st ed. ils. 251p. VG/VG. B10. $40.00

MORTON, Rosalie Slaughter. *Doctor's Holiday in Iran.* 1940. Funk Wagnalls. 1st ed. 8vo. 15 pl. 335p. xl. VG. W1. $15.00

MOSBY, John Singleton. *Memoirs of Colonel John S Mosby.* 1917. Little Brn. 1st ed. 414p. cloth. VG. M8. $275.00

MOSCATI, Sebatino. *Face of the Ancient.* 1961. London. Routledge. 2nd. ils/fld map. 328p. NF/dj. W1. $22.00

MOSELEY, George Clark. *Extracts From the Letters of...* 1923. Chicago. 1st ed. ils/photos. 239p. F/case. B18. $125.00

MOSELY, Leonard. *Power Play: Oil in the Middle East.* 1973. Random. 1st Am ed. 458p. VG. W1. $22.00

MOSER, Barry. *Twelve Wood Engravings of Cirsia & Various Thistles...* 1978. Northampton. Gray Parrot. 1/35. sgn Moser/ils/binder/pub. near miniature. B24. $950.00

MOSES, Robert. *Public Works: A Dangerous Trade.* 1970. McGraw Hill. sgn. 8vo. 952p. full leather. VG. B11. $150.00

MOSHER, Howard Frank. *Stranger in the Kingdom.* 1989. Doubleday. 1st ed. F/F. M23. $25.00

MOSHER, Marlene. *New Directions From Don L Lee.* 1975. Hicksville. Exposition. 1st ed. NF/VG+ clip. B4. $75.00

MOSKOWITZ, Sam. *Editor's Choice in SF.* 1954. McBride. 1st ed. VG/VG. P3. $45.00

MOSKOWITZ, Sam. *Explorers of the Infinite.* 1974. Hyperion. F. P3. $40.00

MOSKOWITZ, Sam. *Horrors Unknown.* 1971. Walker. 1st ed. sgn. VG/VG. P3. $22.00

MOSKOWITZ, Sam. *Immortal Storms.* 1974. Hyperion. F. P3. $40.00

MOSKOWITZ, Sam. *SF by Gaslight.* 1974. Hyperion. F. P3. $40.00

MOSKOWITZ, Sam. *Under the Moons of Mars.* 1970. HRW. 1st ed. VG/VG. P3. $50.00

MOSLEY, Leonard. *On Borrowed Time: How WWII Began.* 1969. NY. BC. 509p. dj. A17. $10.00

MOSLEY, Walter. *Black Betty.* 1994. Norton. 1st ed. sgn. F/F. M22. $35.00

MOSLEY, Walter. *Black Betty.* 1994. Norton. 1st ed. sgn/dtd. F/dj. w/press kit. S9. $50.00

MOSLEY, Walter. *Devil in a Blue Dress.* 1990. Norton. 1st ed. author's 1st book. F/F. H11. $75.00

MOSLEY, Walter. *Little Yellow Dog.* 1996. Norton. 1st ed. F/F. P3. $23.00

MOSLEY, Walter. *Red Death.* 1991. Norton. 1st ed. sgn. 284p. NF/NF. M20. $60.00

MOSLEY, Walter. *White Butterfly.* 1992. Norton. 1st ed. F/NF. B2. $75.00

MOSS, Howard. *Rules of Sleep.* 1984. Atheneum. 1st ed. RS. F/wrp. w/promo sheet. V1. $10.00

MOSS, Howard. *Toy Fair.* 1954. Scribner. 1st ed. poet's 2nd book. F/VG. V1. $45.00

MOSS, Morrie A. *Lillian & Morrie Moss Collection of Paul Storr Silver.* 1972. Miami. Rjoskin Book Prod. sgn. ils/photos. aeg. bl leather. D2. $80.00

MOSS, Thylias. *Small Congregations.* 1993. Ecco. 1st ed. F/NF. V1. $10.00

MOSSA, R.G. *Gulliver's Travels.* ca 1930s. Garden City. 8vo. VG+. M5. $35.00

MOSSE, George L. *Nazi Culture: Intellectual Culture & Social Life...* 1977. Grosset Dunlap. rpt. 386p. wrp. A17. $8.50

MOSSMAN, Samuel. *Japan.* 1880. London. ils/map. 247p. brn cloth. VG. B14. $95.00

MOSSO, Angelo. *Fear.* 1896. London. Longman Gr. 1st ed. 278p. pebbled crimson cloth. w/24p catalog. G1. $75.00

MOSTERT, Noel. *Supership.* 1974. Knopf. BC. 1st ed. VG/VG. P12. $7.00

MOTT, Michael. *Corday.* 1986. Beacham. 1st ed. inscr. F/VG+. V1. $15.00

MOTT, T. Bentley. *Myron T Herick: Friend of France.* 1929. Doubleday. 1st ed. 399p. gilt blk cloth. VG+. B22. $8.00

MOTT-SMITH, Geoffrey. *Contract Bridge & Advanced Auction Bidding.* 1927. NY. 281p. VG. S1. $12.00

MOTT-SMITH, Geoffrey. *Pencil Bridge.* 1928. NY. 161p. VG. S1. $4.00

MOTZ, Lloyd. *This Is Outer Space.* 1960. Archer. 8vo. 10 pl. 199p. VG/dj. K5. $10.00

MOULE, Thomas. *County Maps of Old England.* 1922. London. Studio. 56 maps. M/dj. O7. $40.00

MOURAD, Kenize. *Regards From the Dead Princess.* 1987. Arcade. 1st Am ed. 8vo. 562p. VG/dj. W1. $18.00

MOWAT, Farley. *Serpent's Coil.* 1961. Little Brn. 1st Am ed. 189p. tan brd. F/F. B22. $5.50

MOWAT, Jean. *Meals for Small Families.* nd. Chicago. Laidlaw. probable 1st ed. 188p. NF. B22. $5.50

MOWRY, George D. *Another Look at the Twentieth-Century South.* 1973. LSU. 90p. VG/VG. B10. $10.00

MOWRY, Jess. *Way Past Cool.* 1992. FSG. 1st ed. F/F. M23. $20.00

MOYER, John W. *Famous Frontiersmen.* nd. Northbrook, IL. Hubbard. probable 1st ed. ils Vlasaty 116p. F. C14. $20.00

MOYES, Patricia. *Angel Death.* nd. BC. VG/VG. P3. $8.00

MOYES, Patricia. *Angel Death.* 1981. HRW. 1st Am ed. F/dj. N4. $30.00

MOYES, Patricia. *Black Girl, White Girl.* 1989. Holt. 1st ed. VG/VG. P3. $18.00

MOYES, Patricia. *Black Widower.* 1975. Collins Crime Club. 1st ed. VG/VG. P3. $15.00

MOYES, Patricia. *Coconut Killings.* nd. BC. VG/VG. P3. $8.00

MOYES, Patricia. *Death & the Dutch Uncle.* 1968. HRW. 1st ed. VG/VG. P3. $20.00

MOYES, Patricia. *Helter-Skelter.* 1968. HRW. 1st ed. VG/VG. P3. $25.00

MOYES, Patricia. *Many Deadly Returns.* 1970. HRW. 1st ed. VG. P3. $10.00

MOYES, Patricia. *Night Ferry to Death.* 1985. HRW. 1st ed. F/F. P3. $14.00

MOYES, Patricia. *Season of Snows & Sins.* 1971. HRW. 1st ed. VG. P3. $10.00

MOYES, Patricia. *Six-Letter Word for Death.* nd. BC. VG/VG. P3. $8.00

MOYES, Patricia. *Who Is Simon Warwick.* 1978. HRW. 1st ed. 168p. VG/VG. B10. $25.00

MOZART. *Letters of Mozart & His Family.* 1989. Norton. 2nd. F/F. P3. $75.00

MOZLEY, Charles. *Famous French Fairy Tales.* 1959. Franklin Watts. 1st ed. 8vo. VG/G. B17. $6.50

MRABET, Mohammed. *Love With a Few Hairs.* 1968. NY. 1st Am ed. trans/inscr Paul Bowles. F/F. C6. $150.00

MUDD, Samuel Alexander. *Life of Dr Samuel A Mudd...* 1906. Neale. 1st ed. 326p. cloth. NF. M8. $450.00

MUDGE, Eugene Tenbroeck. *Social Philosophy of John Taylor of Caroline...* 1939. Columbia. 1st ed. 225p. VG. B10. $45.00

MUDGE, Robert W. *Meteorology for Pilots.* 1945. McGraw Hill. 1st ed. ils/9 charts. 259p. G/torn. K5. $15.00

MUDIE, R. *Popular Guide to Observations of Nature.* 1836. NY. 16mo. 343p. blk cloth. G. T3. $20.00

MUELLER, Chester. *Small Arms Lexicon & Concise Encyclopedia.* 1968. Shooter's Bible. 1st ed. ils/photos. gilt gr bdg. NF/VG. P12. $25.00

MUELLER, Rose. *Gay Day for 7.* 1887. Louis Prang. 8vo. ils. VG. M5. $125.00

MUGGLEBEE, Ruth. *Father Coughlin: The Radio Priest...* 1933. NY. photos. 358p. VG. B14. $37.50

MUIR, Augustus. *Shadow on the Left.* 1928. Methuen. 1st ed. VG. P3. $20.00

MUIR, John. *Travels in Alaska.* 1915. Boston. 1st ed. VG/VG. B5. $80.00

MUIR, John. *Two Essays on the Forests & Lakes of the Sierra Nevada.* 1971. Lewis Osborne. 8vo. ils. 63p. gilt gr cloth. F. T10. $75.00

MUIR, Percy. *English Children's Books.* 1969. 2nd. NF/NF. S13. $10.00

MUIR. *Binding & Repairing Books by Hand.* 1978. np. 4to. ils. 120p. NF/NF. A4. $65.00

MUIR. *Natural Trust Guide to Dark Age & Medieval Britain...* 1985. F/VG. D2. $40.00

MUJICA GALLO, Miguel. *Museo Oro del Peru/Museum Gold of Peru.* nd. np. Eng/Spanish text. 109p. VG/wrp. F3. $20.00

MUKERJI, Dhan Gopal. *Gay-Neck: Story of a Pigeon.* 1928 (1927). Dutton. Lib Convention. 1/1000. sgn. ils/sgn Artzybasheff. 197p. VG. P2. $110.00

MULDOON, Paul. *Madoc: A Mystery.* 1991. FSG. UP. RS. NF. V1. $25.00

MULFORD, Clarence E. *Bar-20.* nd. Hodder Stoughton. VG. P3. $15.00

MULFORD, Clarence E. *Coming of Cassidy.* nd. Grosset Dunlap. VG. P3. $15.00

MULFORD, Clarence E. *Corson of the Jc.* 1927. Doubleday Page. 1st ed. G. P3. $30.00

MULFORD, Clarence E. *Hopalong Cassidy Returns.* 1943. Triangle. 2nd. VG/VG. P3. $15.00

MULFORD, Clarence E. *Tex.* nd. Grosset Dunlap. NF/NF. P3. $25.00

MULLALLY, Frederic. *Assassins.* 1965. Walker. 1st ed. NF/NF. P3. $10.00

MULLER, Frederik. *Beredeneerde Beschrijving van Nederlandsche...* 1970. Amsterdam. 3 vol. rpt. M/case. O7. $275.00

MULLER, Herbert J. *Thomas Wolfe.* 1947. New Directions. 1st ed. 196p. 12mo. cloth. A17. $15.00

MULLER, Ingo. *Hitler's Justice, the Courts of the Third Reich.* 1991. London. IB Tauris. M11. $25.00

MULLER, John E.; see Fanthorpe, Lionel.

MULLER, Marcia. *Broken Promise Land.* 1996. Mysterious. 1st ed. hc. F/F. P3. $23.00

MULLER, Marcia. *Cavalier in White.* nd. BC. VG/VG. P3. $8.00

MULLER, Marcia. *Deceptions.* 1991. Mystery Scene. 1st ed. sgn. F/F. P3. $25.00

MULLER, Marcia. *Trophies & Dead Things.* 1990. Mysterious. 1st ed. F/F. P3. $17.00

MULLER, Marcia. *Where Echoes Live.* nd. BC. VG/VG. P3. $8.00

MULLER, Marcia. *Wild & Lonely Place.* 1995. Mysterious. 1st ed. F/F. P3. $20.00

MULLER, Marcia. *Wolf in the Shadows.* 1993. Mysterious. 1st ed. F/F. M23. $20.00

MULLER & PRONZINI. *Deadly Arts.* 1985. Arbor. 1st ed. VG/VG. P3. $16.00

MULLER & PRONZINI. *Web She Weaves.* 1983. Morrow. 1st ed. VG/VG. P3. $18.00

MULLIN, Michael. *MacBeth Onstage.* 1976. Columbia. MO U. 7th ed. obl 4to. F/VG. T10. $50.00

MULLINS, James. *Defense Matrix.* 1986. San Diego. 1st ed. sgn. VG/G. B11. $8.00

MULLINS & REED. *Civil War Books: A Critical Bibliography.* 1996. Broadfoot. 2 vol in 1. AN. B10. $75.00

MULOCK, Dinah. *Little Lame Prince.* 1909. Rand McNally. ils Dunlap. K2. $65.00

MULOCK, Dinah. *Little Lame Prince.* 1964. Whitman. ils Thompson. K2. $10.00

MULOCK, Dinah. *Little Lame Prince.* 1918. 1st ed thus. ils Maria Kirk. VG. S13. $18.00

MUMEY, Nolie. *Friendly Fire & Other Poems.* 1945. Denver. Range. sgn. F/sans. V1. $20.00

MUMFORD, George Saltonstall. *Twenty Harvard Crews.* 1923. Harvard. 22 full-p ils. 154p. VG. B14. $75.00

MUMFORD, John Kimberly. *Oriental Rugs.* 1905. NY. 278p. teg. G. B18. $45.00

MUNARI, Bruno. *Tic, Tac, & Toc.* 1957. World. 1st Am ed. 4to. F. B24. $175.00

MUNBY, A.N.L. *Cult of the Autograph Letter in England.* 1962. London. 125p. F/VG. A4. $85.00

MUNBY, A.N.L. *Earl & the Thief, Lord Ashburnham & Count Libri.* 1968. Houghton Lib. 17p. stapled wrp. M11. $35.00

MUNDELL, E.H. *Erle Stanley Gardner: A Checklist.* 1968. Kent State. F. P3. $15.00

MUNDY, Ralph. *East & West.* 1937. NY. 1st ed. VG. B5. $100.00

MUNDY, Talbot. *Guns of the Gods.* nd. AL Burt. G. P3. $20.00

MUNDY, Talbot. *Hira Singh.* 1918. Bobbs Merrill. 1st ed. VG. P3. $40.00

MUNDY, Talbot. *King of the Khyber Rifles.* 1972. Tom Stacey. VG/VG. P3. $20.00

MUNDY, Talbot. *Nine Unknown.* 1924. Bobbs Merrill. VG. P3. $75.00

MUNDY, Talbot. *Om: Secret of Ahbor Valley.* 1924. Bobbs Merrill. VG. P3. $75.00

MUNDY, Talbot. *Thunder Dragon Gate.* 1937. Appleton Century. 1st ed. G+/dj. P3. $40.00

MUNFORD, Robert. *Candidates; or, Humours of a Virginia Election.* 1948. Wm Byrd Pr. 43p. xl. VG-. B10. $25.00

MUNGO, Raymond. *Confessions From Left Field.* 1983. Dutton. 1st ed. F/F. P8. $35.00

MUNICHKERN & KERTESS. *Brice Marden. Zeichnungen/Drawings: 1964-78.* 1979. Munich. 52 pl. 132p. D2. $85.00

MUNITZ, Milton K. *Theories of the Universe.* 1957. Glencoe, IL. Free Pr. 1st ed. 8vo. 437p. G. K5. $22.00

MUNK, Joseph. *Story of the Munk Library of Arizoiana.* 1927. Times-Mirror Pr. 1st ed. inscr. 78p. gilt brn cloth. xl. T10. $45.00

MUNKACSI, Martin. *Nudes.* 1951. NY. Greenberg. 1st ed. photos. NF/dj. S9. $225.00

MUNNINGS, Alfred. *Autobiography of...* 1950. London. Mus Pr. 3 vol. 1st ed. VG/G. O3. $425.00

MUNRO, Hugh. *Clutha Plays a Hunch.* 1959. Ives Washburn. 1st ed. VG/VG. P3. $15.00

MUNRO, James. *Die Rich Die Happy.* 1966. Knopf. 1st ed. F/F. H11. $25.00

MUNRO, James. *Man Who Sold Death.* 1964. Hammond. 1st ed. VG/fair. P3. $20.00

MUNRO-SMITH, R. *Merchant Ships & Shipping.* 1970. Barnes. ARC/1st Am ed. VG/VG. A16. $20.00

MUNROE, David. *Grand National 1839-1930.* 1931. NY. Huntington. 1st trade ed. VG/G. O3. $45.00

MUNSEY, Frank A. *Boy Broker.* 1889. Munsey. 3rd. VG. P3. $40.00

MUNSON, Edward Lyman. *Soldier's Foot & the Military Shoe.* 1912. Ft Leavenworth. ils. 145p. tan cloth. VG. B14. $150.00

MUNSON, Ronald. *Nothing Human.* 1991. Pocket. 1st ed. F/F. H11. $25.00

MURAKAMI, Haruki. *Wild Sheep Chase.* 1989. Kodansha. 1st ed. NF/F. w/promo postcard. M23. $20.00

MURDOCH, Iris. *Good Apprentice.* 1985. London. 1st ed. 1/250. sgn. F/F tissue dj. C6. $100.00

MURDOCH, Iris. *Green Knight.* 1st Eng ed. AN/dj. B30. $25.00

MURFREE, M.N. *Mystery of Witch-Face Mountain & Other Stories.* 1895. Houghton Mifflin. 1st ed. 279p. G. B10. $15.00

MURIE, A. *Naturalist in Alaska.* 1961. NY. 1st ed. sgn. VG/VG. B5. $27.50

MURPHY, Bud. *Wild Stallion.* 1952. Cleveland. World. VG/G. O3. $12.00

MURPHY, Dallas. *Apparent Wind.* 1991. Pocket. 1st ed. AN/dj. N4. $22.50

MURPHY, Dallas. *Lush Life.* 1994. Pocket. 1st ed. F/F. A20. $12.00

MURPHY, Gloria. *Down Will Come Baby.* 1991. Donald Fine. ARC. F/F. w/promo material. B4. $35.00

MURPHY, Gloria. *Playroom.* 1987. Donald Fine. 1st ed. VG/VG. P3. $18.00

MURPHY, Haughton; see Duffy, James.

MURPHY, Henry C. *Catalogue of an American Library Chronologically Arranged.* 1850? Brooklyn. part 1. inscr. later quarter leather. NF. T10. $200.00

MURPHY, R.C. *Bird Islands of Peru.* 1925. NY. 1st ed. ils. 362p. VG. B5. $65.00

MURPHY, Richard. *World of Cezanne 1839-1906.* 1959. Time Life. NF/case. H4. $15.00

MURPHY, Robert Cushman. *Logbook for Grace: Whaling Brig Daisy 1912-1913.* 1947. Macmillan. 1st ed. inscr. 8vo. VG. B11. $60.00

MURPHY, Robert F. *Robert H Lowie.* 1972. NY. 1st ed. 179p. AN/dj. P4. $17.50

MURPHY, Shirley Rousea. *Castle of Hope.* 1980. Atheneum. 1st ed. F/F. P3. $15.00

MURPHY, Shirley Rousea. *Catswold Portal.* 1992. Roc. 1st ed. F/F. P3. $22.00

MURPHY, Shirley Rousea. *Flight of the Fox.* 1978. Atheneum. 1st ed. F/F. P3. $15.00

MURPHY, Shirley Rousea. *Nightpool.* nd. Harper Row. 3rd. VG/VG. P3. $12.00

MURPHY, Shirley Rousea. *Soonie & the Dragon.* 1979. Atheneum. 1st ed. F/F. P3. $18.00

MURPHY, Shirley Rousea. *Wolf Bell.* 1979. Atheneum. 1st ed. F/F. P3. $15.00

MURPHY, Thomas D. *New England Highways & Byways From a Motor Car.* 1924. Boston. Page. 1st ed. 8vo. 25 pl. 327p. teg. pict cloth. VG. T10. $45.00

MURPHY, Thomas D. *New England Highways & Byways from a Motor Car.* 1924. Page. ils/map. G+. P12. $15.00

MURPHY, Thomas D. *Seven Wonderlands of the American West.* 1925. Page. 1st ed. 8vo. 32 pl/24 photos/7 maps. 352p. gilt bdg. T10. $115.00

MURPHY, Warren. *Forever King.* 1992. Tor. F/F. P3. $22.00

MURPHY, Warren. *Jericho Day.* 1989. Diamond Books. 1st ed. F/F. P3. $18.00

MURRAY, A.S. *Greek Bronzes.* 1898. London. Seeley. 1st ed. 4to. ils. 104p. T10. $125.00

MURRAY, Albert. *Sea League Boots.* 1995. Pantheon. 1st ed. F/F. M23. $25.00

MURRAY, Albert. *Spyglass Tree.* 1991. Pantheon. 1st ed. F/F. M23. $25.00

MURRAY, Arthur. *Dance Secrets.* 1946. NY. 1st ed. pres. sgn. VG/VG. B5. $32.50

MURRAY, Beatrice; see Posner, Richard.

MURRAY, Cromwell. *Day of the Dead.* 1946. McKay. 1st ed. VG/VG. P3. $20.00

MURRAY, Joan. *Poems by...* 1947. Yale. 1st ed. edit WH Auden. F/NF. V1. $20.00

MURRAY, John Ogden. *Immortal Six Hundred: A Story of Cruelty...* 1911. Roanoke, VA. Stone Prt. 2nd ed. 355p. NF. M8. $150.00

MURRAY, John Wilson. *Memoirs of a Great Canadian Detective.* 1978. Collins. 2nd. VG. P3. $15.00

MURRAY, Lindley. *Power of Religion on the Mind, in Retirement, Affliction...* 1802. NY. Collins. 280p. tree calf. VG. B14. $150.00

MURRAY, Max. *Neat Little Corpse.* nd. Detective BC. VG. P3. $8.00

MURRAY, Pauli. *Dark Testament & Other Poems.* 1970. Silvermine. 1st ed. F/NF clip. B4. $100.00

MURRAY, William H.H. *Adventures in the Wilderness.* 1869. Boston. 1st ed. 236p. gilt gr cloth. NF. B14. $75.00

MURRAY, William. *Getaway Blues.* 1990. Bantam. 1st ed. F/F. P3. $18.00

MURRAY, William. *King of the Nightcap.* 1989. Bantam. 1st ed. VG/VG. P3. $17.00

MURRAY, William. *Sweet Ride.* 1967. WH Allen. VG/VG. P3. $18.00

MURRAY, William. *When the Fat Man Sings.* 1987. Bantam. 1st ed. NF/NF. P3. $15.00

MURRAY. *Caught in the Web of Words...* 1978. Yale. 26 photos. F/VG. A4. $25.00

MURRY, Colin. *Golden Valley.* 1958. Hutchinson. 1st ed. xl. dj. P3. $25.00

MUSIL, Robert. *Five Women.* 1966. Delacorte. 1st ed. NF/NF. B2. $85.00

MUSKE, Carol. *Dear Digby.* 1989. Viking. 1st ed. author's 1st book. rem mk. F/F. H11. $20.00

MUSKE, Carol. *Red Trousseau.* 1993. Viking. 1st ed. sgn. F/NF. V1. $30.00

MUSUR, Harold Q. *Attorney.* 1973. Random. 1st ed. VG/VG. P3. $18.00

MUSUR, Harold Q. *Big Money.* nd. BC. VG/VG. P3. $8.00

MUSUR, Harold Q. *Broker.* 1981. Souvenir. 1st ed. VG/VG. P3. $18.00

MUSUR, Harold Q. *Make a Killing.* nd. BC. VG/VG. P3. $8.00

MUSUR, Harold Q. *Mourning After.* 1981. St Martin. 1st ed. VG/VG. P3. $15.00

MUSUR, Harold Q. *Send Another Hearse.* nd. BC. VG/VG. P3. $8.00

MUSUR, Harold Q. *Tall, Dark & Deadly.* nd. BC. VG/VG. P3. $8.00

MUTER, Gladys. *Little Bim, the Circus Boy.* 1924. Volland. ils Janet Laura Scott. NF. P2. $90.00

MUZIK, T.J. *Weed Biology & Control.* 1970. McGraw Hill. 8vo. 273p. cloth. VG. B1. $18.50

MYER, Albert J. *Manual of Signals.* 1868. Van Nostrand. enlarged ed. 30 pl. 417p. rebound cloth. T7. $95.00

MYERS, Gary. *House of the Worm.* 1975. Arkham. 1st ed. F/F. P3. $20.00

MYERS, Jeffrey. *Painting & the Novel.* 1975. Barnes Noble. ils/pl. 180p. dj. D2. $25.00

MYERS, Joan. *Santiago: Saint of Two Worlds.* 1991. Albuquerque. 1st ed. 4to. 73p. F/F. T10. $50.00

MYERS, John Myers. *Deaths of the Bravos.* 1962. Boston. Little Brn. stated 1st ed. 467p. VG. P4. $20.00

MYERS, Louise W. *Santa Claus & the Little Lost Kitten.* 1952. Whitman. Fuzzy Wuzzy Picture Story Book. VG+. M5. $15.00

MYERS, Robert J. *Cross of Frankenstein.* 1975. Lippincott. 1st ed. VG/VG. P3. $25.00

MYERS, Robert Manson. *Children of Pride & True Story of Georgia & the Civil War.* 1972. Yale. 1st ed. 1845p. VG/VG. B5/M8. $55.00

MYERS, Tamar. *Too Many Crooks Spoil the Broth.* 1994. Doubleday. 1st ed. F/F. H11. $20.00

MYERSON, Joel. *Emily Dickinson: A Descriptive Bibliography.* 1984. Pittsburgh. 1st ed. 8vo. F/sans. A11. $45.00

MYKEL, A.W. *Salamandra Glass.* 1983. NY. 1st ed. F/F. H11. $40.00

MYKEL, A.W. *Salamandra Glass.* 1983. St Martin. 1st ed. NF/NF. P3. $25.00

N.E.S.F.A. *NESFA, Index to the SF Magazines 1966-1970.* 1971. NESFA. 1st ed. hc. F. P3. $25.00

NABB, Magdalen. *Marshal & the Madwoman.* 1988. Scribner. 1st ed. VG/VG. P3. $18.00

NABOKOV, Peter. *Two Leggings: The Making of a Crow Warrior.* 1967. Crowell. 2nd. 8vo. ils/maps/photos. 226p. F/dj. T10. $25.00

NABOKOV, Vladimir. *Book of the Bear.* 1926. Nonesuch. trans Harrison/Mirrlees. ils Garnett. VG. M17. $25.00

NABOKOV, Vladimir. *Lolita.* 1955. Paris. Olympia. 2 vol. 1st ed/2nd issue. NF/gr wrp. C6. $2,000.00

NABOKOV, Vladimir. *Lolita.* 1955. Paris. Olympia. 1st ed/1st issue (900 Francs). 2 vol. NF/prt wrp. B24. $3,000.00

NABOKOV, Vladimir. *Nabokov's Congeries.* 1968. Viking. 1st ed. NF/NF. B4. $85.00

NABOKOV, Vladimir. *Nikolai Gogol.* 1944. Norfolk. 1st ed/1st issue. F/F. C2. $150.00

NABOKOV, Vladimir. *Poems.* 1959. Doubleday. 1st ed. F/NF. B4. $350.00

NABOKOV, Vladimir. *Three Russian Poets: Pushkin, Lermontov, Tyutchev.* 1944. New Directions. 1st ed. NF/VG. B4. $175.00

NADELL, Aaron. *Projecting Sound Pictures.* 1931. McGraw Hill. 1st ed/4th prt. 8vo. 265p. F. T10. $100.00

NADER, George. *Chrome.* 1978. Putnam. 1st ed. VG/VG. P3. $15.00

NADER, Laura. *Harmony Ideology.* 1990. Stanford. 1st ed. 343p. dj. F3. $20.00

NAEF, Weston. *Collection of Alfred Stieglitz.* 1978. NY. VG. V4. $150.00

NAGLE, Jacob. *Nagle Journal: Diary of the Life of Jacob Nagle...* 1988. NY. Weidenfeld Nicholson. 20 pl. 402p. dj. T7. $28.00

NAIPAUL, V.S. *Among the Believers: An Islamic Journey.* 1981. Knopf. 1st trade ed. 430p. VG/dj. W1. $18.00

NAIPAUL, V.S. *Turn in the South.* 1989. Knopf. 1st ed. sgn. F/F. M23. $35.00

NAKAYAMA, Shigeru. *History of Japanese Astronomy.* 1969. Harvard. 1st ed. 8vo. 329p. VG/VG. K5. $30.00

NALSON, John. *Impartial Collection of Great Affairs of State...* 1682-83. London. Mearne. only ed. contemporary calf. M11. $350.00

NANCE, John J. *Pandora's Clock.* 1995. Doubleday. 1st ed. F/F. H11. $25.00

NANSEN, Fridtjof. *Farthest North.* 1898. London. Newnes. 2 vol. 8vo. photos/fld maps/pl. F. T10. $200.00

NASH, Anne. *Cabbages & Crime.* 1945. Crime Club. hc. G. P3. $15.00

NASH, Eleanor Arnett. *Footnote to Life.* 1944. Appleton. 1st ed. inscr. G/worn. B11. $15.00

NASH, Garrett. *Bridge Institute Lesson Manual.* 1968. Waltham. 96p. VG/wrp. S1. $3.00

NASH, Jay Robert. *Dark Fountain.* 1982. A&W. 1st ed. VG/VG. P3. $15.00

NASH, John Henry. *Christmasse Tyde. Being a Collection of Seasonable...* 1907. San Francisco. Elder/Tomoye. 8vo. 114p. F/prt wrp/partial box/case. B24. $200.00

NASH, Ogden. *Everybody Ought To Know.* 1961. Lippincott. 1st ed. assn copy. F/NF. V1. $30.00

NASH, Ogden. *Good Intentions.* 1942. Little Brn. 1st ed. pres. bl cloth. NF/dj. B24. $450.00

NASH, Ogden. *Versus.* nd. Little Brn. VG/VG. P3. $15.00

NASH, Ogden. *You Can't Get There From Here.* nd. Little Brn. VG/VG. P3. $15.00

NASH, Ogden. *You Can't Get There From Here.* 1957. Little Brn. 1st ed. 12mo. 190p. gilt cloth. NF. C14. $40.00

NASHE, Thomas. *Pierce Penilesse, His Supplication.* 1924. Bodley Head. hc. VG. P3. $35.00

NASON, Elias. *Life & Public Services of Henry Wilson.* 1876. Boston. 12mo. 452p. gilt gr cloth. G. T3. $25.00

NASR, Seyyed Hossein. *Three Muslim Sages.* 1976. Delmar, NY. Caravan. 8vo. 185p. VG/wrp. W1. $12.00

NASRALLAH. *United States Corporation Histories, a Bibliography...* 1987. 335p. F. A4. $35.00

NASSER, Gamal Abdul. *Egypt's Liberation.* 1955. Public Affairs. 1st ed. 119p. VG/dj. W1. $16.00

NAST. *Index to Signed Engravings by Thomas Nast...* 1985. NCSA. 12mo. 58p. VG/wrp. T3. $5.00

NASTASE, Ilie. *Breaking Point.* 1986. St Martin. 1st ed. F/F. P3. $16.00

NATHAN, George Jean. *Intimate Notebooks of George Jean Nathan.* 1932. Knopf. 1st ed. F/VG. B4. $85.00

NATHAN, Robert. *Barly Fields.* 1938. Literary Guild. VG. P3. $25.00

NATHAN, Robert. *Heaven & Hell & the Megas Factor.* 1975. Delacorte. 3rd. F/F. P3. $10.00

NATHAN, Robert. *Mr Whittle & the Morning Star.* 1947. Knopf. 1st ed. VG/VG. P3. $20.00

NATHAN, Robert. *River Journey.* 1949. Knopf. 1st ed. VG/VG. P3. $25.00

NATHAN, Robert. *Road of Ages.* 1935. Knopf. 1st ed. VG/VG. P3. $45.00

NATIONAL GEOGRAPHIC SOCIETY. *Alaska: High Roads to Adventure.* 1976. WA. 200p. gray cloth. VG/dj. P4. $12.00

NATIONAL GEOGRAPHIC SOCIETY. *Animals Showing Off.* 1988. NGS. ils Tony Chen. F. B17. $15.00

NATIONAL GEOGRAPHIC SOCIETY. *Explore a Tropical Forest.* 1989. NGS. ils Barbara Gibson. VG. B17. $15.00

NATIONAL GEOGRAPHIC SOCIETY. *Isles of the South Pacific.* 1968. WA. NGS. 212p. VG/worn. P4. $17.50

NATIONAL GEOGRAPHIC SOCIETY. *Whales, Mightly Giants of the Sea.* 1990. NGS. ils Seidler. F. B17. $15.00

NAUD, Yves. *Curse of the Pharoahs Vol 1.* 1977. Eds Ferni. 1st ed. VG/VG. P3. $15.00

NAUD, Yves. *UFO's & Extraterrestrials Volume 1.* 1978. Ferni. VG. P3. $18.00

NAUMOFF, Lawrence. *From Thurberama.* 1990. Chapel Hill. 1st ed. 1/100. sgn. F/wrp. C2. $45.00

NAUMOFF, Lawrence. *Rootie Kazootie.* 1990. FSG. UP. sgn. F/wrp. B4. $100.00

NAVRATILOVA, M. *Total Zone.* 1994. Villard. 1st ed. F/F. A20. $10.00

NAYLOR, Gloria. *Bailey's Cafe.* 1991. HBJ. 1st ed. F/F. H11. $25.00

NAYLOR, Gloria. *Bailey's Cafe.* 1991. HBJ. 1st ed. sgn. F/F. B35. $65.00

NAYLOR, Gloria. *Linden Hills.* 1985. Ticknor Fields. 1st ed. author's 2nd book. F/NF. B4. $50.00

NAYLOR, Gloria. *Mama Day.* 1988. Ticknor Fields. 1st ed. F/clip. H11. $35.00

NAYLOR, Gloria. *Mama Day.* 1988. Ticknor Fields. 1st ed. sgn. F/F. B35. $85.00

NAYLOR, Gloria. *Mama Day.* 1992. HBJ. 1st ed. F/F. B4. $45.00

NAYLOR, Gloria. *Women of Brewster Place.* 1983. Viking. UP. sgn. VG/wrp. B4. $400.00

NAYLOR, Phyllis Reynolds. *Dark of the Tunnel.* 1985. Atheneum. 1st ed. F/F. P3. $12.00

NEAL, Bill. *Southern Cooking.* 1985. UNC. ils. 233p. VG/VG. B10. $15.00

NEALE, Walter. *Life of Ambrose Bierce.* 1929. NY. 1st ed. VG/VG. B5. $50.00

NEALE, Walter. *Sovereignty of the States...* 1910. NY/WA. Neale. 1st ed. 143p. cloth. NF. M8. $250.00

NEARING, H. *Sinister Researches of CP Ransom.* 1954. Doubleday. 1st ed. VG/VG. P3. $35.00

NEARING & NEARING. *Living the Good Life & Man's Search for the Good Life.* 1954. Harborside, ME. Social Science Inst. 1st ed. sgns. F/sans/NF case. N3. $75.00

NEAVE, Airey. *On Trial at Nuremburg.* 1978. Boston. 1st Am ed. 348p. dj. A17. $15.00

NEBENZAHL, Kenneth. *Atlas of Columbus & the Great Discoveries.* 1990. Rand McNally. BOMC. folio. 100 maps. gilt bl cloth. F/F. T10. $75.00

NEBENZAHL, Kenneth. *Atlas of the American Revolution.* 1974. Rand McNally. folio. 54 maps. M/dj. O7. $95.00

NEBENZAHL, Kenneth. *Maps of the Holy Land: Images of Terra Sancta...* 1986. Abbeville. 1st ed. folio. NF/dj. W1. $125.00

NECKER. *Four Centuries of Cat Books, a Bibliography 1570-1970.* 1972. 3000 entries. 518p. F. A4. $135.00

NEELY, Richard. *Accidental Woman.* 1981. HRW. 1st ed. VG/VG. P3. $20.00

NEELY, Richard. *Walter Syndrome.* 1970. McCall. VG/VG. P3. $20.00

NEEPER, Cary. *Place Beyond Man.* 1975. Scribner. 1st ed. F/F. P3. $13.00

NEESE, Robert. *Prison Exposures: First Photos Inside Prison...* 1959. Phil. 1st ed. 4to. 135p. F/VG. N3. $25.00

NEFF, Donald. *Warriors at Suez: Eisenhower Takes America Into Middle East.* 1981. Linden/Simon Schuster. 1st ed. ils. 479p. NF/dj. W1. $18.00

NEFF, Renfreu. *Living Theatre: USA.* 1970. Bobbs Merrill. F/NF. D2. $20.00

NEIDER, Charles. *Great Wrest.* 1958. Coward McCann. 1st ed. ils/maps. 457p. NF/dj. T10. $65.00

NEIHARDT, John G. *Eagle Voice: Authentic Tale of the Sioux Indians.* 1953. London. Andrew Melrose. 1st ed. NF/VG. A18. $75.00

NEIKIRK, Mabel. *Oscar the Trained Seal, Story of Oscar on the Radio.* 1948. Whitman. 4to. F/G. M5. $35.00

NEILL, John R. *Lucky Bucky in Oz.* 1942. Reilly Lee. not 1st ed. blank ep. tan cloth. F. B17. $90.00

NEILL, John R. *Raven.* 1910. Chicago. 1st ed thus. VG. B5. $50.00

NEILL, John R. *Scalawagons of Oz.* 1941. Reilly Lee. hc. fair. P3. $50.00

NEILL, John R. *Scalawagons of Oz.* 1941. Reilly Lee. not 1st ed. pict ep. pict red cloth. VG-. B17. $90.00

NEILL, John R. *Scalawagons of Oz.* 1941. Reilly Lee. 1st ed. ils. 309p. cloth. VG. M20. $92.00

NEILL, John R. *Wonder City of Oz.* 1940. Reilly Lee. not 1st ed. pict tan cloth. VG. B17. $100.00

NEILL, John R. *Wonder City of Oz.* 1940. Reilly Lee. 1st ed. 8vo. red cloth/pict label. F. T10. $250.00

NEITZ, John A. *Old Textbooks.* 1961. Pittsburgh. 1st ed. 8vo. 364p. VG/dj. T10. $75.00

NELSON, C.M. *Barren Harvest.* 1949. Crime Club. 1st ed. G. P3. $6.00

NELSON, Christopher. *Mapping the Civil War: Featuring Rare Maps...* 1992. WA. Starwood. 53 maps. M/dj. O7. $40.00

NELSON, Hugh Lawrence. *Dead Giveaway.* 1950. Rinehart. 1st ed. VG. P3. $13.00

NELSON, James Poyntz. *Balla & Other Virginia Stories.* 1914. Richmond. Bell. inscr. 225p. dj. w/sgn letter. B10. $50.00

NELSON, John Young. *Fifty Years on the Trail.* 1969. Norman, OK. 2nd. 12mo. 291p. F/F. T10. $25.00

NELSON, Paul. *Average Nights.* 1977. Colorado. L'Epevier. 1st ed. F/wrp. V1. $10.00

NELSON, Raymond. *Van Wyck Brooks: A Writer's Life.* 1981. NY. Dutton. 1st ed. 332p. F/dj. P4. $15.00

NEMEROV, Howard. *Sentences.* nd. Chicago. 1st ed. F/wrp. V1. $10.00

NENTWIG, W. *Spiders of Panama.* 1993. Gainesville. Sandhill Crane. 8vo. 274p. new cloth. VG. B1. $35.00

NEPO, Mark. *Fire Without Witness.* 1988. British Am Pub. ARC/1st ed. 406p. F/NF. w/pub letter. V1. $35.00

NEPOS, Cornelius. *Perperam Vulgo Aemilus Probus Dictus de Vita Excellentium...* MDCCLXXI. Lipsiae. 4 fld maps. 472p. all edges red. VG. B14. $300.00

NERO, Robert. *Great Gray Owl.* 1980. WA. 1st ed. ils/index. 167p. VG/VG. B5. $22.50

NERUDA, Pablo. *Five Decades: Poems 1925-1970.* 1974. Grove. 1st/bilingual ed. trans Ben Belitt. F/F. B4. $100.00

NERUDA, Pablo. *Fully Empowered.* 1975. Grove. ARC/1st ed. RS. F/dj. S9. $40.00

NERUDA, Pablo. *Heights of Macchu Picchu.* 1967. FSG. 1st ed. 8vo. NF/dj. S9. $75.00

NERUDA, Pablo. *Pablo Neruda: A New Decade.* 1969. Grove. ARC/1st ed. 8vo. RS. F/F. S9. $45.00

NERUDA, Pablo. *Selected Poems: Bilingual Edition.* 1970. Delacorte. 1st Am ed. F/F. C2. $60.00

NESBIT, E. *Wouldbegoods.* 1902 (1901). Harper. ils R Birch. 313p. pict bdg. VG. P2. $75.00

NESBIT, Troy. *Forest Fire.* nd. Whitman. VG. P3. $8.00

NESBIT, Troy. *Fury & the Mystery at Trapper's Hole.* 1959. Racine. ils. 282p. VG. A17. $6.00

NESBIT, Troy. *Wagon Train.* 1959. Whitman. TVTI. VG. P3. $15.00

NESBIT, Wilbur. *Friend or Two.* 1915. Volland. 1st ed. 12mo. VG. M5. $16.00

NESBIT, Wilbur. *Jolly Kid Book.* nd. Volland. 1st ed. 4to. ils. pict brd. VG. M5. $175.00

NESBIT, Wilbur. *Paths of Long Ago.* 1926. Chicago. Reilly Lee. 1/300. sgn. VG/G case. B11. $30.00

NESBIT, William. *How To Hunt With the Camera.* 1926. NY. photos. 337p. gilt cloth. VG. A17. $30.00

NESBIT, William. *Just Because of You.* 1925. Wise Parslow. 12mo. ils. VG/dj. M5. $12.00

NESBITT, Paul H. *Ancient Mimbrenos...Investigations at Mattocks...* 1931. Beloit College. ils/pl/fld map. 105p. NF. A17. $30.00

NESIS, K.N. *Cephalopods of the World.* 1987. Neptune City. TFH Pub. lg 8vo. 351p. pict brd. NF. B1. $50.00

NETANYAHU, Benjamin. *Fighting Terrorism*. 1995. FSG. ARC/1st ed. w/promo material. F/F. B35. $30.00

NETANYAHU, Benjamin. *Terrorism: How the West Can Win*. 1986. FSG. 1st ed. inscr. F/F. B4. $125.00

NEUBERGER, Maurine. *Smoke Screen: Tobacco & the Public Welfare*. 1963. Englewood. 1st ed. 151p. VG. A13. $20.00

NEUMAN, Fredric. *Maneuvers*. 1983. Dial. 1st ed. rem mk. F/NF. H11. $20.00

NEUMANN, G. *Herman the German*. 1984. NY. 1st ed. VG/VG. B5. $30.00

NEUTRA, Richard. *Survival Through Design*. 1954. Oxford. 8vo. NF/dj. S9. $40.00

NEVILLE, Margot. *Murder of a Nymph*. nd. Detective BC. VG. P3. $8.00

NEVILLE, Vera. *Brownie of the Circus & Other Stories of Today*. 1941. McKay. 1st ed. VG. B17. $10.00

NEVIN, Robert P. *Les Trois Rois*. 1888. Pittsburgh. Eichbaum. 1st ed. inscr to Geo Westinghouse. 12mo. gilt gr cloth. T10. $200.00

NEVINS, Allan. *Civil War Books: A Critical Biography*. 1970. np. 4to. bl cloth. VG/dj. T3. $30.00

NEVINS, Allan. *History of the Bank of NY & Trust Co, 1784-1934*. 1934. NY. private prt. 1st ed. ils. NF. T10. $45.00

NEVINS, Allan. *John D Rockefeller*. 1940. 2 vol. 1st ed. sgn. red bdg. VG. S13. $55.00

NEVINS, Allan. *Ordeal of the Union*. 1973. Scribner. 8vo. 500p. VG/VG. T10. $25.00

NEVINS. *Traditional Marbling*. 1985. np. 1/500. sgn. ils/14 orig sample papers. cloth. A4. $165.00

NEW SYDENHAM SOCIETY. *Atlas of Illustrations of Pathology*. 1877. London. lg 4to. 27 full-p pl. morocco/cloth. B14. $475.00

NEWARK, Tim. *Celtic Warriors 400 BC-AD 1600*. 1986. Blanford. F/F. P3. $15.00

NEWBERRY, Clare Turlay. *Cousin Toby*. 1939. Harper. 1st ed. ils. yel pict brd. VG/VG. D1. $120.00

NEWBERRY, Clare Turlay. *Mittens*. (1936). Harper. ils. 29p. pict brd. G+. T5. $30.00

NEWBERRY, Clare Turlay. *Pandora*. 1944. Harper. 1st ed. ils. VG/VG. P2. $75.00

NEWBERRY, Clare Turlay. *T-Bone the Babysitter*. 1950. Harper. probable 1st ed. VG. M5. $45.00

NEWBIGIN, Marion I. *Mediterranean Lands: Intro Study in Human & Hist Geography*. 1924. Knopf. 1st ed. 8vo. 16 maps. VG. W1. $12.00

NEWBY, P.H. *Egypt Story: Its Art, Its Monuments, Its People...* ca 1970. Heritage. 1st ed. 4to. 260p. VG/dj. W1. $16.00

NEWCOMB, Charles G. *Smoke Hole*. 1968. Naylor. 1st ed. 8vo. 198p. F/dj. T10. $35.00

NEWCOMB, Covelle. *Secret Door: Story of Kate Greenaway*. 1946. Dodd Mead. 1st ed. 162p. gr cloth. VG/G+. T5. $75.00

NEWCOMB, Covelle. *Silver Saddles*. 1951. Longman Gr. VG/fair. O3. $18.00

NEWCOMB, Simon. *Compendium of Spherical Astronomy*. 1960. Dover. rpt. pb. 8vo. 444p. K5. $12.00

NEWCOMB, Simon. *Side-Lights on Astronomy*. 1906 (1882). harper. photos. 350p. cloth. K5. $35.00

NEWELL, Gordon. *Ocean Liners of the 20th Century*. 1963. WA. Superior. 1st ed. G/dj. A16. $25.00

NEWELL, Peter. *Hole Book*. 1908. Harper. 1st ed. 8vo. cloth/pict label. F/rare dj/chemise/case. B24. $3,000.00

NEWELL, Peter. *Pictures & Rhymes*. 1899. Harper. 1st ed. 50 pl. VG. P2. $225.00

NEWELL, Peter. *Rocket Book*. nd. np. G+. M17. $100.00

NEWELL, Peter. *Rocket Book*. 1912. Harper. 1st ed. VG. P2. $250.00

NEWELL, Peter. *Slant Book*. 1910. Harper. 1st ed. ils. G. P2. $130.00

NEWELL, Richard S. *Politics of Afghanistan*. 1972. Cornell. 1st ed. 8vo. ils/tables. VG/dj. W1. $18.00

NEWHALL, Beaumont. *Beaumont Newhall: In Plain Sight*. 1983. Salt Lake City. 1st ed. inscr/dtd 1985. VG/clip. S9. $100.00

NEWHALL, Beaumont. *Photographer of the Southwest*. nd. Bonanza. 1st ed thus. 92 pl. F/dj. S9. $65.00

NEWHAN, Ross. *California Angels*. 1982. Simon Schuster. 1st ed. F/F. P8. $20.00

NEWMAN, Bernard. *Turkish Crossroads*. 1951. London. Hale. 1st ed. 8vo. ils/maps. 258p. VG. W1. $20.00

NEWMAN, E.M. *Seeing Egypt & the Holy Land*. 1928. Funk Wagnall. 1st ed. 394p. xl. VG. W1. $35.00

NEWMAN, Edwin. *Civil Tongue*. 1976. Bobbs Merrill. 1st ed. inscr. 207p. F/dj. B14. $60.00

NEWMAN, Eric P. *Early Paper Money of America*. 1976. np. Bicentennial ed. 4to. 416p. brn cloth. F/dj. T3. $30.00

NEWMAN, G.F. *Sir, You Bastard*. 1970. Simon Schuster. 1st ed. stp on ffe. F/F. H11. $20.00

NEWMAN, Kim. *Jago: A Novel of Horror*. 1993. Carroll Graf. 1st Am ed. F/F. T2. $20.00

NEWMAN, Kim. *Night Mayor*. 1989. London. Simon Schuster. 1st ed. author's 1st novel. F/F. T2. $25.00

NEWMAN, Kim. *Night Mayor*. 1989. Simon Schuster. 1st ed. sgn. F/F. P3. $30.00

NEWMAN, Paul S. *Shadowdown on Front Street*. 1969. Whitman. TVTI. VG. P3. $8.00

NEWMAN, Paul. *Hill of the Dragon*. 1979. Bath. Kinsmead. 1st ed. 8vo. 275p. T10. $75.00

NEWMAN, Sharan. *Death Comes As Epiphany*. 1993. NY. Tor. 1st ed. author's 1st mystery. sgn. F/F. T2. $35.00

NEWMAN, Sharan. *Devil's Door*. 1994. Forge. 1st ed. sgn. F/F. T2. $30.00

NEWQUIST, Don. *Counterpoint*. 1st ltd ed. sgn. VG/VG. B30. $30.00

NEWTON, A. Edward. *Amenities of Book Collecting*. 1918. np. 1st imp. 376p. VG+. A4. $65.00

NEWTON, A. Edward. *Bibliograph & Pseudo Bibliography*. 1936. PA U. 1st VG. A4. $55.00

NEWTON, A. Edward. *Derby Day & Other Adventures*. 1934. np. 1/1129. sgn. 726 pl. 1p. VG/dj. A4. $75.00

NEWTON, A. Edward. *Doctor Johnson: A Play*. 1923. np. 9 portraits. 137p. VG. A4. $25.00

NEWTON, A. Edward. *End Papers: Literary Recreations*. 1933. np. 1/1351. inscr. ils. 249p. NF. A4. $85.00

NEWTON, A. Edward. *Greatest Book in the World & Other Papers*. 1925. np. ils. 468p. VG. A4. $15.00

NEWTON, A. Edward. *Magnificent Farce & Other Diversions of a Book Collector*. 1921. np. 50 pl/18 ils. 287p. VG/dj. A4. $25.00

NEWTON, A. Edward. *Newton on Blackstone*. 1937. PA U. 1/2000. sgn. 38p. F/VG. A4. $45.00

NEWTON, A. Edward. *Pope, Poetry & Portrait*. 1936. Oak Knoll. ils. 25p. F/bl wrp. A4. $40.00

NEWTON, A. Edward. *Tourist in Spite of Himself*. 1930. Little Brn. 3rd. 8vo. 252p. F/NF. T10. $35.00

NEWTON, Corsette Faust. *Great American Accident.* 1951. Dallas. Story Book. 1st ed. NF/NF. B4. $85.00

NEWTON, Janet. *Las Positas: Story of Robert & Josefa Livermore.* 1969. Newton. Livermore. 8vo. sgn. ils/map ep. 195p. yel cloth. NF. T10. $35.00

NEWTON, Richard. *Rambles in Bible Lands.* 1892. Nelson. 12mo. ils. 346p. VG. W1. $35.00

NG, Fae Myenne. *Bone.* 1993. Hyperion. 1st ed. author's 1st novel. F/F. B4. $50.00

NICHIREN. *Selected Writings of Nichiren.* 1990. NY. Columbia. 1st ed. 508p. NF/VG. P4. $20.00

NICHOLAS, James Lynn. *Confederate Engineers.* 1957. Confederate Pub. 1st ed. 122p. VG. M8. $150.00

NICHOLAS, Margaret. *World's Greatest Cranks & Crackpots.* 1982. Octopus. VG. P3. $15.00

NICHOLLS, Philip. *Homeopathy & the Medical Profession.* 1988. London. 1st ed. 298p. dj. A13. $30.00

NICHOLLS. *Science Fiction Encyclopedia.* 1979. np. ils. 672p. NF/VG. A4. $125.00

NICHOLS, George Ward. *Story of the Great March From the Diary of a Staff Officer.* 1865. NY. 1st ed. fld map. 394p. half leather. VG. B18. $65.00

NICHOLS, Jeannette. *Emblems of Passage.* 1968. Rutgers. 1st ed. F/NF. V1. $15.00

NICHOLS, John. *American Blood.* 1987. Holt. 1st ed. sgn. F/F. A20. $27.00

NICHOLS, John. *Elegy for September.* 1992. Holt. 1st ed. rem mk. F/closed tear. H4. $25.00

NICHOLS, John. *Ghost in the Music.* 1979. HRW. 1st ed. sgn. VG/VG. A20. $28.00

NICHOLS, John. *Keep It Simple.* 1992. Norton. 1st ed. sgn. F/F. A20. $33.00

NICHOLS, John. *Sterile Cuckoo.* 1965. McKay. 1st ed. author's 1st book. F/dj. A18. $80.00

NICHOLS, Leigh; see Koontz, Dean R.

NICHOLS, Ruth Alexander. *Billy.* 1934. NY. 1st ed. ils. 48p. G. A17. $12.50

NICHOLS, Ruth. *Left-Handed Spirit.* 1978. Macmillan of Canada. VG/VG. P3. $15.00

NICHOLS, Ruth. *Song of the Pearl.* 1976. Macmillan of Canada. 1st ed. F/F. P3. $20.00

NICHOLS & PROULX. *Complete Dairy Foods Cookbook: How To Make Everything...* 1982. Rodale. 1st ed. 4to. F. B4. $375.00

NICHOLS & PROULX. *Sweet & Hard Cider: Making It, Using It & Enjoying It.* 1980. Garden Way. 1st ed. xl. NF. B4. $200.00

NICHOLSEN. *People in Books, a Selective Guide...* 1969. HW Wilson. 4to. 516p. VG. A4. $95.00

NICHOLSON, Kenyon. *Barker.* nd. Grosset Dunlap. MTI. VG. P3. $25.00

NICHOLSON, Lois P. *Babe Ruth: Sultan of Swat.* 1994. Goodwood. 1st ed. AN/dj P8. $20.00

NICHOLSON, Norman. *Five Rivers.* 1945. Dutton. 1st ed. F/NF. V1. $15.00

NICHOLSON, Reynold A. *Mystics of Islam.* 1970. Routledge/Kegan Paul. 12mo. 178p. VG. W1. $20.00

NICHOLSON & SEBERT. *Maps of Canada: Guide to Official Canadian Maps...* 1981. Folkestone. Dawson. 74 ils/tables. M. O7. $50.00

NICHOLSON. *Catalogue of Lib of Brevet Lieutenant-Colonel JP Nicholson.* nd.. 1st/only rpt. 1/150. 1022p. F. A4. $165.00

NICKELL, Joe. *Secrets of the Supernatural.* 1990. Prometheus. 4th. VG. P3. $10.00

NICOL, Eric. *Say Uncle.* 1961. Harper. VG/VG. P3. $10.00

NICOL, Eric. *Space Age Go Home!* 1961. Harper. 3rd. VG/VG. P3. $10.00

NICOL, Walter. *Gardener's Kalendar; or, Monthly Directory of Operations...* 1822. Edinburgh. Constable. 4th. 646p. contemporary cloth. VG. A10. $85.00

NICOLL, M.J. *Three Voyages of a Naturalist.* 1908. London. Witherby. 56p. 246p. VG. T7. $95.00

NICOLSON, Harold. *War Years 1939-45.* 1967. BC. 511p. dj. A17. $9.50

NICOLSON, Iain. *Simple Astronomy.* 1973. Scribner. ils Don Pottinger. 64p. VG/dj. K5. $10.00

NICOLSON, John. *Arizona of Joseph Pratt Allyn: Letters From a Pioneer Judge.* 1974. AZ U. 1st ed. 284p. AN/dj. P4. $18.50

NIDA, Eugene A. *Morphology: Descriptive Analysis of Words.* 1963. Ann Arbor. 2nd ed/8th prt. 342p. VG/stiff wrp. W1. $20.00

NIELSEN, Helen. *Fifth Caller.* 1959. Morrow. VG/fair. P3. $12.00

NIELSEN, Helen. *Killer in the Street.* 1967. Morrow. 1st ed. VG. P3. $13.00

NIELSEN, Helen. *Verdict Suspended.* 1964. Morrow. 1st ed. xl. dj. P3. $6.00

NIELSEN, Torben. *Gallowsbird's Song.* 1976. Collins Crime Club. 1st ed. VG/VG. P3. $15.00

NIERENBERG, W.A. *Encyclopedia of Earth System Science Vol 4, Ri-Z Index.* 1992. San Diego. Academic Pr. 715p. VG. D8. $20.00

NIETZ. *Evolution of American Secondary School Textbooks...* 1966. np. 28 pl. 305p. F. A4. $125.00

NIETZ. *Old Textbooks: Spelling, Grammar, Reading, Arithmetic...* 1961. Pittsburgh. 373p. VG. A4. $125.00

NIGGLI, Josephina. *Mexican Village.* 1945. Chapel Hill. 4th. 491p. dj. F3. $15.00

NIGHTINGALE, Florence. *Notes on Nursing: What It Is & What It Is Not.* 1860. NY. 1st Am ed. 140p. NF. M8. $450.00

NILES, Blair. *Colombia, Land of Miracles.* 1924. NY. Century. 1st ed. sgn. 8vo. 389p. VG/VG. B11. $40.00

NILES, Douglas. *Dungeoneer's Survival Guide.* 1986. Tsr. hc. F. P3. $15.00

NIMS, John Frederick. *Iron Pastoral.* 1947. Wm Sloan. 1st ed. poet's 1st book. sgn. F/NF. V1. $75.00

NIMUENDAJU, Curt. *Apinaye.* 1939. Catholic U of Am. 189p. wrp. F3. $35.00

NIN, Anais. *Children of the Albatross.* 1959. Owen. 1st Eng ed. F/NF. M19. $75.00

NIN, Anais. *Ladders to Fire.* 1946. NY. 1st ed. VG/G. B5. $55.00

NIN, Anais. *Paris Revisited.* Capra. 1st ed. 1/250. sgn. F. M19. $125.00

NININGER, H.H. *Arizona's Meteorite Crater: Past, Present, Future.* 1956. Sedona, AZ. Am Meteorite Mus. 8vo. 232p. VG/dj. K5. $70.00

NISSEN, Claus. *Die Botanische Buchillustration, Ihre Geschiechte...* nd. 2 vol in 1. rpt of 1951-52 ed. 1/225. 4to. F. A4. $165.00

NISSEN, Claus. *Die Illustrierten Vogelbucher, Ihre Geschichte...* nd. rpt of 1953 ed. 1/150. 1031 entries. F. A4. $125.00

NISTER, Ernest. *Toy Model Book.* ca 1850s. Dutton/Nister. 6 cut-out p. VG/wrp. D1. $285.00

NIVEN, David. *Go Slowly, Come Back Quickly.* 1981. Doubleday. 1st ed. w/sgn leaf. F/F. B2. $65.00

NIVEN, Larry. *Archilles' Choice.* 1991. Tor. 1st ed. VG/VG. P3. $16.00

NIVEN, Larry. *Footfall.* 1985. Del Rey. 1st ed. F/F. P3. $18.00

NIVEN, Larry. *Gripping Hand.* 1993. Pocket. 1st ed. F/F. P3. $22.00

NIVEN, Larry. *Integral Trees.* 1984. Del Rey. 1st ed. VG/VG. P3. $15.00

NIVEN, Larry. *Legacy of Heorot.* 1987. Simon Schuster. 1st ed. F/F. P3. $18.00

NIVEN, Larry. *N-Space.* 1990. Tor. 1st ed. F/F. M21/P3. $20.00

NIVEN, Larry. *Playgrounds of the Mind.* 1991. Tor. 1st ed. F/F. P3. $23.00

NIVEN, Larry. *Ringworld Engineers.* 1980. HRW. 1st ed. F/F. P3. $30.00

NIVEN, Larry. *Smoke Ring.* 1987. Del Rey. 1st ed. F/F. P3. $18.00

NIVEN, Larry. *World Out of Time.* nd. HRW. 2nd. VG/VG. P3. $13.00

NIVEN & POURNELLE. *Oath of Fealty.* 1981. Timescape. 1st trade ed. rem mk. F/NF. G10. $10.00

NIXON, Pat. *Century of Medicine in San Antonio.* 1936. San Antonio. 1st ed. 405p. VG. A13. $65.00

NIXON, Richard. *Leaders.* 1982. Warner. 1st ed. sgn. F/F. B2. $150.00

NIXON, Richard. *Memoirs of...* 1978. NY. 1st ed. sgn. NF/case. C6. $195.00

NIZAN, Paul. *Watchdogs: Philosophers & the Established Order.* 1971. Monthly Review. 1st ed. F/F. B35. $31.00

NIZER, Louis. *What To Do With Germany.* 1944. Chicago. Ziff Davis. G/worn. M11. $45.00

NOBILE, V. *Polar Flights.* 1961. NY. 1st ed. F/F. B5. $30.00

NOEL, Arlene. *Cinderella.* 1973. Hallmark. moveables. G+. P2. $25.00

NOEL, Theophilus. *Autobiography & Reminiscences of Theophilus Noel.* 1904. Chicago. Theo Noel. 1st ed. 348p. cloth. VG. M8. $175.00

NOELL, Mae. *History of Noell's Ark Gorilla Show.* 1979. Noell's Ark Pub. sgn. 8vo. 246p. F/VG. B11. $25.00

NOGUERES, Henri. *Munich, Peace for Our Time.* 1965. NY. 423p. F/dj. A17. $15.00

NOLAN, Frederick. *Lincoln County War.* 1992. Norman, OK. 1st ed. lg 8vo. 607p. F/dj. T10. $65.00

NOLAN, William F. *Black Mask Boys: Masters in Hard-Boiled School Dectective...* 1985. Morrow. 1st ed. sgn. F/F. T2. $25.00

NOLAN, William F. *Black Mask Murders.* 1994. St Martin. 1st ed. F/F. P3. $20.00

NOLAN, William F. *Death Is for Losers.* 1968. Los Angeles. Sherbourne. 1st ed. sgn orig drawing on ffe. F/F. T2. $65.00

NOLAN, William F. *Hammett: Life at the Edge.* 1983. Congdon Weed. 1st ed. F/F. T2. $20.00

NOLAN, William F. *Hammett: Life at the Edge.* 1983. NY. 1st ed. sgn. F/F. A11. $45.00

NOLAN, William F. *Ray Bradbury Review.* 1952. San Diego. 1st ed. sgn Nolan/inscr Bradbury. F/clip. C2. $125.00

NOLL, Bink. *Feast.* 1967. Harcourt Brace. 1st ed. assn copy. F/NF. V1. $15.00

NOLL, Edward M. *Hamm & CB Antenna Dimension Charts.* 1977. New Augusta, IN. 5th. 64p. VG. P4. $10.00

NONTE, George C. *Modern Handloading.* 1974. Winchester. ils. NF/VG. P12. $12.50

NONTE, George C. *Pistol & Revolver Guide.* 1975. Stoeger Pub. ils. VG. P12. $10.00

NOON, Jeff. *Vurt.* 1993. Crown. 1st ed. author's 1st book. F/F. H11. $30.00

NOONE, Edwina; see Avallone, Mike.

NORDAN, Lewis. *Welcome to the Arrow Catcher Fair.* 1983. LSU. 1st ed. author's 1st book. F/F. B4. $650.00

NORDHOFF, Charles. *Crossing the Line: Cruise on a Whaler; A Book for Boys.* ca 1899. Edinburgh. 190p. G. A17. $10.00

NORDHOFF, Charles. *History of Playing Cards.* 1977. Buffalo. 1/250. ils. 48p. orang pict cloth. F. B24. $75.00

NORDMANN, Charles. *Tyranny of Time: Einstein or Bergson?* 1925. NY. Internat Pub. trans EE Fournier d'Albe. 217p. cloth. G. K5. $20.00

NORDON, Pierre. *Conan Doyle.* 1966. John Murray. 1st ed. VG/VG. P3. $30.00

NORFOLK, Lawrence. *Lemprierre's Dictionary.* 1991. London. Sinclair-Stevenson. 1st ed. author's 1st book. F/F. B4. $125.00

NORFOLK, William; see Farmer, Philip Jose.

NORMAN, Barry. *Matter of Mandrake.* 1968. Walker. 1st ed. VG/VG. P3. $13.00

NORMAN, Charles. *Case of Ezra Pound.* 1948. NY. 1st ed. F/wrp. A9. $40.00

NORMAN, D. *Illustrated Encyclopedia of Dinosaurs.* 1985. Salamander Books. 208p. cloth. AN/dj. D8. $30.00

NORMAN, Frank. *Too Many Crooks Spoil the Caper.* 1979. St Martin. 1st ed. VG/VG. P3. $15.00

NORMAN, Howard. *Northern Lights.* 1987. Summit. 1st ed. author's 1st novel. RS. F/NF. w/promo letter. C2. $150.00

NORMAN, Howard. *Owl-Scatterer.* 1986. Atlantic Monthly. 1st ed. ils Michael McCurdy. F/F. B4. $175.00

NORMAN, Marc. *Oklahoma Crude.* 1973. Dutton. 1st ed. F/F. A18. $10.00

NORMAN, Philip. *Elton John: The Biography.* 1991. Harmony. 1st ed. VG/VG. P3. $23.00

NORRIS, Kathleen. *Dakota: A Spiritual Geography.* 1993. Ticknor Fields. 1st ed. F/F. M23. $40.00

NORRIS, Kathleen. *Fun of Being a Mother.* 1927. Doubleday. 1st ed. 31p. F/NF clip. B4. $50.00

NORRIS, Kathleen. *Lucky Lawrences.* 1930. Doubleday Doran. 1st ed. F/NF. B4. $60.00

NORTH, Darian. *Criminal Seduction.* 1993. Dutton. 1st ed. author's 1st book. NF/dj. H11. $25.00

NORTH, Eric. *Ant Men.* 1960. HRW. 2nd. VG. P3. $15.00

NORTH, Howard. *Expressway.* 1973. Collins. 1st ed. VG/VG. P3. $20.00

NORTH, Marianne. *Vision of Eden, the Life & Work of Exeter, Webb & Bower.* 1980. np. 240p. AN/dj. A10. $35.00

NORTH, Oliver. *Under Fire.* 1991. NY. 3rd. inscr. F/dj. A15. $20.00

NORTH, Sterling. *Five Busy Bears.* 1962 (1955). Rand McNally. Elf Book. 8vo. VG. M5. $12.00

NORTH, Sterling. *Five Little Bears.* 1955. RAnd McNally. Elf Book. 1st ed thus. 8vo. ils. VG+. M5. $20.00

NORTH, Sterling. *Greased Lightning.* 1940. Winston. 1st ed. ils Kurt Wiese. NF/NF. P2. $75.00

NORTH, Sterling. *Midnight & Jeremy.* 1943. Winston. 1st ed. ils Kurt Wiese. VG/G+. P2. $55.00

NORTHEN, Rebecca Tyson. *Home Orchid Growing.* 1970. Van Nostrand Reinhold. 3rd. sgn. 4to. F/F. B11. $50.00

NORTHEN, Rebecca Tyson. *Miniature Orchids.* 1980. Van Nostrand. 4to. ils/photos. 189p. hc. VG. B1. $25.00

NORTHOUSE. *First Printings of Texas Authors.* 1982. np. 1/500. 4to. ils. 96p. VG. A4. $50.00

NORTHRUP, Marguerite. *Christmas Story From the Gospels of Matthew & Luke.* 1966. NYGS. 4to. VG/VG. B17. $7.50

NORTON, Alice; see Norton, Andre Alice.

NORTON, Andre Alice. *Anroid at Arms.* 1971. HBJ. 1st ed. NF/NF. P3. $85.00

NORTON, Andre Alice. *Dare To Go A-Hunting.* 1990. Tor. 1st ed. VG/VG. P3. $20.00

NORTON, Andre Alice. *Dark Piper.* 1968. HBW. 1st ed. xl. dj. P3. $13.00

NORTON, Andre Alice. *Dread Companion.* 1970. HBJ. 1st ed. 8vo. F/dj. T10. $75.00

NORTON, Andre Alice. *Flight in Yiktor.* 1986. Tor. 1st ed. F/F. P3. $15.00

NORTON, Andre Alice. *Forerunner: The Second Venture.* 1985. Tor. 1st ed. NF/NF. P3. $15.00

NORTON, Andre Alice. *Garan the Eternal.* 1972. Fantasy. 1st ed. F/F. P3. $40.00

NORTON, Andre Alice. *Gate of the Cat.* 1987. Ace. 1st ed. F/F. P3. $17.00

NORTON, Andre Alice. *Iron Cage.* 1974. Viking. 1st ed. F/F. P3. $35.00

NORTON, Andre Alice. *Judgment on Janus.* 1971. Gollancz. 3rd. xl. dj. P3. $10.00

NORTON, Andre Alice. *Lord of Thunder.* nd. HBW. 6th. xl. dj. P3. $10.00

NORTON, Andre Alice. *Opal-Eyed Fan.* 1977. Dutton. 1st ed. VG/VG. P3. $20.00

NORTON, Andre Alice. *Opal-Eyed Fan.* 1977. Dutton. 1st ed. 8vo. F/dj. T10. $50.00

NORTON, Andre Alice. *Operation Time Search.* 1967. HBW. 1st ed. xl. dj. P3. $13.00

NORTON, Andre Alice. *Small Shadows Creep.* 1974. Dutton. 1st ed. F/F. P3. $15.00

NORTON, Andre Alice. *Trey of Swords.* 1977. Grosset Dunlap. 1st ed. VG/VG. P3. $25.00

NORTON, Andre Alice. *Victory on Janus.* 1966. HBW. 1st ed. VG/VG. M20/P3. $80.00

NORTON, Andre Alice. *Wizards' Worlds.* 1989. Tor. 1st ed. NF/NF. P3. $20.00

NORTON, Andre Alice. *Wraiths of Time.* 1976. Atheneum. 2nd. F/F. P3. $15.00

NORTON, Andre; see Norton, Andre Alice.

NORTON, Mary. *Borrowers Afield.* 1955. Harcourt Brace. 1st Am ed. 215p. VG/dj. M20. $57.00

NORTON, Mary. *Borrowers Afloat.* 1959. Harcourt Brace. 1st Am ed. 191p. cloth. VG/dj. M20. $37.00

NORTON, Olive. *Corpse-Bird Cries.* 1971. Cassell. 1st ed. VG/VG. P3. $18.00

NORTON & SHWARTZ. *Imperial Lady.* 1989. Tor. 1st ed. F/F. P3. $20.00

NORTON. *New England Planters in the Maritime Provinces of Canada.* 1993. Toronto. 4to. 2181 annotated entries. 403p. F. A4. $125.00

NORTON. *100 Years of Collecting in America. Story of Sotheby...* 1984. F/F. D2. $35.00

NORVELL, Anthony. *Mind Cosmology.* 1972. Parker. 3rd. VG. P3. $15.00

NORVIL, Manning; see Bulmer, Kenneth.

NORVILLE, Barbara. *Writing the Modern Mystery.* 1987. Writer's Digest Books. 2nd. VG/VG. P3. $20.00

NORWICH, Oscar I. *Maps of Africa: Illustrated & Annotated Carto-Bibliography.* 1983. Johannesburg. Donker Capetown/Delta. 370 maps. M/dj. O7. $300.00

NORWOOD, Frank. *Burning.* 1995. Dial. 1st ed. sgn. F/dj. S9. $35.00

NOTLEY, Alfred. *Letter to Lucian & Other Poems.* 1957. Lippincott. 1st ed. F/F double dj. V1. $25.00

NOTLEY, Alice. *Margaret & Dusty.* 1985. Coffee House. 1st ed. F/wrp. V1. $15.00

NOTT, Charles C. *Sketches of the War.* 1865. NY. 12mo. 174p. teg. G. T3. $45.00

NOTT, Charles Stanley. *Chinese Jades in the Stanley Charles Nott Collection.* 1942. W Palm Beach. Norton Gallery. 1/1000. sgn. 118 pl. later gr morocco. T10. $450.00

NOURSE, Alan E. *Fourth Horseman.* 1983. Harper Row. 1st ed. VG/VG. P3. $18.00

NOURSE, Alan E. *Intern.* nd. BC. VG/VG. P3. $5.00

NOVA, Craig. *Trombone.* 1992. Grove Weidenfeld. 1st ed. F/F. H11. $20.00

NOWARRA, Heinz J. *Pictorial History of Luftwaffe, Vol II 1915-18.* 1964. Genoa, Italy. Eng/Italian/German text. 231p. VG/dj. B18. $25.00

NOWELL, Charles E. *Rose-Colored Map: Portugal's Attempt To Build...* 1982. Lisboa. Junta Investigacoes Cientificas Ultramar. 6 maps. F/dj. O7. $125.00

NOWELL, Elizabeth. *Letters of Thomas Wolfe.* 1956. np. 797p. VG/dj. A4. $65.00

NOWELL, Elizabeth. *Thomas Wolf: A Biography.* 1960. Doubleday. 456p. VG. B10. $15.00

NOXON, Alan. *Attack on Vienna.* 1972. St Martin. 1st ed. F/F. P3. $13.00

NOXON, Alan. *Item 7.* 1970. Simon Schuster. 1st ed. F/F. P3. $13.00

NOY, William. *Principal Grounds & Maxims With an Analysis...* 1821. London. later ed. contemporary quarter calf. G. M11. $350.00

NOYED, Alexander D. *Market Place: Reminiscences of a Financial Editor.* 1938. Little Brn. 1st ed. 384p. gr/yel cloth. F. B22. $9.00

NULAND, Sherwin. *Doctors: The Biography of Medicine.* 1988. NY. 1st ed. 519p. VG. A13. $30.00

NUMBERS, Ronald. *Education of American Physicians.* 1980. Los Angeles. 345p. dj. A13. $35.00

NUNEZ URETA, Teodoro. *La Vida del Gente. Acuarelas y Dibujos del Peru...* 1982. Lima, Peru. Banco de la Nacion. sgn/dtd. 208p. tan leather. D2. $85.00

NUNN, Kem. *Pomona Queen.* 1992. Pocket. 1st ed. F/F. A20. $25.00

NUNN, Kem. *Tapping the Source.* 1984. Delacorte. 1st ed. F/NF. H11. $55.00

NUNN, Kem. *Unassigned Territory.* 1978. Delacorte. 1st ed. F/NF. H11. $35.00

NUTE, Grace. *Lake Superior.* 1944. Indianapolis. 1st ed. VG/VG. B5. $45.00

NUTINI, Hugo. *Tados Santos in Rural Tlaxcala.* 1988. Princeton. 1st ed. 471p. F3. $25.00

NUTT, Alfred. *Studies on the Legend of the Holy Grail...* 1888. London. David Nutt. 1st ed. 8vo. 281p. VG. C2. $100.00

NUTTING, Wallace. *Clock Book.* 1924. Old Am Co. photos. VG. M17. $50.00

NUTTING, Wallace. *Furniture Treasury.* 1948-1949. NY. 3 vol. Vol 1+2 in box. VG/VG. B5. $90.00

NUTTING, Wallace. *Massachusetts Beautiful.* 1935. Garden City. sgn. 8vo. 254p. G/fair. B11. $65.00

NUTTING, Wallace. *Virginia Beautiful.* 1930. Old Am Co. 330 ils. VG. P12. $35.00

NYBERG & ZACKE. *On the Dragon Seas.* 1935. London. Hurst Blackett. sgn Nyberg. 8vo. 287p. VG. B11. $25.00

NYE, Robert. *Falstaff.* 1976. Hamish Hamilton. 1st ed. NF/NF. P3. $25.00

NYE, Robert. *Merlin.* 1979. NY. 1st ed. F/F. N3. $25.00

NYE, Robert. *Merlin.* 1979. Putnam. 1st ed. VG/VG. P3. $20.00

NYE, Robert. *Voyage of Destiny.* 1982. Putnam. 1st ed. hc. VG/VG. P3. $15.00

O

O'BANNON. *Oriental Rugs: A Bibliography.* 1994. np. 2875 entries. 753p. F. A4. $95.00

O'BRIAN, Patrick. *HMS Surprise.* 1973. Lippincott. 1st Am ed. F/NF. B4. $450.00

O'BRIAN, Patrick. *Mauritius Command.* 1977. Stein Day. 1st ed. F/F clip. B4. $450.00

O'BRIAN, Patrick. *Post Captain.* 1972. London. Collins. 1st Eng ed. F/NF. B4. $1,500.00

O'BRIAN, Patrick. *Testimonies.* 1952. Harcourt Brace. 1st Am ed. author's 1st novel. F/F. B4. $750.00

O'BRIAN, Patrick. *Wine-Dark Sea.* 1993. Norton. 1st Am ed. sgn. F/F. w/author's bookmark. B4. $250.00

O'BRIEN, C. *From Three Yachts.* 1950. Rupert Hart Davis. 239p. dj. T7. $24.00

O'BRIEN, Flann. *Poor Mouth: A Bad Story About the Hard Life.* 1974. Viking. 1st Am ed. ils Ralph Steadman. F/NF wht dj. B4. $100.00

O'BRIEN, Flann. *Third Policeman.* 1967. Walker. 1st Am ed. F/NF. B2. $45.00

O'BRIEN, Frederick. *White Shadows in the South Seas.* 1924. NY. Century. 8vo. 7 pl. cloth. VG. W1. $10.00

O'BRIEN, Howard V. *Notes for a Book About Mexico.* 1937. Willett Clark. 1st ed. sgn. 12mo. F/G. B11. $30.00

O'BRIEN, John. *Leaving Las Vegas.* 1990. Wichita. Watermark. 1st ed. sgn. author's 1st novel. AN/dj. B4. $500.00

O'BRIEN, N. *Revolution From the Heart.* 1987. Oxford. 1st ed. sgn. 310p. VG/dj. W1. $18.00

O'BRIEN, Sharon. *Willa Cather: The Emerging Voice.* 1987. Oxford. 1st ed. F/F. P3. $30.00

O'BRIEN, Tim. *In the Lake of the Woods.* 1994. Houghton Mifflin. 1st ed. F/F. T2. $25.00

O'BRIEN, Tim. *Nuclear Age.* 1985. Knopf. 1st ed. F/F. M19. $25.00

O'BRIEN, Tim. *Things They Carried.* 1990. Houghton Mifflin. 1st ed. F/F. M19. $35.00

O'BRIEN. *Herbert Hoover: A Bibliography.* 1993. np. 2643 annotated entries. 401p. F. A4. $75.00

O'CALLAGHAN, E.B. *Documentary History of the State of NY.* 1849880. Albany. Weed Parsons. 3 vol. 1st ed. fld ils. VG+. H7. $85.00

O'CALLAGHAN, E.B. *Lists of Inhabitants of Colonial New York.* 1979. Baltimore. G. V4. $25.00

O'CONNELL, Carol. *Mallory's Oracle.* 1994. Putnam. AP/1st Am ed. author's 1st book. F/wrp. T2. $40.00

O'CONNELL, Carol. *Mallory's Oracle.* 1994. Putnam. UP. RS. F/wrp. M23. $40.00

O'CONNELL, Carol. *Mallory's Oracle.* 1994. Putnam. 1st ed. F/F. M23. $30.00

O'CONNELL, Jack. *Box Nine.* 1992. Mysterious. 1st ed. author's 1st novel. AN/dj. M22. $40.00

O'CONNELL, Jack. *Wireless.* 1993. Mysterious. 1st ed. F/F. P3. $20.00

O'CONNOR, Betty. *Better Homes & Gardens Story Book.* 1950. Meredeth. 4to. VG. B17. $20.00

O'CONNOR, Flannery. *Complete Stories.* 1971. FSG. 1st ed. VG/NF clip. B4. $45.00

O'CONNOR, Flannery. *Habit of Being: Letters of Flannery O'Connor.* 1979. FSG. UP. intro Sally Fitzgerald. F/wrp. B4. $200.00

O'CONNOR, Flannery. *Memoir of Mary Ann.* 1961. FSG. 1st ed. VG/VG. S13. $85.00

O'CONNOR, Flannery. *Running in the Family.* 1982. FSG. 1st ed. NF/VG+. S13. $30.00

O'CONNOR, Jack. *Arms & Ammunition Annual 1952.* 1952. Outdoor Life. sc. G+. P12. $10.00

O'CONNOR, Jack. *Art of Hunting Big Game in North America.* 1967. Outdoor Life. ils. VG. P12. $15.00

O'CONNOR, Jack. *Hunting Rifle.* 1970. Winchester. 1st ed. 314p. cloth. VG+/dj. M20. $25.00

O'CONNOR, John. *Adobe Book.* 1973. Santa Fe. 1st ed. 130p. VG/VG. B5. $45.00

O'CONNOR, R. *Hell's Kitchen.* 1958. NY. 1st ed. VG/VG. B5. $20.00

O'CONNOR, Robert. *Buffalo Soldiers.* 1993. Knopf. 1st ed. author's 1st novel. F/F. B4/H11. $50.00

O'CROULEY. *Description of the Kingdom of New Spain.* 1972. John Howell Books. F/F. D2. $85.00

O'DELL, Scott. *Hawk That Dare Not Hunt.* 1975. Houghton Mifflin. 1st ed. F/F. B17. $20.00

O'DELL, Scott. *Island of the Blue Dolphins.* 1960. Houghton Mifflin. 23rd. VG/VG. B17. $6.50

O'DELL, Scott. *Treasure of Topo-El-Bampo.* 1972. Houghton Mifflin. 8vo. 48p. VG. C14. $6.00

O'DONNELL, Barrett; see Malzberg, Barry.

O'DONNELL, E.P. *Great Big Doorstop.* 1941. Houghton Mifflin. 1st ed. F/NF. B4. $250.00

O'DONNELL, Elliott. *Casebook of Ghosts.* 1969. Taplinger. 1st ed. NF/NF. P3. $20.00

O'DONNELL, K.M.; see Malzberg, Barry.

O'DONNELL, Lillian. *Aftershock.* 1977. Detective BC. VG. P3. $8.00

O'DONNELL, Lillian. *Casual Affairs.* 1985. Putnam. 1st ed. F/F. P3. $17.00

O'DONNELL, Lillian. *Falling Star.* 1979. Putnam. 1st ed. F/F. P3. $20.00

O'DONNELL, Lillian. *Good Night To Kill.* 1989. Putnam. 1st ed. F/F. P3. $18.00

O'DONNELL, Lillian. *Ladykiller.* 1984. Putnam. 1st ed. VG/VG. P3. $18.00

O'DONNELL, Lillian. *Wicked Designs.* 1980. Putnam. 1st ed. VG/VG. P3. $13.00

O'DONNELL, Peter. *Dead Man's Handle.* 1985. London. Souvenir. 1st ed. sgn. F/F. T2. $55.00

O'DONNELL, Peter. *Death of a Jester.* 1987. London. Titan. 1st ed. F/wrp. T2. $15.00

O'DONNELL, Peter. *Dragon's Claw.* 1985. Mysterious. 1st Am ed. 1/250. sgn. F/sans/case. T2. $65.00

O'DONNELL, Peter. *I, Lucifer.* 1975. Pan. 3rd. VG. P3. $5.00

O'DONNELL, Peter. *Iron God.* 1989. London. Titan. 1st ed. F/wrp. T2. $15.00

O'DONNELL, Peter. *Last Day in Limbo.* 1984. Mysterious. 1st Am ed. 1/250. sgn. F/F/case. T2. $35.00

O'DONNELL, Peter. *Modesty Blaise.* 1965. Souvenir. 1st ed. NF/NF. P3. $30.00

O'DONNELL, Peter. *Night of Morningstar.* 1987. Mysterious. 1st Am ed. 1/250. sgn. F/sans/case. T2. $35.00

O'DONNELL, Peter. *Puppet Master.* 1987. London. Titan. 1st ed. ils Romero. F/pict wrp. T2. $15.00

O'DONNELL, Peter. *Silver Mistress.* 1981. Cambridge. Archival. 1st Am ed. F/F. T2. $20.00

O'DONNELL, Peter. *Silver Mistress.* 1984. Mysterious. ltd ed. 1/250. sgn. F/sans/case. T2. $35.00

O'DONNELL, Peter. *Warlords of Phoenix.* 1987. London. Titan. 1st ed. F/pict wrp. T2. $15.00

O'DONNELL, Peter. *Xanadu Talisman.* 1984. Mysterious. 1st Am ed. 1/250. sgn/#d. F/sans/case. T2. $35.00

O'DONOGHUE & SPRINGER. *Adventures of Phoebe Zeit-Geist.* 1968. Grove. 1st ed. 150p. bl cloth. AN/dj. B22. $12.00

O'DONOVAN, Edmond. *Mern Oasis: Travels & Adventures East of Caspian...* 1883. NY. 2 vol. maps. VG. B5. $250.00

O'FAOLAIN, Sean. *Talking Trees & Other Stories.* 1970. Boston. 1st ed. F/F. A17. $20.00

O'FARRELL, William. *Repeat Performance.* 1947. Triangle. VG/VG. P3. $15.00

O'FLAHERTY, Liam. *Fairy Goose & Two Other Stories.* 1927. Crosby Gaige. 1/1190. sgn. F/VG. C6. $75.00

O'GORMAN, Ned. *Harvesters Vase.* 1968. Harcourt Brace. 1st ed. assn copy. F/NF. V1. $20.00

O'GRADY, Timothy. *Motherland.* 1989. Holt. 1st Am ed. F/F. A20. $18.00

O'GRADY, Tom. *In the Room of the Just Born.* 1989. Dolphin Moon. sgn. 72p. VG. B10. $10.00

O'HANLON, Redmond. *Into the Heart of Borneo: Account of a Journey...* 1984. Salamander. 1st ed. F/F. C2. $150.00

O'HARA, Frank. *Homage to Frank O'Hara.* 1980. Creative Age. revised ed. photos. V1. $15.00

O'HARA, John. *Farmers Hotel.* 1951. Random. 1st ed. VG/VG. P3. $60.00

O'HARA, John. *Lockwood Concern.* 1965. NY. 1st ed. 1/300. sgn. F/case. C2. $150.00

O'HARA, John. *North Frederick.* 1955. Random. 1st ed. VG/VG. P3. $50.00

O'HARA, John. *Pipe Night.* 1946. Faber. 1st ed. F/F. M19. $85.00

O'HARA, John. *Sermons & Soda Water.* 1960. Random. 1st ed. 3 vol. F/NF case. B35. $25.00

O'HARA, Kenneth. *View to a Death.* 1958. Cassell. 1st ed. VG/VG. P3. $25.00

O'HARA, Kevin. *Exit & Curtain.* 1952. Hurst Blackett. 1st ed. xl. VG. P3. $10.00

O'HARA, Mary. *Flica's Friend: Autobiography of...* 1982. NY. ils. 284p. F/dj. A17. $10.00

O'HARA. *Making Watercolor Behave.* 1932. VG. D2. $15.00

O HENRY. *Four Million.* 1907. McClure. 3rd ed. VG. P3. $20.00

O'KANE, John. *Ship of Sulaiman.* 1972. Columbian. 1st Am ed. 250p. NF/dj. W1. $22.00

O'KEEFE, John A. *Tektites & Their Origin.* 1976. Amsterdam. Elsevier. ils/pl. 254p. VG/dj. K5. $75.00

O'LEARY, Patrick. *Door Number Three.* 1995. Tor. 2nd. F/F. P3. $24.00

O'MALLEY, Austin. *Ethics of Medical Homide & Mutilation.* 1922. NY. 285p. VG. A13. $75.00

O'MALLEY & SAUNDERS. *Leonardo da Vinci on the Human Body.* 1982. Greenwich/Crown. rpt of 1952 ed. 506p. cloth. dj. D2. $60.00

O'MARIE, Carol Anne. *Missing Madonna.* nd. BC. VG/VG. P3. $8.00

O'NAIR, Mairi. *Girl With the X-Ray Eyes.* 1935. Mills Boon. 1st ed. xl. VG. P3. $15.00

O'NAN, Stewart. *Snow Angels.* 1994. Doubleday. 1st ed. sgn. F/F. B4. $125.00

O'NEAL, Bill. *American Assn.* 1991. Eakin. 1spb. VG+. P8. $15.00

O'NEIL, Daniel J. *Contract Bridge Made Simple.* 1961. NY. revised. lg format. 187p. VG/wrp. S1. $5.00

O'NEIL, Dennis. *Private Files of the Shadow.* 1989. DC Comics. hc. VG/VG. P3. $25.00

O'NEIL, Dennis. *Shadow 1941: Hitler's Astrologer.* 1988. Marvel Graphic Novel. 1st ed. VG/VG. P3. $25.00

O'NEIL, Dennis. *Stacked Deck, the Greatest Joker Story.* 1990. Longmeadow. 1st ed. rpt of comics. aeg. leahter. F. P3. $60.00

O'NEIL, George. *That Bright Heat.* 1928. Boni Liveright. 1st ed. sgn. 12mo. G. B11. $8.00

O'NEILL, Brian. *Easter Week.* 1939. NY. Internat. 1st ed. NF/wrp. B2. $45.00

O'NEILL, Dennis J. *Whale of a Territory.* 1966. NY. 1st ed. 249p. VG/torn. B18. $15.00

O'NEILL, Eugene. *All God's Chillun Got Wings & Welded.* 1924. NY. 1st ed. NF. B4. $75.00

O'NEILL, Eugene. *Before Breakfast: A Play in One Act.* 1916. NY. Shay. 1st ed/only prt. 1/500. NF/gray wrp/bl chemise/case. B24. $850.00

O'NEILL, Eugene. *Days Without End.* 1934. Random. 1st ed. inscr/sgn. gilt navy cloth. F/dj. B24. $1,250.00

O'NEILL, Eugene. *Emperor Jones.* 1928. NY. 1/750. sgn. VG/worn box. B5. $200.00

O'NEILL, Eugene. *Gold: A Play in Four Acts.* 1920. Boni Liveright. 1st ed. inscr/dtd 1938. NF. B24. $750.00

O'NEILL, Eugene. *Great God Brown/The Fountain/Moon of the Caribbees...* 1926. Boni Liveright. 1st ed. F/F. B4. $350.00

O'NEILL, Eugene. *Hughie.* 1959. New Haven. Yale. 1st ed. F/F. B4. $200.00

O'NEILL, Eugene. *Iceman Cometh.* 1946. Random. 2nd. VG+/VG+. P10. $20.00

O'NEILL, Eugene. *Lazarus Laughed.* 1927. NY. VG/VG. C6. $60.00

O'NEILL, Eugene. *Marco Millions.* 1927. Boni Liveright. 1st ed. F/F. B4. $275.00

O'NEILL, Eugene. *Nine Plays.* ca 1931. NY. Novel Prize ed. 867p. cloth. dj. A17. $15.00

O'NEILL, Eugene. *Strange Interlude.* 1928. Boni Liveright. 1st ed. NF/dj. B24. $150.00

O'NEILL, John. *Prodigal Genius.* 1944. NY. sgn. VG/VG. B5. $45.00

O'NEILL, William L. *Everyone Was Brave: Rise & Fall of Feminism in America.* 1969. Quadrangle. 1st ed. F/F. B35. $35.00

O'REILLY, Victor. *Games of the Hangman.* 1991. Grove Weidenfeld. 1st ed. F/F. H11. $35.00

O'REILLY, Victor. *Games of the Hangman.* 1991. Grove Weidenfeld. 1st ed. NF/NF. P3. $20.00

O'REILLY, Victor. *Rules of the Hunt.* 1995. Putnam. 1st ed. F/F. H11. $25.00

O'SHAUGHNESSY, Edith. *Diplomat's Wife in Mexico.* 1917. NY. Harper. 8vo. 356p. VG. P4. $25.00

O'SHAUGHNESSY, Michael. *Monster Book of Monsters.* 1988. Bonanza. 1st ed. F/F. P3. $15.00

O'SHAUGHNESSY, Perri. *Motion to Suppress.* 1995. Delacorte. 1st ed. F/F. H11. $25.00

O'SHEA, Sean; see Tralins, Bob.

OAKLEY, Graham. *Church Mice at Bay.* 1979 (1978). Atheneum. 1st Am ed. ils. unp. tan cloth. NF/NF. T5. $45.00

OAKLEY, Imogen Brashear. *Awake, America! & Other Verse.* 1934. Macrea Smith. sgn. ils/sgn Thornton Oakley. 8vo. 74p. VG. B11. $40.00

OATES, Joyce Carol. *All the Good People I've Left Behind.* 1979. Blk Sparrow. 1st ed. 1/300. sgn. F/glassine dj. B4. $100.00

OATES, Joyce Carol. *Angel of Light.* 1981. Dutton. 1st ed. F/F. P3. $25.00

OATES, Joyce Carol. *Anonymous Sins & Other Poems.* 1969. LSU. 1st ed. F/NF. A15. $40.00

OATES, Joyce Carol. *Assassins.* 1975. Vanguard. 1st ed. F/F. H11. $35.00

OATES, Joyce Carol. *Assignation.* 1988. Ecco. 1st ed. F/F. B4. $45.00

OATES, Joyce Carol. *Childworld.* 1976. Vanguard. 1st ed. inscr. F/F. B4. $125.00

OATES, Joyce Carol. *Edge of Impossibility.* 1972. Vanguard. 1st ed. sgn. F/VG clip. B4. $100.00

OATES, Joyce Carol. *Fabulous Beasts.* 1975. LSU. 1st ed. ils AG Smith. F/F. B4. $125.00

OATES, Joyce Carol. *Foxfire: Confessions of a Girl Gang.* 1993. NY. 2nd. 328p. F/F. A17. $9.50

OATES, Joyce Carol. *Garden of Earthly Delights.* 1967. Vanguard. 1st ed. sgn. NF/NF. B4. $150.00

OATES, Joyce Carol. *Goddess & Other Women.* 1974. Vanguard. 1st ed. VG/VG. P3. $30.00

OATES, Joyce Carol. *Hostile Sun: Poetry of DH Lawrence.* 1973. Blk Sparrow. ARC. sgn. RS. F/wrp. B4. $125.00

OATES, Joyce Carol. *Hostile Sun: Poetry of DH Lawrence.* 1973. Blk Sparrow. ltd ed. 1/300. sgn/#d. F. M19. $125.00

OATES, Joyce Carol. *Hungry Ghosts.* 1974. Blk Sparrow. 1/350. sgn/#d. F/acetate dj. S9. $60.00

OATES, Joyce Carol. *I Lock My Door Upon Myself.* 1990. Ecco. 1st ed. sgn. F/F. B4. $85.00

OATES, Joyce Carol. *Martya: A Life.* 1986. Dutton. 1st ed. F/F. H11. $25.00

OATES, Joyce Carol. *On Boxing.* 1987. Dolphin/Doubleday. 1st trade ed. sgn. F/F. B4. $85.00

OATES, Joyce Carol. *Poisoned Kiss & Other Stories.* 1976. Gollancz. 1st ed. F/F. P3. $20.00

OATES, Joyce Carol. *Raven's Wing.* 1986. 1st ed. VG/VG. K2. $14.00

OATES, Joyce Carol. *Seduction & Other Stories.* 1975. Blk Sparrow. 1st ed. inscr. F/wrp. B4. $85.00

OATES, Joyce Carol. *Solstice.* 1985. Dutton. 1st ed. F/F. H11. $25.00

OATES, Joyce Carol. *Son of the Morning.* 1978. Vanguard. 1st ed. VG/VG. P3. $30.00

OATES, Joyce Carol. *Them.* 1969. Vanguard. 1st ed. NF/VG. M19. $35.00

OATES, Joyce Carol. *Wheel of Love.* 1967. Vanguard. ARC. sgn. F. w/photo & promo material. B4. $200.00

OATES, Joyce Carol. *Will You Always Love Me?* 1994. Huntington Beach. Cahill. 1/26 lettered. sgn. F. marbled brd/leather spine. F. B4. $250.00

OATES, Joyce Carol. *Women Whose Lives Are Food.* 1978. VG/dj. K2. $35.00

OATES, Joyce Carol. *Wonderland.* 1971. Vanguard. ARC. inscr. RS. F/F. B4. $200.00

OATES, Joyce Carol. *Wonderland.* 1971. Vanguard. 1st ed. F/F. H11. $45.00

OATES, Stephen B. *Confederate Cavalry West of the River.* 1961. Austin, TX. 1st ed. 234p. cloth. NF/VG. M8. $165.00

OATES, William Calvin. *War Between the Union & the Confederacy...* 1974. Dayton, OH. Morningside Bookshop. rpt. 808p. NF. M8. $45.00

OBERG, Arthur. *Anna's Song.* 1980. WA U. 1st ed. F/F. V1. $10.00

ODELL & ROSING. *Future of Oil.* 1980. London/NY. Kogan Page/Nichols. 1st ed. ils. 265p. xl. VG/dj. W1. $30.00

ODETS, Clifford. *Clash by Night.* 1942. Random. 1st ed. inscr. NF. B4. $250.00

OEMLER, A. *Truck-Farming at the South.* 1883. NY. Orange Judd. 270p. VG. A10. $50.00

OFFUTT, Chris. *Same River Twice.* 1993. Simon Schuster. 1st ed. F/F. A20. $22.00

OGBURN, Charlton Jr. *Marauders.* 1959. NY. 1st ed. 307p. dj. A17. $10.00

OGDEN, Robert Morris. *Hearing. Illustrated With Diagrams.* 1924. London. Cape. 1st ed. russet buckram. G1. $35.00

OGILVIE, J.S. *Album Writer's Friend.* 1881. NY. 64p. decor cloth. G. B18. $15.00

OGRIZEK, Dore. *United States.* 1950. NY. ils. 518p. G. A17. $10.00

OJIKE, Mbonu. *My Africa.* 1946. John Day. 8vo. 350p. red cloth. VG/worn. P4. $20.00

OKSENBERG, Michel. *China's Developmental Experience.* 1973. Columbia. 1st ed. 8vo. 219p. VG/dj. W1. $20.00

OKUDA, Seiiti. *Japanese Industrial Arts.* 1941. Tokyo. Brd Tourist Industry. 12mo. 106p. VG/wrp. W1. $12.00

OLAFSON, Frederick A. *Society, Law & Morality.* 1961. Englewood Cliffs. M11. $25.00

OLCOTT, Anthony. *Murder at the Red October.* 1981. Chicago. 1st ed. NF/NF. H11. $20.00

OLCOTT, Frances Jenkins. *Adventures of Haroun er Raschid & Other Tales...* 1923. Henry Holt. 1st ed. 363p. red cloth. VG. M20. $75.00

OLDENBURG, Chloe Warner. *Leaps of Faith.* 1985. Pepper Pike, OH. 183p. G+/dj. B18. $15.00

OLDERMAN, Murray. *Nelson's 20th-Century Encyclopedia of Baseball.* 1963. Nelson. 1st ed. VG. P8. $15.00

OLDNALL, William Russell. *Practice of the Court of Great Sessions...* 1814. London. Butterworth. contemporary calf. M11. $650.00

OLDRIN, John. *Chipmunk Terrace.* 1958. Viking. sgn. 79p. VG+/dj. M20. $20.00

OLDRIN, John. *Eight Rings on His Tail.* 1956. Viking. 1st ed. sgn. 79p. VG+/dj. M20. $25.00

OLDRIN, John. *Round Meadow.* 1951. Viking. 1st ed. sgn. 80p. VG+/dj. M20. $25.00

OLDS, C. Burnell. *Trees & Shrubs of Claremont.* 1955. Claremont. VG. B26. $17.50

OLDS, Sharon. *Father.* 1992. Knopf. UP. sgn. F. V1. $35.00

OLEKSAK & OLEKSAK. *Beisbol.* 1991. Masters. 1st ed. F/VG+. P8. $65.00

OLIVELLE, Patrick. *Vasudevasrama Yatidharmaprakasa...Part 2: Translation.* 1977. Vienna. sm 4to. 231p. VG/stiff wrp. W1. $18.00

OLIVER, Chad. *Shadows in the Sun.* 1985. Crown. 1st ed. F/F. P3. $13.00

OLIVER, Chad. *Shores of Another Sea.* 1984. Crown. F/F. P3. $15.00

OLIVER, Katherine Elspeth. *Claw.* 1914. Los Angeles. Out West Magazine. 1st ed. 384p. gilt red cloth. VG. T10. $45.00

OLIVER, Nola Nance. *This Too Is Natchez.* 1953. Hastings. photos. 72p. VG/fair. B10. $12.00

OLIVER, Paul. *Blues Fell This Morning: Meaning of the Blues.* 1960. Horizon. 1st ed. intro Richard Wright. F/VG+ clip. B4. $85.00

OLIVER, Paul. *Shelter in Africa.* 1971. Praeger. F/VG. D2. $65.00

OLIVIER, Charles P. *Comets.* 1930. Baltimore. Williams Wilkins. 1st ed. 8vo. 246p. G/dj. K5. $100.00

OLMSTEAD, A.T. *History of Palestine &* *Syria to the Macedonian Conquest.* 1931. Scribner. 1st ed. 664p. VG. W1. $85.00

OLMSTED, Lorena Ann. *Setup for Murder.* 1962. Avalon. 1st ed. xl. dj. P3. $5.00

OLNEY, Ross R. *Tales of Time & Space.* 1969. Whitman. VG. P3. $5.00

OLSEN, Elder. *Olson's Penny Arcade.* 1975. Chicago. 1st ed. assn copy. F/NF. V1. $10.00

OLSEN, Elder. *Plays & Poems 1948-1958.* 1958. Chicago. 1st ed. assn copy. F/NF. V1. $15.00

OLSEN. *Painting the Marine Scene in Watercolor.* 1967. VG/VG. D2. $10.00

OLSHAKER, Mark. *Einstein's Brain.* 1981. Evans. 1st ed. F/F. P3. $15.00

OLSON, Kenneth E. *Music & Musket:* *Bands & Bandsmen of the American Civil War.* 1981. Greenwood. 1st ed. 299p. VG/VG. B10. $25.00

OLSON, Lyla M. *Improvised Equipment in Home Care of the Sick.* Jan 1944. Phil. Saunders. 419 ils. 264p. VG. B14. $45.00

OLSON, Sigurd. *Lonely Land.* 1961. NY. 1st ed. VG/VG. B5. $25.00

OLSON, Toby. *Changing Appearance:* *Poems 1965-1970.* 1975. Membrane. NF/wrp. V1. $20.00

OLSON, Toby. *Dorit in Lesbos.* 1990. Simon Schuster. 1st ed. F/F. A20. $18.00

OLSON, Toby. *Vectors.* 1972. Ziggurat-Membrane/Albatross. F/wrp. V1. $15.00

OMAN, C. *History of Art of War in Middle Ages.* 1924. London. 2 vol. 2nd. VG+. A15. $125.00

OMMANNEY, F.D. *Isle of Cloves: A View of Zanzibar.* 1956. Phil/NY. Lippincott. 230p. VG/dj. P4. $25.00

OMURA, Bunji. *Last Genro: Prince Saionji,* *Man Who Westernized Japan.* 1938. Lippincott. 1st ed. VG. W1. $25.00

OMWAKE, John. *Conestoga Six-Horse Bell* *Teams of Eastern Pennsylvania.* 1930. Cincinnati. 4to. VG. O3. $195.00

ONDAATJE, Michael. *Cinnamon Peeler.* 1991. Knopf. 1st ed. F/F. M23. $20.00

ONDAATJE, Michael. *English Patent.* 1992. Knopf. 1st ed. rem mk. NF/F. M23. $25.00

ONDAATJE, Michael. *In the Skin of the Lion.* 1987. NY. 1st ed. sgn. F/F. C2. $50.00

OPIE, John Newton. *Rebel Cavalryman With Lee, Stuart & Jackson.* 1899. Chicago. WB Conkey. 1st ed. 336p. cloth. VG. M8. $250.00

OPIE & OPIE. *Tail Feathers From Mother Goose, Opie Rhyme Book.* 1988. Little Brn. 1st ed. ils. 125p. AN/VG. T5. $40.00

OPPENHEIM, E. Phillips. *Battle of Basinghall Street.* 1935. McClelland Stewart. 1st Canadian ed. VG/dj. P3. $30.00

OPPENHEIM, E. Phillips. *Berenice.* 1911. Little Brn. NF. P3. $25.00

OPPENHEIM, E. Phillips. *Curious Happenings to the Rookie Legatees.* 1940. Triangle. 2nd. VG/VG. P3. $20.00

OPPENHEIM, E. Phillips. *Devil's Paw.* 1936. Hodder Stoughton. 12th. VG/VG. P3. $20.00

OPPENHEIM, E. Phillips. *Dumb Gods Speak.* 1937. McClelland Stewart. 1st ed. VG/VG. P3. $30.00

OPPENHEIM, E. Phillips. *Envoy Extraordinary.* 1937. Little Brn. 1st ed. VG. P3. $20.00

OPPENHEIM, E. Phillips. *Evil Shepherd.* nd. Review of Reviews. VG. P3. $10.00

OPPENHEIM, E. Phillips. *Gabriel Samara, Peacemaker.* 1925. McClelland Stewart. 1st ed. VG. P3. $25.00

OPPENHEIM, E. Phillips. *General Besserley's Second Puzzle Box.* 1940. Little Brn. 1st ed. VG. P3. $30.00

OPPENHEIM, E. Phillips. *Golden Beast.* 1926. Little Brn. 1st ed. VG. P3. $20.00

OPPENHEIM, E. Phillips. *Great Impersonation.* 1938. Triangle. 2nd. VG/VG. P3. $15.00

OPPENHEIM, E. Phillips. *Man From Sing Sing.* 1944. Tower. 2nd. VG/VG. P3. $15.00

OPPENHEIM, E. Phillips. *Matorni's Vineyard.* 1928. Little Brn. G. P3. $12.00

OPPENHEIM, E. Phillips. *Ostrekoff Jewels.* 1932. McClelland Stewart. 1st ed. VG/VG. P3. $30.00

OPPENHEIM, E. Phillips. *Passionate Quest.* 1924. Little Brn. 1st ed. VG. P3. $18.00

OPPENHEIM, E. Phillips. *Pawns Count.* 1918. McClelland Goodchild. G. P3. $20.00

OPPENHEIM, E. Phillips. *Pulpit in the Grill Room.* 1939. Little Brn. 1st ed. VG. P3. $20.00

OPPENHEIM, E. Phillips. *Shy Plutocrat.* 1941. Little Brn. 1st ed. VG. P3. $25.00

OPPENHEIM, E. Phillips. *Spymaster.* 1938. Little Brn. 1st ed. VG. P3. $20.00

OPPENHEIM, E. Phillips. *Tempting of Tavernake.* 1912. Little Brn. 1st ed. VG. P3. $20.00

OPPENHEIM, E. Phillips. *Wrath To Come.* 1924. Little Brn. 2nd. 355p. G. B10. $12.00

OPPENHEIM, E. Phillips. *Wrath To Come.* 1924. McClelland Stewart. 1st ed. VG. P3. $25.00

OPPENHEIM, E. Phillips. *Zeppelin's Passenger.* 1918. McClelland Goodchild Stewart. 1st ed. G. P3. $20.00

OPPENHEIM, Janet. *Other World: Spiritism & Psychical Research in England...* 1985. Cambridge. 1st ed. 503p. VG/dj. A13. $45.00

OPPENHEIMER, Joel. *Names & Local Habitations.* 1988. Jargon Soc. 1st ed. F/F. V1. $20.00

OPPENHEIMER, Joel. *Poems 1962-68.* 1969. IN. 1st ed. VG/dj. A17. $9.50

OPPENHEIMER, Joel. *Wrong Season.* 1973. Bobbs Merrill. 1st ed. F/VG. P8. $40.00

ORCHARD, Vincent. *Derby Stakes: A Complete History 1900 to 1953.* (1954). London. 1st ed. ils. 325p. gilt bl cloth. F/G. H3. $80.00

ORCUTT, William Dana. *Book in Italy.* 1928. Harper. 1/750. 128p. T10. $100.00

ORCUTT, William Dana. *In Quest of the Perfect Book.* 1926. Little Brn. 1st ed. 1/365p. sgn. 316p. half vellum. F/split case. T10. $250.00

ORCUTT, William Dana. *Kingdom of Books.* 1927. Little Brn. 1st trade ed. 8vo. ils. gilt brn cloth. NF. T10. $45.00

ORCZY, Baroness. *Beau Brocade.* 1953. Hodder Stoughton. 36th. xl. dj. P3. $5.00

ORCZY, Baroness. *Bronze Eagle.* 1915. Doran. 1st ed. NF. P3. $30.00

ORCZY, Baroness. *Scarlet Pimpernel: Four Complete Novels.* 1950. Hodder Stoughton. 7th. G. P3. $20.00

ORDE, A.J. *Little Neighborhood Murder.* 1989. Doubleday. 1st ed. author's 1st book. F/F. H11. $25.00

ORGA & ORGA. *Ataturk.* 1962. London. Joseph. 1st ed. 304p. VG. W1. $28.00

ORGILL, Douglas. *Man in the Dark.* 1980. Ian Henry. hc. VG/VG. P3. $20.00

ORIOL, Laurence. *Murder To Make You Grow Up.* 1968. MacDonald. 1st ed. VG/VG. P3. $22.00

ORIOL, Laurence. *Short Circuit.* 1967. MacDonald. 1st ed. VG/VG. P3. $15.00

ORLEANS, Ilo. *Funday: A Diary for Judy & Julian.* 1930. Martin. 365p. G+. A17. $17.50

ORLEN, Steve. *Place at the Table.* 1981. HRW. 1st ed. F/G+. V1. $10.00

ORR, A. *In the Ice King's Palace.* 1986. Tor. hc. F/F. P3. $16.00

ORR, A. *World in Amber.* 1985. Bluejay. 1st ed. VG/VG. P3. $20.00

ORR, Bobby. *Bobby Orr: My Game.* 1974. Little Brn. 1st ed. VG/VG. P3. $20.00

ORR, Gregory. *We Must Make a Kingdom of It.* 1986. Wesleyan. 1st ed. F/VG+. V1. $10.00

ORR, H. Winnett. *On the Contributions of Hugh Owen Thomas, Sir Robert Jones.* 1949. Springfield. 1st ed. 253p. VG. A13. $60.00

ORR, James L. *Smithville Days.* 1922. Smithville, OH. 1st ed. 128p. G. B18. $45.00

ORSINI, Abe. *Life of the Blessed Virgin Mary...* 1861. NY. Virtue. 24 pl. 764p. aeg. emb gilt morocco. VG. W1. $65.00

ORTELIUS, Abraham. *Thesaurus Geographicus.* 1596. Antwerp. Ex Officina Plantiniana. folio. unp. K1. $1,000.00

ORTH, Johannes. *Compend of Diagnosis in Pathological Anatomy...* 1882. Boston. Riverside. 8vo. 440p. gr cloth. VG. w/8 orig 1880s Harvard exams. B14. $150.00

ORTLOFF, Henry Stuart. *Garden Bluebook of Annuals & Biennials.* 1931. Doubleday. hc. VG. P3. $8.00

ORUI & TOBA. *Castles in Japan.* 1935. Tokyo. 12mo. 106p. xl. VG. W1. $12.00

ORVIS, Kenneth. *Night Without Darkness.* 1965. McClelland Stewart. VG. P3. $8.00

ORWELL, George. *Dickens, Dali & Others.* 1946. 1st ed. VG/G+. S13. $18.00

ORWELL, George. *Keep the Aspidistra Flying.* 1936. London. Gollancz. 1st ed. bl cloth. F/yel dj. B24. $1,850.00

ORWELL, George. *Shooting an Elephant.* 1950. Harcourt Brace. 1st Am ed. F/VG+. H4. $100.00

ORWELL, George. *Such, Such Were the Joys.* 1953. NY. Harcourt Brace. ARC/1st Am ed. RS. F/NF. H4. $75.00

ORWELL, George. *1984.* 1949. Harcourt. 1st Am ed. VG/VG. M22. $85.00

ORWELL, George. *1984.* 1949. Saunders. 1st Canadian ed. VG/VG. M19. $100.00

OSBORN, David. *Love & Treason.* 1982. NAL. 1st ed. VG/VG. P3. $15.00

OSBORN, Henry S. *Palestine, Past & Present.* 1859. Phil. ils/fld map. VG. M17. $175.00

OSBORN, Marjorie Noble. *Jolly Times Cook Book, Simple Recipes for Beginners.* 1936 (1934). Chicago. Rand McNally. 16mo. VG+. C8. $40.00

OSBORN. *Questioned Documents, Second Edition.* 1929. np. 1052p. NF. A4. $125.00

OSBORNE, Denise. *Murder Offscreen.* 1994. Holt. 1st ed. F/F. M23. $25.00

OSBORNE, John. *Patriot for Me.* 1966. London. Faber. 1st ed. F/F. B4. $125.00

OSBORNE, John. *Time Present & the Hotel in Amsterdam.* 1968. London. Faber. 1st ed. F/F. B4. $125.00

OSBORNE, Lilly de Jongh. *Four Keys to El Salvador.* 1956. Funk Wagnall. 1st ed. 221p. dj. F3. $25.00

OSBORNE, Walter. *Thoroughbred World.* nd. np. Amiel. 4to. VG/fair. O3. $20.00

OSBORNE & WOOD. *Indian Costumes of Guatemala.* 1966. Graz, Austria. Akademische Druck. 1st ed. 8vo. 154p. gray cloth. F/dj. T10. $125.00

OSBORNE & WOOD. *Indian Costumes of Guatemala.* 1966. Graz, Austria. 1st ed. sgn Wood. 60 tippcd in pl. 154p. F3. $200.00

OSKISON, John. *Tecumseh & His Times.* 1938. NY. 1st ed. ils. 244p. VG/G. B5. $45.00

OSLER, Mirabel. *Gentle Plea for Chaos.* 1989. NY. 1st Am ed. ils. 176p. F/dj. B26. $20.00

OSLER, William. *Aphorisms.* 1950. Schuman. 1st ed. edit WB Bean. F/dj. A15. $30.00

OSLER, William. *Diagnosis of Abdominal Tumors.* 1900. London. 1st ed. NF. A9. $95.00

OSLER, William. *Evolution of Modern Medicine.* 1921. New Haven. 1st ed. 243p. VG. A13. $125.00

OSLER, William. *Principles & Practice of Medicine.* 1896. NY. 2nd. calf/cloth. VG+. B14. $250.00

OSLER, William. *Principles & Practice of Medicine.* 1899. NY. 3rd. gr cloth. F. B14. $125.00

OSLER, William. *Principles & Practice of Medicine.* 1912. NY. 8th. 1225p. cracked inner hinge. A13. $75.00

OSLER, William. *Science & Immortality.* 1905. Boston. 1st ed. 12mo. 54p. VG. A13. $125.00

OSMOND, Andrew. *Saladin!* 1976. Doubleday. hc. VG/VG. P3. $10.00

OSSENDOWSKI, Ferdinand. *Beasts, Men & Gods.* 1923. Dutton. 2nd. 8vo. 325p. cloth. VG. W1. $16.00

OSSENDOWSKI, Ferdinand. *Man & Mystery in Asia.* 1924. Dutton. 2nd. 8vo. 343p. VG. W1. $16.00

OSSENDOWSKI, Ferdinand. *Slaves of the Sun.* 1928. Dutton. 1st ed. 5 maps. 489p. xl. VG. W1. $28.00

OSSWALD & REED. *Hundreds of Turkeys.* 1941. Heath. TB. NF. M5. $12.00

OSSWALD & REED. *Little Crow.* 1950. Heath. 8vo. ils. NF/wrp. M5. $12.00

OSTER, Jerry. *Club Dead.* 1988. Harper Row. 1st ed. F/F. P3. $16.00

OSTER, Jerry. *Fixin' To Die.* 1992. Bantam. 1st ed. F/F. A20. $10.00

OSTER, Jerry. *Internal Affairs.* 1990. Bantam. 1st ed. sgn. F/F. P3. $25.00

OSTER, Jerry. *Municipal Bonds.* 1981. Houghton Mifflin. 1st ed. VG/VG. P3. $20.00

OSTER, Jerry. *Nowhere Man.* 1987. Harper Row. 1st ed. F/F. P3. $18.00

OSTER, Jerry. *Rancho Maria.* 1986. Harper Row. 1st ed. F/F. P3. $15.00

OSTER, Jerry. *Saint Mike.* 1987. Harper Row. 1st ed. NF/NF. P3. $16.00

OSTER, Jerry. *Sweet Justice.* 1985. Harper Row. 1st ed. F/F. P3. $18.00

OSTER, Jerry. *Violet Love.* 1991. Bantam. 1st ed. NF/NF. P3. $20.00

OSTRANDER, Isabel. *Twenty-Six Clues.* 1919. WJ Watt. 277p. VG/dj. M20. $45.00

OSTRANDER, Shelia. *Psychic Discoveries Behind the Iron Curtain.* nd. Laffont. VG. P3. $15.00

OSTRANDER, Tobias. *Planetarium & the Astronomical Calculator.* 1834. NY. 8 unusual pl. fld frontis. prt brd/leather spine. NF. B14. $75.00

OSTRIKER, Alicia. *Woman Under the Surface.* 1982. Princeton. 1st ed. sgn/Dtd. F/dj. V1. $35.00

OSTROW, Albert A. *Complete Card Player.* 1945. NY. 2nd. 771p. VG. S1. $5.00

OTIS, James. *Captain Tom the Privateersman.* 1899. Dana Estes. 1st ed. 163p. VG. M20. $17.50

OTIS, James. *Toby Tyler; or, Ten Weeks With the Circus.* 1923. Harper. hc. VG/VG. P3. $15.00

OTT, Gil. *Children.* 1981. Tamarisk. ltd ed. 1/250. VG+/wrp. V1. $10.00

OTTIN, Merry. *Land of Emperors & Sultans.* ca 1964. Crown. 1st ed. folio. ils. 300p. VG/torn. W1. $85.00

OTTO, Whitney. *How To Make an American Quilt.* 1991. Villard. 1st ed. author's 1st book. F/F. C2/M19. $50.00

OTTO, Whitney. *Now You See Her.* 1994. Villard. 1st ed. 8vo. F/dj. w/photo & promo material. S9. $40.00

OTTOS, Svend. *Giant Fish & Other Stories.* 1982. Larousse. trans Joan Tate. VG. B17. $6.50

OTTUM, Bob. *See the Kid Run.* 1978. Simon Schuster. 1st ed. F/F. P3. $15.00

OTWAY, Howard. *Evangelist.* 1954. Harper. 1st ed. F/VG. H11. $40.00

OUELLETTE, Pierre. *Deus Machine.* 1993. Villard. 1st ed. F/NF. G10. $10.00

OUIDA. *Nurnberg Stove.* 1916. Lippincott. 12mo. ils Maria L Kirk. VG. B17. $4.00

OURSLER, William. *Marijuana: The Facts — -The Truth.* 1968. NY. Eriksson. 240p. F/dj. B14. $55.00

OURSLER, William. *Narcotics: America's Peril.* 1952. Doubleday. 1st ed. VG. P3. $25.00

OUSPENSKY, A. *Most Important.* 1940. Moscow. 8vo. ils. 44p. F/prt wrp. B24. $375.00

OUTCAULT, R.F. *My Resolutions: Buster Brown.* 1906. NY. 1st ed. VG. A15. $50.00

OUTHWAITE, Ida. *Bunch of Wildflowers.* 1933. Angus Robertson. 1st ed. ils. VG. M5. $550.00

OUTHWAITE. *Outrolling the Map: Story of Exploration.* 1935. np. ils Gordon Grant/56 maps. 351p. VG. A4. $25.00

OUTRAM, George. *Legal & Other Lyrics.* 1888. Edinburgh. Blackwood. crimson cloth. M11. $85.00

OVENDEN. *Pre-Raphaelite Photography.* 1972. F/F. D2. $45.00

OVERHOLSER, Stephen. *Track of a Killer.* 1982. Walker. 1st ed. F/F. A18. $10.00

OVERHOLSER, Wayne D. *Best Western Stories of...* 1984. S IL U. 1st ed. edit Pronzini/Greenberg. M/M. A18. $20.00

OVERHOLSER, Wayne D. *Gun for Johnny Deere.* 1963. Macmillan. 1st ed. F/F. A18. $12.50

OVERHOLSER, Wayne D. *Trial of Billy Peale.* 1962. Macmillan. 1st ed. F/F. A18. $12.50

OVERMIER & SENIOR. *Books & Manuscripts of the Bakken.* 1992. np. ils. 525p. F. A4. $80.00

OVERTON, Grant. *American Nights Entertainment.* 1923. Appleton Doran. 1st ed. VG. P3. $35.00

OWEN, Dean; see McGaughy, Dudley.

OWEN, Iris M. *Conjuring Up Philip.* 1976. Harper Row. 1st ed. VG. P3. $15.00

OWEN, Mrs. Octavius Freire. *Heroines of History.* 1854. NY. Carlton. ils. 386p. VG. B14. $45.00

OWEN, Robert; see Geis, Richard.

OWEN, Wilfred. *Thriteen Poems.* 1956. Northampton. Gehenna. 1/400. ils Ben Shahn. 31p. brn half morocco. NF. B24. $450.00

OWEN, William. *Pictorial Sunday Readings...* ca 1870. London. Snagster. 8vo. 80 chromolithograph pl. 308p. aeg. morocco. VG. W1. $225.00

OWEN & RAMSAY. *Nuts & Their Uses/Story of Citrus Fruits.* 1928. Dansville, NY. ils. 128p. decor cloth. VG. B26. $20.00

OWEN & SRB. *General Genetics.* 1955. San Francisco. ils. 50p. B26. $17.50

OWENS, Bill. *Working (I Do It for the Money).* 1977. Simon Schuster. 1st ed. VG/wrp. S9. $50.00

OWENS, George. *Judas Pool.* 1994. Putnam. 1st ed. F/F. H11. $20.00

OWENS, Rochelle. *Futz & What Came After: Five Plays.* 1968 (1904). Random. 1st ed. inscr. F/NF. B4. $300.00

OWNBEY, Gerald B. *Monograph of Genus Argemone for North America & W Indies.* 1958. NY. ils. 159p. VG. B26. $30.00

OXENHAM, John. *Carette of Sark.* nd. Hodder Stoughton. VG/G+. P3. $8.00

OXFORD, William. *Ferry Steamers: Story of the Detroit-Windsor Ferry Boats.* 1992. Ontario. Boston Mills. AN/wrp. A16. $15.00

OZ, Amos. *In the Land of Israel.* 1983. HBJ. 1st ed. F/F. B35. $20.00

OZ, Amos. *Touch the Water, Touch the Wind.* 1973. HBJ. 1st ed. F/F. B35. $20.00

OZAKI, Yei Theodora. *Warriors of Old Japan & Other Stories.* 1909. Boston/NY. 1st ed. VG+. C6. $60.00

OZICK, Cynthia. *Bloodshed & Three Novellas.* 1976. Knopf. 1st ed. author's 3rd book. F/F. B4. $45.00

OZICK, Cynthia. *Pagan Rabbi & Other Stories.* 1971. Knopf. 1st ed. author's 2nd book. F/NF. B4. $85.00

OZICK, Cynthia. *Shawl.* 1989. Knopf. 1st ed. F/NF. B4. $35.00

PABOR, William E. *Colorado As an Agricultural State: Its Farms, Fields...* 1883. Orange Judd. 213p. cloth. VG. A10. $80.00

PACE, A. *Luigi Castiglioni's Viaggio.* 1983. Syracuse. trans A Pace/edit Joseph Ewan. F/dj. B26. $38.00

PACE, Mildred Mastin. *Old Bones the Wonder Horse.* 1955. Whittlesey. 3rd. 8vo. F/VG. M5. $12.00

PACE, Tom. *Fisherman's Luck.* nd. BC. F/F. P3. $8.00

PACK, Graham. *Two Kinds of Time.* 1950. Houghton Mifflin. 8vo. ils. 725p. VG/dj. W1. $18.00

PACK, Robert. *Clayfield Rejoyces, Clayfield Laments.* 1987. Godine. 1st ed. F/NF. V1. $10.00

PACK, Robert. *Nothing But Light.* 1972. Rutgers. 1st ed. sgn. F/VG+. V1. $20.00

PACKARD, Frank L. *Broken Waters.* 1925. Copp Clarke. VG. P3. $20.00

PACKARD, Frank L. *Doors of Night.* 1922. Copp Clarke. VG. P3. $25.00

PACKARD, Frank L. *Jimmie Dale & the Blue Envelope.* 1930. Copp Clarke. VG. P3. $20.00

PACKARD, Frank L. *Pawned.* 1921. Copp Clark. 1st Canadian ed. VG. P3. $20.00

PACKARD, Frank L. *Tiger Claws.* 1928. Copp Clarke. 1st ed. VG. P3. $25.00

PACKER, Vin; see Meaker, Marijane.

PADDOCK, Paul. *China Diary: Crisis Diplomacy in Dairen.* 1977. IA State. 8vo. 274p. VG. W1. $18.00

PADEN, Irene. *Wake of the Prairie Schooner.* 1943. Macmillan. 1st ed. 8vo. red cloth. F/NF. T10. $65.00

PADEN, Irene. *Wake of the Prairie Schooner.* 1943. NY. Macmillan. sgn. 8vo. 514p. VG. B11. $40.00

PADFIELD, P. *Titanic & the Californian.* 1966. NY. 1st ed. VG/VG. B5. $35.00

PADGETT, Abigail. *Child of Silence.* 1993. Mysterious. 1st ed. author's 1st novel. F/F. T2. $75.00

PADGETT, Abigail. *Strawgirl.* 1994. Mysterious. 1st ed. author's 2nd novel. sgn. F/F. T2. $40.00

PADGETT, Lewis. *Mutant.* 1953. Gnome. 1st ed. VG/VG. P3. $100.00

PADGETT, Lewis. *Robots Have No Tails.* 1952. Gnome. 1st ed. NF/NF. P3. $150.00

PADGETT, Lewis. *Tomorrow & Tomorrow/Fairy Chessmen.* 1951. Gnome. 1st ed. VG/VG. P3. $85.00

PADGETT, Ron. *Great Balls of Fire.* nd. HRW. 1st ed. F/VG+. V1. $20.00

PADOVER, Saul. *Letters of Karl Marx.* 1979. Englewood Cliffs. 1st ed. 576p. F/F. A17. $15.00

PAGE, Charles N. *Feathered Pets: A Treatise on Food, Breeding & Care...* 1898. Des Moines. self pub. 142p. A17. $25.00

PAGE, Charlotte A. *Under Sail & in Port.* 1950. Peabody Mus. 8 pl. 88p. VG. T7. $70.00

PAGE, Elizabeth. *Tree of Liberty.* 1939. Farrar Rinehart. 1st ed. 985p. G+. B10. $50.00

PAGE, Gertrude Cook. *Illusion & Other Poems.* 1940. Dietz. inscr. 83p. VG. B10. $7.50

PAGE, Irvine. *Speaking to Doctor: His Responsibilities & Opportunities.* 1972. Minneapolis. 1st ed. 320p. VG. A13. $20.00

PAGE, Jesse. *Land of the Peaks & the Pampas.* 1913. London. 1st ed. ils/pl. 368p. VG. H3. $50.00

PAGE, Russell. *Education of a Gardner.* 1983 (1962). London. ils. 381p. VG/dj. B26. $25.00

PAGE, Thomas Nelson. *In Ole Virginia; or, Marse Chan & Other Stories.* 1888 (1887). Scribner. inscr. 230p. VG/case. B10. $200.00

PAGE, Thomas Nelson. *John Marvel Assistant.* 1909. Scribner. 1st ed. 573p. VG. B10. $25.00

PAGE, Thomas Nelson. *Old Gentleman of the Black Stock.* 1901. Scribner. ils HC Christy. teg. G+. B10. $25.00

PAGE, Thomas Nelson. *Red Rock: Chronicle of Reconstruction.* 1898. NY. 1st ed. 584p. gilt cloth. VG-. A17. $17.50

PAGE, Thomas Nelson. *Robert E Lee the Southerner.* 1908. Scribner. 1st ed. sgn. 12mo. 312p. xl. VG. B11. $100.00

PAGE, Thomas Nelson. *Two Little Confederates.* 1932. Scribner. 1st ed. ils JW Thomason. 189p. NF. D1. $85.00

PAGE, Thomas Nelson. *Washington & Its Romance.* 1923. NY gr cloth. xl. VG. B30. $15.00

PAGE, Thomas. *Hephaestus Plague.* 1973. Putnam. 1st ed. xl. dj. P3. $5.00

PAGE, Thomas. *Spirit.* 1977. Rawson. 1st ed. NF/NF. P3. $20.00

PAGE, Warren. *One Man's Wilderness.* nd. HRW. 1st ed. photos. NF/VG. P12. $18.00

PAGE & PAGE. *Hopi.* 1982. Abrams. 1st ed. 137 pl/32 line drawings. blk cloth. F/F. T10. $55.00

PAHIR, C. *Atlantic Salmon Fishing.* 1937. NY. Derrydale. 1/950. fair. B5. $200.00

PAIGE, Richard; see Koontz, Dean R.

PAIN, Barry. *Stories & Interludes.* 1892. Harper. G. P3. $100.00

PAINE, Albert Bigelow. *Hollow Tree Snowed-In Book.* 1924 (1910). ils Conde. VG. S13. $15.00

PAINE, Albert Bigelow. *Tent Dwellers.* 1921. Harper. B-V ed. 279p. VG/dj. M20. $32.00

PAINE, Swift. *Eilly Orrum, Queen of the Comstock.* 1929. Bobbs Merrill. 8vo. photos. 309p. G. T10. $45.00

PAINE, Swift. *Eilly Orrum, Queen of the Comstock.* 1949. Palo Alto. Pacific Books. later ed. 8vo. 309p. red cloth. VG. T10. $35.00

PAINE, Thomas. *Common Sense.* 1928. NY. Rimington Hooper. 1/376. 130p. gilt blk cloth. case. K1. $45.00

PAINE, Thomas. *Complete Writings of...* 1945. NY. 2 vol. 1st ed. 8vo. gilt blk cloth. VG/rpr case. H3. $50.00

PAINTER, A. *Coyote in the Garden.* 1988. Confluence. 1st ed. F/NF. V1. $10.00

PAINTER, F.V.N. *Poets of the South: A Series of Biographical...* 1903. Am Book Co. 237p. G. B10. $25.00

PAINTER, F.V.N. *Poets of Virginia.* 1907. BF Johnson. 336p. NF. B10. $35.00

PALAZZO, Tony. *Bianco & the New World.* 1957. Viking. 1st ed. 64p. VG+/VG+. P2. $30.00

PALAZZO, Tony. *Mister Whistler's Secret.* 1953. Viking. 1st ed. 8vo. 52p. G+. C14. $7.00

PALEY, Grace. *Enormous Changes at the Last Minute.* 1974. FSG. 1st ed. F/F. B4. $85.00

PALEY, Grace. *Little Disturbances of Man.* 1959. Doubleday. 1st ed. sgn. F/NF. B4. $350.00

PALLEN, R. *Birds of Caribbean.* 1961. NY. 1st ed. 98 pl. VG/VG. B5. $45.00

PALLEY, Reese. *Porcelain Art of Edward Marshall Boehm.* 1976. Abrams. sgn. obl 4to. 89 mc pl. 312p. F/VG. B11. $55.00

PALLIS, Marco. *Peaks & Lamas.* 1949. Knopf. revised. 64 pl/4 maps. VG. W1. $45.00

PALLISTER, Charles. *Sensationalist.* 1991. Ballantine. 1st ed. author's 1st book. F/F. H11. $30.00

PALLOTTINO, Massimo. *Etruscan Painting*. 1952. Geneva. Skira. 1st ed. 64 tipped-in pl. 139p. VG/torn. W1. $45.00

PALMER, Albert W. *Orientals in American Life*. 1934. NY. Friendship. 12mo. 212p. VG. W1. $10.00

PALMER, Beverly W. *Selected Letters of Charles Sumner*. 1990. Boston. 2 vol. F/dj. A17. $45.00

PALMER, Drew; see Lucas, Mark.

PALMER, Edwin Henry. *Song of the Reed & Other Pieces*. 1877. London. Truebner. 1st ed. 8vo. 200p. teg. morocco. F. W1. $85.00

PALMER, Eve. *Field Guide to Trees of Southern Africa*. 1983 (1977). London. 2nd. 32 pl/700 drawings, 383p. VG. B26. $30.00

PALMER, Frederick. *Bliss, Peacemaker: Life & Letters of General Tasker H Bliss*. 1934. NY. 1st ed. ils. 476p. xl. G. B18. $25.00

PALMER, Frederick. *So a Leader Came*. 1932. Long Smith. 1st ed. VG. P3. $40.00

PALMER, Joe. *This Was Racing*. 1953. NY. 1st ed. ils. 270p. brn/orange cloth. F/VG. H3. $30.00

PALMER, Joel. *Journal of Travels Over the Rocky Mountains*. 1983. Ye Galleon. 1st ed thus. M/sans. A18. $17.50

PALMER, Robin. *Mickey Never Fails*. (1939). Boston. DC Heath. 1st ed. 8vo. ils Walt Disney Studios. 102p. G+. C14. $20.00

PALMER, Robin. *Wings of the Morning: Verses From the Bible*. 1968. NY. Walck. 1st ed. 8vo. unp. VG+/dj. C14. $7.00

PALMER, Thomas. *Dream Science*. 1990. Ticknor. 1st ed. author's 2nd book. F/F. H11. $25.00

PALMER, William J. *Detective & Mr Dickens*. nd. Quality BC. F/F. P3. $10.00

PALMER, William J. *Highwayman & Mr Dickens*. 1992. St Martin. 1st ed. NF/NF. P3. $19.00

PALMER & PIERCE. *Cambios: Spirit of Transformation in Spanish Colonial Art*. 1992. NM U. 1st ed. 4to. 148p. AN/dj. T10. $50.00

PALMER & WILLIAMS. *Dictionary of National Biography 1951-1960*. 1971. 1176p. xl. VG. A4. $85.00

PALMQUIST, Peter E. *With Nature's Children: Emma B Freemen*. 1976. Interface CA Corp. 8vo. unp. F/wrp. T10. $40.00

PALWICK, Susan. *Flying in Place*. 1992. Tor. F/F. G10. $15.00

PANATI, Charles. *Links*. 1978. Houghton Mifflin. 1st ed. VG/G. P3. $10.00

PANCAKE, John S. *Destructive War: British Campaign in the Carolinas 1780-82*. 1985. AL U. 1st ed. ils/map ep. 293p. VG/dj. B18. $17.50

PANERO, Jose L. *Systematics of Pappobolus*. 1992. Ann Arbor. ils. 195p. VG/wrp. B26. $25.00

PANG, Eul-Soo. *In Pursuit of Honor & Power*. 1988. Tuscaloosa. 1st ed. 341p. dj. F3. $20.00

PANGBORN, Edgar. *Davy*. 1964. St Martin. 1st ed. VG/VG. P3. $60.00

PANGBORN, Edgar. *Good Neighbors & Other Strangers*. 1972. Macmillan. 1st ed. NF/NF. P3. $25.00

PANGBORN, Edgar. *Trial of Callista Blake*. 1961. St Martin. 1st ed. VG/G+. P3. $40.00

PANGBORN, Edgar. *West of the Sun*. 1953. Doubleday. 1st ed. VG/VG. P3. $35.00

PANOFSKY, Erwin. *Life & Art of Albrecht Durer*. 1955. ils. VG/VG. S13. $18.00

PANSHIN, Alexei. *Farewell to Yesterday's Tomorrow*. 1975. Berkeley Putnam. 1st ed. VG/VG. P3. $18.00

PANSHIN, Alexei. *World Beyond the Hill*. 1989. Tarcher. F/F. P3. $60.00

PANTZER, Eugene E. *Antun Gustav Matos*. 1981. Twayne. 1st ed. 144p. xl. VG. A17. $7.50

PANUM, Peter. *Observations Made During the Epidemic on Measles...1846*. 1940. NY. 1st Eng trans. 111p. VG. A13. $60.00

PAPAIOANNOU, Kostas. *Byzantine & Russian Painting*. 1973. Funk Wagnall. 8vo. 207p. F/dj. T10. $45.00

PAPAZOGLOU, Orania. *Sanctity*. 1986. Crown. 1st ed. F/dj. N4. $30.00

PAPE, Max. *Art of Driving*. 1982. London. Allen. 1st ed. VG/VG. O3. $45.00

PAPER, Gordon. *Chain Reaction*. 1978. Viking. 1st ed. hc. F/F. P3. $15.00

PARACELSUS. *Selected Writings, Editied With Intro by Jolande Jacobi*. 1951. NY. 1st Eng trans. 347p. VG. A13. $100.00

PARDEY & PARDEY. *Seraffyn's Mediterranean Adventure*. 1981. NY. Norton. ils/maps. 256p. dj. T7. $22.00

PARDIES, Ignace Gaston. *Dell'anima Delle Bestie, e sue Funzioni*. 1694. Venezia. Per Andrea Poletti. sm 8vo. 187p. G1. $185.00

PARDOE, Julia. *Romance of the Harem*. 1839. Phil. 2 vol. 1st Am ed. VG. C6. $120.00

PARDON & WILKS. *How To Play Solo Whist: Its Methods & Principles...* 1893. London. New ed. VG. S1. $20.00

PARETSKY, Sara. *Bitter Medicine*. 1987. NY. 1st ed. F/F. C2. $40.00

PARETSKY, Sara. *Blood Shot*. 1988. Delacorte. 1st ed. NF/NF. M22. $25.00

PARETSKY, Sara. *Blood Shot*. 1988. Delacorte. 1st ed. sgn. F/F. T2. $45.00

PARETSKY, Sara. *Burn Marks*. 1990. Delacorte. 1st ed. F/F. H11/N4. $30.00

PARETSKY, Sara. *Deadlock*. 1984. Dial. 1st ed. NF/NF. P3. $250.00

PARETSKY, Sara. *Guardian Angel*. nd. Delacorte. 5th. VG/VG. P3. $15.00

PARETSKY, Sara. *Killing Orders*. 1985. Morrow. 1st ed. sgn. F/F. C2. $175.00

PARETSKY, Sara. *Tunnel Vision*. 1994. Delacorte. 1st ed. sgn. F/F. T2. $35.00

PARGETER, Edith Mary. *Confession of Brother Haluin*. 1988. Stoddart. 1st ed. VG/VG. P3. $35.00

PARGETER, Edith Mary. *Dead Man's Ransom*. 1984. Morrow. 1st ed. NF/NF. H11. $30.00

PARGETER, Edith Mary. *Devil's Novice*. 1984. Morrow. 1st Am ed. F/F. B4. $100.00

PARGETER, Edith Mary. *Fallen Into the Pit*. 1990. MacDonald. VG/VG. P3. $30.00

PARGETER, Edith Mary. *Heretic's Apprentice*. 1989. Stoddart. 1st ed. VG/VG. P3. $30.00

PARGETER, Edith Mary. *Hermit of Eyton Forest*. 1987. Stoddart. 1st ed. hc. F/F. P3. $35.00

PARGETER, Edith Mary. *Holy Thief*. nd. Mysterious. 3rd. sgn. VG/VG. P3. $25.00

PARGETER, Edith Mary. *Leper of St Giles*. 1982. Morrow. 1st Am ed. F/F. B4. $100.00

PARGETER, Edith Mary. *Monk's Hood*. 1981. Morrow. 1st Am ed. F/F. B4. $125.00

PARGETER, Edith Mary. *Potter's Field*. 1989. Stoddart. 1st ed. VG/VG. P3. $30.00

PARGETER, Edith Mary. *Sanctuary Sparrow*. 1983. Morrow. 1st ed. VG/VG. P3. $30.00

PARIS, John. *Kimono*. 1921. London. Collins. 1st ed. 12mo. 345p. G. W1. $10.00

PARIS, W. Francklyn. *Napoleon's Legion.* 1928. Funk Wagnall. popular ed. sgn. 8vo. 240p. gr cloth. VG. B11. $75.00

PARISH, Edmund. *Hallucinations & Illusions: Study of Fallacies...* 1897. London. Walter Scott. 12mo. 390p. VG. G1. $75.00

PARISH, Elijah. *Sacred Georgraphy; or, Gazetteer of the Bible...* 1813. Boston. Armstrong. 1st ed. 8vo. unp. contemporary calf. VG. W1. $125.00

PARISH, H.J. *Victory With Vaccines: Story of Immunization.* 1968. Edinburgh. 1st ed. 245p. dj. A13. $50.00

PARISH, James Robert. *Hollywood Character Actors.* 1978. Arlington. 1st ed. VG/VG. P3. $35.00

PARISH, James Robert. *Jeanette MacDonald Story.* 1976. NY. 1st ed. VG/VG. B5. $40.00

PARISH, James Robert. *Leading Ladies.* 1977. Arlington. 1st ed. VG/VG. P3. $35.00

PARK, Jordan; see Kornbluth, Cyril.

PARK, No-Yong. *Oriental View of American Civilization.* 1945. Hale Cushman Flint. 12mo. inscr in Eng/Chinese. 128p. red cloth. T10. $50.00

PARK, Paul. *Coelestis.* 1993. Harper Collins. 1st ed. hc. F/F. P3. $30.00

PARK, Paul. *Sugar Rain.* 1989. Morrow. 1st ed. F/F. G10. $15.00

PARK, Ruth. *Witch's Thorn.* 1952. Houghton Mifflin. 1st ed. VG/VG. P3. $35.00

PARKER, Charles. *Paris Furniture Master Ebenistes.* 1956. Eng. Newport. 1st ed. 1/1000. ils. 104p. VG. B5. $75.00

PARKER, Constance-Anne. *Mr Stubbs, the Horse Painter.* 1971. London. JA Allen. 1st ed. ils. 203p. NF/dj. B14. $55.00

PARKER, Dorothy. *Enough Rope.* 1926. Boni Liveright. 1st ed. F/F. B4. $850.00

PARKER, Dorothy. *Viking Portable Library of Dorothy Parker.* 1944. Viking. 1st ed. intro WS Maugham. F/NF. B4. $55.00

PARKER, Helen F. *Arthur's Aquarium.* 1873. Boston. 152p. red cloth. gilt spine. G. B14. $35.00

PARKER, Herbert. *Courts & Lawyers of New England.* 1931. NY. Am Hist Soc. 4 vol. ils/photos. buckram. worn. M11. $250.00

PARKER, John. *Tidings Out of Brazil.* 1957. NM U. 1st ed. 1/1000. 48p. F3. $35.00

PARKER, Louis N. *Disraeli: A Play.* nd. Copp Clarke. VG. P3. $10.00

PARKER, Pat. *Movement in Black: Collected Poetry of Pat Parker 1961-1978.* 1978. Oakland. Diana. 1st ed. fwd Audre Lord. intro Judy Grahn. F/NF. B4. $85.00

PARKER, Robert B. *All Our Yesterdays.* 1994. Delacorte. ARC/1st ed. sgn. F/pict wrp. T2. $20.00

PARKER, Robert B. *All Our Yesterdays.* 1994. Delacorte. 1st ed. F/F. N4. $25.00

PARKER, Robert B. *Catskill Eagle.* 1985. Delacorte. 1st ed. sgn. rem mk. F/F. T2. $25.00

PARKER, Robert B. *Catskill Eagle.* 1985. Delacorte. 1st ed. VG/VG. P3. $18.00

PARKER, Robert B. *Crimson Joy.* 1988. Delacorte. 1st ed. VG/VG. P3. $20.00

PARKER, Robert B. *Double Deuce.* 1992. Putnam. 1st ed. NF/NF. N4. $25.00

PARKER, Robert B. *Early Autumn.* 1981. Delacorte. 1st ed. NF/dj. P3. $45.00

PARKER, Robert B. *Headquarters Budapest.* 1944. NY. index. 345p. VG/tape rpr. A17. $10.00

PARKER, Robert B. *Judas Goat.* 1978. Houghton Mifflin. 1st ed. F/F. T2. $75.00

PARKER, Robert B. *Judas Goat.* 1978. Houghton Mifflin. 1st ed. VG/VG. P3. $40.00

PARKER, Robert B. *Looking for Rachel Wallace.* 1980. Delacorte. 3rd. NF/NF. P3. $20.00

PARKER, Robert B. *Pale Kings & Princes.* 1987. Delacorte. 1st ed. F/F. P3. $16.00

PARKER, Robert B. *Pastime.* 1991. NY. Putnam. 1st ed. sgn. F/F. B11. $35.00

PARKER, Robert B. *Pastime.* 1991. Putnam. 1st ed. VG/VG. P3. $20.00

PARKER, Robert B. *Perchance To Dream.* 1991. Putnam. F/F. P3. $20.00

PARKER, Robert B. *Playmates.* 1989. Putnam. 1st ed. F/dj. M22. $20.00

PARKER, Robert B. *Playmates.* 1989. Putnam. 1st ed. sgn. VG/VG. B11. $35.00

PARKER, Robert B. *Playmates.* 1989. Putnam. 1st ed. VG/VG. P3. $18.00

PARKER, Robert B. *Poodle Springs.* 1989. Putnam. 1st ed. sgn. F/F. T2. $25.00

PARKER, Robert B. *Promised Land.* 1976. Houghton Mifflin. 1st ed. inscr. F/F. T2. $150.00

PARKER, Robert B. *Savage Place.* 1981. Delacorte/Lawrence. 1st ed. sgn. rem mk. F/F. T2. $40.00

PARKER, Robert B. *Stardust.* 1990. Putnam. 1st ed. F/F. P3. $19.00

PARKER, Robert B. *Stardust.* 1990. Putnam. 1st ed. sgn. AN/dj. N4. $30.00

PARKER, Robert B. *Taming a Sea-Horse.* 1986. Dealcorte. 1st ed. NF/NF. P3. $16.00

PARKER, Robert B. *Taming a Sea-Horse.* 1986. Delacorte/Lawrence. AP. 1/500. sgn/#d. F/prt wrp. T2. $125.00

PARKER, Robert B. *Three Weeks in Spring.* 1978. Houghton Mifflin. 1st ed. sgn. inscr/sgn Joan Parker. F/NF. T2. $75.00

PARKER, Robert B. *Valediction.* 1984. Delacorte/Lawrence. 1st ed. sgn. F/F. T2. $35.00

PARKER, Robert B. *Walking Shadow.* 1994. Putnam. 1st ed. RS. F/F. P3. $20.00

PARKER, Robert B. *Widening Gyre.* 1983. Delacorte. 1st ed. F/F. H11. $35.00

PARKER, Robert B. *Widening Gyre.* 1983. Delacorte/Lawrence. 1st ed. sgn. F/F. T2. $45.00

PARKER, Robert B. *Wilderness.* 1979. Delacorte/Lawrence. AP/1st ed. sgn. F/prt wrp. T2. $125.00

PARKER, Samuel. *Parker's Exploring Tour Beyond the Rocky Mountains.* 1967. Minneapolis. Ross Haines. facsimile. 1/2000. 380p. fld map. AN/dj. P4. $15.00

PARKER, T.J. *Laguna Heat.* 1985. NY. 1st ed. F/NF. H11. $35.00

PARKER, T.J. *Little Saigon.* 1988. St Martin. 1st ed. F/F. P3. $19.00

PARKER, T.J. *Little Saigon.* 1988. St Martin. 1st ed. VG+/VG+. A20. $15.00

PARKER, T.J. *Pacific Beat.* 1991. St Martin. 1st ed. F/F. A20. $12.00

PARKER, Watson. *Gold in the Black Hill.* 1966. Norman. 1st ed. sgn. 259p. VG/VG. B5. $35.00

PARKER & PARKER. *Year at the Races.* 1990. Viking. 1st ed. sgns. F/F. T2. $125.00

PARKER & SMITH. *Modern Turkey.* 1940. London. Routledge. 8vo. 18 pl/maps. 259p. cloth. VG. W1. $22.00

PARKES, Oscar. *British Battleships 1860-1950.* 1970-1973. London. Seeley. revised. 450 plans/photos. 701p. AN. T7. $120.00

PARKHURST. *Painter in Oil: A Complete Treatise...* 1898. VG. D2. $40.00

PARKINSON, C. Northcote. *Law & the Profits.* 1960. Houghton Mifflin. M11. $12.50

PARKINSON, Virginia. *Pointers for Little Persons Book Two: Safety...* 1943. NY. Schilling. ils. 28p. F/NF. A17. $17.50

PARKMAN, Francis. *Journals of Francis Parkman.* 1947. NY. 2 vol. 1st ed. edit M Wade. F/NF. A15. $60.00

PARKS, Gordon. *Gordon Parks: Whispers of Intimate Things.* 1971. Viking. 1st ed. photos. unp. VG+/VG. R11. $18.00

PARKS, Joseph Howard. *John Bell of Tennessee.* 1950. LSU. F/VG. B30. $20.00

PARKS. *Elizabethan Club of Yale University & Its Library.* 1986. Yale. 4to. 280p. F. A4. $85.00

PARLETT, David. *Solitaire: Aces Up & 399 Other Card Games.* 1979. NY. 367p. VG. S1. $5.00

PARNALL, Peter. *Dog's Book of Birds.* 1977. Scribner. 1st ed. 16mo. unp. F/G. C14. $8.00

PARNELL, Frank H. *Monthly Terrors: An Index to Weird Fantasy Magazines.* 1985. Greenwood. VG. P3. $100.00

PARR, Charles McKew. *So Noble a Captain: Life & Times of Ferdinand Magellan.* 1953. Crowell. 1st ed. inscr. 8vo. 15 pl/map ep. 423p. VG/G. B11. $65.00

PARRISH, Frank. *Bird in the Net.* 1988. Harper Row. 1st ed. VG/VG. P3. $16.00

PARRISH, Frank. *Death in the Rain.* 1984. Dodd Mead. 1st ed. lacks ffe. xl. VG/VG. N4. $10.00

PARRISH, Frank. *Fly in the Cobweb.* 1986. Harper Row. F/F. P3. $15.00

PARRISH, Maxfield. *Palgrenes Golden Treasury.* 1941. Garden City. VG/G. B5. $65.00

PARRISH, Peggy. *Amelia Bedelia & the Surprise Shower.* (1966). Harper Row. I Can Read Book. 8vo. ils. VG+/fair. C14. $6.00

PARRISH, Randall. *Case & the Girl.* nd. AL Burt. hc. VG/VG. P3. $25.00

PARRISH, Randall. *Devil's Own.* nd. Donohue. VG/VG. P3. $18.00

PARRY, Judge. *Don Quixote.* 1924. NY. ils Walter Crane. VG. M17. $40.00

PARRY, Michel. *Savage Heroes.* 1980. Taplinger. 1st ed. F/F. P3. $22.00

PARSONS, Allen P. *Complete Book of Fresh-Water Fishing.* 1969. Outdoor Life/Harper Row. photos. VG/G+. P12. $20.00

PARSONS, Elsie Clew. *Isleta Paintings.* 1962. Smithsonian. 1st ed. 4to. 299p. VG/dj. T10. $250.00

PARSONS, Herbert Collins. *Puritan Outpost: History of Town & People of Northfield, MA.* 1937. NY. 1st ed. ils. 546p. VG. B18. $22.50

PARSONS, J. *Smith & Wesson Revolvers.* 1957. NY. 1st ed. VG/G. B5. $60.00

PARSONS, John Herbert. *Introduction to Study of Colour Vision.* 1924. Cambridge. 2nd. tall 8vo. 324p. VG/dj. G1. $60.00

PARTEE, Charles. *Adventure in Africa. Story of Don McClure.* 1990. Ministry. sgn. 8vo. F/F. B11. $12.00

PARTINGTON, J.R. *History of Greek Fire & Gunpowder.* (1960). Cambridge, Eng. ils. 381p. gilt red cloth. VG. H3. $150.00

PARTON, Dolly. *Coat of Many Colors.* 1994. Harper. 1st ed. AN/dj. H4. $15.00

PARTON, James. *Life & Times of Aaron Burr.* 1858. np. VG. M17. $50.00

PARTON, James. *Life of Horace Greeley.* 1869. Boston. 8vo. 598p. gr cloth. xl. T3. $15.00

PARTRIDGE, Norman. *Slippin' Into Darkness.* 1994. Baltimore. CD Pub. 1st ed. 1/500. sgn. ils/sgn AM Clark. F/F. T2. $65.00

PASCALIS, Felix. *Annual Oration, Delivered Before the Chemical Society...* 1802. Phil. 48p. modern wrp. B14. $175.00

PASTERNAK, Boris. *Safe Conduct.* 1959. Elek. 1st ed. VG/VG. M19. $35.00

PATCHEN, Kenneth. *Journal of Albion Moonlight.* 1944. United Book Guild. hc. NF. V1. $25.00

PATCHEN, Kenneth. *Journal of Albion Moonlight.* 1946. NY. sgn twice w/orig poem. VG/VG. B5. $100.00

PATCHEN, Kenneth. *Poemscapes.* 1958. Highlands, NC. Jonathan Williams. 1st ed. 1/42. sgn. F/wrp. B4. $850.00

PATCHEN, Kenneth. *Red Wine & Yellow Hair.* 1949. New Directions. 1st ed. assn copy. RS. F/VG. V1. $55.00

PATCHEN, Kenneth. *Selected Poems.* 1946. New Directions. 1st ed. RS. VG+/VG. V1. $100.00

PATCHETT, M.E. *Adam Troy, Astoman.* 1954. Lutterworth. G+/dj. P3. $15.00

PATCHETT, M.E. *Kidnappers of Space.* 1953. Lutterworth. 1st ed. G+/dj. P3. $15.00

PATCHIN, Frank Gee. *Pony Rider Boys With the Texas Rangers.* nd. Saalfield. VG/VG. P3. $15.00

PATER, Walter. *Greek Studies: A Series of Essays.* 1911. London. Macmillan. Lib ed. crown 8vo. gilt bl cloth. NF. T10. $25.00

PATER, Walter. *Marius the Epicurean.* 1898. NY. G. A17. $15.00

PATERSON, Antionette Mann. *Infinite Worlds of Giordano Bruno.* 1970. Springfield, IL. Charles Thomas. 1st ed. inscr. 8vo. VG/VG. B11. $25.00

PATON, Alan. *Case History of a Pinky.* (1965). Johannesburg. SA Inst Race Relations. NF/stapled wrp. B4. $125.00

PATRICK, Keats. *Death Is a Tory.* 1935. Bobbs Merrill. 1st ed. VG/VG. P3. $45.00

PATRICK, Richard North. *Degree of Guilt.* 1993. Knopf. 1st ed. F/F. H11. $30.00

PATRICK, Richard North. *Escape the Night.* 1983. Random. 1st ed. F/F. H11. $35.00

PATRICK, Vincent. *Family Business.* 1985. Poseidon. 1st ed. F/F. H11. $35.00

PATRICK, Vincent. *Pope of Greenwich Village.* 1979. Seaview. 1st ed. author's 1st book. NF/F. H11. $30.00

PATRICK, William. *Spirals.* 1983. Houghton Mifflin. 1st ed. RS. F/F. P3. $15.00

PATRICK & RANSOME. *Red Dancing Shoes.* 1993. Tambourine. 1st ed. sgn. AN/dj. B4. $45.00

PATROUCH, Joseph F. *SF of Isaac Asimov.* 1974. Doubleday. 1st ed. hc. VG/VG. P3. $22.00

PATTEN, Brian. *Sly Cormorant & the Fishes.* 1977. Middlesex, Eng. Cormorant. 1st ed. NF/VG. C8. $50.00

PATTEN, John. *Pre-Industrial England: Geographical Essays.* 1979. Folkstone. Kent Dawson. 1st ed. 8vo. 245p. F/F. T10. $35.00

PATTEN, Lewis B. *Gene Autry & the Ghost Riders.* 1955. Whitman. G. P3. $12.00

PATTEN, William. *Book of Sport.* 1901. NY. Taylor. ltd ed. 1/1500. folio. binding copy. O3. $185.00

PATTEN. *George Cruikshank: A Revaluation.* 1974. Princeton. ils. 302p. NF. A4. $85.00

PATTERSON, Harry. *Dillinger.* 1983. Hutchinson. 1st ed. F/F. P3. $20.00

PATTERSON, Innis. *Eppworth Case.* 1930. Farrar Rinehart. 1st ed. VG/VG. P3. $30.00

PATTERSON, James. *Along Came a Spider*. 1993. Little Brn. ARC. VG/prt wrp. M22. $25.00

PATTERSON, James. *Along Came a Spider*. 1993. Little Brn. 1st ed. NF/NF. P3. $22.00

PATTERSON, James. *Black Market*. 1986. Simon Schuster. 1st ed. NF/NF. P3. $20.00

PATTERSON, James. *Jericho Commandment*. 1979. Crown. 1st ed. author's 2nd novel. F/F. T2. $40.00

PATTERSON, James. *Midnight Club*. 1989. Little Brn. 1st ed. F/F. T2. $15.00

PATTERSON, Leonardo. *Magic of Middle American Culture Before 1492*. 1992. Austria. Bavariadruck. 1st ed. pl. wrp. F3. $65.00

PATTERSON, Richard North. *Degree of Guilt*. 1993. Knopf. 1st ed. sgn. F/F. T2. $35.00

PATTERSON, Richard North. *Escape the Night*. 1983. Random. 1st ed. VG/VG. P3. $25.00

PATTERSON, Richard North. *Eyes of a Child*. 1995. Knopf. 1st ed. NF/NF. P3. $24.00

PATTERSON, Richard North. *Outside Man*. 1981. Atlantic/Little Brn. 1st ed. NF/NF. H11. $45.00

PATTERSON, Richard North. *Private Screening*. 1985. Villard. 1st ed. F/F. H11. $45.00

PATTISON, Barrie. *Seal of Dracula*. nd. Bounty. F/F. P3. $15.00

PATTON, Frances Gray. *Good Morning, Miss Dove*. 1954. Dodd Mead. 1st ed. F/NF. B4. $175.00

PATTOU, Edith. *Hero's Song*. 1991. HBJ. 1st ed. F/F. P3. $17.00

PAUL, Aileen. *Kid's Gardening: A First Indoor Gardening Book for Children*. 1972. Doubleday. 1st ed. 8vo. ils. F/VG. M5. $12.00

PAUL, Barbara. *But He Was Already Dead When I Got There*. 1986. Scribner. 1st ed. F/F. P3. $14.00

PAUL, Barbara. *Cadenza for Caruso*. 1984. St Martin. 1st ed. VG/VG. P3. $20.00

PAUL, Barbara. *Chorus of Detectives*. 1987. St Martin. 1st ed. VG/VG. P3. $18.00

PAUL, Barbara. *Fare Play*. 1995. Scribner. 1st ed. F/F. P3. $20.00

PAUL, Elliot. *Black & the Red*. 1956. Random. 1st ed. 277p. VG/dj. M20. $27.00

PAUL, Elliot. *Desperate Scenery*. 1954. Random. 1st ed. F/clip VG. A18. $25.00

PAUL, F.W.; see Fairman, Paul.

PAUL, Henry E. *Outer Space Photography for the Amateur*. 1976. NY. Amphoto. 4th. 152 photos. 155p. VG/dj. K5. $18.00

PAUL, Jim. *What's Called Love*. 1993. Villard. ARC. w/promo material. F/F. B35. $18.00

PAUL, Raymond. *Who Murdered Mary Rogers?* 1971. Prentice Hall. hc. VG. P3. $20.00

PAULEY, Bruce F. *Hitler & the Forgotten Nazis: A History...* 1981. NC U. biblio/index. 292p. VG/dj. A17. $20.00

PAULHAN, Frederic. *L'Activite Mentale et les Elements de l'Esprit*. 1889. Paris. Germer Bailliere. 8vo. 588p. later blk cloth. VG. G1. $75.00

PAULL, Mrs. George A. *Marjorie's Doings*. 1900. Jacobs. 12mo. gr cloth. VG. M5. $22.00

PAULLIN, Charles O. *Atlas of the Historical Geography of the United States*. 1932. Carnegie/Am Geographical Soc. 688 maps. F. O7. $300.00

PAULSEN, Martha. *Toyland*. 1944. Saalfield. ils Julian Wehr. spbg. F/chip. T10. $175.00

PAVLOV, Ivan Petrovich. *Lectures on Conditioned Reflexes*. (1928). NY. Internat Pub. 1st Eng-language ed. 414p. blk cloth. VG. G1. $85.00

PAWIAK, Janina. *Historical Atlas of Poland*. 1981. Warsaw. Dept State Cartographical Pub. 54p of maps. F/dj. O7. $35.00

PAXSON, Diana L. *White Raven*. 1988. Morrow. 1st ed. VG/VG. P3. $10.00

PAXSON, Diana L. *Wolf & the Raven*. 1993. Morrow. 1st ed. NF/dj. M21. $15.00

PAXTON, Harry. *Whiz Kids*. 1950. McKay. 1st ed. F/VG+. P8. $250.00

PAXTON, Joseph. *Paxton's Magazine of Botany*. 1834-1879. London. Orr Smith. 16 vol. 717 hand-colored pl. 2 bdg states. NF. A10. $11,000.00

PAYES, Rachel Cosgrove. *Forsythia Finds Murder*. 1960. Avalon. 1st ed. xl. dj. P3. $8.00

PAYNE, David. *Early From the Dance*. 1989. Doubleday. VG+/F. A20. $13.00

PAYNE, Laurence. *Malice in Camera*. 1983. Crime Club. 1st ed. F/F. P3. $15.00

PAYNE, Robert. *Forever China*. 1945. Dodd Mead. 2nd. 8vo. 573p. VG. W1. $18.00

PAYNE, Robert. *Holy Sword: Story of Islam From Muhammad to Present*. 1959. Harper. 1st ed. 16 pl/2 maps. 335p. VG/dj. W1. $20.00

PAYNE, Robert. *Mao Tse-Tung: Ruler of Red China*. 1950. NY. Schuman. 8vo. 4 pl. 303p. VG. W1. $18.00

PAYNE, Robert. *Portrait of a Revolutionary: Mao Tse-Tung*. 1961. Abelard-Schuman. 8vo. 311p. VG/dj. W1. $18.00

PAZ, Ireneo. *Life & Adventures of Celebrated Bandit Joaquin Murieta...* 1925. Chicago. Regan. 1st ed. 1/975. 174p. red ribbed cloth. NF. T10. $85.00

PEABODY, H.G. *Glimpse of the Grand Canyon*. 1900. KS City. worn. V4. $35.00

PEAGRAM, William Mead. *Past-Times*. 1909. Baltimore. Saumenig. 141p. G. B10. $12.00

PEAKE, Mervyn. *Gormenghast*. 1967. Weybright Talley. hc. VG. P3. $20.00

PEAKE, Mervyn. *Ride a Cock-Horse & Other Nursery Rhymes*. 1940. Chatto Windus. 1st ed. 4to. pict brd. NF/NF. D1. $650.00

PEAKE, Mervyn. *Titus Groan*. 1946. Reynal Hitchcock. 1st ed. NF/NF. P3. $250.00

PEARCE, Hamilton. *Story of the Kidnaping of Billy Whitla*. 1909. Cleveland. 204p. fair. B18. $32.50

PEARCE, Michael. *Mamur Zapt & the Camil of Destruction*. 1993. Collins Crime Club. 1st ed. NF/NF. P3. $25.00

PEARING, Blanche. *In the City by the Lake*. 1892. Chicago. 1st ed. 192p. G. A17. $15.00

PEARIS, Leonard M. *Insect Pests of Farm, Garden & Orchard*. 1941. NY. 4th. ils. 549p. VG. B26. $27.50

PEARL, Jack. *Dam of Death*. 1967. Whitman. TVTI. VG. P3. $8.00

PEARL, Jack. *Fear Formula*. 1968. Whitman. TVTI. F. P3. $13.00

PEARL, Jack. *Space Eagle: Operation Star Voyage*. 1970. Whitman. VG. P3. $10.00

PEARMAN, G.I. *Greenhouse*. 1988. Melbourne. 8vo. 752p. pict brd. F. B1. $35.00

PEARS, Tim. *In the Place of the Fallen Leaves*. 1995. Donald Fine. 1st ed. F/F. M23. $35.00

PEARSON, C. *Indomitable Goose*. 1960. Minneapolis. G/G. B5. $40.00

PEARSON, E. *Studies in Murder*. 1924. NY. 1st ed. VG/VG. B5. $37.50

PEARSON, E. *Trial of Lizzie Borden*. 1937. NY. 1st ed. VG/G. B5. $70.00

PEARSON, E.L. *Theodore Roosevelt*. 1925. NY. 12mo. ils. 159p. bl cloth. G. T3. $15.00

PEARSON, John. *James Bond: The Authorized Biography.* 1973. Morrow. 1st ed. VG/VG. P3. $40.00

PEARSON, John. *Kindness of Dr Avicenna.* 1982. HRW. 1st ed. F/F. P3. $15.00

PEARSON, John. *Life of Ian Fleming.* 1966. McGraw Hill. 1st ed. VG/VG. P3. $30.00

PEARSON, Karl. *Grammar of Science.* 1900. London. 2nd. 548p. VG. A13. $50.00

PEARSON, Ridley. *Angel Maker.* 1993. Delacorte. 1st ed. F/F. M22. $15.00

PEARSON, Ridley. *Hard Fall.* 1992. Delacorte. 1st ed. sgn. F/F. T2. $25.00

PEARSON, Ridley. *Probable Cause.* 1990. St Martin. 1st ed. F/F. P3. $20.00

PEARSON, Ridley. *Probable Cause.* 1990. St Martin. 1st ed. sgn. NF/NF. B2. $35.00

PEARSON, Ridley. *Seizing of Yankee Green Mall.* 1987. NY. 1st ed. NF/F. H11. $35.00

PEARSON, Ridley. *Undercurrents.* 1988. St Martin. 1st ed. VG/VG. P3. $18.00

PEARSON, T.R. *Call & Response.* 1989. NY. Linden. 1st ed. sgn. F/F. B4. $45.00

PEARSON, Virginia. *Play a Tune With Betty & Billy.* nd. Boston Music Co. 21p. NF. C14. $20.00

PEARSON, William. *Chessplayer.* 1984. Viking. 1st ed. F/F. H11. $25.00

PEARSON, William. *Chessplayer.* 1984. Viking. 1st ed. hc. VG/VG. P3. $15.00

PEARSON, William. *Hunt the Man Down.* nd. BC. VG/VG. P3. $8.00

PEARSON, William. *Trial of Honor.* 1967. NAL. 1st ed. xl. dj. P3. $5.00

PEARTH, Dorothy L. *Ferns & Flowering Plants of Westmoreland Co, PA.* 1975. Pittsburgh. ils. 115p. sc. B26. $17.50

PEARY, Danny. *We Played the Game.* 1994. Hyperion. 1st ed. F/F. P8. $25.00

PEASE, Arthur S. *Flora of Northern NH.* 1964. Cambridge. New Eng Botanical Club. 2 maps. 278p. wrp. B26. $35.00

PEASE, Howard. *Tod Moran: Fog Horns.* 1937. Doubleday. later ed. 295p. VG/dj. M20. $12.50

PEASE, Josephine Van Dolzen. *This Is the World.* 1956. Chicago. rpt. ils. 72p. F/F. A17. $7.50

PEASE, William D. *Playing the Dozens.* 1990. Viking. 1st ed. author's 1st book. F/F. H11. $25.00

PEAT, Fern Bisel. *Mother Goose, Her Best-Known Rhymes.* 1933. Saalfield. 4to. VG+. C8. $75.00

PEAT, Fern Bisel. *Three Little Kittens.* 1937. Saalfield. 12 pl. VG/stiff wrp. M5. $40.00

PEAT, H.R. *Inexcusable Lie.* 1923. Donnelley. 1st ed? inscr. VG. A15. $15.00

PEATTIE, Donald C. *Audubon's America.* 1940. Boston. 1st ltd ed. sgn. 329p. teg. gilt cloth. VG/case. H3. $75.00

PEATTIE, Roderick. *Look to the Frontier: A Geography for Peace Table.* 1970. Kennikat. 246p. F. A17. $7.50

PECK, George. *Peck's Bad Boy & His Pa.* 1900. WB Conkey. 1st/only complete ed. ils Williams. G+. P12. $15.00

PECK, George. *Peck's Irish Friend.* 1900. WB Conkey. ils Williams. G+. P12. $15.00

PECK, Richard E. *Final Solution.* 1973. Doubleday. 1st ed. VG/VG. P3. $15.00

PEDERSEN & PIHL. *Early Physics & Astronomy.* 1974. NY. Am Elsevier. 1st ed. 8vo. 413p. VG/VG. K5. $40.00

PEDLER, Kit. *Brainrack.* 1974. Souvenir. 1st ed. F/F. P3. $25.00

PEDRAZAS, Allan. *Harry Chronicles.* 1995. St Martin. 1st ed. F/F. M23. $50.00

PEDRETTI, Carlo. *Codex Huygens & Leonardo da Vinci's Art Theory.* 1968. Kraus Rpt. ils. linen. D2. $65.00

PEDRETTI, Carlo. *Leonardo da Vinci Inedito. Tre Saggi.* 1968. Florence. Barbera. ils/pl. 97p dj. D2. $70.00

PEDRETTI, Carlo. *Leonardo: A Study in Chronology & Style.* 1973. Berkeley. sgn. 199 pl. 192p. dj. D2. $55.00

PEEL, Lynnette J. *Rural Industry in the Port Phillip Region 1835-1880.* 1974. Carlton. VG. O7. $20.00

PEET, Bill. *Bill Peet: An Autobiography.* nd. Houghton Mifflin. 2nd. 4to. 190p. xl. VG. C14. $12.00

PEET. *Who's the Author? A Guide to Authorship of Novels...* 1901. np. 321p. VG. A4. $35.00

PEFFER, Nathaniel. *Far East: A Modern History.* 1958. Ann Arbor. 8vo. 489p. VG. W1. $15.00

PEI, Meg. *Salaryman.* 1992. Viking. 1st ed. author's 1st book. F/F. H11. $30.00

PEISSEL, Michel. *Great Himalayan Passage.* 1975. Little Brn. sm 8vo. 32 pl. 254p. VG/dj. W1. $20.00

PEISSEL, Michel. *Lost World of Quintana Roo.* 1963. Dutton. 1st ed. 306p. dj. F3. $20.00

PELHAM, D. *Human Body.* 1983. Viking. 1st ed. moveables. VG. P2. $40.00

PELL, Franklyn. *Hangman's Hill.* 1946. Dodd Mead. 1st ed. VG/VG. P3. $23.00

PELLAPRAT, Henri-Paul. *Modern French Culinary Art.* 1966. np. VG/VG. B30. $60.00

PELLEGRINO, Charles. *Her Name Titanic.* 1988. McGraw Hill. VG/VG. A16. $15.00

PELLEGRINO, Charles. *Unearthing Atlantis.* 1991. Random. 1st ed. VG. P3. $23.00

PELLER, Hugo. *Stork Shee Rose on Christmas Eve.* 1977. Attic Pr. 1/150. miniature. teg. sgn Peller bdg. F/double-clamshell box. B24. $950.00

PELLETIER, C. *Bubble Reputation.* 1993. NY. Crown. 1st ed. F/F clip. B4. $45.00

PELLETIER, C. *Marriage Made at Woodstock.* 1994. Crown. 1st ed. F/F. A20. $10.00

PELLICO, Silvio. *Le Mie Prigioni.* 1869. Milan. Edoardo Sonzogno Editore. ils Tony Johannot. VG. T10. $100.00

PELLOW, Thomas. *Adventures of Thomas Fellow...* 1890. Fisher Unwin/Macmillan. 1st ed. 10 pl. xl. VG. W1. $45.00

PENA, Amado. *Pena on Pena.* 1995. Waco, TX. WRS Pub. 1st ed. ils. AN/dj. T10. $30.00

PENDEXTER, Hugh. *Red Belts.* 1920. Doubleday Page. 1st ed thus. 246p. VG/fair. B10. $15.00

PENDLETON, Louis. *Corona of the Nantahalas: A Romance.* 1895. Merriam. 1st ed. 99p. G. B10. $35.00

PENDRAY, G. Edward. *Men, Mirrors & Stars.* 1935. Funk Wagnalls. 1st ed. 8vo. 339p. G/dj. K5. $28.00

PENFIELD, F.C. *East of Suez.* 1907. NY. Century. 8vo. ils/map. xl. VG. W1. $12.00

PENFIELD & ROBERTS. *Speech & Brain Mechanisms.* 1959. Princeton. ils. maroon cloth. VG/worn. G1. $65.00

PENFOLD. *Africa: Maps & Plans in the Public Record Office.* 1982. London. HMSO. 440p. F/NF. A4. $135.00

PENGUIN BOOKS. *Penguin Book of Comics.* 1967. ils/photos. 256p. F. M13. $25.00

PENICK, I *Empire Strikes Back: A Pop-Up Book.* 1980. Random. VG. P3. $15.00

PENLEY, Norman. *Miss Melbourn's Milton.* nd. Modern Pub. VG. P3. $25.00

PENN, John. *An Ad for Murder.* 1982. Scribner. 1st ed. F/F. P3. $15.00

PENN, John. *Deadly Sickness.* 1985. Scribner. 1st ed. F/F. P3. $15.00

PENN, John. *Outrageous Exposures.* 1988. Collins. 1st ed. VG/VG. P3. $20.00

PENNAK, R.W. *Fresh-Water Invertebrates of the United States.* 1953. Ronald Pr. 8vo. ils. 769p. cloth. xl. B1. $20.00

PENNELL, Francis W. *Scrophulariaceae of Eastern North America.* 1935. Phil. 155 distributional maps/ils. 650p. wrp. B26. $45.00

PENNELL, Joseph Stanley. *History of Rome Hanks & Kindred Matters.* 1944. Scribner. 1st ed. 363p. VG/G. B10. $10.00

PENNELL, Joseph. *Adventures of an Illustrator.* 1925. Little Brn. 1st trade ed. 4to. beige cloth. xl. VG. T10. $75.00

PENNELL, Joseph. *Quaint Corners In Philadelphia.* 1922. Wanamaker. VG. P12. $18.00

PENNEY, Clara Louisa. *List of Books Printed Before 1601 in Lib Hispanic Soc of Am.* 1929. np. 290p. VG. A4. $65.00

PENNY, Marie. *Children's Corner.* 1933. Greenberg. 1st ed. sm 8vo. F/G. M5. $35.00

PENROSE, Margaret. *Campfire Girls on the Program.* nd. NY. 202p. F. A17. $10.00

PENROSE, Margaret. *Dorothy Dale, Girl of Today.* 1908. Cupples Leon. G+. P12. $5.00

PENROSE, Margaret. *Dorothy Dale & Her Chums.* 1909. Cupples Leon. G+. P12. $5.00

PENTECOST, Hugh. *Murder Round the Clock.* 1985. Dodd Mead. 1st ed. F/NF. H11. $25.00

PENTICOST, Hugh; see Phillips, Judson.

PENZER. *Annotated Bibliography of Sir Richard Francis Burton.* nd. rpt. 1/225. ils. 367p. F. A4. $85.00

PENZLER, Otto. *Detectionary.* nd. BC. VG/VG. P3. $10.00

PEPER & RIKOFF. *Hunting Moments of Truth.* 1973. Winchester. 1st ed. ils Milton C Weiler. VG/VG. P12. $15.00

PEPPER, Charles. *Life-Work of Louis Klopsch.* nd. Christian Herald. probable 1st ed. 395p. VG. B22. $12.00

PEPPIN, Brigid. *Golden Age of Fantastic Illustration.* 1975. Watson Guptill. 1st Am ed. ils. 192p. VG+/VG+. P2. $100.00

PEPPIN & MICKLETHWAIT. *Dictionary of British Book Illustrator, the 20th Century.* 1983. London. ils. 336p. VG/VG. A4. $95.00

PEPYS, Samuel. *Diary of Samuel Pepys.* 1970-1983. Berkeley. 11 vol. VG+ or F. B18. $195.00

PERCY, Walker. *Lancelot.* 1977. FSG. 1st ed. NF/F. B35. $29.00

PERCY, Walker. *Lost in the Cosmos.* 1983. FSG. 1st ed. NF/NF. A20/B35. $18.00

PERCY, Walker. *Love in the Ruins.* 1971. FSG. 1st ed. F/NF. B35. $60.00

PERCY, Walker. *Second Coming.* 1980. FSG. 1st ed. VG/VG. P3. $18.00

PERCY, Walker. *Thanatos Syndrome.* 1987. FSG. VG/VG-. P3. $15.00

PERELMAN, S.J. *Dream Department.* 1943. Random. 1st ed. F/NF. B2. $125.00

PERELMAN, S.J. *Rising Gorge.* 1961. Simon Schuster. 1st ed. VG/G. P12. $12.00

PERELMAN & REYNOLDS. *Parlor, Bedlam & Bath.* 1930. NY. Liveright. 1st ed. sgn/dtd 1931. teg. full leather. F. B4. $1,500.00

PEREZ, Bernard. *First Three Years of Childhood.* 1888 (1878). NY. Kellogg. 2nd Eng-language ed. 12mo. 292p. G1. $40.00

PEREZ DE RIBAS, Andres. *My Life Among the Savage Nation of New Spain.* 1968. Ward Ritchie. 8vo. 256p. gilt red cloth. F. T10. $75.00

PERKIN. *Ayn Rand. First Descriptive Bibliography.* 1990. ils. 100p. F/VG. A4. $65.00

PERKINS, Al. *Ian Fleming's Chitty-Chitty Bung-Bung.* nd. Beginner Books BC. VG. P3. $4.00

PERKINS, Charles Elliott. *Pinto Horse.* 1937. Fisher Skofield. ils Edward Borein. F. T10. $150.00

PERKINS, Jack. *Pied Piper of Hamlin.* 1931. McLoughlin. Jr Color Classics. ils. F. M5. $20.00

PERKINS, Lucy Fitch. *Colonial Twins of Virginia.* 1924. Houghton Mifflin. 1st ed. ils. pict cloth. VG+/fair. M5. $40.00

PERKINS, Lucy Fitch. *Filipino Twins.* 1923. Houghton Mifflin. 1st ed. ils. VG+/G. M5. $40.00

PERKINS, Marlin. *Zoo Parade.* 1954. Rand McNally. 1st ed. ils Bransom/Fleishman. 95p. VG. C14. $18.00

PERKINS & TANIS. *Native Americas of North America.* 1975. Scarecrow. 558p. F3. $35.00

PERLES, Alfred. *Great True Spy Adventures.* 1960. Arco. 2nd. VG. P3. $15.00

PERLING, J.J. *President Takes a Wife.* 1959. Denlinger. VG/fair. B10. $10.00

PERLMAN. *Immortal Eight: American Painting From Eakins...* 1979. F/F. D2. $25.00

PERNA, Albert F. *Glider Gladiators of WWII.* 1970. Freeman, SD. 1st ed. ils. 383p. F/dj. B18. $20.00

PERNICK, Martin. *Calculus of Suffering: Pain, Professionalism & Anesthesia...* 1985. NY. 1st ed. 421p. VG. A13. $35.00

PERON, Eva. *My Mission in Life.* 1953. Vantage. 1st Am ed. trans Ethel Cherry. VG+/VG. B4. $125.00

PEROWNE, Barry. *Raffles in Pursuit.* 1934. Cassell. 1st ed. xl. VG. P3. $15.00

PEROWNE, Barry. *Raffles of the MCC.* 1979. St Martin. 1st ed. VG/VG. P3. $15.00

PEROWNE, Stewart. *Jerusalem & Bethlehem.* 1965. London. Phoenix. Cities of the World series. 1st ed. 8vo. VG. W1. $12.00

PERRAULT, Charles. *Beauty & the Beast.* 1980. Gr Tiger. ils Michael Hague. 74p. VG. D1. $85.00

PERRAULT, Charles. *Cinderella.* 1919. London. Heinemann. 1st ed. ils/sgn Rackham. wht brd/vellum back. NF/case. D1. $1,600.00

PERRAULT, Charles. *Histoire De Peau D'Ane.* 1902. Hammersmith. 1st ed thus. 1/230. VG. C6. $400.00

PERRAULT, Charles. *Perrault's Classic French Fairy Tales.* 1967. Meridith. 1st ed. 8vo. 224p. NF. C14. $10.00

PERRAULT, Charles. *Sleeping Beauty.* 1919. London. Heinemann. 1st ed. ils/sgn Rackham. VG/case. D1. $1,500.00

PERRETT, Bryan. *Knights of the Black Cross: Hitler's Panzerwaffe...* 1986. NY. 1st Am ed. 266p. brd. VG/dj. B18. $15.00

PERRY, Anne. *Hyde Park Headsman.* 1994. Fawcett. 1st Am ed. F/F. B4. $35.00

PERRY, Gaylord. *Me & the Spitter.* 1974. Saturday Review. later prt. VG+/VG+. P8. $50.00

PERRY, George Sessions. *Hackberry Cavalier.* 1945. Viking. 1st ed. VG/VG. A18. $20.00

PERRY, George Sessions. *Texas: A World in Itself.* 1942. Whittlesey. 8th. sgn. 293p. NF/dj. T10. $45.00

PERRY, John. *American Ferryboats.* 1957. NY. Wilfred Funk. VG/VG. A16. $35.00

PERRY, Milton Freeman. *Infernal Machines: Story of Confederate Submarine...* 1965. Baton Rouge. LA U. 1st ed. 231p. cloth. F/NF. M8. $75.00

PERRY, Ritchie. *Fall Guy.* 1972. Houghton Mifflin. 1st ed. VG/VG. P3. $18.00

PERRY, Ritchie. *One Good Death Deserves Another.* 1976. Collins Crime Club. 1st ed. VG/VG. P3. $15.00

PERRY, Ronald. *Denizens.* 1980. Random. 1st ed. Nat Poetry Series. F/F. V1. $10.00

PERRY, Thomas. *Island.* 1987. Putnam. 1st ed. VG+/F. A20. $22.00

PERRY, Thomas. *Vanishing Act.* 1995. Random. 1st ed. F/F. P3. $23.00

PERSICO, Joseph E. *Piercing of the Reich.* 1979. Viking. 1st ed. hc. VG/VG. P3. $18.00

PERSICO, Joseph E. *Spiderweb.* 1979. Crown. 1st ed. VG/VG. P3. $15.00

PERTWEE, Roland. *Hell's Loose.* 1929. Houghton Mifflin. VG. P3. $8.00

PERVIVAL, Olive. *Our Old-Fashioned Flowers.* 1947. Pasadena. ils. 245p. VG+. B26. $35.00

PESCE, Angelo. *Colours of the Arab Fatherland.* 1975. Falcon. 1st ed. ils. 143p. VG/dj. W1. $30.00

PESETSKY, Bette. *Author From a Savage People.* 1983. Knopf. 1st ed. author's 2nd book. F/F. B4. $35.00

PESETSKY, Bette. *Stories Up to a Point.* 1981. Knopf. 1st ed. rem mk. F/F. B4. $50.00

PESHA. *Great Lakes Ships Book 2.* Great Lakes Maritime Inst. G/wrp. A16. $20.00

PESOTTA, Rose. *Bread Upon the Waters.* 1944. NY. 1st ed. 435p. VG/torn. B18. $35.00

PETAJA, Emil. *Stardrift.* 1971. Fpci. 1st ed. sgn. F/F. P3. $30.00

PETER, Lily. *Great Riding.* 1966. Robert Moore Allen. sgn. 8vo. 269p. F/G. B11. $20.00

PETER & SOUTHWICK. *Cleveland Park: Early Residential Neighborhood...* 1958. Community Lib Comm. ils/map. 60p. VG/wrp. B10. $12.00

PETERKIN, Julia. *Plantation Christmas.* 1934. Houghton Mifflin. 12mo. VG/VG. B17. $30.00

PETERKIN & ULMANN. *Roll, Jordan, Roll.* 1933. NY. Ballou. 1st trade ed/1st issue. NF/NF. B4. $850.00

PETERS, Elizabeth; see Mertz, Barbara Gross.

PETERS, Ellis; see Pargeter, Edith Mary.

PETERS, Harry. *Currier & Ives, Printmakers to the American People...* 1976. 4 vol. rpt. 4to. ils. cream buckram. box. A4. $400.00

PETERS, Ludovic. *Tarakian.* 1963. Abelard Schuman. 1st ed. VG/G+. P3. $20.00

PETERS, Ludovic. *Two After Malic.* 1966. Walker. 1st ed. VG/VG. P3. $13.00

PETERS, Robert. *Poet As Ice-Skater.* 1975. San Francisco. 1/1000. 52p. wrp. A17. $9.50

PETERS. *Clipper Ship Prints, Including Other Merchant Sailing Ships.* 1930. np. 4to. ils Currier & Ives checklist. 109p. VG. A4. $165.00

PETERS. *Currier & Ives, Printmakers to the American People.* 1976. np. 2 vol. rpt of 1929 & 1931 Arno ed. ils/pl. cream buckram. F. A4. $295.00

PETERSE, Richard G. *Lost Cities of Cibola.* 1980. Chicago. Franciscan Herald. 8vo. ils. 292p. gilt cloth. NF/dj. T10. $50.00

PETERSEN, Eugene T. *Mackinac Island: Its History in Pictures...* 1973. Mackinac Island, MI. State Park Comm. ils. dj. T7. $35.00

PETERSEN, Herman. *Covered Bridge.* 1950. Crowell. 1st ed. VG/VG. P3. $20.00

PETERSEN, Marjorie. *Stornaway East & West.* 1966. Van Nostrand. VG/VG. A16. $10.00

PETERSEN, William. *Hippocratic Wisdom: Modern Appreciation of Ancient Medical.* 1946. Springfield. 1st ed. 263p. VG. A13. $50.00

PETERSHAM & PETERSHAM. *Miki & Mary: Their Search for Treasures.* 1934. Viking. 1st ed. ils. G+. P2. $80.00

PETERSHAM & PETERSHAM. *Off to Bed (7 Stories for Wide-Awakes).* (1954). WI. EM Hale/Cadmus. rpt. unp. VG. T5. $15.00

PETERSHAM & PETERSHAM. *Stories From the Old Testament.* 1938. Winston. 1st ed. ujnp. cloth. VG/dj. M20. $42.00

PETERSHAM & PETERSHAM. *Story Book of Foods From the Field.* 1936. 1st ed. NF/VG+. S13. $20.00

PETERSHAM & PETERSHAM. *Story of the Presidents of the United States of America.* 1953. NY. Macmillan. 1st ed. 4to. 80p. NF. C14. $10.00

PETERSON, Audrey. *Nocturne Murder.* 1987. Arbor. 1st ed. VG/VG. P3. $18.00

PETERSON, Frederick. *Ancient Mexico.* 1961. Putnam. 2nd. 313p. dj. F3. $20.00

PETERSON, Hans. *Liselott & the Quiffin.* 1964. London. Methuen. 1st ed. 12mo. 156p. G+/G+. T5. $20.00

PETERSON, Hans. *Magnus in Danger.* nd. Pantheon. stated 1st Am ed. 8vo. 135p. VG+. C14. $8.00

PETERSON, Harold L. *Pageant of the Gun.* 1967. Doubleday. ils/photos. gilt bdg. VG/VG. P12. $10.00

PETERSON, Keith; see Klavan, Andrew.

PETERSON, Robert. *Leaving Taos.* 1980. Harper Row. 1st ed. Nat Poetry series. F/F. V1. $20.00

PETERSON, Susan. *Living Tradition of Maria Martinez.* 1978. NY. Kodansha. 2nd. VG/VG. B5. $45.00

PETERSON, William J. *Steamboating on the Upper Mississippi.* 1968. Iowa City. State Hist Soc. sgn. 8vo. 64 pl. 575p. map ep. A4/B11. $85.00

PETIEVICH, Gerald. *Earth Angels.* 1989. NAL. 1st ed. NF/NF. P3. $18.00

PETIEVICH, Gerald. *Paramour.* 1991. Dutton. 1st ed. xl. dj. P3. $5.00

PETIEVICH, Gerald. *Quality of the Informant.* 1985. Arbor. 1st ed. F/F. H11. $30.00

PETIEVICH, Gerald. *Shakedown.* 1988. Simon Schuster. 1st ed. F/F. P3. $17.00

PETIEVICH, Gerald. *To Life & Die in LA.* 1984. Arbor. 1st ed. F/F. H11. $55.00

PETIT, Christopher. *Robinson.* 1994. Viking. 1st ed. F/F. P3. $21.00

PETRARCH. *Le Rime del Petrarca.* 1822. Pickering. teg. full brn morocco. miniature. T10. $150.00

PETRY, Ann. *Street.* 1946. Houghton Mifflin. 1st ed. author's 1st book. F/NF. B4. $450.00

PETSOPOULOS, Yanni. *Tulips, Arabesques & Turbans: Decorative Arts...* 1982. Abbeville. 1st ed. 224p. VG/dj. W1. $65.00

PETTEE, F.M. *Palgrave Mummy.* 1929. Payson Clarke. 1st ed. hc. VG. P3. $30.00

PETTEE, F.M. *Who Bird & Other Whimsies.* 1920. Chicago. Whitman. possible 1st ed. unp. F/box lacks end pieces. T5. $35.00

PETTES, G.W. *American or Standard Whist.* 1881. Boston. 2nd. 268p. VG. S1. $10.00

PETTES, G.W. *American Whist Illustrated Containing Laws & Principles...* 1890. Boston. 2nd 367p. VG. S1. $12.00

PETTES, Helen. *Mouse's Tail.* 1917. Cupples Leon. ils Julia Greene. NF. M5. $42.00

PETTIJOHN, F.J. *Sedimentary Rocks.* 1957. Harper. 2nd. 40 pl. 718p. VG. D8. $30.00

PETTIJOHN & POTTER. *Paleocurrent & Basin Analysis.* 1963. Academic Pr. 1st ed. 30 pl/130 figures. 296p. VG/dj. D8. $35.00

PETTY, William. *Hiberniae Delineato-Atlas of Ireland.* 1968. Newcastle-Upon-Tyne. Frank Graham. facsimile. 36 pl. M. O7. $575.00

PETZAL, David. *Experts' Book of the Shooting Sports.* 1972. Simon Schuster. 1st ed. photos. NF/VG. P12. $12.50

PETZINGER, T. *Oil & Honor: The Texaso-Pennzoil Wars.* 1987. Putnam. 1st ed. 495p. VG/dj. D8. $15.00

PEYTON, John Lewis. *Rambling Reminiscences of a Residence Abroad...* 1888. Staunton. SM Yost. 298p. VG. B10. $25.00

PEYTON, Richard. *At the Track.* 1987. Bonanza. hc. F/F. P3. $13.00

PFLUGER, Edward. *Die Sensorischen Functionen des Ruckenmarks...* 1853. Berlin. Hirschwald. 146p. modern brd. VG. G1. $575.00

PHEAR, J.B. *Treatise on Rights of Water, Including Public & Private...* 1859. London. Norton. emb cloth. M11. $250.00

PHELAN, Nancy. *Welcome the Wayfarer: Traveller in Modern Turkey.* 1965. Macmillan. 1st ed. 8vo. 16 pl. NF/dj. W1. $12.00

PHELPS, Earle Bernard. *Disinfection of Sewage & Dewage Filter Effluents.* 1909. GPO. 8vo. fld plan/index. 91p. F/new wrp. T10. $25.00

PHELPS, Earle Bernard. *Pollution of Atreams by Sulphite Pulp Waste.* 1909. GPO. 8vo. 37p. F/new wrp. T10. $25.00

PHELPS, Elizabeth Stuart. *Trixy.* 1904. Houghton Mifflin. 1st ed. inscr. F/NF. B4. $125.00

PHELPS, Richard H. *Newgate of Connecticut, Its Origin & Early History...* 1901. Hartford. Am Pub. gilt maroon cloth. M11. $125.00

PHILBRICK, W.R. *Slow Dancer.* 1984. St Martin. 1st ed. VG/VG. P3. $18.00

PHILIP & UPGREN. *Star Catalogues: Centennial Tribute to AN Vyssotsky.* 1989. NY. Davis. ils. 100p. VG. K5. $25.00

PHILIPS, Shine. *Big Spring: Causual Biography of a Prairie Town.* 1942. Prentice Hall. 1st ed. 8vo. 231p. tan cloth. NF. T10. $35.00

PHILIPSON, John. *Harness: As It has Been, As It Is...* 1882. Newcastle. 1st ed. O3. $85.00

PHILLIPS, Alexander M. *Mislaid Charm.* 1947. Prime. 1st ed. VG/chip 1st state (yellow dj). P3. $25.00

PHILLIPS, Caryl. *Cambridge.* 1992. Knopf. 1st ed. F/F. M23. $20.00

PHILLIPS, Conrad. *Empty Cot.* 1958. Arthur Barker. 1st ed. VG/VG. P3. $25.00

PHILLIPS, Conrad. *Unrepentant.* 1958. Arthur Barker. 1st ed. VG/VG. P3. $25.00

PHILLIPS, Hubert. *Bridge Is Only a Game.* 1959. London. 96p. VG. S1. $10.00

PHILLIPS, Hubert. *Brush Up Your Bridge.* 1939. London. 119p. VG. S1. $8.00

PHILLIPS, Jayne Ann. *Counting.* 1978. NY. Vehicle Eds. 1st ed. 1/526. author's 2nd book. VG/wrp. B4. $150.00

PHILLIPS, Jayne Ann. *Fast Lanes.* 1984. NY. Vehicle Eds. 1/200. sgn. F/wrp. B4. $85.00

PHILLIPS, Jayne Ann. *Machine Dreams.* 1984. Dutton. ARC. F/F. w/photo. B4. $50.00

PHILLIPS, Jayne Ann. *Shelter.* 1994. Houghton Mifflin. ARC. F/F. B4. $45.00

PHILLIPS, Jayne Anne. *Fast Lanes.* 1987. Dutton. 1st ed. F/F. H11. $35.00

PHILLIPS, Jayne Anne. *How Mickey Made It.* 1981. St Paul. Bookslinger. 1/150. sgn/#d. special bdg. F. B2. $150.00

PHILLIPS, Jayne Anne. *Machine Dreams.* 1984. Dutton. 1st ed. author's 1st novel. F/F. H11. $40.00

PHILLIPS, Jayne Anne. *Machine Dreams.* 1984. Dutton. 1st ed. F/F. B35. $42.00

PHILLIPS, Jayne Anne. *Shelter.* 1994. Houghton Mifflin. 1st ed. F/F. H11. $30.00

PHILLIPS, Judson. *Backlash.* 1976. Dodd Mead. 1st ed. VG/VG. P3. $20.00

PHILLIPS, Judson. *Cannibal Who Overate.* 1962. Red Badge Detective. VG+/VG+. P10. $10.00

PHILLIPS, Judson. *Champagne Killer.* 1972. Dodd Mead. 1st ed. VG/VG. P3. $20.00

PHILLIPS, Judson. *Deadly Joke.* 1971. Dodd Mead. 1st ed. VG/VG. P3. $20.00

PHILLIPS, Judson. *Deadly Trap.* 1978. Dodd Mead. 1st ed. NF/NF. P3. $15.00

PHILLIPS, Judson. *Death by Fire.* 1986. Dodd Mead. 1st ed. F/F. P3. $16.00

PHILLIPS, Judson. *Death Syndicate.* 1941. Triangle. VG. P3. $15.00

PHILLIPS, Judson. *Escape a Killer.* 1971. Dodd Mead. 1st ed. VG/VG. P3. $20.00

PHILLIPS, Judson. *Honeymoon With Death.* 1975. Dodd Mead. 1st ed. VG/VG. P3. $15.00

PHILLIPS, Judson. *Judas Freak.* 1974. Dodd Mead. G+/dj. P3. $15.00

PHILLIPS, Judson. *Murder Arranged.* 1978. Dodd Mead. 1st ed. VG/VG. P3. $18.00

PHILLIPS, Judson. *Murder in High Places.* 1983. Dodd Mead. 1st ed. VG/VG. P3. $15.00

PHILLIPS, Judson. *Murder in Luxury.* 1981. Dodd Mead. 1st ed. VG/VG. P3. $18.00

PHILLIPS, Judson. *Past, Present & Murder.* 1982. Dodd Mead. VG/VG. P3. $15.00

PHILLIPS, Judson. *Plague of Violence.* 1970. Dodd Mead. 1st ed. VG/VG. P3. $18.00

PHILLIPS, Judson. *Power Killers.* 1974. Dodd Mead. 1st ed. VG/G+. P3. $13.00

PHILLIPS, Judson. *Remember To Kill Me.* 1984. Dodd Mead. 1st ed. VG/VG. P3. $15.00

PHILLIPS, Judson. *Sniper.* nd. Detective BC. VG. P3. $8.00

PHILLIPS, Judson. *Vanishing Senator.* 1972. Dodd Mead. 1st ed. xl. dj. P3. $8.00

PHILLIPS, Lance. *Saddle Horse.* 1970. Barnes. later prt. VG/VG. O3. $45.00

PHILLIPS, P. Lee. *List of Geographical Atlases in the Library of Congress.* nd. 4 vol. rpt of 1904-1920 ed. 1/100. F. A4. $295.00

PHILLIPS, P. Lee. *List of Works on Cartography.* 1901. WA. GPO. 90p. F. O7. $95.00

PHILLIPS, Paul C. *Medicine in the Making of Montana.* 1962. Missoul. a. 1st ed. 564p. NF. N3. $15.00

PHILLIPS, Stanley S. *Excavated Artifacts From Battlefields & Campsites...* 1986. np. 4to. 199p. VG. T3. $20.00

PHILLIPS, W. Glasgow. *Tuscaloosa.* 1994. Morrow. 1st ed. sgn. F/F. M23. $40.00

PHILLIPS, Wendell. *Oman: A History.* 1967. Reynal/Morrow. 1st ed. ils/2 full-p maps. VG/torn. W1. $45.00

PHILLIPS, Wendell. *Qataban & Sheba: Exploring Ancient Kingdoms...* 1955. Harcourt. 1st ed. sgn. 362p. VG/dj. W1. $22.00

PHILLIPS, Wendell. *Qataban & Sheba: Exploring Ancient Kingdoms...* 1955. Harcourt. 1st ed. 362p. cloth. VG+. B22. $7.00

PHILLIPS, Wendell. *Unknown Oman.* 1966. McKay. 1st Am ed. pres. 8vo. ils. 319p. VG. W1. $30.00

PHILLIPS & STEAVENSON. *Splendour of the Heavens*. 1931. NY. McBride. 4to. 976p. G/tattered. K5. $250.00

PHILLIPS-BIRT, Douglas. *When Luxury Went to Sea*. 1971. St Martin. 1st Am ed. VG/VG. A16. $40.00

PIAGET, Jean. *Child's Conception of Physical Causality*. 1930. London. Kegan Paul. 1st Eng-language ed/later issue. bl-gr cloth. G1. $100.00

PIAGET, Jean. *La Formation du Symbole Chez l'Enfant...* (1945). Paris. Delachaux Niestle. 312p. prt yel wrp. G1. $75.00

PIAGET, Jean. *Moral Judgment of the Child*. 1932. Harcourt Brace/Kegan Paul. 1st Eng-language ed. 418p. G1. $50.00

PICANO, Felice. *Mesmerist*. 1977. Delacorte. 1st ed. F/F. H11. $40.00

PICANO, Felice. *Mesmerist*. 1977. Delacorte. 1st ed. VG/VG. P3. $25.00

PICARD, Barbara. *French Legends, Tales & Fairy Stories*. 1955. Walck. 1st ed. 8vo. VG/VG. B17. $5.00

PICARD, Jean. *De Prisca Celtopaedia, Libri Doctrina, Quam Vel in Graecia*. 1556. Paris. Matthew David. only ed. 4to. suede. VG. B14. $880.00

PICASSO, Pablo. *Hunk of Skin*. 1968. City Lights. 1st Am ed. VG+. V1. $40.00

PICK, Bernhard. *Talmud: What It Is & What It Knows About Jesus...* 1877. NY. John B Alden. 147p. decor tan cloth. VG. B14. $55.00

PICKARD, Nancy. *Afraid of the Time*. 1992. Mystery Scene Short Story. 1st ed. 1/100. sgn. F/sans. P3. $20.00

PICKARD, Nancy. *But I Wouldn't Want To Die There*. 1993. Pocket. 1st ed. F/F. P3. $20.00

PICKARD, Nancy. *27-Ingredient Chile Con Carne Murders*. 1993. Delacorte. 1st ed. F/F. P3. $18.00

PICKERING, James S. *Asterisks, a Book of Astronomical Footnotes*. 1964. Dodd Mead. 8vo. 214p. VG/dj. K5. $25.00

PICKNEY, Darryl. *High Cotton*. 1992. Farrar. 1st ed. F/F. B2. $50.00

PIDDINGTON, R.A. *Limits of Mankind: Philosophy of Population*. 1956. Bristol, Eng. 153p. F/dj. B14. $75.00

PIDGEON, William. *Traditions of De-Coodah & Antiquarian Researches*. 1853. NY. Thayer Bridgman. 8vo. ils/fld map/fld pl. 334p. G. T10. $300.00

PIDGIN, C.F. *Blennerhassett*. 1901. Boston. 1st ed. ils. F. A17. $10.00

PIENKOWSKI, Jan. *Robot*. 1981. Dell. 1st Am ed. 4to. F. B17. $22.00

PIERCE, David M. *Angels in Heaven*. 1992. Mysterious. 1st ed. VG/VG. P3. $18.00

PIERCE, John J. *Old Genre*. 1994. Greenwood. F. P3. $55.00

PIERCE, Josephine H. *Fire on the Hearth*. 1951. Springfield, MA. 254p. VG/dj. B18. $22.50

PIERCE, Ovid Williams. *Devil's Half*. 1968. Doubleday. 1st ed. inscr/dtd 1973. F/NF. M23. $20.00

PIERCE, R.V. *People's Common Sense Medical Advisor*. 1895. Buffalo. 12mo. ils. 1008p. blk cloth. VG. T3. $30.00

PIERCY, Marge. *Available Light*. 1988. Knopf. 1st ed. sgn. F/NF. V1. $25.00

PIERCY, Marge. *Braided Lives*. 1982. Summit. 2nd. VG/VG. P3. $13.00

PIERCY, Marge. *Dance the Eagle to Sleep*. 1970. Doubleday. 1st ed. author's 2nd novel. F/NF. H11. $45.00

PIERCY, Marge. *He, She & It*. 1991. Knopf. 1st ed. F/F. H11. $25.00

PIERCY, Marge. *He, She & It*. 1991. Knopf. 1st ed. VG/VG. P3. $22.00

PIERCY, Marge. *High Cost of Living*. 1978. Harper Row. 1st ed. F/F. H11. $40.00

PIERCY, Marge. *Mars & Her Children*. 1992. Knopf. 1st ed. sgn. F/F. V1. $25.00

PIERCY, Marge. *Moon Is Always Female*. 1989. Knopf sgn. F/wrp. V1. $15.00

PIERCY, Marge. *Summer People*. 1989. Summit. 1st ed. F/F. H11. $30.00

PIERCY, Marge. *Woman on the Edge of Time*. 1976. Knopf. 1st ed. inscr. F/F. B4. $85.00

PIERSOL, George. *Gateway of Honor: American College of Physicians 1915-59*. 1962. Phil. 1st ed. 646p. VG. A13. $35.00

PIERSON, Willard J. *Practical Methods for Observing & Forecasting Ocean Waves*. 1955. Hydrographic Office. 284p. VG. P12. $20.00

PIGGOTT, Stuart. *Earliest Wheeled Transport...* 1983. Cornell. 1st Am ed. 4to. 272p. VG/dj. W1. $18.00

PIKE, Christopher. *Season of Passage*. 1992. Tor. 1st ed. NF/NF. P3. $20.00

PIKE, James A. *Other Side*. nd. Laffont. hc. VG. P3. $15.00

PIKE, James. *Prostrate State: South Carolina Under Negro Government*. 1935. NY. VG. B30. $35.00

PILEGGI, Nicholas. *Wiseguy*. 1985. Simon Schuster. 1st ed. F/F. H11. $25.00

PILGRIM, Mariette S. *Oogaruk the Aleut*. 1949. Caxton. sgn. ils HH Wilson. 8vo. 223p. F/G. B11. $35.00

PILKINGTON, James. *Artist's Guide & Mechanics Own Book...* 1841. Boston. 490p. VG. B14. $100.00

PILLSBURY, W.B. *Attention. Library of Philosophy Series*. 1908. Macmillan. 1st Eng-language ed. 346p. panelled crimson cloth. G1. $75.00

PINCHER, Chapman. *Not With a Bang*. 1965. Weidenfeld Nicolson. hc. G/torn. P3. $10.00

PINCHON, Edgcumb. *Viva Villa!* (1933). Grosset Dunlap. 383p. G. F3. $15.00

PINCHOT, Giffort. *To the South Seas: Cruise of the Schooner Mary Pinchot...* 1930. Winston. 1st ed. sgn. ils/map ep. 500p. gilt bl brd. VG. B11. $85.00

PINI & PINI. *Elfquest Book 1*. 1981. Donning. 1st/ltd ed. sgn. hc. F/box. P3. $225.00

PINI & PINI. *Elfquest Book 2*. 1982. Donning. 1st/ltd ed. sgn. F/box. P3. $150.00

PINI & PINI. *Elfquest Book 3*. 1983. Donning. 1st/ltd ed. sgn. F/box. P3. $100.00

PINI & PINI. *Elquest Book 4*. 1984. Donning. 1st/ltd ed. sgn. F/box. P3. $75.00

PINKERTON, Allan. *Detective & the Somnambulist*. 1877. Belford. 1st Canadian ed. fair. P3. $40.00

PINKERTON, Allan. *Spy of the Rebellion*. 1883. NY. ils. VG. B30. $42.50

PINKERTON, Allan. *Spy of the Rebellion*. 1911. Dillingham. hc. VG. P3. $20.00

PINKWATER, Daniel. *Fish Whistle*. 1939. Addison Wesley. 1st ed. sgn/sketch. F/F. B11. $25.00

PINNER, David. *Ritual*. 1967. New Authors Ltd. 1st ed. F/F. P3. $13.00

PINTER, Harold. *Poems & Prose 1949-1977*. 1978. Grove. 1st ed. F/F. V1. $20.00

PIOZZI, Hester Lynch. *Anecdotes of the Late Samuel Johnson, LLD...* 1786. London. T Cadell. 1st ed. 8vo. modern calf. F. T10. $450.00

PIPER, Evelyn. *Nanny*. nd. BC. VG/VG. P3. $8.00

PIPER, Evelyn. *Stand-In.* 1970. McKay Washburn. 1st ed. VG/VG. P3. $15.00

PIPER, H. Beam. *Murder in the Gun Room.* 1953. Knopf. 1st ed. NF/VG. B2. $150.00

PIPER, John F. *Marine Electrical Installation.* 1943. Cornell. 3rd. ils. gilt red bdg. G+. P12. $10.00

PIPER, Watty. *Brimful Book: A Collection of Mother Goose Rhymes...* 1939. Platt Munk. folio. ils. VG. B17. $17.50

PIPER, Watty. *Children's Hour on the Farm.* 1929. Platt Munk. 16mo. VG. M5. $15.00

PIPER, Watty. *Children's Hour With the Birds.* 1929. Platt Munk. 16mo. VG. M5. $15.00

PIPER, Watty. *Nursery Tales Children Love.* 1933. Platt Munk. lg 4to. VG+. M5. $55.00

PIPER, Watty. *Stories That Never Grow Old.* 1952 (1938). Platt Munk. ils Hauman. unp. VG/torn. T5. $45.00

PIPER. *English Face.* 1975. VG/G. D2. $25.00

PIRIE, David. *Vampire Cinema.* 1977. Crescent. VG/VG. P3. $20.00

PIRSIG, Robert M. *Lila.* 1991. Bantam. 1st ed. F/F. M23. $25.00

PISERCHIA, Doris. *Spaceling.* nd. BC. F/F. P3. $9.00

PITCAIRN, Robert. *Ancient Criminal Trials in Scotland...* 1829-33.. Edinburgh. Bannatyne Club. M11. $1,500.00

PITCHFORD, Kenneth. *Color Photos of the Atrocities.* 1973. Atlantic. 1st ed. assn copy. VG. V1. $15.00

PITTENGER, Peggy Jett. *Back Yard Foal.* 1967. Barnes. sm 4to. VG. O3. $25.00

PITTER, Ruth. *Spirit Watches.* 1940. Macmillan. 1st ed. F/NF. V1. $35.00

PITTS, Lilla Belle. *Singing & Rhyming.* 1950. Ginn. 8vo. ils Eloise Wilkin. VG. B17. $7.50

PITZ, Henry. *Brandywine Tradition.* 1968. Weathervane. 1st ed thus. ils. 252p. G+. T5. $32.00

PITZ, Henry. *Drawing Trees.* 1956. 1st ed. VG/VG. S13. $45.00

PITZ, Henry. *King Arthur & His Noble Knights.* 1949. Lippincott. 1st imp. 8vo. F/VG. B17. $7.50

PIZER. *Theodore Dreiser: A Primary & Secondary Bibliography.* 1975. np. 525p. F. A4. $65.00

PLAIDY, Jean. *Prince of Darkness.* 1978. Hale. 1st ed. VG/VG. P3. $12.00

PLATH, Sylvia. *Bed Book.* 1976. Harper. 1st Am ed. NF/VG. C8. $40.00

PLATH, Sylvia. *Bed Book.* 1976. London. Faber. 1st ed. ils Quentin Blake. F/F. B4. $175.00

PLATH, Sylvia. *Bell Jar.* 1971. Harper Row. 1st Am ed. author's only novel. VG+/NF. B4. $85.00

PLATH, Sylvia. *Colossus & Other Poems.* 1967. Knopf. 2nd. F/NF. V1. $20.00

PLATH, Sylvia. *Crossing the Water.* 1971. Harper Row. 2nd. F/NF. V1. $10.00

PLATH, Sylvia. *Letters Home.* 1975. Harper Row. 1st ed. photos. 402p. NF/clip. S9. $30.00

PLATO. *Collected Dialogues of...* 1987. Princeton. 13th. hc. F/F. P3. $33.00

PLATT, Kin. *Body Beautiful Murder.* 1976. Random. 1st ed. VG/G+. P3. $18.00

PLATT, Kin. *Terrible Love Life of Dudley Cornflow.* 1976. Bradbury. 1st ed. VG/VG. P3. $15.00

PLATT, Rutherford. *Walt Disney Secrets of Life.* 1957. NY. ils. 124p. VG/wrp. A17. $5.00

PLAYLE, Margaret. *Second Rucksack Book.* 1954. London. ils. 192p. VG/dj. A17. $8.50

PLEASANTS, W. Shepard. *Stingaree Murders.* 1932. Mystery League. 1st ed. VG. P3. $15.00

PLEDGE, H.T. *Science Since 1500: A Short History of Mathematics...* 1940. London. 1st ed. 357p. VG. A13. $20.00

PLIMPTON, George. *Paper Lion.* 1966. Harper Row. 1st ed. F/F. B35. $25.00

PLIMPTON, George. *Rabbit's Umbrella.* 1955. Viking. 1st ed. ils Wm Pene DuBois. F/VG+. B4. $250.00

PLOMER, Henry R. *Short History of English Printing 1476-1898.* 1900. London. Kegan Paul. 1/50. 8vo. 330p. full vellum. NF. T10. $250.00

PLOMER, Henry R. *Wynkyn de Worde & His Contemporaries From Death of Caxton...* 1925. London. Grafton. 1st ed. 8vo. ils. 264p. F. T10. $250.00

PLOWDEN, David. *End of an Era.* 1992. Norton. AN. A16. $50.00

PLOWRIGHT, Teresa. *Dreams of an Unseen Planet.* 1986. Arbor. 1st ed. author's 1st novel. F/F. G10/P3. $20.00

PLUM, Jennifer; see Kurland, Michael.

PLUMLY, Stanley. *Boy on the Step.* 1989. Ecco. 1st ed. AN/dj. V1. $20.00

PLUNKET, Robert. *My Search for Warren Harding.* 1983. 1st ed. author's 1st book. VG+/VG+. S13. $18.00

PLUTARCH. *Lives of the Noble Grecians & Romanes.* 1929. London. Nonesuch. 5 vol. 1st ed thus. sm folio. brn buckram. NF. C6. $325.00

PODHAJSKY, Alois. *Die Spanische Hofreitschule.* 1959. Wien. Holzhausens. VG/G. O3. $45.00

PODHAJSKY, Alois. *Lipizzaners.* 1970. Doubleday. 2nd Am. VG/VG. O3. $48.00

PODHAJSKY, Alois. *My Dancing White Horses.* 1966. NY. HRW. 3rd. VG/VG. O3. $35.00

PODHAJSKY, Alois. *Spanish Riding School of Vienna.* 1956. Vienna. Eng text. VG/wrp. O3. $25.00

PODMORE, Frank. *Apparitions & Thought-Transference...* 1894. London. Walter Scott. 12mo. 401p. prt mauve cloth. VG. G1. $65.00

PODRUG, Junius. *Frost of Heaven.* 1992. Arlington Hts. Dark Harvest. 1st ed. inscr. F/F. H11. $45.00

POE, Edgar Allan. *Chapter on Autography.* 1926. NY. 1/750. F/NF. C6. $60.00

POE, Edgar Allan. *Fall of the House of Usher.* 1986. Marshall Cavendish. hc. decor brd. F. P3. $25.00

POE, Edgar Allan. *Masque of the Red Death & Other Tales.* 1932. Halcyon. 1st ed thus. 1/175. ils JB Wright. NF. C6. $300.00

POE, Edgar Allan. *Murders in the Rue Morgue.* nd. JH Sears. VG. P3. $20.00

POE, Edgar Allan. *Seventy-Seven Tales/One Complete Novel/Thirty One Poems.* 1985. Amaranth. aeg. leather. F/sans. G10. $15.00

POE, Edgar Allan. *Tales of Edgar Allan Poe.* 1979. Franklin Lib. gilt bdg/leather spine. NF. P3. $20.00

POE, Edgar Allan. *Tales of Mystery & Imagination.* nd. Brentano. 1/2500. ils Harry Clarke. VG/worn. B5. $135.00

POE, Edgar Allan. *Tales of Mystery & Immagination.* nd. Spencer. VG. P3. $10.00

POE, Edgar Allan. *Tales.* 1928. NY. 1st ed. ils. 520p. F/dj. A17. $9.50

POE, Edgar Allan. *Works...* 1864. NY. 4 vol. G+. M17. $120.00

POESCH. *Art of the Old South: Painting, Sculpture, Architecture.* 1983. F/F. D2. $35.00

POGANY, Willy. *Golden Cockerel.* 1938. NY. 1st ed. ils. VG. B5. $45.00

POGANY, Willy. *Gulliver's Travels.* 1917. Macmillan. 1st ed. 8vo. VG. M5. $75.00

POGANY, Willy. *My Poetry Book, an Anthology of Modern Verse...* 1957. Winston. 2nd ed thus. 8vo. VG. M5. $12.00

POGANY, Willy. *Wimp & the Woodle & Other Stories.* 1935. Sutton House. 1st ed. ils. VG. B5. $45.00

POGANY & POGANY. *Peterkin.* 1940. McKay. 1st ed. ils Willy Pogany. VG+/ragged dj. M20. $110.00

POHL, Frederik. *Best of Frederik Pohl.* nd. BC. VG/VG. P3. $8.00

POHL, Frederik. *Beyond the Blue Event Horizon.* 1980. Del Rey. VG/VG. P3. $18.00

POHL, Frederik. *Black Star Rising.* nd. BC. VG/VG. P3. $8.00

POHL, Frederik. *Chernobyl.* 1987. Bantam. 1st ed. VG/G. P3. $15.00

POHL, Frederik. *Coming of the Quantum Cats.* nd. BC. VG/VG. P3. $8.00

POHL, Frederik. *Cool War.* 1981. Del Rey. 1st ed. VG/VG. P3. $15.00

POHL, Frederik. *Day the Martians Came.* 1989. Easton. 1st ed. sgn. full leather. F/swrp. P3. $60.00

POHL, Frederik. *Heechee Rendezvous.* 1984. Del Rey. 1st ed. F/F. P3. $20.00

POHL, Frederik. *Homegoing.* 1989. Easton. 1st ed. sgn. leather. F/wrp. P3. $60.00

POHL, Frederik. *Jem.* 1979. St Martin. 1st ed. VG/VG. P3. $15.00

POHL, Frederik. *Merchant's War.* 1984. St Martin. 1st ed. NF/VG. N4. $20.00

POHL, Frederik. *Merchants' War.* 1985. Gollancz. 1st ed. F/F. P3. $20.00

POHL, Frederik. *Midas World.* 1983. St Martin. 1st ed. F/F. P3. $20.00

POHL, Frederik. *Narabedla Ltd.* 1988. Ballantine. 1st ed. F/F. H11. $25.00

POHL, Frederik. *Nebula Winners 14.* 1980. Harper. 1st ed. NF/NF. P3. $30.00

POHL, Frederik. *Outnumbering the Dead.* 1990. Legend. 1st ed. hc. F/F. P3. $25.00

POHL, Frederik. *Second If Reader of SF.* 1968. Doubleday. 1st ed. VG/VG. P3. $25.00

POHL, Frederik. *SF Roll of Honor.* 1975. Random. 1st ed. F/F. P3. $15.00

POHL, Frederik. *Starburst.* 1982. Del Rey. 1st ed. VG/VG. P3. $15.00

POHL, Frederik. *Stopping at Slowyear.* 1991. Axolotl. 1st ed. sgn. F/F. P3. $45.00

POHL, Frederik. *Way the Future Was.* 1978. Del Rey. VG/VG. P3. $15.00

POHL, Frederik. *World at the End of Time.* 1990. Del Rey. 1st ed. F/F. P3. $18.00

POHL & KORNBLUTH. *Presidential Year.* 1956. Ballantine. 1st ed. F/F. P3. $400.00

POHL & KORNBLUTH. *Town Is Drowning.* 1955. Ballantine. 1st ed. VG. P3. $375.00

POHL & WILLIAMSON. *Land's End.* nd. BC. VG/VG. P3. $8.00

POHL & WILLIAMSON. *Singers of Time.* 1991. Doubleday. 1st ed. VG/VG. P3. $22.00

POHL & WILLIAMSON. *Starbild Trilogy.* nd. BC. VG/VG. P3. $10.00

POINDEXTER, Miles. *Ayer Incas.* 1930. NY. 2 vol. 1st ed. ils. VG/G+. B5. $65.00

POLASEK, Emily. *Bohemian Girl in America.* 1982. Rollins. inscr. 8vo. 120p. VG/VG repro. B11. $25.00

POLE, William. *Philosophy of Whist.* 1884. London. 2nd. 218p. VG. S1. $8.00

POLE, William. *Pole on Whist. Theory of Modern Scientific Game of Whist.* 1889. NY. Authorized Am ed. 5th. 128p. VG. S1. $6.00

POLEMON. *Physionomia e Graeco in Latium Versa per Carolum...* 1612. Mutinae. Mariae de Verdis. 1st Latin ed. 4to. modern bdg. G1. $475.00

POLIDORI, John William. *Vampyre.* 1973. Hertfordshire. Gubblecote. 1/1000. 8vo. 42p. F. T10. $100.00

POLITE, Carlene. *Les Flagellants.* 1966. Paris. Christian Bourgois. 1/15. author's 1st novel. F/dj. B4. $450.00

POLITE, Carlene. *Sister X & the Victims of Foul Play.* 1975. FSG. 1st ed. F/NF. B4. $45.00

POLITI, Leo. *Bunker Hill.* 1964. Palm Desert. Desert Southwest Inc. 1st ed. ils. gilt gray cloth. dj. T10. $250.00

POLITI, Leo. *Mission Bell.* (1953). Scribner. later prt. 32p. F/dj. T10. $45.00

POLITI, Leo. *Mission Bell.* 1953. Scribner. ils. pict lib bdg. NF/clip. T10. $135.00

POLITI, Leo. *Pedro the Angel of Olivera St.* 1946. Scribner. 1st ed. 12mo. VG/VG. D1. $125.00

POLITZ, Edward A. *Forty-First Thief.* 1975. Delacorte. 1st ed. VG/VG. P3. $15.00

POLITZER, Adam. *Atlas der Beleuchtungbinder des Trommelfells...* 1896. Vienna/Leipzig. 12 chromolithographs. 154p. blk cloth. B14. $475.00

POLK. *Island of California: A History of the Myth.* 1991. np. 57 pl. 398p. F/F. A4. $125.00

POLLACK, Rachel. *Temporary Agency.* 1994. St Martin. 1st ed. F/F. M23. $35.00

POLLARD, A.O. *Unofficial Spy.* 1936. Hutchinson. xl. dj. P3. $13.00

POLLARD, Alfred W. *Romance of King Arthur.* 1917. Macmillan. VG. P3. $40.00

POLLARD, Edward A. *First Year of the War: Southern History of the War.* 1863 (1862). Charles Richardson. 368p. gilt gr cloth. VG. M20. $77.00

POLLARD, Edward A. *Second Year of the War.* 1864 (1863). Charles Richardson. 386p. gilt cloth. VG. M20. $87.00

POLLARD, Edward A. *War in America.* 1864. London. 12mo. 354p. gr cloth. G. T3. $70.00

POLLOCK, Channing. *Fool.* nd. Grosset Dunlap. MTI. VG. P3. $10.00

POLLOCK, Dale. *Skywalking.* nd. Harmony. VG/VG. P3. $15.00

POLLOCK, J.C. *Mission MIA.* 1982. Crown. 1st ed. F/F. P3. $16.00

POLLOCK, John Hackett. *Athens Aflame.* ca 1920. Dublin. Martin Lester. 1/500. 8vo. 49p. NF. T10. $65.00

POLLOCK, John Hackett. *Smoking Flax.* ca 1920. Dublin. Martin Lester. 1/500. 8vo. 59p. NF. T10. $50.00

POLLOCK, John Hackett. *Tale of Thule: Together With Some Poems.* ca 1920. Dublin. Talbot. 1/500. 8vo. 56p. VG. T10. $50.00

POLNER, Murray. *Branch Rickey.* 1982. Atheneum. 1st ed. F/F. P8. $50.00

POLWHELE, Richard. *History of Devonshire.* 1793, 1797 & 1806. London. Caddell Johnson Dilly. 3 vol in 1. 1st ed. C6. $500.00

POLZER, Charles. *Kino Guide.* 1968. Tucson. SW Mission Research Center. 1/200. cloth. F3. $30.00

POMERANCE. *Ludwig Bemelmans, a Bibliography.* 1993. NY. Heinemann. 4to. ils. 413p. F/F. A4. $75.00

POMERANZ, Herman. *Medicine in the Shakespearean Plays & Dicken's Doctors.* 1936. NY. 1st ed. 416p. VG. A13. $100.00

POMEROY, Earl. *Pacific Slope.* 1966. Knopf. 2nd. 8vo. ils/fld map/index. xl. VG. T10. $15.00

PONDER, Zita Inez. *Bandaged Face.* 1929. MacAulay. 1st ed. G. P3. $30.00

PONICSAN, Darryl. *Cinderella.* 1973. Liberty. 1st ed. MTI. VG/VG. S13. $30.00

PONICSAN, Darryl. *Goldengrove.* 1971. Dial. 1st ed. NF/VG. B4. $45.00

PONSOT, Marie. *Fables of La Fontaine.* (1957). Grosset Dunlap. ils. pict ep. VG. T5. $25.00

POOL & POOL. *Who Financed Hitler?* 1978. NY. 1st prt. 535p. dj. A17. $12.50

POOLE, Stafford. *In Defense of the Indians.* 1974. DeKalb, IL. 1st ed. 385p. dj. F3. $45.00

POOR, Charles Lane. *Men Against the Rule.* 1937. Derrydale. 1/950. ils. 157p. VG/dj. B5. $70.00

POORTVLIET, Rien. *Dutch Treat, the Artist's Life...* 1981. Abrams. folio. xl. VG/VG. D17. $7.50

POP, Alexander. *Poetical Works of...* nd. Ward Lock. marbled brd. 3-quarter leather. VG. S13. $50.00

POPE, Alexander. *Works of...* 1871. London. Murray. 10 vol. ils/index. gilt cloth. NF. A17. $95.00

POPE, Dudley. *Buccaneer.* 1981. Musson. 1st ed. F/F. P3. $22.00

POPE, Dudley. *England Expects.* 1959. Weidenfeld Nicolson. 1st ed. VG/VG. P3. $30.00

POPE, Dudley. *Ramage's Devil.* 1982. Secker Warburg. 1st ed. VG/VG. P3. $20.00

POPE, Dudley. *Ramage.* 1965. Weidenfeld Nicolson. 3rd. xl. dj. P3. $8.00

POPE, Edwin. *Ted Williams: The Golden Year 1957.* 1970. Prentice Hall. later prt. sgn. VG+/VG+. P8. $275.00

POPE, Saxton. *Adventurous Bowmen: Field Notes on African Archery.* 1926. NY. ils. 233p. VG. B14. $100.00

POPE, Saxton. *Study of Bows & Arrows.* 1914. Berkeley. 20 pl. 64p. G/G. B5. $145.00

POPE & WNELEY. *China.* 1944. Smithsonian. 85p. VG. P4. $22.50

POPHAM, A.E. *Correggio's Drawings.* 1957. London. Oxford. ils/pl. 218p. cloth. D2. $275.00

POPKIN, Zelda. *Journey Home.* nd. BC. VG/VG. P3. $8.00

PORGES. *Edgar Rice Burroughs.* 2 vol. photos/art/covers/ads. 1309p. F. M13. $40.00

PORTER, Anna. *Mortal Sins.* 1988. NAL. 1st ed. rem mk. NF/dj. N4. $15.00

PORTER, Burton P. *Old Canal Days.* 1942. Columbus, OH. 1st/Premiere ed. sgn. ils. 469p. ES. G+. B18. $65.00

PORTER, Connie. *All-Bright Court.* 1991. Houghton Mifflin. 1st ed. author's 1st novel. F/F. M23. $20.00

PORTER, Eliot. *Galapagos the Flow of Wildness.* 1968. Sierra Club. 2 vol. 1st ed. VG/G box. B5. $125.00

PORTER, Gene Stratton. *Birds of the Bible.* 1909. Cincinnati. Jennings Graham. ils. 467p. VG. A4. $400.00

PORTER, Gene Stratton. *Daughter of the Land.* 1918. Garden City. 1st ed. ils. pict cloth. G. A17. $30.00

PORTER, Gene Stratton. *Freckles.* nd. Grosset Dunlap. VG. P3. $15.00

PORTER, Gene Stratton. *Laddie.* (1913). Tor/Country Life. 1st Canadian ed. 4 pl. VG-. A17. $50.00

PORTER, Gene Stratton. *Magic Garden.* nd. Grosset Dunlap. VG. P3. $20.00

PORTER, Gene Stratton. *Magic Garden.* 1927. Garden City. 1st ed. VG/VG. B5. $80.00

PORTER, Gene Stratton. *Music of the Wild.* 1910. Doubleday Page. 426p. VG. M20. $77.00

PORTER, Gene Stratton. *Song of the Cardinal.* May 1903. Indianapolis. 1st ed. lg 8vo. photos. gilt cloth. NF. A17. $175.00

PORTER, Gene Stratton. *Song of the Cardinal.* 1915. NY. sgn. ils. teg. gilt full red leather. VG. H3. $225.00

PORTER, Gene Stratton. *Tales You Won't Believe.* 1925. NY. G. V4. $125.00

PORTER, Gene Stratton. *White Flag.* 1923. Doubleday Page. 1st ed. F/NF. B4. $350.00

PORTER, Gene Stratton. *White Flag.* 1923. Doubleday Page. 1st ed. 8vo. 483p. VG. H3. $35.00

PORTER, Joyce. *Dead Easy for Dover.* 1979. St Martin. VG/VG. P3. $22.00

PORTER, Joyce. *Dover & the Unkindest Cut of All.* 1967. Scribner. 1st ed. VG/VG. P3. $25.00

PORTER, Joyce. *Dover Goes To Pott.* 1968. Jonathan Cape. 1st ed. VG. P3. $13.00

PORTER, Joyce. *Dover One.* 1964. Scribner. 1st ed. VG/VG. P3. $40.00

PORTER, Joyce. *Dover Three.* 1965. Scribner. 1st ed. VG/VG. P3. $25.00

PORTER, Joyce. *Neither a Candle Nor a Pitchfork.* 1970. McCall. VG/VG. P3. $25.00

PORTER, Katherine Anne. *Christmas Story.* 1967. Delacorte. ARC. inscr. gilt brd. F/dj. w/letter. B24. $275.00

PORTER, Katherine Anne. *Collected Stories of...* 1965. HBW. 2nd. inscr to nephew/dtd 1971. VG/VG. B4. $250.00

PORTER, Katherine Anne. *Days Before.* 1952. Harcourt Brace. 1st ed. NF/F. B4. $85.00

PORTER, Katherine Anne. *Flowering Judas & Other Stories.* 1935. Harcourt Brace. 1st trade ed. F/dj. B24. $450.00

PORTER, Katherine Anne. *French Song Book.* 1933. Harrison of Paris. 1st ed. 1/595. inscr/sgn to LD Wolfe. NF. B4. $400.00

PORTER, Katherine Anne. *Leaning Tower & Other Stories.* 1944. Harcourt Brace. 1st ed. F/NF. B4. $100.00

PORTER, Katherine Anne. *Leaning Tower & Other Stories.* 1944. Harcourt Brace. 1st ed. 242p. VG/VG. B10. $85.00

PORTER, Katherine Anne. *Pale Horse, Pale Rider.* 1939. Harcourt Brace. 1st ed. F/NF. B24. $235.00

PORTER, Katherine Anne. *Ship of Fools.* 1962. Atlantic/Little Brn. 1st ed. F/NF. H11. $55.00

PORTER, Miriane. *Sally Gabble & the Fairies.* 1929. Macmillan. 1st ed. ils Helen Sewell. VG/VG. P2. $110.00

PORTER & PORTER. *All Under Heaven: The Chinese World.* 1983. Pantheon. 1st ed. 192p. decor cloth. VG+/dj. B18. $25.00

PORTER & PORTER. *In Sickness & Health: The British Experience 1650-1850.* 1988. NY. 1st ed. 324p. dj. A13. $40.00

PORTER & WIGGINS. *Flora of the Galapagos Islands.* 1971. Stanford. ils. 998p. VG+/dj. B26. $110.00

PORTER. *Negro in the United States: A Selected Bibliography.* 1970. GPO. 1781 annotated entries. 327p. VG. A4. $75.00

PORTIS, Charles. *Gringos.* 1991. Simon Schuster. 1st ed. F/F. A18. $20.00

PORTIS, Charles. *True Grit.* 1968. NY. 1st ed. F/F. B5. $25.00

POSNER, David. *Sandpipers, Selected Poems 1965-1975.* nd. FL U. 1st ed. F/VG+. V1. $20.00

POST, Emily. *Children Are People.* 1940. NY. 1st ed. 383p. F/dj. A17. $10.00

POST, Emily. *How To Behave Though a Debutant.* 1928. Doubleday Doran. 1st ed. cloth. F/F. B4. $175.00

POST, George E. *Flora of Syria, Palestine & Sinai...* 1932-33. Beirut. 2nd ed. 2 vol. ils/5 maps. B26. $110.00

POST, Kenneth. *Florist Crop Production & Marketing.* 1950 (1949). NY. 427 photos/diagrams. VG. B26. $45.00

POSTON, Charles D. *Building a State in Apache Land.* 1963. Tempe. 1st ed. 8vo. 174p. red cloth. NF. T10. $35.00

POSY, Arnold. *Israeli Tales & Legends.* 1948. Block. 8vo. VG/G. B17. $4.00

POTOK, Chaim. *Chosen.* 1992. Knopf. 1st ed. sgn. rem mk. F/F case. B35. $40.00

POTOK, Chaim. *Promise.* 1969. Knopf. 1st ed. author's 2nd book. F/NF. H11. $30.00

POTTER, Beatrix. *Fairy Caravan.* 1929. Phil. McKay. 1st Am ed. ils Potter. 225p. VG. D1. $450.00

POTTER, Beatrix. *Pie & the Patty-Pan.* 1905. London. 1st ed. VG. M17. $325.00

POTTER, Beatrix. *Roly-Poly Pudding.* 1908. Warne. 1st Am ed. 8vo. 70p. red cloth cloth. VG. D1. $400.00

POTTER, Beatrix. *Tale of Little Pig Robinson.* 1930. McKay. 1st Am ed. 8vo. gr cloth. VG. D1. $350.00

POTTER, Beatrix. *Tale of Peter Rabbit.* 1916. Saalfield. ils Virginia Albert. unp. VG. M20. $10.00

POTTER, Beatrix. *Tale of Peter Rabbit.* 1995. Kingston, NY. Battledore Ltd. 1/250. sgn Sendak/Bain. AN/box. B24. $950.00

POTTER, Dennis. *Ticket To Ride.* 1985. Faber. 1st Am ed. author's 2nd novel. NF/VG. M22. $30.00

POTTER, Jonathan. *Collecting Antique Maps: An Introduction to History...* 1992. London. Studio/ 4to. ils. 192p. F/dj. O7. $35.00

POTTER, Woodburne. *War in Florida: Being an Exposition of Its Causes...* 1836. Baltimore. 1st ed. maps/3 fld maps. 184p. VG. C6. $550.00

POTTER & ROLAND. *Annotated Bibliography of Canadian Medical Periodicals...* 1979. Toronto. 1st ed. 77p. dj. A13. $45.00

POTTERTON, David. *Culpepper's Color Herbal.* 1983. NY. sc. M. B26. $15.00

POTTLE, Frederick A. *Boswell in Holland 1763-1764.* 1952. Heinemann. lg 8vo. 14 pl. 428p. vellum/gilt bl cloth. K1. $75.00

POTTLE, Frederick A. *Boswell in Holland 1763-1764.* 1952. NY. 1st ed. ils. F/dj. A17. $15.00

POTTLE, Frederick A. *Boswell on the Grand Tour: Germany & Switzerland, 1764.* 1953. London. Heinemann. lg 8vo. 1/1000. 354p. gilt bl cloth. K1. $75.00

POULIN, A. *Nameless Garden.* 1978. Croissant. 1st ed. 1/50. sgn/#d. F/wrp. V1. $45.00

POULLE, Emmanuel. *Bibliotheque Scientifique d'un Imprimeur Humaniste...* 1963. Geneva. Libraire Droz SA. 4to. 104p. cream cloth. K1. $35.00

POULSEN, Svend. *Poulsen on the Rose.* 1955 (1941). London. 1st Eng ed. 7 pl. VG/dj. B26. $15.00

POUND, Ezra. *ABC of Reading.* 1934. Yale. 1st Am ed. NF. B4. $85.00

POUND, Ezra. *Cavalcanti Poems.* 1966. London. Faber. 1st ed. sgn. 105p. teg. F/case. B24. $2,250.00

POUND, Ezra. *Ezra Pound & James Laughlin: Selected Letters...* 1994. np. 335p. F/F. A4. $30.00

POUND, Ezra. *Imaginary Letters.* 1930. Blk Sun. 1/50 on Japan vellum. sgn. pub's copy. 56p. F/F/case. C6. $3,000.00

POUND, Ezra. *Lustra.* 1916. London. 2nd. rem bdg. F. C2. $100.00

POUND, Ezra. *Lustra.* 1916. London. Elkin Mathews. 1st ed/1st imp. 1/200. tan cloth. F/case/chemise. B24. $2,500.00

POUND, Ezra. *Personae.* 1909. London. Elkin Mathews. 1st ed. F. B24. $750.00

POUND, Ezra. *Redondillas; or, Something of That Sort.* 1967. New Directions. 1st ed. 1/110. sgn. F/orig plain dj. B24. $1,850.00

POUND, Reginald. *Harley Street.* 1967. London. 1st ed. 198p. dj. A13. $25.00

POURNELLE, Jerry. *Nebula Winners 16.* 1982. HRW. 1st ed. VG/VG. P3. $20.00

POURNELLE, Jerry. *Step Farther Out.* 1980. WH Allen. 1st ed. VG. P3. $20.00

POURNELLE, Jerry. *Storms of Victory.* 1987. Ace. 1st ed. VG/VG. P3. $17.00

POWELL, Anthony. *Kindly Ones.* 1962. Little Brn. 1st ed. F/F. B35. $35.00

POWELL, Anthony. *Soldier's Art.* 1966. London. Heinemann. 1st ed. F/F. C2. $75.00

POWELL, Danny. *Parting the Curtains: Interviews With Southern Writers.* 1994. John K Blair. 1st ed. photos Jill Krementz. F/F. A20. $28.00

POWELL, Dawn. *Golden Spur.* 1962. Viking. 1st ed. F/NF. B4. $400.00

POWELL, Donald M. *Peralta Grant.* 1960. Norman, OK. 1st ed. sgn. ils. 186p. F/NF. T10. $65.00

POWELL, E. Alexander. *Yonder Lies Adventure!* 1932. Macmillan. 1st ed. 452p. VG. W1. $18.00

POWELL, Fay Ellen. *Kitty Colette.* 1988. Saltbush. 1/200. F/sans. B19. $20.00

POWELL, G. Harold. *Letters From the Orange Empire.* 1990. Hist Soc of CA. 1st trade ed. 1/350. 142p. VG. B19. $30.00

POWELL, Gertrude Eliza Clark. *Looking Back & Remembering.* 1987. private prt. 1st ed. ils. 85p. NF. B19. $45.00

POWELL, J.W. *Report of the US Geological Survey...1882-1883.* 1884. WA. folio. 473p. G. T3. $62.00

POWELL, J.W. *Seventh Annual Report of the Bureau of Ethnology...* 1891. GPO. xl. 409p. gr cloth. T10. $50.00

POWELL, J.W. *Sixth Annual Report of the Bureau of Ethnology 1884...* 1888. WA. 669p. gilt olive gr cloth. G+. M20. $95.00

POWELL, J.W. *Thirteenth Annual Report of the US Geological Survey...* 1893. GPO. 4to. 2 fld pocket maps. T10. $150.00

POWELL, Lawrence Clark. *Act of Enchantment.* nd (1961). Stagecoach. 1/300. hc. NF/VG. B19. $32.50

POWELL, Lawrence Clark. *Arizona: A Bicentennial History.* 1976. Norton. 1st ed. ils. 154p. NF/NF. B19. $25.00

POWELL, Lawrence Clark. *Blue Train.* 1977. Capra. 1st ed. author's 1st novel. 128p. VG+/dj. B19. $45.00

POWELL, Lawrence Clark. *Bookman's Progress: Selected Writings of...* 1968. Ward Richie. 255p. F/NF. A4. $45.00

POWELL, Lawrence Clark. *Bookman's Progress: Selected Writings of...* 1968. Ward Ritchie. 1st ed. 246p. AN/as issued. B19. $50.00

POWELL, Lawrence Clark. *Books Are Basis: The Essential Lawrence Clark Powell.* 1986. AZ U. 95p. M. B19. $17.00

POWELL, Lawrence Clark. *Books in My Baggage.* 1960. World. 1st ed. inscr. 257p. NF. B19. $35.00

POWELL, Lawrence Clark. *Books West Southwest.* 1957. Ward Ritchie. 1st ed/1st state (blk cloth backstrip). 157p. NF. B19. $50.00

POWELL, Lawrence Clark. *California Classics: Creative Literature...* 1971. Ward Ritchie. 1st ed. inscr. 393p. NF. B19. $65.00

POWELL, Lawrence Clark. *El Morro.* 1984. Capra. 1st ed. 129p. VG+. B19. $30.00

POWELL, Lawrence Clark. *Eucalyptus Fair.* 1992. Books West Southwest. 1st ed. 1/50. sgn/#d. 277p. M/case. B19. $100.00

POWELL, Lawrence Clark. *Evening Redness.* 1991. Capra. 1/100. sgn/#d. 436p. leather spine. NF/case. B19. $75.00

POWELL, Lawrence Clark. *Ex Libris: Notes on My Family's Bookplates.* 1984. Bajada. 1st ed. 38p. F/sans. B19. $50.00

POWELL, Lawrence Clark. *Fortune & Friendship.* 1968. RR Bowker. 1st ed. inscr. 227p. NF. B19. $40.00

POWELL, Lawrence Clark. *From the Heartland.* 1976. Northland. ils. 167p. NF. B19. $40.00

POWELL, Lawrence Clark. *Holly & the Fleece.* 1993. Capra. 1st ed. 125p. M. D19. $20.00

POWELL, Lawrence Clark. *Land of Fact.* 1992. Hist Soc S CA. 1st ed. 1/150. sgn LCP/Ward Ritchie. M/sans. B19. $100.00

POWELL, Lawrence Clark. *Landscape & Literature.* 1990. DeGolyer Lib. 1st ed. 1/750. sgn. NF/sans. B19. $40.00

POWELL, Lawrence Clark. *Le Monde Passe, la Figure de ce Monde Passe.* 1983. private prt. 1st ed. 81p. F/sans. B19. $25.00

POWELL, Lawrence Clark. *Life Goes On: Twenty More Years of Fortune...* 1986. Scarecrow. ils. 186p. NF/NF. B19. $45.00

POWELL, Lawrence Clark. *Little Package.* 1964. World. 1st ed. 319p. NF. B19. $55.00

POWELL, Lawrence Clark. *My Haydn Commonplace Book.* 1983. private prt. 1st ed. 1/200 (not intended for sale). 50 p. NF. B19. $50.00

POWELL, Lawrence Clark. *My Mozart Commonplace Book.* 1980. private prt. 1/300. 73p. w/pres card. VG+. B19. $35.00

POWELL, Lawrence Clark. *My New Mexico Literary Friends.* 1986. Pr of Palace of Governors. 1st ed. 27p. bl cloth. NF. B19. $95.00

POWELL, Lawrence Clark. *Orange Grove Boyhood.* 1988. Capra. 1st ed. ils. 80p. NF. B19. $25.00

POWELL, Lawrence Clark. *Passion for Books.* 1958. World. ltd ed. 154p. F/NF case. B19. $110.00

POWELL, Lawrence Clark. *Philosopher Pickett.* 1942. CA U. 1st ed. inscr. 178p. NF/clip. B19. $95.00

POWELL, Lawrence Clark. *Portrait of My Father.* 1986. Capra. 1st ed. 111p. NF. B19. $35.00

POWELL, Lawrence Clark. *River Between.* 1979. Capra. 1st ed. sgn. VG/tattered. B19. $20.00

POWELL, Lawrence Clark. *Vein of Silk, Vein of Steel.* 1975. private prt. 1st ed. F/sans. B19. $65.00

POWELL, Lawrence Clark. *Where Water Flows.* 1980. Northland. 1st ed. 64p. NF. B19. $20.00

POWELL, Mary Lucas. *Status & Health in Prehistory: A Case Study...* 1988. Smithsonian. 8vo. ils/tables/pl. F/F. T10. $25.00

POWELL, P.H. *Murder Premeditated.* 1951. Herbert Jenkins. hc. xl. dj. P3. $10.00

POWELL, Padgett. *Edisto.* 1983. FSG. 1st ed. author's 1st novel. F/F. B4. $75.00

POWELL, Padgett. *Edisto.* 1984. FSG. 1st ed. sgn. F/F. B35. $100.00

POWELL, Padgett. *Typical.* 1991. FSG. 1st ed. F/F. A20. $10.00

POWELL, Padgett. *Typical.* 1991. FSG. 1st ed. sgn. F/F. B35. $50.00

POWELL, Padgett. *Woman Named Drown.* 1987. FSG. 1st ed. sgn. F/F. B35. $55.00

POWELL, Philip. *Soldiers, Indians & Silver.* 1952. CA U. 1st ed. 317p. xl. F3. $25.00

POWELL, Richard R. *Compromises of Conflicting Claims, a Century of CA Law...* 1977. Dobbs Ferry. Oceana. M11. $45.00

POWELL, Talmage. *Mission Impossible: Money Explosion.* 1970. Whitman. TVTI. VG. P3. $10.00

POWELL, Talmage. *Mission Impossible: Priceless Particle.* 1969. Whitman. TVTI. w/sgn label. VG. P3. $20.00

POWELL, Talmage. *Smasher.* 1959. Macmillan. 1st ed. VG/VG. P3. w/sgn label. $35.00

POWELL, Thomas Reed. *Compulsory Vaccination & Sterilization, Constitutional...* 1943. np. Annals of Internal Medicine. 10p. wrp. M11. $10.00

POWELL, Thomas Reed. *Constitution in Transition.* 1941. IL U. 15p. stapled self wrp. M11. $25.00

POWELL, Thomas Reed. *Our Academic Heritage.* 1942. np. Vermont Alumnus. rpt. 4p. M11. $5.00

POWER, Susan. *Grass Dancer.* 1994. Putnam. ARC. F/wrp. B4. $50.00

POWER, Susan. *Grass Dancer.* 1994. Putnam. 1st ed. F/F. M23. $40.00

POWERS, J.F. *Prince of Darkness & Other Stories.* 1947. Doubleday. 1st ed. author's 1st book. F/NF. C2. $100.00

POWERS, J.L. *Black Abyss.* 1966. Arcadia. VG/VG. P3. $13.00

POWERS, John R. *Do Black Patent Leather Shoes Really Reflect Up?* 1975. Chicago. Regnery. 1st ed. author's 2nd book. F/F. H11. $50.00

POWERS, John R. *Junk-Drawer Corner-Store Front-Porch Blues.* 1992. Dutton. 1st ed. F/F. H11. $20.00

POWERS, Richard. *Prisoner's Dilemma.* 1988. NY. Beech Tree/Morrow. 1st ed. F/NF. B2. $100.00

POWERS, Stephen. *A Foot & Alone: A Walk From Sea to Sea by Southern Route.* 1872. Hartford. Columbian Book Co. 1st ed. 12 pl. 327p. cloth. VG+. T10. $275.00

POWERS, Tim. *Anubis Gates.* 1989. Shingletown. Mark Ziesing. 1st Am hc ed. inscr. F/F. T2. $35.00

POWERS, Tim. *Dinner at Deviant's Palace.* nd. BC. VG/VG. P3. $10.00

POWERS, Tim. *Dinner at Deviant's Palace.* 1985. Ace. 1st hc ed. F/F. T2. $12.00

POWERS, Tim. *Drawing of the Dark.* 1991. Eugene. Hypatia. 1st hc ed. 1/275. sgn. intro/sgn KW Jeter. F/sans. T2. $70.00

POWERS, Tim. *On Stranger Tides.* 1987. Ace. 1st ed. sgn. F/F. T2. $45.00

POWERS, Tim. *Skies Discrowned.* 1993. Huntington Beach. James Cahill. 1st hc ed. 1/300. sgns. F/F. T2. $75.00

POWERS, Tim. *Stress of Her Regard.* 1989. Ace. 1st ed. inscr. F/F. T2. $45.00

POWYS, John. *Cowper & Llewellyn: Confessions of Two Brothers.* 1916. Rochester. 1st ed. F/F. C2. $75.00

POWYS, T.F. *Black Bryony.* 1923. Chatto Windus. 1st ed. author's 1st book. bl-gr cloth. F. B24. $125.00

POYER, David C. *Stepfather Bank.* 1987. St Martin. 1st ed. F/F. P3. $17.00

POYER, Joe. *North Cape.* 1969. Doubleday. 1st ed. xl. dj. P3. $5.00

POYNTER, Noel. *Medicine & Man.* 1971. London. 1st ed. 195p. VG. A13. $25.00

PRAERAFFAELITEN. *Baden Baden, Staatliche Kunsthalle.* 1974. 2nd. F/F. D2. $95.00

PRAGER, Arthur. *Rascals at Large.* 1971. Doubleday. 1st ed. VG/VG. P3. $25.00

PRASHER. *Indian Library Literature, an Annoted Bibliography.* 1971. New Delhi. 3550 engries. 504p. VG/dj. A4. $65.00

PRATCHETT, Terry. *Strata.* 1994. Doubleday. 1/500. sgn/#d. F/F. P3. $45.00

PRATHER, Richard S. *Amber Effect.* 1986. Tor. 1st ed. F/F. P3. $13.00

PRATHER, Richard S. *Kubla Khan Caper.* 1966. Trident. 1st ed. VG/VG. P3. $25.00

PRATT, Ambrose. *Lore of the Lyrebird.* 1937. Melbourne. 8vo. fwd Colin Mackenzie. 71p. cloth. VG. B14. $30.00

PRATT, Caroll C. *Logic of Modern Psychology.* 1939. Macmillan. inscr. 185p. bl cloth. G1. $35.00

PRATT, Charles Stuart. *Bye-O-Baby Ballads.* nd. Lathrop. later rpt. 8vo. ils Childe Hassam. G+. M5. $90.00

PRATT, Fletcher. *All About Famous Inventors...* 1955. Random. hc. VG. P3. $20.00

PRATT, Fletcher. *Civil War in Pictures.* nd. BC. VG. P3. $10.00

PRATT, Fletcher. *Double in Space.* 1951. Doubleday. 1st ed. NF/NF. P3. $40.00

PRATT, Fletcher. *Fighting Ships of the US Navy.* 1941. Garden City. G/dj. A16. $30.00

PRATT, Fletcher. *Night Work.* 1946. Holt. 1st ed. VG. P3. $30.00

PRATT, Fletcher. *Rockets, Jets, Guided Missiles...* 1951. Random. G. P3. $20.00

PRATT, Fletcher. *Undying Fire.* 1953. Ballantine. 1st ed. F/F. P3. $45.00

PRATT, Fletcher. *Witches Three.* 1952. Twayne. 1st ed. VG/VG. P3. $45.00

PRATT, J.S.B. *Hawaii I Remember.* 1965. Kanoehe. VG/wrp. O7. $20.00

PRATT, Theodore. *Murder Goes to the World's Fair.* nd. Eldon. hc. VG. P3. $25.00

PRAWY, Marcel. *Vienna Opera.* 1969. Praeger. 4to. 224p. wht cloth. dj. K1. $45.00

PREISS, Byron. *Microverse.* 1989. Bantam. 1st ed. F/F. G10. $30.00

PREISS, Byron. *Planets.* 1985. Bantam. hc. F/F. P3. $25.00

PREISS, Byron. *Raymond Chandler's Philip Marlowe.* 1988. Knopf. 1st ed. F/F. P3. $19.00

PREISS, Byron. *Universe.* 1987. Bantam. 4to. 335p. VG/VG. K5. $15.00

PRENTIS, Joseph. *Monthly Kalander.* 1992. Chillicothe, IL. Am Botanist. 65p. stiff wrp. A10. $18.00

PRESCOT, Dray; see Bulmer, Kenneth.

PRESCOTT, Philander. *Recollections of Philander Prescott, Frontiersman...* 1966. Lincoln, NE. 8vo. 272p. NF/NF. T10. $35.00

PRESCOTT, William Hickling. *History of the Conquest of Mexico.* 1957. Heritage. 8vo. ils Miguel Ovarrubias. prt brd/cloth spine. F. T10. $35.00

PRESCOTT, William Hinkling. *History of the Conquest of Peru.* 1874. Lippincott. 2 vol. 12mo. teg. later quarter red leather. T10. $75.00

PRESS & SIEVER. *Earth.* 1978. WH Freeman. 2nd. 649p. F. D8. $20.00

PRESTON, Howard Willis. *Rhode Island & the Sea.* 1932. Providence. State Bureau of Information. T7. $35.00

PRESTON, Thomas W. *Historical Sketches of the Holston Valleys.* 1926. Kingsport. 186p. VG/VG. B10. $50.00

PREUSS, Paul. *Human Error.* 1985. Tor. 1st ed. hc. F/F. P3. $15.00

PREUSS, Paul. *Starfire.* 1988. Tor. 1st ed. F/F. P3. $18.00

PREUSSLER, Otfried. *Satanic Mill.* nd. Macmillan. 3rd. VG/VG. P3. $14.00

PREYER, Wilhelm. *Die Seele des Kindes: Beobachtungen Uber die Geistige...* 1884. Leipzig. Theodor Grieben. 2nd. 488p. rebound. G1. $100.00

PREYER, Wilhelm. *Ein Merkwurdiger Fall von Fascination.* 1895. Stuttgart. Ferdinand Enke. VG/prt yel wrp. G1. $75.00

PRICE, Alfred. *World War II Fighter Conflict.* 1975. London. MacDonald. 160p. VG+/dj. B18. $32.50

PRICE, Anthony. *Colonel Butler's Wolf.* 1973. Crime Club. 1st ed. xl. dj. P3. $6.00

PRICE, Anthony. *For the Good of the State.* 1987. Mysterious. 1st ed. F/F. P3. $17.00

PRICE, Anthony. *Gunner Kelly.* 1984. Doubleday Crime Club. 1st ed. VG/torn. P3. $12.00

PRICE, Derek J. de Solla. *Science Since Babylon.* 1961. New Haven. 1st ed. 149p. VG. A13. $20.00

PRICE, E. Hoffman. *Strange Gateways.* 1967. Arkham. 1st ed. 1/2007. F/F. T2. $125.00

PRICE, Emerson. *Inn of That Country.* 1939. Caldwell. 1st ed. author's 1st book. F/F. A17. $20.00

PRICE, Eugenia. *New Moon Rising.* 1969. Lippincott. 1st ed. sgn. F/NF. B4. $45.00

PRICE, Eva Jane. *China Journal 1889-1900.* 1989. Scribner. 1st ed. 8vo. 289p. AN/dj. P4. $22.50

PRICE, Fred W. *Moon Observer's Handbook.* 1988. Cambridge. photos. 309p. F/F. K5. $35.00

PRICE, Margaret Evans. *Legends of the Seven Seas.* 1929. Harper. 1st ed. 168p. bl cloth. fairl. T5. $15.00

PRICE, Margaret Evans. *Little Red Riding Hood & Other Old-Time Fairy Tales.* 1926 (1921). Rand McNally. lg 4to. VG. M5. $35.00

PRICE, Margaret Evans. *Sleeping Beauty & Other Old-Time Fairy Tales.* 1926 (1921). Rand McNally. lg 4to. ils. VG. M5. $35.00

PRICE, Molly. *Iris Book.* 1966. Princeton. ils/photos. VG/dj. B26. $22.00

PRICE, Nancy. *Sleeping With the Enemy.* 1987. Simon Schuster. 1st ed. F/F. H11. $40.00

PRICE, Reynolds. *Back Before Day.* 1989. 1/400. sgn. VG/VG. C4. $50.00

PRICE, Reynolds. *Blue Calhoun.* 1st ed. NF/NF. B30. $23.00

PRICE, Reynolds. *Clear Pictures.* 1989. np. ils. 304p. F/F. A4. $25.00

PRICE, Reynolds. *Collected Stories.* 1993. Atheneum. 1st ed. sgn. F/F. C2. $75.00

PRICE, Reynolds. *Kate Vaiden.* 1987. London. 1st ed. VG/VG. C4. $45.00

PRICE, Reynolds. *Love & Work.* 1968. Atheneum. 1st ed. F/F. B2. $40.00

PRICE, Reynolds. *Mustian.* 1983. Atheneum. 1st ed. F/NF. B4. $65.00

PRICE, Reynolds. *Use of Fire.* 1990. Atheneum. 1st ed. F/F. M23. $20.00

PRICE, Richard. *Breaks.* 1983. Simon Schuster. 1st ed. xl. dj. P3. $10.00

PRICE, Richard. *Clockers.* 1992. Houghton Mifflin. 1st ed. F/F. H11. $45.00

PRICE, Richard. *Wanderers.* 1974. Houghton Mifflin. 1st ed. author's 1st novel. F/F clip. B35. $60.00

PRICE, Richard. *Wanderers.* 1974. Houghton Mifflin. 1st ed. author's 1st novel. F/F. H11. $90.00

PRICE. *Civl War Handbook.* 1961. Fairfax, VA. 8vo. 72p. G. T3. $9.00

PRICHARD, James B. *Archaeology & the Old Testament.* 1959. Princeton. 2nd. 8vo. ils/map. VG/dj. W1. $22.00

PRICHARD, James Cowles. *Researches Into the Physical History of Mankind.* 1836-1847. Sherwood Gilbert Piper. 5 vol. 3rd. ils/1 fld map. G. W1. $95.00

PRIDDELL, Guy. *We Began at Jamestown.* 1968. Richmond. Dietz. 1st ed. inscr. 8vo. 198p. orange cloth. F/VG. B11. $40.00

PRIDEAUX. *Bibliography of the Works of Robert Louis Stevenson.* 1917. np. 411p. VG. A4. $125.00

PRIDGEN, Tim. *Courage: Story of Modern Cockfighting.* 1938. ils. VG. M17. $40.00

PRIEST, Christopher. *Glamour.* 1984. Jonathan Cape. 1st ed. sgn. F/F. P3. $30.00

PRIESTLY, J.B. *Black-Out in Gretley.* 1943. Clipper Books. F/F. P3. $30.00

PRIESTLY, J.B. *Bright Day.* 1946. Heinemann. 2nd. VG. P3. $15.00

PRIESTLY, J.B. *Carfitt Crisis.* 1976. Stein Day. 1st ed. VG/VG. P3. $15.00

PRIESTLY, J.B. *Doomsday Men.* 1938. London. Heinemann. 1st ed. VG. M22. $20.00

PRIESTLY, J.B. *Faraway.* 1932. Macmillan. 1st ed. hc. VG. P3. $25.00

PRIESTLY, J.B. *Festival at Farbridge.* 1951. Heinemann. 1st ed. VG. P3. $30.00

PRIESTLY, J.B. *Good Companions.* 1929. Harper. 1st ed. VG. P3. $35.00

PRIESTLY, J.B. *It's an Old Country.* nd. BC. VG/VG. P3. $10.00

PRIESTLY, J.B. *Lost Empires.* 1965. Atlantic/Little Brn. 1st Am ed. VG/VG. M22. $15.00

PRIESTLY, J.B. *Magicians.* 1954. Harper. 1st ed. VG/VG. P3. $40.00

PRIESTLY, J.B. *Salt Is Leaving.* 1975. Harper Row. VG/VG. P3. $15.00

PRIESTLY, J.B. *Shapes of Sleep.* 1962. Heinemann. 1st ed. NF/NF. P3. $25.00

PRILL, David. *Unnatural.* 1995. St Martin. 1st ed. author's 1st book. F/F. M23. $40.00

PRINCE, Leslie. *Ferrier & His Craft.* 1980. London. Allen. 1st prt. VG. O3. $35.00

PRINCE, Morton. *Clinical & Experimental Studies in Personality.* 1929. Cambrige. Sci-Art Pub. 8vo. 559p. dj. G1. $125.00

PRINCE, Pamela. *Once Upon a Time.* 1988. Harmony. 1st ed. ils JW Smith. 47p. NF/NF. T5. $30.00

PRINCE, Pamela. *Sweet Dreams, the Art of Bessie Pease Gutmann.* 1985. Harmony. 11th. rem mk. F/VG. B17. $9.00

PRINGLE, Elizabeth W.A. *Chronicles of Chicora Wood.* 1940. Boston. purple cloth. VG. B30. $25.00

PRINGLE, Terry. *Preacher's Boy.* 1988. Algonquin. 1st ed. rem mk. F/F. H11. $35.00

PRINGLE, Terry. *Tycoon.* 1990. Algonquin. 1st ed. F/F. H11. $20.00

PRIOR, M. *Poems on Several Occasions.* 1709. London. Tomson. 1st authorized ed. 8vo. 328p. F. T10. $250.00

PRITCHARD, N.H. *Eecchhooeess.* 1971. U Pr. 1st ed. F/NF. V1. $15.00

PROCTER, Maurice. *Body To Spare.* nd. BC. VG/VG. P3. $8.00

PROCTER, Maurice. *His Weight in Gold.* 1966. Harper Row. 1st ed. F/F. P3. $18.00

PROCTER, Maurice. *Rogue Running.* 1966. Harper Row. 1st ed. F/F. P3. $18.00

PROCTOR, M. *Natural History of Pollination.* 1996. Portland. 39 tables. 487p. sc. M. B26. $25.00

PROCTOR, Mary. *Everyman's Astronomy.* 1939. Scientific BC. 23 pl. 246p. G/dj. K5. $13.00

PROCTOR, Richard A. *Mysteries of Time & Space.* 1883. NY. Worthington. 1st Am ed. 8vo. 418p. G. K5. $45.00

PRODDOW, Penelope. *Hermes, Lord of Robbers.* 1971. Doubleday. 1st ed. ils Barbara Cooney. NF/VG+. P2. $55.00

PROFATT, John. *Curiosities & Law of Wills.* 1884. San Francisco. Whitney. gilt gr cloth. M11. $75.00

PRONZINI, Bill. *Blowback.* 1977. Random. 1st ed. NF/NF. M22. $65.00

PRONZINI, Bill. *Breakdown.* 1991. Delacorte. 1st ed. F/F. P3. $20.00

PRONZINI, Bill. *Cat's Paw.* 1991. Mystery Scene Short Story. 1st ed. 1/100. sgn. F/sans. P3. $20.00

PRONZINI, Bill. *Crime & Crime Again.* 1990. Bonanza. NF/NF. P3. $12.00

PRONZINI, Bill. *Demons.* 1993. Delacorte. 1st ed. F/F. P3. $20.00

PRONZINI, Bill. *Gallows Land.* 1983. Walker. 1st ed. sgn. F/F. A18. $15.00

PRONZINI, Bill. *Hard-Boiled.* 1995. Oxford. 1st ed. F/F. P3. $25.00

PRONZINI, Bill. *Masques.* 1981. Arbor. 1st ed. VG/VG. N4. $30.00

PRONZINI, Bill. *Nightshades.* 1984. St Martin. 1st ed. F/F. P3. $25.00

PRONZINI, Bill. *Panic!* 1972. Random. 1st ed. VG/VG. P3. $40.00

PRONZINI, Bill. *Quicksilver.* 1984. St Martin. 1st ed. F/F. P3. $25.00

PRONZINI, Bill. *Shackles.* 1988. St Martin. 1st ed. VG/VG. P3. $25.00

PRONZINI, Bill. *Shatterbot.* 1982. St Martin. 1st ed. F/F. P3. $30.00

PRONZINI, Bill. *Small Felonies.* 1988. St Martin. 1st ed. F/F. P3. $20.00

PRONZINI, Bill. *Snowbound.* 1974. Putnam. 1st ed. VG/VG. P3. $30.00

PRONZINI, Bill. *Stacked Deck.* 1991. Mystery Scene. 1st ed. 1/50. leather. F/sans. P3. $50.00

PRONZINI, Bill. *Stalker.* 1971. Random. 1st ed. author's 1st book. NF/NF. H11. $55.00

PRONZINI, Bill. *Tales of the Dead.* nd. Bonanza. 3rd. F/F. P3. $12.00

PROPPER, Milton. *Divorce Court Murder.* 1934. Harper. 1st ed. NF/NF double djs. B4. $125.00

PROPPER, Milton. *Handwriting on the Wall.* 1941. Harper. 1st ed. F/NF double djs. B4. $75.00

PROSE, Francine. *Glorious Ones.* 1974. Atheneum. ARC. inscr. RS. F/F. B4. $150.00

PROSE, Francine. *Women & Children.* 1988. Pantheon. 1st ed. F/F. B4. $45.00

PROTTER, Eric. *Harvest of Horrors.* nd. BC. VG/VG. P3. $10.00

PROUDLEY & PROUDLEY. *Heathers in Colour.* 1978 (1974). Poole, Dorset. ils/photos. 192p. F/dj. B26. $16.00

PROULX, E. Annie. *Fences & Gates, Walkways, Walls & Drives.* 1983. 1st ed. author's 2nd book. NF. S13. $75.00

PROULX, E. Annie. *Gardener's Journal & Record Book.* 1983. Rodale. simultaneous wrp ed. F. B4. $185.00

PROULX, E. Annie. *Gourmet Gardner: Growing Choice Fruits & Vegetables...* 1987. Fawcett Columbine. 1st ed. F/wrp. B4. $150.00

PROULX, E. Annie. *Heart Songs & Other Stories.* 1988. Scribner. ARC/1st ed. author's 1st book. RS. F/NF. S9. $750.00

PROULX, E. Annie. *Postcards.* 1992. Scribner. ARC. author's 1st novel. RS. F/F. B4. $500.00

PROULX, E. Annie. *Shipping News.* 1993. Scribner. UP. sgn. F/wrp. B4. $350.00

PROUST, Marcel. *Remembrance of Things Past.* 1934. Random. 2 vol. VG/tattered box. P3. $40.00

PROUST, Marcel. *Swann's Way.* 1954. LEC. 1st ed. ils/sgn Bernard Lamotte. 441p. NF/case. C2. $75.00

PROVENSEN & PROVENSEN. *Animal Fair.* 1952. Simon Schuster. 1st ed. ils. VG. P2. $40.00

PROVENSEN & PROVENSEN. *Golden Bible for Children, the New Testament.* 1953. Golden. folio. G. B17. $4.00

PROVENSEN & PROVENSEN. *Karen's Curiosity.* (1963). Golden. ils. 24mo. unp. G+/torn. T5. $25.00

PROVENSEN & PROVENSEN. *Peaceable Kingdom: The Shaker Abecedarius.* 1978. NY. Viking. 1st ed. F/VG+. C8. $40.00

PROWELL, Sandra West. *By Evil Means.* 1993. Walker. 2nd. F/F. P3. $35.00

PROWELL, Sandra West. *Killing of Monday Brown.* 1994. NY. Walker. AP. 8vo. F/red wrp. S9. $30.00

PROWELL, Sandra West. *Killing of Monday Brown.* 1994. Walker. 1st ed. sgn. F/F. T2. $30.00

PRYOR, William Clayton. *Steamship Book.* 1934. Harcourt Brace. G. A16. $17.50

PSEUDOMAN, Akkad. *Zero to Eighty.* 1937. Scientific Pub. 1st ed. NF/NF. P3. $35.00

PTOLEMAEI, Clavdii. *Cosmographia Tabvlae.* 1900. Leicester. Magna. 27 double-p maps. ils brd. M. O7. $45.00

PTOLEMAEUS, Claudius. *Cosmographia.* 1966. Amsterdam. facsimile. folio. M/dj. O7. $225.00

PTOLEMAEUS, Claudius. *Geographica.* 1966. Amsterdam. facsimile of 1540 ed. 48 double-p maps. M/dj. O7. $295.00

PUBLIUS. *Works...* 1822. Pickering. contemporary calf. miniature. T10. $100.00

PUCKETT, Andrew. *Bloodstains.* 1989. Crime Club. 1st ed. NF/NF. P3. $15.00

PUCKETT, Andrew. *Terminius.* 1990. Collins Crime Club. 1st ed. F/F. P3. $18.00

PUCKETT, David H. *Memories.* 1987. Vantage. 1st ed. F/F. B4. $100.00

PUDNEY, John. *Suez: De Lesseps' Canal.* 1969. London. Dent. 242p. xl. VG/dj. W1. $16.00

PUFENDORF, Samuel. *De Officio Hominis et Civis Juxta Legem Naturalem Libri Duo.* 1715. London. contemporary calf. M11. $250.00

PUFENDORF, Samuel. *Of the Law of Nature & Nations...* 1729. London. Walthoe Wilkin. calf. worn. M11. $750.00

PUFFER, Ethel D. *Psychology of Beauty.* 1905. Houghton Mifflin. 286p. prt pebbled crimson cloth. G1. $35.00

PUHARICH, Andrija. *Sacred Mushroom: Key to the Door of Eternity.* 1959. Doubleday. 1st ed. F/NF. B2. $45.00

PUISEUX, P. *La Terre et la Lune.* 1980. Paris. Gauthier-Villars. sm 4to. 176p. xl. K5. $60.00

PUNCH, Walter. *Keeping Eden.* 1992. Boston. Little Brn/MA Horticulture Soc. 277p. AN/dj. A10. $50.00

PUNER, Helen Walker. *Daddies: What They Do All Day.* 1957. Lee Shepard. 7th. 4to. 95p. VG+/G. C14. $10.00

PUNER, Helen Walker. *Sitter Who Didn't Sit.* 1949. Lee Shepard. 1st ed. ils Duvoisin. unp. VG/torn. T5. $35.00

PUNSHON, E.R. *It Might Lead Anywhere.* 1949. Gollancz. 2nd. VG/VG. P3. $20.00

PURCELL, Richard J. *Connecticut in Transition 1775-1818.* 1963. Middletown, CT. Wesleyan U. 8vo. 305p. F/NF. H4. $40.00

PURDY, Carl. *My Life & Times.* 1976. np. ils/photos. 228p. sc. VG. B26. $25.00

PURDY, Elijah. *I Am Elijah Thrush.* 1972. Doubleday. 1st ed. sgn. F/NF. B4. $125.00

PURDY, James. *Day After the Fair.* 1977. NY. Note of Hand Pub. 1st ed. sgn. F/dj. S9. $35.00

PURDY, James. *Eustace Chisholm & the Works.* 1967. NY. 1st ed. F/F. A17. $15.00

PURDY, James. *Mourners Below.* 1981. Viking. 1st ed. F/F. A20. $8.00

PURSER, Philip. *Four Days to the Fireworks.* 1965. Walker. 1st ed. VG/VG. P3. $13.00

PURVES, David Laing. *English Circumnavigators: Most Remarkable Voyages...* 1874. London. Nimmo. ils/4 fld maps. 831p. VG. T7. $60.00

PURVEY, Margery. *Royal Society: Concept & Creation.* 1967. London. 1st ed. 246p. dj. A13. $30.00

PUSHKAREV & TUNNARD. *Man-Made America: Chaos or Control?* 1967.. Yale. 5th. ils. VG/VG. M17. $25.00

PUSHKIN, Alexander. *Golden Cockerel.* 1950. LEC. 1/1500. ils/sgn Edmund Dulac. 42p. F/chemise/case. B24. $350.00

PUTNAM, George Haven. *Books & Their Makers During the Middle Ages.* 1962. rpt of 1896-97 ed. 2 vol. VG/box. B30. $100.00

PUTNAM, H. Phelps. *Collected Poems.* 1970. FSG. 1st ed. F/NF. V1. $20.00

PUTNAM, Mary Traill Spence. *Record of an Obscure Man.* 1861. Ticknor Fields. 1st ed. 8vo. 216p. gilt brn cloth. K1. $35.00

PUTNAM & UHLE. *Pre-Inca Pottery of Nazca, Peru.* 1994. Falcon Hill. rpt. ils. sbdg. F3. $20.00

PUZO, Mario. *Fools Die.* 1978. Putnam. 1st ed. F/NF. H11. $40.00

PUZO, Mario. *Fools Die.* 1978. Putnam. 1st ed. VG/VG. N4/P3. $25.00

PUZO, Mario. *Godfather.* 1969. Putnam. 1st ed. NF/VG. H11. $120.00

PUZO, Mario. *Sicilian.* 1984. Linden. 1st ed. NF/dj. H11/N4. $20.00

PYE, Henry James. *Summary of the Duties of a Justice of the Peace...* 1810. London. contemporary speckled calf. M11. $350.00

PYE, Peter. *Sail in a Forest.* 1961. London. Hart Davies. ils/map. 174p. dj. T7. $24.00

PYLE, Ernie. *Last Chapter.* 1946. 1st ed. VG+/chip. S13. $15.00

PYLE, Howard. *Book of King Arthur.* 1970. Classic. hc. VG. P3. $10.00

PYLE, Howard. *Garden Behind the Moon.* 1988. Parbola. 8vo. ils. F/G. B17. $7.00

PYLE, Howard. *Merry Adventures of Robin Hood.* 1920. Scribner. ils. VG. M19. $45.00

PYLE, Howard. *Merry Adventures of Robin Hood.* 1966. Golden. 2nd. 4to. 284p. VG+. C14. $10.00

PYLE, Howard. *Pepper & Salt; or, Seasoning for Young Folks.* 1886. NY. Harper. 1st ed. 4to. 121p. tan cloth. NF. B24. $600.00

PYLE, Howard. *Wonder Clock.* (1915). Harper. ils Howard Pyle. 8vo. 318p. VG. T5. $45.00

PYLE, Katharine. *Tales of Folk & Fairies.* 1919. Little Brn. 1st ed. VG. N4. $35.00

PYLE, Katherine. *Katherine Pyle Book of Fairy Tales.* (1925). Dutton. 338p. red cloth. VG. T5. $65.00

PYM, Roland. *Cinderella.* nd. Houghton Mifflin. moveables. VG. P2. $65.00

PYM, Roland. *Sleeping Beauty.* 1951. Houghton Mifflin. Peepshow fld book. VG. P2. $65.00

PYNCHON, Thomas. *Crying of Lot 49.* 1966. Lippincott. 1st ed. F/NF. B2. $125.00

PYNCHON, Thomas. *Gravity's Rainbow.* 1973. Viking. 1st ed. author's 3rd book. NF/clip. C2. $375.00

PYNCHON, Thomas. *V.* 1963. Lippincott. 1st ed. author's 1st book. NF/NF. C2. $750.00

PYRNELLE, Louis Clarke. *Diddie, Dumps & Tot; or, Plantation Child-Life.* 1882. Harper. 1st ed. pl. blk stp olive-gr cloth. G. M5. $275.00

PYRNELLE, Louise Clark. *Diddie, Dumps & Tot; or, Plantation Child-Life.* 1882. Harper. 1st ed. 12mo. rebacked. VG. M5. $200.00

PYTHON, Monty. *Brand New Monty Python Book.* nd. Eyre Methuen. VG/G. P3. $20.00

PYTHON, Monty. *Brand New Monty Python Book.* nd. London. 4to. pict brd. NF/VG. S13. $30.00

PYTHON, Monty. *Just the Words Volume 1.* 1989. Methuen. 1st ed. VG. P3. $18.00

QUACKENBUSH, Robert. *Sherlock Chick & the Peekaboo Mystery.* 1987. Parents Magazine. 1st ed. 8vo. ils. 41p. NF. C14. $8.00

QUACKENBUSH, Robert. *Stairway to Doom: Miss Mallard Mystery.* 1983. Prentice Hall. 1st ed. 8vo. 48p. NF/dj. C14. $12.00

QUAD, Matthias. *Geographisch Handtbuch.* 1969. Amsterdam. rpt. Eng/German intro. 82 double-p maps. M/dj. O7. $135.00

QUAIFE, Milo Milton. *Lake Michigan.* 1944. Bobbs Merrill. 1st ed. American Lake series. 8vo. 384p. VG. H4. $16.00

QUAIFE, Milo Milton. *Pictures of Gold Rush California.* 1967. NY. rpt. 383p. F/VG. E1. $35.00

QUARRY, Nick; see Albert, Marvin H.

QUASEM, Muhammad Abul. *Jewels of the Qur'an.* 1977. Kuala Lumpur. Malaya U. 1st ed. 8vo. 244p. VG/wrp. W1. $12.00

QUATERMAIN, James. *Diamond Hostage.* 1975. Constable. 1st ed. VG/VG. P3. $20.00

QUAYLE, Eric. *Collector's Book of Books.* 1971. NY. 144p. F/dj. A17. $20.00

QUEEN, Ellery. *Challenge to the Reader.* 1940. Bl Ribbon. hc. VG. P3. $20.00

QUEEN, Ellery. *Detective Story.* 1969. NY. 1st ed thus. sgn. F/F. C6. $125.00

QUEEN, Ellery. *Double, Double.* 1950. Little Brn. 1st ed. VG. M22. $15.00

QUEEN, Ellery. *Ellery Queen's Circumstantial Evidence.* 1980. Dial. 1st ed. VG/VG. P3. $16.00

QUEEN, Ellery. *Ellery Queen's Crime Cruise...* 1981. Dial. 1st ed. VG/VG. P3. $15.00

QUEEN, Ellery. *Ellery Queen's Doors to Mystery.* 1981. Dial. 1st ed. VG/VG. P3. $15.00

QUEEN, Ellery. *Ellery Queen's Lost Men.* 1983. Dial. 1st ed. F/F. P3. $15.00

QUEEN, Ellery. *Ellery Queen's Multitude of Sins.* 1978. Dial. 1st ed. VG/VG. P3. $15.00

QUEEN, Ellery. *Ellery Queen's Poetic Justice.* 1967. NAL. 1st ed. VG/VG. P3. $20.00

QUEEN, Ellery. *Ellery Queen's Wings of Mystery.* 1979. Dial. 1st ed. VG/VG. P3. $15.00

QUEEN, Ellery. *Ellery Queen's 10th Series.* 1955. Little Brn. 1st ed. VG. P3. $20.00

QUEEN, Ellery. *Ellery Queen's 15 Mystery Annual.* 1960. Random. 1st ed. hc. VG/VG. P3. $40.00

QUEEN, Ellery. *Ellery Queen's 20th Anniversary Annual.* 1965. Random. 1st ed. VG. P3. $12.00

QUEEN, Ellery. *Four of Hearts.* 1946. Tower. 1st ed. VG. P3. $10.00

QUEEN, Ellery. *Fourth Side of the Triangle.* 1965. 1st ed. VG/VG. M19. $35.00

QUEEN, Ellery. *Murder Is a Fox.* 1945. Little Brn. 1st ed. xl. G. P3. $10.00

QUEEN, Ellery. *Player on the Other Side.* 1963. Gollancz. 1st ed. VG/G+. P3. $35.00

QUEEN, Ellery. *Queen's Awards, Sixth Series.* 1951. Little Brn. 1st ed. VG. M22. $10.00

QUEEN, Ellery. *Queen's Awards 1946.* 1946. Little Brn. 1st ed. VG. P3. $18.00

QUEEN, Ellery. *Roman Hat Mystery.* 1948. Tower. VG/VG. P3. $15.00

QUEEN, Ellery. *There Was an Old Woman.* 1943. Little Brn. 1st ed. VG. P3. $30.00

QUEEN, Ellery. *To the Queen's Taste.* 1946. Little Brn. 1st ed. VG. P3. $30.00

QUEEN, Ellery. *Tragedy of X.* 1978. CA U. VG/sans. P3. $10.00

QUEEN, Ellery. *101 Years' Entertainment.* nd. Modern Lib. VG. P3. $25.00

QUEEN OF ROMANIA. *Dreamer of Dreams.* nd (1915). London. Hodder Stoughton. ils Edmund Dulac. dk bl gilt cloth. VG/dj. D1. $400.00

QUEENY, Edgar. *Cheechako. Alaskan Bear Hunt.* 1941. NY. 1st ed. 1/1200. VG/G box. B5. $105.00

QUENNELL, Peter. *Mayhew's Characters.* nd. London. Spring Books. VG/dj. M20. $15.00

QUESADA MARCO, Sebastian. *La Leyenda Antiespanola.* 1967. Madrid. 79p. stiff wrp. F3. $15.00

QUEST, Erica. *Design for Murder.* 1981. Doubleday. 1st ed. xl. VG/VG. N4. $12.50

QUICK, Herbert. *Invisible Woman.* 1924. Bobbs Merrill. 1st ed. F/VG. A18. $30.00

QUIGG, Lemuel Ely. *Gentleman George Ives, a Montana Desperado.* (1958). Houston, TX. rpt. 1/500. VG/stiff wrp. E1. $35.00

QUIGLEY, Joan. *What Does Joan Say?* 1990. Carol Pub. 1st ed. 218p. AN/dj. B22. $4.50

QUIGLEY, Martin. *Crooked Pitch.* 1984. Algonquin. 1st ed. VG+/VG+. P8. $35.00

QUILICI, Folco. *Children of Allah.* 1979. Chartwell. 1st ed. photos. 231p. NF/dj. W1. $45.00

QUILL, J.J. *Motor Yachting.* 1959. Southampton. Adlard Coles. Bosun Books #12. G/wrp. A16. $10.00

QUILLER-COUCH, Arthur. *Sleeping Beauty & Other Fairy Tales.* 1910. London. Hodder Stoughton. 1st ed. ils Dulac. 129p. F. D1. $750.00

QUIMBY, Myron J. *Scratch Ankle: USA American Place Names & Their Derivation.* 1970. NY. 2nd. 390p. F/chip. E1. $25.00

QUIN, Bernetta. *Introduction to the Poetry of Ezra Pound.* 1972. Columbia. 1st ed. F/VG+. V1. $15.00

QUINBY & STEVENSON. *Catalogue of Botanical Books in Collection of RMM Hunt.* nd. rpt of 1958-1961 ed. 3 vol in 2. ils. 1270p. F. A4. $300.00

QUINBY & STEVENSON. *Catalogue of Botanical Books in Collection of RMM Hunt.* 1958 & 1961. Pittsburgh. 2 vol. ltd ed. ils. F/NF. B26. $1,200.00

QUINBY. *Richard Harding Davis: A Bibliography.* 1924. np. 1/1000. 31 pl. 315p. VG. A4. $135.00

QUINN, Dan; see Lewis, Alfred Henry.

QUINN, Seabury. *Phantom-Fighter.* 1966. Arkham. 1st ed. VG/VG. P3. $60.00

QUINN, Vernon. *50 Card Games for Children With an Easy Lesson...* 1946. Cincinnati. 128p. VG. S1. $3.00

QUINNELL, A.J. *In the Name of the Father.* 1987. NAL. 1st ed. rem mk. F/NF. N4. $17.50

QUIRK, Charles J. *Full Circle.* 1936. Mobile, AL. Duval. 1/200. sgn. VG. M8. $27.50

QUIRK, John. *Hard Winners.* 1965. Random. 1st ed. VG/VG. P3. $22.00

QUITMAN, John A. *Speech of John A Quitman, of Mississippi...1856.* 1856. WA. Union Office. 1st ed. 1p. VG/wrp. M8. $27.50

QUOGAN, Anthony. *Fine Art of Murder.* 1988. St Martin. 1st ed. VG/VG. P3. $16.00

RAAB, Lawrence. *Mysteries of the Horizon.* 1972. Doubleday. 1st ed. F/VG+. V1. $15.00

RAABE, Tom. *Biblioholism: The Literary Addiction.* 1991. Golden. Fulcrum. 1st ed. pb. F/pict wrp. T2. $15.00

RABAN, Jonathan. *Arabia: Journey Through the Labyrinth.* 1979. Simon Schuster. 1st ed. 344p. VG/dj. W1. $20.00

RABAN, Jonathan. *Old Glory: An American Voyage.* 1981. Simon Schuster. 409p. dj. T7. $22.00

RABE, David. *Crossing Guard.* 1995. Hyperion. UP. NF. B35. $30.00

RABELAIS, Francois. *Gargantua & Pantagruel.* 1990. Norton. 2nd. F/F. P3. $30.00

RABKIN, Eric S. *Fantastic Worlds.* 1979. Oxford. 1st ed. VG/VG. P3. $20.00

RABOFF, Ernest. *Paul Klee, Art for Children.* 1969. Doubleday. VG/VG. B17. $5.00

RACE, Elizabeth. *Little Gumdrop.* nd. McNight. 8vo. ils. unp. VG. C14. $10.00

RACINA, Thom. *Great Los Angeles Blizzard.* 1977. Putnam. 1st ed. VG/VG. P3. $15.00

RACKHAM, Arthur. *Arthur Rackham Fairy Book.* 1987. Weathervane. VG/VG. P3. $15.00

RACKHAM, Arthur. *Midsummer-Night's Dream.* 1912. Doubleday Page. 3rd imp. 4to. G. B17. $80.00

RACKHAM, Arthur. *Peter Pan in Kensington Gardens, Retold for Little People.* 1958. Scribner. 12mo. ils. xl. G. B17. $7.50

RACKHAM, Arthur. *Rhinegold & the Valkyrie.* 1939. Garden City. 8vo. bl cloth. VG/G. B17. $45.00

RACKHAM, Arthur. *Some British Ballads.* (1920). Dodd Mead. 1st Am ed. ils Rackham. 170p. gilt bl cloth. F. T10. $250.00

RACKHAM, B. *Book of Porcelain.* 1910. London. Blk. 1st ed. 28 tipped-in pl. VG. B5. $90.00

RACZ, Attila. *Courts & Tribunals, a Comparative Study.* 1980. Budapest. Akademiai Kiado. M11. $45.00

RADCLIFFE, Charles Bland. *Vital Motion As Mode of Physical Motion.* 1876. Macmillan. sm 8vo. 252p. prt cloth. G1. $75.00

RADCLIFFE, J.N. *Friends, Ghosts & Sprites.* 1854. London. early 3-quarter leather. VG. A9. $125.00

RADCLIFFE OF WERNETH, Lord. *Mountstuart Elphinstone.* 1962. Clarendon. 32p. stapled wrp. M11. $20.00

RADDALL, Thomas. *Wings of Night.* 1956. Doubleday. 1st ed. VG/VG. P3. $20.00

RADEKA, Lynn. *Legendary Towns of the Old West.* 1990. NY. 1st ed. photos. 176p. F/F. E1. $30.00

RADER. *South of Forty, From Mississippi to Rio Grande...* 1947. OK U. 4to. describes 3793 titles. 336p. VG/dj. A4. $225.00

RADESTOCK, Paul. *Schlaf und Traum: Eine Physiological-Psychologische...* 1879. Leipzig. Druck Breitkopf Hartel. 330p. contemporary bdg. G1. $185.00

RADFORD, P.J. *Antique Maps.* 1965. Denmead. Radford. 33 maps. NF/rpr. O7. $35.00

RADIGUET, Raymond. *Devil in the Flesh.* 1948. Blk Sun. 1st ed. trans Kay Boyle. VG/VG. M22. $35.00

RADIN, Edward D. *Lizzie Borden: The Untold Story.* 1961. Simon Schuster. cloth. worn. M11. $35.00

RADIN, Paul. *Indians of South America.* 1942. Doubleday Doran. 1st ed. 324p. F. E1. $45.00

RADIN & WEI. *Precision's One Club Complete.* 1981. 169p. VG/wrp. S1. $5.00

RADLEY, Shelia. *Quiet Road to Death.* nd. BC. VG/VG. P3. $10.00

RADLEY, Shelia. *Who Saw Him Die?* 1987. Scribner. 1st ed. VG/VG. P3. $15.00

RADOK, Rainier. *Australia's Coast: Environmental Atlas Guide...* 1976. Adelaide. Rigby. 33 pl. NF. O7. $50.00

RAE, Hugh C. *Harkfast.* 1976. St Martin. 1st ed. hc. F/F. P3. $20.00

RAE, Hugh C. *Sullivan.* 1978. Constable. 1st ed. VG/VG. P3. $18.00

RAE, John. *Statues of Henry VII.* 1869. London. John Camden Hotten, contemporary morocco. M11. $225.00

RAEMAEKERS, Louis. *Kultur in Cartoons.* 1917. NY. dk gr cloth. xl. VG. B30. $20.00

RAFERT, Stewart. *Miami Indians of Indiana.* 1996. IN Hist Soc. 352p. M. M20. $30.00

RAFFERTY, Milton D. *Historical Atlas of Missouri.* 1982. Norman, OK. 1st ed. maps/references. 113p. F/stiff wrp. E1. $25.00

RAFINESQUE, Constantine S. *Ancient History; or, Annals of Kentucky...* 1824. Frankfort, KY. 1st ed. 39p. gray wrp/bl chemise/case. C6. $950.00

RAFIZADEH, Mansur. *Witness: From the Shah to the Secret Arms Deal...* 1987. Morrow. 1st ed. 8vo. 12 pl. 396p. VG/dj. W1. $18.00

RAGO, Henry. *Sky of Late Summer.* 1963. Macmillan. 1st ed. F/NF. V1. $20.00

RAGSDALE, Kenneth Baxter. *Quicksilver, Terlingua & the Chisos Mining Company.* 1976. College Sta, TX. 1st ed. photos. 327p. F/F. E1. $30.00

RAHEB, Barbara J. *Diary of a Victorian Cat.* 1993. Pennywright. 1/300. ils. gilt morocco. miniature. B24. $55.00

RAHEB, Barbara J. *Haunted House.* 1992. Agoura Hills. Pennyweight. gilt leatherette. miniature. F. B24. $250.00

RAHMAN, Fazlur. *Islam.* 1979. Chicago. 2nd. 8vo. 285p. VG. W1. $22.00

RAHT, Carlysle Graham. *Romance of Davis Mountains & Big Bend Country.* 1919. El Paso. Rathbooks. ils/26 pl. 382p. gilt bl cloth. K1. $100.00

RAINE, Richard. *Night of the Hawk.* 1968. Heinemann. 1st ed. VG/VG. P3. $22.00

RAINE, William MacLeod. *Broad Arrow.* 1945. Triangle. VG. P3. $12.00

RAINE, William MacLeod. *For Honor & Life.* 1933. Houghton Mifflin. 1st ed. F/F. A10. $25.00

RAINE, William MacLeod. *Guns of the Frontier: Story of How the Law Came to the West.* (1946). Cleveland, OH. Forum. 1st ed. 282p. F. E1. $35.00

RAINE, William MacLeod. *Gunsight Pass.* 1946. Triangle. VG. P3. $8.00

RAINE, William MacLeod. *Hell & High Water.* 1973. Tom Stacey. hc. VG/VG. P3. $15.00

RAINE, William MacLeod. *Outlaw Trail.* 1947. London. Hodder Stoughton. 1st ed. VG/clip. A18. $20.00

RAINE, William MacLeod. *Plantation Guns.* 1945. Hodder Stoughton. 1st ed. F/VG. A18. $20.00

RAINE, William MacLeod. *This Nettle Danger.* 1947. Houghton Mifflin. 1st ed. F/VG+. A18. $30.00

RAINE, William MacLeod. *Trail's End.* 1947. World. VG/VG. P3. $15.00

RAINE, William MacLeod. *45-Caliber Law: Way of Life of the Frontier Officer.* nd. np. pict bdg. F. E1. $35.00

RAINER, Arnulf. *Arnulf Rainer. Bedkt-Ontdekt.* 1987. Brussels. ils/photos. 143p. stiff wrp. D2. $55.00

RAINEY, George. *Cherokee Strip.* (1933). Guthrie. 1st ed. inscr. 504p. photos/index. F/case. E1. $100.00

RAJAB, Jehan. *Palestinian Costume.* 1989. Kegan Paul. 1st ed. 160p. NF/dj. W1. $45.00

RAK, Mary Kidder. *Cowman's Wife.* 1934. Boston. 1st ed. ils/map ep. 269p. NF/worn. E1. $45.00

RAKOCY, Bill. *Images Paso Del Norte, 400 Years of Pictorial Borderland...* 1980. El Paso. 1st ed. sgn/dtd. 301p. F. E1. $100.00

RAKOSI, Carl. *Ere-Voice.* 1971. New Directions. 1st ed. sgn. NF. V1. $35.00

RALEIGH, Walter. *Cabinet-Council.* 1658. Johnson. 12mo. 200p. rebound calf. K1. $300.00

RALLING, C. *Voyage of Charles Darwin: His Autobiographical Writings...* 1979. Mayflower Books. 1st Am ed. 183p. F/dj. D8. $12.00

RALPHSON, George H. *With the Canadians at Vimy Ridge.* 1919. Donohue. Over There series. G+. P12. $6.00

RAMAGE, Edwin S. *Atlantis: Fact or Fiction?* 1978. IN U. 1st ed. NF/NF. M23. $20.00

RAMANUJAN, A.K. *Striders.* 1966. London. 1st ed. assn copy. F/NF. V1. $20.00

RAMBO, Ralph. *Trailing the California Bandit, Tiburcio Vasquez 1835-75.* 1968. San Jose, CA. 1st ed. sgn. ils/maps. 40p. F/stiff wrp. E1. $45.00

RAME, David. *Road to Tunis.* 1944. Macmillan. 1st ed. 296p. VG. W1. $18.00

RAME, David. *Road to Tunis.* 1944. NY. 1st ed. 296p. VG/VG. B5. $25.00

RAMPLING, Anne; see Rice, Anne.

RAMSAY, Diana. *Deadly Discretion.* 1973. Collins. 1st ed. F/F. P3. $25.00

RAMSAY, Jay; see Campbell, Ramsey.

RAMSAYE, Terry. *Million & One Nights: A History of the Motion Picture.* 1926. Simon Schuster. 2 vol. 1st ed. 8vo. teg. gilt bl cloth. NF. T10. $500.00

RAMSBOTTOM, J. *Book of Roses.* 1941. Middlesex, Eng. ils. 30p. brd. B26. $15.00

RAMSEY, Dan. *How To Forecast the Weather.* 1983. Tab pb. 213p. K5. $10.00

RAMSEY, Guy. *Aces All.* 1955. London. 205p. VG. S1. $15.00

RAMSEY, Jack C. *Thunder Beyond the Razos, Mirabeau B Lamrar: A Biography.* 1985. Austin. 1st ed. 244p. F/F. E1. $25.00

RAMSEY, R.H. *Men & Mines of Newmont: A Fifty-Year History.* 1973. Octagon. 1st ed. 344p. VG/dj. D8. $20.00

RAMSLAND, Katherine. *Prism of the Night: A Biography of Anne Rice.* 1991. NY. 1st ed. 85p. F/F. A17. $20.00

RAMSLAND, Katherine. *Vampire Companion.* 1993. Ballantine. 1st ed. F/F. P3. $30.00

RAND, Ayn. *Atlas Shrugged.* 1957. NY. 1st ed. VG/torn. A15. $150.00

RAND, Ayn. *For the New Intellectual.* 1961. NY. 1st ed. VG/VG. B5. $45.00

RAND, Ayn. *Fountainhead.* nd. Bobbs Merrill. VG. P3. $15.00

RAND, Ayn. *Goal of My Writing.* 1963. Nathaniel Branden Inst. 10p. VG/wrp. B4. $100.00

RAND, Clayton. *Sons of the South.* 1961. HRW. 1st ed. inscr. 212p. NF. T10. $35.00

RAND, Edward. *Popular Flowers & How To Cultivate Them.* 1874 (1870). Boston. Shepard. 208p. VG. A10. $40.00

RAND, George Hart. *Sherman Hale, the Harvard Half-Back.* 1910. Fenno. 326p. VG+/dj. M20. $40.00

RAND MCNALLY. *Commercial Atlas & Marketing Guide. 81st Edition.* 1950. Chicago. xl. G. O7. $45.00

RANDALL, Bob. *Fan.* 1977. Random. 1st ed. VG/VG. P3. $18.00

RANDALL, Homer. *Army Boys in the French Trenches.* 1919. World. VG/G+. P12. $6.00

RANDALL, Homer. *Army Boys on the Firing Line.* 1919. Saalfield. G+/G+. P12. $8.00

RANDALL, J.G. *Lincoln & the South.* 1946. Baton Rouge. 1st ed. 161p. VG/dj. B18. $15.00

RANDALL, Marta. *Sword of Winter.* 1983. Timescape. 1st ed. VG/VG. P3. $20.00

RANDALL, Robert. *Dawning Light.* 1959. Gnome. 1st ed. xl. dj. P3. $15.00

RANDAU, Carl. *Visitor.* 1945. Tower. 1st ed. hc. NF/NF. P3. $20.00

RANDIER, Jean. *Nautical Antiques for the Collector.* 1976. London. Barrie Jenkins. VG/VG. A16. $65.00

RANDISI, Robert J. *Alone With the Dead.* 1995. St Martin. 1st ed. F/F. P3. $22.00

RANDISI, Robert J. *Dead of Brooklyn.* 1991. St Martin. 1st ed. NF/NF. P3. $19.00

RANDISI, Robert J. *Eyes Have It.* 1984. Mysterious. 1st ed. F/F. P3. $25.00

RANDISI, Robert J. *No Exit From Brooklyn.* 1987. St Martin. 1st ed. F/NF. T2. $20.00

RANDISI, Robert J. *Separate Cases.* 1990. Walker. 1st ed. NF/F. N4. $20.00

RANDISI & WALLACE. *Deadly Allies.* 1992. Doubleday Perfect Crime. 1st ed. F/F. P3. $20.00

RANDOLPH, Buckner Magill. *Ten Years Old & Under...1873-1880.* 1935. Ruth Hill. 127p. VG. B10. $45.00

RANDOLPH, J. Ralph. *British Travelers Among the Southern Indians 1660-1763.* 1973. np. 1st ed. 183p. F/dj. E1. $35.00

RANDOLPH, Marion. *Breathe No More.* 1944. Tower. VG/G+. P3. $13.00

RANDOLPH, Mary. *Virginia Housewife; or, Methodical Cook.* 1984. Birmingham. facsimile of 1828 ed. silk moire ep. aeg. A17. $20.00

RANDOLPH, Vance. *Down in the Holler.* 1953. Norman. 1st ed. VG/worn. B5. $32.50

RANKE, Herman. *Art of Ancient Egypt.* 1936. Allen Unwin. 1st ed. tall 8vo. 232 pl. VG/dj. W1. $22.00

RANKIN, E.B. *Modern Base Ball Science.* 1915. Nat Base Ball Reg Bureau. G+. P8. $350.00

RANKIN & SCHEER. *Rebels & Redcoats: Living Story of the American Revolution.* 1957. World. 1st ed. inscr Rankin. 8vo. 572p. F/F. B11. $50.00

RANKINE, John. *Fingalnam Conspiracy.* 1973. Sidgwick Jackson. 1st ed. hc. F/F. P3. $35.00

RANKINE, John. *Never the Same Door.* 1967. Dobson. 1st ed. F/F. P3. $20.00

RANNEY, Edward. *Stonework of the Maya.* 1974. Albuquerque. 1st ed. 119p. wrp. F3. $20.00

RANQUEREL DES PLANCHES, L.J.C. *Lead Diseases: From the French With Notes & Additions...* 1850. Boston. 411p. contemporary sheep. G. B14. $150.00

RANSOM, Bill. *Burn.* 1995. Ace. 1st ed. AN/dj. M22. $20.00

RANSOM, Bill. *Last Call.* 1983. Bl Begonia. 1/300. sgn. F/wrp. V1. $15.00

RANSOM, Bill. *Virvax.* 1993. Ace. 1st ed. NF/VG+. G10. $5.00

RANSOM, J.E. *Fossils in America.* 1964. Harper Row. 1st ed. 402p. F/dj. D8. $18.00

RANSOM, John Crowe. *Armageddon*. 1923. Charleston. Poetry Soc of SC. 1st ed. VG/stapled wrp. C2. $450.00

RANSOM, John Crowe. *Grace After Mead*. 1924. Hogarth. 1st ed. 1/400. F. B24. $650.00

RANSOM, John Crowe. *Poems About God*. 1919. Holt. 1st ed. poet's 1st book. assn copy. F/glassine. V1. $550.00

RANSOM, John Crowe. *Poems About God*. 1919. NY. 1st ed. author's 1st book. VG+. C2. $175.00

RANSOM, M.A. *Sea of the Bear: Journal of a Voyage to Alaska & the Arctic*. 1921. US Naval Inst. 1st ed. 119p. bl cloth. NF/dj. B22. $8.50

RANSOME, Stephen. *Alias His Wife*. 1965. Dodd Mead. 1st ed. VG/G+. P3. $15.00

RANSOME, Stephen. *False Bounty*. 1948. Crime Club. 1st ed. G. P3. $15.00

RANSOME, Stephen. *Frazer Aquittal*. 1955. Crime Club. 1st ed. VG/VG. P3. $20.00

RANSOME, Stephen. *Lilies in Her Garden Grew*. 1973. Lythway. hc. F/F. P3. $15.00

RANSOME, Stephen. *Shroud Off Her Back*. 1953. Doubleday. 1st ed. lacks ffe. VG. P3. $10.00

RANSOME, Stephen. *Warning Bell*. 1960. Crime Club. 1st ed. VG/G+. P3. $20.00

RANSTEAD, Herbert E. *True Story & History of 53rd Regiment...* 1910. np. 1st ed. 104p. VG/wrp. M8. $650.00

RAO, N.S.S. *Biological Nitrogen Fixation*. 1988. Montreaux. Gordon Breach. 337p. brd. F/F. B1. $50.00

RAPER, J.R. *Without Shelter: Early Career of Ellen Glasgow*. 1971. LSU. 273p. VG/VG. B10. $15.00

RAPHAEL, Morris. *Battle in the Bayou Country*. 1976. Detroit. 2nd. sgn. 199p. VG/dj. B18. $15.00

RAPHAEL, Rick. *Thirst Quenchers*. 1966. British SF BC. hc. xl. dj. P3. $5.00

RAPP, George. *Thoughts on the Destiny of Man...* 1824. New Harmony, IN. sm 8vo. 96p. plain bl wrp. C6. $2,000.00

RAPPORT, Leonard. *Fakes & Facsimiles: Problems of Identification*. Jan 1979. Am Archivist. ils. 58p. G/wrp. T3. $20.00

RAPPORT, S. *History of Egypt*. 1904. London. Grollier. 1st ed. 1/200. 1200 ils/pl. 3-quarter morocco. VG. W1. $350.00

RAPPORT & RAPPORT. *America Remembers: Our Best-Loved Customs & Traditions*. 1956. NY. 1st ed. 669p. VG. E1. $25.00

RASA, A. *Mongoose Watch*. 1985. London. John Murray. 8vo. 298p. NF/F. B1. $25.00

RASCOE, Burton. *Belle Starr, the Bandit Queen*. 1941. NY. 1st ed. ils/photos/index. 340p. F. E1. $60.00

RASCOE, Jesse. *Pegleg's Lost Gold*. 1973. Ft Davis, TX. 1st ed. 102p. F/wrp. E1. $25.00

RASHER, Mrs. *Mrs Rasher's Curtain Lectures*. 1884. JS Ogilvie. 1st ed. G+. P12. $18.00

RASMUSSEN, Halfdan. *Halfdan's ABC*. 1982 (1967). Copenhagen. Carlsen Litho. Danish text. unp. NF. C14. $20.00

RASOR, Dina. *Pentagon Underground*. 1985. NY. 1st ed. 310p. E1. $15.00

RASWAN, Carl. *Drinkers of the Wind*. 1961. NY. Ariel. 2nd. VG/G. O3. $35.00

RATCHFORD, Fannie E. *Story of Champ d'Asile, As Told by Two of the Colonists*. 1969. Austin, TX. facsimile. 180p. F/case. E1. $40.00

RATCLIFF, J. *Yellow Magic, the Story of Penicillin*. 1945. NY. 173p. VG. A13. $30.00

RATCLIFFE, J.A. *Physics of the Upper Atmosphere*. 1960. Academic. 8vo. photos/diagrams. 586p. VG/dj. K5. $45.00

RATH, Ida Ellen. *Rath Trail*. 1961. Wichita. 1st ed. 204p. E1. $30.00

RATHBONE, Julian. *Carnival!* 1976. Michael Joseph. 1st ed. VG/VG. P3. $20.00

RATHBONE, Julian. *Diamonds Bid*. 1967. Walker. 1st ed. F/F. P3. $15.00

RATHBONE, Julian. *Euro-Killers*. 1979. Pantheon. 1st ed. VG/VG. P3. $15.00

RATHBONE, Julian. *Ravishing Monarchist*. 1978. St Martin. 1st ed. NF/NF. P3. $20.00

RATHBONE, Julian. *Watching the Detectives*. 1983. Pantheon. 1st ed. VG/VG. P3. $14.00

RATHBONE, Julian. *With My Knives I Know I'm Good*. 1970. Putnam. 1st ed. VG/VG. P3. $25.00

RATHBONE, Julian. *Zdt*. 1986. Heinemann. 1st ed. NF/NF. P3. $22.00

RATHBONE, Perry T. *Mississippi Panorama...* 1950. City Art Mus of St Louis. new/revised. 228p. VG/G. B10. $15.00

RATHJEN, Carl Henry. *Flight of Fear*. 1969. Whitman. TVTI. VG. P3. $8.00

RATHJEN, Frederick W. *Texas Panhandle Frontier*. 1973. Austin, TX. 2nd. 286p. F/dj. E1. $30.00

RATIGAN, William. *Great Lakes Shipwrecks & Survivals*. 1960. Grand Rapids. Eerdmans. 1st ed. VG/VG. A16. $20.00

RATIGAN, William. *Great Lakes Shipwrecks & Survivals*. 1969. Grand Rapids. Eerdmans. new revised ed. VG/VG. A16. $20.00

RATIGAN, William. *Straits of Mackinac!* 1957. Grand Rapids. Eerdmans. G/G. A16. $15.00

RATTAN, Volney. *Popular California Flora...* 1988. San Francisco. 8th revised. ils. VG. B26. $18.00

RAUCHER, Herman. *Maynard's House*. 1980. Putnam. 2nd. F/F. P3. $15.00

RAUCHER, Herman. *Summer of '42*. 1971. Putnam. 1st ed. F/F. B4. $150.00

RAVEN, Neil. *Evidence*. 1987. Scribner. 1st ed. F/F. H11. $20.00

RAVEN, Simon. *Before the Cock Crow*. 1986. Muller Blond Wht. 1st ed. VG/VG. P3. $25.00

RAVEN, Simon. *Rich Pay*. 1965. Putnam. 1st ed. VG/VG. P3. $20.00

RAVEN & RAVEN. *Genus Epilobium (Onagraceae) in Australia...* 1976. Christchurch. sgns. ils/sgn Keith R West. photos/map. 322p. B26. $55.00

RAVEN. *British Fiction 1750-1770, a Chronological Check-List...* 1987. DE U. 1363 entries. 359p. F/VG. A4. $50.00

RAWLINGS, Charles. *In Our Neck O' the Woods*. 1972. Sheridan, WY. F/VG. N3. $20.00

RAWLINGS, Marjorie Kinnan. *Cross Creek Cookery*. 1942. NY. 1st ed. VG/VG. P3. $50.00

RAWLINGS, Marjorie Kinnan. *Cross Creek*. 1942. Scribner. 1st ed. VG/G. H7. $40.00

RAWLINGS, Marjorie Kinnan. *Cross Creek*. 1942. Scribner. 1st ed. VG/VG. M19. $50.00

RAWLINGS, Marjorie Kinnan. *Cross Creek*. 1942. Scribner. 1st ed. 368p. VG/fair. B10. $35.00

RAWLINGS, Marjorie Kinnan. *Secret River*. 1956. Scribner. 2nd. 8vo. ils. NF. C14. $12.00

RAWLINGS, Marjorie Kinnan. *Secret River*. 1967 (1955). Scribner. 8vo. unp. NF/G+. T5. $32.00

RAWLINGS, Marjorie Kinnan. *Sojourner*. 1953. Scribner. 1st ed. VG/VG. P3. $40.00

RAWLINGS, Marjorie Kinnan. *When the Whippoorwill*. 1940. Scribner. 1st ed. NF/VG. B4. $350.00

RAWLINGS, Marjorie Kinnan. *Yearling*. 1938. Scribner. 1st ed. NF/VG+. B4. $300.00

RAWLINGS, Marjorie Kinnan. *Yearling.* 1947. Scribner. ils NC Wyeth. VG/torn dj. P3. $15.00

RAWLINGS, Rover. *Last Airmen.* 1989. NY. 1st ed. 241p. VG+/dj. B18. $15.00

RAWN, Melanie. *Golden Key.* 1966. DAW. 1st ed. F/F. P3. $25.00

RAWN, Melanie. *Stronghold.* 1990. DAW. 1st ed. F/F. P3. $22.00

RAWSON, Clayton. *Footprints on the Ceiling.* 1979. Gregg. VG/VG. P3. $25.00

RAWSON, Clayton. *Headless Lady.* 1940. Putnam. 1st ed. VG. P3. $45.00

RAWSON, Clayton. *No Coffin for the Corpse.* 1979. Gregg. 1st ed. VG/VG. P3. $25.00

RAY, Clarence E. *Rube Burrow, King of Outlaws & Train Robbers.* nd. Chicago. 181p. NF/wrp. E1. $45.00

RAY, David. *Kangaroo Paws.* 1995. Thomas Jefferson U. 1st ed. F/sans. V1. $20.00

RAY, Gordon N. *Buried Life: Study of Relation Between Thackeray...* 1962. Harvard. 148p. dj. A17. $7.50

RAY, Isaac. *Treatise on the Medical Jurisprudence of Insanity.* 1962. Cambridge. 376p. VG. A13. $50.00

RAY, Man. *Man Ray: Self Portrait.* 1963. Boston. 1st ed. ils/photos. 398p. F/dj. A17. $75.00

RAY, Robert. *Cage of Mirrors.* 1980. Lippincott Crowell. 1st ed. VG+/VG. A20. $18.00

RAY, Robert. *Hit Man.* 1988. St Martin. 1st ed. F/F. P3. $19.00

RAY, Robert. *Merry Christmas, Murdock.* 1989. Delacorte. 1st ed. F/VG+. A20. $8.00

RAY, Tom. *Yellowstone Red.* 1948. Dorrance. 1st ed. sgn. VG/VG. P3. $30.00

RAY, Worth S. *Down in the Cross Timbers.* 1947. Austin, TX. 1st ed. 1/500. inscr. ils. 160p. F. E1. $80.00

RAYER, F.G. *Tomorrow Sometimes Comes.* 1951. Home & Van Thal. 1st ed. VG. P3. $15.00

RAYMO, Chet. *In the Falcon's Claw.* 1990. Viking. 1st ed. rem mk. F/F. M23. $15.00

RAYMOND, Alex. *Flash Gordon & the Planet Mongo.* 1974. Nostalgia. 1st ed. VG/VG. P3. $35.00

RAYMOND, Alex. *Flash Gordon.* 1967. Nostalgia. hc. ils. F. M13. $17.00

RAYMOND, Dora Neill. *Captain Lee Hall of Texas.* 1940. Norman, OK. 2nd. ils Louis Lundean/Frederick Remington. 350p. F/F. E1. $35.00

RAYMOND, Jehan. *Le Cur, Compositions Decoratives.* ca 1900. Chicago. G Broes Van Dort. folio. 48 pl. VG. T10. $250.00

RAYMOND, M. *God Goes to Murderer's Row.* 1951. Bruce. 1st ed. VG/VG. P3. $10.00

RAYMOND, Nancy. *Smoky.* 1945. Fideler. 4to. VG/VG. B17. $22.50

RAYMONT, J.E.G. *Plankton & Productivity in the Oceans.* 1967. Pergamon. 2nd. 8vo. 2 fld ils/tables/graphs. dj. B1. $30.00

RAYTER, Joe. *Stab in the Dark.* 1955. Morrow. 1st ed. G+/dj. P3. $15.00

READ, Conyers. *Lord Burghley & Queen Elizabeth.* 1960. Knopf. 1st ed. 603p. VG/dj. M20. $20.00

READ, Herbert. *Herbert Read: An Intro to His Various Works...* nd. Faber. F/NF. V1. $20.00

READ, Opie. *Arkansas Planter.* 1896. Chicago. 1st ed. VG. B5. $75.00

READ, Piers Paul. *Season in the West.* 1988. Random. 1st ed. F/F. H11. $20.00

READE, Hamish. *Comeback for Stark.* 1968. Putnam. 1st ed. NF/NF. P3. $10.00

READING, Robert S. *Indian Civilizations.* 1961. San Antonio, TX. 2nd. 200p. F/F. E1. $20.00

REAGAN, Ronald. *Where's the Rest of Me.* 1965. NY. 1st ed. VG/VG. B5. $35.00

REAGAN, Thomas B. *Caper.* 1969. Putnam. 1st ed. VG/VG. P3. $20.00

REAVER, Chap. *Mote.* 1990. Delacorte. 1st ed. sgn. F/VG. B11. $20.00

REBELL, Fred. *Escape to the Sea.* 1939. London. Murray. ils. 254p. VG. T7. $30.00

REBEN, Martha. *Healing Woods.* 1952. NY. 1st ed. sgn. VG/VG. B5. $25.00

RECHY, John. *This Day's Death.* 1969. Grove. 1st ed. F/F. B2. $35.00

RECORD, S.J. *Ecomomic Woods of the United States.* 1912. Wiley. 8vo. ils. 117p. cloth. NF. B1. $25.00

RED FOX. *Memoirs of Chief Red Fox.* 1971. McGraw Hill. 2nd. 8vo. 209p. F/dj. T10. $25.00

REDFERN, R. *Corridors of Time: 1,700,000,000 of Years of Earth...* 1983. Reader's Digest. 195+p. cloth. F/dj. D8. $20.00

REDFIELD, J.S. *Mineral Resources in Oklahoma.* 1927. OK Geological Survey. 130p. VG/wrp. D8. $15.00

REDFIELD, James. *Celestine Prophecy.* 1994. NY. Warner. 1st ed. F/F. H11. $30.00

REDMOND, Juanita. *I Served on Bataan.* 1943. Phil. 3rd imp. 167p. G. A17. $7.50

REDMOND, Paul J. *Flora of Worchester County, MD.* 1932. WA, DC. 104p. NF/wrp. B26. $20.00

REDONDI, Pietro. *Galileo: Heretic.* 1987. Princeton. trans Raymond Rosenthal. 356p. VG/dj. K5. $30.00

REED, David. *Anna.* nd. BC. VG. P3. $10.00

REED, Earl. *Dune Country.* 1916. John Lane. 1st ed. inscr. VG. A20. $95.00

REED, Earl. *Silver Arrow.* 1926. Reilly Lee. 1st ed. inscr. VG. A20. $75.00

REED, Ennis. *Poems.* 1964. CA U. 1st ed. assn copy. F/NF. V1. $20.00

REED, Ishmael. *Shrovetide in Old New Orleans.* 1978. Doubleday. 1st ed. sgn. F/F. B30. $45.00

REED, John F. *Campaign to Valley Forge: July 1, 1777-December 19, 1777.* 1965. Phil. inscr. 8vo. 11 maps. 448p. F/F. T10. $45.00

REED, John. *Ten Days That Shook the World.* 1919. Boni Liveright. G+. B5. $50.00

REED, Kit. *Catholic Girls.* 1987. Donald Fine. 1st ed. F/F. P3. $15.00

REED, Kit. *Fort Privilege.* 1985. Doubleday. 1st ed. NF/NF. P3. $18.00

REED, Kit. *Tiger Rag.* 1973. Dutton. 1st ed. VG/VG. P3. $20.00

REED, Robert. *Exaltation of Larks.* 1995. Tor. 1st ed. F/F. P3. $22.00

REED, Robert. *Hormone Jungle.* 1987. Donald Fine. 1st ed. F/F. P3. $20.00

REED, Robert. *Leeshore.* 1987. Donald Fine. 1st ed. NF/NF. P3. $17.00

REED, Sarah N. *Romance of Arlington House.* 1908. Chapple. 110p. VG-. B10. $12.00

REED, W. Maxwell. *Patterns in the Sky.* 1951. Morrow. 8vo. 125p. xl. dj. K5. $10.00

REED & SONDERGAARD. *Fun for Fidelia.* 1950. Heath. ils. VG. M5. $12.00

REEDER, Red. *Three Great Pitchers on the Mound.* 1966. Garrard. 1st ed. photos. VG+/G+. P8. $8.00

REEDSTROM, Ernest L. *Scrapbook of the American West.* 1991. Caldwell. ARC/1st ed. 259p. stiff wrp. E1. $30.00

REES, John. *Shaping of Psychiatry by War.* 1945. NY. 1st ed. 158p. VG. A13. $40.00

REES-MOGG. *How To Buy Rare Books: A Practical Guide...* 1985. np. 4to. ils/pl. 160p. F/F. A4. $85.00

REESE, A.M. *Alligator & Its Allies.* 1915. NY. 1st ed. sgn. 358p. VG. B5. $130.00

REESE, John. *Singalee.* 1969. Doubleday. 1st ed. VG/VG. P3. $15.00

REESE, John. *Sunblind Range.* 1968. Doubleday. 1st ed. VG/VG. P3. $15.00

REESE, John. *Sure Shot Shapiro.* 1968. Doubleday. 1st ed. VG/VG. P3. $15.00

REESE, Kitty. *Mystery Trivia Quiz Book.* 1985. Bell. hc. VG. P3. $12.00

REESE, Terence. *Modern Bidding & the ACOL System.* 1960 (1956). London. rpt. 128p. VG. S1. $7.00

REESE, Terence. *Precision Bidding & Precision Play.* 1973. NY. 153p. VG. S1. $4.00

REEVE, Arthur B. *Craig Kennedy Listens in.* 1923. Harper. 1st ed. VG/fair. P3. $45.00

REEVE, J. Stanley. *Foxhunter's Journal.* 1952. Dorrance. 1/550. VG/case. O3. $125.00

REEVE, J. Stanley. *Foxhunting Recollections.* 1928. Lippincott. 1st trade ed. VG. O3. $45.00

REEVE & REEVE. *New Mexico: Land of Many Cultures.* 1969. Boulder, CO. 1st ed. photos/maps. 231p. F/NF. E1. $30.00

REEVES, Hubert. *Stellar Evolution & Nucleosynthesis.* 1968. NY. Gordon Breach. 8vo. 99p. VG. K5. $25.00

REEVES, James J. *History of the Twenty-Fourth Regiment of NJ Volunteers.* 1889. Camden, NJ. Chew. 1st ed. 45p. NF/wrp. M8. $150.00

REEVES, John. *Murder Before Matins.* 1984. Doubleday. 1st ed. F/F. P3. $13.00

REEVES, John. *Murder by Microphone.* 1978. Doubleday. 1st ed. VG/VG. P3. $15.00

REEVES, John. *Murder With Muskets.* 1985. Canada. Doubleday. 1st ed. VG/VG. P3. $18.00

REEVES, P. *Bactericocins.* 1972. NY/Berlin. Springer/Berlag. ils. 142p. orange cloth. F. B14. $75.00

REEVES, Robert. *Doubting Thomas.* 1985. Arbor. 1st ed. author's 1st novel. F/F. H11. $40.00

REEVES, Robert. *Peeping Thomas.* 1990. Crown. 1st ed. sgn. F/F. B4. $35.00

REEVES & THORNTON. *Medical Book Illustration: A Short History.* 1983. NY. 1st ed. 142p. dj. A13. $75.00

REEVES-STEVENS, Garfield. *Nighteyes.* 1989. Doubleday. 1st ed. F/F. G10. $10.00

REGAN, David. *Mourning Glory.* 1981. Devin-Adair. 1st ed. F/F. B4. $100.00

REGAN, Tom. *All That Dwell Therein.* 1982. CA U. 1st ed. VG/VG. P3. $10.00

REGINALD, R. *Cumulative Paperback Index 1939-1959.* 1973. Gale Research. G. P3. $200.00

REICH, John. *Italy Before Rome: The Making of the Past.* 1979. Oxford. Elsevier/Phaidon. 4to. 151p. AN/dj. P4. $25.00

REICH, Oswald. *Dog, Goat & Horse Training.* 1963. NY. Exposition. 67p. VG/VG. O3. $45.00

REICH, Wilhelm. *Psychischer Kontakt und Vegetative Stromung.* 1935. Copenhagen. Sex-Pol-Verlag. inscr. NF/stapled wrp. B4. $1,500.00

REICHARD, Gladys. *Navajo Shepherd & Weaver.* 1936. NY. 1st ed. photos. VG. M17. $75.00

REICHLER, Joseph. *Baseball's Great Moments.* 1985. Bonanza. hc. VG/VG. P3. $10.00

REICHLER, Joseph. *Inside the Majors.* 1952. Hart. ils/photos. 192p. VG. A17. $20.00

REID, Alastair. *Ounce Dice Trice.* 1958. Little Brn. stated 1st ed. 4to. 57p. VG/fair. C14. $14.00

REID, Alastair. *Supposing.* 1960. Little Brn. 1st ed. 8vo. ils Birnbaum. 48p. VG+/G+. C14. $9.00

REID, J.H. Stewart. *Mountains, Men & Rivers.* 1954. Ryerson. 1st ed. VG/VG. P3. $25.00

REID, Jesse Walton. *History of the 4th Regiment of SC Volunteers...* 1892. Greenville, SC. Shannon. 1st ed. 143p. NF/prt wrp. M8. $1,750.00

REID, Mayne. *War-Trail.* 1857. Robert DeWitt. ils. G+. P12. $35.00

REID, Robert Leonard. *Mountains of the Great Blue Dream.* 1991. San Francisco. North Point. 1st ed. 8vo. 184p. maroon cloth. F/dj. T10. $25.00

REIK, Theodore. *Unknown Murderer.* 1945. NY. 1st ed. trans from German. 260p. NF. B14. $45.00

REILLY, Helen. *Compartment K.* 1955. Detective BC. hc. VG. P3. $8.00

REILLY, Helen. *Death Demands an Audience.* 1941. Dial. VG. P3. $20.00

REILLY, Helen. *Follow Me.* 1960. Random. 1st ed. NF/NF. P3. $25.00

REILLY, Helen. *Not Me, Inspector.* 1959. Random. 1st ed. VG/VG. P3. $30.00

REIMAN, Terry. *Vamp Till Ready.* 1954. Harper. 1st ed. NF/NF. P3. $15.00

REIMER, E.F. *Matching Mountains With the Boy Scout Uniform.* 1929. NY. 1st ed. ils. 197p. VG/worn. B5. $95.00

REINA, Ruben. *Gift of Birds.* 1991. Phil. 1st ed. photos. wrp. F3. $40.00

REINACH, Theodore. *Jewish Coins.* 1966. Chicago. Argonaut. 1st Am ed. 8vo. 11 pl. 77p. NF/dj. W1. $20.00

REINER, Carl. *Enter Laughing.* 1958. NY. 1st ed. author's 1st book. VG/G. B5. $30.00

REINHARDT, Richard. *Out West on the Overland Train.* 1967. Palo Alto. 209p. VG. B18. $17.50

REINHARDT, Richard. *Workin' on the Railroad.* 1970. Am W Pub. 1st ed. 318p. F/F. E1. $45.00

REISER, Stanley. *Medicine & the Reign of Technology.* 1978. Cambridge. 1st ed. 317p. dj. A13. $50.00

REITSCH, Hanna. *Flying Is My Life.* 1954. NY. 1st Am ed. 246p. VG/dj. B18. $150.00

REJAUNIER, Jeanna. *Motion & the Act.* 1972. Nash. 1st ed. F/F. B35. $20.00

RELANDER, Click. *Drummers & Dreamers: Story of Smowhala the Prophet...* 1956. Caldwell, ID. sgn. photos/biblio/index. 345p. F/NF. E1. $250.00

RELLING, William. *Deadly Vintage.* 1995. Walker. 1st ed. F/F. M23. $40.00

REMARQUE, Erich Maria. *All Quiet on the Western Front.* 1969. LEC. 1st ed. 1/1500. ils/sgn John Groth. F/case. C2. $75.00

REMENHAM, John. *Going Wrong.* 1990. Mysterious. 1st ed. NF/NF. P3. $19.00

REMENHAM, John. *Peacemaker.* 1947. MacDonald. 1st ed. VG/tape rpr. P3. $23.00

REMEZOV, Semyon. *Atlas of Siberia...* 1958. Gravenhage. Mouton. 4to. 171+ pl. F. O7. $185.00

REMINGTON, Frederic. *Pony Tracks.* 1982. Am Legacy Pr. rpt. 8vo. F/dj. T10. $25.00

RENAUL, Lynn. *Racing Around Kentucky.* 1995. Louisville. 214p. AN. O3. $15.00

RENAULT, Mary. *Kings Must Die.* 1958. Pantheon. 1st ed. F/NF. B2. $45.00

RENDA, Gunsel. *History of Turkish Painting.* 1988. Seattle/London. Palasar. 444p. NF/dj. W1. $145.00

RENDEL, Robert. *That Extra Trick.* 1932. Boston. 126p. VG. S1. $12.00

RENDELL, Ruth. *Asta's Book.* 1993. Bristol. Scorpion. 1/99 (119 total). sgn. quarter leather. F. B4. $150.00

RENDELL, Ruth. *Bridesmaid.* 1989. Doubleday. 1st ed. VG/VG. P3. $23.00

RENDELL, Ruth. *Crocodile Bird.* 1993. Crown. 1st Am ed. sgn. F/NF. N4. $40.00

RENDELL, Ruth. *Fever Tree & Other Stories of Suspense.* 1982. NY. 1st Am ed. VG/G. V4. $15.00

RENDELL, Ruth. *Going Wrong.* 1990. NY. 1st ed. inscr. F/F. V4. $50.00

RENDELL, Ruth. *New Girl Friend.* 1985. Hutchinson. F/F. P3. $20.00

RENDELL, Ruth. *Talking to Strange Men.* 1987. Pantheon. 1st ed. F/F. P3. $17.00

RENDELL, Ruth. *Unkindness of Ravens.* 1985. Pantheon. 1st Am ed. NF/VG clip. M22. $8.00

RENDELL, Ruth. *Veiled One.* 1988. Hutchinson. 1st ed. F/F. P3. $18.00

RENEHAN, E.J. *John Burroughs: American Naturalist.* 1992. Post Mills. Chelsea Gr. 1st ed. photos. 356p. half cloth. F/F. B1. $35.00

RENICK & RENICK. *Tommy Carries the Ball.* 1940. Scribner. later rpt. ils F Machetanz. VG/VG. B17. $4.00

RENNERT, Vincent Paul. *Western Outlaws. Vivid Accounts of the Deeds & Misdeeds...* 1968. np. 152p. F/dj. E1. $35.00

RENOIR, Jean. *Notebooks of Captain Georges.* 1966. Boston. 1st ed. VG/dj. A17. $9.50

RESHAW, Patrick. *Wobblies: Story of Syndicalism in the US.* 1967. NY. ils. 312p. G+/dj. B18. $17.50

RESNICK, Mike. *Dinosaur Fantastic.* nd. BC. F/F. P3. $8.00

RESNICK, Mike. *Eros at Zenith.* 1984. Phantasia. 1st ed. hc. F/F. P3. $25.00

RESNICK, Mike. *Ivory.* 1988. Tor. 1st ed. F/F. P3. $18.00

RESNICK, Mike. *Shaggy BEM.* 1988. Nolacon. 1st ed. hc. F/F. P3. $20.00

RESNICK, Mike. *Will the Last Person to Leave...* 1992. Tor. 1st ed. F/F. P3. $20.00

RESNICOW, Herbert. *Gold Gamble.* 1988. St Martin. 1st ed. VG/VG. P3. $18.00

RESNICOW & TARKENTON. *Murder at the Super Bowl.* 1986. Morrow. 1st ed. VG/VG. P3. $15.00

RESTON, James Jr. *Collision at Home Plate.* 1991. Burlingame. 1st ed. VG+/VG+. P8. $17.50

REVEILLE-PARISE, J.-H. *Hygiene de l'Esprit: Physiologie et Hygiene des Hommes.* (1880). Paris. J-B Bailliere. 12mo. 435p. early bl silk. G1. $50.00

REVERE, Lawrence. *Playing Blackjack As a Business.* 1971. Las Vegas. 171p. VG. S1. $5.00

REVESZ, Gesa. *Psychology of a Musical Prodigy.* 1925. London. Harcourt Brace/Kegan Paul. 180p. gr cloth. dj. G1. $65.00

REVI, Albert C. *American Art Nouveau Glass.* 1968. Nashville. Nelson. ils/drawings/pl. 476p. cloth. dj. D2. $60.00

REVKIN, Andrew. *Burning Season.* 1990. Houghton Mifflin. 1st ed. 317p. dj. F3. $15.00

REXROTH, Kenneth. *100 Poems From the Japanese.* 1955. New Directions. 1st ed. NF/VG. M19. $45.00

REY, H.A. *Stars: A New Way To See Them.* 1962. Houghton Mifflin. 4to. VG/G. B17. $8.50

REY, H.A. *Where's My Baby?* 1943. Houghton Mifflin. sm 4to. scarce. M5. $20.00

REYES, Carlos. *Prisoner.* 1973. Capra. 1st ed. Chapbook series. F/wrp. V1. $15.00

REYNOLDS, Chang. *Pioneer Circuses of the West.* 1966. Los Angeles. photos /biblio/index. 212p. F/F. E1. $30.00

REYNOLDS, Francis J. *Master Tales of Mystery Vol 1.* nd. Collier. hc. VG. P3. $15.00

REYNOLDS, Francis J. *New Encyclopedia Atlas & Gazetter of the World...* 1917. NY. Collier. folio. fld world map (poor). F. O7. $65.00

REYNOLDS, James. *Andrea Palladio.* 1948. NY. 1st ed. VG/VG. B5. $35.00

REYNOLDS, James. *Gallery of Ghosts.* 1965. Grosset Dunlap. VG/VG. P3. $15.00

REYNOLDS, John Lawrence. *Whisper Death.* 1991. Viking. 1st ed. hc. F/F. P3. $19.00

REYNOLDS, John S. *Reconstruction in South Carolina 1865-1877.* 1969. NY. Negro U. rpt of 1905 ed. 522p. NF. M8. $35.00

REYNOLDS, Mack. *Compounded Interest.* 1983. NESFA. 1st ed. 1/1000. NF/NF. G10. $10.00

REYNOLDS, Mack. *Star Trek: Mission to Horatius.* 1968. Whitman. TVTI. G. P3. $15.00

REYNOLDS, Maxine; see Reynolds, Mack.

REYNOLDS, Quentin. *Dress Rehearsal: Story of Dieppe.* 1943. NY. 3rd. 278p. dj. A17. $9.50

REYNOLDS, Sheri. *Bitterroot Landing.* 1994. Putnam. 1st ed. author's 1st book. F/F. M23. $25.00

REYNOLDS, V. *Apes: Gorilla, Chimpanzee, Orangutan & Gibbon...* 1967. NY. Dutton. stated 1st ed. 8vo. ils. 296p. VG/VG. B1. $30.00

REYNOLDS, William J. *Naked Eye.* 1990. Putnam. 1st ed. sgn. F/F. P3. $28.00

RHEIMS, Bettina. *Modern Lovers.* 1990. Paris. Audiovisuel. 1st ed. French text. 57 full-p pl. F/dj. S9. $125.00

RHEIMS, Maurice. *Strange Life of Objects.* 1961. Atheneum. 1st Am ed. 274p. cloth. M20. $27.00

RHINE, J.B. *New Frontiers of the Mind.* 1937. Farrar Rinehart. pl. 275p. gray cloth. VG/dj. G1. $65.00

RHINEHART, Luke. *Book of Est.* 1976. NY. HRW. 1st ed. inscr. NF/NF. B4. $150.00

RHINEHART, Luke. *Dice Man.* 1971. Morrow. 1st ed. VG/VG. P3. $30.00

RHINEHART, Mary Roberts. *Nomad's Land.* 1926. Doran. 8vo. 27 pl. 287p. VG. W1. $18.00

RHODE, Deborah. *Justice & Gender, Sex Discrimination & the Law.* 1989. Harvard. M11. $25.00

RHODES, Daniel. *Adversary.* 1988. St Martin. 1st ed. author's 2nd novel. F/F. T2. $15.00

RHODES, Daniel. *Next, After Lucifer.* 1987. St Martin. 1st ed. author's 1st novel. F/F. T2. $15.00

RHODES, Eugene Manlove. *Bransford in Arcadia; or, The Little Eohippus.* 1914. Holt. 1st ed. VG. A18. $100.00

RHODES, Eugene Manlove. *Bransford in Arcadia; or, The Little Eohippus.* 1975. OK U. 1st ed thus. intro WH Hutchinson. F/clip. A18. $10.00

RHODES, Eugene Manlove. *Copper Streak Trail.* 1970. Norman. new ed. 318p. F/F. E1. $30.00

RHODES, Eugene Manlove. *Proud Sheriff.* 1968. OK U. 1st ed. pref WH Hutchinson. intro HH Knibbs. F/F. A18. $20.00

RHODES, Eugene Manlove. *Rhodes Reader: Stories of Virgins, Villains & Varmits.* 1957. OK U. 1st ed. intro WH Hutchinson. F/clip. A18. $40.00

RHODES, Eugene Manlove. *Stepsons of Light.* 1969. Norman, OK. rpt. 322p. F/F. E1. $30.00

RHODES, Eugene Manlove. *Stepsons of Light.* 1969. OK U. 1st ed. intro WH Hutchinson. rem mk. F/clip. A18. $10.00

RHODES, Eugene Manlove. *West Is West.* 1917. NY. 1st ed. ils Harvey Dunn. F/NF. C2. $175.00

RHODES, Henry T.F. *Alphonse Bertillon, Father of Scientific Detection.* 1956. London. Harrap. M11. $35.00

RHODES, Jack. *Inter-City Bus Lines of the Southwest.* 1988. TX A&M. 8vo. 158p. F/dj. T10. $35.00

RHODES, May D. *Hired Man on Horseback.* 1938. Houghton Mifflin. 1st ed. 263p. cloth. VG/dj. M20. $20.00

RHODES, Richard. *Making Love: An Erotic Odyssey.* 1992. Simon Schuster. 1st ed. F/F. A20. $15.00

RIBOT, Theodule Armand. *Diseases of Personality.* 1887. NY. Fitzgerald. 1st Eng-language ed. 8vo. 52p. bl wrp. G1. $50.00

RIBOT, Theodule Armand. *Diseases of Personality.* 1910. Chicago. Open Court. 1st ed. 12mo. 163p. bl cloth. G1. $37.50

RIBOT, Theodule Armand. *Evolution of General Ideas.* 1899. Chicago. Open Court. 1st Eng-language ed. 231p. prt gr cloth. G1. $65.00

RIBOT, Theodule Armand. *L'Evolution des Idees Generales.* 1897. Paris. Germer Bailliere/Felix Alcan. 260p. later gray cloth. G1. $75.00

RIBOT, Theodule Armand. *La Logique des Sentiments.* 1905. Paris. Felix Alcan. 200p. early marbled brd. G1. $75.00

RIBOUD, Barbara Chase. *Echo of Lions.* 1989. Morrow. 1st ed. F/F. B4. $35.00

RIBOUD, Barbara Chase. *From Memphis & Peking.* 1974. Random. 1st ed. author's 1st book. rem mk. NF/NF clip. B4. $65.00

RICCI. *Films of John Wayne.* 1973. Citadel. 288p. F. M13. $35.00

RICE, Anne. *Beauty's Punishment.* 1984. Dutton. 1st ed. F/F. B4. $250.00

RICE, Anne. *Beauty's Release.* 1985. Dutton. 1st ed. F/F. B4. $200.00

RICE, Anne. *Belinda.* 1986. Arbor. 1st ed. NF/NF. P3. $35.00

RICE, Anne. *Belinda.* 1986. Arbor. 1st ed. sgn. F/F. B4. $100.00

RICE, Anne. *Claiming of Sleeping Beauty.* 1987. London. Macdonald. 1st ed. sgn. F/F. B4. $125.00

RICE, Anne. *Cry to Heaven.* 1982. Knopf. 1st ed. VG/VG. P3. $45.00

RICE, Anne. *Exit To Eden.* 1985. Arbor. 1st ed. VG/VG. P3. $65.00

RICE, Anne. *Feast of All Saints.* 1979. NY. 1st ed. author's 2nd book. F/F. M19. $125.00

RICE, Anne. *Feast of All Saints.* 1979. NY. 1st ed. VG/VG. B5. $40.00

RICE, Anne. *Feast of All Saints.* 1979. Simon Schuster. 1st ed. author's 2nd book. rem mk. NF/NF. H11. $80.00

RICE, Anne. *Interview With the Vampire.* 1976. Knopf. 1st ed. author's 1st book. F/F. B4. $750.00

RICE, Anne. *Lasher.* 1993. Knopf. 1st ed. F/F. H11. $45.00

RICE, Anne. *Lasher.* 1993. Knopf. 1st ed. sgn. F/F. B2/M19. $50.00

RICE, Anne. *Queen of the Damned.* 1988. Knopf. 1st ed. VG/VG. P3. $25.00

RICE, Anne. *Tale of the Body Thief.* 1992. Knopf. 1st ed. sgn. F/F. B4. $100.00

RICE, Anne. *Tale of the Body Thief.* 1992. Knopf. 1st ed. VG/VG. P3. $25.00

RICE, Anne. *Taltos.* 1994. Canada. Knopf. 1st ed. F/F. P3. $25.00

RICE, Anne. *Taltos.* 1994. Knopf. ltd ed. sgn. AN/box. B30. $225.00

RICE, Anne. *Vampire Lestat.* 1985. NY. 1st ed. F/F. B5. $95.00

RICE, Anne. *Vampire Lestat.* 1985. NY. 1st ed. inscr. VG/VG. M19. $250.00

RICE, Anne. *Vampire Lestat.* 1985. NY. 1st ed. NF/NF. S13. $75.00

RICE, Anne. *Witching Hour.* 1990. Knopf. 1st ed. F/F. H11. $45.00

RICE, Anne. *Witching Hour.* 1990. Knopf. 1st ed. sgn. F/F. B4. $100.00

RICE, Anne. *Witching Hour.* 1990. Knopf. 1st ed. VG/VG. P3. $25.00

RICE, Craig. *Having Wonderful Crime.* 1943. Simon Schuster. 1st ed. VG. P3. $20.00

RICE, Craig. *Knocked for a Loop.* 1957. Simon Schuster. G. P3. $15.00

RICE, Craig. *Sunday Pigeon Murders.* 1945. Tower. 2nd. VG/G+. P3. $20.00

RICE, Craig. *Thursday Turkey Murders.* 1943. Simon Schuster. 1st ed. hc. VG. P3. $20.00

RICE, David Talbot. *Constantinople: From Bysantium to Istanbul.* 1965. Stein Day. 1st Am ed. 214p. xl. VG. W1. $25.00

RICE, David Talbot. *Icons.* 1990. Secaucus, NJ. 1st ed. 143p. VG/dj. W1. $65.00

RICE, Elmer. *Flight to the West.* 1941. Coward McCann. 1st ed. F/VG+. B4. $100.00

RICE, John. *Health for 7,500,000 People: Annual Report of the Dept...* 1938. NY. 1st ed. 390p. VG. A13. $45.00

RICE, Philip E. *America's Favorite Fishing.* 1971. Outdoor Life/Harper Row. ils. VG. P12. $9.00

RICE, Philip E. *Game Bird Hunting.* 1982. Outdoor Life. sc. ils/photos. G+. P12. $4.00

RICE, Philip E. *Outdoor Life Gun Data Book.* 1975. Outdoor Life/Harper Row. VG/G+. P12. $8.00

RICE, Prudence. *Macanche Island, El Peten, Guatemala.* 1987. Gainesville, FL. 1st ed. 267p. dj. F3. $40.00

RICE, Robert. *Business of Crime.* 1956. FSC. 1st ed. VG. P3. $15.00

RICH, Adrienne. *On Lies, Secrets & Silence: Selected Prose 1966-1978.* 1979. Norton. 1st ed. F/NF. V1. $15.00

RICH, Adrienne. *What Is Found There: Notebooks on Poetry & Politics.* 1993. Norton. 1st ed. F/F. V1. $20.00

RICH, Ben E. *Mr Durant of Salt Lake City, That Mormon.* 1893. Salt Lake City. George Cannon. 1st ed. 12mo. 320p. gilt bl cloth. VG. T10. $125.00

RICH, Edwin Gile. *Why-So Stories.* nd. Maynard Sm. 2nd. 207p. gilt red cloth. VG. B22. $4.00

RICH, Virginia. *Nantucket Diet Murders.* 1985. Delacorte. 1st ed. F/F. T2. $25.00

RICHARD, Adrienne. *Accomplice.* 1973. Little Brn. 1st ed. 8vo. 174p. F/VG. C14. $15.00

RICHARD, James. *Snow King.* 1957. Lee Shepard. VG/fair. O3. $25.00

RICHARD, John. *Where's Jack? A Christmas Pop-Up Book.* 1993. np. ils/tab-operated mechanicals/popups. F. A4. $30.00

RICHARD, Mark. *Fishboy.* 1993. Doubleday. 1st ed. sgn. F/F. M23. $45.00

RICHARDS, Allen. *To Market To Murder.* 1961. Macmillan. 1st ed. hc. VG/VG. P3. $15.00

RICHARDS, Dorothy. *Beversprite. My Years Building an Animal Sanctuary.* 1977. NY. Chronicle. 1st ed. sgn. 8vo. 191p. VG/VG. B11. $25.00

RICHARDS, Eva Alvey. *Arctic Mood: A Narrative of Arctic Adventures.* 1949. Caldwell, ID. Caxton. 1st ed. 8vo. 282p. map ep. NF. T10. $35.00

RICHARDS, Gregory B. *SF Movies.* 1984. Bison. 1st ed. VG/VG. P3. $15.00

RICHARDS, John R. *Inside Dope on Football Coaching.* 1917. Chicago. TE Wilson. ils. 114p. VG. B14. $45.00

RICHARDS, Laura E. *Daughter of Jehu.* 1918. Appleton. 1st ed. F/NF. B4. $100.00

RICHARDS, Laura E. *Digging Out.* 1966. McGraw Hill. 1st ed. F/VG+. B4. $85.00

RICHARDS, Laura E. *Isla Heron.* 1896. Boston. Estes Lauriat. 5th thousand. 109p. G. A17. $10.00

RICHARDS, Leverett G. *TAC: Story of Tactical Air Command.* 1961. NY. 1st ed. 254p. F/VG. B18. $22.50

RICHARDS, R.R. *Championship Bridge.* 1928. NY. 114p. VG. S1. $15.00

RICHARDS, Robert. *California Crusoe; or, Lost Treasure Found.* 1854. London/NY. 1st ed. 12mo. 162p. gilt cloth. lacks ffe. T10. $500.00

RICHARDSON, A.D. *Personal History of Ulysses S Grant.* 1868. Hartford. 8vo. ils. 560p. VG. T3. $50.00

RICHARDSON, Donald. *Greek Mythology for Everyone.* 1989. Avenel. F/F. P3. $10.00

RICHARDSON, Frederick. *Billy Bunny's Fortune.* 1936. Wise-Algonquin. later reissue. ils. F. M5. $40.00

RICHARDSON, Gladwell. *Two Guns, Arizona.* 1968. Santa Fe, NM. photos/sources. 28p. F/stiff wrp. E1. $30.00

RICHARDSON, H. Edward. *William Faulkner: Journey to Self-Discovery.* 1969. Columbia. MO U. 1st ed. F/dj. C2. $25.00

RICHARDSON, N. *Richardson's New Method for the Piano-Forte.* 1859. Oliver Ditson. 4to. 236p. T3. $20.00

RICHARDSON, Robert. *Bellringer Street.* 1988. St Martin. BC. F/F. N4. $7.50

RICHARDSON & WHITAKER. *Adventure South.* 1942. Detroit. 1st ed. sgns. 330p. VG/VG. B5. $35.00

RICHEAL, Kip. *Pittsburgh Pirates: Still Walking Tall.* 1993. Sagamore. 1st ed. AN/dj. P8. $12.50

RICHELSON, Geraldine. *Star Wars Storybook.* nd. Random. 14th. VG. P3. $10.00

RICHET, Charles. *Our Sixth Sense.* ca 1929. London. Rider. 1st ed. 227p. blk cloth. G1. $37.50

RICHTER, Conrad. *Early Americana & Other Stories.* 1936. Knopf. 1st ed. F/NF. A18/C2. $75.00

RICHTER, Conrad. *Early Americana & Other Stories.* 1978. Gregg. 1st ed thus. intro WA Bloodworth. F/F. A18. $25.00

RICHTER, Conrad. *Fields.* 1946. Knopf. 1st ed. F/NF. A18. $60.00

RICHTER, Conrad. *Free Man.* 1943. Knopf. 1st ed. inscr. NF/NF. A18. $60.00

RICHTER, Conrad. *Lady.* 1957. Knopf. 1st ed. F/clip. A18. $15.00

RICHTER, Conrad. *Rawhide Knot & Other Stories.* 1978. Knopf. 1st ed. fwd Harvina Richter. F/F. A18. $40.00

RICHTER, Conrad. *Town.* 1950. Knopf. 1st ed. F/F. A18. $75.00

RICHTER, Conrad. *Tracy Cromwell.* 1942. Knopf. 1st ed. F/VG. A18. $40.00

RICHTER, Conrad. *Trees.* 1940. Knopf. 1st ed. F/NF. A18. $75.00

RICHTER, Ed. *Making of a Big League Pitcher.* 1963. Chilton. 1st ed. VG+/VG. P8. $45.00

RICKARDS, Colin. *Bowler Hats & Stetsons.* nd. Bonanza. 1st ed thus. VG/dj. E1. $25.00

RICKARDS, Colin. *Buckskin Frank Leslie, Gunman of Tombstone.* 1964. El Paso, TX. 1st ed. 1/450. 45p. E1. $85.00

RICKARDS, Colin. *Mysterious Dave Mather.* 1968. Santa Fe. 1st ed. 1/1500. photos. 42p. F. E1. $65.00

RICKEY & RIGER. *American Diamond: A Documentary of the Game of Baseball.* 1965. Simon Schuster. 1st ed. F/VG. B4. $85.00

RIDDELL, James. *Holy Land.* 1954. Seabury. 1st ed. ils/2 maps. 96p. VG/torn. W1. $22.00

RIDDICK. *Guide to Indian Manuscripts, Materials From Europe...* 1993. 286p. F. A4. $65.00

RIDDLE, Donald W. *Lincoln Runs for Congress.* 1948. Rutgers. 1st ed. 217p. VG/torn. B18. $15.00

RIDDLE, Kenyon. *Records & Maps of the Old Santa Fe Trail.* 1963. Stuart. Southeastern Prt. 8vo. 8 fld map. 147p. M. O7. $100.00

RIDEOUT, Walter. *Radical Novel in the United States, 1900-1954.* 1960. 1/250. sgn. F/VG. A4. $450.00

RIDER, Bevan. *More Expeditious Conveyance.* 1984. London. Allen. 1st ed. F/F. O3. $25.00

RIDER, J.W. *Hot Tickets.* 1987. Arbor. 1st ed. author's 2nd book. F/F. H11. $25.00

RIDER, Rowland W. *Roll Away Saloon, Cowboy Tales of the Arizona Strip.* 1985. Logan, UT. ils/photos. 114p. F/stiff pict wrp. E1. $10.00

RIDGE, John Rollin. *Life & Adventures of Joaquin Murieta, Celebrated CA Bandit.* 1955. Norman, OK. 1st WFL ed. 12mo. 159p. VG/dj. E1/T10. $25.00

RIDGE & RIDGE. *America's Frontier Story: A Documentary History...* 1969. NY. 1st ed. photos/notes. 655p. F/F. E1. $30.00

RIDGELY, Frances S. *Animalitos.* 1959. Pageant. 1st ed. sgn. ils Barry Martin. 63p. VG. B11. $45.00

RIDGELY, Frances S. *City Is Not Builded in a Day.* 1968. Springfield, IL. Vachel Lindsay Assoc. sgn. 8vo. 34p. VG/wrp. B11. $30.00

RIDLEY, Bromfield. *Battles & Sketches of the Army of Tennessee.* 1978. Dayton. F. V4. $35.00

RIDLEY, H. *LM Montgomery: A Biography.* 1956. Toronto. 1st ed. VG/VG. B5. $30.00

RIDLEY, Thomas. *View of the Civile & Ecclesiastical Law...* 1676. Oxford. Hall Davis. 396p. modern gilt calf/morocco spine label. K1. $200.00

RIDPATH, John Clark. *History of the World.* 1890. Jones Bros. 4 vol. ils. VG. P12. $50.00

RIDPATH, Michael. *Free To Trade.* 1994. Harper Collins. 1st ed. author's 1st novel. F/F. M22. $15.00

RIED, P.R. *Men of Colditz.* 1954. Phil. 1st ed. VG/VG. B5. $20.00

RIEFENSTAHL, Leni. *Schonheit im Olympischen Kampf.* 1937. Berlin. Im Deutshen. 261p. cloth. D2. $775.00

RIEGEL, Robert. *Merchant Vessels.* 1921. Appleton. G/dj. A16. $40.00

RIES, Karl. *Die Maulwurte (The Moles) 1919-1935.* 1970. Mainz. 1st ed. 151p. VG. B18. $22.50

RIESE, Randall. *Unabridged Marilyn.* 1990. Bonanza. 1st ed. F/F. P3. $15.00

RIESE, Walther. *Concept of Disease, Its History, Its Versions & Nature.* 1953. NY. 1st ed. 343p. dj. A13. $30.00

RIESEBERG, Harry E. *Adventures in Underwater Treasure Hunting.* 1965. NY. Frederick Fell. ils. 140p. dj. T7. $24.00

RIESENBERG, Felix. *Gold Road: California's Spanish Mission Trail.* 1962. NY. 1st ed. Am Trail series. 315p. F/dj. A17. $25.00

RIFKIN, Shepard. *Murder Vine.* 1970. Dodd Mead. 1st ed. VG/VG. P3. $15.00

RIGELSFORD, Adrian. *Dr Who: The Monsters.* 1992. Dr Who Books. F/F. P3. $25.00

RIGGS, Ellas. *Outline of a Grammar of the Turkish Language.* 1856. Constantinople. AB Churchill. 1st/only ed. 12mo. 56p. brn cloth. VG. C6. $200.00

RIGGS, James. *Hello Doctor: Brief Biography of Charles Bernstein.* 1936. Roycroft. apparant 1st/only ed. 120p. bl bdg. B22. $6.50

RIGNANO, Eugenio. *Upon the Inheritance of Acquired Characters...* 1911. Chicago. 1st Eng trans. 413p. A13. $50.00

RIHANI, Ameen. *Chant of Mystics & Other Poems.* 1921. NY. White. 1st ed. narrow 12mo. lacks part of spine strip o/w VG. W1. $25.00

RIKER, Ben. *Pony Wagon Town Along US 1890.* 1948. Bobbs Merrill. 1st ed. sgn. 8vo. 312p. bl brd. VG. B11. $35.00

RILEY, Edward Miles. *Journal of John Harrower, an Indentured Servant...* 1963. Colonial Williamsburg. 1st ed. sgn. 8vo. 202p. bl cloth. G/G. B11. $45.00

RILEY, J. *Authentic Narrative of Loss of the American Brig Commerce.* 1833. Hartford. 8vo. ils. 271p. leather. G. T3. $42.00

RILEY, James Whitcomb. *Child-World.* 1897. Bowen Merrill. 1st ed/later prt. 209p. VG. M20. $62.00

RILEY, James Whitcomb. *Home Again With Me.* 1908. Bobbs Merrill. ils HC Christy. fair. P12. $75.00

RILEY, James Whitcomb. *Morning.* 1907. Bobbs Merrill. 1st ed. 162p. gilt red cloth. VG. M20. $42.00

RILEY, James Whitcomb. *Riley Roses.* 1909. 1st ed. ils HC Christy. NF. M19. $25.00

RILEY, James Whitcomb. *Riley Songs of Home.* 1910. Grosset Dunlap. 8vo. ils Will Vawter. 190p. cloth. NF. B36. $35.00

RILEY, James Whitcomb. *Runaway Boy.* 1906. Bobbs Merrill. 8 pl. VG+. M5. $85.00

RILKE, Rainer Maria. *Thirty-One Poems.* 1946. NY. Beechhurst. 1st ed. VG/G. V1. $20.00

RINEHART, Mary Roberts. *Album.* 1933. Farrar Rinehart. 1st ed. G. P3. $30.00

RINEHART, Mary Roberts. *Doctor.* 1936. Farrar Rinehart. 1st ed. VG. P3. $20.00

RINEHART, Mary Roberts. *Door.* nd. Farrar Rinehart. VG. P3. $25.00

RINEHART, Mary Roberts. *Lost Ectasy.* nd. Grosset Dunlap. MTI. VG. P3. $20.00

RINEHART, Mary Roberts. *Man in Lower Ten.* 1940. Triangle. VG. P3. $10.00

RINEHART, Mary Roberts. *Red Lamp.* 1925. Doran. 1st ed. G. P3. $20.00

RINEHART, Mary Roberts. *Street of Seven Stars.* 1914. Houghton Mifflin. 1st ed. 377p. VG. M20. $27.00

RINEHART, Mary Roberts. *Swimming Pool.* 1952. Rinehart. 1st ed. VG/VG. P3. $25.00

RINEHART, Mary Roberts. *Temperamental People.* 1924. Doran. 1st ed. F/NF. B4. $85.00

RINEHART, Mary Roberts. *Yellow Room.* 1945. Farrar Rinehart. 1st ed. VG. P3. $15.00

RING, Douglas; see Prather, Richard.

RING, Ray. *Arizona Kiss.* 1991. Little Brn. 1st ed. F/F. P3. $18.00

RING, Ray. *Telluride Smile.* 1988. NY. Dodd Mead. 1st ed. author's 1st book. F/F. H11. $50.00

RINGELBLUM & SLOAN. *Notes From the Warsaw Ghetto.* 1958. NY. 1st ed. maps/index. VG/VG. B5. $35.00

RINGGOLD, Cadwalader. *Series of Charts With Sailing Directions.* 1852. WA. JT Towers. 4th ed. 6 lg fld maps+8 pl. VG+. O7. $2,000.00

RINGGOLD, Jennie Parks. *Frontier Days in Southwest, Pioneer Days in Old Arizona.* 1952. San Antonio. 1st ed. 197p. VG. E1. $40.00

RINGWALD, Donald C. *Hudson River Day Line.* 1965. Howell-North. G/dj. A16. $80.00

RINHART & RINHART. *America's Affluent Age.* 1971. NY. 1st ed. 343p. F/NF. E1. $35.00

RINK. *Technical Americana: A Checklist of Technical Publications.* 1981. np. 6065 entries. 804p. NF. A4. $200.00

RINKER, H.L. *Warman's Americana & Collectibles.* 1984. 8vo. ils. 550p. G. T3. $7.00

RIOS, Eduardo Enrique. *Life of Fray Antonio Margil, OFM.* 1959. Academy Francisco Hist. 1st ed. 8vo. 159p. gilt bl cloth. F. T10. $50.00

RIPLEY, Alexandra. *Charleston.* 1981. Doubleday. 1st ed. NF/NF. B35. $75.00

RIPLEY, Alexandra. *Scarlett.* 1991. Warner. 1st ed. F/F. H11. $30.00

RIPLEY, Alexandra. *Scarlett.* 1991. Warner. 1st ed. VG/VG. P3. $25.00

RIPLEY, K.B. *Sand in My Shoes.* 1931. NY. 1st ed. VG. B5. $30.00

RIPLEY, Robert L. *Believe It or Not!* 1929. Simon Schuster. 1st ed. pres. ils. 172p. red stp gr cloth. K1. $125.00

RIPLEY, W.L. *Dreamsicle.* 1993. Little Brn. 1st ed. F/F. H11. $30.00

RIRINGO, Charles. *History of...Billy the Kid.* 1967. Austin. facsimile. 142p. NF. E1. $65.00

RIRINGO, Charles. *Riata & Spurs.* 1927. NY. 1st ed/1st issue. G. E1. $150.00

RIRINGO, Charles. *Two Evilsims: Pinkertonism & Anarchism.* 1967. Austin. facsimile. 109p. F/sans. E1. $60.00

RISCHBIETER. *Art & the Stage in the 20th Century.* 1968. NYGS. folio. F/VG. D2. $90.00

RISTER, Carl Coke. *Oil! Titan of the Southwest.* 1949. Norman, OK. 1st ed. photos/fld map. 467p. F. E1. $75.00

RISTER, Carl Coke. *South-Western Frontier 1865-1881.* 1928. Cleveland. 336p. F/case. E1. $300.00

RISTER, Carl Coke. *Southern Plainsmen.* 1938. Norman, OK. 1st ed. 298p. F/chip. E1. $100.00

RISTOW, Walter W. *Guide to the History of Cartography...* 1973. WA. Lib of Congress. 3rd. sgn. F/wrp. O7. $45.00

RISTOW & SKELTON. *Nautical Charts on Vellum in Library of Congress.* 1977. WA. Lib of Congress. 33 charts/12 ils. F. O7. $85.00

RITCHIE, Jack. *Adventures of Henry Turnbuckle.* 1987. Carbondale. SIU. 1st ed. F/F. H11. $30.00

RITCHIE. *Masters of British Painting 1800-1950.* 1956-1957. MOMA. VG/G. D2. $25.00

RITTENHOUSE, Jack D. *Carriage Hundred.* 1961. Houston. Stagecoach Pr. 1/450. VG/VG. O3. $165.00

RITTENHOUSE, Jack D. *Disturnell's Treaty Map: Map That Was Part of Guadelupe...* 1985. Santa Fe. Stagecoach. fld map. gilt bl cloth. F. O7. $125.00

RITTENHOUSE, Jack D. *Outlaw Days at Cabezon, New Mexico.* 1964. Santa Fe. ltd ed. sgn. 28p. F/stiff wrp. E1. $50.00

RITTER, Hans. *Die Letzien Karawanen in Der Sahara.* 1985. Atlantis. special ed. folio. ils. 211p. NF/dj. W1. $45.00

RITTER, Mary Bennett. *More Than Gold in California 1849-1933.* 1933. Berkeley. private prt. 1st ed. inscr/dtd. 451p. F. E1. $100.00

RITTER VON RITTERSHAIN, G. *Geistesleben. Betrachtungen Uber die Geistige Thatigkeit...* 1871. Wien. Wilhelm Braumuller. 116p. prt yel wrp. G1. $150.00

RITZ, David. *Blue Notes Under a Green Felt Hat.* 1989. NY. Donald Fine. 1st ed. rem mk. NF/F. H11. $15.00

RIVERA, Diego. *My Art, My Life.* 1960. 1st ed. photos. VG/VG. S13. $20.00

RIVERE, Alec; see Nuetzel, Charles.

RIVES, Amelie. *Barbara Dering.* 1893. Lippincott. reading copy. B10. $8.00

RIVES, Amelie. *Trix & Over-The-Moon.* 1909. Harper. 1st ed. ils F Walter Taylor. 165p. VG. B10. $25.00

RIVES, Reginald. *Coaching Club.* 1935. Derrydale. 1/300. sgn. O3. $995.00

RIZK, Salom. *Syrian Yankee.* 1952. Doubleday. sgn. 8vo. 317p. VG/torn. W1. $16.00

ROAD, Alan. *Doctor Who: Making of a TV Series.* 1982. Andre Deutsch. TVTI. NF. P3. $20.00

ROARK & YOUNG. *Formulas for Stress & Strain.* 1975. McGraw Hill. 5th. 624p. VG. D8. $20.00

ROBACK, A.A. *Popular Psychology With Chapters on Intelligence.* 1928. Cambridge. Sci-Art Pub. 267p. VG/dj. G1. $35.00

ROBACK, A.A. *Psychology of Character...* 1927. Harcourt Brace. 1st ed/Am issue. 596p. gr cloth. VG. G1. $75.00

ROBACKER, Earl F. *Old Stuff in Up-Country Pennsylvania.* 1973. Cranbury, NJ. 1st ed. 283p. F/F. E1. $30.00

ROBACKER, Earl F. *Pennsylvania Dutch Stuff.* 1960. NY. rpt. F/VG. E1. $30.00

ROBARTS, Edith. *Gulliver in Giantland.* nd. London. Sisley's Ltd. 16mo. ils. VG+. M5. $35.00

ROBBINS, A. *Journal...of the Brig Commerce...Upon the Western Coast...* 1818. Hartford. 16mo. fld map. 275p. full leather. G. T3. $40.00

ROBBINS, Harold. *Memories of Another Day.* 1979. Simon Schuster. 1st ed. NF/NF. B35. $20.00

ROBBINS, Harold. *Pirate.* 1974. Simon Schuster. 1st ed. NF/NF. B35. $30.00

ROBBINS, Harold. *79 Park Avenue.* 1955. Knopf. 1st ed. author's 4th book. F/VG. H11. $40.00

ROBBINS, Leonard A. *Index to Adventure Magazine Volume 1 & Volume 2.* nd. Starmont. VG. P3. $150.00

ROBBINS, Leonard A. *Pulp Magazine Index First Series, Volume 1.* nd. Starmont. VG. P3. $100.00

ROBBINS, Leonard A. *Pulp Magazine Index Second Series.* nd. Starmont. VG. P3. $120.00

ROBBINS, Tom. *Jitterbug Perfume.* 1984. Bantam. 1st ed. VG/VG. P3. $16.00

ROBBINS. *Law: A Treasury of Art & Literature.* 1990. np. sm folio. 198 pl. F/NF clip. A4. $85.00

ROBERSON, Jennifer. *Lady of the Forest: Novel of Sherwood.* 1992. Zebra. 1st ed. sgn. F/F. T2. $22.00

ROBERSON, Jennifer. *Smoketree.* 1985. Walker. 1st ed. sgn. F/F. T2. $18.00

ROBERTS, Charles G.D. *In the Morning of Time.* 1922. McClelland Stewart. 1st ed. G. P3. $35.00

ROBERTS, Dan W. *Rangers & Sovereignty.* 1914. San Antonio. 1st ed. photos. 190p. F/case. E1. $200.00

ROBERTS, Dorothy James. *Return of the Stranger.* 1958. Appleton Century Crofts. VG/VG. P3. $20.00

ROBERTS, E.M. *Flying Fighter.* 1918. NY. 1st ed. 338p. G+. B18. $45.00

ROBERTS, E.M. *Great Meadow.* 1930. Viking. 1/295. 338p. teg. VG/lacks glassine wrp/box. B10. $75.00

ROBERTS, E.M. *Kentucky Poetry Review.* Fall 1981. np. Special Roberts issue. NF/stiff wrp. V1. $10.00

ROBERTS, Gail. *Atlas of Discovery.* 1973. London. Aldus. 1st ed. ils. 192p. M/dj. O7. $45.00

ROBERTS, Gillian. *Caught Dead in Phil.* 1987. Scribner. 1st ed. F/F. C2. $75.00

ROBERTS, Gillian. *I'd Rather Be in Philadelphia.* 1992. Ballantine. 1st ed. F/F. H11. $25.00

ROBERTS, Gillian. *With Friends Like These...* nd. BC. VG/VG. P3. $8.00

ROBERTS, Katharine. *Center of the Web.* nd. Collier. VG. P3. $15.00

ROBERTS, Keith. *Furies.* 1966. London. Hart Davis. 1st ed. author's 1st book. VG/VG. scarce. M21. $200.00

ROBERTS, Keith. *Kiteworld.* 1985. Gollancz. 1st ed. F/F. P3. $25.00

ROBERTS, Keith. *Lordly Ones.* 1986. Gollancz. 1st ed. VG/VG. P3. $30.00

ROBERTS, Keith. *Winterwood & Other Hauntings.* 1989. Morrigan. 1st ed. F/F. P3. $30.00

ROBERTS, Kenneth. *Battle of Cowpens.* 1958. Garden City. 1st ed. F/F. B5. $30.00

ROBERTS, Kenneth. *Don't Say That About Maine.* 1951. Waterville, ME. Colby College. F/stapled wrp in dj. B4. $150.00

ROBERTS, Kenneth. *Lydia Bailey.* 1947. Doubleday. 1st ed. 1/1050. sgn. F/glassine dj/case. B24. $250.00

ROBERTS, Kenneth. *Why Europe Leaves Home.* 1922. Bobbs Merrill. 1st ed. inscr. F. B24. $650.00

ROBERTS, Lee; see Martin, Robert.

ROBERTS, Les. *Infinite Number of Monkeys.* 1987. NY. 1st ed. F/F. H11. $30.00

ROBERTS, Les. *Pepper Pike.* 1988. St Martin. 1st ed. F/F. P3. $16.00

ROBERTS, Lionel. *In-World.* 1968. Arcadia. F/F. P3. $20.00

ROBERTS, Martha. *These Go in Flight.* 1970. Golden Quill. inscr. 56p. VG/VG. B10. $8.00

ROBERTS, Nancy. *Appalachian Ghosts.* 1978. Doubleday. 1st ed. VG/VG. P3. $12.00

ROBERTS, Ned H. *Muzzle-Loading Cap Lock Rifle.* 1952. Bonanza. rpt. 308p. F/NF. E1. $40.00

ROBERTS, Paul William. *River in the Desert: Modern Travels in Ancient Egypt.* 1993. Random. 1st ed. 394p. NF/dj. W1. $20.00

ROBERTS, Ruby Altizer. *Forever Is Too Long.* 1946. Wings. inscr. 91p. VG/fair. B10. $10.00

ROBERTS, S.C. *Holmes & Watson: A Miscellany.* 1953. Oxford. 1st ed. VG/VG. P3. $75.00

ROBERTS, Susan. *Magician of the Golden Dawn.* 1978. Comtemporary Books. VG/VG. P3. $20.00

ROBERTS, W. Adolphe. *Brave Mardi Gras.* 1946. Bobbs Merrill. 1st ed. VG/G. P3. $15.00

ROBERTS & ROBERTS. *Moreau de St Merys American Journey 1793-1798.* 1947. Doubleday. 1st ed. VG/G+. P12. $20.00

ROBERTS & SEELY. *Tidewater Dynasty.* 1981. IIDJ. BC. VG/VG. B10. $8.00

ROBERTS. *Jean Stafford: A Biography.* 1988. np. 28 photos. 294p. NF/NF. A4. $25.00

ROBERTSON, Dale. *Son of the Phantom.* 1946. Whitman. G. P3. $15.00

ROBERTSON, Don *By Antietam Creek.* 1960. Prentice Hall. 1st ed. VG/VG. B11. $25.00

ROBERTSON, Don. *Ideal, Genuine Man.* 1987. Philtrum. 1st ed. F/NF clip. G10. $25.00

ROBERTSON, E. Arnot. *Sign Post.* 1944. Canada. Macmillan. 1st ed. VG. P3. $13.00

ROBERTSON, Giles. *Giovanni Bellini.* 1968. Oxford. Clarendon. pl/biblio. 171p. cloth. D2. $125.00

ROBERTSON, James I. *Concise Illustrated History of the Civil War.* 1971. Nat Hist Soc. sm 4to. ils. 50p. G/wrp. T3. $6.00

ROBERTSON, Keith. *Three Stuffed Owls.* 1957 (1954). Viking. 3rd. 8vo. 198p. VG. T5. $20.00

ROBERTSON, Morgan. *Wreck of the Titan.* 1912. NY. VG. B5. $45.00

ROBERTSON, P. *Book of Firsts.* 1974. NY. 4to. ils. 256p. brn cloth. VG/dj. T3. $20.00

ROBERTSON, R.B. *Of Whales & Men.* 1954. Alfred Knopf. 300p. gilt bl bdg. VG. P12. $15.00

ROBERTSON, W. Graham. *Year of Songs for a Baby in a Garden.* 1906. London. John Lane. inscr/dtd 1905. 110p. olive-gr cloth. B24. $450.00

ROBERTSON & ROBERTSON. *Cowman's Country: Fifty Frontier Ranches in TX Panhandle...* 1981. Paramount. 1st ed. sgns. photos/biblio. 184p. F. E1. $75.00

ROBESON, Kenneth; see Goulart, Ron.

ROBIN, Robert. *Above the Law.* 1992. NY. Pocket. 1st ed. F/F. H11. $20.00

ROBINS, George. *Lays of the Hertfordshire Hunt.* 1916. London. Humphreys. 12mo. G. O3. $18.00

ROBINSON, Bob. *Show Your Horse.* 1978. St Louis. Saddle & Bridle. 1st ed. 200p. sc. VG. O3. $12.00

ROBINSON, Brooks. *Putting It All Together.* 1971. Hawthorn. 1st ed. F/VG+. P8. $30.00

ROBINSON, Douglas H. *Dangerous Sky: History of Aviation Medicine.* 1973. Seattle. ils. 292p. VG/dj. B18. $25.00

ROBINSON, E.A. *Amaranth.* 1934. Macmillan. 1st ed. 105p. VG+/dj. M20. $25.00

ROBINSON, E.A. *Critical Study.* 1952. Macmillan. 1st ed. F/NF. V1. $20.00

ROBINSON, E.A. *Man Who Died Twice.* 1924. Macmillan. 1st ed. ltd. sgn. tall 8vo. F. T10. $150.00

ROBINSON, E.A. *Sonnets 1889-1927.* 1928. Macmillan. 1st collected ed. 8vo. F/NF. T10. $50.00

ROBINSON, E.A. *Tristam.* 1927. Macmillan. 1st ed. red cloth. NF. V1. $25.00

ROBINSON, Francis. *Atlas of the Islamic World Since 1500.* 1982. Facts on File. 1st ed. folio. 238p. VG/dj. W1. $65.00

ROBINSON, Frank M. *Power.* nd. BC. VG/VG. P3. $10.00

ROBINSON, Frank. *Extra Innings.* 1988. McGraw Hill. 1st ed. F/F. P8. $17.50

ROBINSON, Henry Morton. *Cardinal.* 1950. Simon Schuster. 1st ed. inscr. F/F. B4. $200.00

ROBINSON, Jane. *Edward G Robinson's World of Art.* 1975. Harper Row. 1st ed. ils/phtos. 117p. cloth. dj. D2. $35.00

ROBINSON, John Louis. *David Lipscomb: Journalist in Texas.* 1872. Nortex. sgn. 60p. F/G. E1. $25.00

ROBINSON, Kim Stanley. *Blue Mars.* 1996. London. Harper Collins. 1st ed. sgn. F/F. M23. $100.00

ROBINSON, Kim Stanley. *Escape From Kathmandu.* 1989. Tor. 1st ed. F/F. P3. $18.00

ROBINSON, Kim Stanley. *Future Primitive: The New Ecotopias.* 1994. Tor. 1st ed. F/F. G10. $20.00

ROBINSON, Kim Stanley. *Gold Coast.* 1988. Tor. 1st ed. F/F. P3. $20.00

ROBINSON, Kim Stanley. *Green Mars.* 1994. Bantam. 1st ed. F/F. M23. $100.00

ROBINSON, Kim Stanley. *Memory of Whiteness.* 1985. Tor. 1st ed. NF/NF. P3. $18.00

ROBINSON, Kim Stanley. *Planet on the Table.* 1986. Tor. 1st ed. F/F. P3. $20.00

ROBINSON, Kim Stanley. *Red Mars.* 1993. Bantam. UP. sgn. F/red wrp. M23. $500.00

ROBINSON, Kim Stanley. *Red Mars.* 1993. Easton. 1st ed. sgn. F. M23. $125.00

ROBINSON, Kim Stanley. *Remaking History.* 1991. Tor. 1st ed. F/F. G10. $25.00

ROBINSON, Kim Stanley. *Short Sharp Shock.* 1990. Ziesing. 1st ed. F/F. P3. $20.00

ROBINSON, Lynda S. *Murder at the God's Gate.* 1995. Walker. 1st ed. F/F. M23. $35.00

ROBINSON, Marilyn. *Housekeeping.* 1980. FSG. 1st ed. inscr. author's 1st novel. F/F. B4. $100.00

ROBINSON, Peter. *Dedicated Man.* 1991. Scribner. 1st Am ed. sgn. F/F. T2. $25.00

ROBINSON, Peter. *Gallows View.* 1987. Viking. 1st ed. VG/VG. P3. $18.00

ROBINSON, Peter. *Necessary End.* 1989. Canada. Viking. 1st ed. VG/VG. P3. $25.00

ROBINSON, Ruth E. *Buy Books Where, Sell Books Where.* 1981-1982. np. 4to. 226p. G. T3. $5.00

ROBINSON, Spider. *Time Pressure.* 1987. Ace. 1st ed. F/F. P3. $20.00

ROBINSON, Thomas. *Common Law of Kent; or, Customs of Gavelkind.* 1788. London. modern quarter calf. M11. $450.00

ROBINSON, Tom. *Buttons.* 1938. Viking. 1st trade ed. ils Peggy Bacon. VG/VG. P2. $60.00

ROBINSON, Tom. *Greylock & the Robins.* 1946. Viking/Jr Literary Guild. 1st ed thus. ils Lawson. VG. M5. $55.00

ROBINSON, Tom. *Trigger John's Son.* 1949. Viking. 1st ed thus. 284p. VG/G. P2. $45.00

ROBINSON, Victor. *Encyclopedia of Sexualis: A Comprehensive Encyclopedia...* 1936. NY. 1st ed. 819p. VG. A13. $100.00

ROBINSON, W.W. *Maps of Los Angeles: From Ord's Survey of 1849 to...* 1966. Los Angeles. Dawson. 1/380. sgn. 27 maps. M/clear plastic. O7. $575.00

ROBINSON, Will G. *Gold Rush Centennial Ed.* 1961. Dakota Territory Centennial Commission. E1. $25.00

ROBINSON, Will H. *Story of Arizona.* 1919. Phoenix. Berryhill Co. 8vo. 458p. ribbed gr cloth. VG. T10. $50.00

ROBINSON, William Albert. *Voyage to Galapagos.* 1936. Harcourt Brace. photos/drawings. 279p. VG. T7. $28.00

ROBINSON, William Morrison. *Confederate Privateers.* 1928. New Haven. Yale. 372p. G. T10. $85.00

ROBISON, Mary. *Amateur's Guide to the Night.* 1983. Knopf. 1st ed. rem mk. F/F. B4. $35.00

ROBISON, Mary. *Days.* 1979. Knopf. 1st ed. author's 1st book. NF/NF. B4. $45.00

ROBYN, Louise. *Technic Tales for the Child at the Piano: Book One.* 1936. Phil. revised. ils Ross/Williams. G. A17. $7.50

ROCHE, John P. *Quest for the Dream: Development of Civil Rights...* 1963. Macmillan. 1st ed. 308p. torn dj. R11. $12.00

ROCHE, Paul. *All Things Considered.* 1968. Weybright Talley. 1st ed. assn copy. F/NF. V1. $20.00

ROCKWELL, Carey. *Danger in Deep Space.* nd. Grosset Dunlap. VG. P3. $15.00

ROCKWELL, Carey. *Sabotage in Space.* nd. Grosset Dunlap. VG. P3. $15.00

ROCKWELL, Carey. *Tom Corbett Space Cadet & Danger in Deep Space.* 1953. Grosset Dunlap. ils. VG/G. P12. $5.00

ROCKWELL, Carey. *Tom Corbett Space Cadet & Stand By for Mars!* 1952. Grosset Dunlap. ils. VG/poor. P12. $5.00

ROCKWELL, Carey. *Tom Corbett: Treachery in Outer Space (#6).* 1954. Grosset Dunlap. lists 8 titles. 210p. cloth. VG/dj. M20. $15.00

ROCKWELL, Norman. *Norman Rockwell: My Adventures As an Illustrator.* 1960. Doubleday. ils. NF/VG. A4. $40.00

ROCKWELL, Norman. *Norman Rockwell: My Adventures As an Illustrator.* 1960. Doubleday. 1st ed. sgn. 437p. xl. VG. B11. $50.00

ROCKWOOD, Roy. *Bomba & the Lost Explorers.* nd. Grosset Dunlap. VG/fair. P3. $12.00

ROCKWOOD, Roy. *Bomba at the Moving Mountain.* nd. Cupples Leon. VG/VG. P3. $18.00

ROCKWOOD, Roy. *Bomba on the Underground River.* nd. Cupples Leon. G. P3. $10.00

ROCKWOOD, Roy. *Bomba the Jungle Boy & the Cannibals.* nd. Cupples Leon. VG. P3. $15.00

ROCKWOOD, Roy. *Bomba the Jungle Boy Among the Slaves.* 1939. Clover Books. G+. P12. $8.00

ROCKWOOD, Roy. *Dave Dashaway, Air Champion.* 1915. Cupples Leon. G+. P12. $5.00

ROCKWOOD, Roy. *On a Torn-Away World.* nd. Whitman. VG. P3. $20.00

RODD, Ralph. *Midnight Murder.* 1931. Collins Crime Club. 1st ed. VG. P3. $20.00

RODDIS, Louis. *Short History of Nautical Medicine.* 1941. NY. 359p. VG. A13. $100.00

RODEN, H.W. *Too Busy To Die.* nd. Detective BC. VG. P3. $10.00

RODEN, H.W. *Wake for a Lady.* 1946. Morrow. 1st ed. VG/VG. P3. $30.00

RODENGEN, Jeffrey L. *Legends of Chris-Craft.* 1988. FL. Write Stuff Syndicate. 1st ed. AN/dj. A16. $100.00

RODENWALDT, Gerhart. *Acropolis.* 1957. Oxford. Blackwell. 2nd. 4to. 104 pl. VG/torn. W1. $35.00

RODINSON, M. *Israel & the Arabs.* 1968. Pantheon. 1st Am ed. sm 8vo. 239p. VG/torn. W1. $18.00

RODKINSON, Michael L. *New Edition of the Babylonian Talmud. Vol VII...* 1918. Boston. Talmud Soc. tall 8vo. xl. VG. W1. $12.00

RODMAN, Selden. *Mexican Traveler.* 1969. Meredith. 1st ed. 264p. dj. F3. $20.00

RODNEY, George B. *Coronado Trial.* nd. Grosset Dunlap. VG/G+. P3. $13.00

RODRIQUEZ, Mario. *Cadiz Experiment in Central America.* 1978. CA U. 1st ed. 316p. dj. F3. $20.00

ROE, A.S. *39th Massachusetts Volunteers 1862-1865.* 1914. Worcester. 1st ed. ils. 493p. VG. B5. $125.00

ROE, Frank Gilbert. *Indian & the Horse.* 1974. Norman, OK. 4th. 433p. E1. $30.00

ROE, Judy. *Same Old Grind.* 1975. Millbrae, CA. Les Femmes. simultaneous wrp ed. B4. $45.00

ROEDER, Ralph. *Juarez & His Mexico.* 1948. Viking. 2nd. 761p. F3. $15.00

ROESSNER, Michaela. *Vanishing Point.* 1993. Tor. 1st ed. F/F. G10. $15.00

ROETHKE, Theodore. *Garden Master.* 1975. Seattle, WA. F/VG. V1. $15.00

ROFF, Joe T. *Brief History of Early Days in North Texas...* 1930. Roff, OK. 40p. VG/stiff wrp. E1. $350.00

ROFFMAN, Jan. *Walk in the Dark.* 1970. Crime Club. 1st ed. VG/VG. P3. $15.00

ROGERS, Dale Evans. *To My Son.* 1957. Revell. 8vo. inscr. 142p. VG. T10. $50.00

ROGERS, Fairman. *Manual of Coaching.* 1900. Lippincott. 1st ed. half leather. VG. O3. $995.00

ROGERS, H.C. *Weapons of the British Soldier.* 1968. London. rpt. 259p. F/F. E1. $35.00

ROGERS, J.E. *Shell Book.* 1951. Boston. Branford. revised. 8vo. ils. cloth. NF. B1. $35.00

ROGERS, J.M. *Topkapi Saray Museum: The Treasury.* 1987. Little Brn. 1st ed. folio. 124 pl. 215p. F/case. W1. $95.00

ROGERS, John William. *Finding Literature on the Texas Plains.* 1931. Dallas. 57p. F. E1. $125.00

ROGERS, John. *Red World: Memories of a Chippewa Boyhood.* 1974. Norman. 2nd ed/1st prt. 153p. F/VG. E1. $30.00

ROGERS, Pat. *Oxford Ils History of English Literature.* 1987. Oxford. readling list/index. F/dj. A17. $25.00

ROGERS, Robert William. *History of Babylonia & Assyria.* 1901. NY/Cincinnati. Eaton Mains/Jennings Pye. 2 vol. 2nd. VG. W1. $75.00

ROGERS, Walter Thomas. *Manual of Bibliography.* 1891. London. Grevel. new ed. 8vo. 213p. teg. VG. T10. $35.00

ROGERS, Walter. *Lone Eagle of the Border.* 1929. Grosset Dunlap. G+. P12. $5.00

ROGERS, Will. *Autobiography of...* 1949. Houghton Mifflin. lacks ffe. G+/dj. P3. $18.00

ROGERS, Will. *GPO Acceptance of Statue of Will Rogers.* 1930. WA. 1st ed. ils. 80p. VG. B5. $25.00

ROGERS, Will. *Letters of a Self-Made Diplomat to His President. Vol I.* 19226. NY. Boni. ils. 263p. VG. A4. $35.00

ROGERS, Will. *Will Rogers Scrapbook.* 1976. Grosset Dunlap. ils. 191p. brn cloth. F/dj. T10. $45.00

ROGERS, William Ledyard. *Greek & Roman Naval Warfare...Strategy, Tactics...* 1964. Annapolis. 555p. F. A17. $25.00

ROHAN, Michael Scott. *Cloud Castles.* 1994. Avonova Morrow. 1st ed. F/F. P3. $22.00

ROHAN, Michael Scott. *Gates of Noon.* 1992. Gollancz. 1st ed. F/F. P3. $25.00

ROHEIM, Gaza. *Hungarian & Vogul Mythology.* 1954. NY. Augustin. 8vo. ils/map. VG. W1. $16.00

ROHMER, Richard. *Exodus UK.* 1975. McClelland Stewart. 1st ed. NF/NF. P3. $10.00

ROHMER, Sax. *Bat Wing.* nd. AL Burt. VG/VG. P3. $35.00

ROHMER, Sax. *Brood of the Witch Queen.* 1924. Doubleday Page. 1st ed. G. P3. $45.00

ROHMER, Sax. *Devil Doctor.* 1973. Tom Stacey. F/F. P3. $20.00

ROHMER, Sax. *Dope.* 1919. AL Burt. 1st ed thus. VG. M21. $20.00

ROHMER, Sax. *Drums of Fu Manchu.* 1939. Crime Club. 1st ed. VG. P3. $75.00

ROHMER, Sax. *Fire Tongue.* 1931. Cassell. 2nd. VG. P3. $20.00

ROHMER, Sax. *Green Eyes of Bast.* 1920. McBride. 1st ed. G. P3. $45.00

ROHMER, Sax. *Insidious Dr Fu Manchu.* nd. AL Burt. 1st ed thus. VG. M21. $10.00

ROHMER, Sax. *Mask of Fu Manchu.* 1932. Crime Club. 1st ed. G. P3. $35.00

ROHMER, Sax. *President Fu Manchu.* 1936. Crime Club. 1st ed. VG. P3. $50.00

ROHMER, Sax. *Wrath of Fu Manchu.* 1973. Tom Stacey. 1st ed. NF/NF. P3. $30.00

ROHMER, Sax. *Yu'an Hee See Laughs.* nd. Collier. 1st ed thus. VG+. M21. $15.00

ROLFE, Edwin. *Collected Poems.* 1993. Urbana, IL. 1st ed. F/F. B2. $35.00

ROLFE, Frank. *Commercial Geography of Southern California.* 1915. Los Angeles. Rolfe. ils/fld maps. ES. NF. O7. $135.00

ROLFE, Fred. *Letter to Claud.* 1964. IA City. 1/150. F/wrp. A15. $50.00

ROLLAND, Sandy. *Raffles: His Sons & Daughters.* 1974. Burlington. 1st ed. 1/1000. sgn. VG. O3. $295.00

ROLLE, Andrew F. *Road to Virginia City: Diary of James Knox Polk Miller.* 1960. OK U. 1st ed. ils Joe Beeler. 142p. F/F. E1. $40.00

ROLLER. *Exhibition of Works by Galileo Galilei...* 1980. Norman, OK. 4to. ils. NF/wrp. A4. $35.00

ROLLERSTON, Humphry. *Some Medical Aspects of Old Age.* 1922. London. 170p. xl. A13. $100.00

ROLLESTON, T.W. *Celtic Myths & Legends.* 1986. Bracken. 1st ed. VG. P3. $25.00

ROLLINS, Philip Ashton. *Cowboy: An Unconventional History of Civilization...* 1936. NY, NY. 3rd. ils/map/index. 402p. F. E1. $65.00

ROLLINS, Philip Ashton. *Gone Haywire: Two Tenderfoots on Montana Cattle Range 1886.* 1939. Scribner. 1st ed. ils Peter Hurd. F/NF. B4. $85.00

ROLLINSON, John K. *Wyoming Cattle Trails: Hist of Migration of OR-Raised Herds.* 1948. Caldwell. 1st ed. 1/1000. sgn/#d. 366p. E1. $200.00

ROLLYSON, Carl. *Lillian Hellman: Her Legend & Her Legacy.* 1988. NY. 1st ed. 613p. F/F. A17. $15.00

ROLLYSON. *Lives of Norman Mailer.* 1991. np. photos. 425p. F/F. A4. $25.00

ROLT-WHEELER, Francis. *Book of Cowboys.* 1921. Lee Shepard. 1st ed. photos. F/chip. A18. $40.00

ROLVAAG, O.E. *When the Wind Is in the South & Other Stories.* 1984. Center for Western Studies. 1st ed. M/M. A18. $30.00

ROMAINE. *Guide to American Trade Catalogs 1744-1900.* 1960. np. 445p. VG. A4. $185.00

ROMANES, George J. *Animal Intelligence.* Internat Scientific Series Vol 44. 1883 (1882). NY. Appleton. 12mo. 520p. xl. VG. G1. $65.00

ROMANES, George J. *Examination of Weismannism.* 1899. Chicago. Open Court. 1st Am ed/2nd prt. 221p. VG. G1. $40.00

ROMANES, George J. *Mind & Motion & Monism.* 1895. Longman Gr. 1st Am ed. 12mo. 170p. panelled gr cloth. VG. G1. $50.00

ROMANO, Deane. *Flight From Time One.* 1972. Walker. 1st ed. VG/VG. P3. $15.00

ROMBAUER, I. *Joy of Cooking.* 1931. St Louis. 1st ed. VG. B5. $800.00

ROMBAUER, Marjorie Dick. *Legal Problem Solving: Analysis, Research & Writing.* 1973. St Paul. West Pub. M11. $35.00

ROMBERGER, J.A. *Meristems, Growth & Development in Woody Plants.* 1963. USDA. 214p. cloth. VG. B1. $27.00

ROME, Anthony; see Albert, Marvin H.

ROME, Jesus. *Civilization of the Maya.* (1979-80). Crescent. 1st ed. 174p. dj. F3. $20.00

RONNS, Edward; see Aarons, Edward S.

ROOME, Annette. *Bad Trip.* 1971. Dodd Mead. 1st ed. VG/VG. P3. $20.00

ROOME, Annette. *Real Shot in the Arm.* 1989. Crown. 1st ed. NF/NF. P3. $18.00

ROOME, Annette. *Requiem for a Blonde.* 1958. Dodd Mead. 1st ed. VG/VG. P3. $25.00

ROOME, Annette. *Triple Threat.* 1949. AA Wyn. 1st ed. VG/torn. P3. $20.00

ROONEY, Andy. *Word for Word.* 1986. Putnam. 1st ed. F/F. B35. $20.00

ROONEY, James. *Lame Horse: Causes, Symptoms & Treatment.* 1975. Barnes. VG/G. O3. $25.00

ROOS & ROOS. *Few Days in Madrid.* 1966. Deutsch. 1st ed. VG/VG. P3. $18.00

ROOSEVELT, Elliott. *Murder & the First Lady.* 1984. St Martin. 1st ed. F/F. B4. $45.00

ROOSEVELT, Elliott. *Murder at the Palace.* nd. BC. VG/VG. P3. $8.00

ROOSEVELT, Elliott. *Murder in the Blue Room.* 1990. St Martin. 1st ed. F/F. P3. $17.00

ROOSEVELT, Elliott. *Roosevelt Letters. Vol 1: Early Years 1887-1904.* 1949. 8vo. 470p. blk cloth. G. T3. $15.00

ROOSEVELT, Selwa 'Lucky.' *Keeper of the Gate.* 1990. Simon Schuster. 1st ed. sgn. VG/VG. B11. $12.00

ROOSEVELT, Theodore. *African Game Trails.* 1910. np. 1st ed. ils. 483p. half leather. VG. A4/S13. $45.00

ROOSEVELT, Theodore. *African Game Trails.* 1910. NY. 1st ed (p78 & p79 are blank). NF. A15. $125.00

ROOSEVELT, Theodore. *Hunting Tales of a Ranchman.* 1908. Current Literay Pub. G+. P12. $10.00

ROOSEVELT, Theodore. *Letters to His Children.* 1919. NF. S13. $15.00

ROOSEVELT, Theodore. *Presidential Addresses & State Papers.* 1910. NY. 8 vol. index. 2359p. VG. A17. $50.00

ROOT, Elihu. *Men & Policies, Addresses by Elihu Root.* 1925. Harvard. M11. $50.00

ROOT, William Pitt. *Fireclock.* 1981. Four Zoas. ltd ed. 1/about 175. NF/wrp. V1. $15.00

ROOT, William Pitt. *Reasons for Going It on Foot.* 1981. Atheneum. 1st ed. F/F. V1. $15.00

ROPER, Allen. *Ancient Eugenics.* 1975. Minneapolis. facsimile of 1913 ed. 76p. VG. A13. $30.00

ROPES, J.C. *Army Under Pope.* 1881. NY. 12mo. fld map. 229p. blk cloth. G. T3. $25.00

ROQUELAURE, A.N.; see Rice, Anne.

ROREM, Ned. *Music From Inside Out.* 1967. NY. 1st ed. inscr. F/clip. C2. $50.00

ROSA, Joseph G. *Gunfighter: Man or Myth?* 1969. Norman, OK. 229p. NF/dj. T10. $25.00

ROSA, Joseph G. *Guns of the American West.* 1985. NY. 1st Am ed. 192p. F/F. E1. $55.00

ROSA, Joseph G. *They Called Him Wild Bill Hickok.* 1964. Norman, OK. 1st ed. photos/index. 278p. F/VG. E1. $75.00

ROSA, Joseph G. *West of Wild Bill Hickok.* 1982. Norman. 1st ed. 23p. F/F. E1. $60.00

ROSAND, David. *Titian: His World & His Legacy.* 1982. Columbian U. ils/pl. 349p. cloth. dj. D2. $75.00

ROSCOE, T. *US Destroyer Operations in WWII.* 1953. Annapolis. 1st ed. VG/VG. B5. $67.50

ROSCOE, Theodore. *I'll Grind Their Bones.* 1936. NY. Dodge. 1st ed. F/VG+. B4. $150.00

ROSCOE, Theodore. *To Live & Die in Dixie.* 1961. NY. 1st ed. VG/VG. B5. $25.00

ROSCOE, Theodore. *Web of Conspiracy.* 1960. Englewood Cliffs. 2nd. 562p. G+/torn. B18. $37.50

ROSCOE, Thomas. *Wanderings & Excursions in North Wales.* 1836. London. Tilt Simpkin. tall 8vo. 262p. aeg. full gr calf. K1. $250.00

ROSCOE, William. *Butterfly's Ball & the Grasshopper's Feast.* 1977. Boston. 1/150. sgn prt/ils Carah Chamberlain. F. B24. $250.00

ROSE, Billy. *Wine, Women & Works.* 1948. 1st ed. ils Salvador Dali. VG/VG. S13. $45.00

ROSE, J. Holland. *Development of European Nations 1870-1900.* 1905. Knickerbocker. 2 vol. 1st ed. maps/plans. teg. VG. W1. $75.00

ROSE, Mrs. Arthur Gordon. *Little Mistress Chicken.* 1925. Columbia, SC. ils. 61p. VG/dj. B18. $22.50

ROSE, Turner. *Marked for Rest.* 1932. Samuel French. 25p. VG/stiff wrp. B10. $15.00

ROSE, Victor M. *Life & Services of General Ben McCulloch.* 1958. Phil. facsimile. photos. 260p. VG/case. E1. $65.00

ROSE, Victor M. *Texas Vendetta on the Sutton-Taylor Feud.* 1956. Houston, TX. rpt. 69p. F. E1. $75.00

ROSE, William K. *Astrophysics.* 1973. HRW. 3rd. 287p. VG. K5. $23.00

ROSEBAULT, Charles J. *Saladin, Prince of Chivalry.* 1930. Cassell. 1st ed. ils/pl/maps. 303p. VG. W1. $30.00

ROSELIEP, Raymond. *Small Rain.* 1963. Newman. 1st ed. assn copy. F/G+. V1. $20.00

ROSEN, Charles. *Mile Above the Rim.* 1976. Arbor. 1st ed. F/F. B35. $20.00

ROSEN, George. *Reception of William Beumont's Discovery in Europe.* 1942. NY. 1st ed. 97p. VG. A13. $55.00

ROSEN, Gerald. *Dr Ebenezer's Book & Liquor Store.* 1980. NY. 1st ed. F/F. H11. $30.00

ROSEN, Marion. *Death by Education.* 1993. NY. 1st ed. F/F. H11. $25.00

ROSEN, Michael. *Down at the Doctor's.* 1987. NY. Simon Schuster. 1st ed. 8vo. unp. NF/NF. C14. $8.00

ROSEN, Richard. *Fadeaway.* 1986. Harper Row. 1st ed. F/F. P3. $16.00

ROSEN, Richard. *Saturday Night Dead.* 1988. Viking. 1st ed. F/F. H11. $30.00

ROSEN, Richard. *Saturday Night Dead.* 1988. Viking. 1st ed. VG/VG. P3. $17.00

ROSENBACH, A.S.W. *Book Hunter's Holiday.* 1936. Houghton Mifflin. 1/760. sgn. F/glassine. T10. $200.00

ROSENBACH, A.S.W. *Collected Catalogues of Dr ASW Rosenbach 1904-1951.* 1967. 10 vol. NF. A4. $650.00

ROSENBACH, A.S.W. *Early American Children's Books...* nd. rpt of 1933 ed. 1/150. 104 ils/816 entries. 413p. F. A4. $85.00

ROSENBAUM, David. *Sasha's Trick.* 1995. Mysterious. 1st ed. F/F. H11. $25.00

ROSENBAUM, David. *Zaddick.* 1993. Mysterious. 1st ed. F/F. H11. $30.00

ROSENBERG, Joel. *Keepers of the Hidden Ways.* 1995. Morrow. 1st ed. F/F. w/pub material. G10. $10.00

ROSENBERG, Joel. *Not for Glory.* 1988. NAL. 1st ed. F/F. P3. $17.00

ROSENBERG, Nancy Taylor. *Interest of Justice.* 1993. Dutton. ARC. F/pict wrp. G10. $30.00

ROSENBERG, Nancy Taylor. *Interest of Justice.* 1993. Dutton. 1st ed. sgn. F/F. H11. $50.00

ROSENBLUM, Robert. *Good Thief.* 1975. Hart Davis MacGibbon. hc. VG/VG. P3. $20.00

ROSENBLUM, Robert. *Sweetheart Deal.* 1976. Putnam. 1st ed. F/F. P3. $15.00

ROSENBLUM. *World History of Photography.* 1984. 803 photos. 671p. F/F. A4. $165.00

ROSENBURG, John. *They Gave Us Baseball.* 1989. Stackpole. 1st ed. M. P8. $12.50

ROSENDORFF, H.G. *Australian Contract Bridge Championships 1964 Perth.* nd. Sydney. VG/wrp. S1. $10.00

ROSENE, Walter. *Bobwhite Quail Life & Management.* 1969. New Brunswick. 2nd. ils. 418p. VG/G. B5. $60.00

ROSENFELD, Lulla. *Death & the I Ching.* 1981. Potter. 1st ed. NF/NF. P3. $18.00

ROSENFELD, Morris. *Sail-Ho!* 1947. NY. Maloney. 1st ed. 4to. ils. 112p. VG. T7. $35.00

ROSENGARTEN, Frederick. *Book of Spices.* 1969. 1st ed. NF/NF. S13. $75.00

ROSENKRANZ, George. *Everything You Always Wanted To Know About Trump Leads...* 1986. Louisville. 158p. F/wrp. S1. $7.00

ROSENQUIST, James. *James Rosenquist.* 1968. Nat Gallery Canada. ils. 92p. D2. $65.00

ROSENTHAL, Franz. *Aramaic Handbook.* 1967. Wiesbaden. Harrassowitz. 1st ed. 4 parts. 2 fld pl. VG/wrp. W1. $60.00

ROSENTHAL, Franz. *Grammar of Biblical Aramaic.* 1983. Wiesbaden. Harrassowitz. 5th. 100p. VG/wrp. W1. $16.00

ROSENTHAL, Jacques. *Bibliotheca Magica et Pneumatica, Geheime Wissenschaften...* nd. rpt. 1/150. 8875 entries. F. A4. $125.00

ROSETTI, Dante Gabriel. *Ballads & Sonnets.* 1881. London. 1st ed. NF. C6. $125.00

ROSKE, Ralph. *Everyman's Eden: History of California.* 1968. Macmillan. 1st ed. 8vo. ils/maps. VG/tattered. T10. $45.00

ROSKILL, S.W. *Strategy of Sea Power.* 1962. London. Collins. VG/VG. A16. $37.50

ROSNER. *Growth of the Book Jacket.* 1954. Harvard. ils. 108p. xl. VG/dj. A4. $95.00

ROSS, A.M. *Blindfold.* 1978. Little Brn. 1st ed. F/F. P3. $13.00

ROSS, Angus. *Bradford Business.* 1974. John Long. 1st ed. F/F. P3. $22.00

ROSS, Christian K. *Father's Story of Charley Ross, the Kidnapped Child.* 1876. Phil. 1st ed. 431p. decor cloth. G. B18. $35.00

ROSS, Clinton. *Zuleka: Being History of Adventure in Life of Am Gentleman.* 1897. Lamson Wolffe. 1st ed. 8vo. 222p. teg. VG. W1. $25.00

ROSS, D.A. *Introduction to Oceanography.* 1970. Appleton Century Crofts. 384p. VG. D8. $8.50

ROSS, David D. *Argus Gambit.* 1989. St Martin. 1st ed. F/F. P3. $19.00

ROSS, Dudley T. *Devil on Horseback: Biography of the Notorious Jack Powers.* 1975. Valley Pub. 1st ed. 185p. F/F. E1. $30.00

ROSS, Frank A. *Bibliography of Negro Migration.* 1934. NY. 251p. VG+. M8. $75.00

ROSS, Frank. *Sleeping Dogs.* 1978. Atheneum. 1st ed. VG/VG. P3. $18.00

ROSS, Harry H. *Enchanting Isles of Erie.* 1949. np. 73p. VG. M20. $27.00

ROSS, Ivan T. *Requiem for a Schoolgirl.* 1961. Heinemann. 1st ed. VG/VG. P3. $28.00

ROSS, James R. *Jesse James.* 1988. Dragon. 1st ed. 280p. E1. $50.00

ROSS, Jonathan. *Burning of Billy Toober.* 1974. Walker. 1st ed. VG/VG. P3. $18.00

ROSS, Lillian. *Takes.* 1983. NY. 1st ed. dj. A17. $7.50

ROSS, Martin. *Last Parallel: Marine's War Journal.* 1957. NY. 3rd. 333p. dj. A17. $8.50

ROSS, Marvin C. *West of Alfred Jacob Miller.* 1968. OK U. revised/enlarged ed. 208p. VG/worn. T10. $65.00

ROSS, Nancy Wilson. *Farthest Reach: Oregon & Washington.* 1949. Knopf. 5th. 8vo. fld map. VG/dj. T10. $25.00

ROSS, Nancy Wilson. *I, My Ancestor.* 1950. Random. 1st ed. VG/VG. P3. $15.00

ROSSELLINI, Roberto. *War Trilogy.* 1973. Grossman. 1st ed. F/dj. A17. $15.00

ROSSER, J. ALlyn. *Bright Moves.* 1990. Northeastern. 1st ed. sgn Charles Simic. F/wrp. V1. $15.00

ROSSHANDLER, Leo. *Man-Eaters & Pretty Ladies.* 1972. NY. 2nd. ils/photos/drawings. F3. $25.00

ROSSITER, Clinton. *Federalist Papers.* 1961. Penguin. 560p. prt wrp. M11. $75.00

ROSSITER, Oscar. *Tetrasomy Two.* 1974. Doubleday. 1st ed. F/F. P3. $13.00

ROSTAND, Robert. *D'Artagnan Signature.* 1976. Putnam. 1st ed. VG/torn. P3. $13.00

ROSTEN, Leo. *Joys of Yiddish.* 1968. NY. 1st ed. VG/VG. B5. $27.50

ROSTEN, Leo. *Silky!* 1979. Harper Row. 1st ed. VG/VG. P3. $20.00

ROSTLER, William. *Hidden Worlds of Zandra.* 1983. Doubleday. 1st ed. F/F. G10. $10.00

ROSTOV, Mara. *Night Hunt.* 1979. Putnam. 1st ed. F/F. P3. $18.00

ROTERBERG, A. *New Era Card Tricks.* nd. NY. 284p. missing cover o/w contents VG. S1. $5.00

ROTH, Henry. *Nature's First Green.* 1979. NY. Targ. 1st ed. 1/350. sgn. F/F. B4. $100.00

ROTH, Holly. *Masks of Glass.* nd. BC. VG. P3. $4.00

ROTH, Holly. *Sleeper.* 1955. Simon Schuster. 1st ed. VG/torn. P3. $10.00

ROTH, Lillian. *I'll Cry Tomorrow.* 1954. Frederick Fell. 1st ed. NF/NF. B35. $40.00

ROTH, Philip. *Anatomy Lesson.* 1983. FSG. 1st ed. 1/300. sgn. F/case. C2. $125.00

ROTH, Philip. *Breast.* 1972. HRW. 1st ed. F/F. B35. $35.00

ROTH, Philip. *Counterlife.* 1986. Franklin Lib. 1st ed. sgn. leather. F. C2. $35.00

ROTH, Philip. *Ghost Writer.* 1979. FSG. 1st ed. NF/NF. B35. $20.00

ROTH, Philip. *Goodbye, Columbus.* 1959. Houghton Mifflin. 1st ed. author's 1st book. F/clip. B24. $500.00

ROTH, Philip. *Goodbye, Columbus.* 1959. Houghton Mifflin. 1st ed. author's 1st book. G/NF. H11. $280.00

ROTH, Philip. *Great American Novel.* 1973. HRW. 1st ed. NF/NF. B35. $20.00

ROTH, Philip. *My Life As a Man.* 1974. HRW. 1st ed/3rd. F/F. B35. $20.00

ROTH, Philip. *Operation Shylock: A Confession.* 1993. NY. ARC. F. w/pub card. C2. $30.00

ROTH, Philip. *Operation Shylock: A Confession.* 1993. Simon Schuster. 1st ed. F/F. H11. $25.00

ROTH, Philip. *Our Gang.* 1971. Random. 1st ed. F/F. B35. $35.00

ROTH, Philip. *Portnoy's Complaint.* 1969. Random. ltd ed. 1/600. sgn. F/dj/case. C2. $300.00

ROTH, Philip. *Portnoy's Complaint.* 1969. Random. 1st ed. F/NF. B35. $38.00

ROTH, Philip. *Portnoy's Complaint.* 1969. Random. 1st ed. NF/NF. M19. $25.00

ROTH, Philip. *Professor of Desire.* 1977. NY. 1st ed. sgn. NF/NF. C6. $55.00

ROTH, Philip. *Sabbath's Theater.* 1995. Houghton Mifflin. ARC. F/pict wrp. G10. $75.00

ROTH, Philip. *Zuckerman Unbound.* 1981. NY. 1st ed. 1/350. sgn. F/case. C2. $100.00

ROTH & ROTH. *James Dean.* 1983. Pomegranate Artbooks. 1st ed. inscr. photos by Sanford Roth. VG+/wrp. S9. $100.00

ROTHA, Paul. *Documentary Film.* 1968 (1952). NY. Communications Arts Books/Hastings. 3rd. F/VG. D2. $25.00

ROTHAUS, James. *Team History Series.* 1987. Creative Education. F. P8. $15.00

ROTHENBERG, Jerome. $B>R>M>T> Z>V>H>$. 1979. Perishable. ltd ed. 1/225. sgn. F. V1. $100.00

ROTHENBERG, Robert. *Group Medicine & Health Insurance in Action.* 1949. NY. 1st ed. 278p. VG. A13. $35.00

ROTHERT, Otto A. *Outlaws of Cave-In-Rock.* 1924. Cleveland. ils/biblio. 364p. VG. E1. $275.00

ROTHERY, Agnes. *Virginia: New Dominion.* 1940. Appleton Century. 1st ed. ils EH Suydam. 368p. VG/fair. B10. $20.00

ROTHSCHILD, A. *Lincoln, Master of Men.* 1906. Riverside. 8vo. 531p. navy cloth. xl. VG. T3. $20.00

ROTHSTEIN, Andrew. *Munich Conspiracy (1938).* 1958. London. 1st ed. 320p. VG/dj. A17. $15.00

ROTHWELL, Richard P. *Mineral Industry in the US & Other Countries...* 1893. NY. inscr to Pres Cleveland. 628p. VG. B14. $125.00

ROUNTHWAITE & SEATON. *Pocket Book of Marine Engineering Rules & Tables.* 1899. London. Griffin. 5th. 128 tables. 471p. full leather. T7. $65.00

ROUNTREE, Harry. *Animal Fun ABC.* ca 1900. Graham. lg 4to. sc. M5. $55.00

ROUSANIERE, John. *America's Cup Book 1851-1983.* 1983. Norton. 1st ed. 4to. VG/dj. T7. $45.00

ROUSE, Blair. *Letters of Ellen Glasgow.* 1958. Harcourt Brace. 1st ed. 384p. VG/G. B10. $35.00

ROUSE, John E. *Criollo Spanish Cattle in the Americas.* 1977. Norman, OK. 1st ed. 301p. F/VG. E1. $40.00

ROUSE, Parke Jr. *Cows on Campus: Williamsburg in Bygone Days.* 1973. Richmond. Dietz. 1st ed. sgn. 8vo. 219p. VG/VG. B11. $40.00

ROUSSEAU, Jean Jacques. *Emilius; or, Essay on Education.* 1763. London. Nourse Vaillant. 2 vol. 1st ed thus. contemporary calf. G1. $575.00

ROUSSEL, Raymond. *How I Wrote Certain of My Books.* 1977. NY. Sun. VG/wrp. V1. $10.00

ROVIN, Jeff. *Mars!* 1978. Corwin. 1st ed. F/NF. G10. $10.00

ROWAN, A.N. *Of Mice, Models & Men.* 1984. Albany. 8vo. 323p. VG. B1. $26.50

ROWBOTHAM, Sally Smith. *Virginia's Historic Trees...* 1931. np. phot. 22p. VG. B10. $45.00

ROWBOTTOM & SUSSKIND. *Electricity & Medicine: History of Their Interaction.* 1984. San Francisco. 1st ed. 303p. VG. A13. $60.00

ROWE, Anne E. *Enchanted Country: Northern Writers in the South 1865-1910.* 1978. LSU. 155p. VG/VG. B10. $15.00

ROWE, Anne. *Century of Change in Guatemalan Textiles.* 1981. NY. 1st ed. 151p. wrp. F3. $30.00

ROWE, John. *Hard Rock Men. Cornish & American Mining Frontier.* 1974. NY. 1st ed. ils/index. 322p. VG/VG. B5. $35.00

ROWLAND, Laura J. *Shinju.* 1994. Random. 1st ed. author's 1st book. F/F. H11. $30.00

ROWLEY, G. *Illustrated Encyclopedia of Succulents.* 1978. Crown. 4to. ils. hc. clip dj. B1. $40.00

ROWLINSON. *Tennyson's Fixations, Psychoanalysis & Topics...* 1994. VA U. 205p. F/F. A4. $35.00

ROWNTREE, Lester. *Flowering Shrubs of California.* 1948. Stanford. 2nd. 317p. VG/dj. A10. $25.00

ROWSE, A.L. *Shakespeare's Southampton.* 1965. Harper Row. 1st ed. 323p. VG/clip. M20. $25.00

ROWSWELL, A.K. *Diamond Laughs.* 1948. Ft Pitt Brewing. 1st ed. ils. G+. P8. $35.00

ROY, Claude. *Modigliani.* 1958. Cleveland. World. ils. 136p. cloth. dj. D2. $25.00

ROYSE, Isaac. *History of 115th Regiment of Illinois Volunteer Infantry...* 1900. Terre Haute. 1st ed. ils/maps. 405p. VG. B5. $175.00

ROYSTER, Vermont. *My Own, My Country's Time.* 1983. Algonquin. 8vo. 351p. brn cloth. VG/clip. P4. $22.50

RUARK, Robert. *Didn't Know It Was Loaded.* 1948. Garden City. 1st ed. VG/G. B5. $37.50

RUARK, Robert. *Honey Badger.* 1965. McGraw Hill. 1st ed. F/VG+. B4. $85.00

RUARK, Robert. *Horn of the Hunter.* 1953. Garden City. 2nd. pres. VG/G. B5. $100.00

RUARK, Robert. *Old Man & Boy.* 1957. NY. 1st ed. VG/VG. B5. $40.00

RUARK, Robert. *Old Man's Boy Grows Older.* 1961. NY. 1st ed. VG/VG. B5. $40.00

RUARK, Robert. *Use Enough Gun.* 1966. NAL. 1st ed. F/NF. H11. $55.00

RUARK, Robert. *Use Enough Gun.* 1966. NAL. 1st ed. 333p. VG/dj. M20. $45.00

RUARK, Robert. *Women.* 1967. NY. 1st ed. VG/VG. B5. $50.00

RUBENS, Jeff. *Win at Poker.* 1968. NY. 218p. VG. S1. $10.00

RUBENSTEIN, Helena. *Food for Beauty.* 1938. Ives Washburn. 1st ed. ils Robert L Leonard. VG/VG+. B4. $85.00

RUBIN, Barry. *Revolution Until Victory?* 1994. Cambridge. Harvard. 1st ed. 271p. NF/dj. W1. $18.00

RUBIN, Louis. *No Place on Earth: Ellen Glasgow, James Branch Cabell...* 1959. TX U. sgn. 81p. VG. B10. $20.00

RUBINSTEIN, Gillian. *Galax-Arena.* 1995. Simon Schuster. 1st Am ed. F/F. G10. $10.00

RUBY & RUBY. *Chinook Indians...Civilization of the Am Indian Series.* 1976. Norman. 1st ed. photos/ils/index. 349p. F/F. E1. $50.00

RUBY & RUBY. *Indians of the Pacific Northwest.* 1981. Norman. 1st ed. biblio/maps. 294p. F/F. E1. $65.00

RUBY & RUBY. *Spokane Indians... Civilization of Am Indian Series.* 1970. Norman, OK. 1st ed. photos/map. 346p. F/F. E1. $50.00

RUDD, RUDD & WHITE. *And Three Small Fishes.* 1974. McClure. F/VG. B10. $8.00

RUDDER. *Literature in Spain in English Translation...* 1975. np. 637p. F/F. A4. $50.00

RUDINGER, N. *Rudinger Atlas of the Osseous Anatomy of the Human Ear.* 1874. Boston. 9 orig mtd photos. trans CJ Blake. red portfolio. B14. $325.00

RUDMAN, Mark. *Rider.* 1994. Wesleyan. 1st ed. F/wrp. V1. $10.00

RUDNIK, Raphael. *Lesson From the Cyclops.* 1967. Random. 1st ed. assn copy. F/NF. V1. $20.00

RUDOLPH, Marguerita. *Magic Sack.* (1967). McGraw Hill. ils Ralph Pinto. pict gr cloth. xl. G. T5. $12.00

RUDOLPH, Wolfgang. *Sailor Souvenirs.* 1985. Leipzig. ils. 151p. VG. T7. $22.00

RUDORFF, Raymond. *Belle Epoque.* 1973. 1st ed. NF/VG. S13. $18.00

RUE, Leonard Lee. *Game Birds of North America.* 1973. Outdoor Life/Harper Row. ils. VG/G+. P12. $14.00

RUEDEBUSCH, Emil F. *Old & New Ideal. Solution of Part of the Social Question...* 1897. Mayville, WI. 2nd. 347p. red cloth. VG. B14. $75.00

RUFF, Ann. *Unsung Heroes of Texas.* 1985. Lone Star. 126p. pb. F. E1. $15.00

RUGE, Friedrich. *Der Seekrieg 1939-45.* 1954. Stuttgart. Koehler. VG. A17. $15.00

RUGGERO, Ed. *28 North Yankee.* 1990. Pocket. 1st ed. F/F. H11. $25.00

RUGGLES, Eleanor. *Prince of Players: Edwin Booth.* 1953. Norton. 1st ed. cloth. VG. D2. $15.00

RUGOFF, Milton. *Beechers.* 1981. NY. 1st ed. 653p. dj. A17. $15.00

RUHEN, Olaf. *Tangaroa's Godchild.* 1962. Little Brn. 1st ed. 346p. VG/worn. P4. $25.00

RUKEYSER, Muriel. *Gates.* 1976. McGraw Hill. 1st ed. F/NF. V1. $20.00

RUKEYSER, Muriel. *Selected Poems.* 1951. New Directions. 1st ed. NF/NF. V1. $35.00

RULFO, Juan. *Burning Plain & Other Stories.* 1970. Austin, TX. 2nd. inscr. 175p. F3. $15.00

RUMBALL. *Rare Bibles: An Introduction for Collectors & a Checklist...* 1954. 2nd/final revised ed. 1/600. F. A4. $165.00

RUNDELL, Walter Jr. *Early Texas Oil.* 1977. TX A&M. 3rd. 4to. 260p. F/dj. T10. $35.00

RUNES, D. *Diary & Sundry Observations of Thomas Alva Edison.* 1948. NY. 247p. F/dj. A17. $20.00

RUNYON, Damon. *In Our Town. Twenty Seven Slices of Life.* 1946. NY. 1st ed. ils Garth Williams. 120p. silvered brn cloth. F. H3. $40.00

RUNYON, Damon. *Tents of Trouble.* 1911. NY. 1st ed. author's 1st book. G/sans. B5. $135.00

RUPORT, A. *Art of Cockfighting: A Handbook for the Beginner...* 1949. Devin-Adair. 1st ed. 211p. NF/dj. M20. $67.00

RUSCH, Kristine Katherine. *Best of Pulphouse: The Hardback Magazine.* 1991. St Martin. 1st ed. F/NF. G10. $10.00

RUSCH, Kristine Katherine. *Pulphouse: The Hardcover Magazine #4, SF.* 1989. Pulphouse. 1/1000. cloth. AN/sans. M21. $20.00

RUSH, Benjamin. *Medical Inquires & Observations.* 1789. Phil. vol 1 only. xl. modern bdg. B14. $350.00

RUSH, James. *Philosophy of the Human Voice.* 1833. Phil. 2nd. ils. 432p. calf. VG. B14. $75.00

RUSH, James. *Philosophy of the Human Voice.* 1859. Lippincott. 5th. 677p. detached spine. G1. $50.00

RUSH, Norman. *Mating.* 1991. Knopf. 1st ed. inscr. F/F. B2. $65.00

RUSH, Oscar. *Open Range & Bunk House Philosophy.* 1930. Denver, CO. 2nd. 118p. professional rpr. w/sgn typewritten note. E1. $65.00

RUSHDIE, Salman. *Haroun & the Sea of Stories.* 1990. Viking. ARC. w/promo material. F/F. B35. $35.00

RUSHDIE, Salman. *Imaginary Homelands.* 1991. Viking/Granta. 1st ed. rem mk. F/F. B35. $35.00

RUSHDIE, Salman. *Jaguar Smile.* 1987. Viking. 1st ed. rem mk. F/F. B35. $25.00

RUSHDIE, Salman. *Moor's Last Sigh.* 1995. NY. ARC/1st Am ed. 1/1000. sgn. F/decor wrp/2-part case. C2. $75.00

RUSHDIE, Salman. *Satanic Verses.* 1988. Viking. 1st ed. F/F. B35. $55.00

RUSHDIE, Salman. *Satanic Verses.* 1989. Viking. 1st ed. NF/F. M23. $40.00

RUSHFORTH, Peters. *Kindergarten.* 1979. Hamish Hamilton. 1st ed. author's 1st ed. AN/dj. C2. $75.00

RUSK, Ralph Leslie. *Literature of the Middle Western Frontier.* 1962. Frederick Ungar. 1st ed thus. VG+. A18. $40.00

RUSKIN, John. *Unto This Last. Four Essays.* 1907. Hammersmith. 1st ed. 1/300. limp vellum. VG. C6. $225.00

RUSS, Joanna. *Zanzibar Cat.* 1983. Arkham. 1st ed. 1/3526. F/F. T2. $55.00

RUSSELL, Alan. *Hotel Detective.* 1994. Mysterious. 1st ed. F/F. H11/M23. $30.00

RUSSELL, Andy. *Grizzly Country.* 1967. Knopf. ils. VG/VG. P12. $7.00

RUSSELL, Andy. *Trails of a Wilderness Wanderer.* 1971. Knopf. 2nd. 8vo. 298p. F/dj. T10. $25.00

RUSSELL, B. *In Praise of Idleness.* 1935. NY. 1st ed. VG/G. B5. $25.00

RUSSELL, Bertrand. *Authority of the Individual.* 1949. Unwin Bros. 1st Eng ed. F/F. B35. $45.00

RUSSELL, Bertrand. *Common Sense & Nuclear Warfare.* 1959. NY. 1st Am ed. NF/NF clip. N3. $15.00

RUSSELL, Bertrand. *Human Society in Ethics & Politics.* 1955. Simon Schuster. NF/VG. M19. $25.00

RUSSELL, Bertrand. *Wisdom of the West.* (1959). Doubleday. 320p. F/dj. B22. $9.00

RUSSELL, Charles Edward. *Greatest Trust in the World.* 1905. NY. 1st ed. 252p. G. E1. $40.00

RUSSELL, Charles Lord. *Diary of a Visit to the USA in the Year 1883.* 1910. NY. 8vo. ils. 220p. gr cloth. x. T3. $20.00

RUSSELL, Charles M. *Good Medicine, Memories of the Real West.* (1930). Garden City. ils. 162p. F/worn. E1. $55.00

RUSSELL, Charles M. *Trails Plowed Under.* (1936). NY. later ed. 211p. F/NF. E1. $45.00

RUSSELL, Don. *Lives & Legends of Buffalo Bill.* 1960. Norman, OK. 1st ed. biblio/index. 514p. VG/dj. E1. $65.00

RUSSELL, Edward C. *Bridge at a Glance: Auction-Contract.* 1930. np. sm format. 28p. VG/wrp. S1. $8.00

RUSSELL, Eric Frank. *Men, Martians & Machines.* 1984. Crown Classic of Modern SF Vol 1. F/F. G10. $10.00

RUSSELL, Florence Kimball. *Woman's Journey Through the Phillipines on a Cable Ship...* 1907. Boston. Page. 1st ed. inscr. 40 pl/fld map. 270p. teg. gr cloth. NF. B11. $85.00

RUSSELL, H. Diane. *Jacques Callot: Prints & Related Drawings.* 1975. np. ils. 351p. D2. $65.00

RUSSELL, Irwin. *Poems.* 1888. Century. 4th. 112p. VG. B10. $25.00

RUSSELL, Jacqueline. *If You Like Horses.* 1932. Houghton Mifflin. 12mo. G+. O3. $25.00

RUSSELL, James. *Evolution of Function of Public Health Administration...* 1895. Glasgow. 1st ed. 141p. xl. A13. $75.00

RUSSELL, Jeffrey Burton. *Devil: Perceptions of Evil From Antiquity...* 1977. Cornell. 1st ed. 8vo. 275p. F. T10. $35.00

RUSSELL, Mary La Fetra. *Mother Goose.* 1924. Gabriel. 4to. 12 linen p. VG. M5. $25.00

RUSSELL, Ray. *Haunted Castles: Complete Gothic Tales.* 1985. Maclay. 1st ed. F/F. R10. $10.00

RUSSELL, Ross. *Jazz Style in Kansas City & the Southwest.* 1971. Berkeley. 1st ed. NF/VG. B2. $30.00

RUSSELL, T. *Diamond Bessie Murder & the Rothschild Trial.* 1971. Waco, TX. 1st ed. sgn. photos/biblio. 183p. F/F. E1. $30.00

RUSSELL, Thomas H. *Sinking of the Titanic.* 1912. LH Walter. ils. 320p. blk stp red bdg/pict label. fair. P12. $12.00

RUSSELL, Thomas H. *Sinking of the Titanic.* 1912. np. 8vo. ils. 320p. red cloth. VG. T3. $30.00

RUSSELL, W. Clark. *Frozen Pirate.* ca 1900. Lupton. gilt bl bdg. G+. P12. $4.00

RUSSELL, W.H. *Atlantic Telegraph.* 1972. David/Charles Rpts. VG/VG. A16. $47.50

RUSSELL, W.L. *Structural Geology for Petroleum Geologists.* 1955. McGraw Hill. 427p. F. D8. $25.00

RUSSELL, Walter. *Age of Innocence.* 1904. Dodd Mead. 1st ed. 8vo. VG. M5. $40.00

RUSSELL, Walter. *Book of Early Whispering.* 1949. Waynesboro, VA. U of Science & Philosophy. ltd ed. sgn. 103p. VG. B11. $15.00

RUSSELL-WOOD, A.J.R. *Fidalgos & Philanthropists: Santa Casa da Misericordia...* 1968. Berkley. 1st ed. 429p. dj. A13. $25.00

RUSSEN, David. *Iter Lunare.* 1976. Gregg. 1st separate Am ed. F/sans. G10. $15.00

RUSSO, Richard. *Nobody's Fool.* 1993. Random. 1st ed. F/F. M23. $25.00

RUST, Edwin Grey. *Those Dexters.* 1929. Michie. 1st ed. 82p. G. B10. $10.00

RUST, Fred Winslow. *Road Ahead & Bypaths.* 1944. Boston. Humphries. sgn. 12mo. VG. B11. $15.00

RUST, Fred Winslow. *Unto the Hills.* 1935. Boston. Humphries. sgn. 12mo. VG. B11. $15.00

RUTH, Babe. *Babe Ruth's Baseball Book for 1932.* 1932. Syndicate. ils/photos. G+. P8. $150.00

RUTH, Babe. *Babe Ruth's Big Book of Baseball.* 1935. Reilly Lee. Quaker Oats premium. photos. VG. P8. $90.00

RUTHERFORD, Ward. *Hitler's Propaganda Machine.* 1978. Grosset Dunlap. 192p. split hinge. A17. $18.50

RUTLEDGE, Archibald. *Deep River: The Complete Poems.* 1960. Columbia, SC. 1st ed. 8vo. 635p. gilt gr buckram. F/VG. H3. $85.00

RUTLEDGE, Archibald. *From the Hills to the Sea.* 1958. Indianapolis. VG/VG. B5. $50.00

RUTLEDGE, Archibald. *Life's Extras.* 1946. Fleming. Revell. sgn. ils. VG. B10. $45.00

RUTLEDGE, Archibald. *Santee Paradise.* 1956. Indianapolis. VG/VG. B5. $50.00

RUTLEDGE, Archibald. *Those Were the Days.* 1955. Richmond, VA. Dietz. 462p. VG. B18. $37.50

RUTT, Richard. *Korean Works & Days.* 1964. Tuttle. 1st ed. sgn. pl. 231p. F/F. B11. $30.00

RUTTER, Owen. *Triumphant Pilgrimage.* 1937. Lippincott. 1st ed. 8vo. pl/map. 296p. xl. VG. W1. $45.00

RUXTON, George F. *Life in the Far West.* 1983 (1849). Time Life. rpt. 312p. leather. E1. $20.00

RYAN, Abram J. *Poems: Patriotic, Religious, Miscellaneous.* 1880. John B Piet. A prt. ils. 347p. G. B10. $75.00

RYAN, Alan. *Night Visions 1: All Original Stories.* 1984. Dark Harvest. 1st ed. 1/300. sgns. F/F/case. G10. $300.00

RYAN, Cheli Duran. *PAZ.* 1971. Macmillan. 1st ed. 12mo. 39p. VG+/G. C14. $7.00

RYAN, David D. *Falls of the James.* 1975. Richmond, VA. 2nd. sgn. 8vo. G. B11. $10.00

RYAN, David D. *Four Days in 1865: Fall of Richmond.* 1993. Cadmus Comm. inscr. 161p. VG/VG. B10. $18.00

RYAN, J.C. *Revolt Along the Rio Grande.* 1964. San Antonio. 1st ed. map ep. 234p. F/NF. E1. $40.00

RYAN, Nolan. *King of the Hill.* 1992. Harper Collins. 1st ed. F/F. P8. $12.50

RYAN. *Civil War Literature of Ohio, a Bibliography...* 1994. rpt of 1991 ed. 1/300. 527p. F. A4. $60.00

RYCAULT, Paul. *History of the Turks...* 1700. London. folio. 626p. 18th-C suede/rebacked. VG. B14. $300.00

RYDELL, Raymond A. *Cape Horn to the Pacific.* 1952. Berkeley. 213p. VG/dj. T7. $40.00

RYDER, Jonathan; see Ludlum, Robert.

RYDIORD, John. *Kansas Placenames.* 1972. OK U. 1st ed. 613p. pb. F. E1. $40.00

RYLANT, Cynthia. *Missing May.* 1992. Orchard Books. 2nd. 89p. F/F. T5. $25.00

RYMAN, Geoff. *Child Garden.* 1989. London. Unwin Hyman. 1st ed. sgn. F/dj. M21. $50.00

RYMAN, Rebecca. *Olivia & Jai.* 1990. NY. 1st ed. NF/F. H11. $20.00

RYNNING, Thomas H. *Gun Notches: Life Story of a Cowboy-Soldier.* 1931. NY. 332p. VG. E1. $45.00

RZEDOWSKI & RZEDOWSKI. *Flora Fanerogamica del Valle de Mexico. Vol I.* 1979. Mexico. sgn. 403p. sc. VG. B26. $36.00

SAAS, Herbert Ravenel. *Look Back to Glory.* 1933. Bobbs Merrill. 1st ed. 1/500. sgn. reading copy. B10. $25.00

SAAVEDRA, Bautista. *Defensa de los Derechos de Bolivia Ante el Gobierno...* 1906. Buenos Aires. Peuser. 2 vol. 24 lg fld maps. xl. poor. O7. $75.00

SABBAG, Robert. *Too Tough To Die.* 1992. NY. 293p. F. E1. $30.00

SABERHAGEN, Fred. *First Book of Lost Swords: Woundhealer's Story.* 1986. Tor. 1st ed. F/F. G10. $10.00

SABERHAGEN, Fred. *Third Book of Lost Swords: Stonecutters Story.* 1988. Tor. 1st ed. NF/dj. M21. $12.00

SABIN, Joseph. *Dictionary of Books Relating to America.* (1868-1874). facsimile. 14 vol in 2. red cloth. VG. T3. $130.00

SABLOFF, Jeremy. *Cities of Ancient Mexico.* 1989. Thames Hudson. 1st ed. 224p. dj. F3. $25.00

SABUDA. *Christmas Alphabet.* 1994. np. popups. F. A4. $50.00

SADAT, Jehan. *Woman of Egypt.* 1987. Simon Schuster. 1st ed. 8vo. 478p. VG. W1. $16.00

SADE, Mark; see Blake, Roger.

SADER, Guy. *Forgotten Soldier.* 1967. NY. 1st ed. VG/VG. B5. $40.00

SADLEIR, Michael. *XIX Century Fiction.* 1951. 2 vol. ltd ed. ils. VG. A4. $450.00

SADLER, Mark; see Lynds, Dennis.

SADLIER, Michael. *Excursions in Victorian Bibliography.* 1974. np. 248p. F/F. A4. $85.00

SAFADI, Yasin Hamid. *Islamic Calligraphy.* 1978. Thames Hudson. 1st ed. 200 ils. 144p. VG/stiff wrp. W1. $18.00

SAFFORD, W.E. *Classification of Genus Annona With Descriptions...* 1914. WA, DC. ils/pl. B26. $17.50

SAFIR, Natalie. *Moving Into Seasons.* 1981. Golden Quill. poet's 1st book. F/F. V1. $20.00

SAFIRE, William. *Eye of Nixon.* 1972. NY. 1st ed. pub bookplate. VG/dj. S9. $40.00

SAFRASTIAN, Arshak. *Kurds & Kurdistan.* 1948. London. Harvill/Mouton. 1st ed. ils/map ep. red cloth. VG. B14. $75.00

SAGAN, Carl. *Comet.* 1985. Random. 2nd. 4to. 398p. VG/VG. K5. $16.00

SAGAN, Carl. *Contact.* 1985. Simon Schuster. 1st ed. F/F clip. H11. $25.00

SAGAN, Carl. *Murmurs of Earth: Voyager Interstellar Record.* 1978. Random. 1st ed. rem mk. NF/F. G10. $18.00

SAGAN, Francoise. *Bonjour Tristesse.* 1955. Dutton. 1st Am ed. F/VG+. B4. $100.00

SAGAN, Hans. *Beat the Odds: Microcomputer Simulations of Casino Games.* 1980. NJ. 210p. VG/wrp. S1. $4.00

SAGENDORF. *Popeye: First 50 Years.* 1979. ils. F. M13. $25.00

SAGON-KING, Alfred F. *Changing Seaway.* 1985. Ontario. Stonehouse. 1st ed. G/wrp. A16. $5.00

SAIKAL, Amin. *Rise & Fall of the Shah.* 1980. Princeton. 1st ed. 8vo. pl/map. NF. W1. $22.00

SAINT, H.F. *Memoirs of an Invisible Man.* 1987. Atheneum. 1st ed. F/F. H11. $35.00

SAINT-AUGUSTINE. *Confessions of St Augustine.* 1962. LEC. 1st ed. 1/1500. ils/sgn Legrand. 296p. F/case. C2. $100.00

SAINT-GAUDENS, Homer. *American Artist & His Times.* 1941. VG. D2. $40.00

SAINT-JOHN, David; see Hunt, E. Howard.

SAINT-JOHN, Harold. *Flora of Southeastern Washington & Adjacent ID.* 1937. Pullman. 1st ed. ils/map. 531p. B26. $30.00

SAINT-JOHN, Harold. *Plants of the Headwaters of the St John River, Maine.* 1929. Pullman. ils/photos/map. red cloth. B26. $25.00

SALAH, Said. *Panorama of Saudi Arabia.* 1975. Beirut. 1st ed. ils. 416p. NF/dj. W1. $45.00

SALAMAN, Redcliffe N. *History & Social Influence of the Potatoe.* 1949. Cambridge. 685p. VG/dj. A10. $75.00

SALANAVE, Leon E. *Lightning & Its Spectrum.* 1980. AZ U. obl 4to. 136p. VG/VG. K5. $40.00

SALE, Roger. *Seattle, Past to Present.* 1976. Seattle. 2nd. 8vo. 273p. F/dj. T10. $25.00

SALES, R.H. *Underground Warfare at Butte.* 1964. Caldwell. 1st ed. VG/VG. B5. $30.00

SALIBA, George. *History of Arabic Astronomy.* 1994. NY U. 1st ed. 8vo. 340p. VG. K5. $40.00

SALINGER, J.D. *Catcher in the Rye.* 1951. Boston. BOMC. F/F 1st state dj. A17. $150.00

SALINGER, J.D. *Franny & Zooey.* 1961. Little Brn. 1st ed. NF/NF. H4. $50.00

SALINGER, J.D. *Franny & Zooey.* 1962. Heinemann. 1st ed. F/NF. A17. $45.00

SALINGER, J.D. *Kit Book for Soldiers, Sailors & Marines.* 1943. Consolidated. 1st ed/2nd state. 336p. NF/box. M20. $175.00

SALINGER, J.D. *Nine Stories.* 1953. Little Brn. 1st ed. VG/G. M19. $500.00

SALINGER, J.D. *Raise High the Roofbeam Carpenters.* 1959. Boston. 1st ed. VG/VG. B5. $35.00

SALINGER, Wendy. *Folly River.* 1980. Dutton. 1st ed. assn copy. F/NF. V1. $15.00

SALISBURY, Harrison. *900 Days: Siege of Leningrad.* 1969. BC. 635p. dj. A17. $10.00

SALISBURY & SALISBURY. *Here Rolled the Covered Wagons.* 1977. Bonanza. rpt. 264p. F/F. E1. $35.00

SALLANDER. *Bibliotheca Walleriana, Books Ils History of Medicine...* nd. 2 vol in 1. rpt of 1955 ed. 1/400. F. A4. $135.00

SALLEY, A.S. *History of Orangeburg, SC.* 1898. SC. fld maps. G. B30. $125.00

SALLIS, James. *Black Hornet.* 1994. Carroll Graf. 1st ed. F/F. H11. $30.00

SALLIS, James. *Long-Legged Fly.* 1992. Carroll Graf. 1st ed. author's 1st book. F/dj H11/M23/T2. $30.00

SALLIS, James. *Moth.* 1993. Carroll Graf. 1st ed. F/F. H11. $35.00

SALMERON, Zarate. *Relaciones.* 1966. Horn Wallace. 1st ed. 122p. F/VG. E1. $30.00

SALTEN, Felix. *Fairy Tales From Near & Far.* 1946. Philosophical Lib. 4to. VG/G. B17. $8.50

SALTER, James. *Chance in a Million: Press deWar.* 1993. facsimile. 1/300. sgn/#d. 4to. F. C4. $125.00

SALTER, James. *Dusk & Other Stories.* 1988. North Point. 1st ed. F/F. B4. $65.00

SALTER, James. *Dusk & Other Stories.* 1988. North Point. 1st ed. VG+/VG+. A20. $20.00

SALTER, James. *Light Years.* 1974. Random. UP. NF/wrp. B4. $250.00

SALTER, James. *Solo Faces.* 1979. Little Brn. 1st ed. rem mk. F/NF. B4. $45.00

SALTER, James. *Solo Faces.* 1979. Little Brn. 1st ed. 8vo. VG/dj. S9. $45.00

SALTER, Mary Jo. *Sunday Skaters.* 1994. Knopf. UP. F/NF yel wrp. V1. $25.00

SALTER, Mary Jo. *Unfinished Painting.* 1989. Knopf. 1st ed. F/F. V1. $25.00

SALTUS, Edgar. *Imperial Orgy: Account of the Tsars From the First to Last.* 1920. Boni Liveright. 237p. bl cloth. VG. B14. $100.00

SALVATORE, R.A. *Sword of Bedwyr.* 1995. Warner. 3rd. VG+/dj. M21. $7.50

SALVERTE, Eusebe. *Philosophy of Magic.* 1846. London. Bentley. 2 vol. 1st ed. 8vo. VG. C6. $175.00

SALZ, Beate. *Human Element in Industrialization.* 1955. WI. 265p. wrp. F3. $15.00

SALZMAN, Mark. *Laughing Sutra.* 1991. Random. 1st ed. F/F. H11. $50.00

SAMBON, Arthur. *Catalogue des Fresques de Boscoreale.* 1903. Paris. Canessa. 4to. 10 chromolithographs. 26p. xl. T10. $300.00

SAMMONS, Sonny. *Keepers of Echowah.* 1995. Atlanta. Cherokee. 1st ed. F/F. M23. $30.00

SAMORA, Julian. *Gunpowder Justice: A Reassessment of the Texas Rangers.* 1979. Notre Dame, IN. 179p. F/F. E1. $20.00

SAMPSON, E.N. *American Stampless Cover Catalog.* 1978. 8vo. 280p. brn cloth. VG. T3. $30.00

SAMPSON, Emma Speed. *Billy & the Major: A Sequel to Miss Minerva's Baby.* 1934 (1920). Chicago. 15th. 12mo. NF/G+. C8. $55.00

SAMPSON, Emma Speed. *Miss Minerva's Baby.* 1920 (1920). Chicago. Reilly Lee. 2nd. ils Donahey. NF/G+. C8. $55.00

SAMPSON, Emma Speed. *Miss Minerva's Neighbors.* 1929. Reilly Lee. possible 1st ed. 12mo. F/VG. C8. $65.00

SAMPSON, Henry T. *Blacks in Black & White: A Source Book on Black Films.* 1977. Scarecrow. 1st ed. 8vo. 333p. F/sans. T10. $25.00

SAMS, Ferrol. *Widow's Mite.* 1987. Peachtree. 1st ed. F/F. B35. $32.00

SAMSON, Joan. *Auctioneer.* 1975. Simon Schuster. 1st ed. F/NF. H11. $20.00

SAMTER, Max. *Excerpts From Classics in Allergy.* 1969. Columbus. 117p. VG. A13. $25.00

SAMUELS, Samuel. *From the Forcastle to the Cabin.* 1924. Lauriat. ils. 308p. VG-. P12. $15.00

SAMUELS & SAMUELS. *Frederic Remington, a Biography.* 1982. Garden City. 1st ed. 537p. F/F. E1. $60.00

SAMUELSON, Nancy B. *Dalton Gang Family: A Genealogical Study...* 1989. np. photos. 20p. wrp. E1. $10.00

SANBORN, B.X.; see Ballinger, Bill.

SANCHEZ, Joseph P. *Spanish Bluecoats: Catalonian Volunteers in Northwestern...* 1990. NM U. 1st ed. 8vo. ils/maps/plans/biblio. 196p. F/sans. T10. $30.00

SANCHEZ, Sonia. *We a BaddDDD People.* 1970. Detroit. Broadside Pr. 1st ed. inscr/dtd 1971. F/stapled wrp. B4. $85.00

SANCHEZ, Thomas. *Mile Zero.* 1989. Knopf. 1st ed. inscr/dtd. F/F. A20. $27.00

SANCHEZ, Thomas. *Native Notes From the Land of Earthquake & Fire.* 1979. Sandpiper. ltd ed. sgn. ils/sgn Stephanie Sanchez. 8vo. F/wrp. B11. $40.00

SANCHEZ, Thomas. *Zoot-Suit Murders.* 1978. Dutton. 1st ed. inscr. F/NF. S9. $60.00

SANDAGE, Allan. *Hubble Atlas of Galaxies.* 1961. WA, DC. ils. 82p text. gilt-silvered cloth. VG. K5. $50.00

SANDBURG, Carl. *Breathing Tokens.* 1978. np. 1st ed. 118 previously unpub poems. F/VG+. V1. $15.00

SANDBURG, Carl. *Lincoln Collector.* 1950. NY. 344p. VG+/dj. B18. $37.50

SANDBURG, Carl. *Lincoln's Devotional.* 1957. Channel. 1st ed. F/NF. V1. $30.00

SANDBURG, Carl. *Rootabaga Pigeons.* 1923. Harcourt Brace. 1st ed. ils/sgn Petersham. VG/G+. P2. $185.00

SANDBURG, Carl. *Rootabaga Stories.* 1988. HBJ. 1st ed. ils Michael Hague. F/VG. B17. $15.00

SANDERS, Alvin Howard. *At the Sign of the Stock Yard Inn...* 1915. Chicago. 1st ed. ils. 322p. 3-quarter leather. professional rpr. E1. $150.00

SANDERS, Charles R. *Carlyle's Friendships & Other Studies.* 1977. Durham. Duke. 342p. NF/NF. M8. $35.00

SANDERS, Charles R. *Strachery Family 1588-1932: Their Writings...* 1953. Duke. 337p. NF/NF. M8. $35.00

SANDERS, Daniel C. *History of the Indian Wars With the First Settlers...* 1812. Montpelier, VT. 1st ed. 16mo. 319p. contemporary calf. VG. C6. $950.00

SANDERS, Dori. *Clover.* 1990. Chapel Hill. Algonquin. ARC. inscr. F/wrp. B4. $85.00

SANDERS, Ed. *Family: Story of Charles Manson's Dune Buggy Attack...* 1971. Dutton. 1st ed. NF/clip. B4. $100.00

SANDERS, James A. *Near Eastern Archaeology in 20th Century.* 1970. Doubleday. 1st ed. 8vo. ils. VG. W1. $25.00

SANDERS, Lawrence. *Anderson Tapes.* 1970. 1st ed. MTI. author's 1st book. NF/VG. S13. $25.00

SANDERS, Lawrence. *McNally's Luck.* 1992. Putnam. 1st ed. F/F. N4. $20.00

SANDERS, Lawrence. *Sixth Commandment.* 1979. Putnam. 1st ed. VG/VG. N4. $20.00

SANDERS, Lawrence. *Sullivan's Sting.* 1990. 1st ed. VG/VG. K2. $10.00

SANDERS, Rosanne. *Remembering Garden.* 1980. NY. ils. F/dj. B26. $15.00

SANDERS & DINSMORE. *History of the Percheron Horse.* 1917. Breeders Gazette. 1st ed. VG. O3. $95.00

SANDERSON, Ruth. *Story of the First Christmas.* 1994. Atlanta. Turner. 8vo. 5 3-D scenes. M/ribbon ties. T10. $25.00

SANDERSON, T.J. Cobden. *Arts & Crafts Movement.* 1905. Hammersmith. 1st ed. pres. full vellum. F. C6. $225.00

SANDERSON, T.J. Cobden. *Journals of...1879-1922.* 1926. np. 2 vol. 1/1050. 862p. xl. VG. A4. $125.00

SANDERSON. *National Maritime Museum, Catalogue of the Library...* 1976. np. 2 parts. 12 pl. 2318 entries. F. A4. $95.00

SANDFORD, John. *Eyes of Prey.* 1991. Putnam. 1st ed. F/F. H11. $40.00

SANDFORD, John. *Fool's Run.* 1989. Holt. 1st ed. as by John Camp. F/F. H11. $50.00

SANDFORD, John. *Rules of Prey.* 1989. Putnam. ARC/1st ed. F/pict wrp. T2. $65.00

SANDFORD, John. *Rules of Prey.* 1989. Putnam. 1st ed. NF/F. H11. $60.00

SANDFORD, John. *Shadow Prey.* 1990. Putnam. 1st ed. F/F. H11. $50.00

SANDFORD, Lettice. *Sappho. The Text Arranged With Translations...* 1932. Manaton. Devon. Christopher Sandford. 1/250. Greek/Eng text. teg. case. B24. $275.00

SANDOR, Marjorie. *Night of Music.* 1989. Ecco. 1st collected ed. F/F. G10. $30.00

SANDOZ, Mari. *Buffalo Hunters.* 1954. NY. 1st ed. biblio. 372p. F. E1. $40.00

SANDOZ, Mari. *Cattlemen: From the Rio Grande Across the Far Marias.* 1958. NY. 1st ed. 527p. F/dj. B5/E1. $40.00

SANDOZ, Mari. *Fantastic Memories.* 1944. Garden City. 1st ed. ils Dali. VG. B5. $35.00

SANDOZ, Mari. *Love Song of the Plains.* 1961. NY. 1st ed. sgn. F/NF. N3. $45.00

SANDOZ, Mari. *Old Jules Country: A Selection From the Works of...* 1965. Hastings. 1st ed. 319p. F/dj. E1/T10. $25.00

SANDOZ, Mari. *Old Jules.* (1935). Boston. 20th-Anniversary ed. 424p. F/NF. E1. $40.00

SANDOZ, Mari. *Old Jules.* 1935. Little Brn. 1st ed. author's 1st book. beige cloth. VG/dj. T10. $125.00

SANDOZ, Maurice. *Pleasures of Mexico.* 1957. Kamin. 1st ed. 171p. dj. F3. $25.00

SANDWEISS, Martha. *Laura Gilpin: An Enduring Grace.* 1986. Ft Worth. Amon Carter Mus. 1st ed. 339p. ils. gilt beige cloth. T10. $75.00

SANDYS, John Edwin. *Speech of Demosthenes Against the Law of Leptines.* 1890. Cambridge. Greek text. orig cloth. M11. $125.00

SANFORD, John. *Rules of Prey.* 1989. Putnam. 1st ed. F/F. A20. $30.00

SANFORD, John. *Silent Prey.* 1992. Putnam. 1st ed. F/F. H11. $30.00

SANFORD, John. *View From the Wilderness: American Literature As History.* 1977. Santa Barbara. Capra. 1st ed. 8vo. inscr. F/F. T10. $35.00

SANFORD, John. *Winter Prey.* 1993. Putnam. 1st ed. F/F. A20. $15.00

SANGUINETTI, E. *Last of the Whitefields.* 1962. NY. 1st ed. sgn. VG/VG. B5. $35.00

SANN, Paul. *Lawless Decade: Pictorial History of Great American...* 1957. Crown. photos/index. 240p. E1. $50.00

SANSOM, William. *Fireman Flower.* (1944). NY. 1st Am ed. author's 1st book. NF/G+. N3. $10.00

SANTEE, Ross. *Bar X Golf Course.* 1971. Northland. 1st ed thus. ils Santee. F/F. A18. $15.00

SANTEE, Ross. *Bubbling Spring.* 1949. Scribner. early ed. inscr. NF/dj. C2. $275.00

SANTEE, Ross. *Hardrock & Silver Sage.* 1951. Scribner. 1st ed. F/VG. A18. $50.00

SANTEE, Ross. *Rummy Kid Goes Home & Other Stories of the Southwest.* 1965. Hastings. 1st ed. ils Santee. F/clip. A18. $40.00

SANTIN, Federico. *Little Red Riding Hood.* 1961. DSP. ils. glazed brd. VG. M5. $15.00

SANTMYER, Helen Hoover. *Ohio Town.* 1962. OH State. 1st ed. NF/VG. B4. $150.00

SANTOS, Sherod. *Accidental Weather.* 1982. Doubleday. 1st ed. 6-line inscr. F/NF. V1. $20.00

SANUDO, Marino. *Liber Secretorum Fidelium Crucis.* 1972. Toronto. facsimile. 4 maps+double-p ep maps. F. O7. $100.00

SANZ, Carlos. *Cartografia Historica de los Descubrimientos Australes.* 1967. Madrid. Aguirre. 96 pl. F/wrp. O7. $45.00

SARG, Tony. *Tony Sarg's Alphabet.* 1945. Greenberg. revised. 8vo. VG. C8. $60.00

SARG, Tony. *Where Is Tommy?* 1932. Greenberg. 1st ed. NF/G+. P2. $55.00

SARG & STODDARD. *Book of Marionette Plays.* 1927. Greenberg. 1st ed. sgns/dtd 1928. 12mo. VG+. C8. $175.00

SARGENT, C.S. *Silva of North America.* 1890-1902. Boston. 14 vol. xl. A15. $750.00

SARGENT, E.N. *African Boy.* 1963. Macmillan. 1st ed. F/clip. V1. $15.00

SARGENT, Frederick L. *Plants & Their Uses.* 1913. NY. ils. 610p. VG+. B26. $15.00

SARGENT, Pamela. *Alien Child.* 1988. Harper Row. 1st ed. F/F. G10. $20.00

SARGENT, Pamela. *Alien Child.* 1988. Harper Row. 1st ed. VG+/dj. M21. $12.00

SARGENT, Pamela. *Eye of the Comet.* 1984. Harper Row. 1st ed. F/F. G10. $20.00

SARGENT, Pamela. *Shore of Women.* 1986. Crown. 1st ed. F/F. G10. $20.00

SARGENT, Walter. *Enjoyment & Use of Color.* 1929. Scribner. ils. gilt cloth. F. B14. $45.00

SARGENT. *British & American Utopian Literature 1516-1975.* 1979. 350p. xl. VG. A4. $95.00

SARJEANT, Thomas. *Elementary Principles of Arithmetic, With Their Application.* 1788. Phil. 1st ed. 16mo. modern full calf. C6. $250.00

SAROYAN, William. *Boys & Girls Together.* 1963. HBW. 1st ed. 153p. VG/dj. W1. $35.00

SAROYAN, William. *Boys & Girls Together.* 1963. London. Peter Davies. AP. 8vo. VG/wrp. S9. $45.00

SAROYAN, William. *Daring Young Man on the Flying Trapeze.* 1934. Random. 1st ed. author's 1st book. inscr/dtd 1934. VG. M19. $375.00

SAROYAN, William. *Time of Your Life.* 1939. Harcourt Brace. 1st ed. 8vo. 247p. VG. W1. $20.00

SAROYAN, William. *3 Times 3.* 1936. Conference Pr. 1/250. F/G. M19. $250.00

SARTON, May. *As We Are Now.* 1973. Norton. 1st ed. F/NF. V1. $20.00

SARTON, May. *At Seventy: A Journal.* 1984. Norton. 1st ed. F/F. B4. $50.00

SARTON, May. *Crucial Conversations.* 1975. Norton. 1st ed. sgn. F/NF. V1. $55.00

SARTON, May. *Encore: Journal of Eightieth Year.* 1993. Norton. 1st ed. AN/dj. B4. $35.00

SARTON, May. *Endgame.* 1992. Norton. 1st ed. F/NF. V1. $15.00

SARTON, May. *Joanne & Ulysses.* 1963. Norton. 1st ed. ils JJ Spanfeller. F/NF clip. B4. $45.00

SARTON, May. *Magnificent Spinster.* 1985. Norton. 1st ed. F/F. B4. $50.00

SARTON, May. *Mrs Stevens Hears the Mermaids Singing.* 1965. Norton. 1st ed. F/F. B4. $65.00

SARTON, May. *Plant Dreaming Deep.* 1968. Norton. 1st ed. sgn. F/VG. B4. $75.00

SARTON, May. *Reckoning.* 1978. Norton. 1st ed. NF/NF. B4. $40.00

SARTON, May. *Small Room.* 1961. Norton. 1st ed. F/NF. H11. $35.00

SARTRE, John Paul. *Being & Nothingness.* 1956. Philosophical Lib. 1st ed. VG/G. M19. $85.00

SASEK, M. *This Is Texas.* 1967. Macmillan. 1st ed. folio. VG/VG. B17. $14.00

SASSON, Jean. *Princess: Sultana's Daughters.* 1994. Doubleday. 1st ed. 8vo. 229p. NF/dj. W1. $20.00

SATTELMEYER. *Thoreau's Reading: A Study in Intellectual History.* 1988. Princeton. 348p. F. A4. $35.00

SATTERFIELD, Archie. *Lewis & Clark Trail.* 1978. Harrisburg. 1st ed. ils. 224p. hc. E1. $30.00

SATTERTHWAIT, Walter. *At Ease With the Dead.* 1990. St Martin. 1st ed. F/F. T2. $95.00

SATTERTHWAIT, Walter. *Flower in the Desert.* 1992. St Martin. 1st ed. F/F. M23. $20.00

SATTERTHWAIT, Walter. *Wilde West.* 1991. St Martin. 1st ed. sgn. F/F. T2. $35.00

SATTLER, H.R. *Illustrated Dinosaur Dictionary.* 1983. Lee Shepard. 1st ed. 315p. VG/dj. D8. $21.00

SAUER, H.W. *Developmental Biology of Physarum.* 1982. London. Cambridge. 8vo. 237p. cloth. dj. B1. $50.00

SAUNDERS, Eileen. *Wagtails Book of Fuchsias. Vols I-IV.* 1971-76. Surrey. ils. VG+. B26. $145.00

SAUNDERS, J.J. *History of Medieval Islam.* 1969. London. Kegan Paul. 3rd. 8vo. 6 maps. 219p. VG. W1. $22.00

SAUNDERS, Leon. *Verterinary Pathology in Russia 1860-1930.* 1930. Ithaca. 1st ed. 327p. VG. A13. $25.00

SAUNDERS, Ripley. *John Kenadie: Being a Story of His Perplexing Inheritance.* 1902. Houghton Mifflin. 1st ed. 295p. VG/VG+. B22. $3.50

SAUNDERS & WILLIS. *Story of Virginia.* 1950. World Book. revised. TB. ils. 392p. VG-. B10. $10.00

SAVAGE, Tom. *Precipice.* 1994. Little Brn. 1st ed. F/F. H11. $30.00

SAVAGE, William W. *Indian Life, Transforming an American Myth.* 1977. Norman, OK. 1st ed. photos. 286p. F/NF. E1. $35.00

SAVAGE, William. *Frontier Comparative Studies Vol 2.* 1979. Norman, OK. 1st ed. 262p. F/VG. E1. $30.00

SAVAGE & SAVAGE. *Andre & Francois Andre Michaux.* 1986. Charlottesville. ils. 435p. F/dj. B26. $35.00

SAVINI, John. *Armies in the Sand: Struggle for Mecca & Medina.* 1981. Thames Hudson. 1st ed. 8vo. 223p. NF/dj. W1. $22.00

SAVOURS, Ann. *Scott's Last Voyage.* 1975. NY. Praeger. ils. 160p. VG/dj. T7. $35.00

SAWARD, Dudley. *Bernard Lovell: A Biography.* nd. London. Hale. 1st ed. ils. 320p. VG/dj. K5. $26.00

SAWDON, Dorothy. *Teddy Bear, My Day.* 1930s. London. Clowes. 4to. ils. 16p. stiff wrp. T10. $100.00

SAWYER, C.W. *US Single Shot Martial Pistols 1776-1945.* 1971. Greenwich. 1st ed. 101p. F/F. E1. $28.00

SAWYER, Edmund Ogden Jr. *Our Sea Saga: Wood Wind Ships.* 1929. San Francisco. inscr. 16 pl/fld map. 8vo. 205p. VG/VG. B11. $75.00

SAWYER, P.H. *Kings & Vikings.* 1982. London. Methuen. 1st ed. 8vo. 182p. gray cloth. F/NF. T10. $25.00

SAWYER, Robert J. *Terminal Experiment.* 1995. Harper Prism. 1st ed. F/wrp. M23. $15.00

SAWYER, Ruth. *Christmas Anna Angel.* 1944. Viking. 1st ed. ils Kate Seredy. 48p. VG/worn. D1. $75.00

SAWYER, Ruth. *Journey Cake, Ho!* (1953). Viking/Weekly Reader. 4to. 45p. VG. C14. $10.00

SAWYER, Ruth. *Way of the Storyteller.* 1942. Viking. 2nd. 8vo. 318p. xl. G+. T5. $25.00

SAXON, A.H. *PT Barnum: The Legend & the Man.* 1989. NY. 1st ed. 327p. F/F. E1. $35.00

SAXTORPH, Niels M. *Warriors & Weapons of Early Times in Color.* 1972. NY. 1st Am ed. 260p. F/F. E1. $30.00

SAYERS, Dorothy. *Omnibus of Crime.* 1929. Payson Clarke. 1st ed. VG. M22. $25.00

SAYERS, Frances. *Tag-Along Tooloo.* 1941. Viking. 1st ed. sgn. ils Helen Sewell. 87p. F/VG. P2. $75.00

SAYERS. *Anne Carroll Moore: A Biography.* 1972. np. photos. 328p. VG/VG. A4. $35.00

SAYLES, J. *Los Gusanos.* 1991. NY. ARC. NF/wrp. A15. $25.00

SAYLES, John. *Union Dues.* 1977. Little Brn. 1st ed. sgn. NF/NF. M19. $65.00

SAYLOR, Steven. *Arms of Nemesis.* 1992. St Martin. 1st ed. sgn. F/F. T2. $30.00

SAYRE, Lewis A. *Practical Manual on Treatment of Club-Foot.* 1869. NY. 1st/only ed. ils. cloth/rebacked. VG. B14. $475.00

SCARBOROUGH, Dorothy. *Wind.* 1925. Harper. 1st ed. F/F. B4. $650.00

SCARBOROUGH, Elizabeth Ann. *Healer's War.* 1988. Doubleday. 1st ed. F/F. B4. $85.00

SCARNE, John. *Odds Against Me: An Autobiography.* 1966. NY. 537p. VG/dj. S1. $8.00

SCARRY, Richard. *Fables of La Fontaine.* 1963. NY. Doubleday. 1st ed. NF/VG+. C8. $150.00

SCARRY, Richard. *Tinker & Tanker.* 1960. Garden City. 1st ed. unp. VG. T5. $55.00

SCERRATO, Umberto. *Monuments of Civilization.* 1976. Grosset Dunlap. 1st ed. folio. 192p. VG/dj. W1. $75.00

SCHAAP, Richard. *Illustrated History of the Olympics.* 1963. Knopf. 1st ed. ils. 319p. VG/VG. B5. $35.00

SCHACHNER, Nathan. *Thomas Jefferson.* 1951. NY. 2 vol. 1st ed. 8vo. gilt bl cloth. F/G/VG case. H3. $65.00

SCHAEFER, Jack. *Adolphe Francis Alphonse Bandelier.* 1966. The Territorian. 1/1000. sgn. 23-pg pamphlet. F. A18. $50.00

SCHAEFER, Jack. *Big Range.* 1953. Boston. 1st ed. VG/VG. B5. $75.00

SCHAEFER, Jack. *Great Endurance Horse Race: 600 Miles on a Single Mount.* 1963. Stagecoach. 1st ltd ed. 1/750. F/clip. A18. $150.00

SCHAEFFER, Susan Fromberg. *Bible of the Beasts of the Little Field.* 1980. Dutton. 1st ed. F/F. B4. $45.00

SCHAEFFER, Susan Fromberg. *Buffalo Afternoon.* 1990. Knopf. 1st ed. F/F. B35. $25.00

SCHAEFFER, Susan Fromberg. *Injured Party.* 1968. St Martin. 1st ed. F/F. B4. $35.00

SCHAEFFER, Susan Fromberg. *Red, White & Blue Poem.* 1977. Ally. ltd ed. 1/26. sgn/lettered. F/wrp. V1. $65.00

SCHAFER, Joseph. *History of Agriculture in Wisconsin.* 1922. Madison, WI. State Hist Soc. 1/1600. inscr. 212p. VG. A10. $55.00

SCHAFFNER, Val. *Algonquin Cat.* 1980. Delacorte. 1st ed (so stated). ils Hilary Knight. VG/VG. D1. $45.00

SCHALDACH, William. *Coverts & Casts.* (1943). NY. ils. 138p. gilt gr cloth. F. H3. $100.00

SCHALDACH, William. *Fish.* 1937. Phil. 1st ed. 1/1500. VG. B5. $95.00

SCHALLER, George B. *Mountain Gorilla: Ecology & Behavior.* 1963. Chicago. photos/diagrams. 431p. gray cloth. F/dj. B14. $125.00

SCHALLER, Michael. *Douglas MacArthur: Far Eastern General.* 1989. NY. 1st ed. 320p. F/dj. A17. $15.00

SCHAPIRO, Boris. *Bridge Analysis.* 1976. NY. 187p. VG. S1. $5.00

SCHARL, Josef. *Josef Scharl.* 1945. NY. Nierendorf. 1/100. ils. 88p. wht/maroon brd. w/sgn etching. K1. $300.00

SCHAT, A.P. *Life Boat Launching Problem. Volumes 1 & 2.* 1931 & 1932. NY. McKay. ils. VG. T7. $110.00

SCHATT, Roy. *James Dean: A Portrait.* 1900. NY. Ruggles deLatour. 4th. sgn. 142p. F/wrp. S9. $45.00

SCHAU, Michael. *JC Leyendecker.* 1974. Watson Guptill. 1st ed. 207p. VG/clip. M20. $85.00

SCHAUKAL, Richard. *Kindergedichte.* 1914. Wien. Bersuchsanstalt. 1/150. sgn author/ils/consignor. F/wrp. B24. $600.00

SCHECHTER, Ruth Lisa. *Double Exposure.* 1978. Barlenmir. 1st ed. F/sans. V1. $15.00

SCHEIDL, Gerda Marie. *Crystal Ball.* 1993. North-South Books. 1st ed. 4to. 26p. F/VG+. C14. $12.00

SCHELE DE VERRE, M. *Studies in English; or, Glimpses of Inner Life of Languages.* 1867. Scribner. 1st ed. 365p. G+. B10. $25.00

SCHENICK, Hilbert. *Chronosequence.* 1988. NY. Tor. 1st ed. F/F. T2. $15.00

SCHENICK, Hilbert. *Rose for Armageddon.* 1984. London. Allison Busby. 1st hc ed. F/F. T2. $15.00

SCHENK, Abe. *Let's Play Train.* ca 1940. Garden City. put-together panorama activity book. VG+. M5. $65.00

SCHERMAN. *Literary America.* 1952. NY. 4to. 176p. red cloth. VG/dj. T3. $20.00

SCHEZEN, Roberto. *Visions of Ancient America.* 1990. NY. Rizzoli. 1st ed. 216p. AN/dj. T10. $50.00

SCHICK. *Paperbound Book in America, History of Paperbacks...* 1958. np. 18 pl. 298p. VG. A4. $125.00

SCHICKEL, Richard. *Disney Version.* 1968. NY. 382p. F/dj. A17. $7.00

SCHICKEL, Richard. *World of Goya 1746-1828.* 1968. Time Life. VG+/case. H4. $10.00

SCHIENCK, Hilbert. *Chronosequence.* 1988. Tor. 1st ed. AN/dj. M21. $15.00

SCHIFF, Stuart David. *Whispers III.* 1981. Doubleday. 1st ed. rem mk. F/NF. G10. $20.00

SCHIFF, Stuart David. *Whispers.* 1979. Jove. ils. NF. R10. $4.00

SCHIFFER, Don. *Major League Baseball Handbook.* 1961. Nelson. 1st ed. VG+/VG. P8. $12.50

SCHIFFMAN, Jack. *Harlem Heyday.* 1984. Buffalo, NY. 272p. F/dj. E1. $25.00

SCHILDER, Gunter. *World Maps of 1624 by Willem Jansz.* 1977. Amsterdam. Nico Israel. lg format. F. O7. $150.00

SCHILDER & WELU. *World Map of 1611 by Pieter Van Den Keere.* 1980. Amsterdam. Nico Israel. 1/600. pres. F/wrp. O7. $150.00

SCHILLING, Vivian. *Sacred Pray.* 1994. Truman. 1st ed. author's 1st novel. F/F. G10. $10.00

SCHINE, Cathleen. *To the Birdhouse.* 1990. FSG. 1st ed. F/F. H11. $35.00

SCHISGAL, Murray. *Typist & the Tiger.* 1963. Coward McCann. 1st ed. F/F. B4. $125.00

SCHJELDAHL, Peter. *White Country.* 1968. Corinth. poet's 1st book. VG+/stiff wrp. V1. $25.00

SCHLEBECKER, John T. *Cattle Raising on the Plains 1900-1961.* 1963. Lincoln, NE. 1st ed. photos/index/notes. 323p. F. E1. $50.00

SCHLEGEL, J.F.W. *Neutral Rights; or, An Impartial Examinatichen...* 1801. Phil. Aurora Office. modern morocco. M11. $250.00

SCHLESINGER, Arthur. *Bitter Heritage: Vietnam & American Democracy 1941-66.* 1967. Houghton Mifflin. 1st ed. 126p. gilt cloth. F/VG+. B22. $10.00

SCHLESINGER, Arthur. *Colonial Merchants & the American Revolution.* 1918. NY. 1st ed. pres. 647p. rebound. B5. $50.00

SCHLESINGER, Arthur. *Thousand Days: John F Kennedy in the White House.* 1965. Boston, MA. 1st ed. 1087p. NF/dj. E1. $40.00

SCHLESINGER, Stephen. *Bitter Fruit.* 1982. Doubleday. 1st ed. 320p. dj. F3. $15.00

SCHLICTING, Hermann. *Boundary Layer Theory.* 1960. McGraw Hill. 647p. VG. P4. $25.00

SCHLOAT, G. Warren. *Andy's Wonderful Telescope.* 1958. Scribner. ils/photos. xl. K5. $6.00

SCHLOSS, Albert. *English Bijou Almanac for 1840.* 1839. London. ils S Lover. 64p. aeg. gilt red morocco. miniature. F. B24. $850.00

SCHLOSSBERG, Dan. *Hammerin Hank.* 1974. Stadia. pb. photos. VG. P8. $10.00

SCHMECKEBIER, Laurence. *Bureau of Internal Revenue: Its History...* 1924. Johns Hopkins. 8vo. 270p. bl buckram. F. B14. $45.00

SCHMIDT, Dana Adams. *Armageddon in the Middle East.* 1974. Day. 1st ed. 8vo. 269p. VG/dj. W1. $18.00

SCHMIDT, Dana Adams. *Yemen the Unknown War.* 1968. HRW. 1st ed. 8vo. 16 pl/maps. VG/dj. W1. $22.00

SCHMIDT, Harrison H. *Equilibrium Diagrams for Minerals at Low Temperature...* 1962. Cambridge. 197p. F/prt wrp. D8. $10.00

SCHMIDT, Leone. *Come Fly to the Prairie.* 1968. Mendota. 1st ed. inscr. F. N3. $15.00

SCHMIDT, Oscar. *Doctrine of Descent & Darwinism.* 1875. NY. ils. 334p. red cloth. VG. B14. $95.00

SCHMITZ, Dennis. *Goodwill Inc.* 1976. Ecco. 1st ed. assn copy. F/NF. V1. $15.00

SCHMITZ, Dennis. *We Weep for Our Strangeness.* 1969. Big Table Pub. 1st ed. poet's 1st book. assn copy. F/VG+. V1. $35.00

SCHMITZ, Joseph W. *Society of Mary in Texas.* 1951. San Antonio, TX. 1st ed. 261p. E1. $35.00

SCHMITZ. *Katalog der Ornamentstich-Sammlung der Staatlichen...* (1936-1939). Berlin. 2 vol in 1. rpt. 1/150. 782p. F. A4. $125.00

SCHMUTZ, Ervin M. *Classified Bibliography on Native Plants of Arizona.* 1978. Tucson. 160p. VG. B26. $30.00

SCHNEEDE, W.M. *Surrealism: The Movement & the Masters.* (1974). Abrams. pl. VG/VG. M17. $50.00

SCHNEIDER, Pierre. *World of Manet 1832-1883.* 1968. Time Life. F/NF. H4. $10.00

SCHNEIDER, Russell J. *Franklin Robinson, Making of a Manager.* 1976. Coward McCann. 1st ed. F/VG+. P8. $35.00

SCHNELL, D.E. *Carnivorous Plants of the United States & Canada.* 1976. John Blair. 8vo. photos. 125p. rpr dj. B1. $28.00

SCHOENDOERFFER, Pierre. *Farewell to the King.* 1970. NY. Stein. 1st ed. NF/NF. I111. $50.00

SCHOFIELD, Eileen K. *Plants of Galapagos Islands.* 1984. NY. ils/maps. 159p. F. B26. $15.00

SCHOLES & SCHOLES. *Maya Chontal Indians of Acalan-T.* 1968. Norman. 1st ed thus (rpt of 1948 Carnegie). 565p. F/F. E1. $40.00

SCHOOLCRAFT, Henry R. *Thirty Years With the Indian Tribes.* 1851. Lippincott Grambo. 1st ed. 703p. F. E1. $300.00

SCHOOLCRAFT, Mentor L. *Narrative Journal of Travels.* 1953. E Lansing, MI. 1st ed thus. VG/torn. B18. $35.00

SCHOOR, Gene. *Ted Williams Story.* 1954. Messner. 1st ed. xl. G. P8. $10.00

SCHORGER, A.W. *Passenger Pigeon.* 1955. Madison. 1st ed. ils/index. VG/VG. B5. $65.00

SCHOW, David J. *Kill Riff.* 1988. Tor. 1st ed. rem mk. NF/NF. G10. $10.00

SCHRAER, H. *Biological Calcification.* 1970. Appleton Century. 8vo. 462p. cloth. dj. B1. $45.00

SCHRAGE, Eltjo. *Unjust Enrichment, the Comparative Legal History...* 1995. Berlin. Duncker Humblot. 333p. prt sewn wrp. M11. $100.00

SCHRANK, Joseph. *Cello in the Belly of the Plane.* 1954. Franklin Watts. 1st prt. 8vo. VG/G. B17. $6.00

SCHREIBER, Flora Rheta. *Sybil.* 1973. Chicago. Regnery. 1st ed. F/VG. B4. $125.00

SCHREIER, Konrad F. *Marble's Knives & Axes.* 1978. N Hollywood, CA. 1st ed. ils. 70p. F/stiff pict wrp. E1. $25.00

SCHREYER, Alice. *History of Books, a Guide to Selected Resources...* 1987. GPO. 221p. NF. A4. $55.00

SCHROEDER, Theodore. *Obscene Literature & Constitutional Law...* 1911. NY. private prt. orig cloth. M11. $125.00

SCHUELER, Donald G. *Incident at Eagle Ranch.* 1980. Sierra Club. 1st ed. 8vo. 296p. map ep. T10. $25.00

SCHULMAN, Grace. *Burn Down the Icons.* 1976. Princeton. 1st ed. sgn. F/F. V1. $25.00

SCHULMAN, Grace. *Hemispheres.* 1984. Sheep Meadow. 1st ed. sgn. F/wrp. V1. $25.00

SCHULT, Friedrich. *Ernst Barlach. Das Plastische Werk.* 1960. Hamburg. Hauswedell. ils/photos. 304p. xl. D2. $850.00

SCHULTES, Richard E. *Native Orchids of Trinidad & Tobago.* 1960. NY. ils/drawings. 275p. VG/dj. B26. $75.00

SCHULTHEIS, Rob. *Night Letters. Inside Wartime Afghanistan.* 1992. Orion. 1st ed. tall 8vo. 155p. NF/dj. W1. $18.00

SCHULTZ, Duane. *Wake Island.* 1978. NY. BC. 192p. dj. A17. $6.00

SCHULTZ, George A. *Indian Canaan, Isaac McCoy & the Vision of an Indian State.* 1972. Norman. 1st ed. 230p. F/dj. E1. $40.00

SCHULTZ, James Willard. *Blackfeet & Buffalo: Memories of Life Among the Indians.* 1962. Norman, OK. 1st ed. photos/index. 384p. VG/dj. E1. $25.00

SCHULTZ, James Willard. *Blackfeet Tales of Glacier National Park.* 1916. Boston. VG. B5. $50.00

SCHULTZ, Philip. *Deep Within the Ravine.* 1984. np. 1st ed. sgn. F/wrp. V1. $20.00

SCHULZ, Charles M. *I Never Promised You an Apple Orchard: Collected Writings...* 1976. HRW. 1st ed. 8vo. unp. F/NF. C14. $16.00

SCHULZ, Charles M. *Peanuts Classics.* 1970. HRW. 1st ed. ils. unp. red cloth. VG/torn. T5. $30.00

SCHULZ, Charles M. *Peanuts Jubilee: My Life & Art.* 1975. Ballantine. 224p. F. M13. $20.00

SCHULZ, Charles M. *Sandlot Peanuts.* 1977. Holt. 1st ed/1st prt. ils. cloth. AN/dj. B14. $55.00

SCHULZ, Charles M. *Snoopy & His Sopwith Camel.* 1969. HRW. 1st ed. 8vo. ils. unp. F/NF clip. C14. $22.00

SCHURKE, Paul. *Bering Bridge: Soviet-American Expedition From Siberia...* 1989. Duluth. Pfeifer-Hamilton. 1st ed. sgn. 8vo. 227p. F. B11. $15.00

SCHUSKY, Ernest L. *Forgotten Sioux: Ethnohistory of Lower Brule Reservation.* 1975. Chicago. 1st ed. photos/biblio/indes. F/F. E1. $35.00

SCHUTT, Arthur. *This Flying Business: Life of Arthur Schutt.* 1976. Melbourne. Nelson. 1st ed. 12mo. inscr/dtd 1978. map ep. F/F. T10. $35.00

SCHUYLER, James. *Few Days.* 1985. Random. 1st ed. F/NF. M23. $20.00

SCHUYLER, James. *Morning of the Poem.* 1980. FSG. 1st ed. F/F. M23. $25.00

SCHUYLER, James. *Selected Poems.* 1988. FSG. ARC. RS. F/NF. w/pub material. V1. $30.00

SCHUYLER, Montgomery. *Index Verborum of the Fragments of the Avesta.* 1965. NY. AMS. 8vo. 106p. VG. W1. $28.00

SCHWAB, Antonia. *Silver Shadows.* 1928. Bozart. G. B10. $15.00

SCHWAB, Rick. *Stuck on the Cubs.* 1977. Sassafras. pbo. G+. P8. $15.00

SCHWARTZ, John Burnham. *Bicycle Days.* 1989. Summit. 1st ed. F/F. H11. $25.00

SCHWARTZ, Joseph. *Creative Moment: How Science Made Itself Alien...* 1992. Harper Collins. 1st ed. VG+/NF. G10. $5.00

SCHWARTZ, Lynne Sharon. *Accounting.* 1983. Penmaen. 1st ed. 1/100. sgn twice/#d. F/glassine. V1. $40.00

SCHWARTZ, Stephen. *Perfect Peach.* 1977. Little Brn. 1st ed. 4to. 48p. NF/G+. C14. $10.00

SCHWARTZ. *1100 Obscure Points: Bibliographies of 25 English...Authors.* 1969. np. ils. 108p. VG. A4. $65.00

SCHWEITZER, Byrd Baylor. *Chinese Bag.* 1968. Houghton Mifflin. 1st prt. 48p. F/VG+. C14. $20.00

SCHWEITZER, Darrell. *Discovering Modern Horror Fiction I.* 1985. Starmont. 1st ed. NF. R10. $6.00

SCHWEITZER, Darrell. *Dream Quest of HP Lovecraft.* 1978. Borgo. 1st ed. F/wrp. R10. $10.00

SCHWEIZER. *William Pitt, Earl of Chatham 1708-1778.* 1993. np. 145p. F. A4. $75.00

SCHWENGEL, Fred. *Republican Party: Its Heritage & History.* 1988. Acropolis. 2nd. sgn. 8vo. VG/VG. B11. $16.00

SCHWINN, Arnold. *50 Years of Schwinn Built Bicycles.* 1945. Chicago. 1st ed. photos. 94p. VG. B5. $65.00

SCIAMA, D.W. *Modern Cosmology.* 1973. Cambridge. 3rd. 8vo. 212p. VG/dj. K5. $16.00

SCMEDDING, Joseph. *Cowboy & Indian Trader.* 1951. Caxton. 1st ed. 364p. NF/dj. E1. $75.00

SCOLLARD, Clinton. *Epic of Golf.* 1923. Boston. 1st ed. 98p. F/NF. A17. $45.00

SCOPPETONE, Sandra. *Creative Kind of Killer.* 1984. Watts. 1st ed. F/F. P3. $18.00

SCOPPETONE, Sandra. *Razzamatazz.* 1985. Franklin Watts. 1st ed. author's 2nd novel. VG/VG. M22. $25.00

SCOPPETONE, Sandra. *Suzuki Beane.* 1961. NY. 1st ed. VG/VG. B5. $95.00

SCORER & WEXLER. *Colour Guide to Clouds.* 1963. Oxford. Pergamon. 8vo. ils. 63p. wrp. K5. $13.00

SCOTT, David. *Epidemic Disease in Ghana 1901-1960.* 1965. London. 208p. dj. A13. $25.00

SCOTT, E.B. *Saga of Lake Tahoe.* 1964. Lake Tahoe. 8th. VG/dj. B5. $55.00

SCOTT, Eleanor. *Fin de Fiesta.* 1974. Santa Fe. Sunstone. 1st ed. unp. wrp. F3. $20.00

SCOTT, Flo Hampton. *Passing Laughter: Stories of the Southland.* 1971. Brimingham. 3rd. ils. VG. B10. $10.00

SCOTT, George. *Scott's New Coast Pilot for the Lakes.* 1890. Detroit Free Pr Prt. fair. A16. $50.00

SCOTT, Melissa. *Burning Bright.* 1993. Tor. 1st ed. NF/NF. G10. $5.00

SCOTT, Milton R. *Supposed Diary of President Lincoln.* 1913. Newark, OH. 140p. G. B18. $22.50

SCOTT, Morgan. *Oakdale Boys in Camp.* 1912. AL Burt. G+. P12. $6.00

SCOTT, Richard. *Jackie Robinson: Baseball Great.* 1986. Chelsea. later prt. M/sans. P8. $15.00

SCOTT, Robert L. *Boring a Hole in the Sky.* 1961. NY. 1st ed. VG/VG. B5. $35.00

SCOTT, Robert L. *Damned to Glory.* 1944. NY. 1st ed. sgn twice. 228p. VG/dj. B18. $95.00

SCOTT, Robert L. *God Is My Co-Pilot.* 1943. NY. later ed. sgn twice. 277p. G+. B18. $55.00

SCOTT, Walter. *Border Antiquities of England & Scotland...* 1814. London. Longman Hurst. 2 vol. 1st ed. 94 engravings. F. T10. $1,000.00

SCOTT, Walter. *Demonology & Witchcraft.* 18686. London. Wm Tegg. ils Cruikshank. 396p. VG. T10. $125.00

SCOTT, Walter. *Lay of the Last Minstrel, a Poem.* 1807. London. Longman Hurst Rees. 6th. 8vo. 340p. aeg. vellum. T10. $100.00

SCOTT, Walter. *Poetical Works.* 1850. Edinburgh. Cadell. 4to. 823p. fore-edge golfing painting. aeg. morocco. B24. $1,350.00

SCOTT, Walter. *Sir Walter Scott 1771-1971: A Bicentenary Exhibition.* 1971. Edinburgh. 60p. prt sewn wrp. M11. $45.00

SCOTT, Walter. *Tales of a Grandfather.* 1988. Edinburgh. 3 vol. brn full leather. VG. B30. $110.00

SCOTT, William Bell. *William Blake: Etchings From His Works.* 1878. London. 1st ed. 10 mtd India proof etchings. G. C6. $250.00

SCOTT, Winifield Townley. *To Marry Strangers.* 1945. Crowell. 1st ed. F/NF. V1. $35.00

SCOTT & SCOTT. *Chrysathemums for Pleasure.* 1953 (1950). Bogota, NJ. 2nd. 318p. VG/dj. B26. $16.00

SCOTT & SCOTT. *Fun & Games With Cards.* 1973. NY. 190p. VG/wrp. S1. $3.00

SCOTT. *Three Contemporary Novelists: An Annotated Bibliography...* 1977. np. 97p. NF. A4. $45.00

SCOVILLE, W. *Revolution in Glass Making.* 1948. Cambridge. 1st ed. ils/index. 398p. VG/G. B5. $50.00

SCOWCROFT & STEGNER. *Stanford Short Stories.* 1952. Stanford. 1st ed. F/torn. A18. $50.00

SCRIPTURE, E.W. *Thinking, Feeling, Doing: Intro to Mental Science.* 1895. Chautauqua-Century. 12mo. 304p. 209p. prt red cloth. VG. C1. $40.00

SCRUTATOR. *On the Management of Hounds.* 1852. London. Bell's Life. 1st ed. fld kennel plan. O3. $225.00

SCULLARD, H.H. *Roman Britain: Outpost of the Empire.* nd. Thames Hudson. 8vo. ils/maps. 192p. orange cloth. F/NF. T10. $35.00

SCWARZENBACH, P.A. *Passionate Shepherd to His Love...* 1902. NY. Russell. 1/500. teg. gilt cream brd/ribbon ties. F/chemise. B24. $385.00

SEAGER, R. *And Tyler Too: President John Tyler.* 1963. NY. 1st ed. F/F. B5. $40.00

SEAL, Basil; see Barnes, Julian.

SEALE, Bobby. *Lonely Rage: Autobiography of Bobby Seale.* 1978. NY Times. 238p. xl. dj. R11. $15.00

SEALE, Bobby. *Seize the Time.* 1970. np. 1st ed. hc. VG/VG. M19. $45.00

SEALE, Bobby. *Seize the Time: Story of the Black Panther Party...* 1970. Vintage. pb/1st ed thus. 429p. R11. $15.00

SEALOCK & SEELY. *Bibliography of Place Name Literature: US, Canada...* 1948. Chicago. Am Lib Assn. 341p. xl. VG. A4. $25.00

SEALSFIELD, Charles. *Making of an American: Adaptation of Memorable Tales...* 1974. SMU. 1st ed. F/F. A18. $17.50

SEAMAN, Louise. *Brave Bantam.* 1946. Macmillan. 1st ed. NF/VG. M5. $15.00

SEAMAN, Louise. *Mr Peck's Pets.* 1947. Macmillan. 1st ed. 8vo. 96p. G. C14. $12.00

SEARLE & MACHIN. *Chrysanthemums the Year Round.* 1968 (1957). London. enlarged/revised ed. ils. 379p. F/dj. B26. $15.00

SEARS, R.W. *Survey of Cycle of Sod & Livestock Industries...* 1941. Los Angeles. 1st ed. photos. 306p. F/VG. E1. $50.00

SEARS, Stephen W. *George B McClellan, the Young Napoleon.* 1988. NY. 8vo. ils. 482p. bl cloth. F/dj. T3. $22.00

SEASHOLES, Craig. *Adrift in the South Pacific.* 1950. Boston. Baker. sgn by survivor. 12mo. 55p. VG/stiff wrp. B11. $10.00

SEAVER, J. *Anthropometry & Physical Examination.* 1909. New Haven. 1st ed. 191p. cracked inner hinge. A13. $45.00

SEAWELL, Molly Elliot. *Midshipman Paulding.* 1893. Appleton. 8vo. ils Geo Wharton Edwards. VG. T10. $50.00

SEBASTIANI, Sylvia. *Sebastiani Family Cookbook.* 1970. Lyle Stuart. sgn. 8vo. 166p. gr cloth. VG. B11. $12.00

SECREST, William B. *Dangerous Men: Gunfighers, Lawmen & Outlaws of Old CA.* 1976. Fresno, CA. 1st ed. photos. 47p. F/stiff pict wrp. E1. $30.00

SECREST, William B. *I Buried Hickok: Memoirs of White Eye Anderson.* 1980. College Sta, TX. 1st ed. sgn. index/biblio/photos. 251p. F/NF. E1. $50.00

SEE, Carolyn. *Dreaming: Hard Luck & Good Times in America.* 1995. Random. ARC. F/wrp. B4. $45.00

SEE, Carolyn. *Making History.* 1991. Houghton Mifflin. ARC. sgn. AN/wrp. B4. $45.00

SEE, Carolyn. *Making History.* 1991. Houghton Mifflin. 1st ed. F/dj. S9. $25.00

SEEGER, Ruth Crawford. *American Folk Songs for Children.* 1948. Doubleday. ils Barbara Cooney. VG/G. B17. $8.50

SEELINGSON, Lelia. *History of Indianola.* 1930. Cuero, TX. 13p. F/stiff wrp. E1. $45.00

SEGAL, Erich. *Acts of Faith.* 1992. Bantam. UP. F. B35. $28.00

SEGAL, Erich. *Love Story.* 1970. Harper. 1st ed. sgn. F/NF. B4. $250.00

SEGAR, E.C. *Popeye the Sailor.* 1971. Woody Gelman Nostalgia. hc. photos. dj. M13. $25.00

SEGAR, E.C. *Popeye With the Hag of the 7 Seas.* 1935. Chicago. Pleasure Book. 4to. 3 popups/ils. pict brd. D1. $500.00

SEGUIN, E. *Myelitis of the Anterior Horns or Spinal Paralysis...* 1877. NY. 120p. orange cloth. VG. B14. $250.00

SEHELL, James Perry. *In the Ojibway Country. Early Missions on MN Frontier.* 1911. Walhalla, ND. 1st ed. 189p. rebound. VG. B5. $100.00

SEIBLE, C.W. *Helium Child of the Sun.* 1968. KS U. 138p. cloth. F/dj. D8. $15.00

SEIBT, Betty Kay. *Millionaire Cowboy.* 1983. Abilene, TX. photos. 89p. F. E1. $10.00

SEIDEL, Frederick. *My Tokyo.* 1993. FSG. 1st ed. F/F. V1. $10.00

SEIDEL, Frederick. *Sunrise.* 1980. Viking. 1st ed. F/NF. V1. $25.00

SEIDMAN, Hugh. *Blood Lord.* 1974. Doubleday. 1st ed. author's 2nd book. sgn. F/F. V1. $55.00

SEIDMAN, Hugh. *Collecting Evidence.* 1970. Yale. poet's 1st book. Younger Poets series. F/F. V1. $85.00

SEIFERT, Jaroslav. *Casting of Bells.* 1983. IA City. Spirit That Moves Us Pr. 1st ed. AN/wrp. V1. $25.00

SEIFERT, Jaroslav. *Eight Days.* 1985. IA City. Spirit That Moves Us Pr. F/wrp. V1. $20.00

SEIFERT, Traudl. *Dokumente Zur Geschichte der Kartographie.* 1973. Unterschneidheim. Walter Uhl. 60p. F. O7. $175.00

SEILER, Emma. *Voice in Singing.* 1879. Phil. ils. trans from German. 192p. VG. B14. $45.00

SEILER, Otto J. *Crossing the Tracks of Columbus.* 1992. Herferd. Mittler. AN/dj. A16. $55.00

SEKKA, Kanzaka. *Flight of Butterflies.* 1979 (1904). NY. 8vo. woodcuts. accordian-style fld book. AN/case. H3. $95.00

SELBY, Hubert Jr. *Last Exit to Brooklyn.* 1964. Grove. 1st ed. author's 1st book. F/F. B24. $300.00

SELDES, George. *Never Tire of Protesting.* 1968. Lyle Stuart. 1st ed. NF/NF. B35. $18.00

SELDON, Reeda. *Little Folks of Other Lands.* 1950. Great Pyramid. 4to. VG/G. B17. $5.00

SELF, Charles R. *Western Horsemanship.* 1979. NY. 1st ed. 232p. F/F. E1. $25.00

SELF, H. *Environment & Man in Kansas.* 1978. np. ils/maps. 288p. NF/dj. D8. $15.00

SELF, Margaret Cabell. *Morgan Horse in Pictures.* 1967. Phil. Macrae Smith. VG/G. O3. $48.00

SELF, Margaret Cabell. *Riding With Mariles.* 1960. McGraw Hill. 1st ed. VG/G. O3. $25.00

SELL, DeWitt. *Collector's Guide to American Cartridge Handguns.* 1963. PA. 1st ed. photos. 244p. F/F. E1. $35.00

SELL, Francis E. *Deer Hunter's Guide.* 1964. Stackpole. photos. G+/G+. P12. $7.00

SELZER, Richard. *Confessions of a Knife.* 1979. Simon Schuster. 1st ed. rem mk. F/F. H11. $25.00

SEMENOFF, W. *Rasplata (In Russian): L'Expiation.* 1910. Paris. Augustin Challamel. 4 vol. various ed. 8vo. NF. T10. $200.00

SEMPLE, George. *Treatise on Building in Water.* 1776. Dublin. 1st ed. 63 pl. 157p. full leather. B5. $700.00

SENDAK, Maurice. *Hector Protector.* 1965. Harper Row. 1st ed. ils Sendak. F/F. D1. $150.00

SENDAK, Maurice. *Hector Protector/As I Went Over the Water.* 1965. Harper Row. 12mo. pict brd. G. B17. $5.00

SENDAK, Maurice. *Higgelti Piggelti Pop!* 1969. Zurich. Diogenes. 1st German pb ed. ils/sgn Sendak. F. D1. $225.00

SENDAK, Maurice. *Higglety Pigglety Pop!; or, There Must Be More to Life.* 1967. Harper Row. 1st ed. 8vo. 69p. F/dj. B24. $250.00

SENDAK, Maurice. *Higglety Pigglety Pop!; or, There Must Be More to Life.* 1991. Bodley Head. London ed. 16mo. F/F. B17. $9.50

SENDAK, Maurice. *In the Night Kitchen.* 1970. Harper Row. 1st ed. ils. unp. VG/VG. D1. $225.00

SENDAK, Maurice. *Love for Three Oranges, the Glyndebourne Version.* 1984. FSG. 1st ed. 4to. F/sans. B17. $22.50

SENDAK, Maurice. *Some Swell Pup or Are You Sure You Wan' a Dog?* 1989. FSG. 2nd. 8vo. F/torn. B17. $6.50

SENDAK, Maurice. *We Are All in the Dumps With Jack & Guy.* 1993. Harper Collins. 1st ed. unp. NF/dj. M20. $25.00

SENEFELDER. *Invention of Lithography.* 1911. np. 4to. trans from German. 239p. NF. A4. $125.00

SENN, Nicholas. *Tahiti: Island of Paradise.* 1906. Chicago. WB Conkey. ils. 254p. T7. $40.00

SENOUR, F. *Morgan & His Captors.* 1864. Cincinnati. CF Vent. 389p. brn cloth. VG. M20. $80.00

SEREDY, Kate. *Chestry Oak.* 1948. Viking. 1st ed. ils. 236p. VG/VG. M5. $32.00

SEREDY, Kate. *Good Master.* 1935. Viking/Jr Literary Guild. 1st ed thus. VG/dj. M5. $75.00

SEREDY, Kate. *Good Master.* 1935. Viking. 1st ed. 8vo. VG/fair. M5. $55.00

SEREDY, Kate. *Philomena.* 1955. Viking. 1st ed. 8vo. ils. beige cloth. VG/VG. D1. $80.00

SEREDY, Kate. *Tree for Peter.* 1941. Viking. 1st ed. cloth. F/VG+. M5. $65.00

SEREDY, Kate. *White Stag.* 1944 (1937). Viking. 4th. 8vo. 94p. red cloth. G+/torn. T5. $25.00

SERGE, Victor. *Year One of the Russian Revolution.* 1972. 1st Am ed. F/F. S13. $25.00

SERGEANT, George. *From Egypt to the Golden Horn.* 1940. Revell. sgn. 8vo. 254p. VG/VG. B11. $24.00

SERVEN, James E. *Colt Firearms From 1836.* 1981. PA. 3rd. ils. 398p. F/dj. E1. $60.00

SERVEN, James E. *Colt Firearms.* 1954. Santa Ana, CA. 1st ed. photos. 385p. NF/dj. E1. $100.00

SERVICE, Robert. *Ballads of a Bohemian.* 1921. Barse Hopkins. 1st ed. NF. V1. $25.00

SERVICE, Robert. *Rhymes of a Red Cross Man.* 1916. Barse Hopkins. ils CL Wrenn. 192p. VG. M20. $47.00

SERVICE, Robert. *Roughneck.* 1924. NY. VG/VG. B5. $40.00

SERVICE, Robert. *Shooting of Dan McGrew.* 1980. Dodd Mead. 1st ed. 12mo. F/wrp. V1. $15.00

SERVISS, Garrett P. *Astronomy in a Nutshell.* 1912. Putnam. 1st ed. 28 pl. 261p. cloth. G. K5. $30.00

SESTAY. *Needlework, a Selected Bibliography With Special Reference.* 1982. np. 153p. F. A4. $25.00

SETCHELL, Brian. *Male Reproduction: Benchmark Papers in Human Psysiology.* 1984. NY. 1st ed. 397p. VG. A13. $40.00

SETON, Anya. *Winthrop Woman.* 1958. Houghton Mifflin. 1st ed. F/NF. B4. $65.00

SETON, Ernest Thompson. *Lives of the Hunted.* 1901. Scribner. 1st Am ed. cloth. M20. $47.00

SETON, Ernest Thompson. *Trail of an Artist-Naturalist.* 1940. Scribner. 1st ed. inscr. ils. 412p. gr buckram. VG. T10. $175.00

SETON, Ernest Thompson. *Trail of the Sandhill Stag.* 1899. Scribner. 6th. 12mo. VG. B17. $12.50

SETON, Ernest Thompson. *Two Little Savages.* 1911. Grosset Dunlap. early rpt. 8vo. VG. B17. $6.00

SETTLE, Mary Lee. *Blood Tie.* 1977. Houghton Mifflin. 1st ed. inscr. F/NF. B4. $85.00

SETTLE, Mary Lee. *Celebration.* 1986. FSG. sgn. bl cloth. G/G. B10. $12.00

SETTLE, Mary Lee. *Charley Bland.* 1989. Franklin Lib. 1st ed. sgn. leather. F. B35. $45.00

SETTLE, Mary Lee. *Charley Bland.* 1989. FSG. 1st ed. F/F. B4. $35.00

SETTLE, Mary Lee. *Choices.* 1995. Doubleday. 1st ed. sgn. AN/dj. B4. $45.00

SETTLE, Mary Lee. *Clam Shell.* 1971. Bodley Head. 1st ed. sgn. F/F. B4. $85.00

SETTLE, Mary Lee. *Killing Ground.* 1982. FSG. ARC. sgn. NF/wrp. B4. $35.00

SETTLE, Mary Lee. *Killing Ground.* 1982. FSG. 1/150. sgn. AN/case/box. B4. $125.00

SETTLE, Mary Lee. *Know Nothing.* 1961. Heinemann. 1st Eng ed. sgn. F/F. B4. $125.00

SETTLE, Mary Lee. *Love Eaters.* 1954. Harper. 1st Am ed. rem mk. F/F clip. B4. $250.00

SETTLE, Mary Lee. *Scapegoat.* 1980. Random. 1st ed. sgn. rem mk. NF/NF. B4. $65.00

SETTLE, William A. *Jesse James Was His Name.* 1966. Columbia, MO. 1st ed. ils/photos/notes. F. E1. $55.00

SETTLE & SETTLE. *Saddles & Spurs: Saga of the Pony Express.* nd. Bonanza. rpt. 217p. F/dj. E1. $25.00

SETTLE & SETTLE. *War Drums & Wagon Wheels.* 1966. Lincoln. NE U. 268p. map ep. VG/dj. B18/M20. $32.50

SEVERANCE, Frank H. *Old Frontier of France. The Niagara Region...* 1917. NY. 2 vol. 1st ed. 8vo. teg. gilt bl cloth. VG. H3. $110.00

SEVIN, Mureddin. *Turk Kiyafet Tarihine Bir Bakis.* 1973. Istanbul. 1st ed. lg 8vo. ils. 151p. VG. W1. $65.00

SEWARD, Olive Risley. *William H Seward's Travels Around the World.* 1873. Appleton. 1st ed. 8vo. 730p. aeg. marbled ep. pub morocco. T10. $300.00

SEWARD, William H. *Life & Public Services of John Quincy Adams.* 1851. Auburn. 12mo. 404p. brn cloth. VG. T3. $30.00

SEWELL, Anna. *Black Beauty.* 1927. Winston. ils Edwin John Prittie. VG. M5. $60.00

SEWELL, Anna. *Black Beauty.* 1952. NY. Scribner. 1st/A ed. ils Paul Brown. VG/G. O3. $295.00

SEWELL, Richard B. *Life of Emily Dickinson.* 1974. FSG. 1st ed. 2 vol. F/case. C2. $75.00

SEXTON, Anne. *Book of Folly.* 1972. Boston. Houghton Mifflin. 1st ed. 1/500. sgn. aeg. F/case. B24. $125.00

SEXTON, Anne. *Death Notebooks.* 1974. Boston. AP. inscr. NF/wrp. C2. $250.00

SEXTON, Anne. *To Bedlam & Part Way Back.* 1960. Houghton Mifflin. 1st ed. F/NF. B4. $200.00

SEXTON, Linda Gray. *Words for Dr Y.* 1978. Houghton Mifflin. 1st ed. NF/VG+. V1. $20.00

SEXTON, R.W. *American Public Buildings of Today.* 1931. NY. Architecural Pub. 1st ed. VG/VG. B5. $70.00

SEXTON, R.W. *Spanish Influence on American Architecture & Decoration.* 1927. NY. Brentano. 1st ed. 4to. 263p. xl. VG. T10. $150.00

SEYBOLT. *Catalogue of the First Editions...of Paul Seybolt.* 1946. private prt. 1/300. ils. 87p. VG. A4. $165.00

SEYFFERT, O. *Spielzeug.* ca 1910. Berlin. Wasmuth. ils Walter Trier. VG. D1. $200.00

SEYMOUR, Flora Warren. *Indian Agents of the Old Frontier.* 1975. NY. rpt. 402p. F. E1. $30.00

SEYMOUR, Flora Warren. *Story of the Red Man.* 1929. Longman Gr. 1st ed. sgn. 8vo. 421p. VG. B11. $40.00

SEYMOUR, Frank C. *Flora of Lincoln County, WI.* 1960. np. ils/maps/photo. gr cloth. VG. B26. $25.00

SEYMOUR, Gerald. *Glory Boys.* 1976. Random. 1st ed. F/NF. H11. $40.00

SEYMOUR, Harold. *Baseball: The Golden Age.* 1971. Oxford. 1st ed. VG+/G+. P8. $65.00

SEYMOUR, Miranda. *Robert Graves: Life on the Edge.* 1995. Holt. ARC. F/F. B35. $35.00

SEYMOUR, Whitney North. *United States Attorney, an Inside View of Justice...* 1975. NY. Morrow. M11. $25.00

SHAARA, Michael. *Killer Angels.* 1974. NY. 1st ed. VG/G+. B5. $135.00

SHAARA, Michael. *Killer Angels.* 1974. NY. 3rd. inscr/dtd 1976. F/NF. C2. $150.00

SHACKLETON, Ernest. *South: Story of Shackleton's Last Expedition 1914-17.* 1983. London. Century. rpt. 375p. T7. $45.00

SHAFFER, Anthony. *Sleuth.* 1970. Dodd Mead. 1st Am ed. F/F. B4. $150.00

SHAFFER, Janet. *Peter Francsico: Virginia Giant.* 1976. Moore. ils. 124p. xl. B10. $15.00

SHAFFER, Peter. *Royal Hunt of the Sun.* 1965. Stein Day. 1st Am ed. F/F. B4. $85.00

SHAGAN, Steve. *Save the Tiger.* 1972. NY. Dial. 1st ed. inscr. F/NF. B4. $275.00

SHAH, Diane K. *Dying Cheek to Cheek.* 1992. Doubleday. 1st ed. F/F. H11. $20.00

SHAH, Idries. *Secret Lore of Magic.* 1958. Citadel. 1st ed. 316p. VG/dj. M20. $47.00

SHAHN, Ben. *Alphabet of Creation.* 1982. 1st ed thus. NF/NF glassine wrp. S13. $25.00

SHAKESPEARE, Bill. *Powerboat Racing.* 1968. London. Cassell. VG/VG. A16. $25.00

SHAKESPEARE, William. *Flowers From Shakespeare's Garden.* 1906. London. Cassell. 1st ed. ils Walter Crane. 40p. VG. D1. $250.00

SHAKESPEARE, William. *Tempest.* 1993. Lexington. Anvil. 1/75. lg 8vo. Holbrook bdg. AN. B24. $150.00

SHAKESPEARE, William. *Tragedy of Hamlet, Prince of Denmark.* 1933. High Wycombe. Hague Gill. 1/1500. ils/sgn Eric Gill. beige morocco. AN/dj/case. B24. $450.00

SHAMES, Laurence. *Florida Straits.* 1992. Simon Schuster. 1st ed. author's 1st novel. B stp on edges. F/F. H11. $45.00

SHAMES, Laurence. *Florida Straits.* 1992. Simon Schuster. 1st ed. author's 1st novel. F/F. B4. $85.00

SHAMES, Laurence. *Scavenger Reef.* 1994. Simon Schuster. 1st ed. NF/NF. N4. $15.00

SHAN, R.H. *Genus Sanicula (Umbelliferae) in the Old World & the New.* 1951. Berkeley. i.s. 78p. wrp. B26. $12.00

SHANE, Elizabeth. *Piper's Tunes.* ca 1954. London. Selwyn Blount. 12mo. F. A17. $10.00

SHANGE, Ntozake. *For Colored Girls Who Have Considered Suicide...* 1977. Macmillan. 1st ed. author's 1st book. F/F. M19. $75.00

SHANGE, Ntozake. *Nappy Edges.* 1978. St Martin. 1st ed. F/dj. B4. $50.00

SHANGE, Ntozake. *Sassafras, Cypress & Indigo.* 1982. St Martin. 1st ed. NF/VG. B4. $45.00

SHANNON, Bill. *Bull Parks.* 1975. Hawthorn. 1st ed. F/VG+. P8. $225.00

SHANNON, Dell. *Murder Most Strange.* 1981. Morrow. 1st ed. F/F. H11. $25.00

SHANNON, James. *Catholic Colonization on the Western Frontier.* 1957. New Haven. Yale. 1st ed. sgn. 10 pl. 8vo. 302p. VG/fair. B11. $40.00

SHANTZ, Bobby. *Story of Bobby Shantz.* 1953. Lippincott. 1st ed. VG/G+. P8. $60.00

SHAPELEY, H. *Climatic Change, Evidence, Causes & Effects.* 1953. Cambridge. 1st ed. 318p. VG. D8. $20.00

SHAPIRO, David. *House (Blown Apart).* 1988. Woodstock. Overlook. 1st ed. F/F. w/pub letter & slip. B4. $100.00

SHAPIRO, Irwin. *Gremlins of Lt Oggins.* nd. NY. ils Donald McKay. unp. VG/dj. B18. $25.00

SHAPIRO, Irwin. *Tall Tales of America.* 1958. Guild Pr. pub sample. ils Al Schmidt. 124p. cloth. A17. $8.00

SHAPIRO, Karl. *Adult Bookstore.* 1976. Random. 2nd. 76p. VG. B10. $8.00

SHAPIRO, Karl. *Collected Poems 1940-1978.* 1979. Random. 1st ed rem mk. NF/VG+. B4. $45.00

SHAPIRO, Karl. *Person, Place & Things.* 1942. Reynal Hitchcock. 2nd. assn copy. NF/VG. V1. $20.00

SHAPIRO, Karl. *Poems 1940-1953.* 1953. Random. rpt. sgn. 8vo. 159p. VG/VG. B11. $45.00

SHAPIRO, Karl. *To Abolish Children & Other Essays.* 1968. Chicago. 1st ed. F/NF. V1. $20.00

SHAPLEN, Robert. *Forest of Tigers.* 1956. Knopf. 1st ed. F/NF. H11. $40.00

SHAPO, Marshall. *Nation of Guinea Pigs: Unknown Risks of Chemical Technology.* 1979. NY. 1st ed. 300p. VG. A13. $30.00

SHARABI, H.B. *Goverments & Politics of the Middle East in 20th Century.* 1963. Van Nostrand. 2nd. ils. 296p. VG/dj. W1. $22.00

SHARDA, S.R. *Sufi Thought.* 1974. New Delhi. 288p. VG/dj. W1. $18.00

SHARER, Robert. *Quirigua.* 1990. Durham, NC. 1st ed. 124p. dj. F3. $50.00

SHARMA, P.V. *Geophysical Methods in Geology.* 1983 (1976). Elsevier. 6th. 8vo. ils/tables/charts. new cloth. VG. B1. $26.50

SHARON, Ariel. *Warrior.* 1989. Simon Schuster. 1st ed. 571p. AN/dj. B22. $5.00

SHARP, Adda Mai. *Gee Whillikins.* 1950. Steck Vaughn. later rpt. 4to. VG/clip. B17. $5.00

SHARP, Anne Pearsall. *Little Garden People & What They Do.* 1938. Saalfield. ils Marion Bryson. pict brd. VG. M5. $20.00

SHARP, Margery. *Miss Bianca & the Bridesmaid.* 1972. Little Brn. 1st Am ed. 123p. VG/dj. M20. $42.00

SHARP, Margery. *Miss Bianca in the Antarctic.* 1971. Little Brn. 1st ed. ils. 134p. F/VG+. P2. $35.00

SHARP, Paul F. *Whoop-Up Country.* 1973. Norman, OK. 1st ed thus. ils/photos/index. 347p. F/dj. E1. $70.00

SHARPE, Philip. *Rifle in America.* 1943. NY. 2nd. ils. 641p. VG. B5. $40.00

SHARPE, Tom. *Great Pursuit.* 1977. Harper. 1st Am ed. NF/NF. B4. $50.00

SHARSMITH, Helen K. *Genus Hesperolinon.* 1961. Berkeley. ils. 80p. wrp. B26. $17.50

SHATNER, William. *TekWar.* 1989. 1st ed. author's 1st book. F/F. M19. $25.00

SHAUB & SHAUB. *Treasures From the Earth: World of Rocks & Minerals.* 1975. Crown. 1st prt. 223p. VG. D8. $10.00

SHAUGHNESSY, Dan. *Curse of the Bambino.* 1990. Dutton. 1st ed. F/F. P8. $25.00

SHAW, Albert. *Cartoon History of Roosevelt's Career.* 1910. NY. red cloth. xl. G. B30. $20.00

SHAW, Andrew; see Block, Lawrence.

SHAW, Bernard. *Saint Joan: A Chronicle & the Apple Cart...* 1932. London. brn full leather/marbled edges. VG. B30. $135.00

SHAW, Bob. *Fugitive Worlds.* 1989. Gollancz. 1st ed. F/NF. G10. $20.00

SHAW, Bob. *Ragged Astronauts.* 1987. BAen. 1st Am ed. F/NF. G10. $10.00

SHAW, Bob. *Wreath of Stars.* 1976. Gollancz. 1st ed. sgn. AN/dj. M21. $35.00

SHAW, Charles. *Indian Life in Texas.* 1987. Austin. 1st ed. photos Reagan Bradshaw. 204p. AN. E1. $24.00

SHAW, George Bernard. *Androcles & the Lion.* 1916. London. Constable. 1st ed. gilt gr cloth. F/dj. B24. $500.00

SHAW, George Bernard. *Bernard Shaw's Rhyming Picture Guide to Ayot Saint Lawrence.* 1950. Leagrave. 1st ed. NF. M19. $17.50

SHAW, George Bernard. *Crime of Imprisonment.* 1946. Phil. 1st ed. F. M19. $17.50

SHAW, George Bernard. *Doctor's Dilemma, Getting Married & Shewing-Up of Blanco...* 1911. Constable. 1st ed. lt gr cloth. F/dj. B24. $500.00

SHAW, George Bernard. *Quintessence of Ibsenism.* 1891. London. Walter Scott. 1st ed. indigo cloth. NF. B24. $300.00

SHAW, George Bernard. *Shaw on Stalin.* 1941. London. Russia Today Soc. 1st ed. 8vo. 11p. NF. B24. $75.00

SHAW, Henry. *Dresses & Decorations of the Middle Ages.* 1851. London. Pickering. 2 vol. 94 engraved pl/98 woodcuts. teg. buckram. T10. $2,500.00

SHAW, Irwin. *Beggarman, Thief.* 1977. Delacorte. 1st ed. F/F. H11. $30.00

SHAW, Irwin. *Young Lions.* 1948. Random. 1st ed. F/F. B4. $400.00

SHAW, Lloyd. *Cowboy Dances: Collection of Western Square Dances.* 1945. Caldwell, ID. 7th. 411p. G. E1. $30.00

SHAW, M.M. *9,000 Miles on Pullman Train.* 1898. Phil. 1st ed. ils. 214p. VG. B5. $50.00

SHAW, Robert. *Man in the Glass Booth.* 1967. HBW. 1st ed. F/NF. H11. $25.00

SHAW. *Childhood in Poetry, a Catalogue...* 1976. FL State. 2 vol. 1965p. VG. A4. $35.00

SHAW. *Childhood in Poetry, the 40-Year History of a Collection...* 1970. np. inscr. 28p. cloth. F. A4. $65.00

SHAW(N), Frank S.; see Goulart, Ron.

SHAY, Frank. *From the Wood, Consolations in Words & Music...* 1929. Gold Label. ils John Held Jr. VG. B17. $7.50

SHAYNE, Mike; see Halliday, Brett.

SHEA, Michael. *Polyphemus.* 1987. Arkham. 1st ed. 1/3528. F/F. T2. $60.00

SHEA & TROYER. *Oriental Literature.* 1901. NY/London. Dunne. 1st ed. 8vo. 411p. teg. VG. W1. $25.00

SHECKLEY, Robert. *Dramoles.* 1983. Holt. 1st ed. F/NF. G10. $8.00

SHEDLEY, Ethan. *Medusa Conspiracy.* 1980. Viking. 1st ed. VG/VG. N4. $17.50

SHEEHY. *Guide to Reference Books, Ninth Edition.* 1976. Am Lib Assn. 4to. 1033p. F. A4. $75.00

SHEFFIELD, Charles. *Cold As Ice.* 1992. Tor. 1st ed. F/F. G10. $10.00

SHEINWOLD, Alfred. *Pocket Book of Bridge Puzzles No 2.* 1970. NY. 191p. VG/wrp. S1. $3.00

SHELDON, Alice Bradley. *Her Smoke Rose Up Forever: Great Years of James Tiptree, Jr.* 1990. Arkham. 1st ed. F/F. M22/T2. $30.00

SHELDON, Alice Bradley. *Tales of the Quintana Roo.* 1986. Arkham. 1st ed. F/dj. G10/T2. $12.00

SHELDON, Raccoona; see Sheldon, Alice Bradley.

SHELDON, Sidney. *Other Side of Midnight.* 1974. Morrow. 1st ed. F/NF. H11. $35.00

SHELDON, Walter J. *Tigers in the Rice: Story of Vietnam...* 1969. NY. Crowell Collier. 1st ed. F/F. B4. $85.00

SHELDON, William. *Penny Whimsey.* 1976. Lawrence, MA. 1t ed. 51 pl. VG/VG. B5. $47.50

SHELL, Ray. *Iced.* 1994. Random. 1st ed. sgn. F/F. M23. $20.00

SHELLER, Roscoe. *Bandit to Lawman.* 1966. Yakima, WA. 1st ed. sgn. photos. 176p. F/worn. E1. $60.00

SHELLER, Roscoe. *Ben Snipes.* 1959. Portland, OR. 3rd. 205p. F/F. E1. $40.00

SHELLEY, Percy Bysshe. *Laon & Cythna.* 1818. London. Sherwood Neely. 1/750. F. B24. $6,500.00

SHELTON, Azariah. *Shelton's American Medicine; or, Improvement...* 1834. Madisonville, TN. 1st ed. 400p. contemporary full sheep. VG. C6. $650.00

SHELTON, Charles E. *Photo Album of Yesterday's Southwest.* 1974. Palm Desert, CA. 1st ed. photos. 191p. E1. $40.00

SHELTON, L. *Charles Marion Russell: Cowboy Artist Friend.* 1962. NY. 1st ed. ils. 229p. VG/VG. B5. $45.00

SHELTON, Robert. *No Direction Home.* 1986. Morrow. AP. 8vo. VG/prt bl wrp. S9. $45.00

SHELTON, V. *Mask for Treason.* 1965. Harrisburg. 1st ed. VG/G. B5. $45.00

SHELTON, William Roy. *Winning the Moon.* 1970. Boston. 1st ed. 230p. VG/dj. A17. $17.50

SHELTON & YEATS. *History of Nolan County, Texas.* 1975. Sweetwater, TX. sgn. 255p. F/F. E1. $25.00

SHEPARD, E.V. *Correct Contract Bridge.* 1930. NY. 265p. VG. S1. $6.00

SHEPARD, E.V. *Win at Bridge.* 1927. NY. 155p. VG. S1. $6.00

SHEPARD, Elaine. *Doom Pussy.* 1967. Trident. 1st ed/2nd prt. inscr. F/NF clip. B4. $75.00

SHEPARD, Ernest H. *Drawn From Memory.* 1957. Lippincott. ARC/1st ed. ils. 190p. VG/dj. D1. $100.00

SHEPARD, Ernest. *Ben & Brock.* 1965. Methuen. 1st ed. 79p. VG+/VG. P2. $36.00

SHEPARD, Lucius. *Ends of the Earth.* 1991. Arkham. 1st ed. sgn. F/F. T2. $45.00

SHEPARD, Lucius. *Golden.* 1993. Mark Ziesing. 1st ed. 1/500. sgn/#d. F/F/case. T2. $85.00

SHEPARD, Lucius. *Jaguar Hunter.* 1987. Arkham. 1st ed. 1/3194. inscr. F/F. T2. $125.00

SHEPARD, Lucius. *Kalimantan.* 1990. London. Century. 1st ed. sgn. F/F. T2. $35.00

SHEPARD, Lucius. *Life During Wartime.* 1988. London. Grafton. 1st hc ed. F/F. T2. $35.00

SHEPARD, Lucius. *Scalehunter's Beautiful Daughter.* 1988. Ziesing. 1st ed. sgn. F/F. T2. $25.00

SHEPARD, Sam. *Rolling Stone Logbook.* 1977. ARC. w/3 publicity photos. NF/VG. S13. $45.00

SHEPARD. *Lore of the Unicorn.* 1982. np. rpt of 1930 ed. 24 pl. 312p. NF/NF. A4. $35.00

SHEPHEARD, William. *Of Corporations, Fraternities & Guilds...* 1659. London. Twyford Dring. only ed. modern unlettered calf. M11. $1,500.00

SHEPHERD, Gordon. *Foundations of the Neuron Doctrine.* 1991. NY. 338p. dj. A13. $40.00

SHEPHERD, John; see Ballard, W.T.

SHEPHERD, Michael; see Ludlum, Robert.

SHEPHERD, Naomi. *Zealous Intruders: Western Rediscovery of Palestine.* 1987. Harper Row. 1st ed. ils/map. 282p. NF/dj. W1. $18.00

SHEPHERD, Shep; see Whittington, Harry.

SHEPPERD, G.A. *History of War & Weapons 1660 to 1918.* 1972. NY. 1st Am ed. 223p. F/F. E1. $33.00

SHEPPERSON, Wilbur S. *Samuel Roberts: A Welsh Colonizer in Civil War Tennessee.* 1961. TN U. 1st ed. ils. VG/G. B10. $25.00

SHERBURNE, Andrew. *Memoirs of Andrew Sherburne.* 1828. Utica. Williams. 262p. half calf/marbled brd. VG. T7. $175.00

SHERBURNE, James. *Hacey Miller.* 1971. Houghton Mifflin. 1st ed. sgn. VG/VG. B11. $30.00

SHERESKY, Norman. *On Trial: Masters of the Courtroom.* 1977. Viking. M11. $45.00

SHERIDAN, Martin. *Comics & Their Creators: Life Stories of Am Cartoonists.* 1942. np. sgn. VG. M17. $25.00

SHERIDAN, Thomas. *Works of the Reverand Doctor Jonathan Swift...* 1784. London. Bathurst. 17 vol. revised/corrected. contemporary bdg. NF. T10. $2,000.00

SHERMAN, Charles Phineas. *Roman Law in the Modern World.* 1924. NY. Baker Voorhis. gr cloth. M11. $250.00

SHERMAN, Delia. *Porcelain Dove.* 1993. Dutton. 1st ed. rem mk. F/F. G10. $20.00

SHERMAN, Fanny Jessop. *Admiral Wags.* 1943. Dodd Mead. 1st ed. inscr. VG. M5. $60.00

SHERMAN, Frances. *Complete Poems.* 1935. Tor. 1st ed. 178p. gilt cloth. VG. A17. $15.00

SHERMAN, Harold M. *Crashing Through!* 1932. Grosset Dunlap. VG/VG. P12. $12.00

SHERMAN, Harold M. *Safe!* 1928. Grosset Dunlap. 308p. cloth. VG/dj. M20. $32.00

SHERMAN, Harold M. *Under the Basket.* 1932. Goldsmith. VG/poor. P12. $7.00

SHERMAN, John. *Recollections of Forty Years in the House, Senate & Cabinet.* 1895. Chicago. Werner. 2 vol. 8vo. ils. dk olive cloth. NF. T10. $50.00

SHERMAN, John. *Recollections of Forty Years in the House, Senate & Cabinet.* 1895. Werner. ils. 949p. VG. B10. $45.00

SHERMAN, William Tecumseh. *Memoirs of..., Written by Himself, With an Appendix...* 1891. NY. Webster. 2 vol. 4th. gr cloth w/shoulder strap insignia. VG+. M8. $150.00

SHERMAN & SHERMAN. *Ghost Towns of Arizona.* 1969. Norman, OK. 1st ed. 208p. F/stiff wrp. E1. $35.00

SHERRINGTON, Charles. *Endeavour of Jan Fernel.* 1946. Cambridge. 1st ed. 223p. VG. A13. $75.00

SHERRINGTON, Charles. *Selected Writings of Sir Charles Sherrington.* 1940. NY. 1st Am ed. 532p. VG. A13. $250.00

SHERROD, Robert. *History of Marine Corps Aviation in WWII.* 1952. WA. 1st ed. 496p. map ep. VG. B18. $25.00

SHERWOOD, Bob. *Hold Yer Hosses.* 1932. NY. 1st ed. inscr. 361p. VG/G. B5. $75.00

SHERWOOD, Elmer. *Ted Marsh, the Young Volunteer.* ca 1900. Whitman. ils Neil O'Keefe. G-. P12. $4.00

SHERWOOD, Elmer. *Ted Marsh on an Important Mission.* ca 1900. Whitman. ils Alice Carsey. G+. P12. $7.00

SHERWOOD, Frances. *Vindication.* 1993. FSG. 1st ed. F/F. M23. $20.00

SHERWOOD, Morgan B. *Alaska & Its History.* 1967. Seattle. 1st ed. photos/biblio. VG. E1. $50.00

SHERWOOD, Robert E. *There Shall Be No Night.* 1940. Scribner. 1st ed. NF/NF. B2. $45.00

SHIEL, Jacob H. *Journey Through the Rocky Mountains & Humboldt Mountains...* 1959. np. 1st ed. trans/edit TN Bonner. 114p. F/F. E1. $40.00

SHIEL, M.P. *Lord of the Sea.* 1981. Souvenir. rpt. F/F. G10. $15.00

SHIEL, M.P. *Prince Zaleski & Cummings King Monk.* 1977. Mycroft Moran. 1st ed thus. 1/4036. F/F. T2. $12.00

SHIEL, M.P. *Xelucha & Others.* 1975. Arkham. 1st ed. 1/4283. F/F. T2. $12.00

SHIELDS, Anna. *Ethiopia's Petition.* 1981. Cambridge. self pub. 1st ed. 12mo. brn stapled wrp. B4. $150.00

SHIELDS, Carol. *Mary Swann.* 1990. London. 1st ed. author's 1st book pub in Eng. F/dj. S9. $75.00

SHIELDS, Carol. *Stone Diaries.* 1994. Viking. 1st ed. F/F. M23. $40.00

SHIMER, J.A. *This Sculptured Earth.* 1959. Columbia. 255p. VG. D8. $14.00

SHINER, Lewis. *Deserted Cities of the Heart.* 1988. Doubleday. 1st ed. author's 2nd novel. NF/NF. M22. $30.00

SHINER, Lewis. *Slam.* 1990. Doubleday. 1st ed. author's 3rd novel. NF/NF. M22. $30.00

SHIPHERD, Jacob R. *History of the Oberlin-Wellington Rescue.* 1859. Boston. 1st ed. 280p. fair. B18. $75.00

SHIPLEY, Robert. *Paddle Wheelers.* 1991. Ontario. Vanwell. AN. A16. $10.95

SHIPLEY, Robert. *Propellers.* 1992. Ontario. Vanwell. AN. A16. $10.95

SHIPMAN, Mrs. O.L. *Letters, Past & Present.* nd. np. 1st ed. inscr. photos/index. 137p. F/stiff wrp. E1. $150.00

SHIPMAN, Mrs. O.L. *Taming the Big Bend: A History...* 1926. Marfa, TX. index. 215p. G. E1. $425.00

SHIPPEY, Lee. *It's an Old California Custom.* 1948. NY. 292p. F/worn. E1. $40.00

SHIPPEY, Tom. *Oxford Book of SF Stories.* 1992. Oxford. 1st ed. F/F. G10. $15.00

SHIRAEFF, Peter. *Flattery's Foal.* 1938. Knopf. 1st Am ed. VG/G. O3. $25.00

SHIRER, William L. *Nightmare Years 1930-1940.* 1984. Boston. BOMC. photos/index. dj. A17. $12.50

SHIRER, William L. *20th-Century Journey: A Memoir of a Life & the Times...* 1976. NY. 1st ed. 510p. F/G. E1. $30.00

SHIRK, Jeannette. *Mr Baxter's Dandelion Garden.* 1940. Dutton. 1st ed. ils. 60p. VG. P2. $18.00

SHIRLEY, Glenn. *Belle Starr & Her Times...* 1982. Norman, OK. 1st ed. 324p. F/F. E1. $50.00

SHIRLEY, Glenn. *Buckskin & Spurs.* 1948. NY. 1st ed. 191p. F/F. E1. $40.00

SHIRLEY, Glenn. *Gunfight at Ingalls: Death of an Outlaw Town.* 1990. Stillwater. 1st ed. sgn. 180p. F/F. E1. $35.00

SHIRLEY, Glenn. *Heck Thomas: Frontier Marshal.* 1962. NY. 1st ed. photos/maps. 231p. F/G. E1. $50.00

SHIRLEY, Glenn. *Heck Thomas: Frontier Marshal.* 1981. Norman OK. 1st ed thus. 285p. F/F. E1. $35.00

SHIRLEY, Glenn. *Henry Starr, Last of the Real Badmen.* 1965. NY. 1st ed. photos/index. F/VG. E1. $45.00

SHIRLEY, Glenn. *Pawnee Bill: A Biography of Major Gordon W Lillie.* 1958. Albuquerque, NM. 1st ed. ils/photos/biblio. 256p. F/VG. E1. $45.00

SHIRLEY, Glenn. *Red Yesterdays.* 1977. Wichita Falls, TX. 1st ed. 298p. F/F. E1. $30.00

SHIRLEY, Glenn. *Temple Houston: Lawyer With a Gun.* 1980. Norman, OK. ARC/1st ed. 339p. F/G. E1. $50.00

SHIRLEY, Glenn. *Temple Houston: Lawyer With a Gun.* 1981. Norman. 1st ed/2nd prt. 339p. M/dj. P4. $25.00

SHIRLEY, Glenn. *West of Hell's Fringe.* 1978. Norman, OK. 1st ed. index/notes/photos. 496p. F/VG. E1. $40.00

SHIRLEY, Rodney W. *Early Printed Maps of the British Isles...* 1980. London. Holland. revised ed. M/dj. O7. $75.00

SHOCKLEY, Ann Allen. *Afro-American Women Writers 1746-1933: An Anthology...* 1988. Boston. GK Hall. 1st ed. 465p. cloth. NF/NF. M8. $45.00

SHOEMAKER, C.E. *Ear: Its Diseases & Their Treatment...* 1882. Reading, PA. ils. F/wrp. B14. $35.00

SHOLOKHOV, Mikhail. *One Man's Destiny & Other Stories...1923-1963.* 1967. Knopf. 1st ed. F/F. B35. $32.00

SHORT, Wayne. *Cheechakoes.* 1964. Random. 1st ed. 244p. VG/dj. P4. $15.00

SHOWKER, Kay. *Fodor's Egypt 1979.* 1979. McKay. 1st ed. 12mo. ils. 246p. VG/dj. W1. $12.00

SHRAKE, Edwin. *Strange Peaches.* 1972. Harper's Magazine Pr. 1st ed. F/F. A18. $20.00

SHRYOCK, Richard. *Medicine in America, Historical Essays.* 1966. Baltimore. 1st ed. 346p. xl. A13. $45.00

SHUBOW, Joseph Shalom. *Brandeis Avukah Annual of 1932...* 1932. NY. Am Student Zionist Fed. w/2 facimile letters. M11. $175.00

SHULEVITZ, Uri. *Oh What a Noise.* nd. NY. Macmillan. 1st ed. 4to. unp. G+. C14. $10.00

SHULL, A.F. *Principles of Animal Biology.* 1946. McGraw Hill. 6th. sgn. 8vo. 425p. cloth. B1. $35.00

SHULMAN, Max. *I Was a Teen-Age Dwarf.* 1959. NY. Geis. 1st ed. F/VG clip. B4. $65.00

SHUMAKER, P.L. *Colt's Variations of the Old Model Pocket Pistol...1872.* 1966. Alhambra, CA. 2nd. 150p. F/F. E1. $45.00

SHUMARD, George. *Ballad & History of Billy the Kid: Facts & Legends.* 1966. np. ils/photos. 31p. NF/wrp. E1. $45.00

SHUMARD, George. *Billy the Kid: Robin Hood of Lincoln Co.* 1969. Deming, NM. 1st ed. 64p. F/stiff pict wrp. E1. $30.00

SHURE, David. *Hester Batemen: Queen of English Silversmiths.* 1959. Garden City. 1st ed. 87 pl. VG. B5. $40.00

SHURLOCK, H.M. *Laws of Contract Bridge Explained.* 1965. London. 88p. F/F. S1. $8.00

SHUTE, H. *Brite & Fair.* 1968. Peterborough. 1st ed. ils Tasha Tudor. VG/VG. P3. $35.00

SHUTE, Neville. *In the Wet.* 1953. NY. 1st ed. VG/VG. B5. $35.00

SHUTE, Neville. *No Highway.* 1948. NY. 1st ed. VG/VG. B5. $40.00

SHUTE, Neville. *On the Beach.* 1957. 1st ed. VG/G+. S13. $25.00

SHUTE, Neville. *Vinland the Good.* 1946. NY. 1st ed. VG/VG. B5. $50.00

SHYROCK & TWENHOFEL. *Invertebrate Paleontology.* 1935. McGraw Hill. 1st ed/11th prt. VG. D8. $30.00

SIBLEY, Celestine. *Children, My Children.* 1981. NY. Harper. 1st ed. inscr. F/F. B4. $65.00

SIBLEY, Marilyn McAdams. *George W Brackenridge, Maverick Philanthropist.* 1973. Austin. 1st ed. 280p. F/VG. E1. $30.00

SIBLEY. *Lone Stars & State Gazettes, Texas Newspapers...* 1983. TX A&M. 431p. VG. A4. $20.00

SICHERMAN. *Notable American Women: The Modern Period.* 1980. Harvard. 795p. VG. A4. $35.00

SIDDONS, Anne Rivers. *Downtown.* 1994. Harper Collins. 1st ed. sgn. AN/dj. B4. $45.00

SIDDONS, Anne Rivers. *Heartbreak Hotel.* 1976. Simon Schuster. 1st ed. rem mk. F/F. B4. $65.00

SIDDONS, Anne Rivers. *Hill Towns.* 1st ed. sgn. F/F. B30. $25.00

SIDDONS, Anne Rivers. *House Next Door.* 1978. NY. 1st ed. sgn. F/NF. C2. $50.00

SIDDONS, Anne Rivers. *King's Oak.* 1992. Harper Collins. ARC. sgn. F/wrp. B4. $35.00

SIDDONS, Henry. *Practical Illustrations of Rhetorical Gesture & Action...* 1922. London. 2nd. 69 full-p pl. 408p. blk calf. VG. B14. $150.00

SIDER, Sandra. *Maps, Charts, Globes: Five Centuries of Exploration.* 1992. NY. Hispanic Soc of Am. new revised ed. 73 full-p pl. M/dj. O7. $45.00

SIDES, Joseph C. *Fort Brown Historical.* 1942. San Antonio. 1st ed. photos/biblio. 160p. E1. $100.00

SIDNEY, George. *For the Love of Dying.* 1969. Morrow. 1st ed. inscr. NF/VG. B4. $125.00

SIDNEY, Margaret. *Five Little Peppers & How They Grew.* 1909. Lee Shepard. 16mo. VG/VG. B17. $10.00

SIEGEL. *Used Book Lover's Guide to New England.* 1933. np. 8vo. ils. 337p. G. T3. $7.00

SIEGLER, S.L. *Fertility in Women.* 1944. Lippincott. ils. 450p. VG. B14. $35.00

SIFAKIS. *Who Was Who in the Civil War.* 1988. np. 4to. ils/photos. 766p. F. A4. $135.00

SIGAL, Clancy. *Zone of the Interior.* 1976. Crowell. 1st ed. F/NF. B35. $20.00

SIGAUD, Louis A. *Douhet & Aerial Warfare.* 1941. NY. 1st ed. 134p. G. B18. $25.00

SIGERIST, Henry. *Experimentelle Untersuchungen Uber die Einwirkung...* 1917. Zurich. 1st ed. 21p. VG/wrp. A13. $35.00

SIGERIST, Henry. *Great Doctors.* 1933. NY. 1st Eng trans. 436p. VG. A13. $100.00

SIGERIST, Henry. *Medicine & Human Welfare.* 1947. New Haven. 148p. w/Christmas card. A13. $60.00

SILEKSY. *Ferlinghetti: Artist in His Time.* 1990. np. 32 photos. 294p. F/F. A4. $35.00

SILK, Dennis. *Punished Land.* 1980. Viking. ARC/1st ed. RS. F/NF. w/pub card. V1. $20.00

SILKO, Leslie Marmon. *Almanac of the Dead.* 1991. Simon Schuster. 1st ed. F/F. A18. $25.00

SILLIMAN, Benjamin. *First Principles of Physics & Natural Philosophy.* 1859. Phil. ils. 720p. blk/brn cloth. VG. B14. $150.00

SILONE, Ignazio. *Bread & Wine.* 1937. Harper. 1st ed. F/VG. A17. $8.50

SILVA, Joseph; see Goulart, Ron.

SILVA, Katharine. *Baja California Bibliography 1965-1966.* 1968. La Jolla, CA. 42p. F3. $25.00

SILVA, Zenaide C.G. *Estudio Sobre Jadeitas y Albititas de Guatemala.* 1969. Guate. ltd ed. 1/300. 4to. 22p. F3. $20.00

SILVERBERG, Robert. *Calibrated Alligator.* 1969. HRW. 1st ed. xl. VG/VG. N4. $12.00

SILVERBERG, Robert. *Ghost Towns of the American West.* 1968. NY. 1st ed. ils/biblio. 309p. E1. $35.00

SILVERBERG, Robert. *Kingdoms of the Wall.* 1993. Bantam. 1st ed. F/NF. G10. $15.00

SILVERBERG, Robert. *Longest Continent.* 1964. Greenwich. NYGS. 1st ed. 279p. VG/dj. P4. $12.50

SILVERBERG, Robert. *New Springtime.* 1990. Putnam. 1st trade ed. VG. M21. $25.00

SILVERBERG, Robert. *Project Pendulum.* 1987. Walker. 1st ed. RS. F/F. G10. $15.00

SILVERBERG, Robert. *Sarnia.* 1974. Hamish Hamilton. 1st ed. NF/NF. P3. $20.00

SILVERBERG, Robert. *Valentine Pontifex.* 1983. Arbor. 1st ed. NF/VG+. G10. $7.50

SILVERMAN, David P. *Masterpieces of Tutankhamun.* 1978. Abbeville. 1st ed. 73 photos. 159p. NF/dj. W1. $25.00

SILVERMAN, Maida. *Dune.* 1984. Grosset Dunlap. ils Daniel Kirk. VG. B17. $15.00

SILVERSTANG, Edwin. *Winning Casino Craps.* 1979. NY. 141p. VG/wrp. S1. $3.00

SILVERSTEIN, Shel. *Missing Piece.* 1976. Harper Row. 1st ed. 8vo. VG/VG. B17. $15.00

SILVERTHORNE, Elizabeth. *Plantation Life in Texas.* 1986. College Sta, TX. 1st ed. 234p. E1. $30.00

SILVETTE, Herbert. *Come Unto Me.* 1958. Johnson. 1st ed. 256p. VG/VG. B10. $20.00

SILVETTE, Herbert. *Eve's Second Apple.* 1946. Dutton. 2nd. inscr. VG/G+. B10. $15.00

SILVETTE, Herbert. *Maiden Voyage.* 1950. Dutton. 1st ed. inscr. xl. G/G. B10. $15.00

SILVIS, Randall. *Luckiest Man in the World.* 1984. Pittsburgh. 1st ed. author's 1st book. F/F. B4. $45.00

SILVIS, Randall. *Occasional Hell.* 1993. Permanent. 1st ed. sgn. F/F. T2. $35.00

SIMENON, Georges. *Glass Cage.* 1973. Harcourt. 1st Am ed. F/F. M22. $15.00

SIMENON, Georges. *Little Saint.* 1965. HBW. 1st Eng-language ed. sgn. trans B Frechtman. NF/NF. A11. $75.00

SIMENON, Georges. *Maigret & the Apparition.* 1976. HBJ. 1st ed. F/F. H11. $20.00

SIMENON, Georges. *Maigret & the Spinster.* 1977. HBJ. 1st ed. F/F. H11. $30.00

SIMENON, Georges. *Maigret's Dead Man.* 1964. Doubleday. 1st Am ed. xl. G+/dj. N4. $12.50

SIMENON, Georges. *Nightclub.* 1979. HBJ. 1st ed. F/F. H11. $25.00

SIMIC, Charles. *Unending Blues.* 1986. HBJ. 1st ed. sgn. F/F. V1. $35.00

SIMIC, Charles. *9 Poems.* 1989. Exact Change. ltd ed. 1/500. F/wrp. V1. $45.00

SIMKINS, Francis Butler. *Virginia: History, Government & Geography.* 1957. Scribner. 1st ed. photos/index. B10. $15.00

SIMMONDS, Posy. *Chocolate Wedding.* 1991. NY. Knopf. 1st Am ed. 4to. unp. VG. C14. $5.00

SIMMONS, Dan. *Carrion Comfort.* 1989. Dark Harvest. 1st ed. F/F. T2. $75.00

SIMMONS, Dan. *Carrion Comfort.* 1989. Dark Harvest. 1st ed. NF/NF. M19. $65.00

SIMMONS, Dan. *Children of the Night.* 1992. Putnam. 1st ed. F/F. M23. $30.00

SIMMONS, Dan. *Fall of Hyperion.* 1990. Doubleday. 1st ed. ES. F/F. T2. $75.00

SIMMONS, Dan. *Fall of Hyperion.* 1990. Doubleday. 1st ed. sgn. ES. F/F. M23. $100.00

SIMMONS, Dan. *Fires of Eden.* 1st ed. F/F. B30. $23.00

SIMMONS, Dan. *Hollow Man.* 1992. Bantam. 1st ed. F/F. M23. $25.00

SIMMONS, Dan. *Hollow Man.* 1992. Northridge. Lord John. ltd ed. 1/500. sgn. F/sans/case. T2. $100.00

SIMMONS, Dan. *Hyperion.* 1989. Doubleday. 1st ed. sgn. F/F. M23. $200.00

SIMMONS, Dan. *Love Death.* 1993. Warner. 1st ed. F/F. M23. $20.00

SIMMONS, Dan. *Summer of Night.* 1991. Putnam. 1st ed. F/F. M23. $40.00

SIMMONS, Dan. *Summer of Night.* 1991. Putnam. 1st ed. rem mk. F/NF. H11. $30.00

SIMMONS, Ernest J. *Dostoevsky: The Making of a Novelist.* 1950. London. Lehmann. 1st ed. 8vo. VG/dj. S9. $25.00

SIMMONS, Herbert. *Man Walking on Eggshells.* 1962. Houghton Mifflin. 1st ed. F/NF. B2. $35.00

SIMMONS, K. *Kriegie.* 1960. NY. 1st ed. sgn. VG/VG. B5. $25.00

SIMMONS, Leo W. *Sun Chief: Autobiography of a Hopi Indian.* 1942. New Haven. 1st ed. 460p. NF. E1. $50.00

SIMMONS, Marc. *Following the Santa Fe Trail: A Guide...* 1984. Santa Fe. 2nd. 215p. G/stiff wrp. E1. $10.00

SIMMONS, Marc. *People of the Sun.* 1979. NM U. 1st ed. ils. 142p. NF. B19. $25.00

SIMON, David. *Homicide.* 1991. Houghton Mifflin. 1st ed. NF/NF. H11. $25.00

SIMON, Howard. *500 Years of Art & Ils From Albrecht Durer to Rockwell Kent.* (1942). np. ils. 476p. VG. A4. $45.00

SIMON, Kate. *Wider World: Portraits in an Adolescence.* 1986. np. 186p. F/F. A4. $30.00

SIMON, Mina Lewiton. *Is Anyone Here?* 1967. Atheneum. 1st ed. unp. NF/VG. T5. $25.00

SIMON, Norma. *Tree for Me.* 1956. Lippincott. ils Helen Stone. unp. gr cloth. VG/torn. T5. $15.00

SIMON, Rachel. *Little Nightmares, Little Dreams.* 1990. Houghton Mifflin. 1st ed. inscr. F/F. B4. $35.00

SIMON, S.J. *Design for Bidding.* 1951. London. 2nd. 268p. VG. S1. $20.00

SIMONDS, William A. *Henry Ford: His Life, His Work, His Genius.* 1943. Bobbs Merrill. 1st ed. inscr. 15 pl. 365p. VG/VG. B11. $50.00

SIMONE, Andre. *Men of Europe.* 1941. NY. 330p. A17. $7.50

SIMPSON, C.H. *Life in the Far West; or, Detective's Thrilling Adventures.* 1898. Chicago. 2nd. ils. 264p. G. E1. $65.00

SIMPSON, Colin. *Lusitania.* 1972. Little Brn. BC. VG/VG. A16. $12.00

SIMPSON, F.A. *Rise of Louis Napoleon.* nd. np. VG. M17. $25.00

SIMPSON, Harold Brown. *Audie Murphy: America's Soldier.* 1975. Hilliboro, TX. 1st ed. 1/5000. VG/worn. B5. $65.00

SIMPSON, Harold Brown. *Hood's Texas Brigade: Lee's Grenadier Guard.* 1970. Waco, TX. Texian Pr. 1st ed. 512p. cloth. F/NF. M8. $125.00

SIMPSON, Harold Brown. *Marshall Guards Harrison County's Contribution to Hood...* 1967. Marshall, TX. Port Caddo. 1st ed. 26p. NF/stiff prt wrp. M8. $45.00

SIMPSON, Lesley Byrd. *Many Mexicos.* 1967. Berkeley. 4th. 8vo. 389p. silvered blk cloth. F/dj. T10. $25.00

SIMPSON, Mona. *Anywhere But Here.* 1987. Knopf. 1st ed. F/F. H11. $40.00

SIMPSON, Mona. *Anywhere But Here.* 1987. London. Bloomsbury. 1st ed. sgn. F/F. B4. $50.00

SIMPSON, Mona. *Lost Father.* 1992. Knopf. 1st ed. F/F. H11. $25.00

SIMPSON, Mona. *Lost Father.* 1992. Knopf. 1st ed. sgn. F/F. B4. $35.00

SIMPSON, Thomas William. *This Way Madness Lies.* 1992. Warner. 1st ed. author's 1st book. F/F. M23. $30.00

SIMPSON, Thomas. *Gypsy Storyteller.* 1993. Warner. 1st ed. F/F. H11. $30.00

SIMPSON, Walter. *Tularemia: History, Pathology, Diagnosis & Treatment.* 1929. NY. 1st ed. 162p. VG. A13. $50.00

SIMS, George; see Cain, Paul.

SIMS, Orland L. *Cowpokes, Nesters & So Forth.* 1970. Austin, TX. 1st ed. 297p. F/F. E1. $45.00

SIMS, P. Hal. *Pinochle Pointers.* 1935. Cincinnati. 111p. VG. S1. $6.00

SINATRA, Frank. *Man & His Art.* 1991. 1st ed. ils. NF/NF. S13. $16.00

SINCLAIR, Andrew. *Project.* 1960. NY. 1st ed. NF/dj. A17. $10.00

SINCLAIR, April. *Coffee Will Make You Black.* 1994. Hyperion. 1st ed. author's 1st novel. F/F. M23. $50.00

SINCLAIR, Upton. *Book of Life, Mind & Body.* 1921. Macmillan. 1st ed. NF. B2. $40.00

SINCLAIR, Upton. *It Happened to Didymus.* 1958. Sagamore. 1st ed. F/F. B2. $35.00

SINCLAIR, Upton. *It Happened to Didymus.* 1958. Sagamore. 1st ed. NF/NF. H11. $25.00

SINCLAIR, Upton. *Mental Radio.* 1930. Pasadena. 1st ed. VG/VG. B5. $65.00

SINCLAIR, Upton. *Millennium.* 1929. Pasadena. self pub. 1st Am hc ed. F. B2. $30.00

SINCLAIR, Upton. *O Shepherd, Speak!* 1949. Monrovia. self pub. 1st ed. sgn. NF/chip. B2. $85.00

SINCLAIR, Upton. *Presidential Mission.* 1947. Viking. 1st ed. F/NF. B2. $40.00

SINCLAIR & SOKOLSKY. *Is the American Form of Capitalism...* 1940. Girard. Haldeman-Julius. NF/wrp. B2. $45.00

SINCLAIR & WILLIAMS. *Good Health & How We Won It.* 1909. Stokes. 1st ed. photos. NF. B2. $85.00

SINCLAIR. *New Jersey & the Negro: A Biography, 1715-1966.* 1967. np. 1601 entries. 196p. VG. A4. $85.00

SINDELL & VENUS. *Dear, Dear Brenda: Love Letters of Henry Miller...* 1986. np. 10 photos. 191p. F/VG. A4. $40.00

SINGER, Brett. *Petting Zoo.* 1979. Simon Schuster. 1st ed. inscr. author's 1st novel. F/F. B4. $45.00

SINGER, I.J. *Steel & Iron.* 1969. Funk Wagnall. 1st Am ed. trans Joseph Singer. F/VG+. B4. $100.00

SINGER, Isaac Bashevis. *Alateh the Goat.* 1966. Harper Row. 1st ed. ils Sendak. 90p. VG/VG. D1. $195.00

SINGER, Isaac Bashevis. *Certificate.* 1992. FSG. 1st ed. F/F. B35. $17.00

SINGER, Isaac Bashevis. *Collected Stories.* 1982. FSG. 1st collected ed. 8vo. 47 stories. F/dj. T10. $35.00

SINGER, Isaac Bashevis. *Collected Stories.* 1982. FSG. 1st ed. F/clip. B35. $28.00

SINGER, Isaac Bashevis. *Elijah the Slave.* 1970. FSG. 1st ed. ils Antonio Frasconi. F/F. P2. $40.00

SINGER, Isaac Bashevis. *Fools of Chelm.* 1973. FSG. 1st ed. ils/sgn Uri Shulevitz. VG/G+. P2. $40.00

SINGER, Isaac Bashevis. *Golem.* 1982. FSG. 1st ed. sgn. ils/sgn Shulevitz. F. B4. $250.00

SINGER, Isaac Bashevis. *Little Boy in Search of God.* 1976. 1st ed. ils Ira Moskowitz. NF/VG. S13. $20.00

SINGER, Isaac Bashevis. *Manor.* 1967. FSG. 1st ed. F/F. H11. $40.00

SINGER, Isaac Bashevis. *Penitent.* 1983. FSG. 1st ed. F/F. B35. $18.00

SINGER, Isaac Bashevis. *Satan in Goray.* 1955. NY. Noonday. 1st ed. F/NF. B4. $250.00

SINGER, Isaac Bashevis. *Tale of Three Wishes.* 1976. FSG. 1st ed. ils Irene Lieblich. 30p. VG/VG. D1. $45.00

SINGER, Isaac Bashevis. *1985.* 1985. Jewish Pub Soc. 1st ed. F/F case. B35. $85.00

SINGER, J. *Unholy Bible.* 1970. NY. 1st ed. VG/VG. B5. $45.00

SINGTON & WEIDENFELD. *Goebell's Experiment: Study of Nazi Propaganda Machine.* 1943. Yale. 1st ed. 274p. G. A17. $14.00

SINISE, Jerry. *Pink Higgins, the Reluctant Gunfighter & Other Tales...* 1973. Quanah, TX. 1st ed. photos/index. F/F. E1. $50.00

SINISTRARI, Ludovico Maria. *Demoniality.* nd. London. Fortune. 1/1200 on Batchelor. teg. VG. T10. $215.00

SIPLE, Paul. *Boy Scout With Byrd.* 1931. NY. 1st ed. sgn. 165p. fair. B18. $22.50

SIPLE, Paul. *Boy Scout With Byrd.* 1931. Putnam. 1st ed. 33 photos. G. A17. $10.00

SIRINGO, Charles. *Texas Cowboy.* 1950. NY. ils Tom Lea. intro J Frank Dobie. F/poor. E1. $75.00

SIRKIS, Ruth. *Taste of Tradition: How & Why of Jewish Cooking.* 1985. Sirkis Pub. 1st ed thus. 128p. F. B22. $5.00

SISLER, George. *Sister on Baseball.* 1954. McKay. 1st ed. VG. P8. $20.00

SITWELL, Edith. *Green Song.* 1946. Vanguard. 1st ed. F/VG. V1. $25.00

SITWELL, Edith. *Poetry & Criticism.* 1926. Holt. 1st Am ed. VG. A15. $25.00

SITWELL, Edith. *Popular Song.* 1928. London. Faber Gwyer. 1st ed. 1/500. sgn. VG+. B4. $75.00

SITWELL, Edith. *Take Care of...* 1965. London. Hutchinson. 1st ed. F/NF. V1. $20.00

SITWELL, Sacheverell *Cupid & the Jacaranda.* 1952. London. 1st ed. VG. A17. $12.50

SITWELL, Sacheverell. *Fine Bird Books 1700-1900.* 1990. Atlantic Monthly. BOMC. 1st prt. 180p. F/dj. A17. $27.50

SITWELL, Sacheverell. *Great Flower Books 1700-1900: A Bibliographical Record.* 1990. Atlantic Monthly. 1st ed. 189p. F/dj. A17. $35.00

SJOBERG, John. *Some Poems on My Day Off.* 1984. Toothpaste Pr. ltd ed. 1/400. sgn. ils/sgn Stuart Mead. F. V1. $20.00

SJOWALL & WAHLOO. *Laughing Policeman.* 1970. Pantheon. 1st Am ed. VG/F. M22. $40.00

SJOWALL & WAHLOO. *Murder at the Savoy.* 1977. Pantheon. 1st Am ed. F/clip. T2. $20.00

SKAZKA. *Ivan Czarevich, the Firebird & Grey Wolf.* 1901. USSR. 1st ed. ils Ivan Bilibine. F/wrp. D1. $1,200.00

SKELTON, R.A. *County Atlases of the British Isles, 1579-1850.* 1978 (1970). Folkestone. Dawson. pl/maps. M. O7. $85.00

SKELTON, R.A. *Decorative Printed Maps of the 15th to 18th Centuries.* 1952. New York/London. ils. NF/rpr. O7. $55.00

SKELTON, Robin. *Begging the Dialect.* 1960. London. 1st ed. inscr/sgn. NF/dj. V1. $40.00

SKELTON, Skeeter. *Handgun Tales.* 1985. Peoria. 1st ed. 114p. F. E1. $25.00

SKENNERTON, Ian D. *British Service Lee.* 1982. London. 1st ed. photos/index. 410p. F/dj. E1. $40.00

SKIDMORE, Hobert Douglas. *Valley of the Sky.* 1944. Boston. 1st ed. VG. B18. $25.00

SKINNER, Cornelia Otis. *Nuts in May.* 1950. Dodd Mead. ils Alajalov. VG/G+. P12. $4.00

SKINNER & SKINNER. *Child's Book of Country Stories.* 1952. Dodde Mead. rpt. ils JW Smith. VG/VG. B17. $22.50

SKIPP & SPECTOR. *Book of the Dead.* 1989. Willimantic. Ziessing. 1st hc ed. 1/500. sgn edit/all contributors. F/dj/case. T2. $195.00

SKIPP & SPECTOR. *Still Dead.* 1992. Shingletown. Ziessing. 1st ed. sgn edit/all contributers except Jetter. F/F. T2. $65.00

SKLEPOWICH, Edward. *Death in a Serene City.* 1990. Morrow. 1st ed. author's 1st book. F/F. H11. $30.00

SKLEPOWICH, Edward. *Farewell to the Flesh.* 1991. Morrow. 1st ed. F/F. H11. $25.00

SKOLLE, John. *Azalai.* 1956. Harper. 1s ed. 8vo. 16 pl/3 maps. 272p. VG/dj. W1. $12.00

SKREBITSKI, G.A. *Forest Echo.* 1967. Braziller. 1st Am ed. 8vo. 72p. VG/VG. C14. $6.00

SKUES, G.E.M. *Way of a Trout With a Fly.* 1949. London. 4th. VG/VG. B5. $35.00

SLACK, Kenneth E. *In the Wake of the Spray.* 1966. Rutgers. 25 pl/3 plans. 274p. dj. T7. $35.00

SLATER, Kitty. *Hunt Country of America Revisited.* 1987. NY. Crowell. ARC/1st ed. VG/VG. O3. $45.00

SLATER, Kitty. *Hunt Country of America.* 1967. Barnes. 1st ed. VG/G. O3. $45.00

SLATKIN, Regina Shoolman. *Francois Boucher in North American Collections.* 1973-74. Art Inst Chicago. ils. 130p. cloth. clear plastic dj. D2. $55.00

SLATTERY, Margaret. *New Paths Through Old Palestine.* 1921. Boston/Chicago. Pilgrim. 1st ed. 8vo. 126p. VG. W1. $12.00

SLAVIN, Arthur J. *Tudor Men & Institutions, Studies in English Law...* 1972. Baton Rouge. 10 essays. M11. $45.00

SLAWINSKI, Lukasz. *Systems in Defence.* 1983. 1st Eng ed. sgn. 74p. VG/wrp. S1. $10.00

SLEIGH, Bernard. *Fairy Pageant.* 1924. Birmingham. Kynoch. 1/475. 12mo. 12 woodcuts. gr brd. F. B24. $150.00

SLESSOR, John. *Central Blue.* 1956. London. 1st ed. 709p. G/torn. B18. $27.50

SLIPHER, Earl C. *Photographic Story of Mars.* 1962. Sky/Northland. 4to. 168p. VG. K5. $100.00

SLOANE, Eric. *Cracker Barrel.* 1967. Funk Wagnall. 1st ed. ils. 110p. VG+/dj. M20. $25.00

SLOANE, T. O'Conor. *Rubber Hand Stamps & Manipulation of India Rubber.* 1912. NY. ils. 167p. VG. B18. $15.00

SLOBODIN, Richard. *WHR Rivers.* 1978. NY. 1st ed. 8vo. 295p. AN/dj. P4. $17.50

SLOBODKIN, Louis. *Colette & the Princess.* 1965. dj. K2. $15.00

SLOBODKIN, Louis. *Momi & the Lovely Animals.* 1960. Vanguard. 1st ed. sgn. VG/dj. M20. $52.00

SLOCUM, Joshua. *Sailing Alone Around the World & the Voyage of Liberdade.* 1948-1950. London. Hart Davis. Mariners Lib No 1. ils/maps. 384p. VG. T7. $24.00

SLOMAN, Joel. *Virgil's Machines.* 1966. Norton. 1st ed. assn copy. F/VG. V1. $15.00

SLONE, Rick. *Brown Shoe.* 1992. Random. 1st ed. author's 1st book. F/F. H11. $25.00

SLYTHE, R. Margaret. *Art of Illustration 1750-1900.* 1970. Lib Assn. 1st ed. sq 4to. 144p. T10. $45.00

SMALL, David. *Alone.* 1991. Norton. 1st ed. F/F. H11. $20.00

SMALL, David. *Eulalie & the Hopping Head.* 1982. Macmillan. 1st ed. sgn/dtd 1982. 8vo. unp. olive brd. NF/NF. T5. $45.00

SMALLBERG, Alfred J. *California Law Review & Quizzer...* 1926. Los Angeles. worn. M11. $50.00

SMALLEY, E.V. *Great Northwest: A Guide-Book & Itinerary...* 1888. St Paul. ils. lg pocket fld map. 390p. prt cloth. VG. B18. $135.00

SMALLWOOD, James. *And Gladly Teach, Reminiscences of Teachers...* 1976. Norman, OK. 1st ed. ils. 262p. E1. $30.00

SMART, Borlase. *Technique of Seascape Painting.* 1947. London. Pitman. 77 mtd pl. 129p. T7. $65.00

SMART, W.M. *Text-Book on Spherical Astronomy.* 1947 (1931). Cambridge. rpt. 8vo. 430p. cloth. G. K5. $30.00

SMEDLEY, H.H. *Fly Patterns & Their Origins.* 1944. Muskegon. VG. B5. $65.00

SMEDLY, Constance. *Tales From Timbuktu.* nd (1923). Chatto Windus. 1st ed. ils M Armfield. 179p. VG. P2. $125.00

SMEE, Alfred. *Instinct & Reason: Deduced From Electro-Biology.* 1850. London. Reeve Benham. 320p. emb ochre cloth. G1. $250.00

SMILEY, Jane. *Age of Grief.* 1987. Knopf. 1st ed. F/F. B4. $100.00

SMILEY, Jane. *Barn Blind.* 1994. London. Flamingo. ARC/1st ed. pb. RS. F/wrp. S9. $75.00

SMILEY, Jane. *Catskill Crafts: Artisans of the Catskill Mountains.* 1988. Crown. 1st ed. 4to. rem mk. F/F. B4. $50.00

SMILEY, Jane. *Duplicate Keys.* 1984. Knopf. 1st ed. F/F. B4. $125.00

SMILEY, Jane. *Greenlanders.* 1988. Knopf. 1st ed. w/promo postcard. F/F. H11. $65.00

SMILEY, Jane. *Ordinary Love & Good Will.* 1989. Knopf. 1st ed. F/F. H11. $45.00

SMILEY, Jane. *Ordinary Love & Good Will.* 1989. Knopf. 1st ed. inscr. F/F. B2. $85.00

SMILEY, Jane. *Thousand Acres.* 1991. Knopf. 1st ed. F/F clip. H11. $70.00

SMILEY, Jane. *Thousand Acres.* 1991. Knopf. 1st ed. F/F. B4. $125.00

SMITH, A.H. *Guide to the Sculptures of the Pentagon.* 1908. London. British Mus. 8vo. 10 pl. paper brd/cloth spine. VG. T10. $25.00

SMITH, A.J.M. *Collected Poems.* 1962. Toronto. ARC/1st ed. F/NF. V1. $15.00

SMITH, Alexander. *Complete History of Lives & Robberies of Most Notorious...* 1933. London. Routledge. 4to. 16 pl. 607p. VG. T7. $85.00

SMITH, April. *Axeman's Jazz.* 1991. St Martin. 1st ed. VG/VG. M22. $10.00

SMITH, April. *North of Montana.* 1994. Knopf. ARC. F/wrp. B4. $45.00

SMITH, April. *North of Montana.* 1994. Knopf. 1st ed. author's 1st novel. AN/dj. M22. $30.00

SMITH, Archibald. *Graphic Method of Correcting Deviations of Ship's Compass...* 1859. London. 8vo. fld prt diagrams. VG/bl prt wrp. B14. $150.00

SMITH, Arthur L. *Mildred the Rain Cloud.* (1963). San Carlos, CA. Golden Gate Jr Books. probable 1st ed. 8vo. 32p. F/VG. C14. $15.00

SMITH, Augusta Owens. *Solon Love Owens: Texas Cowboy.* 1978. Nortex. 131p. F. E1. $45.00

SMITH, Barbara Burnett. *Writers of the Purple Sage.* 1994. St Martin. 1st ed. F/F. M23. $30.00

SMITH, Betty. *Maggie-Now.* 1958. Harper. 1st ed. F/NF. B4. $75.00

SMITH, Betty. *Tomorrow Will Be Better.* 1948. Harper. 1st ed. NF/NF. B4. $100.00

SMITH, Bradford. *Islands of Hawaii.* 1957. Phil. VG. O7. $15.00

SMITH, Bradford. *Yankees in Paradise: New England Impact on Hawaii.* 1956. Lippincott. 8vo. 376p. F/dj. T10. $25.00

SMITH, Bruce. *State Police Organization & Administration.* 1925. Macmillan. 1st ed. NF. H7. $45.00

SMITH, Brydon. *Donald Judd: Catalogue Raisonne of Paintings...* 1975. Nat Gallery Canada. ils/photos. 319p. dj. D2. $750.00

SMITH, C. Harry. *Mennonites of America.* 1909. Mennonite Pub. VG+. M20. $20.00

SMITH, Charles W. *Life & Military Services of Brevet-Major General RS Foster.* 1915. Indianapolis. EJ Hecker. 1st separate ed. lib bookplate. VG/prt wrp. M8. $37.50

SMITH, Charlie. *Canaan.* 1984. Simon Schuster. 1st ed. author's 1st novel. sgn. rem mk. F/NF. M23. $35.00

SMITH, Charlie. *Chimney Rock.* 1993. Holt. 1st ed. F/F. H11. $20.00

SMITH, Charlie. *Crystal River.* 1991. Linden. 1st ed. F/F. H11. $35.00

SMITH, Charlie. *Indistinguisable From the Darkness.* 1990. Norton. 1st ed. F/NF. V1. $20.00

SMITH, Charlie. *Lives of the Dead.* 1990. Linden. 1st ed. F/F. H11. $35.00

SMITH, Charlie. *Shine Hawk.* 1988. Latham. British Am. 1st ed. NF/NF clip. H11. $45.00

SMITH, Clark Ashton. *Rendezvois in Averoigne: Best Fantastic Tales...* 1988. Arkham. 1st ed. 1/5025. F/F. T2. $23.00

SMITH, Clark Ashton. *Spells & Philtres.* 1958. Sauk City, WI. Arkham. 1st ed. 1/519. F/F. B24. $600.00

SMITH, Cordwainer; see Linebarger, Paul.

SMITH, Cornelius C. *Southwestern Vocabulary: The Words They Used.* 1984. Glendale. 1st ed. 168p. F. E1. $30.00

SMITH, Curt. *America's Dizzy Dean.* 1978. Bethany. 1st ed. F/VG. P8. $17.50

SMITH, David Alexander. *Future Boston.* 1994. Tor. 1st ed. F/F. G10. $25.00

SMITH, Dean C. *By the Seat of My Pants.* 1961. Boston. 1st ed. 245p. VG/dj. B5/B18. $35.00

SMITH, E. Delafield. *Perterhoff: Argument of E Delafield Smith, US Attorney...* 1863. NY. Amerman. 1st ed. VG/wrp. M8. $65.00

SMITH, E. Ehrlich. *Our Virginia: Description of Virginia for Young People.* 1923. States Pub. ils. 122p. G. B10. $12.00

SMITH, Edward E. *Gray Lensman.* 1951. Gnome. 1st ed. NF/VG. M19. $85.00

SMITH, Edward E. *Skylark of Space.* 1947. Providence. VG/fair. B5. $60.00

SMITH, Edward E. *Skylark Three.* 1948. Fantasy. 1st ed. NF/VG. M19. $85.00

SMITH, Edward. *Gray Lensman.* 1951. Hicksville. 1st ed. VG/VG. B5. $30.00

SMITH, Evelyn E. *Copy Shop.* 1985. Doubleday. 1st ed. NF/NF. H11. $35.00

SMITH, F. Hopkinson. *Colonel Carter's Christmas.* 1903. Scribner. 1st ed. 12mo. ils FC Yohn. VG. B17. $8.00

SMITH, Frances Rand. *Architectural History of Mission San Carlos Borromeo, CA.* 1921. Berkeley. 1st ed. 45 photos. 81p. gilt bl cloth. F. A17. $75.00

SMITH, Frank E. *Look Away From Dixie.* 1965. LSU. 90p. VG/VG. B10. $10.00

SMITH, Frank. *Yazoo.* 1954. NY. 1st ed. Am River series. VG/VG. B5. $40.00

SMITH, Gene. *Champion.* 1987. Atheneum. 1st ed. VG/VG. O3. $18.00

SMITH, George Adam. *Historical Geography of the Holy Land...* 1903. Hodder Stoughton. 10th. 5 maps. 713p. xl. VG. W1. $22.00

SMITH, George Adam. *Historical Geography of the Holy Land...Third Edition.* 1895. London. Hodder Stoughton. 8vo. 6 maps. VG+. O7. $95.00

SMITH, George O. *Venus Equilateral.* 1947. Prime. 1st ed. sgn. F/F. M19. $125.00

SMITH, Goldwin. *Letter to Whig Member of the Southern Independence Assn.* 1864. London. Macmillan. 1st ed. 76p. NF/cloth wrp. M8. $150.00

SMITH, H.A. *Great Chili Confrontation.* 1968. NY. 1st ed. VG/VG. B5. $50.00

SMITH, H.A. *Mr Klein's Kampf.* 1939. NY. 1st ed. VG/VG. B5. $40.00

SMITH, H.W. *Life & Sport in Aiken.* 1935. NY. Derrydale. 1st ed. 1/950. VG/VG. B5. $145.00

SMITH, Harold S. *I Want To Quit Winners.* 1963. NJ. 7th. sgn. 336p. VG/worn. S1. $10.00

SMITH, Harry B. *First Nights & First Editions*. 1931. Little Brn. 1/250. sgn. teg. F/F case. B35. $65.00

SMITH, Helena Huntington. *War on Powder River: History of an Insurrection*. 1966. NY. 1st ed. 320p. photos/notes/index. NF/dj. E1. $50.00

SMITH, Holland. *Coral & Brass*. 1949. NY. 1st ed. VG/VG. B5. $40.00

SMITH, Howard. *Seneca Men Were There: A Particular History of Civil War...* 1995. Seneca Co Hist Soc. 12p. wrp. M20. $6.00

SMITH, J. Frazer. *White Pillars: Early Life & Architecture of Lower MS Valley*. 1941. Bramhall. 252p. VG/G. B10. $25.00

SMITH, Jessie Willcox. *Mother Goose*. 1986. Derrydale. 6th prt. F/sans. B17. $8.00

SMITH, Jim. *Alphonse & the Stonehenge Mystery*. nd. Beecles/London. Wm Clowes. 1st ed. 4to. ils. unp. VG. C14. $10.00

SMITH, Joan. *Masculine Ending*. 1988. Scribner. 1st ed. author's 1st book. F/F. H11. $25.00

SMITH, John William. *Selection of Leading Cases on Various Branches of the Law...* 1866. Phil. Johnson. 1st Am ed. contemporary calf. M11. $150.00

SMITH, John. *Spearhead in the West 1945*. Frankfurt. 1st ed. VG/VG. B5. $65.00

SMITH, Joseph E. *WHB Smith Classic Book of Pistols & Revolvers*. 1968. Harrisburg, PA. 7th. 816p. F/F. E1. $35.00

SMITH, Josiah W. *Compendium of the Law of Real & Personal Property...* 1856. Phil. Johnson. contemporary sheep. M11. $50.00

SMITH, Julie. *Jazz Funeral*. 1993. Fawcett. 1st ed. F/F. A20. $15.00

SMITH, Julie. *New Orleans Beat*. 1994. Fawcett. 1st ed. F/F. A20. $12.00

SMITH, Julie. *Sourdough Wars*. 1984. Walker. 1st ed. inscr/dtd 1988. F/F. C2. $100.00

SMITH, Ken. *Work, Distance*. 1972. Chicago. Swallow. 1st ed. inscr to fellow poet. F/NF. V1. $25.00

SMITH, L. *Ant Miles To Go*. 1967. Boston. 1st ed. VG/VG. B5. $25.00

SMITH, Laurence Dwight. *Hiram & Other Cats*. 1941. Grosset Dunlap. 4to. ils. pict brd. VG-. B17. $15.00

SMITH, Lawrence Dwight. *Mystery of the Yellow Tie*. 1939. Grosset Dunlap. 220p. cloth. VG/dj. M20. $30.00

SMITH, Lee. *Black Mountain Breakdown*. 1980. NY. AP. sgn. NF/wrp. C2. $90.00

SMITH, Lee. *Black Mountain Breakdown*. 1980. Putnam. UP. sgn. NF/wrp. C2. $150.00

SMITH, Lee. *Cakewalk*. 1981. Putnam. 1st ed. author's 5th book. F/F. B4. $85.00

SMITH, Lee. *Devil's Dream*. 1992. Putnam. 1st ed. F/F. B4. $35.00

SMITH, Lee. *Fair & Tender Ladies*. 1988. Putnam. UP. F/wrp. B4. $65.00

SMITH, Lee. *Family Linen*. 1985. Putnam. 1st ed. F/F. B4. $45.00

SMITH, Lee. *Family Linen*. 1985. Putnam. 1st ed. sgn/dtd 1985. F/F. C2. $65.00

SMITH, Lillian. *Strange Fruit*. 1944. Reynal Hitchcock. 4th. 371p. VG/fair. B10. $12.00

SMITH, Marc. *Enterprising Tales*. 1990. NJ. 275p. VG/wrp. S1. $10.00

SMITH, Martin Cruz. *Gorky Park*. 1981. Random. 1st ed. F/F. H11. $45.00

SMITH, Martin Cruz. *Gorky Park*. 1981. Random. 1st ed. VG+/G. A20. $27.00

SMITH, Martin Cruz. *Nightwing*. 1979. Norton. 1st ed. NF/NF. A20. $30.00

SMITH, Martin Cruz. *Polar Star*. 1989. Random. sc. 386p. VG. P12. $3.00

SMITH, Martin Cruz. *Polar Star*. 1989. Random. 1st trade ed. VG+/F. A20. $20.00

SMITH, Martin Cruz. *Stallion Gate*. 1986. Random. 1st ed. F/F. A20. $25.00

SMITH, Martin Cruz. *Stallion Gate*. 1986. Random. 1st ed. F/F. H11. $40.00

SMITH, Martin Cruz. *Stallion Gate*. 1986. Random. 1st ed. rem mk. F/F. B35. $30.00

SMITH, Maurice. *Short History of Dentistry*. 1958. London. 120p. dj. A13. $30.00

SMITH, Nora Archibald. *Boys & Girls of Bookland*. 1923. 1st ed. ils JW Smith. F. B30. $125.00

SMITH, O.W. *Gold on the Desert*. 1956. Albuquerque. 1st ed. ils/photos. VG/VG. B5. $37.50

SMITH, O.W. *Trout Lore*. 1917. NY. 1st ed. VG. B5. $35.00

SMITH, P.D.W. *Modern Marine Electricity*. 1948. Cornell. 3rd. 384p. VG. P12. $15.00

SMITH, Red. *Views of Sport*. 1954. Knopf. 1st ed. VG. P8. $25.00

SMITH, Robert. *Baseball in America*. 1961. HRW. 1st ed. ils. VG+/VG+. P8. $60.00

SMITH, Robert. *Pioneers of Baseball*. 1978. Little Brn. 1st ed. F/VG+. P8. $40.00

SMITH, Rosamond; see Oates, Joyce Carol.

SMITH, S.E. *United States Navy in World War II*. 1966. NY. 1049p. dj. A17. $16.50

SMITH, Samuel Stanhope. *Essay on Causes of Variety of Complexion & Figure...* 1810. Simpson/Williams Whiting. 2nd. 412p. modern brd. G1. $185.00

SMITH, Samuel Stelle. *Battle of Trenton*. 1965. Monmouth Beach, NJ. Philip Freneau. inscr pres. maps. F. O7. $55.00

SMITH, Scott. *Simple Plan*. 1993. Knopf. 1st ed. author's 1st book. F/F. H11. $40.00

SMITH, Scott. *Simple Plan*. 1993. Knopf. 1st ed. VG/VG. A20. $15.00

SMITH, Stevie. *Scorpion & Other Poems*. 1972. London. Longman. 1st ed. intro P Dickinson. F/NF. H4. $40.00

SMITH, Sydney. *Mostly Murder*. 1959. London. McKay. 1st ed. VG+. M22. $65.00

SMITH, Theodore Clarke. *Life & Letters of James Abram Garfield*. 1925. New Haven. 1st ed. 2 vol. VG. B18. $47.50

SMITH, Thomas H. *Mapping of Ohio, the Delineation of State of Ohio...* 1977. Kent, OH. 1st ed. 252p. VG/dj. B18. $65.00

SMITH, Thorne. *Lazy Bear Lane*. 1931. Doubleday Doran. stated 1st ed. ils George Shanks. 240p. VG. D1. $200.00

SMITH, Tim. *White House Memoir*. 1972. Norton. 1st ed. 250p. brn cloth. AN/dj. B22. $6.50

SMITH, Wallace. *Prodigal Sons*. 1951. Boston, MA. 1st ed. 434p. F. E1. $145.00

SMITH, Wilbur. *Diamond Hunters*. 1972. Doubleday. 1st ed. rem mk. F/F. H11. $40.00

SMITH, William B. *On Wheels & How I Came There: A Real Story for Real Boys...* 1892. NY. Hunt Eaton. 1st ed. 338p. NF. M8. $250.00

SMITH, William Fielding. *Diamond Six: Saga of a Fighting Family From KY to TX*. 1958. Garden City. 1st ed. 383p. F/VG. E1. $40.00

SMITH, William Jay. *Journey to the Dead Sea*. 1979. Omaha. Abatoir. 1/222. VG+/wrp. V1. $30.00

SMITH, William Jay. *Spectra Hoax*. 1961. Wesleyan U. ils. 158p. F/VG. A4. $45.00

SMITH, William Jay. *Tin Can.* 1966. Delacorte. 1st ed. assn copy. F/dj. w/sgn Christmas card. V1. $30.00

SMITH, William. *Brief View of the Conduct of Pennsylvania...* 1756. London. 1st ed. 88p. 19th-C bdg. VG. C6. $1,150.00

SMITH, Winston. *Days of Exile: The Story of the Vine & Olive Colony in Am.* 1967. Tuscaloosa, AL. Drake. 1st ed. 144p. NF. M8. $45.00

SMITH & SMITH. *Book of Rifles.* 1965. Harrisburg. 3rd. 656p. G. E1. $25.00

SMITH & THIERS. *Boletes of Michigan.* 1971. Ann Arbor. 1st ed. 8vo. 157 pl/133 drawings. 428p. cloth. F. B1. $45.00

SMITH & WIGGIN. *Twilight Stories: More Tales for the Story Hour.* 1925. Houghton Mifflin. 1st ed. ils Kayren Draper. 228p. G+. T5. $30.00

SMITH & WILCOX. *Farmer's Cyclopedia of Agriculture.* 1911. Orange Judd. 619p. gilt gr cloth. VG. T10. $50.00

SMITH. *American Travelers Abroad: A Bibliography of Accounts...* 1969. np. 4to. 169p. F/wrp. A4. $55.00

SMITH. *Architecture in English Fiction.* 1970. rpt. F/F. D2. $25.00

SMITH. *Crusoe 250: Being a Catalogue in Celebration...* 1970. np. 1/500. ils. 119p. VG. A4. $125.00

SMITH. *Matting & Hanging of Works of Art on Paper.* 1986. np. sm 4to. 31p. G/wrp. T3. $7.00

SMITHI, Thomae. *De Republica Anglorum Libri Tres...* 1641. Batavorium. Ex Officina Elzeviriana. last complete ed. worn. M11. $350.00

SMITHSONIAN INSTITUTE. *Smithsonian Collection of Newspaper Comics.* 1977. folio. ils. 336p. F. M13. $65.00

SMITHWICK, Noah. *Revolution of a State; or, Recollections of Old TX Days.* 1983. TX U. rpt. ils. 264p. F/F. E1. $30.00

SMOCK, Nell Stolp. *White Tail, King of the Forest.* 1938. Platt Munk. 8vo. VG/G. B17. $5.00

SMOLUCHOWSKI, R. *Solar System.* 1983. Scientific Am Books. 174p. cloth. F/dj. D8. $12.00

SMUCKER, Isaac. *Centennial History of Licking County, OH.* 1876. Newark, OH. 80p. G/wrp. B18. $65.00

SMYTH, Henry D. *Atomic Energy for Military Purposes...* 1945. Princeton. ils. 264p. VG/VG. A4. $395.00

SNAVELY, Tipton Ray. *Taxation of Negroes in Virginia.* 1917. VA U. 97p. wrp. R11. $25.00

SNEAD, Sam. *Natural Golf.* 1953. NY. 1st ed. VG/VG. B5. $30.00

SNELL, Edmund. *Kontrol.* 1928. Lippincott. 1st Am ed. F/NF. B4. $250.00

SNELL, Tee Lofton. *Wild Shores: America's Beginnings.* 1983. WA, DC. 2nd. 203p. F/F. E1. $25.00

SNODGRASS, W.D. *Boy Made of Meat.* 1983. Concord, NH. Ewart. 1/36. sgns. prt brd w/morocco trim. F. B24. $250.00

SNOW, Benjamin. *Currents of High Potential of High & Other Frequencies.* 1905. Scientific Authors Pub. 1st ed. 8vo. 196p. gilt gr cloth. T10. $150.00

SNOW, Edward R. *Famous Lighthouses of New England.* Oct 1945. Boston. 1st ed. pres. ils. 457p. F/pict dj. H3. $50.00

SNOW, Jack. *Magical Mimics in Oz.* 1946. Reilly Lee. ils Frank Kramer. pict label/orange cloth. VG. B17. $100.00

SNOW, Jack. *Shaggy Man of Oz.* 1949. Chicago. 1st ed. ils Frank Kramer. VG+. C6. $95.00

SNOW, Karen. *Wonders.* 1980. Viking. 1st ed. F/NF. V1. $10.00

SNOW, Wilbert. *Sonnets to Steve & Other Poems.* 1957. Exposition. 1st ed. inscr. 8vo. 55p. VG/G. B11. $18.00

SNOWDON, J. *Truth About Mormonism.* 1926. NY. 1st ed. VG/VG. B5. $40.00

SNYDER, Charles. *Massachusetts Eye & Ear Infirmary, Studies on Its History.* 1984. Boston. Alpine. 8vo. 368p. bl cloth. VG. B14. $35.00

SNYDER, Don. *Virginia Boasts.* 1947. Waynesboro. sgn. unp. G. B10. $12.00

SNYDER, Fairmont. *Lovely Garden.* 1919. Volland. 1st ed. 8vo unp. G+. T5. $55.00

SNYDER, Fairmont. *Rhymes for Kindly Children.* 1916. Volland. 1st ed. ils Johnny Gruelle. VG+. P2. $125.00

SNYDER, Gary. *Earth House Hold.* 1969. New Directions. 1st ed. 8vo. 143p. F/dj. S9. $75.00

SNYDER, Gary. *Place in Space: New & Selected Prose.* 1995. Counterpoint. 1st ed. sgn. V1. $40.00

SNYDER, Martin P. *City of Independence: Views of Philadelphia Before 1800.* 1975. NY. Praeger. 4to. ils/maps. F/dj. O7. $95.00

SNYDER & YOST. *Pinnacle Jake.* 1953. Caldwell. 2nd. photos. NF/NF. E1. $35.00

SOBILOFF, Hy. *Breathing of First Things.* 1963. Dial. 1st ed. F/NF. w/author's card. V1. $25.00

SOCOLOFSKY & SELF. *Historical Atlas of Kansas.* 1978. Norman, OK. 3rd. 70p. F/stiff wrp. E1. $30.00

SODERBERGH, Steven. *Sex, Lies & Videotape.* 1990. Harper. 1st ed. AN/dj. B4. $85.00

SOHMER, Steve. *Favorite Son.* 1987. Bantam. 1st ed. author's 1st book. F/F. H11. $40.00

SOHN & TYRE. *Frost: The Poet & His Poetry.* 1967. NY. 8vo. 70p. F/tan wrp. w/33-1/3rpm record. A11. $55.00

SOKOLOVE, Michael. *Hustle.* 1990. Simon Schuster. ARC/1st ed. RS. F/F. P8. $17.50

SOLBRIG, Otto T. *Topics in Plant Population Biology.* 1979. NY. VG/dj. B26. $45.00

SOLEM, Elizabeth. *French-Canadian Children.* 1947. Encyclopedia Brittanica. photos. 40p. glossy wrp. A17. $7.00

SOLLID, Roberta Beed. *Calamity Jane: A Study in Historical Criticism.* 1958. Hist Soc of MT. 1st ed. 147p. F/NF. E1. $75.00

SOLLIER, Paul. *Les Troubles de la Memoire.* 1901. Paris. J Rueff. 2nd. 12mo. 262p. VG. G1. $50.00

SOLOMON, Barbara Probst. *Beat of Life.* 1960. Lippincott. 1st ed. author's 1st book. sgn. F/NF. B2. $60.00

SOLOMON & SOLOMON. *Honey in the Rock: Ruby Pickens Tartt Collection...* 1991. Macon. Mercer U. 176p. F. A17. $12.00

SOLTES, Mordecai. *Yiddish Press: An Americanization Agency.* 1925. NY. 8vo. 242p. bl cloth. F. B14. $55.00

SOLTIS, Jonas F. *Seeing, Knowing & Believing.* 1966. London. Allen Unwin. 1st ed. sgn. 8vo. VG/G. B11. $25.00

SOLZHENITSYN, Alexandre. *August 1914.* 1972. FSG. 1st ed. F/F clip. B35. $21.00

SOLZHENITSYN, Alexandre. *Gulag Archipelago 1929-1956.* 1973. Harper Row. 1st Am ed. F/NF. H4. $35.00

SOLZHENITSYN, Alexandre. *Lenin in Zurich.* 1976. FSG. 1st ed. F/F. B35. $24.00

SOLZHENITSYN, Alexandre. *Rebuilding Russia.* 1991. FSG. 1st ed. rem mk. F/F. B35. $16.00

SOLZHENITSYN, Alexandre. *Stories & Prose Poems.* 1971. FSG. 1st ed. F/F. B35. $26.00

SOLZHENITSYN, Sanya. *Sanya: My Life With Alexandre Solzhenitsyn.* 1975. Bobbs Merrill. 1st ed. 284p. AN/F. B22. $5.50

SOMEKH, Sasson. *Changing Rhythm.* 1973. Leiden. Brill. 1st ed. 8vo. 241p. VG. W1. $22.00

SOMERVILLE, E. *Slipper's ABC of Fox Hunting.* 1903. Longman Gr. 1st ed. folio. G+. O3. $145.00

SOMMERS, Lawrence M. *Atlas of Michigan.* 1978. E Lansing. MI State U. 400 maps. F/dj. O7. $55.00

SOMTOW, S.P. *Forgetting Places.* 1987. NY. Tor. 1st ed. inscr. F/F. T2. $30.00

SOMTOW, S.P. *Shattered Horse.* 1986. NY. Tor. 1st ed. F/F. T2. $17.00

SONNE, Conway B. *World of Wakara.* 1962. San Antonio. 1st ed. 235p. F. E1. $25.00

SONNECK. *Bibliography of Early Secular American Music, 18th Century.* 1971. revised/enlarged ed. 632p. xl. VG. A4. $50.00

SONNENBERG, Maya. *Cartographies.* 1989. Pittsburgh. 1st ed. author's 1st book. F/F. B4. $45.00

SONNICHSEN, C.L. *Alias Billy the Kid.* 1955. Albuquerque. 1st ed. photos/notes. 136p. F/NF. E1. $85.00

SONNICHSEN, C.L. *Ambidextrous Historian.* 1981. Norman, OK. 1st ed. 8vo. 120p. F/dj. P4. $20.00

SONNICHSEN, C.L. *Billy King's Tombstone.* 1951. Caldwell, ID. 3rd. 232p. NF/G. E1. $65.00

SONNICHSEN, C.L. *El Paso Salt War of 1877.* 1973. El Paso. rpt. ils Jose Cisneros. F/F. E1. $30.00

SONNICHSEN, C.L. *From Hopalong to Hud: Thoughts on Western Fiction.* 1978. College Sta, TX. 1st ed. index/biblio. 201p. F/F. E1. $35.00

SONNICHSEN, C.L. *Grave of John Wesley Hardin: Essays on Grassroots History.* 1979. College Sta, TX. 1st ed. 90p. F/F. E1. $35.00

SONNICHSEN, C.L. *I'll Die Before I'll Run: Story of the Great Feuds of TX.* 1951. NY. 1st ed. 294p. F. E1. $40.00

SONNICHSEN, C.L. *Pass of the North: Four Centuries on the Rio Grande.* 1980. El Paso, TX. 1st ed. sgn. ils/photos/maps. 149p. F/F. E1. $60.00

SONNICHSEN, C.L. *Roy Bean: Law West of the Pecos.* 1943. Old Greenwich, CT. rpt. 207p. dj. E1. $30.00

SONNICHSEN, C.L. *State National Since 1881: Pioneer Bank of El Paso.* 1971. El Paso. 171p. F. E1. $45.00

SONNICHSEN, C.L. *Ten Texas Feuds.* 1957. Albuquerque, NM. 1st ed. 248p. F/case. E1. $75.00

SONNICHSEN, C.L. *Tularosa, Last of the Frontier West.* 1960. NY. 1st ed. 336p. F/VG. E1. $60.00

SONTAG, Susan. *Against Interpretation.* 1966. FSG. 1st ed. sgn. NF/NF. B4. $75.00

SONTAG, Susan. *Benefactor.* 1963. Farrar Strauss. 1st ed. author's 1st book. F/F. B4. $100.00

SONTAG, Susan. *Death Kit.* 1967. FSG. 1st ed. NF. B4. $75.00

SONTAG, Susan. *I, Etcetera.* 1978. FSG. 1st ed. F/NF. B4. $45.00

SONTAG, Susan. *On Photography.* 1977. FSG. 1st ed. F/F. B4. $35.00

SONTAG, Susan. *Susan Sontag Reader.* 1967. FSG. UP. sgn. F/wrp. B4. $85.00

SONTAG, Susan. *Volcano Lover: A Romance.* 1992. FSG. 1st ed. NF. B4. $35.00

SOOS, Troy. *Murder at Fenway Park.* 1994. Kensington. 1st ed. F/F. H11. $35.00

SORACCO, Sin. *Edge City.* 1992. Dutton. 1st ed. author's 1st novel. NF/NF. M22. $15.00

SORENSEN, Lorin. *Ford Road, 7th Anniversary of Ford Motor Company 1908-78.* 1978. Silverado Pub. 1st/only ed? 191p. gilt leather. NF. B22. $12.00

SORRENTINO, Gilbert. *Perfect Fiction.* 1968. Norton. 1st ed. NF/stiff wrp. V1. $15.00

SORRENTINO, Gilbert. *Sky Changes.* 1966. Hill Wang. 1st ed. F/NF. B2. $50.00

SOTO, Gary. *Jesse.* 1994. Harcourt Brace. 1st ed. F/F. V1. $15.00

SOUHAMI, Diana. *Gluck.* 1988. London. Pandora. 1st ed. 8vo. 333p. F/dj. T10. $35.00

SOUPAULT, Philippe. *William Blake.* 1928. Dodd Mead. 8vo. 40 ils. VG. T10. $20.00

SOUSA, John Philip. *Marching Along.* 1941. Boston. popular ed. 384p. dj. A17. $9.50

SOUTHERN, Terry. *Texas Summer.* 1991. Arcade/Little Brn. 1st ed. inscr. F/F. B4. $285.00

SOUTHEY, Robert. *Life of Nelson.* 1881. London. Bickers. 8vo. ils Westall. marbled ep. full bl calf. T10. $100.00

SOUTHWART, Elizabeth. *Passowrd to Fairyland.* 1920s. London. Simpkin Marshall Hamilton Kent. 187p. VG+. T5. $125.00

SOWELL, A.J. *Life of Big Foot Wallace.* 1957. Austin, TX. rpt. 123p. pict bdg. F. E1. $75.00

SOWELL, A.J. *Texas Indian Fighters: Early Settlers & Indian Fighters...* 1900. Austin, TX. rpt. 861p. F/F. E1. $40.00

SOWERBY. *Catalogue of the Library of Thomas Jefferson.* 1983. np. 5 vol. 1/400. 4to. 2513p. VG. A4. $195.00

SPACKS, Barry. *Book of Children.* 1969. Doubleday. 1st ed. assn copy. F/VG+. V1. $45.00

SPACKS, Barry. *Something Human.* 1976. Harper. 1st ed. assn copy. F/NF. V1. $15.00

SPAETH, Harold J. *Supreme Court Policy Making, Explanation & Prediction.* 1979. San Francisco. WH Freeman. M11. $35.00

SPAFFORD, H.G. *Gazetteer of the State of New York.* 1813. Southwick. fld map. orig tree calf. VG. H7. $150.00

SPAIGHT, J.M. *Aircraft in War.* 1914. London. 1st ed. 172p. xl. A17. $75.00

SPALDING, A.G. *America's National Game.* 1911. NY. Am Sports Pub. 1st ed. pres. 12mo. 542p. bl cloth. F. B11. $550.00

SPARK, Muriel. *Collected Poems.* 1968. Knopf. 1st ed. NF/NF. B2. $25.00

SPARK, Muriel. *Curriculum Vitae.* 1993. Houghton Mifflin. UP. F/pict wrp. B35. $30.00

SPARK, Muriel. *Hothouse by the East River.* 1973. Viking. 1st ed. 146p. AN/dj. B22. $12.00

SPARKS, Edwin Erle. *Lincoln-Douglas Debates of 1858.* 1908. IL State Hist Lib. 627p. G. S17. $27.50

SPAULDING, Edward Selden. *Adobe Days Along the Channel.* 1957. Santa Barbara. 1/1015. sgn. VG. B5. $60.00

SPEAR, David. *Nugents 'Close to Home' Photographs by David M Spear.* 1993. Jargon Soc. 1st ed. sgn Spear/Williams. AN/dj. C2. $75.00

SPEAR, Roberta. *Silks.* 1980. HRW. 1st ed. assn copy. F/F. V1. $15.00

SPEARE, Elizabeth George. *Bronze Bow.* 1961. Boston. 255p. F/dj. A17. $7.50

SPEARMAN, Frank H. *Whispering Smith.* (1912). NY. later ed. ils NC Wyeth. 421p. reading copy. E1. $20.00

SPEARS, R.S. *Cabin Boat Primer.* 1913. Columbus. Harding. 1st ed. VG. B5. $75.00

SPECK, Ernest B. *Moody Boatright, Folklorist: A Collection of Essays.* 1973. Austin, TX. 198p. F/NF. E1. $30.00

SPEDALE, W.A. *Battle of Baton Rouge, 1862.* 1985. Baton Rouge. ltd ed. sgn. 8vo. ils. 64p. red cloth. VG/dj. T3. $15.00

SPEDALE, W.A. *Historic Treasures of the American Civil War.* 1988. Baton Rouge. 8vo. 193p. red cloth. VG. T3. $20.00

SPEDDING, Charles T. *Reminiscences of Transatlantic Travellers.* 1926. London. Unwin. G. A16. $50.00

SPEED, John Gilmer. *Horse in America.* 1905. McClure Phillips. 1st ed. VG. O3. $45.00

SPEED, John. *Prospect of the Most Famous Parts of the World.* 1961 (1627). Amsterdam. facsimile. 29 double-p maps. F/dj. O7. $275.00

SPEER, Albert. *Inside the Third Reich.* 1970. NY. BC. 705p. dj. A17. $9.50

SPEER, Emory. *Lincoln, Lee, Grant & Other Biographical Addresses.* 1909. NY/WA. Neale. 1st ed. cloth. NF. M8. $150.00

SPEER, Marion A. *Western Trails.* 1931. Huntington Beach, CA. ltd ed. sgn/#d. 377p. E1. $100.00

SPEIDEL, W. *You Can't Eat Mount Rainier.* 1955. Portland. 1st ed. VG/VG. B5. $30.00

SPELMAN, Henry. *English Works...His Posthumous Works Relating to Laws...* 1723. London. early panelled calf. M11. $450.00

SPENCE, Johnny. *Golf Pro for God.* 1965. Hawthorn. inscr. 8vo. 219p. G/G. B11. $35.00

SPENCE, Lewis. *Myths of the North American Indians.* nd. NY. ils. VG/VG. M17. $35.00

SPENCE, Vernon Gladden. *Colonel Morgan Jones, Grand Old Man of Texas Railroading.* 1971. OK U. 1st ed. 240p. F/F. E1. $35.00

SPENCER, Bernard. *With Luck Lasting.* 1963. London. 1st ed. assn copy. F. V1. $10.00

SPENCER, Cornelia Phillips. *Last Ninety Days of the War in North Carolina.* 1866. NY. Watchman Pub. 1st ed. 287p. VG+. M8. $450.00

SPENCER, Elizabeth. *Legacy.* 1988. Chapel Hill. 1st ed. 1/100. sgn. F. C2. $50.00

SPENCER, Elizabeth. *Salt Line.* 1984. Doubleday. 1st ed. F/F. B4. $50.00

SPENCER, Elizabeth. *Snare.* 1972. McGraw Hill. 1st ed. F/F. B4. $85.00

SPENCER, Frank. *Piltdown: A Scientific Forgery.* 1990. London. Oxford. 1st ed. 8vo. ils. 272p. AN. T10. $24.00

SPENCER, Herbert. *Principles of Psychology.* 1855. Longman Gr Brn Longmans. 620p. emb panelled cloth. G1. $550.00

SPENDER, Brenda. *On'y Tony & the Dragon.* 1938. London. Country Life. 1st ed. VG. O3. $18.00

SPENDER, Brenda. *On'y Tony's Circus.* 1936. London. Country Life. 1st ed. VG/G. O3. $20.00

SPENDER, Brenda. *On'y Tony: Adventures of Three Ponies & a Little Boy.* 1935. London. Country Life. 1st ed. 8vo. 96p. VG+. C14. $18.00

SPENDER, Stephen. *Collected Poems 1928-1985.* 1986. Random. 1st ed. F/NF. V1. $20.00

SPENDER, Stephen. *Twenty Five Poems.* 1988. Helsinki. Eurographica. 1/350. sgn/#d. F/F. V1. $100.00

SPENSER, Edmund. *Shephearde's Calendar: Conteyning Twelve Aeglogues...* 1896. Hammersmith. Kelmscott. 1/225. 98p. Leighton vellum. F. B24. $1,350.00

SPERRY, Armstrong. *Call It Courage.* 1940. Macmillan. 30th. Newberry medal. F/VG. B17. $8.00

SPERRY, Armstrong. *One Day With Jambin in Sumatra.* 1934. Phil. Winston. 1st ed. ils A Sperry. VG. D1. $35.00

SPERRY, Armstrong. *River of the West.* 1952. Phil. 1st ed. ils Henry Pitz. 182p. F/dj. A17. $7.50

SPICER, Edward H. *Cycles of Conquest: The Impact of Spain, Mexico & US...* 1962. Tucson. AZ U. 1st ed. 4to. ils Hazel Fontana. F. T10. $150.00

SPIELMANN. *Catalogue of the Library of Miniature Books...* nd. rpt of 1961 ed. 1/150. ils. 304p. F. A4. $85.00

SPIER, Peter. *Tin Lizzie.* 1975. Doubleday. 1st ed. ils. F/VG. P2. $45.00

SPIES, Otto. *Turkische Marchen.* 1967. Dusseldorf/Koln. Diederichs. 1st ed. 12mo. 331p. teg. VG. W1. $30.00

SPIGNESI. *Shape Under the Sheet: Complete Stephen King Encyclopedia.* 1991. np. 1/3000. 4to. ils. 800p. F. A4. $125.00

SPILLANE, John. *Medical Travelers: Narratives From the 17th, 18th...* 1984. London. 1st ed. 236p. dj. A13. $35.00

SPILLANE, Mickey. *By-Pass Control.* 1966. Dutton. 1st ed. F/dj. B2. $25.00

SPILLANE, Mickey. *Day the Sea Rolled Back.* 1979. NY. Windmill. 1st ed. VG/VG. B4. $85.00

SPILLANE, Mickey. *Death Dealers.* 1965. Dutton. 1st ed. AN/dj. M22. $15.00

SPILLANE, Mickey. *Deep.* 1961. Dutton. 1st ed. author's 8th novel. NF/NF. A11. $55.00

SPILLANE, Mickey. *Deep.* 1961. Dutton. 1st ed. author's 8th novel. VG/VG. M22. $30.00

SPILLANE, Mickey. *Kiss Me Deadly.* 1952. Dutton. 1st ed. VG. P10. $25.00

SPILLANE, Mickey. *Kiss Me Deadly.* 1952. Dutton. 1st ed. VG/G. B5. $75.00

SPILLANE, Mickey. *Long Wait.* 1951. Dutton. 2nd. VG. P10. $15.00

SPILLANE, Mickey. *Vengeance Is Mine.* 1950. Dutton. 1st ed. VG. P10. $20.00

SPINA, Lillian. *Fire in the Louvre.* 1979. Swamp Pr. 1/65. sgn. ils Jon Vlakos. F. V1. $100.00

SPINK, Alfred F. *National Game.* 1910. Nat Game Pub. 1st ed. VG. P8. $900.00

SPINK, Alfred F. *Spink Sport Stories. Vol II.* 1921. self pub. 1st ed. VG. P8. $125.00

SPINRAD, Norman. *Child of Fortune.* 1985. Bantam. 1st ed. NF/NF. G10. $10.00

SPINRAD, Norman. *Russian Spring.* 1991. Bantam. 1st ed. F/F. G10. $20.00

SPINRAD, Norman. *Russian Spring.* 1991. Bantam. 1st ed. F/NF. M21. $15.00

SPITZ, Armand, N. *Start in Meteorology.* 1943 (1942). NY. Henley. 2nd. 8vo. 97p. G/tattered. K5. $15.00

SPIVACK, Kathleen. *Flying Island.* 1973. Doubleday. 1st ed. F/VG+. V1. $15.00

SPLAN, John. *Life With the Trotters.* 1889. Chicago. White. 1st ed. O3. $35.00

SPLETE & SPLETE. *Frederic Remington: Selected Letters.* 1988. Abbeville. 8vo. ils. 487p. F/NF. T10. $25.00

SPLITTSTOESSER, W.E. *Vegetable Growing Handbook.* 1990. NY. 3rd. ils. 362p. AN. B26. $22.50

SPOCK, Benjamin. *Psychological Aspects of Pediatric Practice.* 1938. NY. State Comm on Mental Hygiene. 1st ed. NF/wrp. B4. $350.00

SPOCK, L.E. *Guide to the Study of Rocks.* 1953. Harper. 1st ed. 256p. F. D8. $18.00

SPOERKE, David. *Hidden Hazards in House & Garden Plants.* 1993. Missoula. ils. 248p. sbdg. B26. $24.00

SPOOR, Jack. *Heat Sink Applications Handbook.* 1974. Aham. 180p. VG. P4. $10.00

SPRAGUE, Marshall. *Gallery of Dudes.* 1966. Boston, MA. 1st ed. ils/photos. 296p. F. E1. $25.00

SPREE, Richard. *Soziale Ungleicheit vor Krankheit Und Tod.* 1981. Gottingen. 1st ed. 209p. wrp. A13. $15.00

SPRING, Agnes Wright. *Caspar Collins: Life & Exploits of an Indian Fighter...* 1927. NY. 1st ed. ils. 187p. E1. $50.00

SPRING, Gardiner. *Memoirs of the Reverend Samuel J Mills...* 1820. NY. 1st ed. 247p. fair. B18. $125.00

SPRING, James W. *Boston & the Parker House 1630-1927.* 1927. JR Whipple. ils. G+. P12. $15.00

SPRING, Michelle. *Every Breath You Take.* 1994. NY. Pocket. 1st ed. F/F. H11. $25.00

SPRINGER, Nancy. *Chains of Gold.* 1987. London. MacDonald. 1st ed. F/F. M21. $25.00

SPRINGS, Elliott White. *Clothes Make the Man.* 1949. NY. 1st ed. 446p. pict cloth. G. B18. $22.50

SPURZHEIM, J.G. *Anatomy of the Brain...Nervous System.* 1826. London. 1st ed. 11 pl. 234p. cloth. VG. B14. $750.00

SPURZHEIM, J.G. *Phrenology in Connection With Study of Physiognomy, Part 1.* 1826. London. 1st ed. 8vo. 34 pl. 181p. G. B14. $125.00

SPYRI, Johanna. *Gritli's Children.* 1924. Lippincott. ils Maria L Kirk. VG. B17. $7.50

SPYRI, Johanna. *Heidi.* 1922. McKay. 1st ed. ils Jessie W Smith. VG. M19. $100.00

SPYRI, Johanna. *Mazli.* (1921). NY. trans EP Stork. 8vo. 320p. G+. T5. $12.00

SPYRI, Johanna. *Mazli.* 1921. Lippincott. 1st ed. ils Maria Kirk. NF/VG. M19. $45.00

SPYRI, Johanna. *New Year's Carol.* 1924. Houghton Mifflin. 1st ed. ils GE Weston. VG. M19. $35.00

SPYRI, Johanna. *Vinzi: Story of the Alps.* 1923. Phil. Lippincott. 3rd. 8vo. 297p. G+. C14. $6.00

SQUIRE, Norman. *Contract Bridge Bidding Today.* 1976. London. 133p. VG. S1. $10.00

SQUIRE, Norman. *Contract Bridge Card Playing Techniques.* 1976. London. VG. S1. $10.00

SQUIRE, Norman. *Guide to Bridge Conventions.* 1958. London. 136p. VG. S1. $7.00

SQUIRE, Norman. *Theory of Bidding.* 1957. London. 280p. VG/VG. S1. $20.00

STAAL, Julius D.W. *Focus on Astronomy.* 1963. London. Newnes. 8vo. 283p. VG/dj. K5. $9.00

STABLEFORD, Brian M. *Angel of Pain.* 1993. Carroll Graf. 1st Am ed. F/NF. G10. $10.00

STABLEFORD, Brian M. *Empire of Fear.* 1991. Carroll Graf. 1st Am ed. F/F. G10. $10.00

STABLEFORD, Brian M. *Werewolves of London.* 1992. Carroll Graf. 1st Am ed. F/F. G10. $10.00

STACEY, Susannah. *Knife at the Opera.* 1988. Summit. 1st ed. F/VG+. N4. $17.50

STACHURA, Peter D. *Nazi Youth in the Weimar Republic.* 1975. Santa Barbara. 301p. dj. A17. $25.00

STACHURA, Peter D. *Weirmar Era & Hitler 1918-1933.* 1977. Oxford. 276p. VG. A17. $45.00

STACKPOLE, Edward. *From Cedar Mountain to Antietam.* 1959. 1st ed. VG/VG. S13. $35.00

STAFF, Frank. *Transatlantic Mail.* 1956. London. Alard Coles. VG/VG. A16. $50.00

STAFFORD, Ann. *Pony for Sale.* 1939. Knopf. 1st Am ed. VG. O3. $15.00

STAFFORD, Jean. *Elephi: Cat With the High IQ.* 1962. Ariel/FSC. 1st ed. F/NF. B4. $125.00

STAFFORD, Jean. *Mountain Lion.* 1947. Harcourt Brace. 1st ed. F/F. B4. $75.00

STAFFORD, T.J. *Shakespeare in the Southwest: Some New Directions.* 1969. El Paso. 107p. F/stiff wrp. E1. $25.00

STAFFORD, William. *Allegiances.* 1970. Harper Row. 1st ed. inscr/dtd 1972. F/NF. V1. $95.00

STAFFORD, William. *Listening Deep.* 1984. Penmaen. 1/50. sgn/#d. ils/sgn Michael McCurdy. F/glassine. V1. $125.00

STAFFORD, William. *Someday Maybe.* 1973. Harper Row. 1st ed. assn copy. F/F. V1. $30.00

STAFLEU, F.A. *Taxonomic Literature.* 1967. Utrecht. 8vo. 556p. cloth. VG. B1. $65.00

STALLONE, Sylvester. *Paradise Alley.* 1977. Putnam. 1st ed. F/NF. H11. $60.00

STALLWORTHY, Jon. *Anzac Sonata.* 1987. Norton. ARC. RS. F/F. V1. $15.00

STAMMERS, Michael K. *Passage Makers.* 1978. Brighton. Teredo Books. ils. 508p. VG/dj. T7. $75.00

STANARD. *Edgar Allen Poe: Letters Till Now Unpublished...* 1925. np. 1/1500. 4to. ils. 327p. VG. A4. $95.00

STAND, Paul. *Retrosepctive Monograph 1915-1968.* 1971. Aperture. 1st ed. 4to. F/F. S9. $300.00

STANDIFORD, Les. *Spill.* 1991. NY. Atlantic. 1st ed. author's 1st book. F/F. H11. $50.00

STANDISH, Burt L. *Rockspur Nine.* 1900. Street Smith. 287p. VG/pict wrp. M20. $12.00

STANDLEY & WOOTON. *Flora of New Mexico.* 1915. WA, DC. 794p. gr buckram. B26. $37.50

STANEK, V.J. *Pictorial Encyclopedia of Insects.* 1972 (1969). Hamlyn. rpt. 8vo. photos. 544p. cloth. VG/clip. B1. $22.50

STANFORD, Ann. *In Mediterranean Air.* 1977. Viking. 1st ed. F/clip. V1. $20.00

STANG, Alan. *It's Very Simple: The True Story of Civil Rights.* 1965. Boston. Western Islands. 1st ed. sgn. F/chip. B2. $35.00

STANLEY, F. *Ciudad Santa Fe, Mexican Rule 1821-1846.* 1965. Pampa, TX. 1st ed. 1/500. sgn. 432p. F/F. E1. $75.00

STANLEY, F. *Civil War in New Mexico.* 1960. Denver. 1st ed. sgn. 508p. F/VG. E1. $150.00

STANLEY, F. *Desperadoes of New Mexico.* 1953. Denver. 1st ed. sgn. photos/biblio. 320p. F/VG. E1. $90.00

STANLEY, F. *Duke City: Story of Albuquorque, NM 1706-1956.* 1963. Pampa, TX. 1st ed. sgn. 267p. F/F. E1. $55.00

STANLEY, F. *Fort Stanton, New Mexico.* 1964. Pampa, TX. 1st ed. 1/500. sgn. 263p. F/NF. E1. $65.00

STANLEY, F. *Golden (New Mexico) Story.* 1964. Pep, TX. 1/400. sgn. F/stiff wrp. E1. $15.00

STANLEY, F. *Longhair Jim Courtright...* 1957. Denver, CO. 1st ed. 1/500. sgn. 234p. F/NF. E1. $75.00

STANLEY, F. *No Tears for Black Jack Ketchum.* 1958. np. 1/500. sgn. 148p. F/stiff wrp. E1. $65.00

STANLEY, F. *Odyssey of Juan Achibeque.* 1962. private prt. 1/500. sgn. 20p. pb. F. E1. $20.00

STANLEY, F. *One Half Mile From Heaven; or, The Cimarron Story.* 1949. Denver. sgn. photos/notes/biblio. 155p. NF/stiff wrp. E1. $200.00

STANLEY, F. *Private War of Ike Stockton.* 1959. Denver. 1st ed. sgn. 169p. F/worn. E1. $65.00

STANLEY, F. *Rodeo Town Canadian, Texas.* 1953. Denver. 1st ed. sgn. 418p. F/NF. E1. $80.00

STANLEY, Henry Morton. *Congo.* 1885. NY. 2 vol. 1st Am ed. 2 fld pocket maps. pub morocco. VG. C6. $325.00

STANLEY, Henry Morton. *In Darkest Africa; or, Quest, Rescue & Retreat of Emin...* 1891. NY. 2 vol. pict cloth. VG-. B18. $47.50

STANLEY, Henry Morton. *Through the Dark Continent.* 1878. NY. 2 vol. 1st Am ed. marbled brd/half brn morocco. VG. C6. $325.00

STANLEY, Hiram M. *Studies in Evolutionary Psychology of Feeling.* 1895. London. Sonnenschein. 1st Eng ed. 392p. G1. $50.00

STANLEY, S.M. *Extinction.* 1987. Scientific Am Books. 242p. F/dj. D8. $26.00

STANLEY & STANLEY. *Bad Guys of the Old West.* nd. Spiro, OK. 91p. F/stiff wrp. E1. $25.00

STANWICK, Michael. *Iron Dragon's Daughter.* 1994. Morrow. 1st Am ed. F/NF. G10. $15.00

STANWICK, Michael. *Vacuum Flowers.* 1987. Arbor. 1st ed. F/F. M23. $25.00

STANWOOD, Edward. *History of Presidential Elections.* 1884. Boston. Osgood. 407p. brn cloth. G. B14. $30.00

STAPP, William Preston. *Prisoners of Perote.* 1977. Austin, TX. rpt of 1845 ed. 226p. F/F. E1. $35.00

STAR, Max. *In the Lion's Den.* 1964. Tampa, FL. Florida Grower Pr. sgn. 8vo. VG/VG. B11. $35.00

STARBUCK, George. *Bone Thoughts.* 1960. Yale. 1st ed. poet's 1st book. assn copy. F/VG. V1. $65.00

STARBUCK, Mary Eliza. *My House & I.* 1929. Houghton Mifflin. 1st ed. sgn. VG. B11. $35.00

STARGELL, Willie. *Willie Stargell: An Autobiography.* 1984. Harper. 1st ed. F/VG+. P8. $25.00

STARK, Richard; see Westlake, Donald E.

STARKER, Carl. *Carl Starker's Album of Arrangements.* 1953. Seattle. Chieftan. 1st ed. fair. B11. $22.00

STARKIE, Enid. *Arthur Rimbaud.* 1961. New Directions. new ed. 491p. F/F. A17. $12.50

STARKIE, Enid. *Flaubert: Making of Master/Critical & Biographical Study.* 1967 & 1971. FSG. 1st Am ed. 2 vol. F/NF. C2. $60.00

STAROBINSKI, Jean. *History of Medicine.* 1964. NY. 1st ed. 114p. VG. A13. $15.00

STARR, Jimmy. *365 Nights in Hollywood.* 1926. Hollywood. Fischer. 1st ed. 1/1000. sgn. NF. D2. $95.00

STARR, John W. *Lincoln's Last Day.* 1922. NY. 1st ed. ils. 100p. VG. B18. $22.50

STARR, Joyce Shira. *Covenant Over Middle Eastern Waters, Key to Survival.* 1995. Holt. 1st ed. 8vo. 3 maps. 222p. NF/dj. W1. $22.00

STARR, Kevin. *Inventing the Dream: California Through the Progrssive Era.* 1985. NY, NY. 2nd. photos. 380p. F/dj. E1. $25.00

STARR, Louis Morris. *Bohemian Brigade: Civil War Newsmen in Action.* 1987. Madison. WS U. rpt of 1954 ed. 387p. cloth. AN. M8. $35.00

STARZYNSKI, Juliusz. *Aleksander Gierymski.* 1971. Warsaw. 1st ed. 198 pl/24 tipped-in pl. F/dj. A17. $50.00

STASHEFF, Christopher. *Oathbound Wizard.* 1993. Ballantine. 1st ed. F/F. G10. $10.00

STASHEFF, Christopher. *Star Stone.* 1995. Ballantine. 1st ed. F/F. G10. $10.00

STASHEFF, Christopher. *Witch Doctor.* 1994. Ballantine. 1st ed. F/NF. G10. $10.00

STAUFFER, R.C. *Charles Darwin's Natural Selection...* 1975. London. photos of manuscript. 692p. F/dj. B26. $75.00

STAUM, Martin S. *Cabanis: Enlightenment & Medical Philosophy...* ca 1980. Princeton. 430p. NF/dj. P4. $25.00

STAUNFORDE, William. *Exposition of Kinges Prerogative Collected...* 1573. London. Richarde Tottle. modern 3-quarter calf. M11. $1,250.00

STAVRIANOS, L.S. *Balkans Since 1453.* 1965. HRW. 8vo. 16 pl/17 maps. 970p. VG/dj. W1. $24.00

STCHUR, John. *Down on the Farm.* 1987. NY. 1st ed. F/F. H11. $35.00

STEAD, J.C. *Homesteaders.* 1973. Toronto. 1st ed. intro Susan Wood Glicksohn. F/VG+. A18. $10.00

STEADMAN, Ralph. *Big I Am.* 1988. Summit. 1st ed. sq 4to. NF/dj. S9. $75.00

STEADMAN, Ralph. *Cherrywood Cannon.* 1978. Paddington. 1st ed. 4to. F/dj. S9. $75.00

STEADMAN, Ralph. *I Leonado.* 1983. Summit. 1st ed. obl 4to. rem mk. F/dj. S9. $50.00

STEADMAN, Ralph. *Jones of Colorado.* 1995. London. Ebury. 1st ed. sgn/dtd. F/dj. S9. $75.00

STEADMAN, Todd A. *Courtyards to Country Gardens.* 1992. Birmingham. photos. 192p. VG+/dj. B26. $30.00

STEARN, William T. *Botanical Gardens & Botanical Literature in 18th Century.* 1961. Pittsburgh. gilt gr cloth. F. B26. $25.00

STEARNS, Monroe. *Ring-A-Ling.* nd. Lippincott. ils. 117p. VG. P2. $35.00

STEAT, Christina. *Little Hotel.* 1973. HRW. 1st ed. NF/NF. B4. $50.00

STEAT, Christina. *People With the Dogs.* 1952. Little Brn. 1st ed. F/VG. B4. $85.00

STEBBINS, Henry M. *Pistols: A Modern Encyclopedia.* 1961. Harrisburg. 1st ed. photos. 390p. F/F. E1. $65.00

STEBBINS, Henry M. *Rifles: A Modern Encyclopedia.* 1958. Harrisburg. rpt. 376p. F/F. E1. $50.00

STEDMAN, John Gabriel. *Narrative of a 5 Years' Expedition Against Revolted Negroes.* 1806. London. Johnson. 2 vol. 4to. 79 (of 80) pl. contemporary bdg. C6. $2,600.00

STEED, Neville. *Boxed In.* 1991. London. Century. 1st ed. F/F. T2. $15.00

STEED, Neville. *Wind-Up.* 1991. St Martin. 1st Am ed. F/F. T2. $15.00

STEEGMAN. *Artist & the Country House.* 1949. Country Life/Scribner. VG/G. D2. $45.00

STEEGMULLER, Francis. *Stories & True Stories.* 1972. Boston. 1st ed. F/dj. A17. $9.50

STEELE, Adison; see Lupoff, Richard.

STEELE, J. Dorman. *Fourteen Weeks in Descriptive Astronomy.* (1896). NY. Barnes. 8vo. 336p. G. K5. $15.00

STEELE, Mary Q. *Owl's Kiss.* 1978. Greenwillow. 1st ed. VG+/dj. M21. $12.00

STEFANSSON, Vilhjalmur. *Adventure of Wrangel Island.* 1925-1926. London/NY. 1st ed. ils/map. 424p. VG. T7. $50.00

STEGNER, Wallace. *All the Little Live Things.* 1967. Viking. 1st ed. F/VG. A18. $60.00

STEGNER, Wallace. *Gathering of the Zion: Story of the Mormon Trail.* 1964. NY. 1st ed. photos. 331p. F/dj. E1. $100.00

STEGNER, Wallace. *Mormon Country.* 1942. NY. 1st ed. 362p. F. E1. $65.00

STEGNER, Wallace. *On a Darkling Plain.* 1940. Harcourt Brace. 1st ed. NF. A18. $175.00

STEGNER, Wallace. *On the Teaching of Creative Writing.* 1988. Dartmouth. 1st ed. prt brd. F/sans. B4. $85.00

STEGNER, Wallace. *Sound of Mountain Water.* 1969. NY. 1st ed. F/NF. A15. $50.00

STEGNER, Wallace. *Spectator Bird.* 1976. Franklin Lib. ltd ed. 8vo. full leather. F. S9. $85.00

STEGNER, Wallace. *Where the Bluebird Sings to the Lemonade Springs.* 1992. Random. ARC/1st ed. 8vo. RS. F/dj. w/promo material. S9. $85.00

STEGNER, Wallace. *Where the Bluebirds Sings to the Lemonade Springs.* 1992. Random. 1st ed. F/F. A18. $45.00

STEICHEN, Edward. *Life in Photography.* 1963. NY. 249 photos. VG/worn. A17. $30.00

STEICHEN, Edward. *US Navy War Photographs.* ca 1945. NY. US Camera. 108p. G/wrp. A17. $17.00

STEIG, Jeanne. *Consider the Lemming.* 1988. 2nd. VG/dj. K2. $14.00

STEIG, William. *Caleb & Kate.* 1977. FSG. 1st ed. ils. F/VG. P2. $35.00

STEIG, William. *Dreams of Glory.* 1953. Knopf. 1st ed. ils. VG/G-. P2. $40.00

STEIG, William. *Rejected Lovers.* 1951. Knopf. 1st ed. author's 1st book. ils. 153p. VG/G+. P2. $50.00

STEIG, William. *Tiffky Doofky.* 1978. FSG. 1st ed. 4to. unp. VG+. C14. $10.00

STEIN, Aaron Marc. *Days of Misfortune.* 1949. Doubleday. 1st ed. VG/NF. M22. $25.00

STEIN, Aaron Marc. *One Dip Dead.* 1979. NY. 1st ed. rem mk. F/F. H11. $20.00

STEIN, Eugene. *Straitjacket & Tie.* 1994. Ticknor. 1st ed. author's 1st book. F/F. H11. $30.00

STEIN, Gertrude. *Brewsie & Willie.* 1946. NY. 1st ed. F/VG. C6. $50.00

STEIN, Gertrude. *Flowers of Friendship: Letters Written to Gertrude Stein.* 1953. Knopf. 1st ed. F/F. B4. $75.00

STEIN, Gertrude. *Four Saints in Three Acts: An Opera To Be Sung.* 1934. NY. 1st ed. VG/G. B5. $70.00

STEIN, Gertrude. *Four Saints in Three Acts: An Opera To Be Sung.* 1934. Random. 1st ed. inscr. VG+. B4. $250.00

STEIN, Gertrude. *Geography & Plays.* 1922. Boston. 1st ed. 1st issue bdg. w/sgn letters pertaining to book. C6. $650.00

STEIN, Gertrude. *Gertrude Stein on Picasso.* 1970. Liveright. 1st ed. obl folio. F/F. B4. $100.00

STEIN, Gertrude. *Gertrude Stein's America.* 1965. WA. Robert Luce. 1st ed. edit Gilbert Harrison. F/F. B4. $125.00

STEIN, Gertrude. *How To Write.* 1973. West Glover, VT. Something Else. ARC. RS. F/NF. B4. $85.00

STEIN, Gertrude. *In Savoy; or, Yes Is for Yes for a Very Young Man.* 1946. London. Pushkin. 1st ed. F/F. B4. $150.00

STEIN, Gertrude. *Last Operas & Plays.* 1949. NY. Rinehart. 1st ed. F/NF. B24. $150.00

STEIN, Gertrude. *Lectures in America.* 1935. NY. Random. 1st ed. 8vo. 246p. NF/dj. T10. $150.00

STEIN, Gertrude. *Making of Americans.* 1966. NY. Something Else. 1st ed thus. F/F. B4. $200.00

STEIN, Gertrude. *Portraits & Prayers.* 1934. NY. 1st ed. inscr. VG+. C6. $350.00

STEIN, Gertrude. *Useful Knowledge.* nd. London. John Lane. 1st ed. inscr. F/F. B4. $1,500.00

STEIN, Gertrude. *What Are Masterpieces?* 1940. Los Angeles. 1st ed. VG/VG. B5. $80.00

STEIN, Leon. *Triangle Fire.* 1962. Lippincott. 1st ed. F/NF. B2. $35.00

STEINBECK, John. *America & Americans.* 1966. 1st ed. VG/VG. 313. $30.00

STEINBECK, John. *Cannery Row.* 1945. NY. 1st ed. VG/VG. B5. $65.00

STEINBECK, John. *Cup of Gold.* 1929. NY. 1st ed. VG. B5. $195.00

STEINBECK, John. *East of Eden.* (1952). np. facimile 1st ed. 602p. F/NF. A4. $65.00

STEINBECK, John. *Forgotten Village.* 1941. 1st ed. 4to. VG+/VG. S13. $55.00

STEINBECK, John. *Grapes of Wrath.* 1939. Heinemann. 1st Eng ed. F/F. A18. $350.00

STEINBECK, John. *Grapes of Wrath.* 1939. Viking. 1st ed. beige cloth. F/dj. B24. $1,250.00

STEINBECK, John. *Grapes of Wrath.* 1939. Viking. 1st ed. NF/NF. C2. $600.00

STEINBECK, John. *Long Valley.* 1938. NY. 1st ed. VG/VG. C6. $175.00

STEINBECK, John. *Moon Is Down.* (1942). Viking. not 1st ed. VG+/VG. H4. $5.00

STEINBECK, John. *Moon Is Down.* 1942. NY. 1st ed/1st state. VG/VG. N3. $45.00

STEINBECK, John. *Moon Is Down.* 1942. Viking. 1st ed/1st prt. F/NF. B24. $200.00

STEINBECK, John. *Of Mice & Men.* Feb 1937. Covici Friede. 1st ed/3rd prt. F. B14. $45.00

STEINBECK, John. *Of Mice & Men.* 1937. Covici Friede. 1st ed/1st issue. tan cloth. NF/dj. B24. $350.00

STEINBECK, John. *Of Mice & Men.* 1937. NY. 1st ed/2nd state. VG/VG. B5. $90.00

STEINBECK, John. *Red Pony.* ca 1959. Viking. ils Wesley Dennis. 120p. NF. C14. $8.00

STEINBECK, John. *Winter of Our Discontent.* 1961. np. 1st Eng ed. F/VG. M19. $65.00

STEINBECK, John. *Winter of Our Discontent.* 1961. NY. 1st issue. F/F. A17. $75.00

STEINBERG, Dave S. *Cooling Techniques for Electronic Equipment.* 1980. NY. Wiley. 370p. F. P4. $25.00

STEINDLER, R.A. *Firearms Dictionary.* 1970. Stackpole. photos. orange stp gray bdg. VG/G+. P12. $13.00

STEINEL, Alvin. *History & Agriculture in Colorado.* 1926. Ft Collins. State Agricultural College. 659p. VG. A10. $92.00

STEINER, Charlotte. *My Bunny Feels Soft.* 1958. Knopf. early ed. 8vo. unp. VG/torn. T5. $25.00

STEINER, Mona Lisa. *Philippine Ornamental Plants & Their Care.* 1952. Manila. 1st ed. ils. 215p. M/dj. B26. $27.50

STEINER, Nancy Hunter. *Closer Look at Ariel: A Memory of Sylvia Plath.* 1973. Harper's Magazine. 1st ed. F/F. B4. $100.00

STEINER, Rudolph. *Triorganic Social Organism.* 1923. Detroit. 1st Am ed. 135p. wrp. A17. $10.00

STEINER, Stan. *Dark & Dashing Horsemen.* 1981. San Francisco. 1st ed. F/F. E1. $25.00

STEINER, Stan. *New Indians.* 1968. NY. 1st ed. 348p. E1. $35.00

STEINER, Stan. *Waning of the West.* 1989. St Martin. 1st ed. 8vo. 300p. AN. T10. $18.00

STENGEL, Casey. *Casey at the Bat.* 1962. Random. 1st ed. VG+/VG+. P8. $35.00

STENHARDT, Anne. *How to Get Balled in Berkeley: Historical Novel of Sixties.* 1976. Viking. 1st ed. F/NF. B4. $65.00

STENZEL, Franz. *James Madison Allen: Yankee Artist of the Pacific Coast...* 1975. Ft Worth, TX. Amon Carter Mus. 1st ed. ils/pl. 209p. gray cloth. F/F. T10. $25.00

STEPHEN, Homer. *Fragments of History of Erath County...* 1966. Stephenville. 1st ed. photos. 137p. F/worn. E1. $35.00

STEPHENS, Alan. *Tree Meditation & Others.* 1970. Swallow. 1st ed. F/F. V1. $20.00

STEPHENS, Alexander H. *Constitutional View of the Late War Between the States.* 1868. Phil. vol 1 of 2. royal 8vo. 654p. brn cloth. G. T3. $30.00

STEPHENS, C.A. *Great Year of Our Lives at the Old Squires, CA.* (1912). Boston. Youths Companion. apparant 1st ed thus. 312p. bl cloth. VG. B22. $4.50

STEPHENS, Dan V. *Cottonwood Yarns...Mostly Stories Told to Children...* 1935. Fremont. 1st ed. photos. 109p. G. A17. $25.00

STEPHENS, Frederick J. *Fighting Knives: An Illustrated Guide...* 1980. NY. ils. 127p. F/F. E1. $35.00

STEPHENS, James. *Crock of Gold.* 1926. London. Macmillan. 1/525. sgn. ils Thomas Mackenzie. F. T10. $300.00

STEPHENS, James. *Crock of Gold.* 1942. LEC. 1st ed. ils/sgn Robert Lawson. VG/case. M5. $100.00

STEPHENS, John L. *Incidents of Travel in Egypt, Arabia Petraea & Holy Land...* 1853. Harper. 2 vol. 11th. ils. xl. G. W1. $65.00

STEPHENS, Robert W. *Lone Wolf: Story of Texas Ranger, Capt MT Gonzaullas.* nd. Dallas. 1/650. sgn. 79p. F. E1. $55.00

STEPHENS, Robert W. *Texas Rangers Indian War Pensions.* 1975. Quanah, TX. 1st ed. 124p. F. E1. $35.00

STEPHENS, Robert W. *Texas Rangers: An American Legend.* 1973. Rogers, AR. ils/photos. 45p. VG/wrp. E1. $30.00

STEPHENSON, Neal. *Diamond Age.* 1995. Bantam. 1st ed. F/F. M23. $60.00

STEPHENSON, Neal. *Zodiac.* 1988. Atlantic Monthly. 1st ed. sgn. author's 2nd book. VG/VG. B11. $40.00

STEPHENSON, Richard W. *Cartography of Northern Virginia: Facsimile Reproductions...* 1981. Farifax County. ils. 145p. VG. B10. $85.00

STERLING, Bruce. *Artificial Kid.* 1980. Harper Row. 1st ed. author's 2nd book. F/F. T2. $85.00

STERLING, Bruce. *Crystal Express.* 1989. Arkham. 1st ed. author's 1st collection. F/F. T2. $35.00

STERLING, Bruce. *Gobalhead.* 1992. Ziesing. 1st ed. sgn. F/F. T2. $45.00

STERLING, Bruce. *Heavy Weather.* 1994. Bantam. 1st ed. F/F. M23. $30.00

STERLING, George. *Lilith.* 1926. Macmillan. 1st trade ed. F. M19. $50.00

STERLING, George. *Sonnets to Craig.* 1928. Boni. 1st ed. 12mo. 120p. red stp gray cloth. NF/dj. T10. $75.00

STERLING, William Warren. *Trails & Trials of a Texas Ranger.* 1959. np. 1/500. inscr. ils Bob Schoenke. 524p. dj. w/promo flyer. E1. $200.00

STERN, Howard. *Private Parts.* 1993. Simon Schuster. 1st ed. F/F. B4. $75.00

STERN, J. David. *Eidolon: Philosophical Phantasy Based on a Syllogism.* 1952. NY. Messner. 1st ed. inscr to author John Gunther. F/VG+. B4. $125.00

STERN, Norton B. *California Jewish History: A Descriptive Bibliography.* 1967. Glendale. Arthur H Clark. 1st ed. 8vo. 438 entries. gilt bl cloth. F/F. T10. $100.00

STERN, Paul. *Sorry, Partner.* 1947. London. 4th. 141p. VG. S1. $8.00

STERN, Paul. *Vienna System of Contract Bridge.* 1947. Leeds, Eng. 1st ed. 243p. VG. S1. $10.00

STERN, Philip Van Doren. *Confederate Navy: A Pictorial History.* 1962. Garden City. 1st ed. 253p. G+/worn. B18. $27.50

STERN, Richard Martin. *Bright Road to Fear.* 1958. Ballantine. 1st ed. sgn. NF/VG. B4. $150.00

STERN, Richard. *Packages.* 1980. Coward. 1st ed. sgn. F/NF. H11. $30.00

STERN, Roger. *Death & Life of Superman.* 1993. Bantam. 1st ed. F/F. G10. $10.00

STERNE, Laurence. *Life & Opinions of Tristram Shandy, Gentleman.* 1832. London. Cochrane. 2 vol. 1st Cruikshank ed. 12mo. contemporary calf. F. T10. $500.00

STERNE, Laurence. *Works of...* 1795. London. Prt for Booksellers. 8 vol. 12mo. contemporary calf. C6. $275.00

STERNE. *Sentimental Journey Through France & Italy.* 1936. LEC. 1/1500. designed/sgn Eric Gill. ils/sgn Denis Tegetmeier. VG. A4. $200.00

STERRETT, Virginia. *Arabian Nights.* 1928. Penn. lg 4to. VG+. M5. $195.00

STETCHKAREV. *Gogol: His Life & Works.* 1965. NYU. 1st ed. NF/VG. S13. $15.00

STETSON, Harlan True. *Sunspots in Action.* 1947. Ronald. 8vo. 252p. G/worn. K5. $20.00

STEUART, Henry. *Planter's Guide; or, Practical Essay on Best Method...* 1828. Edinburgh. Murray. 2nd. 3-quarter leather/marbled brd. 527p. VG. A10. $115.00

STEVENS, Carla. *Stories From a Snowy Meadow.* 1976. Seabury/Clarion. 8vo. 48p. VG. T5. $10.00

STEVENS, Denis. *Tudor Church Music.* 1966. London. Faber. 2nd. ed. inscr. w/EP record. F/dj. T10. $75.00

STEVENS, Garfield Reeves. *Dark Matter.* 1990. Doubleday. 1st ed. F/F. P3. $20.00

STEVENS, Garfield Reeves. *Nighteyes.* 1989. Doubleday. 1st ed. F/F. P3. $19.00

STEVENS, J.C. *Surface Water Supply of Nebraska.* 1909. GPO. 8vo. 251p. F/new wrp. T10. $25.00

STEVENS, James. *Big Jim Turner.* 1948. Doubleday. 1st ed. F/VG+. A18. $17.50

STEVENS, Mark. *Summer in the City.* 1984. Random. 1st ed. F/NF. H11. $25.00

STEVENS, Orin A. *Handbook of North Dakota Plants.* 1950. Fargo. ils/drawings/photos. 324p. VG/dj. B26. $25.00

STEVENS, Reba Mahan. *Old Town Clock.* 1931. Lee Shepard. ils Florence Liley Young. VG. B17. $8.50

STEVENS, Ruth. *Hi-Ya Neighbor.* 1947. NY. Tupper Love. 1st ed. sgn. 122p. G/G. B11. $25.00

STEVENS, Wallace. *Auroras of Autumn.* 1950. NY. 1st ed. VG/VG. B5. $145.00

STEVENS, Wallace. *Celebration.* 1980. Princeton. 1st ed. assn copy. F/NF. V1. $20.00

STEVENS, Wallace. *Harmonium.* 1947. NY. 3rd. VG/VG. B5. $25.00

STEVENS, Wallace. *Necessary Angel: Essays on Reality & the Imagination.* 1951. Knopf. 1st ed. gilt gr cloth. F/red dj. B24. $235.00

STEVENS, Wallace. *Notes Toward a Supreme Fiction.* 1942. Cummington. 2nd ed. 1/330. F. B24. $300.00

STEVENS, Wallace. *Palm at the End of the Mind.* 1971. NY. Knopf. 1st ed. F/NF. B2. $75.00

STEVENS, Wallace. *Relations Between Poetry & Painting.* 1951. NY. MOMA. 1st ed. F/prt wrp. B24. $275.00

STEVENSON, Allan. *Bibliographical Method for Description of Botanical Books.* 1961. Pittsburgh. ils. 1961p. F. B26. $25.00

STEVENSON, Allan. *Problem of the Missale Speciale.* 1967. London. Bibliographical Soc. 8vo. 400p. F. T10. $75.00

STEVENSON, Robert Louis. *Catriona: Sequel to Kidnapped.* 1893. Cassell. 1st ed. NF. M19. $85.00

STEVENSON, Robert Louis. *Child's Garden of Verses.* nd. Scribner. rpt of 1905 ed. 8vo. 105p. VG. C14. $12.00

STEVENSON, Robert Louis. *Child's Garden of Verses.* 1895. Scribner. 1st ed. 12mo. teg. gr cloth. VG. M5. $125.00

STEVENSON, Robert Louis. *Child's Garden of Verses.* 1905. Scribner. ils JW Smith. teg. VG. M5. $75.00

STEVENSON, Robert Louis. *Child's Garden of Verses.* 1919. Rand McNally. 1st ed/2nd prt. VG+. M5. $80.00

STEVENSON, Robert Louis. *Child's Garden of Verses.* 1924. 1st ed. ils Frances Brundage. VG. S13. $25.00

STEVENSON, Robert Louis. *Child's Garden of Verses.* 1926. McKay. 1st Am ed. ils H Willebeek LeMair. G. P2. $150.00

STEVENSON, Robert Louis. *Child's Garden of Verses.* 1929. np. 1st ed thus. ils Eulalie. VG+. S13. $45.00

STEVENSON, Robert Louis. *Child's Garden of Verses.* 1929. Saalfield. ils Clara Burd. F. M5. $65.00

STEVENSON, Robert Louis. *Child's Garden of Verses.* 1930. Saalfield. ils Clara M Burd. VG. B30. $30.00

STEVENSON, Robert Louis. *Child's Garden of Verses.* 1943. Saalfield. ils FB Peat. VG/VG. C8. $100.00

STEVENSON, Robert Louis. *Child's Garden of Verses.* 1947. Oxford. 1st ed. sm 8vo. ils Tasha Tudor. VG/VG. C8. $200.00

STEVENSON, Robert Louis. *Ebb Tide.* 1894. Chicago/Cambridge. Stone/Kimball. VG. C6. $95.00

STEVENSON, Robert Louis. *Jolly Jump-Ups: A Child's Garden of Verses.* 1944. McLoughlin. mechanical. VG. C8. $75.00

STEVENSON, Robert Louis. *Kidnapped.* 1913. Scribner. 1st ed. ils NC Wyeth. blk cloth. NF. M20. $100.00

STEVENSON, Robert Louis. *Land of Nod & Other Poems for Children.* 1988. Holt. 1st ed. folio. ils Michael Hague. F/sans. B17. $20.00

STEVENSON, Robert Louis. *Master of Ballantrae.* 1911. London. Cassell. 8vo. ils. VG. B17. $10.00

STEVENSON, Robert Louis. *Songs of Travel & Other Verses.* 1896. London. 1st ed. NF. C6. $55.00

STEVENSON, Robert Louis. *Strange Case of Dr Jekyll & Mr Hyde.* 1886. London. Longman Gr. early ed. 8vo. VG/wrp/early custom cloth envelope. T10. $500.00

STEVENSON, Robert M. *Music in El Paso 1919-1939.* 1970. El Paso. 1st ed. photos. 40p. F/wrp. E1. $15.00

STEWARD, Dwight. *Acupuncture Murders.* 1973. Harper. 1st ed. F/F. B4. $65.00

STEWARD, Harold D. *First Was First.* 1945. Manila. Santo Tomas U. 18p. fair/wrp. B18. $65.00

STEWART, Frank. *Bridge Player's Comprehensive Guide to Defense.* 1988. NY. 404p. VG/wrp. S1. $10.00

STEWART, Frank. *Frank Stewart's Contract Bridge Quiz Book.* 1986. NJ. 234p. VG/wrp. S1. $8.00

STEWART, George R. *American Place-Names: A Conscise & Selective Dictionary.* 1970. NY. 1st ed. 550p. F/dj. E1. $30.00

STEWART, George R. *California Trail.* 1962. NY. 1st ed. 339p. F/dj. A17. $25.00

STEWART, George R. *California Trail.* 1983. Lincoln, NE. 1st Bison Book prt. 339p. stiff pict wrp. E1. $10.00

STEWART, George R. *Names on the Land.* 1958. Houghton Mifflin. 1st revised ed. 8vo. 511p. VG/dj. T10. $30.00

STEWART, James L. *Campfire Girls at Long Lake.* 1914. Saalfield. G+. P12. $5.00

STEWART, James L. *Campfire Girls on Hurricane Island.* 1921. Reilly Lee. 1st ed. VG. P12. $8.00

STEWART, John D. *Gibraltar the Keystone.* 1967. Boston. Houghton Mifflin. 1st ed. 335p. xl. VG. W1. $16.00

STEWART, Mary. *Crystal Cave.* 1970. Morrow. 1st ed. NF/clip. H11. $30.00

STEWART, Mary. *Merlin Cycle: Crystal Cave, Hollow Hills, Last Enchantment.* 1970-1983. London. 4 vol. Hodder Stoughton. 1st ed. djs. T10. $450.00

STEWART, Robert Armistead. *History of Virginia's Navy of the Revolution.* 1933. Richmond. private prt. 279p. VG. T7. $95.00

STEWART, Susan. *Yellow Stars & Ice.* 1981. Princeton. 1st ed. F/NF. V1. $15.00

STICK, David. *Graveyard of the Atlantic: Shipwrecks of the NC Coast.* 1987. Chapel Hill. sgn. 8vo. 276p. VG/G. B11. $20.00

STIEGLITZ, Alfred. *America & Alfred Stieglitz.* 1934. NY. Literary Guild. 1st ed. 8vo. photos. VG/dj. S9. $75.00

STIGAND, C.H. *Hunting the Elephant in Africa.* 1913. NY. 1st ed. xl. VG. N3. $95.00

STILES, George K. *Dragonman.* 1913. Harper. 1st ed. 8vo. 312p. VG. W1. $18.00

STILLE, Charles Janeway. *How a Free People Conduct a Long War...* 1863. NY. Anson DF Randolph. 1st ed thus. 35p. M8. $15.00

STILLMAN, Jacob D.B. *An 1850 Voyage: San Francisco to Baltimore by Sea...* 1967. Palo Alto. Lewis Osborne. 8vo. gilt bl cloth. VG. T10. $45.00

STILLMAN, Peter. *That Happy Feeling of Thank You.* nd. Norwalk, CT. Gibson. 12mo. unp. NF/VG. C14. $8.00

STILWELL, Hart. *Border City.* 1945. Doubleday Doran. 1st ed. F/clip. A18. $20.00

STIMSON, Henry L. *Prelude to Invasion.* 1944. Public Affairs Pr. 332p. stiff wrp. A17. $9.50

STINE, G. Harry. *Starship Through Space.* 1954. Holt. 2nd. author's 1st novel. VG+. M21. $25.00

STIRLING, James Hutchinson. *Lectures on the Philosophy of Law...* 1873. London. Longman Gr. orig gr cloth. M11. $250.00

STIRLING, Monica. *Wild Swan.* 1965. HBW. 1st Am ed. 384p. NF/VG. P2. $25.00

STITH, John E. *Manhattan Transfer.* 1993. Tor. 1st ed. F/F. G10. $15.00

STOCK, Dennis. *Haiku Journey.* 1974. 1st ed. F/F. S13. $45.00

STOCKING, Hobart E. *Road to Santa Fe.* 1971. NY. 1st ed. ils/maps. 372p. E1. $45.00

STOCKLEY, C.H. *African Camera Hunts.* 1948. London. 1st ed. VG/worn. B5. $40.00

STOCKTON, Frank R. *Bee-Man of Orn.* 1964. HRW. 1st ed (so stated). ils Sendak. 46p. NF/NF. D1. $100.00

STOCKTON, Frank. *Ardis Claverden.* 1890. Dodd Mead. VG. A17. $9.50

STOCKTON, J. Roy. *Gashouse Gang.* 1945. Barnes. 1st ed. G. P8. $25.00

STODDARD, William O. *Inside the White House in War Times.* 1890. NY. Webster. ils Dan Beard. 244p. silvered cloth. VG. B14. $35.00

STOFFLET. *Dr Seuss From Then to Now.* 1986. ils. cloth. F/F. A4. $45.00

STOKER, Bram. *Snake's Pass.* 1891. Sampson Low. authorized facsimile. NF/wrp. M22. $30.00

STOKES, Thomas L. *Savannah.* 1951. NY. 401p. F/NF. E1. $35.00

STOKES, W.L. *Essentials of Earth History.* 1960. Prentice Hall. 502p. VG. D8. $17.50

STOKES, William N. *Oil Mill on the Texas Plains: A Study in Agricultural...* 1979. TX A&M. 173p. E1. $25.00

STOLZ, Mary. *Ready or Not.* 1953. Harper. 1st ed. 243p. VG/G. P2. $20.00

STOLZ, Preble. *Judging Judges, the Investigation of Rose Bird...* 1981. Free Pr. M11. $35.00

STOMMEL. *Lost Islands: Story of Islands That Have Vanished...* 1984. U of British Columbia. ils. 146p. F/F. A4. $65.00

STONE, Carol. *Sentimental Education.* MCMLXXI. Swamp. 1/100. sgn. padded bdg. V1. $25.00

STONE, George Cameron. *Glossary of the Construction, Decoration & Use of Arms...* 1961. NY. Brussel. 2nd. sm 4to. 694p. VG/dj. W1. $100.00

STONE, Irving. *Agony & the Ecstacy.* 1961. Doubleday. 1st ed. sgn. F/NF. B4. $100.00

STONE, Irving. *Depths of Glory.* 1985. Doubleday. 8vo. inscr. F/NF. T10. $150.00

STONE, Irving. *Depths of Glory.* 1985. Franklin Lib. 1st ed. sgn. leather. F. B35. $55.00

STONE, Irving. *Manana Land: Irving Stone's Southern California.* 1991. Hist Soc of S CA. rpt. 8vo. 28p. AN/wrp. T10. $15.00

STONE, Irving. *Passions of the Mind.* 1971. NY. 1/500. sgn. F/case. w/sgn letter. A9. $75.00

STONE, Irving. *President's Lady.* 1951. Doubleday. 1st ed. G/G. B35. $18.00

STONE, John. *Practice of the Petty Sessions.* 1844. London. Robert Baldock. 5th. pebbled cloth. M11. $175.00

STONE, Phil. *Young Settler.* nd. Dodd Mead. stated 1st ed. ils Kurt Wiese. VG. M5. $45.00

STONE, Robert. *Children of Light.* 1986. Knopf. 1st ed. F/NF. H11. $40.00

STONE, Robert. *Children of Light.* 1986. Knopf. 1st ed. rem mk. F/F. B35. $20.00

STONE, Robert. *Dog Soldiers.* 1974. Houghton Mifflin. 1st ed. author's 2nd book. F/F. B35. $90.00

STONE, Robert. *Dog Soldiers.* 1974. Houghton Mifflin. 1st ed. author's 2nd book. VG/dj. S9. $35.00

STONE, Robert. *Flag for Sunrise.* 1981. Knopf. 1st ed. rem mk. F/F. B35. $32.00

STONE, Robert. *Outerbridge Reach.* 1992. Franklin Lib. 1st ed. sgn. ils. VG. C4. $125.00

STONE, Robert. *Outerbridge Reach.* 1992. Ticknor Fields. 1st ed. F/F. A20. $28.00

STONE, Stuart. *Kingdom of Why.* 1913. Bobbs Merrill. 1st ed. ils Peter Newell. 275p. G. P2. $85.00

STONE, Thomas H.; see Harknett, Terry.

STONEHOUSE, Frederick. *Munising Shipwrecks.* 1989. MI. Avery Color Studios. G/wrp. A16. $15.00

STOPES, Marie. *Contraception: Its Theory, History & Practice.* 1924. London. 1st ed/3rd prt. 418p. VG. A13. $100.00

STOPPARD, Tom. *Lord Malquist & Mr Moon.* 1966. London. 1st ed. author's 1st book. F/NF. C6. $175.00

STORER, D. Humphreys. *Report of the Committee on Obstetrics...* May 1851. Phil. pres. 63p. wrp. B14. $175.00

STORER, H.R. *Criminal Abortion: Its Prevelance, Its Prevention...* 1897. NY. rpt from Atlantic Medical Weekly. 34p. gr wrp. B14. $50.00

STOREY, Moorfield. *Reform of Legal Procedure.* 1912. New Haven. orig cloth. G. M11. $85.00

STORKE, Thomas M. *California Editor.* 1958. Los Angeles. Westernlore. ils. 489p. brn cloth. VG/worn. P4. $20.00

STORM, Hyemeyohsts. *Lightningbolt.* 1994. Ballantine. 1st ed. sgn. AN/dj. C2. $50.00

STORM, Hyemeyohsts. *Seven Arrows.* 1972. Harper. 1st ed. sgn. 373p. NF/NF. C2. $150.00

STORY, Joseph. *Commentaries on the Law of Bills of Exchange...* 1843. London. Maxwell. 1st Eng ed. emb cloth. M11. $650.00

STORY, Joseph. *Power of Solitude.* 1804. Salem. Macanulty. contemporary sheep. M11. $350.00

STOUDT, J.J. *Pennsylvania Folk Art.* 1948. Allentown. 1st ed. 403p. VG/G. B5. $45.00

STOUT, G.F. *Analytic Psychology.* 1896. London. 2 vol. 1st ed. 314p. pebbled russet cloth. G1. $85.00

STOUT, G.F. *Manual of Psychology.* 1901. London. College Correspondence College. 2nd. 661p. bl cloth. G1. $40.00

STOUT, Joseph A. *Apache Lightning: Last Great Battles of the Ojo Calientes.* 1974. NY. 1st ed. photos/biblio/notes/index. 210p. F/NF. E1. $30.00

STOUT, Neil R. *Perfect Crisis: Beginning of the Revolutionary War.* 1976. NY U. 8vo. ils. 206p. bl cloth. F. T10. $25.00

STOUT, Rex. *Champagne for One.* 1958. Viking. 1st ed. NF/VG. H11. $90.00

STOUT, Rex. *Family Affair.* 1975. Viking. 1st ed. F/F. M22. $30.00

STOUT, Rex. *In the Best of Families.* 1950. Viking. 1st ed. NF/VG. M22. $105.00

STOUT, Rex. *Murder by the Book.* 1951. Viking. 1st ed. NF/NF. M22. $125.00

STOUT, Rex. *Please Pass the Guilt.* 1973. Viking. 1st ed. NF/F. H11. $25.00

STOUT, Rex. *Three Aces.* 1971. Viking. 1st ed. F/NF. B4. $125.00

STOUT, Rex. *Too Many Women.* 1947. Viking. 1st ed. VG/G. M22. $70.00

STOUT, Rex. *Triple Jeopardy.* 1952. Viking. 1st ed. VG/VG. M22. $95.00

STOUTENBURG, Adrien. *Heros Advise Us.* 1964. Scribner. 1st ed. poet's 1st book. F/dj. V1. $25.00

STOUTENBURGH, John L. *Dictionary of the American Indian.* (1950). NY Philosophical Lib. later prt. 8vo. 459p. F/dj. E1/T10. $25.00

STOVALL, Pleasant Alexander. *Robert Toombas: Statesman, Speaker, Soldier, Sage...* 1892. NY. Cassell. 1st ed. 396p. cloth. NF. M8. $175.00

STOVER, Elizabeth M. *Son-of-a-Gun Stew: Sampling of the South-West.* 1945. Dallas. 1st ed. ils HD Bugbee. 216p. VG/dj. E1. $50.00

STOVER, Laren. *Pluto, Animal Lover.* 1994. Harper Collins. 1st ed. rem mk. F/F. G10. $10.00

STOWE, Charles Edward. *Life of Harriet Beecher Stowe.* 1890. Boston. 1st ed. 530p. bl cloth. VG. B14. $95.00

STOWE, Harriet Beecher. *Key to Uncle Tom's Cabin.* mid 1800s. London. modern bdg. VG. M17. $75.00

STOWE, Harriet Beecher. *Pink & White Tyranny: A Society Novel.* 1871. Boston. 1st Am ed/1st prt. VG. C6. $100.00

STOWE, Harriet Beecher. *Pink & White Tyranny: A Society Novel.* 1871. Boston. Roberts. 1st ed. 331p. G+. M20. $62.00

STOWE, Harriet Beecher. *Uncle Tom's Cabin; or, Life Among the Lowly.* 1852. Boston/Cleveland. John P Jewett Proctor Worthington. 2 vol. 1st ed. VG. M8. $3,500.00

STOWE, Harriet Beecher. *Uncle Tom's Cabin; or, Life Among the Lowly.* 1891. Houghton Mifflin. new ed. inscr/sgn. 12mo. 500p. gilt gr cloth. VG. B11. $2,250.00

STOWE, Harriet Beecher. *Women in Sacred History.* (1873). NY. 1st ed. ils/pl. 400p. aeg. full leather. VG+. H3. $125.00

STRACK, L. H. *Swords & Iris.* 1937. Harper. 1st ed. ils Bunji Tagawa. beige cloth. VG. D1. $50.00

STRAIGHT, Susan. *I Been in Sorrow's Kitchen & Licked Out All the Pots.* 1992. Hyperion. 1st ed. F/F. M23. $40.00

STRAIGHT, Susan. *I Been in Sorrow's Kitchen & Licked Out all the Pots.* 1992. NY. Hyperion. 1st ed. sgn. author's 2nd novel. F/F. B4. $45.00

STRALEY, John. *Woman Who Married a Bear.* 1992. Soho. 1st ed. F/F. H11. $45.00

STRAND, Mark. *Dark Harbor.* 1993. Knopf. 1st ed. rem mk. F/F. B35. $18.00

STRAND, Mark. *Mr Baby & Other Stories* 1985. Knopf. 1st ed. rem mk. F. G10. $35.00

STRAPAROLA, Giovanni. *Italian Novelists.* 1909. London. Soc of Bibliophiles. 7 vo. 1/300. teg. F. A17. $150.00

STRATEMEYER, Edward. *Colonial Series: At the Fall of Montreal.* 1903. Lee Shepard. 212p. gilt red cloth. VG. M20. $25.00

STRATEMEYER, Edward. *Colonial Series: Fort in the Wilderness.* 1905. Lee Shepard. 306p. gilt red cloth. VG. M20. $25.00

STRATEMEYER, Edward. *Colonial Series: With Washington in the West.* 1901. Lee Shepard. 302p. VG. M20. $25.00

STRATEMEYER, Edward. *Old Glory Series: Under Dewey at Manila.* 1898. Lee Shepard. 282p. gilt red cloth. VG. M20. $25.00

STRATEMEYER, Edward. *On to Pekin.* 1900. Boston. 1st ed. ils. pict cloth. G. A17. $15.00

STRATEMEYER, Edward. *Ship & Shore Series: Last Cruise of the Spitfire.* 1901 (1894). Lee Shepard. 245p. VG-. M20. $20.00

STRATEMEYER, Edward. *Stratemeyer Popular Series: Reuben Stone's Discovery.* 1900 (1895). Lee Shepard. 260p. rust cloth. VG+. M20. $20.00

STRATEMEYER, Edward. *Stratemeyer Popular Series: True to Himself.* 1900 (1891). Lee Shepard. 280p. VG+/dj. M20. $25.00

STRATFORD, Esme Wingfield. *They That Take the Sword.* 1931. Morrow. 1st ed. 424p. blk cloth. NF/dj. B22. $8.50

STRATTON, Helen. *Book of Myths.* nd. Nelson. 8vo. 16 pl. bl cloth. VG. M5. $50.00

STRATTON. *Pioneer Women: Voices From the Kansas Frontier.* 1981. np. 38 photos. 352p. VG/VG. A4. $65.00

STRAUB, Peter. *Floating Dragon.* 1983. Putnam. 1st ed. NF/dj. N4. $40.00

STRAUB, Peter. *Ghost Story.* 1979. CMG. 1st ed. NF/VG. H11. $45.00

STRAUB, Peter. *Ghost Story.* 1979. CMG. 1st ed. VG/VG. N4. $27.50

STRAUB, Peter. *Houses Without Doors.* 1990. Dutton. 1st Am ed. rem mk. F/NF. G10. $15.00

STRAUB, Peter. *Koko.* 1988. Dutton. 1st ed. F/F. H11. $40.00

STRAUB, Peter. *Throat.* 1993. NY. 1st ed. sgn. VG/VG. B5. $25.00

STRAUSS, Botho. *Devotion.* 1979. FSG. 1st Am ed. F/F. B4. $35.00

STRAWBERRY, Darryl. *Darryl.* 1992. Bantam. 1st ed. F/F. P8. $12.50

STRAWSON, John. *Battle for Berlin.* 1974. NY. ils/maps. 182p. F/dj. A17. $9.50

STRAWSON, John. *Italian Campaign.* 1988. NY. 1st Am ed. 221p. F/dj. A17. $10.00

STREAMER. *Book Titles From Shakspere (sic).* 1911. private prt. 1/800. inscr. identifies 400 works. 79p. F. A4. $95.00

STREATFIELD, Noel. *Circus Shoes.* 1939. Random. 1st ed. 401p. VG. P2. $25.00

STREATFIELD, Noel. *First Book of the Ballet.* 1953. Franklin. 1st ed. 8vo. ils. F/VG. M5. $30.00

STREATFIELD, Noel. *New Shoes.* 1960. Random. 1st ed. ils Vaike Low. 314p. NF/VG. P2. $30.00

STREET, Charles Stuart. *Whist Up to Date Revised, Enlarged & Explained.* 1897. Boston. 4th. 147p. VG. S1. $15.00

STREET, Donald M. *Ocean Sailing Yacht.* 1973. Norton. 4th. 703p. F/dj. A17. $20.00

STREET, Donald M. *Seawise: Helpful Hints, Warings & Common Sense...* 1979. Norton. ils/drawings, 320p. dj. T7. $22.00

STREET, George G. *Che! Wah! Wah!; or, The Modern Montezumas in Mexico.* 1883. Rochester, NY. fld map/mtd photos/woodcuts. 115p. T10. $1,500.00

STREET, James. *Oh Promised Land.* 1940. NY. 1st ed. VG/VG. B5. $40.00

STREET, James. *Tap Roots.* 1946. NY. Dial. later prt. pres. VG/VG. B5. $40.00

STREET, P. *Animal Reproduction.* 1974. Taplinger. 8vo. 263p. VG/G. B1. $22.50

STREET, P. *Crab & Its Relatives.* 1966. London. Faber. 8vo. 167p. cloth. dj. B1. $35.00

STREETER, Floyd B. *Ben Thompson, Man With a Gun.* 1957. Frederick Fell. 1st ed. 8vo. 217p. NF/dj. T10. $85.00

STREETER, Thomas W. *Bibliography of Texas 1795-1845.* 1996. Stoors-Mansfield. 5 vol. rpt. M8. $175.00

STREETER. *Eighteenth-Century English Novel in French Translation.* 1936. NY. Inst French Studies. 273p. VG. A4. $135.00

STREIBER, Whitley. *Transformation.* 1988. London. Century. 1st ed. VG/VG. M22. $12.00

STRETE, Craig. *Death in the Spirit House.* 1988. Doubleday. 1st ed. F/F. B4. $50.00

STRIBLING, Robert Mackey. *Gettysburg Campaign & Campaigns of 1864 & 1865 in VA* 1905. Petersburg, VA. Franklin. 1st ed. 308p. cloth. M8. $150.00

STRICKLAND, Agnes. *Lives of the Queens of England.* 1882. London. 8 vol. 8vo. teg. 3-quarter tan leather. VG to F. H3. $225.00

STRICKLER, Harry M. *Old Tenth Legion Marriages: Marriages in Rockingham County.* 1928. JK Reubush. 128p. G. B10. $45.00

STRIEBER, Whitley. *Black Magic.* 1982. Morrow. 1st ed. VG/VG. N4. $40.00

STRIKER, Cecil L. *Myrelaion Mesopotamien.* 1962. Munich. Hirmer. 1st ed. folio. 280 pl. NF/dj/case. W1. $150.00

STRIKER, Fran. *Lone Ranger (#1).* 1936. Grosset Dunlap. lists 2 titles. 218p. VG/tattered. M20. $20.00

STRIKER, Fran. *Lone Ranger & Gold Robbery (#3).* 1939. Grosset Dunlap. 1st ed. lists 2 titles. 185p. VG/dj. M20. $40.00

STRIKER, Fran. *Lone Ranger & the Outlaw Stronghold (#4).* 1939. Grosset Dunlap. 1st ed. lists 2 titles. 214p. VG/ragged. M20. $30.00

STRIKER, Fran. *Lone Ranger & Tonto (#5).* 1940. Grosset Dunlap. 1st ed. lists 3 titles on dj. 214p. VG/dj. M20. $62.00

STRIKER, Fran. *Lone Ranger on Red Butte Trail.* 1956. Grosset Dunlap. 1st ed. last title in series/lists to itself. VG/dj. M20. $190.00

STRIKER, Fran. *Lone Ranger Traps the Smugglers (#7).* 1941. Grosset Dunlap. lists to this title. 214p. VG/dj. M20. $47.00

STRINDBERG, August. *Getting Married.* 1972. NY. 1st Eng-language ed. 384p. F/F. A17. $17.50

STRINGER, George A. *Shakespeare's (sic) Draughts From the Living Water.* 1883. np. self pub. 1/65. 4to. teg. pebbled gilt gr cloth. VG+. H7. $125.00

STRONG, Charles. *Story of American Sailing Ships.* 1957. Grosset Dunlap. ils Gordon Grant/HB Vestal. VG/VG. B17. $5.00

STRONG, Phil. *Censored, the Goat.* 1945. Dodd Mead. probable 1st ed. 78p. NF/G. C14. $35.00

STRONG, Phil. *Horses & Americans.* 1946. Garden City. VG/G. O3. $20.00

STRONG, Phil. *Missouri Canary.* 1943. Dodd Mead. 1st ed. 78p. VG/G+. T5. $35.00

STRONG, Phil. *Young Settler.* 1938. 1st ed. ils Kurt Wiese. VG/tattered. B30. $30.00

STROTHER, David Hunter. *Virginia Illustrated: Containing a Visit...* 1857. Harper. 1st ed. ils. 300p. G. B10. $125.00

STROUD, Robert. *Stroud's Digest of Diseases of Birds.* 1943. St Paul. 1st ed. VG. B5. $40.00

STRUNG, Norman. *Misty Mornings & Moonless Nights.* 1974. Macmillan. 1st ed. ils. NF/VG. P12. $15.00

STRUSS, H.W. *Ring-Riding.* 1891. NY. Appleton. 1st ed. diagrams. VG. O3. $65.00

STUART, Dabney. *Diving Bell.* 1966. Knopf. 1st ed. poet's 1st book. F/VG. V1. $30.00

STUART, Dabney. *Particular Place.* 1969. Knopf. 1st ed. assn copy. F/worn. V1. $20.00

STUART, David Schiff. *Best of Whispers.* 1994. Baltimore/Binghamton. Borderlands/Whispers. 1st ed. 1/500. sgns. F/F/case. T2. $65.00

STUART, J.E.B. *Letters of Major General James EB Stuart.* (1990). np. inscr JEB Stuart IV. 442p. F/NF. M8. $65.00

STUART, Jesse. *Album of Destiny.* 1944. NY. 1st ed. VG/VG. B5. $50.00

STUART, Jesse. *Hie to the Hunters.* 1950. NY. 1st ed. VG. B5. $50.00

STUART, Jesse. *Mongrel Mettle.* 1944. NY. 1st ed. VG/G. B5. $50.00

STUART, Jesse. *Penny's Worth of Character.* 1954. Whittlesey. 1st ed. ils Henneberger. 62p. G+/G. P2. $50.00

STUART, Jesse. *Red Mule.* 1955. Whittlesey. 1st ed. inscr. ils Henneberger. 123p. VG/G+. P2. $65.00

STUART, Jesse. *Taps for Private Tussie.* 1943. NY. BC. ils Benton. dj. A17. $9.50

STUART, Sidney; see Avallone, Mike.

STUBBS, John Heath. *Charity of the Stars.* 1949. Wm Sloane. 1st ed. F/NF. V1. $35.00

STUMPF, Carl. *Tonpsychologie.* 1883. Leipzig. Hirzel. 2 vol. buff wrp. F. G1. $425.00

STURGES, Henry C. *Chronologies of the Life & Writings of Wm Cullen Bryant...* 1968 (1903). NY. Franklin. facsimile. xl. VG. A17. $12.50

STURGES, Katharine. *Mimi, Momo & Miss Tabby Tibbs.* 1927. Volland. 4th. ils K Struges. VG/VG box. D1. $175.00

STURTEVANT & TAYLOR. *Native Americans: The Indigenous People of North America.* 1991. London. Salamander. 3rd. 4to. 256p. F/dj. T10. $35.00

STYRON, William. *American Academy of Arts & Letters.* 1990. 1st ed. 1/633. VG/VG. C4. $65.00

STYRON, William. *Confessions of Nat Turner.* 1967. Random. 1st ed. F/F. H11. $75.00

STYRON, William. *Darkness Visible: A Memoir of Madness.* 1990. NY. 1st ed. F/F. M23. $30.00

STYRON, William. *Darkness Visible: A Memoir of Madness.* 1990. NY. 1st ed. sgn. F/F. M23. $40.00

STYRON, William. *Lie Down in Darkness.* 1951. Indianapolis. 1st ed. VG/VG. B5. $95.00

STYRON, William. *Sophie's Choice.* 1979. Random. 1st ed. F/F. B35. $35.00

STYRON, William. *Sophie's Choice.* 1979. Random. 1st ed. sgn. F/F. B2. $45.00

STYRON, William. *This Quiet Dust & Other Writings.* 1982. Random. 2nd. 305p. VG/VG. B10. $12.00

SUCKOW, Ruth. *Country People.* 1924. NY. 1st trade ed. author's 1st book. inscr. F/F. C2. $75.00

SUCKOW, Ruth. *Folks.* 1934. Farrar Rinehart. 1st ed. F/chip. A18. $30.00

SUCKOW, Ruth. *John Wood Case.* 1959. Viking. 1st ed. F/F. A18. $15.00

SUDWORTH, G.B. *Forest Trees of the Pacific Slope.* 1967. NY. Dover. 8vo. 455p. VG. B1. $18.00

SUKENICK, Lynn. *Houdini.* 1973. Capra. 1st ed. Chapbook series. inscr. F/wrp. V1. $10.00

SULLIVAN, Dulice. *LS Brand: Story of a Texas Panhandle Ranch.* 1968. Austin, TX. 1st ed. 178p. F/NF. E1. $50.00

SULLIVAN, Eleanor. *Alfred Hitchcock's Tales To Keep Yourself Spellbound.* 1976. BC. VG/dj. M21. $7.50

SULLIVAN, Leon H. *Build, Brother, Build.* 1969. Phil. Macrae Smith. 192p. dj. R11. $13.00

SULLIVAN, Marion F. *Westward the Bells.* 1971. Alba. 1st ed. 8vo. 220p. F/dj. T10. $35.00

SULLIVAN, Maurice S. *Jedediah Smith, Trader & Trail Blazer.* 1936. NY. Pr of Pioneers. 1st ed. ils Howard Simon. 233p. F/VG. B18. $125.00

SULLIVAN, T.R. *Boston Old & New.* 1912. Houghton Mifflin. 1/785. 8vo. teg. NF. T10. $100.00

SULLIVAN, Thomas. *Phases of Harry Moon.* 1988. Dutton. 1st ed. author's 1st book. F/F. H11. $35.00

SULLIVAN, Walter. *Black Holes: Edge of Space, End of Time.* 1979. Anchor. 1st ed. NF/VG+. G10. $5.00

SULLIVAN, Walter. *Continents in Motion: New Earth Debate.* 1974. NY. 1st ed. sgn. 399p. VG/VG. B11. $30.00

SULLIVAN, Walter. *Recollection (Allen Tate).* nd. LSU. 1st ed. VG/G. V1. $20.00

SULLIVAN, Winona. *Sudden Death at the Norfolk Cafe.* 1993. St Martin. 1st ed. AN/dj. N4. $25.00

SULLIVAN. *British Literary Magazines, Modern Age 1914-1984.* 1986. np. 658p. F. A4. $55.00

SULLIVAN. *British Literary Magazines, Victorian & Edwardian...* 1984. np. 586p. F. A4. $55.00

SULLY, James. *Human Mind: TB of Psychology.* 1892. Longman Gr. 2 vol. 1st ed/2nd issue. emb brn cloth. G. G1. $100.00

SULLY, James. *Illusions: Psychological Study.* 1888. Appleton. 12mo. 372p. red cloth. G1. $50.00

SULLY, James. *Outlines of Psychology With Special Reference to Theory...* 1887 (1884). Appleton. thick 8vo. 711p. bevvled ruled brn cloth. G1. $35.00

SULZBERGER, C.L. *Long Row of Candles: Memoirs & Diaries 1934-1954.* 1968. BC. VG. A17. $10.00

SUMER & WALKER. *Stargazer to the Sultan.* 1967. Parents Magazine. 1st ed. ils. VG+. C14. $15.00

SUMMERHAYES, R.S. *Observers Book of Horses & Ponies.* 1958. London. 12mo. ils. 256p. F/VG. H3. $40.00

SUMMERS, Bart; see Fox, Gardner F.

SUMMERS, Hollis. *Sit Opposite Each Other*. 1970. Rutgers. 1st ed. assn copy. F/VG+. V1. $15.00

SUPERVIELLE, Jules. *Horses of Time*. 1985. Tamarack. 1/26. sgnlettered. sewn handmade papers. V1. $75.00

SUPERVIELLE, Jules. *Selected Writings*. 1967. New Directions. ARC. RS. F/NF. w/photo. V1. $20.00

SUPREE, Burton. *Bear's Heart: Scenes From the Life of a Cheyenne Artist...* 1977. Lippincott. 1st ed. 8vo. F/G. B17. $35.00

SURTEES, Robert. *Analysis of the Hunting Field*. 1923. London. 1st ed thus. tall 8vo. aeg. NF. C2. $150.00

SURTEES, Robert. *Sporting Novels of RS Surtees*. 1929-1931. Eyre Spottiswoode/Scribner. 12 vol. 1/976. teg. VG+. H3. $475.00

SURTEES, Robert. *Sporting Novels*. 1847-1888. Lodnon. 7 vol. 8vo. ils Leech. teg. full calf. T10. $2,000.00

SUSKIND, Patrick. *Perfume*. 1986. Knopf. 1st ed. B stp on edges. F/F. w/promo card. H11. $40.00

SUTCLIFF, Rosemary. *Arthurian Trilogy*. 1979-1982. NY. Dutton. 3 vol. later prt. F/dj. T10. $150.00

SUTCLIFF, Rosemary. *Warrior Scarlet*. 1970 (1958). London. Oxford. rpt. 207p. xl. dj. T5. $28.00

SUTERMEISTER, Edwin. *Story of Papermaking*. 1954. Boston. SD Warren. Anniversary ed. 8vo. 209p. bl cloth. T10. $25.00

SUTTON, David. *Complete Book of Model Railroading*. 1964. 1st ed. 4to. ils. NF/VG+. S13. $30.00

SUTTON, Ernest V. *Life Worth Living*. 1948. Pasadena, CA. 1st ed. photos/index. 350p. F/VG. E1. $65.00

SUTTON, Felix. *Big Book of Dogs*. nd. Grosset Dunlap. 4to. unp. NF. C14. $12.00

SUTTON, Margaret. *Ghost Parade*. (1933). Grosset Dunlap. 217p. red bdg. F/VG+. P2. $15.00

SUTTON, Margaret. *Judy Bolton: Black Cat's Clue (#23)*. 1952. Grosset Dunlap. 210p. pict brd. VG. M20. $52.00

SUTTON, Margaret. *Judy Bolton: Haunted Fountain (#28)*. 1957. Grosset Dunlap. lists 29 titles. 180p. VG/dj. M20. $52.00

SUTTON, Margaret. *Judy Bolton: Whispered Watchword (#32)*. 1961. Grosset Dunlap. 1st ed. lists to this title. 180p. VG+/clip. M20. $125.00

SUTTON, Margaret. *Lollypup: True Story of a Little Dog*. nd. Grosset Dunlap. 8vo. ils. unp. G+. C14. $12.00

SUTTON, Stephen. *Tales To Tremble By*. 1966. Whitman. 1st ed thus. VG+. M21. $10.00

SUTTON, Willie. *Where the Money Was*. 1973. Viking. 1st ed. F/F. A20. $20.00

SUTTON & SUTTON. *American West: A Natural History*. 1976. Promontory. 194 ils/16 maps. 272p. F/dj. T10. $50.00

SUVIN, Darko. *Positions & Presuppositions in SF*. 1988. Kent State. 1st ed. F/F. T2. $15.00

SUYIN, Han. *Fron One China to the Other*. 1956. 1st ed. photos Henri Cartier Bresson. VG+/VG+. S13. $75.00

SVEVO, Italo. *As a Man Grows Older*. 1963. London. Secker Warburg. Uniform ed. F/NF. H4. $30.00

SVEVO, Italo. *Life*. 1963. London. Secker Warburg. 1st Eng ed. F/F. H4. $75.00

SWALLOW, Alan. *Nameless Sight*. 1956. IA City. Prairie Pr. 1st ed. assn copy. F/NF. V1. $35.00

SWALLOW, Alan. *Wild Bunch*. 1966. Denver, CO. 136p. F/worn. E1. $50.00

SWAN, Jon. *Door to the Forest*. 1979. Random. 1st ed. F/F. V1. $15.00

SWAN, Oliver G. *Frontier Days*. 1928. Phil. 1st ed. ils/pl. 512p. VG. B18. $22.50

SWAN. *Gregory Dexter of London & New England 1610-1700*. 1949. np. 157p. VG/VG. A4. $25.00

SWANSON, Doug J. *Big Town*. 1994. Harper Collins. 1st ed. author's 1st book. rem mk. F/F. H11. $35.00

SWANSON, Gloria. *Swanson on Swanson*. 1980. Random. 1st ed. w/sgn leaf. F/NF. B2. $85.00

SWANSON, Henry F. *Countdown for Agriculture in Orange County Florida*. 1975. Orlando. 1st ed. sgn. 8vo. 338p. F/F. B11. $30.00

SWANSON, Logan; see Matheson, Richard.

SWANTON, John R. *Indian Tribes of North America*. 1952. WA. GPO. 8vo. lg fld maps. gilt olive cloth. VG. T10. $150.00

SWANWICK, Michael. *Gravity's Angels*. 1991. Arkham. 1st ed. F/F. T2. $22.00

SWARD, Robert. *Thousand Year Old Fiance & Other Poems*. 1965. Cornell. 1st ed. F/NF. V1. $15.00

SWARG, Leopold F. *Apparatus Work for Boys & Girls...* 1923. Phil. McVey. photos. 8vo. wht ils buckram. VG. B14. $35.00

SWARTHOUT, Glendon. *Homesman*. 1988. Weidenfeld Nicolson. 1st ed. F/F. M23. $20.00

SWEENEY, James B. *Pictorial History of Oceanographic Submersibles*. 1971. NY. Crown. 4to. ils. 308p. VG/dj. T7. $30.00

SWEETSER, M.F. *King's Handbook of the United States*. 1891. Buffalo. Moses King. 8vo. 51 maps. 393p. F. O7. $75.00

SWENSON, Peggy; see Geis, Richard.

SWIFT, Graham. *Ever After*. 1992. Knopf. 1st ed. sgn. F/F. B2. $50.00

SWIFT, Jonathan. *Gulliver's Travels to Lilliput & Brobdingnag*. nd. Garden City. ils RG Mossa. VG/G. B17. $6.50

SWIFT, Jonathan. *Gulliver's Travels*. ca 1885. Routledge. thick 8vo. ils. VG. M5. $45.00

SWIFT, Jonathan. *Gulliver's Travels*. ca 1910. McLoughlin Brothers. 8vo. pict cloth. VG. T10. $45.00

SWIFT, Jonathan. *Gulliver's Travels*. 1917. Macmillan. 1st ed thus. ils Willy Pogany. VG. M5. $75.00

SWIFT, Jonathan. *Gulliver's Travels*. 1931 (1912). Rand McNally. ils Milo Winter. blk cloth/pl. F/G. M5. $45.00

SWIFT, Jonathan. *Travels of Lemuel Gulliver*. 1929. NY. LEC. ils Alexander King. VG/case. T10. $300.00

SWINBURNE, Algernon Charles. *Chastelard: A Tragedy*. 1865. London. Moxon. 1st ed. 12mo. 219p. F. B24. $750.00

SWINBURNE, Algernon Charles. *Laux Veneris*. 1866. NY. Author's Ed. gilt cloth. VG. A17. $20.00

SWINBURNE, Algernon Charles. *Pilgrimage of Pleasure, Essays & Studies, With Bibliography*. 1913. np. 1/500. 181p. VG. A4. $75.00

SWINBURNE, Algernon Charles. *Shelley*. 1973. Worcester. St Onge. 1/500. aeg. gilt stp red leather. miniature. T10. $50.00

SWINDELL, L. *Screwball*. 1975. NY. 1st ed. VG/VG. B5. $40.00

SWINDELLS, P. *Overlook Water Gardener's Handbook*. 1984. Woodstock. Overlook. 172p. VG/VG. B1. $27.00

SWINFORD, A. *Clays & Clay Minerals*. 1963. Macmillan. Earth Sience series. 509p. F/dj. D8. $25.00

SWINK & WILHELM. *Plants of the Chicago Region.* 1994. IN Academy of Science. 4th. 921p. dj. B1. $70.00

SYDNOR, Caroline. *Bridge Made Easy, Volume 1.* 1978 (1975). Alexandria, VA. pb. 165p. F. w/deck of cards. S1. $8.00

SYERS, William E. *Texas: The Beginning 1519-1834.* 1978. Waco, TX. 1st ed. photos/index. 172p. F/F. E1. $25.00

SYKES, Al. *Pulp & Paper Fleet.* 1988. Canada. Stonehouse. A16. $15.00

SYKES, C.A. *Service & Sport on the Tropical Nile.* 1903. London. ils/fld map. 306p. G. B5. $75.00

SYLVESTER, Jerry. *Salt-Water Fishing Is Easy.* 1956. Stackpole. sgn. 208p. cloth. VG/dj. M20. $15.00

SYME, M. Herbert. *National Labor Relations Act & National Defense.* 1941. NY. rpt. 41p. M11. $25.00

SYMONDS, Arthur. *Study of Walter Pater.* 1932. London. 1/100. sgn. teg. bl buckram. VG. B14. $250.00

SYMONDS, Arthur. *Study of Walter Pater.* 1932. London. Sawyer. 1st ed. 1/350. 8vo. 112p. cloth/brd. VG. T10. $100.00

SYMONDS, John Addington. *Problem in Modern Ethics.* 1896. London. private print. 1/100. xl. VG. B2. $60.00

SYMONDS, John Addington. *Wine, Women & Song: Mediaeval Latin Students' Songs.* 1884. London. Chatto Windus. 1st ed. 12mo. teg. later morocco/ribbon marker. F. T10. $250.00

SYMONDS, R.D. *Where the Wagon Led.* 1973. NY. 1st ed. 343p. F/VG. E1. $30.00

SYMONS, Julian. *Criminal Comedy.* 1985. Viking. 1st Am ed. AN/dj. M22. $15.00

SYMONS, Julian. *Name of Annabel Lee.* 1983. Viking. 1st ed. AN. M22. $15.00

SZAPARY, Le Comte F. *Magnetism Et Magnetotherapie.* 1854. Paris. inscr. 492p. marbled brd/morocco spine. VG. B14. $250.00

SZEKERES, Cindy. *Thumpity Thump Gets Dressed.* 1984. Golden. 1st ed. 8vo. VG. C14. $10.00

SZENT-GYORGYI, Albert. *Crazy Ape.* 1970. NY. 1st ed. 8vo. 93p. red cloth. VG/dj. B14. $45.00

SZYK, Arthur. *La Tentation de Saint Antoine, by Gustave Flaubert.* (1926). Paris. Reynaud. 1/30 on Japan. 293p. F/chemise/case. w/extra suite. B24. $3,000.00

TABACHNICK, Stephen E. *Explorations in Doughty's Arabia Deserta*. 1987. Athens, GA. 1st ed. 8vo. map. VG. W1. $25.00

TABAK, Herman D. *Cargo Containers: Their Stowage, Handling & Movement*. 1970. Cambridge. Maritime. VG/VG. A16. $15.00

TABB, Warner. *Pondering Muse*. 1973. Whittet Sheperson. 17p. VG. B10. $8.00

TABER, Gladys. *Especially Dogs*. 1968. Phil. 1st ed. 191p. F/dj. A17. $15.00

TABER, Gladys. *Especially Dogs...Especially at Stillmeadow*. 1968. Lippincott. 2nd. sgn. 191p. VG/dj. M20. $87.00

TABER, Gladys. *First Book of Dogs*. 1949. Franklin Watts. ils Bob Kuhn. VG/VG. S13. $25.00

TABER, Gladys. *One Dozen & One*. 1966. Lippincott. 1st ed. sgn. 239p. cloth. VG+/dj. M20. $60.00

TABER, Gladys. *Stillmeadow Kitchen*. 1947. Macrae Smith. revised/1st prt. 311p. VG/dj. M20. $30.00

TABORI, Paul. *Private Life of Adolf Hitler...* 1949. London. 1st ed. 171p. VG. A17. $15.00

TAFF, Laurence G. *Celestial Mechanics: Computational Guide...* 19854). John Wiley. 1st prt. 8vo. 520p. VG/VG. K5. $45.00

TAFT, Robert. *Artists & Illustrators of the Old West 1850 1900*. 1953. Scribner. 1st ed. ils. map ep. VG/dj. T10. $75.00

TAIBO, Paco Ignacio II. *An Easy Time*. 1990. Viking. 1st Am ed. AN/dj. M22. $20.00

TAINE, Hippolyte Adolph. *De L'Intelligence*. 1870. Paris. Hachette. 2 vol. contemporary bdg. VG. G1. $225.00

TAINE, Hippolyte Adolph. *On Intelligence*. 1872. Holt Williams. 1st Am ed. thick 8vo. xl. G1. $85.00

TAITS, S.W. *Wildcatters: Informal History of Oil-Hunting in America*. 1946. Princeton. 218p. VG. D8. $12.00

TALBERT, Bill. *Tennis Observed*. 1967. Barre. 1st ed. sgn. VG. B5. $45.00

TALBOT-BOOTH, E.C. *Merchant Ships 1939*. 1939. London. Sampson Low Marston. G/dj. A16. $175.00

TALBOYS, W.P. *West Indian Pickles*. 1876. NY. ils. G+. B18. $22.50

TALESE, Gay. *Unto the Sons*. 1992. Knopf. 1st trade ed. F/F. B35. $20.00

TALIAFERRO. *Cartographic Sources in Rosenberg Library*. 1988. TX A&M. 10 maps. 247p. F/F. A4. $45.00

TALLANT, Edith. *David & Patience*. 1940. Lippincott. sgn. ils Dorothy Bayler. VG/tattered. M20. $27.00

TALLANT, Edith. *Girl Who Was Marge*. 1939. Lippincott. sgn. ils Dorothy Bayley. VG/dj. M20. $27.00

TAMURA, Naomi. *Japanese Bride*. 1893. NY. 1st ed. ils. 92p. VG. B14. $60.00

TAN, Amy. *Hundred Secret Senses*. 1995. Putnam. 1/175. sgn. F/case/swrp. S9. $175.00

TAN, Amy. *Hundred Secret Senses*. 1995. Putnam. 1st ed. sgn. F/F. M23. $40.00

TAN, Amy. *Hundred Secret Senses*. 1995. Putnam. 1st ed. sgn. M/M. B4. $50.00

TAN, Amy. *Joy Luck Club*. 1989. Putnam. 1st ed. author's 1st book. NF/F. H11. $160.00

TAN, Amy. *Kitchen God's Wife*. 1991. NY. 1st ed. sgn. F/F. C2. $30.00

TAN, Amy. *Kitchen God's Wife*. 1991. Putnam. 1st ed. F/F. G10. $25.00

TANGIER. *Lu Singulieree Zone de Tungier*. 1955. Paris. Eurafricaines. 8vo. 313p. VG/wrp. P4. $25.00

TANNER, Clara Lee. *Southwest Indian Painting: A Changing Art*. 1973. Tucson. AZ U. 2nd. lg 4to. 477p. gr cloth. F/dj. T10. $75.00

TANNER, Helen Hornbeck. *Atlas of Great Lakes Indian History*. 1987. OK U. 1st ed. 33 maps/80 ils. M/dj. O7. $85.00

TARBELL, Harlan. *Tarbell Course in Magic. Vol 4*. 1945. Louis Tannen. revised ed. inscr. 8vo. 418p. gilt gr brd. F. B11. $65.00

TARBELL, Ida. *History of the Standard Oil Company*. 1904. np. 2 vol. sgn. VG. A4. $300.00

TARG, William. *American West*. 1946. Cleveland. World. sgn. 8vo. 595p. VG. B11. $35.00

TARG, William. *Bibliophile in the Nursery*. 1957. World. 503p. cloth. VG/dj. M20. $62.00

TARG, William. *Bouillabaisse for Bibliophiles*. 1955. Cleveland. 1st ed. VG/VG. B5. $40.00

TARG, William. *10,000 Rare Books & Their Prices*. 1940. VG+. S13. $18.00

TARKENTON, Fran. *Murder at the Super Bowl*. 1986. Morrow. 1st ed. F/NF. H11. $20.00

TARKINGTON, Booth. *Beasley's Christmas Party*. 1909. Harper. 1st ed/1st state. ils RS Clements. 99p. VG. M20. $37.00

TARKINGTON, Booth. *Gentleman From Indiana*. 1899. Doubleday McClure. 1st ed. inscr/dtd 1934. VG. B4. $275.00

TARKINGTON, Booth. *Penrod Jashber*. 1929. Doubleday. stated 1st ed. ils Gordon Grant. VG+. M5. $25.00

TARKINGTON, Booth. *Penrod*. 1914. Garden City. 1st ed. VG. B5. $50.00

TARKINGTON, Booth. *Seventeen*. 1916. Harper. 1st (B-Q) ed. 329p. VG. M20. $105.00

TARKINGTON, Booth. *Two Vanrevels*. 1902. 1st ed. teg. VG. w/sgn. S13. $40.00

TARN, Nathaniel. *Old Savage Young City*. 1964. London. Cape. 1st ed. inscr. F/nf. w/sgn note. V1. $65.00

TARRANT, Margaret. *Favourite Fairy Tales*. 1920s. London. Ward Lock. 1st ed. 24 pl. VG/G. P2. $120.00

TARRANT, Margaret. *Margaret Tarrant Christmas Book*. 1940. Hale Cushman Flint. lg 4to. VG. M5. $25.00

TARRANT, Margaret. *Margaret Tarrant's Christmas Garland*. 1942. Boston. 19 mtd pl. silvered red cloth. VG+. M5. $60.00

TARTT, Donna. *Secret History*. 1992. Knopf. 1st ed. author's 1st book. F/F. B35. $38.00

TARTT, Donna. *Secret History*. 1992. Knopf. 1st ed. sgn. F/F. B2. $65.00

TARVIN, A.H. *Century of Baseball*. 1938. Standard Prt. G+. P8. $45.00

TASHLIN, Frank. *Bear That Wasn't*. 1946. Dutton. 1st ed. sm 4to. NF/G. C8. $75.00

TASSIN, Ray. *Stanley Vestal: Champion of the Old West*. 1973. Glendale. 299p. F/NF. P4. $18.00

TATE, Allen. *Collected Poems 1919-1976*. 1988. LSU. 1st ed. F/wrp. V1. $15.00

TATE, Allen. *Constant Defender*. 1983. Ecco. 1st ed. F/NF. w/pub card. V1. $30.00

TATE, Allen. *Fragment of a Meditation*. 1947. Cummington. VG/hand-tied gray wrp. V1. $100.00

TATE, Allen. *Hovering Fly & Other Essays*. 1949. Cummington. 1st ed. 1/245. NF. B24. $650.00

TATE, Allen. *Man of Letters in the Modern World*. 1957. Meridian. 2nd imp. 352p. VG/VG. B10. $45.00

TATE, Allen. *Mr Pope & Other Poems*. 1928. Minton Balch. 1st ed. F/NF. B2. $600.00

TATE, Allen. *Poems 1922-1947*. 1948. Scribner. 1st ed. assn copy. F/VG. V1. $40.00

TATE, Allen. *Selected Poems.* 1937. Scribner. 1st ed. F/dj. V1. $45.00

TATE, Allen. *Winter Sea, a Book of Poems.* 1944. Cummington. 1st ed. 1/330. blk cloth/paper label. B24. $325.00

TATE, Florence Lee. *Random Reveries, True Incidents & Echoes.* 1942. np. 204p. VG/fair. B10. $8.00

TATNALL, Robert R. *Flora of Delaware & the Eastern Shore.* 1946. Wilmington. ils. 313p. F. B26. $55.00

TATON, R. *Reason & Chance in Scientific Discovery.* 1957. London. 171p. VG. A13. $30.00

TAUBENHAUS, J.J. *Culture & Diseases of the Sweet Pea.* 1917. NY. 232p. cloth. scarce. B26. $22.00

TAUBER, Gerald E. *Man & the Cosmos.* 1979. Greenwich. 4to. photos/diagrams. 352p. VG/VG. K5. $30.00

TAVERNIER, John Baptista. *Collection of Several Relations & Treatises...* 1680. London. Godbid Playford. 1st ed. 2 parts in 1. lg fld map/7 fld pl. full calf. C6. $2,500.00

TAVERNIER, John Baptista. *Collections of Travels Through Turky (sic) Into Persia...* 1684. London. Moses Pitt. 3 vol in 1. 1st Eng-language ed. ils. modern full calf. C6. $4,000.00

TAVERS, P.L. *Maria Poppin AB A-Z.* 1968. Harcourt Brace. 1st ed. 12mo. trans GM Lyne. F/F. C8. $50.00

TAX, Sol. *Penny Capitalism.* 1963. Chicago. rpt of 1953 ed. VG. F3. $20.00

TAXAY, Don. *Money of the American Indians & Other Primitive Currencies.* 1970. NY. Mummus. 8vo. ils. 158p. F/dj. T10. $50.00

TAYLER, Zack; see Marshall, Mel.

TAYLOR, Alan R. *Arab Balance of Power.* 1982. Syracuse. 1st ed. 8vo. map. VG/wrp. W1. $12.00

TAYLOR, Bayard. *At Home & Abroad.* 1889. NY. 12mo. 500p. red cloth. G. T3. $20.00

TAYLOR, Charles F. *Pathology & Treatment of Lateral Curvature of the Spine.* 1868. NY. 18p. prt gray wrp. B14. $125.00

TAYLOR, Charles H. *Simplified Review of the Important Laws of Bridge.* nd. NY. sm format. 22p. VG/wrp. S1. $5.00

TAYLOR, Frank J. *High Horizons.* 1962. NY. new revised ed. ils. 266p. VG/dj. B18. $12.50

TAYLOR, George H. *Massage: Principles & Practice of Remedial Treatment...* 1884. NY. 1st ed. 203p. tan cloth. F. B14. $35.00

TAYLOR, Hannis. *Due Process of Law & Equal Protection of the Laws.* 1917. Chicago. Callaghan. prospectus. 1 sheet/fld. orig mailing envelope. M11. $25.00

TAYLOR, Henry J. *Big Man.* 1964. Random. 1st ed. inscr. 311p. VG/G+. B10. $15.00

TAYLOR, Henry. *Afternoon of Pocket Billiards.* 1978. UT U. 1st ed. F/VG. V1. $10.00

TAYLOR, Jane. *Little Ann: A Book.* nd. Warne. early prt. ils Kate Greenaway. VG+. S13. $55.00

TAYLOR, John. *All the Works of John Taylor, the Water Poet.* 1630. Menston, Yorkshire. 4to. 146p. gilt gr cloth. dj. K1. $75.00

TAYLOR, Louis. *Harper's Encyclopedia for Horsemen.* 1973. NY. Harper Row. VG/G. O3. $25.00

TAYLOR, Lucy. *Close to the Bone.* 1993. Seattle. Silver Salamander. 1st ed. sgns. F/F. T2. $35.00

TAYLOR, Meadows. *Confession of a Thug.* 1968. NY. 338p. F/worn. A17. $12.50

TAYLOR, Peter. *Conversations With Peter Taylor.* 1987. Jackson, MS. 1st ed. F/F. C2. $25.00

TAYLOR, Peter. *Summons to Memphis.* 1986. Knopf. 1st ed. F/F. B4. $75.00

TAYLOR, Peter. *Tennessee Day in St Louis: A Comedy.* 1957. Random. 1st ed. sgn. NF/NF. C2. $150.00

TAYLOR, Robert Lewis. *Niagara.* 1980. Putnam. 1st ed. F/F clip. B4. $50.00

TAYLOR, Robert Lewis. *Travels of Jaimie McPheeters.* 1958. NY. 1st ed. VG/VG. B5. $30.00

TAYLOR, Samuel W. *Line Haul.* 1959. San Francisco. 1st ed. 307p. NF. B18. $15.00

TAYLOR, Sidney. *More All-Of-A-Kind Family.* 1954. Follett. ils Mary Stevens. 149p. VG/dj. M20. $22.00

TAYLOR, Telford. *Munich the Price of Peace.* 1979. NY. 1st ed. photos. cloth. G. A17. $14.50

TAYLOR, Thomas E. *Running the Blockade: A Personal Narrative of Adventures...* 1897. London. John Murray. 3rd. fld map. 180p. cloth. VG. M8. $150.00

TAYLOR, W. *Historic Survey of German Poetry I.* 1828-1830. London. 1st ed. later 19th-C half morocco. VG. C6. $120.00

TAYLOR, W.C. *WC Fields: His Follies & Fortunes.* 1949. Doubleday. brd. VG. D2. $10.00

TAYLOR, W.R. *Marine Algae of the Northeastern Coast of North America.* 1962. Ann Arbor. 2nd revised/2nd prt. 8vo. 509p. cloth. F. B1. $55.00

TAYLOR, Welford. *Virginia Authors Past & Present.* 1972. VA Assn Teachers of Eng. inscr. 125p. VG. B10. $50.00

TAYLOR, William H. *Yachting in North America.* 1948. Van Nostrand. VG/dj. A16. $50.00

TAYLOR, William. *California Life Illustrated.* ca 1885. NY. 12mo. ils. 404p. brn cloth. xl. VG. T3. $45.00

TAYLOR & TAYLOR. *Black Dutch.* 1991. NY. Walker. 1st ed. F/F. H11. $20.00

TAYLOR & TAYLOR. *Neon Dancers.* 1991. Walker. 1st ed. author's 3rd novel. AN/dj. M22. $15.00

TAYLOR. *Art Nouveau Book in Britain.* 1966. MIT. 176p. VG/VG. A4. $95.00

TAYLOR. *From the White House Inkwell: Am Presidential Autographs.* 1968. ils. 147p. F/NF. A4. $125.00

TAYLOR. *Introduction to Cartooning.* 1947. F/F. D2. $25.00

TAYLOR-HALL, Mary Ann. *Come & Go, Molly Snow.* 1995. Norton. 1st ed. author's 1st book. F/F. M23. $45.00

TAZEWELL, Charles. *Littlest Angel.* 1946. Chicago. 1st ed. 50p. F/dj. A17. $16.00

TAZEWELL, William L. *Down to the Sea With Jack Woodson.* 1987. Algonquin. ils. 72p. VG/dj. T7. $40.00

TEASDALE, Sara. *Sonnets to Duse & Other Poems.* 1907. Boston. 1st ed. 1/1000. author's 1st book. ils. w/photo. F. B24. $250.00

TEASDALE, Sara. *Stars To-Night: Verses New & Old for Boys & Girls.* 1930. Macmillan. 1st ed. 8vo. VG/G. M5. $75.00

TEASDALE, Sara. *Strange Victory.* 1933. Macmillan. 1st ed. xl. F. V1. $25.00

TEBBEL & ZUKERMAN. *Magazine in America 1741-1990.* 1991. Oxford. 433p. F/F. A4. $35.00

TEBBEL. *American Magazine, a Compact History.* 1969. np. 287p. RS. NF/VG. A4. $45.00

TEMIANKA. *Jack Vance Lexicon, From Ahulph to Zipangote...* 1992. np. 136p. F. A4. $55.00

TEMPEST, Margaret. *Little Lamb of Bethlehem.* 1963. Medici Soc. 3rd imp. 16mo. VG. B17. $7.50

TEMPLE, Shirley. *Shirley Temple's Favorite Tales of Long Ago.* 1958. NY. Random. 1st prt. unp. NF. C14. $20.00

TEMPLE, Shirley. *Storybook.* 1958. 1st ed. 4to. NF/VG. S13. $30.00

TENGGREN, Gustaf. *Tenggren's Cowboys & Indians.* 1948. Simon Schuster. 1st ed. lg 4to. VG. M5. $45.00

TENGGREN, Gustaf. *Tenggren's Story Book.* 1944. Simon Schuster. stated 1st ed. ils. VG/dj. M5. $40.00

TENISON, Robin Hansbury. *Worlds Apart: An Explorer's Life.* 1984. Boston. Little Brn. 1st Am ed. sm 4to. dj. F3. $20.00

TENN, William; see Klass, Philip.

TENNANT, Eleanor A. *ABC of Bridge.* ca 1904. Toronto. 5th. 128p. VG. S1. $6.00

TENNEY, Jack. *Red Fascism: Boring From Within...* 1947. Los Angeles. Federal Prt. 1st ed. 700+p. NF. B2. $45.00

TENNYSON, Alfred Lord. *Enoch Arden.* 1864. London. 2nd issue. VG. C6. $75.00

TENNYSON, Alfred Lord. *Idylls of the King.* 1859. London. Moxon. 1st ed. Arthur Machen's copy. 12mo. emb cloth. T10. $1,000.00

TENNYSON, Alfred Lord. *Morte d'Arthur.* 1912. Chatto Windus. 4to. sgn Alberto Sangorski. NF. T10. $100.00

TENNYSON, Alfred Lord. *Seven Poems & Two Translations.* 1902. Hammersmith. 1/325. 8vo. 55p. full limp vellum. NF. B24. $350.00

TENNYSON, Alfred Lord. *Tennyson's Guinevere & Other Poems.* 1912. Blackie. 1st ed. ils Florence Harrison. VG+. M5. $250.00

TENNYSON, Alfred Lord. *Tennyson's Poems.* 1897. Crowell. gilt red cloth. F. V1. $20.00

TEPFER, Sanford S. *Floral Anatomy & Oteogeny in Aquilegia Formosa...* 1953. Berkeley. 136p. wrp. B26. $15.00

TERENTIUS AFER, Publius. *Comoediae Sex en Recensione Frid.* 1820. London. Priestley. 2 vol. 8vo. teg. gilt gr calf. K1. $175.00

TERHUNE, Albert Payson. *Real Tales of Real Dogs.* (1955). Saalfield. ne. 4to. 92p. F/VG. C14. $20.00

TERHUNE, Albert Payson. *Real Tales of Real Dogs.* 1955. Saalfield. 1st ed. ils Diana Thorne. VG. B30. $35.00

TERHUNE & THORNE. *Dog Book.* 1932. Saalfield. 4to. ils. NF/fair. M5. $45.00

TERKEL, Studs. *Good War.* 1984. Pantheon. 1st ed. sgn. F/F. B2. $50.00

TERKEL, Studs. *Great Divide.* 1988. Pantheon. 1st ed. F/F. B2. $45.00

TERRACE, Edward L.B. *Egyptian Paintings of the Middle Kingdom.* 1968. Braziller. 1st ed. folio. 172p. xl. VG/dj. W1. $65.00

TERZIAN, James. *Kid From Cuba.* 1967. Doubleday. 1st ed. VG/G+. P8. $40.00

TESICH, Steve. *Summer Crossings.* 1982. Random. 1st ed. F/F. H11. $25.00

TESNOLIDEK, Rudolf. *Cunning Little Vixen.* 1985. FSG. 1st ed. 8vo. ils Sendak. F/F. B17. $15.00

TESSIER, Thomas. *Nightwalker.* 1980. Atheneum. 1st Am ed. F/VG. M21. $75.00

TEUKOLSKY, Roselyn. *How To Play Bridge With Your Spouse...And Survive.* 1991. NY. 192p. VG/wrp. S1. $10.00

TEVIS, Walter. *Far From Home.* 1981. Doubleday. 1st ed. NF/NF. R10. $10.00

TEVIS, Walter. *Queen's Gambit.* 1983. NY. 1st ed. VG/VG. B5. $25.00

TEVIS, Walter. *Steps of the Son.* 1983. Doubleday. 1st ed. VG/VG. M22. $15.00

THACKERAY, William Makepeace. *Doctor Birch & His Young Friends.* 1849. London. 16 pl. NF/orig pk wrp/Zachnsdorf bdg. C6. $175.00

THACKERAY, William Makepeace. *Four Georges: Sketches of Manners, Morals, Court...* 1861. London. Smith Elder. 1st ed/1st issue. 8vo. 226p. gr cloth. F. B24. $375.00

THACKERAY, William Makepeace. *Rose & the Ring; or, History of Prince Giglio...* 1937. Macmillan. 16mo. 212p. VG. C14. $15.00

THACKERAY, William Makepeace. *Thackeray's Letters to an American Family...* 1904. Merrymount. ils. VG. A4. $45.00

THACKERAY, William Makepeace. *Thackery Alphabet.* 1930. Harper. 1st ed. ils. VG/G. P2. $25.00

THACKERAY, William Makepeace. *Works...* 1871. London. Smith Elder. 12 vol. half leather/marbled brd. NF. T10. $500.00

THACKREY, Ted. *Gambling Secrets of Nick the Greek.* 1968. 1st ed. VG/VG. K2. $12.00

THALL, Michael. *Let Sleeping Afghans Lie.* 1990. Walker. 1st ed. F/F. H11. $25.00

THANE, Edith. *Marionettes Are People.* 1948. DSP. 1st ed. VG/VG. P3. $8.50

THANE, Elswyth. *Ever After.* 1945. DSP. 2nd. 334p. VG. B10. $8.00

THARP, Louise Hall. *Baroness & the General.* 1962. Little Brn. 1st ed. ils. 458p. VG/VG. B10. $12.00

THATCHER, Margaret. *Path to Power.* 1995. Harper Collins. 1st ed. w/sgn bookplate. NF/F. B2. $85.00

THATCHER. *First Christmas Pop-Up Press-Out Characters...Storybook.* nd. np. opens to panorama. pull tab to play Silent Night. F. A4. $45.00

THAWAITES, Reuben Gold. *Original Journals of Lewis & Clark Expedition 1804-1806.* 1969. Arno. 8 vol. 54 fld maps. F/cloth clamshell case. A4. $395.00

THAYER, Bert Clark. *Horses in the Blue Grass.* 1940. DSP. 2nd. photos. 78p. VG. O3. $20.00

THAYER, Bert Clark. *Thoroughbred: Pictorial Highlights...* 1964. DSP. 1st ed. VG/fair. O3. $25.00

THAYER, Emma Homan. *Wild Flowers of the Pacific Coast.* 1887. NY. Cassell. 24 chromolithographs. aeg. cloth. F. T10. $350.00

THAYER, Jane. *Part Time Dog.* 1965. Morrow. ils Seymour Fleishman. VG/G. B17. $5.00

THAYER, Steve. *Saint Mudd.* 1992. Viking. 1st ed. author's 1st book. rem mk. F/F. H11. $30.00

THAYER, W.M. *From Tannery to White House: Life of Ulysses S Grant.* 1885. NY. 12mo. 480p. bl cloth. G. T3. $20.00

THAYER, W.M. *Marvels of the New West.* 1888. Norwich, CT. thick royal 8vo. ils/maps. 715p. gilt gr cloth. G. T3. $30.00

THAYER, William Roscoe. *Life & Letters of John Hay.* 1915. Boston. 2 vol. 10th. VG. V4. $60.00

THEINER, George. *Let's Go to the Circus.* 1963. London. Bancroft. 8vo. ils Rudolf Lukes/5 moveables. unp. T10. $150.00

THEODOR, O. *Fauna Palaestina. Insecta I: Diptera Pupipara.* 1975. Jerusalem. tall 8vo. 168p. cloth. NF. B1. $40.00

THERNSTROM, Mel. *Dead Girl.* 1990. Pocket. 1st ed. F/F. A20. $15.00

THEROUX, Alexander. *Adultery.* 1987. Simon Schuster. UP. sgn. John Updike's copy (sgn). F/wrp. B4. $200.00

THEROUX, Alexander. *Darconville's Cat.* 1981. Doubleday. 1st ed. 704p. VG/G. B10. $20.00

THEROUX, Alexander. *Lollipop Trollops.* 1992. Dalkey Arch. 1st ed. F/wrp. V1. $10.00

THEROUX, Alexander. *Three Wogs.* 1972. Boston. 1st ed. author's 1st book. sgn. F/NF. C2. $200.00

THEROUX, Paul. *Chicago Loop.* 1990. Random. 1st ed. F/F. H11. $30.00

THEROUX, Paul. *Half Moon Street.* 1984. Houghton Mifflin. 1st ed. F/NF. H11. $30.00

THEROUX, Paul. *My Secret History.* 1989. Putnam. 1st ed. 8vo. F/dj. T10. $25.00

THEROUX, Paul. *O-Zone.* 1986. Putnam. 1st ed. F/VG. A20. $20.00

THEROUX, Paul. *Pillars of Hercules: Grand Tour of the Mediterranean.* 1995. Putnam. 1st ed. sgn. AN/dj. B4. $65.00

THEROUX, Peter. *Sandstorms: Days & Nights in Arabia.* 1990. Norton. 1st ed. 8vo. 281p. NF/dj. W1. $20.00

THESIGER, Wilfred. *Arabian Sands.* 1959. Dutton. 1st ed. 8vo. ils/fld map. 326p. VG. W1. $25.00

THIFFAULT, Mark. *Fisherman's Digest.* 1984. DBI Books. photos. VG. P12. $5.00

THOMAS, Alan G. *Great Books & Book Collectors.* 1988. London. Spring. rpt. 280p. F/dj. A17. $25.00

THOMAS, Alfred Barnaby. *Teodoro de Croix & the Northern Frontier of New Spain...* 1968. Norman. 2nd. 273p. red cloth. VG/dj. P4. $25.00

THOMAS, Benjamin P. *Lincoln's New Salem.* 1954. Knopf. new/revised ed. sgn. 166p. VG/dj. B18. $30.00

THOMAS, D. Gourlay. *Simple, Practical Hybridising for Beginners.* 1962. BC. 127p. F/dj. B26. $15.00

THOMAS, D.M. *Shaft.* 1973. Dalkey Arch. 1/400. ils. NF/wrp. w/promo sheet. V1. $20.00

THOMAS, Dylan. *Child's Christmas in Wales.* 1985. Holiday House. 1st ed. ils Trina Hyman. AN/dj. C8. $75.00

THOMAS, Dylan. *Conversations About Christmas.* 1954. New Directions. 1st ed. 12mo. F/wrp. B24. $200.00

THOMAS, Dylan. *Letters to Vernon Watkins.* 1957. London. 1st ed. F/VG+ clip. N3. $20.00

THOMAS, Dylan. *Twenty-Five Poems.* 1939. London. Dent. 1st ed. 1/730. gray brd. F/prt gray dj. B24. $950.00

THOMAS, Dylan. *Under Milk Wood.* 1954. New Directions. 1st Am ed. 12mo. F/VG. T10. $50.00

THOMAS, Frederick W. *Emigrant; or, Reflections While Descending the Ohio.* 1872. Cincinnati. 48p. cloth. G. B5. $45.00

THOMAS, Graham S. *Flowering Plants of the Riviera.* 1914. London. ils. 249p. cloth. B26. $30.00

THOMAS, Graham S. *Garden of Roses.* 1987. Topsfield. 160p. F. B26. $27.50

THOMAS, Graham S. *Shrub Roses of Today.* 1962. London. 1st ed. ils. 241p. VG/dj. B26. $20.00

THOMAS, Ianthe. *Lordy, Aunt Hattie.* 1973. Harper. 1st ed. 8vo. AN/dj. C8. $20.00

THOMAS, Isaiah. *Diary of Isaiah Thomas 1805-1828.* 1909. Am Antiquarian Soc. 2 vol. portrait. F. A4. $185.00

THOMAS, John. *British Railways, Steamers of the Clyde.* 1948. London. Ian Allan Ltd. G/wrp. A16. $25.00

THOMAS, Joseph. *Hounds & Hunting Through the Ages.* 1937. Garden City. rpt. G+. O3. $35.00

THOMAS, L. *Lives of a Cell.* 1974. Viking. 5th. 12mo. 153p. half cloth. clip dj. B1. $15.00

THOMAS, Leslie. *Some Lovely Islands.* 1969. Coward McCann. 1st Am ed. F/NF. B4. $65.00

THOMAS, Lewis. *Long Line of Cells: Collected Essays.* 1990. NY. 361p. VG. A13. $20.00

THOMAS, Lowell. *Count Luckner, the Sea Devil.* 1927. Garden City. ils. 308p. G+. P12. $20.00

THOMAS, Lowell. *Seeing Canada With Lowell Thomas.* 1936. Akron. 1st ed. photos. 108p. pict brd. VG. A17. $12.50

THOMAS, Lowell. *Wreck of the Dumaru.* 1930. Doubleday Doran. 1st ed. sgn by survivor. 8vo. 271p. VG. B11. $75.00

THOMAS, Norman. *Conscientious Objector in America.* 1923. NY. Huebsch. 1st ed. F/NF. B2. $125.00

THOMAS, Patricia. *There Are Rocks in My Socks!* 1979. Lee Shepard. 1st ed. ils Mordicai Gerstein. unp. G+/dj. T5. $24.00

THOMAS, R.S. *Old Brick Church Near Smithfield Virginia Built in 1632.* (1892). VHS. rpt. hc. 37p. VG. B10. $15.00

THOMAS, Ross. *Briarpatch.* 1984. Simon Schuster. 1st ed. rem mk. NF/NF. H11. $20.00

THOMAS, Ross. *Eighth Dwarf.* 1979. Simon Schuster. 1st ed. F/F. T2. $35.00

THOMAS, Ross. *Mordida Man.* 1981. Simon Schuster. 1st ed. F/F. T2. $35.00

THOMAS, Ross. *No Questions Asked.* 1976. Morrow. 1st ed. F/NF. T2. $130.00

THOMAS, Ross. *Out on the Rim.* 1987. Mysterious. 1st ed. F/F. N4. $22.50

THOMAS, Ross. *Out on the Rim.* 1987. Mysterious. 1st ed. VG/VG. M22. $10.00

THOMAS, Ross. *Procane Chronicle.* 1972. Morrow. 1st ed. 3rd novel as Oliver Beeck. F/NF. B4. $150.00

THOMAS, Ross. *Thumbsuckers, Etc.* 1989. Northridge, CA. Lord John. 1st ed. 1/300. sgn/#d. F/sans. A11. $75.00

THOMAS, Ross. *Twilight at Mac's Place.* 1990. Mysterious. 1st ed. rem mk. F/F. N4. $15.00

THOMAS, Ross. *Voodoo, Ltd.* 1992. Mysterious. ARC. NF/wrp. M22. $20.00

THOMAS, Ross. *Voodoo, Ltd.* 1992. Mysterious. 1st ed. AN/dj. N4. $20.00

THOMAS, Witts. *Enola Gay.* 1977. np. 1st ed. NF/VG. w/mtd photo sgn by Tibbets & Caron. S13. $40.00

THOMAS & THOMAS. *Nature, a Quote by John Muir.* 1996. Santa Cruz. brn morocco w/inset onlay flower. miniature. M. B24. $300.00

THOMAS & THOMAS. *Our Flight to Adventure.* 1956. Doubleday. 1st ed. sgn Lowell Thomas Jr. 8vo. 318p. F/clip. B11. $45.00

THOMAS & WITTS. *San Francisco Earthquake.* 1971. Stein Day. 316p. F/dj. D8. $10.00

THOMAS. *History of Printing in America.* 1970. rpt. F/F. D2. $45.00

THOMAS. *With Bleeding Footsteps: Mary Baker Eddy's Path...* 1994. np. 363p. F/F. A4. $25.00

THOMASON, John W. *Fix Bayonets!* 1926. NY. later prt. 245p. G+. B18. $22.50

THOMASON, John W. *Gone to Texas.* 1937. 1st ed. VG/fair. S13. $75.00

THOMASON, John W. *Jeb Stuart.* 1934. Scribner. early prt. 512p. cloth. VG/dj. M8. $35.00

THOMLINSON, H.M. *Norman Douglas.* 1931. Harper. 1st ed. 77p. VG/VG. B18. $22.50

THOMPSON, Blanche Jennings. *All the Silver Pennies.* 1967. NY. 1st ed. VG/VG. B5. $30.00

THOMPSON, Blanche Jennings. *Silver Pennies: A Collection of Modern Poems...* 1925. Macmillan. 1st ed. sm 8vo. bl pict cloth. VG. M5. $95.00

THOMPSON, Craig. *Since Spidletop: A Human Story of Gulf's 1st Half Century.* nd. np. private prt. 104p. gilt emb bdg. F. B22. $8.00

THOMPSON, D.W. *Men & Meridians: History of Surveying & Mapping Canada...* 1966. Ottawa. Roger Duhamel. 1st ed. 37 maps. G. D8. $18.00

THOMPSON, Dorothy. *I Saw Hitler!* 1932. NY. 1st ed. inscr. NF/VG. B4. $250.00

THOMPSON, Dunstan. *Poems.* 1943. Simon Schuster. 1st ed. F/NF. V1. $55.00

THOMPSON, Edgar T. *Perspectives on the South: Agenda for Research.* 1967. Duke. 231p. VG/G. B10. $12.00

THOMPSON, Edmund. *Maps of Connecticut Before the Year 1800.* 1940. Hawthorn. 1/250. sgn. 4 maps. F. O7. $325.00

THOMPSON, Fresco. *Every Diamond Doesn't Sparkle.* 1964. McKay. later prt. VG/VG. P8. $30.00

THOMPSON, G.A. *Geographical & Historical Dictionary of America...* 1970. Burt Franklin. 5 vol. 4to. F3. $250.00

THOMPSON, H.T. *Ousting the Carpetbagger From South Carolina.* 1926. Columbia. 1st ed. ils. 182p. VG. B5. $75.00

THOMPSON, Hunter S. *Fear & Loathing in Las Vegas.* 1971. Random. 1st ed. F/F. B4. $300.00

THOMPSON, Hunter S. *Fear & Loathing in Las Vegas.* 1971. Random. 1st ed. NF/dj. S9. $275.00

THOMPSON, Hunter S. *Generation of Swine.* 1988. Summit. 1st ed. 304p. NF/dj. M20. $37.00

THOMPSON, Hunter S. *Generation of Swine.* 1988. Summit. 1st ed. 304p. VG/dj. M20. $18.00

THOMPSON, Hunter S. *Great Shark Hunt.* 1979. Summit. 1st ed. F/NF. B4. $85.00

THOMPSON, Hunter S. *Great Shark Hunt. Gonzo Papers, Vol 1.* 1979. NY. Summit. 1st ed. 8vo. 600+p. VG/dj. S9. $40.00

THOMPSON, Hunter. *Fear & Loathing on the Campaign Trail.* 1963. San Francisco. 1st ed. F/F. B5. $60.00

THOMPSON, J. Eric. *Thomas Gage's Travels in the New World.* 1958. OK U. 1st ed. 8vo. 379p. gr cloth. VG. T10. $50.00

THOMPSON, Jim. *Black Box Thrillers: 4 Novels by Jim Thompson.* 1983. London. Zomba. 1st hc ed. F/F. T2. $35.00

THOMPSON, Jim. *End of the Book.* 1937. Viking. 1st ed. NF/VG+. A11. $300.00

THOMPSON, Jim. *Heed the Thunder.* 1991. Armchair Detective. NF/NF. P10. $15.00

THOMPSON, Jim. *King Blood.* 1993. Armchair Detective. 1st Am ed. NF/NF. P10. $20.00

THOMPSON, Jim. *More Hardcore.* 1986. NY. Donald Fine. 1st ed. F/F. B4. $65.00

THOMPSON, Jim. *Mourn the Hangman.* 1952. Hasbrouck Hts, NJ. F. A11. $40.00

THOMPSON, Jim. *Now & on Earth.* 1986. Bellen, NM. Dennis McMillan. 1/400. F/F. A11. $95.00

THOMPSON, Josiah. *Six Seconds in Dallas.* 1967. NY. 1st ed. VG/VG. B5. $55.00

THOMPSON, Kay. *Eloise.* nd. Simon Schuster. 22nd. VG/VG. B17. $8.50

THOMPSON, Kay. *Eloise at Christmastime.* 1958. NY. Random. 1st prt. 4to. VG/VG+. C8. $150.00

THOMPSON, Kay. *Eloise in Moscow.* 1959. NY. 1st ed. VG/fair. B5. $95.00

THOMPSON, Kay. *Eloise in Moscow.* 1959. Simon Schuster. 1st ed. ils Hilary Knight. orange cloth. VG/dj. D1. $200.00

THOMPSON, Kay. *Eloise in Moscow.* 1959. Simon Schuster. 1st ed. ils/sgn Hilary Knight. F/VG. P2. $225.00

THOMPSON, Kay. *Eloise in Moscow.* 1960. Max Reinhardt Ltd. 1st ed. ils Hilary Knight. unp. gr cloth. VG/dj. M20. $175.00

THOMPSON, Kay. *Eloise in Paris.* 1957. Simon Schuster. 1st ed. ils Hilary Knight. unp. NF/NF. D1. $225.00

THOMPSON, Kay. *Eloise in Paris.* 1957. Simon Schuster. 1st ed. 4to. G. M5. $45.00

THOMPSON, Kay. *Eloise in Paris.* 1957. Simon Schuster. 1st ed/4th prt. xl. VG/VG. C8. $100.00

THOMPSON, Kay. *Kay Thompson's Miss Pooky Peckinpaugh.* 1970. Harper Row. 1st ed. 4to. F/VG. B17. $20.00

THOMPSON, L.M. *Soils & Soil Fertility.* 1957. McGraw Hill. 2nd. 451p. VG. D8. $15.00

THOMPSON, Lawrence. *Essays in Hispanic Bibliography.* 1970. Shoe String. 1st ed. 117p. F3. $25.00

THOMPSON, Lawrence. *New Sabin.* 1974-1975. 4 vol. describes 5802 items. xl. VG. A4. $125.00

THOMPSON, Mark L. *Steamboats & Sailors of the Great Lakes.* 1991. Detroit. Wayne State. AN. A16. $27.50

THOMPSON, Morton. *Joe, the Wounded Tennis Player.* 1945. Garden City. 1st ed. VG/VG. B5. $25.00

THOMPSON, Ruth Plumley. *Grampa in Oz.* 1924. Reilly Lee. 1st ed. ils JR Neill. VG/tattered. D1. $300.00

THOMPSON, Ruth Plumley. *Kabumpo in Oz.* nd. Reilly Lee. 1st ed/later state. ils JR Neill. pict bl cloth. G. D1. $285.00

THOMPSON, Ruth Plumley. *Royal Book of Oz.* 1921. Reilly Lee. 1st ed. ils JR Neill. VG. D1. $275.00

THOMPSON, Ruth Plumley. *Speedy in Oz.* 1934. Reilly Lee. 1st ed. ils J Neill. orange stp blk cloth. VG. D1. $375.00

THOMPSON, Ruth Plumly. *Giant Horse of Oz.* 1928. Reilly Lee. 1st ed/1st state. F/G+. P2. $600.00

THOMPSON, Silvanus P. *Magnetizer to the Sette of Odd Volumes.* nd. Bedford Pr. 1/199. sgn. F/gray prt wrp. B14. $150.00

THOMPSON, Silvanus P. *Pied Piper of Hamelin.* 1905. London. 1/199. inscr. 40p. F/prt gray wrp. B14. $200.00

THOMPSON, Slason. *Eugene Field: A Study in Heredity & Contradictions.* 1901. Scribner. 2 vol. 8vo. NF. M5. $125.00

THOMPSON, W.M. *Land & the Book. Volume I.* 1860. NY. 12mo. 557p. xl. T3. $10.00

THOMPSON, William Irwin. *Islands Out of Time.* 1985. Dial/Doubleday. ARC/1st ed. NF/F. M23. $25.00

THOMSON, Allen. *History of the Walker Horse.* 1893. Woodstock. woodcuts. 95p. VG/wrp. O3. $195.00

THOMSON, James. *Seasons, With the Castle of Indolence.* 1814. Georgetown. Richards Mallory/Wm Fry. full calf. B18. $250.00

THOMSON, James. *Seasons.* 1927. London. 1/1500. 8vo. ils Jacquier. Riviere bdg. F/case. B24. $750.00

THOMSON, Origen. *Crossing the Plains.* 1983. Ye Galleon. 1st ed thus. ils. M/sans. A18. $17.50

THOMSON, Richard. *Old Roses for Modern Gardens.* 1959. Princeton. ils/photos. 154p. VG/dj. B26. $32.50

THOMSON, William. *Mathematical & Physical Papers: Volume II.* 1884. Cambridge. 1st collected ed. 8vo. 407p. gilt gr cloth. VG. T10. $50.00

THON, Melanie Rae. *Girls in the Grass.* 1991. Random. 1st ed. F/F. A20. $20.00

THON, Melanie Rae. *Iona Moon.* 1993. Poseidon. 1st ed. F/F. A20. $15.00

THON, Melanie Rae. *Meteors in August.* 1990. Random. 1st ed. F/F. A20. $22.00

THORBURN, Archibald. *British Birds.* 1925-1926. Longman Gr. 4 vol. new ed. 8vo. 192 pl. red cloth. F. T10. $400.00

THOREAU, Henry David. *Excursions.* 1863. Boston. 1st ed. NF. A9. $450.00

THOREAU, Henry David. *Letters to Various Persons.* 1965. Boston. 1st ed. 1st issue. NF. C2. $400.00

THOREAU, Henry David. *Summer: From the Journal of Henry David Thoreau.* 1884. Boston. 1st ed. cloth. VG. C2. $200.00

THOREAU, Henry David. *Wild Apples. History of the Apple Tree.* 1956. Worcester, MA. St Onge. 1/950. sgn Pierre Thielen/dtd 1994. miniature. F/box. B24. $3,000.00

THORNDIKE, Joseph J. *Discovery of Lost Worlds.* 1979. Simon Schuster. 1st ed. 352p. NF/dj. W1. $12.00

THORNDIKE. *History of Magic & Experimental Science.* nd. Columbia. 8 vol. F. A4. $450.00

THORNDYKE, Helen. *Honey Bunch: Her First Visit to the City.* 1923. Grosset Dunlap. ils. 182p. VG. T5. $15.00

THORNDYKE, Helen. *Honey Bunch: Her First Visit to the Seashore.* 1924. Grosset Dunlap. ils. 180p. VG. T5. $15.00

THORNE, Diana. *101 Favorite Animals & Birds.* 1953. Sterling. 1st ed. 4to. ils. VG/dj. M5. $25.00

THORNTON, Ian. *Darwin's Islands: Natural History of Galapagos.* 1971. Garden City. ils/photos. 322p. VG+/dj. B26. $22.50

THORNTON, Lawrence. *Under the Gypsy Moon.* 1990. Doubleday. 1st ed. F/F. M23. $20.00

THORP, Roderick. *Detective.* 1966. Dial. 1st ed. F/F. B4. $150.00

THORP, Roderick. *Nothing Lasts Forever.* 1979. Norton. 1st ed. F/rem mk sticker. B4. $250.00

THORPE, Carlye. *Journey to the Walnut Sections of Europe & Asia.* 1923. Los Angeles. private prt. sm 8vo. 102p. khaki cloth/gray brd. K1. $30.00

THORPE, Thomas B. *Master's House; or, Scenes Descriptive of Southern Life.* 1855. Derby. 3rd. 391p. gr cloth. fair. B10. $35.00

THRAPP. *Encyclopedia of Frontier Biography.* 1990. np. 3 vol. 2nd. 1698p. VG. A4. $250.00

THROWER, Norman. *Sir Francis Drake & the Famous Voyage 1577-1580.* 1984. Berkeley. ils/maps. 314p. VG/dj. T7. $36.00

THUBRON, Colin. *Jerusalem.* 1969. Little Brn. 1st ed. 256p. VG/dj. W1. $45.00

THURBER, James. *Beast in Me & Other Animals.* 1948. NY. 1st ed. VG/VG. B5. $45.00

THURBER, James. *Further Fables for Our Time.* 1956. Simon Schuster. 1st ed/1st prt. inscr. ils. gilt bdg. NF/pict dj. B24. $450.00

THURBER, James. *Great Quillow.* 1944. NY. 1st ed. VG/VG. B5. $75.00

THURBER, James. *Last Flower: A Parable in Pictures.* 1939. Harper. 1st ed. inscr/dtd 1939. F/dj. B24. $1,000.00

THURBER, James. *Let Your Mind Alone...* 1937. NY. Armed Services ed. 256p. wrp. B18. $17.50

THURBER, James. *Middle-Aged Man on the Flying Trapeze.* 1935. Harper. 1st ed. ils. NF/dj. B24. $250.00

THURBER, James. *Middle-Aged Man on the Flying Trapeze.* 1935. NY. Armed Services ed. 282p. G+. B18. $17.50

THURBER, James. *Thurber's Dogs.* 1955. Simon Schuster. 1st ed. NF/VG. B2. $65.00

THURBER, James. *Thurber's Men, Women & Dogs.* 1943. NY. 1st ed. 211p. VG/dj. B18. $125.00

THURBER, James. *Wonderful O.* 1957. Simon Schuster. 1st ed. 72p. VG/dj. M20. $32.00

THURMAN, Wallace. *Negro Life in New York's Harlem.* ca 1928. Girard, KS. 1st ed. author's 1st book. VG/wrp. C6. $350.00

THURSTON, Hazel. *Cyprus: Traveller's Guide.* 1971. London. Cape. revised ed. ils. 286p. VG. W1. $14.00

THURSTON, Lucy Meacham. *Girl of Virginia.* 1902. Little Brn. 305p. reading copy. B10. $8.00

THURSTON, P.C. *Geology of Ontario. Special Vol 4, Part 1.* 1991. Toronto. 4to. ils. 711p. brd. B1. $85.00

THURSTON, Robert. *Alicia II.* 1978. Berkley. 1st ed. F/NF. G10. $8.00

TIBBETS, Paul W. *Tibbets Story.* 1978. NY. 1st ed. ils. 316p. VG/VG. B5. $50.00

TIBURZI, Bonnie. *Take Off! The Story of America's First Woman Pilot...* 1984. NY. 1st ed. ils. 299p. VG/dj. B18. $25.00

TICE, George A. *Artie Van Blarcum.* 1977. Addison. 1st ed. inscr/dtd 1979. VG/wrp. S9. $45.00

TICKNER, John. *Tickner's Hunting Field.* 1970. London. Putnam. 1st ed. VG/VG. O3. $25.00

TIDESTROM, Ivar. *Flora of Utah & Nevada.* 1925. WA, DC. 1st ed. fld map. 665p. brn buckram. VG. B26. $65.00

TIDESTROM & KITTELL. *Flora of Arizona & New Mexico.* 1941. WA, DC. fld map. 897p. VG. B26. $65.00

TIDYMAN, Ernest. *Shaft.* 1973. 1st ed. inscr. MTI. author's 1st book. NF/VG+. S13. $40.00

TIEDE, Tom. *Coward.* 1968. NY. Trident. 1st ed. F/NF. B4. $85.00

TIEMANN & TIEMANN. *Boy Named John.* 1948. Platt Munk. 4to. VG. B17. $6.50

TIERNANN, Terence. *Adventures of Michael & the Pirates.* 1939. Little Brn. 1st ed. ils. cloth. G. M5. $15.00

TIGER, John; see Wager, Walter.

TILGHMAN, Christopher. *Father's House Place.* 1990. 1st ed. author's 1st book. VG/VG. C4. $50.00

TILLINGHAST, Richard. *Sewanee in Ruins.* 1981. Sewanee, TN. 1/1500. assn copy. NF/stiff wrp. V1. $10.00

TILLMAN, Lynne. *Absence Makes the Heart.* 1980. London. Serpent's Trail. 1st ed. sgn. F/self wrp. B4. $45.00

TILLMAN, Lynne. *Motion Sickness.* 1991. London. Serpent's Trail. 1st ed. sgn. F/self wrp. B4. $35.00

TILLOTSON, Harry Stanton. *Beloved Spy.* 1948. Caxton. 1st ed. 199p. VG/torn. B18. $25.00

TIMBERLAKE, R.E. *Somewhere in Time. Paintings & Commentary by Bob Timberlake.* 1989. Raleigh, NC. 1st ed. photos/pl. 159p. cloth/leather spine. D2. $225.00

TIMBERLAKE, R.E. *World of Bob Timberlake.* 1979. Oxmoor. pres. ils/137 pl. 141p. dj. D2. $200.00

TIME-LIFE EDITORS. *Old West: The Soldiers.* 1973. NY. 4to. 239p. emb simulated leather. F. T3. $17.00

TIMERMAN, Jacabo. *Chile. Death in the South.* 1987. Knopf. 1st ed. 134p. dj. F3. $10.00

TIMLIN, William M. *Ship That Sailed to Mars.* 1923. London. Harrap. 1st ed. 4to. 48 pl. prt brd. F. B24. $2,200.00

TIMM. *American Library Directory, 39th Edition.* 1985. Bowker. 2 vol. 4to. 2220p. F. A4. $125.00

TIMMEN, Fritz. *Blow for the Landing.* 1973. Caxton. ils. 235p. VG/dj. T7. $65.00

TINDALL, George Brown. *Disruption of the Solid South.* 1972. GA U. 98p. G/G. B10. $8.00

TINE, Robert. *Uneasy Lies the Head.* 1982. Viking. 1st ed. author's 2nd book. F/F. H11. $20.00

TIPPETT, James S. *Picnic.* 1936. NY. Grosset Dunlap. ils Samuel J Brown. NF. C8. $125.00

TIPPETT, Tom. *When Southern Labor Stirs.* 1931. NY. Cape Smith. 1st ed. 2nd tan bdg. NF/NF. B2. $40.00

TIPTREE, James; see Sheldon, Alice Bradley.

TISSOT, V. *Unknown Switzerland.* nd. NY. 19 tipped-in photos. 2-tone cloth. VG+. A15. $225.00

TITCOMBE, Marianne F. *Bookbinding Career or Rachel McMasters Miller Hunt.* 1974. Pittsburgh. ils. 63p. marbled cover. VG. B26. $12.00

TITIEV, Mischa. *Araucanian Culture in Transition.* 1951. Ann Arbor. 164p. wrp. F3. $25.00

TITLEY, Norah M. *Persian Miniature Painting & Its Influence on Art...* 1984. TX U. 1st ed. ils/pl. NF/dj. W1. $35.00

TITTLE, Walter. *First Nantucket Tea Company.* 1907. Doubleday. 1st ed. VG. M5. $40.00

TOBEY, James A. *Medical Department of the Army: Its History, Activities...* 1927. Johns Hopkins. 161p. bl buckram. F. B14. $75.00

TOBIAS, Thomas J. *Hebrew Benevolent Society of Charleston, SC, Founded 1784.* 1965. The Society. 62p. B10. $45.00

TOBIN, Brian. *Missing Person.* 1994. St Martin. 1st ed. author's 2nd novel. AN/dj. M22. $25.00

TODD, Frank M. *Story of the Exposition. Official History...1915.* 1921. Putnam/Knickerbocker. 5 vol. teg. coth. VG to F. D2. $355.00

TODD, Henry John. *Works of Edmund Spenser...With the Principal Illustrations.* 1805. London. Rivington. 8 vol. 8vo. contemporary calf/marbled brd. NF. T10. $1,500.00

TODD, J. *Moral Influence, Dangers & Duties...* 1841. Northampton. 16mo. 267p. xl. T3. $17.00

TODD, Paul; see Posner, Richard.

TODD, Ruthven. *Mantlepiece of Shells.* 1954. Bonacio Saul/Grove. 1st ed. sgn. NF/VG+. V1. $35.00

TOFTE, Arthur. *Survival Planet.* 1977. Bobbs Merrill. 1st ed. F/F. G10. $10.00

TOKLAS, Alice B. *Aromas & Flavors of Past & Present.* 1958. Harper. 1st ed. F/F clip. B35. $60.00

TOLAND, John. *Ships of the Sky.* 1957. NY. 1st ed. ils. 352p. VG/dj. B18. $37.50

TOLKIEN, J.R.R. *Adventures of Tom Bombadil.* 1962. London. Allen. 1st ed. ils Pauline Baynes. NF/NF. M22. $75.00

TOLKIEN, J.R.R. *Annotated Hobbit.* 1988. Houghton Mifflin. 1st ed. ils. 329p. F/F. T10. $75.00

TOLKIEN, J.R.R. *Devil's Coach-Horses.* 1925. London. 1st ed. VG/wrp. C6. $275.00

TOLKIEN, J.R.R. *Father Christmas Letters.* 1976. Houghton Mifflin. 1st ed. ils. F/VG. P2. $75.00

TOLKIEN, J.R.R. *Lord of the Rings Trilogy: Fellowship of the Rings...* nd. Ace. 1st Am pb ed. VG/wrp. M20. $62.00

TOLKIEN, J.R.R. *Lord of the Rings.* 1967. Houghton Mifflin. 2nd/1st Am prt. F/NF dj/NF box. M21. $300.00

TOLKIEN, J.R.R. *Middle English Losenger.* 1953. Paris. 1st ed. 14p. F/wrp. C6. $200.00

TOLKIEN, J.R.R. *Pictures by JRR Tolkien.* 1978. Houghton Mifflin. 1st Am ed. F/case. C10. $100.00

TOLKIEN, J.R.R. *Poems & Stories.* 1994. Houghton Mifflin. 8vo. 342p. AN/dj. T10. $20.00

TOLKIEN, J.R.R. *Road Goes Ever On.* 1967. Houghton Mifflin. 1st ed. NF/dj. M21. $75.00

TOLKIEN, J.R.R. *Sagan Om De Tva Tornen.* 1960. Stockholm. Gebers. 1st Swedish ed. inscr. F/NF wrp. B4. $850.00

TOLKIEN, J.R.R. *Silmarillion.* 1977. Houghton Mifflin. 1st ed. F/NF. B30. $25.00

TOLKIEN, J.R.R. *Sir Gawain & the Green Knight; Pearl & Sir Orfeo.* 1975. Houghton Mifflin. 1st Am ed. 8vo. 149p. gilt bl cloth. F/dj. T10. $45.00

TOLKIEN, J.R.R. *Sir Gawain & the Green Knight; Pearl & Sir Orfeo.* 1975. London. Allen Unwin. 1st ed. 8vo. gr cloth. F/clip. T10. $75.00

TOLKIEN, J.R.R. *Smith of Wooton Major.* 1967. Houghton Mifflin. 2nd. ils Pauline Barnes. NF/NF. M22. $12.00

TOLKIEN, J.R.R. *Some Contributions to Middle-English Lexicography.* 1925. London. 1st ed. VG/wrp. C6. $250.00

TOLKIEN, J.R.R. *Unfinished Tales.* 1980. Allen Unwin. 1st ed. F/F. M21. $35.00

TOLKIN, Michael. *Player.* 1988. Atlantic Monthly. 1st ed. author's 1st book. AN/dj. M22. $40.00

TOLLES, Frederick B. *George Logan of Philadelphia.* 1953. Oxford. VG+/VG+. H4. $25.00

TOLNAY, Tom. *Celluloid Gangs.* 1990. NY. Walker. 1st ed. rem mk. F/F. H11. $25.00

TOLSTOY, Leo. *Anna Karenina.* 1951. LEC. 1/1500. 2 vol. ils/sgn Freedman. dj/case. w/complete proof set. B24. $1,250.00

TOLSTOY, Nikolai. *Coming of the King: First Book of Merlin.* 1989. Bantam. 2nd. 8vo. 630p. F/F. T10. $35.00

TOMALIN, Claire. *Katherine Mansfield: A Secret Life.* 1988. NY. 1st ed. 282p. F/dj. A17. $10.00

TOMAN, Rolf. *High Middle Ages in Germany.* 1990. Cologne. Benedikt Taschen. 4to. 140p. F/dj. T10. $25.00

TOMES, Margaret A. *Julia Chester Emery.* 1924. Women's Auxiliary. photos. VG. P12. $8.00

TOMKINS, Calvin. *Inter-Mission.* 1951. 1st ed. author's 1st book. VG/VG. S13. $18.00

TOMLINSON, H.M. *Gallions Reach.* 1927. Harper. 1st ltd ed. sgn. 12mo. 283p. F/G case. B11. $15.00

TOMLINSON, H.M. *South to Cadiz.* 1934. Harper. 1st ed. 8vo. 195p. red cloth. P4. $22.50

TOMPKINS, Peter. *Secrets of the Great Pyramids.* 1971. Harper Row. 1st ed. NF/NF. G10. $20.00

TOMPKINS, S.R. *Alaska.* 1940. Norman. 1st ed. VG/VG. B5. $32.50

TONEY, Marcus Breckenridge. *Privations of a Private: Campaign Under General RE Lee...* 1907. Nashville. ME Church. 2nd. 133p. cloth. VG. M8. $125.00

TOOLE, John Kennedy. *Neon Bible.* 1989. Grove. 1st ed. rem mk. F/F. B35. $18.00

TOOLE, K. Ross. *Montana: An Uncommon Land.* 1977. Norman, OK. 8th. 278p. brn cloth. NF/dj. T10. $25.00

TOOLEY, R.V. *Maps & Map-Makers.* 1952. London. Batsford. 2nd. 104 ils. F. O7. $75.00

TOOMAY, Pat. *On Any Given Sunday.* 1984. Donald Fine. 1st ed. F/F. B35. $20.00

TOOMER, Jean. *Essentials.* 1931. Chicago. private prt. 1/1000. NF/VG. C6. $600.00

TOOZE, Ruth. *Nikkos & the Pink Pelican.* 1964. Viking. 1st ed. ils Janina Domanska. VG/G+. P2. $15.00

TOPEROFF, Sam. *Crazy Over Horses.* 1969. Little Brn. 1st ed. VG/VG. O3. $15.00

TOPKINS, Katherine. *Kotch.* 1965. McGraw Hill. 1st ed. inscr. F/VG+. B4. $150.00

TOPPING, E.S. *Chronicles of the Yellowstone.* 1968. Minneapolis. rpt. 279p. AN/dj. P4. $20.00

TORJESEN, Elizabeth Fraser. *Captain Ramsey's Daughter.* 1953. Lee Shepard. 1st ed. 8vo. 223p. NF/G. C14. $20.00

TORME, Mel. *It Wasn't All Velvet.* 1988. Viking. 1st ed. sgn. F/F. B2. $50.00

TORREY, Marjorie. *Artie & the Princess.* 1945. Howell Soskin. 1st ed. lg 8vo. NF. M5. $28.00

TOSCHES, Nick. *Cut Numbers.* 1988. Harmony. 1st ed. F/F. B4. $65.00

TOURGEE, Albion W. *Bricks Without Straw.* 1880. Fords Howard Hulbert. 2nd. 521p. G+. B10. $15.00

TOUSEY, Sanford. *Trouble in the Gulch.* 1944. Whitman. 12mo. VG. B17. $12.50

TOVEY, Doreen. *New Boy.* 1970. Norton. 1st ed. ils. 162p. NF/VG. C14. $15.00

TOWLE, Tony. *North.* 1970. Columbia. 1/1150. F/NF. V1. $35.00

TOWNSEND, John T. *Code of Procedure, of the State of New York. Fifth Edition.* 1857. NY. Voorhies. modern quarter calf. M11. $150.00

TOWNSEND, William H. *Lincoln the Litigant.* 1925. Boston. 1st ed. 1/1050. 116p. brd. VG. B18. $25.00

TOWNSEND. *Memorial Life of William McKinley, Our Martyred President.* 1901. np. 8vo. ils. 528p. gilt bl cloth. G. T3. $15.00

TOWNSLEY, John A. *Book of Poetry Composed by...* 1840. Cuyahoga Falls. 1st ed. 40p. VG/plain bl wrp. B18. $95.00

TRACHTMAN, Paula. *Disturb Not the Dream.* 1981. Crown. 1st ed. NF/NF. G10. $8.00

TRACIES, INC. *Tracie's Toons: Draw Your Own Funnies.* ca 1935. Holyoke. 6 double-sided color sheets/tracing paper. NF. A17. $20.00

TRACY, David F. *Psychologist at Bat.* 1951. Sterling. 1st ed. VG/G. P8. $50.00

TRACY, Edward B. *Great Horse of the Plains.* 1954. Dodd Mead. 1st ed. inscr/sgn. F/fair. M5. $18.00

TRAHERNE, Thomas. *One Hundred Meditations & Devotions...* 1975. Pownal, VT. 1/75. ils Mark Livingston. 55p. bl brd/gilt vellum. F. B24. $750.00

TRAKL, Georg. *Transfigured Autumn.* 1984. Tamarack. 1/26. ils/sgn Wand. trans/sgn Allen Hoey. F. V1. $65.00

TRAPHAGEN, Ethel. *Costume Design & Illustration.* 1918. NY. Wiley. VG. D2. $40.00

TRASK, P.D. *Applied Sedimentation.* 1950. John Wiley. 707p. cloth. F. D8. $20.00

TRAVER, Robert. *Jealous Mistress.* 1967. Boston. 1st ed. F/NF. A17. $35.00

TRAVER, Robert. *Laughing Whitefish.* 1965. NY. 1st ed. F/dj. A17. $50.00

TRAVER, Robert. *Trout Madness.* 1960. St Martin. 1st ed. 178p. VG/clip. M20. $35.00

TRAVERS, P.L. *Maria Poppina AB A-Z.* 1968. Harcourt Brace. 1st ed. lg 12mo. F/F. B5. $50.00

TRAVERS, P.L. *Mary Poppins Comes Back.* 1935. Reynal Hitchcock. 1st ed. ils Mary Shepard. G+. M5. $55.00

TRAVERS, P.L. *Mary Poppins Opens the Door.* 193. Reynal Hitchcock. 3rd. 8vo. 239p. G+. T5. $20.00

TRAVIS, Tristan Jr. *Lamia.* 1982. Dutton. 1st ed. F/F. H11. $30.00

TRAXEL. *American Saga: Life & Times of Rockwell Kent.* 1980. np. 40 pl. 256p. VG/worn. A4. $85.00

TREAT, Roger. *Walter Johnson.* 1948. Messner. Special Ltd WA ed. sgn/#d. G+/G+. P8. $200.00

TREATT, Stell Court. *Sudan Sand: Filming the Baggara Arabs.* 1930. Harrap. 1st ed. 8vo. 63 pl. 252p. G. W1. $28.00

TREDREY. *House of Blackwood 1804-1954.* 1954. np. 4to. 308p. VG. A4. $45.00

TREECE, Henry. *Crusades.* 1963. Random. 1st Am ed. 334p. VG. W1. $18.00

TREECE, Henry. *New Romantic Anthology.* 1949. London. Gray Walls. 1st ed. VG/VG. V1. $20.00

TREMBLAY, Bill. *Crying in the Cheap Seats.* 1971. MA U. 1st ed. assn copy. F/NF. V1. $20.00

TRESS, Arthur. *Shadow.* 1975. Avon. 1st ed. sgn/photo credit stp. VG+/wrp. S9. $125.00

TREVANIAN. *Loo Sanction.* 1973. NY. Crown. 1st ed. NF/NF clip. H11. $20.00

TREVANIAN. *Shibumi.* 1979. NY. Crown. 1st ed. F/F. H11. $40.00

TREVANIAN. *Summer of Katya.* 1983. Crown. 1st ed. F/F. N4. $30.00

TREVATHAN, Charles. *American Thoroughbred.* 1905. Macmillan. 1st ed. VG. O3. $40.00

TREVELYAN, George Otto. *American Revolution.* 1917. Longman Gr. 4 vol. later ed. 8vo. maroon cloth. VG. T10. $100.00

TREVELYAN, Humphrey. *Middle East in Revolution.* 1970. Boston. Gambit. 1st ed. map ep. VG/dj. W1. $18.00

TREVELYAN, Raleigh. *Shades of the Alhambra.* 1984. London. Folio Soc. 1st Folio ed. tall 8vo. ils. F/sans. T10. $40.00

TREVOR-BATTYE, Aubyn. *Ice-Bound on Kolguev.* 1895. London. Constable. 25 pl/3 maps/75 drawings. 458p. rebound. T7. $125.00

TREW, Cecil. *Accoutrements of the Riding Horse.* (1951). London. Seeley. 1st ed. ils. VG. O3. $85.00

TREYMAYNE, Peter; see Ellis, Peter Beresford.

TRIBBLES, Thomas Henry. *Buckskin & Blanket Days.* 1957. Doubleday. 1st ed. 336p. cloth. VG+/ragged. M20. $22.00

TRIBUTSCH, H. *When the Snakes Awake.* 1982. Cambridge. MIT. 8vo. 248p. cloth. clip dj. B1. $25.00

TRIGG, Emma Gray. *After Eden: Poems.* 1937. Putnam. 1st ed. 110p. VG/VG. B10. $15.00

TRIGG, Emma Gray. *Paulownia Tree.* 1969. Golden Quill. inscr. 80p. VG/VG. B10. $8.00

TRIGG, Roberta. *Haworth Idyll: A Fantasy.* 1946. Whittet Shepperson. sgn. 88p. VG. B10. $12.00

TRIMBLE, Joe. *Yogi Berra.* 1952. Barnes. 1st ed. photos. VG/G+. P8. $40.00

TRIMINGHAM, J. Spencer. *Islam in West Africa.* 1978. Clarendon. 7th. 8vo. 262p. VG/dj. W1. $22.00

TRIMMER, Eric. *Rejuvenation: The History of an Idea.* 1970. NY. 189p. dj. A13. $40.00

TRIPP, Wallace. *Great Big Ugly Man Came Up & Tied His Horse to Me.* 1973. Little Brn. 1st ed. ils. VG+/VG. P2. $30.00

TRITTEN, Charles. *Heidi Grows Up.* 1938. Grosset Dunlap. 1st ed. 8vo. VG+/worn. M5. $35.00

TROBETZKOY, Amelie Rives. *Selene.* 1905. Harper. 1st ed. 89p. G. B10. $15.00

TROCHECK, Kathy Hogan. *Every Crooked Nanny.* 1992. Harper Collins. 1st ed. author's 1st book. rem mk. F/NF. H11. $90.00

TROCHECK, Kathy Hogan. *To Life & Die in Dixie.* 1993. Harper Collins. 1st ed. F/F. M23. $20.00

TROLLOPE, A. *Claverings.* 1866. NY. 1st Am ed. VG+. A15. $200.00

TROSCLAIR. *Cajun Night Before Christmas.* 1976. Gretna. 1st ed. VG/VG. B5. $25.00

TROTTER, I. Lilias. *Between the Desert & the Sea.* ca 1920. Marshall Morgan Scott. 1st ed. ils. 63p. VG/dj. W1. $75.00

TROUT, Kilgore; see Farmer, Philip Jose.

TRUDEAU, Gary. *Doonesbury Deluxe.* 1987. Holt. ils. F. M13. $15.00

TRUEBLOOD, Ted. *Ted Trueblood Hunting Treasury.* 1978. McKay. 1st ed. photos. NF/VG. P12. $15.00

TRUESDELL, S.R. *Rifle: Its Development for Big Game Hunting.* 1947. Harrisburg. 1st ed. photos. 274p. VG. B5. $80.00

TRUMAN, Margaret. *Murder at the Kennedy Center.* 1989. Random. 1st ed. F/F. A20. $10.00

TRUMAN, Margaret. *Murder in the White House.* 1980. Arbor. 1st ed. F/NF. M22. $25.00

TRUMAN, Pearl S. *General's Boss.* 1941. House of Field. sgn. 12mo. G. B11. $10.00

TRUMBO, Dalton. *Harry Bridges.* 1941. League Am Writers. 1st ed. F/wrp. B2. $45.00

TRUSCOTT, Alan. *Doubles & Redoubles.* 1987. NY. 152p. VG/wrp. S1. $6.00

TRUSCOTT, Alan. *Grand Slams.* 1985. NY. 133p. F/wrp. S1. $5.00

TRYON, Thomas. *Adventures of Opal & Cupid.* 1992. Viking. 1st ed. F/NF. G10. $10.00

TRYON, Thomas. *Other.* 1971. Knopf. 1st ed. author's 1st book. NF/VG. H11. $35.00

TU, A.T. *Marine Toxins & Venoms. Handbook of Natural Toxins, Vol 3.* 1988. NY. Marcel Dekker. lg 8vo. 587p. pict brd. NF. B1. $125.00

TUCHMAN, Barbara. *Distant Mirror.* 1978. NY. Knopf. 11th. 677p. map ep. VG/dj. P4. $20.00

TUCHMAN, Barbara. *First Salute.* 1988. BC. 347p. M/dj. P4. $10.00

TUCHMAN, Barbara. *Stillwell & the American Experience in China 1911-45.* 1971. BC. dj. A17. $10.00

TUCHMAN, Barbara. *Zimmerman Telegram.* 1958. NY. 1st ed. 244p. VG/dj. B18. $22.50

TUCK. *Encyclopedia of Science Fiction & Fantasy Through 1968.* 1974 & 1978. np. 2 vol. xl. VG. A4. $75.00

TUCKER, Glenn. *Zeb Vance: Champion of Personal Freedom.* 1965. Bobbs Merrill. 1st ed. 564p. NF/NF. M8. $75.00

TUCKER, Henry St. George. *Commentaries on Laws of Virginia...* 1846. Shepherd Colin. 2 vol. G. B10. $175.00

TUCKER, Jerry. *Bermuda's Story.* 1970. Bermuda Bookstores. rpt. sgn. 8vo. 213p. F/VG. B11. $35.00

TUCKER, Kerry. *Still Waters.* 1991. Harper Collins. 1st ed. inscr. F/F clip. H11. $40.00

TUCKER, Philip Thomas. *History of the Irish Brigade: A Collection...* 1995. Fredericksburg, VA. Sgt Kirkland's Mus. 1st ed. sgn. 223p. stiff wrp. M8. $20.00

TUCKER, St. George. *Devoted Bride; or, Faith & Fidelity, a Love Story.* 1878. Peterson. 370p. fair. B10. $25.00

TUCKER, St. George. *Hansford: A Tale of Bacon's Rebellion.* 1857. GM West. 356p. fair. B10. $35.00

TUCKER, Wilson. *Ice & Iron.* 1974. Doubleday. BC. sgn. VG/g. B11. $20.00

TUCKEY, H.B. *Dwarfed Fruit Trees.* 1964. Macmillan. 8vo. 562p. cloth. dj. B1. $50.00

TUDOR, Tasha. *Corgiville Fair.* 1971. Crowell. 1st ed. 8vo. unp. gilt turquoise cloth. G+. T5. $85.00

TUDOR, Tasha. *Corgiville Fair.* 1971. Harper Collins. 5th. 8vo. F/F. B17. $18.00

TUDOR, Tasha. *Corgiville Fair.* 1971. NY. 2nd. VG/VG. B5. $50.00

TUDOR, Tasha. *Dorcas Porkus.* 1942. Oxford. not 1st ed. lists to A Tale for Easter. polka-dot brd. VG. M5. $150.00

TUDOR, Tasha. *First Delights, a Book About the Five Senses.* 1966. Platt Munk. early prt. 8vo. unp. NF. T5. $35.00

TUDOR, Tasha. *First Graces.* 1989. Random. ils. rem mk. F/F. B17. $7.00

TUDOR, Tasha. *First Poems of Childhood.* 1967. Platt Munk. ils. 8vo. 45p. pict ep. gray brd. VG. T5. $30.00

TUDOR, Tasha. *Jenny Wren Book of Valentines.* 1988. Jenny Wren. 1st ed. F/wrp. B17. $6.00

TUDOR, Tasha. *Mother Goose.* 1944. Oxford. 2nd. 87p. VG/tattered. M20. $47.00

TUDOR, Tasha. *Mother Goose.* 1989. Random. 16mo. Caldecott Honor. F/F. B17. $11.00

TUDOR, Tasha. *Pumpkin Moonshine.* 1989. Random. 16mo. ils. rem mk. F/wrp. B17. $4.50

TUDOR, Tasha. *Pumpkin Moonshine.* 1993. Jenny Wren. 55th Aniversary ed. sgn. F/F. B17. $35.00

TUDOR, Tasha. *Springs of Joy.* 1979. Rand McNally. 1st ed. 4to. VG. B17. $30.00

TUDOR, Tasha. *Take Joy.* 1966. Cleveland. 1st ed. VG/G. B5. $50.00

TUDOR, Tasha. *Tale for Easter.* 1989. Random. 16mo. rem mk. F/sans. B17. $7.00

TUDOR, Tasha. *Tasha Tudor Book of Fairy Tales.* 1969. Platt Munk. folio. VG. B17. $15.00

TUDOR, Tasha. *Tasha Tudor's Bedtime Book.* 1977. Platt Munk. folio. VG. B17. $14.00

TUDOR, Tasha. *Tasha Tudor's Fairy Tales.* 1989. Platt Munk. 4to. F. B17. $10.00

TUDOR, Tasha. *Tasha Tudor's Seasons of Delight.* 1986. Philomel. 1st probable ed. mechanical. NF. C8. $30.00

TUDOR, Tasha. *Time To Keep, the Tasha Tudor Book of Holidays.* 1978. Rand McNally. 4th prt. VG. B17. $14.00

TUDOR, Tasha. *Twenty Third Psalm.* 1965. Achille J St Onge. miniature ed. aeg. gr polished calf. F/F. B17. $50.00

TUDOR, Tasha. *Wings From the Wind.* 1964. Lippincott. 3rd. 119p. VG. T5. $65.00

TUER, Andrew W. *Forgotten Children's Books.* 1898-99. Leadenhall Pr. 1st ed/later issue. ils. gilt cloth. VG. D1. $185.00

TUER, Andrew W. *History of the Horn Book.* 1968. np. ils. 486p. xl. VG. A4. $40.00

TUER, Andrew W. *Stories From Old-Fashioned Children's Books.* 1989. Bracken. 8vo. F/F. B17. $6.50

TUFFY, Barbara. *1001 Questions Answered About Hurricanes...* 1987 (1970). Dover. pb. 8vo. ils. 381p. K5. $8.00

TUGWELL, Rexford Guy. *Chronicle of Jeopardy 1945-55.* 1955. Chicago. 489p. dj. A17. $15.00

TUKER, Francis. *Pattern of War.* 1948. London. 1st ed. 159p. VG. A17. $12.50

TULLY, Jim. *Beggars of Life.* 1924. NY. Boni. 1st ed. 8vo. gilt bl cloth. VG. S9. $35.00

TULLY, Richard. *Narrative of a Ten Years' Residence at Tripoli in Africa.* 1817 (1816). London. Colburn. 7 full-p pl/fld map. 376p. modern calf. C6. $650.00

TUNIS, Edwin. *Colonial Craftsmen & the Beginnings of American Industry.* 1965. Cleveland. F/F. D2. $30.00

TUNIS, John R. *Keystone Kids.* 1943. Harcourt Brace. 209p. VG/dj. M20. $20.00

TUNIS, John R. *Kid From Tomkinsville.* 1945 (1940). Harcourt Brace. ils JH Barnum. 355p. red cloth. G+. T5. $12.00

TURBERVILLE, A.S. *Johnson's England: Account of His Life & Manners...* 1933. Clarendon. 1st ed. 2 vol. bl cloth. F. C2. $150.00

TURNBULL, Andrew. *F Scott Fitzgerald: Letters to His Daughter.* nd. 1st ed. VG/VG. M17. $40.00

TURNBULL, Andrew. *Thomas Wolfe.* 1967. Scribner. 1st ed. 374p. VG/VG. B10. $15.00

TURNBULL, Archibald Douglas. *Commodore David Porter, 1780-1843.* 1929. NY. Century. 1st ed. ils. 326p. VG. T7. $45.00

TURNBULL, Colin M. *Man in Africa.* 1976. Anchor. 1st ed. ils John Morris. F/VG. T10. $25.00

TURNBULL, Robert. *World We Live In; or, Home & Foreign Traveler.* 1851. Hartford. 8vo. 544p. VG. T3. $45.00

TURNBULL. *Correspondence of Isaac Newton; Vol I, II & III.* 1959, 1960 & 1961. Cambridge. Royal Soc of London. 3 vol. F/VG. A4. $435.00

TURNER, Ann. *Heron Street.* 1989. Harper Row. inscr/dtd 1989. 4to. unp. NF/VG+. C14. $20.00

TURNER, Dawson. *Radium: Its Physics & Therapeutics.* 1911. NY. ils. 86p. gr cloth. VG. B14. $125.00

TURNER, E.S. *All Heaven in a Rage.* 1965. St Martin. 1st ed. 324p. NF/clip. M20. $22.00

TURNER, E.S. *Phoney War.* 1962. NY. 1st Am ed. 311p. dj. A17. $9.50

TURNER, E.S. *Taking the Cure.* 1967. London. 1st ed. 284p. A13. $35.00

TURNER, Frederick. *April Wind & Other Poems.* 1991. VA U. 1st ed. F/F. V1. $20.00

TURNER, Josephine M. *Courageous Caroline: Founder of UDC.* 1965. Paragon. sgn. ils. 63p. VG/G+. B10. $15.00

TURNER, Nancy Byrd. *Magpie Lane.* 1927. Harcourt Brace. ils Merwin. 88p. VG. B10. $12.00

TURNER, Nancy Byrd. *Poems Selected & New.* 1965. Golden Quill. 122p. G/G. B10. $10.00

TURNER, Nancy Byrd. *Star in a Well.* 1935. NY. sgn. 8vo. 175p. VG. B11. $15.00

TURNER & VERHOOGEN. *Igneous & Metamorphic Petrology.* 1951. McGraw Hill. 1st ed. VG. D8. $20.00

TUROW, Scott. *Burden of Proof.* 1990. FSG. 1st trade ed. sgn. F/F. B11. $25.00

TUROW, Scott. *Pleading Guilty.* 1993. FSG. 1st ed. F/F. N4. $22.50

TUROW, Scott. *Pleading Guilty.* 1993. FSG. 1st ed. NF/NF. M22. $15.00

TUROW, Scott. *Presumed Innocent.* 1987. Farrar. 1st ed. F/F. H11. $60.00

TURPIN, Edna. *Lost Covers.* 1937. Random. ils Victor Perard. 281p. VG/G. B10. $12.00

TURVILLE-PETRE, Ed. *Viga-Clums Saga.* 1940. London. Oxford. 8vo. 112p. F. B14. $55.00

TUTTLE, Lisa. *Catwitch.* 1983. Doubleday. 1st ed. ils. F/clip. B17. $25.00

TWAIN, Mark; see Clemens, Samuel L.

TWENHOFEL, W.H. *Principles of Sedimentation.* 1939. McGraw Hill. 1st ed/2nd imp. 610p. F. D8. $40.00

TWENHOFEL, W.H. *Treatise on Sedimentation.* 1932. Williams Wilkins. 2nd. 926p. VG. D8. $35.00

TWINING, W.J. *Reports on Survey of the Boundary Between Territory of US...* 1878. WA. ils/7 fld maps. G. B5. $400.00

TYACKE, Sarah. *English Map-Making 1500-1650.* 1983. London. British Lib. 4to. ils. M/ils dj. O7. $95.00

TYACKE, Sarah. *London Map-Sellers 1660-1720: A Collection...* 1978. Tring. Map Collector Pub. 19 maps. M. O7. $40.00

TYLEE, Mrs. George. *Amy's Wish & What Came of It.* 1870. London. Griffith Farran. 1st ed. 12mo. VG. M5. $40.00

TYLER, Anne. *Accidental Tourist.* 1985. Knopf. 1st ed. F/F. B30. $65.00

TYLER, Anne. *Accidental Tourist.* 1985. Knopf. 1st ed. F/NF. H11. $40.00

TYLER, Anne. *Accidental Tourist.* 1985. Knopf. 1st ed. sgn. F/NF. B4. $150.00

TYLER, Anne. *Breathing Lessons.* 1988. Chatto Windus. 1st ed. F/clip. B4. $50.00

TYLER, Anne. *Breathing Lessons.* 1988. Franklin Lib. 1st ed. sgn. full leather. F. B4. $125.00

TYLER, Anne. *Breathing Lessons.* 1988. Knopf. UP. sgn. VG/wrp. B4. $95.00

TYLER, Anne. *Breathing Lessons.* 1988. Knopf. 1st ed. F/F. H11. $30.00

TYLER, Anne. *Celestial Navigation.* 1974. Knopf. 1st ed. author's 5th novel. F/F. B4. $350.00

TYLER, Anne. *Dinner at the Homesick Restaurant.* 1982. Knopf. 1st ed. F/clip. B4. $85.00

TYLER, Anne. *Dinner at the Homesick Restaurant.* 1982. NY. 1st ed. 303p. VG+/dj. B18. $35.00

TYLER, Anne. *Dinner at the Homesick Restaurant.* 1982. NY. Knopf. 1st ed. F/NF. B4. $100.00

TYLER, Anne. *Earthly Possessions.* 1977. Knopf. 1st ed. NF/NF. B4. $60.00

TYLER, Anne. *Earthly Possessions.* 1977. NY. 1st ed. inscr/dtd 1977. NF/F. C6. $175.00

TYLER, Anne. *If Morning Ever Comes.* 1964. Knopf. 1st ed. author's 1st book. F/NF. S9. $2,000.00

TYLER, Anne. *Morgan's Passing.* 1980. Knopf. ARC. RS. AN/dj. B4. $175.00

TYLER, Anne. *Saint Maybe.* 1991. Knopf. 1st ed. F/F. H11. $30.00

TYLER, Anne. *Saint Maybe.* 1991. Knopf. 1st ed. sgn. F/F. B4. $85.00

TYLER, Anne. *Saint Maybe.* 1991. Knopf. 1st ed. w/sgn leaf. F/F. B2. $65.00

TYLER, Anne. *Saint Maybe.* 1991. Knopf. 1st trade ed. rem mk. F/F. B35. $20.00

TYLER, Anne. *Searching for Caleb.* 1976. Knopf. 1st ed. F/F. B4. $450.00

TYLER, Anne. *Slipping-Down Life.* 1970. NY. 1st ed. author's 3rd book. VG+/NF. C6. $325.00

TYLER, Anne. *Tin Can Tree.* 1965. NY. 1st ed. author's 2nd book. VG/NF clip. C6. $525.00

TYLER, David Budlong. *Steam Conquers the Atlantic.* 1939. Appleton Century. ils. G. A16. $75.00

TYLER, Gillian. *Perhaps a Poem.* 1967. Thetford. Cricket. 1/42. 4to. ils after Leonard Baskin. NF. B24. $275.00

TYLER, K.S. *Telecasting & Color.* 1946. NY. 1st ed. 213p. NF/VG. N3. $55.00

TYLER, Parker. *Three Faces of the Film.* 1960. NY. Yoseloff. 4to. dj. A17. $15.00

UBELAKER, Douglas. *Ayalan Cementary.* 1981. Smithsonian. 175p. xl. wrp. F3. $10.00

UBELAKER, Douglas. *Bones: A Forensic Detective's Casebook.* 1992. Burlinghame. later prt. F/F. N4. $15.00

UDRY, Janice May. *Tree Is Nice.* 1956. Harper. possible 1st ed. ils. VG. M5. $18.00

UKERS, William. *Trip to Brazil.* 1935. Tea & Coffee Trade Journal Co. 37p. wrp. F3. $15.00

ULANOV, Barry. *Incredible Crosby.* 1948. NY. 1st ed. VG/VG. B5. $30.00

ULPH, Owen. *Leather Throne.* 1984. Dream Garden. 1st ed. sgn. F/dj. A18. $25.00

UMBLE, John. *Ohio Mennonite Sunday Schools: Studies in Anabaptist...* 1941. Goshen College. 522p. dj. A17. $17.50

UNDERHILL, Ruth. *Here Come the Navaho!* 1953. Lawrence, KS. 4to. 285p. NF/pict wrp. N3. $30.00

UNDERWOOD, Adin B. *Three Years' Service of the 33rd MA Infantry Regiment...* 1881. Boston. xl. w/record. B18. $95.00

UNDERWOOD, F.H. *Quabbin: Story of a Small Town.* 1893. Boston. VG. M17. $40.00

UNDERWOOD, J.L. *Women of the Confederacy.* 1906. Neale. 1st ed. 313p. VG. B10. $175.00

UNDERWOOD, Tom. *Thoroughbred Racing & Breeding.* nd. NY. Coward McCann. VG. O3. $25.00

UNDERWOOD, Tom. *Thoroughbred Racing & Breeding. Story of the Sport...* 1945. NY. 1st ed. ils. pict gr cloth. F/G. H3. $95.00

UNGER, Douglas. *Leaving the Land.* 1984. Harper Row. 1st ed. F/F. A20. $30.00

UNGERER, Tomi. *Christmas Eve at the Mellops.* 1960. Harper. ils. VG. P2. $25.00

UNGERER, Tomi. *Crictor.* 1958. Harper. ils. 32p. G+. P2. $20.00

UNGERER, Tomi. *Emile.* 1960. Harper. BC. orange brd. VG/G. B17. $7.50

UNGERER, Tomi. *Hat.* nd. Parents Magazine. possible 1st ed. 4to. unp. VG+. C14. $10.00

UNGNAD, Arthur. *Babylonish-Assyrische Grammatik.* 1926. Munich. Beck'sche. 2nd. 184p. VG/torn. W1. $20.00

UNITED NATIONS. *Fun Around the World.* 1955. Pelham, NY. Seahorse Pr. 1st ed. 4to. ils. 128p. F. C14. $20.00

UNNERSTAD, Edith. *Pysen.* 1955. Macmillan. 1st ed. ils Louis Slobodkin. 172p. VG/G. P2. $18.00

UNRUH, John D. *Plains Across.* 1979. Urbana. 3rd. ils/index. 565p. NF/VG. T10. $45.00

UNSWORTH, Barry. *Hide.* 1970. London. Gollancz. 1st ed. NF/VG. B4. $250.00

UNSWORTH, Barry. *Sacred Hunger.* 1992. Doubleday. 1st ed. F/F. M23. $30.00

UNTERMEYER, Jean Starr. *Love & Need: Collected Poems.* 1940. Viking. 1st ed. VG/G. V1. $15.00

UNTERMEYER, Louis. *More Poems From the Golden Treasury of Poetry.* (1959). Golden. 12mo. 80p. VG. C14. $8.00

UNTERMEYER & UNTERMEYER. *Grimm's Fairy Tales.* 1962. LEC. 4 vol. 1/1500. 8vo. ils Lucille Corcos. linen. F/case. T10. $250.00

UNZER, John Augustus. *Principles of Psysiology.* 1851. London. Sydenham Soc. 1st Eng-language ed. emb gr cloth. NF. G1. $225.00

UPDEGRAFF, Allan. *Native Soil.* 1930. NY. 1st ed. dj. A17. $7.50

UPDIKE, John. *Bech Is Back.* 1982. Knopf. 1st ed. NF/VG. B35. $32.00

UPDIKE, John. *Bech Is Back.* 1982. NY. 1st ed. 1/500. sgn. F/F/case. C2. $75.00

UPDIKE, John. *Bech: A Book.* 1970. NY. 1st ed. 1/500. sgn. F/F/case. C2. $75.00

UPDIKE, John. *Bottom's Dream.* 1969. Knopf. 1st ed. F/NF. B2. $85.00

UPDIKE, John. *Brazil.* 1994. Knopf. 1st trade ed. as issued. A20. $28.00

UPDIKE, John. *Buchanan Dying.* 1974. NY. 1st ed. F/F. C6. $40.00

UPDIKE, John. *Carpentered Hen & Other Tame Creatures.* 1958. Harper. 1st ed. author's 1st book. NF/NF clip 1st state dj. C6. $500.00

UPDIKE, John. *Carpentered Hen.* 1982. Knopf. 1st ed thus. assn copy. F/VG+. V1. $20.00

UPDIKE, John. *Collected Poems 1953-1993.* 1993. Knopf. 1st ed. F/F. V1. $25.00

UPDIKE, John. *Coup.* 1978. Knopf. 1st ed. F/F. B35. $24.00

UPDIKE, John. *Facing Nature.* 1985. Knopf. 1st ed. F/F. B35. $23.00

UPDIKE, John. *In the Beauty of the Lilies.* London. 1st ed. VG/VG. C4. $60.00

UPDIKE, John. *In the Cemetery High Above Shillington.* 1995. 1st ed. 1/100. sgn. ils/sgn Barry Moser. VG/VG. C4. $175.00

UPDIKE, John. *Just Looking.* 1989. NY. AP. 4to. F/wrp. C2. $60.00

UPDIKE, John. *Marry Me.* 1976. Knopf. 1st ed. F/F. H11. $40.00

UPDIKE, John. *Memories of the Ford Administration.* 1992. KNopf. 1st trade ed. rem mk. F/F. B35. $24.00

UPDIKE, John. *Midpoint & Other Poems.* 1969. Knopf. 1st ed. F/NF. H11. $65.00

UPDIKE, John. *Poorhouse Fair.* 1959. Knopf. 1st ed. F/NF. B4. $450.00

UPDIKE, John. *Problems.* 1979. Knopf. 1st ed. F/NF. B35. $30.00

UPDIKE, John. *Rabbit at Rest.* 1990. Knopf. 1st ed. F/F. B35. $28.00

UPDIKE, John. *Rabbit at Rest.* 1990. London. 1st ed. VG/VG. C4. $45.00

UPDIKE, John. *Rabbit Is Rich.* 1981. Knopf. 1st ed. F/F. B35/H11. $35.00

UPDIKE, John. *Rabbit Redux.* 1971. Knopf. 1st ed. NF/NF. B35. $45.00

UPDIKE, John. *Roger's Version.* 1986. Franklin Lib. 1st ed. sgn. leather. F. C2. $40.00

UPDIKE, John. *Roger's Version.* 1986. Knopf. 1st trade ed. F/F. B35. $28.00

UPDIKE, John. *Roger's Version.* 1986. NY. 1st ed. 1/350. sgn. quarter calf. F/case. C2. $75.00

UPDIKE, John. *Telephone Poles & Other Poems.* 1963. NY. 1st ed. F/F. C6. $65.00

UPDIKE, John. *Trust Me.* 1987. Knopf. 1st ed. F/F. H11. $40.00

UPDIKE, John. *Witches of Eastwick.* 1984. Knopf. 1st ed. F/F. H11. $30.00

UPDYKE, James; see Burnett, W.R.

UPHAM, C.W. *Life, Explorations & Public Services of John Chas Fremont.* 1856. Boston. 12mo. 356p. G. T3. $42.00

UPHAM, C.W. *Life, Explorations & Public Services of John Chas Fremont.* 1856. Ticknor Fields. 356p. VG. M20. $52.00

UPHAM, Thomas C. *Elements of Intellectual Philosophy.* 1827. Portland, ME. Wm Hyde. 504p. early patterned mauve cloth. G1. $375.00

UPHAM, Thomas C. *Elements of Mental Philosophy Embracing Two Departments...* 1828. Portland, ME. Shirley Hyde. 2nd. 576p. contemporary calf. G1. $125.00

UPHAM, Thomas C. *Outlines of Imperfect & Disordered Mental Action.* 1840. harper. 16mo. 400p. pub pebbled dk brn cloth. G1. $85.00

UPTON, Bertha. *Adventures of Two Dutch Dolls.* 1898. Longman Gr. 1st ed. ils F Upton. pict brd. VG. D1. $350.00

UPTON, Bertha. *Golliwog's Bicycle Club.* 1896. London. Longman Gr. 1st ed. 4to. ils Florence Upton. VG. T10. $250.00

UPTON, Bertha. *Golliwogg's Circus.* 1903. Longman Gr. 1st ed. ils F Upton. D1. $240.00

URDANG, Constance. *Only the World.* 1983. Pittsburgh U. 1st ed. F/wrp. V1. $10.00

URE, James M. *Benedictine Office: Old English Text.* 1957. Edinburgh. 8vo. 141p. gilt maroon cloth. NF. T10. $45.00

URIS, Leon. *Exodus.* 1958. Garden City. Doubleday. 1st ed. 8vo. 2 maps. 626p. VG/torn. W1. $18.00

URIS, Leon. *Mila 18.* 1961. Doubleday. 1st ed. F/NF clip. H11. $40.00

URIS, Leon. *Milta Pass.* 1988. Doubleday. 1st ed. w/sgn leaf. F/F. B2. $40.00

URIS, Leon. *OB VII.* 1970. Doubleday. 1st ed. F/NF. H11. $25.00

URIS, Leon. *Topaz.* 1967. McGraw Hill. 1st ed. NF/VG. M22. $30.00

URNER, Clarence H. *Thrush.* 1927. Henkel. 88p. VG-. B10. $25.00

UTLEY, Robert M. *Four Fighters of Lincoln County.* 1986. NM U. 1st ed. 8vo. 3 maps. 116p. NF/dj. T10. $35.00

UTTLEY, Alison. *Traveller in Time.* 1973 (1939). London. Faber. ils Phyllis Bray. 331p. gr brd. NF/NF. T5. $30.00

UZANNE, Octave. *Chronique, Scandaleuse.* 1879. Paris. Quantin. ils/index. 325p. half red cloth/marbled brd. K1. $150.00

VACHSS, Andrew. *Blossom*. 1990. Knopf. 1st ed. F/F. A20. $28.00

VACHSS, Andrew. *Blue Belle*. 1988. Knopf. 1st ed. author's 3rd novel. NF/NF. M22. $20.00

VACHSS, Andrew. *Flood*. 1985. Donald Fine. 1st ed. author's 1st book. F/NF. M23. $30.00

VACHSS, Andrew. *Flood*. 1985. Donald Fine. 1st ed. F/F. A20. $35.00

VACHSS, Andrew. *Hard Candy*. 1989. Knopf. 1st ed. sgn. F/NF. M23. $20.00

VACHSS, Andrew. *Sacrifice*. 199. Knopf. 1st ed. F/F. A20. $25.00

VACHSS, Andrew. *Strega*. 1987. Knopf. 1st ed. F/F. A20. $33.00

VAETH, J. Gordon. *Blimps & U-Boats: US Navy Airships in Battle of Atlantic*. 1992. Annapolis. 1st ed. ils. 205p. VG/dj. B18. $22.50

VAGO, Bela. *Shadow of the Swastika: Rise of Facsism...* 1975. London. Inst for Jewish Affairs. 1st ed. 431p. dj. A17. $25.00

VALE, R.B. *Wings, Fur & Shot*. 1936. Harrisburg. 1st ed. VG. B5. $32.50

VALENTINE, Benjamin Bachelder. *Old Marster & Other Verses*. 1921. Whittet Shepperson. 117p. VG. B10. $25.00

VALENTINE, Jean. *Pilgrims*. 1969. FSG. 1st ed. F/NF. V1. $30.00

VALENTINE, Laura. *Aunt Louisa's London Gift Book* ca 1880. London. Warne. chromolithographs. pict cloth. T10. $75.00

VALENTINE, Laura. *Aunt Louisa's Sunday Book*. ca 1871. London. Warne. ils Kroheim. gilt/red decor gr cloth. VG. T10. $215.00

VALENTINE. *Noah's Ark*. nd. Dundee. Valentine. shaped book. 23p. VG. D1. $95.00

VALLEJO, Doris. *Boy Who Saved the Stars*. 1978. NY. O'Quinn Studios. 1st ed. ils Boris Vallejo. NF/VG. B4. $85.00

VALLIER, Dora. *Henri Rousseau*. 1962. Abrams. ils. 382p. yel stp gr cloth. dj. K1. $100.00

VAN ALLSBURG, C. *Ben's Dream*. nd. Houghton Mifflin. 1st ed. ils Van allsburg. VG/dj. D1. $150.00

VAN ALLSBURG, C. *Jumanji*. 1981. Houghton Mifflin. 1st ed. ils. unp. F/F. D1. $225.00

VAN ALLSBURG, C. *Just a Dream*. 1990. Houghton Mifflin. 3rd. VG/VG. B17. $9.00

VAN ALLSBURG, C. *Mysteries of Harry Burdick*. 1984. Houghton Mifflin. 1st ed. ils. unp. F/F. D1. $135.00

VAN ALLSBURG, C. *Polar Express*. 1985. Houghton Mifflin. 1st ed. ils. VG/VG. D1. $150.00

VAN ALLSBURG, C. *Stranger*. 1986. Houghton Mifflin. 1st ed. ils. NF/NF. D1. $85.00

VAN ALLSBURG, C. *Z Was Zapped*. 1987. Houghton Mifflin. 1st ed. ils. unp. F/F. D1. $85.00

VAN ANTWERP, William C. *Collectors' Comment on His First Editions...Walter Scott*. 1932. San Francisco. Gelber. Lilienthan. 1st ed. 1/400. sgn. NF. T10. $125.00

VAN ARSDALE, G.D. *Hydrometallurgy of Base Metals*. 1953. McGraw Hill. 1st ed. 370p. F. D8. $25.00

VAN ASH, Clay. *Fires of Fu Manchu*. 1987942. Harper Row. 1st ed. F/F. H11. $30.00

VAN ASH, Clay. *Ten Years Beyond Baker Street*. 1984. Harper Row. 1st ed. author's 1st novel. F/F clip. H11. $40.00

VAN BEEK, Gus W. *Hajar Bin Humeid*. 1969. Johns Hopkins. 1st ed. 4to. 69 pl. 421p. VG/dj. W1. $45.00

VAN DE GOHM, Richard. *Antique Maps for the Collector*. 1973. NY. Macmillan. 1st Am ed. F/F. O7. $45.00

VAN DE KAMP, Peter. *Elements of Astromechanics*. 1964. Freeman. San Francisco. 8vo. 140p. VG. R5. $25.00

VAN DE WATER, F. *Lake Champlain-Lake George*. 1946. Indianapolis. 1st ed. VG/VG. B5. $40.00

VAN DE WETERING, Janwillem. *Blond Baboon*. 1978. Houghton Mifflin. 1st ed. sgn. F/NF. T2. $45.00

VAN DE WETERING, Janwillem. *Hard Rain*. 1986. Pantheon. 1st ed. sgn. F/NF. B2. $40.00

VAN DE WETERING, Janwillem. *Inspector Saito's Small Satori*. 1985. Putnam. 1st ed. F/F. H11. $25.00

VAN DE WETERING, Janwillem. *Inspector Saito's Small Satori*. 1985. NY. Putnam. 1st ed. sgn. F/F. T2. $40.00

VAN DE WETERING, Janwillem. *Just a Corpse at Twilight*. 1994. Soho. 1st ed. F/F. T2. $25.00

VAN DE WETERING, Janwillem. *Mangrove Mama & Other Tropical Tales of Terror*. 1995. Tucson. McMillan. 1st ed. sgn. F/F. T2. $30.00

VAN DE WETERING, Janwillem. *Rattle-Rat*. 1985. Pantheon. 1st ed. F/clip. A20. $17.00

VAN DE WETERING, Janwillem. *Rattle-Rat*. 1985. Pantheon. 1st ed. sgn. F/NF. B2. $45.00

VAN DE WETERING, Janwillem. *Sergeant's Cat & Other Stories*. 1987. Pantheon. 1st ed. sgn. F/F. T2. $40.00

VAN DE WIELE, Annie. *West in My Eyes*. 1956. Dodd Mead. 4 plans/9 maps. VG/dj. T7. $24.00

VAN DEN BORREN, Charles. *Sources of Keyboard Music in England*. nd. London. Noello. ltd ed. Peter Warlock's copy. 378p. VG. T10. $250.00

VAN DEN KEER, Pieter. *Germania Inferior*. 1966. Amsterdam. Theatrvm Orbis Terrarvm. facsimile. AN/dj. O7. $175.00

VAN DER BURCH, Lambert. *Sabavdorvm Cvcvm Principvmq*. 1634. Leyden. Elzevier. 2nd. engraved frontis. vellum. VG+. H7. $250.00

VAN DER LINDEN, Peter. *Great Lakes Ships We Remember. Vol I*. 1992. Freshwater. rpt of 1979 ed. AN/dj. A16. $27.00

VAN DER LINDEN, Peter. *Great Lakes Ships We Remember. Vol III*. 1994. Freshwater. AN. A16. $35.00

VAN DER MEULEN, D. *Aden to the Hadhramaut*. 1947. London. Murray. 2nd. xl. VG. W1. $65.00

VAN DER POST, Laurens. *Lost World of the Kalahari*. 1958. Morrow. 1st ed. map. 279p. VG/torn. W1. $14.00

VAN DERVEER, Helen. *Little Sallie Mandy Story Book*. 1935. Platt Munk. 4to. red brd. VG+. M5. $55.00

VAN DINE, S.S. *Green Murder Case*. 1928. Scribner. 1st ed. sgn. 388p. VG/dj. M20. $180.00

VAN DOREN, Carl. *Benjamin Franklin*. 1938. Viking. 1/625. 1st ed. 3 vol set. sgn. 8vo. VG/case. B11. $75.00

VAN DOREN, Carl. *James Branch Cabell*. 1932. np. revised. ils. 95p. VG. A4. $25.00

VAN DOREN, Mark. *Henry David Thoreau: A Critical Study*. 1916. Boston/NY. 1st ed. author's 1st book. VG. C6. $95.00

VAN DOREN, Mark. *Noble Voice: Study of Ten Great Poems*. 1946. 1st ed. VG+/VG. S13. $14.00

VAN DUYN, Mona. *Fireball*. 1993. Knopf. 2nd. F/NF. V1. $10.00

VAN DUYN, Mona. *Merciful Disguises.* 1973. Atheneum. 1st ed. assn copy. sgn. F/NF. V1. $45.00

VAN DUYN, Mona. *Near Changes.* 1990. Knopf. 1st ed. F/NF. V1. $10.00

VAN DYKE, Henry. *Spirit of Christmas.* 1905. Scribner. 1st ed. VG. M19. $17.50

VAN DYKE, John C. *In Egypt: Studies & Sketches Along the Nile.* 1931. Scribner. 1st ed. 8vo. 206p. xl. VG. W1. $22.00

VAN GILESON, Judith. *Lies That Blind.* 1993. Harper Collins. 1st ed. sgn. VG+/VG+. A20. $30.00

VAN GILESON, Judith. *Other Side of Death.* 1991. Harper Collins. 1st ed. rem mk. F/F. A20. $25.00

VAN GULIK, Robert. *Chinese Bell Murders.* 1958. Harper. 1st Am ed. 8vo. NF/dj. T10. $200.00

VAN GULIK, Robert. *Poets & Murder.* 1968. Scribner. 1st ed. NF/NF. N4. $65.00

VAN GULIK, Robert. *Red Pavilion.* 1968. Scribner. 1st Am ed. F/F. B2. $50.00

VAN GULIK, Robert. *Red Pavilion.* 1968. Scribner. 1st Am ed. F/NF. T2. $45.00

VAN HINTE, J.E. *Proceedings of Second West African Micropaleontological...* 1966. Leiden. EJ Brill. 294p. F/dj. D8. $30.00

VAN HOESEN, Henry. *Brown University Library 1767-1782.* 1938. Providence. private prt. brn brd/wht label. F. B14. $45.00

VAN INGEN, Phillip. *New York Academy of Medicine: Its First Hundred Years.* 1949. NY. 1st ed. 573p. A13. $40.00

VAN LOON, Gerard. *Story of Hendrick Willem Van Loon.* 1972. np. ils. 410p. F/F. A4. $45.00

VAN LOON, Hendrik Willem. *My School Books.* 1939. Du Pont De Nemours. 8vo. 24p. gray fabricoid w/bl & gilt trim. AN. H4. $7.50

VAN LUSTBADER, Eric. *Angel Eyes.* 1991. Fawcett. 1st ed. F/F. N4. $25.00

VAN LUSTBADER, Eric. *Black Heart.* 1983. NY. Evans. 1st ed. NF/NF. H11. $20.00

VAN LUSTBADER, Eric. *Dai-San.* 1978. Doubleday. 1st ed. NF/NF. P3. $25.00

VAN LUSTBADER, Eric. *Miko.* 1984. Villard. 1st ed. NF/NF. P3. $30.00

VAN LUSTBADER, Eric. *Ninja.* 1980. Evans. 1st ed. F/F. N4. $35.00

VAN LUSTBADER, Eric. *Sirens.* 1981. Evans. 1st ed. VG/VG. P3. $15.00

VAN LUSTBADER, Eric. *Zero.* 1988. Random. 1st ed. VG/VG. P3. $20.00

VAN METRE, T.W. *Tramps & Liners.* 1931. Doubleday Doran. 1st ed. 8vo. 324p. gr cloth. NF. T10. $75.00

VAN PAASSEN, Pierre. *Forgotten Ally.* 1943. Dial. 1st ed. 8vo. 343p. map ep. VG/torn. W1. $12.00

VAN RIPER, Guernsey. *Mighty Macs.* 1972. Garrard. 1st ed. photos. F/VG. P8. $17.50

VAN STOCKUM, Hilda. *Mitchells.* 1945. Viking. ils. 246p. VG/G+. P2. $25.00

VAN THIENEN, F. *Great Age of Holland 1600-1660.* 1951. London. Harrap. VG/G. D2. $15.00

VAN TRAMP, John C. *Prairie & Rocky Mountain Adventures; or, Life in the West.* 1869 (1867). Segner Condit. 775p. leather. VG. M20. $87.00

VAN WATERS, George. *Illustrated Poetical Geography.* 1864. NY. 96p. fair. B18. $20.00

VAN WORMER, Joe. *World of the Black Bear.* nd. NY Times. 442p. F/dj. B22. $5.00

VAN ZANDT, J. Parker. *Geography of World Air Transport.* 1944. Brookings Inst. 67p. G/tape rpr. B18. $19.50

VANCE, Eleanor. *Tall Book of Fairy Tales.* 1947. VG. K2. $18.00

VANCE, Jack. *Blue World.* 1979. Underwood Miller. 1st hc ed. 1/700. F/F. T2. $35.00

VANCE, Jack. *Five Gold Bands.* 1993. Underwood Miller. rpt of The Space Pirate. F/NF. G10. $15.00

VANCE, Jack. *Mad Man Theory.* 1988. London. Kindell. 1st hc ed. sgn. F/F. T2. $35.00

VANCE, Jack. *Room To Die In.* 1987. London. Kinnell. 1st hc ed. sgn. F/F. T2. $35.00

VANCE, Marguerite. *Martha, Daughter of Virginia: Story of Martha Washington.* 1947. Dutton. 1st ed. ils Nedda Walker. 190p. G+. B10. $8.00

VANDENBELD, J. *Nature of Australia.* 1988. NY. Facts on File. 8vo. photos. brd. dj. B1. $28.00

VANDENBURG, Arthur H. *Private Papers of Senator Vandenburg.* 1952. Boston. 599p. A17. $10.00

VANDENBURGH, Jane. *Failure to Zigzag.* 1989. North Point. 1st ed. F/F. H11. $35.00

VANDENBUSCHE, Duane. *Gunnison Country.* 1980. Gunnison. B&B Prt. 3rd. 4to. 472p. F. S9. $75.00

VANDERBILT, Gloria. *Once Upon a Time.* 1983. Knopf. 1st ed. inscr. F/F. w/sgn letter. $45.00

VANDERBILT, Harold S. *Club Convention System of Bidding at Contract Bridge.* 1964. NY. inscr. 186p. VG. S1. $20.00

VAS DIAS, Robert. *Ode.* nd. Abattoir. 1/225 on Hodomura paper. F/sgn wrp. V1. $20.00

VASILOFF, Mary Jean. *Alone With Your Horse.* 1978. Harper Row. 1st ed. sgn. VG/G. O3. $25.00

VASSILTCHIKOV, Marie. *Berlin Diaries 1940-1945.* 1991. London. Folio Soc. 1st ed. 8vo. 3 maps. 296p. full red buckram. F/case. T10. $40.00

VASSOS, Ruth. *Ultimo.* 1930. NY. 1st ed. F/VG. H7. $60.00

VATIKIOTIS, P.J. *Modern History of Egypt.* 1969. Praeger. 1st ed. 8vo. 16 pl. 512p. VG. W1. $25.00

VAUGHN, Elizabeth Dewberry. *Break the Heart of Me.* 1994. Doubleday. 1st ed. sgn. F/F. M23. $50.00

VAUGHN, Elizabeth Dewberry. *Many Things Have Happened Since He Died.* 1990. Doubleday. 1st ed. sgn. author's 1st book. F/F. H11. $45.00

VAUX, W.S.W. *Ancient History From the Monuments.* ca 1876. London. 1st ed. 12mo. 190p. VG. W1. $20.00

VAVRA, Robert. *Tiger Flower.* 1968. London. Collins. 1st ed. 4to. olive cloth. VG+/VG. T5. $45.00

VAVRA, Robert. *Vavra's Horses.* 1989. Morrow. 1st prt. F/F. O3. $45.00

VECESY, George. *Joy in Mudville.* 1970. McCall. 1st ed. VG+/G+. P8. $20.00

VECESY, George. *One Sunset a Week. Story of a Coal Miner.* 1974. NY. Saturday Review. 2nd. NF/NF. B2. $25.00

VELIMIROVIC, Nicholas. *Servia in Light & Darkness.* 1916. Longman Gr. 1st ed. 20 pl. 147p. VG. W1. $20.00

VENABLE, Charles L. *American Furniture in the Bybee Collection.* 1989. Austin. 1st ed. 80+ pl. 192p. F/dj. A17. $25.00

VENABLE, William Henry. *June on the Miami.* 1912. Cincinnati. 1st ed. 35p. VG/VG. B5. $35.00

VENKUS, Robert E. *Raid on Qaddafi: The Untold Story...* 1992. NY. 1st ed. 197p. VG+/dj. B18. $25.00

VENTURA, Piero. *Magic Well.* 1976. Random. 1st ed. 4to. unp. gray cloth/bl spine. NF/G+. T5. $20.00

VENZI, G. *Little Angel With the Pink Wings.* (1963). Boston. Daughters of St Paul. 12mo. 21p. VG. C14. $6.00

VER BECK, Frank. *Donkey Child.* 1917. Oxford. 1st ed. 12mo. ils. VG+/pict wrp. C8. $65.00

VER WEIBE, W.A. *Oil Fields in the United States.* 1930. McGraw Hill. 1st ed/2nd imp. sgn. VG. D8. $30.00

VERBRUGGE, Frank. *Whither Thou Goest.* 1979. Minneapolis. private prt. sgn. 8vo. photos. 120p. gr cloth. F. B11. $30.00

VERDELLE, A.J. *Good Negress.* 1995. Algonquin. 1st ed. author's 1st book. F/F. M23. $40.00

VERDERY, Katherine. *Little Dixie Captain.* 1930. Dobbs Merrill. stated 1st ed. ils Winifred Bromhall. VG+/dj. M5. $85.00

VERGA, Giovanni. *Cavalleria Rusticana & Other Narratives.* 1950. Emmaus, PA. Story Classics. 1/3000. 8vo. prt buckram. NF/case. T10. $40.00

VERKLER & ZEMPEL. *Book Prices: Used & Rare.* 1993. 4to. 613p. F. A4. $60.00

VERLAINE, Paul. *Forty Poems.* 1948. London. 1st ed. F/dj. A17. $15.00

VERLAINE, Paul. *Selected Poems.* 1948. Berkeley. trans CF MacIntyre. F/NF. B2. $30.00

VERMEULE, Emily. *Greece in the Bronze Age...* 1966. Chicago. 2nd. 406p. NF/dj. W1. $30.00

VERNE, Jules. *From the Earth to the Moon.* 1918. Scribner. 4 pl. F. A17. $35.00

VERNE, Jules. *Fur Country.* 1876. Montreal. 1st Canadian ed. ils Ferat. VG. C6. $60.00

VERNE, Jules. *Michael Strogoff: Courier of the Czar.* ca 1930. Grosset Dunlap. 1st ed. ils. F/dj. B14. $75.00

VERNE, Jules. *Mysterious Island.* 1924. Scribner. ils NC Wyeth. VG. B17. $40.00

VERNE, Jules. *20,000 Leagues Under the Sea.* 1993. Annapolis. Naval Inst. 1st ed thus. F/F. M23. $50.00

VERNER, Elizabeth O'Neill. *Stonewall Ladies.* 1963. Tradd Street. 2nd. 144p. VG/VG. B10. $12.00

VERNEY, Richard. *Student Life: Philosophy of Sir William Osler.* 1957. Edingburgh. 1st ed. 214p. VG. A13. $60.00

VERNON, Bowen. *Lazy Beaver.* 1948. McKay. early ed. VG/VG. B17. $14.00

VERRILL, A. Hyatt. *Romantic & Historical Virginia.* 1935. Dodd Mead. 1st ed. ils/map ep. VG/G. B10. $25.00

VESALIUS, Andreas. *Epitome of Andreas Vesalius.* 1949. NY. 1st Eng trans. trans LR Lind. 103p. A13. $75.00

VESALIUS, Andreas. *Icones Anatomicae.* 1934. Bremer Presse. NY Adacemy Medicine/Lib of U of Munich. F/dj/box. B24. $6,800.00

VICKER, Ray. *Kingdom of Oil. The Middle East: Its People & Its Power.* 1974. Scribner. 1st ed. 8vo. 264p. VG/dj. W1. $22.00

VICTORIA, R.I. (Queen). *More Leaves From the Journal of a Life in the Highlands.* 1884. London. 404p. ils cloth. G. B18. $25.00

VIDAL, Gore. *Burr.* 1973. Random. 1st ed. NF/F. B35. $25.00

VIDAL, Gore. *Creation.* 1981. NY. Random. 1st ed. F/F. M23. $25.00

VIDAL, Gore. *Evening With Richard Nixon.* 1972. Random. 1st ed. F/F. B35. $28.00

VIDAL, Gore. *Hollywood.* 1990. Random. 1st ed. 1/200. sgn. F/case. B35. $70.00

VIDAL, Gore. *Lincoln.* 1984. Random. 1st ed. NF/NF. H11. $25.00

VIDAL, Gore. *Second American Revolution.* 1982. Random. 1st ed. rem mk. F/F. B35. $20.00

VIERECK, Peter. *Archer in the Marrow.* 1987. np. 1st ed. F/VG+. V1. $15.00

VIERECK, Peter. *First Morning.* 1952. Scribner. 1st ed. F/G. V1. $15.00

VIERECK, Peter. *Metsa-Politics: Roots of the Nazi Mind.* 1961 (1941). NY. rpt. 364p. wrp. A17. $5.00

VIERECK, Peter. *New & Selected Poems.* 1967. Bobbs Merrill. ARC. sgn. assn copy. F/NF. V1. $25.00

VIERECK, Peter. *Tree Witch.* 1961. Scribner. 1st ed. F/VG+. V1. $20.00

VIERTEL, Salka. *Kindness of Strangers: A Theatrical Life.* 1969. Holt. 1st ed. 338p. slate cloth. AN/glassine. B22. $6.00

VIETS, Henry. *Brief History of Medicine in Massachusetts.* 1930. Boston. 194p. VG. A13. $50.00

VILLA, Jose Garcia. *Have Come Am Here.* 1942. Viking. 1st ed. VG+/VG. V1. $35.00

VILLA-REAL, Ricardo. *Alhambra & the General Life.* 1989. Granada. Sanchez. 1st ed. 56p. VG. W1. $16.00

VILLARD, Henry Serrano. *Contact! Story of the Early Birds.* 1968. NY. 1st ed. ils. 263p. VG/torn. B18. $22.50

VILLIERS, Alan. *Men, Ships & the Sea.* 1973. NGS. G/torn. A16. $10.00

VILLIERS, Alan. *Men, Ships & the Sea.* 1973. NGS. ils. 434p. VG/G+. P12. $12.00

VILLIERS, Alan. *Sons of Sinbad: An Account of Sailing With the Arabs...* 1940. Scribner. 1st ed. ils/maps. 429p. xl. VG. W1. $50.00

VILLIERS, Alan. *Whalers of the Midnight Sun.* 1934. Scribner. 1st ed. ils. 285p. VG. T7. $30.00

VINCENT, Leon H. *Bibliotaph & Other People.* 1898. Boston. Houghton Mifflin. 1st ed. 8vo. 233p. teg. F. T10. $75.00

VINCENT, Thomas MacCurdy. *Abraham Lincoln & Edwin M Stanton.* 1892. WA, DC. 1st ed. 35p. NF/prt wrp. M8. $37.50

VINCENT, William. *Voyage de Nearque...* 1799. Paris. Imprimerie Republique. folio. contemporary bdg. VG. W1. $650.00

VINE, Barbara; see Rendell, Ruth.

VINE, Peter. *Jewels of the Kingdom.* 1987. London. Immel. 1st ed. folio. ils. 159p. xl. F/dj. W1. $28.00

VINGE, Joan. *Psion.* 1982. Delacorte. 1st ed. F/NF. G10. $25.00

VINGE, Joan. *Return of the Jedi: Storybook Based on the Movie.* 1983. Weekly Reader. 1st ed. 8vo. VG. M21. $10.00

VINGE, Joan. *World's End.* 1984. Bluejay. 1st ed. F/F. G10. $15.00

VINGE, Venor. *Fire Upon the Deep.* 1992. Tor. 1st ed. F/F. G10. $50.00

VIORST, Milton. *Sandcastles: The Arabs in Search of the Modern World.* 1994. Knopf. ARC. RS. F/F. B35. $22.00

VIPONT, Elfrida. *Pavilion.* 1970 (1969). HRW. 1st Am ed. 8vo. 218p. pk brd. G+/G. T5. $25.00

VISINTIN, Luigi. *Atlante Geografico Metodico.* 1935. Novarra. Istituto Geografico de Agostini. 69 maps. F. O7. $85.00

VIVA. *Superstar.* 1970. Putnam. 1st ed. NF/VG clip. B4. $65.00

VIZCAYNO, Sebastian. *Jornada Principal des Las Californias.* 1963. Liberia Anticuaria. 1/300. full red leather/raised bands. miniature. T10. $125.00

VIZENOR, Gerald. *Darkness in Saint Louis Bearheart.* 1978. St Paul. Truck Pr. 1st ed. NF/wrp. B4. $85.00

VLIET, R.G. *Events & Celebrations.* 1966. Viking. 1st ed. assn copy. F/VG. V1. $15.00

VOEGELIN, C.F. *Shawnee Stems & Jacob P Dunn Miami Dictionary.* 1940. Indianapolis. IN Hist Soc. 478p. VG/wrp. B18. $12.50

VOGEL, Ilse-Margret. *Willy, Willy, Don't Be Silly.* 1965. Atheneum. 1st ed. 8vo. unp. G+. T5. $20.00

VOGEL, John. *This Happened in the Hills of Kentucky.* 1952. Zondervan. 382p. VG. B10. $15.00

VOGEL, S. *Role of Scent Glands in Pollination.* 1990. New Delhi. Amerind. 8vo. trans from German. 202p. cloth. VG/VG. B1. $48.00

VOIGHT, Ellen Bryant. *Two-Trees.* 1992. Norton. 1st ed. F/NF. V1. $15.00

VOIGT, Cynthia. *Solitary Blue.* 1984. Atheneum. 3rd prt. 8vo. Newberry Honor. VG/VG. B17. $6.50

VOINOVICH, Vladimir. *Pretender to the Throne.* 1981. FSG. UP. F. B35. $26.00

VOLLMAN, William T. *You Bright & Risen Angels.* 1987. NY. 1st Am ed. author's 1st book. F/F. C6. $100.00

VOLNEY, Constantin F. *View of the Climate & Soil of the USA...* 1804. London. missing 1 fld map. 504p. full calf. B18. $125.00

VOLTAIRE. *Candide.* 1928. Random. 1/1470. 8vo. ils/sgn Rockwell Kent. Riviere bdg. F. w/drawing. B24. $1,500.00

VOLTAIRE. *Jeannot et Colin.* 1895. Paris. 1/50 in red on Japon. F/wrp/chemise/case. B24. $200.00

VON ABELE, Rudolph Radama. *Alexander H Stephens: A Biography.* 1946. Knopf. 1st ed. 337p. cloth. NF/NF. M8. $75.00

VON ALENITCH, Victor. *Dressage.* 1982. Chicago. Adams. 1st ed. sgn. 205p. VG. O3. $15.00

VON BECHTEREW, W. *Die Funktionen der Nervencentra.* 1909-1911. Jena. Gustav Fisher. 3 vol. 1st German ed. gr buckram. VG. G1. $400.00

VON ECKARDT, Hans. *Russia.* 1932. Knopf. 1st ed. VG+. B2. $40.00

VON ELSNER, Don. *Cruise Bridge.* 1980. Hawthorne, CA. 187p. VG/wrp. S1. $5.00

VON FOERSTER, Heinz. *Cybernetics: Circular Causal & Feedback Mechanisms...* 1951. NY. Josiah Macy Jr Foundation. 252p. prt gr cloth. VG/dj. G1. $40.00

VON HAGEN, Victor Wolfgang. *Aztec & Maya Papermakers.* 1944. NY. Augustin. 1st trade ed. 8vo. 39 pl. prt cloth. VG/dj. T10. $100.00

VON HAGEN, Victor Wolfgang. *Frederick Catherwood, Architect.* 1950. NY. 1st ed. ils. 177p. gilt bl cloth. F/VG. H3. $75.00

VON KLEIST, Heinrich. *Gesammelte Schriften.* 1826. Berlin. 12mo. 3 vol. gilt leather/marbled brd. VG. A17. $50.00

VON KRIES, Johannes. *Allgemeine Sinnesphysiologie.* 1923. Leipzig. Vogel. 300p. emb mauve cloth. VG. G1. $40.00

VON KRUSENTSTERN, Adam J. *Atlas of the Voyage Round the World.* 1974 (1813). Amsterdam/NY. Israel/DaCapo. 104 pl. ribbon ties. M. O7. $475.00

VON LIPPERHEIDE. *Katalog der Freiherrlich von Lipperheide'schen Kostumbiblio.* nd. 2 vol. rpt of 1895-1905 ed. 5000 entries. ils. 840p. F. A4. $150.00

VON MATT, Leonard. *Ancient Crete.* 1968. Praeger. 1st ed. 4to. ils. 238p. VG/dj. W1. $65.00

VON MUELLER, Fred. *Select Extra-Tropical Plants...* 1881. Sydney, Australia. T Richards. enlarged NSW ed. inscr. 403p. gr cloth. VG. B14. $150.00

VON SAVIGNY, Frederick C. *Of the Vocation of Our Age for Legislation & Jurisprudence.* 1986. Birmingham. facsimile of 1831 London ed. modern leather. M11. $65.00

VON SCHMERTZING, Walt. *Outlawing the Communist Party: A Case History.* 1957. Bookmailer. 1st ed. F/wrp. B2. $25.00

VON STEIN, Heinrich. *Ueber Wahrnehmung.* 1877. Berlin. Gustav Schade. sq 8vo. 48p. modern gr linen. G1. $35.00

VON TRAPP, Maria. *Maria.* 1972. Carol Stream. Creation. 1st ed. sgn. F/NF. H11. $30.00

VON WOLFF, Christian. *Psychologia Rationalis Methodo Scientifica Pertracata...* 1734. Francofurti Lipsiae. 680p. modern leather. G1. $850.00

VON WOLFF, Christian. *Psychologia Rationalis...* 1734. Veronae. Typis Dionyssi Ramanzini Bibliopolae. 2nd. 397p. G1. $500.00

VONNEGUT, Kurt Jr. *Slaughterhouse-Five; or, Children's Crusade.* 1969. Delacorte. 2nd. NF/NF. B35. $40.00

VONNEGUT, Kurt. *Bluebird.* 1987. Delacorte. 1st ed. F/F. H11. $30.00

VONNEGUT, Kurt. *Deadeye Dick.* 1982. Delacorte. 1st ed. F/NF. H11. $30.00

VONNEGUT, Kurt. *Jailbird.* 1979. Delacorte. 1st ed. NF/VG clip. B35. $25.00

VONNEGUT, Kurt. *Slapstick.* 1976. Delacorte. 1st ed. NF/NF. M22. $25.00

VONNEGUT, Kurt. *Slapstick; or, Lonesome No More.* 1976. Delacorte. 1st ed. F/NF. H11. $30.00

VONNEGUT, Kurt. *Slaughterhouse Five; or, Children's Crusade.* 1969. Lawrence/Delacorte. 1st ed. sgn bookplate. NF/F. M22. $275.00

VOOUS, K.H. *Atlas of European Birds.* 1960. London. Nelson. 284p. cloth. xl. B1. $22.00

VORHEES, Oscar. *History of Phi Beta Kappa.* 1945. NY. 372p. A13. $30.00

VORRES, I. *Last Grand Duchess.* 1965. NY. 1st ed. VG/VG. B5. $45.00

VORSE, M.H. *Time & the Town.* 1942. NY. 1st ed. VG/VG. B5. $35.00

VOZNESENSKY, Andrei. *Nostalgia for the Present.* 1978. Doubleday. 1st ed. inscr. NF/NF. V1. $45.00

WACE, Robert. *Notice Sur la Vie et les Escrits.* 1824. French text. marbled ep. VG. S13. $20.00

WACHTEL, Curt. *Idea of Psychosomatic Medicine.* 1951-27. NY. 239p. dj. A13. $45.00

WADDELL, Helen. *Peter Abelard.* 1947. NY. 1st ils ed. 277p. F/F. A17. $10.00

WADDELL, Helen. *Stories From the Holy Writ.* 1949. Macmillan. 1st ed. 244p. gray cloth. F/dj. B22. $4.50

WADE, Blanche Elizabeth. *Ant Ventures.* 1924. Rand McNally. 1st ed. 12mo. VG/tattered. M5. $110.00

WADE, David. *Pattern in Islamic Art.* 1976. Woodstock. Overlook. 1st ed. ils. 144p. VG/dj. W1. $45.00

WADE, Wyn Craig. *Titanic: End of a Dream.* 1979. Rawson Wade. BC. ils. 366p. VG/G. P12. $5.00

WADE. *Fiery Cross: Ku Klux Clan in America.* 1987. np. ils. 526p. F/F. A4. $35.00

WADE. *Journals of Francis Parkman.* 1947. np. 2 vol. ils. 750p. VG. A4. $85.00

WADSWORTH, H.A. *Quarter-Centennial History of Lawrence, MA.* 1878. Lawrence. Hammon Reed. 180p. gilt/blk stp brn cloth. K1. $50.00

WADSWORTH, W. Austin. *Hunting Diaries of 1984 Genesee Valley Hunt.* 1/950. F. O3. $45.00

WADSWORTH, William. *Ode on the Intimations of Immortality.* 1903. London. Arnold/Essex. 1/150. 8vo. ftspc Walter Crane. 12p. all vellum. F. B24. $525.00

WAGENKNECHT, Edward. *William Dean Howells, the Friendly Eye.* 1969. NY. 1st ed. 340p. VG/worn. A17. $12.50

WAGER, Walter. *Designated Hitter.* 1982. Arbor. 1st ed. F/F. H11. $20.00

WAGER, Walter. *Viper Three.* 1971. Macmillan. 1st ed. F/F. H11. $25.00

WAGERIN, William. *Book of the Dun Cow.* 1978. Harper Row. 1st ed. NF/VG. N4. $15.00

WAGHENAER, Lucas Jansz. *Mariners Mirrour.* 1966. Amsterdam. facsimile. lg folio. 2 parts in 1. 45 double-p charts. M. O7. $300.00

WAGLEY, Charles. *Amazon Town: Study of Man in the Tropics.* 1953. Macmillan. 1st ed. 305p. dj. F3. $20.00

WAGLEY, Charles. *Social & Religious Life of a Guatemalan Village.* 1949. Am Anthro Assoc. 3 pl. 150p. wrp. F3. $25.00

WAGNER, Enrique R. *Nueva Bibliografia Mexicana del Siglo XVI.* 1946. Mexico. Editorial Polis. only ed. 1/1000. 548p. T10. $600.00

WAGNER, Henry R. *California Voyages 1539-1541.* 1925. San Francisco. John Howell. 8 full-p maps. F. O7. $250.00

WAGNER, Henry R. *Cartography of the Northwest Coast of America to Year 1800.* 1937. Berkeley. CA U. 2 vol. 1st ed. folio. NF/dj/case. O7. $750.00

WAGNER, Henry R. *Juan Rodriguez Cabrillo.* 1941. CA Hist Soc. 1st ed. 1/750. 94p. decor brd. NF. T10. $250.00

WAGNER, Henry R. *Peter Pond: Fur Trader & Explorer.* 1955. Yale. ltd ed. 1/500. 3 fld maps. M/case+map portfolio. O7. $395.00

WAGNER, Henry R. *Spanish Expeditions in the Strait of Juan de Fuca.* 1933. Santa Ana. Fine Arts. 1st ed. 1/425. gilt bdg. F. O7. $750.00

WAGNER, Jack R. *Gold Mines in California.* 1989. San Diego. ils/maps/index. 259p. F/dj. A17. $25.00

WAGNER, Karl Edward. *Echoes of Vallor II.* 1989. Tor. 1st ed. AN/dj. M21. $15.00

WAGNER, Richard. *Parsifal.* 1918. Vienna. Munch. ils Willy Pogany. F/pict wrp. B24. $575.00

WAGNER, Richard. *Ring of the Niblung.* 1939. NY. ils Arthur Rackham. VG. A17. $35.00

WAGONER, David. *Baby, Come on Inside.* 1968. FSG. 1st ed. sgn. F/VG+. V1. $25.00

WAGONER, David. *Hanging Garden.* 1980. Little Brn. ARC. sgn. RS. V1. $25.00

WAGONER, David. *Rock.* 1958. Viking. 1st ed. F/NF. V1. $25.00

WAGONER, David. *Staying Alive.* 1966. IN. 1st ed. RS. F/F. V1. $30.00

WAGONER, David. *Travelling Light.* 1976. Graywolf. 1/150. sgn. F/F. V1. $40.00

WAGONER, Don M. *Conditioning To Win.* 1974. Grapevine. VG. O3. $25.00

WAGONER, Don M. *Feeding To Win.* 1973. Grapevine. VG. O3. $25.00

WAGONER, Don M. *Quine Genetics & Selection Procedures.* 1978. Tyler. VG. O3. $35.00

WAHAB, Farouk Abdel. *Modern Egyptian Drama: An Anthology.* 1974. Bibliotheca Islamica. 1st ed. 492p. VG. W1. $30.00

WAHL, Jan. *Howards Go Sledding.* 1964. HRW. 1st ed. sgn. VG/dj. M20. $22.00

WAHL, Jan. *Little Blind Goat.* 1981. Owings Mills, MD. Stemmer House. 1st ed. 4to. F/F. C8. $85.00

WAHL, Jan. *Muffletumps, the Story of Four Dolls.* 1966. HRW. 1st ed. 16mo. unp. xl. G. T5. $24.00

WAHLSTRUM, E. *Optical Crystallography.* 1969. John Wiley. 4th. VG. D8. $20.00

WAIN, John. *Letters to Five Artists.* 1970. Viking. 1st ed. F/NF. V1. $15.00

WAINER, Cord; see Dewey, Thomas B.

WAINWRIGHT, John. *All Through the Night.* 1985. St Martin. 1st Am ed. F/VG+. N4. $20.00

WAITE, Arthur Edward. *Belle & the Dragon: An Elfin Comedy.* 1894. London. ils. VG-. M17. $100.00

WAITE, Frederick C. *History of the New England Female Medical College 1848-74.* 1950. Boston. ils. 132p. red cloth. VG. B14. $55.00

WAITE, Terry. *Taken on Trust.* 1993. Harcourt Brace. 1st ed. 8vo. 16 pl. 370p. NF/dj. W1. $18.00

WAITEM, Robert G.L. *Psychopathic God, Adolf Hitler.* 1977. NY. Basic. 1st ed. 482p. G. A17. $10.00

WAITZ, Julia Ellen. *Journal of Julia Le Grand, New Orleans, 1862-63.* 1911. Richmond. Everett Waddey. 1st ed. 318p. cloth. VG+. M8. $150.00

WAJNTRAUB. *Hebrew Maps of the Holy Land.* 1992. np. 277p. F/F. A4. $95.00

WAKEFIELD, John A. *History of the War Between the States...* 1834. Jacksonville, IL. 1st ed. 12mo. 142p. Riviere bdg. C6. $1,000.00

WAKEFIELD, Lawrence. *Sail & Rail.* 1980. Traverse City. Village. 1/1500. VG. A16. $65.00

WAKELEY, Cecil. *Great Teachers of Surgery in the Past.* 1969. Bristol. 147p. A13. $40.00

WAKOSKI, Diane. *Discrepancies & Apparitions.* 1966. Doubleday. 1st ed. sgn. F/VG clip. V1. $45.00

WAKOSKI, Diane. *Fable of the Lion & the Scorpion.* 1975. Pentagram. 1/100. sgn/#d. F/wrp. V1. $75.00

WAKOSKI, Diane. *Inside the Blood Factory.* 1968. Doubleday. 1st ed. sgn. 1st state red ep. F/NF. V1. $40.00

WALBRIDGE, William. *American Bottles, Old & New.* 1920. Toledo, OH. Owens Bottle Co. 112p. VG. M20. $25.00

WALD, A. *Sequential Analysis.* 1947. John Wiley. 1st ed. 212p. F/dj. D8. $10.00

WALDEN, Howard T. *Native Inheritance.* 1966. NY. 1st ed. 199p. F/VG. B18. $17.50

WALDMAN, Diane. *Anthony Caro.* 1982. Abbeville. ils/photos. 232p. cloth. dj. D2. $165.00

WALDMAN, Diane. *Kenneth Nolan: A Retrospective.* 1977. Guggenheim Mus. ils/photos. 160p. cloth. dj. D2. $75.00

WALDORF, John Taylor. *Kid on the Comstock.* 1970. Palo Alto. Am West. 198p. gr cloth. VG+/dj. P4. $25.00

WALDRON, Ann. *Close Connections: Caroline Gordon & Southern Renaissance.* 1987. Putnam. 1st ed. 416p. VG/VG. B10. $15.00

WALDROP, Keith. *Poems From Memory.* 1975. Providence. 1st ed. 1/500. wrp. A17. $15.00

WALDROP, Keith. *Windmill Near Calvary.* 1968. MI U. 1st ed. NF/NF. V1. $15.00

WALDROP, R. *Peculiar Motions.* 1990. Kelsey. 1st ed. inscr/sgn. F/wrp. V1. $20.00

WALDROP, R. *Reproduction of Profiles.* 1987. New Directions. 1st ed. inscr. F/wrp. V1. $15.00

WALDROP & WALDROP. *Since Volume.* 1975. Burning Deck. 1/500. sgn. NF. V1. $20.00

WALFORD. *Guide to Reference Material, Third Edition, Vol I.* 1973. London. Lib Assn. 4to. 4300 entries. 622p. xl. VG. A4. $45.00

WALKE, Henry. *Naval Scenes & Reminiscences of the Civil War in the US...* 1877. NY. FR Reed. 1st ed. 38 pl/2 diagrams. 480p. cloth. VG. M8. $650.00

WALKER, Alice. *Color Purple.* 1982. NY. HBJ. 1st ed. F/F. B4. $600.00

WALKER, Alice. *Finding the Greenstone.* 1991. Hodder Stoughton. 1st ed. ils Catherine Deeter. AN/dj. C8. $40.00

WALKER, Alice. *Good Night, Willie Lee, I'll See You in the Morning.* 1979. Dial. UP. F/yel wrp. B4. $850.00

WALKER, Alice. *In Search of Our Mothers' Gardens.* 1983. HBJ. 1st ed. sgn. F/F. B4. $125.00

WALKER, Alice. *Meridian.* 1976. HBJ. 1st ed. B stp on edges. VG/VG. H11. $140.00

WALKER, Alice. *Possessing the Secret of Joy.* 1992. HBJ. 1st ed. sgn. F/F. B4. $75.00

WALKER, Alice. *Third Life of Grange Copeland.* 1970. HBJ. 1st ed. sgn. author's 2nd book. F/F. B4. $450.00

WALKER, Alice. *You Can't Keep a Good Woman Down.* 1981. HBJ. 1st ed. F/F. B4. $275.00

WALKER, Anne. *Once Long Ago.* 1989. Paris. self pub. 12mo. sgn/dtd. AN/box. B24. $475.00

WALKER, Barbara M. *Little House Cookbook.* 1979. Harper Row. ils Garth Williams. 240p. AN/dj. T5. $35.00

WALKER, Barbara M. *Little House Cookbook.* 1979. Harper Row. 1st ed. ils. 240p. VG/dj. B18. $25.00

WALKER, David. *Moving Out.* 1976. VA U. 1st ed. F/dj. V1. $25.00

WALKER, Elizabeth. *In the Mist & Other Uncanny Encounters.* 1979. Arkham. 1st ed. 1/4053. F/F. T2. $12.00

WALKER, Jeanie Mort. *Life of Capt Joseph Fry, the Cuban Martyr...* 1875. Hartford. JB Burr. 1st ed. 589p. cloth. VG-. M8. $85.00

WALKER, M. *Curlews Cry.* 1955. NY. 1st ed. VG/VG. B5. $25.00

WALKER, Martin. *Daily Sketches: A Cartoon History of 20th-C Britain.* 1978. Frederick Muller. 1st ed. ils. NF/VG. P12. $10.00

WALKER, Mary Willis. *Red Scream.* 1994. Doubleday. 1st ed. sgn. F/F. T2. $60.00

WALKER, Mildred. *Southwest Corner.* 1951. Harcourt Brace. probable rpt. inscr to author Samuel Hopkins. F/VG. B4. $75.00

WALKER, Robert Harris. *Cincinnati & the Big Red Machine.* 1988. IN U. 1st ed. sgn. VG/wrp. P8. $12.50

WALKER, William J. *Essay on the Treatment of Compound & Complicated Fractures.* 1845. Boston. 46p. wrp. B14. $175.00

WALKOWITZ, Judith. *Prostitution & Victorian Society: Women, Class & the State.* 1980. Cambridge. 1st ed. 347p. A13. $40.00

WALL, Bernhardt. *Following Abraham Lincoln, 1809-1865.* 1943. NY. ils. 415p. VG/dj. B18. $35.00

WALL, George. *Natural History of Thought in Its Practical Aspect.* 1887. London. Trubner. 416p. gr cloth. G1. $35.00

WALL, John. *Horseman's Handbook of Practical Breeding.* 1939. Myrtle Beach. 1st ed. flexible bdg. O3. $35.00

WALLACE, Alexander. *Heather in Lore, Lyric & Lay.* 1903. NY. DeLaMare. 245p. cloth. VG. A10. $75.00

WALLACE, Alfred R. *Wonderful Century.* 1898. Dodd Mead. 1st Am ed. VG. A15. $35.00

WALLACE, Andrew. *Sources & Readings in Arizona History.* 1965. AZ Pioneers' Hist Soc. 8vo. xl. silvered gray cloth. NF. T10. $25.00

WALLACE, Cornelia. *C'nelia.* 1976. NY. Holman. 1st ed. inscr. 8vo. VG/VG. B11. $25.00

WALLACE, David Foster. *Broom of the System.* 1987. Viking. 1st ed. author's 1st book. F/NF. B2. $200.00

WALLACE, David Foster. *Girl With Curious Hair.* 1989. Norton. 1st ed. sgn. F/F. B2. $75.00

WALLACE, Dillon. *Lure of the Labrador Wild.* 1905. NY. Revell. photos/fld map. 339p. VG. T7. $60.00

WALLACE, Edgar. *Day of Uniting.* 1930. Mystery League. 1st ed. VG. M21. $15.00

WALLACE, George C. *Stand Up for America.* 1976. Doubleday. 1st ed. photos. 183p. F/VG. B10. $8.00

WALLACE, George Selden. *Charters of Blenheim: A Genealogy...* 1955. self pub. 1/300. 139p. VG. B10. $50.00

WALLACE, Irving. *Fan Club.* 1974. Simon Schuster. 1st ed. NF/F. H11. $25.00

WALLACE, Irving. *Man.* 1964. NY. 1st ed. F/F. A17. $12.50

WALLACE, Irving. *R Document.* 1976. Simon Schuster. 1st ed. NF/NF. H11. $20.00

WALLACE, Ivy L. *Pookie at the Seaside.* 1940s?. Collins. ils. VG. B17. $20.00

WALLACE, Lew. *First Christmas.* 1899. Harper. 1st ed. VG. M19. $25.00

WALLACE, P.B. *Colonial Ironwork in Old Philadelphia.* 1930. NY. Architectural Pub. 1st ed. VG/VG. B5. $70.00

WALLACE, Robert. *Ungainly Things.* 1968. Dutton. 1st ed. NF/NF. V1. $20.00

WALLACE, Robert. *World of Leonardo 1452-1519.* 1967. Time Life. NF/case. H4. $15.00

WALLACE. *Bibliography of William Carlos Williams.* 1968. Wesleyan U. ils. 381p. F/VG clip. A4. $125.00

WALLEGHEN, Michael V. *More Trouble With the Obvious.* 1981. IL U. 1st ed. F/NF. V1. $20.00

WALLER, R.J. *Slow Waltz in Cedar Bend.* 1993. NY. ARC. F/wrp. A15. $30.00

WALLER, Robert James. *Bridges of Madison County.* 1992. NY. 1st ed. F/F. w/sgn promo sheet. B5. $200.00

WALLER, Robert James. *Bridges of Madison County.* 1992. Time Warner. 1st ed/1st prt. photos. AN/dj. B24. $250.00

WALLER, Robert James. *Bridges of Madison County.* 1992. Warner. 1st ed. NF/F. H11. $175.00

WALLIN, Homer N. *Pearl Harbor: Why, How. Fleet Salvage & Final Appraisal.* 1968 (1976). Naval Hist Div. 377p. VG. A17. $17.50

WALLIS, Helen. *Discovery of the World: Maps of the Earth & the Cosmos...* 1985. Montreal. 66 maps. F. O7. $65.00

WALLIS, Helen. *Raleigh & Roanoke.* 1985. NC Dept Cultural Resources. 1st ed. 4to. 116p. F3. $35.00

WALLON, H. *Jeanne d'Arc.* 1892. Paris. Firmin-Didot. 16 pl. 556p. VG. A17. $150.00

WALMSLEY, Lee. *Light Sister, Dark Sister.* 1994. Random. 1st ed. author's 1st book. F/F. H11. $25.00

WALPOLE, Horace. *Catalogue of Royal & Noble Authors of England, Scotland...* 1806. London. John Scott. 5 vol. enlarged/continued by Thomas Park. aeg. F. T10. $975.00

WALPOLE, Hugh. *Harmer John.* 1926. 1st ed. VG/VG. w/sgn. S13. $20.00

WALSDORF, John J. *Printers on Morris.* 1981. Beaverdam Pr. 1/326 ils Barry Moser. miniature. F. B24. $200.00

WALSH, Christy. *Baseball's Greatest Lineup.* 1952. Barnes. 1st ed. VG/G+. P8. $35.00

WALSH, J.H. *Horse in the Stable & the Field.* nd. Winston. VG. O3. $45.00

WALSH, John Evangelist. *Into My Own: English Years of Robert Frost 1912-1915.* 1988. Grove. 1st ed. F/F. A17. $15.00

WALSH, John. *Poe the Detective: Curious Circumstances...* 1968. Rutgers. 1st ed. VG/VG. N4. $30.00

WALSTROM, E.E. *Igneous Minerals & Rocks.* 1955 (1947). John Wiley. 4th. VG. D8. $25.00

WALTER, Elizabeth. *In the Mist & Other Uncanny Encounters.* 1979. Arkham. 1st ed. ils/sgn Stephen Fabian. 12mo. F/F. B11. $45.00

WALTER, Ellery. *World on One Leg.* 1929. Putnam. sgn. fld map/pl. 8vo. 325p. VG. B11. $25.00

WALTER, Lutz. *Japan: A Cartographic Vision: European Printed Maps...* 1993. Munich. Prestel. 265 ils. 232p. M/dj. O7. $75.00

WALTERS, D.W. *Rutters of the Sea: The Sailing Directions of Pierre Garcie.* 1967. Yale. sgn. fwd HC Taylor. 8 maps. 478p. F. O7. $250.00

WALTERS, Eurof. *Serpent's Presence.* 1954. London. Golden Cockerel. 1/50. ils Clifford Webb. 105p. morocco-backed cloth. F. B24. $400.00

WALTERS, Frank. *Colorado.* 1946. Rinehart. 1st ed. 8vo. 400p. VG/partially separated. H4. $25.00

WALTERS, L. *Year's at the Spring.* 1920. Brentano. 1st Am ed. ils Henry Clarke. VG/G. P2. $300.00

WALTERS, Minette. *Sculptress.* 1993. St Martin. 1st ed. author's 2nd book. F/dj. S9. $50.00

WALTON, Ed. *Rookies.* 1982. Stein Day. 1st ed. F/VG+. P8. $12.50

WALTON, Isaak. *Compleat Angler.* nd. McKay. 1st Am trade ed. ils Rackham. 223p. gr cloth. VG+. M20. $160.00

WALTON, Isaak. *Compleat Angler.* 1815. London. ils. recent full leather. VG. M17. $300.00

WALTON, Isaak. *Compleat Angler.* 1931. London. Harrap. 1/775. ils/sgn Rackham. gilt vellum. NF. T10. $1,750.00

WALTON, Todd. *Forgotten Impulses.* 1980. Simon Schuster. 1st ed. rem mk. F/NF. H11. $20.00

WALWORTH, Jeannette. *History of the State of NY in Words of One Syllable.* 1888. Belford Clarke. 180p. gilt bdg. VG. P2. $45.00

WALZ & WALZ. *Bizarre Sisters.* 1950. DSP. 370p. reading copy. B10. $12.00

WAMBAUGH, Joseph. *Black Marble.* 1978. Delacorte. 1st ed. VG/F. A20. $27.00

WAMBAUGH, Joseph. *Blooding.* 1989. Morrow. 1st ed. F/F. A20. $20.00

WAMBAUGH, Joseph. *Echoes in the Darkness.* 1987. Morrow. 1st ed. F/F. N4. $25.00

WAMBAUGH, Joseph. *Finnegan's Week.* 1993. Morrow. 1st ed. F/NF. N4. $20.00

WAMBAUGH, Joseph. *Glitter Dome.* 1981. Morrow. 1st ed. VG/dj. A20/N4. $25.00

WAMBAUGH, Joseph. *Golden Orange.* 1990. Morrow. 1st ed. VG+/F. A20. $18.00

WAMBAUGH, Joseph. *Golden Orange.* 1990. Perigord. 1st ed. F/F. N4. $22.50

WAMBAUGH, Joseph. *Secrets of Harry Bright.* 1985. Morrow. 1st ed. F/F. A20. $20.00

WANDREI, Donald. *Donald Wandrei: Collected Poems.* 1988. W Warwick. Necronomicon. 1st ed. ils Howard Wandrei. F/pict wrp. T2. $20.00

WANDREI, Howard. *Time Burial: Collected Fantasy Tales of...* 1995. Minneapolis. Fedogan Bremer. 1st ed. ils. F/F. T2. $30.00

WANG, Loretta H. *Chinese Purse: Embroidered Purses of the Ch'ing Dynasty.* 1991. Hilit Pub. 2nd. 120p. stiff wrp. A17. $15.00

WANGERIN, Walter. *Book of the Dun Cow.* 1978. Harper Row. 1st ed. F/dj. M21. $30.00

WARBASSE, James. *Medical Sociology: A Series of Observations...* 1909. NY. 1st ed. 355p. A13. $100.00

WARBURG, Fredric. *All Authors Are Equal.* 1973. London. 1st ed. 310p. dj. A17. $10.00

WARD, Andrew. *Blood Seed.* 1985. Viking. 1st ed. sgn. F/F. B11. $35.00

WARD, Anne G. *Quest for Theseus.* 1970. Praeger. 1st ed. ils. 281p. VG. W1. $45.00

WARD, Arch. *Green Bay Packers: Records 1919-1945.* 1946. Putnam. 1st ed. photos. 240p. VG/VG. B5. $30.00

WARD, Cindy. *Cookies Week.* 1988. Putnam. 1st ed. unp. NF. C14. $10.00

WARD, Colin. *Chartres: Making of a Miracle.* 1986. London. Folio Soc. 1st ed. 8vo. ils. F/case. T10. $45.00

WARD, Grace E. *In the Mix.* 1904. Boston. ils Clara E Atwood. VG. M17. $25.00

WARD, James. *Naturalism & Agnosticism.* 1899. London. Blk. 2 vol. gr cloth. G. G1. $65.00

WARD, Jonas (some); see Ard, William (Thames).

WARD, Lester. *Psychic Factors of Civilization.* 1893. Boston. Ginn. 369p. maroon cloth. VG. G1. $40.00

WARD, Lynd. *Mad Man's Drum.* 1930. NY. Cape Smith. 1st ed. woodcuts. NF. B14. $125.00

WARD, Lynd. *Nic of the Woods.* 1967 (1965). Great Britain. World's Work Ltd. 1st ed. 95p. VG/tattered. T5. $25.00

WARD, Lynd. *Silver Pony, a Story in Pictures.* 1973. Houghton Mifflin. 1st ed. F/F. C8. $150.00

WARD, Nanda. *Black Sombrero.* 1952. Ariel Books. 1st ed. VG/VG. P2. $35.00

WARD, R. *Records of Big Game.* 1962. London. 11th. 375p. G. B5. $75.00

WARD, Ralph T. *Steamboats.* 1973. Bobbs Merrill. 1st ed. VG/VG. A16. $22.50

WARD, Robert DeCourcey. *Climates of the United States.* 1925. Boston. Ginn. ils. 518p. G. K5. $30.00

WARD. *Abraham Lincoln: Tributes From His Associates.* 1895. NY. 12mo. 295p. gilt gr cloth. G. T3. $20.00

WARE, Francis. *Driving.* 1903. Doubleday Page. 1st ed. VG. O3. $395.00

WARE, Francis. *First-Hand Bits of Stable Lore.* 1903. Little Brn. 1st ed. VG. O3. $45.00

WARE, George W. *German & Austrian Porcelain.* 1963. NY. Crown. ils/178 pl/2 photos. 244p. gilt gray cloth. dj. K1. $35.00

WARE, I.D. *Coach-Makers' Illustrated Hand-Book, Second Edition...* 1875. Phil. 1st prt this ed. O3. $595.00

WARGA, Wayne. *Fatal Impressions.* 1989. Arbor/Morrow. 1st ed. F/F. T2. $20.00

WARHOL, Andy. *Philosophy of Andy Warhol.* 1975. HBJ. 1st trade ed. 8vo. VG/dj. T10. $50.00

WARING, Gilchrist. *City of Once Upon a Time, Children's True Story...* 1965 (1946). VA. Dietz. 3rd. 4to. unp. VG/torn. T5. $20.00

WARING, William R. *Report to the City Council of Savannah on Epidemic Disease.* 1820. Savannah. 1st ed. 8vo. 78p. orig prt self wrp. C6. $585.00

WARNER, Charles. *Roundabout Journey.* 1891. Houghton Mifflin. 5th. 8vo. cloth. VG. W1. $20.00

WARNER, E.J. *Generals in Blue: Lives of Union Commanders.* 1989. LSU. lg 8vo. 680p. F/dj. T3. $25.00

WARNER, E.J. *Generals in Gray: Lives of Confederate Commanders.* 1991. LSU. lg 8vo. ils. 420p. F/dj. T3. $25.00

WARNER, Francis. *Nervous System of the Child: Its Growth & Health.* 1900. Macmillan. 1st Am ed. 233p. pebbled gr buckram. G1. $50.00

WARNER, Francis. *Study of Children & Their School Training.* 1898. Macmillan. 1st Am ed/2nd prt. ils/tables. gr buckram. G1. $35.00

WARNER, Gertrude Chandler. *Boxcar Children.* 1950. Scott Foresman. ils Kate Deal. VG+. S13. $25.00

WARNER, Gertrude Chandler. *Surprise Island, a Sequel to Boxcar Children.* 1949. Scott Foresman. 4th. ils Mary Gehr. 8vo. 178p. gr cloth. G+. T5. $22.00

WARNER, Ken. *Gun Digest.* 1984. DBI Books. sc. P12. $5.00

WARNER, Langdon. *Craft of the Japanese Sculptor.* 1936. NY. 1st ed. ils. NF. A17. $40.00

WARNER & WHITE. *Shakespeare's Flowers.* 1987. Wilmington, DE. ils. 96p. F. B26. $25.00

WARREN, B.S. *Health Insurance: Its Relation to the Public Health.* 1916. WA. 1st ed. 76p. wrp. A13. $75.00

WARREN, J. Mason. *Cases of Occlusion of the Vagina...* 1853. Boston. offprint. 28p. F/prt wrp. B14. $150.00

WARREN, J. Mason. *Lithotrity & Lithotomy, With Use of Ether...* 1849. Boston. 15p. bl prt wrp. NF. B14. $475.00

WARREN, John C. *Comparative View of the Sensoral & Nervous Systems...* 1822. Boston. 8 pl. 157p. modern bdg. VG. B14. $475.00

WARREN, John. *Official Price Guide to Paperbacks, First Edition.* 1991. np. ils. 934p. F/wrp. A4. $25.00

WARREN, Joseph. *What a Widow!* 1930. Grosset Dunlap. 264p. VG+/dj. M20. $20.00

WARREN, Robert Penn. *All the King's Men.* 1946. NY. 1st ed. NF. C2. $100.00

WARREN, Robert Penn. *Band of Angels.* 1955. Random. 1st ed. VG/VG. V1. $20.00

WARREN, Robert Penn. *Cave.* 1959. Putnam. 1st ed. F/NF. H11. $40.00

WARREN, Robert Penn. *Chief Joseph of the Nez Perce.* 1983. Random. 1st ed. F/VG+. V1. $25.00

WARREN, Robert Penn. *New & Selected Poems 1923-1985.* 1985. Random. 1st ed. F/NF. V1. $35.00

WARREN, Robert Penn. *Or Else Poems 1968-1971.* 1974. Random. 1st ed. xl. NF. V1. $25.00

WARREN, Robert Penn. *Place To Come To.* 1977. Random. 1st ed. F/F. H11. $40.00

WARREN, Robert Penn. *Rumor Verified.* 1981. Random. 1st ed. F/NF. V1. $25.00

WARREN, Robert Penn. *Selected Poems, New & Old 1923-1966.* 1966. Random. 1st ed. NF/NF. B35. $28.00

WARREN, Robert Penn. *Selected Poems 1923-1943.* 1944. Harcourt Brace. 1st ed. assn copy. F/G+. V1. $95.00

WARREN, Rosanna. *Stained Glass.* 1993. Norton. 1st ed. F/F. V1. $10.00

WARRENER. *Picnic for Bunnykins.* 1984. Middlesex, Eng. Viking Kestrel. 8vo. unp. NF. C14. $10.00

WARRICK, Patricia S. *Mind in Motion: Fiction of Philip K Dick.* 1987. S IL U. 1st ed. F/F. T2. $25.00

WARRINGTON, William. *History of Wales, in Nine Books.* 1786. London. J Johnson. 1st ed. quarter sheep/marbled brd. C6. $275.00

WARWICK, Ronald. *QE2.* 1985. NY. Norton. VG/dj. A16. $30.00

WASHINGTON, Booker T. *Character Building.* 1902. Toronto. Wm Briggs. 1st Canadian ed. xl. VG. B2. $50.00

WASHINGTON, Booker T. *Future American Negro.* 1900. Boston. 2nd. ils. 244p. G. B5. $32.50

WASHINGTON, Booker T. *Up From Slavery.* 1901. Doubleday. 1st ed. inscr/dtd 1901. F. B4. $2,000.00

WASHINGTON, George. *Official Letters to Honorable American Congress...* 1795. London. 2 vol. 1st ed. VG. M8. $350.00

WASHINGTON, George. *Washington's Farewell Address to the People...* 1922. San Francisco. 1/50 (of 175). sgn Grabhorn/others. F. B24. $375.00

WASHINGTON NATIONAL GALLERY. *Mary Cassatt 1844-1926.* 1970. WA. ils/pl. 119p. stiff wrp. D2. $40.00

WASSON, R.G. *Hall Carbine Affair.* 1948. NY. 1/750. VG/VG. B5. $60.00

WATERHOUSE, Keith. *Billy Liar.* 1960. Norton. 1st Am ed. 191p. VG/VG. M20. $42.00

WATERS, B. *Modern Training & Handling.* 1894. Boston. 1st ed. ils. 332p. VG. B5. $45.00

WATERS, Frank. *Colorado.* 1946. NY. Rivers of Am series. 1st ed. VG/VG. B5. $50.00

WATERS, Frank. *Masked Gods: Navaho & Pueblo Ceremonialism.* 1950. Albuquerque. 1st ed. 8vo. 438p. beige cloth. NF/defective. T10. $150.00

WATERS, Frank. *People of the Valley.* 1941. NY. 1st ed. VG/VG. B5. $50.00

WATERTON, Charles. *Wanderings in South America, the NW of the United States...* 1825. London. 1st ed. 4to. 326p. contemporary morocco/raised bands. C6. $400.00

WATKINS, John V. *Gardens of Antilles.* 1952. Gainesville. ils. 244p. VG. B26. $25.00

WATKINS, Paul. *Calm at Sunset, Calm at Dawn.* 1989. Houghton Mifflin. 1st ed. F/F. H11. $50.00

WATKINS, Paul. *In the Blue Light of African Dreams.* 1990. Houghton Mifflin. 1st ed. F/NF. H11. $40.00

WATKINS, Paul. *Night Over Day Over Night.* 1988. Knopf. 1st ed. author's 1st book. rem mk. F/F. M23. $25.00

WATKINS, Paul. *Promise of Light.* 1992. Random. 1st ed. F/F. H11. $30.00

WATKINS, T.H. *Mark Twain's Mississippi: Pictorial History...* 1974. Weathervane. 1st ed. photos. 221p. F/F. B10. $35.00

WATKINS, Vernon. *Affinities.* 1963. New Directions. 1st ed. assn copy. F/VG. V1. $20.00

WATKINS-PITCHFORD, Denys. *Little Grey Men.* 1949. Jr Literary Guild. 1st/A ed. 8vo. VG/worn. B17. $30.00

WATSON, Aldren. *Village Blacksmith.* 1968. NY. Crowell. 1st ed. VG/VG. O3. $45.00

WATSON, Clyde. *Father Fox's Pennyrhymes.* 1971. Crowell. 2nd. 56p. VG. T5. $18.00

WATSON, E.W. *Watercolor Demonstrated by 23 American Artists.* 1946. NY. 1st ed. VG/VG. B5. $25.00

WATSON, Harold Francis. *Sailor in English Fiction & Drama 1550 1800.* 1931. Columbia. 241p. VG. T7. $40.00

WATSON, Ian. *Gardens of Delight.* 1980. London. Gollancz. 1st ed. AN/dj. M21. $20.00

WATSON, James. *Double Helix: A Personal Account of the Discovery of...DNA.* 1968. NY. 1st ed. 226p. A13. $22.50

WATSON, Jane Werner. *Golden History of the World.* 1955. Golden. ils Cornelius DeWitt. 4to. 156p. glossy brd. VG. T5. $30.00

WATSON, John. *Comte, Mill & Spencer: Outline of Philosophy.* 1895. Glasgow. Maclehouse. 12mo. 302p. pebbled maroon cloth. G1. $50.00

WATSON, Larry. *Montana 1948.* 1993. Milkweed. 1st ed. F/F. B4. $100.00

WATSON, Nancy Dingman. *Blueberries Lavender: Songs of the Farmer's Children.* (1977). Reading, MA. Addison Wesley. 1st ed. 8vo. unp. F/VG+. C14. $10.00

WATSON, Robert. *Advantages of Dark.* 1966. Atheneum. 1st ed. assn copy. F/dj. V1. $20.00

WATSON, Robert. *Night Blooming Cactus.* 1980. Atheneum. 1st ed. assn copy. F/NF. V1. $20.00

WATSON, Virginia. *Princess Pocahontas.* 1916. Hampton. ils GW Edwards. 306p. VG+. T5. $25.00

WATSON, Wendy. *Jamie's Story.* 1981. Philomel. 1st ed. ils. NF/VG. T5. $15.00

WATSON. *New Cambridge Bibliography of English Literature.* 1969-1977. Cambridge. 5 vol. 4to. F/NF. A4. $500.00

WATSON. *Supplement to Bitters Bottles.* 1968. np. ils. 160p. VG. A4. $35.00

WATT, Leilani. *Caught in the Conflict.* 1984. Harvest. 1st ed. sgn. 191p. VG/VG. B11. $8.50

WATTERS, Pat. *Down to Now!* 1971. Pantheon. 1st ed. 426p. NF/NF. R11. $18.00

WATTERS, Pat. *Fifty Years of Pleasure: Ils Hist of Publix Super Markets.* 1980. Lakeland. Publix. inscr Jenkins (creator of chain). F/VG. B11. $30.00

WATTS, Mabel. *Patchwork Kilt.* 1954. Aladdin. 1st ed. ils Winifred Bromhall. unp. VG+. T5. $25.00

WAUGH, Evelyn. *Brideshead Revisited.* 1946. Little Brn. 1st Am trade ed. NF/NF. B4. $450.00

WAUGH, Evelyn. *Edmund Campion.* 1946. Little Brn. 1st Am ed. F/NF clip. B4. $175.00

WAUGH, Evelyn. *Helena.* 1950. Little Brn. 1st ed. VG/VG. M19. $45.00

WAUGH, Evelyn. *Loved One.* 1948. Chapman Hall. 1st ed. sgn. ils/sgn Stuart Boyle. F/tissue dj. B4. $1,500.00

WAUGH, Evelyn. *Loved One.* 1948. London. Chapman Hall. 1st ed. 1/250 lg paper issue. inscr. NF. B4. $1,250.00

WAUGH, Evelyn. *Men at Arms.* 1952. Little Brn. 1st ed. NF/G. M19. $45.00

WAUGH, Evelyn. *Msgr Ronald Knox.* 1959. Little Brn. 1st ed. F/VG. M19. $25.00

WAUGH, Evelyn. *Officers & Gentlemen.* 1955. Chapman Hall. 1st ed. F/dj. C2/C6. $125.00

WAUGH, Evelyn. *Officers & Gentlemen.* 1955. Little Brn. 1st ed. F/VG. M19. $45.00

WAUGH, Evelyn. *Scott-King's Modern Europe.* 1947. London. 1st ed. F/NF. B4. $85.00

WAUGH, Evelyn. *They Were Still Dancing.* 1931. Cape Smith. 1st Am ed. F/NF. C2. $450.00

WAUGH, Hillary. *Death in a Town.* 1989. Carroll Graf. 1st ed. inscr. F/F. B11. $25.00

WAUGH, Hillary. *Shadow Guest.* 1971. Doubleday. 1st ed. VG/VG. M22. $20.00

WAUGH, John C. *Class of 1846.* 1994. Warner. 1st ed. F/F. M23. $35.00

WAUGH & WAUGH. *South Builds: New Architecture in the Old South.* 1960. UNC. photos. 173p. F/G. B10. $35.00

WAVLE, Ardra Soule. *Rain & Shine.* 1947. Heath. revised ed. 119p. F. A17. $5.00

WAY, F. *Log of the Betsy Ann.* 1933. NY. 1st ed. sgn. VG/VG. B5. $55.00

WAY, F. *Pilotin' Comes Natural.* 1943. Farrar Rinehart. 1st ed. ils John Cosgrove. G/G. A16. $65.00

WAYLAND, Anne Rutherford. *Poems.* nd. self pub. 47p. VG. B10. $10.00

WAYLAND, Francis. *Elements of Political Economy.* 1843. Boston. 406p. blk cloth. T3. $27.00

WAYLAND, Francis. *Limitations of Human Responsibility.* 1838. Boston. Gould Kendall Lincoln. 24mo. xl. VG. G1. $50.00

WAYLAND, John Walter. *Battle of New Market Memorial Address...* 1926. New Market, VA. Henkel. 1st ed. 2 maps. NF/wrp. M8. $75.00

WAYLAND, John. *Hopewell Friends History 1734-1834.* 1936. Frederick County, MD. 1st ed. ils/index. VG. B5. $75.00

WAYNE, Jenifer. *Kitchen People.* 1964. Bobbs Merrill. ils Leonard Shortall. 156p. VG/torn. T5. $15.00

WEATHERLY, F.E. *Punch & Judy & Some of Their Friends.* 1987. Sidney, Australia. View Productions. 1st ed thus. F/VG. B17. $8.50

WEATHERLY, Fred J. *Holly Boughs.* ca 1885. NY. EP Dutton. ils ME Edwards/Staples. pict brd/cloth spine. VG. T10. $75.00

WEAVER, John V.A. *Finders.* 1924. Knopf. 3rd. VG. V1. $10.00

WEAVER, John V.A. *To Youth.* 1928. Knopf. 1st ed. VG. V1. $15.00

WEBB, Charles. *Graduate.* 1963. NY. NAL. 1st ed. F/VG clip. B4. $150.00

WEBB, Jack. *Big Sin.* 1952. Rinehart. 1st ed. F/NF. B4. $65.00

WEBB, Jack. *Deadly Sex.* 1959. Rinehart. 1st ed. VG/VG. P10. $20.00

WEBB, James. *Fields of Fire.* 1978. Prentice Hall. 1st ed. author's 1st book. 344p. VG/VG. M20. $37.00

WEBB, Joe. *Care & Training of the Tennessee Walking Horse.* 1962. Searcy. 1st ed. VG/VG. O3. $48.00

WEBB, Sharon. *Halflife.* 1989. Tor. 1st ed. F/NF. G10. $10.00

WEBB, T.W. *Celestial Objects for Common Telescopes.* 1899 & 1917. London. Longman Gr. 2 vol. unmatched. xl. K5. $70.00

WEBB, William. *Henry & Friends: The California Years 1946-1977.* 1991. Capra. ltd ed. 1/100. sgn. F. w/photo. M19. $45.00

WEBB. *American Landmarks & Popular Places.* 1989. F/F. D2. $30.00

WEBBER, Everett. *Escape to Utopia.* 1969. NY. 1st ed. ils/index. 444p. VG/VG. B5. $30.00

WEBER, Carl J. *Fore-Edge Painting: A Historical Survey...* 1966. np. 4to. ils. 238p. F/VG. A4. $325.00

WEBER, Carl J. *Thousand & One Fore-Edge Paintings.* 1949. Colby College. 1/1000. sm 4to. 194p. F/VG. H4. $350.00

WEBER, F.E. *Summary of Preliminary Designs, Estimates & Surveys...* 1930. Metro Water District. 4 vol. only ed. 4to. prt wrp/cloth spine. VG. T10. $500.00

WEBER, Francis J. *Rose: America's Flower.* 1988. San Fernando. Junipero Serra. 1/200. aeg. red leather. miniature. T10. $50.00

WEBER, Francis J. *San Xavier del Bac.* 1975. San Fernando. Junipero Serra. 1/300. aeg. gray leather. miniature. T10. $50.00

WEBER, Walter Alois. *Homes & Habits of Wild Animals.* 1934. Donohue. folio. ils. VG/G. B17. $8.00

WEBER, Walter Alois. *Traveling With the Birds.* 1933. Donohue. folio. ils. VG. B17. $6.50

WEBER, William A. *Handbook of Plants of the Colorado Front Range.* 1953. Boulder. ils/glossary. 232p. VG/dj. B26. $22.00

WEBER, William A. *Theodore dru Alison Cockerell, 1866-1948.* 1965. Boulder. 126p. VG/wrp. B26. $22.50

WEBSTER, Frank V. *Newsboy Partners.* 1909. Cupples Leon. 203p. VG/dj. M20. $42.00

WEBSTER, H.T. *Best of...* 1953. Simon Schuster. ils/photos. 225p. F. M13. $30.00

WEBSTER, H.T. *Webster's Bridge.* 1924. NY. VG. S1. $15.00

WEBSTER, John. *Displaling of Supposed Witchcraft...* 1677. London. Prt for JM. folio. 346p. G. rare. G1. $1,750.00

WEBSTER, Noah. *Compendious Dictionary of English Language, a Facsimile...* 1970. np. intro Philip Gove. 446p. NF/VG. A4. $45.00

WEBSTER, Noah. *Webster's Biographical Dictionary.* 1943. np. 8vo. 1697p. brn cloth. VG. T3. $15.00

WEBSTER, W.H.B. *Narrative of a Voyage to the South Atlantic.* 1834. London. 2 vol. maps/pl. contemporary sheepskin. VG. B14. $225.00

WEED, Clarnece M. *Insects & Insecticides.* 1911 (1895). NY. 2nd. 334p. VG+. B26. $20.00

WEEDON, Howard. *Bandana Ballads.* 1909. NY. intro JC Harris. G+. B5. $80.00

WEEDON, Howard. *Songs of the Old South.* 1901 (1900). Doubleday Page. 94p. G+. B10. $125.00

WEEDON, L.L. *Child Characters From Dickens.* ca 1900. Nister Dutton. ils Arthur A Dixon. VG+. M5. $135.00

WEEDON, L.L. *Life of Our Lord.* 1934. London. 1st ed. ils. VG/VG. M17. $32.50

WEEKS, Edward. *Lowells & Their Institute.* 1966. Atlantic Little Brn. 1st ed. 4-line inscr. 202p. F. B14. $55.00

WEEMS, John Edward. *If You Don't Like the Weather...* 1986. TX Monthly. ils. 121p. VG/dj. K5. $14.00

WEEMS, M.L. *Life of George Washington: With Curious Anecdotes...* 1812. Phil. Mathew Carey. 12th. 12mo. 228p. new full sheep. T10. $150.00

WEESNER, Theo. *True Detective.* 1987. Summit. 1st ed. sgn. rem mk. VG/VG. A20. $14.00

WEGELIN. *Early American Fiction 1774-1830.* 1929. np. 3rd. 40p. VG. A4. $85.00

WEHR, Julian. *Animated Animals.* 1943. Akron. Saalfield. 4 moveables. VG/dj. D1. $150.00

WEHR, Julian. *Animated Story Rhymes.* 1944. Garden City. 4 moveables. sbdg. VG. D1. $125.00

WEHR, Julian. *Jack & the Beanstalk.* 1944. Duenewald. 5 moveables. prt brd/comb bdg. F/dj. T10. $300.00

WEHR, Julian. *Little Red Riding Hood.* 1944. NY. Duenewald. mechanical. NF/partial. C8. $95.00

WEHR, Julian. *Puss in Boots.* 1944. Dunewald. 1st ed thus. 6 moveables. VG/VG. D1. $200.00

WEHR, Julian. *Snow White.* 1949. Duenewald. 4 moveables. sbdg. VG. D1. $150.00

WEICHMANN, Louis J. *True History of the Assassination of Abraham Lincoln...* 1975. Knopf. 1st ed. 498p. cloth. VG/dj. M20. $32.00

WEIDMAN, Jerome. *I'll Never Go There Anymore.* 1941. Simon Schuster. 1st ed. F/VG. B4. $100.00

WEIER, T.E. *Botany.* 1974 (1950). NY. 5th. VG. B26. $17.50

WEIL, Ann. *Red Sails to Capri.* 1952. Viking. 1st ed. sgn. cloth. G. B11. $15.00

WEINBERG, Larry. *Star Wars: The Making of the Movie.* 1980. Random. 1st ed. 8vo. 69p. NF. C14. $10.00

WEINBERG, Robert E. *Far Below & Other Horrors.* 1974. Fax Collectors. 1st ed. F/F. G10. $20.00

WEINBERG, Steven. *Discovery of Subatomic Particles.* 1983. Scientific Am Lib. 1st ed. 206p. cloth. VG+/dj. M20. $28.00

WEINTRAUB, Stanley. *Savoy: Nineties Experiement.* 1966. PA U. 1st ed. 294p. VG+/dj. M20. $70.00

WEISBACH, Werner. *Die Kunst Des Barock in Italien, Frankreich, Deutschland...* 1924. Berlin. 44 pl. 596p. modern half leather. A17. $40.00

WEISBORD, Albert. *Conquest of Power.* 1937. Covici Friede. 2 vol. NF/NF. B2. $125.00

WEISHAUPT, C.G. *Vascular Plants of Ohio.* 1971. Dubuque. Kendall/Hunt. 3rd. 4to. 293p. worn wrp. B1. $22.00

WEISING, George. *Ice & Snow Sculpturing.* 1954. Fairfield. ltd ed. sgn. ils/photos. xl. A17. $20.00

WEISMILLER, Edward. *Deer Come Down.* 1936. Yale. 1st ed. inscr. assn copy. NF/VG. V1. $35.00

WEISS, Dianne. *Carrousel.* nd. Mill Valley. 1/100. sgn. miniature. music box plays/ties. F. B24. $375.00

WEISS, Harry B. *Whaling in New Jersey.* 1974. NJ Agriculture Soc. 148p. NF. P12. $17.50

WEISS, Malcolm E. *Storms: From the Inside Out.* 1976 (1973). Messner. 3rd. xl. K5. $8.00

WEISS, Theodore. *Catch.* 1951. Twayne. 1st ed. poet's 1st book. inscr. F/clip. V1. $65.00

WEISS, Theodore. *World Before Us: Poems 1950-1970.* 1970. London. 1st ed. F/NF. V1. $25.00

WEISSBERGER, L. Arnold. *Famous Faces.* 1972. Abrams. inscr pres. 4to. 444p. bl linen. dj. K1. $60.00

WEISSMANN, Adolf. *Der Virtuose.* 1920. Berlin. Paul Cassirer. ils. 174p. gilt red cloth. K1. $150.00

WEISSMANN, Adolf. *Die Primadonna.* 1920. Berlin. Paul Cassirer. ils. 224p. gilt beige cloth. K1. $150.00

WELCH, Galbraith. *North African Prelude.* 1949. Morrow. 1st ed. 8vo. 5 maps. VG. W1. $15.00

WELCH, James. *Death of Jim Loney.* 1979. Harper. 1st ed. F/NF. B2. $75.00

WELCH, James. *Fools Crow.* 1986. Viking. 1st ed. F/F. A18. $35.00

WELCH, James. *Indian Lawyer.* 1990. Norton. 1st ed. sgn. F/F. A18. $50.00

WELCH, James. *Indian Lawyer.* 1990. Norton. 1st ed. xl. VG/F. A20. $18.00

WELCH, Stuart Cary. *Wonders of the Age: Masterpieces of Early Safavid Painting.* 1980. Cambridge. Fogg Art Mus/Harvard. ils. VG/wrp. W1. $30.00

WELCOME, John. *Fred Archer: His Life & Times.* 1967. London. 1st ed. ils. 208p. gilt gr cloth. H3. $85.00

WELDON, Fay. *...And the Wife Ran Away.* 1968. McKay. 1st Am ed. NF/NF. B2. $45.00

WELDON, Fay. *Life & Loves of a She-Devil.* 1983. Pantheon. 1st ed. F/NF. H11. $30.00

WELLARD, James. *Waters of Babylon.* 1973. Readers Union. 2nd 8vo. 223p. VG/dj. W1. $18.00

WELLER, J.M. *Course of Evolution.* 1969. McGraw Hill. ils. 696p. NF. D8. $35.00

WELLER, J.M. *Stratigraphic Principles & Practice.* 1960. Harper. 1st ed. F/dj. D8. $30.00

WELLMAN, Manly Wade. *School of Darkness.* 1985. Doubleday. 1st ed. F/F. G10. $15.00

WELLMAN, Manly Wade. *They Took Their Stand: Founders of the Confederacy.* 1959. Putnam. 1st ed. 258p. F/NF. M8. $55.00

WELLMAN, Paul. *Portage Bay.* 1957. NY. pres. VG/VG. B5. $25.00

WELLMAN, William A. *Go, Get 'Em!* 1918. Boston. 1st ed. ils. 284p. pict cloth. VG. B18. $195.00

WELLS, Carolyn. *Book of American Limericks.* 1925. 1st ed. VG/G. w/sgn. S13. $45.00

WELLS, Carolyn. *Patty's Motor Car.* 1922 (1911). Dodd Mead. ils Mayo Bunker. 279p. VG. T5. $20.00

WELLS, Carolyn. *Patty's Romance.* 1924 (1915). Dodd Mead. 8vo. 303p. VG. T5. $20.00

WELLS, Carolyn. *Prillilgirl.* 1924. Lippincott. 1st ed. VG. M22. $15.00

WELLS, Carolyn. *Rubaiyat of Bridge.* 1908. NY. ils May Wilson Preston. unp. VG. S1. $20.00

WELLS, Dean Faulkner. *Ghosts of Rowan Oak: William Faulkner's Ghost Stories...* 1980. Yoknapatawpha. 1st ed. inscr/sgn twice. F/F. C2. $25.00

WELLS, Dorothy. *Editor on the Comstock Lode.* 1936. NY. 1st ed. VG/worn. B5. $35.00

WELLS, Ellen. *Book Collecting & Care of Books.* 1987. Smithsonian. sm 4to. 23p. G/wrp. T3. $10.00

WELLS, Ellen. *Rare Books & Special Collections of Smithsonian Inst Lib...* 1995. WA, DC. 1st ed. 4to. 107p. F3. $20.00

WELLS, Evelyn. *Fremont Older.* 1936. NY. Appleton Century. 407p. VG. P4. $20.00

WELLS, H.G. *Croquet Player.* 1937. Viking. 1st ed. 8vo. VG/dj. S9. $30.00

WELLS, H.G. *Crux Ansata: Indictment of the Roman Catholic Church.* 1953. NY. Freethought. 1st ed. VG/wrp. B14. $35.00

WELLS, H.G. *George Gissing & HG Wells: A Record of Their Friendship...* 1961. IL U. 1st ed. F/F. R10. $30.00

WELLS, H.G. *Time Machine.* 1895. London. Heinemann. 1st ed. 12mo. pres. contemporary calf. F. T10. $1,000.00

WELLS, H.G. *War of the Worlds.* 1898. Harper. 1st Am ed. NF. H4. $650.00

WELLS, H.G. *World of William Clissold.* 1926. London. 3 vol. 1/198. sgn. NF/case. C6. $300.00

WELLS, H.P. *American Salmon Fisherman.* 1886. NY. 1st ed. G. B5. $50.00

WELLS, Helen. *Cherry Ames' Book of First Aid & Home Nursing.* 1959. Grosset Dunlap. 250p. VG+/dj. M20. $35.00

WELLS, Helen. *Cherry Ames, Camp Nurse.* 1957. Grosset Dunlap. VG. P12. $5.00

WELLS, Helen. *Vicki Barr: Clue of the Carved Ruby (#14).* 1961. Grosset Dunlap. lists to this title. VG/dj. M20. $52.00

WELLS, Rosemary. *Benjamin & Tulip.* 1973. NY. Dial. 1st prt. obl 12mo. NF/VG+. C8. $40.00

WELMAN, C.W. *Native States of the Gold Coast: History & Constitution.* 1969. London. Dawsons. rpt of 1925-30 ed. 8vo. 3 fld maps. VG. W1. $20.00

WELMERS, William Everett. *Descriptive Grammar of Fanti.* 1946. Baltimore, MD. Linguistic Soc of Am. 78p. VG. W1. $14.00

WELTNER, Charles Longstreet. *Southerner.* 1966. Lippincott. 1st ed. VG/G. B10. $10.00

WELTY, Eudora. *Acrobats in a Park.* 1980. Lord John. 1/100. sgn. F. B4. $350.00

WELTY, Eudora. *Delta Wedding.* 1946. NY. 1st ed. VG/G. B5. $95.00

WELTY, Eudora. *In Black & White.* 1985. Lord John. 1/100. sgn/#d. marbled brd/leather spine. AN/case. B30. $300.00

WELTY, Eudora. *Losing Battles.* 1970. Random. ltd ed. 1/300. sgn. F/NF case. S9. $275.00

WELTY, Eudora. *Music From Spain.* 1/750. sgn/#d. VG. B30. $625.00

WELTY, Eudora. *On Short Stories.* 1949. NY. 1/1500. VG/glassine dj. B5. $95.00

WELTY, Eudora. *One Time, One Place.* Silver Anniversary ed. fwd Wm Maxwell. VG/VG. C4. $30.00

WELTY, Eudora. *Robber Bridegroom.* 1942. NY. 1st ed. inscr/dtd 1983. F/F. A9. $450.00

WELTY, Eudora. *Shoe Bird.* 1964. HBJ. 1st ed. 4to. ils Beth Krush. F/F. B4. $250.00

WENTWORTH, Lady. *Swift Runner.* 1957. London. Allen Unwin. 1st ed. VG. W1. $45.00

WENTWORTH, Patricia. *Gazebo.* 1956. Lippincott. 1st ed. VG/VG. M22. $40.00

WENTWORTH, Patricia. *Red Shadow.* 1932. Lippincott. 1st ed. VG. N4. $35.00

WERNER, Alfred. *Amedeo Modigliani.* 1966. Abrams. Lib of Great Painters. ils/photos/pl. cloth. dj. D2. $95.00

WERNER, Herbert. *Iron Coffins.* 1969. Holt Rinehart. ils. 364p. VG/dj. T7. $22.00

WERNER, Jane. *Child's Book of Bible Stories.* 1944. NY. 1st ed. 54p. VG/VG. A17. $17.50

WERNER, Jane. *Tall Book of Make-Believe.* 1950. Harper. early ed. ils Garth Williams. NF/VG+. C8. $150.00

WERNER, Jane. *Tall Book of Make-Believe.* 1950. Harper. VG/VG. K2. $85.00

WERNER, Jane. *Walt Disney's Living Desert.* 1954. Simon Schuster. 124p. VG. A17. $10.00

WERT, J. Howard. *Poems of Camp & Hearth.* 1887. Harrisburg. 176p. VG. B10. $15.00

WERTHEIM, M. *Salmon of the Dry Fly.* 1948. Woodstock. 1/500. photos. VG. B5. $75.00

WERTMULLER, Lina. *Head of Alvise.* 1982. Morrow. 1st ed. sgn. F/F. B11. $20.00

WEST, Charles. *Lectures on the Diseases of Infancy & Childhood.* 1859. London. 4th. 755p. rebacked. A13. $100.00

WEST, Charles. *Rat's Nest.* 1990. Walker. 1st Am ed. NF/NF. M22. $10.00

WEST, Dorothy. *Dot & Dash at the Maple Sugar Camp (#1).* 1938. Cupples Leon. lists 3 titles. 210p. VG/dj. M20. $25.00

WEST, Edwin; see Westlake, Donald E.

WEST, Geoffrey. *Charles Darwin: A Portrait.* 1938. Yale. 359p. VG/dj. A10. $25.00

WEST, Herbert Faulkner. *Mind on the Wing.* 1947. Coward McCann. 1st ed. 308p. cloth. VG/dj. M20. $25.00

WEST, Jessamyn. *Crimson Ramblers of the World, Farewell.* 1970. HBJ. 1st ed. sgn. F/F. B4. $125.00

WEST, Jessamyn. *Friendly Persuasion.* 1945. NY. 1st ed. F/VG. H7. $75.00

WEST, John Anthony. *Call Out the Malicia.* 1963. NY. 1st ed. author's 1st book. dj. A17. $10.00

WEST, Michael Lee. *Crazy Ladies.* 1990. Atlanta. Longstreet. 1st ed. author's 1st book. sgn. F/F. M23. $45.00

WEST, Michael Lee. *She Flew the Coop.* 1994. Harper Collins. 1st ed. sgn. F/F. M23. $35.00

WEST, Michael. *Clair de Lune & Other Troubadour Romances.* ca 1920. Saynt Albans, Eng. Harrup. ils Evelyn Paul. F. T10. $125.00

WEST, Morris L. *Tower of Babel.* 1968. NY. Morrow. 1st ed. 361p. VG/torn. W1. $18.00

WEST, Nathanael. *Day of the Locust.* 1939. Random. 1st ed. F/VG. B4. $1,000.00

WEST, Owen; see Koontz, Dean R.

WEST, Ray B. Jr. *Kingdom of the Saints.* 1957. NY. 1st ed. 389p. NF/reinforced. E1. $35.00

WEST, Rebecca. *Black Lamb & Grey Falcon: Journey Through Yugoslavia.* 1943. Viking. 1st 1-vol ed. 1181p. VG. W1. $25.00

WEST, Rebecca. *Judge.* 1922. NY. 1st ed. NF. A17. $10.00

WESTBROOK, Robert. *Left-Handed Policeman.* 1986. Crown. 1st ed. F/F. H11. $25.00

WESTBROOK, Robert. *Nostalgia Kills.* 1988. Crown. 1st ed. NF/dj. H11. $20.00

WESTCOTT, Glenway. *Pilgrim Hawk: A Love Story.* 1940. NY. 1st ed. inscr. F/VG. C2. $175.00

WESTCOTT, Katherine Roberts. *Salt & Sand.* 1963. Onacock. Eastern Shore News. VG. B10. $12.00

WESTERMAN, Percy F. *Rival Submarines.* ca 1920. London. Partridge. ils. 432p. VG. T7. $16.00

WESTERMAN, Percy F. *Unconquered Wings.* 1920s?. London. Blackie. ils. 320p. pict cloth. G+. B18. $17.50

WESTLAKE, Donald. *Busy Body.* 1966. Broadman. 1st Eng ed. F/VG. M19. $75.00

WESTLAKE, Donald. *Good Behavior.* 1986. Mysterious. 1st ed. F/F. M22. $20.00

WESTLAKE, Donald. *High Adventure.* 1982. Mysterious. 1st ed. sgn. F/F. B11. $35.00

WESTLAKE, Donald. *High Jinx.* 1987. Dennis McMillan. 1st ed. intro Martin C Smith. F/wrp. A20. $20.00

WESTLAKE, Donald. *I Know a Trick Worth Two of That.* 1986. Tor. 1st ed. VG/VG. P3. $15.00

WESTLAKE, Donald. *Slayground.* 1971. Random. ARC. inscr w/both names. F/VG. M19. $100.00

WESTLAKE, Donald. *Split.* 1985. London. Allison Busby. 1st hc ed. AN/dj. M22. $25.00

WESTLAKE, Inez B. *American Indian Designs.* nd. Phil. HC Perleberg. 36 silver photos. loose in portfolio/ties. xl. T10. $900.00

WESTMORELAND, William C. *Soldier Reports.* 1976. NY. 1st ed. inscr/dtd. maps/photos/index. 446p. bl cloth. F/dj. B14. $125.00

WESTON, Brett. *Brett Weston: Photographs From Five Decades.* 1980. NY. Aperture. 1st ed. sgn. F/dj. S9. $200.00

WESTON, Jack. *Real American Cowboy.* 1985. NY. New Amsterdam. 8vo. rem mk. F/wrp. T10. $11.00

WETMORE, Alexander. *Birds of the Past in North America.* 1929. Smithsonian. removed. 8vo. 11 pl. F. P4. $15.00

WETMORE. *Last of the Great Scouts: Life Story of Col Wm E Cody...* 1899. inscr/dtd Buffalo Bill. ils. 296p. VG-. A4. $395.00

WETZEL, George T. *Gothic Horror & Other Weird Tales.* 1978. np. 1st ed. ils Tim Kirk. wrp. R10. $5.00

WEXLEY, John. *Judgement of Julius & Ethel Rosenberg.* 1955. Cameron Kahn. 1st ed. 672p. cloth. VG+/dj. M20. $77.00

WHALEY, Miriam. *Four American Settlers.* 1979. Baltimore. VG. V4. $20.00

WHAN, Mabel Dodge. *Edge of Taos Desert.* 1937. Harcourt Brace. 1st ed. VG/G. B5. $95.00

WHARTON, Edith. *Artemis to Actaeon.* 1909. London. Macmillan. 1st Eng ed from Am sheets. inscr/dtd 1909. VG. B4. $5,000.00

WHARTON, Edith. *Certain People.* 1930. Appleton. 1st ed. 8vo. gilt bl cloth. VG. S9. $25.00

WHARTON, Edith. *Children.* 1928. Appleton. 1st ed. 346p. VG/dj. M20. $82.00

WHARTON, Edith. *Ethan Frome.* 1911. Scribner. 2nd. VG. B4. $65.00

WHARTON, Edith. *French Ways & Their Meaning.* 1919. London. Macmillan. 1st ed. F. B4. $45.00

WHARTON, Edith. *Fruit of the Tree.* 1907. Scribner. 1st ed. 633p. VG. M20. $47.00

WHARTON, Edith. *God's Arrive.* 1932. Appleton. 1st ed. VG+. B4. $75.00

WHARTON, Edith. *House of Mirth.* 1905. Scribner. 1st ed. 8vo. VG+. M5. $75.00

WHARTON, Edith. *Hudson River Bracketed.* 1929. Appleton. 1st ed. VG. B4. $100.00

WHARTON, Edith. *Italian Villas & Their Gardens.* 1904. Bodley Head. 1st Eng ed. ils Parrish. A bdg (gr cloth). VG. B4. $750.00

WHARTON, Edith. *Madame de Treymes.* 1907. NY. 1st ed. NF. C6. $60.00

WHARTON, Edith. *Mother's Recompense.* 1925. Appleton. 1st ed. VG. B4. $125.00

WHARTON, Edith. *Son at the Front.* 1923. Scribner. 1st ed. VG. B4. $125.00

WHARTON, Edith. *Twilight Sleep.* 1927. Appleton. 1st ed. G. B4. $60.00

WHARTON, Edith. *Valley of Decision.* 1902. Scribner. 2 vol. 2nd issue (lacks Updike imprint on c p). VG. B4. $175.00

WHARTON, Edith. *Xingu.* 1916. Scribner. 1st ed. G. B4. $65.00

WHARTON, William. *Dad.* 1981. NY. 1st ed. F/clip. A17. $8.50

WHATELY, Mary L. *Letters From Egypt.* ca 1970. Dodd Mead. 12mo. 4 pl. 289p. VG. W1. $25.00

WHATMAN, Susannah. *Susannah Whatman, Her Housekeeping Book.* 1952. Cambridge. 1/250. 8vo. 40p. cloth. F. B24. $175.00

WHEAT, Carl. *Mapping the Transmississippi West.* 1957-1963. Grabhorn. 5 vol in 6. 1/1000. maps. cloth/linen brd. F. A4. $4,850.00

WHEAT, Carl. *Mapping the Transmississippi West.* 1957-1963. San Francisco. Inst for Hist Cartography. 5 vol in 6. 1st ed. NF. T10. $4,500.00

WHEAT, Carl. *Maps of California Gold Region, 1848-1857...* nd (1995). revised. 1/350. 26 facsimile maps. 262p. F. A4. $125.00

WHEATLEY, Dennis. *Man Who Killed the King.* 1965. NY. 1st Am ed. dj. A17. $7.50

WHEELER, F.G. *Billy Whiskers at the Circus.* 1913. Akron. 6 pl. VG/G. B5. $30.00

WHEELER, Helen. *Womanhood Media: Current Resources About Women.* 1972. Scarecrow. 335p. red cloth. F. B22. $5.50

WHEELER, Opal. *HMS Pinafore.* 1946. Dutton. 1st ed. 4to. 96p. VG/G. T5. $25.00

WHEELER, Richard. *Dodging Red Cloud: An Evans Novel of the West.* 1987. Evans. 1st ed. 12mo. F/F. T10. $10.00

WHEELOCK, John Hall. *Black Panther: Book of Poems.* 1922. Scribner. 1st ed. inscr w/5-line poem. VG+. V1. $50.00

WHEELOCK, John Hall. *Poems Old & New.* 1956. Scribner. 1st ed. assn copy. F/NF. V1. $30.00

WHEELOCK, John Hall. *Poems 1911-1936.* 1936. NY. 1st ed. dj. A17. $10.00

WHEELOCK, John Hall. *What Is Poetry?* 1963. Scribner. ARC. 1st ed. F/NF. V1. $30.00

WHEELWRIGHT, John. *Selected Poems.* 1941. Norfolk. 1st ed. 30p. dj. A17. $15.00

WHERRY, Joseph. *Indian Masks & Myths of the West.* 1969. NY. 1st ed. VG/VG. V4. $35.00

WHICHARD, Rogers Dey. *History of Lower Tidewater Virginia.* 1959. Lewis Hist. 3 vol. photos. VG. B10. $300.00

WHIDDEN, John D. *Ocean Life in the Old Sailing Ship Days.* 1908. Little Brn. 1st ed. sgn. 12mo. cloth. G. B11. $45.00

WHIGHTMAN, W.P.D. *Growth of Scientific Ideas.* 1953. New Haven. 495p. A13. $15.00

WHIPPLE, A.B.C. *Fighting Sail.* 1978. Time Life. ils. 184p. G+. P12. $12.00

WHIPPLE, A.B.C. *Storm.* 1982. Alexandria, VA. Time Life. 176p. pict cloth. VG. K5. $12.00

WHITAKER, Harold. *Harold Whitaker Collection of County Atlases...* 1947. Leeds. Brotherton Lib. 10 maps. NF. O7. $95.00

WHITCOMB, Jon. *Coco, the Far-Out Poodle.* 1963. Random. 1st prt. VG/VG. B17. $10.00

WHITE, A. *Come Next Spring.* 1990. Clarion. 1st ed. 8vo. 170p. NF/G+. T5. $20.00

WHITE, A. *Golden Sunbeams for the Young People.* 1956. Zarephath. 6th. 135p. VG. A17. $8.50

WHITE, Annie Randall. *Twentieth Century Etiquette.* 1901. np. 100 full-p engravings. decor gr cloth. G. B30. $20.00

WHITE, Colin. *World of the Nursery.* 1984. Dutton. 1st ed. 224p. NF/NF. T5. $45.00

WHITE, Diana. *Descent of Ishtar.* 1903. Hammersmith. Eragny. 1/226. 12mo. silk ep. dk gr full-crushed morocco. F. B24. $3,500.00

WHITE, E.B. *Annotated Charlotte's Web.* 1994. Harper Collins. AP. 8vo. NF/wrp. S9. $25.00

WHITE, E.B. *Charlotte's Web.* 1952. Harper. 1st ed. ils Garth Williams. 184p. F/NF. B14. $350.00

WHITE, E.B. *Charlotte's Web.* 1952. Harper. 1st ed. sm 8vo. VG+/G+. C8. $200.00

WHITE, E.B. *Poems & Sketches.* 1981. Harper Row. 1st ed. F/VG+. A20. $18.00

WHITE, E.B. *Stuart Little.* 1945. 1st ed. ils Williams. VG/worn. S13. $50.00

WHITE, E.B. *Wild Flag.* 1946. Houghton Mifflin. 1st ed. VG/VG. A20. $23.00

WHITE, Edmund. *Boy's Own Story.* 1982. Dutton. UP. F/wrp. B4. $125.00

WHITE, Edmund. *Genet: A Biography.* 1993. Knopf. 1st ed. AN/dj. C2. $35.00

WHITE, Edward A. *American Orchid Culture.* 1927. NY. 1st ed. 227p. VG-. B26. $40.00

WHITE, Eliza Orne. *Joan Morse.* 1926. Houghton Mifflin. 1st ed. ils. 176p. VG. P2. $15.00

WHITE, Eliza Orne. *When Esther Was a Little Girl.* 1944. Houghton Mifflin. 1st ed. inscr. 141p. VG/G+. P2. $40.00

WHITE, Ethel Lina. *War.* 1935. Doubleday Crime Club. 1st ed. NF/VG+. B4. $200.00

WHITE, Gilbert. *Natural History of Selborne.* 1924. London. 248p. G. B18. $19.50

WHITE, J. Samuel. *Shipbuilding.* nd. London. Albion. folio. ils. rebacked. T7. $125.00

WHITE, J.F. *Study of the Earth.* 1962. Prentice Hall. 2nd. 408p. F/dj. D8. $15.00

WHITE, Katharine S. *Onward & Upward in the Garden.* 1979. NY. ils. 362p. VG/dj. B26. $25.00

WHITE, Kathryn. *They Loved To Laugh.* 1942. Garden City. ils DeAngeli. VG/VG. B5. $30.00

WHITE, Lawrence G. *Dante: The Divine Comedy.* 1948. Pantheon. 187p. purple brd/tan cloth. VG. B22. $7.00

WHITE, Margaret Bourke. *Portrait of Myself.* 1963. NY. 1st ed. sgn. photos. F/NF. A17. $100.00

WHITE, Margaret Bourke. *They Called It Purple Heart Valley.* 1944. NY. 1st ed. VG/VG. B5. $40.00

WHITE, Margaret Bourke. *They Called It Purple Heart Valley. War in Italy.* 1944. 2nd. VG/chip. S13. $20.00

WHITE, Minor. *Mirrors, Messages, Manifestations.* 1969. NY. 1st ed. VG/VG. B5. $150.00

WHITE, Paul Dudley. *Heart Disease.* 1931. NY. 1st ed. 931p. F. B14. $300.00

WHITE, Randy Wayne. *Heart Islands.* 1992. St Martin. 1st ed. F/F. B4. $125.00

WHITE, Randy Wayne. *Sanibel Flats.* 1990. NY. 1st ed. author's 1st book. F/NF. H11. $625.00

WHITE, Randy Wayne. *Sanibel Flats.* 1990. St Martin. 1st ed. author's 1st hc novel. VG+/VG+. M22. $425.00

WHITE, Richard G. *New Gospel of Peace According to St Benjamin.* 1863-1864. NY. 4 parts in 1. NF. M8. $350.00

WHITE, Sol. *Sol White's Official Base-Ball Guide.* 1984. Camden. rpt of 1907 ed. F/sans. P8. $125.00

WHITE, Steve. *Privileged Information.* 1991. Viking. 1st ed. author's 1st novel. AN. M22. $20.00

WHITE, Stewart Edward. *African Camp Fires.* 1913. Doubleday Page. 1st ed. 8vo. VG. T10. $50.00

WHITE, Stewart Edward. *Daniel Boone: Wilderness Scout.* (1922). Garden City. later prt. 274p. NF. C11. $10.00

WHITE, Stewart Edward. *Land of Footprints.* ca 1920. Thomas Nelson. ils/photos. 462p. gilt brn cloth. VG. T10. $50.00

WHITE, Teri. *Bleeding Hearts.* 1984. Mysterious. 1st ed. F/NF. N4. $25.00

WHITE, Theodore H. *America in Search of Itself.* 1982. Harper. 1st ed. w/sgn leaf. F/F. B2. $50.00

WHITE, William Allen. *Real Issue.* 1896. Chicago. Way Williams. 1st separate book. 16mo. VG-. A17. $25.00

WHITE-STEVENS, R. *Pesticides in the Environment.* 1976. Marcel Dekker. 8vo. 458p. brd. B1. $48.00

WHITED, Charles. *Knight, a Publisher in the Tumultuous Century.* 1988. NY. 1st ed. 405p. VG+/dj. B18. $15.00

WHITEFIELD, Shelby. *Kiss It Goodbye.* 1973. Abelard-Schuman. 1st ed. F/VG. P8. $25.00

WHITEHEAD, Don. *Journey Into Crime.* 1960. Random. 1st ed. VG/VG. M22. $12.00

WHITEHEAD, Wilbur C. *Championship Bridge Hands.* 1924. NY. 120p. worn. S1. $7.00

WHITEHEAD, Wilbur C. *Contract Bridge Yellow Book...* 1930. London. 129p. VG. S1. $15.00

WHITEHOUSE, Arch. *Years of the War Birds.* 1960. NY. 1st ed. 384p. VG/dj. B18. $15.00

WHITELEY, Rocky. *Crazy Charlie's Crew.* 1977. Exposition. 1st ed. xl. F/F. B4. $150.00

WHITFIELD, Philip. *Macmillan Illustrated Animal Encyclopedia.* 1984. NY. 1st ed. 2000+ ils. 600p. F/dj. A17. $25.00

WHITFORD, David. *Extra Innings.* 1991. Burlinghame. 1st ed. F/F. P8. $20.00

WHITFORD, Genevieve Smith. *Sound of the Harp.* 1987. Harp Pr. sgn. 8vo. 52p. F/VG. B11. $10.00

WHITFORD, William. *Art Stories for Young Children. Book Two.* (1934). Reilly Lee. 1st ed thus. 168p. VG. B22. $5.50

WHITING, Charles. *Bloody Aachen.* 1976. NY. BC. 191p. dj. A17. $6.00

WHITING, Charles. *Hitler's Werewolves: Story of Nazi Resistance...* 1972. NY. 208p. F/dj. A17. $10.00

WHITMAN, Edmund S. *Those Wild West Indies.* 1938. Sheridan. 1st ed. inscr. 8vo. 316p. G/G. B11. $40.00

WHITMAN, George Washington. *Civil War Letters of...* 1975. Duke. 1st ed. ils. 173p. VG/VG. B10. $25.00

WHITMAN, Ruth. *Marriage Wig.* 1968. HBW. 1st ed. F/NF. V1. $10.00

WHITMAN, Walt. *American Bard.* 1982. Viking. 1st ed. F/VG. V1. $25.00

WHITMAN, Walt. *Franklin Evans; or, The Inebriate: A Tale of the Times.* 1842. NY. Winchester. 1st ed. 31p. morocco clamshell box. C6. $2,500.00

WHITMAN, Walt. *Franklin Evans; or, The Inebriate: A Tale of the Times.* 1929. Random. 1st hc ed. author's 1st book/only novel. 1/700. NF. B4. $200.00

WHITMAN, Walt. *Half-Breed & Other Stories.* 1927. NY. Columbia. 1st ed/A prt. 1/155. ils Allen Lewis. B18. $195.00

WHITMAN, Walt. *Leaves of Grass.* 1882. Phil. VG. A9. $10.00

WHITMAN, Walt. *November Boughs.* 1888. McKay. 1st ed/lg paper issue. inscr/dtd 1906. gr cloth. F. B4. $950.00

WHITMAN, Walt. *Out of the Cradle Endlessly Rocking.* 1978. Torrance, CA. Labyrinth. 1/65. prt/sgn Richard Bigus. linen brd. F. B24. $550.00

WHITMAN, Walt. *There Was a Child Went Forth.* 1943. Harper. stated 1st ed. ils Zhenya Gay. VG. M5. $35.00

WHITNEY, Cornelius Vanderbilt. 1951. NY. sgn pres. 314p. G+/tattered. B18. $45.00

WHITNEY, Leon F. *How To Breed Dogs.* 1937. NY. 1st ed. ils. 338p. bl cloth. VG. B14. $45.00

WHITNEY, Phyllis A. *Ebony Swan.* 1992. Doubleday. 1st ed. 269p. VG/VG. B10. $15.00

WHITNEY, T.R. *Defence of the American Policy.* 1856. NY. 12mo. 369p. gilt pict cloth. G. T3. $30.00

WHITTEMORE, Reed. *Feel of the Rock.* 1982. Dryad. 1st ed. F/wrp. V1. $10.00

WHITTEMORE, Reed. *From Zero to the Absolute.* 1967. Crown. F/NF. V1. $10.00

WHITTEN, Norman. *Sacha Runa.* 1976. Urbana, IL. 1st ed. index/biblio. 348p. dj. F3. $20.00

WHITTIER, John Greenleaf. *At Sundown.* 1892. Houghton Mifflin. VG. M19. $25.00

WHITTIER, John Greenleaf. *Early Poems of...* 1885. Boston. Houghton Mifflin. 1st ed. gilt navy cloth. NF. V1. $20.00

WHITTIER, John Greenleaf. *In War Time & Other Poems.* 1864. Ticknor Fields. 1st ed/1st state. teg. NF. T10. $200.00

WHITTIER, John Greenleaf. *Vision of Echard.* 1878. 1st ed. VG. M19. $25.00

WHITTINGSTALL-FEARNLEY, Jane. *Rose Gardens.* 1989. NY. ils/photos. 202p. F/dj. B26. $32.00

WHITTON, Blair. *Paper Toys of the World.* 1986. Hobby House. F/F. B17. $25.00

WHYMPER, Edward. *Scrambles Amongst the Alps.* 1986. Salt Lake City. index. 262p. F/dj. A17. $20.00

WHYTE. *Great Comic Cats.* ils. F. M13. $20.00

WIATER, Stanley. *After the Darkness.* 1993. Maclay. 1st ed. 1/750. sgn all 18 contributors. F/case. G10. $40.00

WIBERLEY, Leonard. *Young Man From the Piedmont.* 1965 (1963). FSG/Ariel. 3rd. 8vo. 184p. xl. VG. T5. $18.00

WICK. *George Washington: American Icon.* 1982. F/F. D2. $40.00

WICKES, George. *Amazon of Letters.* 1976. NY. 286p. F/VG. B18. $17.50

WICKES, George. *Henry Miller & the Critics.* 1963. Carbondale. 1st ed. 8vo. NF/dj. S9. $25.00

WIDEMAN, John Edgar. *Glance Away.* 1967. HBJ. 1st ed. F/NF. B4. $225.00

WIDMER, Jack. *Practical Guide for Horse Owners.* 1957. Scribner. VG/fair. O3. $20.00

WIEBE, Rudy. *Mad Trapper.* 1980. McClelland Stewart. 1st Canadian ed. F/VG. A18. $30.00

WIEBE, Rudy. *Peace Shall Destroy Many.* 1962. McClelland Stewart. 1st Canadian ed. F/VG. A18. $30.00

WIEBE, Rudy. *Peace Shall Destroy Many.* 1962. McClelland Stewart. 1st Canadian ed. sgn. F/F. A18. $40.00

WIEBE, Rudy. *Scorched-Wood People.* 1977. McClelland Stewart. 1st Canadian ed. F/clip. A18. $25.00

WIEBELT, J.A. *Engineering Radiation Heat Transfer.* 1966. HRW. 278p. F. P4. $20.00

WIEDEMANN, Alfred. *Plants of the Oregon Coastal Dunes.* 1969. Corvallis. ils/photos. 117p. sbg. B26. $15.00

WIEGAND, M. Gonsalva. *Sketch Me, Berta Hummel.* 1978. Eaton, OH. Miller. 3rd. sgn. 98p. w/pamphlets. VG/dj. M20. $37.00

WIEGERT, W.J. *Lords of the Leaf.* 1988. NY. Carlton. 1st ed. author's 1st book. F/F. H11. $25.00

WIENERS, John. *Cultured Affairs in Boston: Poems & Prose 1956-1985.* 1988. BSP. 1/226. sgn Wieners/Creeley/Raymond Foye. F/NF. V1. $65.00

WIENERS, John. *Nerves.* 1970. Cape Goliard. 1st ed. photos Gerard Malanga. F/NF. V1. $65.00

WIENERS, John. *Unhired.* 1968. Perishable. 1st ed. 1/250. sgn. F/self wrp. V1. $75.00

WIESE, Arthur James. *Discoveries of America to the Year 1525.* 1884. Putnam. 12 maps. xl. VG+. O7. $75.00

WIESE, Kurt. *Liang & Lo.* 1930. Doubleday Doran. 1st ed. ils. VG. P2. $125.00

WIESEL, Elie. *Beggar in Jerusalem.* 1970. Random. 1st ed. F/F. B35. $18.00

WIESEL, Elie. *Golem.* 1983. Summit. 1st ed. F/F. B35. $35.00

WIESEL, Elie. *Testament.* 1981. Summit. 1st ed. NF/F. B35. $30.00

WIESNER, William. *Three Good Friends.* 1946. Harper. ils. VG/dj. B17. $7.50

WIEST & WIEST. *Down the River Without a Paddle.* 1973. Chicago. Children's Pr. 1st ed. 47p. VG. T5. $15.00

WIGGAM, Lionel. *Landscapes With Figures.* 1936. NY. Viking. 2nd. sgn. ils Thomas W Nason. 76p. G. B11. $30.00

WIGGETT, Howard. *Great Man.* 1953. Garden City. 1st ed. VG/VG. B5. $35.00

WIGGIN, Kate Douglas. *Bird's Christmas Carol.* 1912. Houghton Mifflin. 1st ed thus. ils Katharine Wireman. gr cloth. VG/VG. D1. $125.00

WIGGIN, Kate Douglas. *Bluebeard, a Humorous Musical Fantasy.* 1914. Harper. 1st ed. 16mo. NF/G. C8. $200.00

WIGGIN, Kate Douglas. *Chronicles of Rebecca.* 1907. Houghton Mifflin. 1st ed. ils FC Yohn. VG. M5. $25.00

WIGGIN, Kate Douglas. *New Chronicles of Rebecca.* 1907. Houghton Mifflin. 1st ed. 12mo. pict cloth. VG. M5. $25.00

WIGGIN, Kate Douglas. *Old Peabody Pew.* 1907. Boston. 1st ed. ils Alice Stephens. gilt cloth. G. A17. $10.00

WIGGIN, Kate Douglas. *Rebecca of Sunnybrook Farm.* 1903. Houghton Mifflin. 1st ed. F. M19. $175.00

WIGGIN, Kate Douglas. *Romance of a Christmas Card.* 1916. Houghton Mifflin. 1st ed. ils Alice Ercle Hunt. 124p. VG+. M20. $50.00

WIGGINS, Marianne. *Bet They'll Miss Us When We're Gone.* 1991. Harper Collins. 1st ed. sgn. F/F. B4. $65.00

WILBER, Donald N. *Riza Shah Pahlavi. Resurrection & Reconstruction of Iran.* 1975. NY. Exposition. 1st ed. 301p. VG/dj. W1. $24.00

WILBUR, Richard. *Analekta 1924-1954.* June 1954. Amherst. anthology. sgn. NF. V1. $35.00

WILBUR, Richard. *Ceremony & Other Poems.* 1950. NY. 1st ed. VG/VG. B5. $90.00

WILBUR, Richard. *Tartuffe.* 1964. London. Faber. trans/sgn Wilbur. F/NF. V1. $50.00

WILBUR, Richard. *Walking To Sleep.* 1969. Harcourt Brace. 1st ed. sgn. F/NF. V1. $45.00

WILCOX, Ella Wheeler. *Worlds & I.* 1918. NY. Doran. VG/VG. B5. $40.00

WILCOX, James. *Modern Baptists.* 1983. Dial. 1st ed. F/F. B4. $100.00

WILDE, Kelley. *Makoto.* 1990. Tor. 1st ed. author's 2nd novel. rem mk. NF/VG. G10. $7.50

WILDE, Oscar. *Birthday of the Infanta & Other Tales.* 1982. Atheneum. 1st Am ed. 4to. 73p. red cloth. F/F. C14. $18.00

WILDE, Oscar. *Happy Prince & Other Tales.* 1940. Winston. 1st ed thus. 148p. VG/G. P2. $38.00

WILDE, Oscar. *Happy Prince.* 1968. Feltham, Middlesex. Paul Hamlyn. 1st ed thus. F/NF. C8. $40.00

WILDE, Oscar. *Happy Prince.* 1980. Oxford. 1st ed thus. ils Jean Claverie. NF. C8. $40.00

WILDE, Oscar. *House of Pomegranates.* nd. Brentano. ils Jessie King/16 pl. expert rebacked. VG. P2. $400.00

WILDE, Oscar. *Salome.* 1938. NY. LEC. 2 vol. 1/1500. ils/sgn Derain. F/glassine/case. B24. $450.00

WILDER, Gerrit Parmile. *Fruits of the Hawaiian Islands.* 1911 (1906). Honolulu. revised ed. 247p. tan buckram/red leather label. B26. $75.00

WILDER, Laura Ingalls. *Little House in the Big Woods.* 1953. Harper. 1st ed thus. ils Garth Williams. VG/G. M5. $40.00

WILDER, Laura Ingalls. *Little House on the Prairie.* 1953 (1935). NY. 12mo. 335p. F/clip. H3. $45.00

WILDER, Laura Ingalls. *West From Home, Letters of Wilder, San Francisco 1915.* 1915. Harper Row. 1st ed. 8vo. VG/VG. B17. $12.50

WILDER, Louise B. *Garden in Color.* 1937. NY. 327p. cloth. B26. $27.50

WILDER, Louise B. *My Garden.* 1916. Garden City. 1st ed. 308p. decor cloth. B26. $27.50

WILDER, Thornton. *Bridge of San Luis Rey.* 1929. NY. 1st ed thus. sgn. ils/sgn Rockwell Kent. VG+/case. C6. $200.00

WILDER, Thornton. *Ides of March.* 1948. Harper. 1st ed. F/F. M19. $75.00

WILDER, Thornton. *Ides of March.* 1948. Harper. 1st ed. 8vo. F/NF. T10. $50.00

WILDER, Thornton. *Woman of Andros.* 1930. Boni. 1st ed. F/VG. M19. $75.00

WILDES, Newlin. *Horse That Had Everything.* 1966. Rand McNally. 1st prt. VG. O3. $10.00

WILDING, Suzanne. *Horse Tales.* 1976. St Martin. 1st ed. VG/G. O3. $22.00

WILDMANN, Otto. *Preliminary Catalog of Birds of Missouri.* 1907. St Louis Acad Science. 288p. VG. A10. $45.00

WILDSMITH, Brian. *Brian Wildsmith's Puzzles.* 1971. Franklin Watts. 1st Am ed. ils. unp. G+. C14. $10.00

WILDSMITH, Brian. *Python's Party.* 1974. Watts. 2nd. 4to. ils. VG/VG. B17. $6.50

WILEY, Bell Irvin. *Plain People of the Confederacy.* 1943. LA U. ARC. 104p. NF/VG. M8. $85.00

WILEY, Bell Irvin. *Role of the Archivist in the Civil War Centennial.* ca 1960. np. author's offprint. F/prt wrp. M8. $22.50

WILEY, George E. *Plantation Tales.* 1906. Broadway. ils WL Hudson. 157p. VG-. B10. $50.00

WILEY, Harvey W. *Foods & their Adulterations.* 1907. Phil. 11 pl. 625p. red cloth. NF. B14. $200.00

WILEY. *Life of Johnny Reb: Common Soldier of the Confederacy.* 1992. LSU. 8vo. ils. 444p. VG. T3. $10.00

WILHELM, Kate. *More Bitter Than Death.* 1963. Simon Schuster. 1st ed. author's 1st book. xl. G/VG. N4. $35.00

WILHELM, Kate. *Seven Kinds of Death.* 1992. St Martin. 1st ed. AN/NF. N4. $25.00

WILHELM, W. *Last Rig to Battle Mountain.* 1970. NY. 1st ed. VG/VG. B5. $40.00

WILHELMASON, Carl. *Speed of the Reindeer.* 1954. Viking. 1st ed. ils R Busoni. 220p. F/NF. P2. $25.00

WILHELMY, Herbert. *Kartographie in Stichworten.* 1966. Kiel. Hirt. 4 vol. ils. F/wrp. O7. $35.00

WILKES, J.J. *History of Province of Roman Empire.* 1969. Cambridge. Harvard. 1st ed. 4to. ils. VG. W1. $45.00

WILKIN, Eloise. *Busy ABC.* 1950. Whitman. 8vo. VG. M5. $32.00

WILKINS, Mary E. *New England Nun & Other Stories.* 1891. Harper. 12mo. 468p. gilt bl cloth. reading copy. T10. $25.00

WILKINS. *First & Early American Editions of Works of Charles Dickens.* 1968. np. ils. 51p. F. A4. $85.00

WILKINSON, Alan C. *Drawings of Henry Moore.* 1977. Tate Gallery. ils. 157p. VG. D2. $45.00

WILKINSON, Helen Hunscher. *Gates Mills & a History of Its Village Church.* 1955. Gates Mills. 1st ed. sgn. ils. 123p. VG/dj. B18. $22.50

WILKINSON. *Bibliography of Pennsylvania History.* 1957. np. 2nd. 856p. VG. A4. $85.00

WILKS, A.S. *Handbook of Solo Whist.* 1898. NY. 204p. VG. S1. $20.00

WILLAN, Robert. *On Vaccine Inoculation.* 1806. London. 2 hand-colored pl. 108p. contemporary bdg. B14. $900.00

WILLARD, Barbara. *Surprise Land.* 1966. Meredith. 1st ed. 8vo. 110p. xl. VG. T5. $12.00

WILLARD, Nancy. *Simple Pictures Are Best.* 1977. HBJ. 1st ed/2nd prt. 4to. unp. wht brd. VG+/VG. T5. $25.00

WILLARD, Nancy. *Sister Water.* 1993. Knopf. 1st ed. rem mk. F/F. G10. $25.00

WILLARD, Nancy. *Visit to William Blakes Inn.* nd. London. Methuen. possible 1st Eng ed. 4to. 45p. VG/dj. C14. $25.00

WILLARD, Sylvester D. *Report on the Condition of the County Poor Houses of NY.* 1865. Albany. 8vo. 70p. G/prt wrp. B14. $175.00

WILLCOCKS, Tim. *Green River Rising.* 1994. Morrow. ARC. author's 1st book. F/wrp. S9. $25.00

WILLCOX, Faith Mellen. *In Morocco: Travelers in a New & Ancient Land.* 1971. HBJ. 1st ed. 8vo. 16 pl/double-p map. 295p. VG/dj. W1. $18.00

WILLCOX. *Rock Art of Africa.* 1984. Holmes Meier. VG/VG. D2. $70.00

WILLE, Jeurg. *Benno Achenbach.* 1991. Switzerland. Iska. 104p. VG+. O3. $45.00

WILLEFORD, Charles. *Burnt Orange Heresy.* 1971. Crown. ARC/1st ed. RS. F/F. A11. $235.00

WILLEFORD, Charles. *High Priest of California.* 1953. NY. Universal Pub. 1st ed. author's 1st novel. NF/VG wrp. A11. $225.00

WILLEFORD, Charles. *Proletarian Laughter.* 1948. Alicat. 1st ed. author's 1st book. NF. M19. $150.00

WILLEFORD, Charles. *Shark-Infested Custard.* 1993. Underwood Miller. 1st ed. F/F. T2. $25.00

WILLEFORD, Charles. *Sideswipe.* 1987. St Martin. 1st ed. F/F. M19/T2. $25.00

WILLEFORD, Charles. *Something About a Soldier.* 1986. Random. 1st ed. F/F. T2. $40.00

WILLEFORD, Charles. *Something About a Soldier.* 1986. Random. 1st ed. NF/F. H11. $35.00

WILLEFORD, Charles. *Way We Die Now.* 1988. Random. 1st ed. F/F. M22. $40.00

WILLEFORD, Charles. *Way We Die Now.* 1988. Random. 1st ed. F/NF. T2. $30.00

WILLEFORD, Charles. *Way We Die Now.* 1988. Random. 1st ed/2nd prt. rem mk. F/F. R10. $10.00

WILLEMS, Emilio. *Buzios Island.* 1952. Seattle. 1st ed. 116p. VG. F3. $15.00

WILLETT, John. *Art & Politics in the Weimar Period...* 1978. Pantheon. 1st Am ed. 272p. F. A17. $25.00

WILLEY, Benjamin G. *Incidents in White Mountain History.* 1856. 3rd thousand. ils. G. M17. $50.00

WILLEY, Elizabeth. *Sorcerer & a Gentleman.* 1995. Tor. 1st ed. author's 2nd novel. AN/dj. M22. $15.00

WILLIAMS, Alan. *Presence.* 1983. Knopf. 1st ed. F/NF. V1. $10.00

WILLIAMS, Beryl. *Young Faces in Fashion.* 1956. Phil. Lippincott. VG. D2. $15.00

WILLIAMS, C.K. *Poems 1963-1983.* 1988. FSG. 1st ed. F/F. V1. $20.00

WILLIAMS, C.K. *Women of Trachis.* 1978. Oxford. 1st ed. trans Williams/Dickerson. F/NF. V1. $20.00

WILLIAMS, Caroline. *Cincinnati Scenes.* 1966. Doubleday. 1st ed. sgn. VG/VG. B11. $28.00

WILLIAMS, Charles Richard. *Life of Rutherford Birchard Hayes.* 1914. Houghton Mifflin. 2 vol. 1st ed. VG+. M20. $85.00

WILLIAMS, Charles. *All Hallows' Eve.* 1948. Pellegrini Cudahy. 2nd. 8vo. 273p. F/dj. T10. $35.00

WILLIAMS, Charles. *Big Bite.* 1956. Dell. 1st ed. NF. B4. $85.00

WILLIAMS, Charles. *Place of the Lion.* 1952. London. Faber. 1st ed/2nd prt. 12mo. gilt red cloth. F/NF. T10. $125.00

WILLIAMS, David A. *David C Broderick: a Political Portrait.* 1969. San Marino. Huntington Lib. 1st ed. 274p. F/dj. P4. $20.00

WILLIAMS, Florence White. *Tadwinkle Twins.* ca 1920s. Saalfield. ils Williams. VG. M5. $45.00

WILLIAMS, Garth. *My Bedtime Book.* 1973. Golden. rth. 4to. unp. VG+. C14. $20.00

WILLIAMS, George. *Bullet & Shell: War As the Soldiers Saw It...* 1882. NY. 1st ed. 454p. A13. $150.00

WILLIAMS, Gordon. *Pomeroy.* 1982. Arbor. 1st ed. F/NF. H11. $25.00

WILLIAMS, H. *Geologic Observations on the Ancient Human Footprints...* 1952. np. wrp. F3. $25.00

WILLIAMS, Henry T. *Ladies' Complete Manual of Home Duties.* 1885. NY. G+. M17. $40.00

WILLIAMS, Iolo. *Points in 18th-Century Verse.* 1934. np. 1/500. VG. A4. $165.00

WILLIAMS, J.G. *Field Guide to Birds of East & Central Africa.* 1967. London. Collins. 3rd. 12mo. 459p. cloth. dj. B1. $25.00

WILLIAMS, J.H. *Bandoola: True Story of Lifelong Loyalty...* 1954. Doubleday. 1st ed. 254p. cloth. VG+/dj. B22. $6.50

WILLIAMS, J.R. *Bull of the Woods.* 1944. NY. VG/VG. B5. $40.00

WILLIAMS, J.R. *Cowboys Out Our Way.* 1951. NY. 1st ed. VG/VG. B5. $85.00

WILLIAMS, J.R. *Out Our Way.* 1943. NY. 1st ed. cartoons. F/VG. w/sgn card. H3. $150.00

WILLIAMS, J.R. *Redrawn by Request.* 1955. NY. 1st ed. 8vo. cartoon ils. yel stp blk cloth. 2 djs. H3/P3. $150.00

WILLIAMS, J.X. (some); see Offutt, Andrew.

WILLIAMS, Jay. *Battle for the Atlantic.* 1959. NY. 1st prt. 178p. A17. $6.00

WILLIAMS, Joan. *Pay the Piper.* 1988. Dutton. 1st ed. sgn. F/NF. B4. $65.00

WILLIAMS, John. *Agustus.* 1972. Viking. 1st ed. F/clip. A20. $32.00

WILLIAMS, John. *Butcher's Crossing.* 1960. Macmillan. 1st ed. F/VG+. A18. $35.00

WILLIAMS, John. *Dr John Williams' Last Legacy to People of the US...* 1811. Prt for Author. 1st ed. 12mo. 28p. 87 homeopathic cures. VG/case. T10. $500.00

WILLIAMS, Joy. *Taking Care.* 1982. Random. 1st ed. F/F. M23. $20.00

WILLIAMS, Judith R. *Youth of Hadouch el Harimi.* 1968. Harvard. 1st ed. 8vo. ils. 146p. VG/wrp. W1. $12.00

WILLIAMS, M. *Velveteen Rabbit.* 1983. Holt. 13th. ils Michael Hague. F/VG. B17. $9.00

WILLIAMS, Martin. *Jazz Panorama.* 1962. Crowell Collier. 1st ed. NF/NF. B2. $65.00

WILLIAMS, Mona. *Voices in the Dark.* 1968. Doubleday. 1st ed. F/NF. V1. $15.00

WILLIAMS, Philip Lee. *Slow Dance in Autumn.* 1988. Atlanta. Peechtree. 1st ed. rem mk. F/F. H11. $30.00

WILLIAMS, Ralph. *United States Public Health Service 1798-1950.* 1951. WA. inscr/dtd 1951. ils. 890p. VG. B14. $60.00

WILLIAMS, Roger Q. *To the Moon & Halfway Back.* 1949. San Angelo, TX. Newsfoto. 1st/ltd ed. sgn. 4to. 282p. VG/G. B11. $50.00

WILLIAMS, Sherley Anne. *Dessa Rose.* 1986. Morrow. 1st ed. sgn. F/F. B4. $45.00

WILLIAMS, Stephen. *American Medical Biography; or, Memoirs...* 1854. Greenfield. 1st ed. 664p. A13. $175.00

WILLIAMS, T. Harry. *Huey Long.* 1970. Knopf. BC. 5th. 884p. VG/VG. B10. $12.00

WILLIAMS, Tennessee. *Cat on a Hot Tin Roof.* 1956. London. Secker Warburg. 1st ed. 8vo. NF/dj. S9. $30.00

WILLIAMS, Tennessee. *Milk Train Doesn't Stop Here Anymore.* 1951. Norfolk. 1st ed. F/F. C2. $275.00

WILLIAMS, Tennessee. *Roman Spring of Mrs Stone.* 1950. New Directions. 1st ed. author's 1st novel. inscr. F/rpr dj. B24. $375.00

WILLIAMS, Tennessee. *Steps Must Be Gentle.* 1980. NY. 1/350. sgn. F/F. C2. $200.00

WILLIAMS, Tennessee. *Two Plays: Summer & Smoke; Eccentricities of a Nightingale.* 1964. 1st ed. MTI. VG+/VG. S13. $35.00

WILLIAMS, Walter Jon. *Angel Station.* 1989. NY. Tor. 1st ed. sgn. ES. F/F. T2. $30.00

WILLIAMS, Walter Jon. *Aristoi.* 1992. NY. Tor. 1st ed. F/F. T2. $20.00

WILLIAMS, Walter Jon. *Facets.* 1990. NY. Tor. 1st ed. sgn. F/F. T2. $25.00

WILLIAMS, Walter Jon. *Hardwired.* 1986. NY. Tor. 1st ed. sgn. F/F. T2. $35.00

WILLIAMS, Walter Jon. *Voice of the Whirlwind.* 1987. NY. Tor. 1st ed. sgn. F/F. T2. $30.00

WILLIAMS, William Carlos. *Collected Later Poems of William Carlos Williams.* 1950. New Directions. 1st ed. 1/50 for Horace Mann School. sgn. F/cb case. B4. $1,500.00

WILLIAMS, William Carlos. *Desert Music & Other Poems.* 1954. Random/Spiral. 1st ed. 1/100. sgn. NF/tissue dj/cb case. B4. $1,500.00

WILLIAMS, William Carlos. *In the Money. White Mule Part II.* 1940. Norfolk. ARC/1st ed. NF/NF. C2. $100.00

WILLIAMS, William Carlos. *Poems of..., a Critical Study.* 1964. Wesleyan. 1st ed. assn copy. F/NF. V1. $30.00

WILLIAMS, William Carlos. *Selected Letters With James Laughlin.* 1989. Norton. 1st ed. edit Hugh Witemeyer. NF/NF. V1. $20.00

WILLIAMS, William Carlos. *Wedge.* 1944. Cummington. 1st ed. 1/380. F/VG glassine. C6. $500.00

WILLIAMS, William Carlos. *White Mule.* 1937. Norfolk. New Directions. 1st ed. wht cloth. F/NF. B24. $250.00

WILLIAMS. *Biograhical Dictionary of Scientists.* 1969. np. 592p. F/VG. A4. $65.00

WILLIAMS. *Dictionary of Homographs.* 1992. np. 144p. F/F. A4. $35.00

WILLIAMS. *Early English Watercolours & Some Cognate Drawings...* 1970. Kingsmead. rpt. F/F. D2. $50.00

WILLIAMS. *Pan Books 1945-1966, a Bibliographical Checklist...* 1990. np. 1/200. 72p. F/wrp. A4. $75.00

WILLIAMSON, Alan. *Muse of Distance.* 1988. Knopf. 1st ed. F/F. w/promo sheet. V1. $15.00

WILLIAMSON, E.M. *Confederate Reminiscences.* 1935. Danville, VA. McDaniel Prt. 1st ed. 39p. xl. NF. M8. $750.00

WILLIAMSON, J.N. *Bloodlines.* nd. Longmeadow. UP. NF/prt wrp. M22. $15.00

WILLIAMSON, J.N. *Masques IV.* 1991. Maclay. 1st ed. 1/750. sgn by 26 (of 27) contributors. F/dj/case. C10. $45.00

WILLIAMSON, J.N. *Masques.* 1984. Maclay. 1st ed. F/NF. R10. $20.00

WILLIAMSON, James J. *Mosby's Rangers...Forty-Third Battalion Virginia Cavalry.* 1982. Time Life. facsimile of 1896 ed. 511p. aeg. F. A17. $25.00

WILLIAMSON, Julia. *Stars Through Magic Casements.* 1931 (1930). Appleton. ils Edna Reindel. 246p. G. K5. $25.00

WILLIAMSON, Robert W. *Essays in Polynesian Ethnology.* 1975. Cooper Sq. facsimile of 1939 ed. 10 pl/2 maps. red cloth. F. T10. $50.00

WILLIAMSON, Robert. *Cruise of the Schooner Driftwood.* 1962. London. Cape. ils. 160p. VG/dj. T7. $18.00

WILLIAMSON, Thomas. *Illustrations of Indian Field Sports.* 1892. Westminster. Constable. 10 chromolithographs. gilt cloth. NF. T10. $100.00

WILLIARD, Nancy. *Visit to William Blake's Inn.* 1981. 1st ed. ils Alice/Martin Provensen. NF/clip. S13. $15.00

WILLINGHAM, C. *Geraldine Bradshaw.* 1950. NY. 1st ed. author's 2nd book. VG+/VG. A15. $35.00

WILLIS, Bailey. *El Norte de la Patagonia: Naturaleza y Riquezas.* 1914. Buenos Aires. 2 vol. ils/maps. teg. F. O7. $375.00

WILLIS, Connie. *Lincoln's Dreams.* 1987. Bantam. 1st ed. F/NF. G10. $50.00

WILLIS, Fritz. *Muffin.* 1945. Cherokee. ils. VG/VG. P2. $45.00

WILLISTON, S.W. *University Geological Survey of Kansas Vol IV. Paleontology.* 1898. 594p. cloth. G. D8. $40.00

WILLISTON, Teresa Pierce. *Japanese Fairy Tales.* 1923 (1904). Rand McNally. ils Sanchi O Gawa. VG-. M5. $20.00

WILLOUGHBY, David. *Empire of Equus.* 1974. Barnes. 1st ed. VG. O3. $25.00

WILLS, Brian Steel. *Battle From the Start: Life of Nathan Bedford Forrest.* 1992. Harper Collins. 1st ed. 457p. F/F. M8. $30.00

WILLS, Garry. *Second Civil War.* 1968. NAL. 169p. VG/VG. R11. $15.00

WILLS, Maury. *How To Steal a Pennant.* 1976. Putnam. 1st ed. F/VG+. P8. $12.50

WILLSON, Dixie. *Honey Bear.* 1923. Algonquin. Sunny Book. 8vo. ils Maginel Wright. VG. M5. $55.00

WILLSON, Dixie. *Pinky Pup & Empty Elephant.* 1928. Volland. 1st combined ed. ils Erick Berry. VG. M5. $40.00

WILLSON, Marcus. *Third Reader of the School & Family Series.* 1860. Harper. 1st ed. ils. VG. M5. $60.00

WILMERDING. *American Views: Essays on American Art.* 1991. F/F. D2. $50.00

WILOCKS, Tim. *Green River Rising.* 1994. Morrow. 1st ed. F/F. H11. $25.00

WILSON, A.N. *Eminent Victorians.* 1989. Norton. 1st Am ed. 4to. ils. F/F. B4. $65.00

WILSON, Barbara Ker. *Willow Pattern Story.* 1981 (1978). Australia. Angus Robertson. ils Lucienne Fontannaz. xl. VG. T5. $20.00

WILSON, Charles L. *World of Terrariums.* 1975. Middle Village. ils/photos. VG/torn. B26. $15.00

WILSON, Charles William. *Picturesque Palestine, Sinai & Egypt.* 1881-1883. Appleton. 1st ed. 480p. aeg. VG/dj. W1. $65.00

WILSON, Colin. *Adrift in Soho.* 1961. Houghton Mifflin. 1st Am ed. F/VG+. B4. $75.00

WILSON, Colin. *Personality Surgeon.* 1986. Mercury House. 1st Am ed. F/F. R10. $20.00

WILSON, Colin. *Strength To Dream: Literature & the Imagination.* 1962. Houghton Mifflin. 1st Am ed. xl. reading copy. R10. $8.00

WILSON, Dorothy Clarke. *Lady Washington.* 1984. Doubleday. 376p. F/G+. B10. $12.00

WILSON, Edmund. *Boys in the Back Room: Notes on California Novelists.* 1941. Colt. 1st ltd ed. 1/1500. NF. A18. $150.00

WILSON, Edmund. *Forties.* 1983. FSG. 1st ed. F/F. B35. $25.00

WILSON, Edmund. *Patriotic Gore: Studies in Literature of Am Civil War.* 1962. Oxford. 1st ed. F/VG. B4. $65.00

WILSON, Edmund. *Shock of Recognition.* 1955. NY. 1st revised ed. ils Robert Hallock. F/tape rpr. A17. $20.00

WILSON, Edmund. *Upstate.* 1971. NY. 1st ed. F/F. A17. $20.00

WILSON, Edward. *Pirate's Treasure.* 1926. Volland. 1st ed. ils Edward Wilson. unp. VG/torn box. D1. $95.00

WILSON, Ella Grant. *Famous Old Euclid Avenue of Cleveland, Ohio. Vol 2.* 1937. Wilson. 8vo. assoc copy. 265p. VG. H4. $40.00

WILSON, Ernest H. *Aristocats of the Trees.* 1930. Boston. 1st ed. 279p. VG. B5. $60.00

WILSON, Ernest H. *More Aristocrats of the Garden.* 1928. Boston. 1st ed. 288p. VG. B5. $45.00

WILSON, F. Paul. *Black Wind.* 1988. Tor. 1st ed. F/F. H11. $25.00

WILSON, F.W. *Kansas Landscapes: A Geologic Diary.* 1978. KS Geological Survey. 50p. VG. D8. $5.00

WILSON, Frazier Ells. *Advancing the Ohio Frontier.* 1937. Blanchester, OH. 1st ed. 124p. xl. VG. B18. $17.50

WILSON, H.W. *Battleships in Action.* nd. London. Sampson Low. 2 vol. 19 tables/22 pl/22 plans. VG. T7. $140.00

WILSON, Harriette. *Memoirs of...* 1924. London. 2 vol. teg. VG/dj. B18. $35.00

WILSON, Harry Leon. *Ruggles of Red Gap.* 1915. Garden City. 1st ed. NF. N3. $35.00

WILSON, Hugh D. *Wild Plants of Mt Cook National Park.* 1978. Christchurch. ils. 294p. sc. B26. $17.50

WILSON, James. *Rod & Gun, Being Two Treatises on Angling & Shooting.* 1840. Adam & Chas Black. sgn. ils. fair. B11. $50.00

WILSON, Margaret. *Kenworthys.* 1925. Harper. 1st ed. author's 2nd novel. F/VG. B4. $125.00

WILSON, Marjorie. *Children's Rhymes of Travel.* 1924. Boston/NY. Houghton Mifflin. possible 1st ed. 56p. VG/VG. C14. $20.00

WILSON, Richard L. *Art of Ogata Kenzan: Persona & Production...* 1991. Weatherhill. 1st ed. 271p. F/dj. A17. $30.00

WILSON, Robert. *Modern Book Collecting.* 1980. np. ils. 286p. F/NF. A4. $55.00

WILSON, Sloan. *Man in the Gray Flannel Suit II.* 1984. Arbor. 1st ed. F/F. B35. $18.00

WILSON, Sloan. *Man in the Gray Flannel Suit II.* 1984. Arbor. 1st ed. sgn. VG/VG. B11. $40.00

WILSON, Violet. *Coaching Era.* nd. Dutton. 1st Am ed. VG. O3. $58.00

WILSON, Warren. *Rediscovery of Jerusalem.* 1872. Appleton. 8vo. 435p. xl. G. W1. $45.00

WILSON, Winifred. *Playground & Indoor Games for Boys & Girls.* ca 1900. London. Brn. 142p. gr cloth. VG. D1. $95.00

WILSTACH, Paul. *Hudson River Landing.* 1933. Bobbs Merrill. 1st ed. ils. 311p. VG. T7. $40.00

WILSTACH, Paul. *Tidewater Maryland.* 1945 (1931). Tudor. photos. VG/G. B10. $15.00

WINBERGER, Bernhard Wolf. *Introduction to History of Dentistry.* 1948. St Louis. 2 vol. ils. red cloth. F. B14. $500.00

WINCHELL, Alexander. *Preadamites; or, Demonstration of the Existence of Men...* 1880. Chicago. ils/woodblocks/maps. VG. B14. $125.00

WINCHESTER, Clarence. *Shipping Wonders of the World.* 1936-1937. London. Amalgamated. 2 vol. 28 pl/40 plans/photos. VG. T7. $120.00

WINCHESTER, Elhanan. *Lectures on the Prophecies.* 1800. Walpole. rebound. V4. $60.00

WINDHAM, William. *Speech...Delivered in the House of Commons...1801...* 1801. London. Cobbett Morgan. new quarter calf. M11. $650.00

WINEGARDNER, Mark. *Prophet of the Sandlots.* 1990. Atlantic Monthly. 1st ed. F/clip. M23. $20.00

WINEGARDNER, Mark. *Prophet of the Sandlots.* 1990. Atlantic Monthly. 1st ed. F/F. P8. $25.00

WINER, Paul. *Among Five Miles of Country Road.* 1967. Vermont Stoveside Pr. 2nd. sgn. 12mo. 40p. VG/stiff wrp. B11. $10.00

WINFIELD, Arthur M. *Rover Boys in Camp (#8).* 1904. Grosset Dunlap. lists to Fortune. 263p. orange cloth. VG/worn. M20. $30.00

WINFIELD, Arthur M. *Rover Boys on Snowshoe Island (#22).* 1918. Grosset Dunlap. lists to #30. 308p. VG+/dj. M20. $35.00

WINFIELD, Dave. *Winfield: A Player's Life.* 1988. Norton. 1st ed. F/F. P8. $35.00

WING, Camilla. *Talking Milstones.* 1945. Pillsbury. 1st ed. 8vo. VG. M5. $22.00

WINGROVE, David. *Broken Wheel.* 1991. Delacorte. 1st ed. F/F. H11. $25.00

WINGROVE, David. *Chung Kuo.* 1990. Delacorte. 1st ed. F/NF. H11. $30.00

WINGROVE, David. *White Mountain.* 1992. Delacorte. 1st ed. F/F. H11. $25.00

WINNAN, A.H. *Catalogue Raisonne of Wanda Gag.* nd. Smithsonian. 1st ed. ils/wood engravings/etchings. 315p. F/F. D1. $95.00

WINNICK, R.H. *Letters of Archibald MacLeish 1907-1982.* 1983. Houghton Mifflin. 1st ed. assn copy. F/VG. V1. $35.00

WINNINGTON, Richard. *Film Criticism & Caricatures 1943-1953.* 1976. Barnes Novle. F/F. D2. $20.00

WINOCOUR, Jack. *Story of the Titanic.* 1960. Dover. G/wrp. A16. $10.00

WINSLOW, Anne Goodwin. *Cloudy Trophies.* 1946. Knopf. 1st ed. F/F. B4. $50.00

WINSLOW, Ola. *Destroying Angel: Conquest of Smallpox in Colonial Boston.* 1974. Boston. 1st ed. 137p. dj. A13. $27.50

WINSOR, Frederick. *Space Child's Mother Goose.* 1958. Simon Schuster. 1st ed. ils Marian Parry. 45p. NF/VG. P2. $50.00

WINSOR, Justin. *Memorial History of Boston 1630-1880.* 1881. Osbood. vol 4 of 4. ils. G. P12. $18.00

WINSTEDT, Richard. *Malaya & Its History.* 1951. London. Hutchinson. map/index. 158p. F. B14. $35.00

WINSTON, Richard. *Thomas Beckett.* 1967. Knopf. 1st ed. 8vo. plan/map/notes/index. NF/NF. T10. $35.00

WINTER, Douglas E. *Prime Evil.* 1988. Donald Grant. ltd ed. 1/1000. sgns. F/sans/case. T2. $350.00

WINTER, Douglas E. *Prime Evil.* 1988. NAL. 1st ed. F/dj. N4. $25.00

WINTER, Douglas E. *Prime Evil.* 1988. NAL. 1st trade ed. NF/dj. M21. $20.00

WINTER, Gerald Arthur. *Knight & the Unicorn.* 1989. Todd Honeywell. 1st ed. sgn. w/sgn note. VG/VG. B11. $20.00

WINTER, Milo. *Animal Pets in Picture.* nd. Donohue. lg 4to. ils. F. M5. $30.00

WINTERBURN, George William. *Value of Vaccination...* 1886. Phil. 182p. blk cloth. NF. B14. $150.00

WINTERICH. *Lantern Slides: Books, Book Trade, Some Related Phenomena...* 1949. IL U. 125p. VG/VG. A4. $45.00

WINTERS, Nancy. *Talking to Birds.* 1994. Robert Barth. ltd ed. 1/300. Chapbook series. F/wrp. w/card. V1. $25.00

WINTERS, Roy Lutz. *Francis Lambert of Avignon (1487-1530).* 1938. United Lutheren Pub House. 1st ed. sgn. F. B35. $30.00

WINTERS, Yvor. *Anatomy of Nonsense.* 1943. New Directions. 1st ed. 8vo. VG/dj. s9. $25.00

WINTERS, Yvor. *In Defense of Reason.* 1947. New Directions. 1st ed. NF/dj. V1. $20.00

WINTERSON, Jeanette. *Oranges Are Not the Only Fruit.* 1985. Atlantic Monthly. 1st Am ed. AN/wrp. B4. $100.00

WINTERSON, Jeanette. *Passion.* 1987. Atlantic Monthly. 1st Am ed. F/F. C2. $35.00

WINTHER, Sophus Keith. *Take All to Nebraska.* 1936. Macmillan. 1st ed. F/clip VG. A18. $30.00

WINWARD, Walter. *Seven Minutes Past Midnight.* 1980. Simon Schuster. 1st ed. rem mk. VG/VG. N4. $15.00

WIRT, Mildred A. *Brownie Scouts in the Circus.* 1949. Cupples Leon. ils. 212p. F/NF. A17. $8.00

WIRT, Mildred A. *Madge Sterling: Deserted Yacht (#2).* 1932. Goldsmith. 123p. VG/dj. M20. $10.00

WIRT, Mildred A. *Painted Shield.* 1950s. World Jr Lib ed. 207p. VG+/dj. M20. $25.00

WIRT, Mildred A. *Penny Parker: Saboteurs on the River (#9).* 1943. Cupples Leon. lists 10 titles. 211p. red cloth. VG/dj. M20. $30.00

WIRT, Mildred A. *Penny Parker: The Vanishing Houseboat (#2).* 1939. Cupples Leon. lists 6 titles. 204p. VG/dj. M20. $42.00

WIRT, Mildred A. *Penny Parker: Wishing Well (#8).* 1942. Cupples Leon. 1st ed. 206p. VG/dj. M20. $52.00

WIRT, Mildred A. *Sky Racers.* 1940. Books Inc. 224p. VG+/dj. M20. $40.00

WISE, Jennings C. *On the Way to Perignan.* 1937. Paisley. 1st ed. inscr. 251p. G/G. w/inscr photo. B10. $35.00

WISE, John. *Through the Air: Narrative of 40-Years Experience...* 1873. Phil. woodcuts. 650p. gilt cloth/new spine & ep. G. B18. $350.00

WISSLER, Clark. *American Indian.* 1938. Oxford. 3rd. 8vo. ils/maps. cloth. VG. T10. $55.00

WISTER, Stanley. *Dark Dreamers: Conversations With Masters or Horror.* 1990. Underwood Miller. 1st ed. 1/350. sgn Wiester & interviewees. F/case. T2. $350.00

WITHNER, Carl L. *Cattleyas & Their Relatives.* 1990. Portland. 87 photos. 154p. VG/dj. B26. $32.50

WITKIN, Joel-Peter. *Gods of Earth & Heaven.* 1989. Twelvetrees. 4to. 52 duotone pl. w/sgn letter. F/case. S9. $500.00

WITKIN, Lee D. *Photograph Collector's Guide.* 1979. Boston. 4to. 438p. red cloth. G. T3. $22.00

WITKOWSKI, Walt. *Civil War Trivia.* 1987. Boston. 12mo. 184p. VG. T3. $10.00

WITMAN, Mabel. *Golden Book of Flowers.* 1944 (1943). Simon Schuster. 2nd. bl cloth. VG. M5. $12.00

WODEHOUSE, P.G. *Angel Cake.* 1952. Doubleday. 1st ed. 8vo. F/VG. T10. $100.00

WODEHOUSE, P.G. *Binkley Manor: A Novel About Jeeves.* Oct 1934. Little Brn. 1st Am ed. NF. H4. $40.00

WODEHOUSE, P.G. *Catnappers.* 1974. Simon Schuster. 1st Am ed. 190p. VG/dj. M20. $25.00

WODEHOUSE, P.G. *Girl in Blue.* 1971. Simon Schuster. 1st ed. VG+/dj. M21. $40.00

WODEHOUSE, P.G. *Intrusion of Jimmy.* 1910. NY. 1st ed. VG. C6. $250.00

WODEHOUSE, P.G. *Jeeves & the Tie That Binds.* 1971. Simon Schuster. 1st ed. 189p. cloth. dj. M20. $52.00

WODEHOUSE, P.G. *Little Nugget.* 1941. NY. 1st Am ed. NF. C6. $225.00

WODEHOUSE, P.G. *Nothing But Wodehouse.* nd. NY. edit Ogden Nash. 1200p. G. A17. $12.50

WODEHOUSE, P.G. *Sam in the Suburbs.* 1925. Doran. 1st ed. 346p. gr cloth. VG. M20. $125.00

WODEHOUSE, P.G. *Wodehouse Nuggets.* 1983. London. 231p. F/F. A4. $25.00

WOIWODE, Larry. *Born Brothers.* 1988. FSG. 1st ed. F/VG. A20. $24.00

WOIWODE, Larry. *Even Tide.* 1977. FSG. 1st ed. F/NF. V1. $20.00

WOLF, Edwin. *Rosenbach.* 1960. 1st ed. VG/VG. S13. $25.00

WOLFE, Aaron; see Koontz, Dean R.

WOLFE, Don. *Purple Testament: Life Stories of Disabled Veterans.* 1946. Stackpole. 1st ed. 361p. dj. A17. $8.00

WOLFE, Edward C. *Play of the Cards at Contract Bridge.* 1932. Phil. 251p. VG. S1. $8.00

WOLFE, Gene. *Gene Wolfe's Book of Days.* 1981. Doubleday. 1st ed. VG+/dj. M21. $30.00

WOLFE, Gene. *Soldier of the Mist.* 1986. Tor. 1st ed. rem mk. F/F. G10. $25.00

WOLFE, Richard J. *Marbled Paper: Its History, Techniques & Patterns.* 1990. Phil. PA U. 1st ed. 4to. 245p. AN/dj. T10. $135.00

WOLFE, Thomas. *From Death to Morning.* 1935. Scribner. 1st ed/1st prt (A on c p). NF/clip. B24. $200.00

WOLFE, Thomas. *Hills Beyond.* 1941. NY. 1st ed. VG/VG. B5. $60.00

WOLFE, Thomas. *Look Homeward, Angel.* 1929. NY. Scribner. 1st ed. author's 1st book. bl cloth. F/dj. B24. $750.00

WOLFE, Thomas. *Look Homeward, Angel.* 1929. Scribner. 1st ed. inscr/dtd 1935. F/NF. C2. $4,000.00

WOLFE, Thomas. *Mannerhouse.* 1948. NY. 1/500. VG/VG. B5. $90.00

WOLFE, Thomas. *Note on Experts: Dexter Vespasian Joyner.* 1939. House of Books. 1st ed. 1/300. gilt brn cloth. F. B24. $275.00

WOLFE, Thomas. *Stone, a Leaf, a Door.* 1945. NY. 1st ed. VG/VG. B5. $50.00

WOLFE, Thomas. *Story of a Novel.* 1936. NY. 1st ed. VG/VG. B5. $60.00

WOLFE, Thomas. *Story of a Novel.* 1936. Scribner. 1st ed. F/NF. B2. $85.00

WOLFE, Thomas. *Web & the Rock.* 1939. Harper. 1st ed. 695p. VG. B10. $35.00

WOLFE, Thomas. *Welcome to Our City.* 1983. LSU. 1st ed. F/F. B4. $85.00

WOLFE, Thomas. *You Can't Go Home Again.* 1940. Harper. 1st ed. bl cloth. F. B24. $150.00

WOLFE, Tom. *Bonfire of the Vanities.* 1987. FSG. 1st ed. F/F. H11/N4. $35.00

WOLFE, Tom. *Electric Kool-Aid Acid Test.* 1968. FSG. 1st ed. F/clip. B4. $225.00

WOLFE, Tom. *Kandy-Kolored Tangerine-Flake Streamline Baby.* 1965. FSG. 1st ed. F/F clip. B4. $300.00

WOLFE, Tom. *Mauve Gloves & Madmen, Clutter & Vine.* 1976. FSG. 1st ed. F/F. H11. $50.00

WOLFE, Tom. *Painted Word.* 1975. NY. 1st ed. inscr. NF/NF. C6. $100.00

WOLFE, Virginia. *Contemporary Writers.* 1965. HBW. ARC/1st ed. 8vo. RS. F/dj. S9. $35.00

WOLFERT, Ira. *Battle for the Solomons, Oct-Nov 1942.* 1943. Boston. 1st ed. 200p. map ep. dj. A17. $9.50

WOLFF, Geoffrey. *Final Club.* 1990. Knopf. 1st ed. F/F. B35. $20.00

WOLFF, Geoffrey. *Inklings.* 1978. Random. 1st ed. F/F. B35. $25.00

WOLFF, Tobias. *In Pharaoh's Army.* 1994. Knopf. 1st ed. sgn. F/dj. S9. $60.00

WOLFF. *Nineteenth-Century Fiction, a Bibliographical Catalogue...* 1981-1986. 5 vol. ils. 1610p. F. A4. $950.00

WOLFRAM, Herwig. *History of the Goths.* 1988. CA U. 1st Am ed. ils/maps. 613p. VG/dj. W1. $25.00

WOLLHEIM, Donald A. *Men From Ariel.* 1982. NESFA. 1st ed. 1/1200. #d. F/F. G10. $15.00

WOLLHEIM, Donald A. *Operation Phantasy: Best From the Phantagraph.* 1967. Rego Park. Phantagraph. 1st ed. 1/420. sgn. F/F. T2. $50.00

WOLLS, William. *Plants of New South Wales...* 1885. Sydney. 121p. wrp. B26. $29.00

WOLSELEY, Garnet Joseph. *Story of a Soldier's Life.* 1903. Westminister. Archibald Constable. 2 vol. 1st ed. cloth. NF. M8. $275.00

WOLSTENHOLME, G.E.W. *Royal College of Physicians of London. Portraits, Catalog 2.* 1977. Amsterdam. 1st ed. 239p. A13. $20.00

WOMACK, Bob. *Echo of Hoofbeats.* 1973. Walking Horse Pub. pres. VG/G. O3. $185.00

WOMACK, Jack. *Ambient.* 1987. NY. Weidenfeld Nicolson. 1st ed. 8vo. F/dj. S9. $45.00

WONDERING, Imgaard. *Art of Egypt: Time of the Pharoahs.* 1963. Greystone. 1st ed. 8vo. ils/pl. 256p. VG/dj. W1. $12.00

WOOD, C.F. *Yachting Cruise in the South Seas.* 1875. London. King. 221p. VG. T7. $70.00

WOOD, Casey. *Introduction to Literature of Vertebrate Zoology...* nd. rpt of 1931 ed. 1/300. 4to. F. A4. $125.00

WOOD, F.W. *Six Years a Priest & a Decade a Protestant.* 1876. Cleveland. Crocker's Pub. 289p. G. B18. $27.50

WOOD, H. *Intellectual Pup, Extracts From His Diary.* 1908. Dillingham. 12mo. G+. B17. $10.00

WOOD, J.G. *Common Objects of the Country.* 1866. London. Routledge. ils/pl. 182p. gilt bl cloth. F. B14. $65.00

WOOD, J.G. *Lane & Field.* 1889. London. SPCK. 12mo. ils. 246p. F. T10. $100.00

WOOD, Lawson. *Lawson Wood's Animal Book.* 1936. Racine. 4to. stiff wrp. T10. $50.00

WOOD, Michael. *In Search of the Trojan War.* 1985. NY/Oxford. Facts on File. 1st ed. 8vo. ils. 272p. VG/dj. W1. $22.00

WOOD, Robert Williams. *How To Tell the Birds From the Flowers.* 1938 (1917). Dodd Mead. ils. VG+/dj. M5. $20.00

WOOD, Rosa Aubrey. *Banjo & Pistols: Tale of the Blue Ridge.* 1929. McBride. 228p. VG. B10. $25.00

WOOD, S. *Over the Range to the Golden Gate.* 1891. Chicago. 8vo. ils. 351p. brn cloth. G. T3. $39.99

WOOD, Samuel. *Infancy.* ca 1820. NY. Wood. 8 wood engravings. F. B24. $110.00

WOOD, Ted. *Corkscrew.* 1987. London. Collins. 1st ed. 245p. VG/dj. M20. $20.00

WOOD, Theodore. *Natural History for Young People.* late 1800s. London/NY. 12 chromolithographs/ils. VG. M17. $60.00

WOOD, William P. *Gangland.* 1988. NY. 1st ed. F/F. H11. $25.00

WOOD. *Of Lasting Interest: Story of Reader's Digest.* 1958. np. 32 pl. NF/G. A4. $35.00

WOOD. *Power of Maps.* 1992. np. ils/248p. F/wrp. A4. $17.00

WOODALL, Sally Lee. *Animal ABC.* 1946. US Camera. 8vo. ils. VG. M5. $20.00

WOODARD, David. *Art & Cartography: Six Historical Essays.* 1987. Chicago. 4to. 34 pl/193 halftones. 249p. F/dj. O7. $65.00

WOODARD, David. *Five Centuries of Map Printing.* 1975. Chicago. 65 maps. F/dj. O7. $55.00

WOODARD, Lt., M.D. see Silverberg, Robert.

WOODBURY, George. *Great Days of Piracy in the West Indies.* 1951. Norton. BC. index/biblio. 232p. dj. A17. $7.50

WOODCOTT, Keith; see Brunner, John.

WOODRELL, Daniel. *Ones You Do.* 1992. Holt. 1st ed. F/F. M23. $20.00

WOODRELL, Daniel. *Under the Bright Lights.* 1986. Holt. 1st ed. author's 1st book. F/F. M23. $35.00

WOODS, Jo. *Advanced Bridge Course: Defensive Play.* 1956. np. lg format pb in ring binder. ca 120p. VG. S1. $10.00

WOODS, Jo. *Bridge Teacher's Manual: Basic Course.* nd. np. lg format sbdg pb. VG. S1. $12.00

WOODS, Lawrence M. *British Gentlemen in the Wild West...* 1989. NY. Free Pr. 1st ed. 245p. F/dj. T10. $30.00

WOODS, Robert Archey. *English Social Movements.* 1891. Scribner. 1st ed. inscr. F. B2. $85.00

WOODS, Sara. *Enter Certain Murderers.* 1966. 1st ed. F/F. M19. $17.50

WOODS, Stuart. *Grassroots.* 1989. Simon Schuster. 1st ed. VG+/VG+. A20. $18.00

WOODS, Stuart. *LA Times.* 1993. Harper Collins. 1st ed. F/F. H11. $20.00

WOODS, Stuart. *Palidrome.* 1991. Harper Collins. 1st ed. F/F. A20. $16.00

WOODSON, Carter. *Negro Makers of History.* 1928. ASsoc Pub. G+. B2. $75.00

WOODWARD, Alice. *Goody Two Shoes.* 1924. Macmillan. Little Library series. ils. F/G. M5. $22.00

WOODWARD, Alice. *History of Little Goody Two Shoes.* 1924. Macmillan. 1st ed thus. 12mo. F/G. M5. $38.00

WOODWARD, W.E. *Meet General Grant.* 1928. Literary Guild. 512p. gilt blk cloth. F. B22. $7.00

WOODWARD. *All-American Map, Wax Engraving & Its Influence...* 1977. Chicago. ils. 184p. F/F. A4. $35.00

WOOLF, Virginia. *Between the Acts.* 1941. London. Hogarth. 1st ed. bl cloth. NF. B24. $475.00

WOOLF, Virginia. *Common Reader: Second Series.* 1932. London. Hogarth. 1st ed. gr cloth. F/dj. B24. $375.00

WOOLF, Virginia. *Mark on the Wall.* 1919. Hogarth. 1st separate ed. 1/1000. F/wrp. B24. $950.00

WOOLF, Virginia. *Nurse Lugton's Curtain.* 1991. Bodley Head. 1st ed. ils Julie Vivas. F/F. C8. $35.00

WOOLF, Virginia. *Orlando.* 1928. NY. 1/861. sgn. VG. C6. $400.00

WOOLF, Virginia. *Roger Fry: A Biography.* 1940. NY. 1st ed. VG/VG. B5. $50.00

WOOLF, Virginia. *Writer's Diary.* 1954. Harcourt Brace. 1st Am ed. 356p. VG/clip. M20. $52.00

WOOLF, Virginia. *Years.* 1937. Hogarth. 1st ed. jade-gr cloth. F/NF. B24. $425.00

WOOLMAN, John. *Journal of the Life & Service of the Gospel.* 1901. London. 1/250. 16mo. 400p. full vellum. F. B24. $375.00

WOOLRICH, Cornell. *Cover Charge.* 1926. Boni Liveright. 1st ed. VG. A11. $275.00

WOOLRICH, Cornell. *Deadline at Dawn.* 1944. Lippincott. VG. P3. $30.00

WOOLRICH, Cornell. *Deadline at Dawn.* 1946. Tower. hc. MTI. VG. P3. $20.00

WOOLRICH, Cornell. *Night Has a Thousand Eyes.* 1945. Farrar Rinehart. 1st ed. as by George Hopley. VG+/VG. A11. $80.00

WOOLRICH, Cornell. *Nightwebs.* 1971. Harper. 1st ed. edit FM Nevins. F/NF. B4. $200.00

WOOLRICH, Cornell. *Phantom Lady.* 1944. Tower. MTI. VG/VG. P3. $25.00

WOOLSEY, Kit. *Partnership Defense in Bridge.* 1980. Shelbyville. 303p. VG/wrp. S1. $6.00

WOOLVIN, Eleanor K. *Barbie & the Ghost Town Mystery (#11).* nd. np. 180p. VG. M20. $20.00

WORDSWORTH, William. *Prelude.* 1850. London. 1st ed. later Riviere full morocco. VG+. C6. $450.00

WORDSWORTH, William. *Yarrow Revisited & Other Poems.* 1835. Longman Rees Orme Brn Gr. 1st ed. 12mo. w/12-p Longman catalog. NF/case/chemise. B24. $850.00

WORK, Milton C. *Auction Declarations.* 1917. Phil. 288p. VG. S1. $6.00

WORKS, Milton. *Whist of Today.* 1897. Phil. 6th. 201p. VG. S1. $10.00

WORMSER, Baron. *White Words.* 1983. Houghton Mifflin. 1st ed. F/VG+. V1. $10.00

WORRILOW, William H. *James Lick (1796-1876): Pioneer & Adventurer...* 1949. NY. Newcomen Soc of Eng. 2nd. 8vo. 36p. wrp. K5. $25.00

WORSFOLD, W. Basil. *Redemption of Egypt.* 1899. Allen. 1st ed. 333p. xl. W1. $28.00

WORTH, C. Brooke. *Mosquito Safari: A Naturalist in Southern Africa.* 1971. Simon Schuster. 1st prt. 274p. AN/F. P4. $16.00

WOUK, Herman. *Caine Mutiny Court-Martial.* 1954. Doubleday. 1st ed in play form. F/NF. B24. $110.00

WOUK, Herman. *Caine Mutiny.* 1952. Doubleday. 1st ils ed. sgn. NF. w/2 facsimile letters. B4. $150.00

WOUK, Herman. *Inside, Outside.* 1985. Little Brn. 1st ed. w/sgn leaf. F/NF. B2. $50.00

WOUK, Herman. *Winds of War.* 1971. London. Collins. 1st ed. 806p. gray cloth. NF. B22. $7.00

WPA WRITERS PROGRAM. *California: Guide to the Golden State.* 1949. Hastings. 6th. 8vo. 713p. pocket map. red cloth. VG/worn. T10. $15.00

WPA WRITERS PROGRAM. *Nevada: A Guide to the Silver State.* 1940. Portland. 1st ed. F. N3. $35.00

WPA WRITERS PROGRAM. *State Guide to Minnesota.* 1938. NY. 1st ed. map. VG. B5. $50.00

WPA WRITERS PROGRAM. *State Guide to Utah.* 1941. NY. 1st ed. w/pocket map. VG/VG. B5. $62.50

WPA WRITERS PROGRAM. *Texas: Guide to the Lone Star State.* 1947. NY. 4th. 718p. F/G. A17. $25.00

WREN, M K. *Gift Upon the Shore.* 1990. Ballantine. 1st ed. rem mk. F/NF. G10. $15.00

WRIGHT, Albert Hazen. *Our Georgia-Florida Frontier. The Okefinokee Swamp...* 1945. Ithaca. Wright. ils/maps. F. O7. $95.00

WRIGHT, Austin Tappin. *Islandia.* 1942. NY. 1st ed. VG/VG. B5. $70.00

WRIGHT, Barton. *Kachinas: A Hopi Artist's Documentary.* 1980. Flagstaff Northland. 4th. obl 4to. F/F. T10. $45.00

WRIGHT, Barton. *Unchanging Hopi.* 1975. Northland. 1st ed. sq 4to. 107p. F/NF. T10. $115.00

WRIGHT, Blanche Fisher. *Jumping Joan.* 1914. Rand McNally. 1st ed. 62p. VG. P2. $28.00

WRIGHT, Blanche Fisher. *Real Mother Goose.* 1916. Rand McNally. 1st ed. ils. VG+. P2. $125.00

WRIGHT, Celeste. *Etruscan Princess.* 1964. Alan Swallow. 1st ed. assn copy. F/NF. V1. $20.00

WRIGHT, Charles. *Southern Cross.* 1981. Random. 1st ed. F/F. V1. $15.00

WRIGHT, Dare. *Holiday for Edith & the Bears.* 1958. Doubleday. 4to. VG/worn. M5. $65.00

WRIGHT, Dare. *Lonely Doll.* 1957. Doubleday. 1st ed. 4to. unp. B17/C14. $35.00

WRIGHT, Dare. *Look at the Gull.* 1967. Random. photos. unp. VG. T5. $25.00

WRIGHT, Esmond. *Fire of Liberty.* 1983. Folio Soc. 1st ed thus. 8vo. ils. 256p. F/case. T10. $45.00

WRIGHT, Eugene. *Great Horn Spoon.* 1928. Garden City. 2nd. 8vo. 4 pl. 320p. VG. W1. $12.00

WRIGHT, Frank Lloyd. *American Architecture.* 1955. Horizon. 1st ed. VG. B5. $55.00

WRIGHT, Frank Lloyd. *Autobiography.* 1933. NY. 2nd. pres. water stained. B5. $285.00

WRIGHT, Frank Lloyd. *Future of Architecture.* 1953. NY. 1st ed. VG/VG. B5. $70.00

WRIGHT, Frank Lloyd. *Natural House.* 1954. Horizon. 2nd. 223p. new ep. F/NF. A17. $27.50

WRIGHT, Frank Lloyd. *Natural House.* 1954. NY. 1st ed. VG. B5. $55.00

WRIGHT, G.F. *Man & the Glacial Period.* 1897. Appleton. 2nd. complete. G. D8. $18.00

WRIGHT, Gordon. *Horsemanship.* 1958. Tryon. ils Sam Savitt. VG/G case. O3. $48.00

WRIGHT, H.G. *Headaches: Their Causes & Their Cure.* 1856. NY. 1st Am ed. 140p. brn cloth. VG. B14. $125.00

WRIGHT, Harold Bell. *Devil's Highway.* 1932. NY. not 1st ed. VG/G. B5. $175.00

WRIGHT, Harold Bell. *Mine With the Iron Door.* 1923. Appleton. 1st ed. 338p. VG/dj. M20. $62.00

WRIGHT, Harold Bell. *Uncrowned King.* 1910. Chicago. 1st ed. gold/red bdg. VG. B5. $45.00

WRIGHT, Harold Bell. *When a Man's a Man.* 1916. AL Burt. photoplay ed. 348p. VG/dj. M20. $22.00

WRIGHT, J.F.C. *Slava Bohu.* 1940. NY. 1st ed. VG/G. B5. $30.00

WRIGHT, Jack. *On the Forty-Yard Line.* 1948. World. ils. G+. P12. $5.00

WRIGHT, James. *Green Wall.* 1958. Yale. 2nd. poet's 1st book. assn copy. F/worn. V1. $30.00

WRIGHT, James. *To a Blossoming Pear Tree.* 1977. FSG. 1st ed. assn copy. NF/NF. V1. $20.00

WRIGHT, Kenneth. *Mysterious Planet.* 1953. Winston. 1st ed. NF/VG. H11. $35.00

WRIGHT, Marcus J. *Social Evolution of Woman.* 1912. Phil. inscr/dtd 1913. NF. M8. $250.00

WRIGHT, Mrs. Frank Lloyd. *Roots of Life.* 1963. NY. 1st ed. VG/VG. B5. $50.00

WRIGHT, Olgivanna. *Shining Brow.* 1960. NY. 1st ed. VG/VG. B5. $50.00

WRIGHT, Olgivanna. *Struggle Within.* 1955. NY. 1st ed. VG/VG. B5. $55.00

WRIGHT, R.C.M. *Roses.* 1961 (1957). London. ils. 160p. F/dj. B26. $17.50

WRIGHT, Richard. *Long Dream.* 1958. NY. 1st ed. VG/VG. B5. $40.00

WRIGHT, Richard. *Native Son.* 1940. Harper. 1st ed. NF/NF later dj. M19. $100.00

WRIGHT, Richard. *Native Son.* 1940. Harper. 1st ed. 1st bdg. F/1st issue dj. B24. $500.00

WRIGHT, Robin. *Sacred Rage.* 1986. London. Deutsch. 1st ed. 8vo. 315p. cloth. NF/dj. W1. $22.00

WRIGHT, W.H.K. *Journal of the Ex Libris Society.* 1970. np. 8 vol in 9. rpt. fld genealogy. VG. A4. $595.00

WRIGHT, William H. *Black Bear.* 1910. NY. 1st ed. ils. gilt blk cloth. F. H3. $65.00

WRIGHT & WRIGHT. *At the Edge of the Universe.* 1991. NY. Horwood. 2nd. 8vo. 230p. VG. K5. $25.00

WRIGHT. *American Fiction 1774-1850, a Contribution...* 1969. San Marino. Huntington Lib. 2nd. 429p. F/F. A4. $40.00

WRIGHTSON, Bernie. *Bernie Wrightson's Frankenstein.* 1994. Lancaster. Underwood Miller. 1st ed thus. F/F. T2. $25.00

WROTH, Lawrence C. *First Century of the John Carter Brown Library.* 1946. np. 23 pl. 119p. VG. A4. $45.00

WU, William. *Hong on the Range.* 1989. Walker. 1st ed. F/NF. G10. $10.00

WUERTHNER, G. *Yellowstone: A Visitor's Companion.* 1992. Stackpole. 1st ed. 218p. AN/wrp. D8. $12.00

WUERTHNER, J.J. Jr. *Businessman's Guide to Practical Politics.* 1961. np. revised ed. sgn. VG/G. B11. $10.00

WULFF, Lee. *Sportsman's Companion.* 1968. Harper Row. 1st ed. ils. NF/VG. P12. $12.00

WULKOP, Elsie. *Social Worker in a Hospital Ward.* 1926. Houghton Mifflin. 347p. red cloth. F/dj. B14. $125.00

WUNDT, Wilhelm Max. *Ethical Systems. Ethics: Investigation of the Facts & Laws.* 1897. Macmillan. 1st Eng ed. 196p. VG. G1. $75.00

WUNDT, Wilhelm Max. *Grundriss der Psychologie.* 1896. Leipzig. Wilhelm Engelmann. 392p. prt brn cloth. xl. VG. G1. $100.00

WUNDT, Wilhelm Max. *Handbuch der Medicinische Physik.* 1867. Erlangen. Verlag. thick 8vo. 556p. F. G1. $375.00

WUNDT, Wilhelm Max. *Lehrbuch der Physiologie des Menschen.* 1878. Stuttgart. 4th. 8vo. 851p. xl. reading copy. G1. $75.00

WUNDT, Wilhelm Max. *Outlines of Psychology.* 1907. Leipzig. Engelmann/Williams Norgate. 3rd. 392p. bl cloth. VG. G1. $75.00

WYCKOFF, Capwell. *Sea Runners' Cache.* 1935. AL Burt. 253p. VG/dj. M20. $37.00

WYE, Deborah. *Louise Bourgeois.* 1983. NY. MOMA. 124p. stiff wrp. D2. $55.00

WYETH, John. *Devil Forest.* 1959. NY. VG/tattered. B30. $40.00

WYETH, N.C. *Boy's King Arthur.* 1936. Scribner. 4to. black cloth. VG+. M5. $45.00

WYETH, N.C. *Boy's King Arthur.* 1947. Scribner. ils. blk cloth. VG. M5. $30.00

WYETH, N.C. *Pike Country Ballads.* 1912. Boston. 1st ed. VG. B5. $95.00

WYETH, N.C. *Robinson Crusoe.* 1920. Cosmopolitan. 1st ed. VG/VG. B5. $135.00

WYETH, N.C. *Scottish Chiefs.* 1923 (1921). Scribner. 9 pl. blk cloth. VG+. M5. $70.00

WYETH, N.C. *Wyeths: Intimate Correspondence of NC Wyeth 1901-1945.* 1971. np. 1st ed. VG/VG. M17. $75.00

WYLIE, C.R. *Advanced Engineering Mathematics.* 1960. McGraw Hill. 8vo. 696p. gray cloth. worn. P4. $22.50

WYLIE, Elinor. *Venetian Glass Nephew.* 1925. NY. Doran. 1st ed. 1/250. sgn. F/dj/defective case. B24. $125.00

WYLIE, Philip. *They Both Were Naked.* 1965. NY. 1st ed. F/VG. A17. $10.00

WYLIE, Philip. *Whe Worlds Collide+After Worlds Collide: 2 in One.* 1933. Phil. 1st ed. VG/VG. B5. $30.00

WYLIE, Phillip. *Best of Crunch & Des.* 1954. NY. 1st ed. F/F. B5. $40.00

WYMAN, L.P. *Bolden Boys & Their New Electric Cell (#1).* 1923A. AL Burt. lists 7 titles. 203p. VG/dj. M20. $30.00

WYNDER, E.L. *Biologic Effects of Tobacco.* 1955. Boston. 1st ed. F/NF. N3. $25.00

WYNDHAM, John. *Jizzle.* 1954. London. Dennis Dobson. 1st/Currey A ed. VG/1st state dj. M21. $75.00

WYNDHAM, Lee. *Susie & the Ballet Horse.* 1961. Dodd Mead. il Jean MacDonald. lib bdg. xl. T5. $15.00

WYNETTE, Tammy. *Stand by Your Man.* 1979. Simon Schuster. 1st ed. sgn. VG/VG. B11. $30.00

WYNMALEN, Henry. *Horse Breeding & Stud Management.* 1966. London. Country Life. VG/VG. O3. $20.00

WYNNE, Anthony. *Fourth Finger.* 1929. Lippincott. 1st Am ed. VG/VG. B4. $75.00

WYNNTON, Pattrick. *Third Messenger.* 1927. Doran. 1st ed. NF/NF. B4. $85.00

WYRICK, E.L. *Strange & Bitter Crop.* 1994. St Martin. 1st ed. author's 1st book. sgn. NF/VG+. P10. $25.00

XYZ

XAVIER, Paul. *Anarchist Papers*. 1969. Berkeley. Undermine. 1/1000. F/wrp. B2. $25.00

XENOPHON. *Art of Horsemanship*. 1987. London. Allen. rpt. 12mo. VG/VG. O3. $15.00

XENOPHON. *Art of Riding*. 1968. NY. Vantage. 1st ed thus. VG/VG. O3. $15.00

XERXES SOCIETY. *Butterfly Gardening*. 1990. San Francisco. 192p. sc. AN. B26. $16.00

XU, H. Mike. *Origin of the Olmec Civilization*. 1966. Edmond, OK. 1st ed. 4to. 52p. wrp. F3. $20.00

YADEUN, Juan. *Towina*. 1993. Mexico/Madrid. ils/map. 158p. F3. $75.00

YADIN, Yigael. *Art of Warfare in Biblical Lands*. 1963. np. 2 vol. photos. VG/VG case. M17. $45.00

YAGODA, Ben. *Will Rogers*. 1993. Knopf. ARC/1st ed. RS. F/dj. S9. $35.00

YALE, William. *Near East: Modern History*. 1958. Ann Arbor. 1st ed. 8vo. 486p. VG/dj. W1. $22.00

YAN, Mo. *Red Sorghum*. 1993. London. Heinemann. AP. 8vo. F/wrp. S9. $75.00

YANDELL, Elizabeth. *Henry*. 1976. St Martin. 1st Am ed. 8vo. 136p. NF/VG. C14. $12.00

YANG, Hongxun. *Classical Gardens of China*. 1982. NY. photos. F/dj. B26. $25.00

YARBROUGH, Camille. *Cornrows*. 1979. Coward McCann. 1st ed. sgn. AN/dj. C8. $60.00

YARBWOOD, Edmund. *Vselod Garshin*. 1981. Boston. Twayne. 1st prt. 147p. xl. VG. A17. $7.50

YARDLEY, H. *Education of Poker Player*. 1957. NY. 1st ed. VG/VG. B5. $25.00

YASTRZEMSKI, Carl. *Play Ball*. 1969. Grow Ahead. 1st ed. VG+/wrp. P8. $15.00

YASTRZEMSKI, Carl. *Yaz, Baseball, the Wall & Me*. 1990. Doubleday. 1st ed. photos. F/F. P8. $20.00

YASTRZEMSKI, Carl. *Yaz*. 1968. Viking. 1st ed. sgn. VG+/F. P8. $75.00

YATES, Elizabeth. *Carolina's Courage*. 1964. Dutton. 1st ed. sgn. ils/sgn NS Unwin. 96p. VG+/dj. C14. $45.00

YATES, Elizabeth. *Christmas Story*. 1949. Aladdin. 1st ed. ils Nora S Unwin. VG/G. B17. $12.50

YATES, Elizabeth. *Once in the Year*. 1947. sgn. ils/sgn Nora Unwin. VG/VG. M17. $25.00

YATES, Gayle Graham. *Harriet Martineau on Women*. 1985. Rutgers. 283p. F/F. A17. $12.50

YBARR, T.R. *Lands of the Andes, Peru & Bolivia*. 1947. Coward McCann. 1st ed. 273p. dj. F3. $20.00

YEAGER, Charles. *Across the High Frontier*. 1955. NY. 1st ed. VG/VG. B5. $50.00

YEATS, William Butler. *Countess Kathleen. And Various Legends & Lyrics*. 1892. Fisher Unwin. 1st ed. 1/30 (530 total). sgn/#d pub. 141p. F. B24. $5,000.00

YEATS, William Butler. *Discoveries: A Volume of Essays*. 1903. Dundrum. 1/200. rpt. F/NF. V1. $20.00

YEATS, William Butler. *Full Moon in March*. 1935. London. Macmillan. 1st ed. F. C2. $50.00

YEATS, William Butler. *Full Moon in March*. 1935. London. Macmillan. 1st ed. gilt gr coth. F/dj. B24. $250.00

YEATS, William Butler. *If I Were Four & Twenty*. 1940. Dublin. 1st ed. 1/450. NF. C2. $100.00

YEATS, William Butler. *Memoirs: Original Previously Unpublished Text...* 1972. edit D Donoghue. VG/VG. M17. $25.00

YEATS, William Butler. *Packet for Ezra Pound*. 1929. Cuala. 1st ed. 1/425. F. C2. $200.00

YEATS, William Butler. *Permanence of Yeats*. 1950. Macmillan. 1st ed. assn copy. NF/VG. V1. $20.00

YEATS, William Butler. *Stone Cottage*. 1988. Oxford. 1st ed. F/F. V1. $15.00

YEATS, William Butler. *Wanderings of Oisin & Other Poems*. 1889. London. Kegan Paul Trench. 1st ed. author's 2nd book. F. B24. $2,500.00

YENSER, Stephen. *Fire in All Things*. 1993. LSU. 1st ed. F/F. V1. $20.00

YEPSEN, Roger B. *Organic Plant Protection*. 1976. Emmaus, PA. 1st ed. 688p. VG. B26. $15.00

YERGEN, D. *Prize: Epic Quest for Oil, Money & Power*. 1991. Simon Schuster. 1st ed. 877p. F/dj. D8. $20.00

YEVTUSHENKO, Yevgeny. *Almost at the End*. 1987. Holt. 1st ed. F/F. B35. $22.00

YEVTUSHENKO, Yevgeny. *From Desire to Desire*. 1976. Doubleday. 1st ed. F/VG+. V1. $20.00

YEVTUSHENKO, Yevgeny. *Precocious Autobiography*. 1963. Dutton. 1st ed. F/F clip. B35. $45.00

YEVTUSHENKO, Yevgeny. *Selected Poems*. 1962. Dutton. ARC. author's 1st book in Eng. F/NF. V1. $35.00

YEVTUSHENKO, Yevgeny. *Wild Berries*. 1981. Morrow. 1st ed. F/F. B35. $18.00

YGLESIAS, Jose. *Home Again*. 1987. Arbor. 1st ed. sgn. F/F. B11. $30.00

YGLESIAS, Rafael. *Fearless*. 1993. Warner. 1st ed. rem mk. F/F. H11. $35.00

YOLEN, Jane. *Dove Isabeau*. 1989. HBJ. B prt. ils Dennis Nolan. F/F. B17. $7.50

YOLEN, Jane. *Girl Who Cried Flowers & Other Tales*. 1974. Crowell. 1st ed. ils David Palladini. 55p. G/G. P2. $12.50

YOLEN, Jane. *Girl Who Cried Flowers & Other Tales*. 1974. Crowell. 1st ed. 55p. xl. VG+/G+. T5. $18.00

YOLEN, Jane. *Inway Investigators*. 1969. Seabury. 1st ed. ils. 80p. F/VG. P2. $30.00

YOLEN, Jane. *Owl Moon*. 1987. Philomel. 1st ed. F/F. C8. $50.00

YOLEN, Jane. *Sister Light, Sister Dark*. 1988. Tor. 1st ed. NF/NF. G10. $10.00

YOLEN, Jane. *Sultan's Perfect Tree*. 1977. Parents Magazine. probable 1st ed. ils Barbara Garrison. G+. T5. $15.00

YOLEN, Jane. *White Jenna*. 1989. Tor. 1st ed. F/F. G10. $25.00

YOLEN, Jane. *Wizard Islands*. 1973. Crowell. 1st ed. ils Robert Quackenbush. 115p. VG/G. P2. $25.00

YOLEN, Jane. *World on a String, the Story of Kites*. 1968. Cleveland. World. 1st ed. 8vo. 143p. F/NF. T5. $25.00

YORK, Jeremy; see Creasey, John.

YOSHIMOTO, Banana. *Kitchen*. 1993. Grove. 1st ed. F/F. M23. $20.00

YOST. *Bibliography of Works of Edna St Vincent Millay*. 1937. np. ils. 255p. VG. A4. $125.00

YOUATT. *History, Treatment & Diseases of the Horse*. 1883. Lippincott. 470p. cloth. VG. A10. $55.00

YOUNG, A.S. *Great Negro Baseball Stars*. 1953. Barmes/ 1st ed. sgn. G+. P8. $145.00

YOUNG, A.S. *Mets From Mobile*. 1970. HBW. 1st ed. VG/VG. P8. $30.00

YOUNG, Agatha. *Blaze of Glory.* 1950. Random. 1st ed. NF/NF. B35. $20.00

YOUNG, Al. *Geography of the Near Past.* 1976. HRW. 1st ed. assn copy. F/VG. V1. $15.00

YOUNG, Andrew W. *First Lessons in Civil Government.* 1846. Cleveland. MC Younglove. 224p. full calf. B18. $25.00

YOUNG, Arthur. *Travels During Years 1787, 1788 & 1789...* 1793. Dublin. 2 vol. maps. xl. rebound. A10. $175.00

YOUNG, Clarence. *Motor Boys Across the Plains.* 1907. Cupples Leon. 1st ed. VG. P12. $7.00

YOUNG, Clarence. *Motor Boys in Mexico (#3).* 1906. Cupples Leon. lists 9 titles. 237p. VG/dj. M20. $45.00

YOUNG, Clarence. *Motor Boys Overland.* 1906. Cupples Leon. ils. VG. P12. $7.00

YOUNG, Collier; see Bloch, Robert.

YOUNG, Edward. *Complaint; or, Night Thoughts on Life, Death & Immortality.* 1743. London. R Dodsley. 1st ed. ca 1900 leather. VG. M19. $250.00

YOUNG, Edward. *Complaint; or, Night Thoughts.* 1817. London. aeg. gilt stp bdg. VG. V4. $75.00

YOUNG, Everild. *Rogues & Raiders of the Caribbean & the South Sea.* 1959. Jarrolds. 1st ed. VG/dj. M20. $25.00

YOUNG, Everild. *Rogues & Raiders of the Caribbean & the South Sea.* 1959. London. Jarrolds. 1st ed. inscr. photos. 240p. VG/VG. B11. $45.00

YOUNG, J. Harvey. *Toadstool Millionaires: A Social History...* 1961. Princeton. 282p. A13. $50.00

YOUNG, J.P. *Seventh Tennesse Calvary.* 1976. Dayton. NF. V4. $25.00

YOUNG, James C. *Harvey S Firestone, 1868-1938.* nd. np. 82p. teg. quarter leather. VG. B18. $22.50

YOUNG, James C. *School Days & Schoolmates of Harvey S Firestone.* 1929. np. 48p. VG. B18. $48.00

YOUNG, James. *What Price Sex in Hollywood?* 1932. NY. 1st ed. F/dj. A17. $12.50

YOUNG, John Richard. *Schooling for Young Riders.* 1977. Norman, OK. 3rd. sgn. VG/VG. O3. $35.00

YOUNG, Margaret B. *First Book of American Negroes.* 1966. Franklin Watts. 1st ed. photos. NF. B2. $35.00

YOUNG, Marguerite. *Moderate Fable.* 1944. NY. 1st ed. assn copy. NF/dj. V1. $40.00

YOUNG, Martha. *Plantation Bird Tales.* 1902. Russell. 1st ed. J Conde. 249p. VG. P2. $125.00

YOUNG, Miriam. *Bear Named George.* 1969. NY. Crown. ils Harold Berson. 8vo. unp. VG. T5. $18.00

YOUNG, Paul H. *Making & Using the Dry Fly.* 1934. Birmingham. VG. B5. $95.00

YOUNG, T. Cuyler. *Near Eastern Culture & Society.* 1951. Princeton. 1st ed. 8vo. 14 pl. VG. W1. $28.00

YOUNG, Thomas Daniel. *John Crow Ransom: An Annotated Bibliography.* 1982. Garland. ARC. VG/VG. B10. $25.00

YOUNG, Thomas. *Bakerian Lecture. Experiments & Calculations...* 1803. London. Bulmer. 190p. rare. G1. $350.00

YOUNGSON, A.J. *Scientific Revolution in Victorian Medicine.* 1979. London. 1st ed. 237p. dj. A13. $22.50

YOURCENAR, Marguerite. *Dark Brain of Piranesi & Other Essays.* 1984. FSG. 1st ed. 8vo. F/dj. S9. $40.00

YOUSSOUPOFF, Felix. *Lost Splendor.* 1954. NY. 1st ed. VG/G. B5. $45.00

YUILL, P.B.; see Williams, Gordon.

ZABEL. *Frigoli Detective.* 1947. Paris. Bias. 4to. ils Andre Jourcin. 2 moveable wheels. prt brd. NF. B24. $265.00

ZAEHNSDORF, Joseph W. *Art of Bookbinding: A Practical Treatise.* 1914. London. Bell. 8th. 12mo. Zaehnsdorf bdg. NF. T10. $400.00

ZAFFO, George J. *Your Police.* 1956. 1st ed. VG. K2. $15.00

ZAFFO, George. *Tommy on the Train.* 1946. Akron. Saalfield. mechanical. sbdg. NF. C8. $125.00

ZAHARIAS, Babe Didrikson. *Life I've Led.* 1955. NY. 1st ed. VG/VG. B5. $35.00

ZAHN, Timothy. *Cascade Point & Other Stories.* 1986. Bluejay. 1st ed. NF/NF. G10. $10.00

ZAISER, Marion. *Beneficent Blaze.* 1960. Pageant. 1st ed. sgn. 8vo. 347p. VG/VG. B11. $40.00

ZANGER, Jack. *Brooks Robinson Story.* 1967. Messner. 1st ed. xl. G/G. P8. $15.00

ZANGER, Jack. *Ken Boyer.* 1965. Nelson. 1st ed. VG+. P8. $40.00

ZANZOTTO, Andrea. *Selected Poetry.* 1975. Princeton. 1st ed. Italian/Eng text. F/VG+. V1. $15.00

ZAPF, Hermann. *Hermann Zaph & His Design Developments...* 1987. Chicago. Society of Typographic Arts. ils. 254p. F/F. A4. $235.00

ZARA, Louis. *Rebel Run.* 1951. Crown. 2nd. 270p. VG/VG. B10. $45.00

ZATURENSKA, Marya. *Collected Poems.* 1965. Viking. 1st ed. F/VG. V1. $20.00

ZATURENSKA, Marya. *Hidden Waterfall.* 1974. Vanguard. 1st ed. assn copy. F/VG. V1. $15.00

ZEBROWSKI, George. *Stars Will Speak.* 1985. Harper. 1st ed. F/F. B11. $45.00

ZEHREN, Erich. *Crescent & the Bull.* 1962. NY. Hawthorn. 1st ed. 366p. VG. W1. $24.00

ZEIER, Franz. *Books, Boxes & Portfolios; Binding, Construction & Design...* 1983. np. ils. 304p. F/NF. A4. $65.00

ZELAZNY, Roger. *Courts of Chaos.* 1978. Doubleday. rpt. sgn. F/F. B11. $20.00

ZELAZNY, Roger. *Knight of Shadows.* 1989. Morrow. 1st ed. F/F. M21. $30.00

ZELAZNY, Roger. *Lord of Light.* 1967. Doubleday. 1st ed. xl. VG-/VG. M21. $75.00

ZELAZNY, Roger. *Nebula Award Stories Three.* 1968. Doubleday. 1st ed. VG/VG. M22. $20.00

ZELL, Steve. *WiZrD.* 1994. St Martin. 1st ed. RS. F/F. G10. $5.00

ZELLER, D.E. *Short Papers on Reasearch in 1968.* 1968. KS State Geological Survey Bulletin #194. F/wrp. D8. $12.50

ZEMACH & ZEMACH. *A Penny a Look — An Old Story.* 1971. FSG. 1st ed. ils. brn cloth. NF/F. D1. $35.00

ZEMAN, Zbynek. *Heckling Hitler.* 1987. Hanover. 2nd. ils. 128p. VG+/dj. B18. $27.50

ZERNO, Eugene. *Annals of Cleveland.* 1897. Cleveland. 114p. G+/wrp. B18. $25.00

ZETTERLING, Mai. *Night Games.* 1966. Coward McCann. 1st Am ed. NF/VG+. B4. $75.00

ZETTERLUND. *Bibliografiska Anteckningar om August Strindberg.* 1968. rpt of 1913 Stockholm ed. VG. A4. $85.00

ZIADEH, Nicola A. *Syria & Lebanon.* 1957. London. Benn. 1st ed. 8vo. 312p. VG/dj. W1. $32.00

ZIEGLER, Tom. *Zen of Base & Ball.* 1964. Simon Schuster. 1st ed. VG+/VG. P8. $35.00

ZIEHEN, Theodor. *Leitfaden in der Physiologischen Psychologie 15 Vorlesungen.* 1892. Jena. Gustav Fischer. 2nd. 220p. pub cloth. G1. $40.00

ZIEROLD, Norman. *Little Charley Ross: America's 1st Kidnapping for Ransom.* 1967. Boston. later prt. 301p. brd. VG/dj. B18. $15.00

ZIGMOND, M.L. *Kawaiisu Ethnobotany.* 1981. Salt Lake City. UT U. 4to. 102p. F/wrp. B1. $37.00

ZIGROSSER, Carl. *Multum in Parvo.* 1965. Braziller. 1st ed. inscr. VG+/dj. S9. $60.00

ZIMBALIST, Andrew. *Baseball & Billions.* 1992. Basic. 1st ed. F/F. P8. $12.50

ZIMMER, Heinrich. *Celtic Church in Britain & Ireland.* 1902. London. David Nutt. 8vo. 131p. gilt bl cloth. VG. T10. $75.00

ZIMMERMAN, Paul. *Year the Mets Lost Last Place.* 1969. World. 1st ed. F/G+. P8. $20.00

ZIMMERMAN, Tom. *Working at the Stadium.* 1989. Pacific Tides 1st ed. F. P8. $10.00

ZINN, Howard. *Southern Mystique.* 1964. Knopf. 1st ed. VG/VG. B10. $10.00

ZINNES, Harriet. *Book of Ten.* 1981. Bellevue. ltd ed. 1/350. F/wrp. V1. $15.00

ZINSSER, William *Spring Training.* 1989. Harper Row. 1st ed. F/F. P8. $20.00

ZIOCK, Hermann. *Lehnert & Landrock's Guide to Egypt.* 1962. Cairo. Lehnert Landrock. 16mo. 46 pl/4 map. 367p. VG/dj. W1. $20.00

ZITZMAN, A. *Iron Ore Deposits of Europe & Adjacent Areas, Vol I.* 1977. Federal Inst Geosciences & Natural Rescources. 418p. D8. $10.00

ZOGNER, Lothar. *Karten in Bibliotheken: Festgabe fur Heinrich Kramm...* 1971. Bonn-Bad Godesberg. Institut fur Landeskunde. 8 maps. F/wrp. O7. $75.00

ZOLLERS, George D. *Thrilling Incidents on Sea & Land.* 1892. Mt Morris, IL. rebound. V4. $200.00

ZOLOTOW, Charlotte. *My Grandson Lew.* 1974. Harper Row. probable 1st ed. 8vo. unp. VG/G+. T5. $25.00

ZOLOTOW, Charlotte. *Sky Was Blue.* 1963. Harper Row. 1st ed. ils/sgn Garth Williams. unp. G+. T5. $95.00

ZOLOTOW, M. *Marilyn Monroe.* 1960. NY. 1st ed. VG/VG. B5. $40.00

ZON, Raphael. *Chestnut in Southern Maryland.* 1904. WA, DC. 5 pl. 31p. NF/wrp. B26. $150.00

ZUCKER, Harvey. *Sports Films: A Complete Reference.* 1987. McFarland. 1st ed. F/sans. P8. $27.50

ZUCKERMAN, Solly. *Nuclear Illusion, Nuclear Reality.* 1982. Viking. 1st ed. NF/NF. G10. $12.00

ZUELKE, Ruth. *Horse in Art.* 1964. Minneapolls. Lerner. ils. 64p. VG. O3. $25.00

ZUG, G.R. *Lizards of Fiji: Natural History & Systematics.* 1991. Honolulu. Bishop Mus. 8vo. ils/maps/references. 136p. wrp. B1. $36.00

ZUILICHEM, B.H. *Twelve Months.* 1990. Catherijne. 1/150. Trevor Jones bdg. F/bl buckram box. B24. $2,500.00

ZUKOFSKY, Louis. *'A' 1-12.* 1967. Doubleday. 1st Am ed. NF/VG. V1. $25.00

ZUKOFSKY, Louis. *'A' 13-21.* 1969. Doubleday. 1st Am ed. F/VG. V1. $25.00

ZUKOFSKY, Louis. *'A'-24.* 1972. Grossman. 1st ed. 8vo. F/dj. S9. $40.00

ZUKOFSKY, Louis. *Barely & Widely.* 1958. NY. CZ. 1st ed. 1/300. sgn. F/wrp. B24. $225.00

ZUKOFSKY, Louis. *Little.* 1970. NY. Grossman. 1st ed. author's 1st novel. F/NF. V1. $25.00

ZUKOFSKY, Louis. *Test of Poetry.* 1948. Objectivist. 1st ed pres. NF/dj. B24. $300.00

ZUKOR, Adolph. *Public Is Never Wrong: My 50 Years in Motion Pictures.* 1953. Putnam. 1st ed. F/F. B4. $200.00

ZUMBERGE, J.H. *Elements of Geology.* 1959. John Wiley. 1st ed/2nd prt. VG/dj. D8. $12.50

ZWEIG, Stefan. *Old-Book Peddler & Other Tales for Bibliophiles.* 1938. Evanston, IL. Chas Deering Lib/Northwestern. 2nd. trans Koch. NF. B4. $100.00

ZWEIG, Stefan. *Royal Game & Other Stories.* 1981. Harmony. 1st ed. F/NF. H11. $35.00

ZWEIG, Stefan. *Royal Game With Amok & the Letter From an Unknown Woman.* 1944. Viking. 1st ed. F/F. B4. $125.00

ZWINGER, Ann. *Desert Country Near the Sea.* 1983. NY. 1st ils. 399p. VG/dj. B26. $25.00

PSEUDONYMS

Listed below are pseudonyms of many paperback and hardcover authors. This information was shared with us by some of our many contributors, and we offer it here as a reference for our readers. This section is organized alphabetically by the author's actual name (given in bold) followed by the pseudonyms he or she has been known to use. (It is interesting to note that 'house names' were common with more than one author using the same name for a particular magazine or publishing house.)

If you have additional information (or corrections), please let us hear from you so we can expand this section in future editions.

Aarons, Edward S.
Ayres, Paul; Ronns, Edward

Albert, Marvin H.
Conroy, Albert; Jason, Stuart; Quarry, Nick; Rome, Anthony

Ard, William (Thomas)
Kerr, Ben; Ward, Jonas (some)

Auster, Paul
Benjamin, Paul

Avallone, Mike
Carter, Nick (a few); Conway, Troy (a few); Dalton, Priscilla; Jason, Stuart; Noone, Edwina; Stuart, Sidney; Walker, Max

Ballard, W.T.
Hunter, D'Allard; MacNeil, Neil; Shepherd, John

Ballinger, Bill
Sanborn, B.X.

Barnard, Robert
Bastable, Bernard

Barnes, Julian
Kavanagh, Dan; Seal, Basil

Blake, Roger
Sade, Mark

Blassingame, Lurton
Duncan, Peter

Beaumont, Charles
Grantland, Keith

Beck, Robert
Iceberg Slim

Bedford-Jones, H.
Feval, Paul; Pemjion, L.

Bloch, Robert
Young, Collier

Block, Lawrence
Ard, William; Emerson, Jill; Harrison, Chip; Lord, Sheldon; Morse, Benjamin, M.D.; Shaw, Andrew

Bradley, Marion Zimmer
Chapman, Lee; Dexter, John (some); Gardner, Miriam; Graves, Valerie; Ives, Morgan

Brunner, John
Woodcott, Keith

Bulmer, Kenneth
Hardy, Adam; Norvil, Manning; Prescot, Dray

Burnett, W.R.
Monachan, John; Updyke, James

Burroughs, William S.
Lee, William

Byrne, Stuart
Bloodstone, John

Cain, Paul
Sims, George

Campbell, Ramsey
Dreadstone, Carl; Ramsay, Jay

Carr, John Dickson
Dickson, Carter; Fairbairn, Roger

Cooper, Basil
Falk, Lee

Cooper, Clarence
Chestnut, Robert

Creasey, John
Ashe, Gordon; Carmichael, Harry; Deane, Norman; Frazier, Robert Caine; Gill, Patrick; Holliday, Michael; Hope, Brian; Hughes, Colin; Hunt, Kyle; Marric, J.J.; York, Jeremy

Crichton, Michael
Lange, John

Cross, David
Chesbro, George B.

Daniels, Norman
Daniels, Dorothy; Wade, David

Davidson, Avram
Queen, Ellery (about 2 titles only)

Derleth, August
Grendon, Stephen

Dewey, Thomas B.
Brandt, Tom; Wainer, Cord

Disch, Thomas
Demijohn, Thomas; Cassandra, Knye (both with John Sladek)

Duffy, James
Murphy, Haughton

Ellis, Peter Beresford
Tremayne, Peter

Ellison, Harlan
Merchant, Paul

Etchison, Dennis
Martin, Jack

Fairman, Paul
Paul, F.W.

Fanthorpe, Lionel
Muller, John E.

Farmer, Philip Jose
Norfolk, William; Trout, Kilgore

Fearn, John Russell
Del Martia, Aston

Foster, Alan Dean
Lucas, George

Fox, Gardner F.
Chase, Glen; Cooper, Jefferson; Gardner, Jeffrey; Gardner, Matt; Gray, James Kendricks; Jennings, Dean; Majors, Simon; Matthews, Kevin; Morgan, John Medford; Morgan, Rod; Summers, Bart

Gardner, Erle Stanley
Fair, A.A.; Kendrake, Carleton; Kinney, Charles

Garrett, Randall
Bupp, Walter; Gordon, David;
1/2 of Mark Phillips and
Robert Randall

Geis, Richard
Owen, Robert; Swenson, Peggy

Geisel, Theodor Seuss
Dr. Seuss

Gibson, Walter B.
Brown, Douglas; Grant, Maxwell

Goulart, Ron
Falk, Lee; Kains, Josephine;
Kearney, Julian;
Robeson, Kenneth;
Shaw(n), Frank S.; Silva, Joseph

Grant, Charles L.
Andrew, Felicia; Lewis, Deborah

Haas, Ben
Meade, Richard

Haldeman, Joe
Graham, Robert

Hall, Oakley
Hall, O.M.

Halliday, Brett
Shayne, Mike

Hansen, Joseph
Brock, Rose; Colton, James

Harknett, Terry
Hedges, Joseph; Stone, Thomas H.

Harris, Timothy
Hyde, Harris

Highwater, Jamake
Marks, J.; Marks-Highwater, J.

Hochstein, Peter
Short, Jack

Hodder-Williams, C.
Brogan, James

Holt, John Robert
Giles, Elizabeth; Giles, Raymond

Hoppley-Woolrich, Cornell
Hopley, George; Irish, William;
Woolrich, Cornell

Hunt, E. Howard
St.John, David

Hunter, Evan
Cannon, Curt; Collins, Hunt;
Hannon, Ezra; Marsten, Richard;
McBain, Ed

Jacks, Oliver
Gandley, Kenneth R.

Jakes, John
Ard, William; Payne, Alan;
Scotland, Jay

Jenkins, Will F.
Leinster, Murray

Jones, H. Bedford
Pemjean, Lucien

Kane, Frank
Boyd, Frank

Kane, Henry
McCall, Anthony

Kent, Hal
Davis, Ron

King, Stephen
Bachman, Richard

Klass, Philip
Tenn, William

Klavan, Andrew
Peterson, Keith

Knowles, William
Allison, Clyde; Ames, Clyde

Koontz, Dean R.
Axton, David; Coffey, Brian;
Dwyer, Deanna; Dwyer, K.R.;
Hill, John; Nichols, Leigh;
North, Anthony; Paige, Richard;
West, Owen; Wolfe, Aaron

Kornbluth, Cyril
Eisner, Simon; Park, Jordan

Kosinski, Jerzy
Somers, Jane

Kubis, P.
Scott, Casey

Kurland, Michael
Plum, Jennifer

L'Amour, Louis
Burns, Tex; Mayo, Jim

Lariar, Lawrence
Knight, Adam

Laumer, Keith
LeBaron, Anthony

Lesser, Milton
Marlowe, Stephen

Lessing, Doris
Somers, Jane

Lewis, Alfred Henry
Quinn, Dan

Linebarger, Paul
Smith, Cordwainer

Long, Frank Belknap
Long, Lyda Belknap

Lovesey, Peter
Lear, Peter

Lucas, Mark
Palmer, Drew

Ludlum, Robert
Ryder, Jonathan;
Shepherd, Michael

Lupoff, Richard
Steele, Adison

Lynds, Dennis
Collins, Michael; Crowe, John;
Grant, Maxwell (some);
Sadler, Mark

Malzberg, Barry
Berry, Mike; Dumas, Claudine;
Johnson, Mel; Johnson, M.L.;
O'Donnell, Barrett;
O'Donnell, K.M.

Manfred, Frederick
Feikema, Feike

Marshall, Mel
Tayler, Zack

Martin, Robert
Roberts, Lee

Mason, Van Wyck
Coffin, Geoffrey

Masterton, Graham
Luke, Thomas

Matheson, Richard
Swanson, Logan

McGaughy, Dudley
Owen, Dean

Meaker, Marijane
Aldrich, Ann; Packer, Vin

Menken, H.L.
Hatteras, Owen

Mertz, Barbara Gross
Michael, Barbara; Peters, Elizabeth

Millar, Kenneth
MacDonald, Ross;
MacDonald, John Ross

Moorcock, Michael
Barclay, Bill; Bradbury, Edward P.

Moore, Brian
Mara, Bernard; Michael, Bryan

Morris, James
Morris, Jan (after sex change)

Nasby, Petroleum
Locke, David R.

Norton, Andre Alice
North, Andrew; Norton, Alice;
Norton, Andre

Nuetzel, Charles
Augustus, Albert Jr.;
Davidson, John; English, Charles;
Rivere, Alec

Oates, Joyce Carol
Smith, Rosamond

Offutt, Andrew
Cleve, John; Giles, Baxter;
Williams, J.X. (some)

Patterson, Henry
Fallon, Martin; Graham, James;
Higgins, Jack; Patterson, Harry;
Marlowe, Hugh

Philips, James Atlee
Atlee, Philip

Phillips, Dennis
Chambers, Peter; Chester, Peter

Phillips, Judson
Pentecost, Hugh

Posner, Richard
Foster, Iris; Murray, Beatrice;
Todd, Paul

Pargeter, Edith Mary
Peter, Ellis

Prather, Richard
Knight, David; Ring, Douglas

Radford, R.L.
Ford, Marcia

Pronzini, Bill
Foxx, Jack

Rabe, Peter
MacCargo, J.T.

Rawson, Clayton
Towne, Stuart

Rendell, Ruth
Vine, Barbara

Reynolds, Mack
Belmont, Bob; Harding, Todd;
Reynolds, Maxine

Rice, Anne
Rampling, Anne; Roquelaure, A.N.

Rosenblum, Robert
Maxxe, Robert

Ross, W.E.D.
Dana, Rose; Daniels, Jan;
Ross, Clarissa; Ross, Dan;
Ross, Dana; Ross, Marilyn

Rossi, Jean-Baptiste
Japrisot, Sebastien

Scoppetone, Sandra
Early, Jack

Sellers, Con
Bannion, Della

Sheldon, Alice Bradley
Bradley, Alice; Sheldon, Raccoona;
Tiptree, James

Silverberg, Robert
Beauchamp, Loren;
Burnett, W.R. (some only);
Drummond, Walter;
Elliott, Don (some); Ford, Hilary;
Hamilton, Franklin; Knox, Calvin;
Lt. Woodard, M.D.

Smith, George H.
Deer, J.M.; Hudson, Jan;
Jason, Jerry; Knerr, M.E.;
Summers, Diana

Stacton, David
Clifton, Bud

Sturgeon, Theodore
Ewing, Frederick R.;
Queen, Ellery (1 book only)

Thomas, Ross
Bleeck, Oliver

Tracy, Don
Fuller, Roger

Tralins, Bob
Miles, Keith; O'Shea, Sean

Tubb, E.C.
Kern, Gregory

Vance, Jack
Held, Peter;
Queen, Ellery (some/few)

Vidal, Luther
Box, Edgar; Vidal, Gore

Wager, Walter
Tiger, John; Walker, Max

Ward, Harold
Zorro

Webb, Jack
Farr, John

Weiss, Joe
Anatole, Ray; Dauphine, Claude;
Mirbeau, Ken

Westlake, Donald E.
Allan, John B.; Clark, Curt;
Culver, Timothy;
Cunningham, J. Morgan;
Holt, Samuel; Marshall, Alan;
Stark, Richard; West, Edwin

Williams, Gordon
Yuill, P.B

Whittington, Harry
Harrison, Whit; Shepherd, Shep

Williamson, Jack
Stewart, Will

Wollheim, Don
Grinnell, David

Worts, George F.
Brent, Loring

BOOKBUYERS

In this section of the book we have listed buyers of books and related material. When you correspond with these dealers, be sure to enclose a self-addressed stamped envelope if you want a reply. Do not send lists of books for appraisal. If you wish to sell your books, quote the price you want or send a list and ask if there are any on the list they might be interested in and the price they would be willing to pay. If you want the list back, be sure to send a SASE large enough for the listing to be returned. When you list your books, do so by author, full title, publisher and place, date, edition, and condition, noting any defects on cover or contents.

Advance Review Copies
Paperbacks
The American Dust Co.
47 Park Ct.
Staten Island, NY 10301
718-442-8253

Adventure
The Silver Door
P.O. Box 3208
Redondo Beach, CA 90277
310-379-6005

African-American
Children's Book Adoption Agency
P.O. Box 643
Kensington, MD 20895-0643
310-565-2834 or fax 301-585-3091
e-mail: KIDS_BKS@interloc.com

Fran's Bookhouse
6601 Greene St.
Phil., PA 19119
215-438-2729 or fax 215-430-0997

Recollection Books
4519 University Way NE
Seattle, WA 98105
206-548-1346
http://www.mediastream.com/m
payson/recollection/

Alaska
Artis Books
201 N Second Ave.
P.O. Box 822
Alpena, MI 49707
517-354-3401

Albania
W.B. O'Neill-Old & Rare Books
11609 Hunters Green Ct.
Reston, VA 22091
703-860-0782 or fax 703-620-0153

Alcoholics Anonymous
The Book Baron
1236 S Magnolia Ave.
Anaheim, CA 92804
714-527-7022 or fax 714-527-5634

1939-1954
Paul Melzer Fine Books
12 E Vine St.
Redlands, CA 92373
902-792-7299

Americana
Amaranth Books
P.O. Box 421
Wilmette, IL 60091-0421
708-328-2939

The Book Inn
6401 University
Lubbock, TX 79413

The Bookseller, Inc.
521 W Exchange St.
Akron, OH 44302
216-762-3101

Bowie & Co. Booksellers, Inc.
314 First Ave. S
Seattle, WA 98104
206-624-4100 or fax 206-223-0966

Woodbridge B. Brown
P.O. Box 445
Turners Falls, MA 01376
413-772-2509 or 413-773-5710

The Captain's Bookshelf, Inc.
P.O. Box 2258
Asheville, NC 28802-2258
704-253-6631

Chapel Hill Rare Books
P.O. Box 456
Carrboro, NC 27510
919-929-8351

Duck Creek Books
Jim & Shirley Richards
P.O. Box 203
Caldwell, OH 43724
614-732-4856 (10 am to 10 pm)

Terry Harper, Bookseller
P.O. Box 312
Vergennes, VT 05491-0312
802-877-9262

Susan Heller, Pages for Sages
22611 Halburton Rd.
Beachwood, OH 44122-3939
216-283-2665 or fax 216-991-2665

Jim Hodgson Books
908 S Manlius St.
Fayetteville, NY 13066
315-637-6264

M & S Rare Books, Inc.
P.O. Box 2594, E Side Sta.
Providence, RI 02906
401-421-1050 or fax 401-272-0831
(attention M & S)

Parmer Books
7644 Forrestal Rd.
San Diego, CA 92120-2203
619-287-0693 or fax 619-287-6135
e-mail: ParmerBook@aol.com

Randall House
835 Laguna St.
Santa Barbara, CA 93101
805-963-1909 or fax 805-963-1650

Thorn Books
P.O. Box 1244
Moorpark, CA 93020
805-529-3647 or fax 805-529-0022
e-mail: thornbooks@aol.com

18th & 19th C
Gordon Totty
Scarce Paper Americana
347 Shady Lake Pky.
Baton Rouge, LA 70810
504-766-8625

Yesterday's Books
229 Riverview Dr.
Parchment, MI 49004
616-345-1011

Anarchism
Nutmeg Books
354 New Litchfield St. (Rte. 202)
Torrington, CT 06790
203-482-9696

Angling
Book & Tackle Shop
29 Old Colony Rd.
P.O. Box 114
Chestnut Hill, MA 02167
617-965-0459 (winter) or
401-596-0700 (summer)

Anthropology
The King's Market Bookshops
P.O. Box 709
Boulder, CO 80306-0709
303-447-0234

Anthologies
Cartoonists from 1890-1960
Craig Ehlenberger
Abalone Cove Rare Books
7 Fruit Tree Rd.
Portuguese Bend, CA 90275

Antiquarian
A.B.A.C.U.S.®
Phillip E. Miller
343 S Chesterfield St.
Aiken, SC 29801
803-648-4632

Antiquarian Book Arcade
110 W 25th St., 9th Floor
New York, NY 10001

Fine & hard-to-find books
Arnold's of Michigan
511 S Union St.
Traverse City, MI 49684

The Book Baron
1236 S Magnolia Ave.
Anaheim, CA 92804
714-527-7022 or fax 714-527-5634

Pre-1900 leatherbound, any subject
Arthur Boutiette
410 W 3rd St., Ste. 200
Little Rock, AR 72201

Bowie & Co. Booksellers, Inc.
314 First Ave. S
Seattle, WA 98104
206-624-4100 or fax 206-223-0966

Children's Book Adoption Agency
P.O. Box 643
Kensington, MD 20895-0643
310-565-2834 or fax 301-585-3091
e-mail: KIDS_BKS@interloc.com

Terry Harper, Bookseller
P.O. Box 312
Vergennes, VT 05491-0312
802-877-9262

Murray Hudson
Antiquarian Books & Maps
The Old Post Office
109 S Church St.
P.O. Box 163
Halls, TN 38040
901-836-9057 or 800-748-9946

Jeffrey Lee Pressman, Bookseller
3246 Ettie St.
Oakland, CA 94608
510-652-6232

Robert Mueller Rare Books
8124 W 26th St.
N Riverside, IL 60546
708-447-6441

Scribe Company
Attn: Bonnie Smith
P.O. Box 1123
Flippin, AR 72634

Printed before 1800
Gordon Totty
Scarce Paper Americana
347 Shady Lake Pky.
Baton Rouge, LA 70810
504-766-8625

Antiques & Reference
Antique & Collectors
  Reproduction News
Box 17774-OB
Des Moines, IA 50325
515-270-8994

Bohemian Bookworm
110 W 25th St., 9th Floor
New York, NY 10001
212-620-5627

Collector's Companion
Perry Franks
P.O. Box 24333
Richmond, VA 23224

Galerie De Boicourt
6136 Westbrooke Dr.
W Bloomfield, MI 48322
810-788-9253

Henry H. Hain III
Antiques & Collectibles
2623 N Second St.
Harrisburg, PA 17110
717-238-0534

Appraisals
J. Sampson Antiques & Books
107 S Main
Harrodsburg, KY 40330
606-734-7829

Lee and Mike Temares
50 Hts. Rd.
Plandome, NY 11030
516-627-8688

Arabian Horses
Worldwide Antiquarian
P.O. Box 391
Cambridge, MA 02141
617-876-6220 or fax 617-876-0939
e-mail: mbalwan@aol.com

The Arabian Nights
Worldwide Antiquarian
P.O. Box 391
Cambridge, MA 02141
617-876-6220 or fax 617-876-0939
e-mail: mbalwan@aol.com

Archaelogy
Flo Silver Books
8442 Oakwood Ct. N
Indianapolis, IN 46260
317-255-5118

Architecture
Cover to Cover
P.O. Box 687
Chapel Hill, NC 27514

Armenia
W.B. O'Neill-Old & Rare Books
11609 Hunters Green Ct.
Reston, VA 22091
703-860-0782 or fax 703-620-0153

Art
AL-PAC
Lamar Kelley Antiquarian Books
2625 E Southern Ave., C-120
Tempe, AZ 85282
602-831-3121 or fax 602-831-3193

Bohemian Bookworm
110 W 25th St., 9th Floor
New York, NY 10001
212-620-5627

Book & Tackle Shop
29 Old Colony Rd.
P.O. Box 114
Chestnut Hill, MA 02167
617-965-0459 (winter) or
401-596-0700 (summer)

Books West Southwest
Box 6149, University Sta.
Irvine, CA 92616-6149
or 14 Whitman Ct.
Irvine, CA 92612
714-509-7670 or fax 714-854-5102
e-mail: bkswest@ix.netcom.com

The Captain's Bookshelf, Inc.
P.O. Box 2258
Asheville, NC 28802-2258
704-253-6631

Fine & applied
L. Clarice Davis Art Books
P.O. Box 56054
Sherman Oaks, CA 91413-1054
818-787-1322

Galerie De Boicourt
6136 Westbrooke Dr.
W Bloomfield, MI 48322
810-788-9253

Edison Hall Books
5 Ventnor Dr.
Edison, NJ 08820
908-548-4455

Heritage Book Shop, Inc.
8540 Melrose Ave.
Los Angeles, CA 90069
213-659-3674

David Holloway, Bookseller
7430 Grace St.
Springfield, VA 22150
703-659-1798

Significant Books
3053 Madison Rd.
P.O. Box 9248
Cincinnati, OH 45209
513-321-7567

Lee and Mike Temares
50 Hts. Rd.
Plandome, NY 11030
516-627-8688

Xanadu Records, Ltd.
3242 Irwin Ave.
Kingsbridge, NY 10463
212-549-3655

Arctic
Artis Books
201 N Second Ave.
P.O. Box 822
Alpena, MI 49707
517-354-3401

Parmer Books
7644 Forrestal Rd.
San Diego, CA 92120-2203
619-287-0693 or fax 619-287-6135
e-mail: ParmerBook@aol.com

Arthurian
Camelot Books
Charles E. Wyatt
P.O. Box 2883
Vista, CA 92083
619-940-9472

Astronomy
Knollwood Books
Lee and Peggy Price
P.O. Box 197
Oregon, WI 53575
608-835-8861 or fax 608-835-8421

Atlases
Murray Hudson
Antiquarian Books & Maps
The Old Post Office
109 S Church St.
P.O. Box 163
Halls, TN 38040
901-836-9057 or 800-748-9946

Before 1870
Gordon Totty
Scarce Paper Americana
347 Shady Lake Pky
Baton Rouge, LA 70810
504-766-8625

Atomic Bomb
Key Books
P.O. Box 58097
St. Petersburg, FL 33715
813-867-2931

Autobiography
Wellerdt's Books
3700 S Osprey Ave. #214
Sarasota, FL 34239
813-365-1318

Autographs
Ads Autographs
P.O. Box 8006
Webster, NY 14580
716-671-2651

Michael Gerlicher
1375 Rest Point Rd.
Orono, MN 55364

Susan Heller, Pages for Sages
22611 Halburton Rd.
Beachwood, OH 44122-3939
216-283-2665 or fax 216-991-2665

Heritage Book Shop, Inc.
8540 Melrose Ave.
Los Angeles, CA 90069
213-659-3674

Key Books
P.O. Box 58097
St. Petersburg, FL 33715
813-867-2931

McGowan Book Co.
39 Kimberly Dr.
Durham, NC 27707
919-403-1503 or fax 919-403-1706

Paul Melzer Fine Books
12 E Vine St.
Redlands, CA 92373
909-792-7299

Randall House
835 Laguna St.
Santa Barbara, CA 93101
805-963-1909 or fax 805-963-1650

Autobiographies
Herb Sauermann
21660 School Rd.
Manton, CA 96059

Aviation
The Bookseller, Inc.
521 W Exchange St.
Akron, OH 44302
216-762-3101

Cover to Cover
P.O. Box 687
Chapel Hill, NC 27514

Baedeker Handbooks
W.B. O'Neill-Old & Rare Books
11609 Hunters Green Ct.
Reston, VA 22091
703-860-0782 or fax 703-620-0153

Barbie
Glo's Books & Collectibles
906 Shadywood
Southlake, TX 76092
817-481-1438

Baseball
Brasser's
8701 Seminole Blvd.
Seminole, FL 34642

R. Plapinger, Baseball Books
P.O. Box 1062
Ashland, OR 87520
503-488-1200

Bibliography

About Books
6 Sand Hill Ct.
P.O. Box 5717
Parsippany, NJ 07054
201-515-4591

Books West Southwest
Box 6149, University Sta.
Irvine, CA 92616-6149
or
14 Whitman Ct.
Irvine, CA 92612
714-509-7670 or fax 714-854-5102
e-mail: bkswest@ix.netcom.com

Big Little Books

Jay's House of Collectibles
75 Pky. Dr.
Syosset, NY 11791

Biographies

Herb Sauermann
21660 School Rd.
Manton, CA 96059

Black Americana

Especially Little Black Sambo
Glo's Books & Collectibles
906 Shadywood
Southlake, TX 76092
817-481-1438

History & literature
David Holloway, Bookseller
7430 Grace St.
Springfield, VA 22150
703-569-1798

Mason's Bookstore, Rare Books
 & Record Albums
115 S Main St.
Chambersburg, PA 17201
717-261-0541

Black Fiction & Literature

Almark & Co., Booksellers
P.O. Box 7
Thornhill, Ontario
Canada L3T 3N1
phone or fax 905-764-2665

Black Studies

Recollection Books
4519 University Way NE
Seattle, WA 98105
206-548-1346
http://www.mediastream.com/m
payson/recollection/

Black Hills

James F. Taylor
515 Sixth St.
Rapid City, SD 57701
605-341-3224

Book Search Service

Authors of the West
191 Dogwood Dr.
Dundee, OR 97115
503-538-8132

Avonlea Books
P.O. Box 74, Main Sta.
White Plains, NY 10602
914-946-5923

Bookingham Palace
Rosan Van Wagenen
 & Eileen Layman
52 North 2500 East
Teton, ID 83451
209-458-4431

Heritage Book Shop, Inc.
8540 Melrose Ave.
Los Angeles, CA 90069
310-659-3674 or fax 310-659-4872

Hilda's Book Search
Hilda Gruskin
199 Rollins Ave.
Rockville, MD 20852
301-948-3181

Lost 'N Found Books
Linda Lengerich
3214 Columbine Ct.
Indianapolis, IN 46224
phone or fax 317-298-9077
e-mail: lindalen@interloc.com

Passaic Book Center
594 Main Ave.
Passaic, NJ 07055
201-778-6646 or fax 201-778-6738

Recollection Used Books
David Brown
4519 University Way NE
WA 98105
206-548-1346
e-mail: eskimo.com
http://www.eskimo.com/~recall/

The Silver Door
P.O. Box 3208
Redondo Beach, CA 90277
310-379-6005

*Especially children's out-of-print
books*
Treasures from the Castle
Connie Castle
1720 N Livernois
Rochester, MI 48306
810-651-7317

Books About Books

About Books
6 Sand Hill Ct.
P.O. Box 5717
Parsippany, NJ 07054
201-515-4591

Books West Southwest
Box 6149, University Sta.
Irvine, CA 92616-6149
or
14 Whitman Ct.
Irvine, CA 92616
714-509-7670 or fax 714-854-5102
e-mail: bkswest@ix.netcom.com

Bowie & Co. Booksellers, Inc.
314 First Ave. S
Seattle, WA 98104
206-624-4100 or fax 206-223-0966

First Folio
1206 Brentwood
Paris, TN 38242
phone or fax 901-644-9940

Susan Heller, Pages for Sages
22611 Halburton Rd.
Beachwood, OH 44122-3939
216-283-2665 or fax 216-991-2665

Key Books
P.O. Box 58097
St. Petersburg, FL 33715
813-867-2931

Randall House
835 Laguna St.
Santa Barbara, CA 93101
805-963-1909 or fax 805-963-1650

George H. Tweney
16660 Marine View Dr. SW
Seattle, WA 98166
206-243-8243

Botany

Brooks Books
Philip B. Nesty
P.O. Box 21473
1343 New Hampshire Dr.
Concord, CA 94521
510-672-4566 or fax 510-672-3338

Bottles
Homebiz Books & More
2919 Mistwood Forest Dr.
Chester, VA 23831-7043

Charles Bukowski
Ed Smith Books
P.O. Box 66
Oak View, CA 93022
805-649-2844 or fax 805-649-2863
e-mail: edsbooks@aol.com

California
Books West Southwest
Box 6149, University Sta.
Irvine, CA 92616-6149
or 14 Whitman Ct.
Irvine, CA 92616
714-509-7670 or fax 714-854-5102
e-mail: bkswest@ix.netcom.com

Paul Melzer Fine Books
12 E Vine St.
Redlands, CA 92373
909-792-7299

Thorn Books
P.O. Box 1244
Moorpark, CA 93020
805-529-3647 or fax 805-529-0022
e-mail: thornbooks@aol.com

Cartography
Overlee Farm Books
P.O. Box 1155
Stockbridge, MA 01262
413-637-2277

Cartoon Art
Jay's House of Collectibles
75 Pky. Dr.
Syosset, NY 11791

Catalogs
Glass, pottery, furniture, doll, toy, jewelry, general merchandise, fishing tackle
Bill Schroeder
P.O. Box 3009
Paducah, KY 42002-3009

Antiques or other collectibles
Antique & Collectors
  Reproduction News
Box 17774-OB
Des Moines, IA 50325
515-270-8994

Hillcrest Books
Rt. 3, Box 479
Crossville, TN 38555-9547
phone or fax 615-484-7680

Celtic
Camelot Books
Charles E. Wyatt
P.O. Box 2883
Vista, CA 92083
619-940-9472

Central America
Flo Silver Books
8442 Oakwood Ct. N
Indianapolis, IN 46260
317-255-5118

Marc Chagall
Paul Melzer Fine Books
12 E Vine St.
Redlands, CA 92373
909-792-7299

Children's Illustrated
Noreen Abbot Books
2666 44th Ave.
San Francisco, CA 94116
415-664-9464

Book & Tackle Shop
29 Old Colony Rd.
P.O. Box 114
Chestnut Hill, MA 02167
617-965-0459 (winter) or
401-596-0700 (summer)

Books of the Ages
Gary Overmann
4764 Silverwood Dr.
Batavia, OH 45103
513-732-3456

Bromer Booksellers
607 Boylston St.
Boston, MA 02116
617-247-2818 or fax 617-247-2975

19th & 20th C
Children's Book Adoption Agency
P.O. Box 643
Kensington, MD 20895-0643
301-565-2834 or fax 301-585-3091
e-mail: KIDS_BKS@interloc.com

Free search service
Steven Cieluch
15 Walbridge St., Ste. #10
Allston, MA 02134
617-734-7778

Ursula Davidson
Children's & Illustrated Books
134 Linden Ln.
San Rafael, CA 94901
414-454-3939 or fax 415-454-1087

Drusilla's Books
859 N Howard St.
Baltimore, MD 21201
401-225-0277

Edison Hall Books
5 Ventnor Dr.
Edison, NJ 08820
908-548-4455

Circa 1850s through 1970s
Encino Books
Diane Yaspan
5063 Gaviota Ave
Encino, CA 91436
818-905-711 or fax 818-501-7711

First Folio
1206 Brentwood
Paris, TN 38242
phone or fax 901-644-9940

Fran's Bookhouse
6601 Greene St.
Phil., PA 19119
215-438-2729 or fax 215-438-8997

Madeline, Eloise, Raggedy Ann & Andy, Uncle Wiggly, Wizard of Oz
Glo's Books & Collectibles
906 Shadywood
Southlake, TX 76092
817-481-1438

Susan Heller, Pages for Sages
22611 Halburton Rd.
Beachwood, OH 44122-3939
216-283-2665 or fax 216-991-2665

Ilene Kayne
1308 S Charles St.
Baltimore, MD 21230
410-347-7570
e-mail: IleneGold@aol.com

Bob Lakin
3021 Lavita Ln.
Dallas, TX 75234
214-247-3291

Marvelous Books
P.O. Box 1510
Ballwin, MO 63022
314-458-3301 or fax 314-273-5452
e-mail: marvlous@interloc.com

Much Ado
Seven Pleasant St.
Marblehead, MA 01945
617-639-0400

Nerman's Books
410-63 Albert St.
Winnipeg, Manitoba
Canada R3B 1G4
fax 204-947-0753

Page Books
HCR 65, Box 233
Kingston, AR 72472
501-861-5831

Jo Ann Reisler, Ltd.
360 Glyndon St., NE
Vienna, VA 22180
703-938-2967 or fax 703-938-9057

Scribe Company
Attn: Bonnie Smith
P.O. Box 1123
Flippin, AR 72634

Barbara Smith Books
P.O. Box 1185
Northampton, MA 01061
413-586-1453

Nancy Stewart, Books
1188 NW Weybridge Way
Beaverton, OR 97006
503-645-9779

Yesterday's Books
229 Riverview Dr.
Parchment, MI 49004
616-345-1011

Treasures from the Castle
Connie Castle
1720 N Livernois
Rochester, MI 48306
810-651-7317

Children's Series
Children's Book Adoption Agency
P.O. Box 643
Kensington, MD 20895-0643
301-565-2834 or fax 301-585-3091
e-mail: KIDS_BKS@interloc.com

Circa 1900s through 1970s
Encino Books
Diane Yaspan
5063 Gaviota Ave
Encino, CA 91436
818-905-711 or fax 818-501-7711

*Judy Bolton, Nancy Drew, Rick
Brant, Cherry Ames, etc.; also Dick &
Jane readers*

Glo's Books & Collectibles
906 Shadywood
Southlake, TX 76092
817-481-1438

Ilene Kayne
1308 S Charles St.
Baltimore, MD 21230
410-347-7570
e-mail: IleneGold@aol.com

Bob Lakin
3021 Lavita Ln.
Dallas, TX 75234
214-247-3291

Nerman's Books
410-63 Albert St.
Winnipeg, Manitoba
Canada R3B 1G4
fax 204-947-0753

Scribe Company
Attn: Bonnie Smith
P.O. Box 1123
Flippin, AR 72634

Bob and Gail Spicer
R.D. 1 Ashgrove Rd., Box 82
Cambridge, NY 12816
518-677-5139

Lee and Mike Temares
50 Hts. Rd.
Plandome, NY 11030
516-627-8688

Yesterday's Books
229 Riverview Dr.
Parchment, MI 49004
616-345-1011

Christian Faith
Books Now & Then
Dennis Patrick
P.O. Box 337
Stanley, ND 58784
701-628-2084

Christmas
Especially illustrated antiquarian
Drusilla's Books
859 N Howard St.
Baltimore, MD 21201
410-225-0277

Sir W.S. Churchill
Chartwell Booksellers
55 E 52nd St.
New York, NY 10055
212-308-0643

Robert L. Merriam
Rare, Used & Old Books
Newhall Rd.
Conway, MA 01341
413-369-4052

Cinema, Theatre & Films
Cinemage Books
105 W 27th St.
New York, NY 10001
212-243-4919

Xanadu Records, Ltd.
3242 Irwin Ave.
Kingsbridge, NY 10463
212-549-3655

Civil War
The Book Corner
Michael Tennero
728 W Lumsden Rd.
Brandon, FL 33511
813-684-1133

Brasser's
8701 Seminole Blvd.
Seminole, FL 34642

Chapel Hill Rare Books
P.O. Box 456
Carrboro, NC 27510
919-929-8351

Elder's Book Store
2115 Elliston Pl.
Nashville, TN 37203
615-327-1867

Rick Harmon
Military Books & Relics
910 Sullivan Dr.
Belvidere, IL 61008
815-547-7580

Jim Hodgson Books
908 S Manlius St.
Fayetteville, NY 13066
315-637-6264

Mason's Bookstore, Rare Books
  & Record Albums
115 S Main St.
Chambersburg, PA 17201
717-261-0541

K.C. Owings
P.O. Box 19
N Abington, MA 02351
617-857-1655

Also ephemera before 1900
Gordon Totty
Scarce Paper Americana
347 Shady Lake Pky.
Baton Rouge, LA 70810
504-766-8625

Cobb, Irvin S.
Always paying $3.00 each plus shipping. Send for immediate payment:
Bill Schroeder
5801 KY Dam Rd.
Paducah, KY 42003

Collectibles
Henry H. Hain III
Antiques & Collectibles
2623 N Second St.
Harrisburg, PA 17110
717-238-0534

Color Plate Books
Bowie & Co. Booksellers, Inc.
314 First Ave. S
Seattle, WA 98104
206-624-4100 or fax 206-223-0966

Drusilla's Books
859 N Howard St.
Baltimore, MD 21201
410-225-0277

Worldwide Antiquarian
P.O. Box 391
Cambridge, MA 02141
617-876-6220 or fax 617-876-0839
e-mail: mbalwan@aol.com

Comics
Passaic Book Center
594 Main Ave.
Passaic, NJ 07055
201-778-6646 or fax 201-778-6738

Cookery & Cookbooks
Book & Tackle Shop
29 Old Colony Rd.
P.O. Box 114
Chestnut Hill, MA 02167
617-965-0459 (winter) or
401-596-0700 (summer)

The Book Corner
Mike Tennero
728 W Lumsden Rd.
Brandon, FL 33511
813-684-1133

RAC Books
R.R. #2
P.O. Box 296
Seven Valleys, PA 17360
717-428-3776

Barbara Smith Books
P.O. Box 1185
Northampton, MA 01061
413-586-1453

Crime
The Silver Door
P.O. Box 3208
Redondo Beach, CA 90277
310-379-6005

Cyprus
W.B. O'Neill-Old & Rare Books
11609 Hunters Green Ct.
Reston, VA 22091
703-860-0782 or fax 703-620-0153

Decorative Arts
Robert L. Merriam
Rare, Used & Old Books
Newhall Rd.
Conway, MA 01341
413-369-4052

Detective
First editions
Karl M. Armens
740 Juniper Dr.
Iowa City, IA 52245

Mordida Books
P.O. Box 79322
Houston, TX 77279
713-467-4280 or fax 713-467-4182

Pulphouse
J.H. James
P.O. Box 481
Elberton, GA 30635
706-213-9280
e-mail: Pulpmaster@msn.com

Thomas Books
P.O. Box 14036
Phoenix, AZ 85063
602-247-9289

The Silver Door
P.O. Box 3208
Redondo Beach, CA 90277
310-379-6005

Earth Science
Used, out-of-print, rare
Patricia L. Daniel, Bookseller
13 English Ave.
Wichita, KS 62707-1005
316-683-2079 or fax 316-683-5448

Emily Dickinson
Robert L. Merriam
Rare, Used & Old Books
Newhall Rd.
Conway, MA 01341
413-369-4052

Disney
Cohen Books & Collectibles
Joel J. Cohen
P.O. Box 810310
Boca Raton, FL 33481
407-487-7888

Jay's House of Collectibles
75 Pky. Dr.
Syosset, NY 11791

Documents
McGowan Book Co.
39 Kimberly Dr.
Durham, NC 27707
919-403-1503 or fax 919-403-1706

Dogs
Kathleen Rals & Co.
211 Carolina Ave.
Phoenixville, PA 19460
610-933-1388

Thomas Edison
Edison Hall Books
5 Ventnor Dr.
Edison, NJ 08820
908-548-4455

Ephemera
Antique valentines
Kingsbury Productions
4555 N Pershing Ave., Ste. 33-138
Stockton, CA 95207
209-467-8438

The Mulberry Cat
Yvonne Davis
Jan Davis Martel
P.O. Box 3573
Boone, NC 28607
704-963-7693

Espionage
The Silver Door
P.O. Box 3208
Redondo Beach, CA 92077
310-379-6005

Estate Libraries
The Book Collector
2347 University Blvd.
Houston, TX 77005
713-661-2665

Exhibition Catalogs
L. Clarice Davis Art Books
P.O. Box 56054
Sherman Oaks, CA 91413-1054
818-787-1322

Exploration
Western
Terry Harper, Bookseller
P.O. Box 312
Vergennes, VT 05491-0312
802-877-9262

Heritage Book Shop, Inc.
8540 Melrose Ave.
Los Angeles, CA 90069
213-659-3674

Key Books
P.O. Box 58097
St. Petersburg, FL 33715
813-867-2931

Paul Melzer Fine Books
12 E Vine St.
Redlands, CA 92373
909-792-7299

Flo Silver Books
8442 Oakwood Ct. N
Indianapolis, IN 46260
317-255-5118

Fantasy
The Book Baron
1236 S Magnolia Ave.
Anaheim, CA 92804
714-527-7022 or fax 714-527-5634

Camelot Books
Charles E. Wyatt
P.O. Box 2883
Vista, CA 92083
619-940-9472

Farming
First editions
Karl M. Armens
740 Juniper Dr.
Iowa City, IA 52245

Also gardening
Hurley Books
1752 Rt. 12
Westmoreland, NH 03467-4724
603-399-4342 or fax 603-399-8326

Henry Lindeman
4769 Bavarian Dr.
Jackson, MI 49201
517-764-5728

Fiction
American, European, detective or crime
Ace Zerblonski
Malcolm McCollum, Proprietor
1419 North Royer
Colorado Springs, CO 80907
719-634-3941

Bob Lakin
3021 Lavita Ln.
Dallas, TX 75234
214-247-3291

19th & 20th-C American
Mason's Bookstore, Rare Books
   & Record Albums
115 S Main St.
Chambersburg, PA 17201
717-261-0541

Fine Bindings & Books
The Book Collector
2347 University Blvd.
Houston, TX 77005
713-661-2665

Bromer Booksellers
607 Boylston St.
Boston, MA 02116
617-247-2818 or fax 617-247-2975

Heritage Book Shop, Inc.
8540 Melrose Ave.
Los Angeles, CA 90069
310-659-3674 or fax 310-659-4872

Terry Harper, Bookseller
P.O. Box 312
Vergennes, VT 05491-0312
802-877-9262

George Robert Kane Fine Books
252 Third Ave.
Santa Cruz, CA 95062
phone or fax 408-426-4133

Kenneth Karimole, Bookseller, Inc.
P.O. Box 464
509 Wilshire Blvd.
Santa Monica, CA 94001
310-451-4342 or 310-458-5930

Mason's Bookstore, Rare Books
   & Record Albums
115 S Main St.
Chambersburg, PA 17201
717-261-0541

Paul Melzer Fine Books
12 E Vine St.
Redlands, CA 92373
909-792-7299

Also sets
Randall House
835 Laguna St.
Santa Barbara, CA 93101
805-963-1909 or fax 805-963-1650

Fine Press
Susan Heller, Pages for Sages
22611 Halburton Rd.
Beachwood, OH 44122-3939
216-283-2665 or fax 316-991-2665

Heritage Book Shop, Inc.
8540 Melrose Ave.
Los Angeles, CA 90069
310-659-3674 or fax 310-659-4872

Randall House
835 Laguna St.
Santa Barbara, CA 93101
805-963-1909 or fax 805-963-1650

Firearms
Melvin Marcher, Bookseller
6204 N Vermont
Oklahoma City, OK 73112

First Editions
After 1937
A.B.A.C.U.S.®
Phillip E. Miller
343 S Chesterfield St.
Aiken, SC 29801
803-648-4632

Hyper-modern
Almark & Co.-Booksellers
P.O. Box 7
Thornhill, Ontario
Canada L3T 3N1
phone or fax 905-764-2665

Modern or signed
AL-PAC
Lamar Kelley Antiquarian Books
2625 E Southern Ave., C-120
Tempe, AZ 85282
602-831-3121 or fax 602-831-3193

Amaranth Books
P.O. Box 421
Wilmette, IL 60091-0421
708-328-2939

Karl M. Armens
740 Juniper Dr.
Iowa City, IA 52245

Modern
Bella Luna Books
P.O. Box 260425
Highlands Ranch, CO 80126-0425
800-497-4717 or fax 303-794-3135

Between the Covers
35 W Maple Ave.
Merchantville, NJ 08109
609-665-2284 or fax 609-665-3639
e-mail: BetweenCov@aol.com

The Book Baron
1236 S Magnolia Ave.
Anaheim, CA 92804
714-527-7022 or fax 714-527-5634

Modern
Chapel Hill Rare Books
P.O. Box 456
Carrboro, NC 27510
919-929-8351

Modern
Bernard E. Goodman, Bookseller
7421 SW 147 Ct.
Miami, FL 33193
305-382-2464

Edison Hall Books
5 Ventnor Dr.
Edison, NJ 08820
908-548-4455

Literary
Janet Egelhofer
36 Fairfield Ave.
Holyoke, MA 01040
413-532-1295

Modern
Susan Heller, Pages for Sages
22611 Halburton Rd.
Beachwood, OH 44122-3939
216-283-2665 or fax 216-991-2665

Modern
David Holloway, Bookseller
7430 Grace St.
Springfield, VA 22150
703-569-1798

Heritage Book Shop, Inc.
8540 Melrose Ave.
Los Angeles, CA 90069
310-659-3674 or fax 310-659-4872

Modern
Ken Lopez, Bookseller
51 Huntington Rd.
Hadley, MA 01035
413-584-4827 or fax 413-584-2045

Much Ado
Seven Pleasant St.
Marblehead, MA 01945
617-639-0400

Robert Mueller Rare Books
8124 W 26th St.
N Riverside, IL 60546
708-447-6441

Jeffrey Lee Pressman, Bookseller
3246 Ettie St.
Oakland, CA 94608
510-652-6232

Pulphouse
J.H. James
P.O. Box 481
Elberton, GA 30635
706-213-9280
e-mail: Pulpmaster@msn.com

American & British
Quill & Brush
Box 5365
Rockville, MD 20848
301-460-3700 or fax 301-871-5425

*Especially fiction, cookery, children's,
business, sports & illustrated*
Eileen Serxner
Box 2544
Bala Cynwyd, PA 19004
610-664-7960

Modern
Ed Smith Books
P.O. Box 66
Oak View, CA 93022
805-646-2844 or fax 805-649-2863
e-mail: edsbooks@aol.com

Scribe Company
Attn: Bonnie Smith
P.O. Box 1123
Flippin, AR 72634

Modern
The Early West/Whodunit Books
P.O. Box 9292
College Sta., TX 77842
409-775-6047 or fax 409-764-7758

Harrison Fisher
Parnassus Books
218 N 9th St.
Boise, ID 83702

Fishing
Artis Books
201 N Second Ave.
P.O. Box 208
Alpena, MI 49707
517-354-3401

Edison Hall Books
5 Ventnor Dr.
Edison, NJ 08820
908-548-4455

Jim Hodgson Books
908 S Manlius St.
Fayetteville, NY 13066
315-637-6264

Melvin Marcher, Bookseller
6204 N Vermont
Oklahoma City, OK 73112

Mason's Bookstore, Rare Books
& Record Albums
115 S Main
Chambersburg, PA 17201
717-261-0541

Yesterday's Books
229 Riverview Dr
Parchment, MI 49004
616-345-1011

Florida
Brasser's
8701 Seminole Blvd.
Seminole, FL 34642

Football
Brasser's
8701 Seminole Blvd.
Seminole, FL 34642

Fore-Edge Painted Books
Susan Heller, Pages for Sages
22611 Halburton Rd.
Beachwood, OH 44122-3939
216-283-2665 or fax 316-991-2665

George Robert Kane Fine Books
252 Third Ave.
Santa Cruz, CA 95062
phone or fax 408-426-4133

Freemasonry

Mason's Bookstore, Rare Books
  & Record Albums
115 S Main St.
Chambersburg, PA 17201
717-261-0541

Gambling & Gaming

Gambler's Book Shop
630 S Eleventh St.
Las Vegas, NV 89101
800-634-6243

Especially on cheating
John A. Greget-Magic Lists
2631 E Claire Dr.
Phoenix, AZ 85032-4932
602-971-5497

Games

Card or board; Whist & Bridge
Bill and Mimi Sachen
927 Grand Ave.
Waukegan, IL 60085
847-662-7204

Gardening

The American Botanist Booksellers
P.O. Box 532
Chillicothe, IL 61523
309-274-5254

The Book Corner
Mike Tennero
728 W Lumsden Rd.
Brandon, FL 33511
813-684-1133

Brooks Books
Philip B. Nesty
P.O. Box 21473
1343 New Hampshire Dr.
Concord, CA 94521
510-672-4566 or fax 510-672-3338

The Captain's Bookshelf, Inc.
P.O. Box 2258
Asheville, NC 28802-2258
704-253-6631

Gazetteers

Murray Hudson
Antiquarian Books & Maps
The Old Post Office
109 S Church St.
P.O. Box 163
Halls, TN 38040
901-836-9057 or 800-748-9946

Genealogy

Elder's Book Store
2115 Elliston Pl.
Nashville, TN 37203
615-327-1867

General Out-of-Print

Best-Read Books
122 State St.
Sedro-Wooley, WA 98284
206-855-2179

Bicentennial Book Shop
820 S Westnedge Ave.
Kalamazoo, MI 49008
616-345-5987

The Book Baron
1236 S Magnolia Ave.
Anaheim, CA 92804
714-527-7022 or fax 714-527-5634

Book Den South
2249 First St.
Ft. Myers, FL 33901
813-332-2333

The Bookseller, Inc.
521 W Exchange St.
Akron, OH 44302
216-762-3101

Cinemage Books
105 W 27th St.
New York, NY 10001

Antiquarian
Eastside Books & Paper
P.O. Box 1581, Gracie Sta.
New York, NY 10028-0013
212-759-6299

Edison Hall Books
5 Ventnor Dr.
Edison, NJ 08820
908-548-4455

Fran's Bookhouse
6601 Greene St.
Phil., PA 19119
215-438-2729 or fax 215-438-8997

Grave Matters
P.O. Box 32192-08
Cincinnati, OH 45232
513-242-7527 or fax 513-242-5115
e-mail: GraveMatrs@aol.com

George Robert Kane Fine Books
252 Third Ave.
Santa Cruz, CA 95062
phone or fax 408-426-4133

McGowan Book Co.
39 Kimberly Dr.
Durham, NC 27707
919-403-1503 or fax 919-403-1706

Robert L. Merriam
Rare, Used & Old Books
New Hall Rd.
Conway, MA 01341
413-369-4052

The Mulberry Cat
Yvonne Davis
Jan Davis Martel
P.O. Box 3573
Boone, NC 28607
704-963-7693

Passaic Book Center
594 Main Ave.
Passaic, NJ 07055
201-778-6646 or fax 201-778-6738

RAC Books
R.R. #2
P.O. Box 296
Seven Valleys, PA 17360
717-428-3776

J. Sampson Antiques & Books
107 S Main
Harrodsburg, KY 40330
606-734-7829

Significant Books
3053 Madison Rd.
P.O. Box 9248
Cincinnati, OH 45209
513-321-7567

A.A. Vespa
P.O. Box 637
Park Ridge, IL 60068
708-692-4210

Genetics

The King's Market Bookshops
P.O. Box 709
Boulder, CO 80306-0709
303-447-0234

Geographies

Murray Hudson
Antiquarian Books & Maps
The Old Post Office
109 S Church St.
P.O. Box 163
Halls, TN 38040
901-836-9057 or 800-748-9946

Overlee Farm Books
P.O. Box 1155
Stockbridge, MA 01262
413-637-2277

Golf
Brasser's
8701 Seminole Blvd.
Seminole, FL 34642

David Goodis
The American Dust Co.
47 Park Ct.
Staten Island, NY 10301
718-442-8253

The Great Lakes
Artis Books
201 N Second Ave.
P.O. Box 822
Alpena, MI 49707
517-354-3401

Sue Grafton
Glo's Books & Collectibles
906 Shadywood
Southlake, TX 76092
817-481-1438

Thomas Books
P.O. Box 14036
Phoenix, AZ 85063
602-247-9289

Greece
W.B. O'Neill-Old & Rare Books
11609 Hunters Green Ct.
Reston, VA 22091
703-860-0782 or fax 703-620-0153

Herbals
The American Botanist Booksellers
P.O. Box 352
Chillicothe, IL 61523
309-274-5254

Brooks Books
Philip B. Nesty
P.O. Box 21473
1343 New Hampshire Dr.
Concord, CA 94521
510-672-4566 or fax 510-672-3338

Heritage Press
Lee and Mike Temares
50 Hts. Rd.
Plandome, NY 11030
516-627-8688

History
American & natural
Ace Zerblonski
Malcolm McCollum, Proprietor
1419 North Royer
Colorado Springs, CO 80907
719-634-3941

Science & medicine
Amaranth Books
P.O. Box 421
Wilmette, IL 60091-0421
708-328-2939

Camelot Books
Charles E. Wyatt
P.O. Box 2883
Vista, CA 92083
619-940-9472

Early American &Indian
Duck Creek Books
Jim and Shirley Richards
P.O. Box 203
Caldwell, OH 43724
614-732-4856 (10 am to 10 pm)

Postal & postal artifacts
McGowan Book Co.
39 Kimberly Dr.
Durham, NC 27707
919-403-1503 or fax 919-403-1706

Local & regional
Significant Books
3053 Madison Rd.
P.O. Box 9248
Cincinnati, OH 45209
513-321-7567

Hollywood
Cinemage Books
105 W 27th St.
New York, NY 10001
212-243-4919

Horse Books
October Farm
2609 Branch Rd.
Raleigh, NC 27610
919-772-0482 or fax 919-779-6265

Horticulture
The American Botanist Booksellers
P.O. Box 532
Chillicothe, IL 61523
309-274-5254

Ornamental
Brooks Books
Philip B. Nesty
P.O. Box 21473
1343 New Hampshire Dr.
Concord, CA 94521
510-672-4566 or fax 510-672-3338

Woodbridge B. Brown
P.O. Box 445
Turners Falls, MA 01376
413-772-2509 or 413-773-5710

Horror
The Book Baron
1236 S Magnolia Ave.
Anaheim, CA 92804
714-527-7022 or fax 714-527-5634

Kai Nygaard
19421 Eighth Place
Escondido, CA 92029
619-746-9039

Pandora's Books, Ltd.
P.O. Box BB-54
Neche, ND 58265
204-324-8548 or fax 204-324-1628

L. Ron Hubbard
AL-PAC
Lamar Kelley Antiquarian Books
2625 E Southern Ave., C-120
Tempe, AZ 85282
602-831-3121 or fax 602-831-3193

Humanities
Reprint editions
Dover Publications
Dept. A 214
E. Second St.
Mineola, NY 11501

Hunting
Artis Books
201 N Second Ave.
P.O. Box 822
Alpena, MI 49707
517-354-3401

Edison Hall Books
5 Ventnor Dr.
Edison, NJ 08820
908-548-4455

Jim Hodgson Books
908 S Manlius St.
Fayetteville, NY 13066
315-637-6264

Melvin Marcher, Bookseller
6204 N Vermont
Oklahoma City, OK 73112

Yesterday's Books
229 Riverview Dr.
Parchment, MI 49004
616-345-1011

Idaho
Parnassus Books
218 N 9th St.
Boise, ID 83702

Illustrated
Noreen Abbot Books
2666 44th Ave.
San Francisco, CA 94116
415-664-9464

Bowie & Co. Booksellers, Inc.
314 First Ave. S
Seattle, WA 98104
206-624-4100 or fax 206-223-0966

Books of the Ages
Gary Overmann
4764 Silverwood Dr.
Batavia, OH 45103
513-732-3456

Bromer Booksellers
607 Boylston St.
Boston, MA 02116
617-247-2818 or fax 617-247-2975

George Robert Kane Fine Books
252 Third Ave.
Santa Cruz, CA 95062
phone or fax 408-426-4133

Old or new; may subjects
Gary R. Smith
517 Laurel Ave.
Modesto, CA 95351

Barbara Smith Books
P.O. Box 1185
Northampton, MA 01061
413-586-1453

Randall House
835 Laguna St.
Santa Barbara, CA 93101
805-963-1909 or fax 805-963-1650

Irvin S. Cobb
*Always paying $3.00 each plus ship-
ping. Send for immediate payment to:*
Bill Schroeder
5801 KY Dam Rd.
Paducah, KY 42003

Indians
Wars
K.C. Owings
P.O. Box 19
N Abington, MA 02351
617-857-1655

Plains, Black Hills, etc.
Flo Silver Books
8442 Oakwood Ct. N
Indianapolis, IN 46260
317-255-5118

Iowa
Karl M. Armens
740 Juniper Dr.
Iowa City, IA 52245

Jazz
Chartwell Booksellers
55 E 52nd St.
New York, NY 10055
212-308-0643

James Joyce
Paul Melzer Fine Books
12 E Vine St.
Redlands, CA 92373
909-792-7299

John Deere
Henry Lindeman
4769 Bavarian Dr.
Jackson, MI 49201
517-764-5728

Judaica
Stanley Schwartz
1934 Pentuckett Ave.
San Diego, CA 92104-5732
619-232-5888 or fax 619-233-5833

Juvenile
Cover to Cover
P.O. Box 687
Chapel Hill, NC 27514

Edison Hall Books
5 Ventnor Dr.
Edison, NJ 08820
908-548-4455

Susan Heller, Pages for Sages
22611 Halburton Rd.
Beachwood, OH 44122-3939
216-283-2665 or fax 216-991-2665

Page Books
HRC 65, Box 233
Kingston, AR 72472
501-861-5831

Jo Ann Reisler, Ltd.
360 Glyndon St., NE
Vienna, VA 22180
703-938-2967 or fax 703-938-9057

Nancy Stewart, Books
1188 NW Weybridge Way
Beaverton, OR 97006
503-645-9779

Lee and Mike Temares
50 Hts. Rd.
Plandome, NY 11030
516-627-8688

Kentucky Authors
Bill Schroeder
P.O. Box 3009
Paducah, KY 42002-3009

Kentucky History
Bill Schroeder
P.O. Box 3009
Paducah, KY 42002-3009

King Arthur
Also early Britain
Thorn Books
P.O. Box 1244
Moorpark, CA 93020
805-529-3647 or fax 805-529-0022
e-mail: thornbooks@aol.com

Labor
Volume I Books
1 Union St.
Hillsdale, MI 49242
517-437-2228

Landscape Architecture
The American Botanist Booksellers
P.O. Box 532
Chillicothe, IL 61523
309-274-5254

Brooks Books
Philip B. Nesty
P.O. Box 21473
1343 New Hampshire Dr.
Concord, CA 94521
510-672-4566 or fax 510-672-3338

Latin American Literature
Almark & Co.-Booksellers
P.O. Box 7
Thornhill, Ontario
Canada L3T 3N1
phone or fax 905-764-2665

Flo Silver Books
8442 Oakwood Ct. N
Indianapolis, IN 46260
317-255-5118

Law & Crime
Meyer Boswell Books, Inc.
2141 Mission St.
San Francisco, CA 94110
415-255-6400 or fax 415-255-6499
e-mail: rarelaw@myerbos.com
http://www.meyerbos.com

T.E. Lawrence
Denis McDonnell, Bookseller
653 Park St.
Honesdale, PA 18431
717-253-6706 or fax 717-253-6785
e-mail:
denis.mcdonnell@microserve.com

Lawrence of Arabia
Denis McDonnell, Bookseller
653 Park St.
Honesdale, PA 18431
717-253-6706 or fax 717-253-6785
e-mail:
denis.mcdonnell@microserve.com

Lebanon
W.B. O'Neill-Old & Rare Books
11609 Hunters Green Ct
Reston, VA 22091
703-860-0782 or fax 703-620-0153

Lewis & Clark Expedition
George H. Tweney
16660 Marine View Dr. SW
Seattle, WA 98166
206-243-8243

Limited Editions
Scribe Company
Attn: Bonnie Smith
P.O. Box 1123
Flippin, AR 72634

Lee and Mike Temares
50 Hts. Rd.
Plandome, NY 11030
516-627-8688

Literature
Amaranth Books
P.O. Box 421
Wilmette, IL 60091-0421
708-328-2939

In translation
Almark & Co., Booksellers
P.O. Box 7
Thornhill, Ontario
Canada L3T 3N1
phone or fax 905-764-2665

First editions
Karl M. Armens
740 Juniper Dr.
Iowa City, IA 52245

18th- & 19th-C English
The Book Collector
2347 University Blvd.
Houston, TX 77005
713-661-2665

First editions
Bromer Booksellers
607 Boylston St.
Boston, MA 02116
617-247-2818 or fax 617-247-2975

African-American
Between the Covers
35 W Maple Ave.
Merchantville, NJ 08109
609-665-2284 or fax 609-665-3639
e-mail: BetweenCov@aol.com

The Captain's Bookshelf, Inc.
P.O. Box 2258
Asheville, NC 22802-2258
704-253-6631

Chapel Hill Rare Books
P.O. Box 456
Carrboro, NC 27510
919-929-8351

Southern
Elder's Book Store
2115 Elliston Pl.
Nashville, TN 37203
615-327-1867

Susan Heller, Pages for Sages
22611 Halburton Rd.
Beachwood, OH 44122-3939
216-283-2665 or fax 216-991-2665

Ken Lopez, Bookseller
51 Huntington Rd.
Hadley, MA 01035
413-584-4827 or fax 413-584-2045

Mason's Bookstore, Rare Books
  & Record Albums
115 S Main St.
Chambersburg, PA 17201
717-261-0541

Much Ado
Seven Pleasant St.
Marblehead, MA 01945
617-639-0400

Randall House
835 Laguna St.
Santa Barbara, CA 93101
805-963-1909 or fax 805-963-1650

Thorn Books
P.O. Box 1244
Moorpark, CA 93020
805-529-3647 or fax 805-529-0022
e-mail: thornbooks@aol.com

Wellerdt's Books
3700 S Osprey Ave. #214
Sarasota, FL 34239
813-365-1318

Xanadu Records, Ltd.
3242 Irwin Ave.
Kingsbridge, NY 10463
212-549-3655

Magazines
Mystery only
Grave Matters
P.O. Box 32192-08
Cincinnati, OH 45232
513-242-7527 or fax 513-242-5115
e-mail: GraveMatrs@aol.com

Robert A. Madle
4406 Bestor Dr.
Rockville, MD 20853
301-460-4712

The Magazine Baron
1236 S Magnolia Ave.
Anaheim, CA 92804
714-527-0358 or fax 714-527-5634

Relating to decorative arts
Mordida Books
P.O. Box 79322
Houston, TX 77279
713-467-4280 or fax 713-467-4182

Passaic Book Center
594 Main Ave.
Passaic, NJ 07055
201-778-6646 or fax 201-778-6738

Magic
Especially tricks
John A. Greget-Magic Lists
2631 E Claire Dr.
Phoenix, AZ 85032
602-971-5497

Manuscripts
Susan Heller, Pages for Sages
P.O. Box 2219
Beachwood, OH 44122-3939
216-283-2665 or fax 216-991-2665

Heritage Book Shop, Inc.
8540 Melrose Ave.
Los Angeles, CA 90069
310-659-3674 or fax 310-659-4872

Key Books
P.O. Box 58097
St. Petersburg, FL 33715
813-867-2931

Asiatic languages
Worldwide Antiquarian
P.O. Box 391
Cambridge, MA 02141
617-876-6220 or fax 617-876-0839
e-mail: mbalwan@aol.com

Randall House
835 Laguna St.
Santa Barbara, CA 93101
805-963-1909 or fax 805-963-1650

Maps
State, pocket-type, ca 1800s
The Bookseller, Inc.
521 W Exchange St.
Akron, OH 44302
216-762-3101

Bowie & Co. Booksellers, Inc.
314 First Ave. S
Seattle, WA 98104
206-624-4100 or fax 206-223-0966

Pre-1900 Florida
Brasser's
8701 Seminole Blvd.
Seminole, FL 34642

Elegant Book & Map Company
815 Harrison Ave.
P.O. Box 1302
Cambridge, OH 43725
614-432-4068

Maritime
Book & Tackle Shop
29 Old Colony Rd.
P.O. Box 114
Chestnut Hill, MA 02167
617-965-0459 (winter) or
401-596-0700 (summer)

Overlee Farm Books
P.O. Box 1155
Stockbridge, MA 01262
413-637-2277

J. Tuttle Maritime Books
1806 Laurel Crest
Madison, WI 53705
608-238-SAIL (7245)
fax 608-238-7249

Martial Arts
Nutmeg Books
354 New Litchfield St. (Rte. 202)
Torrington, CT 06790
203-482-9696

Masonic History
Mason's Bookstore, Rare Books
  & Record Albums
115 S Main St.
Chambersburg, PA 17201
717-261-0541

Mathematics
Significant Books
3053 Madison Rd.
P.O. Box 9248
Cincinnati, OH 45209
513-321-7567

Medicine
Amaranth Books
P.O. Box 421
Wilmette, IL 60091-0421
708-328-2939

Book & Tackle
29 Old Colony Rd.
P.O. Box 114
Chestnut Hill, MA 02167
617-965-0459 (winter) or
401-596-0700 (summer)

Key Books
P.O. Box 58097
St. Petersburg, FL 33715
813-867-2931

M & S Rare Books, Inc.
P.O. Box 2594, E Side Sta.
Providence, RI 02906
401-421-1050 or fax 401-272-0831
(attention M & S)

Smithfield Rare Books
20 Deer Run Trail
Smithfield, RI 02917
401-231-8225

Medieval
Camelot Books
Charles E. Wyatt
P.O. Box 2883
Vista, CA 92083
619-940-9472

Metaphysics
AL-PAC
Lamar Kelley Antiquarian Books
2625 E Southern Ave., C-120
Tempe, AZ 85282
602-831-3121 or fax 602-831-3193

Meteorology
Knollwood Books
Lee and Peggy Price
P.O. Box 197
Oregon, WI 53575
608-835-8861 or fax 608-835-8421

Mexico
Flo Silver Books
8442 Oakwood Ct. N
Indianapolis, IN 46260
317-255-5118

Michigan
Artis Books
201 N Second Ave.
P.O. Box 822
Alpena, MI 49707
517-354-3401

Yesterday's Books
229 Riverview Dr.
Parchment, MI 49004
616-345-1011

Middle Eastern Countries
Denis McDonnell, Bookseller
653 Park St.
Honesdale, PA 18431
717-253-6706 or fax 717-253-6785
e-mail:
denis.mcdonnell@microserve.com

Worldwide Antiquarian
P.O. Box 391
Cambridge, MA 02141
617-876-6220 or fax 617-876-0839
e-mail: mbalwan@aol.com

Militaria
The Book Corner
Mike Tennero
728 W Lumsden Rd.
Brandon, FL 33511
813-684-1133

The Bookseller, Inc.
521 W Exchange St.
Akron, OH 44302
216-762-3101

Brasser's
8701 Seminole Blvd.
Seminole, FL 34642

Edison Hall Books
5 Ventnor Dr.
Edison, NJ 08820
908-548-4455

Rick Harmon
Military Books & Relics
910 Sullivan Dr.
Belvidere, IL 61008
815-547-7580

Robert L. Merriam
Rare, Used & Old Books
Newhall Rd.
Conway, MA 01341
413-369-4052

Significant Books
3053 Madison Rd.
P.O Box 9248
Cincinnati, OH 45209
513-321-7567

Before 1900
Gordon Totty
Scarce Paper Americana
347 Shady Lake Pky.
Baton Rouge, LA 70810
504-766-8625

Histories
Tryon County Bookshop
2071 State Hwy. 29
Johnstown, NY 12905
518-762-1060

Volume I Books
1 Union St.
Hillsdale, MI 49242
517-437-2228

Miniature Books
Bromer Booksellers
607 Boylston St.
Boston, MA 02116
617-247-2818 or fax 617-247-2975

Foreign atlases
Murray Hudson
Antiquarian Books & Maps
The Old Post Office
109 S Church St.
P.O. Box 163
Halls, TN 38040
901-836-9057 or 800-748-9946

Hurley Books
1752 Rt. 12
Westmoreland, NH 03467-4724
603-399-4342 or fax 603-399-8326

Miscellaneous
Bridgman Books
906 Roosevelt Ave.
Rome, NY 13440
315-337-7252

Montana
Nancy C. May
Bygone Books 'n Things
1720-C S Peaceable Rd.
McAlester, OK 74501

Movies
Cinemage Books
105 W 27th St.
New York, NY 10001
212-243-4919

Mystery
Karl M. Armens
740 Juniper Dr.
Iowa City, IA 52245

First editions
Island Books
P.O. Box 19
Old Westbury, NY 11568
516-921-9408

Mordida Books
P.O. Box 79322
Houston, TX 77279
713-467-4280 or fax 713-467-4182

Mail order; primarily first editions
Norris Books
2491 San Ramon Vly. Blvd.
Ste. #1-201
San Ramon, CA 94583
phone or fax 510-867-1218
www.slip.net/cgchav/norrisbooks
e-mail: norrisbooks@slip.net

Pandora's Books, Ltd.
P.O. Box BB-54
Neche, ND 48265
204-324-8548 or fax 204-324-1628

Pulphouse
P.O. Box 481
Elberton, GA 30635-0481
706-213-9280
e-mail: Pulpmaster@msn.com

RAC Books
R.R. #2
P.O. Box 296
Seven Valleys, PA 17360
717-428-3776

The Silver Door
P.O. Box 3208
Redondo Beach, CA 90277
310-379-6005

Napoleonic Memorabilia
The Book Collector
2347 University Blvd.
Houston, TX 7005
713-661-2665

Narcotics
Nutmeg Books
354 New Litchfield St. (Rte. 202)
Torrington, CT 06790
203-482-9696

Natural History
Thomas C. Bayer
85 Reading Ave.
Hillsdale, MI 49242
517-439-4134

Bohemian Bookworm
110 W 25th St., 9th Floor
New York, NY 10001
212-620-5627

Woodbridge B. Brown
P.O. Box 445
Turners Falls, MA 01376
413-772-2509 or 413-773-5710

Noriko I. Ciochon
Natural History Books
1025 Keokut St.
Iowa City, IA 52240
319-354-4844

Melvin Marcher, Bookseller
6204 N Vermont
Oklahoma City, OK 73112

Nautical
Much Ado
Seven Pleasant St.
Marblehead, MA 01945
617-639-0400

Overlee Farm Books
P.O. Box 1155
Stockbridge, MA 01262
413-637-2277

Needlework
Stanley Schwartz
1934 Pentuckett Ave.
San Diego, CA 92104-5732
619-232-5888 or fax 619-233-5833

Neuroscience
John Gach Books
5620 Waterloo Rd.
Columbia, MD 21045
410-465-9023 or fax 410-465-0649

New England
Book & Tackle
29 Old Colony Rd.
P.O. Box 114
Chestnut Hill, MA 02167
617-965-0459 (winter) or
401-596-0700 (summer)

Non-Fiction
Pre-1950
Brasser's
8701 Seminole Blvd.
Seminole, FL 34642

Novels
The Silver Door
P.O. Box 3208
Redondo Beach, CA 90277
310-379-6005

Occult
AL-PAC
Lamar Kelley Antiquarian Books
2625 E Southern Ave., C-120
Tempe, AZ 85282
602-831-3121 or fax 602-831-3193

Ohio
The Bookseller, Inc.
521 W Exchange St.
Akron, OH 44302
216-762-3101

Omar Khayyam
Worldwide Antiquarian
P.O. Box 391
Cambridge, MA 02141
617-876-6220 or fax 617-876-0839
e-mail: mbalwan@aol.com

Original Art
By children's illustrators
Kendra Krienke
230 Central Park W
New York, NY 10024
201-930-9709 or 201-930-9765

Paperbacks
The American Dust Co.
47 Park Ct.
Staten Island, NY 10301
718-442-8253

For Collectors Only
2028B Ford Pky. #136
St. Paul, MN 55116

Michael Gerlicher
1375 Rest Point Rd.
Orono, MN 55364

Bernard E. Goodman, Bookseller
7421 SW 147 Ct.
Miami, FL 33193
305-382-2464

Vintage
Grave Matters
P.O. Box 32192-08
Cincinnati, OH 45232
513-242-7527 or fax 513-242-5115
e-mail: GraveMatrs@aol.com

Modern Age Books
P.O. Box 325
E Lansing, MI 48826
517-351-9334

Originals
Mordida Books
P.O. Box 79322
Houston, TX 77279
713-467-4280 or fax 713-467-4182

Olde Current Books
Daniel P. Shay
356 Putnam Ave.
Ormond Beach, FL 32174
904-672-8998
e-mail: PEAKMYSTER@aol.com

Pandora's Books, Ltd.
P.O. Box BB-54
Neche, ND 58265
204-324-8548 or fax 204-324-1628

Pulphouse
J.H. James
P.O. Box 481
Elberton, GA 30635
706-213-9280
e-mail: Pulpmaster@msn.com

Also trades; want lists welcomed
Roger Reus
9412 Huron Ave.
Richmond, VA 23294
Mail order only

Tom Rolls
640 E Seminary #2
Greencastle, IN 46135

Robert B. Parker
Thomas Books
P.O. Box 14036
Phoenix, AZ 85063
602-247-9289

Pennsylvania
Mason's Bookstore, Rare Books
  & Record Albums
115 S Main
Chambersburg, PA 17201
717-261-0541

Performing Arts
Bowie & Co. Booksellers, Inc.
314 First Ave. S
Seattle, WA 98104
206-624-4100

Philosophy
The Book Corner
Mike Tennero
728 W Lumsden Rd.
Brandon, FL 33511
813-684-1133

John Gach Books
5620 Waterloo Rd.
Columbia, MD 21045
410-465-9023 or fax 410-465-0649

Photography
Cary Loren
The Captain's Bookshelf, Inc.
P.O. Box 2258
Asheville, NC 28802-2258
704-253-6631

Significant Books
3053 Madison Rd.
P.O. Box 9248
Cincinnati, OH 45209
513-321-7567

19th-C Middle & Far East Countries
Worldwide Antiquarian
P.O. Box 391
Cambridge, MA 02141
617-876-6220 or fax 617-876-0839
e-mail: mbalwan@aol.com

Playing Cards
Bill and Mimi Sachen
927 Grand Ave.
Waukegan, IL 60085
847-662-7204

Poetry

Edison Hall Books
5 Ventnor Dr.
Edison, NJ 08820
908-548-4455

Janet Egelhofer
36 Fairfield Ave.
Holyoke, MA 01040
413-532-1295

Ed Smith Books
P.O. Box 66
Oak View, CA 93022
805-649-2844 or fax 805-649-2863
e-mail: edsbooks@aol.com

VERSEtility Books
P.O. Box 1133
Farmington, CT 06034-1133
860-677-0606

Polar Explorations & Ephemera

Alaskan Heritage Bookshop
174 S Franklin, P.O. 22165
Juneau, AK 99802

Parmer Books
7644 Forrestal Rd.
San Diego, CA 92120-2203
619-287-0693 or fax 619-287-6135
e-mail: ParmerBook@aol.com

Political

Realm of Colorado
P.O. Box 24
Parker, CO 80134

Radical
Volume I Books
1 Union St.
Hillsdale, MI 49242
517-437-2228

Post Cards

Book & Tackle Shop
29 Old Colony Rd.
P.O. Box 114
Chestnut Hill, MA 02167
617-965-0459 (winter) or
401-596-0700 (summer)

Posters

The Mulberry Cat
Yvonne Davis
Jan Davis Martel
P.O. Box 3573
Boone, NC 28607
704-963-7693

Pre-Colombian Art

Flo Silver Books
8442 Oakwood Ct. N
Indianapolis, IN 46260
317-255-5118

Press Books

Heritage Book Shop, Inc.
8540 Melrose Ave.
Los Angeles, CA 90069
213-659-3674

Randall House
835 Laguna St.
Santa Barbara, CA 93101
805-963-1909 or fax 805-963-1650

Prints

The Mulberry Cat
Yvonne Davis
Jan Davis Martel
P.O. Box 3573
Boone, NC 28607
704-963-7693

Private Presses

American
Richard Blacher
209 Plymouth Colony, Alps Rd.
Branford, CT 06405

First Folio
1206 Brentwood
Paris, TN 34842
phone or fax 901-644-9940

Susan Heller, Pages for Sages
22611 Halburton Rd.
Beachwood, OH 44122-3939
216-283-2665 or fax 216-991-2665

Promoters of Paper, Ephemera & Book Fairs

Kingsbury Productions
Katherine and David Kreider
4555 N Pershing Ave., Ste. 33-138
Stockton, CA 95207
209-467-8438

Psychedelia

Nutmeg Books
354 New Litchfield St. (Rte. 202)
Torrington, CT 06790
203-482-9696

Psychiatry

John Gach Books
5620 Waterloo Rd.
Columbia, MD 21045
410-465-9023 or fax 410-465-0649

Psychoanalysis

Also related subjects
John Gach Books
5620 Waterloo Rd.
Columbia, MD 21045
410-465-9023 or fax 410-465-0649

Psychology

John Gach Books
5620 Waterloo Rd.
Columbia, MD 21045
410-465-9023 or fax 410-465-0649

The King's Market Bookshops
P.O. Box 709
Boulder, CO 80306-0709
303-447-0234

Pulps

Science fiction & fantasy before 1945
Robert A. Madle
4406 Bestor Dr.
Rockville, MD 20853
301-460-4712

Quaker

Vintage Books
181 Hayden Rowe St.
Hopkinton, MA 01748
517-437-2228

Also Shakers, Christians & Collectivists
Duck Creek Books
Jim & Shirley Richards
P.O. Box 203
Caldwell, OH 43724
614-732-4856 (10 am to 10 pm)

Quilt Books

Bill Schroeder
P.O. Box 3009
Paducah, KY 42002-3009

Galerie De Boicourt
6136 Westbrooke Dr.
W Bloomfield, MI 48322
810-788-9253

Arthur Rackham

Books of the Ages
Gary Overmann
4764 Silverwood Dr.
Batavia, OH 45103
513-732-3456

R.R. Donnelley Christmas Books

Linda Holycross
109 N Sterling Ave.
Veedersburg, IN 47987

Railroading
Mason's Rare & Used Books
115 S Main St.
Chambersburg, PA 17201
717-261-0541

Rare & Unusual Books
First Folio
1206 Brentwood
Paris, TN 38242
phone or fax 901-644-9940

Susan Heller, Pages for Sages
22611 Halburton Rd.
Beachwood, OH 44122-3939
216-283-2665 or fax 216-991-2665

Kenneth Karimole, Bookseller, Inc.
P.O. Box 464
509 Wilshire Blvd.
Santa Monica, CA 94001
310-451-4342 or 310-458-5930

M & S Rare Books, Inc.
P.O. Box 2594, E Side Sta.
Providence, RI 02906
401-421-1050 or fax 401-272-0831
(attention M & S)

Reprint editions
Dover Publications
Dept. A 214
E Second St.
Mineola, NY 11501

Terry Harper, Bookseller
P.O. Box 312
Vergennes, VT 05491-0312
802-877-9262

Heritage Book Shop, Inc.
8540 Melrose Ave.
Los Angeles, CA 90069
213-659-3674

Paul Melzer Fine Books
12 E Vine St.
Redlands, CA 92373
909-792-7299

Thorn Books
P.O. Box 1244
Moorpark, CA 93020
805-529-3647 or fax 805-529-0022
e-mail: thornbooks@aol.com

Reference
About Books
6 Sand Hill Ct.
P.O. Box 5717
Parsippany, NY 07054
201-515-4591

Religion
Chimney Sweep Books
419 Cedar St.
Santa Cruz, CA 94060-4304
408-458-1044

Reptiles
Mason's Bookstore, Rare Books
  & Record Albums
115 S Main St.
Chambersburg, PA 17201
717-261-0541

Revolutionary War
K.C. Owings
P.O. Box 19
N Abington, MA 02351
617-857-1655

Roycroft Press
Richard Blacher
209 Plymouth Colony, Alps Rd.
Branford, CT 06405

Scholarly Books
Reprint editions
Dover Publications
Dept. A 214
E Second St.
Mineola, NY 11501

Science & Technology
Thomas C. Bayer
85 Reading Ave.
Hillsdale, MI 49242
517-439-4134

Book & Tackle Shop
29 Old Colony Rd.
P.O. Box 114
Chestnut Hill, MA 02167
617-965-0459 (winter) or
401-596-0700 (summer)

Key Books
P.O. Box 58097
St. Petersburg, FL 33715
813-867-2931

M & S Rare Books, Inc.
P.O. Box 2594, E Side Sta.
Providence, RI 02906
401-272-0831 or fax 401-272-0831
(attention M & S)

Smithfield Rare Books
20 Deer Run Trail
Smithfield, RI 02917
401-231-8225

Science Fiction
AL-PAC
Lamar Kelley Antiquarian Books
2625 E Southern Ave., C-120
Tempe, AZ 85282
602-831-3121 or fax 602-831-3193

Karl M. Armens
740 Juniper Dr.
Iowa City, IA 52245

Bernard E. Goodman, Bookseller
7421 SW 147 Ct.
Miami, FL 33193
305-382-2464

First editions
Island Books
P.O. Box 19
Old Westbury, NY 11568
516-759-0233

Horror & Occult
Bob Lakin
3021 Lavita Ln.
Dallas, TX 75234
214-247-3291

Robert A. Madle
4406 Bestor Dr.
Rockville, MD 20853
301-460-4712

Also fantasy
Kai Nygaard
19421 Eighth Place
Escondido, CA 92029
619-746-9039

Pandora's Books, Ltd.
P.O. Box 54
Neche, ND 58265
204-324-8548 or fax 204-324-1628

Pulphouse
P.O. Box 481
Elberton, GA 30635-0481
706-213-9280
e-mail: Pulpmaster@msn.com

Also fantasy
Xanadu Records, Ltd.
3242 Irwin Ave.
Kingsbridge, NY 10463
212-549-3655

Sciences
Cover to Cover
P.O. Box 687
Chapel Hill, NC 27514

Reprint editions
Dover Publications
E Second St.
Mineola, NY 11501

Significant Books
P.O. Box 9248
3053 Madison Rd.
Cincinnati, OH 45209
513-321-7567

Series Books
Glo's Children's Series Books
906 Shadywood
Southlake, TX 76092
817-481-1438

Set Editions
Bowie & Weatherford, Inc.
314 First Ave. S
Seattle, WA 98104
206-624-4100

Sherlockiana
The Silver Door
P.O. Box 3208
Redondo Beach, CA 90277
310-379-6005

Ships & Sea
Book & Tackle Shop
29 Old Colony Rd.
P.O. Box 114
Chestnut Hill, MA 02167
617-965-0459 (winter) or
401-596-0700 (summer)

Parmer Books
7644 Forrestal Rd.
San Diego, CA 92120-2203
619-287-0693 or fax 619-287-6135
email: ParmerBook@aol.com

J. Tuttle Maritme Books
1806 Laurel Crest
Madison, WI 53705
608-238-SAIL(7245)
fax 608-238-7249

Signed Editions
Chapel Hill Rare Books
P.O. Box 456
Carrboro, NC 27510
919-929-8351

Janet Egelhofer
36 Fairfield Ave.
Holyoke, MA 01040
413-532-1295

Dan Simmons
Thomas Books
P.O. Box 14036
Phoenix, AZ 85063
602-247-9289

Socialism
Volume I Books
1 Union St.
Hillsdale, MI 49242
517-437-2228

South America
Flo Silver Books
8442 Oakwood Ct. N
Indianapolis, IN 46260
317-255-5118

South Dakota
Also any pre-1970 Western-related books
James F. Taylor
515 Sixth St.
Rapid City, SD 57701
605-341-3224

Space Exploration
Knollwood Books
Lee and Peggy Price
P.O. Box 197
Oregon, WI 53575
608-835-8861 or fax 608-835-8421

Speciality Publishers
Arkham House, Gnome, Fantasy, etc.
Robert A. Madle
4406 Bestor Dr.
Rockville, MD 20853
301-460-4712

Sports
Baseball or boxing
Ace Zerblonski
Malcolm McCollum, Proprietor
1419 North Royer
Colorado Springs, CO 80907
719-634-3941

Adelson Sports
13610 N Scottsdale Rd. #10
Scottsdale, AZ 85254
602-596-1913 or fax 602-598-1914

Randall House
835 Laguna St.
Santa Barbara, CA 93101
805-963-1909 or fax 805-963-1650

Statue of Liberty
Mike Brooks
7335 Skyline
Oakland, CA 94611

Surveying
Also tools, instruments and ephemera
David and Nancy Garcelon
10 Hastings Ave.
Millbury, MA 01527-4314
508-754-2667

Technology
Thomas C. Bayer
85 Reading Ave.
Hillsdale, MI 49242
517-439-4134

Cover to Cover
P.O. Box 687
Chapel Hill, NC 27514

Significant Books
3053 Madison Rd.
P.O. Box 9248
Cincinnati, OH 45209
513-321-7567

Tennessee History
Elder's Book Store
2115 Elliston Pl.
Nashville, TN 37203
615-327-1867

Tennis
Brasser's
8701 Seminole Blvd.
Seminole, FL 34642

Texana Fiction & Authors
Bob Lakin
3021 Lavita Ln.
Dallas, TX 75234
214-247-3291

Textiles
Galerie De Boicourt
6136 Westbrooke Dr.
W Bloomfield, MI 48322
810-788-9253

Stanley Schwartz
1934 Pentuckett Ave.
San Diego, CA 92104-5732
619-232-5888 or fax 619-233-5833

Theology
Chimney Sweep Books
419 Cedar St.
Santa Cruz, CA 94060-4304
408-458-1044

Hurley Books
1752 Rt. 12
Westmoreland, NH 03467-4724
603-399-4342 or fax 603-399-8326

Jim Thompson
The American Dust Co.
47 Park Ct.
Staten Island, NY 10301
718-442-8253

Trade Catalogs
Eastside Books & Paper
P.O. Box 1581, Gracie Sta.
New York, NY 10028-0013
212-759-6299

Trades & Crafts
19th C
Cover to Cover
P.O. Box 687
Chapel Hill, NC 27514

Hillcrest Books
Rt. 3, Box 479
Crossville, TN 38555-9547
phone or fax 615-484-7680

Travel
Bohemian Bookworm
110 W 25th St., 9th Fl.
New York, NY 10001
212-620-5627

Also exploration
Duck Creek Books
Jim and Shirley Richards
P.O. Box 203
Caldwell, OH 43724
614-732-4856 (10 am to 10 pm)

Terry Harper, Bookseller
P.O. Box 312
Vergennes, VT 05491-0312
802-877-9262

Heritage Book Shop, Inc.
8540 Melrose Ave.
Los Angeles, CA 90069
213-659-3674

Jim Hodgson Books
908 S Manlius St.
Fayetteville, NY 13066
315-637-6264

Flo Silver Books
8442 Oakwood Ct. N
Indianapolis, IN 46260
317-255-5118

Discoveries before 1900
Gordon Totty
Scarce Paper Americana
347 Shady Lake Pky.
Baton Rouge, LA 70810
504-766-8625

Turkey
W.B. O'Neill-Old & Rare Books
11609 Hunters Green Ct.
Reston, VA 22091
703-860-0782 or fax 703-620-0153

Tasha Tudor
Books of the Ages
Gary Overmann
4764 Silverwood Dr.
Batavia, OH 45103
513-732-3456

UFO
AL-PAC
Lamar Kelley Antiquarian Books
2625 E Southern Ave., C-120
Tempe, AZ 85282
602-831-3121 or fax 602-831-3193

Vargas
Parnassus Books
218 N 9th St.
Boise, ID 83702

Vietnam War
Rick Harmon
Military Books & Relics
910 Sullivan Dr.
Belvidere, IL 61008
815-547-7580

Voyages, Exploration & Travel
Chapel Hill Rare Books
P.O. Box 456
Carrboro, NC 27510
919-929-8351

Terry Harper, Bookseller
P.O. Box 312
Vergennes, VT 05491-0312
802-877-9262

Heritage Book Shop, Inc.
8540 Melrose Ave.
Los Angeles, CA 90069
213-659-3674

Jim Hodgson Books
908 S Manlius St.
Fayetteville, NY 13066
315-637-6264

Key Books
P.O. Box 58097
St. Petersburg, FL 33715
813-867-2931

Overlee Farm Books
P.O. Box 1155
Stockbridge, MA 01262
413-627-2277

George H. Tweney
16660 Marine View Dr. SW
Seattle, WA 98166
206-243-8243
813-666-1133

Western Americana
Bowie & Co. Booksellers, Inc.
314 First Ave. S
Seattle, WA 98104
206-624-4100

Terry Harper, Bookseller
P.O. Box 312
Vergennes, VT 05491-0312
802-877-9262

K.C. Owings
P.O. Box 19
N Abington, MA 02351
617-857-1655

Scribe Company
Attn: Bonnie Smith
P.O. Box 1123
Flippin, AR 72634

Thorn Books
P.O. Box 1244
Moorpark, CA 93020
805-529-3647 or fax 805-529-0022
e-mail: thornbooks@aol.com

George H. Tweney
16660 Marine View Dr. SW
Seattle, WA 98166
206-243-8243

Nonfiction 19th-C outlaws, lawmen, etc.
The Early West/Whodunit Books
P.O. Box 9292
College Sta., TX 77842
409-775-6047 or fax 409-764-7758

Charles Willeford
The American Dust Co.
47 Park Ct.
Staten Island, NY 10301
718-442-8253

Wine
Second Harvest Books
P.O. Box 3306
Florence, OR 97439
phone or fax 541-902-0215

Women's History
Volume I Books
1 Union St.
Hillsdale, MI 49242
517-437-2228

World War I
The Book Corner
Mike Tennero
728 W Lumsden Rd.
Brandon, FL 33511
813-684-1133

Denis McDonnell, Bookseller
653 Park St.
Honesdale, PA 18431
717-253-6706 or
fax 717-253-6785
e-mail:
denis.mcdonnell@microserve.com

World War II
Cover to Cover
P.O. Box 687
Chapel Hill, NC 27514

BOOKSELLERS

This section of the book lists names and addresses of used book dealers who have contributed the retail listings contained in this edition of *Huxford's Old Book Value Guide*. The code (A1, S7, etc.) located before the price in our listings refers to the dealer offering that particular book for sale. (When more than one dealer has the same book listing their code is given alphabetically before the price.) Given below are the dealer names and their codes.

Many book dealers issue catalogs, have open shops, are mail order only, or may be a combination of these forms of business. When seeking a book from a particular dealer, it would be best to first write (enclose SASE) or call to see what type of business is operated (open shop or mail order).

A1
A-Book-A-Brac Shop
6760 Collins Ave.
Miami Beach, FL 33141
305-865-0092

A2
Aard Books
31 Russell Ave.
Troy, NH 03465
603-242-3638

A3
Noreen Abbot Books
2666 44th Ave.
San Francisco, CA 94116
415-664-9464

A4
About Books
6 Sand Hill Ct.
P.O. Box 5717
Parsippany, NJ 07054
201-515-4591

A5
Adelson Sports
13610 N Scottsdale Rd. #10
Scottsdale, AZ 85254
602-596-1913 or fax 602-596-1914

A6
Ads Autographs
P.O. Box 8006
Webster, NY 14580
716-671-2651

A7
Avonlea Books Search Service
P.O. Box 74, Main Sta.
White Plains, NY 10602
914-946-5923
fax 914-946-5924 (allow 6 rings)

A8
AL-PAC
Lamar Kelley Antiquarian Books
2625 E Southern Ave., C-120
Tempe, AZ 85282
602-831-3121 or fax 602-831-3193

A9
Amaranth Books
P.O. Box 421
Wilmette, IL 60091-0421
708-328-2939

A10
The American Botanist
P.O. Box 532
Chillicothe, IL 61523

A11
The American Dust Co.
47 Park Ct.
Staten Island, NY 10301
718-442-8253 or fax 718-442-2750

A12
Antiquarian Book Arcade
110 W 25th St., 9th Floor
New York, NY 10001

A13
Antiquarian Medical Books
W. Bruce Fye
1607 N Wood Ave.
Marshfield, WI 54449
715-384-8128 or fax 715-389-2990

A14
Almark & Co.-Booksellers
P.O. Box 7
Thornhill, Ontario
Canada L3T 3N1
phone or fax 905-764-2665

A15
Karl M. Armens
740 Juniper Dr.
Iowa City, IA 52245
319-337-7755

A16
Arnold's of Michigan
218 S Water St.
Marine City, MI 48039
313-765-1350

A17
Artis Books
201 N Second Ave.
P.O. Box 822
Alpena, MI 49707-0822
517-354-3401

A18
Authors of the West
191 Dogwood Dr.
Dundee, OR 97115
503-538-8132

A19
Aplin Antiques & Art
HC 80, Box 793-25
Piedmont, SD 57769
605-347-5016

A20
Ace Zerblonski
Malcolm McCollum, Proprietor
1419 North Royer
Colorado Springs, CO 80907
719-634-3941

B1
Thomas C. Bayer
85 Reading Ave.
Hillsdale, MI 49242
517-439-4134

B2
Paul and Beth Garon
Beasley Books
1533 W Oakdale, 2nd Floor
Chicago, IL 60657
312-472-4528 or fax 312-472-7857
e-mail: beasley@mcs.com
web page: http://www.abaa-
booknet.com/usa/beasley/

B3
Bela Luna Books
P.O. Box 260425
Highlands Ranch, CO 80126-0425
800-497-4717 or fax 303-794-3135

B4
Between the Covers
35 W Maple Ave.
Merchantville, NJ 08109
609-665-2284 or fax 609-665-3639
e-mail: BetweenCov@aol.com

B5
Bicentennial Book Shop
820 S Westnedge Ave.
Kalamazoo, MI 49008
616-345-5987

B6
Bibliography of the Dog
The New House
216 Covey Hill Rd.
Havelock, Quebec
Canada J0S 2C0
514-827-2717 or fax 514-827-2091

B7
Best-Read Books
122 State St.
Sedro-Woolley, WA 98284
206-855-2179

B8
Bohemian Bookworm
110 W 25th St., 9th Floor
New York, NY 10001
212-620-5627

B9
The Book Baron
1236 S Magnolia Ave.
Anaheim, CA 92804
714-527-7022 or fax 714-527-5634

B10
Book Broker
P.O. Box 1283
Charlottesville, VA 22902
804-296-2194

B11
The Book Corner
Michael Tennero
728 W Lumsden Rd.
Brandon, FL 33511
813-684-1133

B12
The Book Emporium
235 Glen Cove Ave.
Sea Cliff, LI, NY 11579
516-671-6524

B13
The Book Inn
6401-D University
Lubbock, TX 79413

B14
Book & Tackle Shop
29 Old Colony Rd.
P.O. Box 114
Chestnut Hill, MA 02167
617-965-0459 (winter)
401-596-0700 (summer)

B15
Book Treasures
P.O. Box 121
E Norwich, NY 11732

B16
The Book Den South
Nancy Costello
2249 First St.
Ft. Myers, FL 33901
813-332-2333

B17
Books of the Ages
Gary J. Overmann
Maple Ridge Manor
4764 Silverwood Dr.
Batavia, OH 45103
513-732-3456

B18
The Bookseller, Inc.
521 W Exchange St.
Akron, OH 44302
216-762-3101

B19
Books West Southwest
Box 6149, University Sta.
Irvine, CA 92616-6149
714-509-760 or fax 714-854-5102
e-mail: bkswest@ix.netcom.com
or
14 Whitman Ct.
Irvine, CA 92612
714-509-7670

B20
Bowie & Co. Booksellers, Inc.
314 First Ave. S
Seattle, WA 98104
206-624-4100 or fax 206 223 0966

B21
Brasser's
8701 Seminole Blvd.
Seminole, FL 34642

B22
Bridgman Books
906 Roosevelt Ave.
Rome, NY 13440
315-337-7252

B23
British Stamp Exchange
12 Fairlawn Ave.
N Weymouth, MA 02191

B24
Bromer Booksellers
607 Boylston St.
Boston, MA 02116
617-247-32818 or fax 617-247-2975
e-mail: books@bromer.com

B25
Mike Brooks
7335 Skyline
Oakland, CA 9461

B26
Brooks Books
Phil and Marty Nesty
1343 New Hampshire Dr.
P.O. Box 21473
Concord, CA 94521
510-672-4566 or fax 510-672-3338
e-mail: brooksbk@interloc.com

B27
The Bookstall
570 Sutter St.
San Francisco, CA 94102
fax 415-362-1503

B28
Woodbridge B. Brown
312 Main St.
P.O. Box 445
Turner Falls, MA 01376
413-772-2509 or 413-773-5710

B29
Books Now & Then
Dennis Patrick
P.O. Box 337
Stanley, ND 58784
701-628-2084

B30
Burke's Bookstore
1719 Poplar Ave.
Memphis, TN 38104-6447
901-278-7484

B32
Richard Blacher
209 Plymouth Colony, Alps Rd.
Branford, CT 06405

B34
Bygone Books 'n Things
Nancy C. May
1720-C S Peaceable Rd.
McAlester, OK 74501

B35
Brillance Books
Morton Brillant, Bookseller
313 Meeting St. #21
Charleston, SC 29401
803-722-6643
http://members.aol.com/brill-books/catalogue.html

B36
Thomas J. Bindas
12 Stone St., Apt C06
Brunswick, ME 04011
207-729-8093

C1
Camelot Books
Charles E. Wyatt
P.O. Box 2883
Vista, CA 92083
619-940-9472

C2
The Captain's Bookshelf, Inc.
Cary Loren
31 Page Ave.
Asheville, NC 22801
704-254-5733 or fax 704-253-4917

C3
Cattermole
20th-C Children's Books
9880 Fairmount Rd.
Newbury, OH 44065

C4
Bev Chaney, Jr. Books
73 Croton Ave.
Ossining, NY 10562
914-941-1002

C5
Chimney Sweep Books
419 Cedar St.
Santa Cruz, CA 95060-4304
408-458-1044

C6
Chapel Hill Rare Books
P.O. Box 456
Carrboro, NC 27510
919-929-8351

C7
Chartwell Booksellers
55 E 52nd St.
New York, NY 10055
212-308-0643

C8
Children's Book Adoption Agency
P.O. Box 643
Kensington, MD 20895-0643
301-565-2834 or fax 301-585-3091
e-mail:KIDS_BKS @interloc.com

C9
Cinemage Books
105 W 27th St.
New York, NY 10001
212-243-4919

C10
Cohen Books & Collectibles
Joel J. Cohen
P.O. Box 810310
Boca Raton, FL 33481
407-487-7888

C11
Cover to Cover
P.O. Box 687
Chapel Hill, NC 27514

C12
Noriko I. Chichon
Natural History Books
1025 Keokut St.
Iowa City, 52240
319-354-4844

C13
Creatures of Habit
403 Jefferson
Paducah, KY 42001
502-442-2923

C14
Steve Cieluch
15 Walbridge St., Ste. #10
Allston, MA 02134
617-734-7778

D1
Ursula Davidson
Children's & Illustrated Books
134 Linden Ln.
San Rafael, CA 94901
415-454-3939 or fax 415-454-1087

D2
L. Clarice Davis
Fine & Applied Art Books
P.O. Box 56054
Sherman Oaks, CA 91413-1054
818-787-1322

D4
Carol Docheff, Bookseller
1390 Reliez Vly. Rd.
Lafayette, CA 94549
510-935-9595

D5
Dover Publications
Dept. A 214
E Second St.
Mineola, NY 11501

D6
Drusilla's Books
859 N Howard St.
P.O. Box 16
Baltimore, MD 21201
410-225-0277

D7
Duck Creek Books
Jim & Shirley Richards
P.O. Box 203
Caldwell, OH 43724
614-732-4856

D8
Patricia L. Daniel, Bookseller
13 English Ave.
Wichita, KS 62707-1005
316-683-2079 or fax 316-683-5448
e-mail: pldaniel@Southwind.net

E1
The Early West/Whodunit Books
P.O. Box 9292
College Sta., TX 77842
409-775-6047 or fax 409-764-7758

E2
Edison Hall Books
5 Ventnor Dr.
Edison, NJ 08820
908-548-4455

E3
Janet Egelhofer
36 Fairfield Ave.
Holyoke, MA 01040
413-532-1295

E4
Elder's Book Store
2115 Elliston Pl.
Nashville, TN 37203
615-327-1867

E5
Elegant Book & Map Company
815 Harrison Ave.
P.O. Box 1302
Cambridge, OH 43725
614-432-4068

E6
Eastside Books & Paper
P.O. Box 1581, Gracie Sta.
New York, NY 10028-0013
212-759-6299

F1
First Folio
1206 Brentwood
Paris, TN 38242-3804
phone or fax 910-944-9940

F2
Fisher Books & Antiques
345 Pine St.
Williamsport, PA 17701

F3
Flo Silver Books
8442 Oakwood Ct. N
Indianapolis, IN 46260
phone or fax 317-255-5118

F4
For Collectors Only
2028B Ford Pky. #136
St. Paul, MN 55116

F5
Fran's Bookhouse
6601 Greene St.
Phil., PA 19119
215-438-2729 or fax 215-438-8997

F6
Frontier America
P.O. Box 9193
Albuquerque, NM 87119-9193

G1
John Gach Fine & Rare Books
5620 Waterloo Rd.
Columbia, MD 21045
410-465-9023 or fax 410-465-0649
e-mail: john.gach@clark.net

G2
Galerie De Boicourt
6136 Westbrooke Dr.
W Bloomfield, MI 48322
810-788-9253

G3
Gambler's Book Shop
630 S Eleventh St.
Las Vegas, NV 89101
800-634-6243

G4
David & Nancy Garcelon
10 Hastings Ave.
Millbury, MA 01527-4314

G5
Michael Gerlicher
1375 Rest Point Rd.
Orono, MN 55364

G6
Glo's Children's Series Books
Gloria Stobbes
906 Shadywood
Southlake, TX 76092
817-481-1438

G7
James Tait Goodrich
Antiquarian Books & Manuscripts
214 Everett Pl.
Englewood, NJ 07631
201-567-0199 or fax 201-567-0433

G8
Grave Matters
P.O. Box 32192-08
Cincinnati, OH 45232
513-242-7527 or fax 513-242-5115
e-mail: GraveMatrs@aol.com

G9
John A. Greget-Magic Lists
2631 E Claire Dr.
Phoenix, AZ 85032
602-971-5497

G10
Bernard E. Goodman, Bookseller
7421 SW 147 Ct.
Miami, FL 33193
305-382-2464

H1
Henry F. Hain III
Antiques & Collectibles
2623 N Second St.
Harrisburg, PA 17110
717-238-0534

H2
Rick Harmon
Military Books & Relics
910 Sullivan Dr.
Belvidere, IL 61008
815-547-7580

H3
Terry Harper, Bookseller
P.O. Box 312
Vergennes, VT 05491-0312
802-877-9262

H4
Susan Heller, Pages for Sages
22611 Halburton Rd.
Beachwood, OH 44122-3939
216-283-2665 or fax 216-991-2665

H5
Heritage Book Shop, Inc.
8540 Melrose Ave.
Los Angeles, CA 90069
310-659-3674 or fax 310-659-4872

H6
Hillcrest Books
Rt. 3, Box 479
Crossville, TN 38555-9547
phone or fax 615-484-7680

H7
Jim Hodgson Books
908 S Manlius St.
Fayetteville, NY 13066
315-637-6264

H8
Homebiz Paper
2919 Mistwood Forest Dr.
Chester, VA 23831-7043

H9
Murray Hudson
Antiquarian Books & Maps
The Old Post Office
109 S Church St.
P.O. Box 163
Halls, TN 38040
901-836-9057 or 800-748-9946

H10
Hurley Books / Celtic Cross Books
1753 Rt. 12
Westmoreland, NH 03467
603-399-4342 or fax 603-399-8326

H11
Ken Hebenstreit, Bookseller
813 N Washington Ave.
Royal Oak, MI 48067
phone or fax 810-548-5460
e-mail: Kensbooks@aol.com

I1
Island Books
P.O. Box 19
Old Westbury, NY 11586
516-759-0233

J1
Jay's House of Collectibles
75 Pky. Dr.
Syosset, NY 11791

K1
Kenneth Karmiole, Bookseller, Inc.
P.O. Box 464
1225 3rd St. Promenade
Santa Monica, CA 90401
310-451-4342 or fax 310-458-5930

K2
Ilene Kayne
1308 S Charles St.
Baltimore, MD 21230
410-347-7570
e-mail: IleneGold@aol.com

K3
Key Books
P.O. Box 58097
St. Petersburg, FL 33715-8097

K4
The King's Market Bookshop
P.O. Box 709
Boulder, CO 80306-0709
303-447-0234

K5
Knollwood Books
Lee and Peggy Price
P.O. Box 197
Oregon, WI 53575-0197
608-835-8861 or fax 608-835-8421
e-mail: books@tdsnet.com

K6
Kendra Krienke
230 Central Park West
New York, NY 10024
201-930-9709 or 201-930-9765

K7
George Robert Kane Fine Books
252 Third Ave.
Santa Cruz, CA 95062
phone or fax 408-426-4133

L1
Bob Lakin
3021 Lavita Ln.
Dallas, TX 75234
214-247-3291

L2
Henry Lindeman
4769 Bavarian Dr.
Jackson, MI 49201
517-764-5728

L3
Ken Lopez, Bookseller
51 Huntington Rd.
Hadley, MA 01035
413-584-4827 or fax 413-584-2045

L4
Liberty Historic Manuscripts, Inc.
300 Kings Hwy. E
Haddonfield, NJ 08033

M1
M & S Rare Books, Inc.
P.O. Box 2594, E Side Sta.
Providence, RI 02806
401-421-1050 or fax 401-272-0831
(attention M & S)

M2
Robert A. Madle
4406 Bestor Dr.
Rockville, MD 20853
301-460-4712

M3
The Magazine Baron
1236 S Magnolia Ave.
Anaheim, CA 92804
714-527-0358 or fax 714-527-5634

M4
Melvin Marcher, Bookseller
6204 N Vermont
Oklahoma City, OK 73112

M5
Marvelous Books
Dorothy (Dede) Kern
P.O. Box 1510
Ballwin, MO 63022
314-458-3301 or fax 314-273-5452
e-mail: marvlous@interloc.com

M6
Mason's Bookstore, Rare Books
   & Record Albums
115 S Main St.
Chambersburg, PA 17201
717-261-0541

M7
Denis McDonnell, Bookseller
653 Park St.
Honesdale, PA 18431
717-253-6706 or fax 717-253-6786

M8
McGowan Book Co.
39 Kimberly Dr.
Durham, NC 27704
919-403-1503 or fax 919-403-1706

M9
Paul Melzer Fine & Rare Books
12 E Vine St.
Redlands, CA 92373
909-792-7299

M10
Robert L. Merriam
Rare & Used Books
39 Newhall Rd.
Conway, MA 01341-9709
413-369-4052

M11
Meyer Boswell Books, Inc.
2141 Mission St.
San Francisco, CA 94110
415-255-6400 or fax 415-255-6499
e-mail: rarelaw@myerbos.com
http://www.meyerbos.com

M12
Frank Mikesh
1356 Walden Rd.
Walnut Creek, CA 94596
510-934-9243

M13
Ken Mitchell
710 Conacher Dr.
Willowdale, Ontario
Canada M2M 3N6
416-222-5808

M14
Modern Age Books
P.O. Box 325
E Lansing, MI 48826
517-351-9334

M15
Mordida Books
P.O. Box 79322
Houston, TX 77279
713-467-4280 or fax 713-467-4182

M16
The Mulberry Cat
Yvonne Davis
Jan Davis Martel
P.O. Box 3573
Boone, NC 28607
704-963-7693

M17
Much Ado
Seven Pleasant St.
Marblehead, MA 01945
617-639-0400

M19
My Book Heaven
2212 Broadway
Oakland, CA 94612
510-893-7273 or 510-521-1683

M20
My Bookhouse
27 S Sandusky St.
Tiffin, OH 44883
419-447-9842
httpc//www.brightnet/-tinfoill

M21
Brian McMillan, Books
1429 L Ave.
Traer, IA 50675
319-478-2360 (Mon.-Sat., 9 am to
9pm CDT)

M22
M/S Books
53 Curtiss Rd.
New Preston, CT 06777
860-868-0627 or fax 860-868-0504

M23
McGee's First Varieties
8012 Brooks Chapel Rd., Ste. 247
Brentwood, TN 37027
615-373-5318
e-mail: Bibliopole@aol.com

N1
Nerman's Books
410-63 Albert St.
Winnipeg, Manitoba
Canada R3B 1G4
fax 204-947-0753

N2
Nutmeg Books
354 New Litchfield St. (Rte. 202)
Torrington, CT 06790
203-482-9696

N3
Kai Nygaard
19421 Eighth Pl.
Escondido, CA 92029
619-749-9039

N4
Norris Books
2491 San Ramon Vly. Blvd.
Ste. #1-201
San Ramon, CA 94583
phone or fax 510-867-1218
www.slip.net/cgchav/norrisbooks
e-mail: norrisbooks@slip.net

O1
David L. O'Neal, Antiquarian
Bookseller
234 Clarendon St.
Boston, MA 02116

O2
W.B. O'Neill
Old & Rare Books
11609 Hunters Green Ct.
Reston, VA 22091
703-860-0782 or fax 703-620-0153

O3
October Farm
2609 Branch Rd.
Raleigh, NC 27610
919-772-0482 or fax 919-779-6295

O4
The Old London Bookshop
111 Central Ave.
P.O. Box 922
Bellingham, WA 98227-0922
206-733-RARE or fax 206-647-8946

O5
The Old Map Gallery
Paul F. Mahoney
1746 Blake St.
Denver, CO 80202
303-296-7725

O6
Old Paint Lick School Antique
Mall
Raymond P. Mixon
11000 Hwy. 52 West
Paint Lick, KY 40461
606-925-3000 or 606-792-3000

O7
Overlee Farm Books
P.O. Box 1155
Stockbridge, MA 01262
413-637-2277

O8
K.C. Owings
P.O. Box 19
N Abington, MA 02351
617-857-1655

O9
Olde Current Books
Daniel P. Shay
356 Putnam Ave.
Ormond Beach, FL 32174
904-672-8998
e-mail: PEAKMYSTER@aol.com
http://members.aol.com/peak-
myster/aolwp.htm

P1
Pacific Rim Books
Michael Onorato
P.O. Box 2575
Bellingham, WA 98227-2575
206-676-0256

P2
Maggie Page
Page Books
H.C.R. 65, Box 233
Kingston, AR 72472
501-861-5831

P3
Pandora's Books Ltd.
P.O. Box 54
Neche, ND 58265
204-324-8548 or fax 204-324-1628

P4
Parmer Books
7644 Forrestal Rd.
San Diego, CA 92120-2203
619-287-0693 or fax 619-287-6135
e-mail: ParmerBook@aol.com

P5
Parnassus Books
218 N 9th St.
Boise, ID 83702

P6
Passaic Book Center
594 Main Ave.
Passaic, NJ 07055
201-778-6646 or fax 201-778-6738

P7
Pauper's Books
206 N Main St.
Bowling Green, OH 43402-2420
419-352-2163

P8
R. Plapinger, Baseball Books
P.O. Box 1062
Ashland, OR 97520
514-488-1220

P9
Prometheus Books
59 John Glenn Dr.
Buffalo, NY 14228-2197
716-691-0133 or fax 716-691-0137

P10
Pulphouse
J.H. James
P.O. Box 481
Elberton, GA 30635
706-213-9280
e-mail: Pulpmaster@msn.com

P11
Pelanor Books
7 Gaskill Ave.
Albany, NY 12203

P12
Popek's Pages Past
R.D. 3, Box 44-C
Oneonta, NY 13820
607-432-0836

Q1
Quill & Brush
Patricia & Allen Ahearn
Box 5365
Rockville, MD 20848
301-460-3700 or fax 301-871-5425

R1
Raintree Books
432 N Eustis St.
Eustis, FL 32726
904-357-7145

R2
Kathleen Rais & Co.
Rais Place Cottage
211 Carolina Ave.
Phoenixville, PA 19460
610-933-1388

R3
Randall House
835 Laguna St.
Santa Barbara, CA 93101
805-963-1909 or fax 805-963-1650

R4
Reference Books
C. Scott Hall
P.O. Box 7076
Salem, OR 97305
503-399-6185

R5
Jo Ann Reisler, Ltd.
360 Glyndon St., NE
Vienna, VA 22180
703-938-2967 or fax 703-938-9057

R6
Wallace Robinson Books
RD #6, Box 574
Meadville, PA 16335
800-653-3280 or 813-823-3280
814-724-7670 or 814-333-9652

R7
Tom Rolls
640 E Seminary #2
Greencastle, IN 46135

R8
RAC Books
R.R. #2
P.O. Box 296
Seven Valleys, PA 17360
717-428-3776

R9
Realm of Colorado
P.O. Box 24
Parker, CO 80134

R10
Roger Reus
9412 Huron Ave.
Richmond, VA 23294
Mail order only

R11
Recollection Books
4519 University Way NE
Seattle, WA 98105
206-548-1346
http://www.mediastream.com/m
payson/recollection/

S1
Bill and Mimi Sachen
927 Grand Ave.
Waukegan, IL 60085-3709
847-662-7204

S2
J. Sampson Antiques & Books
107 S Main
Harrodsburg, KY 40330
606-734-7829

S3
Stanley Schwartz
1934 Pentuckett Ave.
San Diego, CA 92104-5732
619-232-5888 or fax 619-233-5833

S4
Scribe Company
Attn: Bonnie Smith
P.O. Box 1123
Flippin, AR 72634
501-453-7387

S5
Significant Books
3053 Madison Rd.
P.O. Box 9248
Cincinnati, OH 45209
513-321-7567

S6
The Silver Door
P.O. Box 3208
Redondo Beach, CA 90277
310-379-6005

S7
K.B. Slocum Books
P.O. Box 10998 #620
Austin, TX 78766
800-521-4451 or fax 512-258-8041

S8
Barbara Smith Books
P.O. Box 1185
Northampton, MA 01061
413-586-1453

S9
Ed Smith Books
P.O. Box 66
Oak View, CA 93022
805-649-2844 or fax 805-649-2863
e-mail: edsbooks@aol.com

S10
Smithfield Rare Books
20 Deer Run Trail
Smithfield, RI 02917
401-231-8225

S11
Nancy Stewart, Books
1188 NW Weybridge Way
Beaverton, OR 97006
503-645-9779

S12
Sweet Memories
Sharyn Laymon
400 Mulberry St.
Loudon, TN 37774
615-458-5044

S13
Eileen Serxner
Box 2544
Bala Cynwyd, PA 19004
610-664-7960

T1
Lee and Mike Temares
50 Hts. Rd.
Plandome, NY 11030
516-627-8688

T2
Thomas Books
4425 W Olive, Ste. 168
Glendale, AZ 85302
602-435-5055 (10 am to 5 pm) or
602-247-9289 (after hours)

T3
Gordon Totty
Scarce Paper Americana
347 Shady Lake Pky.
Baton Rouge, LA 70810
504-766-8625

T4
Trackside Books
8819 Mobud Dr.
Houston, TX 77036
713-772-8107

T5
Treasures From the Castle
Connie Castle
1720 N Livernois
Rochester, MI 48306
810-651-7317

T6
H.E. Turlington Books
P.O. Box 190
Carrboro, NC 27510

T7
J. Tuttle Maritime Books
1806 Laurel Crest
Madison, WI 53705
608-238-SAIL (7245)

T8
George H. Tweney
16660 Marine View Dr. SW
Seattle, WA 98166
206-243-8243

T9
Typographeum Bookshop
The Stone Cottage
Bennington Rd.
Francestown, NH 03043

T10
Thorn Books
P.O. Box 1244
Moorpark, CA 93020
805-529-36647 or fax 805-529-0022
e-mail: thornbooks@aol.com

V1
VERSEtility Books
P.O. Box 1133
Farmington, CT 06034-1133
860-677-0606

V2
A.A. Vespa
P.O. Box 637
Park Ridge, IL 60068
708-692-4210

V3
Vintage Books
Nancy and David Haines
181 Hayden Rowe St.
Hopkinton, MA 01748
508-435-3499

V4
Volume I Books
1 Union St.
Hillsdale, MI 49242
517-437-2228

W1
Worldwide Antiquarian
P.O. Box 391
Cambridge, MA 02141
617-876-6220 or fax 617-876-0839
e-mail: mbalwan@aol.com

Y1
Yesterday's Books
229 Riverview Dr.
Parchment, MI 49004
616-345-1011

X1
Xanadu Records, Ltd.
3242 Irwin Ave.
Kingsbridge, NY 10463
718-549-3655

Reach **Thousands** with Your **Free Listing** in Our Next Edition!

☛ **Book Sellers!** If you publish lists or catalogs of books for sale, take advantage of this *free* offer. Put us on your mailing list right away so that we can include you in our next edition. We'll not only list you in our Bookbuyers section under the genre that best represents your special interests (please specify these when you contact us), but each book description we choose to include from your catalog will contain a special dealer code that will identify you as the book dealer to contact in order to buy that book. Please send your information and catalogs or lists right away, since we're working on a first-come, first-served basis. Be sure to include your current address, just as you'd like it to be published. You may also include a fax number or an e-mail address. Our dealers tell us that this service has been very successful for them, both in buying and selling.

Send your listings to:

Huxford's Old Book Value Guide
1202 Seventh Street
Covington, IN 47932-1099